W9-CPP-138

HURON COUNTY LIBRARY

2 008 235419 0

LANDMARKS OF CANADA

WHAT ART HAS DONE FOR CANADIAN HISTORY

A GUIDE TO THE

J. ROSS ROBERTSON

HISTORICAL COLLECTION

IN THE

PUBLIC REFERENCE LIBRARY

TORONTO, CANADA

WINGHAM PUBLIC LIBRARY

THIS CATALOGUE OF THE COLLECTION COVERS THREE THOUSAND SEVEN HUNDRED ILLUSTRATIONS AND INCLUDES ORIGINALS AND REPRODUCTIONS IN EVERY FORM OF ART OF ALL KNOWN PICTURES IN CONNECTION WITH CANADIAN HISTORY FROM THE LANDING OF WOLFE AT LOUISBURG IN 1758 TO THE PRESENT TIME.

PRESENTED TO THE TRUSTEES OF THE PUBLIC LIBRARY

BY J. ROSS ROBERTSON

TORONTO,
DECEMBER, 1917

CONTENTS OF THIS VOLUME

THIS COLLECTION, IN THE LOWER ART ROOM OF THE REFERENCE LIBRARY, COLLEGE ST., COMPRISES PAINTINGS, ENGRAVINGS, PORTRAITS, PRINTS, ETC., IN MEZZOTINT, LINE AND STIPPLE, BY AND AFTER PAINTERS AND ENGRAVERS OF THE ENGLISH SCHOOL, WITH WATER COLORS, PASTELS, PENCIL, SEPIA AND WASH DRAWINGS, PEN AND INK SKETCHES, LITHOGRAPHS AND AQUATINTS BY WELL-KNOWN BRITISH AND CANADIAN ARTISTS ON SUBJECTS RELATING TO CANADA AND NEWFOUNDLAND—WITH VIEWS OF NOTED LANDMARKS OF ALL PRINCIPAL CITIES AND TOWNS FROM THE ATLANTIC TO THE PACIFIC, AND PARTICULARLY THE LANDMARKS OF THE TOWN OF YORK, NOW TORONTO, THE CAPITAL OF ONTARIO.

THE OVERFLOW OF THE HISTORICAL COLLECTION, CONSISTING OF ABOUT ONE THOUSAND HISTORICAL PICTURES, NOT YET CATALOGUED, IS ON EXHIBITION IN THE UPPER ART ROOMS OF THE LIBRARY. IN THESE ROOMS MAY BE SEEN ALSO THE J. ROSS ROBERTSON ORNITHOLOGICAL COLLECTION, EMBRACING THE POPE COLLECTION OF TWO HUNDRED AND TWENTY EXAMPLES IN WATER COLOR AND ONE HUNDRED AND TWENTY-FIVE PICTURES OF A SPECIAL COLLECTION—ALL OF CANADIAN BIRDS.

CONDITION FOR COPYING

ANY OF THE PICTURES IN THE COLLECTIONS MAY BE COPIED ON CONDITION THAT PERMISSION IS GRANTED BY THE CHIEF LIBRARIAN AND THAT EACH REPRODUCTION IS CREDITED TO THE "J. ROSS ROBERTSON HISTORICAL COLLECTION, PUBLIC LIBRARY, TORONTO."

INTRODUCTORY

In a young country, where the struggle for existence seems to be only too soon followed by the struggle for the mighty dollar, we are but little concerned with history.

History is supposed to be the work of the teachers, the professors in the universities, the antiquarians and archivists. And yet, how are we to understand ourselves and our position as a nation unless there are preserved the evidences of our growth and of the struggles of our fathers to the end that a strong nation might be established? And these evidences of struggle and growth, so eagerly sought after and so carefully preserved by the older nations of the world, are not revealed in books, but in reproductions of scenes of the times. These prints tell a story, by the side of which the printed word is cold and dead, and to see the faces of the men who accomplished great things for our country, and to see the pictures of the houses in which they lived and worked, and of the villages and towns as they were in those times, gives us a thrill of "ancestor worship" which a discovery in Debrett could never produce.

The Dominion Government has recognized the necessity for the conservation and preservation of historical documents by the establishment of the Archives Department, which is doing a work too little recognized. This is a great storehouse of national history, but it has the disadvantages of a storehouse in that its treasures cannot be accessible to all.

Here and there in our country are persons who collect this historical material as an avocation or hobby, and among these stands pre-eminently Mr. J. Ross Robertson, whose interest in this intellectual pleasure is known to collectors the world over. Mr. Robertson believed that the value of such material lay, not in the hoarding of it, the mere possession of it, but in allowing all those who had similar interests to share in the pleasure of looking at and enjoying these illustrations of the age that has gone.

The value in money expended on this collection is very considerable, as those know who are in the market for such illustrations as are treasured in this collection. These are exceedingly hard to obtain, and there are at least one hundred important exhibits in this collection which have not been on the London market in complete form for over twenty years, and dealers do not know where to look for them.

The collection is impressive even to the man who thinks in dollars; it is interesting to those who find in it scenes and persons familiar to them and recalling the early days of Canada; it is illuminating to the student of our history; but, above all, it is the national character of the collection that awakens the deepest emotions—that here is the history of a young nation, the background of men and events which have brought us to this critical period in the world's history, and have made us active participators in the solution of a great world problem and crisis.

To the boy and girl at school; to the young man and woman at college, whose knowledge of Canadian history is but an acquaintance with the dry details of a text-book; to the elderly man and woman, who can remember some of the people and some of the scenes depicted; and even to the people from other lands who have adopted this country as their home, and wish to know something of its history—to all these the J. Ross Robertson Historical Collection will be a means of education as well as recreation, and the name of the donor will live in everlasting remembrance for this practical, local and national gift to the city of Toronto.

The history of this collection is very interesting. In a letter to the Public Library Board in 1910, Mr. Robertson stated that for many years he had been collecting examples of the history of Canada from 1758 up to the present time as exhibits in pictorial form, and that he was anxious that the public should have the benefit of it. He knew of no more fitting place than the Public Library, and informed the Board that he was willing to instal this collection, and, eventually, to give to the Board another collection of Canadian prints and photos contained in portfolios in his private library, numbering about 15,000 pieces, to be held by the Board in trust for the people of Canada. The only condition made by Mr. Robertson was that the pictures should be placed in a suitable room, with skilled attendants, covered by insurance, catalogued, and that they should not be loaned to any person or persons, or removed from the Library building on College street. The collection was to be known as the "J. Ross Robertson Historical Collection," and if any one wished to copy a picture of the collection this might be done only on condition that permission to do so was obtained from the Librarian, and that the collection was given due credit on each copy of a picture made, or if published in book or other form, each reproduction should be credited to the collection.

The formal opening took place 29th January, 1912. The collection at that time comprised 560 pictures, for these were all that were ready for hanging. Since then the growth has been marvellous, and to-day. (1917) there are 3,700 pictures in the art room. Indeed, it is the largest collection of Canadian pictures gathered by any one person, and that a private person, and in many respects compares favorably with the collection accumulated by Dr. Doughty, in the Dominion Archives at Ottawa.

What might be called the central figure is the magnificent oil portrait of Governor Simcoe, by E. Wyly Grier, showing the General in the uniform he wore during the time that he was Lieutenant-Governor (1792-6). It was fitting that this portrait should be unveiled by Sir John M. Gibson, Lieutenant-Governor of Ontario, when this collection was opened.

A unique feature is the reproduction of about ninety pen and pencil drawings and water colors, made by Mrs. Simcoe. Were it not for the gifted hand of the wife of our first Governor, we would never have had the faithful pictures of places and scenes in Upper and Lower Canada from 1791-6, nor of the early days of the Toronto, Niagara and Kingston settlements that were then, and are now, important places in the history of the Province of Upper Canada.

The collection has been made up by levying upon practically all the print shops of the world, and while it covers all Canada it is particularly rich in the illustrations of Toronto and vicinity. This, of course, can be well understood when one remembers that Mr. Robertson is a native of Toronto, and during his whole life has devoted a great deal of his wonderful energy towards building up institutional work within the city.

This is a National Gallery of Canada, where the pictures tell the stories and link together the men and events so that one can see the evolution of a nation. This is the visualization of history, and is an endowment for the boys and girls of to-day who will have an historical background to enable them to set in proper perspective the national problems that will soon press for solution.

This is the outcome of the hobby of a great man. Hobbies are incidental to real greatness, and when these hobbies are socialized and applied to the public good they are the greatest legacy one can leave to mankind.

GEO. H. LOCKE,
Chief Librarian.

December, 1917.

PORTRAITS

GENERAL INDEX

2

3

CATALOGUE OF THE COLLECTION

1—LOUIS RIEL AND HIS COUNCIL AT FORT GARRY—An insurrectionary council was created in the autumn of 1869, with John Bruce as president and Louis Riel as secretary. The latter, however, was really the leading spirit of the movement, and was elected president of a "Provisional Government" the following February. The members of the council were: 1, Le Roc; 2, Pierre de Lorme; 3, Thomas Bunn; 4, Xavier Page; 5, Andre Beauchemin; 6, Baptiste Tereaux; 7, Thomas Spence; 8, Pierre Poitras; 9, John Bruce; 10, Louis Riel; 11, W. B. O'Donoghue; 12, Francois Dauphinais; 13, Bob O'Lane; 14, Paul Prue. Photograph, colored. Size 5 x 7.

2—DOORWAY OF MANITOBA PENITENTIARY, 1887—Stoney Mountain, fourteen miles from Winnipeg. The group is composed of the following: 1, Very Rev. Albert Lacombe, one of the first Roman Catholic missionaries in Manitoba; 2, Chief Little Bear; 3, Sam Bedson, warden of the penitentiary; 4, Rev. Father Clouthier, of Winnipeg; 5, Poundmaker, an Indian; 6, Priest, unknown. Photograph, colored. Size 5 x 6.

3—RIEL, LOUIS, 1844-85—Leader of the Manitoba and Northwest Rebellions. In October, 1869, he became Secretary of the Comite National des Metis, and the following December was elected President of Provisional Government at Fort Garry. He was returned by acclamation to the House of Commons for Provencher, Man., in 1873, but never allowed to take his seat. Appeared in 1884 in Saskatchewan district, resulting in breaking out of Northwest Rebellion. Taken prisoner after Batoche. Executed 16th Nov., 1885. Photograph, colored. Size 4 x 5. Head and shoulders.

4—CHIEF DAVID SAWYER OF THE CREDIT—Painted by the Rev. James Spencer, M.A. Oil painting. Size 26 x 30. Head and shoulders.

5—"VIEW OF VICTORIA, VANCOUVER ISLAND—Drawn by H. O. Tiedemann. T. Picken, lith. London. Published by Day & Son, lithographers to the Queen, June 13th, 1860." Victoria, on the Strait of Juan de Fuca, formerly the capital of Vancouver Island, and now of the Province of British Columbia, was named by the officers of the Hudson's Bay Company after her late Majesty, Queen Victoria. In the summer of 1843, the building of the fort, which was the foundation of the future city of Victoria, was commenced. The place selected was known to the Indians as Camosun or Camosack. It was given the name of Fort Albert, then Fort Victoria, and finally in 1852, when the town site was laid out, the name Victoria obtained. The city was incorporated in 1862, and the old fort finally demolished in 1864. Chromo lithograph, with key. Size 8 x 34.

6—FORT OSBORNE BARRACKS, WINNIPEG, MAN.—A "Hut Encampment" of the old style. Built in 1873 on a site of slightly over fifteen acres. The barracks lie three-quarters of a mile due west of Main street and the Old Fort Garry site. All the buildings on the property are new, the last of the old structures having been destroyed in 1912. No. 1, in the sketch, was the commanding officer's quarters; 2, building set aside for ⁿther officers; 3, garrison hospital. Pen drawing. Size 8 x 17.

7—SIMPSON—"Thomas Simpson, the Arctic Discoverer. G. P. Green, pinxit. J. Cook, sculpt." Born in Scotland, 1808. Entered the service of the Hudson's Bay Company, and on arriving in Canada became secretary to his cousin, Sir George Simpson, then Governor of the Company's territories. On the decision of the Honourable Adventurers to further explore the Arctic Coast, young Simpson was asked to undertake the arduous task. He accordingly set out from Fort Garry in the winter of 1836-7, travelling on foot to Lake Athabasca, where he joined Peter Warren Dease. In recognition of his valuable services on this expedition he was awarded a gold medal by the Royal Geographical Society, while the British Government bestowed upon him a pension of £100 per annum. Simpson's later discoveries far excelled his early ones. His death took place in 1840. Line engraving. Size 4 x 5. Head and shoulders.

8—THE CITADEL, LOUISBURG, 1731—Situated in the gorge of the King's Bastion. In the early days Louisburg was known as Havre a l'Anglois. No important settlements, however, were made here until after the surrender of Newfoundland and Acadia to Great Britain by the Treaty of Utrecht, when the French troops and inhabitants evacuated Placentia, Newfld., and came to Louisburg. In 1714 M. de St. Ovide de Brouillan was appointed Governor, and some six years later the fortress was commenced. It was 350 feet long, built of solid masonry, and so constructed that in time of trouble it could be surrounded by walls and moats as means of defence. Duke d'Anville, who commanded the French Armada, 1746, was buried in the citadel, near the chapel. Copied from a plan in the National Library, Paris, France, by Albert Almon, of Glace Bay, N.S. Size 3 x 9.

9—TURQUAND, BERNARD—Although an Englishman by birth, he came of Huguenot stock. He was born in London, 2nd February, 1790, and came to Canada in 1820, holding office, under Hon. John Henry Dunn, in the Receiver-General's Department, and, in later years, in the Crown Lands Department. He was Grand Secretary of Provincial Grand (Masonic) Lodge in U.C., 1822-42. Water color. Size 9 x 10. Head and shoulders.

10—BEIKIE, JOHN—He came to York (Toronto) at an early date, and from 1810-15 was Sheriff of the Home District. Elected a member of the Legislature, Upper Canada, 1813, and Clerk of the Executive Council, succeeding John Small in 1832. For many years he attended St. James' Church (Anglican), Toronto. Mr. Beikie was a prominent member of the Masonic fraternity, serving as Deputy Grand Master, Second Provincial Grand Lodge, 1825-39. His death took place in March, 1839. Water color. Size 10 x 12. Head and shoulders. See 897.

11—FORT VANCOUVER—On the northern bank of the Columbia River, ninety miles inland from the sea. It was built in 1824-5 by John McLoughlin, first great leader of the Hudson's Bay Company in the Oregon. Primarily the site of the fort was about a mile from the river. This location, however, was found to be disadvantageous to transport and communication, and after a few years a removal was made to within a quarter of a mile of the Columbia. For nearly a quarter of a century Fort Vancouver was an emporium of the Hudson's Bay Company; for its central location gave access to interior trade as well as sea traffic. In 1846, on the determination of the Oregon boundary question, this fort passed into American territory, but until 1849 remained as a post of the company. To-day (1917) the place, known as Vancouver, capital of Clarke County, Washington, is the headquarters of the military department of the Columbia. Chromo lithograph. Size 8 x 12.

12—INDIAN TOMB—A memorial to the dead, erected by Indians in the pioneer days of Canada. H. J. Warre, del.; Dickinson & Co., lith. Chromo lithograph. Size 7 x 12.

13—"THE LAUNCH OF THE NORTHWEST AMERICA AT NOOTKA SOUND—Being the first vessel that was ever built in that part of the globe. C. Metz, del. R. Pollard, sculpt. Publish'd Augt. 16, 1790, by J. Walter & Son, No. 160 Piccadilly." The scene in picture took place in July, 1788, at Nootka Sound, west coast of Vancouver Island, where Capt. Meares, who arrived at the sound the previous May, had the "Northwest America" built. It was the first vessel, other than natives' canoes, constructed on the shores of what is now British Columbia. The word "Nootka" means "to go around," or "make a circuit." Line engraving. Size 8 x 10.

14—McGILLIVRAY, WILLIAM, MONTREAL—Elder brother of Simon McGillivray, and one of the founders of the Northwest Company. He was an active Mason in the early part of the nineteenth century, and from 1823-26 was Provincial Grand Master of the Montreal and William Henry districts of the Grand (Masonic) Lodge of England. Water color. Size 8 x 11. Head and shoulders.

15—SMART, REV. WILLIAM—Presbyterian missionary at Elizabethtown (Brockville). Early in life he resolved to devote himself to missionary work and became a student of the London Missionary Society. In April, 1811, in response to a petition from the inhabitants of Elizabethtown, Yonge and Augusta, he came to Canada, arriving at Elizabethtown (Brockville) in October following. For thirty-eight years he was pastor of the congregation of Brockville. He was an enthusiastic Free Mason and Grand Chaplain of the Second Provincial Grand Lodge of Upper Canada, 1823-5. Mr. Smart died at Gananoque 9th Sept., 1876. Knox College, Toronto, has a collection of letters and papers presented by Mrs. Smart, which are of great interest in connection with the early Presbyterian Church in Canada. Water color. Size 10 x 12. Head and shoulders.

16—McGILLIVRAY, SIMON—London, Montreal and Toronto—Born at Stratherrick, Inverness-shire, in 1783. About 1800 he emigrated to Canada, becoming actively interested in the North-West Company, gaining so much experience in connection with its business that he was entrusted with arranging the fusion of the Company with the Hudson's Bay Company. He was Provincial Grand Master of the Grand (Masonic) Lodge of Upper Canada, 1822-40. After the amalgamation of the North-West and Hudson's Bay Companies he joined the firm of McTavish, McGillivray & Co., of Montreal, returning to England when the firm retired from business. His death took place near London, England, in 1840. Water color from the original oil portrait in possession of the family of his son-in-law, the late Rear-Admiral Dawkins, of Stoke Gabriel, Devon, England. Size 9 x 10. Head and shoulders.

17—FACSIMILE OF ROBERT BURNS' MASONIC APRON—The apron is now in the possession of the Grand Secretary of the Grand Lodge A.F. and A.M. of Scotland, at Edinburgh. It is made of lambskin, the flap embroidered with blue thread, but both the face of the lambskin and the ornamental work are nearly all worn off. The celebrated Scottish bard was born at Kirk Alloway, near Ayr, January 25th, 1759. In 1781 he was initiated in St. David's Lodge (Masonic), Tarbolton; Deputy Master of the Lodge, July 27th, 1784. Affiliated with St. James' Lodge, Tarbolton. Exalted in St. Abbs R.A. Lodge, May 19th, 1787. Poet Laureate of Canongate Kilwinning Lodge, Edinburgh. Died July 21st, 1796. Photograph by W. E. Carnegie Dickson, son of R. W. Bro. G. Dickson, W.M. Lodge No. 1, Scotland; colored by Miss Bessie Dickson, daughter of the latter, presented to M.W. Bro. J. Ross Robertson by R.W. Bro. Dickson. Size 9 x 12.

18—RIDOUT, THOMAS GIBBS—Second son of Hon. Thomas Ridout, born at Sorel, L.C., 1792, accompanying his parents to York in 1796. In 1806 he was sent to school at Cornwall. From 1813-20 filled the position of Deputy Assisstant Commissary-General. He subsequently turned his attention to banking, and after studying the system in New York and Boston, was appointed cashier of the Bank of Upper Canada. Ridout was the first president of the Mechanics' Institute, Toronto, and as president of St. Andrew's Society welcomed Lord Elgin on his arrival in Toronto in 1849. He was Deputy Grand Master of the Provincial Grand (Masonic) Lodge of Upper Canada, 1845-57, and Honorary Past Grand Master of the Grand Lodge of Canada, 1859-61. His death took place in the latter year. Water color. Size 8 x 10. Head and shoulders.

19—MAXWELL—"Sir Murray Maxwell, Kt., C.B., 1775-1831. Drawn and etch'd by Richd. Dighton. Pub'd by Humphrey, St. James's St."—Born near Perth, Scotland, in 1775, the third son of Captain James Maxwell, of the 42nd Regiment. Entered the navy in 1790; accompanied Lord Amherst on his mission to China, exploring the Gulf of Pechili, west coast of Korea, and the Loo Choo Islands. In 1818 he received a knighthood. From 1821-2 was captain of the "Bulwark," and in 1823 commanded the "Briton" on the South American Station. Appointed Lieutenant-Governor of Prince Edward Island, May, 1831, and was preparing for his departure when he died suddenly, July 26th of that year. Etching in color. Size 9 x 12. Full length.

20—DUNCOMBE, DR. CHARLES—As a man of education, a medical practitioner, a politician and a member of the Masonic Fraternity, he commanded a prominent position in the western part of Upper Canada. He was born in Connecticut in 1794 and emigrated to Canada in 1820. Practised his profession in Burford, London and St. Thomas, and represented the County of Oxford in the Provincial Legislature. His influence was widespread as a leader of the Reform party. Forced on account of his views to leave the country in 1837, residing for many years in the United States. He died in Hicksville, California, 1st October, 1875. Water color. Size 8 x 10. Head and shoulders.

21—FRANKLIN, SIR JOHN, 1786-1847—Distinguished navigator and Arctic Explorer—He was born at Spilsby, Lincolnshire, Eng.; entered the navy as midshipman, about 1800. Served at Trafalgar in the Bellerophon. Franklin led his first overland expedition from York Factory, near the mouth of the Hayes River, to the Arctic Coast, in 1819-22; continued his explorations of the northern coast, 1825-7. He sailed with the "Terror" and "Erebus" in May, 1845, to make the North-West Passage, but never returned. Several expeditions were sent in search of him by England and America, without success. In the summer of 1859 a record, deposited by survivors of Franklin's party, was found in a cairn on the north-west shore of King William Land. It was supposed to have been built there in 1831 by James Ross. The record, bearing date 25th April, 1848, stated that Sir John had died 11th June, 1847, that the "Terror" and "Erebus" were abandoned 22nd April, 1848, when the survivors, numbering about a hundred, started for the Great Fish River. They evidently perished after leaving the vessels. Photogravure from painting by T. Phillips, in National Portrait Gallery, London, Eng. Size 5 x 6. Head and shoulders.

22—RADSTOCK, LORD WILLIAM WALDEGRAVE, FIRST BARON—"William, Lord Radstock, Admiral of the White. From a Painting in Water Colours by F. W. Wilkin. Drawn and engraved by C. Wilkin. Published Feb. 16, 1810, by T. Cadell and W. Davies, Strand, London." Admiral in the Pomone; captured the American privateer "Cumberland," and in the "Prudente" took "L'Americain." Accompanied Admiral Darby to the relief of Gibraltar; Colonel of Marines, 1794; third in command off Cape St. Vincent, 1797. Commander-in-Chief of Newfoundland, 1797-1800. G.C.B., 1815. Born in 1753 and died in 1825. Engraving. Size 8x9. Head and shoulders.

23—**KERR, DR. ROBERT**—A connection of Sir Robert Ker, afterwards Duke of Roxburghe, in the peerage of Scotland. Was born in 1755. He was an army surgeon in Sir John Johnson's 2nd Battalion, and settled at Niagara about 1789. Was judge of the Surrogate Court, Niagara, and served in War of 1812-15. Dr. Kerr was an active Mason in Niagara, and was Grand Master of the Provincial Grand Lodge, Niagara, 1807-20. Died in Albany, N.Y., 1824. Married Elizabeth, daughter of Molly Brant and Sir William Johnson, Bart. Water color from original miniature in possession of the Gillespie family, of Montreal, Que. Size 8 x 10. Head and shoulders.

24—**DUNN, HON. JOHN HENRY**—Born in St. Helena, 1794. Died in England, 21st April, 1854. Between 1817-20 he held an appointment in the Old East India Service Office, London, and in the latter year became Receiver-General; was member of Executive and Legislative Councils of Upper Canada, 1820-41; Grand Treasurer of the Provincial Grand Lodge of Masons of Upper Canada, 1822-24. His son, Alex. Roberts, fought bravely at Balaclava, and on his return to Canada was presented with a sword of honor by the Corporation of Toronto. Water color by Lady Green, wife of Major-General Sir Henry Rodes Green, and daughter of Hon. John Henry Dunn, from an oil painting in her possession. Size 6 x 8. Head and shoulders. See 244.

25—**"BIRD'S-EYE VIEW OF VICTORIA, VANCOUVER ISLAND, B.C.,** 1878—Drawn by E. S. Glover. Published by M. W. Waitt & Co., Victoria, B.C. A. L. Bancroft & Co., lithographers, San Francisco, Cal., U.S. Entered according to Act of Congress, in the year 1878, by E. S. Glover, in the office of the Librarian of Congress at Washington, D.C. Entered according to Act of Parliament of Canada, in the year 1878, by M. W. Waitt, in the office of the Minister of Agriculture." Chromo lithograph, with key. Size 19 x 32.

26—**MACNAB, SIR ALLAN NAPIER**—Born at Niagara, 1798, died in Hamilton, August, 1862—Was educated at the Home District School in York. After the surrender of York, Macnab accompanied the retreating forces to Kingston. He joined the 100th Regiment under Col. Murray, and for his conduct in connection with the taking of Fort Niagara was honored with ensigncy in the 49th Regiment. He was Speaker of the Legislative Assembly, Upper Canada, 1837-41, and Speaker of the first Parliament of United Canada, and Prime Minister in 1854. He was knighted in 1838, created a baronet in 1856, and in 1857 retired from public life. He was Grand Master Provincial Grand (Masonic) Lodge, Canada West, 1845-57, and Grand Master Ancient Grand Lodge of Canada, 1857-8. Water color. Size 8 x 10. Head and shoulders. See 1388.

27—**PHILLIPS, DR. ZIBA MARCUS**—Born at Oswego, N.Y., in 1787, the son of a U.E. Loyalist, who settled subsequent to the Revolutionary War in the Township of Augusta. Practised medicine from about 1816. He fought at Queenston Heights and Lundy's Lane, and in 1842 was Lieut.-Colonel of the 2nd Regiment, Grenville County Militia. He was the leading Freemason of Midland District, 1817-47. Died September, 1847, at Tin Cap, in Elizabethtown (Brockville). In St. Peter's Church, Brockville, is a mural Masonic tablet to his memory. Water color. Size 8 x 10. Head and shoulders.

28—**"LA PEROUSE**—From a miniature in possession of La Perouse's niece at Alby. Engraved by T. Woolnoth, under the superintendence of the Society for the Diffusion of Useful Knowledge. London. Published by Charles Knight, Ludgate street, and Pall Mall, East." Jean Francois Galoup de la Perouse, the eminent French navigator, was born at Albo (Tarn) in 1741. In 1756 he entered the navy; became lieutenant, 1775. Fought against English in the American War, 1778-83. Was senior captain of the victorious

French vessels in a naval battle with the English off Sydney Harbor, 21st July, 1781. In the following year captured the British Forts Churchill and York, on the Hudson's Bay coast. While on an exploring expedition in 1788, he, with his party, perished by shipwreck at Vanicoro (Wanicoro), an island in the Pacific. Size 4 x 5. Line engraving. Head and shoulders.

29—ALLEN—"John Carter Allen, Esqr., Admiral of the White Squadron. J. Northcote, Pinxt. H. R. Cook, Sculp. Published March 31, 1810, by J. Gold, Shoe Lane, Fleet Street." Present at capture of Louisburg, 1758; in command of the "Repulse," 32 guns, in the British fleet employed in the expedition against Martinique, 1762. Commanded the "Egremont," 74 guns, in the action off Ushant, July, 1778, and at the relief of Gibraltar, 1782. Admiral of the White, 1799. His death took place in 1800. Line engraving. Size 3 x 4. Head and shoulders.

30—DALY HON. SIR DOMINICK—Lieutenant-Governor of Prince Edward Island, 1854-9. Came to Canada as secretary to Sir Francis Burton. In 1827 became Provincial Secretary for L. C., and from the Union until 1848 held the same office for Canada. He was born in Co. Galway, Ireland, in 1798. Died in South Australia, 1868, during his term as Governor there. Original silhouette taken at Saratoga, Sept. 1st, 1840. Size 6 x 9. Full length.

31—HEARNE—"Mr. Samuel Hearne, late Chief at Prince of Wales's Fort, Hudson's Bay"—For several years a midshipman in the Royal Navy. He subsequently entered the service of the Hudson's Bay Company, and in 1769 was sent on an expedition to discover a North-West passage. Because of unsurmountable difficulties, the expedition was a failure, as was a second attempt. In December, 1770, however, he made a third essay and was this time successful, being the first European to penetrate to the Arctic Ocean from the interior. In 1774 he established Cumberland House, on the west shore of Cumberland or Pine Island Lake. It is still in existence, and at one time was the chief depot or fort of the Cumberland District of the Hudson's Bay Company. In 1782 during Hearne's governorship of Fort Prince of Wales, on the Churchill River, and one of the most impregnable strongholds on the continent, the fort was attacked and taken by La Perouse. Hearne was born in London, Eng., 1745. Died in 1792. Line engraving. Size 4 x 5. Head and shoulders. See 2758.

32—BRITISH COLUMBIA MINER, 1864—The dress of early miners in British Columbia is here accurately represented. The only natives of B.C. at that time were Indians and half-breeds, the very earliest settlers being employes of the Hudson's Bay Company, many of whom married Indian women. The men who were working in the country at the date of painting, attracted by the discovery of gold, came from all parts of the world. They were all adventurers and for the most part a superior class of men. In Cariboo one frequently met Oxford and Cambridge men. Most of the old-timers have passed away, and since the advent of the railways a new class has come in from all parts. The first Mines Report in British Columbia was published in 1874, so that it is difficult to estimate the number of miners in the country during the sixties, but it is said that there were about five hundred. To-day (1917) there are nearly ten thousand. Oil painting by William G. R. Hind. Size 3 x 5. Half length.

33—IMPERIAL BLUE BOOK MAP, 1819—Facsimile of section showing important points in events in the Red River Settlement, 1812-18. A—Seven Oaks, where massacre took place 19th June, 1816. B—Point from which the "Metis" left for Frog Plain (Kildonan). C—Kildonan, where Selkirk settlers from east coast of Sutherlandshire, Scotland, settled in 1812 and later. E-F—De Meuron settlers on the Seine River. They finally emigrated to United States in 1826. G—French half-breed settlement and church (St. Boniface). H—Fort Douglas, built 1813, mile below site of Fort Garry. I—Colony Gardens, where Selkirk colonists settled 1812, and later—now (1917) part of Winnipeg. J—Fort Gibraltar, built 1806 at forks of Red and Assiniboine. K—Road followed by "Metis" at Frog Plain. L—Plain rangers' dry cart trail, west of settlers' lots. Size 7 x 9.

34—VICTORIA, B.C., 1862—To the left is the bridge leading to the Songhees Reserve, and towards the upper right-hand corner of picture the Victoria District Church. The paddle-wheel steamer with the two funnels is the "Labouchere" (H.B. Co.'s), and the other paddle-wheel steamer is the "Pacific," alongside of which may be seen the "Forward." It is a difficult matter, in fact, almost an impossibility, states Mr. Edgar Fawcett, of Victoria, to define correctly the various points in this picture, which was made from a sketch taken from several positions. Water color. Size 6 x 9. See 2306, 2338.

35—SIMPSON—"Sir George Simpson, K.B. Painted by Stephen Pearce. Engraved by James Scott. London: Published by Henry Graves & Compy. March 5th, 1857. Printsellers to the Queen; 6 Pall Mall." He was born in Ross-shire, Scotland, 1792, later removing to London. Entered the service of the Hudson's Bay Company, and in 1820 left England to take up his duties in that connection in Canada. When the Hudson's Bay and North-West Companies coalesced, Simpson was made Governor of the Northern Department, later known as Rupert's Land, and general superintendent of the Hudson's Bay Company's affairs in North America. Active in exploring projects, and for his services in this respect he received a knighthood from Her Majesty Queen Victoria. He welcomed the Prince of Wales at Lachine, Que. (where Sir George latterly resided) in July, 1860. Died at Lachine in Sept. of that year. Engraving. Size 13 x 17. Half length.

36—VANCOUVER, COMMANDER GEORGE, R.N., of H.M.S. DISCOVERY—Navigator, discoverer and surveyor. Born at King's Lynn, England, 1757. In 1771 entered the Navy and sailed with Cook on his second and third voyages. Appointed lieutenant on the "Martin" sloop, 1780; removed to the "Fame" and sailed with Rodney for the West Indies, taking part in the victory over the French fleet, 12th April, 1782. In December, 1790, was promoted commander and given charge of the expedition along the north-west coast of America. In 1792 he met at Nootka Captain Quadra, in the service of Spain, commandant of Nootka, to carry out certain provisions of the Britannic-Spanish agreement. As a compliment to him Vancouver named the largest island on west coast of America "Quadra and Vancouver." It is now, however, known as Vancouver. Vancouver's exploring survey, which lasted from 1792-94, was zealously carried on and most successful. His death occurred in 1798. Oil painting from original by Lemuel F. Abbott, in the National Portrait Gallery, London, Eng. Size 14 x 17. Half length.

37—DARLING, SIR CHARLES HENRY—"His Excellency Charles Henry Darling, Esquire (late Governor of New Foundland), Captain General and Governor in Chief of the Island of Jamaica and its Dependencies—Governor of the Bay Islands, etc., etc., etc. Painted by Henry Phillips, London. Lith. of Sarony, Major and Knapp, 449 Broadway, N.Y." Born at Annapolis Royal, N.S., 1809, and educated at the Royal Military College, Sandhurst. In 1827 he was appointed assistant private secretary, and in 1830 military secretary to his uncle, Lieut.-Gen. Ralph Darling, then Governor of New South Wales. In 1833 appointed to the staff of Sir Lionel Smith; Lieutenant-Governor of St. Lucia, 1847, and in 1851 Lieutenant-Governor of Cape Colony, in the absence on military duty of the Governor, Sir George Cathcart. Sent to administer the Government of

Newfoundland and to inaugurate the system of "responsible government" there. Afterwards served as Captain-General and Governor-in-Chief of Jamaica, including the Government of the Honduras and the Bay Islands. In 1862 was made a K.C.B. in recognition of his long and effective public service. Died in 1870 at Cheltenham, England. Lithograph. Size 12 x 18. Full length.

38—"ENTRANCE TO DIGBY (N.S.) FROM THE NORTH—M. G. Hall, delt., Pendleton's Lithography, Boston." The view shows in the distance the Joggin shore and one of the entrances to the Bear River. Contiguous to where this picture was taken is the Gut of Digby. Chromo lithograph Size 6 x 9. See 2143.

39—"PARTRIDGE ISLAND AND THE HARBOUR OF ST. JOHN, N.B.— M. G. Hall, delt. Pendleton's Lithography, Boston." A quarantine station. The beacon light seen in the view between the island and the city of St. John stands on the outer point of a natural bar, which at low water becomes perfectly dry. The high lands of Nova Scotia are said to be distinctly seen from this island, previous to a storm, or at low water. Chromo lithograph. Size 6 x 9.

40—"FALLS OF THE ST. JOHN RIVER, NEAR INDIAN TOWN— Taken from the Carleton side. M. G. Hall, delt. Pendleton's Lithography, Boston." These falls are occasioned by the compression of the river waters into the gorge near the city. The rush of the upward tide and the Falls, which become visible at low tide, fill the stream with eddies which render navigation impossible. At a certain stage of flood-tide, and for a few minutes only, the gorge may be passed by vessels. Chromo lithograph. Size 6 x 9. See 1732.

41—TOWN AND HARBOR OF ST. JOHN'S, NEWFOUNDLAND, 1811—(With key). Water color from old sketches, showing the town and harbor, made by J. W. Hayward, an old resident of the place. Original in possession of the late Archbishop Howley, of St. John's. Size 10 x 27.

42—ST. JOHN'S, NEWFOUNDLAND, 1798—From the south-east. (With key). A unique view of one of the pioneer towns of the British American continent. From a drawing in water color, by R. P. Brenton, in the British Museum. Size 10 x 14.

43—OLD SPAR HOUSE AND DOCK, HALIFAX, N.S., 1888—Looking about north-north-west, towards the citadel. This view was evidently inspired by John Flemming's old spar yard, near what is now Geo. S. Campbell & Co.'s wharf, Lower Water street, near foot of Salter street. The spar house has been demolished. To be accurate topographically, the space below the citadel, in the distance to the right, should be shown filled with buildings, as here lies the heart of the city. For artistic purposes it has been left devoid of buildings. No such church is in the locality shown in background to the left; but the spire of St. Mary's Cathedral (R.C.) in that direction probably suggested its introduction. A most artistic pen drawing made for J. Ross Robertson, by F. Leo. Hunter, Ossining, N.Y. Size 14 x 24.

44—"THE GREAT FIRE AT ST. JOHN, N.B., JUNE 20TH, 1877—The fire broke out on York Point at half-past two p.m. and burned furiously until after midnight, consuming several hundred buildings, among which were the Post Office, Custom House, Academy of Music, eleven churches, a number of hotels, banks and various public buildings, the entire business portion of the city, and vessels at the wharves. Thirteen lives were lost. The total loss is estimated at $25,000,000. Published by Currier & Ives, 115 Nassau St., New York. Copyright, 1877, by Currier & Ives, N.Y." Chromo lithograph. Size 8 x 13.

45—ST. JOHN'S, NEWFOUNDLAND—"To his Excellency Sir Thomas John Cochrane, Knt., Governor and Commander-in-Chief of the Island of Newfoundland, etc., etc. This plate of the town and harbor of St. John's, is, with permission, respectfully dedicated by his Excellency's obliged, humble servant, William Eagar. Taken from Signal Hill, June 1st, 1831. London: Pub'd for the Proprietor, 1831, by H. Pyall, 115 London road." The harbor is small, but deep, and so landlocked that the water is always smooth, while the entrance is so narrow that it bears the name, "Narrows." Signal Hill, on the north side of the channel, is the grand observatory of the country. Aquatint, in color. **Size 16 x 23.**

46—"OFFICERS' BARRACKS AT FREDERICTON, WINTER, 1834— W. P. Kay, delt., from a sketch by Captn. Campbell. S. Russell, lith. Day and Haghe, Lithrs. to the King." Up to the point marked on the picture these barracks, or officers' quarters, are still standing. A portion was re-built in stone some time previous to Confederation, and the intention was to have the remainder rebuilt. The British soldiers, having removed from the Province, the project was not proceeded with. Chromo lithograph. Size 7 x 12.

47—ST. JOHN'S (PROVINCE OF QUEBEC)—"A south-west view of St. John's, shewing the fort and the detach'd redoubt, with the blockhouse opposite. J. Peachey, Ensn. 60th Regt., from the original view taken by J. Hunter. R. Regt. Arty. (v) Montgomery's Mortar Battery; (vv) Mont-gomery's Battery for Guns; (a) South Redoubt and Commanding Officer's Quarters; (b) North Redoubt, Magazine & Artillery Storehouses; (c) De-tached Redoubt, Officers' and Soldiers' Barracks; (d) Market Place; (v) Inflexible; (vv) Royal George." Water color. Size 13 x 24.

48—HALIFAX, N.S., FROM THE GLACIS LOOKING OVER THE HARBOR IN A NORTH-EASTERLY DIRECTION—"To the Right Honour-able George Dunk, his Majesty's Principal Secretary of State, etc., etc., etc. This plate, representing part of the town and harbour of Halifax in Nova Scotia, looking down George street to the opposite shore, called Dartmouth, is most humbly inscribed by his Lordship's most devoted servant, R. Short. Serres, pinxit. R. Short, delint. Jas. Mason, sculpsit. Published Ap. 25th, 1777, by John Boydell, engraver in Cheapside, London. 1. King's Yard; 2, Barracks; 3, Printing House; 4, Pontack's." With key. Line engraving. Size 13 x 20.

49—HALIFAX, N.S., AND THE HARBOUR FROM THE NORTH END OF GEORGE'S ISLAND, LOOKING NORTH-WESTWARD—"To the Right Honourable George Dunk, Earl of Halifax, his Majesty's Principal Secretary of State, etc., etc., etc. This plate, representing the town and harbour of Halifax, in Nova Scotia, as it appears from George Island, looking up to the King's Yard and Bason, is most humbly inscribed by his Lordship's most devoted servant, R. Short. Serres, pinx. R. Short, delint. Jas. Mason, sculp. Published Ap. 25th, 1777, by John Boydell, engraver in Cheapside, London." With key. Line engraving. Size 13 x 20.

50—"KINGSTON, CANADA WEST, FROM FORT HENRY. Drawn from nature by E. Whitefield, Kingston, published by E. Whitefield, 1855." With key. Lithograph. Size 20 x 34.

51—HALIFAX, N.S., FROM THE DARTMOUTH SHORE, LOOKING WEST-SOUTHWEST—"To the Rt. Honourable George Dunk, Earl of Halifax, his Majesty's Principal Secretary of State, etc., etc., etc. This plate, repre-senting the town and harbour of Halifax, in Nova Scotia, as they appear from the opposite shore, called Dartmouth, is most humbly inscribed by his Lordship's most devoted servant, R. Short. Serres, pinxt. R. Short, delint.

Mason, sculp. Published Ap. 25th, 1777, by John Boydell, engraver in Cheapside, London. 1. St. Paul's. 2. St. Mather's. 3. Governor's House. 4. Market Place. 5. George Street. 6. Duke Street. 7. Major's Houses and Wharf. 8 8 8, South, Middle and North Batteries." Line engraving. Size 13 x 20.

52—HALIFAX, N.S., FROM THE GLACIS OF THE CITADEL LOOKING OVER THE HARBOR IN A SOUTHEASTERLY DIRECTION—"To the Right Honorable George Dunk, Earl of Halifax, his Majesty's Principal Secretary of State, etc., etc., etc. This plate, representing part of the town and harbor of Halifax, in Nova Scotia, looking down Prince street to the opposite shore, shews the Eastern Battery, George and Cornwallis Islands, Thrum Cap, etc., to the sea off Chebucto Head, is most humbly inscribed by his Lordship's most devoted servant, R. Short. Serres, pinxt. R. Short, delin. Jas. Mason, sculpsit. Published Ap. 25th, 1777, by John Boydell, engraver in Cheapside, London. 1. Pontack's; 2. Governor's Summer House and Gardens; 3, Work House." Line engraving. Size 13 x 20.

53—HALIFAX, N.S.—View Looking Southwestward—"To the Right Honourable George Dunk, Earl of Halifax, his Majesty's Principal Secretary of State, etc., etc., etc. This plate, representing the Governor's House and St. Mather's Meeting House, in Holles street, also looking up George street, shews part of the Parade and Citadel Hill at Halifax, in Nova Scotia, is must humbly inscribed by his Lordship's most devoted servant, R. Short. Serres, pinx. R. Short, delint. Aveline, sculp. Published Ap. 25th, 1777, by John Boydell, engraver in Cheapside, London." Line engraving. Size 13 x 20.

54—GILBERT, SIR HUMPHREY—Founder of the first British Colony in North America. Scion of an ancient Devonshire family and step-brother of Sir Walter Raleigh; born in 1539. Educated at Eton and Oxford; afterwards distinguished himself in several military enterprises. M.P. for Plymouth, 1571. As Commander-in-Chief of the Province of Munster, Ireland, defeated the Spaniards off the Irish coast in 1579. Arrived at St. John's, Newfoundland, Aug. 5th, 1583, taking possession of the surrounding country in the name of Queen Elizabeth. Lost in a storm off the Southern Azores in 1583. Line engraving. Size 4 x 5. Head and shoulders.

55—RODNEY, LORD GEORGE BRYDGES—Governor of Newfoundland, 1748-9. Born at Walton-upon-Thames in 1718, and educated at Harrow, England, subsequently entering the Navy. Blockaded Havre, 1759-60; Commander-in-Chief of the Leeward Islands the following year. Reduced Martinique, St. Lucia, Grenada and Cape St. Vincent, 1762. For five years was Governor of Greenwich Hospital. Represented Northampton, Eng., in Parliament, 1768. Commander-in-Chief at Jamaica from 1771-4. Defeated Spanish off Cape St. Vincent; captured St. Eustatius, and in 1782 defeated the French off Dominica. Sir Joshua Reynolds, pinxt. P. W. Tomkins, pupil of F. Bartolozzi, sculpt. Stipple engraving. Size 3 x 4. Head and shoulders.

56—HURON CHIEFS AT LORETTE—"Michel Tsioui, Teacheandale, Chief of the Warriors; Stanislas Coska, Aharathaha, Second Chief of the Council; Andre Romain, Tsouhahissen, Chief of the Council. Three Chiefs of the Huron Indians Residing at La Jeune Lorette, near Quebec, in their National Costume. From a painting by E. Chatfield. Printed by C. Hullmandel. Published by J. Dickinson, 144 New Bond Street, 1825." The remnant of the Huron tribe which survived the massacres of 1648-9, since 1697, has made its home at Indian, or Jeune Lorette, some eight miles northwest of Quebec. The descendants of the ancient warlike tribe have largely intermarried with the French-Canadians, and French is the language principally spoken in the peaceful little village on the banks of the St. Charles. Lithograph, in color. Size 15 x 18.

57—"HALIFAX FROM McNAB'S ISLAND—Drawn from nature by W. Lyttleton, S. W. Chandler and Bro., Lith. Boston. Published by E. G. Fuller, Halifax, N.S." The capital and largest city of Nova Scotia is situated on the south-east coast of the Province, on the slope of a rocky peninsula. It is enclosed by a splendid harbor six miles long and a mile wide. McNab's Island, from which this view was made in 1862, by Capt. Westcote W. Lyttleton, of the 64th Regt., is three miles in length and lies at the mouth of Halifax Harbor, affording, with George's Island, an excellent shelter for it. On McNab's Island are Fort McNab and other batteries, which cross fire with that of York Redoubt on the west shore. Lithograph. Size 13 x 19.

58—ALEXANDER, SIR WILLIAM—"A true portrait of William, Earl of Stirling, at the age of fifty-seven. Published Novr. 1, 1795, by Wm. Richardson, No. 2 Castle street, Leicester Square." The celebrated poet, courtier and colonist was born in Scotland, near Stirling. The date of his birth is uncertain, some authorities giving 1567, and others, 1580. In 1621 he became interested in colonization and persuaded James I. to grant him a charter covering a large territory in North America—practically what is now Nova Scotia, New Brunswick, and Prince Edward Island. The colony was named "New Scotland." Shortly after the accession to the throne of Charles I., Sir William was made a Privy Councillor and Secretary of State for Scotland, which offices he held until his death. Created a peer in 1630, under the title of Viscount of Stirling and Lord Alexander of Tullibody; three years later was raised to the dignity of Earl of Stirling. Viscount Canada, etc. He contributed largely to the literature of his time, first coming into prominence as the author of "The Tragedies of Darius." He also completed the version of the Psalms of David, under-taken by King James I. His death took place in 1640. Line engraving. Size 5 x 7. Head and shoulders.

59—"SLEIGH MEETING ON THE ST. LAWRENCE—Quebec in the distance. Wildrake, del. W. Radcliffe, sc. London. R. Ackermann, 191 Regent St., Feby. 1, 1841." Chromo lithograph. Size 4 x 5.

60—SCHANK—"Captn. John Schank, Royal Navy. I. J. Masquerier, pinxt. C. Turner, sculpt. London, published Octr. 19, 1799, by C. Turner, No. 40 Castle St., Oxford Road." Born in Fifeshire, Scotland, 1740. En-tered the Navy in 1758, on board the "Duke." Promoted in 1776 to lieuten-ancy, and put in command of the "Canso," employed in the St. Lawrence. Fitted out several vessels on Canadian lakes, and had control of establish-ments at Quebec, St. John and Detroit. Built at Quebec the "Inflexible," commanding her on Lake Champlain, October, 1776. Schank, who was a talented seaman and engineer, retired in 1802, became Rear-Admiral, 1805, and in 1822 Admiral of the Blue. Died at Dawlish Devonshire, 1823. Photograph. Size 6 x 7. Head and shoulders. See 1682.

61—PRENTICE'S PERILOUS JOURNEY FROM QUEBEC—"The departure of S. W. Prentice, ensign of the 84th Regiment, and five others, from their shipwrecked companions in the depth of winter, 1781. Mr. Prentice was sent with public despatches from Govr. Haldiman at Quebec, to Sir Heny. Clinton at New York, who, with 18 seamen and passengers, were cast away on a desolate, uninhabited part of the Island of Cape Breton, Decr. 5, 1780. Five perished and several lost their fingers and toes by the severity of the cold. The survivors continued in this place several weeks, when Mr. Prentice and such as were able, embarked in a small, shatter'd boat to seek some inhabited country. They stopped the leakes of their boat by pouring water on its bottom till the holes were closed up with ice. During a voyage of two months, in which they suffered incredible hardships, and at length, worn out with fatigue, benumbed, diseased and famished, they were discovered by some of the native Indians. These friendly savages afterwards went to assist those who had been left at the wreck, of whom 5 only were found alive, and they had subsisted many days on the bodies of their dead companions. (See Ensign Prentice's Narrative). Painted by Robt. Smirke. Engraved by Robt. Pollard. Aquatinta by F. Jukes. London: Pub'd March 8, 1784, by R. Pollard, No. 15 Brayne's Row, Spa Fields, and R. Wilkinson, No. 58 Cornhill." Size 15 x 21.

62—"THE QUEBEC DRIVING CLUB MEETING AT THE PLACE D'ARMES is humbly dedicated by permission to the Rt. Honourable the Earl of Dalhousie, Patron of the Club, by a member, his Lordship's most obedient and very humble servant, William Wallace, Ensign 71st Lt. Inf. Sketched by W. Wallace. Engraved by J. Smillie, Junr. Published by D. Smillie & Sons, Quebec, 1826." The Place d'Armes, in the time of the French called the Grande Place, was the scene of military parades and a fashionable promenade. It was the regular meeting place of the Tandem Club, which flourished in Quebec when it was a garrison town. In 1650, the Huron Indians, who had been driven from Lake Simcoe, encamped here. To the left of the picture (No. 2) is shown an old French building, used as militia headquarters, formerly a commissariat building, where in the early part of the century was kept the specie to be paid out to the troops and army contractors. The Church of England Cathedral is on the right, while in the foreground is the Place d'Armes. The habitant, in the lower left hand corner, is driving his sleigh exactly opposite the site of old Castle Haldimand. Photograph of an engraving. Size 6 x 10.

63—"QUEBEC—Engraved by permission, from the picture painted for Her Majesty, Queen Victoria, by L. R. O'Brien, President Royal Canadian Academy of Arts. Engraved by A. Willmore." Size 5 x 9.

64—RAPIDS OF WHITE EARTH LAKE, THUNDER BAY DISTRICT —A picturesque spot. White Earth Lake, White Clay Lake and White Water Lake are all tributaries of the Ogoki River, which falls into the Albany River in the northern section of Thunder Bay District. These rapids are at the west end of White Earth Lake, about 160 miles north of Port Arthur. Water color. By Wm. Armstrong, C.E., 1869. Size 8 x 12.

65—"A VIEW OF THE FALL AT MONTMORENCI, and the Attack made by Genl. Wolfe, on the French Intrenchments near Beauport, with the Grenadiers of the Army, July 31st, 1759. 1. Quebec. 2. Point Levy. 3. Orleans. Capt. Smith, del. J. Smith, sculp. London. Printed for Robt. Sayer, Print and Mapseller, No. 53 Fleet street." Engraving, printed in color. Size 6 x 10. See 2082.

66—"VIEW OF THE VILLAGE OF ST. THOMAS, RIVIERE DE SUD, AND REGENT'S BRIDGE—J. Bouchette, Esqr., del. Engrav'd by W. J. Bennett." This place, now (1917) known as Montmagny, is the county town of Montmagny. Its proper designation is St. Thomas de Montmagny. The town is one of the oldest on the banks of the St. Lawrence, a parish having been first established there in 1679. Many of the original inhabitants were Bretons. Riviere du Sud is a small but beautiful stream, rising in the hills to the south-west in Bellechasse Co., joining the St. Lawrence at Montmagny. Size 5 x 9.

67 to 71—These pictures comprise views of Quebec, published in Germany about 1775—four engraved and printed in color by F. X. Habermann, and one by B. F. Leizelt. They are imaginary, and were made for panoramic representation. No mention is made of these prints by P. Lee Phillips, F.R.G.S., of the Library of Congress, Washington, in his work cataloguing the maps, plans, etc., of America, while Dr. A. G. Doughty, Dominion Archivist, briefly catalogues them in his "Bibiliography of the Siege of Quebec." Mr. Phileas Gagnon, however, the keeper of the Judicial Archives of Quebec, says with regard to them:—"These very curious views are rather the fruit of an inventive imagination than pic-

tures of the localities indicated; but, in spite of this, they are desirable additions to a collection of Canadian views. Four views of Boston and two of New York, of a similar character to these, were made at the same time by the same German designers." The inscriptions on the pictures are in French and in German.

67—**VIEW OF THE UPPER TOWN OF QUEBEC**—Showing the route leading to the Cavalier of the Windmill. Sold at Augsburg, at the general establishment of the Imperial Academy of Fine Arts, by the privilege granted by his Imperial Majesty, and with a prohibition to make or sell copies. Engraved by Francois Xav. Habermann." Printed in color. Size 10 x 16.

68—**QUEBEC**—"A town of Canada in North America, near the left bank of the River St. Lawrence. It was the capital of New France, but the English took it in 1759, and by the treaty of peace which followed it was ceded to the Crown of England with whole of Canada. Sold at Augsburg, at the general establishment of the Imperial Academy of Fine Arts, by the privilege granted by his Imperial Majesty, and with a prohibition to make or sell copies. Engraved by Balth. Frederic Leizelt." Mr. E. T. D. Chambers, of Quebec, thinks this is a "complete fake picture." None of the buildings can be identified, simply because they never existed, except in the imagination of the artist. Printed in color. Size 10 x 16.

69—**VIEW OF THE RECOLLETS STREET IN THE UPPER TOWN OF QUEBEC**—Sold at Augsburg at the general establishment of the Imperial Academy of Fine Arts, by the privilege granted by his Imperial Majesty, and with a prohibition to make or sell copies. Engraved by Francois Xav. Habermann." No record of any Recollets street can be found in Quebec. If the buildings in the picture bore any resemblance to the Recollets church or convent, which they do not, then the street would be Anne, but none of the buildings or surroundings as shown can be identified by views of the period. Printed in color. Size 10 x 16.

70—**VIEW OF THE LOWER TOWN OF QUEBEC**—Near the St. Lawrence River. Sold at Augsburg, at the general establishment of the Imperial Academy of Fine Arts, by the privilege granted by his Imperial Majesty, and with a prohibition to make or sell copies. Engraved by Francois Xav. Habermann." No architecture of the magnificence shown in the picture ever marked the river front of Quebec in olden time. Printed in color. Size 10 x 16.

71—**VIEW OF THE PRINCIPAL SQUARE IN THE LOWER TOWN OF QUEBEC**—Sold at Augsburg at the general establishment of the Imperial Academy of Fine Arts by the privilege granted by his Imperial Majesty, and with a prohibition to make or sell copies. Engraved by Francois Xav. Habermann." The "Place Capitale" of the Lower Town in the eighteenth century was Sault au Matelot street, then, as now, little more than a narrow lane, and bearing no resemblance at all to this picture. Printed in color. Size 10 x 16.

72—**FULFORD**—"Rt. Rev. Francis Fulford, D.D., Lord Bishop of Montreal, 1850. Drawn, Engraved and Published July 15th, 1851, by Mr. Skelton, 118 Albany St., Regents Park." In 1850 Bishop Mountain's wish that Montreal should be formed into a separate diocese was realized. Rev. Francis Fulford, of Curzon Chapel, Mayfair, was chosen as the new bishop. His consecration took place in Westminster Abbey, in July, his enthronement taking place 15th Sept., following, at Christ Church, Montreal, which thereafter became the Anglican Cathedral of the diocese. Bishop Fulford was a tireless worker. He endeavored to establish a church school for girls in Montreal, wrote letters to and delivered lectures to mechanics at their institutes and to library associations. When the Montreal cemetery was set apart his Lordship advocated that the entire ground be dedicated to a common purpose instead of separating on denominational lines. In 1859 he was appointed Metropolitan of Canada. He was born at Sidmouth, Eng., 1803, and died in Montreal, 9th September, 1868. Line engraving. Size 10 x 13. Half length.

73—CAPTURE OF LOUISBOURGH, 26TH JULY, 1758—"Captn. Laforey, with 25 boats, attack'd and took the 'Prudent,' of 74 guns; but finding her aground, was obliged to burn her. Captn. Balfour, with 25 boats, attack'd, took and towed off the 'Bienfaisant,' of 64 guns, into the n.e. harbour, then in possession of the British troops. To the captains, other officers and seamen, who (with a detachment of boats from the fleet commanded by Admiral Boscawen), burnt the 'Prudent' and took the 'Bienfaisant' into Louisbourgh Harbour about 1 o'clock in the morning of the 26th July, 1758. In memory of that singular and brave action this representation is humbly inscribed by their most obedient servant, Richd. Paton. R. Paton, pinxit. P. C. Canot, sculp. Publish'd according to Act of Parliament, 14th Feb., 1771." Line engraving. Size 14 x 23. See 2433-4, 2442-3.

74—KIDD, REV. ADAM, 1802-31—Author of "The Huron Chief" and other poems. The works of Kidd exhibit considerable powers of versification. "The Huron Chief" was published at the office of the Herald and New Gazette, Montreal, in 1830. Mr. Kidd died at Quebec, 5th July, 1831. Water color. By E. H., 1828. Size 4 x 6. Half length.

75—DE SALABERRY, IGNACE-MICHEL L.A.—Born at the Manor House, Beauport, July, 1752, and educated in France. Father of the "Hero of Chateauguay." He was a personal friend of the Duke of Kent during the latter's sojourn in Canada with his regiment. M. de Salaberry died March 22nd, 1825. From silhouette in possession of M. Hertel La Rocque, Montreal. Size 3 x 5. Head and shoulders.

76—DE SALABERRY, MADAME (Catherine Francois de Hertel)— Wife of Ignace Michel L. A. de Salaberry, and mother of the "Hero of Chateauguay." Her death occurred at Beauport, Quebec, 1824. From silhouette in possession of M. Hertel La Rocque, Montreal. Size 3 x 4. Head and shoulders.

77—DE SALABERRY, COL. HON. CHARLES MICHEL D'IRUM-BERRY, C.B.—Born at the Manor House of Beauport, Que., 1778; died at Chambly, 1829. Member of the Legislative Council, Quebec. Served in the West Indies under Prescott. Present at the conquest of Martinique, 1794; stationed in Ireland, 1809, and in the following year took part in the Walcheren expedition. Returned to Canada in 1811, as aide-de-camp to Major-General de Rottenburg. Called the "Hero of Chateauguay" for his bravery on October 26th, 1813, when he defeated the United States troops under General Hampton. Photograph from a portrait in the Chateau de Ramezay collection, Montreal. Size 5 x 7. Head and shoulders.

78—PAPINEAU, HON. LOUIS JOSEPH, 1786-1870—Drawn by Maurin. Lithographed by Maurin, Rue de Vaugirard, 72, Paris. Size 11 x 14. Head and shoulders. See 1675.

79—HABITANT OVEN, 1860—Ovens similar to that shown in the picture are to be seen in the majority of French-Canadian parishes in the Province of Quebec, and are operated exactly as the ovens of professional bakers in the towns. They are built of brick with an arched top. In fact, except that the bottom of the oven is flat, they are shaped like half an egg. They are covered with mortar or cement on the outside for better preservation of the structure, and have usually an outer wooden covering as shown in the picture. Almost every house is provided with one of these ovens. A fire of wood is made in the oven, and, when the latter has become well heated, the fire is raked out, the oven carefully swept, and the loaves of dough inserted. The splendid home-made bread thus produced by a skilful housewife is baked through in about an hour. Water color, by Charles E. Moss, near Murray Bay, 1860. Size 10 x 13. See 1909.

80—TACHE, SIR ETIENNE PASCAL—Celebrated political leader prior to Confederation—Born at St. Thomas, C.E., 1795. On the outbreak of hostilities in 1812 he entered the Incorporated Militia of Lower Canada as an ensign. During the war was promoted to a lieutenancy in the Canadian Chasseurs. When peace was declared young Tache studied medicine and practised his profession successfully until 1841. In that year he entered Parliament, and six years later was appointed Deputy Adjutant-General, holding that office until his entrance to the Lafontaine-Baldwin Ministry as Commissioner of Public Works, 1848. Became Receiver-General in 1849, and Speaker of the Legislative Council, 1856. In recognition of his distinguished services received a knighthood in 1858. Aide-de-camp to her late Majesty Queen Victoria, and as such was attached to the suite of H.R.H. Prince of Wales during his tour through Canada, 1860. Lithograph. Size 7 x 9. Half length.

81—CARTIER, SIR GEORGE ETIENNE—Provincial Secretary in the Macnab-Tache Ministry. Born at St. Antoine, Vercheres Co., L.C., 1814. Educated at the College of St. Sulpice, Montreal. Studied law and successfully practised his profession in that city. Entered Parliament in 1848, first representing Vercheres, and later Montreal. Assisted in carrying the bill for the abolition of seigniorial tenures. Died in London, Eng., 1873. Lithograph. Size 7 x 9. Head and shoulders.

82—QUEBEC PAGEANT, 1908—Samuel de Champlain, Governor of New France, 1612-29 and 1633-5, as represented at the Pageant. Reproduction in color from sketch by George Agnew Reid, Toronto. Size 4 x 6. Full length. See 1641.

83—QUEBEC PAGEANT, 1908—Champlain at the Court of Henri IV. of France, 1603. Champlain had left Canada in August, 1603, for France, and while there visited Court, where he was always welcome. He made his report and presented maps in connection with his expedition, to the King, who at once recognized the importance of peopling the New World and securing rights already obtained by France. Reproduction in color by George Agnew Reid. Size 4 x 6.

84—QUEBEC PAGEANT, 1908—Le Don de Dieu (the Gift of God), the ship in which Champlain came to Canada in 1608. Reproduction in color from sketch by George Agnew Reid, Toronto. Size 4 x 6. See 1161.

85—QUEBEC PAGEANT, 1908—Review of the Historic Armies on the Plains of Abraham before H.R.H. the Prince of Wales (King George V.), July, 1908. Reproduction in color from an oil painting in the Dominion Archives, by Frank Craig. Size 4 x 6.

86—QUEBEC PAGEANT, 1908—Bishop Laval (first Roman Catholic Bishop of Quebec) receiving the Marquis de Tracey, and the Intendant Talon, 1665. Reproduction in color. Size 4 x 6.

4

87—ICE PONT, QUEBEC—"This View of the Ice Pont formed between Quebec and Point Levi in the Year 1831, is by special permission dedicated to his Most Excellent Majesty William the Fourth. From a drawing by Lieut.-Col. Cockburn. Engraved by J. Stewart. London. Pubd. 1833, by Ackermann & Co., 96 Strand. Plate 2." Line engraving. Size 17 x 27.

88—LOWER CITY, QUEBEC—"This View of the Lower City of Quebec from the parapet of the Upper City, is by special permission dedicated to his Most Excellent Majesty William the Fourth. From a drawing by Lieut.-Col. Cockburn. Aquatint by C. Hunt. London. Pubd. 1833, by Ackermann & Co., 96 Strand. Plate 6." Engraving. Size 17 x 27.

89—CAPE DIAMOND AND WOLFE'S COVE—"This View of Quebec, from Cape Diamond and Wolf's Cove from Point a Pizeau is by special permission dedicated to his Most Excellent Majesty William the Fourth. From a drawing by Lieut.-Col. Cockburn. Engraved by C. Hunt. London. Pubd. 1833, by Ackermann & Co., 96 Strand. Plate 1." Line engraving. Size 17 x 27.

90—SOUTHEAST VIEW OF QUEBEC—Chromo xylograph from the Atlantic Neptune. Size 12 x 22.

91—QUEBEC FROM PT. LEVI—"This View of Quebec, from below Aubigny Church, Point Levi, is by special permission dedicated to his Most Excellent Majesty William the Fourth. From a drawing by Lieut.-Col. Cockburn. Engraved by H. Pyall. London: Pubd. 1833, by Ackermann & Co., 96 Strand. Plate 3." Line engraving. Size 17 x 27.

92—CONE OF MONTMORENCY—"This View of the Cone of Montmorency, as it appeared in 1829, is by special permission dedicated to his Most Excellent Majesty William the Fourth. From a drawing by Lieut.-Col. Cockburn. Aquatint by C. Bently. London. Pubd., 1833, by Ackermann & Co., 96 Strand. Plate 5." The gentleman and lady in the centre are Lieut.-Col. and Mrs. Cockburn, and the two young men on the right and left are their sons. The features of the Colonel can be readily distinguished with the aid of a glass. Line engraving. Size 17 x 27. See 1998.

93—FALLS OF MONTMORENCY—"This View of the Falls of Montmorency (Quebec in the Distance), is by special permission dedicated to his Most Excellency Majesty William the Fourth. From a drawing by Lieut.-Col. Cockburn. Engraved by C. Hunt. London. Pubd., 1833, by Ackermann & Co., 96 Strand. Plate 4th." Line engraving. Size 17 x 27. See 1961.

94—QUEBEC PAGEANT, 1908—The arrival of the Ursulines at Quebec, 1639. Madame de la Peltrie with two Ursulines from Tours, France, and one from Dieppe, sailed on 4th May, 1639, for Quebec, in company with the Hospitalieres. They arrived at Quebec, 1st August, and shortly afterwards were established on the banks of the St. Charles River. Their first convent was completed in 1641. The order was founded on St. Catharine's Day, 1537, and in 1544 its constitution was approved of by the Sovereign Pontiff, Paul III. Reproduction in color. Size 4 x 6.

95—QUEBEC PAGEANT, 1908—Arrival of Madame de Champlain at Quebec in 1620—Helene Boulle, wife of the founder of Quebec and Montreal, was the daughter of Nicholas Boulle, secretary of the King's Chamber. She was born in 1598, and in 1610 her marriage to Champlain took place. Owing to her extreme youth, however, she returned to her parents' home for a time. In 1620 she came to Quebec with her husband, remaining only four years in this country. Originally a Calvinist, she was converted to the Roman Catholic faith by her husband, and, after his death, entered the Monastery of St. Ursula, Paris. In 1648 she founded an Ursuline monastery at Meaux, where she died in 1654. Reproduction in color. Size 4 x 6.

96—QUEBEC PAGEANT, 1908—Return of the Iroquois from the Massacre at the Long Sault, 1660—In the spring of 1660 several hundred Iroquois gathered at the mouth of the Ottawa for the purpose of invading Montreal, Quebec and Three Rivers. Dollard, a young French officer, and a company of sixteen, joined by forty Hurons, determined to put up a defence at the Sault. Dollard and his companions were killed, but the Iroquois had received such a surprise that for the time being they gave up the project of invasion. Reproduction in color. Size 4 x 5.

97—QUEBEC PAGEANT, 1908—Jacques Cartier recounting the story of his discoveries in Canada to Francis I., King of France, 1534. Reproduction in color. Size 4 x 6.

98—MONTCALM, M. DE—Last descendant in a direct line of the great French General. In appreciation of the part taken by Hon. P. J. O. Chauveau at the inauguration of the St. Foye monument, 19th Oct., 1862, M. de Montcalm sent him a photograph. The writing on the left-hand card may be translated:—"This portrait was given me by M. Quibusque in behalf of M. de Montcalm, who sent it in acknowledgment of my oration at the laying of the corner-stone of the St. Foye monument and who placed his autograph on the portrait." This monument was erected about a mile from the city by the St. Jean Baptiste Society of Quebec, to the memory of those who fell on both sides in the battle of St. Foye, 1760. The French were commanded by de Levis, and the English, who were defeated, by Murray. Photograph. Size 4 x 7. Full length.

99—YORK PIONEER AND HISTORICAL SOCIETY, 1915—Photo, with key. Size 14 x 19. See 1135, 1141, 1145.

100—ISAACSON, ROBERT PHILIP—"Dolly of the Chop House, Montreal. Lith. of Sarony and Major, New York." Isaacson, who was born in London, Eng., named his eating-house after "Dolly's Chop House" of that city. He kept his establishment, first on St. Francois-Xavier St., north side, opposite Hospital St. (1845-8), and later on the west side of St. James St., where the Royal Bank now stands, next door west of the old St. Lawrence Hotel. His Chop House was one of the popular resorts and the most famed of all Montreal restaurants down to his death, and a favorite resort of the officers of the large British Garrison. "Dolly" used to sit in front of his place and lay down the law—a typical and very handsome "John Bull," always dressed in knee breeches and suit of old-time cut. Chromo lithograph. Size 11 x 15. Full length, sitting.

101—PORTEOUS, ANDREW—Postmaster of Montreal, 1832-43—He was born in 1780, and became a well-known merchant in Montreal; a partner in the firm of Porteous, Hancock and McGill (later Hon. Peter McGill). The last-named member of the firm was originally a McCutcheon, but assumed the surname of McGill in order to inherit the property of his uncle, Hon. Peter McGill. Mr. Porteous was one of the founders of St. Paul's Presbyterian Church, Montreal. His death occurred Dec. 16th, 1849, in Toronto. Charles Morgan, of the Merchants' Bank, Montreal, is a grandson. Water color. Size 3½ x 4. Head and shoulders.

102—McGILL, HON. JAMES, 1744-1813—Founder of McGill University, Montreal—At an early age he came to Canada from Scotland, engaging for some years in western fur trade. Represented Montreal in Parliament of Lower Canada, and was a member of the Legislative and Executive Councils. He was also an officer of the militia, rising to the rank of brigadier-general in the War of 1812. As a philanthropist and benefactor

Mr. McGill was well known. He devoted a great deal of his wealth to institutions in Montreal, which owes much to his liberality in leaving property and money for the purpose of founding the college that bears his name. Photogravure from engraving in Library of McGill University, Montreal. Size 4 x 5. Half length.

103—"QUEBEC FROM BEAUPORT—Drawn from nature and on stone by E. Whitefield. Printed in tint by Maclear & Co., Toronto, C.W. Published by E. Whitefield, 16 King St., Toronto., in 1855. Entered according to the Act of the Provincial Legislature in the year of our Lord, 1855, by Edwin Whitefield in the office of the Registrar of the Province of Canada." With key. Size 20 x 36.

104—"VICTORIA BRIDGE, MONTREAL, CANADA—Summer View to accompany Hunter's Hand Book of Victoria Bridge. Dedicated by permission to the Grand Trunk Railway Co., of Canada. W. S. Hunter, Del. Sarony, Major & Knapp, Liths., 449 Broadway, N.Y. Entered according to Act of Congress in the year 1860 by Sarony, Major & Knapp, in the Clerk's Office of the District Court of the Southern District of New York. Description—Length of Bridge, $1\frac{3}{4}$ miles. Length of Tube, 6,600 feet, $1\frac{1}{4}$ miles. Height of centre tubes, 22 feet. Height of end tubes, 19 feet. Width of tubes, 16 feet. Length of side spans, 242 feet. Length of centre span, 330 feet. Number of spans, 25. Cost of bridge, $6,300,000." Lithograph, in color. Size 8 x 26. See 115, 1866-7.

105—"SAINT JAMES'S STREET, MONTREAL—R. A. Sproule, Delt. W. L. Leney, Sc. Published by A. Bourne, Montreal, 1830." Engraved in aquatint. Size 9 x 14. See 107.

106—"NORTH-EAST VIEW, NOTRE DAME STREET, MONTREAL— Drawn by John Murray. Bourne, Engr." One of the oldest streets in Montreal. The Parish Church of Ville Marie, the first Church of Notre Dame, formerly stood directly in the centre of Notre Dame Street, in front of the present Cathedral. To the left is seen Nelson's Column, erected by the English and French residents of the city in 1809 to the memory of the hero of Trafalgar. It is strange that the renowned Admiral has his back to the sea. Engraved and printed in color. Size 9 x 11. See 110, 113.

107—"GREAT ST. JAMES STREET, MONTREAL—Drawn by John Murray. Bourne, Engr." Dollier de Casson, first historian of Montreal, laid out the streets in 1672. St. James street, or Rue St. Jacques, was so named in honor of Jean Jacques Olier, a courtier abbe of Paris, who felt called to leave his social sphere in the gay city and found a mission in the Island of Montreal. He was one of the party who, with Maisonneuve, landed on 18th May, 1642, at Montreal. Engraved and printed in color. Size 9 x 11. See 105.

108—"VIEW OF THE CHAMP DE MARS, MONTREAL—R. A. Sproule, Delt., W. L. Leney, Sc. Published by A. Bourne, Montreal, 1830." Engraved and printed in color. Size 9 x 14.

109—"PLACE D'ARMES, MONTREAL—R. A. Sproule, Delt. W. L. Leney, Sc. Published by A. Bourne, Montreal, 1830." In 1836 the City of Montreal purchased the ground from the gentlemen of the Seminary, and some years later the square was paved and enclosed. In the centre is a bronze statue, erected in 1892, of Maisonneuve, the founder of the city. Facing the square is seen the parish church of Notre Dame, built in 1824 to replace the church of 1672. The towers are 227 feet high and contain a magnificent set of bells, including "Le Gros Bourdon." Engraved and printed in color. Size 9 x 14. See 112.

110—"NOTRE DAME STREET, MONTREAL—R. A. Sproule, Delt. W. L. Leney, Sc. Published by A. Bourne, Montreal, 1830." Engraved and printed in color. Size 9 x 14. See 113.

111—"VIEW OF THE HARBOR, MONTREAL—R. A. Sproule, Delt. W. L. Leney, Sc. Published by A. Bourne, Montreal, 1830." Engraved and printed in color. Size 9 x 14.

112—"PLACE D'ARMES, MONTREAL—Drawn by John Murray. Bourne, Engr." Engraved and printed in color. Size 9 x 10. See 109.

113—"SOUTH-WEST VIEW NOTRE DAME STREET, MONTREAL— Drawn by John Murray. Bourne, Engr." On the right is shown the Parish Church of Notre Dame, facing on the street; in the distance, to the left, is the old St. Gabriel Street Presbyterian Church, adjoining the Champ de Mars. This was the first Protestant church erected in Montreal, having been built in 1792. A new church was afterwards built on St. Catharine street, the congregation holding their first service in it in 1886. The old structure was demolished in 1903 to make room for an extension of the Court House. Engraved and printed in color. Size 9 x 11. See 110.

114—"VIEW OF MONTREAL FROM SAINT HELEN'S ISLAND— R. A. Sproule, Delt. W. L. Leney, Sc. Published by A. Bourne, Montreal, 1830." Engraved and printed in color. Size 9 x 14. See 203.

115—"VICTORIA BRIDGE, MONTREAL, CANADA—Winter View— To Accompany Hunter's Hand Book of Victoria Bridge. Dedicated by permission to the Grand Trunk Railway Co., of Canada. W. S. Hunter, Del. Sarony, Major & Knapp, Liths., 449 Broadway, N.Y. Entered according to Act of Congress in the year 1860 by Sarony, Major & Knapp in the Clerk's Office of the District Court of the Southern District of N.Y." Lithograph in color. Size 8 x 26. See 104, 1866-7.

116—"SLEIGHING IN CANADA—On the River St. Lawrence, facing Montreal, 1841—No. 1, Captn. Sandeman; 2, Captn. Clitherow, A.D.C.; 3, Mr. Warre, A.D.C.; 4, Mr. Baring, A.D.C.; 5, Lt.Coll. Whyte, 7th Huzzars; 6, Mrs. Murdock; 7, Mrs. Shirley; 8, Major Dickson, A. Adjt.-Genl.; 9, Mr. Raynier, Rl. Artly.; 10, Earl of Mulgrave, A.D.C.; 11, Coll. The Honble. C. Gore. Drawn by Mrs. Shirley and Mr. Warre, A.D.C. C. Warren, Lith." Chromo lithograph. Size 10 x 30.

117—BOUNDARY BETWEEN UNITED STATES AND CANADA— Iron Post at St. Regis, Que—At St. Regis, in Huntingdon Co., Que., on the St. Lawrence and St. Regis Rivers, may be seen one of the cast iron obelisks, three and a half feet high, placed as boundary monuments at certain intervals along that frontier line. Upon the four sides of the obelisk were inscriptions in raised letters giving the name of the treaty, the date, and the names of the commissioners, and the fact that the obelisk marked the boundary between the United States and Canada. On the west face—"Boundary, August 9, 1842"; on the east—"Treaty of Washington"; on the north, the name of the British Commissioner, "Lieutenant-Colonel J. B. B. Estcourt, H.B.M., Com."; on the south face, "Albert Smith, U.S. Com." Photograph, colored. Size 5 x 5.

118—THORNTON, LT.-GEN. WILLIAM—Military Secretary to Sir James H. Craig, Governor of Canada, 1807-11; elected M.P. for Woodstock, Eng., 1st October, 1812. Lithograph. Size 7 x 9. Half length.

119—LAFONTAINE, SIR L. H., BART., 1807-64—Of Lafontaine-Baldwin Ministry—He was born at Boucherville, Que., educated at the College of Montreal; studied law, the practice of which he began in Montreal. In 1830 LaFontaine was elected a member of the Assembly for Terrebonne. He did not sympathize with the Rebellion; left the country, and on his return was arrested, but released without trial, as there were no legal grounds for his arrest. The union of the Provinces was strongly opposed by him. He became Attorney-General of Lower Canada, formed with Baldwin, the LaFontaine-Baldwin Administrations, the second of which was called the "great ministry." His efforts to carry a bill for redistributing seats in the Legislature were unsuccessful. LaFontaine, who was responsible for the introduction of the Rebellion Losses Bill, retired from public life in 1851, again taking up his profession. He was in 1853 appointed Chief Justice, Court of Queen's Bench, L.C., and the following year created a baronet in recognition of his distinguished career. Died in Montreal. Photogravure from a painting in the Chateau de Ramezay, Montreal. Size 4 x 5. Head and shoulders.

120—RYLAND, HERMAN WITSIUS—Born in England in 1770. Took part in the American Revolutionary War, returning to England with Sir Guy Carleton. On the latter's appointment as Governor-General, Mr. Ryland, as Civil Secretary, accompanied him to Canada, filling the position, not only while Dorchester was in office, but during the terms of succeeding Governors. He resigned in 1811, continuing to fill, however, his position as Clerk of the Executive Council until his death in 1838. His son, George Herman Ryland, then held the office until the union of the Canadas. Photograph from a portrait in possession of his granddaughter, Mrs. Henry J. Low, Montreal. Size 9 x 12. Head and shoulders.

121—PRESENTATION OF A NEWLY-ELECTED CHIEF OF THE HURON TRIBE, CANADA, 1839—"Dedicated by special permission to her Majesty Adelaide, the Queen Dowager (widow of William IV. of Great Britain) by her very grateful humble servant, H. D. Thielcke. H. D. Thielcke, pinxt., Historical-Portrait Painter to H.R.H. the late Duchess of York. On stone by H. Lynch. Day and Haghe, Lithrs. to the Queen. Published for the Proprietors by Messrs. Colnaghi & Puckle, Cockspur St., 1st of July, 1841. Proof." The election of a white to the honorary chieftainship of an Indian tribe is the highest honor his Indian friends can confer upon him. The election must be preceded by the adoption or ceremony of giving the name. By this ceremonial the person becomes a member of the tribe and of a particular family of the tribe. Adoption of an honorary chief must have the unanimous consent of the chiefs present in council. Lithograph in color. Size 16 x 19.

122—ARMS OF THE GRAND LODGE OF CANADA, A. F. and A. M., in the Province of Ontario—Adopted 14th July, 1858, at the union of the Ancient Grand Lodge of Canada, of which Sir Allan Macnab was Grand Master, and the Grand Lodge of Canada, of which Col. Wm. Mercer Wilson was Grand Master. The arms are described: Per pale; dexter, per fesse; the upper part gules, a chevron between the castles, argent; on the chevron a pair of compasses extended, the lower part gules, a beaver proper; sinister, a cross (vert) voided argent, the field beneath the cross quartely azure and or; (1) a lion rampant; (2) ox passant; (3) a man with arms uplifted; (4) an eagle displayed. The dexter side of the shield is formed by ears of wheat, and the sinister by an olive branch. On a ribbon below, Audi, Vide, Tace (Hear, See, Be Silent). Crest: the Ark of the Covenant, over which two cherubs are bending, supporting two cherubim, each having one wing extended over the shield and crest. Between their wings, over the ark, are Hebrew letters, Legend: Grand Lodge of Ancient, Free and Accepted Masons of Canada. Original drawing in water color. 1858. Size 11 x 12.

123—JOHNSON, LADY JOHN (Mary Watts)—Daughter of John Watts, for some time President of the Council, New York. She was born in New York, 27th Oct., 1753. In 1773 married Sir John Johnson, Bart. Her death took place at Mount Johnson, near Montreal, 7th August, 1815. From original oil in possession of Sir Gordon Johnson, Bart., Montreal. Size 8 x 10. Head and shoulders.

124—RESIDENCE OF SIR JOHN JOHNSON, BART., MONTREAL— St. Mary street, now Notre Dame—In an old plan of Montreal, 1846, the house and grounds are shown opposite the Molson Distillery, but there is no trace of the Johnson home to-day, the grounds having been built upon. Sir John Johnson, Bart., had, before Simcoe's appointment as Lieut.-Governor of Upper Canada, been recommended by Dorchester for the position. Wash drawing in black and white. Size 6 x 8.

125—JOHNSON, SIR JOHN, BART., 1742-1830—Son of Sir William Johnson, Bart. Served in the American Revolutionary War. After the war he became Superintendent of Indian Affairs in British North America, and member of the Legislative Council. He had been recommended by Lord Dorchester as first Lieutenant-Governor of Upper Canada, but his appointment, owing to his local interests and the policy of the British Government, was considered inadvisable. Sir John, who had been knighted during his father's lifetime, died at his seat, Mount Johnson, Montreal. Photograph of an engraving by H. Robinson. Published by Baldwin & Cradock, Paternoster Row, London, Eng., 1836. From the miniature by Abbott, 1793, drawn from original by W. Harvey. Size 4 x 6.

126—FRASER, GENERAL SIMON—Eldest son of Lord Lovat. In 1757 he was nominated Colonel of the Second Highland Battalion, afterwards known as the 78th or Fraser's Highlanders, which served with distinction during the Seven Years' War, especially at Louisburg, C.B., where Fraser was wounded, and at the capture of Quebec. In 1762, when the French and Spanish troops invaded Portugal, one of the officers in command in the English army was the "Master of Lovat," at that time holding rank of Major-General. While in America he had been elected M.P. for Inverness, representing that place until his death in 1782. Although he raised the regiment of the 71st Highlanders at the outbreak of the Revolutionary War, he did not come to America. He had in 1772 petitioned the Government for the restoration of his ancestral estates, and his request was only to a certain extent granted, for the General had to pay thousands of pounds in legal and other expenses before he received his property. Water color from a copy of a picture in possession of Dr. Arthur Doughty, Dominion Archivist, Ottawa. Size 13 x 16. Head and shoulders.

127—MACAULAY, DR. JAMES—Born in Scotland in 1759; entered the Army as a surgeon to the 33rd Regiment about 1785. He came to Canada with the Queen's Rangers in 1792, and was stationed at Kingston and Niagara. Subsequently he received the appointment as Deputy Inspector-General of Hospitals. When Toronto became the seat of Government instead of Niagara, Dr. Macaulay settled in the former place with his family. Teraulay street, Toronto, preserved the last syllable of Hayter (his wife's name) and the two last syllables of Macaulay. Photo from an oil in possession of his grandaughters, the Misses Macaulay, Exmouth, Devon, Eng. Size 11 x 14. Half length.

128—SEIGNIORIAL TENURE—"View of the Special Court Assembled Under the Authority of the Seigniorial Act of the Provincial Parliament, 1854, at its opening on the 4th day of September, 1855. Entered according to Act of the Provincial Legislature in the year 1856 by W. W. Smith, Esq., of St. John, L.C., editor and proprietor of the News, in the office of the registrar of the Province of Canada. Entered according to Act of

Congress in the year 1856 by W. W. Smith, Esqr., in the Clerk's Office of the District Court of the United States for the Southern District of New York. Arranged and drawn on stone by William Lockwood. Print of A. Weingartner's Lithy. This historical picture of the Seigniorial Court is respectfully dedicated by his very obedient and humble servant, W. W. Smith." The tenure of land in New France (Canada) was a modification of the feudal system. Grants of land were made and held on condition of paying fealty to the King. In 1854 the system of seigniorial tenure was abolished at a cost to the Government of Lower Canada of $2,500,000. The picture shows the faces of the men appointed by the Government to settle this vexed question. Lithograph. Size 16 x 31.

129—TABLET COMMEMORATING CONFEDERATION OF CANADA, 1867—In the Westminster Palace Hotel, London, Eng. During the winter of 1866-7 delegates representing Canada, Nova Scotia and New Brunswick assembled in conference at the Westminster Palace Hotel, for the purpose of framing the British North America Act, under which was formed the Dominion of Canada. In the room where they met a tablet was erected, with the following inscription:—"Dominion of Canada. In this room in 1866-7 delegates representing the Provinces of Canada, Nova Scotia and New Brunswick, under the chairmanship of the late Right Hon. Sir John A. Macdonald, P.C., G.C.B., framed the Act of Union under which all British North America, except Newfoundland, is now united under one government as the Dominion of Canada. This tablet was affixed with the approval of the Rt. Hon. Sir Charles Tupper, Bart., P.C., G.C.M.G., C.B., one of the delegates from Nova Scotia, A.D. 1911." Photograph. Size 11 x 14. See 130, 131.

130—FATHERS OF CONFEDERATION—The question of a union between the Provinces of British North America was first brought up in 1808 by Robt. J. Uniacke, a member of the Nova Scotia Legislature. He was followed along similar lines by Chief Justice Sewell, of Quebec, in 1814, Attorney-General John Beverley Robinson in 1822, and later by Robert Gourlay, Lord Durham, Sir A. T. Galt, and others. To Nova Scotia also belongs the honor of taking the first legislative action in the matter by the passing in 1861 of a resolution in favor of federal union. Three years later the Maritime and Quebec conferences were held, and these paved the way for the conference at London, resulting in the framing of the British North America Act, under which the "Dominion of Canada" came into being. With the picture is a key giving the names of the statesmen who inaugurated the union, July 1st, 1867. Lithograph. Size 19 x 34. See 129, 131.

131—MAKING OF THE BRITISH NORTH AMERICA ACT, 1866-7— The Conference Chamber in the Westminster Palace Hotel, London, Eng., in which the delegates to the London Council, assisted by the Colonial Secretary, the Earl of Carnarvon, his Excellency Lord Monck, Governor-General of Canada, and several law officers of the Crown, framed the British North America Act, under which was formed "The Dominion of Canada." A key gives the list of the delegates present. Hon. (Sir) J. A. Macdonald was chairman of the Conference. Photograph. Size 12 x 14. See 129, 130.

132—BURY, RT. HON. VISCOUNT WILLIAM COUTTS—Superintendent-General of Indian Affairs, Canada, 1854-6. Born in London, Eng., in 1832, the only son of the Earl of Albermarle. Entered Scots Fusilier Guards, 1849, and served in India as aide-de-camp to Lord Frederic Fitzclarence. Left the army, 1854; came to Canada in December of that year as Civil Secretary and Superintendent-General of Indian Affairs, and did much in his official capacity to better conditions among the Indians. He was first returned to the Imperial Parliament at the General Election of 1857, for the borough of Norwich. In conjunction with Mr. Roebuck brought the question of the Hudson's Bay Territory before the House of Commons. Appointed Treasurer to the Queen's Household, 1859. Viscount Bury is identified as the originator of the Canadian peerage scheme. His death occurred August 28th, 1894. Original drawing for "Vanity Fair" by C. Pelligrini (Ape) May 1st, 1875. Size 8 x 12. Full length.

133—OLD CODE OF SHIP SIGNALS, ST. JOHN'S, NEWFOUND-LAND, 1770—Made, it is said, by a Highlander of the 72nd Regiment, showing the flags of the mercantile firms of St. John's prior to 1800, as well as the signals used at the signal station. It was customary for a soldier on Southern Head (Fort Amherst), lighthouse and fort, to go between the flagstaffs seen at the head of the picture, to the right, and with a speaking trumpet (the present day megaphone) as vessels passed in the Narrows, ask the usual questions, "What ship is that?" etc. For instance, the brig shown is from Weymouth, Eng. The red burgee or pennant signifies that fact, which is repeated at the Signal Hill Block House. At that time the light at Fort Amherst was simply a couple of lanterns burning penny dips. By J. W. Hayward, St. John's, Newfoundland. Drawings in water color. Size 15 x 18.

134—MACAULAY, MRS. (Elizabeth Tuck Hayter)—Of Devonshire, Eng., who in 1790 became the first wife of Dr. James Macaulay, of the Queen's Rangers. She was an intimate friend of Mrs. Simcoe during the latter's sojourn in both Niagara and York. Photo from an oil portrait in possession of her granddaughters, the Misses Macaulay, Exmouth, Devon, England. Size 11 x 14. Half length.

135—"NAVAL BATTLE, 21ST JULY, 1781—By M. de la Perouse, Captain of the Fleet. This engagement took place at Louisburg, between two frigates of the King, the 'Astree,' 26 guns, commanded by M. de la Perouse, captain of the fleet, and the 'Hermoine,' with same number of guns, in command of M. the Count de la Touche, also captain, against six English warships, of which one was taken. After having been dismasted, and having lowered his flag, the English commander made his escape in the darkness, and the enemy's convoy was put to flight. Engraved from the original picture, 5 feet long by 3½ feet high, belonging to the King, and forming part of the collection of eighteen sea battles of the last war. Painted by order of His Majesty, by Marquis Rossel, formerly captain of the fleet, Knight of the Royal and Military Order of St. Louis. Dedicated to the King. Rossel, Pinxt., 1788. Dequevauviller, Sculpt., 1790. A.P.D.R. (By the King's permission.) Pere Livraison, and to be found at Merigot's the younger, Paris. Publisher, 4 Quai des Augustins, at the corner of Rue Pavee No. 38. Printed by Robbe." This battle, fought off Sydney Harbor, was stubbornly contested. The "Little Jack," 6 guns, of the British fleet, surrendered, and the remainder of the fleet would have shared the same fate had it not been for the approach of night. Eighteen British were killed and twenty-eight wounded. Line engraving. Size 19 x 29.

136—JOHNSON, COL. GUY—Son-in-law of Sir William Johnson, **Bart.**—Entered the Indian Department about 1756; accompanied Amherst up the lakes in 1759; appointed Deputy Superintendent of the Indian Department, 1761; succeeded his father-in-law as Superintendent, but this commission coming from the colony of New York and other colonies leagued together against the Indians, was dropped after the Revolutionary War. His property in the State of New York was confiscated by the Act of 1779. Born in Ireland; died in London, Eng., 5th March, 1788. Drawing in water color. Size 8 x 12. Head and shoulders.

137—**WASHINGTON, GEORGE**—"Washington (Virginia). Commander-in-Chief of the American forces during the War of Independence; first President of the United States (from 16th April, 1789, to 4th March, 1797). Painted from life by G. Stuart. Drawn by S. F. Dubourjal, Painter, in New York. Lithographed by Alophe. Paris and New York, Goupil, Vibert & Co., Publishers. Imp. Lith. by Cattier." Lithograph in color. Size 9 x 11. Half length. See 209.

138—**ARMSTRONG, LIEUT-GEN. SIR RICHARD, COMMANDER OF THE FORCES IN UPPER CANADA**—He received rank of Major-General, Royal Canadian Regiment, in 1841, and in 1842 was at Kingston, U.C. Subsequently he was at Niagara, U.C., and Sorel, Que. In 1850 he became Major-General, and Lieutenant-General, 11th November, 1851. Original silhouette taken by August Edouart at Saratoga, N.Y., 25th July, 1844. Size 6 x 9. Full length.

139—**ROCHEFOUCAULD-LIANCOURT**—"Francois Alexandre Frederic de la Rochefoucauld-Liancourt—T. Goutiere, Sc." Born in 1747; died 1827. A clever politician. On account of his loyalty to Louis XVI. he was compelled to leave France. Spent several years in England and America. Made a tour of Upper Canada, 1795. Visited Navy Hall, Niagara, June of that year, where he was warmly welcomed by Governor Simcoe. His account of the visit was severely and justly criticized by (Sir) D. W. Smith, Surveyor-General of Upper Canada. Lord Dorchester, Governor-General, did not think it advisable to allow the Duke to visit Quebec on his tour. He returned to France under the Consulate, and was made a peer. Line engraving. Size 3 x 3. Head and shoulders.

140—**JOHNSON, SIR WILLIAM, BART.**, 1715-74—Warraghiyagey, as he was known to the Indians, came to America from Ireland in 1738. In November, 1747, he had command of the northern frontier of New York, and in 1750 was appointed to a seat in His Majesty's Council for the Province of New York. Superintendent of Indian Affairs. Major-General in 1755, and created a baronet in November of the same year. He commanded Fort Niagara in 1759, defeating the French under General D'Aubry. Johnstown, N.Y., formerly Caughnawaga, was founded by Sir William Johnson. Photo from line engraving by J. C. Buttre, N.Y. Size 4 x 6. Head and shoulders.

141—**NELSON**—"Admiral Lord Nelson. Painted by J. Hoppner, Esq., R.A., portrait painter to H.R.H. the Prince of Wales. Engraved by C. Turner." Went to sea about the age of thirteen; served several years in the East Indies, and took part in the Revolutionary War. Was at Quebec in 1782 in command of H.M.S. 'Albemarle.' Gained the decisive battle of the Nile in 1798, for which service he was rewarded with a pension and the title of Baron Nelson of the Nile. Hostilities were renewed with France in 1803, and Nelson took command of the Mediterranean fleet, failed to overtake the French; proposed to suspend his active service, was reappointed in 1805, and on 21st October of that year gained a complete victory at Trafalgar, over the combined French and Spanish fleets. He was, however, mortally wounded in the encounter. Mezzotint, printed in color. Size 16 x 23. Full length.

142—**PRESCOTT, ROBERT**, 1725-1815—"Robert Prescott, Esqr. Captain-General and Governor-in-Chief of the Provinces of Upper and Lower Canada, Nova Scotia and New Brunswick, etc., etc. General of his Majesty's Forces, Colonel of the 28th Regiment of Foot." He was born in Lancashire, Eng., where his family lost their estates owing to their opposition to the revolution of 1688; served in the expedition against Rochefort, 1757, and Louisburgh, 1758. He was ordered in 1793 to Barbadoes, afterwards being appointed Civil Governor of the island. In April,

1796, he received instructions to succeed Lord Dorchester as Governor-General of Canada. The latter did not know he was to be recalled until Prescott arrived in Quebec. General Prescott made considerable additions to the fortifications of Quebec, and in 1797 was appointed Governor of Nova Scotia, remaining at the head of the Government of that colony as well as of Canada and New Brunswick till 1799, when he returned to England. He, however, continued to hold office as Governor until 1807. His death took place at Battle, Sussex, Dec., 1815. Mezzotint engraving. Size 9 x 10. Half length, oval. See 1689.

143—SHERBROOKE, SIR JOHN COAPE—Born in England, 1764, the son of William Coape, J.P., who on his marriage had taken his wife's name of Sherbrooke. Young Sherbrooke entered the army and was subsequently in Canada with the 33rd Foot. In 1794 he became second Lieutenant-Colonel of the regiment, and served under the Duke of York in the latter part of the campaign in the Netherlands the same year. In 1796 the 33rd went to the Cape, and thence to India, taking part in the Mysore War of 1799. In 1805, Sherbrooke was sent to Sicily, where he was given command of the troops at Messina. Two years later went to Egypt to negotiate with the Beys, after the failure of Fraser's expedition. In 1810, after a further varied military career, he returned to England, broken in health, but the next year he received the appointment of Lieutenant-Governor of Nova Scotia, and in 1816 he was appointed Governor-in-Chief of Canada. His arduous duties told on him severely, and in 1818 he suffered a paralytic stroke, which forced him to resign. The rest of his life was spent in retirement at Calverton, Nottinghamshire, Eng., where he died in 1830. Line engraving. Size 9 x 13. Full length.

144—"DETROIT IN 1820, WITH A VIEW OF 'WALK-IN-THE-WATER' —The vessel from an original painting. Corrie's Lithographic Office, Detroit. The "Walk-in-the-Water," built at Buffalo, was the first steamboat to ply on Lake Erie. Lithograph. Size 15 x 22.

145—"PLAN OF THE MILITARY AND NAVAL OPERATIONS BEFORE QUEBEC—Under the command of the immortal Wolfe and Vice-Admiral Saunders. To the members of the United Services of the British Empire, whose daring achievements this plan is designed to commemorate and honor, and to whom it is respectfully dedicated by their obedient servant, Alfred Hawkins, Quebec, 1841. J. Wyld, Sculp. London. Published by Jas. Wyld, Geographer to the Queen, and to H.R.H. Prince Albert, Charing Cross East, May 1st, 1841, for Alfred Hawkins, Esqe., Quebec. Proof." The plan gives a list of the defences of Quebec, the names of the ships in the British naval force under Admiral Saunders, and the British military force under command of Major-General Wolfe, with the commanding officers of the three brigades, etc. There is also a list of the encampments with defences at Montmorency, 9th July, encampment upon the point of Orleans, 29th June, and encampment upon Point Levy, 30th June, with batteries and works at and near the Point Des Peres. In the lower centre of the plan is a "detail of the action fought on the Plains of Abraham, Sept. 13th, 1759." To the right is a vignette showing Britannia standing by the monument in honor of Wolfe and Montcalm. To the left of the picture the vignette shows the Highlanders scaling the cliffs. At the top of the plan is a vignette of West's "Death of Wolfe." Size 24 x 30.

146—WELLINGTON—"Field Marshal the Duke of Wellington. From the original picture presented by His Grace to his distinguished friend and companion in arms, the Marquis of Anglesey. Painted and engraved by John Lucas. London. Published, 1854, by Thos. McLean, 26 Haymarket." Arthur Wellesley, first Duke of Wellington, the celebrated British General and statesman, was born in Ireland in 1769. Educated at

Eton and at a military academy in France, and received in 1787 an ensign's commission in the 73rd Regiment of Foot. Returned to the House of Commons for the borough of Rye in 1806, and appointed Chief Secretary for Ireland in 1807. He was most successful in the Wars of the Peninsula, the culminating victory, of course, being that of Waterloo, on 18th June, 1815. His character presents a striking contrast to that of his great antagonist, Napoleon, in that he never indulged in the slightest misrepresentation, even to save his own fame. It is a coincidence that both were born in the same year. The "Iron Duke" died in 1852. Mezzotint, printed in color. Size 18 x 28. Full length.

147—GREY—"Sir Charles Grey, K.B. Painted by T. Lawrence, R.A., Principal Painter in Ordinary to His Majesty. Engraved by J. Collyer, A.R.A., Portrait Engraver to Her Majesty. Published as the Act directs, 29 May, 1797, by Wm. Austin, Drawing Master at Turnham Green." Sir Charles, the first Earl Grey, and great-grandfather of the fourth earl, who was Governor-General of Canada, 1904-11, was born at Howick, England, in 1729, and died there, 1807. He was actively engaged in the Revolutionary War; returned to England in 1782, and was appointed Commander-in-Chief in America, an appointment, however, which was rendered inoperative owing to the close of the war. In 1793, appointed with Jervis (subsequently Earl St. Vincent), Commander of an expedition to the French West Indies. Stipple engraving. Size 12 x 15. Half length.

148—GREY, RIGHT HON. HENRY, K.G., THIRD EARL AND VISCOUNT HOWICK—The eldest son of the second Earl Grey, born, 1802. In 1832 took his seat in the Reformed House of Commons for North Northumberland, and was appointed Under Secretary for the Colonies. Became Minister at War, 1835, and from 1846-52 was Secretary of State for the Colonies. His death occurred in 1894. Photograph from a portrait at Howick House, Lesbury, England. Size 9 x 11. Head and shoulders.

149—GREY, RIGHT HON. ALBERT HENRY GEORGE, 4TH EARL—In Sept., 1904, he received his commission as Governor-General of Canada. His term expired, therefore, in 1909, but various circumstances caused an extension in his governorship, which ended in Sept., 1911; Administrator of Rhodesia, 1896-97; Director of British South Africa Company, 1898-1904. During his stay in Canada he travelled from coast to coast, became thoroughly conversant with men and affairs. In fact, it is said that no man of the time knew as much of Canada as the former Governor-General whose career in the Dominion was successful in the highest sense of the term. He was born Nov. 28th, 1851. Died Aug. 29th, 1917. Replica of crayon by John S. Sargent; autographed. Size 9 x 12. Head and shoulders.

150—GREY, MAJOR-GENERAL SIR CHARLES—Second son of Charles, second Earl Grey, whose character he was supposed to resemble, and father of fourth Earl; was born in 1804, and in 1839 was quartered in Canada. He was sent by Lord Durham to Washington to complain of the action of the United States Government in not keeping in order the unruly spirits who were at the time causing annoyance to his Majesty's subjects on the frontier. His knowledge of Bytown (Ottawa) and its qualifications as a federal capital were probably communicated to the Prince Consort, whose private secretary General Grey was. Head in profile, with facsimile of autograph. Drawn by G. Thomas. On stone by J. Bacon. Size 6 x 8.

151—GREY, CHARLES—Second Earl Grey and Viscount Howick, 1764-1845. Entered Parliament, 1786; Prime Minister, Great Britain, 1830; eldest son of first Earl Grey. He became First Lord of the Admiralty under Grenville in 1806. In 1833 he carried a bill abolishing slavery throughout the British Empire, and in 1834 passed the Poor Law Amendment Act. Painted by J. Jackson. Engraved by J. Ward. Size 8 x 10. Head and shoulders.

152—"HIS ROYAL HIGHNESS PRINCE EDWARD, Duke of Kent and Strathearn, Earl of Dublin, Field Marshal of his Majesty's Forces, K.G., G.C.B., K.S.P., Governor of Gibraltar and Colonel of the 1st or the Royal Scots Regiment of Foot, etc., etc., etc. Painted by Sir Willm. Beechey, R.A., Portrait Painter to her Majesty. Engraved by Willm. Skelton. Published Novr. 1, 1816, by W. Skelton, 1 Stafford place, Pimlico." Line engraving. Size 11 x 12. Half length. See 2464-5, 2472-5.

153—METCALFE, SIR CHARLES THEOPHILUS—"The Rt. Honble. Charles Theophilus, Baron Metcalfe, G.C.B., Captain-General and Governor of Canada. Bengal Civil Service. From the picture by F. R. Say, Esqr. Painted for the Oriental Club. Engraved by F. C. Lewis, Esqr., Engraver to the Queen, 53 Charlotte Street, London. Published for the Proprietor by W. W. Watson on Vere Street, 1845." From March 30th, 1843, to November 26th, 1845, he was Governor-General of Canada. Born in Calcutta, India, 30th Jan., 1785, was educated at Eton and subsequently entered the service of the East India Company as a writer. He was a member of the Superior Council of Bengal, Resident of Delhi, 1811-20, and Resident of Hyderabad, 1820-27. Returned to England in 1837, and two years later was appointed Governor of Jamaica. Resigned the Governor-Generalship of Canada owing to ill-health. Died at Basingstoke, Eng., Sept., 1846. Line engraving. Size 16 x 26. Full length. See 1629.

154—SOCIAL GATHERING OF SIR JOHN A. MACDONALD'S SUPPORTERS—The Dinner of the "Old Guard" at Ottawa, Ont., 4th May, 1882—With key. A reunion of those Liberal-Conservative members of the House of Commons in 1882, who were also members during the period the party was in Opposition (1874-1878), was held in the House of Commons Restaurant, Ottawa, on the evening of the 4th of May, 1882. The gathering was a large one, including many ladies. Sir John A. Macdonald proposed a toast to the "Old Guard," to which Mr. Alonzo Wright and Mr. J. B. Plumb responded. This photograph is a fine production by Topley, of Ottawa, and is a composite picture, from individual photographs which were afterwards rephotographed. Size 17 x 32.

155—ARGYLL—John Douglas Sutherland Campbell, 9th Duke of Argyll, K.G., K.T., P.C., G.C.M.G., G.C.V.O., LL.D. Born Aug. 6th, 1845, at Stafford House, London, Eng., and educated at Eton and at Trinity College, Cambridge. In 1871 he married H.R.H. Princess Louise, fourth daughter of H.M. Queen Victoria. A State Councillor for Scotland; Lord-Lieutenant of the County of Argyll; Governor-General of the Dominion of Canada, 1878-83; Governor and Constable of Windsor Castle, 1892-1914. From 1868-78 he was M.P. for Argyllshire, and from 1895-1900 represented South Manchester in Parliament. At the coronation of Edward VII. and George V., in 1902 and 1911 respectively, his Grace bore the King's sceptre with the Cross. His death occurred May 2nd, 1914. Line engraving. Size 12 x 16. Half length.

156—BAGOT—"The Right Honble. Sir Charles Bagot, G.C.B. Late Governor-General of Canada, etc., etc., etc. Published by J. Ryman, Oxford, March 1, 1844. H. W. Pickersgill, R.A. J. Burnet, F.R.S." Born in Staffordshire, Eng., 1781. Educated at Rugby and Oxford. Admitted to Lincoln's Inn, Nov. 12th, 1801. In 1807 entered Parliament, becoming Under-Secretary for Foreign Affairs under Canning. Minister Plenipotentiary to France, 1814, and to the United States, 1815-20. Privy Councillor in 1815. In 1820 Sir Charles was appointed Ambassador to St. Petersburg (Petrograd), and to The Hague, four years later. Declined Governor-Generalship of India, in succession to Lord Amherst, 1828. Governor-General of Canada, 1841-3. His death occurred at Kingston, U.C., May 19th, 1843. Besides settling the irritation consequent on the War of 1812-14, and improving trade relations between the United States and British Provinces, Bagot secured the neutrality of the Great Lakes. Mezzotint engraving. Size 13 x 16. Three-quarter length.

157—**TOWNSHEND**—"The Most Noble George, Marquis Townshend, Field Marshall of his Majesty's Forces, Colonel of the 2nd Regiment of Dragoon Guards, Governor of Jersey, Steward of Tamworth and Yarmouth, Lord-Lieutenant and Vice-Admiral of the County of Norfolk, etc., etc., etc. Painted by Sir Jos'a Reynolds. Engraved by C. Turner. London: Published Jan. 1, 1801, for the proprietor by Charles Turner, No. 30 Warren Street, Surrey Square." Born 1724, died 1807. Succeeded Gen. Wolfe as Commander-in-Chief at Quebec when the latter was killed. Line engraving. Size 15 x 24. Full length.

158—**BRANT**—"Joseph Tayadaneega, called the Brant, the Great Captain of the Six Nations. Engraved from an original painting of G. Romney, in the collection of the Right Honble. the Earl of Warwick, by J. R. Smith." He was born on the banks of the Ohio in 1742. His father, a full-blooded Mohawk of the Wolf tribe, died when the lad was quite young. The widow married a second time, an Indian whose Christian name was Barnet, hence the contraction Brant. Joseph was educated at "Moor Charity School," in Lebanon, Conn. Accompanied Sir William Johnson during several expeditions against the French, and took part in many of the encounters between the revolutionists and Indians. His allegiance to Britain so provoked the Americans that the valley of the Mohawks, the original home of his people, suffered more than any other part of the country during the war. In 1776 he visited England and was presented at court. He proudly declined to kiss the King's hand, but remarked that he would gladly thus salute the Queen. While in England he was initiated into Freemasonry in "the Falcon Lodge," in Princess Street, Leicester Fields, London, and presented by George III. with a Masonic apron. After the war, he, with the greater part of the Mohawks, and a number of Indians from the other five tribes, withdrew to Canada, where the Six Nations subsequently received grants of land near Wellington Square, now Burlington, Ont. Here he built a dwelling long known as Brant House. In 1785, through his efforts, a wooden church was erected at the Mohawk village, near Brantford, where was placed the first "Church-going bell" that ever tolled in Upper Canada. He died in Brant House, 24th Nov., 1807, and his remains were interred in a vault at the Mohawk church on the Grand River. Brant, although a chief by courtesy and ability, and always so called, was not such by descent. A very rare mezzotint. Size 14 x 18. Three-quarter length. See 159, 1673-4.

159—**BRANT**—Joseph Tayadaneega, called the Brant, the Great Captain of the Six Nations. Water color of original painting of G. Romney in the collection of the Right Honble. the Earl of Warwick. Size 14 x 18. Three-quarter length. See 158, 1673-4.

160—**SEATON**—"Field Marshal Lord Seaton, G.C.B., G.C.H., G.C.M.B.; Colonel of the 2nd Life Guards; Colonel-in-Chief of the Rifle Brigade; Governor-General and Commander of the Forces in British North America; Lord High Commissioner of the Ionian Islands, and Commander of the Forces in Ireland. Engraved from the original picture painted for and dedicated to the members of the United Service Club. Painted by G. W. Fisher, Esqr. Engraved by James Scott. London: Published April 11th, 1864, by Henry Graves & Co., the Proprietors, Publishers to the Queen, 6 Pall Mall." Line engraving. Size 15 x 24. Full length. See 417, 834.

161—**SIMCOE, MAJOR-GENERAL JOHN GRAVES**—First Lieut.-Governor of Upper Canada, 1792-96. Life size oil painting by E. Wyly Grier, ex-President Ontario Society of Artists, and R.C.A. Size 54 x 94. Full length. See 406, 3265, 3370.

162-8—**UNIFORMS WORN BY OFFICERS AND SEAMEN OF THE BRITISH NAVY FROM 1748-68**—This is a companion set to the drawings in the collection of the 1768-86 period. The uniforms of British naval officers, 1748-68, never having been made in one set, Mr. Robertson secured the services of Commander Charles N. Robinson, editor of the Army and Navy Gazette. Under his careful direction and by aid of old prints, the naval drawings of this period are given. The first uniform for the executive officers of the Royal Navy was prescribed by regulations issued 13th April, 1748. Only patterns were issued, however, but it is known from portraits of Anson and other admirals, that the full dress was ornamental and expensive. In 1767 new regulations were issued, discontinuing the full dress, altering the "frock uniform cloathing," or what would now be called undress, and making this the only uniform to be worn. In 1768 and 1774 some further alterations were made. The uniforms of the Post Captain of over three years' standing, and Junior Captain, were copied from coats and waistcoats in the Royal United Service Institution, Whitehall, London, The uniforms worn by the British navy at Quebec under Admiral Saunders in 1758 were the same as here shown. Water colors. Size of each picture 7 x 7. Full length. See 1192-7.

169—CONNAUGHT AND STRATHEARN, H. R. H., DUKE OF— Prince Arthur William Patrick Albert, K.G., P.C., K.T., K.P., etc., etc., Governor-General of Canada, 1911-16, son of Queen Victoria and uncle of George V., was born 1st May, 1850, appointed lieutenant Royal Engineers, 1868, became general in 1893, and field marshal in 1902. He served during the Fenian Raid in Canada, 1870; was with Egyptian Expeditionary Force, 1882; Commander-in-Chief in Bombay Presidency in 1886-90, and in Ireland, 1900-1. Was a personal aide-de-camp to her late Majesty, Queen Victoria; initiated into Freemasonry 19th March, 1874, by his brother, the late King Edward, then Prince of Wales, and in 1901 H.R.H. Duke of Connaught became Grand Master of the Grand Lodge of England. Published by George Kenning & Son, London, Liverpool, Glasgow, Manchester. Photogravure. Size 15 x 22. Three-quarter length.

170—GRANT, SIR WILLIAM—"The Right Hon. Sir William Grant, Master of the Rolls. From the portrait painted by Sir Thomas Lawrence, P.R.A., for the gentlemen of the Chancery Bar. Ric. Golding, Sc." He was descended from the Grants of Beldornie, so long distinguished in the history of Scotland; born in 1754 at Elchies, on the banks of the Spey; appointed third Attorney-General of Quebec, 10th May, 1776. His talents were generally recognized, on one occasion in particular, when the question of a new code of laws for Quebec was under discussion. He distinguished himself in 1791 in the great debate relating to the laws of Canada; Master of the Rolls, 1801-17. Died 25th May, 1832, at Barton House, Dawlish, Eng., the home of his sister, the widow of Admiral Schank. Line engraving. Size 14 x 22. Full length.

171—DAVISON—"Alexander Davison, Esqr. L. F. Abbott, Pinxt., 1797. Engraved by W. Barnard. Published June 15, 1804, by G. Andrews, No. 7 Charing Cross, London." Davison was the intimate friend of Lord Nelson. This life-long friendship was formed in Quebec, when he was the head of the firm of Davison & Lees, and Nelson was captain of H.M.S. "Albemarle," of 24 guns, in 1782. Davison, who is supposed to have had a distrust of marriage in general, interfered with Nelson's love affair with Mary Simpson, a Quebec belle of the period. Line engraving. Size 14 x 17. Half length.

172—ELGIN—Rt. Hon. James Bruce, Earl of Elgin and Kincardine, 1811-63. Governor of Jamaica, 1842-6, and Governor-General of Canada, 1847-54. It was, therefore, during his term of office in Canada that the Reciprocity Treaty with the United States, signed June 5th, 1854, by Lord Elgin and Hon. W. L. Marcy, to continue in force for ten years from March, 1855, terminable on twelve months' notice from either party, was passed. Painted by F. Grant, R.A. Engraved by James Faed. London: Published June 7th, 1864, by Henry Graves & Co., the Proprietors, Publishers to the Queen, 6 Pall Mall. Line engraving. Size 16 x 26. Full length. See 1600.

173—DENISON, SIR WILLIAM THOMAS, 1804-71—Born in London, Eng., entered the Royal Military Academy at Woolwich, 1819, and passed for the Royal Engineers in 1823. He was sent to Canada in 1827, being employed during the next four years in the construction of the Rideau Canal. His headquarters were at Ottawa. During this time he made a series of experiments for the purpose of testing the strength of various kinds of American timber. Originated the publication of the professional papers of the Royal Engineers, and in 1846, for his services under the Admiralty, was knighted. In 1866 he returned to England from Madras, where he had filled the office of Lieutenant-Governor since 1861. Died at East Sheen, Eng., 19th January, 1871. Painted by Fredk. R. Say, Esqr. Engraved by W. Giller. Proof. Size 14 x 23. Full length.

174—DALHOUSIE—"George, Earl of Dalhousie, etc., G.C.B. Captain-General Royal Company of Archers, the King's Body Guard for Scotland. As he appeared on 23rd July, 1832, when he received for the Royal Company two standards, the gift of his Majesty King William the Fourth. Engraved from a portrait painted at the request of the Royal Company, and dedicated by generous permission to his Majesty by his dutiful subject and servant, Alexr. Hill. Painted by John Watson Gordon, S.A. Engraved by Thomas Lupton, 4 Leigh Street, Burton Crescent. Published by Alexr. Hill, 50 Princes Street, Edinburgh. Proof." Governor-General of Canada, June 19th, 1820-Sept 8th, 1828. Born in 1770 and succeeded to the Earldom of Dalhousie, 1787; in the same year entered the army as cornet in the 3rd Dragoon Guards. Commanded the 2nd Foot at Martinique, 1792. After a varied service at home and abroad Lord Dalhousie was appointed to Wellington's staff in the Peninsula. Served with distinction at Vittoria, the battle of the Pyrenees, Waterloo, and elsewhere. In 1816 was appointed lieutenant-general commanding in Nova Scotia. Afterwards became commander-in-chief in the East Indies. His death occurred at Dalhousie Castle, Scotland, March 21st, 1838. Mezzotint engraving. Size 17 x 25. Full length.

175—OLD-TIME WHARF ON THE HARBOR FRONT, HALIFAX, N.S., 1888—The place of business of John Fleming, mast and spar maker, is here shown. It formerly stood on what was then known as Corbett's south wharf, on Lower Water Street. The old building has since been demolished and the whole character of the water front has changed since the picture was made in 1888. Original etching by F. Leo Hunter, Ossining, N.Y. Size 15 x 21.

176—"CANADIAN PARENTS AT THEIR CHILD'S GRAVE—A scene in the early days, when husband and wife visited the grave of a child, and the mother, after six months, pours out her tears, while the milk flows again from her breasts. Painted by Le Barbier, Sen., Painter to the King, 1781. Engraved by Ingouf, Jun., 1786. At Paris, in the author's home, rue Poupee St. Andre, No. 5. Beauble, Scrip. Lithographed by Sampier. Philosophical and Political History, Geneva edition. T. 8, page 43." Size 14 x 18.

177—MACDONALD, RT. HON. SIR JOHN ALEXANDER, G.C.B., D.C.L., Q.C.—Born in Glasgow, 11th Jan., 1815; came to Canada with his parents five years later. Called to the bar in 1836; elected member for Kingston in the second Parliament of United Canada, 1844. Receiver-General in 1847; Attorney-General, Upper Canada, 1854-62, 1864-7; Government Leader in the Assembly, 1864-7. On 1st July, 1867, when the new constitution came into force, having been elected to the Parliament of Canada for Kingston, he was called upon to form the first Government for the Dominion, and appointed Minister, of Justice and Attorney-General of Canada, and held office until 1873. In 1878 he formed the new Government, being Premier and Minister of the Interior. The latter office he exchanged for the Presidency of the Council and Superintendent-Generalship of Indian Affairs, 1883. Died at Ottawa, 6th June, 1891. Engraved from the painting by A. D. Patterson, 1886. Photogravure, Goupil & Co. Size 11 x 15. Half length. See 1354.

178—MILLER'S DOCK AND MORAN'S WHARF, HALIFAX, N.S., 1888 —It is almost impossible to identify positively the locality as so many changes have taken place along the water front since 1888, but Mr. Harry Piers, of the Provincial Museum, Halifax, is of the opinion that the scene depicted is at the foot of Stevens' Lane, showing the extreme south end of Lower Water Street, adjoining H. M. Lumber Yard. A number of years ago all the buildings there were razed, and the southern portion of the Halifax Electric Tram Company's car shed occupies the site. Original etching by Leo Hunter, Ossining. N.Y. Size 15 x 21.

179—HEAD—"His Excellency Sir Francis Bond Head, Bart., K.C.H., Lieutenant-Governor of Upper Canada., etc., etc., etc. From an original picture painted at the solicitation of the inhabitants of the City of Toronto. This plate is respectfully dedicated to her Most Gracious Majesty's loyal Canadian subjects by their fellow citizen and most obt. hum'le servt., Frederick Chase Capreol. Painted by Nelson Cook, Esqre. Engraved by C. Turner, A.R.A." Appointed by the Melbourne ministry to succeed Sir John Colborne as Lieutenant-Governor of Upper Canada. He entered military service at an early age in the Royal Engineers; was at Waterloo, and subsequently made a tour of exploration in South Africa. In 1836 he arrived in Toronto; resigned his office in 1837, though he administered the affairs of the Province till March, 1838. He was created a member of the Privy Council in order to assist in connection with the British North America Act. Line engraving. Size 10 x 12. Half length. See 418.

180—RAE, JOHN—"This portrait of Dr. Rae, F.R.G.S., Chief Factor, etc., etc., etc., is respectfully dedicated by permission to the Hudson's Bay Company by their obedient servants, Henry Graves & Compy. Painted by Stephen Pearce. Engraved by James Scott. London: Published by Henry Graves & Compy., Jany. 26, 1858, printsellers to the Queen, 6 Pall Mall." Arctic explorer, born near Stromness, in the Orkney Islands, 30th Sept., 1813. Studied medicine in Edinburgh, and in 1833 was appointed surgeon to the Hudson's Bay Company's ship which visited Moose Factory every year. From 1835-45 he was the Company's resident surgeon at Moose Fort. In June, 1846, he set out on his first journey of exploration, and the following year joined the first land expedition in quest of Sir John Franklin. The coast between the Mackenzie and Coppermine Rivers was searched in vain. A second expedition, in 1850, was also unsuccessful. For geographical results of the latter expedition and for the survey of 1847, Dr. Rae was in 1852 awarded the Founder's Gold Medal of the Royal Geographical Society. He later proposed to the Hudson's Bay Co. that the survey of the northern coasts of America should be completed, and in 1853 undertook the expedition. In 1858 he walked from Hamilton to Toronto on snow shoes in seven hours, and showed no signs of fatigue. Conducted in 1864 a difficult telegraph survey from Winnipeg across the Rocky Mountains to the Pacific Coast. Died 22nd July, 1893, at his home in London, Eng. Line engraving. Size 9 x 11. Head and shoulders.

181—GRANT, HON. ALEXANDER, 1734-1813—Commodore British armed vessels between Niagara and Mackinaw. Water color from an oil painting from life, in possession of Ian Robert James Murray Grant, the Chief of the Clan, of Glenmoriston, Inverness-shire, Scotland. Size 13 x 15. Three-quarter length. See 408.

182—ARMS AND AUTOGRAPHS OF FRENCH GOVERNORS OF CANADA—From Champlain, 15th Oct., 1612--20th July, 1629, and 23rd May, 1633, till his death, 1635, to Pierre Rigaud, Marquis de Vaudreuil-Cavagnal. last French Governor, 1st Jan., 1755-8th Sept., 1760. Painted by the late Alfred Sandham, in water color, and presented by him to the Toronto Public Library. Size of each Coat of Arms, 3 x 4.

183—WILLIAMS, WM. FENWICK—"Major-General Sir William Fenwick Williams, of Kars, Bart., K.C.B., M.P. for Calne, etc. Dedicated by special permission to her Most Gracious Majesty. London, 18th March, 1857. W. Walker, Excudit, 64 Margaret St., Cavendish Square. Engraved by W. Walker from a photograph by John Watkins. Enlarged and completed by the engraver from subsequent sittings." Second son of Commissary-General Thomas Williams, barrack master at Nova Scotia, born at Annapolis, N.S., 4th Dec., 1800. He entered the Royal Military Academy at Woolwich in 1815, and became lieutenant in Royal Artillery, 1827. Was elected for post of British Commissioner with the Turkish Army in Anatolia, visited Kars, Sept., 1854, and the following January was made a ferik, or Lieut.-General in the Turkish Army, and also a pasha. The Russians were repulsed in their attack on Kars, 15th June, 1855, but succeeded in establishing a blockade of the fortress. In September, General Williams gave battle to his besiegers, defeating them.* He became known as the "hero of Kars," and almost immediately gazetted a Knight Commander of the Bath. He accepted in 1858 the position of Commander-in-Chief of the Forces in British North America, and from 12th Oct., 1860, to 22nd Jan., 1861, administered the Government of Canada during the absence of Sir Edmund W. Head. In 1865 he was given the Governorship of Nova Scotia, and in 1870 made Governor and Commander-in-Chief of Gibraltar. Died 26th July, 1883. Line engraving. Size 13 x 17. Three-quarter length, sitting.

184—SAUNDERS, SIR CHARLES—"Charles Saunders, Esqr., Vice-Adml. of the Blue Squadron of his Majesty's Fleet, and Lieutt.-General of his Majesty's Marine Forces. J. Reynolds, pinxt. Js. McArdell, fecit." First won distinction in action off Cape Finisterre, 1747. Five years later went out in Penzance for protection of Newfoundland Fishery. Rear-Admiral of the Blue, 1756; Admiral, 1759. Commanded squadron acting with British army at Quebec, 1759, when the fleet rendered valuable service to Wolfe. Vice-Admiral of the White, 1762; four years later sworn in Privy Council and appointed First Lord of the Admiralty. Admiral of the White, 1770. Died 1775. Line engraving. Size 11 x 14. Half length.

185—HARVEY—"His Excellency Lieut.-Gen. Sir John Harvey, K.C.B., K.C.H. Colonel of Her Majesty's 59th Regt. and Governor and Commander-in-Chief of Nova Scotia and its dependencies, etc." Entered the army as an ensign in the 80th Regiment. In June, 1812, he was appointed Deputy Adjutant-General to the army in Canada, with the rank of Lieutenant-Colonel, and during the War of 1812-15 served with distinction, his advice regarding methods of defence being followed with success in almost every instance. In 1841 he became Governor and Commander-in-Chief of Newfoundland, and from 1846-52 was Governor of Nova Scotia. Original lithograph. Size 12 x 14. Head and shoulders.

186—LITTLEHALES, LIEUT.-COL. E. B. (SIR EDWARD BAKER BAKER), 1763-1825—Crayon, from a portrait from life in the possession of his grandson, Sir Randolph Littlehales Baker, Bart., Dorset, Eng. Size 13 x 16. Head and shoulders. See 2844.

187—AGRICULTURAL ASSOCIATION OF UPPER CANADA—Member's Ticket to Exhibition, Kingston, Sept. 27th-30th, 1859—Signed by William Ferguson, President. The Provincial Agricultural Association and Board of Agriculture for Upper Canada was formed in 1846, with E.

W. (Col.) Thompson as president. The first exhibition was held in Toronto, 22nd October, of that year, in the grounds attached to the old Government House, several of the exhibits being located in the House itself. Fairs, at which one saw almost every conceivable article used in Canada, were held at different places, and with great success. The present Canadian National Exhibition, in the erection of the old Crystal Palace, 1858, on Garrison Commons, had its beginnings in the Provincial Agricultural Association and Board of Agriculture for Upper Canada. (Nos. 187 to 190 are in one frame).

188—TICKET OF ADMISSION TO DINNER OF THE YORK PIONEER SOCIETY, 17TH APRIL, 1871—Held in St. Lawrence Hall, to celebrate the formation of the Society, the oldest of its kind in Canada. The first meeting was held 17th April, 1869, in the Mechanics' Institute Building, corner Church and Adelaide streets.

189—MINIATURE PAGE OF TORONTO DAILY MAIL, 30TH AUGUST, 1887—The Mail, now (1917) The Mail and Empire, founded in 1872, is an organ of the Conservative Party. It publishes a morning edition, which has a large local and provincial circulation. Size 6 x 8.

190—AGRICULTURAL SOCIETY—Member's Badge, Provincial Agricultural Exhibition, Brantford, C.W. 1857.

191—SCARBORO CENTENNIAL EXECUTIVE COMMITTEE, 1896— This executive was formed for the purpose of producing a history of the township of Scarboro, and the preparation of a fitting celebration of the hundredth anniversary of the settlement of the township, June, 1896. The first actual settler was David Thomson, who, in 1795, came with his wife from Scotland to Canada, and a few months later took up land in the valley of Highland Creek, about two miles from the lake shore. To this day Mrs. Thomson is called "The Mother of Scarboro." Photo. Size 8 x 10.

192—"A VIEW OF BROCKVILLE, UPPER CANADA, FROM UMBRELLA ISLAND—Respectfully dedicated to his patrons, Sir Peregrine Maitland, Lt.-Governor, and the gentlemen of Upper Canada, by their obedient servt., James Gray. Drawn by J. Gray; outlined by J. Allen; aquatinted by J. Pyall, London: Published by Willett & Blandford. Bouverie Street, Fleet Street, 1828." The town of Brockville was founded in 1785, when William Buell, senior, a U.E.L., received from the Crown a grant of land, on which he settled. He erected the first house in what at that time was a veritable wilderness, but which subsequently became the central portion of Brockville. Size 12 x 22.

193—"KINGSTON, FROM FORT HENERY—Respectfully dedicated to his Patrons, Sir Peregrine Maitland, Lt.-Governor, and the Gentlemen of Upper Canada by their obedient servt., James Gray. Drawn by J. Gray; aquatinted by J. Gleadah, London; published by J. Willett and Blandford, Bouverie Street, Fleet Street. Decr. 1st, 1828." Size 12 x 22.

194—"OTTAWA CITY, CANADA WEST (LATE BYTOWN)—View of the Uppertown, looking up the Ottawa River from Government Hill. Drawn from nature by E. Whitefield. Lith. of Endicott & Co., New York. Ottawa. Published by E. Whitefield, 1855. Copyright secured. 1. French Church. 2. English Church. 3. Timber Slide. 4. Suspension Bridge and Chaudiere Falls. 5. Hull." Size 20 x 36.

195—"YORK—From Gibraltar Point. Respectfully dedicated to his patrons, Sir Peregrine Maitland, Lt.-Governor, and the gentlemen of Upper Canada, by their obedient servt., James Gray. Drawn by J. Gray. Aquatinted by J. Gleadah. London: Published Decr. 1st, 1828, by J. Willett and Blandford, Bouverie Street, Fleet Street." The present Hanlan's Point, Toronto Island, was in the early days known as Gibraltar Point, and is so designated in all Government maps from 1796. Governor Simcoe gave the point the name. Size 11 x 22.

196—RED CROSS FLAG—Improvised during the Northwest Rebellion by Surgeon-General G. Sterling Ryerson, M.D., M.L.A., and used at the engagements at Fish Creek, 24th April, and Batoche, 9th-12th May, 1885. Presented by Dr. Ryerson, 1887, to the Public Library.

197—LE MOINE, SIR JAMES MACPHERSON, KT., with Autograph— Born in the city of Quebec, 1825. Called to the bar in 1850, and successfully practised his profession. In 1869 he was appointed Inspector of Inland Revenue, District of Quebec, retiring from that position in 1899. Author of many books relating to his native city, notable among them being "Picturesque Quebec." Knighted in 1897 for his literary services. One of the original members of the Royal Society of Canada, selected by the Marquis of Lorne (Duke of Argyll). His death occurred at "Spencer Grange," Quebec, Feb. 5th, 1912. Lithograph. Size 13 x 16. Three-quarter length, sitting.

198—"HORSESHOE FALL OF FALLS OF NIAGARA—From the Upper Bank of the British shore. Respectfully dedicated to his patrons, Sir. Peregrine Maitland, Lt.-Governor, and the gentlemen of Upper Canada, by their obedient servt., James Gray. Drawn by J. Gray; aquatinted by J. Gleadah. London. Published Decr. 1st, 1828, by J. Willett & Blandford, Bouverie St., Fleet St." By the interposition of two islands the River Niagara is separated into three falls, that of the Great Horseshoe, on the west or British side, and those of Fort Schlosser and Montmorency, on the eastern or American side. The three falls, with the islands describe a crescent. Size 12 x 22.

199—KINGSTON, ONT., 1860—View from the harbor, with key. Line engraving. Size 7 x 25.

200—"GENERAL VIEW OF THE FALLS OF NIAGARA—From the British shore. Respectfully dedicated to his patrons, Sir Peregrine Maitland, Lt.-Governor, and the gentlemen of Upper Canada, by their obedient servt., James Gray. Drawn by J. Gray. Aquatinted by J. Gleadah. London: Published Decr. 1st, 1828, by Willett & Blandford, Bouverie Street, Fleet Street." The height of the American Falls is about 167 feet, while the perpendicular descent of the Horseshoe Falls is 158 feet. Size 11 x 21.

201—DWIGHT, HARVEY PRENTICE, 1828-1913—President Great North-Western Telegraph Co. Born in Belleville, Jefferson County, N.Y. Came to Canada in 1847 and entered the service of the Montreal Telegraph Co., remaining in the employ of that company until 1881. In the latter year he became associated with the Great North-Western, as general manager, becoming president in 1892. During the North-West Rebellion rendered the Government signal service, which was acknowledged in Parliament by the Minister of Militia. He died in Toronto. Lithograph. Size 11 x 13. Head and shoulders.

202—LIGHTHOUSE AT MISSISSAGUA POINT, NIAGARA—Plan, Elevation and Section—In 1803 an Act was passed by the Provincial Assembly at York (Toronto) to erect a lighthouse at this point. Dominic Henry, a veteran of the 4th Battalion, Royal Artillery of Cornwallis, was keeper up to 1814, when the beacon was taken down. It is said that Fort Mississagua was built from the ruins of Fort Niagara and the material of the lighthouse. Size 12 x 14.

203—"MONTREAL, FROM ST. HELEN'S ISLAND—Respectfully dedicated to his patrons, Sir Peregrine Maitland, Lt.-Governor, and the gentlemen of Upper Canada, by their obedient servt., James Gray. Drawn by J. Gray. Aquatinted by J. Gleadah. London: Published Decr. 1, 1828, by Willett & Blandford, Bouverie Street, Fleet Street." The picture is taken from opposite the east end of the city. Size 12 x 21. See 114.

204—REPLICA OF JOSEPH BRANT'S MASONIC CERTIFICATE— Captain Brant (Thayendanegea) visited England in 1776, and on 26th April was initiated into Masonry in "The Falcon Lodge," London. On the certificate is inscribed the following: "These are to certify that Brother Joseph Thayeadanegee was made a Mason and admitted to the third degree of Masonry as appears by the Register of the Lodge of Free and Accepted Masons, regularly constituted and meeting at the Falcon, Princess Street, Leicester Fields. Signed by the Master, Wardens and Secretary of the said Lodge hereunto annexed and you are desired to receive him as a Brother after due examination. Given under the Seal of the Grand Lodge. Jas. Heseltine, Grand Secretary, London, 26th April, A. 5776, D. 1776." Photograph of certificate in possession of his great-granddaughter, Mrs. Donald Kerby, Morden, Man.

205—"OTTAWA CITY, CANADA WEST (LOWER TOWN)—From Government Hill, looking down the Ottawa River, showing the locks of the Rideau Canal. Drawn from nature by E. Whitefield. Lith. of Endicott & Co., N.Y., Ottawa. Published by E. Whitefield. 1855. Copyright secured." The picture gives a key of the principal buildings. Lithograph. Size 20 x 36.

206—"FALLS OF MONTMORENCI—From the East Bank. Respectfully dedicated to his patrons, Sir Peregrine Maitland, Lt.-Governor, and the gentlemen of Upper Canada, by their obedient servt., James Gray. Drawn by J. Gray; aquatinted by J. Gleadah. London: Published Decr. 1, 1828, by J. Willett and J. Blandford, Bouverie Street, Fleet Street." A beautiful spot, about eight miles northeast of Quebec. Although higher than Niagara, it has nothing of the latter's grandeur, on account of its narrowness. Prince Edward, afterwards Duke of Kent, made the Montmorency House, in the vicinity of the Falls, his home during the summers of 1791-4. Now Kent House (as the old-time mansion is known), is a summer hotel, the home of many a tourist who visits the rushing waters of the Montmorency. Size 12 x 22.

207—"QUEBEC, FROM POINT LEVI—Respectfully dedicated to his patrons, Sir Peregrine Maitland, Lt.-Governor, and the gentlemen of Upper Canada, by their obedient servt., James Gray. Drawn by J. Gray. Aquatinted by J. Gleadah. London: Published Decr. 1st, 1828, by J. Willett and J. Blandford, Bouverie Street, Fleet Street." Size 12 x 22.

208—AN OLD GUEST BILL—This bill against a guest for a two days' stay at the Clifton House, Niagara Falls, Ont., in May, 1853, was signed by Samuel Shears, brother of George P. Shears, proprietor of the hostelry from 1850-7.

209—WASHINGTON, GEORGE—First President of the United States, 1789-97. Wood engraving. Size 5 x 6. Head and shoulders. See 137.

210—PICKERING, TIMOTHY—An American statesman, born in Massachusetts. July, 1745. He graduated at Harvard in 1763, and became Judge of the Common Pleas in 1775. Joined the army of Washington in 1776, and took part in the battles of Brandywine and Germantown. Appointed Postmaster-General of the United States by Washington, 1791, Commissioner Indian Boundary, Niagara, 1793, and Secretary of War, 1794. From 1814-1817 he was a member of the National House of Representatives. Line engraving. Size 2½ x 4. Head and shoulders.

211—LINCOLN, GENERAL BENJAMIN, 1733-1810—U.S. Commissioner Indian Boundary, Niagara, 1793—Born in Massachusetts. He was a member of the Provincial Congress, assembled in 1775 at Cambridge and Watertown, and one of the secretaries of that body. In 1776, appointed a Major-General of Militia, and joined the army of Washington in 1777. Appointed to the chief command of the Southern Department, 1778, and defended Charleston against Prevost the following year. Later besieged by Sir Henry Clinton in that place and compelled to surrender. From 1781-4 was Secretary of War, and Lieutenant-Governor of Massachusetts, 1787. Line engraving. Size 4 x 4. Three-quarter length.

212—AUTOGRAPHS of President Washington and Secretaries Pickering and Lincoln.

213—MACKINAW ISLAND, 1837—"Indian Lodges on the Beach of the Island of Mackinaw. Anna Jameson, fecit." This view, at the northwest extremity of Lake Huron, was taken by Anna Jameson, artist and authoress, and wife of Chancellor Robert Jameson. In the summer of her sojourn in Canada the lady ventured on an expedition up Lake Huron, making her way to Sault Ste. Marie. The trip occupied two months, and during this time Mrs. Jameson saw a good deal of freedom and roughness of life amongst the Indians. One of her achievements was the shooting of the rapids of Sault Ste. Marie in an Indian birch bark canoe. Pen drawing. Size 6 x 8.

214—BOUCHETTE, R. S. M.—Son of Col. Joseph Bouchette. Took an active part in the suppression of the Lower Canada insurrection. On his return to Canada held office as Commissioner of Customs until 1875. Private plate, with autograph, from a painting by Arminius Meyer, R.A., London, Eng., 1832. Line engraving. Size 5 x 6. Head and shoulders.

215—BOUCHETTE, LIEUT.-COLONEL JOSEPH—Born in Canada, 1774, the son of Commodore Jean Bouchette. As early as 1790 Joseph was employed as a draftsman in the office of his uncle, the Hon. Major Holland, then Surveyor-General of British North America. The following year he entered the provincial navy, sailing the Great Lakes until 1796. Surveyed the harbor of Toronto in 1793. The following year succeeded in raising H.M. war vessel "Onondaga," 14 guns, which had been cast away in York (Toronto) harbor and abandoned; taking command ne sailed with her to Niagara. This service elicited the unqualified approbation of Lord Dorchester, and Bouchette was raised to the rank of second-lieutenant. On the reduction of the navy he obtained a lieutenancy in the Royal Canadian Volunteers. In 1803 he was appointed Deputy Surveyor-General, and the ensuing year Surveyor-General of Lower Canada. Served with merit in the War of 1812. Besides publishing maps of Canada he was the author of a "Topography of Lower Canada," London, 1815, and "Topography of the British Dominions in North America," London, 1831-2. The boundary line between Canada and the United States, as laid down by Col. Bouchette, is generally conceded to be a much fairer one than that determined by the Ashburton Treaty. His death occurred at Montreal, April 9th, 1841. Englehart, pinxt. J. Thomson, sc. Line engraving. Size 6 x 8. Head and shoulders.

216—"GRAND MILITARY STEEPLECHASE AT LONDON, CANADA WEST, 9TH MAY, 1843—Lt. Burnaby, R.E., on Fanny, pink and white; Lt. Romer, 14th Regt., on Moose, blue and white; Lt. Anderson, 83rd Regt., on Murat, black and blue; Lt. Patton, on Francis, lt. blue; Lt. Windham, Royals, on Wild Boy, purple and black; Lt. Lysons, Royals, on Red Indian, crimson and blue. Stewards—Capt. Davenport, Royal Regt.; Lieut. Fisher, R.A.; Lieut. Douglas, 14th Regt., to whom this print is most respectfully dedicated by their obliged and obedient servant, R. Ackermann. Drawn by Lady Alexander. Engraved by J. Harris. London: Published February 21st, 1845, for the Proprietor by Rudolph Ackermann, 191 Regent Street." Lithograph in color. Size 14 x 20.

217—AMERICAN REGIMENTAL COLORS—Taken by the British forces in the War of 1812-14. That on the left was captured, with others, at Fort Detroit, Aug. 16th, 1812. It bears the arms of the United States, and the words, "4th Regiment of Infantry," and was the national color of that regiment. That on the right was taken at Queenston Heights, Oct. 13th, 1812. It bears on one side the arms of the United States, and on the other (shown above) the arms of New York, with its motto, "Excelsior"— the colors of a New York regiment (militia). These colors were sent to England, and placed in the Chapel Royal, Whitehall, London, whence all trophies—French eagles, standards and colors—were by order of the King, transferred to the Royal Hospital, Chelsea, in 1834. The original water color was copied by the kind permission of Mrs. Robinson, widow of the late Christopher Robinson, K.C., third son of the Chief Justice. The late Sir John Beverley Robinson, Bart., as a lieutenant of volunteers, was present in 1812 at the capture of both these colors. Water color. Size 9 x 13.

218—"SKETCH OF THE NIAGARA FALLS SUSPENSION BRIDGE (Now in progress)—Shewing the Basket Ferry and the Temporary Towers of the Foot Bridge. Span 800 ft. Height 230 ft. Hall & Mooney, Lith., Buffalo. Entered according to Act of Congress, A.D. 1848, by Henry Filkins in the Clerk's Office of the Northern District of New York. Halloway, del." Lithograph in color. With description of bridge. Size 9 x 14.

219—"THE RAILROAD SUSPENSION BRIDGE, NEAR NIAGARA FALLS—John A. Roebling, Esqre., Engineer. Length of bridge 822 feet. Height above water 240 feet. Entered according to Act of Congress in the year 1856 by N. Currier, in the Clerk's Office of the District of the Southern District of New York. C. Parsons, del. Published by N. Currier, 152 Nassau Street, New York." The bridge is in full view of the Falls, connecting the U.S. and Canada, the New York Central and Great Western Railways. Chromo lithograph. Size 10 x 15.

220—OLD MASONIC CERTIFICATE—Issued at Niagara in 1787. This is a photo copy of the oldest Masonic certificate known in Upper Canada. It was issued to John Wrong, July 1st, 1787, by Freemasons' Lodge No. 322, "of the Registry of Ireland, held in his Majesty's twenty-ninth Regiment of Foot," stationed at that day in Niagara. The certificate is the property of J. E. Wrong, Niagara Falls, Ont., a great-grandson of Brother John Wrong.

221—"A BIRDSEYE VIEW OF THE RIVER NIAGARA—From Lake Erie to Lake Ontario, shewing the situation and extent of Navy Island, and the towns and villages on the banks of the river, in Canada and the United States, with the situation of the Caroline steamboat off Schlosser. From a drawing by W. R. Callington, engineer, Boston, from an actual survey made in 1837. Published by J. Robins, Bride Court, Fleet Street, London." With key. Lithograph in color. Size 9 x 15.

222—SLEIGHING IN NORTH AMERICA—London, published by G. S. Tregear, 96 Cheapside. Aquatint in color. Size 8 x 11.

223—NIAGARA FALLS, 1850—With river bank in foreground. Water color by Gen. A. R. V. Crease, R.E. Size 7 x 11.

224—ENTRANCE TO THE NIAGARA RIVER FROM THE CANADIAN FORT, 1849—The steamer shown is the Chief Justice Robinson, 400 tons, owned and commanded by Capt. Hugh Richardson; was built at Niagara in 1842, and for many years was on the route between Lewiston and Toronto. Water color by Gen. A. R. V. Crease, R.E. Size 7 x 10.

225—INTERIOR OF ST. ANDREW'S PRESBYTERIAN CHURCH, NIAGARA—Water color, by Owen Staples. Size 20 x 26. See 1253, 1273.

226—"LONDON, CANADA WEST—Drawn from nature by E. Whitefield, London. Published by E. Whitefield, 1855. Entered according to Act of Congress in the year 1855 by E. Whitefield, in the clerk's office of the district court of New York." Lithograph with key. Size 20 x 36.

227—"PROPOSED TUBULAR BRIDGE FOR CROSSING THE NIAGARA GORGE—S. Russel, Del.. Kell Bros., Lithrs., Castle St., Holborn. Published by John Weale, London, 1860." The proposed bridge was never erected. Chromo lithograph. Size 14 x 20.

228—"NAVY ISLAND AND THE VILLAGE OF CHIPPEWA—Looking towards the Falls of Niagara, Chippewa Village, Niagara Falls and Goat Island, Navy Island. G. Tattersall. G. Barnard, lit." Navy Island is situated just above the mouth of the Chippawa River. The village is at the confluence of the Chippawa River with the Niagara, and is memorable for the battle fought there, July 5th, 1814, between the British and Americans. Lithograph. Size 11 x 14.

229—"THE BATTLE OF QUEENSTON, 13TH OCT., 1812—Which ended in a complete victory on the part of the British, having captured 927 men, killed or wounded about 500, taken 1,400 stand of arms, a six-pounder and a stand of colours. Drawn by Major Dennis. Engraved by T. Sutherland. London: Pubd. April 12th, 1836, for I. W. Laird's Martial Achievements, at 1 Leadenhall Street." Line engraving. Size 13 x 19.

230—NIAGARA, 1854—With key. The "Chief Justice Robinson," which for a number of years plied between Toronto and Lewiston, is seen entering the river. Water color by F. H. Granger. Size 7 x 24.

231—ST. MARK'S ANGLICAN CHURCH, NIAGARA, 1834—The first church was opened in 1809, destroyed by Americans in 1813, rebuilt later, and transepts added in 1843. The steamer in the river is the "Queenston," built in 1824, and continued as a regular packet between that point, Toronto and Prescott until 1831. Drawn from nature and on stone by G. D'Almaine. In color. Size 11 x 17. See 1270, 1274.

232—FORT MISSISSAGA, NIAGARA—On west side of the entrance to Niagara River. Little but the ramparts, tower and magazines remain of this fort, the earthworks of which were erected about 1793. At different points where there were batteries during the War of 1812, and after the war, the fort was constructed, the walls being built of bricks brought from the ruins of the town. For many years the fort and buildings within the enclosure were occupied by British soldiers. Water color by Gen. A. R. V. Crease. Size 6 x 9.

233—FORT NIAGARA, N.Y.—Built by De Nonville in 1687, abandoned a year later. In 1716 a recommendation for a fort at Niagara was sent from Quebec to France, and the French in 1725 built the first permanent fort. It was besieged by the British in 1759, and captured by Sir William Johnson. At the end of the "hold over" period, 1796, the fort was given up by the British to the United States. Water color by Gen. A. R. V. Crease. Size 6 x 9.

234—SERVOS FARM, PALATINE HILL, NIAGARA TOWNSHIP, 1910 —From the site of the Servos Mill, the first Government grist mill, erected on the Servos farm about 1777. The Four-Mile Creek is shown in the foreground, and running into the picture. Water color by Owen Staples. Size 22 x 29.

235—"HAMILTON, CANADA WEST, FROM THE MOUNTAIN—
Drawn from nature by E. Whitefield, Hamilton. Published by E. White-
field, Hamilton, 1854. Lith. of Endicott & Co., N.Y. Entered according to
Act of Congress in the year 1854, by E. Whitefield, in the clerk's office
of the district court of the southern district of N.Y. Lithograph with key.
Size 20 x 35.

236—SHIPMAN, PAUL, 1756-1825—Son of Paul Shipman, who, with
ten other members of the family, fought in the Revolutionary War. Paul
Shipman, jun., emigrated to Canada, settling at "The Twelve" (St.
Catharines). The first tavern in the place was built by George Adams
in 1797, at what is now the junction of Ontario and St. Paul streets. He
owned it for a considerable time, but Shipman, shortly after his arrival,
acquired it, and St. Catharines, which had been so named on its first
survey in 1809, bore the name "Shipman's Corners" for a time. In the
early days Shipman's Tavern was a favorite rendezvous and pleasure resort. A tablet to the memory of Paul Shipman is in St. George's Church,
St. Catharines. From a silhouette in possession of his great-granddaughter,
Mrs. C. Van Auda, New York. Size 3 x 4. Head, in profile. See 237.

237—SHIPMAN, MRS. ELIZABETH—Wife of Paul Shipman, a St.
Catharines pioneer. From a silhouette in possession of her great-granddaughter, Mrs. C. Van Auda, New York. Size 3 x 4. Head, in profile.

238—ANCIENT INVITATION—Reproduction of an invitation to Miss
Catharine Rodman Prendergast, daughter of Dr. Prendergast, one of the
earliest physicians on the Niagara peninsula, to attend a ball at Shipman's
Tavern, Twelve-Mile Creek (now St. Catharines, Ont.), 18th Feb., 1811. Miss
Prendergast afterwards became the wife of Hon. Wm. Hamilton Merritt,
who in 1816 purchased the greater part of the land upon which the present
city of St. Catharines is built. From original in possession of her granddaughter, Miss Merritt, St. Catharines.

239—NIAGARA FALLS—Canada—This view of the Falls was engraved
from a "Map of the Dominions of the King of Great Britain in North
America," by Herman Moll, geographer, 1711. From an old engraving in
the British Museum, London, England, with description. Size 9 x 9.

240—MAP OF LAKE ONTARIO—With English and French Fleets in
1757—The original by Labroquerie, a French engineer at Fort Frontenac
(Kingston, U.C.), 4th Oct., 1757, is the first hand-made map of Lake Ontario,
and gives not only the principal ports and places from east to west on both
sides of the lake, but also pictures of the English and French fleets. A
full description of the map, with ports and places, and the fleets will be
found in Robertson's Landmarks of Toronto, Vol. III., pp. 88-90. Labroquerie
(La Broquerie) died in 1762 at Boucherville, Que. Reproduction from
original in the King's Library, British Museum. Size 9 x 11.

241—"VIEW OF THE RAILWAY DISASTER AT HAMILTON, C.W.,
on Thursday Evn., March 12th, 1857—Drawn & Lith. by H. Gregory,
Hamilton, from a daguerreotype by D. Preston." Size 11 x 15. See 242.

242—SCENE OF THE GREAT WESTERN RAILWAY ACCIDENT,
12TH MARCH, 1857—A passenger train proceeding from Toronto to
Hamilton crashed through the bridge over the Desjardins Canal, near
Hamilton, and, as a result, seventy lives were lost. This was the first
serious railway accident that had ever occurred in the Province of Ontario.
The accident was caused by the deck or flooring of the bridge giving way.
A steel structure stands here to-day (1917). Wood engraving. Size 6 x 10.
See 241.

243—ZIMMERMAN, SAMUEL—In 1842 came to Canada from Pennsylvania, where he was born in 1815. Settled at Thorold and became a celebrated financier and railway contractor, building 120 miles of the Great Western Railway, as well as several other railways in Canada. Also constructed four locks and an aqueduct on the Welland Canal. He lost his life in the Desjardins Canal accident, March 12th, 1857. Lithograph. Size 8 x 9. Head and shoulders.

244—DUNN, HON. JOHN HENRY, 1794-1854—Water color, by his daughter, Lady Green, wife of Major-General Sir Henry Rodes Green, of London, from an oil painting made about 1834. Size 9 x 11. Head and shoulders. See 24.

245—GALE—"Revd. Alexander Gale, First Presbyterian Minister of Hamilton, Canada West. Obt. 6 April, 1854. Aet. 54. From a daguerreotype by A. Hoenisch. Schenck & McFarlane, lithographers, Edinburgh." He was a native of Coldstone, Aberdeenshire, Scotland; came to Lower Canada in 1827, and subsequently settled as minister in Amherstburgh, U.C., where he remained three years. From 1833-46 he was in Hamilton, and was then called to occupy the positions of principal of the Toronto Academy and classical professor in Knox College. Lived at Logie-on-the-Mountain, near Cook's Mills, where for some years he had a private school. He died there 6th April, 1854. Lithograph. Size 6 x 7. Head and shoulders. See 2797.

246—SWALE, MRS. HOGARTH J.—Foundress of Holy Trinity Church, Toronto. In 1845 Mrs. Swale, who resided in England, through the Bishop of Ripon, afterwards Archbishop of Canterbury, gave £5,000 sterling to Bishop Strachan for the purpose of erecting a church in his diocese. Her express conditions were that the church be called the "Church of the Holy Trinity," that the seats be "free and unappropriated forever," and that her name remain secret. The church was opened and consecrated in 1847. For nearly fifty years the secret of who built Holy Trinity Church was well kept, but about 1894 the name became known, and in 1897 the church-wardens, feeling it was then no breach of confidence, alluded to the matter in most fitting terms in their report. Water color from the original in England. Size 4 x 5. Head and shoulders.

247—BOOTH, REV. WILLIAM ("GENERAL"), 1829-1912—Founder of the Salvation Army. He was born in Nottingham, England, and at an early age became a member of the Methodist Church. Was much interested in evangelistic work, continuing it after his ordination as minister. In 1865 he formed the Christian Mission, which developed into a large organization on military lines, and in 1878 became known as the Salvation Army. Mr. Booth, commonly called "General," was an indefatigable worker and organizer, and kept constantly in touch with the international work of the Army, established the "War Cry" in 1880, and ten years later published "Darkest England and the Way Out." In 1907, Oxford conferred upon him the degree of D.C.L. In Washington he was invited to open the U.S. Senate with prayer, and, as a mark of honor, the City of London presented him with its freedom. His death took place in London, England. Original drawing for "Vanity Fair," by L. Ward (Spy), Nov. 25th, 1882. Size 8 x 12. Full length.

248—LAVAL, HIS GRACE FRANCOIS DE, 1622-1708—First Roman Catholic Bishop of Canada (Quebec)—He was ordained priest at Paris, 23rd Sept., 1645, and made Archdeacon of Evreux in 1653. Appointed Vicar Apostolic of Nouvelle France, by Pope Alexander VII., 5th July, 1658. He arrived in Canada the following June, founded the Seminary of Quebec, consecrated the Parochial Church of Quebec, and in 1674 returned to

France, when he was named Bishop of Quebec, a suffragan Bishop of the Holy See. His Grace de Laval resigned his Bishopric of Quebec in Paris, 24th Jan., 1688 (he had visited France several times since 1659), and left that city some time after for Quebec. He afterwards retired to his Seminary, to which he made over his entire effects. Line engraving. Size 4 x 5. Head and shoulders. See 1650.

249—CHARBONNEL, THE RT. REV. ARMAND FRANCIS MARIE, COMTE DE—Second Roman Catholic Bishop of Toronto, 1850-60. Belonged to an old and illustrious family; was born 1st December, 1802, near Monistrol-sur-Loire, France; ordained priest in 1825; entered Society of St. Sulpice the following year. He came to Canada in 1839. During the succeeding years he was frequently offered episcopal honors, which he declined. In 1850 Father Charbonnel, as successor to Bishop Power, was consecrated Bishop of Toronto by Pope Pius IX., taking formal possession of the See in September of that year. During his episcopate the House of Providence, Toronto, was founded, and the Diocese of Hamilton and London erected. His repeated appeal that he be allowed to resign was at last sustained, and in 1860 he returned to France. Died 29th March, 1891. Photo from lithograph. Size 7 x 9. Head and shoulders. See 2535.

250—McMAHON, REV. PATRICK—Founder of St. Patrick's Church, Quebec—He was born at Abbeylix, Ireland. Came to Canada in 1818, and was ordained by Mgr. Plessis, 6th Oct., 1822. In 1825 he labored as a missionary at St. John, N.B., but was recalled to Quebec three years later to minister to the Irish Catholics of that city. Accommodation offered in Church of Notre Dame des Victoires, in which Father McMahon held special services was totally inadequate, so that subscriptions were taken up for construction of an independent church. To this fund the Protestants of the city liberally subscribed. On 7th July, 1833, the first service was held in St. Patrick's. Father McMahon, who died 3rd October, 1851, is the only individual honored by burial in the church, which also contains a mural monument to his memory. Lithograph. Size 13 x 21. Full length.

251—MECHANICS' INSTITUTE DIPLOMA—The Mechanics' Institute, fashioned after the Mechanics' Institute in Edinburgh and London, was in 1830 established in York (Toronto) under the title of the York Mechanics' Institute. Its object was the mutual improvement of mechanics and others who were members, and, with this end in view, annual exhibitions were held by the Institute, at which the best efforts of manufacturers were shown. The first exhibition was held in 1848. The honors awarded were diplomas, those in 1850 being made by Scobie & Balfour's lithographing and printing establishment, Toronto, and designed and lithographed by Sandford Fleming (late Sir Sandford Fleming), Land Surveyor, on stone. The diploma shown was won by W. & R. Edwards, saddlers, on Yonge street, near Temperance street.

252—STRACHAN, BISHOP—"The Honourable and Right Rev. John Strachan, D.D., Lord Bishop of Toronto. To the Clergy and Laity of the United Church of England and Ireland and Canada, this engraving is most respectfully dedicated by the publisher, Henry Rowsell, Toronto. Painted by Berthon. Engraved by Warner. Proof." Born in Aberdeen, 1778; entered the university of that place in 1794. Through the late Hon. Richard Cartwright and Hon. Robert Hamilton, he received an offer to come to Canada, which he did in 1799. Opened a school at Kingston, and, subsequently, resolved to enter the Church of England (he was of the Presbyterian faith). Accordingly he was ordained deacon by Bishop Mountain, and appointed to the Mission of Cornwall. In 1812 he became rector of York. Member Executive and Legislative Councils. In the summer of that year he was consecrated first Bishop of Toronto, a diocese comprising the whole of Upper Canada. He labored in this field until the western division of the province was erected into a diocese, under Rev. Dr. Cronyn. Bishop Strachan passed away on 1st November, 1867, in Toronto. Line engraving. Size 10 x 12. Half length, sitting. See 2732, 2805, 3199.

253—FIRST CATHOLIC PROVINCIAL COUNCIL OF FATHERS AND THEOLOGIANS, HELD IN ST. MICHAEL'S PALACE, TORONTO, 1875— The object of the Council was to lay down rules in directing priests in their general administration and to regulate their lives in keeping with their sacred calling. The following key gives the names of those present: 1, Right Rev. P. T. Crinnon, D.D., Bp. of Hamilton. 2, Right Rev. John Walsh, D.D., Bp. of London. 3, Most Rev. John Jos. Lynch, D.D., Archbp. of Toronto. 4, Right Rev. J. F. Jamol, D.D., Bp. of Peterborough. 5, Right Rev. John O'Brien, D.D., Bp. of Kingston. 6, Rev. Father Williams, of Kingston. 7, Rev. Dr. Chisholm, of Kingston. 8, Rev. Father Stafford, of Kingston. 9, Very Rev. Father J. Farley, V.G., of Kingston. 10, Rev. C. Rouman, S.J. 11, Rev. Father J. M. Laurent, of Toronto. 12, Very Rev. F. C. Rooney, V.G., Toronto. 13, Very Rev. Laurent, V.G., London. 14, Very Rev. E. Funcken, Supt. St. Jerome's, (Berlin) College. 15, Very Rev. Heenan, V.G., Hamilton. 16, Rev. John Furlong, Sacristan, Toronto. 17, Rev. F. F. Rohleder, Toronto. 18, Rev. J. J. McEntee, Toronto. 19, Very Rev. Bruyere, V.G., Hamilton. 20, Rev. J. B. Proux, Toronto. 21, Rev. John Shea, Toronto. 22, Rev. P. Conway, Toronto. 23, Very Rev. C. Vincent, Supt. St. Michael's College. Photograph, hand colored. Size 9 x 14.

254—GREEN—"Revd. Anson Green, D.D., President of the Canada Conference in 1842. Painted by W. Gush, Esq. Engraved by J. Cochran." Entered the work of the Methodist ministry in 1824, and ordained at Ancaster three years later. For many years he labored in various Ontario circuits, and in 1854 was superannuated. He, however, resumed active work, being finally superannuated in 1865. Elected President of the Canada Conference in 1842, and in 1846 and 1854 acted as representative to the British Conference. Dr. Green was from 1845-53 Book Steward of the Methodist Book Room, King street east, Toronto, and again from 1859-64. He died February, 1879. Line engraving. Size 4 x 5. Head and shoulders.

255—MEDLEY—"The Right Revd. the Lord Bishop of Fredericton. Painted by John Bridges. Engraved by Saml. Bellin. Published Aug. 1st, 1849, by J. Hogarth, 5 Haymarket, London. H. J. Wallace, Exeter. Printed by W. Hatton. Proof." Most Rev. John Medley, D.D., was born in London, Eng., 19th Dec., 1804; educated at Wadham College, Oxford, graduating with honors, 1826. In 1828 he was ordained deacon, and priest in 1829. He became incumbent of St. John's Chapel, Truro, Cornwall, 1831, seven years later being transferred to Exeter, where in 1842 he became prebendary of Exeter Cathedral. When the Diocese of Fredericton, N.B., was formed in 1845, the Archbishop of Canterbury appointed Dr. Medley as first Bishop, his See to comprise the whole Province of New Brunswick. For many years he labored diligently, seldom leaving his diocese. In 1879, as oldest Bishop in the Dominion, he became Metropolitan of Canada. Bishop Medley wrote several books of a religious character. He died 9th Sept., 1892. Line engraving. Size 12 x 16. Three-quarter length, sitting.

256—MACKENZIE, WILLIAM LYON, 1795-1864—Photo from a portrait by J. W. L. Forster. Size 12 x 16. Head and shoulders. See 363.

257—HUT-GOH-SO-DO-NEH (LEWIS BENNETT)—Known as Deerfoot, the Seneca Indian runner. He was born in 1830 at the Cattaraugus Reserve, a few miles southwest of Buffalo, N.Y. In 1865-6 he toured England, and in 1871 ran at Listowel, Ont. In England and occasionally in the States he ran in moccasins and Indian head-dress, but performed best in the regulation costume, the moccasins and feathers being worn for the entertainment of the spectators to whom he was somewhat of a circus sensation. He ran with the "flat-footed" action common to the Indians, but it was not as pronounced as the "shamble" of the Canadian runner, Tom Longboat. Bennett's death occurred in 1896 at the Cattaraugus Reservation. The name, "Deerfoot," was given to Bennett because of his prowess in running down and killing deer when the hard crust of the winter's snow was softened by the sun and the speed of the quarry thus retarded. London: Published November 9th, 1861, by Geo. Newbold, 303 and 304 Strand, W.C. Lithograph. Size 12 x 16. Full length.

258—TORONTO HARBOR—Original entrance at Queen's Wharf, north Channel, at west end of Bay, in use from 1790-1911. A new channel from the lake is now cut about 1,000 feet south, and is the regular steamer channel. Chromo lithograph, by Coke Smyth. Size 11 x 15.

259—MENU OF DINNER TO ROBERT STEPHENSON, C.E., M.P., D.C.L., F.R.S.—Son of George Stephenson, who built the first locomotive. Born in England, 1803. After studying at the University of Edinburgh for one session he assisted his father in the construction of the Stockton and Darlington Railway, and in the manufacture of locomotives. In 1824 he went to South America to examine gold and silver mines there. Was the designer of the Victoria Bridge, Montreal, which was first opened for traffic in 1860. Completed the 140 miles of railway between Cairo and Alexandria, with two tubular bridges, and also constructed an immense bridge across the Nile. Represented Whitby, Yorkshire, in Parliament from 1847 until his death, in 1859. When in Canada in 1853 he visited Toronto, and was entertained by the engineering profession at a dinner held in the Parliament Buildings, August 26th, 1853. The guests were received in the Legislative Assembly Chamber, and the dinner was held in the Council Chamber. In the chair was the Hon. H. H. Killaly, then Assistant Commissioner of the Board of Public Works.

260—ST. STEPHEN'S CHURCH (ANGLICAN)—"N.E. View of the Church of S. Stephen, Toronto, Canada, W. To Robert Brittain Denison, Esq., of Toronto. This view is dedicated by his faithful servant, the Architect. T. Fuller, Architect, Toronto. Fuller & Bencke, Lithographers, Victoria Hall, Toronto." The church, which was erected by Lieut.-Col. R. B. Denison, at the corner of Bellevue avenue and College street, was opened for service November 28th, 1858, and was the first church in the city west of Spadina avenue. In 1865 it was destroyed by fire, but was immediately rebuilt, and has since been enlarged several times. It is of red brick with stone facings, and is designed after the Early English Gothic style of architecture. The first rector was the Rev. J. H. McCollum, who had charge from 1858-61, when he was succeeded by the Rev. A. J. Broughall, rector, 1861-98. The present (1916) incumbent is the Rev. Thos. G. Wallace. Lieut.-Col. Denison, the donor, was also one of the first Church Wardens of St. Stephen's. Lithograph in color. Size 16 x 20.

261—ORIGINAL PLAN OF TORONTO PURCHASE FROM THE INDIANS, 1787-1805—The site on which Toronto stands was sold by the Mississaga Indians to the Crown. There were two interviews in connection with the sale, the first in September, 1787, when the purchase was formally discussed, and at the second meeting, 1st August, 1805, the bargain was completed. For the sum of $9,500 the extent of 250,808 acres were sold, of which Toronto at present (1916) occupies 25,330.4 acres. Of this, 20,418.8 acres is land, and 4,911.6 is water. The latter is made up of harbor area, 1,759.5 acres, Ashbridge's Bay, 1,385 acres, and other waters. Pen and ink drawing from original in Crown Lands Dept. Size 12 x 18.

262—KING STREET, TORONTO, 1836—Depicting the north side of the street, between Toronto and Church, and the south side from opposite the south end of Toronto street, to East Market street. Among the buildings shown are St. James' Church (Cathedral), northeast corner of King and Church, built 1831, destroyed by fire, 1839; the Court House, Jail and Market House. (See key to picture). T. Young, Archt. Delt. Bufford, on stone. N. Currier's Lith., No. 1 Wall St., N.Y. Size 12 x 18.

263—LADY ELGIN CUTTING THE FIRST SOD OF THE ONTARIO, SIMCOE AND HURON RAILWAY—The late F. C. Capreol, of Toronto, conceived the idea of carrying through a railroad from Toronto to Lake Huron. He met with many obstacles and difficulties in his plans. Nothing daunted, however, he persevered, and, finally, on the 15th October, 1851, Lady Elgin, wife of the then Governor-General, in the presence of a large number of people on the south side of Front street, just west of Simcoe street, opposite the old Parliament Buildings, turned the first sod of Canada's first railroad. The scene was a gala one. Flags floated, banners flew, while Mayor Bowes was resplendent in cocked hat, knee breeches, silk stockings, and shoes with silver buckles. In 1859 the system was known as the Northern Railway. On amalgamation with the Hamilton and North Western Railway, the company in 1888 became the Grand Trunk. Water color by Gen. A. R. V. Crease, R.E. Size 12 x 25. See 518, 782.

264—OLD-TIME BUGGY—The first constructed in North York. It was made early in 1844 by James Charles and the Wilkins Brothers, at Cosford's Corners, about a mile and a half north of present (1916) Wellington street, Aurora. Seth Heacock, members of whose family lived on farm lots 26, 27, concession 3, King Township, from 1806-1910, owned the vehicle, which was considered a fine one and figured in many weddings of the countryside. It was presented in 1910 to the York Pioneer Society, by G. W. and F. W. Heacock. The vehicle known as the "buggy" had its origin in India. The name comes from the Hindustani "baggi." In India it was a two-wheeled vehicle with a hood, in England the same, with or without a hood, and in the United States and Canada a four-wheeled vehicle with one seat, with or without a hood. Drawing in water color. Size 5 x 7.

265—CHURCH OF THE HOLY TRINITY, TORONTO—Interior View. In 1835 the locality of Holy Trinity Church was known as "the fields," and comprised the garden and clear space around the residence of Dr. James Macaulay, formerly of the Queen's Rangers. Through funds supplied by Mrs. Hogarth J. Swale (see No. 246), the church was built on a site given by Col. John Simcoe Macaulay, son of Dr. Macaulay. The building is a large brick structure, cruciform in shape, with two narrow transepts adjoining the chancel. It runs east and west. The foundation stone was laid 1st July, 1846, and the church opened and consecrated, 1847. The Church of the Holy Trinity still (1917) stands, enclosed on all sides by buildings, within a few rods of Yonge street, one of Toronto's busiest thoroughfares. Sketch plan by C. E. Thomas, son of Wm. Thomas, the architect. Size 6 x 8.

266—WRIT OF SUMMONS, 1816—This writ, which is now (1916) in the office of Sheriff Mowat, of Toronto, was issued against Donald McArthur, a merchant of the town of York, on complaint of Michael Stoben, for trespass. It is signed by John Small, Clerk of Crown and Pleas, 1806-25. Samuel Jarvis, a cousin of William Botsford Jarvis, was the plaintiff's attorney. Photograph.

267—BAINES RESIDENCE—The dwelling, which stood on the west side of Simcoe street, on what is now the site of No. 190 (AB) 192-6, was the home of Thomas Baines, of Baines and Thompson, brewers, 1850-8

Queen street west. Mr. Baines was the father of Dr. Allen Baines, of Toronto. The view shown is from the garden at the rear of the house. Pen drawing. Size 6 x 9.

268—BALDWIN, HON. W. W.—"William Warren Baldwin, of Spadina, in the County of York, Upper Canada. Formerly M.P. for the United Counties of York and Simcoe, and afterwards for the County of Norfolk in the Parliament of Upper Canada, and many years Treasurer of the Honourable the Law Society of that section of the Province. To the Treasurer and Benchers of which Society this plate, taken by their permission from the original in their Convocation Chambers at Osgoode Hall, is most respectfully dedicated by their most obedt. servt., the Publisher. Painted by Theople. Hamel. Printed by Nagel & Weingaertner, N.Y. F. Davignon, Lithr., 323 Broadway." Lithograph. Size 10 x 12. Head and shoulders.

269—BALDWIN, HON. ROBT.—"Robert Baldwin, of Spadina, in the County of York, Upper Canada. Her Majesty's Attorney-General for Upper Canada, and P.M. for the North Riding of the County of York in the Parliament of Canada. Painted by Theophle. Hamel." Lithograph. Size 11 x 13. Half length, sitting. See 271, 461, 1050.

270—UPPER CANADA COLLEGE, TORONTO—This institution was founded by Sir John Colborne in 1829. The ground on which the buildings were erected was known as Russell Square, bounded by John, King, Simcoe and Adelaide streets. During erection, classes were held in the "Old Blue School," in the block directly north of St. James' Cathedral. On 8th Jan., 1830, the buildings on King street west were opened, and in 1876-77 additions were made. The College moved into the present (1917) buildings, Deer Park, Toronto, in 1891. Water color. Size 6 x 8. See 3666.

271—BALDWIN, HON. ROBERT, 1804-58—"This portrait of the Honorable Robt. Baldwin is dedicated to the Reformers of Canada by their obt. servant, H. Meyer. Painted and engraved by Hoppner Meyer." Size 9 x 10. Head and shoulders. See 269, 461, 1050.

272—GIVINS HOMESTEAD, "PINE GROVE"—Rear view. The residence was situated near North road, now Givens street. Etching by Wm. J. Thomson. Size 4 x 6. See 280, 675, 681.

273—KING'S COLLEGE, TORONTO—East side of Queen's Park, present site of east wing of Legislative Buildings. The charter was granted in 1827 and the building erected 1842-3, but not occupied till 1845. While it was in the process of erection the first sessions of the University were held in the Parliament Buildings, Front street. The structure shown was occupied from 1845-53. A second charter was issued in 1849, and the institution became the University of Toronto, the faculty of divinity being abolished. In 1853 the faculties of law and medicine were also abolished, and in the same year the site of this hall of learning was appropriated for the Parliament of Upper and Lower Canada. The University was thus compelled to again hold lectures in their old quarters on Front street, but in 1855 they returned to the Medical Building, on the site now (1917) occupied by the Biological Department. Two years later they removed to the new University Buildings. Water color. Size 5 x 7. See 2815.

274—TORONTO IN 1841-3—"To the Right Honorable Lord Stanley, her Majesty's Principal Secretary of State for the Colonies, etc., etc., etc. This print of the west view of the city of Toronto, in the Province of Canada, is most respectfully dedicated by his Lordship's very obedient and humble servant, the Publisher. Drawn by John Gilespie, Toronto. Dodson, Lith. Day & Haghe, Lithrs. to the Queen, London: Published by F. C. Capreol,

24th Jany., 1842." With key. The picture gives a glimpse of King street from Leslie Bros.' Building, site (1917), north-east corner of Victoria and King Sts. Lord Stanley was in 1833-4 and from 1841-5 Colonial Secretary. He was created Baron Stanley in 1844. Lithograph. Size 13 x 24.

275—GRASETT—"Rev. Henry James Grasett, Rector of St. James' Church, Toronto, C.W." Son of Dr. Grasett, of the 48th Northamptonshire Regiment, was born at Gibraltar, 18th June, 1808. He entered St. John's College, Cambridge, in 1831, took his B.A. in 1834, and M.A. eight years later, and D.D. in 1869. His first charge was in Quebec, after being ordained deacon by Bishop Stewart. In 1835 he was appointed assistant to Archdeacon Strachan at St. James' Church, Toronto. The latter in 1839 became first Anglican Bishop of Toronto, but remained rector of St. James' until 1847, when Mr. Grasett succeeded him. For many years he was examining and domestic chaplain and private secretary to the Bishop. Became first Dean of Toronto, 1867. He died in 1882 and was buried in the chancel of the church where for so many years he had ministered. Lithograph. Size 12 x 15. Head and shoulders. See 3200.

276—RAVEN PLUME—The first bazaar in York (Toronto) was held 27th December, 1833, under the patronage of Lady Colborne, and was given to obtain funds for the relief of distress occasioned by a recent visitation of cholera. The "Raven Plume" was written for the York Bazaar and sung on that occasion by J. E. Goodson, Esq. The song, a romance from a Welsh legendary tale, was dedicated to Miss Mary Powell, and was composed by Mr. I. W. Cawdell, who later was librarian and secretary to the Law Society of Upper Canada at Osgoode Hall. Original MSS of music.

277—A LEAPING FIN-BACK—Whaling off the British Columbia Coast, 1912—The artist, who spent some time with the whalers on the north coast of Vancouver Island, has here depicted a seventy-foot fin-back whale leaping into the air after having been harpooned. These fin-backs average seventy feet in length, yielding some forty barrels of oil. During the whaling season, which covers nine months of the year, a fleet of small vessels is employed, bringing in as many as a dozen prizes a day. Oil, in black and white, by Arthur Heming, Toronto. Size 14 x 21.

278—PROPOSED FIRST GAS LAMP, TORONTO, 1840—"To the Right Honorable the Mayor, Aldermen and Common Council of the City of Toronto, this elevation of an obelisk suggested to be erected at the junction of King and Yonge Streets, is most respectfully inscribed by their obedient humble servant, Thomas Glegg, Architect, July, 1840. It is proposed that this obelisk be lighted with oil until it is decided to introduce gas into the city. The requisite number of lamps similar to the above to be made and the lamp posts to be cast of a pattern as near as possible to agree in design with the obelisk." This lamp post was never erected. Toronto's streets were first lighted with gas on 28th Dec., 1841. Photograph from original in Board of Works Office, City Hall. Size 10 x 13.

279—CUTTING UP A BLUE WHALE—At Kyuquot, Vancouver Island, 1912—The men at the whaling station, the most weasterly on the island— are engaged in cutting up the bone taken from the skull of an eighty-two foot blue whale, captured by a whaling party which Mr. Heming accompanied. The blubber is first stripped off, cut into pieces about a foot square, thrown into a chopping machine and the minced fat carried to the rendering tanks. It is then boiled in these steam tanks, allowed to settle and cool, filtered and barrelled. The sediment, or stearine remaining, which resembles lard, is valuable in the making of soap and candles. The flesh is cooked, dried, screened and blown into sacks, to be sold as fertilizer. The bones, after having been boiled, are broken up, dried and pounded fine, and then also sold as fertilizer. Oil, in black and white, by Arthur Heming, Toronto. Size 14 x 22.

280—GIVINS HOMESTEAD—Front view, 1888—There is some doubt as to when this house was built by Col. James Givins, Supt. Indian Department, Upper Canada, who bought the land, one of twentyeight park lots, consisting of one hundred acres each, from Col. Joseph Bouchette in 1802. The homestead was situated on what was known as Pine Grove, North road, and the house was reached from Dundas street, north of Queen, east side, near the first turn. It was demolished in 1891, and the site is now (1916) 28 Halton street, while the property at the back, on the south side of Arthur street, is occupied by houses Nos. 259-279, opposite North Givins street. Givins street, north of College, is now Roxton road. Pen drawing by Owen Staples. Size 10 x 15. See 272, 675, 681.

281—"TORONTO HARBOUR IN 1820—Facsimile of an original drawing by Sir Peregrine Maitland, K.C.B., Lieutt.-Governor of Upper Canada. W. C. Chewett & Co., Litho., Toronto." Size 5 x 10.

282—JONES, REV. PETER—"Kahkewaquonaby, Peter Jones. Painted by Matilda Jones. Engraved by T. A. Dean. Published by Mason, 14 City Road and 66 Paternoster Row." An Ojibway missionary and chief, who for thirty-one years labored in the ministry of the Wesleyan Methodist Church. Born January 1st, 1802, in the woods at Burlington Heights, C.W. His father, Augustus Jones, who was of Welsh extraction, is notable as the man who made the earliest surveys in Northumberland County. Peter, or, according to his Indian designation, Kahkewaquonaby (Sacred Waving Feathers), until he reached the age of fourteen, was brought up in the customs and superstitutions of his Indian mother. His death occurred in Toronto, June 29th, 1856. Line engraving. Size 4 x 5. Half length.

283—THE GRANGE—Head of John street, Toronto—The main building was erected about 1820 by D'Arcy Boulton, eldest son of Justice Boulton. The gate, now crowded back to the head of John street, was originally at Queen street, and the house was reached by a central drive through the grounds, beginning at the east side of McCaul street. In the social life of York and Toronto the Grange played an important part, many notables having been entertained there. After the death of D'Arcy Boulton in 1844, his widow continued to reside there with her eldest son, William Henry Boulton. The widow of the latter married Prof. Goldwin Smith. Mrs. Smith died 9th Sept., 1909, and her husband in 1910. By the terms of her will, The Grange passed to the recently-formed Art Museum of Toronto. Etching by Henry S. Howland, jr., 1887. Size 5 x 8.

284—COLBORNE LODGE, HIGH PARK—Residence of J. G. Howard, architect and surveyor; one of the early settlers of York. Pen drawing by Owen Staples. Size 10 x 16.

285—GOVERNMENT HOUSE, TORONTO, C.W., 1828-62—Southwest corner King and Simcoe streets. Water color. Size 12 x 19. See 296.

286—PRICE—"The Hon. James Hervey Price, M.P. for the South Riding of York, and her Majesty's Commissioner of Crown Lands, Canada. First City Clerk of Toronto in the Year of its Incorporation, 1834. Painted by Theople. Hamel. Lith. by F. Davignon. Print by Nagel, N.Y." Size 10 x 10. Half length. See 750.

287—CELEBRATED MURDER TRIAL—Grace Marks, alias Mary Whitney, and James McDermott, as they appeared in the Court House, Church street, Toronto, 3rd Nov., 1841, accused of murdering Mr. Thomas Kinnear, a resident of Yonge street road, near Richmond Hill, and his housekeeper, Nancy Montgomery. Reproduction of pen sketches made at trial. Size 5 x 6.

6

288—**ELMSLEY VILLA, TORONTO**—Situated on what is now the northwest corner of Grosvenor and St. Vincent streets. View looking east and north. This charming roughcast villa was built, 1839-40, by Hon. John Simcoe Macaulay, and during Lord Elgin's residence in Toronto, 1849-54, was used for the gubernatorial mansion, as the real Government House was at that time undergoing extensive repairs. Lord Elgin was particularly attracted by the surroundings of Elmsley Villa, and when he came from Montreal in the autumn of 1849 expressed himself as highly pleased with his new home. From 1855-75 Knox College held its sessions here, and a considerable addition was made to the original building to provide dormitories for the students. Finally the site was occupied by the Central (Grosvenor Street) Presbyterian Church, which, in 1916, is still standing. Photo of pencil drawing in possession of the Misses Macaulay, Exmouth, England. Size 5 x 8. See 289.

289—**ELMSLEY VILLA**—View looking west. Photo of pencil drawing in possession of the Misses Macauley, Exmouth, Eng. Size 6 x 8. See 288.

290—**"ROSEDALE," TORONTO**—The residence of Sheriff Wm. Botsford Jarvis. Built in 1821 by Hon. J. E. Small, on the north side of Rosedale Ravine, opposite the "white bridge," which crossed the ravine from the northerly limit of Gwynne St. (Park Road), where it united with Little James St. (Collier). The property was purchased in 1824 by the late Sheriff Wm. Botsford Jarvis. At that time the hillsides thereabout were covered with roses, hence the origin of the name, "Rosedale," which was given by Mrs. Jarvis, who was a granddaughter of Chief Justice Powell. During Sheriff Jarvis' occupation of the house, verandahs and a conservatory were added and extensions made. All this, however, was subsequently removed. A part of the house was moved and made into a dwelling on Roxboro St. E., but this has also disappeared. The main entrance to the Jarvis property to-day is No. 12 Rosedale Road. Original water color by James Hamilton, London, Ont. Size 9 x 14.

291—**UNION STATION, TORONTO, 1859**—In 1858 the original Union Station, a frame building, situated about 200 feet west of the west line of York St., below Front, was opened. It was considered a fine depot for those days. The old station at the corner of Bay and Front streets was torn down, all tracks moved from the bay shore bank and the new building at the foot of York street made the Union Station for the Grand Trunk, Great Western and Northern Railways. In 1871 it was demolished and a temporary shed put up at the western side of Simcoe street for the accommodation of passengers until the completion of the second Union Station, which was opened on Dominion Day, 1873. The present (1916) structure was built, 1896. Water color by William Armstrong. Size 15 x 22.

292—**"HOUSES OF PARLIAMENT AND GOVERNMENT OFFICES, FRONT STREET, WEST, TORONTO, U.C., 1835**—To his Excellency Major-General Sir John Colborne, K.C.B., etc., etc., etc., Governor of Upper Canada. This plate is by permission inscribed by his obt. hble. servant, Thomas Young, archt. delt. Toronto, U.C., 1835. W. K. Hewitt, delt., on stone. N. Currier's lith., No. 1 Wall St., N.Y." Size 8 x 18. See 1060.

293—**TORONTO STREET RAILWAY TICKETS**—The first tickets for the Sunday service, inaugurated Sunday, May 23, 1897.

294—**BROWN, PETER, 1800-63**—Came to America from Edinburgh in 1838. He was an accomplished writer and a keen politician on the side of Liberalism; edited for a time the British Chronicle, New York; resided in Toronto for many years, where he continued the publication of the Banner after his son, the late Hon. George Brown, assumed managership of the Toronto Globe in March, 1844. Photo, hand colored, from a portrait in possession of his grandson, E. B. Brown, K.C., Toronto.

295—BROWN, MRS. PETER (Marianne Mackenzie)—Only daughter of George Mackenzie, of Stornoway, in the Island of Lewis, Scotland. Died in 1861. Photo, hand colored, from a portrait in possession of her grandson, E. B. Brown, K.C., Toronto. Size 8 x 10. (Including foregoing). Half length.

296—"GOVERNMENT HOUSE AND GROUNDS, TORONTO, C.W., ON THE QUEEN'S BIRTHDAY, 1854—Lucius O'Brien, del. Litho., J. Ellis, King St., Toronto." Government House, southwest corner King and Simcoe Streets, Toronto, was built in 1828; burnt Jan., 1862; rebuilt 1867, and finally demolished in 1912 to make room for C.P.R. freight sheds and offices. On 24th May, 1854, a procession was formed at the City Hall, headed by police, members of the corporation, fire brigade, national societies, and the citizens generally. The procession was escorted by Col. Denison's demi-troop of Provincial Cavalry. Triumphal arches were erected at different points on King Street. On arrival at Government House grounds a public meeting was held, presided over by the Mayor. Sheriff Jarvis, Henry Sherwood, M.P.P., Hon. J. H. Cameron, G. P. Ridout, M.P.P., Dr. McCaul, William Cawthra and other prominent citizens were present, and an address to the Queen was prepared for presentation. Over 5,000 persons were present, and great enthusiasm prevailed. At the conclusion cheers were given for the Queen, the Emperor of the French and the Turks. The Crimean War was on at the time. Lithograph. Size 17 x 23. See 285.

297—TORONTO IN 1908—Key to. See 298.

298—TORONTO IN 1908—From an oil painting in the J. Ross Robertson collection of pictures of Toronto in the City Hall, by Owen Staples, O.S.A. Water color copy. Size 14 x 60. See 297.

299—THE PIONEER WIMBLEDON RIFLEMEN, 1871—First team to represent Canada in England—with key. The first Wimbledon Team was financed by private subscriptions from military men all over Ontario. Col. Skinner, of Hamilton, was largely responsible for assembling the team. The members were chosen by competition at their own headquarters, and were then sent to Hamilton to shoot for position on the team at the Victoria Rifle Range of the 13th Battalion. Photograph, colored, from a half-tone. Size 6 x 12.

300—OSGOODE—"Hon. William Osgoode, First Chief Justice of Upper Canada. British American Bank Note Co., Montreal." Line engraving. Size 4 x 4. Head and shoulders. See 1684.

301—FALCONBRIDGE, CHIEF JUSTICE HON. SIR WILLIAM GLENHOLME—Born at Drummondville, Ont. 1846. Educated at Barrie Grammar School, U. C. Model Grammar School and the University of Toronto; gold medalist in moderns. Became a barrister in 1871, and as a member of the firm of Harrison, Osler & Moss successfully practised his profession here. Appointed Registrar of Toronto University, 1872, and subsequently a senator. K.C., 1885. In Nov., 1887, was appointed Judge of the Queen's Bench Division of the Supreme Court of Judicature, Ontario. In 1900 elevated to the Chief Justiceship. Was a member of the commission appointed in 1896 to revise the Statutes of Ontario, and of the commission chosen in 1901 to collect and revise the Imperial Statutes affecting civil rights in the Province. Knighted in 1908. President High Court of Justice, 1916. Has written metrical translations of the Latin and German poets. Photograph. Size 4 x 5. Three-quarter length, sitting.

302—WATKINS AND HARRIS CURRENCY, TORONTO—In 1838-9 Upper Canada suffered great inconvenience from the scarcity of fractional currency, caused by the suspension of specie payments in consequence of the Rebellion. Due bills of merchants increased to such an extent that people became shy of accepting them. Mr. T. D. Harris, of the hardware firm of Watkins & Harris, King street east, on permission of the Mayor, issued fractional currency, an example of which is here given. The bills were redeemable at the "Sign of the Anvil and Sledge," the well-known sign of the firm, and were guaranteed. The total amount put out was several thousand dollars. Mr. Watkins subsequently sold his share in the business, which was commenced in 1829, and discontinued in 1860. The place of occupancy during that time was a brick building, No. 158 King street east. It was destroyed by fire, and when re-built became the Clyde Hotel.

303—TICKET OF ADMISSION TO JENNY LIND CONCERT IN ST. LAWRENCE HALL, TORONTO, 21ST OCT., 1851—Jenny Lind was a Swedish vocalist of exceptional ability, who began to sing on the stage at ten years of age. In 1850-2 she toured the United States and Canada, and then returned to Europe. When she visited Toronto she gave a concert in St. Lawrence Hall, the proceeds of which were to be devoted to the founding of some charity commemorative of the event. The Protestant Orphans' Home was the result.

304—OLDEST LOG HOUSE IN PEEL COUNTY, ONT., 1842 1916—Home of Miss Margaret Higgiston, picturesquely situated on the second concession, Caledon Township, near Inglewood, and built by Malcolm Higgiston, who emigrated from Scotland in the early thirties. The quaint old cottage, which was altered and repaired in the summer of 1912, was occupied by Miss Higgiston until her death in March, 1916. Water color by Owen Staples. Size 13 x 20.

305—MOSS PARK, TORONTO—Residence of the late Hon. G. W. Allan. Original pen drawing, made in 1842. Size 10 x 16. See 508.

306—JACOBI, OTTO R., 1812-1901—President Royal Canadian Academy—Born in Koenigsburg, Prussia. At an early age devoted himself to art, and for twenty years held the position of court painter at Wiesbaden. In 1860 he was invited to Canada to paint a picture of Shawinigan Falls, to be used in connection with the reception of the Prince of Wales. On the organization of the Royal Canadian Academy of Art, 1880, Mr. Jacobi was chosen as one of the first members of that body by the Marquis of Lorne, and in 1891 was elected President. Photo. Size 4 x 5. Full length, sitting.

307—CROOKSHANK, RACHEL—Sister of Hon. George Crookshank, Commissary-General, second wife (1817) of Dr. James Macaulay, of the Queen's Rangers. Miss Crookshank was an intimate friend of Mrs. Simcoe. From a silhouette in possession of her niece, the late Mrs. Stephen Heward, daughter of the Hon. George Crookshank. Size 3 x 4. Head, in profile.

308—"HOUSE OF PROVIDENCE, TORONTO, CANADA WEST—Lith. par Courtois, Imp. Villain, 45 rue de Sevres, Paris, 1855. Wm. Hay, Architect." One of the largest charitable institutions in the Province of Ontario is that known as the House of Providence, Power St., Toronto. It is an imposing edifice, the main building being 130 x 60 feet and four storeys high, founded by Mgr. Armand, Comte de Charbonnel, second Roman Catholic Bishop of Toronto. In 1857 the building was opened under the direction and management of the Sisters of St. Joseph for the care of the aged and infirm of both sexes. Becoming overcrowded, the Sisters erected a new wing in 1874, and in 1881 built a chapel. Later a large wing was added to the south, together with a Community House. Again to relieve the congested condition of the house it became necessary, in 1906, to erect a fifth addition on the east side for the accommodation of neglected infants of the city. This house is known as St. Vincent's Infant Home. Lithograph in color. Size 15 x 23.

309—YORK (TORONTO), 1824—Key to. See 310.

310—YORK (TORONTO), 1824—From a water color by a British army officer stationed in York at that time. View shows from the north-east corner of East Market Square (Jarvis St.) and east along Palace (Front St.) to Parliament, afterwards known as Berkeley St. In 1824 Parliament ran from Palace to King St. Water color copy by Owen Staples. Size 16 x 40. See 309.

311—"SLEIGH SCENE, TORONTO BAY, CANADA WEST—This print is dedicated by permission to the officers of the 83rd Regiment by the artist. Painted by Mr. J. T. Downman. Lithographed by Mr. E. Walker, London. Published by the proprietor, March 26th 1853 (private plate), Ackermann & Co., Direxnt. Printed by Day & Son, Lithrs. to the Queen." The picture depicts a scene between Yonge street and the Garrison, when the 83rd Regiment was stationed at the Old Fort. The foreground, showing the Bay, is correct, and is the only part of the drawing made by Downman. The picture was finished in England, and the background north from the shore line faked—that is, it was drawn from memory, and is in no particular like Front street, Toronto, or the city in 1841-2. Lithograph in color. Size 21 x 31.

312—OATES, RICHARD H.—Born in Belfast, Ireland, in 1809. Came to Canada in 1817. Educated here and in England. Subsequently entered the millstone business at Bradford. It was he who in 1868 conceived the idea of forming the York Pioneer Society, the first meeting of which was held on April 17th of the following year. Mr. Oates was a son of Captain Edward Oates, and a direct descendant of John Hampden, the great English political reformer in the reign of Charles I. He died in 1881. Line engraving. Size 4 x 4. Head and shoulders.

313—DUGGAN, HON. GEORGE, 1813-76—Born in Malon, Ireland; studied law in Canada. At the time of the Rebellion in 1837 he was in charge of some troops at Toronto, and upon going out to reconnoitre was taken prisoner. Represented 2nd Riding of York, 1841-44. While Recorder of the City of Toronto in 1865 he tried the celebrated case of Bennett G. Burley for extradition to United States. In 1868 received appointment as Senior Judge of the County of York. From a portrait in possession of his son, Henry Duggan, Clerk 10th Division Court, Toronto. Size 5 x 6. Head and shoulders.

314—SCADDING, REV. HENRY, D.D., 1813-1901—Third son of John Scadding; born in Devonshire, Eng.; came to Canada, 1824. Educated at U. C. C., Toronto, and a graduate of St. John's College, Cambridge, 1837. Classical master, U. C. C., 1838-62; rector of Holy Trinity Church, Toronto, 1847-75. Photograph. Size 7 x 10. Three-quarter length, sitting. See 2509, 2511, 3698.

315—ROBINSON, SIR JOHN BEVERLEY, Bart., D.C.L.—Second son of Christopher Robinson, born at Berthier, L.C., July, 1791; died at Toronto, January 1863. He served under General Brock at Detroit and Queenston Heights, and in the same year was appointed Acting Attorney-General of Upper Canada, and subsequently became Solicitor-General and Attorney-General of the Province. In 1821 became first representative of York in Provincial Legislature. Chief Justice of Upper Canada, 1829-63. From the first sketch for an oil painted in 1856 by James Richmond, a celebrated British artist. Size 12 x 16. Head and shoulders. See 1683.

316—DESIGN OF PRINCE OF WALES' ARCH—At foot of John St., Toronto, 1860, to welcome H.R.H. The late King Edward, when Prince of Wales, visited Canada in the summer of 1860. From Brockville his party sailed in the steamer Kingston, and after touching at several places en route, arrived in Toronto on 7th September. The steamer landed at a dock at the foot of John St. Near the edge of the bank at the foot of the street was erected a handsome arch, under which the procession which received the Prince passed on its way to Government House, corner Simcoe and King streets, where H.R.H. sojourned during his stay in Toronto. Original water color. Size 18 x 26.

317 to 330—"BISHOPS OF THE ECCLESIASTICAL PROVINCE OF QUEBEC, 1884—Publie par Asselin & Dumont, Manchester, N.H. Copyrighted 1884 by Asselin & Dumont at Washington, D.C. S. C. Carbee, England, 576 Washington St., Boston, Mass., U.S.A." Lithograph. Size 20 x 24.

317—LAROQUE, S.G., MGR. JOSEPH—Bishop of Germanicopolis. Born at Chambly, Que., Aug. 28th, 1808. Ordained to the priesthood, 1835, and consecrated titulary Bishop of Cydonia, 1852; Coadjutor of Montreal; transferred to St. Hyacinthe, 1860. In 1865 he resigned and two years later was named Titulary Bishop of Germanicopolis. Died Nov. 18th, 1887. Head and shoulders.

318—LAFLECHE, S.G., MGR. LOUIS FRANCOIS, D.D.—Second Bishop of Three Rivers. Born at Ste. Anne de la Perade, Que., 1818, and educated at the Seminary, Nicolet; ordained at Quebec, 1844. For a time he labored as a missionary among the Indians of the North-West and later occupied the chair of Mathematics and Philosophy at Nicolet, eventually becoming prefect of studies and Superior of the College. In 1861 he was appointed Vicar-General of the Diocese. Created titulary Bishop or Anthedon and at the same time named Coadjutor to Mgr. Cooke, Bishop of Three Rivers. He subsequently became Administrator of the Diocese, and succeeded to the Bishopric, April 30th, 1870. His death occurred July 14, 1898. Head and shoulders.

319—FABRE, S.G., MGR. EDOUARD CHARLES, D.D.—First Archbishop of Montreal. Born at Montreal, Feb. 28th, 1827; ordained a priest, 1850. In 1873 appointed Coadjutor-Bishop cum jure successionis of Montreal, and in the same year consecrated titulary Bishop of Gratianopolis. Bishop of Montreal, May 11th, 1876, and raised to the Archiepiscopal dignity, June 8th, 1886. His death occurred December 30th, 1896. Head and shoulders.

320—DUHAMEL, S.G., MGR. JOSEPH THOMAS, D.D.—Archbishop of Ottawa. He was born at Contrecoeur, Que., in 1841, but shortly afterwards removed with his parents to Ottawa. Educated at St. Joseph's College in that city, and ordained to the priesthood in 1863. Consecrated second R.C. Bishop of Ottawa, Oct. 28th, 1874. In 1886 he was made Archbishop, and Metropolitan of the Ecclesiastical Province of Ottawa the following year. Was the means of securing for the College of Ottawa the powers of a Catholic University, and also established "Les Conferences Ecclesiastiques" for the better management of the affairs of the diocese. Died June 5th, 1909. Head and shoulders.

321—BOURGET, S.G., MGR. IGNACE, D.D—Archbishop of Martianopolis Born at Pointe Levis, 1799. Educated at Nicolet and Seminary of Quebec. Subsequent to his ordination appointed Vicar-General and in 1837 nominated Coadjutor Bishop of Montreal, with the title of Bishop of Telmessa. Became Bishop of Montreal, 19th April, 1840. In 1862 he was created a Roman Count and Assistant at the Pontifical throne. Raised to the rank of Archbishop of Martianopolis. His closing years were spent at Sault au Recollet, where he died, June 8th, 1885. Head and shoulders. See 2827.

322—LAFORCE-LANGEVIN, S.G., MGR. JEAN PIERRE FRANCOIS— Bishop of Rimouski. Born at Quebec, Sept. 22, 1821. Ordained to the priesthood, 1844, and consecrated first Bishop of Saint Germain de Rimouski, May 1st, 1867; resigned and was nominated Archbishop of Leontopolis, 1891. He died in January of the following year. Head and shoulders.

323—MOREAU, S.G., MGR. LOUIS ZEPHIRIN—Bishop of St. Hyacinthe. He was born at Becancourt (Nicolet), Que., April 1st 1824, and educated at the Seminary, Nicolet. After his ordination to the priesthood became Assistant Secretary and Master of Ceremonies at the Bishop's Palace, Montreal. In 1852 he accompanied Mgr. Prince to St. Hyacinthe as Secretary, and was later appointed Vicar-General of that diocese. Raised to the episcopate as fourth Bishop of St. Hyacinthe, 1875. His death took place May 24th, 1901. Head and shoulders.

324—SMEULDERS, S. E., DOM HENRI—Apostolic Delegate. A Belgian ecclesiastic. He was appointed Apostolic Delegate to Canada by Pope Leo XIII., to report upon matters affecting University education in Quebec, chiefly in connection with Laval, and also to investigate certain diocesan difficulties which had arisen. The result of his mission has never been made public. Head and shoulders.

325—S. S. POPE LEO XIII.—Born at Carpineto, Diocese of Anagni, in the Papal States, March 2nd, 1810. He was the son of Count Louis Pecci, a scion of an ancient noble house of Sienna. In 1818 he was sent with his oldest brother to the College of the Jesuits in Viterbo, and later studied at Rome. Afterwards studied law and diplomacy at the Academy of Noble Ecclesiastics. In 1837 he was named by Gregory XVI. Prelate of his household and Referendary of the Segnatura. After a somewhat varied career he was preconized Archbishop of Dalmatia in partibus, and sent in the quality of apostolic nuncio to the Court of Belgium. Preconized Bishop of Perugia in 1846, and at the same time named a Cardinal. On the death of Pius IX. in 1878 he became Pope, with the title of Leo XIII. Died 1903. Half length.

326—TASCHEREAU, S.G., MGR. ELZEAR ALEXANDRE, D.D.—Archbishop of Quebec. Born in 1820 at Ste. Marie de la Beauce, Que., and educated at the Quebec Seminary and the Grand Seminary. Ordained to the priesthood, 1842. Elected Superior, 1860. Became Vicar-General of the Archdiocese, 1862, and consecrated sixteenth Archbishop of Quebec, March 19th, 1871. Founder of the Hotel Dieu du Sacre-Coeur, Quebec. In 1886 created a Cardinal Priest of the Holy Roman Church, being the first Canadian to be elevated to the Sacred College. He retired from active work in 1894, and died four years later. Head and shoulders. See 1656.

327—RACINE, S.G., MGR. ANTOINE, D.D.—First Bishop of Sherbrooke. He was born at St. Ambroise de la Jeune Lorette, Que., January 26th, 1822. On completing his studies he was ordained to the priesthood in September, 1844. Consecrated first Bishop of Sherbrooke, October 18th, 1874. His death took place in 1893. Head and shoulders.

328—LORRAIN, S.G., MGR. NARCISSE ZEPHIRIN, D.D.—Titulary Bishop of Cythere. Received his education at the College of Ste. Therese and at Laval University (B.Sc., 1864). Ordained a priest three years later, and became assistant director at Ste. Therese. Appointed Vicar-General of the Diocese of Montreal, 1880. On erection of the new Vicariate-Apostolic of Pontiac, 1882, he was consecrated to it. Received the degree of D.D. from Rome in the same year. In 1898 the Diocese of Pembroke was formed from the Apostolic Vicariate of Pontiac, and he became Bishop of Pembroke. He was born at St. Martin, Que., in 1842. His death took place at Pembroke, Dec. 17th, 1915. Head and shoulders.

329—BOSSE, MGR. FRANCOIS XAVIER—Apostolic Prefect of the Gulf of St. Lawrence. Born at Ste. Anne de Lapocatiere, Kamouraska Co., Que., 6th September, 1838; ordained to the priesthood, 4th October, 1863. In 1895 the Apostolic Prefecture became the Vicariate-Apostolic of the Gulf of St. Lawrence. Head and shoulders.

330—RACINE, S.G., MGR. DOMINIQUE, D.D.—Bishop of Chicoutimi. Consecrated Bishop, August 4th, 1878, by Mgr. Taschereau. He was born at Saint Ambroise de la Jeune Lorette, Que., January 24th, 1828. Ordained to the priesthood in 1853. Died January 28th, 1888. Head and shoulders.

331—SOUTH SIDE KING STREET EAST, TORONTO, 1858—From store of A. & S. Nordheimer, No. 14 King street east to St. Lawrence Market. The stores shown are those of A. & S. Nordheimer, Maclear & Co., Wylie & Murray, Thomas & Arthurs, J. W. Skelton, Merrick & Wilson, Robert Walker & Son, J. C. Collins and Charles Cook. Chromolithograph. Size 3 x 5.

332—HOMESTEAD OF THE HELLIWELL FAMILY, YORK, (TO-RONTO)—On the bank of the Don, north of Taylor's Mills. The house was built by Thomas Helliwell in 1820, and is still in a good state of preser-vation. Mr. Helliwell came to this country in 1818, and for a time resided at Lundy's Lane. He determined, however, to settle at York, and in 1820, built a brewery and distillery on the Don. Pencil drawing in color, by Owen Staples. Size 5 x 8.

333—BLOCKHOUSE AT THE HEAD OF SHERBOURNE STREET, TORONTO—This was one of three modern blockhouses (the others being at College st. and Spadina ave., and at Yorkville, east of Yonge st.) which surrounded the city. It stood on the exact line of Bloor street, going east, at the east end of this road, and in the middle just over the steep descent to the valley of the Don, to avoid which precipitous descent the road turned aside southwards towards Sherbourne street. Mr. Hirschfelder's house and grounds were immediately south of this blockhouse. It was built 1837-8, at time of the rebellion troubles, in order to protect the city from the north, and was demolished in 1875. Water color by Henry Perre, of Toronto, 1863. Size 5 x 7.

334—OLDEST PLANTED TREE IN TORONTO—A native white elm—This noted landmark of the northern part of Toronto stands in the grounds of Rosedale House, residence of the late Wm. Botsford Jarvis, who from 1827-56 was Sheriff of the Home District. It was two years old when planted, on 24th May, 1822, by Amelia Jarvis, eldest daughter of Frederick Starr Jarvis, a brother of the Sheriff. The event commemorated the birth-day of Princess Victoria (her Majesty Queen Victoria), 24th May, 1819, which was also the birthday of Amelia Jarvis. The fused tree, which comes from one root, has the remarkable girth of 26 feet, due to branching very low. This measurement includes the main trunk, (1) which is by itself 21½ feet, and a branch, (2) by itself of 8 feet. The crown is ex-tremely broad, having a sweep greater than the height of the tree, which is 75 feet. The average increase in radius of half an inch a year shows that its age is 95 years. The main entrance to the Jarvis property to-day is No. 12 Rosedale road. The original residence was demolished many years ago and nothing remains (1916) to mark the site except a few out-houses. Photograph, colored. Size 5 x 7.

335—"THE CRICKET MATCH PLAYED AT TORONTO, CANADA, ON THE 2ND AND 3RD OF SEPTEMBER, 1872—Between Twelve of the Gentlemen of England and Twenty-two of the Toronto Club. Dedicated by permission to T. C. Patteson, Esq., the Originator and Promoter of the Expedition. Designed and lithographed by Rolph, Smith & Co., Toronto. Entered according to Act of Parliament of Canada in the year one thousand eight hundred and seventy-five, by Rolph, Smith & Co., in the office of the Minister of Agriculture." This picture was presented to J. Ross Robertson by the William Rennie Co., Limited, 130-6 Adelaide street east, Toronto. Lithograph. Size 20 x 35. See 336.

336—CRICKET MATCH, TORONTO, SEPT. 2ND AND 3RD, 1872—
Between the Gentlemen of England and Twenty-two of the Toronto Club.
Key. It will be noted that N. Kirchhoffer appears twice in the key, Nos.
23 and 60. The former number shows him fielding and the latter gives his
full portrait. See 335.

337—TORONTO STREET R. R. TICKETS—Set of first of each class
of street railway tickets issued in Toronto when city assumed possession
of street railway, 19th May, 1891; and also first of each series issued by
the Kiely and Everitt Syndicate the following August.

338—"TORONTO, CANADA WEST, FROM THE TOP OF THE JAIL—
Drawn from nature by E. Whitefield. Lith. of Endicott & Co., N.Y. Entered according to Act of Congress in the year 1854, by E. Whitefield, in
the Clerk's Office of the District Court of the Southern District of New
York." The jail, which was the third structure of the kind in Toronto, was
built in 1840, near the corner of Front and Berkeley streets, the entrance
being on the north from Front street. It overlooked the harbor, and a
green running to the water's edge was a favorite playground for the boys
of Toronto sixty years ago. Several of the city's principal educational and
ecclesiastical buildings of the period are shown, and indeed some of them
may be seen to-day (1917) as they appeared in 1854. The buildings indicated are: 1. City Hall. 2. Lunatic Asylum. 3. Trinity College. 4. Osgoode Hall. 5. St. Lawrence Hall. 6. St. James' Cathedral. 7. Congregational Church. 8. St. Andrew's Church. 9. United Presbyterian Church.
10. St. George's Church. 11. Knox Church. 12. Mechanics' Institute. 13.
Holy Trinity Church. 14. St. Michael's Cathedral. 15. Normal School.
16, Unitarian Church. Lithograph. Size 20 x 36.

339—MEMBERS OF ST. ANDREW'S SOCIETY, TORONTO, 1874-75—
With key. The Society was founded in May, 1836, with Hon. Wm. Allan
as President. As early as 1822, however, Scotsmen in York (Toronto) met
in reunion on St. Andrew's Day, for in the Upper Canada Gazette of 12th
Dec., 1822, is the following:—"The Sons of St. Andrew, residing in York,
celebrated the anniversary of the Saint by giving a dinner to the principal
gentlemen of the place on the 30th ult. The Company, consisting of nearly
forty persons, sat down to an elegant dinner at Forest's Hotel, about six
o'clock, the Venerable Chief Justice Scott in the chair, having the Hon.
Chief Justice Powell and the Hon. James Baby on the left and right hands."
The Portrait gives as many members as it was possible to assemble together at the time. Mr. John MacKenzie, Toronto, prepared the key,
which gives the years of joining. The names marked (x) indicate those
who were alive in 1913, and the blanks are unknown. Col. J. Forbes
Michie is President, 1913-16. Photograph. Size 13 x 18.

340—OPENING OF CITY HALL, QUEEN STREET WEST, TORONTO
—The present City Hall, on Queen street west, at the head of Bay, was
formally opened, September 18th, 1899, Mayor John Shaw presiding. The
key accompanying the picture gives the names of the City Council, officials of the Corporation, and a large number of leading citizens who were
photographed immediately after the close of the proceedings. Photograph.
Size 15 x 18.

341—TORONTO, C.W., IN THE SUMMER OF 1851—From Gooder-
ham's Windmill at the east end of the city, showing Palace (Front) street
and Front west to the Old Fort, the then western limit of Toronto, with
key to picture. Water color, made on the spot, by Frederick H. Granger,
scenic artist of the Royal Lyceum Theatre, Toronto. Size 17 x 54.

342—"SWORDS' HOTEL—Front street, Toronto, between York and Bay streets. P. Swords, Proprietor." The buildings in the picture were four dwelling houses, called the Ontario Terrace, erected about 1845, on the north side of Front, between York and Bay streets. They were occupied from 1848-53 by Knox College, and a year later became Swords' Hotel, under the proprietorship of P. Swords. From 1860-62 the business was carried on by J. B. Riley, as the Revere House. Since 1862 the hotel has been known as the Queen's under the proprietorship of Capt. Thos. Dick up to 1874, McGaw and Irish, 1875, and 1876-1916 McGaw and Winnett. Lithographed by Maclear & Co., Toronto. Size 19 x 29.

343—JOHNSON, PETER—Eldest son of Sir William Johnson, Bart., and Molly Brant, sister of Captain Joseph Brant (Thayendanegea). Oil painting. Size 23 x 30. Half length.

344—OLD FORT, TORONTO, 1879—Showing officers' house and office of Lieut.-Col. William S. Durie, who from 1868-80 was Deputy Adjutant-General, Military District No. 2. This sketch was begun in 1878 and finished some months later, after a storm had knocked off the top of the poplar tree shown. Sepia drawing by J. O. Fowler. Size 7 x 8.

345—HAMILTON'S WHARF, FOOT OF SCOTT STREET, TORONTO, 1879—The city map of 1842 shows seven wharves, one of which was that owned by James Browne, east of Scott street. In 1840-56 the Royal Mail steamers sailed from this wharf, which has been leased to Mr. J. Borst & Co., Robert Hamilton and others. It is now (1917) the Toronto Electric Light Company's wharf, but when the harbor improvements are made these works will be removed. Sepia drawing by J. O. Fowler. Size 7 x 8.

346—OLD FORT, TORONTO, 1879—The blockhouse shown was built by Gov. Simcoe when the Fort was laid out. It was in the centre of the Old Fort, and at the west end of Front street. In 1813 it was destroyed by the Americans, but was rebuilt two years later, and between 1820-25 a second blockhouse, to the east of the first one, was erected. The "Old Well" of the Fort, used in 1812-13, is also shown. Sepia drawing by J. O. Fowler. Size 7 x 9.

347—QUEEN'S PARK, TORONTO, 1879—South of the culvert leading to the little streamlet that emptied into the pool east of the University. A miniature lake was constructed in the ravine, and remained in existence for some time, but finally, the water becoming stagnant, it was drained off and the ravine regained its former appearance. Sepia drawing by J. O. Fowler. Size 7 x 8.

348-59—LEGISLATURES OF ONTARIO—With keys. First Legislature, 1867-71; Second, 1871-4; Third, 1875-9; Fourth, 1879-83; Fifth, 1883-6; Sixth, 1886-90, met in the old Parliament Buildings, Front street west, Toronto. The sessions of 1890-92 of the Seventh Legislature also met on Front street, while those of 1893-94 were held in Queen's Park. The Eighth Legislature, 1894-98; Ninth, 1898-1902; Tenth, 1902-4; Eleventh, 1905-8; Twelfth, 1908-11; Thirteenth, 1911-14, have met in the Parliament Buildings, Queen's Park, Toronto. In 1867 when Confederation became an accomplished fact, Provincial Legislatures were again organized, and The Sixth Parliamentary era began. Ontario was divided into eighty-two electoral districts, with the same number of representatives. To-day (1916) there are a hundred and eleven members with a hundred and seven constituencies. From 1867-92 the sessions of the Ontario Legislature were held in the old Front street Parliament Buildings, and on April 4th, of the latter year, the formal opening of the building in Queen's Park took place. This series gives the members of the different Legislatures since 1867, with the exception of the fifth, 1883-6, which is unobtainable, and it is believed, never photographed. With regard to the Second Legislature, the closing is given, 12th Nov., 1874. It is noteworthy that many of Toronto's prominent women are in this picture.

348—FIRST LEGISLATURE, 1867-71—Photograph. Size 12 x 20.

349—SECOND LEGISLATURE—Closing of—12th Nov., 1874—Photograph. Size 10 x 16.

350—THIRD LEGISLATURE, 1875-9—Photograph. Size 9 x 20.

351—FOURTH LEGISLATURE, 1879-83—Photograph. Size 14 x 18.

352—SIXTH LEGISLATURE, 1886-90—Photograph. Size 16 x 20.

353—SEVENTH LEGISLATURE, 1890-4—Photograph. Size 15 x 20.

354—EIGHTH LEGISLATURE, 1894-8—Photograph. Size 15 x 19.

355—NINTH LEGISLATURE—1898-1902—Photograph. Size 13 x 17.

356—TENTH LEGISLATURE, 1902-4—Photograph. Size 15 x 19.

357—ELEVENTH LEGISLATURE, 1905-8—Photograph. Size 15 x 20.

358—TWELFTH LEGISLATURE, 1908-11—Photograph. Size 16 x 20.

359—THIRTEENTH LEGISLATURE, 1911-14—Photograph. Size 15 x 19.

360—EDWARDS, ROBERT—Secretary, 1848-58, of the old Mechanics' Institute, now Toronto Public Library. After his death in 1858 the members of the Institute subscribed for a memorial portrait. This portrait, until 1883, hung in the reading-room of the Institute. When the Institute was merged into the Public Library, the directors presented the portrait to Mr. William Edwards, brother of the late Robert Edwards, and himself a former secretary. Shortly afterwards he offered the portrait to the Public Library, who accepted the offer gratefully. Oil painting. Artist unknown. Size 29 x 35. Half length, sitting.

361—SECOND TOLL GATE, ON YONGE STREET, TORONTO, 1870— View looking south, near Hogg's Hollow Hill. The toll house stood on the left or east side of Yonge street, and the gateway, which was a covered one, was on the right or west side. The house to the right of the picture was the dwelling of the gatekeeper, while a lean-to is seen on the left. About 1883 this gate was removed. W. J. Hill, Reeve of York Township, moved in York County Council, in 1896, a by-law for the abolition of toll gates. It was passed, and the by-law came into effect 31st December, 1896. This was done by the County Council in consideration of the City Council abolishing market fees of the farmers. Oil painting by J. McPherson Ross, Toronto. Size 27 x 36.

362—GORE, FRANCIS—LIEUT.-GOVERNOR UPPER CANADA— Aug. 25th, 1806-Oct. 9th, 1811, and from Sept. 21st, 1815-Jan. 6th, 1818— This picture is said to have been painted by Thomas (Sir) Lawrence in 1814, and, it is claimed, was brought to Canada in 1815 and presented to Col. James Givins when Gov. Gore returned to England. It hung for about forty-five years on the walls of the drawing-room of the Givins Cottage, known as "Pine Grove," near North road (Givins street). After the death of Miss Cecil Givins, daughter of the Colonel, the portrait, a fine piece of artistic work, was given to the Mechanics' Institute, now the Toronto Public Library. Oil portrait. Size 25 x 30. Head and shoulders. See 409, 1669.

363 to 400—MAYORS OF TORONTO, since its incorporation in 1834, to 1916:

363—MACKENZIE, WILLIAM LYON—Mayor of Toronto, 1834—A Scotsman, born near Dundee, Forfarshire, Scotland, 1795. Came to Canada as a young man, settling in York (Toronto), and in 1829 was elected member of the Provincial Legislature. He was a prominent figure in the Rebellion of 1837, after which he left the country, and was unable to return until the general amnesty in 1849. About 1850 he again obtained a seat in Parliament. Died in Toronto, 28th August, 1861. Mr. Mackenzie was first Mayor, not only of Toronto, but in the Province. Water color. Size 5 x 6. Head and shoulders. See 256.

364—SULLIVAN, ROBERT BALDWIN—Mayor of Toronto, 1835— Barrister-at-law. Born at Bandon, near Cork, Ireland, 1802. Appointed to the Executive Council, U.C., 1836, and was a member of the first Executive Council formed after the Union; Justice, Court of Queen's Bench, 1848, and subsequently transferred to the Common Pleas. Judge Sullivan was distinguished as a lawyer, statesman and orator. Died at Toronto, 1853. Water color. Size 5 x 6. Head and shoulders.

365—MORRISON, DAVID THOMAS—Mayor of Toronto, 1836—Born at Quebec, 1796; died at Toronto, 1856. He was the only medical man who has ever occupied the Mayor's chair in Toronto. In the early days he was clerk in the Surveyor-General's Office; vice-president of the Bible Society, 1831; member of the first Municipal Council, and an active politician. Was compelled to leave Canada after the Rebellion of 1837, but returned to Toronto in 1843. Water color. Size 5 x 6. Head and shoulders.

366—GURNETT, GEORGE—Mayor of Toronto, 1837, 1848-50—Proprietor and editor of the "Courier," in the early thirties. Entered the City Council as Councilman for St. George's Ward in 1834; became alderman in 1835. To Mr. Gurnett belongs the honor of having had the longest period of uninterrupted municipal service in the city. Accepted position of Police Magistrate in 1851. He was born at Horsham, Sussex, England, in 1791. Died at Toronto, 17th November, 1861. Water color. Size 5 x 6. Head and shoulders. See 600.

367—POWELL, JOHN—Mayor of Toronto, 1838-40—Son of Chief Justice Powell. Born at Niagara, U.C., 19th June, 1809. He was a barrister, practising in Toronto. Alderman for St. Andrew's Ward, 1837-41. He took active part in Rebellion of 1837. As Registrar of the County of Lincoln, he lived at Niagara and St. Catharines. Died at the latter place, 24th February, 1881. Water color. Size 5 x 6. Head and shoulders.

368—MONRO, GEORGE—Mayor of Toronto, 1841—Came to Canada in 1814 from Scotland, where he was born 1801. He carried on a wholesale business, southwest corner King and George streets. Was a member of the first City Council, represented St. Lawrence Ward almost uninterruptedly from 1834-45. Retired in 1857. Died in Toronto, 5th January, 1878. Water color. Size 5 x 6. Head and shoulders.

369—SHERWOOD, HENRY—Mayor of Toronto, 1842-44—He was a son of Judge Livius Peters Sherwood, of Brockville, Ont. Entered politics early in life, first representing Brockville and then Toronto in the old Parliament of Canada. He was successively Solicitor and Attorney-General in 1842 and 1847, respectively. Was a member of the City Council from 1842-49. Born at Augusta, Co. Leeds, Ont., July, 1809. Died at Kissingen, Germany, in the late fifties. Water color. Size 5 x 6. Head and shoulders.

370—**BOULTON, WILLIAM HENRY**—Mayor of Toronto, 1845-7 and 1858—Born at York (Toronto), 19th April, 1812. He was an enthusiastic sportsman. Represented Toronto in Parliament continuously from 1844-53. Alderman for St. Patrick's Ward, 1838-1842, and again in 1844. Mr. Boulton was largely instrumental in building St. George's Anglican Church, Toronto. Retired from municipal politics, 1858. Died in Toronto, 1st February, 1873. Water color. Size 5 x 6. Head and shoulders.

371—**BOWES, JOHN GEORGE**—Mayor of Toronto, 1851-3 and 1861-3— His birthplace was Clones, Ireland, 1812. Came to Canada in 1840, settling in Toronto, where he carried on business as a wholesale and retail merchant. Represented Toronto in the Canadian Parliament, 1854-8. During his first term of office of Mayor, the first sod of the Ontario, Simcoe & Huron, afterwards the Northern Railway, was turned by Lady Elgin. Mr. Bowes died at Toronto, 20th May, 1864. Water color. Size 5 x 6. Head and shoulders.

372—**BEARD, JOSHUA GEORGE**—Mayor of Toronto, 1854—With the exception of the years 1848 and 1853, he sat in the Council either as alderman or councilman for St. Lawrence Ward since 1834. He was an iron founder, had an interest in Beard's Hotel, and was a considerable propertyholder in the city. He also for many years filled the position of Clerk to the Sheriff of York. Retired from municipal life on expiration of his term as Mayor. He was born in England, 1797, and died in Toronto 9th November, 1866. Water color. Size 5 x 6. Head and shoulders.

373—**ALLAN, GEORGE WILLIAM**—Mayor of Toronto, 1855—He was a son of Hon. Wm. Allan, an early postmaster of York. Born in York (Toronto), 1822, and one of the first pupils in Upper Canada College. In 1849, and again in 1855, was elected alderman for St. David's Ward; from 1858-67 a member of the Legislative Council; at Confederation was selected for the Senate of the Dominion. Chancellor Trinity University, 1877-1901. His death took place in Toronto, 27th July, 1901. Water color. Size 5 x 6. Head and shoulders. See 956.

374—**ROBINSON, (HON.) JOHN BEVERLEY**—Mayor of Toronto, 1856 —Water color. Size 5 x 6. Head and shoulders. See 425, 1006, 3228.

375—**HUTCHISON, JOHN**—Mayor of Toronto, 1857—He was born in Ayrshire, Scotland, in 1817. Came to Toronto in 1851, and was associated with Mr. H. Black, of Montreal, as commission merchant, under the name of Hutchison, Black & Co. Their place of business was on the east side of Church, near Front street. Later Mr. Hutchinson moved to Wellington street, where he went into a more extensive business. He was alderman for St. James' Ward, 1852-3 and 1856-7. After his retirement from politics he removed to Montreal. He died at Metis, on the St. Lawrence, 2nd July, 1863. Water color. Size 5 x 6. Head and shoulders.

376—**READ, DAVID BREAKENRIDGE**—Mayor of Toronto, 8th November to 31st December, 1858, on the resignation of W. H. Boulton—Called to the bar 1845. Appointed a commissioner for the revision of the Consolidated Statutes of Canada and Upper Canada, 1856. Created a Q.C. in 1858. Author of works of a biographical and historical nature. He was of U.E.L. descent. Born at Augusta, County of Leeds, Ontario, in 1823. Died at Toronto, 11th May, 1904. Water color. Size 5 x 6. Head and shoulders.

377—**WILSON (SIR) ADAM, Q.C.**—Mayor of Toronto, 1859-60—He was the first mayor who had the honor of being elected by the people. He was a well-known barrister, and afterwards raised to the justiciary as Chief Justice of the Court of Queen's Bench. First elected to the Council as alderman for St. Patrick's Ward, 1858. As mayor, received H.R.H. the

Prince of Wales (King Edward VII) on his visit to Toronto in 1860. Knighted in 1888. Sir Adam was a Scotsman, born in Edinburgh, 1813. Died at Toronto, 28th December, 1891. Water color. Size 5 x 6. Head and shoulders.

378—CARR, JOHN—Mayor of Toronto, 1860—Born in Ireland in 1813, and came to Canada in 1836. For a number of years he took an active part in the civic affairs of Toronto, and in 1860 became President of the Council, in the absence of Mayor Adam Wilson, in Parliament. From 1865-71 he acted as City Clerk, and from 1871-2 City Commissioner. His death occurred in Toronto in 1881. Water color. Size 5 x 6. Head and shoulders. See 591, 752, 3513.

379—MEDCALF, FRANCIS H.—Mayor of Toronto, 1864-6, and 1874-5 —Carried on business as an iron founder, north side of King street, just west of Don bridge, Mr. Medcalf was a prominent member of the Orange Order. He was of Irish birth, having been born in County Wicklow, Ireland, 1803. First entered the City Council as alderman for St. Lawrence Ward, 1860. Represented St. David's Ward, 1863, and St. John's Ward in 1870-71. Died at Toronto, 26th March, 1880. Water color. Size 5 x 6. Head and shoulders.

380—SMITH, JAS. EDWARD—Mayor of Toronto 1867-8—Wholesale grocer—For many years he was manager of the British Empire Life Insurance Co. Came to Toronto at an early age from London, England, where he was born 25th December, 1831. Sat for St. John's Ward from 1857-67. After filling the office of Mayor, he again was elected an alderman for St. John's Ward. Remained in Council until 1870. Died in Toronto, 9th March, 1892. Water color. Size 5 x 6. Head and shoulders. See 3549.

381—HARMAN, SAMUEL BICKERTON—Mayor of Toronto, 1869-70— Was born in Brompton, west of London, Eng., 1819. Spent a large portion of his early life in Antigua, B.W.I., where his father was Chief Baron of the Court of Exchequer. Studied law, practised in Toronto, holding, among other appointments, that of Chancellor of the Diocese of Toronto. Assessment Commissioner 1873-4, and City Treasurer from 1874-88. Died at Toronto, 26th March, 1892. Water color. Size 5 x 6. Head and shoulders. See 1008, 3556, 3568.

382—SHEARD, JOSEPH—Mayor of Toronto, 1871-2—He was born in Yorkshire, England, 1813, coming to York (Toronto) in 1832, where for many years he carried on business as a contractor. Mr. Sheard first entered the Council as an alderman for St. Patrick's Ward in 1851. Sat for St. John's Ward 1854-5, and for St. James' Ward in 1859, and from 1865-70. Withdrew from municipal life in 1877. His death took place at Toronto, 30th August, 1883. Water color. Size 5 x 6. Head and shoulders.

383—MANNING, ALEXANDER—Mayor of Toronto, 1873 and 1885— His municipal career extended over a period of thirty years. Elected alderman for St. Lawrence Ward in 1856, continuing to sit for that constituency, though with several absences, until 1872. After his second term as mayor (1885) he retired. Mr. Manning was born in Dublin, Ireland, 1819. As a contractor he was engaged in the erection of the Lambton Flour Mills, the Normal School, Toronto, and a portion of the Parliament Buildings, Ottawa. He also had a part in the construction of the Welland Canal, 1842-3. Died at Toronto, 20th October, 1903. Water color. Size 5 x 6. Head and shoulders.

384—MORRISON, ANGUS, Q.C.—Mayor of Toronto, 1876-8—Represented Simcoe (N. R.) three times in the United Parliament, and was member for Niagara in 1864. In 1853 he entered the Town Council as alderman for St. James' Ward, and was re-elected the ensuing year. Twenty-two years later he became Mayor. He was born in Scotland in 1820. His death occurred in Toronto, 1882. Water color. Size 5 x 6. Head and shoulders. See 947.

385—BEATY, JAMES—Mayor of Toronto, 1879-80—A lawyer by profession. Elected to the Council as alderman for St. James' Ward in 1877. On the expiration of his second year as mayor, he retired from municipal life. Mr. Beaty was prominent in political circles, and represented West Toronto in the Dominion Parliament, being elected in 1880 and again in 1882. Beaty avenue, Toronto, is called after his family. He was born in Halton County, 1831, and died at Toronto, 1899. Water color. Size 5 x 6. Head and shoulders.

386—McMURRICH, WILLIAM BARCLAY—Mayor of Toronto, 1881-2— A barrister. Born in Toronto in 1842, the eldest son of Hon. John Mc-Murrich. He was educated at Upper Canada College and Toronto University, and was called to the bar in 1866. In 1879 he was chosen to represent St. Patrick's Ward, which he did until his election to the mayoralty. During his term of office he had the honor of receiving H.R.H. Princess Louise and the Marquis of Lorne, on their first official visit to the city. His death took place in 1908. Water color. Size 5 x 6. Head and shoulders. See 949.

387—BOSWELL, ARTHUR RADCLIFFE, K.C.—Mayor of Toronto, 1883-4—A son of the late Judge Boswell, of the County Court of Northumberland. He was called to the bar in 1865, and was twice chairman of the Public Library Board. In 1877 he became a member of the City Council, and in 1883 was elected as Mayor. In 1911 appointed Superintendent of Insurance for Ontario and Registrar of Loan Companies. He was born in Cobourg. Ont., in 1838. Water color. Size 5 x 6. Head and shoulders.

388—HOWLAND, WILLIAM HOLMES—Mayor of Toronto, 1886-7— Elected to the mayoralty on the temperance platform; was largely instrumental in having the work of straightening the Don commenced. He was the eldest son of Sir William Pearce Howland, Lieutenant-Governor of Ontario, and was born at Lambton Mills, Ont., in 1844. His death occurred in Toronto, 1893. Water color. Size 5 x 6. Head and shoulders.

389—CLARKE, EDWARD FREDERICK—Mayor of Toronto, 1888-91— Born at Bailieboro', County Cavan, Ireland, 1850. On coming to Canada he learned the printing trade on the Globe. Subsequently he became editor of the Orange Sentinel, and in 1887 was elected D.G.M. of the Orange Order, British North America. From 1886 to 1894 he sat in the Provincial House for one of the Toronto constituencies, and from 1896, until 1905 (the year of his death) represented West Toronto in the Dominion House. Water color. Size 5 x 6. Head and shoulders.

390—FLEMING, ROBERT JOHN—Mayor of Toronto, 1892-3 and 1896-7—Entered the City Council in 1886, representing St. David's Ward. In August, 1897, he became Assessment Commissioner, holding that position until 1905, when he resigned to accept the managership of the Toronto Street Railway Company, a position he still (1917) holds. He was born in Toronto in 1854. Water color. Size 5 x 6. Head and shoulders. See 3515, 3571.

391—KENNEDY, WARRING—Mayor of Toronto, 1894-5—Born at Waterask, County Down, Ireland, in 1827. Came to Toronto in 1858, and established in 1869 the wholesale dry goods firm of Samson, Kennedy & Gemmell. Opposed Angus Morrison for the mayoralty in 1877, but was defeated, winning over R. J. Fleming, however, in 1894-5. He died in Toronto in 1904. Water color. Size 5 x 6. Head and shoulders.

392—**SHAW, JOHN**—Mayor of Toronto, 1897-9—When Mayor Fleming resigned to accept the Assessment Commissionership, he was succeeded by John Shaw, a lawyer. The latter sat in the Council continuously from 1884 to 1900, with the exception of the year 1896, when he ran unsuccessfully for Mayor. In 1904-5 he was elected controller, and in 1908 was returned to the Provincial Legislature, representing North Toronto. Water color. Size 5 x 6. Head and shoulders.

393—**MACDONALD, ERNEST ALBERT**—Mayor of Toronto, 1900— Born in Oswego, N.Y., in 1858, but removed to Brockville when very young, later coming to Toronto and taking part in the boom of the "eighties." Through his instrumentality sections of Riverdale and Chester were opened up. For several years he sat in the City Council as representative of St. Matthew's Ward, St. James' Ward and Ward One, and was elected mayor in 1900. His death took place in 1902. Water color. Size 5 x 6. Head and shoulders.

394—**HOWLAND, OLIVER AIKEN, K.C., C.M.G.**—Mayor of Toronto, 1901-2—Second son of Sir William P. Howland and brother of W. H. Howland (mayor 1886-7). Was called to the bar in 1875, and in 1894 defeated Sir Charles Moss in South Toronto in the Provincial elections. On the occasion of the visit of the Prince and Princess of Wales, in 1902, he was created a C.M.G. He was born at Lambton Mills, Ont., in 1847, and died in Toronto in 1905. Water color. Size 5 x 6. Head and shoulders.

395—**URQUHART, THOMAS**—Mayor of Toronto, 1903-5—Born in Wallacetown, Elgin Co., Ont., in 1858; became Township Clerk of Dunwich at the age of 21, and in 1886 was called to the bar, subsequently practising in Toronto. He represented Ward Four from 1900-2, and in the following year defeated Daniel Lamb and O. A. Howland in the mayoralty race. In 1903 he ran for North Toronto in the Dominion elections, but was defeated by Hon. Geo. E. Foster. Water color. Size 5 x 6. Head and shoulders.

396—**COATSWORTH, EMERSON**—Mayor of Toronto, 1906-7—A son of City Commissioner Emerson Coatsworth; born in 1854. Subsequent to learning the carpentering trade he studied law, and in 1875 was called to the bar. He represented East Toronto in the Dominion Parliament from 1891-6, was elected to the City Council in 1904-5. In 1909 he was appointed chairman of the Board of License Commissioners by the Provincial Government. Water color. Size 5 x 6. Head and shoulders.

397—**OLIVER, JOSEPH**—Mayor of Toronto, 1908-9—Born in Erin, Ont., in 1852, but removed to Toronto three years later. Early in life he entered the lumber business, and in 1885 he became a member of the School Board. Ten years later he was elected to the City Council, and was again chosen in 1901, serving until 1904, and being on the Board of Control in the latter year. Water color. Size 5 x 6. Head and shoulders.

398—**GEARY, GEORGE REGINALD, K.C.**—Mayor of Toronto, 1910-12 —Born in Strathroy, Ont., 1873, son of Theophilus Jones Geary; educated at Upper Canada College and Toronto University, subsequently studying law and successfully practising in Toronto. Represented Ontario in the insurance investigation ordered by the Dominion Government. He was elected to the School Board in 1903, and represented Ward Three from 1904-7; became controller in 1909. At the funeral of Edward VII., and later at the coronation of King George V., he represented the city of Toronto. In 1911 he was appointed a member of the Toronto Power Commission, and in October of the following year resigned from the mayoralty to become Corporation Counsel for Toronto. Water color. Size 5 x 6. Head and shoulders. See 3208.

399—HOCKEN, HORATIO CLARENCE—Mayor of Toronto, 1912-14, following Mayor Geary's resignation to become Corporation Counsel—He learned the trade of compositor at the Globe, later going with the Evening News, where he became successively foreman compositor, municipal reporter and managing editor. He was owner and manager of the Orange Sentinel. In 1907 he became controller, and was re-elected in 1908-9 and 1911-12. Water color. Size 5 x 6. Head and shoulders.

400—CHURCH, THOMAS LANGTON—Mayor of Toronto, 1915-16—Born in the city of Toronto, 1872, of Irish parentage. Educated in the Public schools here, Jarvis Collegiate and Toronto and Trinity Universities (B.C.L.) Studied law and was called to the bar in 1897, subsequently successfully practising his profession in the city of his birth. Interested in civic affairs; elected alderman in Ward Two, 1905-9; controller, 1910-14. In 1915 became mayor of Toronto by a large majority. A member of the Harbor Commission since 1905; vice-president of Hydro Radial Union, and of Great Waterways Union; president Great Lakes and St. Lawrence Improvement Association. Water color. Size 4 x 5. Head and shoulders.

401—SECOND MEETING PLACE OF TORONTO'S MUNICIPAL FATHERS—The old City Hall on the south side of Front street, between Jarvis and West Market streets. The building, designed by J. G. Howard after the Italian style of architecture, was erected in 1844, altered in 1851, occupied until 1899, and demolished in 1901. The South St. Lawrence or Lower Market now (1917) stands on the site. In 1833 a market building and town hall of brick was erected on the King street front to replace the frame structure in the market square, set apart previously for municipal and market purposes. The upper rooms of the new building were used as city offices and by the City Council for meetings. This building was burnt in the great fire of 1849. Water color. Size 10 x 12.

402—THE CITY HALL, 1912—Situated on Queen street west, at the head of Bay street. On 21st November, 1891, the foundation stone was laid, and the building was completed and declared open 18th September, 1899. It is built of stone and occupies the square bounded on the north by Albert street, south by Queen, east by James, and west by Teraulay. Platinum print, hand colored. Size 10 x 12.

403—For future Mayor.

404—For future Mayor.

405—For future Mayor.

406 to 431—LIEUTENANT-GOVERNORS OF UPPER CANADA, 1792-1841, AND OF ONTARIO, 1867-1917—Two portraits are missing, those of Peter Hunter, the first regularly appointed Lieut.-Covernor to succeed Simcoe, and Major-General de Rottenburg, who from June-December, 1813, acted as Administrator. It is supposed that no portraits of these men are in existence. From the Union until Confederation Upper Canada was without a Lieutenant-Governor. The two provinces were governed by a Governor-General, and the seat of Government changed from place to place. From 1867, however, the Federal Government had the power of appointing lieutenant-governors of the provinces, and in July of that year Major-General Henry Stisted held the reins of office for Ontario. These portraits, with the exceptions of Hon. Alex. Grant and Sir J. M. Gibson, are water colors from oil paintings in Government House, Toronto.

406—SIMCOE, GEN. JOHN GRAVES—First Lieut.-Governor Upper Canada, 8th July, 1792-20th July, 1796—Son of Captain John Simcoe, R.N.— Was born at Cotterstock, England, in 1752. In 1771 he entered the army as an ensign in the 35th Regiment of Foot, afterwards purchasing a captaincy

7

in the 40th Regiment. From 1777 he was in command of the Queen's Rangers, in the War of the Revolution, receiving the rank of lieutenant-colonel in the army. After the war he returned to England, but in 1792 came to Canada as the first Lieutenant-Governor of Upper Canada, his term of office extending until 1796, when in the usual form of "leave of absence" he again went to England. In 1796 he was appointed Civil Governor and Commander-in-Chief of the British Forces in San Domingo. In 1801 he was gazetted as "lieutenant-general in the army," and in 1806 was directed to join Earl St. Vincent at Lisbon. He was taken ill on the voyage, brought back to England, where he died, at Exeter, 26th October. Water color from painting by G. T. Berthon. Size 6 x 8. Half length. See 161, 3265, 3370.

407—RUSSELL, HON. PETER—President and Administrator Upper Canada, 20th July, 1796-17th Aug., 1799—Was a member of the Irish branch of the family of Russell, of which the Duke of Bedford was the head. He was educated for the church, but preferred to enter the army. He served as secretary to Sir Henry Clinton during the Revolutionary War, after which he returned to England. He came to Upper Canada as Inspector-General of the Province in 1792. When Governor Simcoe returned to England, Hon. Peter Russell succeeded him as Administrator, convening the first Parliament held at York, 1st June 1797. The government of the province was handed over by President Russell to Governor Hunter in 1799. Water color from painting by G. T. Berthon. Size 6 x 8. Half length, sitting.

408—GRANT (COMMODORE), HON, ALEXANDER—President and Administrator Upper Canada, 11th Sept., 1805-25th Aug., 1806, during the interval between Lieut.-Governor Hunter and Lieut.-Governor Gore. He was second son of Patrick, 8th Laird of Grant of Glenmoriston, Inverness-shire. Born in 1734. Served in the Royal Navy as a midshipman, and was with Amherst in the Lake Champlain expedition in the Seven Years' War. Later he was placed in command of lake vessels from Niagara to Mackinaw, and was known as Commodore Grant. He was a member of the first Executive and Legislative Council. The Commodore's death took place in May, 1813, at his residence, Grant Castle, at Grosse Point, on Lake St. Clair. Photograph colored by White, Inverness, Scotland, from oil portrait in possession of Ian Robert James Murray Grant, the chief of the Clan, of Glenmoriston, Inverness-shire, Scotland. Size 6 x 7. Three-quarter length. See 181.

409—GORE, FRANCIS—Lieut.-Governor Upper Canada, Aug. 25th, 1806-Oct. 9th, 1811, and Sept. 21st, 1815-Jan. 6th, 1818—Succeeded General Peter Hunter. He held a commission in the 47th Regiment in 1787; was in service on the continent in 1794. On the recommendation of George III. in 1804, became Governor of Bermuda, retaining that office until his appointment in Canada, 1806. So severely attacked by the House of Commons in 1810, in connection with a Militia Act previously passed in the Provinces, that he asked for leave of absence, and went to England the following year. He, however, returned to Canada in 1815, his second administration terminating in 1818, although he left the country earlier. Water color from a painting by Lawrence. Size 6 x 8. Half length, sitting. See 362, 1669.

410—BROCK, GENERAL SIR ISAAC, K.B.—President and Administrator Upper Canada, 9th October, 1811-Oct. 13th, 1812—Eighth son of John Brock, was born at St. Peter's Port, Guernsey, 1769. When sixteen years of age he received a commission as ensign in 8th Regiment. On obtaining his lieutenancy he exchanged into the 49th, and was with it at Copenhagen, after which he received orders to proceed to Canada. Stationed at York 1803. Returned to England on leave. Came again to Canada, and was given command of the troops in both provinces. Built dock-yards at York. Planned new Parliament Buildings; prepared township maps showing state of roads and bridges. War with the United States was inevitable, so Brock had many problems to solve, chief of which were the defence of the frontier and the Indian question. On 12th June, 1812, war was declared. Brock took Detroit the following August (gold medal), and on 13th Oct., 1812, fell at Queenston Heights. Water color from painting by G. T. Berthon. Size 6 x 8. See 1225, 1690.

411—SHEAFFE, MAJOR-GENERAL SIR ROGER HALE—President and Administrator Upper Canada, 20th Oct., 1812-June 19th, 1813—He was born in 1763 in Boston, and was a son of William Sheaffe, Deputy Collector of Customs at that port. Entered the army as an ensign in 1778, and rose to rank of lieutenant in 1780. Served in Canada from 1787-97, having been made a captain in 1795. In 1811 he became Major-General, and in recognition of his services at Queenston Heights was made a Baronet. He was in command at York in April, 1813, and was severely, and, in the opinion of many, justly, criticized for his conduct in not remaining at the town in order to assist the local militia. Made a General in 1828. His death took place in Edinburgh, 1851. Water color from painting by G. T. Berthon. Size 4 x 6. Half length, sitting.

412—DRUMMOND, LIEUT.-GENERAL SIR GORDON, K.B.—President and Administrator, Upper Canada, 13th Dec., 1813-25th April, 1815—Born in Quebec, 1771, where his father held position of Paymaster-General of the Forces. He entered the Army in 1789 and became lieutenant-colonel in 1794. In 1805 he was second in command in Jamaica. He performed important service in Ireland in 1812, and in 1813, still retaining his post on the staff in Ireland, was sent to Canada as second in command to Lieut.-General Sir George Prevost. General Drummond was in command at Lundy's Lane, 25th July, 1814, and in August attacked Fort Erie. Late in the year he succeeded Prevost as Commander-in-Chief, and became Administrator-in-Chief of Upper and Lower Canada. He asked to be recalled to England in 1816, and died in London in 1854. Water color from painting by G. T. Berthon, Toronto. Size 6 x 8. Half length.

413—MURRAY, GENERAL SIR GEORGE, G.C.B., G.C.H.—Provisional Lieut.-Governor Upper Canada, 25th April, 1815-1st July, 1815—Served in Flanders, 1793, and in Egypt, 1801; went as quartermaster-general to Portugal with Sir John Moore, in 1808. Was made Major-General, 1812; appointed Adjutant-General to the Forces in Ireland, 1814, and subsequently sent to Canada. Whether he was entitled to rank of Lieutenant-Governor does not seem clear, for Governor Gore was still acting. Soon after Murray's arrival in York he heard of Napoleon's escape from Elba, and, applying for active service, left the country without having met the Legislature of the Province. General Murray was born at Ochtertyre, Perthshire, Scotland, 6th Feb., 1772, and died in London, Eng., July, 1846. Water color from a painting by G. T. Berthon. Size 6 x 8. Half length. See 1676.

414—ROBINSON, MAJOR-GENERAL SIR FREDERICK PHILIPSE—Provisional Lieutenant-Governor Upper Canada, 1st July, 1815-21st Sept., 1815—A son of Col. Beverley Robinson of New York, who in the Revolutionary War raised a regiment called "The King's Loyal Americans." Sir Frederick entered the army in 1777 as ensign in his father's regiment. He served with distinction in West Indies and in Peninsular campaign, commanding a brigade at Vittoria. The short period of his governorship did not give opportunity for administrative action. In 1838 he was nominated Knight Grand Cross of the Bath, and in 1846 became lieutenant-general. He died in England, 1852. Water color from a painting by G. T. Berthon. Size 6 x 8. Half length.

415—SMITH, LT.-COL. HON. SAMUEL—Administrator Upper Canada, June 11th, 1817-Aug. 12th, 1818, and March 8th-June 30th, 1820—Joined the Rangers during the Revolutionary War, subsequently becoming captain. At the close of the war he retired to New Brunswick. In 1792 he joined the new regiment of Rangers, under Simcoe, being with the Lieut.-Governor at Niagara and York, later becoming colonel. In Oct., 1815, he was appointed a member of the Executive Council, and on the retirement of Governor Gore became Administrator of the Province. He opened the second session of Parliament in Feb., 1818, which dealt chiefly with acts on inland revenue. During Governor Maitland's absence he was again Administrator for a short time. Col. Smith was born in 1756 and died at Toronto, 20th Oct., 1826. Water color. From a painting by G. T. Berthon, Toronto. Size 6 x 8. Half length.

416—MAITLAND, MAJOR-GENERAL SIR PEREGRINE, K.C.B.— Lieut.-Governor Upper Canada, 13th Aug., 1818-23rd Aug., 1828—Born in Hampshire, Eng., 1777. He served throughout the campaign in Flanders. In 1803 became lieutenant-colonel, and major-general in 1814. At Waterloo commanded 2nd and 3rd Battalions of 1st Foot Guards. Through the influence of his father-in-law, the Duke of Richmond, he received the appointment of Lieutenant-Governor of Upper Canada in 1818. During his administration both Gourlay and Mackenzie were to the fore. Sir Peregrine was criticized for his action in refusing to allow the Superintendent of Indian Affairs and the Adjutant-General to give evidence before a committee of the House of Assembly, for which he had not much respect. In 1820 he acted as Commander-in-Chief of the Forces for three months. He was recalled in 1828, filled several appointments subsequently, and died in London, Eng., 30th May, 1854. Water color from painting by G. T. Berthon, Toronto. Size 6 x 8. Half length.

417—COLBORNE, SIR JOHN, G.C.B., G.C.H. (LORD SEATON)— Lieut.-Governor Upper Canada, 4th Nov., 1828-30th Nov. 1835—Born in England, 1778. Served in Egypt, 1801; in Sicily, 1808; joined Wellington's Army and was present at the Battle of Ocana, Nov., 1809. He led the attack of the 52nd Light Infantry on Marshal Soult's position at the Battle of Orthes in 1814, and at Waterloo was in command of his old regiment, the 52nd. Founded Upper Canada College, Toronto, and was the means of having new Parliament Buildings erected in York. Sir John Colborne was deeply interested in everything pertaining to the benefit of the Province, and never over-stepped the bounds of constitution under which the Province was governed. Although his term expired in 1835 he remained in Toronto until after the new House met in January, 1836. He was appointed Commander-in-Chief of the two Provinces, suppressed the rebellion in Lower Canada, remained as Administrator and acted as Governor from Jan.-Oct., 1839, when he returned to England, and was created Lord Seaton. He died in 1863. Water color from painting by G. T. Berthon. Size 6 x 8. Half length. See 160, 834.

418—HEAD, SIR FRANCIS BOND—Lieut.-Governor Upper Canada, 25th Jan., 1836-23rd March, 1838—He entered military service at an early age, serving in the Royal Engineers. Was at Waterloo, and subsequently made a tour of exploration in South Africa. His appointment by the Melbourne Ministry as Lieut.-Governor was entirely unsolicited, and came as a surprise. In 1836 he arrived in Toronto; resigned his office in 1837, though he administered the affairs of the Province till March, 1838. On the outbreak of the Rebellion of 1837 advanced to meet the rebels, and succeeded in quelling the rising, so far as the Toronto district was concerned, with little difficulty. He was created a member of the Privy Council in order to assist in framing the British North America Act. Sir Francis wrote several books, amongst the number being "The Emigrant" and "A Fortnight in Ireland." He was born in Kent, Eng., 1793, and died at Croydon, 20th July, 1875. Water color from painting by G. T. Berthon. Size 6 x 8. Half length. See 179.

419—THOMSON, RT. HON. CHARLES EDWARD POULETT (BARON SYDENHAM)—Acting Lieut.-Governor Upper Canada, Nov. 22nd, 1839-18th Feb., 1840, during his term as Governor-General—He entered political life in 1826, becoming in 1830 Vice-President of the Board of Trade in Lord Grey's Ministry. Was appointed Gov-General, October, 1839. Arrived in Toronto in November; opened the Legislature on 3rd December. His Government introduced the Union resolutions, which were carried.. His next step was to settle the Clergy Reserves question, his measure being subsequently adopted by the Imperial Parliament. He saw the importance of establishing local or municipal government. While dealing with the politicians of Upper Canada he endeavored to steer a middle course; was elevated to the peerage in 1840; made the proclamation of the Union 1841, and opened the first Parliament of the United Canadas at Kingston. He resigned in July, 1841, and died the following September, from injuries received by being thrown from his horse. Water color from painting by G. T. Berthon. Size 6 x 8. Three-quarter length, sitting. See 1626.

420—ARTHUR, COL. SIR GEORGE—Lieut.-Governor Upper Canada, 23rd March, 1838-9th Feb., 1841—He was born in 1784, and entered the army twenty years later, in the 91st Highlanders. Promoted to a lieutenancy in the 35th Foot, serving with that regiment in Italy in 1806. In 1808 he served as a captain in Sicily, and in 1809 in the expedition to Walcheren; was employed in the attack upon Flushing, and for his services on this occasion was thanked in general orders. He recommended the settlement of Clergy Reserves in Canada and the promotion of education by improvement in the Common School System. In 1841 the two Provinces were united under Lord Sydenham, then Governor-General, at whose request Sir George Arthur continued for a time to conduct the administration of Upper Canada. His services in Canada were rewarded with a baronetcy shortly after his return to England in the summer of 1841. Water color from a painting by G. T. Berthon. Size 6 x 8. Three-quarter length, sitting.

421—STISTED, MAJOR-GENERAL HENRY WILLIAM—First Lieut.-Governor (Provisional) Ontario, 8th July, 1867-14th July, 1868—Served with the 78th Highlanders in the Persian War, 1857; was at the Relief of Lucknow, holding the command of the 1st Brigade during the defence of the Residency. In 1864 he was made Major-General, and in the latter part of 1866 was given divisional command of Upper Canada. From the Union of the Canadas in 1841 to Confederation, Upper Canada was without a Lieut.-Governor, as both Provinces were under the jurisdiction of the Governor-General. In 1867 General Stisted was made provisional Lieut.-Governor of Ontario. His term of office lasted a year, during which he presided over the first Parliament of Ontario, which dealt with the Act regarding free grants and homesteads. Died in England, 10th Dec., 1875. Water color from painting by G. T. Berthon. Size 6 x 8. Half length, sitting.

422—HOWLAND, HON. SIR WILLIAM PEARCE—Lieut-Governor Ontario, 22nd July, 1868-11th Nov., 1873—Born in Paulings, N.Y., 1811. In 1830 he came to Canada, settling at Cooksville, where he assisted in a general store. His next venture was a business in partnership with his brother, Peleg Howland. Although a prominent man in Toronto at the time of the Rebellion, he took no part in it. In 1841 he became naturalized, interested himself in the election of 1848, was a firm believer in reform, and at the general election of 1857 was returned to the Assembly as representative of West York. He succeeded Hon. Oliver Mowat as Postmaster-General, and became a member of the Executive Council. On the formation of the first Dominion Government, 1st July, 1867, he was appointed a member of the Privy Council and Minister of Inland Revenue. He was a firm supporter of the scheme to attain Confederation. July, 1868, saw his retirement from the Government and his appointment as Lieutenant-Governor of Ontario. On 24th May, 1879, he was created a Knight of the Order of St. Michael and St. George. Water color from a painting by Berthon. Size 6 x 8. Half length.

423—CRAWFORD, HON. JOHN WILLOUGHBY—Lieut.-Governor Ontario, 12th Nov., 1873-13th May, 1875—Came to Canada from Ireland when seven years of age, having been born at Manor Hamilton, County Leitrim, 1817. Educated in Toronto, and called to the bar in 1839; applied himself especially to banking and commercial law. He was Lieutenant-Colonel of the 5th Battalion, Canadian Militia, President of the Toronto and Nipissing Railway, and President of the Royal Canadian Bank. In 1861 he was elected for East Toronto, representing this constituency until the general election in 1863. After Confederation he represented South Leeds, until Nov. 5th, 1873, when he was appointed Lieut.-Governor of Ontario. He died at Government House, 13th May, 1875. Water color. Size 5 x 6. Half length sitting.

424—MACDONALD, HON. DONALD ALEXANDER—Lieut.-Governor Ontario, 21st May, 1875-29th June, 1880—Was born at St. Raphael's, Quebec, in 1816. He entered Parliament in 1835, being returned for the County of Glengarry as member to the Upper Canada House of Assembly, retaining his seat until the Union in 1841. After Confederation he was in 1867 and again in 1872 elected to represent Glengarry in the Commons. In the latter year he was appointed Postmaster-General, holding the position until 1875, when he was offered the Lieutenant-Governorship of Ontario, which he accepted. His appointment was a popular one with all classes, and at the end of his term he left Government House with the respect of the community. His death took place in Montreal, 10th June, 1896. Water color from painting by G. T. Berthon. Size 6 x 8. Half length, sitting.

425—ROBINSON, HON. JOHN BEVERLEY—Lieut.-Governor Ontario, July 8th, 1880-May 31st, 1887—The second son of Sir John Beverley Robinson, Chief Justice of Ontario. Born in Toronto in 1820 and received his education at Upper Canada College. In 1837 he was appointed aide-de-camp to Sir Francis Bond Head, and as such took part in the Rebellion. On its suppression young Robinson began the study of law, and was called to the bar in 1844. In 1858 he was elected to represent one of the Toronto divisions in Parliament, and from 1872-8 sat for Algoma. In the latter year he was again returned for Toronto. He was also City Solicitor for the city of his birth from 1864-80. Continued to represent West Toronto until his appointment as Lieutenant-Governor. His death occurred suddenly while he was attending a political meeting in Toronto in 1896. Water color from a painting by Berthon. Size 5 x 7. Head and shoulders. See 374, 1006.

426—CAMPBELL, HON. SIR ALEXANDER, K.C.M.G.—Lieut.Governor Ontario, 1st June, 1887-24th May, 1892—When two years of age he came to Canada from England, with his parents, and settled near Montreal. Studied law and was called to the bar in 1843. Became a partner of Sir John A. Macdonald. In 1858 he was elected to the Legislative Council of the Cataraqui Division, and Speaker in 1863. Mr. Campbell was a staunch advocate of Confederation, and in recognition of his services in the cause, elected to the Senate, sworn in the Privy Council, 1st July, 1867, and took office as Postmaster-General. Six years later he became first Minister of the Department of the Interior. In 1880 he accepted office of Minister of Militia. Died at Government House, Toronto, 24th May, 1892. Water color from painting by Robert Harris. Size 6 x 8. Three-quarter length, sitting.

427—KIRKPATRICK, HON. SIR GEORGE AIREY—Lieut.-Governor Ontario, 1st June, 1892-Nov. 18th, 1897—Canadian by birth, a son of Thomas Kirkpatrick, Q.C., of Kingston, Ont. Studied law, and was called to the bar in 1865. He was an ardent supporter of the Volunteer Militia, and served during the Fenian Raid; became Lieut.-Colonel of the 47th Battalion in 1872. Represented the County of Frontenac for many years; was Chairman of the Standing Committee on Public Accounts, and Speaker of the House of Commons, 1883-7. Interests of sailors were watched by him while in the House, and in educational matters he always took an active part. His appointment as Lieutenant-Governor of Ontario was well received by all parties. Sir George's death took place in Toronto, 13th December, 1899. Water color from painting by A. D. Patterson. Size 6 x 8. Half length.

428—MOWAT, HON. SIR OLIVER—Lieut.-Governor Ontario, 18th Nov., 1897-19th April, 1903—Received his early education in Kingston, Ont. He entered the office of John A. Macdonald as a law student; studied with him for four years, and was called to the bar in 1841. Shortly after this he came to Toronto; created a Q.C. in 1855, and afterwards elected a Bencher of the Law Society. He was elected to Parliament in 1857 as representative for South Ontario, continuing to represent that constituency until 1864. Was one of the "Fathers of Confederation." In 1872 he succeeded Mr. Blake as Premier, and from that time until 1896 was also Attorney-General. He did much towards shaping the laws of Ontario, while his success in obtaining a large increase of territory for this Province is a monument to his administration. In 1896 he resigned his seat in the Provincial House, and was elected to the Dominion Parliament by North Oxford. Sir Oliver was born in Kingston, 1820, and died at Toronto, April 19th, 1903. Water color from painting by J. W. L. Forster. Size 5 x 6. Head and shoulders. See 468.

429—CLARK, HON. SIR WM. MORTIMER, K.C.—Lieut.-Governor Ontario, 20th April, 1903-21st Sept., 1908—He was born in Aberdeen, Scotland, 24th May, 1836, and educated in Scotland. Practised law in Toronto; was one of the founders and first directors of St. Andrew's College for Boys. He was in 1878-9 President of the County York Law Association, and formerly a vice-president of the "Equal Rights" Association. In 1907 he was knighted. His interests educationally and in the business sphere were broad and varied. Sir Mortimer wrote several sketches of travel in Europe and the East. His death took place Aug. 10th, 1917, at Prout's Neck, Me., where he had been summering. Water color from painting by J. W. L. Forster. Size 6 x 8. Half length, sitting. See 967.

430—GIBSON, HON. SIR JOHN MORISON, K.C.M.G.—Lieut.-Governor Ontario, 22nd Sept., 1908-24th Sept., 1914—Born in Township of Toronto, Peel Co., in 1842; a graduate of Toronto University; M.A. in 1864; practised his profession of law in Hamilton for many years; a bencher of the Law Society of Upper Canada, 1899. Chairman Hamilton Board of Education; was an active member of the 13th Regiment, Hamilton, from 1860-95, being appointed in that year Hon. Lieut.-Colonel, and in 1901 Hon. Colonel. Served at Ridgeway in 1866; a fine rifle shot, having been a member of Canadian Wimbledon Teams for several years, winning in 1879 the Prince of Wales Prize. He was Provincial Secretary, 1889-96. Commissioner of Crown Lands, 1896-9, and Attorney-General, 1899-1905. Was Grand Master of Grand Lodge of Canada, 1892-4. An honorary A.D.C. to the Gov.-General. Platinum print from life, hand colored. Size 5 x 8. Full length.

431—HENDRIE, LIEUT-COL., HON. SIR JOHN STRATHEARN—Lieut.-Governor Ontario, Sept. 25th, 1914—Born at Hamilton, Ont., 1857; educated at a private school, Hamilton Grammar School and Upper Canada College, Toronto. Was Mayor of Hamilton, 1901-3; elected to represent that city in the Provincial House, 1902. Minister without portfolio in the

Whitney Administration from its formation; appointed member of the Royal Hydro-Electric Commission, 1906. Commanded the Canadian Artillery on the occasion of Queen Victoria's Diamond Jubilee, London, England; holds long service decoration. Water color from painting by E. Wyly Grier. Size 5 x 8. Half length, sitting. See 3490.

432—For future Lieut.-Governor.

433 to 453—GOVERNMENT HOUSE, TORONTO, 1867-1912—Views, interior and exterior, of the old Government House, Simcoe, Dorset, King and Wellington streets. The gubernatorial residence was built in 1828, destroyed by fire in 1862, and rebuilt, as it is shown in the series, in 1867. In 1912 the mansion was torn down to make way for the railways, the district in which it was situated having long ceased to be a residential one. Prior to the completion of the palatial structure in Rosedale, the Lieutenant-Governor's household took up temporary residence at the north-east corner of College and St. George streets. Sir John Morison Gibson was the last administrator to occupy the Simcoe street mansion, leaving it in 1912.

433—BUSINESS OFFICE OF THE LIEUTENANT-GOVERNOR— North-east corner of the ground floor. This is the first room to the right on coming in through the principal entrance. Through the open doorway one catches a glimpse of the small reception room across the hall. Platinum print in color. Size 8 x 10.

434—PRINCIPAL RECEPTION AND BALLROOM—At the west end may be seen the coat of arms of the Province of Ontario. On the left are the conservatory openings, and on the right the table is set for a small reception. In this apartment the State dinners were given, as was also the last dance, held on the evening of the dinner in honor of the descendants and connections of former Lieutenant-Governors, April 29th, 1912. Platinum print, in color. Size 8 x 10.

435—LAST STATE DINNER GIVEN AT THE OLD GOVERNMENT HOUSE, April 29th, 1912—The dinner was served in the dining-room at the end of the west or right side of the main entrance hall. The guests on the right hand or east side of the table, reading from right to left, were: 1, Dr. Goldwin Howland; 2, Mrs. D. D. Young; 3, Mr. H. M. Mowat; 4, Mrs. Harcourt Vernon; 5, Mr. W. M. Kirkpatrick; 6, Mrs. Wallace Jones; 7, Sir John Beverley Robinson; 8, Mrs. Law; 9, Sir John M. Gibson; 10, Lady Clark; 11, Mr. George S. Crawford; 12, Mrs. Forsyth Grant; 13, Mr. J. Ross Robertson; 14, Miss Mowat; 15, Capt. Forsyth Grant; 16, Mrs. Henry Watson; 17, Lieut.-Col. Macdonald; 18, Miss Elise Clark; 19, Mr. Hope Gibson, A.D.C., at end of table. The guests on the left hand, or west side of the table, reading from right to left, were: 1, Mrs. H. M. Mowat; 2, Capt. D. D. Young; 3, Miss Clark; 4, Mr. Wallace Jones; 5, Miss Gibson; 6, Sheriff Mowat; 7, Lady Robinson; 8, Hon. J. O. Reaume; 9, Lady Gibson; 10, Sir Mortimer Clark; 11, Mrs. George S. Crawford; 12, Prof. Ramsay Wright; 13, Mrs. A. S. Hardy; 14, Commander Law; 15, Mrs. Ramsay Wright; 16, Mr. Henry Watson; 17, Miss Meta Gibson; 18, Mr. Harcourt Vernon; 19, Mr. Fellowes, A.D.C., at end of table. Photograph. Size 10 x 13.

436—GOVERNMENT HOUSE—View from the south, showing the mansion, driveway, grounds, conservatories and flower beds. Platinum print, in color. Size 6 x 8.

437—GOVERNMENT HOUSE, 1867-1912—Front view, facing Simcoe street, from the south-east.The fine old mansion of red brick with stone facings was a reminder of the days when the neighborhood, now given over to manufacturers and railroads, was the aristocratic section of the Queen City. Platinum print, in color. Size 6 x 9.

438—RECEPTION ROOM—On the south-east corner, on the left of the entrance hall, ground floor. Platinum print, in color. Size 8 x 10.

439—BLUE GUEST CHAMBER—North side of the upper hall. Her Majesty Queen Mary occupied this room during her visit to Toronto as Duchess of York. Platinum print, in color. Size 8 x 10.

440—VIEW OF THE EAST END OF THE UPPER HALL—With the staircase leading to the second floor at the west. The first door on the right opens into the room occupied by Her Majesty Queen Mary as Duchess of York, during her visit to Toronto in 1901. Adjoining are toilet and dressing rooms. The first apartment on the left was the morning-room used as a sitting-room by Lady Aberdeen, Lady Grey and the Duchess of Connaught. The last door on the left, near the staircase, opens into the green guest chamber. Platinum print, in color. Size 8 x 10.

441—GOVERNMENT HOUSE—A bird's-eye view of the south-east side of the residence and grounds from the entrance on Simcoe street. At right angles to Simcoe street is seen King street, with its large factory buildings. Platinum print, in color. Size 6 x 8.

442—EAST END OF THE DRAWING-ROOM—Windows looking south. The mantel was a unique piece of marble work. Platinum print, in color. Size 8 x 10.

443—BEDROOM OF HIS HONOR THE LIEUT.-GOVERNOR—North-east corner of the upper hall. This room was occupied by Sir William Mortimer Clark, and also as the chamber of the Duke of York (His Majesty George V.) during his visit to Toronto in 1901. Platinum print, in color. Size 8 x 10.

444—FAMILY GROUP—Miss Margaret (Meta) Gibson, now Mrs. Robert Waldie (1); Miss Eugenia (2); Sir John Morison Gibson (3); Lady Gibson (4); Mr. Hope Gibson (5). Taken in May, 1912. Platinum print, in color. Size 8 x 12.

445—SPACIOUS DRAWING-ROOM—Looking west into the conservatories. The picture is from the east, on the south or left side of the entrance hall. All the New Year's receptions and also those prior to State dinners were held in this room. Platinum print, in color. Size 8 x 10.

446—MORNING-ROOM—On the south side of the upper hall—The windows are not shown; a favorite sittingroom of H.R.H. Princess Louise, Marchioness of Lorne. Platinum print, in color. Size 8 x 10.

447—GOVERNMENT HOUSE—South-west view showing the grounds from Wellington Street, St. Andrew's Church, Simcoe Street (Presbyterian), is shown to the right of the picture. Platinum print, in color. Size 6 x 8.

448—MAIN STAIRCASE—At the west end of the entrance hall, leading to the first floor. The door to the left, at the foot of the staircase, is that of the dining-room. Platinum print, in color. Size 8 x 10.

449—ENTRANCE HALL—Ground floor, looking west from the official entrance on Simcoe Street, and showing the main staircase. The first door on the right (not shown) opens into the office of his Honor the Lieutenant-Governor; the second door to the right leads to the steward's office and the private entrance from King Street, the third into the private dining-room. The first door to the left (not shown) opens into a small reception room; the second leads to the east end of the principal drawing and reception room; while the fourth opens into a small sitting-room, connected on the north with the drawing-room and on the south with the conservatories. Platinum print, in color. Size 8 x 10.

450—**MAIN STAIRCASE**—Looking down the main hall to the principal entrance of the Lieutenant-Governor's residence. Platinum print, in color. Size 8 x 10.

451—**GREEN GUEST CHAMBER**—In the south-west corner of the upper hall, occupied by Lady Grey and the Duchess of Connaught when visiting Toronto. Platinum print, in color. Size 8 x 10.

452—**DINING-ROOM**—At the end of the west or right side of the entrance hall, windows looking north; used as a private dining-room or for small State dinners. The table is shown laid for the last official dinner, 29th April, 1912, at the old gubernatorial mansion to descendants and connections of its former occupants. On the wall are seen the portraits of some of the early Lieutenant-Governors and Administrators of Ontario. Platinum print, in color. Size 8 x 10.

453—**"LAST DANCE" IN OLD GOVERNMENT HOUSE, 29TH APRIL,** 1912—Held in the principal reception and ballroom at the west end of the main entrance to Government House, and in which large dances and State dinners were held. The group in the foreground is composed of (1) Lady Gibson, (2) Mr. J. Ross Robertson, (3) Mrs. John King, daughter of the late Wm. Lyon Mackenzie. (4) Sir John Morison Gibson. Photograph. Size 10 x 13.

454—**RESIDENCE OF SIR WILLIAM MORTIMER CLARK, WELL- INGTON STREET WEST, TORONTO**—This handsome residence was erected about 1871 by Mr. John Gordon, brother of the late Lady Clark, but never occupied until purchased from his executors by Sir Mortimer Clark (then Mr. Clark) in 1884. During the period that Government House was being renovated, the Clarks resided in the old mansion. Demolished in 1912 to make room for railways. Photograph, colored. Size 7 x 9.

455—**CLARK, LADY (HELEN GORDON)**—Wife of Sir William Mortimer Clark, K.C., Lieutenant-Governor of Ontario, 1903-8. Born in Caithness, Scotland, in 1839, the daughter of Gilbert Gordon, and sister of John Gordon, of Gordon, Mackay & Co., Toronto. In 1866 she married Sir William Mortimer Clark, who was knighted in 1907. Lady Clark was one of the promoters of the Female Immigrants' Receiving Home, and first directress of the Home for Incurables, the success of the latter charity being largely due to her efforts. She died in Toronto, 1913. Photograph, colored. Size 6 x 9. Full length, sitting.

456—**GOVERNMENT HOUSE, TORONTO,** 1912-15—North-east corner College and St. George streets. The residence was erected by Lieut.-Col. Frederick W. Cumberland, well-known engineer and architect, and occupied by him from 1861 until his death in 1881. It subsequently passed into the hands of Alfred Cosby, and from 1905 to 1912 was occupied by Walter D. Beardmore. In May of the latter year it became the residence of Sir John M. Gibson, Lieutenant-Governor of Ontario, 1908-14, the old Government House at the south-west corner of King and Simcoe streets being demolished at that time. In December, 1915, Sir John Strathearn Hendrie, Sir John Gibson's successor in office, removed to the handsome new gubernatorial mansion in Rosedale and now (1916) Mrs. Walter D. Beardmore has resumed occupancy of the College street residence. Photograph, colored. Size 5 x 7.

457—**HOME OF JUDGE (SIR) WM. BUELL RICHARDS**—South-east corner Ann and Yonge sts., Toronto—Erected about 1845 by Mr. John Willoughby Crawford (afterwards Lieut.-Governor of Ontario), and sold by him to Judge Richards in 1850. The latter lived there during the whole of his residence in Toronto. The large, frame, roughcast house was, at the time of its erection, quite in the country, but many years ago it was torn down to make way for stores. Judge Richards, a native of Brockville, entered Parliament in 1848 as member for Leeds County. Held post of Attorney-General, U.C., in Hincks-Morin Ministry, retiring to take a puisne judgeship in the Court of Common Pleas. Succeeded Chief Justice Draper in same court, and again succeeded him when Draper was transferred from the Queen's Bench to the Court of Appeal. On the creation of the Supreme Court of Canada, 1875, Richards was appointed Chief Justice of that court. Knighted, 1877; retired two years later. Died, 1889. Water color. Size 5 x 7.

458—"WILLOWS," TORONTO, 1908—Built by James McDonell, a son of Hon. Alexander McDonell, member of the Legislative Council of Upper Canada. The "Willows," so called because the grounds surrounding it were covered with willow trees, was the first substantial house on Bathurst street, north of Queen. It was erected in 1853-4, and in its day was one of the best residences of Toronto. The property was leased by the Western Hospital, 1899, and purchased in 1903. To-day (1917) the "Willows" stands in rear of the new hospital, opened November, 1911, and is still used for the care of patients. Water color. Size 5 x 7.

459—SIMONS, COL. TITUS GEER—Son of Titus Simons, who after the Revolutionary War settled at Kingston and then at Niagara, York and Flamboro West, U.C., successively. The younger Simons had a distinguished career in the war of 1812, although, strange to say, his name has not been mentioned by historians. He was in command of the volunteer armed militia at the burning of Black Rock, December 29th, 1813, and was severely wounded at Lundy's Lane. Became colonel of the 2nd Gore Militia 1824. In 1797 Col. Simons purchased the Upper Canada Gazette from the Tiffanys at Niagara and shortly afterwards, with William Waters as partner, published the first Gazette in York. He died at Flamboro West, U.C., August 20th, 1829. Water color. Size 4 x 5. Head and shoulders.

460—BONNYCASTLE, SIR RICHARD H., 1791-1847—Served in the War of 1812-15—In 1825 became a captain in the Royal Engineers; commanding Royal Engineer in Canada West, 1837-9; knighted for services in connection with the defence of Kingston, 1837, and was subsequently commanding Royal Engineer in Newfoundland. Water color from a miniature. Size 5 x 6. Head and shoulders.

461—BALDWIN, HON. ROBERT, 1804-58—Closely associated with Responsible Government of Canada, eldest son of Dr. William Warren Baldwin; in 1819 began the study of law and elected a Bencher in 1830. In January of that year he took his seat in Parliament, and ten years later became Solicitor-General. In 1842 the Hincks-Baldwin Administration came into existence, and in 1847 the Baldwin-Lafontaine Administration was formed. Mr. Baldwin held office for eleven years, laboring enthusiastically in the cause of reform. He contributed largely to the establishment of the municipal system, remodelled the Law Courts, and aided materially in University reform. In 1854 Queen Victoria conferred upon him the degree of Companion of the Bath. His death occurred in 1858 at his residence, "Spadina," Toronto. Water color from an oil portrait by T. Hamel, in possession of his grandson, Robert W. Y. Baldwin, Paris, Ont. Size 4 x 6. Head and shoulders. See 269, 271, 1050.

462—O'HARA, LIEUT.-COL. WALTER —At Twenty-two Years of Age—Born 3rd Feb., 1787, in Dublin, Ireland; died in Toronto, 13th Jan., 1874; educated at Trinity College, Dublin, and afterwards studied for the Bar at the Inner Temple, London. In 1806 he accepted an Ensigncy in the 91st Regiment, and subsequently obtained a Captaincy in the 47th. In 1808, O'Hara accompanied Walter Savage Landor to Spain. He was selected to serve, with rank of Major, in the Portuguese army and attached to the 6th Cacadores. His Peninsular career included all the great actions, and for his services he received the Order of the Tower and Sword, and the Peninsula medal with eight clasps. He emigrated to Canada in 1831, holding the post for several years of Adjutant-General, Upper Canada. For many years he resided in Toronto. Water color from a miniature by Sir Wm. Charles Ross, R.A., in possession of his daughter. Miss Mary O'Hara, Toronto. Size 4 x 5. Head and shoulders. See 463.

463—O'HARA, LIEUT.-COL. WALTER—At Eighty-two Years of Age—Water color from a portrait in possession of his daughter, Miss Mary O'Hara, Toronto. Size 4 x 5. Head and shoulders. See 462.

464—JARVIS, LIEUT.-COL. R. E. COLBORNE—Youngest son of William Botsford Jarvis, born in Toronto, 1842, and educated at Upper Canada College. Entered army as ensign in 100th Prince of Wales' Regiment, Royal Canadians (now Leinster Regiment) in 1859; subsequently joined 69th. Served with distinction throughout Franco-Prussian War in Red Cross Ambulance Corps, receiving a decoration. After passing through the Staff College at Sandhurst, served in Afghan War, 1878-80. Accompanied the late Lord Roberts in march from Cabul to Khandahar. Mentioned in despatches. On his retirement in 1882, returned to Canada, where he died in 1903. Water color. Size 4 x 5. Head and shoulders.

465—THOMSON, COL. E. W., 1794-1865—Son of Archibald Thomson, of Kingston; served in the War of 1812-15. He was elected a member of the Provincial Legislature, for the Second Riding of York, 1836, but was more interested in agriculture than politics. First President of the Provincial Agricultural Association and Board of Agriculture for Upper Canada. His farm, known as Aikinshaw, was on the Dundas road, the eastern boundary being the concession, now (1917) Keele street, West Toronto. Col. Thomson resided here from 1844-65. Water color. Size 4 x 7. Full length.

466—OATES, CAPT. EDWARD—Born near Cork, Ireland, 1772. Captain in the naval service of Great Britain; was captured by a French privateer in the Mediterranean and carried as a prisoner of war to Algiers. He was subsequently ordered to Quebec, and in 1817 finally settled in Canada. Commanded the "Richmond," a sloop of 100 tons burthen, which ran between York and Niagara, and which was built by Oates himself. It was launched in 1820, and wrecked six years later. Capt. Oates died at Port Dalhousie, Ont., in 1827. He was a cousin of Hon. Peter Russell, Administrator of Upper Canada, 1796-9. Water color from photograph in Niagara Historical Museum. Size 7 x 10. Head and shoulders.

467—CAMERON, DUNCAN, C.B., 1775-1842—Born at Camisky, Inverness-shire, Scotland. Received commission as ensign in 79th, or Cameron Highlanders, 1798, and was continuously engaged in campaigns in Europe until after Waterloo. Was severely wounded at Quatre Bras. Came to Canada in 1835, on the recommendation of his cousin, Bishop Macdonell, and settled on a farm on Yonge street, near York Mills. From 1838-41 was colonel of First Regiment of North York Militia. Water color from a miniature in Windsor, N.S. Size 4 x 6. Head and shoulders.

468—MOWAT, SIR OLIVER, 1820-1903—Water color by F. V. Poole. Size 12 x 12. Half length, sitting. See 428.

469—YONGE—"The Right Honorable Sr. George Yonge, Bt., Secretary at War, Knight of the Bath, one of His Majesty's Most Honorable Privy Council, F.R.S., F.A.S. and M.P. Mather Brown, pinxt. E. Scott, sculpt., Engraver to the Duke of York and Prince Edward. Published May 1, 1792, by S. W. Fores, No. 3 Piccadilly." Born in 1732. Died 1812. Was the chief representative of an ancient Devonshire family, and sat in Parliament for the borough of Honiton, England, from 1754-96; was Secretary at War 1782-94. In 1797 he became Governor and Commander-in-Chief at Cape of Good Hope. Governor Simcoe gave the name Yonge (now Yonge street, Toronto), to the road hewn out in 1793-1800, through the woods from Lake Ontario to Lake Huron, as a compliment to the Secretary at War, who was an authority on Roman roads. Stipple engraving, printed in color. Size 7 x 9. Half length.

470—JARVIS, WILLIAM DUMMER—Born 4th Aug., 1834, the eldest son of William Botsford Jarvis. Became lieutenant in the 12th Regiment, and later lieut.-colonel in the 12th York Rangers. Resided for a time in Toronto, but subsequently removed to Manitoba, where he acted as Inspector of the Northwest Mounted Police. He now (1917) resides in Nelson, B.C. Water color. Size 4 x 5. Head and shoulders.

471—DR. GRANT POWELL'S COTTAGE, TORONTO, 1826-59—North side of Richmond street, east of Simcoe. Dr. Powell, third son of Chief Justice William Dummer Powell, was educated in England and afterwards migrated to the United States, settling at Stillwater, N.Y., and practising his profession there until 1811, when he removed to Montreal. The following year he settled in York and was subsequently appointed surgeon in charge of all hospital arrangements on the Niagara frontier. At the close of the war Dr. Powell resumed the practice of his profession in York, and some years later was appointed Clerk of the Assembly and Judge of the Home District Court. In 1828 he became Clerk of the Legislative Council. On receiving these appointments he transferred his medical practice to Dr. Widmer. Dr. Powell also had the direction of the building of the old General Hospital, corner of King and John streets. On his death the Richmond street house was occupied until 1859 by Mrs. Seymour, daughter of Dr. Powell, and widow of Charles Seymour. The late Mr. Grant Seymour, of Ottawa, a Government official, was a grandson of the well-known physician. Water color. Size 5 x 7.

472—LIGHTHOUSE, TORONTO ISLAND—A dignified landmark, 1809-1917—In 1803 an Act was passed providing for a lighthouse on what was then York Peninsula, and in 1809 the present hexagonal structure was built of limestone, brought from Queenston for the purpose. When first built it was 52 feet in height, but in 1832 the Government added twelve feet of Kingston stone, built in cement. Above the stone work is the lantern cage with gallery surrounding it, and a weather vane, making the actual height of the lighthouse 82 feet. To the left is the Lakeside Home for Little Children, the summer sanitarium of the Hospital for Sick Children, Toronto. Water color. Size 5 x 7.

473—LIGHTHOUSE, TORONTO ISLAND, 1809-1917—Overlooking Lake Ontario. The several buildings shown are:—1, The lighthouse; 2, Keeper's dwelling, built as a one-storey cottage in 1838, and made a two-storey house in 1875. It was first occupied by James Durnan. 3, One-storey dwelling of plank, the oldest house in Toronto still standing, built 1809, for the first lightkeeper, J. P. Radenmuller; 4, Workshop built by the late George Durnan. These buildings all face south. Water color. Size 5 x 7.

474—BROWN, JOHN GORDON—Born in Alloa, Clackmannanshire, Scotland, 16th Nov., 1827. Youngest son of Peter Brown, and brother of Hon. George Brown; was managing editor of Globe for many years; a leading Liberal writer; subsequently appointed registrar Surrogate Court of Toronto. Died 13th June, 1896. From a portrait in possession of his son, E. B. Brown, K.C., Toronto. Size 6 x 8. Head and shoulders.

475—BROWN, HON. GEORGE—Eldest son of Peter Brown; born in Edinburgh, 1818. In 1838 he emigrated to America with his father, settling in New York, where in 1842 they published the British Chronicle. The following year Mr. Brown, Jr., visited Canada for the purpose of advertising and obtaining support for the paper. During his visit he came into contact with leading Liberals of Upper Canada, and in 1843 he and his father came to Toronto, commencing the publication of the Banner, a weekly paper of the Free Church party. George Brown was, however, pressed to publish a purely political paper, the outcome being the appearance of the Globe, 5th March, 1844. He entered Parliament in 1852 for Haldimand, defeating William Lyon Mackenzie, and during his Parliamentary career favored all reform. Entered the Coalition Government for the purpose of accomplishing Confederation, but subsequently resigned. In 1873 he was called to the Senate. A discharged employe of the Globe shot him, 25th March, 1880, resulting in his death, 9th May. Photograph. Size 9 x 13. Half length. See 969, 3385.

476—DURNAN, GEORGE—Lighthouse-keeper at Toronto Island, 1853-1905, being interviewed in June, 1907, by J. Ross Robertson, when writing a history of the lighthouse for "Robertson's Landmarks" of Toronto. It is a coincidence that Mr. Durnan, during the interview, happened to sit in front of a picture of Toronto, showing the lighthouse, in the art room of The Evening Telegram. Photograph. Size 4½ x 5.

477—LINDSEY, CHARLES—Born in Lincoln, Eng., 1820, died in Toronto, 1908. Arrived in Canada, 1842. Editor of Toronto Examiner; started Canadian Farmer with Hon. Wm. Macdougall, 1848; wrote History of Clergy Reserves, 1851; editor of Toronto Leader, 1853-67; wrote Life of William Lyon Mackenzie, whose eldest daughter he married; wrote Rome in Canada, 1877; contributed to The Nation, Canadian Monthly, and other publications. One of the leading writers on the Conservative press for many years. In 1867 he was appointed Registrar of Deeds for the City of Toronto. Photograph from a portrait in possession of his son, G. G. S. Lindsey, barrister, Toronto. Size 5½ x 6. Head and shoulders.

478—ROBERTSON, JOHN, 1802-75—A well known Scotsman of Toronto—Born in Moraystown, Parish of Petty, Nairnshire, Scotland. He emigrated to Canada in 1832, and was a prominent wholesale dry goods merchant on the west side of Yonge street, near the corner of Melinda, from 1839-75. He was a member of St. Andrew's Society, a Vice-President of the Board of Trade, a leading member of the Clan Donnachaidh (Robertson) in Toronto, and a descendant of Struan Robertson, Chief of the Clan. Mr. Robertson's eldest son, J. Ross Robertson, proprietor of The Evening Telegram, Toronto, is the only member of the family living in 1917. Photograph, colored, from a portrait in possession of his son, J. Ross Robertson, Toronto. Size 3 x 6. Full length.

479—ROBERTSON, MARGARET SINCLAIR, WIFE OF JOHN ROBERTSON—She was the daughter of Hector Sinclair, of Kerrowaird, in the Parish of Petty, Nairnshire, born in 1810 at the farm of Goathill, near Stornoway, Scotland. Her marriage to John Robertson took place in 1841, and in the same year she came to Canada with him, residing in Toronto until her death in 1865. Photograph, colored, from a portrait in possession of her son, J. Ross Robertson, Toronto. Size 3 x 6. Full length.

480—ROLPH, DR. JOHN, 1793-1870—Born at Thornbury, Gloucestershire, Eng. Came to Canada at the beginning of the War of 1812, during which he acted as paymaster in the London District. After the War he returned to England, engaging in the study of law and medicine. He became a member of the Royal College of Surgeons, England, and in 1821 was called to the Bar of Upper Canada. For a time he resided in the township of Charlotteville, then in the Talbot District, and at the general elections of 1824 became a member for Middlesex. About this time he removed to Dundas, whence he came to Toronto in 1831, a year later abandoning law for medicine. Dr. Rolph was elected one of the first aldermen of the city on its incorporation. Becoming involved in the Rebellion of 1837, he was compelled to leave Canada. Subsequent to his return, he formed "Rolph's School," which in 1853 was incorporated as the "Toronto School of Medicine." From 1851-4 he was a member of Hon. Francis Hinck's Administration. His death took place at Mitchell, Ont. Photograph, colored. Size 4 x 5. Head and shoulders.

481— SCOBIE, HUGH—Editor of "The British Colonist"—Mr. Scobie, a son of Capt. James Scobie, 93rd Highlanders, was born at Fort George, Inverness-shire, Scotland, April 29th, 1811. Educated at the Academy of Tain, subsequently engaging in the office of Messrs. Gordon and Stuart, Writers to the Signet, Edinburgh. In 1832 he came to Canada, shortly afterwards purchasing a farm in West Gwillimbury. Acted as agent of Dr. Bartlett, for the New York Albion, until 1837, when he started the Scotsman, which, after two numbers, became the British Colonist. Mr. Scobie continued the publication of the journal until his death, which occurred in Toronto, Dec. 4th, 1853. Water color from original by Hoppner Meyer, in possession of Mr. Scobie's granddaughter, Mrs. Calderwood, Barrie, Ont. Size 6 x 8. Head and shoulders. See 497.

482—BROUGH, SECKER, 1813-79—Born in Ireland and educated at Trinity College Dublin. While a young man he emigrated to Canada, joining his uncle, Gen. Brough, R.A., Commandant at Halifax. He afterwards came to Toronto and entered the office of Messrs. Hagerman and Draper; called to the Bar, 1840,, and later Mr. Draper's partner. On the establishment of the Court of Probate for Upper Canada he was appointed Judge, continuing to hold the office until the abolition of the Court. For several years Mr. Brough had one of the most extensive practices at the Chancery Bar, and took a very active and prominent part as a Bencher of the Law Society. In 1859 he was made Queen's Counsel, and in 1866 became Judge of the County Court of Huron. Owing to ill-health he resigned his position eleven years later. His death occurred at Goderich, Ont., in 1879. Water color. Size 4 x 5. Head and shoulders.

483—MORRISON, MR. AND MRS. DANIEL—Mr. Morrison, one of the most brilliant editorial writers on the Canadian press from about 1853-69, was born in Inverness, Scotland, 1827, the son of the Rev. Mr. Morrison. In the early fifties he emigrated to Canada, engaging in farming for a time, and later editing the Dundas (Ont.) Warder in conjunction with S. T. Jones. In 1854 he assumed the editorship of the Toronto Leader; three years later became editor of the Toronto Daily Colonist, and in 1859 was appointed by the Government as a Provincial Arbitrator in connection with the Public Works Department, resigning the following year to become editor of the Quebec Morning Chronicle. In 1861 he edited the London Prototype, and then joined the staff of the New York Times. Returned to Toronto in 1868 and became editor of the Toronto Daily Telegraph, remaining with that paper until his death in 1870. In 1858 he married Miss Charlotte Nickinson, the celebrated and accomplished actress and daughter of the well-known actor, John Nickinson. Water color from a daguerreotype in possession of their daughter, Mrs. Edward B. Brown, Toronto. Size 5 x 6. Half length, sitting.

484—SHEPPARD, GEORGE—In 1859 Mr. Sheppard was on the Toronto Globe, but subsequently joined the editorial staffs of the Toronto Colonist and Leader. From 1863-80 also he was editor of the New York Times. The celebrated article, "Whither Are We Drifting?" which created considerable discussion at the time of its appearance, was written by Mr. Sheppard. He at one time, too, did actuarial work for the Canada Life

Assurance Company. Born at Newark-on-Trent, Eng., in 1819. His death occurred in 1912 at Jamaica Plain, near Boston. Photograph. Size 5 x 7. Head and shoulders.

485—DENISON, COLONEL GEORGE TAYLOR, HEYDON VILLA, TORONTO, 1839-1916—Water color from oil portrait in Heydon Villa. Size 5 x 7. Half length. See 603.

486—DENISON, LIEUT.-COL. GEORGE TAYLOR, BELLEVUE, TO-RONTO—A son of Captain John Denison, in whose company of the 3rd Regiment of York Militia he served as sergeant in 1812, later joining Ridout's Company. In the Rebellion of 1837 he commanded the volunteer cavalry troop organized by him, and now known as the Governor-General's Body Guard. Colonel Denison was a member of the first City Council of Toronto. His property, Bellevue, purchased by him in 1815, consisted of park lot 17 and half of lot 18. The original drive is now known as Denison avenue, Toronto. Water color from an oil portrait in possession of his grandson, Colonel George Taylor Denison, Heydon Villa, Toronto. Size 5 x 7. Half length.

487—JARVIS, WILLIAM—First Provincial Secretary, Upper Canada. He was born in Stamford, Conn., 11th September, 1756, and died in York (Toronto), 13th August, 1817. At an early age he was sent to England, where he received his education. He was a cornet in the Queen's Rangers, commanded by Lieut.-Col. Simcoe (first Lieut.-Governor of Upper Canada, 1792-6); served in the Revolutionary War, and in 1785 again went to England. In 1789 Jarvis was commissioned as a lieutenant in the "Western Regiment of Militia" in Middlesex, Eng., and on 1st January, 1791, as a captain in the same regiment. In March, 1792, he was appointed Provincial Grand Master of Masons in Upper Canada, having been made a Mason the month previous, and later in the same year he came to Canada as "Secretary and Registrar of the Records of the Province of Upper Canada," which position he held until his death. Water color from an oil painting in possession of his grandson, Aemilius Jarvis, Toronto. Size 4 x 5. Head and shoulders.

488—REES, DR. WILLIAM—First Superintendent Provincial Lunatic Asylum, Toronto, 1841-4—Came from England, 1819; practised in Quebec, removing to York toward the close of 1829, where he purchased Dr. Daly's practice. Some years later he was made surgeon to the 1st West York Battalion. As a result of his efforts the old jail near the northwest corner of King and Toronto streets was acquired by the Provincial authorities for the reception of the insane, there being no such institution in Upper Canada up to 1841. Further accommodation was soon required, and the eastern wing of the Parliament Buildings appropriated. Dr. Rees constructed a wharf at the foot of Graves (Simcoe) street, which was known for many years as Rees' Wharf. Water color from original portrait. Size 4 x 5. Head and shoulders.

489—LEE, GRAVES SIMCOE, 1829-1912—A well-known Canadian actor, as he appeared at twenty-four years of age. The son of Dr. Hiram Davis Lee, of London, Ont. Young Lee became enamored of the stage through the private theatricals which were a favorite pastime in the military circles of the day in London. He subsequently adopted acting as a profession, and in 1855 was a popular member of John Nickinson's Stock Company, which played in the Royal Lyceum, Toronto, and drew enthusiastic audiences while here. Lee afterwards starred in various parts of the United States. In 1892 he retired. Water color from a daguerreotype in possession of his niece, Miss A. Daly, Kingston, Ont. Size 4 x 5. Head and shoulders. See 490.

490—LEE, GRAVES SIMCOE, AT SEVENTY YEARS OF AGE—Water color from a portrait in possession of his sister, Mrs. J. B. Strathy, Toronto. Size 4 x 5. Head and shoulders. See 489.

491—DENNIS HOUSE, YORK (TORONTO)—Northeast corner King and Yonge streets—The cottage was a frame structure, painted white, with a paling in front, and shaded by large willow trees; erected about 1820 and enlarged 1823. It was demolished about 1830, and superseded by a four-storey red brick building, occupied for forty years by Ridout Bros., and afterwards the office of the Cunard Steamship Company. John Dennis, a U.E. Loyalist, was, prior to his removal to York, superintendent of the dockyard at Kingston. The site of the Dennis cottage is now (1916) occupied by the Royal Bank building. Water color. Size 5 x 7.

492— BELFORD, CHARLES—Editor Toronto Leader—Born in the city of Cork, Ireland, April 25th, 1837; educated on the Island of Valentia. In 1856 Mr. Belford came to Canada, joining the staff of the Toronto Leader the following year. On the retirement of Mr. Charles Lindsey, in 1867, was appointed editor-in-chief, resigning Oct. 4th, 1871. Editor of the first issue of the Toronto Mail, March, 1872. His death took place at Ottawa, Ont., December 19th, 1880. Water color from portrait in possession of his son, Mr. C. A. Belford, Ottawa. Size 3 x 4. Head and shoulders.

493—DENISON, CAPTAIN JOHN, 1754-1824—An officer in 2nd West York Regiment, England. Was induced to come to Canada from Heydon, Yorkshire, in 1792, by his friend, Hon. Peter Russell. He first settled in Kingston, but four years later came to York, living at Castle Frank for a time, by permission of Hon. Mr. Russell, the Administrator, U.C. He afterwards lived on Front street, near Bay, and at Petersfield, north side of what is now (1916) Queen street, near Soho. In the War of 1812 he was captain of the 3rd Regiment of York Militia. Water color from a portrait in possession of his great-grandson, Colonel George Taylor Denison, Heydon Villa, Toronto. Size 5 x 7. Half length.

494—DENISON, COLONEL GEORGE TAYLOR, RUSHOLME, TORONTO—Born in 1816, the son of George Taylor Denison, of Bellevue. Although a lawyer by profession, he devoted his energies chiefly to the Canadian volunteer service. In 1838 he was appointed lieutenant in the Governor-General's Body Guard, then commanded by his father, and in 1846 obtained command of the troop. Colonel Denison may be called the founder of the militia in Toronto, having organized cavalry, artillery and rifles, including the Queen's Own Corps, the second battalion of Volunteer Militia Rifles of Canada, in 1860. He was also for some time alderman for St. Patrick's Ward. In 1839 he built Rusholme, a handsome roughcast house on Dundas street, and here he resided until his death in 1873. Water color from an oil portrait in possession of his son, Col. G. T. Denison, Heydon Villa, Toronto. Size 6 x 8. Half length.

495—SHANLY, WALTER, C.E., 1817-99—A prominent engineer on railway works. He was a son of James Shanly, Norman's Grove, near Dublin, Ireland; a brother of James Shanly, London, Ont., Master in-Chancery, and of Francis Shanly, C.E., one-time City Engineer for Toronto. As a young man Walte Shanly was employed by the Government on the Beauharnois and Welland Canals; in 1851-3 was engineer of the Ottawa and Prescott Railway, and of the Western Division of the Grand Trunk, 1851-9. He was also general manager of the latter from 1858-62. His most important work as a railway contractor was the Hoosac Mountain Tunnel, Massachusetts, which he, in conjunction with his brother, Francis, success-

8

fully constructed, 1869-75. From 1863-7 he sat in the old Parliament of Canada, and also in the House of Commons after Confederation. Water color. Size 5 x 7. Head and shoulders.

496—SHANLY, FRANCIS, C.E., 1820-82—From 1875-80 he was City Engineer of Toronto. In conjunction with his brother, Walter Shanly, successfully constructed the Hoosac Mountain Tunnel, Massachusetts, 1869-75; also engaged on the Grand Trunk Railway from Toronto to Guelph. He was a son of James Shanly, a member of the Irish Bar, who came to Canada in 1836, from Norman's Grove, near Dublin, and settled with his family in the vicinity of London, C.W., in Co. Middlesex. Water color. Size 5 x 7. Head and shoulders. See 2789.

497— SCOBIE, HUGH, 1811-53—Well-known newspaper man of the early days, and editor of "The British Colonist." Water color from miniature in possession of his granddaughter, Mrs. Calderwood, Barrie, Ont. Size 4 x 5. See 481.

498—AGRICULTURAL HALL, TORONTO—This building occupied the lot on the northwest corner of Queen and Yonge streets. It was a noted site from 1830. The commodious frame building which stood there was known as the "Sun" Tavern, and later as the "Craven Heifer." About 1857 the building was burned, and some years later the Government purchased the land, and in 1866 the Board of Agriculture erected what was known as the Agricultural Hall. The tenants of the stores on the Yonge street front were James Fleming & Co., the well-known seedsmen, and William Bilton, an oyster and fruit dealer. The building was subsequently remodelled for Philip Jamieson, tailor, and is now (1917) occupied by the F. W. Woolworth Company. Water color. Size 4 x 5.

499—JUSTICE POWELL'S HOUSE, TORONTO—A two-storey, white frame dwelling, erected about 1812, on the east side of York street, near Front, and occupied by Chief Justice William Dummer Powell from 1820. The Chief Justice died in 1834, but his wife survived him until 1849. Dr. Gwynne afterwards occupied the residence, which later became a cheap lodging house, and was eventually purchased by Mr. Verral, a one-time alderman of the city, who had it demolished in 1894 to make way for the stables of the Verral Transfer Company. Water color. Size 6 x 8.

500—SEVENTH CUSTOM HOUSE, TORONTO, 1870-6—When the sixth Custom House was burned the Government rented the large three-storey brick building which stood at about No. 26 Front street west. It had been built as a residence by Judge Jones, and later turned into a hotel known as the Rochester House, by John Hanlan, an uncle of the famous oarsman, Ned Hanlan. In this building the customs business was carried on until 1876, when the present structure was completed on the site of the sixth Custom House, southwest corner Front and Yonge streets. The site of the Rochester House is now (1917) a fine business block. Water color. Size 5 x 6.

501—GREAT WESTERN RAILWAY STATION, TORONTO—In 1834 an Act was passed by the Legislature to incorporate the "London and Gore Railway Company." Nothing, however, being accomplished until 1845, a second Act reviving that of 1834 was passed, with an amendment to change the name of the railway to the Great Western. A reorganization of the company took place, and on 3rd December, 1855, the Toronto and Hamilton branch of the line was opened for traffic. For a time the Great

Western used the Union Station at the foot of York street. In March, 1866, their own depot at the eastern angle of Esplanade and Yonge street was opened. On 11th August, 1882, the Great Western amalgamated with the Grand Trunk. The old station of the former is now (1917) used as the G.T.R. fruit depot. Water color. Size 5 x 7.

502—BANK OF UPPER CANADA, TORONTO, 1822-30—Situated on the southeast corner of King and Frederick streets; demolished in 1915, and now site of the warehouse of A. Muirhead & Co., Ltd. Although an Act was passed in 1819 for the institution of a bank in York, the Bank of Upper Canada did not commence operations until about 1822. For many years it did a flourishing business, but finally became embarrassed, burdened with unsaleable lands taken as security, and in 1866 failed. Hon. William Allan, one of the incorporators, was the first president, and it was in the substantial brick building erected by him in 1818, at the corner of King and Frederick streets, that the bank for a number of years did business, removing from there about 1830 to the northeast corner Duke and George, and in the early sixties to the southeast corner of Yonge and Colborne streets. Water color. Size 6 x 7. See 522.

503—DR. WIDMER'S HOUSE, TORONTO—North side of Front street east, now (1916) the site of Nos. 228-32. After living for many years on King street, nearly opposite Ontario, Dr. Christopher Widmer, an eminent physician and surgeon of York in the early days, erected on the lower part of his lot the dwelling shown in the picture. It was a commodious, double-gabled, red brick two-storey dwelling, with a large wing at the west side. After Dr. Widmer's death in 1858 the Front street residence became the home of his son-in-law, Captain John Clarke, well-known as an officer of the 100th Regiment, and also of the Royal Canadian Rifles. It was torn down in 1900 and is now part of the site of the Copland Brewery plant. Water color. Size 5 x 7.

504—COTTAGE HOME ON THE BEACH AT THE FOOT OF BAY STREET, TORONTO—Here lived Michael, popularly known as "Fisty," Masterson and his wife. From 1847-62 they kept boats for hire and were well patronized by the boys of Upper Canada College, which was then on King street. Masterson had a small schooner, the "Christina," with which he is said to have done considerable smuggling in the early days. His nickname originated from the fact that he lost his left arm while firing a salute at Kingston on the Queen's Birthday. Water color. Size 5 x 7.

505—QUEEN STREET WEST, TORONTO, 1890—North side, from James to Teraulay streets. With key. Water color. Size 7 x 11.

506—DWELLING OF LIEUT. ZACHARIAH MUDGE, YORK (TORONTO)—West side of Emily street, near Wellington. The cottage was one of the early houses in York, being considered quite an old house in 1825. In its latter days it was used as a barn. For some years the cottage was occupied by Lieut. Mudge, an artillery officer, and one of the aides-de-camp of Sir John Colborne, K.C.B., Lieut.-Governor of Upper Canada, 1828-1836. Water color. Size 6 x 7.

507—THIRD PARLIAMENT BUILDINGS—View of rear from northeast corner Simcoe and Wellington streets. The buildings were commenced in 1826, and from 1832-41 were occupied by the Legislature. At different times until 1867 they were used as a court of law, university, asylum and military barracks. In 1867 the sessions of the Ontario Legislature met within the walls of the red brick pile, continuing to do so until

1892, the 100th anniversary of the first Parliament of old Upper Canada. The buildings were demolished in 1903, and the site is now occupied by freight sheds of the G.T.R. Water color by W. J. Thomson. Size 8 x 11. See 519.

508—MOSS PARK, TORONTO—Residence of the Hon. William Allan, at one time Postmaster of York (Toronto), and of his son, Hon. G. W. Allan. The old brick mansion was situated on the west side of Sherbourne street, between Queen and Shuter, and was occupied for many years by the Allans. In 1904 the city purchased the property; the house was demolished and the land used for a public square. Water color, from a pen drawing in 1842. Size 7 x 10. See 305.

509—FIRST CUSTOM HOUSE, YORK (TORONTO), 1801-20—When York was made a customs port in 1801 Col. (Hon.) William Allan was appointed first customs collector, and in a small, one-storey frame building on the east side of Frederick street, south of King, established his official headquarters. Mr. Allan later removed the custom house to the Merchants' Wharf, at the foot of Frederick street, on the bay front. Water color. Size 4 x 7.

510—FOURTH CUSTOM HOUSE, YORK, 1829-35—Scott street, near Wellington. In 1829 Mr. George Savage removed the custom offices from the temporary quarters in Isaac Columbus' shop to the brick cottage of Mr. Thomas Carfrae on the east side of Scott street. The latter occupied one end of the cottage as a dwelling, while the other end was used as the custom house. Mr. Carfrae himself afterwards became customs collector. Water color. Size 5 x 7.

511—UNIVERSITY OF TORONTO, 1862—With the expropriation of old King's College in 1853 it became necessary to provide proper accommodation for University College, the name given by legislation to the Arts teaching faculty of the University in that year. In 1858 the handsome freestone pile, of Norman architecture, was completed, but, unfortunately, the February of 1890 saw its destruction by fire. It was rebuilt, however, in 1890-2 in practically the same external form as it stands to-day (1917), but with various internal changes. The main doorway, which is a copy of an ancient English entrance, is said to be the most perfect example of Norman architecture on the continent. Water color. Size 5 x 7.

512—THIRD CUSTOM HOUSE, YORK, 1828-9—The second collector of the port of York was Mr. George Savage, who received his appointment in 1828. He established a temporary office in the shop of Isaac Columbus, the well-known gunsmith, on the southeast corner of Duke and Caroline (Sherbourne) streets, afterwards removing to Scott, near Wellington. Water color. Size 5 x 7.

513—SIXTH CUSTOM HOUSE, TORONTO, 1841-70—Southwest corner of Front and Yonge streets. A brick structure erected by the Government after the plans of Kivas Tully, the Toronto architect and civil engineer. In 1870 the building was destroyed by fire. Mr. Carfrae was succeeded in the collectorship by William Moore Kelly. In 1843 Mr. Kelly was followed by Robert Stanton, who resigned 1849. William F. Meudell was appointed collector in 1850, remaining in office eight years, when he was succeeded by Robert Spence, who acted until his death in 1868. James E. Smith was then appointed and continued in the position until 1879. Water color. Size 5 x 7.

514—ST. PATRICK'S MARKET, TORONTO, 1836-1912—In 1836 Mr. D'Arcy Boulton presented to the city the land on which St. Patrick's Market now stands, on condition that the corporation should erect a market there, and that it should be maintained as such perpetually. Just after the presentation a frame building was erected on the site. About 1854 it fell into decay and was replaced by a white brick structure two storeys high in front and surmounted by a tower. This building was demolished in 1912, and the present market erected in 1913. Water color by F. V. Poole. Size 6 x 10.

515—SECOND CUSTOM HOUSE, YORK, 1820-8—It was established by Col. (Hon.) William Allan, first customs collector of York, in a frame storehouse erected by him on the Merchants' Wharf. This wharf, at the foot of Frederick street, was one of the earliest landing places for the larger lake craft, and belonged to Mr. Allan. The storehouse in question was subsequently used as a malt house. Water color. Size 5 x 6.

516—EIGHTH CUSTOM HOUSE, TORONTO, 1876-1916—Erected at the southwest corner of Front and Yonge streets, facing the former, on the site of the sixth custom house, which was severely damaged by fire in 1870. The structure, which is of stone, is designed after the Renaissance style of architecture, and was first occupied November, 1876. The vacant lot west of the building was purchased by the Government as a protective measure. Mr. John Bertram, who succeeded the late John Small, is the present (1917) customs collector. Photograph, colored. Size 6 x 7.

517—STEAMER CHIEF JUSTICE ROBINSON—Landing her passengers in the winter of 1852-3 on the ice in Toronto Bay, east of Queen's Wharf, and about 1,500 feet south of the then north shore of Toronto Bay. The route from Toronto to Montreal in 1852 was by boat to a point on the Niagara River, probably Lewiston; rail, Niagara Falls to Whitehall via Albany; boat, Plattsburg; rail to Caughnawaga via West Chazy, Moore's Junction and St. Isidore Junction; ferry to Lachine, and rail to Montreal. At that time there were nine railway lines used from Montreal to Niagara Falls, several of which were consolidated into the New York Central in 1853. The "Chief Justice Robinson," 400 tons burthen, was built at Niagara, 1842. She was owned and commanded by Captain Hugh Richardson, and was a well-known packet on the route between Lewiston and Toronto for several years. Subsequently she was sold, her engine eventually being put into a new steamer, the "Marine City." Water color by Wm. Armstrong, C.E., Toronto. Size 8 x 13.

518—SCENE AT CUTTING OF FIRST SOD OF THE ONTARIO, SIMCOE AND HURON RAILWAY, TORONTO, 15TH OCT., 1851—Water color by General A. R. V. Crease, taken from a window on the west side of John street. Size 7 x 11. See 263, 782.

519—THIRD PARLIAMENT BUILDINGS, TORONTO—View of rear from northwest corner of John and Wellington streets. Water color by W. J. Thomson. Size 7 x 13. See 507.

520—FIRST BRIDGE OVER THE DON RIVER, TORONTO, 1803— Erected by the Government of Upper Canada at the east end of King street. William Smith, an early settler of York, was the contractor. Water color. Size 6 x 11.

521—MARYVILLE LODGE, YORK (TORONTO), 1794-1854—The home of Surveyor-General (Sir) David W. Smith, who came to York in the train of Governor Simcoe. Mr. Smith, who was a member of the Executive Council and Surveyor-General of Upper Canada, became the possessor of some 20,000 acres in the Province, and was the original owner of the park lot which constituted the Moss Park estate. Maryville Lodge was a one-storey frame structure, facing the north side of King street, near the northeast corner of King and Ontario streets. At one end was Mr. Smith's office. From the fact that the house was painted yellow it acquired the appellation of "The Yellow House." It subsequently became a school and now (1916) stores occupy the site. Water color by F. V. Poole. Size 3 x 7.

522—BANK OF UPPER CANADA, TORONTO, 1830-66—On the north-east corner of Duke and George streets. The building is now (1917) a part of the De La Salle Institute. Water color. Size 5 x 6. See 502.

523—CANADA COMPANY'S OFFICE, YORK (TORONTO)—North-east corner of King and Frederick streets. The building was erected in 1807 by Quetton St. George, who in 1805 established himself in business in York. For its construction Mr. St. George brought from Oswego or Rochester the first bricks ever seen in York. The ground floor and part of the cellar were used by the builder for carrying on his general mercantile business, while the remainder of the building was occupied as a residence. In 1817 Mr. St. George transferred this property to Mr. John Spread Baldwin, who conducted the business for a number of years. Subsequently the corner came into possession of the Canada Company, which was established in York in 1826, its first office being a room in the Steamboat Hotel, east of the market block in Front street. In the colonization of Canada this company played an important part. The site of the old Canada Company's Building is (1917) occupied by Adams Bros., saddlers, Water color. Size 5 x 7. See 823.

524—SHAKESPEARE HOTEL, TORONTO, 1831-70—It was a medium-sized, two-storey, white frame structure, on the north-east corner of York and King streets, fronting on York street. It was occupied as a Mechanics' Boarding House till 1843, when James Mirfield, an Englishman. kept it as the Shakespeare Hotel. After his death Mr. Thomas Kerr, an enterprising citizen, was the landlord. The house was patronized largely by the theatrical profession. For a time plays were put on in a small frame theatre at the rear and east of the hotel, entrance to which was gained by a lane from King street. It continued open until John Ritchey built the Royal Lyceum on the south side of King street. The hotel was demolished about 1870 and later rebuilt. It continued as an hotel under various names for 45 years, and was last known as the Imperial. It is now (1917) vacant. Water color. Size 5 x 7.

525—ANDREW MERCER'S COTTAGE, YORK (TORONTO)—At the south-east corner of Bay and Wellington streets, erected about 1811-12 by Andrew Mercer, who came to York with Chief Justice Scott, acquiring large tracts of land from the Crown. During the War of 1812 the printing office of the Upper Canada Gazette was removed to this house, and for a time Mr. Mercer had charge of the publication of the paper. On the occupation of York by the Americans the place was entered and the printing press demolished. At Mr. Mercer's death, in 1871, a legal dispute arose regarding the validity of the will purported to have been made by him, and the result was that the valuable properties were escheated to the Crown. The Ogilvie Building now (1917) stands on the site of the old cottage. Water color. Size 5 x 7.

526—FIFTH CUSTOM HOUSE (TORONTO'S FIRST), 1835-41—A small, one-storey, hip-roofed, brick building, on the north side of Front street, east of Scott, between the Coffin Block and the Newbigging House, now (1917) the site of the rear of John Macdonald & Co.'s warehouse, 32-6 Front street east. In 1835 Mr. Thomas Carfrae succeeded Mr. George Savage as collector of customs. He will be remembered as the originator of the Potter's Field in Toronto. Water color. Size 6 x 7.

527—**SEVERN'S BREWERY, YORKVILLE**—On the east side of Yonge street, just north of Davenport road. In 1835 John Severn, a York blacksmith, removed to Yorkville, establishing there a smithy in which he worked for a short time prior to his taking over the brick and stone brewery erected by John Baxter. The brewery was enlarged from time to time by Severn, and on his death by his son George, who conducted the business until 1890. John Severn was one of the first five councillors or aldermen of Yorkville at the time of its incorporation in 1853. Water color. Size 5 x 7.

528—**WEST LODGE, TORONTO**—The residence of Lieutenant-Colonel Walter O'Hara; built in 1832, on "the lake shore road," now (1917) West Lodge avenue. Several additions have been made to the original red brick house. The building is now occupied by the Monastery of Our Lady of Charity. Lieut.-Col. O'Hara, for many years a well-known citizen of Toronto, served with distinction throughout the whole of the Peninsular Campaign, and for a time was in the Canadian Militia. From a water color by his son, Robert O'Hara, and now in possession of Miss Mary O'Hara, a daughter of the first owner of West Lodge. Size 6 x 9.

529—**GEORGE DUGGAN'S STORE, TORONTO**—About 1805 the Rev. George O'Kill Stewart, first rector of St. James' Church (Cathedral), erected on the south-east corner of King and George streets a small frame residence as a rectory. Attached to it he constructed a small stone building, afterwards clapboarded, and in this unpretentious place the first District school in York was conducted from 1807-13. In that year, on Dr. Stewart's removal to Kingston, Mr. George Duggan, father of Recorder Duggan, became the occupant of the old rectory, keeping a general store there. With him resided his brother, Dr. Thos. Duggan, a well-known York physician. At a later date, Hughes Bros., clothiers, occupied the building. From 1856 until the early seventies, when the building was demolished, John Kitson and others conducted a tavern there. A brick hostelry, the York Hotel, now (1917) stands on the site. Water color. Size 5 x 6.

530—**JORDAN'S "YORK" HOTEL, TORONTO**—South side of King, between Princes street to the west and Berkeley street to the east. Firstbrook's Box Factory, 283 King east, is now located on the site. It was a storey and a half frame building, with dormer windows along its roof, and in the early days was the first-class hotel, not only of York, but of all Upper Canada. It was one of the oldest houses in York, and as far back as 1820 presented a dilapidated appearance. Before the completion of the Legislative Buildings which succeeded those burned by the Americans when they occupied York in 1813, the Parliament of U.C. met for one session in the ball room of the hotel, and here also public dinners and assemblies were held. John Jordan was a pew holder in St. James' Church (Cathedral) from its inception, and was one of the signatories to a congratulatory address presented to Lieut.-Governor Sir Francis Gore on his return from England in 1815. Water color by F. V. Poole. Size 6 x 8.

531—**MIRROR PRINTING OFFICE, TORONTO, 1856**—Erected by Joshua G. Beard about 1825, on the south-east corner of King and East Market streets. For about ten years the ground floor was used as a combined tailoring establishment and tavern, known as the Crown Inn, and conducted by Thomas Moore. During his occupancy the upper floor was the office of the Courier, edited by George Gurnett, and from 1836-58 the Mirror was published there by Charles Donlevy. On Moore's removal the ground floor was occupied as a grocery store by William Henderson. The second door south on East Market street was William Gibson's saddlery, the third was Thomas Berkinshaw's grocery, and at the right of the picture is shown the Albion Hotel, kept by George Platt. Water color. Size 4 x 6.

532—NORTH SIDE OF FRONT STREET, FROM PETER TO JOHN STREETS, YORK (TORONTO) 1810—The picture shows the home (two views) of Hon. George Cruickshank, Deputy Commissary-General, a colonial cottage building, built about 1800, and a two-storey frame building filled in with brick, erected in front of the cottage, 1821. Both houses were demolished in 1881. In the centre of the picture may be seen the home of John Beikie, Clerk of the Executive Council. The Commissariat, or military storehouse, on the bay shore, a frame building, painted in ordnance grey and containing militia stores, and the Half-Way House, a resort for soldiers from the garrison, are on extreme right. Water color, by E. Wyly Grier, from original in possession of the late Mrs. Stephen Heward, Toronto. Size 13 x 20.

533—VIEW FROM SOUTH SIDE OF FIRST ROYAL CANADIAN YACHT CLUB HOUSE, TORONTO ISLAND—To the left of the picture is shown the city. The water in the foreground is the deep lagoon south of the Yacht Club grounds, now used as a slip for the yachts. Water color by J. T. Rolph, Toronto. Size 11 x 14. See 741.

534—SIGNING OF THE ONTARIO HYDRO-ELECTRIC POWER CONTRACT—The contract for 10,000 h.p. for 30 years was between the City of Toronto and the Ontario Hydro-Electric Power Commission, of which Hon. Adam Beck was chairman. He signed on Tuesday, 5th May, 1908. The picture shows those present at the signing of the contract by the Mayor and City Treasurer on 7th May, 1908. 1, Joseph Oliver, Mayor of Toronto. 2, R. T. Coady, Treasurer of Toronto. 3, Controller Hocken. 4, Robert Staton, City Contract Clerk. 5, Controller Church. 6, Wm. A. Littlejohn, City Clerk. 7, A. F. Lobb, Solicitor, Ontario Hydro Commission. 8, Controller F. S. Spence. Photograph, colored. Size 6 x 9.

535—TENTH ROYALS REGIMENT, TORONTO—Presentation of Colors, 1863—F. W. Cumberland (afterwards Lieut.-Colonel), Managing Director of the Northern Railway, organized the Tenth Royals in 1861-2. Early in January, 1862, drill began for the officers, and in March the official list of appointments was compiled. On 6th July, 1863, a set of colors was presented by the ladies of Toronto, the event taking place on the commons which were in those days bounded by Spadina avenue, College, Cecil and Huron streets. Mrs. Cumberland read the presentation address, after which Col. Robertson, commandant of the garrison, handed first the Queen's and then the regimental colors to her. She in turn presented them to the ensigns, who received them kneeling. Rev. Dr. McCaul, President of Toronto University, consecrated the colors. The regimental color is of heavy blue silk; near the top is a crown beautifully embroidered with the motto, "Ready, aye ready." The number of the regiment is encircled by a beautiful wreath in appropriate colors and composed of the Rose, Thistle, Shamrock and Maple Leaf, while underneath are the words "Tenth Royal Regiment T.V." On the Union Jack is a crown of bullion, with "X Regiment T.V. Canada" of the same material. The staff of each color is surmounted by a lion and crown in solid silver, and a shield inserted into each staff contains the legend that the colors were "Presented to the Tenth Royals by the Ladies of Toronto." The Tenth Royals in 1881 became known as Tenth Battalion Royal Grenadiers. Water color. Size 5 x 7.

536—PIONEER SKATING RINK OF TORONTO—THE VICTORIA— 1863—The rink was located at the south-west corner of Gerrard and Sherborne streets, opposite the Horticultural Gardens (Allan Gardens), and was built by P. Arnold and Orin Wardell. It extended west on Gerrard to Pembroke st., and 120 feet south on Sherbourne. The picture was made March 7th, 1863, when a grand prize skating match came off. Miss Alice Worts (Mrs. E. Strachan Cox), a daughter of Mr. James Worts, won the first prize, and Miss Elliot, daughter of Mr. Wm. Elliot, the second. The Gardens are shown to the north, and to the left in the Gardens may be seen the original pavilion and the caretaker's house. Water color. Size 5 x 6.

537—WYKEHAM HALL, BISHOP STRACHAN SCHOOL FOR GIRLS, COLLEGE ST., TORONTO—A view of the main hallway in the spring of 1915. Photograph, colored. Size 5 x 7. See 538, 543, 553.

538—WYKEHAM HALL, BISHOP STRACHAN SCHOOL FOR GIRLS, COLLEGE ST., TORONTO—A view of the drawing room in the spring of 1915. Photograph, colored. Size 5 x 7. See 537, 543, 553.

539—INAUGURAL MEETING OF THE TORONTO CITY COUNCIL, CITY HALL, JANUARY 11TH, 1915—The following ladies and gentlemen were present:—1, Mayor T. L. Church. Controllers—2, J. E. Thompson; 3, Thomas Foster; 4, John O'Neill, jun.; 5, F. S. Spence. Aldermen—6, R. H. Cameron; 7, L. M. Singer; 8, S. M. Wickett; 9, W. H. Weir; 10, Sam Ryding; 11, J. W. Meredith; 12, John Dunn; 13, J. G. Ramsden; 14, Sam McBride; 15, D. Spence; 16, W. D. Robbins; 17, J. J. Gibbons; 18, John Cowan; 19, C. A. Maguire; 20, H. H. Ball; 21, C. A. Risk; 22, J. W. Somers, Chief Clerk; 23, Thomas Sanderson, Assistant City Clerk; 24, W. A. Littlejohn, City Clerk; 25, Albert Smart, Clerk; 26, The Press Table. The Mayor's sisters—27, Miss Rebecca Church; 28, Mrs. Scadding; 29, Mrs. Byfield. Aldermen A. E. Walton, R. M. Yeomans, J. M. Warren and Thomas Roden, who were present, are not in the picture, as they were sitting outside the range of the camera. Photograph. Size 13 x 20.

540—TORONTO BOARD OF TRADE—Members representing the Council and other officers of the Board, 1888. The Act incorporating the Board of Trade of the City of Toronto was passed by the Legislature of Canada on the 10th of February, 1845. George Percival Ridout, the first President, continued in office until 1851. In 1884 the Toronto Corn Exchange amalgamated with the Board of Trade by Act of Parliament. Two years later negotiations were entered into for the purchase of a building site, and on 29th January, 1891, the annual meeting was held in the new home of the Board, corner Front and Yonge streets. They removed to the Royal Bank Building in 1915. It is a noteworthy fact that the Toronto Board of Trade has not only played a part in the legislation of the country, but conserves the local interests of the people. The present President (1917) is Mr. Arthur Hewitt, manager of the Consumers' Gas Co. Photograph, colored. Size 8 x 12.

541—PROVINCIAL LUNATIC ASYLUM, QUEEN STREET WEST, TORONTO—"North view. J. G. Howard, Architect. On stone by J. Johnston. Scobie and Balfour, Lith." The building was begun in 1846 and the print, showing it as Mr. Howard primarily planned it, was made about 1847. In the actual erection, however, the original scheme was not strictly adhered to. This was the first institution of its kind to be built in Western Canada. Previous to its erection the insane were housed in the old jail near the north-west corner of King and Toronto streets, and in a wing of the Parliament Buildings, Front street. Lithograph. Size 5 x 8. See 548, 832.

542—ARMS OF ONTARIO—"'Ut incepit fidelis sic permanet'—the armorial bearing of the Province of Ontario in the Dominion of Canada. College of Arms, London, 22nd March, 1909. Charles H. Athell, Richmond Herald." Upon a wreath of the colors a bear passant sable, and the supporters on the dexter side a moose, and on the sinister side the Canadian deer, both proper, together with the motto quoted above, the translation of which is, "As loyal she began, so loyal she remains." More freely, but not so accurately, "Loyal in the beginning, loyal still." Print in color. Size 7 x 10. See 3394.

543—WYKEHAM HALL, BISHOP STRACHAN SCHOOL FOR GIRLS, COLLEGE ST., TORONTO—Rear view. Photograph, colored. Size 5 x 7. See 537-8, 553.

544—FRONT STREET, TORONTO, 1820—From the Bay, showing the Garrison, on the west, to Parliament Buildings, on the east. Water color by E. Wyly Grier, Toronto, from the original in possession of the late Mrs. Stephen Heward, Toronto, daughter of the late Hon. George Cruickshank. Size 7 x 34.

545—EASTERN VIEW OF YORK (TORONTO), 1810—Showing blockhouse destroyed by Americans in 1813. There has been some dispute as to the exact spot on which this blockhouse stood. Some writers claim that it was on the east side of the Don, but the best authorities state that it was on the west side of "The Little Don," for, in 1796-1815, the river was a delta at its mouth, one entrance being known as "The Little Don," and the other as "The Don." The blockhouse stood east of Berkeley street, south of Palace (Front) street, near the point where the Little Don entered the Bay. It was designed to protect the road or track leading to the peninsula, where there was a landing place on the south shore. There is now no double entrance or delta, as the river, by dredging, has been made to flow in one stream into Toronto Bay. Water color by E. Wyly Grier. Size 13 x 17.

546—CRISPIN'S TAVERN, NORTH-EAST CORNER YORK AND RICHMOND STREETS—This was a popular place of resort for many years, kept by Richard Crispin, first as a grocery shop, and about 1836 converted into a tavern. The house, a one and a half storey structure, with entrance on Richmond street, at that time known as Hospital street, was built on the corner of a plot of ground owned by John Long. Crispin, who had come to York in 1828 with Sir John Colborne, as his coachman, was a well-known, genial character in the locality, and was familiarly called "Coachman Crispin." The tavern, after his death, again became a shop. Water color. Size 5 x 7.

547—ONTARIO HYDRO-ELECTRIC POWER COMMISSION—Contract between them and the City of Toronto. Photograph of the last page of the contract containing the signature of Hon. (Sir) Adam Beck, chairman of commission, who signed Tuesday, 5th May, 1908; Joseph Oliver, Mayor of Toronto, and R. T. Coady, Treasurer of Toronto. The two latter signed on Thursday, 7th May, 1908. Size 6 x 9.

548—PROVINCIAL LUNATIC ASYLUM, TORONTO—"South view. J. G. Howard, Architect. On stone by J. Johnston. Scobie and Balfour, Lith." Size 5 x 8. See 541, 832.

549—TOWNSLEY HOME, ROXBOROUGH ST., TORONTO, 1850— Away back about the mid-forties Mr. James Townsley, who owned the large brickyards in Tannery Hollow, on Yonge street, built for himself a brick dwelling. The picture shows the rear of the residence and property on Roxborough street, at the south-west corner of Yonge. The buildings at the corner are now (1917) 1086-88 Yonge. The dwelling does not face Yonge; its front is on a lane which runs east and west, with the front looking south. Water color by J. T. Rolph, Toronto. Size 10 x 14.

550—BANK OF BRITISH NORTH AMERICA, TORONTO—The first Toronto branch of this bank was established in 1837 at the south-east corner of King and Frederick streets, in the old Bank of Upper Canada building. The structure in the picture was erected in 1843 at the north-east corner of Yonge and Wellington streets. In 1871 it was torn down and rebuilt as it stands to-day (1917). Water color by F. V. Poole. Size 5 x 7.

551—SOUTH-WEST CORNER OF BAY AND WELLINGTON STREETS, TORONTO, 1843-78—The building on the corner was the residence of Chancellor Blake from 1849-57. It was then occupied by John Salt, a Toronto hatter, and from 1865-75 by a branch of the City Bank of Montreal. The building to the south was the residence of Dr. Adams, 1855-65. It was afterwards, until 1873, occupied by the Grand Trunk Railway. Both buildings were demolished in 1878 to make way for W. R. Brock & Co.'s warehouse, which was destroyed by fire in 1904, but re-erected on the same site. Water color. Size 5 x 6.

552—OLD CRYSTAL PALACE, TORONTO, 1858-66—It was the first permanent Exhibition building, and stood on what was then known as Garrison Common, just south of the Provincial Lunatic Asylum. It was erected for the housing of exhibits other than live stock or heavy agricultural implements. When H.R.H. the Prince of Wales (King Edward VII.) visited Toronto during the Exhibition of 1860, a ball was held in this building in his honor. The site is now (1917) occupied by manufacturing firms and the C.P.R. yards. Water color. Size 4 x 6.

553—WYKEHAM HALL (WICKHAM LODGE), TORONTO—Residence of Hon. James B. Macaulay, and later the Bishop Strachan School for Girls—This brick residence on the south side of College street, near the present Yonge street, was erected about 1843 by Chief Justice Macaulay and by him called Wickham Lodge, after the village of Wickham, in Hampshire, Eng., where some of his relatives lived. Lady Macaulay adopted the spelling "Wykeham," which obtains to-day (1917). From 1869-1915 the building was occupied by the Bishop Strachan School, founded in 1867, for a time held at "Pinehurst," Grange road, and then in the Palace, residence of Bishop Strachan, Front street. The old home of the Chief Justice has been altered and enlarged considerably. The entire property, from its eastern extremity, west of Yonge, to its western boundary at Teraulay street, was sold in 1914 for business purposes, the school retaining the use of the buildings till the completion of their new structure on Russell Hill road, Toronto. The building is now a Military Convalescent Hospital. Water color. Size 6 x 7. See 537-8, 543.

554—OSGOODE HALL, TORONTO—Home of the Superior Courts of Ontario—In 1826 the Law Society of Upper Canada (incorporated 1797) purchased from Attorney-General Sir John Beverley Robinson six acres of land, at what is now (1917) the n.e. corner of Queen street and University avenue. In the midst of this plot, and facing Queen street, stands Osgoode Hall, named in honor of Hon. Wm. Osgoode, first Chief Justice of Upper Canada. The east wing, a square, brick, two-and-a-half storey structure, was begun in 1829, under supervision of Dr. Wm. Warren Baldwin, then treasurer of the Law Society, and completed in 1832. In 1844-6 a corresponding wing was built to the west, and the two buildings connected by a dome surmounted structure. In 1857-60 the entire edifice was renovated, the dome removed, a handsome facade of cut stone, inner area of Caen stone, court rooms, library and offices added. From time to time since, further additions have been made at the rear and other improvements effected. On the occasion of the Prince of Wales' visit to Toronto in 1860 an entertainment was given in his honor at Osgoode Hall, when the architectural lines of the exterior were brilliantly marked out by rows of minute gas-jets. The fence—classical in design—enclosing the grounds was erected just before the Prince's visit, and is one of the best pieces of iron work in Toronto. The entrance gate faces the Queen street frontage of 495 feet; the two flanks on University and Chestnut streets each measure 163 feet. The cost of the fence was approximately $20 a running foot, and $40 for each post, making a total of about $20,000, there being 16 posts on each flank and 50 on the front. Water colors (three in one frame). Sizes—buildings, 4 x 7; gates and fence, 5 x 6.

555—CRUICKSHANK (CROOKSHANK) AND BEIKIE RESIDENCES, YORK (TORONTO), 1821—On Front street, between Peter and Windsor streets. At that date these two residences were the most prominent buildings on Front street. The Cruickshank house, used by invading officers during the occupation of York by the Americans, became the rear part of the later and more commodious residence shown in the picture. In 1863 the house was divided into two dwellings, and in 1881 was finally demolished. The builder, Hon. George Cruickshank, was Deputy Commissary-General of U.C. from 1797-1815. The residence to the right, behind the poplars, was that of John Beikie, Clerk of the Executive Council of Upper Canada, 1820-37. This site is now (1917) occupied as railway yards. Pen drawing, colored. Size 6 x 10. See 532, 556.

556—BAY FRONT, YORK (TORONTO), 1820—Showing some noted houses of the early days. The view shows Front street to the water's edge, from Peter street to within a hundred feet of John street: 1, The original (1800) Cruickshank House before it was moved back and a new dwelling erected in front in 1821. 2, The John Beikie residence, of frame, where Windsor street opens. 3, The military storehouse. 4, The Half-Way Tavern, a popular resort of the soldiers from the fort. The site is now (1917) part of the G.T.R. freight yards. Pen drawing, colored. Size 6 x 10. See 532, 555.

557—KING STREET, TORONTO, FROM TORONTO STREET TO YONGE, 1881—To the left, on the south side of the street, is the old building of the business office of the Leader, a daily paper that ceased publication about 1872. Standing out in relief is Glover Harrison's China Hall, No. 49 King east, and the "Golden Lion" dry goods emporium, Nos. 33-7. In the distance, on the south-east corner of King and Yonge streets, John Kay's dry goods and carpet establishment is shown. The business has since been amalgamated with that of W. A. Murray & Company, now (1917) the Murray-Kay Co., dry goods merchants, 17 King east and 36 King west. To the right of the picture, north side of King, is the Birmingham House and Rice Lewis & Son, Nos. 52-4. At the north-west corner of Toronto and King streets is the exchange office of C. S. Gzowski, jr. West, toward Yonge street, is the Globe office and stores to No. 24, Paterson & Sons, hardware merchants. Drawing in water color. Size 7 x 10.

558—SOUTH-WEST AND SOUTH-EAST CORNERS YONGE AND KING STREETS, TORONTO, 1873-4—The south-west corner shows part of the Yonge street side of the W. H. Dow building; next south, Bacon and Phillips, and the St. Charles Restaurant, then kept by Geo. Brown. South across Melinda street, at the corner, was No. 62, Hughes Bros. The south-east corner of Yonge and King shows the Yonge street side of John Kay's and several leading mercantile establishments down to Bank of British North America, north-east corner Wellington street. Across Wellington at south-east corner of Yonge is the Royal Insurance building, now (1917) the Gutta Percha Company. Drawing in water color. Size 8 x 10.

559—LAKE SHORE ROAD AT THE HUMBER RIVER, 1875—With key—Near the Humber River bridge—Where the solitary apple tree stands on One-Tree Point (near the ship) is now (1917) the village of Mimico (the Indian equivalent for "flying pigeon"). The shore around the river mouth was yellow sand, and boats could unload here. In Gamble's storehouse flour and lumber were stored. Captain James McLean, owner of the vessel "Indian Chief," carried on extensive trading here with the Indians. Water color, from a drawing by Rev. W. Johnston, Weston. Size 6 x 10.

560—VIEW OF THE OLD WHITE BRIDGE, ROSEDALE, TORONTO, 1854-78—It crossed the Rosedale Ravine from the northerly limit of Gwynne street (Park road), where it unites with James, now Collier street. To the left, north-east of the bridge, may be seen the house of Charles Jarvis near the site of the present Cawthra House, Huntley street. On the hill to the right, at the south-east corner of James street and Gwynne street, stood the residence of Chief Justice Draper. The shack to the right in the foreground was the boathouse of Charles Thom, a well-known rifle shot in the early days. The water was known as Severn Creek, and the west end of it as Bloor Pond. The entire front of the pond is now (1917) filled up, the hill to the left terraced and the site of the handsome residence of Mr. Cawthra. Water color. Size 6 x 11.

561—OLD WADSWORTH MILL, WESTON, ONT., 1854-1917—The village of Weston, on the Humber River, was practically founded during the War of 1812-14 by the Government, which erected a mill there for the purpose of providing flour for the troops in active service. In 1814 the mill was leased by James Farr, and in turn transferred by him to Charles and William Wadsworth, in 1828. Subsequently the Wadsworth brothers purchased the freehold of the property from the Government. A second mill, the present (1917), was erected in 1854, four miles from the Humber's mouth as the crow flies. The first had four run of Burr millstones, while the present was designed for eight run of Burr stones. Water color by J. W. Cotton. Size 5 x 7.

562—BONNYCASTLE RESIDENCE, YORK (TORONTO)—Opposite the south-west corner of Front and Peter streets. This old-time house was in turn the residence of Colonel N. Coffin, Captain Philpotts, Captain Bonnycastle (afterwards Sir Richard, author of "Canada and the Canadians in 1846" and "Canada As It Was, Is and May Be,") and Raymond Baby, all of whom were military officials. It was used by the Royal Engineers as an office for a time. During Captain Bonnycastle's residence here in the forties, the beach below the house on the bay shore was the favorite bathing spot for the boys of Upper Canada College. About 1857 the dwelling was torn down. The land on which this residence stood was originally part of Front street, south of the south line of the street, where the Esplanade was made in 1854-7. The part south of Front street was cut away down to the level of the Esplanade. It is now part of the railway yards. Pen drawing, colored. Size 4 x 10.

563—OAKHILL, YORK (TORONTO)—The little log building was one of the earliest houses in York. It stood about half a mile north of what is now Queen street, a short distance northwest of the present (1917) site of Trinity College, and was built by Captain (Major-General) Aeneas Shaw, a member of the Executive Council of Upper Canada, shortly after he settled in York in 1793. It was in this log cabin that Major-Gen. Shaw had the honor of entertaining H.R.H. the Duke of Kent, father of Queen Victoria, on the occasion of his visit to York. A larger and more pretentious residence, said to have been the first private house of frame erected in York, was afterwards built, a little to the west of the log house. Up to 1871 Oakhill was occupied by Capt. Alexander Shaw, a descendant of the first owner. Water color. Size 5 x 7.

564—NORTH-WEST AND SOUTH-WEST CORNERS YONGE AND KING STREETS, TORONTO, 1873-4—This view does not take in the actual corner, but within thirty feet of it. On the north side to the right are stores of M. Staunton, Joseph McCausland and Edward Bach, and west in the distance is the English Chop House. On the south side to the left is the shop of Fulton, Michie & Co. (now, 1917, Michie & Co.), the Royal Saloon, next west, R. T. Pocknell, confectioner, Felix Drouillard and the Sheffield House of Joseph Robinson (now site of Standard Bank Building). Drawing in water color. Size 7 x 10.

565—NORTH-WEST AND NORTH-EAST CORNERS YONGE AND ADELAIDE STREETS, TORONTO, 1856—The block on the west side of Yonge street, extending from Adelaide almost to Temperance, was known as the Elgin Buildings. The picture shows from No. 79, J. & W. McDonald, dry goods, to No. 93, J. Belton, boot and shoe maker, across Temperance street. On the east side of Yonge are shown the stores from No. 78, S. Shaw & Son, hardware, to No. 88, C. Mabley, tailor. The corner is now occupied by the Lumsden Building. Water color. Size 8 x 13.

566—SOUTH SIDE KING STREET, EAST OF CHURCH, TORONTO, 1873-4—The stores at the south-east corner of Church and King streets are not in picture. With this exception the entire block, from No. 109, J. H. Rogers, hatter, to No. 153, Latham, Trebilcock & Liddell, dry goods, at south-west corner of West Market street, is given. Across West Market is the St. Lawrence Hall, with shops of Lyman Bros., C. A. Backas, Shaver & Bell, and the Toronto Tea Co. Drawing in water color. Size 7 x 10.

567—FOUR CORNERS OF WELLINGTON AND SCOTT STREETS, TORONTO, 1873—On the north side of Wellington street, to right of picture, was the wholesale grocery establishment of Robert Jordan & Co. and Molsons Bank. The Cooper's Arms Tavern was in those days situated on the north-west corner of Scott and Wellington, now the site of the Western Insurance building. On the east side of Wellington, to the left of the picture, was the four-storey building of John Macdonald & Co., and on the south-west corner of Wellington and Scott the Montreal Telegraph building, now (1917) that of the Great North-Western Company. Water color. Size 7 x 10.

568—YONGE STREET, FROM FRONT TO WELLINGTON, TORONTO, 1873-4—The actual north-east corner of Front is not shown, but is the American Hotel, remembered as the stopping-place of Charles Dickens when he visited Toronto. North of the hostelry are the stores of G. W. Smith, H. Shorey, Joseph Wey & Co., Dunn, Cowan & Co., Hodgson & Boyd, T. Brownlow, W. Myles and R. C. Brayley. On south-east corner of Yonge and Wellington stood the Royal Insurance Co., while the Bank of British North America occupied the north-east corner, as it still (1917) does. The Gutta Percha Co. is now on site of the old Royal Insurance Co. On the west side of Yonge, to the left of the picture, are stores from No. 34, Bryce, McMurrich & Co., to No. 46, J. C. Joseph & Co., at the south-west, and Robt. Wilkes, 48-50, at the north-west corner of Wellington and Yonge. The offices of the Richelieu & Ontario Navigation and the Dominion Express Companies occupy these sites. Drawing in water color. Size 6 x 10.

569—FRONT STREET, AT THE JUNCTION OF CHURCH AND WELLINGTON, TORONTO, 1873-4—In the centre stands the Coffin Block, so called from its shape, in which were the original offices of the Montreal and of the Dominion Telegraph Companies. The north-east corner of Front and Church was No. 62, W. & R. Griffith & Co., wholesale grocers, and across the road, No. 58, the Bank of Toronto; further west was a vacant lot, and adjoining, warehouses. the Toronto Exchange building, which after entire remodelling is now (1917) the head office of the Imperial Bank. Water color. Size 5 x 9.

570—FIRST COURT HOUSE, YORK (TORONTO)—West and north of the north-west corner of Richmond and Upper George (Victoria) streets, and approached from Richmond, although nearer Queen. After the destruction in 1813, by the Americans, of the Government buildings at York, the Court House was removed to the building shown in picture, a plain two-storey structure, previously occupied as a residence by Alexander Montgomery. On being abandoned as a Court House it was used occasionally for religious purposes, "The Children of Peace" utilizing it as a place of worship. Later it became the House of Industry. Water color. Size 5 x 7.

571—DUCK'S HOTEL AT THE HUMBER, 1873-1912—This popular roadhouse was originally on a part of the Gamble estate, from which it was purchased by John Strathy. Until its disposal by Mr. Strathy to John Duck in 1873 it was tenanted by Shepherd, the shoemaker. Duck conducted it as a tavern until his death in 1891, and for two years afterwards his widow carried on the business. During the next eight years it was run by various persons, and in 1901 was converted into a tenement house by Richard West, who in 1910 transferred it to Mrs. Crow. It was destroyed by fire in 1912. The entire vicinity has been entirely changed by the erection of new buildings and other improvements. Water color. Size 5 x 9.

572—NORTH-EAST COR. KING AND YORK STS., TORONTO, 1858— On the corner, to the right of the picture, stood the Shakespeare Hotel, once a favorite rendezvous of actors playing in Toronto. The Imperial Hotel, 144 King west, now (1917) vacant, occupies the site. The row of buildings seen in the background is Ritchey's Terrace, Adelaide street, built in 1854. Water color. Size 6 x 10.

573—FOUR CORNERS OF KING AND BAY STREETS, TORONTO, 1864-5—On the north side of King street, to right of picture, was the shop of Charles Baker, and the King street side of Wm. Cawthra's residence, which faced on Bay street, while on the north-west corner Bay and King was the Metropolitan Hotel, now the site of the Mail Building. On the south side of King, to the left of the picture, are the stores of Philip Jacobi, Thos. Flynn, R. S. Thompson, D. S. & B. Adams, and Jacques & Hay (Union Bank of Canada). Across Bay street, on the south-west corner of King, is the grocery of Robert Davis & Co., now (1917) site of the Bank of Toronto building. Water color. Size 7 x 10.

574—SOUTH-EAST CORNER OF BAY AND MELINDA STREETS, TORONTO—Now (1917) the site of The Evening Telegram building. The dwellings shown were built in 1841, and used as such until the eighties, when they were converted into places of business. The Telegram building was erected on the site in 1900, when the office of that journal was removed from the south-west corner of King and Bay streets. Water color. Size 5 x 7.

575—ON THE BAY SHORE, TORONTO, 1850—View from the north-east corner of Front and Peter streets. No. 1 is the guardhouse; No. 2, military storehouse. In the distance to the right is the lighthouse on Toronto Island. The locality, in the early days a residential district of the city, is now (1917) a part of the Grand Trunk Railway property. Water color. Size 6 x 7.

576—SECOND COURT HOUSE, YORK (TORONTO), 1824-52—Situated on Church street, near the north-west corner of King, in what was at the time of its erection known as Court House Square. It was built in 1824, at the same time as the second York Jail, n.e. corner King and Toronto streets, sixty feet north of the King street line. Both buildings were of red brick with stone trimmings, two storeys in height and in exactly the same style of architecture. After the erection of the new Court House on Adelaide street, in 1852, the old Court Room was used as an assembly room by teachers of dancing. Two well-known professors of the terpsichorean art, Mr. McIndoe and Mr. James Thomson, taught from 1852-58. The Church street front of the building was in the sixties extended to the street line, and is now (1917) shops and offices. The north gable can yet be seen on Court street. To the left of picture will be observed a small cabin with a woman sitting in it. She is in the stocks, punished for disorderly conduct, and was the last person in Toronto, so the late Rev. Dr. Henry Scadding informed Mr. Robertson, to suffer that kind of punishment. Water color. Size 5 x 7.

577—THIRD COURT HOUSE, TORONTO, 1853-1900—South side of Adelaide street east, Nos. 57-65. A substantial building with cut stone dressings, erected in 1852-3 and used until 1900, when the courts were transferred to the present (1917) City Hall, Queen street west, the architect of which was Fred Cumberland, father of the late Barlow Cumberland. The building on Adelaide street is now York County Municipal Hall and other offices. Water color. Size 5 x 7.

578—RIGNEY, THOMAS—An old-time merchant of Toronto—He was born in Ferbane, King's Co., Ireland, and at an early age came to Canada. He was with Levi, Cook & Co., in Montreal, and in 1837 carried on a wholesale comb factory and fancy store at the corner of King and Toronto streets, and later, on the same site, occupied the first four-storey business building in the city. Mr. Rigney subsequently, as a produce merchant, was at the north-east corner of Yonge and Wellington streets, in the British North America Bank building. He was also interested in business in New York from the early fifties, and at the time of his death in 1900 was the oldest member of the New York Produce Exchange. Photograph, colored. Size 4 x 9. Head and shoulders.

579—RITCHEY, JOHN, 1796-1866—A pioneer builder and contractor in Toronto—He came to Canada from Ireland in 1819. In the early days he did a good deal of Government work, including the Lount and Matthews gallows. Many buildings in Toronto were erected by him, amongst them St. George's and Trinity Anglican Churches, the Court House and Ritchey's Terrace, both on Newgate (now Adelaide) street, a row of houses on the east and west sides of Bay street, south of the present Telegram Office, and the Royal Lyceum, ninth playhouse in Toronto. The residences in Ritchey's Terrace were some years ago converted into factories and are used to-day as such. Photograph, colored. Size 4 x 5. Head and shoulders.

580-82—Managers of Consumers' Gas Company, Toronto, 1849-1916.

580—THOMPSON, HENRY—Manager Consumers' Gas Company, 1849-75—He came to Canada in 1834, first going to Stratford. On locating in Toronto he entered the employ of Benjamin Thorne & Co., importers of oils, 38-40 Front street, and for some years was junior partner. He was born in London, Eng., 1814. Died in Toronto, 19th Nov., 1880. A younger brother of Mr. Thompson was Christopher Thompson, a well-known English and writing master of Upper Canada College. Photograph, colored. Size 4 x 5. Head and shoulders.

581—PEARSON, WILLIAM H.—Manager Consumers' Gas Company, 1875-1909—He was born in 1831 in London, Eng. In his youthful days was a post office employe, under Charles Berczy; entered the Gas Company's service as clerk, 1854; appointed secretary, 1874. As secretary he managed the affairs of the company until 1888, the title of general manager then being added. He retired in 1909, and still (1917) resides in Toronto. Photograph, colored. Size 4 x 5. Head and shoulders.

582—HEWITT, ARTHUR—Manager Consumers' Gas Company, 1909-16 —He was born in Wolverhampton, Eng., 18th August, 1868, educated there and in Toronto. Became secretary to Mr. W. H. Pearson in 1886; was appointed chief clerk and accountant four years later; assistant general manager in 1907, and general manager 1909. President Board of Trade, 1916. Photograph, colored. Size 4 x 5. Head and shoulders.

583—**CAMERON, JOHN,** 1810-67—Manager Commercial Bank of Midland District, later called the Merchants' Bank. While connected with that institution was stationed at Kingston and Toronto. Water color from portrait in possession of his daughter, Mrs. Gamsby, Ocala, Fla. Size 4 x 6. Head and shoulders. See 944.

584—**CAMERON, MRS. JOHN (ROSA ROGERS)**—The daughter of an Englishman, she was born in Schenectady, N.Y., in 1814, and married, at Niagara, Mr. Cameron, of the Commercial Bank. For a time they lived in Kingston, and later came to Toronto, where Mrs. Cameron died November 23rd, 1890. Water color from an oil painting in possession of her daughter, Mrs. Gamsby, Ocala, Fla. Size 4 x 6. Head and shoulders.

585—**NICKINSON, JOHN**—Born in London, Eng., in 1808; at an early age he enlisted in the 24th Regiment, receiving his discharge with the rank of color-sergeant in 1835. He thereupon entered the theatrical profession, his first engagement being at Albany, N.Y. He then went to New York City, where he remained for several years, coming to Canada in 1852. From 1853-8 he managed the Royal Lyceum, King street west, Toronto. Mr. Nickinson possessed histrionic ability of a high character, and displayed wonderful versatility. He died in 1864 in Cincinnati, Ohio. His only son, John, an American Custom House official, died in New York in 1916. His eldest daughter, Charlotte, married Daniel Morrison, and his two granddaughters, Miss Charlotte Morrison and Miss Agnes Morrison, married Mr. E. B. Brown, son of the late Gordon Brown, and the late Mr. Raynald Gamble, of the Dominion Bank, respectively. Photograph, colored. Size 4 x 5. Head and shoulders. See 1121.

586—**SMALL, MAJOR JOHN**—Born in Gloucestershire, Eng., 1746. Came to Canada about 1792, filling the position of first Clerk of the Executive Council of Upper Canada, 1793-1831. He was also Clerk of the Crown and Pleas, 1806-25, retiring from the duties of the latter position at his own request. Married Eliza Goldsmith, a native of the County of Kent, Eng. Major Small died at Berkeley House, York (Toronto), 18th July, 1831. Water color from an oil painting in possession of Mrs. Small, Berkeley House, Toronto. Size 4 x 5. Head and shoulders.

587—**SMALL, MRS. JOHN (ELIZA GOLDSMITH)**—Born in Kent, England, 30th April, 1760. Lived for many years in York (Toronto). She was the grandmother of the late John Small, Collector of Customs, Toronto. Died at Berkeley House, 31st May, 1837. Water color from an oil painting in possession of Mrs. Small, widow of the late collector, Berkeley House, Toronto. Size 4 x 5. Head and shoulders.

588—**SOMERVILLE, ALEXANDER—"The Whistler at the Plough"**— Born at Springfield, Scotland, 1811. He began life as a cowherd, but early became interested in political questions, and in 1831 published his first letter in a newspaper. In 1832 he joined the Scots Greys. They received instructions to leave Birmingham for London to quell the Reform Riots, and Somerville, protesting strongly, was flogged. However, those who had ordered the punishment were reprimanded. In 1835 he took service in the British Legion in Spain, under Sir George de Lacy Evans, serving with credit for two years. On his return to England he contributed letters to the London Morning Chronicle, thus attracting the notice of Cobden, who sent him through the country districts of England to collect information for the Anti-Corn Law League. In 1844 Somerville became correspondent for the Manchester Examiner. Came to Canada in 1858 and engaged in journalistic work, for a time editing the Canadian Illustrated News at Hamilton. Amongst his writings are "Autobiography of a Working Man" and "Canada as a Battle Ground." His death occurred in Toronto, 17th June, 1885. Water color. Size 4 x 5. Head and shoulders.

9

589-93—Harbor Masters of Toronto, 1850-1917.

589—RICHARDSON, CAPT. HUGH—Harbor Master, 1850-69—Born in London, Eng., in 1784, the son of Thomas Richardson, a West India merchant; came to Canada in 1820. Six years later he became captain of the "Canada," a vessel plying between York and Niagara, planned and constructed by Richardson. The "U. E. Loyalist" of 12th Aug., 1826, states that "The new steamboat, 'Canada,' Capt. Richardson, made her first trip to Niagara on Monday last, and went out of the harbor in fine style." Capt. Richardson's death occurred in Toronto, 2nd August, 1870. Photograph, colored. Size 3 x 4. Head and shoulders.

590—HARRIS, THOMAS DENNIE—Harbor Master, 1870-2—He was at one time engaged in the hardware business on the north side of King street, east of St. James' Cathedral, and was well-known in Toronto business circles. From 1838-41 he was chief engineer of the fire brigade. His death took place in Toronto, 18th Jan., 1873. Photograph, colored. Size 3 x 4. Head and shoulders. See 3186.

591—CARR, JOHN—Harbor Master, 1873-9. Photograph, colored. Size 3 x 4. Head and shoulders. See 378, 752, 3513.

592—BALDWIN, MORGAN—Harbor Master, 1880-96—A son of John Spread Baldwin; born in Toronto in 1834 and received his education at Upper Canada College. He died in the city of his birth, March 15th, 1898. Photograph, colored. Size 3 x 4. Head and shoulders.

593—POSTLETHWAITE, COLIN W.—Harbor Master, 1896-1917— Came to Canada in 1857, and was for some time private secretary to the general manager of the Grand Trunk Railway. From 1862-83 he was purchasing agent for the Northern Railway, and in 1884 received the appointment of Deputy Harbor Master. He is an Irishman by birth, first seeing the light of day at Manor-Hamilton, November 29th, 1836. Photograph, colored. Size 3 x 4. Head and shoulders.

594—RESIDENCE OF REV. HENRY SCADDING, D.D., TORONTO— View of study and library—He resided for many years on the north side of Trinity street, in the district at one time known as Macaulay Town, so called from Dr. James Macaulay, of the Queen's Rangers. It was in the room shown that Dr. Scadding wrote "Toronto of Old." Water color. Size 5 x 7.

595—ALLAN, MRS. WILLIAM (LEAH TYRER GAMBLE)—She was born in New Brunswick, 1790, the daughter of John Gamble, M.D., who came to America in 1799, serving as a regimental surgeon during the Revolutionary War. He settled in New Brunswick in 1783, and resided there until his appointment to the Queen's Rangers. In 1809 Miss Gamble married Hon. William Allan at Kingston. Hon. George W. Allan was a son of this marriage. Mrs. Allan died in Toronto, October 20th, 1848. Water color. Size 4 x 5. Head and shoulders.

596—GOWAN, OGLE R.—Founder of Orangeism in America—Born at Mount Nebo, Co. Wexford, Ireland, 13th July, 1803. For a time he edited a political newspaper known as the Antidote, published in the city of Dublin. Emigrated to Canada with his family about 1829, settling at Escott Park, Leeds Co. He was four times elected to Parliament for that county, and subsequently represented Leeds and Grenville. On the outbreak of the Rebellion of 1837 appointed captain in the 2nd Regiment of Leeds Militia by Sir Francis Bond Head; subsequently was promoted by Lord Seaton to a company in the Queen's Own Rifles. In the same year he was appointed to command the ninth provisional battalion of embodied militia, as lieutenant-colonel. Was present at the engagement at the "Windmill," near

Prescott, November, 1838; subsequently commanded the 2nd Regiment of Leeds Militia. Again sat in Parliament, finally retiring in 1861, as "the father of the House." Held various public positions. Organized the Grand Lodge of British North America (Orange) at Brockville in 1830. Died in 1876. Two of his grandsons are T. R. Ferguson, K.C., and Judge Ferguson, of Toronto, and a granddaughter is Mrs. Murphy ("Janey Canuck"), Edmonton, Alta. Photograph, colored. Size 4 x 5. Head and shoulders.

597—FREELAND, PETER—A native of Glasgow, Scotland, he emigrated to America in 1819, crossing the Atlantic in the first passenger ship run by the Allan line of steamships. Shortly after his arrival at New York he went on to Montreal, where he and his brother, Mr. William Freeland, conducted a soap and candle business. In 1830 the former removed to York, erecting a large and well-appointed factory on the wharf at the foot of Yonge street. Mr. Freeland was one of the originators of Congregationalism in Toronto. His death occurred here in 1861. Water color, Size 4 x 5. Head and shoulders.

598—CROOKSHANK, HON. GEORGE, 1763-1859—Born in New York, of Scottish parentage. At the conclusion of the American Revolutionary War the family emigrated to New Brunswick, and later settled in York (Toronto), where Mr. Crookshank received a grant of three hundred acres of land, and where, during his term in the commissariat, he had charge of the building of the fort. He was Deputy Commissary-General from 1796 until the end of the War of 1812, when he retired on half-pay. During the occupation of York by the Americans in 1813 the Crookshank home, Front and Peter streets, was used by American officers. Mr. Crookshank was a member of the Legislative Council of Upper Canada. His death took place in Toronto. Water color. Size 3 x 4. Head and shoulders.

599—HEWARD, MRS. STEPHEN (Catherine Crookshank)—Only daughter of Hon. George Crookshank, Deputy Commissary-General during the War of 1812. She was born at her mother's (Sarah Susannah Lambert) home, Wilton, Conn., in 1829, was educated in Toronto, residing there almost all her life, in Front street, and subsequently Peter street. Miss Crookshank married in 1858 Mr. Stephen Heward, of Toronto. Her death took place 11th Jan., 1917. Mrs. John McGill, aunt of Catherine Crookshank, was a personal friend of Mrs. Simcoe during the latter's sojourn in York. Water color from portrait in possession of her son, C. E. Heward, Toronto. Size 4 x 5. Three-quarter length, sitting.

600-03—Police Magistrates of Toronto, 1851-1917.

600—GURNETT, GEORGE—Police Magistrate, 1851-61. Water color. Size 3 x 4. Head and shoulders. See 366.

601—BOOMER, GEORGE—Police Magistrate, 1862-5—Born at Hill Hall, near Lisburn, Co. Down, Ireland, in 1819, the son of George Boomer. About 1832 he came to Canada; studied law, subsequently entering into partnership with Richard Miller, of the then County Town of Niagara. He practised his profession there until the firm moved to St. Catharines. Later he removed to Toronto, where he became a partner of Skeffington Connor (afterwards Judge). His death occurred in Toronto in 1866. Water color. Size 4 x 5. Head and shoulders.

602—MACNABB, ALEXANDER—Police Magistrate, 1866-77—The son of Donald MacNabb, a non-commissioned officer in the 71st Highlanders. Born in Barracks at Fort George, Niagara, U.C., in 1830. After graduating from Toronto University he studied law in the office of Henry Eccles, a prominent Toronto attorney, and on being called to the bar in 1853, commenced the practice of law on his own account. After holding the office of Police Magistrate for eleven years he resumed the practice of his profession, finally retiring in 1887, and removing to San Angelo, Texas. In 1902 he again changed his residence, going to Los Angeles, Cal., where his death took place in 1907. Photograph, colored. Size 3 x 4. Head and shoulders.

603—DENISON, COL. GEORGE TAYLOR—Police Magistrate, 1878-1917—Born in Toronto in 1839, and educated at Upper Canada College and Toronto University. Became a barrister in 1861, and successfully practised his profession in Toronto, in partnership with his brother, the late Col. F. C. Denison. In 1872-3 he acted as special Immigration Commissioner from Ontario to Great Britain. He is one of the oldest living officers in the Canadian volunteer militia service, having entered the Governor-General's Body Guard as a Cornet in 1855, and becoming Colonel in 1907. He was on active service in the Fenian Raid, 1866, and again in the North-West Rebellion of 1885, and is well known as a contributor to military literature. He still (1917) continues to hold office as Police Magistrate. Photograph, colored. Size 3 x 4. Head and shoulders. See 485.

604—HODDER, EDWARD MULBERRY, M.D.—Born in England, 30th Dec., 1810; son of Capt. Hodder, R.N. He entered the navy in 1822 as a midshipman under his father, but left the service, preferring the medical profession. Studied in England, France and Scotland, and in 1835 visited Canada. Three years later he returned, determining to settle here. He made his home near Queenston, where he remained five years, removing in 1843 to Toronto. He established in 1850, with Dr. Bovell, the Upper Canada School of Medicine, which in that year became the medical department of Trinity College; was a member of the active staff of the Toronto General Hospital, and in 1875 was president of the Canada Medical Association. Dr. Hodder was one of the founders of the Toronto Boat Club, afterwards the Royal Canadian Yacht Club, and the latter's third commodore, serving in that capacity from 1856-9 continuously, and at different periods from 1862-77. He died Feb. 20th, 1878. Water color from portrait in possession of his youngest daughter, Miss Olivia Hodder, Jersey, Channel Islands. Size 4 x 5. Three-quarter length, sitting. See 605.

605—HODDER, EDWARD MULBERRY, M.D., 1810-78—Commodore R.C.Y.C., Toronto. Water color from a portrait in possession of his youngest daughter, Miss Olivia Hodder, Jersey, Channel Islands. Size 4 x 5. Three-quarter length, sitting. See 604.

606-09 and 638—Officers Commanding Toronto Military District, 1868-1914—Previous to Confederation there was no militia officer in command in a district or area in Canada, although in 1862 an amendment of the Militia Act divided the country into brigade divisions, a brigade major being appointed for each division. These brigade majors, however, were not given command, but were merely staff officers. In 1868 a consolidated Militia Act was passed for the Dominion, dividing the country into military districts, and providing for the appointment of a deputy adjutant-general for each district. Under this authority the counties and cities in the vicinity of Toronto were created the 2nd Military District.

606—DURIE, LIEUT.-COL. WILLIAM SMITH—Deputy Adjutant-General, Military District No. 2, 1868-80. The son of William Durie, K.H., Inspector-General of Hospitals, Woolwich, Eng. He was born at Gibraltar, and after his military training at Sandhurst received a commission in the 94th Regiment of Foot. In 1838 he came to Canada and was appointed adjutant, with the rank of captain in the militia. He subsequently raised the Barrie Rifles, commanding that regiment until he was appointed First

Commanding Officer of the Queen's Own Rifles in 1860. In 1864 he was appointed to serve with the 2nd Administrative Battalion on the Niagara Frontier, and the following year was made D.A.G. at Toronto. He died in Toronto in 1885. Water color. Size 4 x 5. Head and shoulders.

607—DENISON, LIEUT.-COL. ROBERT BRITTAIN—Deputy Adjutant-General, Military District No. 2, 1881-6. Born at York (Toronto) in 1821, the third son of Lieut.-Col. George Taylor Denison, of Bellevue. In 1843 he joined Denison's troop as Cornet, and in 1857 became Major, commanding the Toronto Field Battery in that year. In 1862 he became Brigade-Major of the 10th Military District, and was commander of a provisional battalion at Clifton during the Fenian Raid in 1866. His death occurred 4th Aug., 1900. Water color. Size 4 x 5. Head and shoulders.

608—OTTER, MAJOR-GENERAL WILLIAM DILLON—Inspector-General Canadian Militia, 1910-12—Born near Clinton, Ont., in 1843; he entered the volunteer militia service in 1861, and in the winter of 1864-5 served as Lieutenant in 2nd Administrative Battalion on Niagara frontier; saw active service also in the Fenian Raid. In 1875 he commanded his regiment in the "Pilgrimage Riots," Toronto, and two years later in the Grand Trunk Ry. Riots, Belleville. He also went through the Riel and North-West Rebellions. From 1886-1908 was Deputy Adjt.-Gen., Military District No. 2. Served in South African War, 1899-1900; mentioned in the despatches twice; C.B.; Queen's medal with four clasps. From 1908-10 was chief of the general staff at headquarters, and in 1910 was made Major-General; K.C.B., 1913. Water color on platinum. Size 4 x 5. Head and shoulders.

609—COTTON, MAJOR-GENERAL WILLIAM HENRY—Inspector-General Canadian Militia, 1912-14—Son of Henry Cotton, chief clerk of the Governor-General's office in the days of Lord Monck, 1867-8. He was born in Montreal, Que., in 1848, and at the age of eighteen was gazetted Lieutenant in the Quebec Garrison Artillery. In 1866 served in the Fenian Raid, and again saw active service at the Riel Rebellion, 1870. Received general service medal with two clasps. From 1908-12 he was G.O.C. for Western Ontario, including 2nd Military District, vacating this appointment to become Inspector-General. His death took place in 1914. Water color on platinum. Size 4 x 5. Head and shoulders.

610-15—Postmasters of York and Toronto, 1816-1917.

610—ALLAN (HON.) WILLIAM—Postmaster, 1816-27. Water color. Size 3½ x 4. Head and shoulders. See 941, 3541.

611—HOWARD, JAMES SCOTT—Postmaster, York (Toronto), 1827-38—Born at Bandon, Co. Cork, Ireland, in 1798, of Huguenot ancestry. At the age of twenty-one he left Ireland, accompanying Chief Justice Sullivan to Canada, and settling in Fredericton, N.B. Later he removed to York (Toronto), where he held office under the Hon. William Allan, and on the latter's retirement, succeeded him as Postmaster. Was Treasurer of the Home District, 1842, and subsequently of the Counties of York and Peel. He was also for several years a corresponding secretary of the U.C. Bible Society. Died 1866. Water color. Size 3½ x 4. Head and shoulders. See 641.

612—BERCZY, CHARLES ALBERT—Postmaster 1839-53—Son of William Berczy, who by arrangement with Governor Simcoe made settlements in the township of Markham, U.C. Was born at Niagara in 1794. During the War of 1812 he entered the Commissariat, rising to the position of Acting Deputy Assistant Commissary-General. For a time he acted as Justice of the Peace, and was also one of the projectors of the Northern Railway. Died in Toronto, 1858. Pencil drawing,, in color, from a portrait in possession of Mrs. Charles de Moll Berczy, Fort Scott, Kansas. Size 3½x 4. Head and shoulders. See 623.

613—LESSLIE, JOSEPH—Postmaster, 1853-79—Born at Dundee, Scotland, in 1813; came to Canada with his father, Edward Lesslie, when nine years of age, and subsequently engaged in the drug and stationery business with his father and brothers. He died in Toronto, January 6th, 1904. Water color. Size 3½ x 4. Head and shoulders.

614—PATTESON, THOMAS CHARLES—Postmaster, 1879-1907—Born at Patney, Wilts, Eng., 1836; educated at Eton and Merton College, Oxford. Won an open postmastership at the latter and graduated with honors in 1858. Came to Canada immediately afterwards; studied law, first in the office of the Hon. J. H. Cameron, and later with the Hon. James Cockburn at Cobourg. In 1863 he was called to the bar, and afterwards formed a partnership with the Hon. John Ross. Four years later was appointed Assistant Provincial Secretary for Ontario, but on establishment of the Mail in 1872 resigned office to become manager. This position he occupied until his appointment as Postmaster. He died in Toronto in 1907. Photograph, colored. Size 3½ x 3. Head and shoulders.

615—ROGERS, WILLIAM BROWN—Postmaster, 1908-1917—Son of Charles Rogers, a Scotsman; born in Toronto in 1852, and educated at the Public and Model schools and Upper Canada College. Entered the service of Rice Lewis & Co., hardware merchants, Toronto, and later the Upper Canada Furniture Co. For twenty-three years was a member of the firm of Charles Rogers & Sons Co., furniture manufacturers; was one of the originators of the Penny Bank. He still (1916) holds the position of Postmaster in the city of his birth. Photograph, colored. Size 3½ x 4. Head and shoulders.

616-22—Superintendents of Toronto General Hospital, 1848-1917.

616—CLARK, DR. EDWARD—Superintendent, 1848-56—Born at Belturbet, Co. Cavan, Ireland, in 1814, the son of Lieut. Clark. Studied medicine at Trinity College, Dublin, and came to Canada when about twenty-one years of age. In 1848 was appointed Resident Surgeon and Superintendent of the Toronto General Hospital, and was also Secretary of the Medical Board of Canada West. His death occurred in Toronto, 17th Oct., 1856. Water color. Size 4 x 5. Head and shoulders.

617—GARDINER, DR. CHARLES—Superintendent, 1857-63—Born in England about 1823; subsequently came to Canada and was appointed assistant at the Toronto General Hospital. Two years later became Resident Surgeon and Superintendent. His death took place in Toronto in 1863. He was an uncle of Dr. W. B. Hampton, who succeeded him as Superintendent. Water color from a painting by C. G. Goeffler. Size 4 x 5. Head and shoulders.

618—HAMPTON, DR. WILLIAM B.—Superintendent, 1864-71—Succeeded his uncle, Dr. Charles Gardiner, as Superintendent of the Toronto General Hospital. Was born in Canada and studied the profession of medicine in Toronto. Married Miss Taylor, daughter of John Taylor, of the Don Mills. Died when only twenty-nine years of age. Photograph, colored. Size 4 x 5. Head and shoulders.

619—McCOLLUM, DR. JOHN HENRY—Superintendent, 1871-5—Born in Tullamore, Chinguacousy Township, near Brampton, in 1841. Prosecuted his medical studies at Toronto University, graduating with honors. After practising in his native village for two years, came to Toronto to take up work at the General Hospital, resigning the position in 1875 to devote his entire attention to his private practice. For many years he was regimental surgeon for the Royal Grenadiers. His death took place in Toronto in 1888. Photograph, colored. Size 4 x 5. Head and shoulders.

620—O'REILLY, DR. CHARLES—Superintendent, 1876-1905—Born in Hamilton, Ont., 1846; received his education in that city and at McGill University (M.D., C.M., 1867). From 1867-75 was resident physician in the Hamilton City Hospital. He effected many reforms and improvements in the General Hospital, Toronto. During the Rebellion of 1885 organized and sent to the front the Toronto General Hospital Ambulance Corps. Photograph, colored. Size 4 x 5. Head and shoulders.

621—BROWN, DR. J. N. E.—Superintendent, 1905-11—Born in 1864 at Nissouri, Oxford Co., of U.E. Loyalist descent; received his education at St. Mary's High School and later at Toronto University, winning his M.B., with a silver medal, in 1892. Six years later was appointed by the Dominion Government to accompany Governor Ogilvie to the Yukon, filling the office of Territorial Secretary and later Medical Health Officer in that country. In 1912 he was appointed Superintendent of the Detroit General Hospital, which on 28th June, 1914, was taken over by Henry Ford. Dr. Brown was transferred with the Hospital, and still (1917) retains the superintendency. Photograph, colored. Size 4 x 5. Head and shoulders.

622—CLARKE, DR. CHARLES KIRK—Superintendent, appointed 1911—Born at Elora, Ont., in 1857; studied medicine at Toronto University, graduating in 1879. Became Medical Superintendent of the Hamilton Insane Asylum the following year, and from 1885-1905 was at Rockwood, Kingston, establishing there a convalescent and nurses' home. In 1905 received the appointment of Medical Superintendent of the Toronto Asylum, resigning six years later to accept the General Hospital position. Photograph, colored. Size 4 x 5. Head and shoulders.

623-31—Presidents of Consumers' Gas Company, Toronto, 1847-1917—Gas was first supplied in Toronto in 1841 by Mr. Albert Furniss, under the name "The City of Toronto Gas, Light and Water Company." In 1847 a new company known as "The Consumers' Gas Company," was founded, with Mr. Charles Berczy as President, and the following March was incorporated. Subsequently negotiations with Mr. Furniss were entered into, and his works purchased in June, 1848. To-day (1917) the Consumers' Gas Co. is known as one of the most successful on this continent.

623—BERCZY, CHARLES ALBERT—President Consumers' Gas Company, 1847-56—Water color. Size 4 x 5. Head and shoulders. See 612.

624—WHITTEMORE, E.F.—President Consumers' Gas Company, 1856-9 —In 1846 he was a member of the firm of Thomas Rigney & Co., wholesale merchants, north-west corner King and Toronto streets. About 1850 he became principal partner of Whittemore, Rutherford (E. H.) & Co. in the old Rigney premises. The firm dissolved in 1855, Mr. Rutherford retiring, and the business was carried on by E. F. Whittemore & Co., bankers and brokers. Mr. Whittemore died in Toronto, 19th February, 1859. Photograph, colored. Size 4 x 5. Head and shoulders.

625—YATES, RICHARD—President Consumers' Gas Company, 1859-67 —He was a well-known tea merchant, whose place of business in 1846 was No. 52 King street east, Toronto, about the present (1917) 71-3 King street east. A familiar sign in his "East India Tea House" was a Chinese mandarin, who in a friendly manner continually bowed to passersby. Mr. Yates retired from business about 1860. He died in Toronto, 11th March. 1867. Photograph, colored. Size 4 x 5. Head and shoulders.

626—RUTHERFORD, E. H.—President Consumers' Gas Company, 1867-74—His birthplace was Manor-Hamilton, Co. Leitrim, Ireland, 15th May, 1820. Educated in Toronto and Ireland. From 1850 he was the junior partner of the firm of Whittemore, Rutherford & Co., Toronto.

Was vice-president of the Bank of Upper Canada, an active member of the House of Industry Board, and a director of the Canada Permanent Building Society. Died 30th September, 1885. Photograph, colored. Size 4 x 5. Head and shoulders.

627—AUSTIN, JAMES—President Consumers' Gas Company, 1874-97— He was born at Tanderagee, Ireland, 6th March, 1814, and for many years resided in Toronto, where he died 27th Feb., 1897. He was fifth president of the Gas Company, which position he held for twenty-three years. He was a pioneer merchant of Toronto, for many years in the firm of Foy & Austin, north-east corner Nelson (Jarvis) and King streets. From 1871-97 he was president of the Dominion Bank. Photograph, colored. Size 4 x 5. Head and shoulders.

628—SMITH, LARRATT WILLIAM—President Consumers' Gas Company, 1897-1905—Born at Stonehouse, Devon, Eng., 29th November, 1820. He was educated at Upper Canada College and King's College, Toronto (B.C.L., 1848; D.C.L., 1858), and was called to the bar in 1843, practising in Toronto. He served as a lieutenant in the North York militia during the Rebellion of 1837, and later became major of the Reserve Militia. In 1876 he acted as chairman of a Royal Commission appointed to enquire into the affairs of the Northern Railway. Died 18th September, 1905. Photograph, colored. Size 4 x 5. Head and shoulders.

629—COCKBURN, GEORGE R. R.—President Consumers' Gas Company, 1905-6—He was a Scotchman, born in Edinburgh; educated at Edinburgh High school and University (M.A. and Stratton prizeman, 1857). In 1861 he was appointed principal of Upper Canada College and a senator of Toronto University. Represented Centre Toronto in House of Commons from 1887-96. He was a warm supporter of Imperial Federation. Elected president of the Ontario Bank in 1894. Died in London. Eng., 18th January, 1912. Photograph, colored. Size 4 x 5. Head and shoulders. See 966, 3653.

630—BLAIKIE, JOHN LANG—President Consumers' Gas Company, 1906-12—A Scot, born near St. Boswell's, Roxburghshire, Scotland, receiving his early education at Melrose and Edinburgh. Came to Canada in 1858, and established in Toronto the financial brokerage firm of Blaikie & Alexander. From 1871 until his death in February, 1912, he was president of the Canada Landed and National Investment Co. Photograph, colored. Size 4 x 5. Head and shoulders.

631—AUSTIN, ALBERT W.—President Consumers' Gas Company, 1912-16—He was born in Toronto, 27th March, 1857, and educated at Upper Canada College, is a director of the Dominion Bank, and present president of the Gas Company. Mr. Austin is a son of James Austin, a former president of the Gas Company, and is also engaged in financial business in Toronto. Photograph, colored. Size 4 x 5. Half length.

632—GIVINS, GEORGE EDWARD—Youngest son of Colonel James Givins, Superintendent of Indian Affairs. He was on the medical staff in India for many years, and died in Toronto in the sixties. Photograph, colored. Size 4 x 5. Head and shoulders.

633—DICK, CAPTAIN THOMAS, 1809-74—A well-known lake mariner. Captain Dick from the early forties plied to and fro on Lake Ontario, having had command of various vessels prominent in lake shipping, such as the "Chief Justice Robinson," and from 1852-8 the "Peerless," which afterwards became a transport in the Civil War, and in November, 1861, was wrecked off Cape Hatteras. Captain Dick retired about 1860, and two years later became proprietor of the Queen's Hotel (originally Swords'), Toronto, conducting the hostelry until his death in 1874. Photograph, colored. Size 4 x 5. Head and shoulders.

634—CONNOR, HON. GEORGE SKEFFINGTON, 1810-63—Born in Dublin, Ireland; took his D.L. degree at Trinity College, there. In 1832 he emigrated to Canada with William Hume Blake (afterwards Chancellor), first settling in Oro Township. He was called to the Canadian Bar in 1842, and some time afterwards became a partner in the firm, Blake, Morrison and Connor. Later he formed a partnership with Mr. George Boomer, afterwards Police Magistrate. Dr. Connor was one of the Commissioners appointed for consolidating the Statutes of Canada and Upper Canada in 1858. On that Commission he made it a specialty to consolidate and revise the Real Property Acts. In 1848 he was lecturer in law in Toronto University, and ten years later received appointment of Solicitor-General. From 1858-62 represented Oxford in Parliament. In January, 1863, he accepted a puisne judgeship of the Court of Queen's Bench, and a few months later died at his residence in Toronto. Photograph, colored. Size 3 x 4. Head and shoulders.

635—RIDOUT, HON. THOMAS, 1754-1829—Born in Sherborne, Dorsetshire, Eng., 1754. When twenty years of age he emigrated to America, proceeding to Annapolis, Md., where an older brother had already settled. In 1788 he came to Montreal and determined to settle in Canada. Became Sergeant-at-Arms, House of Assembly, 1794; two years later Registrar for the County of York; Clerk of the Peace, Home District, 1800; Surveyor-General, 1810; M.P.P., West York, 1812, and a member of the Legislative Council, 1824. His death occurred at York in 1829. Water color. Size 4 x 5. Head and shoulders.

636—HOWARD, MRS. JAMES SCOTT (SALOME MACLEAN)—A daughter of Captain Maclean, of the New York Loyalist Corps; born at Nashwaak, York Co., N.B. She subsequently married Mr. J. S. Howard, in Fredericton, N.B., where he settled in 1819. They later resided in Toronto for many years. Mrs. Howard's death took place here in 1857. The late Allan Maclean-Howard, clerk of the Division Court, was a son. Water color. Size 3 x 4. Head and shoulders. See 640.

637—ROBINSON, HON. PETER—Eldest son of Christopher Robinson, of the Queen's Rangers, and brother of Sir John Beverley Robinson, Bart., Chief Justice; was born in New Brunswick, 1785. He commanded a volunteer rifle company at the capture of Detroit in 1812; was representative of East Riding of York in Provincial Legislature, 1817-20, and afterwards member of Legislative Council. In 1827 was appointed Commissioner of Crown Lands, which position he held until his death in Toronto in 1838. Hon. Peter Robinson had a great deal to do with the settlement of Peterboro, Ont., which is named after him. From silhouette in color, in possession of Mrs. Christopher Robinson, Toronto. Size 4 x 5. Head, in profile.

638—LESSARD, MAJOR-GENERAL FRANCOIS LOUIS—Inspector-General Eastern Canadian Forces, 1915—Born in Quebec, 1860; educated at St. Thomas' College and the Commercial Academy at Quebec. In 1878 he entered the volunteer militia as a private in the Queen's Own Canadian Hussars at Quebec; gazetted as a lieutenant in the Quebec Garrison Artillery, 1879; from there transferred to the 65th Regiment of Montreal, 1884. Four years later he entered the Royal Canadian Dragoons as captain. In 1907 was made Substantive-Colonel and Brigadier-General, 1911. Served in the North-west Rebellion in 1885, and commanded the Royal Canadian Dragoons in the South African War; present at the relief of Kimberley. Received Queen's medal with five clasps. Promoted to be Major-General, and made Commander of the 2nd Military Divisional Area, Dec., 1912. On January 1st, 1915, received appointment as Inspector-General of the Eastern Canadian Forces. Chief staff officer Quebec Tercentenary Celebration, 1908, when he was presented to his Majesty King George V. Water color on platinum. Size 3½ x 4. Head and shoulders.

639—WILKIE, D. R., 1846-1914—President Imperial Bank, Toronto. Photograph, colored. Size 4 x 5. Head and shoulders. See 954.

640—HOWARD, MRS, JAMES SCOTT—Water color. Size 4 x 5. Head and shoulders. See 636.

641—HOWARD, JAMES SCOTT, 1798-1866—Treasurer Home District and United Counties of York and Peel. Water color. Size 3 x 4. Head and shoulders. See 611.

642—KETCHUM, JESSE, 1782-1867—"The Children's Friend" was born at Spencetown, N.Y.; came to York (Toronto) when a young man and engaged in the tannery business at the s.w. corner of Newgate (Adelaide) and Yonge streets. Mr. Ketchum was a most liberal citizen, especially in matters pertaining to secular education and religious instruction. The Bible and Tract Society owes a great deal to his generosity; he also gave the old Queen street site to Knox church, and very largely assisted in the building of the edifice. Several acres of land were given, too, by Mr. Ketchum for a children's park at Yorkville, in the neighborhood of the present Jesse Ketchum school. As a result of his bounty books are annually distributed in the Public and Sunday schools of the city. In 1845 he removed to Buffalo, where he continued his interest in children until his death in 1867. Water color. Size 4 x 5. Head and shoulders.

643—HORWOOD, GEORGE C.—He was born in 1808 and spent his early days in the Royal Navy. In 1840 he came to Toronto, and some two years later built the North American Hotel, a leading hostelry of the day, on Front street, near Scott. This establishment he conducted until 1855. It is now (1917) the site of the Pacific building and the John Macdonald warehouse. Mr. Horwood's death occurred in 1856. Water color. Size 4 x 5. Head and shoulders.

644—WRIGHT, EDWARD GRAVES SIMCOE—First white child born at York (Toronto), 1794. Son of Edward Wright, of the Queen's Rangers, Niagara and York, 1792-1802, who emigrated to America before the Revolutionary War. On its expiration he returned to the old land, where he remained for several years, but in 1792 came to Canada with the Queen's Rangers. His son, Edward Graves Simcoe Wright, in after years kept the Greenland Fisheries Tavern, north-west corner of Front and John streets, Toronto. Water color, from an oil in possession of his great-grandson, Edward H. Rodden, Toronto. Size 4 x 5. Head and shoulders.

645—BAIN, JAMES, D.C.L.—Chief Librarian, Toronto Public Library, 1883-1908—Photograph, colored, from portrait in possession of his son, Prof. J. Watson Bain, Toronto. Size 4 x 5. Head and shoulders. See 977.

646—SCADDING, JOHN, JR.—Eldest son of John Scadding, Sr., of Wolford, Devon, who emigrated to Canada in 1792. The Scadding home in York was just over the Don. The late Rev. Dr. Henry Scadding was a brother of John Scadding, Jr., while H. Crawford Scadding, M.D., of Toronto, is his grand-nephew. Water color from a portrait in possession of Dr. H. Crawford Scadding, Toronto. Size 3½ x 4. Head and shoulders.

647—GOODWIN, LT.-COL. HENRY—Born in Ireland in 1794. Enlisted in the army and served in Bull's Brigade, Royal Horse Artillery, at Quatre Bras and Waterloo. He afterwards came to Canada, and on the formation of the County of York Volunteer Militia Field Battery, December, 1856, was appointed sergeant-major and drill instructor. From 1855-65 he was fencing master at Upper Canada College, and was a member of the Queen's Own Rifles. His death occurred at the Old Fort, Toronto, February 17th, 1877. Photograph, colored. Size 4 x 6. Full length.

648—ROBINSON, WILLIAM B., M.P.P.—Third son of Christopher Robinson, of Queen's Rangers, and brother of Sir John Beverley Robinson, Bart., Chief Justice; born at Kingston, Upper Canada, 22nd December, 1797. He represented the county of Simcoe in House of Assembly for twenty-five years, was Inspector-General for Canada with a seat in the Executive

Council. Held the office of Chief Commissioner of Public Works, 1846-7. Also a commissioner of the Canada Company. Died at Toronto in 1873. Water color from a portrait in possession of Mrs. Christopher Robinson, Toronto. Size 4 x 5. Head and shoulders.

649—ARMSTRONG, WILLIAM, C.E.—In 1851 Mr. Armstrong, then a young man, thirty years of age, came to Canada from Dublin, his native place, and settled in Toronto. Under Mr. A. M. Ross he was one of the engineers employed in connection with the narrow gauge Grand Trunk Railway. In 1870 he went out as chief engineer with the Wolseley expedition, and while a member of the party made many sketches. Mr. Armstrong was one of the early members of the Canadian Yacht Club, whicn afterwards became the Royal Canadian Yacht Club, and was for many years a moving spirit in that organization. In addition to his work as an engineer, William Armstrong was an artist of considerable merit. His death occurred at his residence, the "Priory," Augusta avenue (formerly Esther street), Toronto, 1914. Water color. Size 3 x 4. Three-quarter length, sitting. See 1116.

650—HIND, DR. HENRY YOULE, 1823-1908—He was born in Nottingham, England, and came to Canada in 1846. In 1848 he was appointed mathematical master and lecturer in chemistry in the Normal School, Toronto, and later professor of chemistry and geology, Trinity University, Toronto. While still a professor at Trinity, he was in 1857 named by the Canadian Government as geologist to the first Red River Expedition, and the following year placed in command of the Assiniboine and Saskatchewan exploring expedition. He explored part of Labrador, made a survey of New Brunswick, examined gold districts of Nova Scotia and the mineral field of the north-eastern part of Newfoundland. He wrote many books; was granted the degree of D.C.L., by King's College, Windsor, in 1890. His death took place at Windsor, N.S. Photograph, colored, from a portrait in possession of his daughter, Miss Margaret Hind, Windsor, N.S. Size 3 x 4. Head and shoulders.

651—SMALL, CHARLES COXWELL—Son of Major John Small: was born at York (Toronto), in 1800. In 1825 he succeeded his father as clerk of the Crown and Pleas. He was a member of the Agricultural Society of York County, and was connected with the militia of the county, being for many years colonel of the Fourth Regiment of North York Militia. His death took place at Berkeley House, Toronto, 17th March, 1864. Water color from a drawing in possession of Mrs. Small, Berkeley House, Toronto. Size 4 x 5. Head and shoulders.

652—MUIR, ALEXANDER—Author of "The Maple Leaf"—He was born in Lesmahagow, Lanarkshire, Scotland, 5th April, 1830; died in Toronto, 26th June, 1906. His parents emigrated to Canada in 1834. Alexander received his early training in his father's school in Scarboro township, attended Queen's College, Kingston, from 1847-50, receiving his degree of B.A. there in April, 1851. He taught in Scarboro, Newmarket, Beaverton and Toronto; was extremely patriotic and very fond of sports. Water color. Size 3 x 4. Head and shoulders.

653—MUIR, JOHN, 1802-65—Father of Alexander Muir, author of "The Maple Leaf Forever"—John Muir was born in the village of Crawford-John, Lanarkshire, Scotland. He, however, removed to Lesmahagow, or, as it is also known, Abbey Green. For some years he taught school near here, and in 1833 emigrated to Canada, with his wife and children. He settled in the Township of Scarboro, where he followed his profession, teaching first in a log building erected in 1817, on lot 31, concession 3, of the township. He retired about 1855. Mr. Muir was fond of quoits, an enthusiastic checker player, and at one time was captain of the Scarboro

Cricket Club. The pupils of his early schools, as a token of their regard and respect, erected in the churchyard of St. Andrew's, Scarboro, a monument to his memory. Water color from a daguerreotype in possession of Mrs. Muir, widow of Alexander Muir. Size 4 x 5. Head and shoulders.

654-661—Post Offices, York and Toronto, 1816-1917.

654—FIRST POST OFFICE, 1816-27—A small, unpretentious log house on the east side of Frederick street, south of King. Hon. William Allan was the first postmaster. In the early days the mails were extremely irregular, communication being by stage and sailing vessel only, and letters and papers mailed in England in November did not arrive in York until the following spring. Water color. Size 5 x 7.

655—SECOND POST OFFICE, 1828-9—On the south side of Duke, between George and New (Jarvis) streets. On the retirement of Mr. Allan from the Postmastership in 1828, James Scott Howard, father of Allan McLean Howard, was appointed in his stead. Pending the completion of Mr. Howard's new residence on the west side of George street, the post office was removed temporarily to the small one-storey house on Duke street, shown in the picture. The site is now Nos. 9 and 11 Duke, Toronto. Water color. Size 5 x 7.

656—THIRD POST OFFICE, 1830-4—When Mr. Howard's new residence was completed, about 1830, the post office was transferred to it. The new building was a commodious two-storey one on the west side of George street, a little below Duke, just behind the Nipissing Hotel. The south end was used as the post office, while the Howard family resided in the remainder of the house. Water color by F. V. Poole. Size 6½ x 7.

657—FOURTH POST OFFICE, 1836-38—North side of Duke street, a little east of George, and just east of the Bank of Upper Canada. It was built by Mr. Howard about 1834, as a private residence, and the post office removed from George street to the east corner of the new dwelling about 1836. On Mr. Howard's resignation from the postmastership the family discontinued residence here. The house is now the east part of De La Salle Institute, Toronto. Water color. Size 5 x 7.

658—FIFTH POST OFFICE, 1839-45—On the north-west corner of Yonge and Front streets. When Mr. Charles Berczy became postmaster he established the post office in a one-storey structure, occupying as a residence a red brick building immediately west, and in off the street about fifty feet. This was previously the residence of Chief Justice Macaulay. In 1845 the site was purchased by the Bank of Montreal and the first bank building erected there. It was subsequently demolished and the present (1917) structure built. Water color. Size 4 x 7.

659—SIXTH POST OFFICE, 1845-52—Situated on the north side of Wellington street east, west of Berczy street, now Leader lane. It was a one-storey white brick building, afterwards painted red; two storeys of red brick were also added subsequently. A part of the Imperial Bank now occupies the site. Up to 1852 the Post Office Department was under the Imperial Government, but almost simultaneously with the introduction of the bonding system through the United States the business was transferred to the Canadian Government and the mails began to arrive once a week via Boston and New York, alternately. Water color. Size 4½ x 5.

660—SEVENTH POST OFFICE, 1852-73—On the appointment of Mr. Joseph Lesslie as postmaster, the post office was removed to the handsome new structure with cut stone front, built after the Ionic style of architecture, on the west side of Toronto street. Although the building was larger than its predecessors it was soon tried to its utmost capacity. Water color. Size 5 x 7.

661—EIGHTH POST OFFICE, 1873-1917—Nos. 36-42 Adelaide, at the head of Toronto street. It was erected in 1873, during the postmastership of Mr. Joseph Lesslie, and is of white brick, faced with cut stone. Although almost doubled in size on the north, or Lombard street side, it is quite inadequate to the present needs of Toronto and a new building is being projected (1917). Water color. Size 6 x 8.

662—BALDWIN RESIDENCE, YORK (TORONTO), 1804-13—North-west corner of Front (Palace) and Frederick streets—The property originally belonged to the Hon. Peter Russell, and was for some time occupied by Captain John Denison, the first of the Denison family to settle in Canada. The house shown in the picture became the home of Dr. William Warren Baldwin in 1804, and in that year his son, Hon. Robert Baldwin, was born there. At a later date the house was the printing office of William Lyon Mackenzie, when he published the Colonial Advocate. Water color by D. M. G. Whyte. Size 5½ x 6. See 717.

663—OLD FORT, YORK (TORONTO)—View looking towards the north-west. During Governor Simcoe's administration a fort was built at York by the Queen's Rangers, the first regiment to be quartered at the garrison. It was situated on the west side of Garrison Creek, east of the site of old Fort Toronto, or as its official name was, Fort Rouille, built by order of Louis XV. The large frame building shown was used as barracks for the soldiers, while the officers were quartered in the brick cottages. Water color. Size 5 x 9.

664—GARDENER'S ARMS INN, YORK (TORONTO)—Second building east side of Yonge street, below Charles. The land on which the hostelry was built was originally a part of the Elmsley estate, and was a two-storey frame structure, having a narrow one-storey extension in front and a small wing at the northern end. Just north of it, and conducted in connection with the inn, was the "Vauxhall Gardens," deriving its name from the famous London resort. Water color by F. V. Poole. Size 5 x 7.

665—TECUMSEH WIGWAM, TORONTO—A small one-storey log cabin on the north-west corner of Bloor street and Avenue road. It was built about 1850 by David King, a Yorkville laborer, for many years was a popular drinking place. It was demolished in 1874 and the Albert Nordheimer residence erected on the site. Now (1917), however, the lot is vacant. Water color. Size 5 x 7.

666—SUN TAVERN, TORONTO—About 1825 John McIntosh, one of three brothers, each of whom commanded a vessel on the Great Lakes, erected as a hotel a large square, white frame structure at the north-west corner of Yonge and Queen streets, opposite Good's foundry. It was at first known as the "Sun Tavern," and occupied successively by Charles Thompson and a Mr. Wilson. About 1830 the builder's brother-in-law, Thomas Elliott, assumed management. It did a thriving business and became the headquarters of the leaders of the Radical party, McIntosh being a brother-in-law of William Lyon Mackenzie. The name of the inn was later changed to the "Falcon," and then to the "Craven Heifer." In 1855, while under the proprietorship of Mr. Henry Fulljames, it was destroyed by fire. Water color. Size 5 x 7.

667—OLD FORT—View at the west end about 1860—The cottages shown north and south of the gateway were for the accommodation of the officers of the regiments stationed in the Fort from 1816-70. The gate at which the people are standing is the western entrance. Water color. Size 5 x 10.

668—**EASTERN AND MAIN ENTRANCE TO THE OLD FORT, YORK (TORONTO)** 1796-1812—It was reached by an ascent from the Garrison Creek Ravine. Strong, iron-studded portals protected the arched gateway. The Queen's Rangers' Masonic Lodge (Lodge No. 3 of Ancient York Masons) met from 1799-1800 in the southernmost of the row of log houses, near the flagstaff. When York was occupied by the Americans in 1813 these houses were unharmed. Water color. Size 4 x 7.

669—**HOME OF WILLIAM LYON MACKENZIE**—On the west side of York street, half way between Queen and Richmond, Toronto—In this modest two-storey, red brick dwelling William Lyon Mackenzie lived during the stormiest part of his career. It was the home of Mackenzie and his family from early in 1836, and it was here that he edited "The Constitution." Here also the Rebellion of 1837 was planned. On the collapse of the uprising Mackenzie fled to the United States. The family, however, remained in the house for a short time, Mrs. Mackenzie joining her husband at Navy Island, 29th Dec., 1837. The York street house was for a time occupied by Andrew Patton, Barrack Master, and father of the late Hon. James Patton. Water color by F. V. Poole. Size 6 x 7.

670—**JONATHAN SCOTT'S HOUSE, TORONTO**—It was built about 1825 by Jonathan Scott, a butcher in the market, and was situated at what is now the south-east corner of Yonge and McGill (Magill) streets, on land purchased by Mr. Scott from Capt. John McGill, whose name is perpetuated in McGill street. The Scott home was the only house of any size, for a time, between the Green Bush Tavern, Yonge and Shuter streets, and the Red Lion Hotel, Yorkville. It was torn down to make room for the old Y.M.C.A. building, erected 1888, used at present as a store and office building. A new Y.M.C.A. building was opened in October, 1913, on College street. Water color. Size 6 x 7.

671—**OLD FORT, YORK (TORONTO)**—View from the west side— The two blockhouses in the picture were built in 1816. The battery on the south, or lake side, is also shown. Water color. Size 6 x 10.

672—**BATTERY ON THE SOUTH SIDE OF OLD FORT, YORK (TORONTO)**—Overlooking Lake Ontario. The guns shown were not those used during the War of 1812-15. About 1860 they were removed to Kingston. Water color. Size 4 x 8.

673—**BERCZY COTTAGE, TORONTO**—It was situated on the north side of Carlton street, just east of Yonge street. The cottage itself was destroyed about 1870, but the foundations have been rebuilt upon and Nos. 6 and 8 Carlton stand on site. Mr. Berczy, third postmaster of Toronto, was the son of William Berczy, who took an active part in connection with the settlement of Markham, Ont. Water color from a photo in possession of Mrs. Charles de Moll Berczy, Fort Scott, Kansas. Size 4 x 6.

674—**SMITH HOMESTEAD TORONTO (YORK),** 1794—North-east corner Duke (King) and Caroline (Sherbourne) streets. About the time of Governor Simcoe's arrival from Niagara, William Smith, Sr., an experienced builder, settled in Toronto. He assisted in laying out the town and was one of the first to draw a building lot, erecting thereon a log cabin, which shortly afterwards was pulled down and a frame dwelling built. Smith, who built many of the earlier houses in York, lived here until 1819. Water color by F. V. Poole. Size 5 x 7.

675—**GIVINS HOMESTEAD, "PINE GROVE,"** 1804-91—Front view. Water color. Size 6 x 8. See 272, 280, 681.

676—HOME OF JOHN LOGAN, A PIONEER TORONTO FLORIST— It was a small, picturesque, one-storey-and-a-half cottage, the first dwelling erected at the north-east corner of Church and Shuter. In the garden at the rear Logan cultivated vegetables and flowers, while his wife sold the produce at the market. Subsequently the cottage fell into decay and was replaced by a storey-and-a-half building, occupied for a number of years as a saloon by John Elliott. This, however, was demolished many years ago and a brick residence erected by the late Dr. J. F. W. Ross. Water color. Size 4 x 7.

677—RICHMONDS' BLACKSMITH SHOP—North-east corner of Queen and William (Simcoe) streets, Toronto—It was owned by William Richmond, wheelwright, and Robert Richmond, blacksmith, from 1850-60. The site is now (1917) occupied by Nos. 170-2 Queen street west. It was within a few yards of the old shop that the celebrated Brown-Cameron election riot took place in 1858. Water color by F. V. Poole. Size 5 x 7.

678—BLOCKHOUSE AND ENTRANCE TO OLD FORT, YORK (TO-RONTO)—The row of buildings to the right of picture were guard houses, occupied by the military from 1816-69. The large blockhouse stood in the centre of the parade ground. The entire front outside of the pickets has been completely changed since 1870. Water color. Size 5 x 7.

679—YONGE STREET, BELOW KING, TORONTO, 1850-70—View of part of the west side, north from Melinda street. The buildings shown are the commercial salesrooms of F. C. Capreol (now site of south end of Dominion Bank building), the wholesale dry goods warehouse of John Robertson, father of J. Ross Robertson, and the auction rooms of Andrew Henderson, father of Charles M. Henderson, the well-known Toronto auctioneer. The Robertson building was afterwards a part of the St. Charles, with its front remodelled, and the Henderson building became the southern portion of the old Dominion Bank building. The new (1917) structure of the Dominion Bank occupies the whole of the Yonge street block from King to Melinda streets. Water color by F. V. Poole. Size 4 x 7.

680—GIVINS HOMESTEAD, TORONTO—View of the drawing-room— To the left is seen Miss Cecil Givins, in the early days one of the belles of York military and Government circles, a daughter of Col. James Givins, and a sister of the Rev. Saltern Givins. She was a life-long resident of the old homestead. Resting on the ottoman to the right of the picture is Col. Givins' sword, worn by him on April 27th, 1813, when at the head of a force of sixty Glengarry Fencibles and a few Indians he ineffectually strove to stem the tide of the American invasion. It is said that more dignitaries visited this cottage from 1804-30 than any other home in York. Water color. Size 6½ x 7.

681—GIVINS HOMESTEAD, "PINE GROVE"—Rear view. Water color. Size 5 x 7. See 272, 280, 675.

682—JESSE KETCHUM'S HOUSE, YORK (TORONTO)—Opposite his tannery, which stood on the south-east corner of Newgate (Adelaide) street and Yonge. Mr. Jesse Ketchum erected a large, white frame, square-turreted residence after the American style. The exact date of building is unknown, but it was probably 1813-14. About 1838-9 the dwelling was destroyed and the site cut up into building lots. The site is now the row of brick stores on the west side of Yonge from Adelaide to Temperance streets. Water color. Size 5 x 7.

683—COLLEGE AVENUE LODGE, TORONTO, 1830—One of four lodges of similar design erected by John G. Howard, the well-known Toronto architect. It stood on the north side of Queen street, at the corner of College avenue (west side of the present University avenue), and was occupied for many years by Mark Fitzpatrick, a one-time caretaker of the University property, and afterwards by his widow. Water color. Size 4 x 7.

684—JOHN SLEIGH'S HOUSE, TORONTO—This two-storey rough-cast house on the north side of Duke street, between George and Caroline (Sherbourne), was erected in 1835 by John Sleigh, one of the best-known local cattlemen and butchers of his time. About 1870 he removed to Yorkville, where he died some years later. The house was demolished in 1912. Water color by F. V. Poole. Size 5 x 6.

685—BISHOP STRACHAN'S RESIDENCE, YORK (TORONTO), 1818-1900—Front street west, directly opposite the main entrance of the Union Station. The "Palace," a handsome structure of red brick, occupying, with its grounds, the entire square bounded by Graves (Simcoe), Market (Wellington), York and Palace (Front) streets, was the third brick building in York, the first being the Parliament buildings, and the second the St. George, or Canada Company building, n.e. corner King and Frederick streets. The residence was built by Rev. John Strachan, first Anglican Bishop of Toronto, and occupied by him until his death in 1867, then being rented for a boarding house. About 1900 it was demolished to make way for warehouses. Mr. J. Ross Robertson had a chair made of the oak threshold of the Bishop's home, and in 1904 presented it to the University of Trinity College, which was founded by Bishop Strachan. The chair stands in the Convocation Hall of the College. Water color. Size 5 x 7.

686—BIRD, LENNOX AND CHARLTON HOTEL, TORONTO—A Queen street view—It was a frame building, situated between James and Teraulay streets, and erected in 1827 by John Bird, who occupied it as a store and residence. After Mr. Bird's death the property became a tavern, and was kept by his son, Joseph, for some years. It subsequently passed through various hands, and finally came into the possession of William Charlton, who continued the business until about 1860. After his decease his widow carried it on for two years, when she remarried and transferred the property to James Spence, who in turn conveyed it to James Lennox. The site is now a part of the City Hall Square. Water color. Size 5 x 7.

687—RICHARD HARPER'S HOUSE—A pioneer Toronto residence, south-east corner Queen and Simcoe streets. Richard Harper, with his son John, came to York in 1818, and on his arrival purchased an acre of land at the s.e. cor. Lot (Queen) and Graves (Simcoe) streets. Some time afterwards he erected the frame dwelling shown in the picture, which, for a time, was the residence of the Rev. Joseph Hudson, chaplain to the forces. At a later date it served as the home of the Rev. John Wenham, curate of St. James' Church (Cathedral), and in 1849-51 was occupied by Mr. Owen, of the firm of Owen, Miller & Mills, King street, carriage manufacturers. About 1855 the dwelling was converted into a shop. It was altered considerably in the summer of 1912, and now is a gents' furnishing store. Water color by F. V. Poole. Size 5 x 7.

688—DOEL'S HOMESTEAD AND BREWERY, YORK (TORONTO)—In 1827 John Doel, an Englishman who came to York from the United States in 1818, erected a two-storey frame residence at the north-west corner of Bay and Adelaide streets. At the rear he built a frame "L"-shaped structure which was used as a brewery until 1847, when it was burned. Mr. Doel was associated with the leaders of the Reform party, and during the exciting days preceding the Rebellion of 1837 the house and brewery formed the principal rendezvous of the agitators. Doel and Mackenzie, however, disagreed as to the method of procedure, and the former withdrew his support from the party. The residence still (1917) stands. Water color by F. V. Poole. Size 4 x 7.

689—HOME OF HON. PETER RUSSELL, YORK (TORONTO)— Russell Abbey, as the charming one-storey frame dwelling was known, was built in 1798, near the bay shore, on Palace (Front) street, at the foot of what is now (1917) Princess street (formerly Princes). Here Mr. Russell, who was Administrator of Upper Canada from 1796-99, died in 1808. The residence was afterwards for many years occupied by his sister, Miss Elizabeth Russell. She in turn willed the entire property of her late brother, to her cousins, the daughters of Wm. Willcocks, one of whom was the wife of Dr. William Warren Baldwin. After Miss Russell's death the house became the residence of Bishop Macdonell, and then of Dr. Bradley, immigration agent. When the latter vacated it a negro family named Truss came into possession, carrying on a shoemaking business there. The Abbey was burned October, 1856. Water color. Size 4 x 7.

690—BELLEVUE HOMESTEAD, TORONTO—An early residence of the Denison family. In 1815 Lieut.-Colonel George Taylor Denison, son of Captain John Denison, purchased park lot 17 and part of 18, adjoining "Petersfield," the property of the Hon. Peter Russell, and occupied by Captain John Denison. On the land (part of Bellevue square) purchased by the younger Denison, "Bellevue" was built. It was a large, comfortable house, lying far back from Queen street, but visible from it through the trees. The present (1917) Denison avenue was originally the drive up to the old residence. Water color. Size 6 x 7.

691—BERKELEY HOUSE, TORONTO—Homestead of the Small family, south-west corner King and Berkeley streets. The homestead was originally built of hewn timber by Major John Small, first Clerk of Executive Council, U.C., and was one of the earliest dwellings in York (Toronto). It was subsequently re-constructed by Major Small's son, Charles Coxwell Small, and although elevated and enlarged, the design and even a portion of the inner substance of the original structure was preserved. The residence, known as Berkeley House, was later converted into three dwellings, the central one containing the remains of the original log house. It still (1917) stands. Water color. Size 5 x 7. See 693.

692—ONTARIO HOUSE—North-west corner Church and Market (Wellington) streets, York (Toronto)—In 1834 it was conducted by William Campbell, who at one time kept the North American Hotel, Front street. In 1845 the Ontario House became the Wellington Hotel, with Russel Inglis as proprietor. It is said that the first room William Lyon Mackenzie entered on his return to Toronto from exile was the private sitting-room of this hostelry. Under Mr. Inglis' management the Wellington became so popular that he was forced to rent the two upper floors of the Coffin House Block, at the gore formed by Wellington, Front and Church streets, to supply adequate accommodation for his patrons. After giving up the Wellington, Mr. Inglis for a long time conducted the Western Hotel, north side of Wellington, between Scott and Yonge streets. His former hostelry became a tenement house and was eventually demolished to make way for the Bank of Toronto. Water color. Size 5 x 6.

693—BERKELEY HOUSE—Residence of the Small family. Water color from an old sketch. Size 4 x 7. See 691.

694—OLD ST. LAWRENCE MARKET, TORONTO—Front Street Entrance—The St. Lawrence Market was first opened for business in April, 1851. The main entrance was then in the centre of the frontage on King street, and consisted of a corridor with a line of shops stretching to the east and west on both sides through to Front. In addition there was a transverse piazza, one hundred feet deep, over which, on the first floor, were various public rooms. In 1904 the present market south of Front was completed and the lower part of the market remodelled, the shops

10

being removed and made into an arena. In 1912 the arena was altered and portions rented on the east and west sides to meat companies, and used by farmers' wagons on market days. Water color. Size 5 x 6. See 701-2.

695-7—Market Places of York and Toronto, 1803-1917.

695—FIRST MARKET PLACE, YORK (TORONTO), 1803-31—On the site of the present St. Lawrence Hall and Upper Market. The first market, which was established by Lieutenant-Governor Peter Hunter in 1803, was simply wooden shambles, forty-five feet long and thirty feet wide, running north and south, and situated in the middle of the block now occupied by the north part of the present (1917) St. Lawrence Market. In 1807 the Market Square was enclosed on the east, west and south sides with a picketing and oak ribbon, and in 1831 the building was demolished. Water color from a pen drawing by Rev. Dr. Henry Scadding, Toronto. Size 4 x 7.

696—SECOND MARKET PLACE, YORK (TORONTO), 1831-49—On the north part of the block facing King street, and now (1917) occupied by the St. Lawrence Hall and Upper Market. It was a quadrangular brick building, which was completed in 1833. Around all four sides of it, above the butchers' stalls, ran a wooden gallery, which at a political meeting in 1834 was so overcrowded that a portion of it fell, resulting in loss of life and severe injuries to numbers of the audience. The front of the building was destroyed in the great fire of 1849, and this led to the demolition of the entire market. Water color from a pen drawing made in 1848 by Rev. Dr. Henry Scadding. Size 5 x 7.

697—THIRD MARKET PLACE, 1851-1917—After the great fire of 1849, in which the front portion of the second market was destroyed, the present (1917) St. Lawrence Hall and Market was built, occupying the entire square bounded by King, Jarvis, Front and West Market streets. The St. Lawrence Hall was from its erection the finest hall in Toronto. Every public meeting, concert, oratorio, ball, bazaar, minstrel show, soiree, panorama, assembly or public dinner, down to 1871, was held in this hall. Great singers and speakers have also been heard within its walls—Jenny Lind, Mlle. Piccolomini, Anna Bishop, Adelina Patti, Elihu Burritt, "the learned blacksmith," Horace Greeley, D'Arcy McGee, Sir John A. Macdonald, George Brown, Bayard Taylor. The upper market, built 1902-3, in rear of the main structure on King street, is now used for farmers' wagons, while the butchers' stalls have been removed to the new or Lower Market, south of Front street, which was commenced in the summer of 1899 and completed in 1901. Water color by F. V. Poole. Size 6 x 7.

698—McLEAN HOMESTEAD, YORK (TORONTO)—Formerly known as Dunnstable. About 1820 the Hon. John Henry Dunn, Receiver-General of Upper Canada, built the two-storey red brick mansion of the picture at the head of Catharine street (Richmond), and here he lived until the death of his wife. In 1837 Chief Justice McLean, who had come to York from Cornwall, bought the residence, occupying it until his death in 1865, when it became the home of his son, Mr. A. G. McLean. In 1900 it was demolished, and Catharine street, which ran along the south side of the property, was opened up, connecting Richmond with Spadina avenue. Water color. Size 5 x 6.

699—HOME OF MAJOR HILLIER, YORK (TORONTO)—An English rustic cottage at the north-east corner of Bay and Front streets. Major Hillier, who was attached to the 74th Regiment, was aide-de-camp and military secretary to Sir Peregrine Maitland. He also belonged to the Masonic Order, being a well-known member of St. Andrew's Lodge. The cottage was originally a part of the property of the Hon. Peter Russell; in 1838 Dr. W. Warren Baldwin erected his town residence on the site, and this dwelling was subsequently conducted as a private hotel by Mrs. John Ellah; from 1863-4 it was used as a military hospital, and afterwards as offices for the Toronto, Grey, Bruce and Nipissing Railroad. Later it was the site of a large warehouse, destroyed in the great fire of 1904, and since that date has been vacant. Water color. Size 4 x 7.

700—SOUTH-EAST CORNER YONGE AND GOULD STREETS, TORONTO—About 1834 the two-storey brick building at the corner, on part of the McCutcheon property, was erected by John Wesley, who kept a seed store there for several years. The property was subsquently purchased by William Reynolds, a baker. Since then it has passed through various hands, as have the two brick buildings south of and adjoining the corner, also erected by Mr. Reynolds about 1848. In 1889 these buildings were demolished, and a hotel and several stores now (1917) occupy the site. Water color. Size 5 x 7.

701—OLD ST. LAWRENCE MARKET ARCADE, 1851-1904—Looking north from Front street. One of the most attractive features of the old market was the arcade, two hundred feet long by twenty feet wide. On both sides, running north and south from King to Front, were fruit and fancy shops at the north end, and butcher shops at the south. At the Christmas season during the fifties the arcade was one of the sights of Toronto, with its glittering toy stalls, profusion of evergreens and well-stocked, gaily decorated butcher shops. In 1904 the old market was converted into an arena, and is now used for farmers' wagons and the butcher shops were removed to the new building south of Front. Water color. Size 4 x 7. See 694, 702.

702—OLD ST. LAWRENCE MARKET—View on East Market (Jarvis) street. Water color. Size 5 x 7. See 694, 701.

703—RUSSELL'S HOTEL—A pioneer Toronto hostelry at the north-east corner of Church and Colborne streets. In the early days there stood at this corner a frame hotel kept by a colored man named Snow; but about 1848 the frame building was demolished and a brick structure erected by Joshua Beard, a one-time Mayor of Toronto. The new hotel was occupied successively by Snow & Wright, Robert Beard, Azro Russell and John Montgomery, proprietor of the famous Montgomery's Tavern of Rebellion times. During the tenancy of Beard and Russell the upper floors of the building were occupied by the Masonic and Orange Orders. Subsequent to Montgomery's retirement the structure was converted into stores. Water color. Size 6 x 7.

704—HOLLAND HOUSE—Wellington street west, Toronto—View from the garden. Water color. Size 5 x 7. See 722.

705—HOUSE OF PAUL BISHOP, TORONTO—Paul L'Eveque, or Bishop (the name having been Anglicized in Upper Canada), was a skilled French-Canadian mechanic, accounted the best lock-maker in Canada. It was he who built for Thornton Blackburn the first cab in Upper Canada. The Bishop cottage was a small red brick dwelling on the south side of Duke, a hundred feet east of Caroline (Sherbourne) streets. Water color by D. M. G. Whyte. Size 6 x 7.

706—LAMB'S HOTEL, TORONTO, 1855-8—North side King street west—This was one of the popular hotels of the city for a number of years. The buildings shown are William Harris' china shop, 1851-5, Angus Blue's house, in rear of which was his bath house, and the Racquet Court, of which he was manager. Mr. Thomas Lamb, after 1858, kept the Fountain restaurant on King street west. Water color. Size 6 x 8.

707—GLOBE OFFICE, TORONTO, 1853-60—King street west, on the site of the present (1917) Bank of Commerce. The building was originally the home of the old Commercial Bank of the Midland District (now the Merchants'), and then became the third office of the Globe. The first office of the Globe was on Yonge street, west side, next door to its present building. The second office was over the Nordheimer music store, King east. The fourth is on the south-west corner of Yonge and Melinda streets. During the Globe regime the east end of the King west structure was occupied by Angus Dallas, woodenware dealer, the outbuilding to the left, or east, by L. D. Campbell, an American, who established the first news depot in Toronto, and Wm. Faulkner, shoe dealer. The store to the west was that of John Goedike, grocer. Water color. Size 7 x 7.

708—GREENLAND FISHERIES TAVERN—North-west corner Front and John streets, York (Toronto). The tavern, erected in 1825, was conducted for many years by Edward Graves Simcoe Wright, who was the first white child born in York, and who afterwards became one of the first aldermen of the corporation, when the town of York became the City of Toronto. Subsequent to its construction, the hostelry was renovated throughout and somewhat enlarged. It was latterly known as the Beauchamp House. In 1902 it was demolished, the site now being part of the G.T.R. freight yards. Water color by F. V. Poole. Size 5 x 7.

709—RED LION HOTEL, YORK (TORONTO)—A rear view of the old building, showing the yard used by the farmers and their wagons on their way to and from the city. Water color. Size 5 x 8. See 710, 716, 718.

710—RED LION HOTEL, YORK (TORONTO)—On the east side of Yonge street, just north of Bloor, now Nos. 749-63. It was a large, white stuccoed building, originally clap-boarded, and was the first place for the accommodation of travellers in the district, subsequently known as Yorkville, being built some time between 1808-10 by Daniel Tiers, and very popular as a meeting room and ball room for more than a quarter of a century. The old hostelry continued its hospitality for nearly eighty years, passing through many hands during its long period of usefulness. Water color. Size 6 x 7. See 709, 716, 718.

711-14—Jails of York and Toronto, from 1800-1917.

711—FIRST JAIL, 1800-24—Situated on the south side of King street, at the corner of Leader lane. "It was," says Dr. Scadding in "Toronto of Old," "a squat, unpainted, wooden building with hipped roof concealed from persons passing in the street by a tall cedar stockade, such as those we see surrounding a Hudson's Bay post or a military woodyard." On different occasions the sheriff complained that the condition of the building was detrimental to the health of the persons confined there, and in 1824 a new jail was built. The brick buildings, erected about 1840, now (1917) occupy the site of the first jail, as does Leader lane, which runs south from King street. Water color. Size 4 x 7.

712—SECOND JAIL, 1824-40—A plain, substantial, two-storeyed red brick building, near the north-east corner of King and Toronto streets, at what would now be the corner of Toronto and Court streets. On three sides it was enclosed by a fifteen-foot picket fence, and in the jail yard so formed was erected the gallows on which Lount and Matthews were hanged in 1838. The gallows stood to the east of the building, and just about thirty feet south of the south line of the present Court street. A Court House was also built in 1824. the corner-stones of both it and the Jail being laid by the Lieut.-Governor on the same date. The former stood on the northwest corner of King and Church streets, about a hundred feet north of King. The parish stocks stood just west of the Court House. The Jail building was remodelled, and is now (1917) the York Chambers, Toronto and Court streets. Water color from a drawing by J. G. Howard. Size 5 x 7.

713—THIRD JAIL, 1840-60—The large, new jail, built of Kingston grey cut limestone, and surrounded by a stone wall about twelve feet high, was situated on Palace street (Front east), at the foot of Berkeley, the latter street being in those days continued down to the waterside in a narrow road. It was almost on the site of the third jail that the first frame buildings in York were erected before the end of the eighteenth century for the use of Parliament and the Law Courts. These buildings, with the books, documents and records contained in them, were destroyed in 1813, when the town was captured by the Americans. Five years later a plain, cubical, brick block was erected on the same site for the use of the Legislature, but this was accidentally destroyed by fire in 1824. The third jail, after being superseded, was occupied by a safe manufacturing company for a time, later being purchased by the Consumers' Gas Company and new buildings erected on the site. Water color. Size 7 x 8.

714—FOURTH JAIL, 1865-1917—On the north side of Gerrard street east, at Riverdale Park, just east of the Don. It is a massive-looking structure of white brick and cut stone, and is (1917) still in use. It was in the process of erection in 1858, but partly burned five years later, before being completed, and was not occupied as a jail until 1865. Water color. Size 6 x 7.

715—FIRST SPADINA HOUSE, RUSSELL HILL, YORK (TORONTO), 1830-37—Built in 1830 by the late Dr. William Warren Baldwin, surgeon-in-chief of the military forces in 1812. The property originally belonged to Hon. Peter Russell, Administrator of Upper Canada on Simcoe's return to England. On his death it came into possession of his sister. The estate finally became Dr. Baldwin's, through his wife and her sister, cousins of Miss Russell. Soon after falling heir to the estate, Dr. Baldwin laid out Spadina on a large scale, and on the hill, nearly three miles from the lake, he built his new home. The house was destroyed by fire in 1837 and rebuilt the following year. "Spadina" is an Indian word, signifying "A view from the hill." Water color by F. V. Poole. Size 6 x 7. See 720.

716—RED LION HOTEL, YORK (TORONTO)—A view of the barroom. Water color. Size 4 x 7. See 709, 710, 718.

717—BALDWIN RESIDENCE, TORONTO, 1838—Finding it inconvenient at certain seasons of the year to reside at "Spadina," Dr. William Warren Baldwin erected as a town house a substantial brick mansion at the north-east corner of Front and Bay streets, on the site of the picturesque old cottage occupied by Major Hillier. Hon. Robert Baldwin also occupied the paternal residence, and later the dwelling became in turn Ellah's Hotel, a military hospital, and the offices of the Toronto, Grey, Bruce and Nipissing R.R. It was demolished about 1884. A large warehouse stood on the site until the great fire of 1904, when it was destroyed, and up to 1917 has not been rebuilt. Water color by F. V. Poole. Size 6 x 8. See 662.

718—RED LION HOTEL, YORK (TORONTO)—Ballroom and public room—The great, old-fashioned assembly-room was a favorite social rendezvous for the young people of the day. It was in this room that William Lyon Mackenzie was presented with a cable chain and medal of gold, Jan. 2nd, 1832, by his admirers, in approbation of his political career. Water color. Size 5 x 7. See 709-10-16.

719—SHOP OF PAUL BISHOP, TORONTO—It was a large frame building, a little distance back from the street, and fronting southward on Duke, at the north-east corner of Duke and Caroline (Sherbourne) streets. Here Bishop plied his trade as a blacksmith for many years. When T. D. Harris came into possession of the property he enlarged and remodelled the shop, moving it to the street line and dividing it into two two-storey dwellings. Water color by D. M. G. Whyte. Size 6 x 8.

720—SECOND SPADINA HOUSE, RUSSELL HILL, TORONTO, 1838-66—Subsequent to the death of Dr. William Warren Baldwin, "Spadina" passed into the hands of his sons, Hon. Robert Baldwin and Captain Augustus Baldwin. The former died there in 1858. It is somewhat of a coincidence that Dr. Baldwin wished to establish a family in Canada whose head was to be maintained by the proceeds of an entailed estate, and his son, Hon. Robert Baldwin, carried through the Legislature of Canada the abolition of the rights of primogeniture. In 1866 the property was purchased by the late James Austin, president of the Dominion Bank and of the Consumers' Gas Company. Water color. Size 5 x 7. See 715.

721—GEORGE RIDOUT'S RESIDENCE, 1820—North-west corner of Dorset and Wellington streets, York, (Toronto)—The house, in its day considered a very stately mansion, was built by Mr. Ridout in the centre of a large block of beautifully wooded land. On Mr. Ridout's disposing of the property, it became the home of Bishop Stewart, second bishop of Quebec. Later Capt. Philpotts, R.E., Judge Jones, Dr. Boys, Bursar of King's College, and Samuel Sherwood, City Registrar, lived there. The mansion eventually became a lodging house, and in 1887 was demolished. The C.P.R. freight yards now occupy the site. Water color. Size 5 x 7.

722—HOLLAND HOUSE, TORONTO—South side of Wellington street west, now (1917) No. 63. Built in 1831 by the Hon. Henry John Boulton, and named after Holland House, Kensington, London, Eng., where the Hon. Mr. Boulton was born. The Toronto mansion was a large, turreted, castle-like building, stuccoed and lined in imitation of brownstone. Mr. Boulton was from 1831-2 Solicitor-General for U.C., and in 1833 was appointed Chief Justice of Newfoundland. On his departure from Toronto, Holland House became the residence of Mr. Truscott, the first private banker of Toronto, and afterwards of the Elmsley and Sherwood families. It was then sold by the Boultons to Alexander Manning, and subsequently became the quarters of the Reform Club. In 1904 it was demolished. When the Earl and Countess Dufferin were in Toronto in 1872 they stayed at Holland House. Water color by F. V. Poole. Size 5 x 7. See 704.

723—RESIDENCE OF JAMES AUSTIN, TORONTO—When the late Mr. James Austin took possession of "Spadina" in 1866 the property included eighty acres of land, used chiefly for farming. The house was almost entirely demolished and rebuilt on the old foundations. In the eighties Mr. Austin disposed of the western half of "Spadina," his son, A. W. Austin, and daughter, Mrs. G. A. Arthurs, inheriting the remainder. Sir John Eaton now (1917) occupies a new residence on the site of Mrs. Arthurs' home, while to the west of the Austin house, enlarged and occupied by Mr. A. W. Austin, is "Casa Loma," residence of Sir Henry Pellatt. The view gives the homestead during the lifetime of Mr. James Austin. Photograph, colored. Size 5 x 7.

724—HOME OF WILLIAM SMITH, JR., ON THE DON—Queen street east, near the Don Bridge, Toronto. William Smith, Jr., acquired the western portion of his father's lot at the north-east corner of Duke (King) and Caroline (Sherbourne) streets, and built a frame addition to his father's house. After the latter's death in 1819, the son occupied the property until 1832. In the meantime George Playter had erected a dwelling near the Don, and this was purchased by William Smith, Jr., who moved it across the road to land bought from John Scadding. An addition was made to the house for the accommodation of employes of a tannery erected by Mr. Smith, and when he decided to remove from King street, another addition was made on the east side. John Smith came into possession of the property on his father's death. Water color. Size 6 x 7.

117

725—"CATHEDRAL OF METHODISM" IN UPPER CANADA—South side Richmond street, between Yonge and Bay, Toronto—The corner-stone of Richmond Street Methodist Church was laid 20th August, 1844, and the dedication took place 29th June, 1845. It was a plain structure, the unique portico with four pillars being its only external ornamentation. In 1888 the building was dismantled, and since 1890 has been occupied with additions by the Methodist Book Room. The site is now (1917) Nos. 29-33 Richmond street west. This old place of worship was succeeded by "New Richmond," or "McCaul Street Church." Water color. Size 6 x 7.

726—TATTLE HOMESTEAD, TORONTO—South side of St. Clair avenue, opposite Forest Hill road. Mr. George Tattle, in 1839, bought a ten-acre lot on the south side of St. Clair avenue from a Mr. Burns, at that time a market gardener on the south-east corner of Bloor street and Spadina road. The property, on part of which the Tattle homestead was built, extended from Avenue road on the east, to Poplar Plains road on the west. In 1880 Mrs. Tattle, who survived her husband quite a number of years, sold the property to Joseph Francis, a son-in-law, who in 1907 laid it out in building lots, and on it now stand the homes of some of Toronto's most prominent citizens. Water color by J. T. Rolph. Size 7 x 14.

727—HOMESTEAD OF WILLIAM WARD, 1871—Rear view from Island Park—William Ward was the second son of David Ward, Sr., a pioneer settler on Toronto Island. The homestead in picture was built in 1870 and demolished about 1885. In the latter year William Ward bought the frame building of the Parkdale Canoe Club at Parkdale, removed it to the Island, and re-erected it on the site of his old home. It is now (1917) a restaurant. Mr. Ward died in Toronto, 1912. Water color. Size 7 x 12.

728—TORONTO, C.W., 1851—View of west end of city from the light-house on the peninsula (now Toronto Island). Water color by Wm. Armstrong, Toronto. Size 13 x 26.

729—THOMAS BRYAN'S LOCKSMITH SHOP, TORONTO, 1881— Front view—Colborne street, head of Scott street; built about 1859. A unique sign over the doorway told the passers-by that all business received attention on "the shortest notice." Water color by George Barker. Size 7 x 9. See 730.

730—THOMAS BRYAN'S LOCKSMITH SHOP, TORONTO—Rear view, 1881. Water color by George Barker. Size 6 x 9. See 729.

731—TORONTO (CENTRE) ISLAND, 1880—View of Long Pond and the first bridge erected crossing it, just west of John Hanlan's boathouse. The eastern part of the Island is shown, and behind it is the city, seen above the bridge at the left side of the picture. The bridge was a wooden one, built by the city, to replace a crossing of planks, used to provide a passage over the marsh at the east end of Long Pond before the place was dredged deep. It was in turn replaced by the present Hallam's Bridge in 1893. To the right of the picture is a two-storey house with a flat roof, built about 1879, and at one time owned by Patrick Gray, who lived at Hanlan's Point, and also had an hotel there. The house was torn down about 1894, and on its site the city built a house for the superintendent of Island Park. The small white cottage to the right of the Gray house was a fowl house for the swans at the pond in Island Park. Water color by J. T. Rolph, Toronto. Size 7 x 10.

732—HEAD OF ST. GEORGE STREET, TORONTO, 1890—West side, between Davenport road and Bernard avenue. To the left may be seen the tower of the Church of the Messiah, built in 1890. The buildings with the gables were on Davenport road. Water color by J. T. Rolph, Toronto. Size 11 x 14.

733—TORONTO ISLAND, 1866—Showing schooner "Sophia" at Gray's Wharf. Gray's, afterwards Heber's, Wharf, was situated in Blockhouse Bay, Toronto Island, where the schooner "Sophia," of which James Kidd was master in the fifties, was dismantled in 1864. Immediately to the south of the wharf, which has not been in existence for several years, is situated (1917) the City Park Department boathouse. Water color by Wm. Armstrong. Size 11 x 16.

734—COLLISION OF THE OLD TORONTO STEAMER "PEERLESS" WITH THE "STAR OF THE SOUTH"—In 1852 the "Peerless" was built on the Clyde, and launched 6th Jan., 1853. In the following June she commenced daily trips to Niagara and return. She left Toronto on 10th May, 1861, under Capt. Robert Kerr, having been purchased by J. T. Wright, of New York. Eventually she became a transport vessel in the Civil War, one of the Burnside expedition; was on 2nd Nov., 1861, while laden with cattle, caught in a gale off Hatteras, and the "Star of the South," in coming to her aid, ran too close, and collided, resulting in the wreck of the "Peerless." Water color from a sketch by an artist of Frank Leslie's Weekly, N.Y., on board "Star of the South." Size 6 x 12.

735—YACHTING ON LAKE ONTARIO, 1880—Showing the "Arrow" and "Gorilla," of the R.C.Y.C. fleet. The "Arrow" was a contestant in the famous regatta of 1860 in honor of the visit to Toronto of the late King Edward VII., then Prince of Wales. During his visit H.R.H. presented the R.C.Y.C. with a handsome champion cup, which is still styled the Prince of Wales' Cup, and sailed for annually. In 1865 the "Arrow" won the cup, her owner at that time being G. H. Wyatt, of Toronto. She was later owned by the late Judge Hamilton, of Kingston. The "Gorilla" was winner of the Prince of Wales' Cup in 1862-3-4, R. W. Standley being her owner in those years, and in 1872 she again appears as winner under the ownership of Capt. Gifford, of Cobourg. She was originally the American yacht "George Steers," designed by and named after the designer of the famous schooner "America," and for several years was one of the fastest yachts on Lake Ontario. Water color by Wm. Armstrong, C.E., Toronto. Size 10 x 14.

736—WINTER SCENE ON TORONTO BAY, 1869—Showing wreck of old "Provincial," formerly a freight steamer. She was sold to the R.C.Y.C. in 1860, fitted up as a clubhouse, and moored on the bay shore near the foot of Simcoe street. In the winter of 1869 she broke away from her moorings and was frozen in the bay, becoming a wreck, which was blown up by order of the Corporation. Water color by Wm. Armstrong, C.E., Toronto. Size 9 x 13.

737—YORK (TORONTO), 1823—Showing Palace (now Front street east) from the corner of Front and East Market Square, down to the old blockhouse that stood near the jail at the foot of Palace street. Water color copy, by E. Wyly Grier, of a sketch by an army officer of H.M. forces, stationed in York. Size 4 x 10.

738—YORK (TORONTO) HARBOR, 1793—North side of the bay, near the Old Fort. Water color, by E. Wyly Grier, from a drawing by Mrs. Simcoe. Size 4 x 7.

739—SCADDING BRIDGE AND HOUSE ON THE DON RIVER, YORK, 1794—John Scadding, Sr., the manager of Wolford, the Simcoe estate near Honiton, Devon, emigrated to Canada in 1792, his home or farm being just east of the Don River, near the Queen street crossing, Toronto. Mrs. Simcoe, in her diary, writes of this house being burned in January, 1794. Water color by E. Wyly Grier, Toronto, from a drawing by Mrs. Simcoe. Size 6 x 15.

740—GARRISON (OLD FORT), TORONTO, 1845-50—From a picture by J. Passmore; lithographed by Hugh Scobie. Water color by E. Wyly Grier, Toronto. Size 6 x 14.

741—FIRST ROYAL CANADIAN YACHT CLUB HOUSE, TORONTO ISLAND—Showing outbuildings on edge of pond. This club house was built in 1880, burned in 1904, and the present institution erected a year later. Water color by J. T. Rolph, Toronto. Size 10 x 13. See 533.

742—LIGHTHOUSE AND THE LAKESIDE HOME FOR LITTLE CHILDREN, TORONTO ISLAND, 1892—The Lighthouse, erected on Lighthouse Point, 1809, is the first and only example of a stone and mortar structure, that remains intact, of pioneer labor in York. Queenston and Kingston stone were the materials used. The Lakeside Home for Little Children, the summer sanitarium of the Hospital for Sick Children, Toronto, was founded in 1882, by J. Ross Robertson, and in July of that year the first detachment of convalescents from the mother hospital (then on Elizabeth street) was sent over. In 1891 a new up-to-date home was erected by Mr. Robertson, and on the 5th September formally transferred to the trustees of the Hospital for Sick Children. Since that time thousands of Ontario's little ones have been placed on the road to health by their summer stay at the Lakeside Home. The main building was destroyed by fire, April 22nd, 1915, and later rebuilt. Water color by J. T. Rolph, Toronto. Size 9 x 11.

743—REAR VIEW OF THE RIDOUT HOMESTEAD, YORK (TORONTO)—South side of Duchess street, between Ontario and Caroline (Sherbourne) streets, 1804-58. Mr. Thomas Ridout, who came to this country about 1788, was in 1810 appointed Surveyor-General of Upper Canada. Water color copy by E. Wyly Grier, Toronto, from original, by Gen. A. R. V. Crease, R.E. Size 14 x 18. See 747.

744—EASTWOOD HOUSE, TORONTO—A stone dwelling, built by John Eastwood, opposite the present (1917) Todmorden Hotel, on the old Mill road leading to the Don Paper Mills, and now known as Broadview avenue. After the death of Parshall Terry, in 1808, his grist mills came into possession of Colin Skinner and John Eastwood, brother-in-law of the Helliwells, and in 1825, in addition to the grist mills erected by Terry, Skinner and Eastwood started a paper mill, the only one in Upper Canada, with the exception of that of Matthew Crooks at Flamboro'. It was Mr. Eastwood who gave the English name of Todmorden to the village overlooking the mills. Water color by Owen Staples. Size 12 x 14.

745—"CITY OF TORONTO—From the Northern Railway Elevator." Lithographed by Alexander Craig, Toronto. The key which accompanies the picture gives some of the main points in 1873. Lithograph. Size 13 x 28.

746—TAYLOR PAPER MILL ON DON RIVER, TORONTO—The mill, primarily a grist mill, built in 1794, is just below Todmorden, on lot 13, township of East York. It was operated by Mr. Timothy Skinner for some years, and then Mr. Colin Skinner, who took Mr. John Eastwood into partnership; they used the building as a paper mill. It is said that the first paper in Upper Canada was made in this mill in 1826. The Flamboro' mill also claimed the prize offered by the Provincial Government, and the claim was compromised by a division of the money. In 1847 the property passed into the hands of the Taylor Bros. During their time it was twice destroyed by fire, and once during the ownership of the present owner, Mr. Robert Davies. The walls, which were of stone, stood, however, and a new roof and floors made the building as it was first built. Water color, by Owen Staples, Toronto. Size 18 x 22.

747—RIDOUT HOMESTEAD AND GROUNDS, YORK (TORONTO), 1804-58—Fronting on the north side of Duke street, a little east of the head of Princess (Princes street). On the right of the property was the old Indian burial ground, on the bank of the stream running through the valley from Moss Park. Water color copy by E. Wyly Grier, Toronto, from original by Gen. A. R. V. Crease, R.E. Size 13 x 18. See 743.

748—THIRD DON BRIDGE, TORONTO—Erected 1851, and covered in twenty years later. In 1878 it was swept away, and in October of the same year an iron bridge constructed, which was partially rebuilt and strengthened in 1893. In 1910 this bridge was removed about sixty feet south, and a new one erected on its site. Water color by R. Baigent. Size 10 x 14.

749—BROWNE, JOHN OLDSWORTH, F.S.A.—Civil Engineer and Deputy Provincial Surveyor, was born in Norwich, England, 1808, and came to Toronto in 1849. Was engaged in pioneer railway work in this country. In 1852 he published a fine map of the township of York, and did a large amount of survey work in and for the City of Toronto. In 1850 he delivered a lecture on railways in the old Mechanics' Institute, Court street, exhibiting a complete miniature locomotive made by Parks & Brothers, iron founders. Mr. Browne was one of the best-known surveyors in Canada West. He died in Toronto, 7th April, 1881. Photograph, colored. Size 4 x 5. Head and shoulders.

750-6—City Clerks of Toronto, 1834-1917.

750—PRICE (HON.) JAMES HERVEY—City Clerk, 1834—In 1828 he came to Canada from England, first settling in Dundas, U.C., but subsequently removing to Toronto, where he entered into a law partnership with John Roaf. In 1834 he acted as City Clerk, and in 1841 was elected by the Reformers to represent York in the United Parliament of Canada, being returned three times. Appointed, 1848, a member of the Executive Council of the Province of Canada, and also Commissioner of Crown Lands. Later he returned to England, where he died in 1882, at Shirley, Southampton. He was born in Wiltshire in 1799. Photograph, colored. Size 3½ x 4. Head and shoulders. See 286.

751—DALY, CHARLES—City Clerk, 1835-64—Born in Ireland in 1808, and received his education in Belgium and France. For a time he was engaged in library work at the Athenaeum, London. Came to Canada early in life. In 1835 he became City Clerk of Toronto, holding that position until his death in 1864. Silhouette. Size 3½ x 4.

752—CARR, JOHN—City Clerk, 1865-71. Photograph, colored. Size 3½ x 4. Head and shoulders. See 378, 591, 3513.

753—RADCLIFFE, STEPHEN—City Clerk, 1871-6—He was born in the township of Adelaide, Middlesex County, Ont., in 1837, and was the son of Colonel Hon. Thomas Radcliffe, of the 27th Inniskillen Regiment. Subsequently came to Toronto, and entered the service of the Corporation in 1851. In 1871 received the appointment of City Clerk, which office he held until his death in 1876. Photograph, colored. Size 3½ x 4. Head and shoulders.

754—RODDY, ROBERT—City Clerk, 1876-84—Entered the service of the City of Toronto in 1852, and for two years prior to his appointment as City Clerk acted as Assistant Clerk. He was born in Toronto in 1837, and was a son of Charles Roddy, of Clones, Monaghan, Ireland. He died in the city of his birth in 1885. Photograph, colored. Size 3½ x 4. Head and shoulders.

755—**BLEVINS, JOHN**—City Clerk, 1885-1900—The fifth City Clerk was a barrister, having been called to the bar in 1854. Twenty years later he was elected to represent St. David's Ward, continuing to do so until 1884. He was born in 1822, and died in Toronto, January 9th, 1900. Photograph, colored. Size 3½ x 4. Head and shoulders.

756—**LITTLEJOHN, WILLIAM A.**—City Clerk, 1900-17—The son of John Wilson Littlejohn, born in Plymouth, North Carolina, U.S.A., his ancestors having immigrated to Carolina from Inverness, Scotland, in the eighteenth century. Came to Canada when nine years of age, and for a time lived at Oil Springs, near Sarnia, removing in 1869 to Toronto. Here he received his education in the Public schools and at Upper Canada College. In 1874 he entered the service of the Corporation of Toronto and has been connected with it ever since. Photograph, colored. Size 3½ x 4. Head and shoulders.

757-9—**Registry Offices, County of York, 1829-1917.**

757—**REGISTRY OFFICE, COUNTY OF YORK,** 1829-50—In 1796 a registry office was established for the Home District—there was no County of York at the time—and Mr. Thomas Ridout appointed first registrar. During his term of office and that of his immediate successors the records were kept in private dwellings. Later Samuel Ridout, too, conducted affairs of the registry office in private houses for a time, but in 1829 built at his own expense a small brick building at 18 Newgate street, north side, now (1917) No. 102 Adelaide street east. A law was passed in 1849 that the registry office should no longer be kept in a private residence, but must be maintained in a public building, and at the same time the office was established as the county registry. The cottage in rear of the Newgate street building was that of Henry Mulholland, caretaker. Water color by John W. Cotton. Size 5 x 6.

758—**REGISTRY OFFICE, COUNTY OF YORK,** 1850-75—In accordance with the Act of 1849, the county built this one-storey, stone, fireproof building next and north of the present (1917) office of the Gas Company, on the east side of Toronto street, just north of Court street. The county and city registrarships were divided in 1859, when the office of the latter was removed to the Royal Insurance building, southeast corner Wellington and Yonge streets. Water color by John W. Cotton. Size 5 x 6.

759—**REGISTRY OFFICE, COUNTY OF YORK,** 1875-1917—A brick building erected at the northeast corner of Richmond and Clare (Berti) streets. The first registrar in this building was John Ridout, his term of office extending from 1855-94. His successors have been J. T. Gilmour, 1894-6; James Massie, 1896-1904, and W. J. Hill, 1904 to date. Water color. Size 5 x 6.

760—**CANADIAN (ROYAL) INSTITUTE, TORONTO**—North-west corner of Richmond and Berti (Clare) streets. In 1849 a number of gentlemen, chiefly architects, land surveyors and civil engineers, met in the office of Kivas Tully to consider the advisability of forming an organization which would unite the three professions throughout the country. In 1850 a constitution was adopted, Mr. (Sir) Sandford Fleming and Mr. E. R. Passmore being the leading organizing spirits. From 1864-76 the Canadian Institute so formed met in the building shown in the picture. It was built in 1850 by George Bilton, and first occupied by Dr. Primrose, who was followed by Thos. Haworth, hardware merchant. In 1876 it was torn down and a brick building erected, which was used by the institute until 1905. When the latter removed to its present (1917) home, 198 College street, in order to make its valuable library more accessible to the University professors and students, the old property was sold to the Sons of England. On April 2nd, 1914, the institute had its title formally changed to "Royal Canadian Institute." Water color. Size 4 x 7.

761—"ZION CHAPEL, ADELAIDE ST., TORONTO—Wm., Thomas architect. Printed in colours by Maclear & Co., King St., Toronto." Zion Congregational church (second) stood on the north-east corner of Bay and Adelaide streets, on the same site as the first church, burned in February, 1855; was dedicated 26th September, 1856. It had a spire (its predecessor having had a tower) which was blown down about two o'clock on the afternoon of the 12th April, 1865, in a terrific wind storm that swept Toronto. The spire was not rebuilt, but replaced by the lower portion being made into a square tower. The last service in the old church was held 3rd Dec., 1882, and the following March the congregation moved to College street, near Elizabeth. The Bay street building was used by a lithographing company, and as a theatre, until 1884. It was then demolished. The site is now (1917) an office building. Lithograph in color. Size 11 x 15. See 797, 1146.

762—RESIDENCE OF T. D. HARRIS, TORONTO—When Duke street was fashionable—In 1832, Mr. J. S. Howard, at that time postmaster of York (Toronto), built, as a residence for himself, a large three-storey red brick building on the north side of Duke street, No. 28, just east of George street. For a time part of the building was used as a post office. Mr. Howard vacated about 1838, and Mr. M. Davidson Murray lived there until 1845. Later, Mr. T. D. Harris occupied the residence, which was one of the best equipped of early Toronto homes. Mr. Harris was prominent in civic matters. He was chief engineer of the fire brigade, 1838-41; carried on the leading hardware business in Toronto, and from 1870-2, after his retirement, filled the position of harbor master. His death took place in January, 1873. The old residence is still standing (1917) as No. 42 Duke street, a part of De La Salle Institute. Water color. Size 4 x 5.

763—BARRETT'S HOTEL, NEWTONBROOK, 1790—On the south-east corner of lot 30, west side of Yonge street, near Thornhill. In the early part of 1811 Royal Arch Lodge No. 16 and its chapter removed from York to "Yonge street," selecting as a meeting place the home of Bro. Alfred Barrett, which was used as a tavern and frequented by farmers on their way to and from the town. It is not improbable that the anticipated trouble with the United States had something to do with the removal of the lodge from York; also a large proportion of the brethren lived on Yonge street. The old tavern was altered and improved in 1840, and until 1856 the lodge room was in existence. Now (1917) the site is vacant. Water color by John W. Cotton. Size 4 x 7. See 764.

764—BARRETT'S HOTEL, NEWTONBROOK, 1790—Interior of the lodge room of Royal Arch Lodge, No. 16. The room was in existence as late as 1856. The benches still remained around the room, as did the raised platforms at the stations of the Worshipful Master, Senior Warden and Junior Warden. Water color by John W. Cotton. Size 4 x 6. See 763.

765—OLD HOUSE ON CROOKSHANK'S FARM, TORONTO—Mr. Arthur Coffin lived in the cottage for over sixty years. It was built about 1820 on the west side of Crookshank's lane, now Bathurst street, at what would now be the south-west corner of Bathurst and Herrick streets. The Hon. George Crookshank (Cruickshank) owned property extending from Queen street to the north of Davenport road, which remained in his possession until 1851. Drawing in water color by J. O. Fowler, 1871. Size 6 x 8.

766—BAIN HOMESTEAD, SHERBOURNE ST., TORONTO—View in 1870—This pretty roughcast residence was built in 1851 by the late James Bain, bookseller, who died in 1908. It stood on the east side of Sherbourne street on a plot of ground between the n.e. and s.e. corners of Sherbourne street and the present Wilton avenue. Beech street (Wilton avenue) was extended from Seaton to Sherbourne, according to a plan dated 1857, and filed in the registry office. The property for this extension had been purchased, one parcel from James Bain on 13th Oct., 1855, and the rest from James Humphrey on 23rd Nov. of the same year. The Bain residence was moved about 50 feet to the n.e. corner of Beech and Sherbourne, and was occupied by Mr. Bain until 1900, when he moved to Kew Beach. In 1878 a by-law was passed changing Crookshank street, which ran from Yonge to George streets, and Beech street, running east from Sherbourne, to Wilton avenue. Wilton crescent, which connected Crookshank and Beech streets, was always known by that name. Mr. Bain sold the remainder of his property in 1906. Three years later the house was demolished and an apartment house erected on the site. During Mr. Bain's residence in the old house the garden at the south side was much admired, for he was a master florist and an expert in horticulture. Water color. Size 6 x 8.

767—NORTH-WEST CORNER YONGE AND COLLEGE STS., TO-RONTO, 1864—The old gates and caretaker's lodge—Under the lease in 1859, between the trustees of the University and the Corporation of Toronto, College street and University avenue were protected by gates to prevent these streets from being used as public thoroughfares. With the agreement of 2nd March, 1889, however, the gates were removed and the two main approaches to Queen's Park dedicated to the city as public streets. Although not stipulated in the agreement, it is understood that the reserved rights of the University apply on both sides of University avenue, from Queen to Bloor streets, and on both sides of College street, from Yonge street to a point a short distance east of Beverley street. In the foreground of the picture is seen the street railway track on Yonge street, constructed in 1861. The rails on College street were put down in 1869. Water color. Size 5 x 6.

768—HOOPER, EDWARD, 1808-1900—Proprietor of the oldest drug store in Toronto—Born in London, Eng., came to Canada in 1832, settling first in Kingston and then in Toronto, where he began his business career with Mr. Joseph Beckett, druggist, south side King street, just east of Jordan. When Mr. Beckett retired the firm name was changed to E. Hooper & Co. Mr. Hooper was on the Board of the Canada Permanent Society for years, and was one of the first members of the Board of the Confederation Life, and its vice-president until his death. Photograph, colored. Size 4 x 5. Head and shoulders.

769—HOOPER, MRS. EDWARD—She was a resident of Kingston and then of Toronto, where in 1836 she married (as Mrs. Binley) Edward Hooper, of the firm of J. G. Beckett & Co., druggists. Mrs. Hooper died in Toronto, 1893. Photograph, colored. Size 4 x 5. Head and shoulders.

770—STEGMANN, JOHN—Born in Germany, 1754, and came to America in 1776 with the Hanoverian troops. About 1800 he removed to York; commenced a survey of the town and township of York. He lost his life in the wreck of the schooner "Speedy," which went down off Presqu' Isle in October, 1804. The late John Stegmann, an official in the Courts of Assize, Toronto, was a grandson. Water color. Size 4 x 5. Head and shoulders.

771—GRANGER, FRANCIS HINCKS, 1829-1906—A well-known scenic artist in Toronto. He was born in Toronto, where for several years he was scenic artist at the Royal Lyceum Theatre, King street. He made an excellent water color of the city's water front, 1849-50, which has been reproduced in oils and presented to the Corporation of Toronto. During his residence in Niagara, from 1856, Granger did many pictures of the old town and surrounding district. Unfortunately, however, most of these were destroyed after his death, which took place at Niagara in 1906. Photograph, colored. Size 3 x 4. Head and shoulders.

772—**VETERANS OF** 1812—On the lawn of Sheriff Wm. Botsford Jarvis' house in Rosedale, Oct. 23rd, 1861. The occasion was the distribution of prizes of the Fifth Militia District Rifle Association, by Gen. Williams, "Hero of Kars." Reading from left to right, the group consists of:—Col. George Duggan, who at one time conducted a general store, corner King and George streets. Served in the militia; member of the first City Council. Died in Toronto, 1863. Rev. George Ryerson, lieutenant in First Norfolk Regiment. Captured at Detroit under Brock; later joined Incorporated Militia of U.C. as lieutenant; present at Stoney Creek, Beaver Dams, Lundy's Lane, and attack on Fort Erie. Also served in Rebellion of 1837. Died in 1882. Wm. Roe, a Toronto confectioner. Saved from capture a considerable portion of the public funds on taking of York by Americans, 1813, being at the time an employe in the Receiver-General's office. Jacob Snyder. Born in New Brunswick, 1790. With Brock at Detroit. Prominent in pressing into service teams of horses for conveying stores, ammunition and troops to Holland Landing and other points where it was feared Americans might attempt to land. Died 1879. Rev. Jas. Richardson. Born in Kingston, 1791. Master of warship in attack on Oswego. Afterwards became a bishop of the M.E. Church. Died 1875. Joseph Dennis, son of a U.E. Loyalist; owned and commanded a vessel on Lake Ontario in 1812. At the outbreak of the war his ship was attached to the Provincial marine, and subsequently captured by the enemy. Dennis was made a prisoner of war and held for fifteen months. Wm. J. Woodall came from England in 1807, settled in Kingston in 1825, and later in York. In Irish Dragoons for a number of years; was at Queenston Heights and served in Rebellion of 1837. Died in 1862. James Ross. Taken prisoner at capture of York, 1813. Afterwards settled in York Township. Removed to Toronto in 1858, and died at Newmarket ten years later. Col. Bridgeford, of Richmond Hill, came to Canada as a child. Colonel of the sedentary militia and captain in 3rd Incorporated Militia. Served at Lundy's Lane, Chippawa, Fort Erie, Detroit and Little York. Took part in Rebellion of 1837, and was made prisoner by Wm. Lyon Mackenzie. George Ridout was born in 1791; second son of Hon. Thos. Ridout. At Queenston Heights. Taken prisoner at capitulation of York, 1813. Died at Clinton, 1871. Tempera painting by Owen Staples from small photograph. Size 12 x 24.

773—**LAST MEETING OF THE CITY COUNCIL (TORONTO) IN THE OLD CITY HALL**—The former municipal building was on Front street, opposite the St. Lawrence Market. The last meeting in it was held on July 10th, 1899—Mayor John Shaw in the chair. With key. Photograph, colored. Size 13 x 20.

774-81—**High Constables and Chief Constables of Toronto, 1834-1917.**

774—**HIGGINS, WILLIAM**—High Constable, 1834—Born in the north of Ireland, 1794, came to Canada at an early age. He was high constable of the town of York from about 1825, and of Toronto in 1834. Subsequently he acted as high constable for the County of York for many years. His death took place 24th Sept., 1871, at his home, Kingston road, near Toronto. Photograph, colored. Size 3 x 4. Head and shoulders.

775—**KINGSMILL, GEORGE**—High Constable, 1835 and 1837-46—Emigrated to Canada about 1830, from his birthplace, Queen's Co., Ireland. For a number of years he was connected with the old Crown Lands Department of Upper Canada, but subsequently carried on an extensive provision business, supplying many of the principal sailing vessels and steamers trading at Toronto. Appointed high constable in 1835, being succeeded in that office by James Stitt. On the latter's resignation Kingsmill was again appointed, holding the position from 1837-46. Retired from business in 1847. Was born in 1808, and died at Galt, Ont., 1852. Photograph, colored. Size 3 x 4. Head and shoulders.

776—**STITT, JAMES**—High Constable, 1836—He was born in Ireland, 1804, emigrated to Canada about 1830, and was engaged for some years in general business. Subsequent to his retirement as high constable he went into the cartage business. About 1850 he was appointed locker in her Majesty's Customs at Toronto, and held office until 1874. He died 23rd November, 1891, and was buried in the Toronto Necropolis. Later his remains were removed to Mount Pleasant Cemetery. Photograph, colored. Size 3 x 4. Head and shoulders.

777—**ALLEN, GEORGE LITTLETON**—High Constable, 1847-52—Born in Sligo, Ireland, 1811, son of Wm. Allen, for forty years recorder of the city of Sligo. His mother was Anne Cartwright, daughter of Col. W. Cartwright. His father's mother was Anne French, sister of John French, of Rosscommon, Ireland, grandfather of General Sir John French, commander of the British Forces in France, 1915-16, through whom he was also related to Edmund Burke, the Irish orator. He arrived in New York, aged fifteen, and was employed for a time in a wholesale house in Fulton street. Later came to Toronto. On his retirement as high constable he became governor of the jail, retaining the position until 1872. His death took place in 1882. Mr. Allen's son, Thomas, was for some years in the office of Sir John A. Macdonald in Ottawa. Water color. Size 3 x 4. Head and shoulders.

778—**SHERWOOD, SAMUEL**—Chief Constable, 1852-8—He was a son of Judge Livius Peters Sherwood, who in 1841 was elected Speaker of the Legislative Council; born in Brockville, U.C., 1819; died in 1867. He married a daughter of Capt. Hugh Richardson, who in 1850-69 was harbor master of Toronto. Photograph, colored. Size 3 x 4. Head and shoulders.

779—**PRINCE, CAPT. WM. STRATTON**—Chief Constable, 1859-73—He was a son of John (Col.) Prince, barrister, of Cheltenham, Eng., who emigrated with his family to Canada in 1833 and settled on the Park Farm, near Sandwich. William Stratton Prince joined the army in 1837 and went to England, where he received a commission in the 71st Regiment of Light Infantry. He was in the Crimea, invalided home in 1854, returning to Canada two years later. After his retirement as chief constable he became warden of the Central prison, Toronto, which position he held until 1881. He married Charlotte, daughter of Samuel Risley, Government inspector of steamboats on the lakes. Capt. Prince died in Toronto. 1881. His father was a member of the Legislature of Upper Canada, and also of the United Parliament. Photograph, colored. Size 3 x 4. Head and shoulders.

780—**DRAPER, MAJOR FRANK C.**—Chief Constable, 1874-86—He was educated at Upper Canada College and at Troy, N.Y. He commanded the Upper Canada College company, attached to the Queen's Own Rifles, of which he was a member. In 1874 Major Draper, who was a barrister by profession, succeeded Capt. W. S. Prince as chief constable. During the term of the former, "Orders and Regulations of the Toronto Police Force" were published and distributed for the information and guidance of the members of the force. Owing to ill-health Major Draper resigned. He was a son of Chief Justice Draper, born at "The Lawn," a quaint old cottage at the n.w. corner Wellington and York streets, Toronto. Died 2nd July, 1894. Photograph, colored. Size 3 x 4. Head and shoulders.

781—**GRASETT, LT.-COL. HENRY JAMES**—Chief Constable, 1886-1916—A son of the late Dean Grasett, Toronto; born here, June 18th, 1847, and educated at Leamington College, England. In 1857 entered H.M. 100th Regiment (Royal Canadians), retiring as lieutenant in 1875. Gazetted lieutenant-colonel 10th Royal Grenadiers, Toronto, 1880, and commanded that regiment in the North-west Rebellion of 1885; present at Fish Creek,

Batoche, and in operations against Chief Big Bear's band. (Despatches; medal and clasp). In Fenian Raid, 1866, served with the Queen's Own Rifles; at Limeridge. (General service medal with one clasp). In 1886 he was appointed chief constable. Toronto, which office he still holds. Photograph, colored. Size 3 x 4. Head and shoulders.

782—FIRST RAILWAY SOD TURNED IN CANADA WEST—Inauguration of Ontario, Simcoe and Huron Railway, Oct. 15th, 1851, at Toronto. Water color from an old print. Size 5 x 7. See 263, 518.

783—BURIAL OF THE DEAD FROM RIDGEWAY—Some of the Queen's Own in Fenian Raid, 2nd June, 1866—Corporal Mark Defries, of No. 3 Company, and Private Christopher Alderson, of No. 7 Company, were buried in St. James' Cemetery, Toronto, 5th June, 1866. The bodies of Ensign Malcolm McEachern, No. 5 Company, and Private W. F. Tempest, No. 9 Company, were, after the service at St. James', sent to the Necropolis. Rev. H. J. Grasett, assisted by Rev. Alexander Williams, chaplain of the forces, officiated. The remains were escorted to the cemetery by the Provincial Battalion of Volunteers of the 5th Military District. Col. George T. Denison was in command. Gen. Napier and Lieut.-Col. Durie were present. The engagement between the Fenians and the Canadians was sharp and severe while it lasted, until finally the latter were forced to retire, hotly pursued to the Ridgeway station by the Fenians. In the years that have elapsed blame for the mistake in command, which for a time caused confusion in the ranks, has never been placed. Water color from old print. Size 5 x 7.

784—McCLAIN, CAPT. WILLIAM—A pioneer of the Great Lakes— He was born in County Monaghan, Ireland, 1823, and came to Canada in 1827. When quite a lad he shipped as cook on the old schooner "Ploughboy," Not for long did he stay, however, but went on the "Lord Nelson," a "big vessel" for her day. After that he sailed in the "Columbus," of Cleveland, and in 1844 launched out for himself in the "Jane Harper," which he bought from John Harper, Toronto. In 1848, Capt. McClain and Capt. Archibald Taylor bought the "Clarissa," another of the old-time "topsail schooners," and carried stone in her from Cleveland for the building of St. James' church, Toronto. In the mid-fifties, Capt. McClain took up farming in Essa Township, Simcoe County. Shortly afterwards he was appointed a magistrate, and in 1857 received a captaincy in the second battalion, Simcoe Militia, followed by the appointment as major in the ninth Simcoe Militia. For many years after his retirement Capt. McClain lived in Toronto, where he was well known in marine circles. His death took place in winter of 1914. Photograph, colored. Size 4 x 5. Head and shoulders.

785—HAMILTON, ALEXANDER—First Secretary of the York Pioneer Society. Born in County Cavan, Ireland, 1802, coming to Canada as an infant, with his parents. For many years he conducted a flourishing business as a decorator in Toronto. In 1832 he was on Newgate (Adelaide) street, north side, nearly opposite George (Toronto st. was then known as George, or Upper George). In 1856 his place of business was on Church street, near the corner of Court, and later on King near George. From 1840-2 he represented St. David's Ward as Councillor. His death took place in Toronto, 1883. Water color. Size 4 x 5. Head and shoulders.

786—BIRTHPLACE OF PROF. GOLDWIN SMITH—No. 15 Friar Street, Reading, England—The building with the entrance was the residence of Dr. Smith, father of Prof. Goldwin Smith. It is an old-fashioned, plain, red brick dwelling, partly covered with ivy, on one of the principal streets of Reading. It is commodious and in excellent condition, and is now (1917) occupied by the Reading Agency of the Royal Insurance Company of England. Mr. Smith resided in Toronto from 1871 until his death in 1910. Photograph, colored. Size 5 x 6.

787—UNWIN, CHARLES, O.L.S.—Born at Mansfield, Eng., in 1829. In 1843 he came to Canada, his uncle, Charles Unwin, being at that time a clerk in the Toronto Registry Office. Subsequent to his coming to Canada, young Unwin attended Upper Canada College for several years, and on leaving that institution, went to Weston to learn surveying with Colonel John Stoughton Dennis. In 1877 he was appointed attorney for the city to settle disputes between the corporation and property owners, with reference to the boundary between the Marsh, a survey of which he had made in 1872, and the broken front lots. From 1872-1905 he held the position of assessor, and city surveyor, 1905-10. He still (1917) resides in Toronto. Photograph, colored. Size 4 x 5. Three-quarter length, sitting. See 3577.

788—KILLALY, HON. HAMILTON H.—Born in Dublin, Ireland, January 2nd, 1800, and educated at Trinity College, being a gold medalist of that institution. In 1829 he came to Canada, where he pursued his calling of civil engineer. First lived in London and St. Catharines, Ont.; came to Toronto in 1853. From 1841-3 he was a member of the Executive Council and represented London, Ont., in the first Parliament of United Canada. Was President of the Board of Public Works, 1841-6, and Assistant Commissioner of Public Works, 1851-8. Engineer Welland Canal and Inspector of Railways, 1859. His death took place at Picton, Ont., March 28th, 1874. Photograph, colored. Size 3 x 4. Head and shoulders.

789—KILLALY, MRS (MARTHA JANE HANDY)—Born 8th Nov., 1808, at Bellbrook House, Abbeylix, Queen's County, Ireland. She subsequently married Hamilton H. Killaly (afterwards Hon. H. H. Killaly) and came to Canada with him in 1829. Her death occurred January 9th, 1906. Photograph, colored. Size 3 x 4. Head and shoulders.

790—ROMAIN, CHARLES EDWARD—Of Italian descent, the son of Pierre Romain, he was born at Point Levis, Que., in 1820. The family subsequently removed to Toronto, and young Romain received his education at Upper Canada College. For some time he conducted business at Cooksville, Ont., as general merchant and grain dealer, later returning to Toronto. He took an active interest in civic affairs, sitting in the Council as councillor, and from 1854-5 as alderman. The Romain building, now (1916) 83-93 King street west, was erected by him in 1857. Later, on his removal to Guelph, he was appointed collector of inland revenue, and afterwards inspector. His death occurred in Guelph, Ont., in 1902. Photograph, colored. Size 3½ x 4. Head and shoulders.

791—GAMBLE, MRS. JOHN (ISABELLA ELIZABETH CLARKE)—She was born at Stratford, Conn., 24th Oct., 1767, a daughter of Dr. Joseph Clarke, who in 1776 joined the British army in New York, and at the close of the Revolutionary War removed to New Brunswick (then a part of Acadia). In 1783 Miss Clarke married Dr. John Gamble, who ten years later went to Niagara as assistant surgeon in the Queen's Rangers, Mrs. Gamble remaining with her father until 1798. In that year she joined her husband at York, he having become surgeon of his regiment. When the Queen's Rangers were disbanded in 1802, Dr. and Mrs. Gamble went to Kingston. She remained there for some years after her husband's death, and then came to York (Toronto), where she died, 9th March, 1859. Water color, oval. Size 4 x 5.

792—CLARKSON, THOMAS, 1798-1872—A pioneer Toronto merchant. In 1835 he emigrated to Canada from England, where he was born, near Hull, Yorkshire, and settled in Toronto. Here he married Miss Sara Helliwell, daughter of Thomas Helliwell, of the Don Mills. Mr. Clarkson was engaged in the grain trade and shipping and was at one time a partner of Thomas Brunskill. From 1852-8 he was president of the Toronto Board of Trade. Mr. E. R. C. Clarkson, of the firm of E. R. C. Clarkson & Sons, is a son. Photograph, colored. Size 4 x 5. Head and shoulders.

11

793—**JOHN STREET, TORONTO**, 1852—From north-west and north-east corners of Queen street. The water color shows St. George's church, built 1845, and "The Grange," at the head of John street, residence of W. H. Boulton, Mayor of Toronto, 1845-6-7 and 1858. Commencing at the lane on the east or right of picture is the cottage of William Armstrong, C.E., a well-known artist. Then north are the residences of James Browne, Bank of Upper Canada; William Stanton, Commissariat Department; the third is vacant; then James Nation, Bank of Upper Canada; James Bovell, surgeon; Thos. Metcalfe, bailiff. The house on the north-west corner of Queen and John was Lord Nelson Inn, kept by Jane Dill. Water color by General A. R. V. Crease, R.E. Size 6 x 11.

794—**QUEEN STREET WEST, TORONTO**, 1852—St. Patrick's Market was built in 1836-7 on land granted by D'Arcy Boulton of "The Grange." The occupants of houses to the west on the north side of Queen street were W. H. Brayley, grocer; Daniel Bell, tailor; W. H. Smith, druggist; Arthur Farrall, cabinetmaker; Wm. Siver, shoemaker; Richard Brown (colored), shoemaker. The buildings on the south-east corner of Queen and John streets were the stables of Beverley House, the residence of Chief Justice J. B. Robinson. Water color by General A. R. V. Crease, R.E. Size 6 x 10.

795—**JOHN FARR'S BREWERY, YORK (TORONTO)**, 1819—On the south side of Queen street west, just west of Bellwoods avenue, in the valley of the Garrison Creek, which at this point was called Gore Vale Brook. It was a long, low, dingy-looking building of hewn logs, built about 1817 by John Farr, a widely-respected Englishman, who, after having conducted the business for many years, retired, transferring his interests to Wallis & Moss. Moss died in 1866, and in his stead John Wallis, who once represented West Toronto in the Dominion Parliament, took into partnership John Cornell. Wallis' death occurred in 1872, but his partner continued to conduct the business until his decease in 1879. The building, which had, some time subsequent to its erection, been rebuilt of brick, was left vacant and was demolished in 1887-8. The site is now (1917) occupied by a row of brick stores. To the left of the picture is seen the residence of Mr. Cornell. The Farr descendants live in Guelph. Water color. Size 4 x 7.

796—**SOUTH SIDE KING STREET WEST, TORONTO**, 1846—Built 1842-3, and in 1843-5 the hotel in the centre of the block, known as the Waterloo buildings, was occupied by Mr. J. Stone. In 1844 it was called Macdonald's Hotel. The buildings extended from No. 68 (now No. 77), R. Score & Son, Limited, to No. 80 (now No. 101), F. W. Lyonde, and the "stables" were those in rear of the hotel. At the south end of the entrance at the west under "stables" the Royal Lyceum was erected in 1849. From 68-74 are now (1917) situated the Romain buildings erected in 1856 by the late Charles E. Romain. Drawing in water color. Size 4 x 9.

797—**ZION CONGREGATIONAL CHURCH**, 1839-55—North-east corner Adelaide and Bay streets, Toronto—The first house north of the church was the residence of Thomas Harding, and the next building, the fire hall, of No. 6 Provincial Fire Engine Co. (south door), and No. 3 British America Fire Company (centre door) and station of the hose company (north door). The church with the square tower, south-east corner Bay and Richmond streets, was the United Presbyterian church. Drawing in water color. Size 5 x 6. See 761, 1146.

798—**ST. JAMES' RECTORY, TORONTO**, 1825-1903—It was an old-fashioned red brick house of two storeys, on the south side of Adelaide, west of Jarvis street, built, it is said, for an hotel. From 1837-82 Rev. Henry J. Grasett, who became rector of St. James' Church in 1847 and first Dean of Toronto, 1867, resided here. In the spring of 1903 the building was demolished and the new building completed on the same site in 1904. It is still the home of the rectors of St. James', the present (1917) occupant being Rev. Canon Plumptre. Water color. Size 5 x 7.

799—BANK OF MONTREAL, TORONTO, 1842-5—North-west corner King and Bay streets. This was originally the Bank of the People, one of the earliest financial institutions in Upper Canada. About 1840 the Bank of Montreal purchased the charter of the sister bank, converting the latter into one of its branches in 1842. After the institution's removal to its present headquarters, north-east corner of Front and Yonge streets, in 1845, the old building was used as club chambers, and later as law offices. It was afterwards known as the Metropolitan Hotel, subsequently being leased by the Mail Printing Co'y. The building of the Mail and Empire is on the site. Water color. Size 5 x 6.

800—STANTON HOUSE, YORK (TORONTO)—Built by Robert Stanton, the son of a British naval officer, and one of the pioneers of Upper Canada. His residence, which stood on the west side of Peter street at the head of Hospital (Richmond), was a substantial building of the secondary brick period of York. For many years Mr. Stanton was King's Printer, with office on King street, now the site of the Canada Life building. He also edited the U.C. Gazette and U.E. Loyalist, and afterwards became collector of customs. Up to the time of his death he occupied the Peter street residence, which then became the home of Mr. Charles Magrath, barrister, who married his widow. The house is now the site of a factory. Water color. Size 5 x 6.

801—HOME OF SAMUEL ROGERS—On the east side of Bay street, north of the north-east corner of King, next to the Sterling Bank. The old-time cottage was erected 1840-1 by Samuel Rogers, who resided here until his death. Rogers was a painter, a tradesman of the old school, and highly respected by his fellow-citizens. The dwelling was demolished in 1876 to make way for the Jarvis Building, 99-103 Bay street, which still (1917) stands. Water color. Size 5 x 6.

802—FIRST FIRE HALL, YORK (TORONTO), 1831—West side of Church street, between Court and Adelaide. On the north-west corner of Court and Church is shown the British America Insurance building. Next north is the two-storey brick fire hall of the first engine company of York, instituted in 1826 by Mr. Carfrae, Jr., who was captain for the six years he remained in the company. To the right of the picture is the old Scottish Kirk of St. Andrew's, south-west corner of Church and Adelaide. The buildings to the south have been converted into offices. Water color. Size 5 x 7.

803—MERCANTILE ROW IN YORK (TORONTO), 1833—South-west corner of King and Frederick streets. In the thirties this part of King east was a busy thoroughfare. William Proudfoot, No. 45 King street east; Robert McKay, No. 51, and John Sproule, No. 53, did about the best retail trade in Toronto. The last named was also a Government contractor. On the floor above the Proudfoot shop was Clarke Gamble's law office. Water color by F. V. Poole. Size 6 x 10.

804—SCADDING HOMESTEAD—East side of the River Don, near Gerrard street, Toronto. John Scadding, Sr., came to Canada in 1792 from Wolford, the estate of Governor Simcoe, in Devonshire, Eng., where prior to coming to Canada he had been manager. The Scadding farm originally consisted of a lot extending from the water's edge of the bay to the present Danforth avenue, and was bounded on the east by the present Broadview avenue, formerly known as the Mill road, and on the western side by the River Don. The dwelling shown in the picture was the second erected by

Mr. Scadding, the first having been a log house adjacent to the Kingston road. The lean-to shown at the rear of the house was constructed from plank and flooring taken from Castle Frank, the Simcoe summer home on the Don. Water color, Size 4 x 5.

805—"GOLDEN LION"—King street east, Nos. 33-7, on site now (1917) occupied by the King Edward Hotel and Victoria street extended. In 1846 Robert Walker, in conjunction with Thomas Hutchinson, founded the dry goods firm of Walker & Hutchinson. In 1853 the partnership was dissolved and Hutchinson opened a rival store several doors below, known as the "Pantechnetheca," the Walker store being known as the "Golden Lion." About 1859 the firm of Robert Walker & Son was formed. In 1898 the business was closed. Water color. Size 6 x 7.

806—HOME OF CHIEF JUSTICE SIR WILLIAM CAMPBELL, YORK (TORONTO), 1822-34—A large red brick mansion on Duke street, at the head of Frederick, erected by Sir William Campbell, after the colonial style of architecture prevailing in York from about 1807-25. He was a Scotsman who emigrated to Nova Scotia in 1783, and in 1811 became Chief Justice of Upper Canada. On his death the house became the property of Hon. James Gordon, formerly of Amherstburg, and was his home for many years. After his death it was occupied by various tenants, and thirty years later was purchased by John Strathy, who resided there until his death. It was sold to Mr. John Fensom for elevator factory purposes, and is now the works of the Capewell Horse Nail Company. Water color. Size 6 x 7.

807—BLOOR'S BREWERY, YORK (TORONTO)—Established by Joseph Bloor, 1830, in the ravine north of the first concession line, now Bloor street, and just east of Yonge street. The brewery was reached by a roadway running down the ravine from Bloor street at the head of Huntley street. After being given up by its original occupant, the business was conducted for a time as Castle Frank Brewery, under the proprietorship of Mr. John Rose. About 1864 brewing was discontinued there, and the east end of the building was tenanted by an old Irishman, and after him by an old negro named Cassidy. It was torn down about 1875. Water color, by R. Baigent, 1865. Size 9 x 13.

808—KING STREET WEST, TORONTO, 1856—North side, from Yonge to Bay streets—Showing King street west, from the north-west corner of Yonge, now (1917) the Grand Trunk Railway offices, to the residence of the late William Cawthra, now the Sterling Bank, at the north-east corner of Bay and King. The cottage, No. 11, is site of Star newspaper building. The Davis (No. 17), and Wilson (No. 19) buildings are site of Manning Arcade, and the Pagerit building (in which was located the English Chop House) is present Hotel Teck. The Baker, Hickman and Lasher stores, immediately west, are the site of the Murray-Kay building and the Canada Life. The Chop House and Cawthra residence are the only two buildings extant in 1917. Water color. Size 5 x 25.

809—FANCY DRESS BALL, 19TH APRIL, 1870—With key. The ball, a brilliant gathering of Toronto's leading citizens, was held in the Music Hall (later the Public Library building), north-east corner of Church and Adelaide streets, in aid of the Protestant Orphans' Home. The home, then on Sullivan street, and now on Dovercourt road, was founded in commemoration of Jenny Lind's visit to Toronto in 1851. About two hundred couples were present at the ball, ninety of whom have been identified. (See key). Financially the function was most successful. Photograph, colored. Size 14 x 20.

810—NORTH-EAST CORNER YONGE AND RICHMOND STREETS, TORONTO, 1888—The view shows the buildings almost to Queen street, and along the north side of Richmond to Victoria. Those shown on Yonge street, up to the Globe Hotel (now the Tremont House), were erected in 1841, and in 1890 together with property on Richmond, were torn down to make way for the Confederation Life building. Water color. Size 5 x 10.

811—DR. STOYELL'S HOUSE, YORK (TORONTO)—On the north side of King street, east of Ontario. Dr. Thomas Stoyell came to York from the United States, where he had received his degree. He never practised his profession here, however. For some time an innkeeper in York, afterwards conducting a brewery at the south-east corner of Sherbourne and Duchess streets. At an early date he built for himself a frame dwelling on the King street site, but about 1829 had the old building torn down and on almost the exact site erected a more commodious, two-storey brick residence. On Dr. Stoyell's death the house was occupied by a Roman Catholic priest until its purchase by Mr. Thomas Helliwell, who made it his residence. The Victor Inn, No. 282A King street east, is now (1917) on the site. Water color by F. V. Poole. Size 4 x 5.

812—CHARLES ROBERTSON'S STORE—South side of King street (No. 42), Toronto—Charles Robertson, who was the younger brother of John Robertson, the Yonge street dry goods merchant, and uncle of J. Ross Robertson, erected the King street store in 1850, and there for many years carried on a dry goods business. On his retirement he removed to Sharon, where he died in 1871. The building was most attractive and was about the first new one from 1840-51, in the block from Leader lane to Yonge street. It was demolished in 1894, and the site is now (1917) No. 61, the eastern portion of Catto's dry goods establishment. Water color. Size 4 x 6.

813—OLD LAW OFFICE, YORK (TORONTO)—North side of Front street, west of Sherbourne—This two-storey brick building, with gable roof, was the office of Hon. (Sir) John Beverley Robinson during his term of office as Attorney-General of Upper Canada, 1818-28. The blacksmith shop shown on the right was erected many years later. The site is now (1917) occupied by Toronto Street Railway buildings. Water color. Size 5 x 7.

814—THOMAS MERCER JONES' VILLA, YORK (TORONTO), 1833-93—North-west corner Front and York streets. The picturesque old residence was designed by John G. Howard for Mr. Jones, who lived here for a time. The property afterwards passed into the hands of Captain James McGill Strachan, son of Bishop Strachan, and was occupied as a residence by him until about 1860, when it was purchased by John Skae, who in 1887 sold out to David Walker. It is now the site of W. R. Johnson & Co., Limited. Water color. Size 5 x 7.

815—FREELAND'S SOAP FACTORY, 1832-65—Shortly after his arrival in York (Toronto), Peter Freeland erected a factory for the manufacture of soap, at the foot of Yonge street on the east side, on property purchased from Judge Sherwood and Peter McDougall. Owing to the fact that almost the whole property was land covered with water, the soap works had to be built on cribs sunk with stone. On the death of the first owner, in 1861, the business was carried on by Robert Freeland, a son, until the demolition of the building in 1865 to make room for the Great Western Railway passenger station, which is now (1917) the Grand Trunk fruit depot. Water color. Size 5 x 7.

816—RESIDENCE OF HON. C. A. HAGERMAN, NORTH-EAST CORNER OF WELLINGTON AND SIMCOE STREETS, TORONTO—York House, the main building to the right of the picture, was built by Hon. C. A. Hagerman shortly before the Rebellion of 1837, and was used as the family residence, while the addition was Mr. Hagerman's law office. Mr.

132

Nanton, a rich West Indian, later occupied the mansion until his decease in 1847, Mr. Hagerman moving into the next house east on Wellington street, where he died shortly afterwards. York House subsequently came into the possession of Hon. John Willoughby Crawford, one-time partner of Chief Justice Hagarty. Mr. Crawford resided there until his appointment as Lieutenant-Governor of Ontario, 1873, and on his removal to Government House transferred the old mansion to the Provincial Government. For some years the property was used as the Attorney-General's office and immigration bureau. It was demolished in 1906. The Randall-Johnston building now (1917) occupies the site. Water color by F. V. Poole. Size 5 x 7.

817—FIRST STONE HOUSE IN YORK (TORONTO)—Built in 1820 at the north-west corner of Church and March (Lombard) streets, and first occupied by James Hunter, a tailor. Then Dr. Macaulay resided there. Later it became the home of the Rev. Thomas Phillips, D.D., headmaster of the Home District school, 1823-30, and subsequently of Weston. In 1834 Dr. Daly occupied the dwelling, and for a time it was used as an hotel, known as the Kingston House. The site is now (1917) No. 114 Church street. Water color. Size 5 x 7.

818—BLACK BULL HOTEL, TORONTO—An old inn at the north-east corner of Queen and Maria (Soho) streets. Originally a frame building, but later succeeded by one of brick, bearing the same name for a time, and afterwards the Clifton Hotel. It was a favorite stopping-place for farmers on their way to town from the west and north-west. The land originally was part of lot No. 14, patented to Hon. Peter Russell in 1798. Water color. Size 5 x 6.

819—HUMBER BRIDGE AND NURSE'S HOTEL (TORONTO), 1883—Lake Shore road. On the south side of the road (left of picture) is Nurse's Hotel, built by Charles Nurse, 1874-5, and destroyed by fire in 1912. The bridge shown spanning the Humber was erected in 1874, and in that year also Mr. O. L. Hicks built boathouses shown, which from time to time were torn down and enlarged. In 1893 Mr. Hicks sold out to his brother, Samuel Hicks, who five years later transferred them to Capt. Robert Maw. A number of years ago the present (1917) owner, Mr. I. N. Devins, purchased them. In the distance to the right is seen the peak of the hotel built by John McDowell, 1852-3. On McDowell's death, in 1870, the hostelry came into the possession of his son, William, and since has passed through many hands. The G.T.R. acquired the property in 1911. The railway and other improvements have entirely changed the appearance of this vicinity. Water color. Size 7 x 10.

820—OLD-TIME RESIDENCES ON EAST SIDE OF SIMCOE STREET, NEAR QUEEN, TORONTO—The house with the arched doorway was the home of John Joseph, Clerk of the Executive Council, and the birthplace in 1838 of Frank Joseph. Mr. Joseph, sr., was at one time private secretary to the philanthropist, William Wilberforce. In 1836 he came to Canada with Sir Francis Bond Head as private secretary. From 1841-50 the house was occupied by Mr. John Robertson, dry goods merchant, and father of Mr. John Ross Robertson. Here the latter was born, Dec. 28th, 1841. The family removed to the next house north (shown in the picture), remaining there until their removal in 1857 to John street. From 1851-4 Col. Page, of the Royal Engineers, and from 1854-5, Mrs. Justina Scobie, widow of Hugh Scobie, the well-known publisher of the British Colonist, occupied the first-mentioned Simcoe street residence. It then became the home of Dr. Lucius O'Brien, and is now (1917) an express office. Water color. Size 5 x 7.

821—MRS. McLEAN'S TAVERN, 1851—The quaint old "Inn," popularly known as "Mother" McLean's Tavern, stood on the east side of the Humber River, at its junction with the Lake Shore road, Mrs. Margaret McLean having been granted lot 40 and the west part of lot 39 of the broken front by the Crown. The road allowance in the rear of the broken front would now (1917) be Queen street, if extended that far. Water color from original drawing by F. H. Granger. Size 5 x 9.

822—ICE HUMMOCKS ON THE LAKE—View of the Lake Shore road in front of High Park, Toronto. Through the trees may be seen Colborne Lodge, the home of Mr. J. G. Howard, and to the left is the Great Western Railway (now the G.T.R.) train going east towards the city. The large ice cone shown is eleven feet high. Water color from the original by J. G. Howard, in the City Hall, Toronto. Size 5 x 8.

823—CANADA COMPANY BUILDING—N.E. corner King and Frederick streets, now site of Adams Bros.' building. Water color from the original by J. G. Howard, in the City Hall, Toronto. Size 5 x 8. See 523.

824—MEIKLE, JAMES—The father of Miss Jemima Frances Meikle, who became the wife of Mr. John G. Howard. Water color from portrait by Hoppner Meyer, in City Hall, Toronto. Size 4 x 5. Head and shoulders.

825—KING STREET, TORONTO, 1835—Looking east from west of York street—1. Fence of King's College Land Office, n.w. cor. York and King. 2. Shakespeare Inn, n.e. cor. King and York streets, partly destroyed by fire, 1843. 3. The stores east on King street were occupied by John G. Howard, surveyor; Richard Turton, chemist; Henry Searle, paperhanger; George Walton, clerk of peace; Thomas Dalton, publisher of the "Patriot"; Dr. Wood, dentist, and others. 4. Chewett's buildings (now, 1916, site of Prince George Hotel), the block at south-east corner of King and York streets, which included the British Coffee House, with its entrance on York street. 5. The British Coffee House. 6. South-west corner of King and York streets. Water color from the original by J. G. Howard, in the City Hall, Toronto. Size 5 x 8.

826—FRONT STREET, YORK (TORONTO), 1834—Looking northwest from the corner of Front and Simcoe streets. 1. Immigration Sheds. 2. Creek, which had its origin in the north-west part of York (Toronto), beyond College and Spadina. It passed in a south-east direction to Queen and the corner of John, then through the Macdonell property, the Upper Canada College and Government House grounds, along the east side of the Parliament Buildings, and then emptied into the bay at Front street. 3. Greenland Fisheries Tavern, north-west corner Front and John streets, 1825. 4. Third Parliament Buildings. Centre buildings erected 1829-31; east and west wings erected 1833. Vacated 1892. Now the site of the Grand Trunk Railway freight sheds. 5. Simcoe street. Water color from the original, by J. G. Howard, in the City Hall, Toronto. Size 5 x 8.

827—A GALLANT RESCUE, DECEMBER, 1861—On Lake Ontario, between Sunnyside and Humber Bay, Toronto. This view was made from the lake shore by Mr. J. G. Howard, donor of High Park, and shows Thomas Tinning, a well-known Toronto oarsman, rescuing the crew from the wrecked schooner "Pacific." In the distance may be seen the lighthouse on Toronto Island. Water color from original, by J. G. Howard, in City Hall, Toronto. Size 5 x 8.

828—WINTER SCENE ON TORONTO BAY, 1835—In the background of picture may be seen: 1. Residence of Bishop Strachan, Front street. 2. Parliament Buildings. 3. Greenland Fisheries Tavern, north-west corner Front and John. 4. Home of John Beikie, just east of Windsor street. 5.

Military storehouse wharf. 6. Hon. Geo. Cruickshank's house, north-east corner Front and Peter. 7. Government wood yards. 8. 8. 8. Buildings of old Fort. 9. Queen's Wharf. Water color from original, by J. G. Howard, in City Hall, Toronto. Size 5 x 8.

829—FIRST DESIGN FOR A GOVERNMENT HOUSE—Although this building was not nearly so large or so elaborate, in elevation, the estimated cost of erection, $50,000, was the same as a later design, also by J. G. Howard. The building was never erected. Water color from the original, by J. G. Howard, in City Hall, Toronto. Size 6 x 8.

830—DESIGN FOR GUILD HALL, 1834—The design covered the entire plot on the north side of King street east, Toronto, between Toronto and Church streets, and provided for the erection of a Guild Hall, Court House, Post Office, Public Library and Merchants' Exchange. Had these plans been carried out the old jail and court house on the north-east corner of King and Toronto, and the north-west corner of King and Church streets, respectively, erected in 1824, were to have been converted into the city and district jails, police office, and temporary lock-up room. The estimated cost of erecting the buildings was £60,000. About 1842 the open space known as Court House Square, between King, Toronto, Church and Court streets, was sold and shops built thereon. Water color from original, by J. G. Howard, in City Hall, Toronto. Size 4 x 8.

831—HOWARD, MRS. JOHN G. (JEMIMA FRANCES MEIKLE)—A Scotswoman, born 18th August, 1802. In 1827 she married Mr. John G. Howard, and emigrated to Canada with her husband in 1832. Her death took place at Colborne Lodge, High Park, Toronto, 1st September, 1877. Water color from portrait in City Hall, Toronto. Size 3 x 4. Head and shoulders. See 847.

832—PROVINCIAL LUNATIC ASYLUM, TORONTO—North view— Water color from original, by J. G. Howard, in City Hall, Toronto. Size 4 x 8. See 541.

833—ENTRANCE GATE TO COLBORNE LODGE, TORONTO, 1870—In 1836 Mr. John G. Howard purchased one hundred and sixty-five acres of land on the east bank of the Humber River, giving his property the name of High Park. On the western side of this piece of land he erected in the same year, Colborne Lodge, so named after Sir John Colborne, Lieutenant-Governor of Upper Canada, 1828-35, and Mr. Howard's first benefactor and friend in York. On the 23rd December, 1837, Mr. Howard moved from Chewett's building, King street, to his new abode, where he lived for many years. Water color from original, by J. G. Howard, in City Hall, Toronto. Size 5 x 8.

834—COLBORNE, MAJOR-GENERAL SIR JOHN—After suppressing the rebellion in Lower Canada, and on the retirement of Lord Durham, Sir John Colborne remained as Administrator of Lower Canada, acting for a time as Governor. Upon his return to England he was created Lord Seaton. Water color from original oil, by Berthon, in the Howard Collection. Size 11 x 18. Full length. See 160, 417.

835—HOWARD, J. G.—Making a survey in front of the Parliament Buildings, foot of Simcoe street. The columns shown in centre of the building were never erected. In the left is seen the Greenland Fisheries Tavern, north-west corner of Front and John streets. Many plans and surveys stand to the credit of Mr. Howard, notable among the latter being a "Chart of the North Shore of Toronto Harbour" in 1846. Water color from original, in the City Hall. Portrait by D'Almaine, landscape by Howard. Size 6 x 7. See 837, 841, 846, 2781, 3575, 3660.

836—DESIGN FOR A GOVERNMENT HOUSE AT YORK (TORONTO), 1833—At this date the "Governor's Residence," as it was called, was situated at the south-west corner of King and Simcoe streets, being originally the home of Chief Justice Elmsley, and subsequently purchased by the Government. The design shown was made in 1833 by John G. Howard, the well-known Toronto architect, and was intended "for the information of Sir John Colborne to shew the impropriety of spending money in repairing the old Government House." The site suggested was on "the military reserve to the west of Peter street, on Front street," and the estimated cost of erection was £50,000. The structure shown was never erected. Water color from original, by J. G. Howard, in City Hall, Toronto. Size 4 x 8.

837—HOWARD, JOHN G., R.C.A., 1803-90—Born near London, Eng. At the age of fifteen was sent to sea, but compelled to abandon the life; took up land surveying, engineering and architecture. In 1832 emigrated to Canada, with his wife, settling in York. The following year Sir John Colborne obtained for Mr. Howard the appointment of drawing master at U.C.C., and in 1843 he was appointed City Surveyor, subsequently becoming City Engineer. Laid out the Island in 1846, and also surveyed the ground and made plans for St. James' Cemetery. In 1873 Mr. Howard conveyed 120 acres of High Park to the Corporation of Toronto by gift as a public park forever, and the remaining 45 acres of his estate were added after his death. He was buried with Masonic honors in High Park. Water color from portrait in City Hall, Toronto. Size 3 x 4. Head and shoulders. See 835, 841, 846, 2781, 3575, 3660.

838—DESIGN FOR UNIVERSITY, 1835—The plan was drawn by Mr. John G. Howard, the Toronto architect, and presented by him to Sir John Colborne, K.C.B., Lieutenant-Governor of Upper Canada, 1828-35. It was intended for King's College, to be erected in Queen's Park, Toronto. With some alterations it gained the £50 premium in competition for Queen's College, Kingston, but was not adopted. Water color from original, by J. G. Howard, in City Hall, Toronto. Size 5 x 8.

839—HOWARD TOMB AND CAIRN—North view. In a reserved portion of High Park, Toronto, Mr. J. G. Howard erected a tomb and cairn in memory of his wife, whose death occurred in 1877. He himself was also buried there in 1890. The cairn is situated a little to the north-west of Colborne Lodge, at the summit of a picturesque ravine. It is constructed of granite boulders bedded in Portland cement, topped with a double pedestal which terminated in a Maltese cross. On the north side of this bit of consecrated ground is a portion of the iron railing which for one hundred and sixty years surrounded St. Paul's Cathedral, London, Eng. Water color from original, by J. G. Howard, in City Hall, Toronto. Size 5 x 8.

840—KING STREET, TORONTO, 1835—Looking north from south side of King street. 1. Second jail, n.e. cor. King and Toronto streets, 1824-40. 2. First fire hall, situated just south of St. Andrew's church, west side of Church street, near Adelaide, 1831-77. 3. Second Court House, north-west corner King and Church streets, 1824-53. 4. Church street, running north between the Court House and St. Andrew's church. 5. Second St. James' church (Cathedral), north-east corner King and Church streets, 1830-9. Water color from original, by John G. Howard, in the City Hall, Toronto. Size 5 x 8.

841—HOWARD, J. G.—In his eightieth year. The cloak shown in the portrait is one which the venerable surveyor wore for fifty years. Water color from portrait in Howard Collection. Size 4 x 7. Full length. See 835, 837, 846, 2781, 3575, 3660.

842—WINTER SCENE ON TORONTO BAY, 1835—View from Taylor's Wharf, south side Palace street. The principal points shown are: 1. Houses on Dr. Widmer's property. 2. Dr. Widmer's dwelling, north side Palace (Front) street, just east of Ontario. 3. Taylor's Wharf. 4. Windmill (Gooderham's). 5, Ashbridge's Bay. Water color from original, by J. G. Howard, in City Hall, Toronto. Size 6 x 8.

843—GAOL AND COURT HOUSE, BROCKVILLE, ONT.—Erected in 1841-3 from a plan by J. G. Howard, the well-known Toronto architect. Mr. Howard also superintended the building of the structure, which replaced the second Brockville Court House, a brick edifice erected in 1824. The naming of the figure of Justice, which surmounts the present building, is an amusing incident. Among the crowd assembled to see the figure raised, were Major Alexander Grant, a man about 6 ft. 5 in. in height, and otherwise large in proportion, and Paul Glassford, small of stature, who had been chairman of the Building Committee. The former was a practical joker and liked nothing better than to have a joke on Glassford. He laughingly called the crowd's attention to the difference in size between Mr. Glassford and his "child." But, when the figure was in position, Mr. Glassford, in response to the cry, "name, name," looked at it, then at Major Grant, and, touching his hat, said, "Her name is Sally Grant." The joke was turned on the notorious joker, and through the heat of summer and snows of winter "Sally Grant" has held the scales of justice on Brockville's Court House since 1845. Water color from original, by J. G. Howard, in City Hall, Toronto. Size 5 x 8.

844—TORONTO BAY—From Browne's Wharf, 1835—The wharf, which was owned by James Browne, a prominent Toronto business man and wharfinger, was situated between Church and Scott streets, and was a landing place for the Royal Mail steamers. This view shows a typical winter scene on the bay in the thirties. At the west end of the peninsula, now Toronto Island, is the lighthouse, while at the east end are some fishermen's dwellings. Water color from original, by J. G. Howard, in City Hall, Toronto. Size 6 x 8.

845—GRENADIER POND, HIGH PARK, TORONTO—View from the east—This pond, one of the ancient outlets of the Humber River, lies in a valley towards the west side of High Park, and in winter is a favorite skating resort for the young people of the city. Water color from original, by J. G. Howard, in City Hall, Toronto. Size 5 x 8.

846—HOWARD, JOHN G.—At the age of forty-five. Water color from a miniature, by Thomas H. Stevenson, in Howard Collection. Size $4\frac{1}{2}$ x 5. Half length. See 835, 837, 841, 2781, 3575, 3660.

847—HOWARD, MRS. J. G.—At forty-five. Water color from a miniature, by Thomas H. Stevenson, in Howard Collection. Size $4\frac{1}{2}$ x 5. Half length. See 831.

848—DEJEUNER AT UPPER CANADA COLLEGE, TORONTO—On the occasion of the laying of the foundation stone of King's College in Queen's Park, by his Excellency, Sir Charles Bagot, Governor-General of the United Canadas and Chancellor of the University, a dejeuner was given in the Prayer Hall of Upper Canada College, April 23rd, 1842. The east wing of the Legislative Buildings is now (1917) on the site of old King's College. Water color from original, by J. G. Howard, in City Hall, Toronto. Size 5 x 10.

849-58—Theatres of York and Toronto, 1820-74.

849—FIRST THEATRE, 1820-29—The first theatrical performance in York was given in the ball room of Frank's Hotel, a two-storey frame building on the north-west corner of West Market street and Market lane

(Colborne street). Mr. Allan Macnab, afterwards Sir Allan, was one of the amateur performers in the pioneer theatre, acquitting himself so well that he was seriously advised to become a professional actor. The playhouse, although its appointments were of the most unpretentious character, was very popular. Water color, by F. V. Poole. Size 4 x 4.

850—**SECOND THEATRE,** 1829-34—On the north side of Colborne street, west of the St. Lawrence Market. It was a two-storey frame building, the ground floor of which was used as a shop, while the upper part was fitted up as a theatre about 1829. Performances were given here by a local amateur club. Water color, by F. V. Poole. Size 3½ x 4.

851—**THIRD THEATRE,** 1834-7—South side King street, west of Jordan, on part of site of Bank of Commerce. It was a frame building 40 x 60, erected in 1818, by Mr. Petch, as the first place of public worship of the Wesleyan Methodists in York. In the same building where the eloquence of early Methodist ministers resounded, playgoers of York also attended ere long, for on the completion of the Adelaide Street Methodist church, Waugh Bros., confectioners on King street, obtained possession of the old chapel and fitted it up as a place of amusement. The first representation given here was a panorama of the "Burning of Moscow," exhibited in the latter part of 1834. Water color, by J. W. Cotton. Size 5 x 7.

852—**FOURTH THEATRE,** 1834-8—From time to time theatrical performances were given in a barn-like frame building, some sixty feet long, situated on the north side of Front street, east of Church. There was no gallery, but the ground floor seated an audience of between two and three hundred. The appointments of the place were of the most primitive sort, candles being the illuminants; nevertheless the acting was at times very Good. Mr. and Mrs. Thorne, who played comedy here, were favorites and always drew full houses. Water color. Size 3½ x 4.

853—**FIFTH THEATRE,** 1836-40—On the north side of King street, near York, on the lot adjoining the Shakespeare Hotel, n.e. corner of King and York. The Theatre Royal, as the new playhouse was named, was of a more pretentious character than its predecessors. It was a large frame structure, erected shortly before the Mackenzie Rebellion of 1837, and was originally a cabinet or carpenter workshop. The seats were arranged in tiers, in much the same fashion as they are at the present day. The popular Thornes graced the boards at this theatre also. In the days of the old Royal ladies had not begun to frequent theatres much. Water color, by F. V. Poole. Size 5 x 7.

854—**SIXTH THEATRE,** 1841-3—This theatre, known as Deering's, was owned by the then proprietor of the Ontario House. It was situated on the east side of Scott, and extended from Front to Wellington streets, the main entrance being on Front street. The building, which was of frame, was well patronized, but its existence as a playhouse was short. It was used subsequently as an immigration office and later became a tavern. Water color. Size 5 x 7.

855—**SEVENTH THEATRE,** 1840-50—On the west side of William street, above Queen. A company of amateurs, notable among them being Alexander Jacques, printer, fitted up an old barn for theatrical performances, giving various plays there for about four years. This theatre had its inception in an old barn on Colborne street, near the corner of Leader lane, owned by Mr. John Munn, but this building was destroyed by fire, and the company had to seek quarters elsewhere. From 1845 the William street theatre was used for local negro minstrel shows. Water color. Size 5 x 7.

856—**EIGHTH THEATRE,** 1849-53—This theatre, a frame building, about seventy feet long, and having a lean-to at the south end to make room for the stage, had been used as a coach and guard house for Government House. It was situated on the south side of King street west, near the ravine or creek that at one time crossed between Simcoe and John streets, and was managed by T. P. Besnard, subsequently manager of the Royal Lyceum. A number of performances were given in this building by the Garrison amateurs; but it never became popular, being too far from the town of those days. Water color. Size 5 x 7.

857—**NINTH THEATRE,** 1848-73—Known as the Royal Lyceum, south side King street, between Bay and York. It was built by John Ritchey, the first occupant being John S. Potter. About 1850 T. P. Besnard undertook the management of the house. He persuaded John Nickinson and his daughters to come over from Buffalo. A managerial partnership was entered into between Mr. Besnard and Mr. Nickinson, the latter in 1853 assuming sole management of the Royal Lyceum, which he considerably altered and improved. He it was who induced the great actors of the day to visit Toronto. In 1872 Mrs. Morrison (Charlotte Nickinson) took the management of the Lyceum. About a year later the building was burned, but was rebuilt. During Mrs. Morrison's management many stars played here. Water color by J. W. Cotton. Size 5 x 7.

858—**TENTH THEATRE,** 1874—North side King street west, between Bay and York, now (1917) Nos. 90-4, about a hundred feet back from the street. It was reached by a passageway nearly opposite that leading to the Royal Lyceum. The playhouse shown, in which were seen some good performances, was known as the Queen's Theatre. Tom C. King, a great Macbeth, played there in tragedy. Water color. Size 5 x 7.

859—**WELLS RESIDENCE, TORONTO**—The comfortable, old-fashioned residence on the high ground overlooking Davenport road, just north-east of Bathurst, was erected by Col. Joseph Wells, of the 43rd Monmouthshire Regiment, and a veteran of the Peninsular War. It was built on the site of a smaller dwelling purchased by Colonel Wells in 1820, and, after his retirement from the army, he lived here until his death in 1853. Until 1873 Colonel Frederick Wells, a son, occupied the residence, which afterwards passed into the hands of the second occupant's daughter, Mrs. De Pencier. Water color. Size 5 x 7.

860—**AMERICAN HOTEL, TORONTO,** 1841-89—About 1840 Mr. Rennie purchased the north-east corner of Front and Yonge streets, formerly owned by the late Chief Justice Scott, erecting thereon a brick building. It was known for many years as the American Hotel, and was one of the best-known hostelries in Canada until its demolition in 1889 to make room for the Board of Trade building. When Charles Dickens visited Toronto in 1842 he was a guest in this house. Mr. Pearson, an American, was the popular landlord for many years, and he was succeeded by the late David Walker, before the days of the Walker House. Pen drawing, colored. Size 5 x 7.

861—**MAIN STREET, WESTON,** 1908—Looking west. The town, which is situated on the Humber River, several miles north-west of the City of Toronto, was founded by the Government in 1813. This view shows the present Eagle House, built in 1870 by the late John Eagle. It was formerly known as Bellis' Hotel. West of the Eagle House is the Assembly Room, erected 1849-50. Pen drawing, colored. Size 5 x 7.

862—**DAVENPORT STATION ON THE NORTHERN RAILWAY,** 1857—This was one of the prettiest stations on the old Northern Railway, now the Grand Trunk. It stood almost in the woods when it was built in

1857, and a couple of miles outside the then city limits of Toronto. To-day, however, commerce has made sad havoc with the beautiful surroundings of nearly sixty years ago, for the station is now (1917) in the city limits, on the north side of Davenport road. It faces west, and Station street runs north and south behind the building, while to the north is St. Clair avenue. Near the station are the works of the Canada Foundry. Water color. Size 4 x 7.

863—OLD FORT, YORK (TORONTO), 1832—Situated at the western part of the town. The view shows: 1. The eastern entrance to fort. 2. Cutting at the entrance. 3. Blockhouse erected after War of 1812. 4. Blockhouse in centre of parade ground, also erected after the war. 5. Row of buildings used by officers. 6. Barracks for soldiers. To the left is a portion of Queen's Wharf, and in the background the lighthouse on Toronto Island is seen. The foreground has been entirely altered in appearance by railways and manufacturing buildings. Drawing in water color by James Hamilton, London, C. W. Size 5 x 18.

864—OLD ROW OF BRICK HOUSES—East side of James street, Toronto, 1845—This row of two-storey brick dwellings was erected about 1842. Reading from right to left, the occupants at the time of the picture were: No. 4, Hugh Reid; No. 6, Robert Kerr, captain of the steamer "America," and father of Mr. Robert Kerr, of Toronto, late traffic manager of the C.P.R.; No. 8, Anthony Blachford, whose descendants are the well-known shoe firm of Toronto; No. 10, William Forbes. Part of the T. Eaton Co. store now (1917) stands on the site of the old-time row. Drawing in water color. Size 5 x 7.

865—SOUTH-EAST CORNER YONGE AND GERRARD STREETS, TORONTO, 1881—An old-time business row—These buildings, originally of frame, but in later years roughcast, were all erected between 1840-50, and in 1917 some of those, from 389 to 367, are still standing. The Forum building, erected in 1890, occupies the site of Nos. 391-5. With key. Water color. Size 6 x 10.

866—HOME OF DAVID WILLIAMSON—An East End landmark of Toronto—Typical workingman's home of the day. It was situated at the north-east corner of South Park (now Eastern avenue) and Trinity street, and was occupied by David Williamson, known as "Long Davy," a carter, who worked for Gooderham & Worts. Williamson was accidentally killed many years ago at the Pape avenue crossing of the G.T.R. The old dwelling was torn down in 1880. Sketch in water color by J. O. Fowler, 1871. Size 7 x 9.

867—HOME OF (SIR) ALLAN NAPIER MACNAB, YORK (TORONTO) —North side of King street, near its intersection with Queen, now Nos. 520-522 King street east. It was in this house that Lieutenant MacNab, formerly of the Queen's Rangers, and father of the eminent Sir Allan Napier MacNab, first Queen's Counsel in Canada, lived for some years after leaving Niagara, and here also the future Sir Allan spent the greater part of his early days. Water color. Size 5 x 8.

868—MEAD'S HOTEL, TORONTO ISLAND, 1882—About 1850 Reuben Parkinson, a carriage builder, built a hotel at Maskelonge Point (Mugg's Landing), Toronto Island, moving it some three years later to the west side of the Privat Hotel grounds. This hotel was washed away, and about 1859 Mrs. Parkinson erected a hostelry on what is now part of Island Park. In 1873 Mrs. Parkinson assigned her lease to Robert Mead, and on the latter's death the business was carried on by his widow. In 1887 the city purchased Mrs. Mead's holdings, consisting of twelve acres, and incorporated them in the park. The wharf shown ran in a northwesterly direction, into the bay, a distance of 283 feet, the end being opposite the extremity of the present (1917) Island ferry. Water color by W. J. Thomson. Size 12 x 18.

869—RUSHOLME—North-west corner Dundas street and Rusholme road, Toronto—Erected of roughcast, in 1839, by George Taylor (Colonel) Denison, son of Lieut.-Col. George Taylor Denison, of Bellevue. The residence was subsequently enlarged by Colonel Denison, who occupied it until his decease in 1873. It is still (1917) standing. Water color. Size 5 x 7.

870—RITCHEY TERRACE, TORONTO—North side of Adelaide, near York street. In 1856 John Ritchey erected the six fine white brick houses known as Ritchey Terrace, adjoining his own residence. Some years ago the dwellings were remodelled and are now (1917) used as factories and warehouses, Nos. 112-22. The walls, ceilings, roof joists, doors and stairways have stood the test of time so well that they will bear the weight of machinery as present-day residences will not do. Only one of the houses has been torn down, its site being occupied by the factory of Douglas Brothers, No. 124 Adelaide street. John Ritchey was the builder who erected the spire of the first St. Paul's church, Bloor street, and the original row of brick buildings on the east side of Bay, between Melinda and Wellington streets. Pen drawing, colored. Size 5 x 7.

871—SOUTH SIDE OF KING STREET WEST, TORONTO, 1866—The view gives a part of King street, between Bay and York, and shows the west end of No. 73, Edward Dack, boot shop; No. 75, D. W. Smith, Toronto Dye Works; No. 77, George Harding, plumber; No. 79, R. W. Laird, gilder. Nos. 81-93 are the Romain buildings, erected in 1856 by Charles E. Romain. The shopkeepers in the buildings at this period were: No. 81, H. J. Kerby, restaurant; No. 83-5, Walter Rose, dry goods; No. 87, C. S. Gzowski & Co. and D. L. McPherson's office, upper floors; No. 89, B. Saunders, tailor; No. 93, A. K. Boomer. In the distance is the Rossin House. Water color. Size 5 x 6.

872—BROCKTON POST OFFICE, 1853—It was first known as Denison Terrace Office, then as Lippincott, and finally as Brockton. A Mrs. Larkin, who kept a small general store, was also postmistress. The old building stood on the south side of Dundas street, Toronto, nearly opposite the Appii Forum, or Three Taverns, Collard's, Church's and James', but it is almost impossible to identify the exact site now as the entire locality has changed. It was probably about the present (1917) Nos. 577-583 Dundas street. Church's Hotel is still standing, as is also a portion of Collard's. Water color. Size 5 x 7.

873—LAMBTON FLOUR MILLS, 1843—At Lambton Mills, on the Humber; the second erected in Toronto Township. The original mills, which were very primitive, being almost entirely of wood with an undershot wheel, were the property of Thomas Cooper, who at one time owned a wharf in Toronto. In 1843 they were purchased by Mr. (Sir) William Pearce Howland, and practically rebuilt by him. Ten years afterwards Mr. Peleg Howland entered the business, which was conducted under the firm name of P. & W. P. Howland. Two years later Mr. F. A. Howland purchased Sir W. P. Howland's interest, and the firm name became P. & F. A. Howland. The senior member died in 1882 and the mills were continued by Mr. F. A. Howland until his death in 1885. The first purchaser and Thomas Elliott succeeded to the business the following year, the firm being then known as Howland and Elliott. In 1895 Mr. Elliott purchased his partner's interest, but kept the old firm name. The property was sold in 1909 to Mr. Home Smith, and the next year the business passed into the hands of Mr. H. Phillips. The old mill had been converted by Mr. Home Smith into a restaurant, patronized principally by Toronto motorists. It was burnt down in 1916. Pen drawing, colored. Size 4 x 6.

874—MUSEUM IN AN OLD TORONTO MANSION—For some time the apartment, originally the dining-room of Hon. William Allan's residence, Moss Park, Sherbourne street, was used as an ornithological museum. The flags shown in the picture belonged to the Third Regiment, East York Militia, and were carried by that regiment in the War of 1812. Only a corner of the room is depicted. Water color by Owen Staples Size 5 x 7.

875—DOVERCOURT, TORONTO—Second residence of Lieut.-Col. Richard Lippincott Denison, now (1917) No. 36 Churchill avenue, looking down Lakeview avenue. A lane, now Ossington avenue, once led through the woods and fields to Dovercourt, which was erected in 1853. Col. R. L. Denison was the eldest son of Lieut.-Col. George T. Denison (1st) of "Bellevue," Toronto. Water color. Size 5 x 7.

876—FIRST BREWERY, YORK (TORONTO)—South-east corner Sherbourne and Duchess streets—In 1815 the brewery was erected by one Henderson. It consisted, in 1820, of a stone malt house and granary (this, the only building remaining, is shown in picture), a range of small frame buildings along Duchess street, where the malt was ground in a handmill, and a row of arches dug in the bank, finished with masonry and covered with earth. These arches, which extended fifty feet along the south side of the lot, were used for storing the beer and fermenting tubs. Just south of the granary, on Sherbourne street, was the entrance to the brewery yard. The property passed through various hands during its long existence. Dr. Thos. Stoyell took it over in 1822, but only retained it for two or three years. John Doel, prior to the erection of the brewery adjoining his house, corner Bay and Adelaide streets, carried on the Sherbourne street business. The granary, years later, was used as a storehouse by John Walz & Co., brewers. It is (1917) used as an automobile supply shop. Water color. Size 5 x 7.

877—NORTHERN RAILWAY OFFICES, TORONTO—Situated on the north-west corner of Front and Brock streets (Spadina avenue)—The first offices of the railway, in 1853 (then the Ontario, Simcoe & Huron), were at 52 Bay street (west side), near Front. In 1864 the company, which had become the Northern in 1859, erected the handsome brick building shown in picture. It was vacated in 1889, about a year after the amalgamation of the Northern and North Western with the Grand Trunk, used for a time by the Y.M.C.A. for railway men, afterwards becoming the British Welcome League. Water color. Size 5 x 6.

878—HOME OF HON. DONALD McDONALD—A popular Toronto residence on the south side of Queen street, west of Spadina avenue. It was a roughcast frame building, erected by William Botsford Jarvis in 1836, and occupied successively by R. G. Turner, W. B. Jarvis and Hon. Donald McDonald, a member of the Legislative Council. The last-named and his wife were noted for their hospitality, and in the fifties and sixties entertained many military men, politicians and other celebrities. After Mr. McDonald's death his widow continued to reside in the house for a time. On her departure for California from Toronto it was put to various uses, and in 1887 was demolished. Water color. Size 4 x 6.

879—COOPER RESIDENCE, TORONTO—About 1853 Mr. George Cooper, a well-known resident of north-west York in the early days, and one of the contractors who took down the Island blockhouse in 1818, erected a large brick residence, north of Davenport road, on the hill overlooking the Davenport Station, on the then Northern, now the northern division of the Grand Trunk Railway. In this house, after a long and useful career, Mr. Cooper died. Water color. Size 5 x 7.

880—AT THE HUMBER RIVER, 1845—The Lake Shore road is here shown just east of the bridge. The building beyond the bridge and on the west side of the Humber, was the storehouse of William Gamble, who owned the mills on the river, built previous to 1830 by Thomas Fisher. The schooners are lying at the entrance to the Humber. The sheds to the left are in the rear of Mother McLean's tavern, which stood behind the willow tree. Water color from a drawing by J. Gillespie, 1845. Size 4 x 7.

881—THE CROOKSHANK FARM HOUSE, YORK (TORONTO)—Crookshank's lane (Bathurst street)—The lane was a semi-private thoroughfare, connecting the farm with York. Its southerly portion received the name of Bathurst street, in honor of Earl Bathurst, Secretary for the Colonies during George IV.'s reign. Even up to 1860, however, the upper part was known as Crookshank's lane. The farm extended from Queen street to the north of Davenport road, the present Bathurst street running through the eastern half. The house shown in the picture dated from before the War of 1812, and was occupied by Mr. George Crookshank (Cruickshank) prior to the erection of his Front street residence, and the property remained in his hands until 1851. In 1864 the house was moved eastward and enlarged. In 1900 it was demolished. Water color. Size 5 x 7.

882—HOUSE FOR TRAVELLERS, RIVER CREDIT, U.C.—Built by the Government in 1793, as a military storehouse and barracks, and for the accommodation of travellers passing to and from Niagara and York, through the Mississauga tract of land. It was a one-storey structure, built of logs, clap-boarded, and stood about thirty yards from the River Credit. It subsequently became a tavern and was conducted as such for many years. In 1861 the house was pulled down and rebuilt on a farm about a mile and a half north of Port Credit, but was destroyed by fire eighteen months later. Pen drawing, colored. Size 4½ x 5.

883—COUNTRY STORE OF W. P. HOWLAND—A Lambton Mills Landmark—Erected in the early forties by W. P. Howland (knighted May 24th, 1879). The store, which also served as a post office, was conducted under the firm name of Peleg and W. P. Howland. In 1855 the firm became P. and F. A. Howland, and on the death of these two gentlemen, Sir W. P. Howland and Thomas Elliott succeeded to the business in 1886. Some years later Elliott bought it, and in 1909 it was purchased by Home Smith, who in turn sold out to H. Phillips. The first mill at Lambton was just west of this store, and was owned by Robert Cooper. It was built some years prior to Howland's coming. Subsequently the Cooper property also passed into the Howlands' hands. The old store was burned in the summer of 1915. Pen drawing, colored. Size 5 x 6.

884—LYNDHURST—The Widder Residence, Toronto, 1845-65—Mr. Frederick Widder, a director of the Canada Company, came to Toronto in 1845 as commissioner of the company, and took up residence at "Lyndhurst." The entrance to this stately mansion was on Wellington place, the grounds extending south to Front, west of Brock street. The view given is that of the drawing-room, looking west. Mr. and Mrs. Widder were widely known for their hospitality, and entertained lavishly here until Mr. Widder's resignation from the Canada Company in 1865. The building has been for many years, and still (1917) is, the home of Loretto Abbey, Wellington street, west of Brock (Spadina) avenue. This part of Wellington street was known as Wellington place up to 1910. Pen drawing, colored. Size 5 x 7.

885—WILLIAM GAMBLE'S STORE, ETOBICOKE, 1888—Also known as Milton Mills Depot. The building, situated on Etobicoke side of the village, on the north side of Dundas street, half way up the hill from the Humber River, was originally owned by William Gamble, who gave up business in 1856, and was succeeded by Charles Bell and others. It was during the occupancy of J. G. Rogers, who conducted the business from 1888-98, that this picture was taken. Since 1902 the business has been carried on by Fitzpatrick & Co. The post office used to be kept in this store, and was called Etobicoke. Pen drawing, colored. Size 5 x 6.

886—YORK MECHANICS' INSTITUTE—North-east corner Church and Adelaide streets, York (Toronto). The York Mechanics' Institute, or Society for Mutual Improvement in the Arts and Sciences, was established in 1830, and was organized on the principle of the Mechanics' Institutes of Edinburgh and London. "The object of this society," the organizers announced, "shall be the mutual improvement of mechanics and others who become members of the society in arts and sciences by the formation of a library of reference and circulation, by the delivery of lectures on scientific and mechanical subjects, the establishment of classes for the instruction of members in the various branches of study and for conversation on subjects embraced by this constitution from which all discussion on political or religious matters is to be carefully excluded." The first meetings of the Institute were held in the old Masonic Hall, on Colborne street, near Church. Later the police building on Court street was used. About 1856, however, the Institute removed to the building shown in the picture, which is the front part of the present Central Public Library. On the passing of the Free Library By-law, January 1st, 1883, the Mechanics' Institute was merged with the Public Library. Water color. Size 5 x 7.

887—HOMESTEAD OF DAVID WARD, SR., TORONTO ISLAND— Rear view from the Bay side, showing also the outbuildings—The original homestead was built about 1839 and washed away in 1855. The following year John Quinn built the present dwelling, which stands 1,500 feet north of the old site. The water shown in the foreground has been cleaned and dredged, and is now used as a waterway for boats. In the early days if the weather was bad and the bay could not be crossed by boats, Ward would hitch his horse to a little waggon and drive around the east end of the peninsula (now Toronto Island) and by way of Woodbine avenue reach the city. William Ward, second son of David Ward, Sr., was born in the first homestead and died in Toronto, 24th January, 1912. David Ward, Jr., died 18th February, 1912. Water color by J. T. Rolph, Toronto. Size 10 x 12. See 906.

888—WELLER STAGE LINE FROM YORK TO KINGSTON, 1829— Founded by William Weller—According to a notice in the Upper Canada Gazette of January 14th, 1830, the Weller stages left York and Kingston at noon on Mondays and Thursdays, arriving on Wednesdays and Saturdays. In 1834 they left the coach office in the east end of the old Coffin Block, corner of Front and Market (Wellington) streets, for Cobourg and the Carrying Place. A steamboat met the stage to and from Kingston at the Carrying Place, which was at a point five miles from Trenton, Ont., between the head of the Bay of Quinte and Weller's Bay. The stage service was discontinued in 1856, after the opening of the Grand Trunk Railway. Water color by J. W. Cotton. Size 7 x 9.

889—"TORONTO—Drawn from nature by Aug. Kollner. Lith. by Deroy. Printed by Jacomme & Co., New York and Paris. Published by Goupil & Co. Entered according to Act of Congress in the year 1851 by William Schaus in the clerk's office of the district court for the southern district of New York." This is one of a series of pictures of British and American cities by Kollner. Lithograph, in color. Size 7 x 11.

890—NORTHERN RAILWAY PASSENGER AND FREIGHT STATION —Foot of Brock street (Spadina avenue), Toronto—The buildings, which were erected in 1856, stood on the land below the embankment, Brock

12

street. In 1868 the passenger station was removed to the foot of West Market street, but after the amalgamation with the Grand Trunk, in 1888, the trains ran from the Union Station. Water color. Size 5 x 9.

891—MONTGOMERY, JOHN, 1784-1879—Prominent in Rebellion of 1837—He was of Scottish descent, a son of Alexander Montgomery, who emigrated from the neighborhood of Inverness, Scotland, to Stamford, Conn. After the Revolutionary War he settled at Gagetown, N.B., and here his son, John, was born. The family removed to York (Toronto) in 1798. John Montgomery served on the Niagara frontier during the War of 1812. He succeeded his father in the hotel business on Yonge street, near the present Newtonbrook, and later moved to what is now Eglinton. Here he built the hotel which figured so prominently in the rebellion, and which was burned to the ground. Montgomery was identified with the cause, arrested, taken to Kingston, and, with others, imprisoned at Fort Henry. He escaped, resided at Rochester for some years, but returned to Canada after the passing of the Amnesty Act. His death took place at Barrie, Ont. Water color. Size 3 x 4.

892—WHITE RIVER, ALGOMA DISTRICT—A cold spot in winter and hot in summer—White River, a post village of Northern Ontario, about three hundred miles east of Sudbury, is frequently quoted in the official weather reports, for the thermometer at times registers about 95° in summer and 59° below in winter. It is a divisional point on the C.P.R. (the headquarters are at Schreiber), and is in district No. 3 of the Lake Superior division, which runs from White River to Fort William. Water color. Size 4 x 9.

893—BURGESS, COLIN (COOL)—Famous Canadian minstrel and comedian—He was the pioneer in blackface monologue, his first appearance, travelling with the minstrels, being in the fall of 1858, when he toured with Denman Thompson, Pat Redmond, Harry Collins, and others. When at the height of his career he received a salary of $350 a week. Born in Toronto, 20th Dec., 1840; his death occurred in his native city, 20th Oct., 1905. Water color from original portrait made in 1878. Size 3 x 4. Head and shoulders.

894—CAER HOWELL, TORONTO—Home of Chief Justice William Dummer Powell. Water color. Size 5 x 6. See 895.

895—CAER HOWELL—First house on Queen street avenue—Home of Chief Justice Powell—On 1st May, 1798, park lot No. 12, consisting of 100 acres, west side of Queen's avenue, bounded on the south by Queen street, and on the north by College, was granted to Hon. William Dummer Powell. The house in picture is said to have been built in 1810, and occupied by the Chief Justice until 1820, when he removed to the north-east corner of York and Front streets. As early as 1845, Henry Layton kept an hotel at Caer Howell, the old Powell home forming a part of it. In later years this house was remodelled and eventually rebuilt. The portion of the property on which Caer Howell Hotel stood, was sold in June, 1911, by a descendant of Henry Layton, and resold the following November. The old building, the site of which was north of the present Orde street, was demolished in 1915. Pencil and pen drawing by William D. Powell, grandson of Chief Justice Powell. Size 10 x 14.

896-904—Sheriffs of Home District, Toronto and York, 1792-1917—The Home District was formerly Nassau, Que., constituted by Lord Dorchester's Proclamation of 24th July, 1788. In 1792 the Home District was organized and described as being between the Bay of Quinte and Long Point, Lake Erie. D. W. Smith, in his "Gazetteer of the Province of Upper Canada," 1813, says, with regard to the district, that it "Is now bounded easterly by a line running northward from between Whitby and Darlington townships, on the Lake Ontario, to Talbot River, and from thence to the Lake Nipissing, westerly by the London district, and on the south by the district of Niagara and the Lake Ontario." From time to time the union of the various counties was dissolved, Simcoe leaving in 1843, Ontario in 1853, and Peel in 1867, and independent corporations formed, until in 1887 York and Toronto separated, with Mr. Frederick Mowat as sheriff of the city. It has been impossible up to the present (1917) to locate portraits of Joseph Willcocks, sheriff of the Home District, 1804-09, and his successor, Miles Macdonell, 1809-10.

896—MACDONELL, ALEXANDER (HON.)—Sheriff Home District, 1792-1804—He was second son of Allan Macdonell, of Collachie, and was born at Fort Augustus, in Glengarry, Scotland, 1762. Served as lieutenant in Butler's Rangers during the Revolutionary War, member of the Legislative Assembly for Glengarry and Prescott, 1800-1804, and Speaker, 1805. After his retirement as Sheriff of the Home District, he became agent for Lord Selkirk in establishing a Highland settlement at the Red River. In 1812 he was Colonel of Militia, Deputy Paymaster-General, and later Assistant Secretary Indian Department. His death took place 18th March, 1842. Water color from a portrait in possession of his grandson, Claude Macdonell, K.C., Toronto. Size 3 x 4. Head and shoulders.

897—BEIKIE, JOHN—Sheriff, Home District, 1810-15—Water color. Size 3 x 4. Head and shoulders. See 10.

898—RIDOUT, SAMUEL—Sheriff, Home District, 1815-27—Eldest son of Hon. Thomas Ridout, was born 7th Sept., 1778, in Hancock, Va., and educated there. He came to Canada in 1797. His father, who was a junior official in the Government and later Surveyor-General of Upper Canada, obtained for him a post in the Surveyor-General's office, where he served many years. About 1800 Mr. Ridout bought for $2,400 the park lot of 200 acres between what is now Seaton, Sherbourne, Queen and Bloor streets, and sold the west half to his brother, Thomas Gibbs Ridout. The old home of the Ridouts was "Sherborne," in Dorset, Eng., hence the name of the street that bounded the west side of the park lot—"Sherbourne" street. In 1827 Sheriff Ridout succeeded Col. Stephen Jarvis as registrar of the Home District, retaining the position until his death in 1855. Water color from a daguerreotype in possession of J. Grant Ridout, Toronto. Size 3 x 4. Head and shoulders.

899—JARVIS, WILLIAM BOTSFORD—Sheriff, Home District (York, Simcoe, Ontario), 1827-56—Commanded a regiment of militia during the Rebellion of 1837, married in 1829 Mary Boyles Powell, granddaughter of Chief Justice Wm. Dummer Powell, and for many years resided at "Rosedale," on the north side of Rosedale ravine, Toronto. Colonel Jarvis, who was the third son of Col. Stephen Jarvis, was born 4th May, 1799, and died 26th July, 1864. Photograph, colored. Size 3 x 4. Head and shoulders.

900—JARVIS, FREDERICK W.—Sheriff, Counties York and Peel, 1857-67, and of York until 1887—Eldest son of Frederick Starr Jarvis, born 7th Feb., 1818. Died April, 1887. He was deputy sheriff to his uncle, W. B. Jarvis, whom he succeeded as sheriff of the united counties of York and Peel. Simcoe and Ontario had in 1843 and 1853, respectively, left the union of the counties. Photograph, colored. Size 3 x 4. Head and shoulders.

901—MOWAT, FREDERICK—Sheriff, City of Toronto, 1887-1916—In 1867 the Corporation of the County of Peel met for the first time, and in 1887 York and Toronto divided, with Mr. Mowat as first sheriff of the city. He is a son of the late Sir Oliver Mowat, Lieut.-Governor of Ontario, 1897-1903, and was born at Toronto, 23rd Feb., 1851, educated at Upper Canada College, Toronto, and Galt Grammar School. Photograph, colored. Size 3 x 4. Head and shoulders.

902—WIDDIFIELD JOSEPH H.—Sheriff of York, 1888-1906—Born on lot 32, concession 3, Whitchurch County, 12th June, 1845; a graduate in medicine of Victoria University, 1869, of the Royal College of Surgeons, London, Eng., 1870, and of the Royal College of Physicians, Edinburgh, the same year. From that time until 1888 he practised in Newmarket, Ont. As Liberal member for North York, Dr. Widdifield was elected in 1875 and re-elected 1880, '84 and '87. For seven years he was Parliamentary whip. His death occurred 2nd June, 1906. Photograph, colored, from a portrait in possession of his brother, W. C. Widdifield, Newmarket. Size 3 x 4. Head and shoulders.

903—DAVILLE, FRANK TURNER—Sheriff of York, 1906-1913—He was born at Middleport, Welland County, 8th May, 1846, educated there, and subsequently became engaged in the tannery business. His death took place in Toronto, 27th June, 1913. Photograph, colored. Size 3 x 4. Head and shoulders.

904—McCOWAN, ALEXANDER—Sheriff of York, 1913-17—He was born 27th May, 1853, in the township of Scarboro, first concession, lot 32, and was educated at Section No. 8 school, there. For many years he led the life of a farmer. He was in 1905 elected member for East York in the Ontario Legislature, resigning in 1913 to take the position of Sheriff of York. Photograph, colored. Size 3 x 4. Head and shoulders.

905—YORK, U.C. (TORONTO), APRIL 27TH, 1813—The picture shows the American fleet, commanded by Commodore Isaac Chauncey, landing troops prior to the bombardment of the Fort, at the west end of the town, on the day of the capture of York. A detailed key gives the properties of many of the principal residents of York at that time; also the location of all the military buildings and the residences of private citizens on the day of capitulation. The drawings of the United States armed vessels shown in the picture are exact in every detail, having been copied from originals in possession of the U.S. naval authorities at Annapolis, Md., and in Washington, D.C. Water color. Size 18 x 24.

906—HOMESTEAD OF DAVID WARD, SR., TORONTO ISLAND— Rear view from Lake Ontario side—This dwelling, the second Ward homestead, was built in 1856, and is still (1917) standing. Water color by J. T. Rolph, Toronto. Size 10 x 13. See 887.

907—SITE OF PRICE'S MILL, ROXBOROUGH STREET, TORONTO— The artist chose a pretty subject when he selected a spot near the ravine drive, Rosedale, where a bridge, which crosses Price's Creek, leads the pedestrian up the road to Toronto Lacrosse Grounds. The picture shows at the left hand corner the site of Price's old mill, and its water wheel, just east of where Roxborough street turns east to descend Mather's Hill. The creek was called Price's because it ran through the grounds of the late Hon. James Hervey Price, north of the Toronto Waterworks Reservoir, crossing Yonge street at Mount Pleasant Cemetery, and then finding its way through the Rosedale ravine. Water color by J. T. Rolph, Toronto. Size 10 x 14.

908—OLD GENERAL HOSPITAL, YORK (TORONTO)—About 1820 a General Hospital was built in York from funds supplied by the Loyal and Patriotic Society of Upper Canada. It was a large, two-storey, brick structure, situated at the north-west corner of King and John streets. At a subsequent date two other buildings, in the rear of the main structure, were added for fever patients. After the Houses of Parliament were burned in 1824 the Legislature met in the hospital until 1828, and from 1856-9 it was used as Government offices. It was then unoccupied for several years, and in 1862 torn down and replaced by a row of brick dwellings. These were converted into the Arlington Hotel, which still (1917) stands. Pen drawing. Size 5 x 7.

909—**BRIGHT HOUSE, TORONTO,** 1820-94—The home of a York pioneer on Queen street east. The site is now (1917) occupied by Nos. 696-712 Queen east. For nearly sixty years the old one-storey frame dwelling was the home of John Bright, a veteran of the War of 1812, and at the time of his death, in 1885, the oldest inhabitant of Toronto. Early in life he acquired the plot of land on the north-west corner of Yonge street, which he afterwards traded for the lot on which the house shown in the picture was built. Water color by J. W. Cotton. Size 5 x 7.

910—**KNOX, OR TORONTO ACADEMY**—It was a frame structure at the rear of the third home of Knox College, now (1917) the site of the Queen's Hotel, Front street west, and was intended as preparatory for Knox College. In 1846 the first principal of the academy was appointed in the person of the Rev. Alexander Gale, an eminent Presbyterian clergy-man, who afterwards kept a school at Logie Farm, Cook's Mills, six miles south-east of Hamilton, for many years. When Knox College was removed to Elmsley Villa the academy building was moved still further to the rear and was used as an outhouse, storeroom and kitchen for the hotel con-ducted by Mr. P. Swords. Water color. Size 4 x 5.

911—**McGILL COTTAGE, TORONTO,** 1803-68—At an early date Capt. John McGill obtained the park lot just east of Yonge street on part of which the Metropolitan Methodist Church and St. Michael's R.C. Cathedral now (1917) stand, the former on what was known as McGill Square, which was bounded by Church, Queen, Shuter and Bond streets. In this square Capt. McGill built the residence shown in picture. For a long period it was occupied by Mr. McCutcheon, who, in accordance with his uncle's (Peter McGill) will, assumed the name of McGill. Further north, running east from Yonge street, is McGill street, named after the original owner of the pro-perty. Capt. John McGill was an officer of the Queen's Rangers, the corps commanded by Lieut.-Col. Simcoe, afterwards first Lieut.-Governor of Upper Canada, and was with that corps during the American Revolutionary War. He became Commissioner of Stores for Upper Canada, 1793. In 1805 he was Inspector-General for Provincial Parliament accounts, and in 1818 Receiver-General and Auditor-General of Land Patents. Water color. Size 5 x 7.

912—**BELL'S (GERRARD STREET) BRIDGE OVER THE DON,** 1860— Below the Riverdale bridge, on the west side of the river, looking south-east. The structure received its name from Mr. John Bell, Q.C., of the firm of Bell & Crowther, and a director of the Don & Danforth Road Co. He was the owner of the property on the west side of Don street, facing the river, and was the moving spirit in having the bridge erected. The building, with the smoke stack, to the right, was William Parsons' oil refinery, No. 9 Don street, now (1917) the site of the Kemp Mfg. Company. The houses to the south were on Don street, in the vicinity of the present Munro and Hamilton streets. In the immediate foreground is a marsh. When Bell's bridge was erected, Gerrard, from Parliament to the Don, was known as Don street. Water color by J. Hoch, Toronto. Size 6 x 13.

913—**OLD LOG DWELLING, YORK (TORONTO)**—West side of Broadview avenue, north of Queen street—It was at the time of its de-molition, in 1894, one of the oldest houses in Toronto, and for forty-two years the residence of Captain James Sparks, who purchased the unpre-tentious, one-and-a-half-storey, low dwelling in 1840, clap-boarding it a few years later. There is a tradition which fixes the date of its erection at or about the same time as that of Castle Frank, one-time residence of Governor Simcoe. Captain Sparks, a Scotsman, emigrated to Canada in 1818, and at an early age began work as a sailor on Lake Ontario, continu-ing that calling until his retirement. In his day he commanded many lake schooners, his last being the "Beaver," which was wrecked at Rochester about 1865. For many years during the winter months, especially from 1822-50, Capt. Sparks acted as tyler for the Masonic Lodge meeting in the Market Lane Hall. Water color. Size 5 x 6.

914—OLD PEACOCK TAVERN, TORONTO—It was a popular stopping-place for farmers on their way to and from the city, and was built about 1845 on Dundas street, near the red brick cottage of Mr. John Scarlett, "father" of West Toronto Junction. It was long ago torn down and replaced by an hotel of the same name, corner Bradd and Dundas streets. Water color by J. W. Cotton. Size 5 x 7.

915—FIRST SCHOOLHOUSE ON TORONTO ISLAND—This view is from the east of the lighthouse, on the ridge east of the Public school; built 1888; burnt, 24th May, 1909, and rebuilt the same year a short distance west of the old site. Water color by J. T. Rolph, Toronto. Size 4½ x 5.

916—PRIVAT'S HOTEL, TORONTO ISLAND—In 1843 Louis Privat opened as a hotel the summer residence built on the Island by Lord Sydenham in 1839. A year later he was joined by his brother, Louis Joseph Privat, with his family. In connection with the hotel the brothers operated the "Peninsula Packet," invariably known simply as "the horse boat," and later the "Victoria," with a steam engine of 25 h.p., was built. In 1853 Louis Privat removed to Durham, Grey County, where he kept a hotel until his death in 1860; and toward the end of 1855 his brother migrated to Bentinck Township, County Grey. When the brothers left the Island they were succeeded by John Quinn; but the site on which their house stood is now covered by the waters of the eastern entrance to Toronto Bay. Water color. Size 5 x 7.

917—SLEEPY HOLLOW, TORONTO—The home of Hon. John Beverley Robinson, built by him in 1849. It was a white, frame, roughcast house, surrounded by woods stretching down to Caer-Howell, and was situated on the south-west corner of College street and University avenue. With the exception of the years of his term as Lieutenant-Governor of Ontario, 1880-7, Mr. Robinson occupied Sleepy Hollow from 1849 until his death in 1895. The old residence stood west of the present (1917) Toronto Conservatory of Music. Water color. Size 5 x 7.

918—SOUTH-EAST CORNER KING AND BAY STREETS, TORONTO, 1868-76—A business centre from the early days. In 1820 Jordan Post, watchmaker, had his store on this corner. From 1840-67 Jacques & Hay occupied a warehouse on site. Then James W. Gale, gents' furnishings, and R. Phillips, carver, carried on business, and rear of building, on Bay street, was used by Wm. Halley as a printers' emporium. These buildings were torn down in 1876, others erected, and in turn demolished. The Union Bank now (1917) stands on the corner. Water color. Size 5 x 7.

919—UNITED PRESBYTERIAN CHURCH, TORONTO—South-east corner Bay and Richmond streets. The congregation met first in the March or Stanley (Lombard) Street Baptist Chapel, up to 1840. In 1841 they purchased the Methodist Episcopal Chapel, Richmond street, and in 1848 the new church at the corner of Bay and Richmond streets was erected. Rev. John Jennings, who came to Canada in 1838, was inducted pastor, 9th July, 1839. He resigned his pastorate in 1874. The church was in the perpendicular English Gothic style of architecture, of white brick with cut stone facings, having a square tower at the went end. William Thomas was the architect. In 1880 the property was sold to the College of Physicians and Surgeons, who installed offices therein. It was demolished in 1886 to make room for a new building, which was occupied by the College of Physicians and Surgeons, and also as an office building. In 1907 it passed into the hands of the Continental Life Co., some storeys were added, and the structure became a prominent office building. Water color by F. V. Poole. Size 6 x 7.

920—MASHQUOTEH (FIRST) HOUSE, TORONTO—This residence, built by William Augustus Baldwin in 1851, stood on what is now (1917) Avenue road, just south of Heath street. The building, demolished in 1890, was of hewn timber, from the Baldwin estate, filled in with brick and roughcast. An elm tree, which stands in front of the site of the house, had a chain attached to a staple driven into the tree, to which horses were tethered. The chain was about a foot long when placed there about fifty years ago. To-day the tree has grown round all the links save one, which may still be seen by passers-by. "Mashquoteh" means in the original Indian, "a meadow," or "a clearing in the forest." Water color. Size 4 x 6.

921—RUSSELL HILL, TORONTO—Home of Captain (Admiral) Augustus Baldwin—The residence shown was built by Captain Baldwin in the forties, on the west side of what is now (1917) Poplar Plains road, and on the site of the Nordheimer home. Augustus Baldwin entered the Royal Navy in 1794; was at Copenhagen, 1807; appointed to the "Tyrian" brig in 1812. On his retirement, in 1846, settled at Toronto, where he built Russell Hill. Water color. Size 5 x 6.

922—OLD NATIONAL CLUB, TORONTO—On the west side of Bay street, south of King. The club was originally organized, and headquarters established, to give the "Canada First" party a local "habitation." In July, 1874, the charter was issued, the club rooms being opened the following March, with Prof. Goldwin Smith as first president. Membership increased to such an extent that new club rooms became necessary, and the Robinson House property, on the east side of Bay street, north of King, was purchased. The present building was erected there, the club formally taking possession on December 17th, 1907. Water color. Size 5 x 7.

923—WRECK OF THE "MONARCH"—The disaster occurred off Toronto Island about five o'clock in the morning of Saturday, November 29th, 1856. A heavy storm had arisen, and, in the darkness, Captain Sinclair, misjudging his position, turned the vessel towards the city. Discovering his mistake, he endeavored to turn out towards the lake again, but a heavy sea drove the freighter on to the shelving clay in rear of Privat's Hotel, not more than fifteen yards from the beach, and she stuck fast. Her deck load was completely washed off, the hold filled with water, and it was with difficulty that the crew got ashore. On the Tuesday and Wednesday following a violent storm broke the "Monarch's" hull in three places and all hope of saving her was abandoned. A part of her machinery was removed, but the cargo was almost a total loss. In 1862 Captain Hugh Richardson, then Harbor Master, reported that the breach in the late peninsula was about half a mile wide, and that the old line of the beach had moved so far that the boiler of the wrecked "Monarch," once high and dry on the beach, was then in deep water about one hundred yards out in the lake. The "Monarch" was a new freight and passenger steamer, plying between Montreal and Hamilton, stopping at Toronto. With key. Water color. Size 9 x 11.

924—KEARSNEY HOUSE ("DUNDONALD"), TORONTO—East side of Yonge street, north of Wellesley—Built in 1848 by the late William Proudfoot, a prominent merchant in Toronto, and president of the old Bank of Upper Canada. It was a large white brick residence, always noted for hearty hospitality and sumptuous entertainments. On one occasion Mr. Proudfoot presided over quite an extensive fancy fair, which was held in the drawing-room, a magnificent apartment, seventy-five feet in length by twenty-five feet wide. In 1862 Mr. Robert Cassels acquired the property, disposing of it in 1869 to Mr. Donald Mackay, who renamed the house "Dundonald." During the latter's occupancy the members of the General Assembly of the Church of Scotland in Canada were entertained there. In June, 1904, on the opening of the street now known as Dundonald, the dwelling was demolished. Water color. Size 5 x 7.

925—BISHOP MACDONELL'S HOUSE, YORK (TORONTO)—For some years after Miss Russell's death (sister of Hon. Peter Russell) her home on Palace (Front) street was occupied by Hon. and Right Rev. Alexander Macdonell, first Roman Catholic Bishop of Upper Canada. On his return from Europe in 1826 the brick dwelling on the south-east corner of Jarvis and Duchess streets became his residence. His private chapel,. once renowned as the "soup kitchen," was a large frame building nearly opposite. The old house, which faces on Jarvis street, is still (1917) standing. Water color. Size 5 x 7.

926—ST. PAUL'S HALL—The old Town Hall of Yorkville—On the west side of Yonge street, north of Bloor; erected 1859-60 by William Hay, architect, and William McGinnis, contractor. Until February, 1883, the municipal offices and Council Chamber were in use as such, but at that date Yorkville was incorporated with Toronto, being designated as St. Paul's Ward. From 1884 until 1907, when the new library building on Yorkville avenue was completed, the Council room was used as a public library. The clock in the tower was installed in 1889. Now (1917) the south wing, No. 856 Yonge street, is Dobson's stationery store; No. 858 is St. Paul's Hall, and 860, Police Station No. 5. Water color. Size 4 x 7.

927—BOSTWICK HOUSE AND WAGON SHOP—On what is now Toronto's busiest thoroughfare—Mr. Lardner Bostwick, a U.E.L., came to Canada from Baltimore in 1810, settling in York. He purchased, shortly after his arrival, about two acres on the south-east corner of King and Yonge streets, extending from King to Colborne, and from Yonge to the site of the King Edward Hotel. On part of this property, the present site of the hotel, his residence and wagon shop were located. Both buildings were of frame. Mr. Bostwick in his business did for the farmers of Upper Canada what in later years the Speight Co., of Markham, and the Bain Wagon Co., of Woodstock, did for the farmers of their day in Ontario. Water color by F. V. Poole. Size 5 x 7.

928—AIKINSHAW—Residence of Col. E. W. Thomson. It was occupied by Col. Thomson, a veteran of the War of 1812, from 1844-65, and enjoyed the distinction of being the first brick house built on Dundas road (street) between Toronto and the Humber. What is now Keele street ran as a concession from the present St. Clair avenue, west to Dundas, forming the eastern boundary of the farm of Aikinshaw. Water color. Size 5 x 7.

929—OLD BLUE SCHOOL, YORK (TORONTO)—Centre "Block D," built 1816. In April, 1807, after the passing of "An Act to establish Public Schools in each and every district of this Province," the Home District school was opened in York, at s.e. corner George and King streets. In 1813 it was removed to a barn, corner King and Yonge streets, Dr. Strachan taking charge. A new building became necessary, and in 1816 the school was removed to the centre of College Square, north of present St. James' Cathedral. It was painted a bluish color, and for this reason was known as the Old Blue School, afterwards the Toronto Grammar School. In 1829 the building was removed to the s.e. corner of New (Jarvis) and March (Lombard) streets, and used by Upper Canada College until 1831. The Grammar School was closed for some years and re-opened in 1834 in the old building. In January, 1864, it was held on the east side of Dalhousie street, just north of Gould, and in 1870 in old King's College, Queen's Park. The school was opened in 1871 in a new building on Jarvis street, now (1917) Jarvis Street Collegiate Institute. Water color. Size 5 x 6. See 2812.

930—SOUTH-WEST CORNER KING AND BAY STREETS, TORONTO, 1898—No. 55 King street, corner of Bay, is The Evening Telegram; No. 57, George Harcourt & Sons, tailors; 59, R. Parker & Co., dyers; 61, National Watch Co.; 63, McIlroy & Co., tailors; 65, P. Dwyer, tailor; 67, J. Hunter

& Co., tailors; 69, Bilton Bros., tailors; 71, R. Dack & Son, boots and shoes. South of The Telegram building, on Bay street, was The Telegram Annex (the McGinn Restaurant), No. 102; then the old National Club, No. 98. J. H. Ames, tailor, was No. 96. Immediately south, No. 94, was vacant, and the Toronto Engraving Company occupied No. 92. The Bank of Toronto is now (1917) built upon the site of the old building of The Telegram and adjoining properties on Bay and King streets. Water color. Size 9 x 12.

931—FIRST RESIDENCE OF LIEUT.-COL. R. L. DENISON—Northwest corner Dundas street and Ossington avenue, Toronto. It was a pretty roughcast cottage, with verandah, facing on Dundas street, and occupied by Lieut.-Col. Richard Lippincott Denison until the completion of Dovercourt in 1853. The old homestead was afterwards the residence of Dr. Thomas Savage for several years. Stores, Nos. 216-20 Dundas street, now (1917) stand on the site. Water color by J. W. Cotton. Size 5 x 7.

932—BROCKTON TOLL BAR, TORONTO, 1852—North side of Dundas street, between the present (1917) Sheridan and Brock avenues, close to the line between park lots 29 and 30. It disappeared when the boundaries of the city were extended to the north-west. The first owner of the land on the north-eastern side of Dundas street, from Ossington to Brock avenues, was Lieut.-Col. G. T. Denison, of Bellevue, Toronto. Water color by J. W. Cotton. Size 5 x 7.

933—GWYNNE COTTAGE, TORONTO, 1848—Dr. W. C. Gwynne, an Irishman by birth, was, during the Rebellion of 1837, surgeon to one of the regiments of incorporated militia here, and for many years took an active interest in the medical department of Toronto University. The picturesque one-and-a-half-storey cottage shown in the picture was erected by him on the west side of Dufferin street, below King. In style it resembled an Indian bungalow. Here Dr. Gwynne died in 1875, and his widow eight years later. A daughter, Miss Gwynne, died in the old homestead in 1910. The cottage was demolished in July, 1917. Water color. Size 5 x 7.

934—PROTESTANT ORPHANS' HOME, TORONTO, 1864—When Jenny Lind visited Toronto in 1851, she gave a concert in St. Lawrence Hall, the proceeds of which were to be devoted to some charity commemorative of the event. After some deliberation it was decided to found the Protestant Orphans' Home, and in 1854 a permanent site on Sullivan street was presented by Hon. Robert Baldwin and Hon. William Cayley, and a building erected. Rev. Stephen Lett, rector of St. George's Anglican church, and Dr. Rees, at one time Superintendent of the Hospital for the Insane, were among the founders of the institution. In 1882 the home was removed to Dovercourt road, and dwellings were built on the Sullivan street property. Pen drawing, colored. Size 5 x 7.

935—CHECK TOLL GATE, 1857—It was one of the four toll gates on Dundas street, and for forty years stood on the north side of that highway at its junction with the concession now known as St. Clair avenue west, which extends from Dundas on the west to Yonge street on the east. In 1894 the toll system was abolished in Ontario, and three years later the old check gate at Lambton disappeared. Water color. Size 5 x 6.

936—OLD ARMORY AND DRILL SHED, TORONTO—East side of West Market street, south of Front. When the old drill shed on the east side of Simcoe, which had its entrance from Wellington street, fell down about 1875, a movement to erect a new armory took definite form. In 1877 the Queen's Own and 10th Royals (Grenadiers) used the West Market street building until the completion in 1895 of the present (1917) Armories on University avenue, to the rear of Osgoode Hall. Pen drawing, colored. Size 5 x 7.

937—RESIDENCE AND BROOM FACTORY OF J. B. CAULKINS, TORONTO—West side of Yonge street, near College, 1865. The site formerly belonged to Dr. James Macaulay, as did all the land on the west side of Yonge street from Lot (Queen) street to College. On his death it was sold to Dr. Clark, Yonge street, who built the substantial brick structure shown in the picture, selling it almost immediately after its completion to J. B. Caulkins, of Smith and Caulkins, brush and broom manufacturers. Later the firm, which carried on an extensive business, became Caulkins and Sanderson. Stores now (1917) occupy the site. Water color. Size 5 x 7.

938—"BLIND" TOLL GATE, TORONTO—North-east corner of Dundas street and the concession now (1917) known as Bloor street. It was a peculiar two-storey structure, with a covered way extending across Dundas street. Tolls were never exacted here from teams proceeding direct along Dundas, the gate having been erected for the purpose of catching people who drove along Dufferin street, north to the concession, thence proceeding west to Dundas on their way from Toronto, and thus avoiding the Brockton gate. With the extension of the city the "blind" toll gate disappeared. Water color. Size 5 x 7.

939—NORTH SIDE OF KING STREET EAST, TORONTO, 1866—This view shows No. 24, the store of P. Paterson & Sons, hardware merchants; No. 26-8, the Globe office; No. 30, Forbes & King, exchange office; No. 34, J. E. Spafford, sewing machines. In the first floor of No. 34 were the rooms of the Y.M.C.A. in 1866. No. 36-8 were Lyman & Macnab, general hardware; No. 40, E. Harris, chinaware. The site is now (1917) Nos. 26-38 King street east. Water color. Size 5 x 6.

940—WEST SIDE OF TORONTO STREET, TORONTO, 1858—Showing the Post Office and Canada Permanent buildings. The structure with the Ionic columns was the seventh Post Office, 1852-73. The next building to the north is that of the Canada Permanent, the ground floor of which is now occupied by financial offices, and from 1857-98 the upper floor was used as a Masonic Hall. The red brick buildings to the north were the offices of the Toronto Mutual Fire Insurance Co. and F. P. Stow, broker. The Excelsior Life Co. building now (1917) occupies the site of the buildings up to the s.w. corner of Toronto and Adelaide streets. Water color. Size 5 x 6.

941-82—Presidents of the St. Andrew's Society, Toronto, 1836-1917.

941—ALLAN, HON. WILLIAM—President St. Andrew's Society, 1836-7 —Born at Moss Farm, near Huntley, Scotland, in 1770. On coming to Canada he settled at Niagara, but removed to York (Toronto) during the Simcoe regime. He was Post Master of York, 1816-27, and also fulfilled the duties of Collector of Customs. When the British America Assurance Company was incorporated in 1833 the first governor to be elected was the Hon. Mr. Allan. In the War of 1812-14 he served as lieut.-colonel in the militia. Was a member of the Legislature for many years, and of the Executive Council, 1837-8. He died in Toronto in 1853. Photograph, colored. Size 3 x 4. See 610, 3541.

942—BUCHANAN, ISAAC—President St. Andrew's Society, 1837-8, 1840-1—Born in Glasgow, Scotland, in 1810, came to Canada twenty years later, as a partner of the firm William Guild, Jr., Sons & Co. He was very much interested in reform, and as a Reformer was elected to a Toronto seat in the Legislature in 1841. He was well-known as a member of the firm Buchanan, Harris & Co., wholesale dry goods, of Hamilton, Montreal and Liverpool, which he established in Hamilton early in the forties. In 1858, 1861 and 1863 Mr. Buchanan represented the constituency of Hamilton in the United Parliament of Canada. His death occurred in Hamilton, Ont., in 1883. Photograph, colored. Size 3 x 4. Head and shoulders. See 1413.

943—McLEAN, HON. ARCHIBALD—President St. Andrew's Society, 1838-40, 1841-6—Came to York (Toronto) in 1808 to study law, and pursued his studies until the outbreak of the War of 1812, when he received a commission in the 3rd York Militia; fought at Queenston Heights and Lundy's Lane. Called to the bar in 1815, afterwards returning to Cornwall, where he had received his early education, and practised there until 1837. In 1820 he was elected to represent Stormont in the Legislative Assembly. He took up the duties of Puisne Judge of the King's Bench in March, 1837; in 1850 became Puisne Judge in the Common Pleas Court, but six years later returned to the Court of the Queen's Bench, becoming Chief Justice in 1862. He was born in St. Andrew's, Stormont. son of Col. Neil McLean, a noted soldier of Scottish birth. Judge McLean died in 1865. Photograph, colored. Size 3 x 4. Head and shoulders.

944—CAMERON, JOHN—President St. Andrew's Society, 1846-8— Born at Berwick-on-Tweed in 1810, of Scottish parents, his father being of the Clan Cameron of Lochiel. Subsequent to his emigrating to Canada he was teller in the Commercial Bank at Kingston, Ont., later coming to Toronto as first manager of that bank here. His death occurred in 1867. Water color. Size 3 x 4. Head and shoulders. See 583.

945—RIDOUT, THOMAS GIBBS—President St. Andrew's Society, 1848-50—Born at Sorel, L.C., in 1792, and came to York (Toronto) with his parents four years later. In 1813 he became Deputy Assistant Commissary-General, holding that position until 1820; was one of the organizers of the Bank of Upper Canada, and filled the position of cashier in the bank. He was also the first president of the Mechanics' Institute, which later became the Toronto Public Library. Died in 1861. Water color. Size 3 x 4. Head and shoulders.

946—MORRISON, HON. JOSEPH CURRAN—President St. Andrew's Society, 1850-2—Studied law as a fellow student of Chancellor Blake, subsequently forming a partnership with him, which continued until Mr. Blake's elevation to the Bench in 1846. In 1843 Mr. Morrison became Clerk of the Executive Council, and was prominent in Political Reform circles. In 1853 he was appointed Solicitor-General for Upper Canada, and in 1856, Receiver-General. Made Registrar of Toronto, 1859, and three years later became Puisne Judge of the Common Pleas, being transferred to the Queen's Bench the following year. Mr. Morrison was born in Ireland, 1816, though of Scottish descent. Died in Toronto, 1885. Photograph, colored. Size 3 x 4. Head and shoulders. See 3518.

947—MORRISON, ANGUS—President St. Andrew's Society, 1852-4— Born in Edinburgh, Scotland. in 1820. Was well-known lawyer in Toronto,' and Mayor of the city from 1876-8. Previous to Confederation he sat in the Parliament of Canada as member for North Simcoe and Niagara. His death took place in Toronto in 1882. Photograph, colored. Size 3 x 4. Head and shoulders. See 384.

948—ARTHURS, WILLIAM—President St. Andrew's Society, 1874-6— He was born in Toronto in 1832, and on arriving at maturity became a member of the firm of Thomas & Arthurs, dry goods merchants. He was active in local militia circles, being made ensign in the Queen's Own Rifles in 1865, and retiring as brevet lieutenant-colonel in 1881, having attained that rank some years previously. During the Fenian Raid Mr. Arthurs saw active service. His death occurred in 1887. Photograph, colored. Size 3 x 4. Head and shoulders.

949—McMURRICH, WILLIAM BARCLAY—President St. Andrew's Society, 1876-8—Born in Toronto in 1842, the eldest son of the Hon. John McMurrich. In 1866 he was called to the bar, and in 1879 represented St.

Patrick's Ward in the City Council; two years afterwards became Mayor for two terms. During his mayoralty he had the municipal by-laws consolidated, and it was he who instituted the system of deposits by contractors and duplicate contracts as a guarantee. At the time of the Trent affair he joined the volunteer militia, and afterwards became captain of the Toronto Garrison Artillery. His death occurred in 1908. Photograph, colored. Size 3 x 4. Head and shoulders. See 386.

950—RAMSAY, WILLIAM—President St. Andrew's Society, 1879-81—Born at Dalkeith, near Edinburgh, Scotland, in 1835; came to Canada in 1854, and carried on business as a wholesale grocer in Toronto. In 1882 he retired and returned to Scotland, where he now (1917) resides. He was vice-president of the Toronto, Grey and Bruce Railway, which later merged with the C.P.R., and was also a director of the Imperial Bank. During his residence in Canada he took an active part in military matters. Photograph, colored. Size 3 x 4. Head and shoulders.

951—MICHIE, JAMES—President St. Andrew's Society, 1881-3—Born in Aberdeenshire, Scotland, in 1828; he later came to Canada and entered the service of Alexander Ogilvie & Company, wholesale grocers, on King street west, Toronto, becoming a partner in the firm in 1852. Mr. Michie's name was prominently associated with the progress and development of the Toronto of his time. Founded the Home for Incurables here, and was also a member of the Council of Queen's College, Kingston. He died in 1883. Photograph, colored. Size 3 x 4. Head and shoulders.

952—GRAHAM, JAMES—President St. Andrew's Society, 1883-4—Born in Scotland and returned to that country about 1886. He was for many years manager of the Toronto agency of the City Bank of Montreal. His death occurred in Edinburgh, Scotland. Photograph, colored. Size 3 x 4. Head and shoulders.

953—CATTENACH, A. J.—President St. Andrew's Society, 1884-7—Born at Laggan, Glengarry, Ont.; educated at L'Orignal, Que., and the University of Toronto. He studied for the bar, and from 1859-83 was a member of the law firm of Crooks, Kingsmill & Cattenach, and later of Kingsmill, Cattenach & Symonds. In 1889 he was made a Queen's Counsel. Died 1890. Photograph, colored. Size 3 x 4. Head and shoulders.

954—WILKIE, DANIEL ROBERT—President St. Andrew's Society, 1887-9—Born in Quebec in 1846. In 1862 he entered the service of the Quebec Bank, becoming manager of the St. Catharines branch, 1867, and of the Toronto branch in 1872. On the foundation of the Imperial Bank of Canada in 1875 he was made general manager, and in 1906 was elected president. He also acted as president and vice-president of the Canadian Bankers' Association, and president of the Toronto Board of Trade; was prominent in advocating the establishment of a branch of the Royal Mint in Canada. During the Trent affair served in the volunteer militia. His death occurred in Toronto, Nov. 17th, 1914. Photograph, colored. Size 3 x 4. Head and shoulders. See 639.

955—CAMERON, HON. J. HILLYARD—President St. Andrew's Society, 1854-5—Served with the militia on the Niagara frontier in 1837-8; was called to the bar in the latter year, and became reporter in the Court of the Queen's Bench in 1843. Three years later he became Queen's Counsel and Solicitor-General in Upper Canada, and from 1854-7 sat in Parliament as a member for Toronto. When Trinity University was founded, Mr. Cameron was appointed to the Faculty of Law. He was also president of the Provincial Insurance Co., of Canada. Born at Beaucaire, Languedoc, France, in 1817; died in Toronto in 1876. Photograph, colored. Size 3 x 4. Head and shoulders.

956—**ALLAN, (HON.) GEORGE WILLIAM**—President St. Andrew's Society, 1855-6—Born in York (Toronto), 1822; a son of Hon. William Allan. Called to the bar in 1846. Elected Mayor of Toronto, 1855, and from 1858-67 was member for York Division in Legislative Council of old Canada. In the latter year he was called to the Senate. He was also Chancellor of the University of Trinity College from 1877-1901, and one of the original members of the Canadian Institute (Royal Canadian Institute, 1914). Filled the position of chief commissioner of the Canada Company. Died in 1901. Water color. Size 3 x 4. Head and shoulders. See 373.

957—**EWART, JOHN**—President St. Andrew's Society, 1856-7—Born at York (Toronto), 25th Feb., 1822. Died 2nd July, 1861. Educated at Market Lane Private School and Upper Canada College, of which he was head boy in his final year. He presented St. Andrew's Society, when president, with a ram's head snuff mull, which is still (1917) in use at he society's dinners. Photograph, colored. Size 3 x 4. Head and shoulders.

958—**MACDONALD, ALEXANDER**—President St. Andrew's Society, 1857-8—He was born in Ross-shire, Scotland, 1810, the oldest son of Hugh Macdonald; graduated from Aberdeen and Glasgow Universities, and in 1835 came to this country as solicitor for the Canada Company. For some years he was a member of the firm of Macdonald & Brother, north-west corner King and Bay streets, Toronto, site of the present Mail building. Died Feb., 1863. Water color. Size 3 x 4. Head and shoulders.

959—**HENDERSON, WILLIAM**—President St. Andrew's Society, 1858-9 Carried on a grocery business in Toronto, and for some years acted as representative of the Hartford Fire Insurance Co. in Canada. In 1855-6 represented St. David's Ward in the City Council. He was born in Halkirk, Scotland, in 1815, and in 1833 he emigrated to Canada. His death occurred in October, 1891. Photograph, colored. Size 3 x 4. Head and shoulders.

960—**MILLER, ROBERT SCHAW**—President St. Andrew's Society, 1859-61—Son of John Miller, Alloa, a small town on the River Forth, Scotland. In 1841, when quite a young man, he emigrated to Canada, and for a time was in the employ of Messrs. Cavillier & Sons, Montreal. Four years later he entered the service of J. D. Bernard, commission merchant, subsequently removing to Toronto, where he became a member of the firm of Miller & Foulds, wholesale dry goods merchants, Wellington street east. He died in Montreal in 1862. His son is Sir John O. Miller, Arkley, Herts, Eng. His eldest grandson, Godfrey Lyall Miller, of the Royal Engineers, King's Medalist at Woolwich, was killed at the Battle of the Aisne, Sept. 14, 1914. Photograph, colored. Size 3 x 4. Head and shoulders.

961—**MICHIE, GEORGE**—President St. Andrew's Society, 1861-2—Born in Scotland in 1811, subsequently came to Canada, settling in Toronto. In 1840 he became a partner in the business of Alexander Ogilvie & Co., the firm later becoming George Michie & Company, now (1917) known as Michie & Company, Limited. Mr. Michie's death occurred in London, England, in 1866. Photograph, colored. Size 3 x 4. Head and shoulders.

962—**CLARK, DR. DANIEL**—President St. Andrew's Society, 1889-91—Born at Granton, Inverness-shire, Scotland, in 1835, and came to Canada in 1841. Studied medicine and practised at Princeton, Ont., having previously been a volunteer surgeon in the army of Potomac, under General Grant, during a part of the American Civil War. From 1875 until 1905 he was superintendent of the Provincial Lunatic Asylum at Toronto. He also wrote a number of books on medical and other subjects. Died in 1912. Photograph, colored. Size 3 x 4. Head and shoulders.

963—**THORBURN, DR. JAMES**—President St. Andrew's Society, 1891-3 —Born at Queenston, U.C., in 1830; studied at Toronto and Edinburgh Universities, graduating from the latter institution in 1855, and practising medicine subsequently in Toronto. Was at Ridgeway in 1866 with the Queen's Own Rifles, in the capacity of surgeon, and retired as surgeon-major in 1879. In 1895 he was elected president of the Canadian Medical Association, and two years later became president of the Ontario Medical Council. His death took place in 1905. Photograph, colored. Size 3 x 4. Head and shoulders.

964—**CASSELS, ALLAN**—President St. Andrew's Society, 1893-5— Born in Quebec in 1847, the son of Robert Cassels, banker; called to the bar in 1871, and for a number of years was a member of the legal firm of Beaty, Hamilton & Cassels, later becoming senior partner in the firm of Cassels & Standish. His death occurred in Toronto in 1909. Photograph, colored. Size 3 x 4. Head and shoulders.

965—**COSBY, ALFRED MORGAN**—President St. Andrew's Society, 1895-7—Born in Pelham, Welland County, Ontario, in 1840, of U.E. Loyalist stock. In 1861 he entered the service of the Bank of Toronto and became manager of the Port Hope branch, but resigned in 1876 to become managing director of the London and Ontario Investment Co. In 1882 he was also one of the charter directors of the Gooderham & Worts Co. He aided in the raising of the 48th Highlanders in 1891, and held the rank of senior major of the regiment from its formation. His death took place in Toronto in 1900. Photograph, colored. Size 3 x 4. Head and shoulders.

966—**COCKBURN, G. R. R.**—President St. Andrew's Society, 1897-9— Born in Edinburgh, Scotland, in 1834; educated at Edinburgh University, continuing his classical studies in France and Germany. In 1858 he became rector of the Model Grammar School for Upper Canada. Shortly afterwards he was appointed to inspect the higher educational institutions of Ontario. In 1861 became president of Toronto University, which position he held for over twenty years. From 1887-96 he sat for Centre Toronto in Dominion Parliament. At the World's Fair, Chicago, 1893, represented Canada as Chief Commissioner, and the following year became president of the Ontario Bank. He died in London, England, in 1912. Photograph, colored. Size 3 x 4. Head and shoulders. See 629, 3653.

967—**CLARK, SIR WILLIAM MORTIMER**—President St. Andrew's Society, 1899-1901—Born in Aberdeen, Scotland, son of John C. Clark, general manager of the Scottish Providential Assurance Co.; educated at Aberdeen and Edinburgh Universities, became a barrister in 1861, and a Q.C. in 1887; was one of the founders and first directors of St. Andrew's College for Boys, Toronto; was also director of the Metropolitan Bank, Consumers' Gas Co., and the Canadian General Electric Co. From 1903-8 he served as Lieutenant-Governor of Ontario, and in 1907 received a knighthood. His death occurred Aug. 10th, 1917, at Prout's Neck, Me., where he was spending the summer. Photograph, colored. Size 3 x 4. Head and shoulders. See 429.

968—**KENNEDY, GEORGE**—President St. Andrew's Society, 1901-3— Born at By-town (Ottawa) in 1838; graduated from Toronto University in 1857, and was called to the bar in 1865, practising his profession in Ottawa, and becoming a K.C. in 1902. In 1872 he received the appointment of law clerk in the Department of Crown Lands, Ontario, which position he held until his death in 1916. Dr. Kennedy wrote various works, "The Relation of Law to Science" being one of them. Photograph, colored. Size 3 x 4. Head and shoulders.

969—**BROWN, HON GEORGE**—President St. Andrew's Society, 1862-4, 1878-9—Photograph, colored. Size 3 x 4. Head and shoulders. See 475, 3385.

970—McBRIDE, JOHN—President St. Andrew's Society, 1864-5—Born at Prescott, Ont., in 1836; studied law and was called to the bar in 1855, subsequently practising his profession in Toronto until his decease in 1878. Photograph, colored. Size 3 x 4. Head and shoulders.

971—CASSELS, ROBERT—President St. Andrew's Society, 1865-6—Born in Quebec in 1843; died in Toronto, 18th Feb., 1882. Was called to the bar in Lower Canada in 1864, and two years later called to the bar of Upper Canada. On the organization of the Supreme Court of Canada in 1875, he was appointed its registrar, and a decade afterwards became a Queen's Counsel. He was one of the founders of St. Luke's Hospital, Ottawa. Photograph, colored. Size 3 x 4. Head and shoulders.

972—SMITH, ALEXANDER MORTIMER—President St. Andrew's Society, 1866-7—Carried on business as wholesale grocer in Toronto for many years, and was also well known in banking circles. Sat in the Parliament of Canada in 1862 as representative of East Toronto. Died in 1895. Photograph, colored. Size 3 x 4. Head and shoulders.

973—MACPHERSON, (HON. SIR) DAVID LEWIS—President St. Andrew's Society, 1867-70—Born in Inverness-shire, Scotland, in 1818; came to Canada in 1835. He represented Saugeen Division, L.C., from 1864 until 1867, when he was called to the Senate. In 1883 became Minister of the Interior, resigning in 1885. In 1868 he was appointed arbitrator for Ontario under the British North America Act, for the division and adjustment of debts, credits, liabilities and properties of Upper and Lower Canada, and in 1884 was created a K.C.M.G. He was also a director of Molson's Bank, of Western Canada Permanent Loan & Savings, president of the Inter-Oceanic Railway Co., and a member of the firm of Gzowski & Co. Died 1896. Photograph, colored. Size 3 x 4. Head and shoulders.

974—WILSON, DR. (SIR) DANIEL—President St. Andrew's Society, 1870-2—Born in Edinburgh, Scotland, in 1816; died in Toronto in 1892. In 1843 he came to Canada and was appointed to the chair of history and English literature in Toronto University, becoming president of that institution in 1881. Seven years later he was knighted. Sir Daniel was well-known as a writer of books, and was also prominent in philanthropic circles, the Newsboys' Home, Toronto, having originated with him. Photograph, colored. Size 3 x 4. Head and shoulders.

975—GORDON, JOHN—President St. Andrew's Society, 1872-4—Born at Latheron, Caithness, Scotland, in 1822, but came to Canada when thirteen years of age, settling in Grenville and then in Peterboro. Later he moved to Hamilton and established a wholesale dry goods business there, subsequently taking his uncle into partnership with him, the firm being known as Gordon, Mackay & Co. Later the business was moved to Toronto. Mr. Gordon was the first to establish cotton manufacturing in Canada, and was the founder of the Lybster Cotton Mills at Welland. He was also president of the Toronto, Grey & Bruce Railway, and director of many public companies. His death occurred in Paris, France, in 1875. Photograph, colored. Size 3 x 4. Head and shoulders.

976—NAIRN, ALEXANDER—President St. Andrew's Society, 1903-5—Born in Glasgow, Scotland, in 1832. On the death of his father in 1851 he conducted the paternal business for several years, and in 1857 came to Canada. The following year he commenced business as grain commissioner and general merchant at Rockwood, Wellington County, Ont., and in 1874 removed to Toronto, four years later forming a partnership with his brother, the firm being known as A. & S. Nairn, wharfingers and coal merchants. In 1884 the partnership was dissolved, and Mr. Alex. Nairn practically retired from active business. In encouraging the development of the country and the promotion of branch railways, he was active, being one of the first to ship grain over the Wellington County section of the Grand Trunk. He died in June, 1914. Photograph, colored. Size 3 x 4. Head and shoulders.

977—BAIN, JAMES—President St. Andrew's Society, 1905-7—Born in London, Eng., in 1842, of Scottish parents; came to Canada with them early in life. Later joined firm of John Nimmo & Son, which became Nimmo & Bain, publishers, London, England. On the dissolution of the firm in 1882 he returned to Toronto, becoming first Chief Librarian of the Toronto Public Library a year later. He died in Toronto in 1908. Photograph, colored. Size 3 x 4. Head and shoulders. See 645.

978—DAVIDSON, LIEUT-COL. JOHN I.—President St. Andrew's Society, 1907-9—Born in 1854 at Wartle, Aberdeenshire, Scotland, the son of Dr. Samuel Davidson. He came to Canada in his early days and subsequently became senior partner in the firm of Davidson & Hay, wholesale grocers, Toronto; was president of the Toronto Board of Trade, 1890-91. In 1891 was appointed to the command of the 48th Highlanders with rank of lieutenant-colonel, having organized the regiment. He died in Toronto in 1910. Photograph, colored. Size 3 x 4. Head and shoulders.

979—McMURRICH, GEORGE—President St. Andrew's Society, 1909-11 —Born in Toronto in 1844, the second son of the Hon. John McMurrich, and was engaged in the fire insurance business for the greater part of his life. From 1891-1913 he sat almost continuously in the City Council, and was for a time a member of the Technical School Board. His death occurred in Toronto in 1913. Photograph, colored. Size 3 x 4. Head and shoulders.

980—ALEXANDER, JAMES MACKENZIE—President St. Andrew's Society, 1911-13—Born in Aberdeenshire, Scotland, in 1840, and subsequently removed to Glasgow, where he was for a time employed in several large mercantile houses. At close of the American Civil War he emigrated to Boston, Mass., later coming to Canada and carrying on a dry goods business in Cobourg and Brantford. Afterwards he became associated with a wholesale millinery business, known as Alexander & Reid. Some time later Mr. Alexander formed a connection with S. F. McKinnon Co., Ltd.; president until his death, Sept. 19th, 1917. Photograph, colored. Size 3 x 4. Head and shoulders.

981—MICHIE, HON. LIEUT.-COL. J. FORBES—President St. Andrew's Society, 1913-16—Born at Strathdon, Aberdeenshire, Scotland, 1867; came to Canada in 1889, joining his brothers in the business of Michie & Company. On incorporation of the company in 1905 he became president. Following the formation of the 48th Highlanders, in 1891, he was appointed an officer, becoming hon. lieutenant-colonel in 1913. In 1911 was granted the Colonial and Auxiliary Forces Long Service Medal, and in the following year received the Colonial and Auxiliary Forces Officers' decoration. Photograph, colored. Size 3 x 4. Head and shoulders.

982—MOWAT, HERBERT M.—President St. Andrew's Society, 1916-17 —Son of Rev. Prof. J. B. Mowat, of Queen's University. Born in Kingston, April 9th, 1860; educated at Queen's (B.A., 1881; LL.B., 1886). Called to the bar, 1886; Q.C., 1899. Practises his profession in Toronto, and, for a time, was Assistant City Solicitor. Vice-President Crown Life Insurance Co. Water color. Size 3 x 4. Head and shoulders.

983—JAMESON, MRS. (ANNA BROWNELL MURPHY)—Distinguished authoress—Born in Dublin, Ireland, in 1794; eldest daughter of D. Brownell Murphy, a miniature painter. She labored for the development of usefulness and mental culture of women in England, wrote many books and essays, chief amongst which are "Companion to the Public Picture

Galleries of London" and "Sacred and Legendary Art," and was herself an excellent artist. She married, about 1822, Robert S. Jameson, a barrister, who in 1833 became Speaker of the Legislature, Upper Canada,, was appointed Attorney-General of the Province, and subsequently Vice-Chancellor. Mrs. Jameson joined him in Toronto, 1836, their home being on the west corner of Brock and Front streets. In 1838 they separated, and after travelling through United States and on the continent, Mrs. Jameson returned to England, where she died in 1860. Drawing in water color from a photograph in the Niagara Historical Museum. Size 7 x 9. Half length.

984-1040—**Presidents St. George's Society, 1835-1917**—According to Walton's Directory of Toronto, 1837, the society was "instituted in 1835," and in that year Col. Joseph Wells became president. In 1824, however, the Festival of St. George was celebrated in York by a ball and supper at Thompson's Hotel, "numerously attended, nearly 200 ladies and gentlemen being present." (U.C. Gazette, April 29th, 1824). From small beginnings the society is now (1917) a power amongst Englishmen in Canada.

984—**WELLS, (COL.) HON. JOSEPH**—President St. George's Society, 1835—Born in England in 1773, and entered the 43rd Regiment of Foot when very young, serving in the Peninsular War and coming to Canada after the Battle of Waterloo. On retiring from the army he was appointed Bursar to Upper Canada College, and was also a member of the Legislative Council previous to the union of the Canadas in 1841. His death occurred in 1853. Water color from portrait by Hoppner Meyer, in possession of his granddaughter, Mrs. A. U. de Pencier, Vancouver, B.C. Size 3 x 4. Head and shoulders. See 3668.

985—**MACAULAY, CAPT. (COL.) JOHN SIMCOE**—President St. George's Society, 1836—Born in London, Eng., 13th Oct., 1791, the eldest son of Dr. James Macaulay, a Scotsman, who came to Canada about 1792 with the Queen's Rangers, and when York (Toronto) became the seat of Government instead of Niagara, settled in the former place. The son served in the Peninsular War at the sieges of Cadiz and Badajoz and Battle of Barrosa; became a colonel in the Royal Engineers, and afterwards a member of the Legislative Council of Upper Canada. He died, December, 1855. Water color from a portrait in possession of his daughters, the Misses Macaulay, Exmouth, Eng. Size 3 x 4. Head and shoulders. See 1668, 3317.

986—**DRAPER, HON. WILLIAM HENRY**—President St. George's Society, 1837-8—Born in London, Eng., 1801. Nineteen years later he came to Canada, and prior to taking up the study of law taught school. In 1828 he was called to the bar and the following year appointed reporter of the King's Bench. In 1837 he became Solicitor-General, afterwards achieving the office of Attorney-General, U.C. Mr. Draper's Parliamentary career commenced in 1836, and he continued to take an active interest in political matters until 1847, in which year he became a puisne judge of the Queen's Bench. In 1854 he was created a Companion of the Bath; in 1856 became Chief Justice of the Common Pleas, and later Chief Justice of the Queen's Bench. His death occurred at Yorkville in 1877. Photograph, colored. Size 3 x 4. Head and shoulders.

987—**JAMESON, HON. R. S.**—President St. George's Society, 1839-41 and 1848—Admitted into the Society of the Middle Temple in 1818, and in 1824 was appointed as a reporter in Lord Eldon's Court, five years later accepting a puisne judgeship in the Island of Dominica, B.W.I. Mr. Jameson married in 1826, Anna Murphy, daughter of an Irish artist. In 1833 he removed to Upper Canada, having been appointed Attorney-General of the Province, and four years later became Vice-Chancellor. Died in Toronto in 1854. Photograph, colored. Size 3 x 4. Head and shoulders.

13

988—WAKEFIELD, WILLIAM—President St. George's Society, 1842-44—Born in England in 1802, he later came to Canada and was one of the pioneer auctioneers of Toronto, his establishment for some years being at 40 King street east, on what is now (1917) the site of the store occupied by John Catto & Sons, dry goods merchants. Mr. Wakefield's death occurred at Beechgrove Grange, Weston, Ont., 31st August, 1873. Photograph, colored. Size 3 x 4. Head and shoulders. See 3376.

989—RIDOUT, GEORGE PERCEVAL—President St. George's Society, 1845-7—Born in Bristol, Eng., in 1807. He came to America in 1820 with his father, residing for a time in Philadelphia and New York, forming in the latter city a partnership in the hardware business with his brother and Messrs. Tarratt, of Wolverhampton, Eng. He afterwards came to York (Toronto), taking an active part in the Rebellion of 1837, and was captain, later becoming colonel of the 7th Battalion York Volunteers. From 1851-3 he represented Toronto in Parliament. He was also one of the founders and a president of the Toronto Board of Trade. His death occurred in 1873. Photograph, colored. Size 3 x 4. Head and shoulders.

990—WHITLEY, JOHN—President St. George's Society, 1867—Practised the profession of law in Toronto, being a member of the firm of Whitley & Esten, with offices on Church street. He subsequently removed to Denver, Col., and died there in 1892. Photograph, colored. Size 3 x 4. Head and shoulders.

991—CRICKMORE, JOHN—President St. George's Society, 1868—The Parish of Hales, Norfolk Co., England, was his birthplace in 1815. He subsequently came to Canada, and, after studying law, was called to the bar at Toronto in 1846, becoming prominent in legal circles here. His death occurred at Lakefield, Ont., on January 25th, 1894. Photograph, colored. Size 3 x 4. Head and shoulders.

992—YOUNG, JAMES—President St. George's Society, 1869—He came to Canada from England, having been born at Bury Saint Edmunds, Eng., in 1821. Subsequently he became a produce and commission merchant on Wellington street east, Toronto, and died in this city in 1906. Photograph, colored. Size 3 x 4. Head and shoulders.

993—WOOD, SAMUEL GEORGE—President St. George's Society, 1870—Born 10th May, 1835, at Three Rivers, Que., where his father, the Rev. S. S. Wood, M.A., was rector. He was educated at Richmond Grammar School, Yorkshire, and at Trinity College, Toronto. Subsequently became a barrister, for many years being in partnership with Larratt Smith. Received LL.D., Toronto University. He died in Toronto in 1906. Photograph, colored. Size 3 x 4. Head and shoulders.

994—MASON, J. HERBERT—President St. George's Society, 1871 and 1891-2—Son of Thomas Mason; he came to Canada with his parents in 1842, and was for some years an accountant with the Farmers' and Mechanics' Building Society, Toronto. In 1855 he organized the Canada Permanent Loan & Savings Co., eventually becoming president of that organization. He took a prominent part in the organization of the Canada Land Law Amendment Association, of which he was elected president in 1883, and was a councillor of the Toronto Board of Trade for some years. He was born at Ivy Bridge, Devon, Eng., in 1827, and died in Toronto in 1911. Photograph, colored. Size 3 x 4. Head and shoulders.

995—DAY, JAMES E.—President St. George's Society, 1872—London, Eng., was his birthplace in 1825. A quarter of a century later he came to Canada, settling first in Hamilton, where he remained for about fifteen years, being secretary of the Hamilton Waterworks for the greater part of that time. In Toronto he was well known as the proprietor of Day's Commercial College. His death occurred in November, 1890. Photograph, colored. Size 3 x 4. Head and shoulders.

161

996—SPOONER, JAMES—President St. George's Society, 1888—England was the land of his birth in 1823. He subsequently came to Canada, being a pioneer tobacconist in Toronto, and in art circles had a reputation as an excellent judge of pictures. He died in Toronto in 1907. Photograph, colored. Size 3 x 4. Head and shoulders.

997—WELLINGTON, W. E.—President St. George's Society, 1889—Born in Oshawa, Ont., in 1856. He formed the firm of Stone & Wellington, now carried on by his sons, in Toronto. He also took a military course and served in both the Fenian Raid and North-west Rebellion. Died in Toronto in 1910. Photograph, colored. Size 3 x 4. Head and shoulders.

998—PLEWS, DAVID—President St. George's Society, 1890—He was born in 1846, and died in Toronto in 1910, as the result of injuries received in a street car accident. At one time he was a pumpmaker, and later became connected with the Post Office Department. Photograph, colored. Size 3 x 4. Head and shoulders.

999—DRAYTON, PHILIP HENRY—President St. George's Society, 1893—The son of English parents, born in Barbadoes, B.W.I., in 1846; educated at Cheltenham College and the Royal Military College, England. He was formerly an officer in the 16th Regiment, later becoming attached to the Royal Canadian Rifles and H.M. 76th Regiment. After completing his law studies in the firm of Bethune, Osler & Moss, Toronto, he was admitted to the bar in 1881. In 1907 he was appointed official arbitrator and referee for Ontario, which position he still (1917) holds, and is also Chairman of the Court of Revision. Appointed K.C., 1908. His son is Sir Henry L. Drayton. Photograph, colored. Size 3 x 4. Head and shoulders.

1000—DAVID T. SYMONS—President St. George's Society, 1894—He was born in 1862, and was the son of John Symons, founder of the Canada Landed Credit Company. He studied law, was admitted to the Ontario bar, and is now (1917) a member of the firm of Kingstone & Symons, barristers, Toronto. Photograph, colored. Size 3 x 4. Head and shoulders.

1001—RIDOUT, PERCIVAL F.—President St. George's Society, 1895-6 Born in Toronto in 1856, the son of George Ridout. He was educated at Upper Canada College, and subsequently married a daughter of Sir David L. Macpherson, at one time a member of the Executive Council of Lower Canada. After a banking career, he retired, and now resides in London, England. Photograph, colored. Size 3 x 4. Head and shoulders.

1002—WIDDER, FREDERICK—President St. George's Society, 1849-50 —He was born in England in 1801, and came to Canada about 1845 as commissioner of the Canada Company, of which company his father, Charles Ignatius Widder, was a director, and the offices of which were situated at the north-east corner of King and Frederick streets. Mr. Widder's death occurred in Montreal in 1865. Water color. Size 3 x 4. Head and shoulders.

1003—RIDOUT, JOSEPH D.—President St. George's Society, 1851-4—Born in Bristol, Eng., in 1809. In 1831 he came to York (Toronto), and the following year became a partner with his brother, George Perceval Ridout, and Messrs. Tarratt, of Wolverhampton, Eng. On the retirement of his brother, James Aikenhead and Alexander Crombie were taken into the firm, and in 1876 he himself retired. He was associated with the founding of the Toronto Board of Trade, and was vice-president of the Farmers' and Mechanics' Building Society, which closed its business successfully in 1853, and from which originated the Canada Permanent Loan & Savings Co. From 1833-67 he was an officer in the East York Militia, retiring as major. His death took place in 1884. Photograph, colored. Size 3 x 4. Head and shoulders.

1004—CUMBERLAND, LIEUT-COL. FREDERICK W.—President St. George's Society, 1855-6—Born April 10th, 1821, and came to Canada in 1847; was well known as an engineer and architect. He was for many years managing director of the Northern Railway, and from 1867-71 represented Algoma in the Provincial Legislature. He also held the rank of lieutenant-colonel in the 10th Royals, being the first to do so. His death occurred in Toronto, Aug. 5th, 1881, at his residence, north-east corner College and St. George streets, used 1912-15 as a temporary Government House. Photograph, colored. Size 3 x 4. Head and shoulders. See 3711.

1005—BILTON, GEORGE—President St. George's Society, 1857—Born in York, England, in 1800, and subsequently came to Toronto, where he and his brother, Thomas, commenced a tailoring business on King street east about 1835. On the partnership being dissolved, George Bilton opened a dry goods business, known as the "Golden Fleece," at the corner of Yonge and Richmond streets, now (1917) the site of Childs' Restaurant. After conducting the business alone for some years he formed a partnership, the firm becoming Bilton & Blakely. He died in Toronto in 1858. Photograph, colored. Size 3 x 4. Head and shoulders.

1006—ROBINSON, HON. JOHN BEVERLEY—President St. George's Society, 1858—Photograph, colored. Size 3 x 4. Head and shoulders. See 374, 425, 3228.

1007—BROWN, THOMAS—President St. George's Society, 1859—Born in Leeds, Eng., 1824; died in 1875. Came to Canada early in life, entering the employ of the Furniss Waterworks and becoming secretary of that company. About 1852 he engaged in the wholesale and retail grocery business, entering into partnership with Albert Berczy, the firm being known as Thomas Brown & Co. Later he opened the Metropolitan Hotel, King and Bay streets, Toronto, and in 1871 moved to the old Palace Hotel on Front street west. From 1858-9 he was a member of the Public School Board; also president of the West Toronto Conservative Association for several years. Photograph, colored. Size 3 x 4. Head and shoulders.

1008—HARMAN, SAMUEL BICKERTON—President St. George's Society, 1860. Photograph, colored. Size 3 x 4. Head and shoulders. See 381, 3556, 3568.

1009—WRIGHT, FREDERICK—President St. George's Society, 1873—Eldest son of Capt. Francis Wright, Walworth Manor, Surrey, Eng.; born at Walworth Manor in 1822, and educated for the East Indian service; came to Canada when a lad with his parents, settling near Belleville. Entered as a solicitor, May 26th, 1866, and called to the bar, Sept. 4th, 1880. Died in Toronto in 1893, after having practised his profession here for a number of years. Water color. Size 3 x 4. Head and shoulders.

1010—COOPER, JAMES—President St. George's Society, 1874—Came to Canada in 1847 from England, where he was born at Gainsborough, Lincolnshire, in 1825. For a time he lived in Quebec, later removing to Toronto. Became a partner in the firm of Sessions, Turner & Cooper, which eventually became Cooper & Smith, with branches in Montreal and Quebec. Afterwards returned to the land of his birth, residing for many years in Boston, Eng., where he died in October, 1915. Until his death he retained his membership in the Toronto Board of Trade. Photograph, colored. Size 3 x 4. Head and shoulders.

1011—OSLER, (SIR) EDMUND BOYD—President St. George's Society, 1875—Born in Tecumseh, Simcoe County, Ont., in 1845. He commenced his business career in the Bank of Upper Canada, and on the failure of the institution entered into partnership with Henry Pellatt, father of Sir

Henry Pellatt. Later he formed the firm of Osler & Hammond, financiers and stock brokers. He was president of the Toronto Board of Trade in 1896, and has sat for Toronto in the House of Commons since that year. He received a knighthood in 1912. Photograph, colored. Size 3 x 4. Head and shoulders.

1012—MARSH, HERBERT T.—President St. George's Society, 1876—Born in Hamilton, Ont., in 1849, the son of the Rev. Thomas Marsh, of Norval, Ont. He was for a time a member of the hardware firm of McNab, Marsh & Coen, who in 1876 did business on Front street, Toronto. He now (1917) resides in England, where he is in business in London. Photograph, colored. Size 3 x 4. Head and shoulders.

1013—TREES, SAMUEL—President St. George's Society, 1877—Born in Walsall, Staffordshire, England, in 1838, and came to Canada in 1866, immediately engaging in the saddlery business. From 1880-3 he represented St. Thomas' Ward in the City Council. He has also been actively connected with many financial organizations in Toronto. Photograph, colored. Size 3 x 4. Head and shoulders.

1014—WALTON, BENJAMIN—President St. George's Society, 1878—He was the son of the Rev. Jonathan Walton; born at Huddersfield, Eng., in 1819, and died in 1885. On coming to Canada, he successfully engaged as a builder and stonecutter, erecting amongst other Toronto buildings, the Customs House of 1841, the Bank of British North America, and a considerable portion of St. James' Cathedral. He also developed the Melbourne Slate Quarries in Quebec Province. Photograph, colored. Size 3 x 4. Head and shoulders.

1015—OSLER, HON. FEATHERSTON—President St. George's Society, 1880—Born at Newmarket, Ont., in 1838. In 1860 he became a barrister and fifteen years later a bencher of the Law Society. From 1879-83 he was puisne judge of the Common Pleas Court, and from 1883 until his retirement from the bench, in 1910, was a justice in the Court of Appeal. He was also appointed as a commissioner for the revision of the Ontario Statutes, 1885 and 1896. He still (1917) resides in Toronto. Photograph, colored. Size 3 x 4. Head and shoulders.

1016—STANWAY, GEORGE—President St. George's Society, 1897—Stoke-upon-Trent, Staffordshire, Eng., was his birthplace, in 1846. In 1858 he emigrated to Montreal with his father; later engaged in the wholesale grocery brokerage business, and in 1867 opened a branch in connection with his father's firm in Toronto. He continued to be identified with the concern until his decease in 1913. Photograph, colored. Size 3 x 4. Head and shoulders.

1017—GOODERHAM, GEORGE H.—President St. George's Society, 1898—Born in Toronto in 1868. During an active business life he has been connected with many of the financial institutions of the city. Commodore Royal Canadian Yacht Club, 1900-03, and subsequently vice-commodore. From 1899-1903 he was a member of the Public School Board, and since 1908 has sat in the Provincial House as representative for South Toronto, seat "A." Photograph, colored. Size 3 x 4. Head and shoulders.

1018—MUSSON, GEORGE—President St. George's Society, 1899-1900—He was born in Toronto in 1836 and received his education at Toronto Academy and Upper Canada College. He is interested in military matters, being at one time a captain in the 10th Royals. In 1887 was appointed Vice-Consul for Brazil, and in 1898 became president of the "Veterans of 1866 Association." Photograph, colored. Size 3 x 4. Head and shoulders.

1019—**TAYLOR, JOHN**—President St. George's Society, 1901-2—His birth occurred in 1840, and he died in 1908. For many years he was the head of the well-known firm of John Taylor & Company, Limited, manufacturers of soaps and perfumes. Photograph, colored. Size 3 x 4. Head and shoulders.

1020—**COPP, JOHN CHARLES**—President St. George's Society, 1903 —Born in Great Torrington, England, in 1839, and came to Canada with his parents in 1842, settling with them in Toronto. He was for many years connected with the firm of Jacques & Hay, and in 1884 became secretary-treasurer of the Toronto Silver Plate Co., resigning from the latter company eleven years later to become manager of the Toronto Land & Investment Corporation. This position he held until his death in 1904. Photograph, colored. Size 3 x 4. Head and shoulders.

1021—**TIPPET, WILLIAM H.**—President St. George's Society, 1904— Born in 1851 at Bear Island, York County, New Brunswick, the fourth son of the rector of the Parish of Queensbury, Rev. W. H. Tippet. He was engaged in various mercantile pursuits in Canada, and England, and also in Central America. In 1892 he was made and still (1917) is Toronto representative of the firm of Arthur P. Tippet & Company, Montreal. Photograph, colored. Size 3 x 4. Head and shoulders.

1022—**HARMAN, GEORGE F.**—President St. George's Society, 1905-6— Came to Toronto with his parents shortly after his birth in the Island of Grenada, B.W.I. He was educated at Trinity College, Toronto, and subsequently called to the bar. During the lifetime of his father, Samuel B. Harman, he was associated with him in the practice of his profession; took part in the revision of the Statutes of Ontario. He still (1917) resides in Toronto. Photograph, colored. Size 3 x 4. Head and shoulders.

1023—**DODGSON, ROBERT**—President St. George's Society, 1861— Was born in Carlisle, Cumberland, Eng., in 1832. From 1853-68 he was prominent in Toronto business circles, being a member of the firm of Dodgson, Shields & Morton, grocers and confectioners, south-west corner of Yonge and Temperance streets. He died in England in 1889. Photograph, colored. Size 3 x 4. Head and shoulders.

1024—**BEACHALL, JAMES**—President St. George's Society, 1862—He was born in England in 1810, and subsequently came to Toronto where he was engaged as a railway contractor for many years. His death occurred in Toronto, 17th May, 1867. Water color. Size 3 x 4. Head and shoulders.

1025—**PHIPPS, WILLIAM B.**—President St. George's Society, 1863— He was the son of Thomas Phipps, a York pioneer, and was well known as a banker and exchange broker on Toronto street, Toronto, conducting his business at the old York Chambers, opposite the Quebec Bank. He was born in 1808, and died in Toronto in 1881. Photograph, colored. Size 3 x 4. Head and shoulders.

1026—**KINGSFORD, WILLIAM**—President St. George's Society, 1864— Born in London, Eng., 1819. Came to Canada with 1st Dragoon Guards. In 1841 he left the army and became attached to the City Surveyor's office, Montreal, subsequently becoming Deputy City Surveyor, which position he held for three years. For a time he was part proprietor of the Montreal Times, and on its discontinuance, was for two years on the engineering staff of the Department of Public Works, during this time completing an important survey in connection with the Lachine Canal. In 1849 he went to the United States, and, on his return to Canada, entered the service of the Grand Trunk, resigning to become Chief Engineer of Toronto. A few months later, however, he returned to the Grand Trunk. For some years he had charge of the harbors of Ontario and Quebec. Wrote a history of Canada in ten volumes, and a number of other works. Died in 1898. Photograph, colored. Size 3 x 4. Head and shoulders. See 2783.

1027—SPRATT, ROBERT—President St. George's Society, 1865 and 1879—Born in 1821. For some years conducted business as a flour dealer and commission merchant on Church street, Toronto, and also was a member of the Board of Trade. His death occurred in Toronto in 1899. Photograph, colored. Size 3 x 4. Head and shoulders.

1028—BOYD, WILLIAM THOMAS—President St. George's Society, 1866—He was a native of England, being born there in 1829, and came to Canada with his parents about 1836. Received his education at Upper Canada College, and later at Toronto University. Took up the study of law, and called to the bar in Hilary term, 1857. Mr. Boyd's death occurred in Toronto, Aug. 23rd, 1916. Photograph, colored. Size 3 x 4. Head and shoulders.

1029—ALLWORTH, JOHN J.—President St. George's Society, 1881— His birthplace was Greenwich, County of Kent, England, where he first saw the light of day in 1821. He subsequently came to Canada and engaged in business in Bond street, Toronto, as a publisher and bookseller. His death occurred in Toronto in May, 1900. Photograph, colored. Size 3 x 4. Head and shoulders.

1030—VIRTUE, GEORGE—President St. George's Society, 1882—He came to America in 1870, and engaged in the publishing business in New York. Later removed to Toronto, following the same line of business here, and continuing it until his death in March, 1894. He was born at Bristol, Eng., in 1828. Photograph, colored. Size 3 x 4. Head and shoulders.

1031—CUMBERLAND, F. BARLOW—President St. George's Society, 1883—Son of Lieut.-Col. F. W. Cumberland, was born in Portsmouth, Eng., 1846, and came to Canada with his parents in 1847; studied law, but abandoned it for a business career in 1870. He was one of the founders of the Niagara Navigation Co. in 1880, and was for some years in the service of the Great Western Railway, later becoming freight and passenger agent for the Northern Railway, and traffic manager of the Lake Superior Steamship Line (afterwards amalgamated with the C.P.R.); served during the Fenian Raid, and was a captain in 10th Royals. He was the author of "The Northern Lakes of Canada," "History of the Union Jack," and "Flags of the Empire." His death occurred in 1914. Photograph, colored. Size 3 x 4. Head and shoulders. See 3712.

1032—ELLIOT, ROBERT WATT—President St. George's Society, 1884—He was the eldest son of William Elliot, and was born in 1835 in the Township of Eramosa, in what was then known as Canada West. His education was received at the Dundas Academy and Toronto Medical School. For many years he was a member of the firm of Elliot & Company, druggists. He died in Toronto in 1905. Photograph, colored. Size 3 x 4. Head and shoulders.

1033—SYMONS, HARRY—President St. George's Society, 1885-6—He was born at Dartmouth, Devon, Eng., in 1854, and was educated in England and at the York County Grammar School; studied law, and in 1875 was called to the Ontario bar, becoming advocate in the North-west Territories in 1890. For a number of years he practised his profession in Toronto, and was at one time M.P. for Stratford, Ont. He was also president of the National Agency Co., and of the Niagara Welland Power Co., and an officer in the 10th Royals. Photograph, colored. Size 3 x 4. Head and shoulders.

1034—**BEARDMORE, GEO. W.**—President St. George's Society, 1887— He was born in Hamilton, Ont., in 1851, and was educated at Upper Canada College and in England. He was one of the originators and a director of the National Life Assurance Co., which was organized in 1899. He was also a promoter of the Ottawa & French River Railway, and a promoter and director of the Ontario Jockey Club. He still (1917) resides in Toronto. Photograph, colored. Size 3 x 4. Head and shoulders.

1035—**GANDER, JOHN M.**—President St. George's Society, 1907-8— He was born in London, Eng., 1844, and came to Toronto in 1870. Seven years later returned to England, but after spending a decade in the Old Land removed again to Toronto. President Toronto Builders' Exchange and a trustee of the Technical School. He died at Bournemouth in 1910. Photograph, colored. Size 3 x 4. Head and shoulders.

1036—**HUDSON, R. S.**—President St. George's Society, 1909-10—Born at Chelsea, Que., in 1843, of U.E. Loyalist ancestry; educated at U.C.C. and Toronto University. Mathematical master at Brockville Grammar School, and, later, head master at Lyn school, and manager of the Lyn Tannery and Mills. Subsequently superintendent of the Canada Permanent Loan & Savings Co., and now (1917) is joint general manager of the Canada Permanent. Photograph, colored. Size 3 x 4. Head and shoulders.

1037—**HARMAN, DAVIDSON M.**—President St. George's Society, 1911-12—Born at Croydon, Surrey, Eng.; educated at U.C.C., and served with the Q.O.R. during the Fenian Raid. Now (1917) he is associated with the firm of Osler & Hammond, stock brokers, Toronto. Photograph, colored. Size 3 x 4. Head and shoulders.

1038—**FRANKLAND, H. R.**—President St. George's Society, 1913-14— Born in Collingwood, Ont., 1858, and educated at Collingwood Grammar School and Todmorden Public school. For some time engaged in the wholesale butcher and cattle business, but since 1899 has been collector of Inland Revenue, Toronto. Photograph, colored. Size 3 x 4. Head and shoulders.

1039—**NICHOLSON, JAMES**—President St. George's Society, 1915-16— Born in Liverpool, England, 1861; educated at a private school in Cheshire. Came to Canada in 1891, four years later locating in Toronto, where he still resides. He is (1917) head of the firm of Nicholson & Brock. Photograph, colored. Size 3 x 4. Head and shoulders.

1040—**RAWLINSON, MARMADUKE**—President St. George's Society, 1917—Born at Sepsey, Lincolnshire, Eng., May 5th, 1853; educated at a Church school, Mintin Park, near Lincoln. In 1883 came to Canada, settling in Toronto, where he commenced his present (1917) cartage and storage business. Elected to the Board of Education, 1901, continuing on the Board for nine years. Member City Council, 1912-13. Water color. Size 3 x 4. Head and shoulders.

1041—**JACKES, FRANKLIN, YORK (TORONTO)** 1804-52—In 1824 Mr. Jackes emigrated from England to York. Removed to Eglinton twelve years later. In 1834 represented St. David's Ward as alderman, and on taking up residence in Eglinton became Reeve of York Township, Warden of the County, and in 1837 Justice of the Peace. Water color. Size 3 x 4. Half length.

1042—**ROSS, CHARLES SMITH,** 1815-76—For many years cashier and manager of the Commercial Bank, Kingston, and from 1871-6 held the appointment of Asst. Receiver-General at Toronto. During his term the Provincial Government was given control of the management of the Toronto General Hospital, and Mr. Ross became a member of the Board of Trustees. In 1875 he assumed the chairmanship. Amongst other things, he decided that municipalities must pay a daily rate, allotted a certain number of free beds and induced the Ontario Government to give a per diem grant. After the death of Mr. Ross his colleagues adopted his policy, which had proven very satisfactory. Water color from a portrait in possession of his son, Charles Ross, of Newmarket, Ont. Size 3½ x 4. Head and shoulders.

1043—MACKENZIE, MRS. WM. LYON (ISABEL BAXTER), 1802-73— A native of Dundee, Scotland—In 1822 she came to Canada, and that same year married, at Montreal, Wm. Lyon Mackenzie, then of the firm of Mackenzie & Lesslie, Dundas, U.C. When the storm of the Rebellion of 1837-8 burst, and Mackenzie and his fellow insurgents ensconced themselves on Navy Island, Mrs. Mackenzie joined her husband, being the only woman on the island. She arrived there shortly before the destruction of the steamer "Caroline," and for a time made cartridges for the rebels with her own hands. In 1868 the Ontario Legislature voted Mrs. Mackenzie, then a widow, $4,000 in payment of a debt due her late husband by the old Province of Upper Canada. Water color from oil in possession of her daughter, Mrs. John King, Toronto. Size 5 x 7. Head and shoulders.

1044—POWELL, MRS. WILLIAM DUMMER (ANN MURRAY)—Born in 1758, the daughter of Dr. J. Murray, Norwich, Eng., of the family of Murray, of Philiphaugh. In 1773 she married Wm. Dummer Powell (Chief Justice). During Mrs. Simcoe's sojourn at Niagara she and Mrs. Powell were personal friends. For many years the latter resided in Toronto. Died 6th March, 1849. Water color from portrait in possession of her great-grandson, Aemilius Jarvis, Toronto. Size 5 x 6. Head and shoulders.

1045—MASSEY, HART A., 1823-96—Founder and donor of Massey Music Hall, Toronto—Born in Township of Haldimand, Northumberland County, Ont. At the age of nineteen entered Victoria College, and two years later took charge of his father's extensive farm, teaching during the winter. In 1851 he became superintendent of the agricultural implement works of his father, Newcastle, Ont., and on the retirement of Mr. Massey, sr., in 1855, sole proprietor. In 1870 he was made president of the Massey Manufacturing Co., incorporated that year. The entire business was removed to Toronto in 1879, and in 1891 the firm became the Massey-Harris Co., Ltd., Mr. Massey still retaining the presidency. The first mowing machine manufactured in Canada was produced at the Newcastle works in 1852, as were the first self-rake reaper and first automatic self-dumping horse-rake several years later. Mr. Massey was a munificent philanthropist. Water color from portrait in possession of his son, Chester D. Massey, Toronto. Size 3 x 4. Head and shoulders.

1046—GOODERHAM, WILLIAM, SR., 1790-1881—A native of Scole, Norfolk, Eng., but spent his early days under the care of a relative engaged in the East India trade in London. As a young man, enlisted in the Royal York Rangers, and went with that regiment to the West Indies; at Martinique and Guadaloupe. On leaving the army in 1832, emigrated to Canada. Almost immediately formed a partnership in York, with his brother-in-law, Jas. Worts. After the death of the latter he took into partnership James G. Worts, son of his first partner, and this connection continued until Mr. Gooderham's death. Water color. Size 3 x 4. Head and shoulders.

1047—GOODERHAM, WM., JR.—Born in England, April 14th, 1824; came to York (Toronto) with his father. Was engaged in various business enterprises. For a time managing director of the Toronto & Nipissing (Midland) Railway, but devoted his later years entirely to religious and philanthropic work. On his death, Sept. 12th, 1889, he left his entire estate for charitable purposes. Water color. Size 3 x 4. Head and shoulders.

1048—GOODERHAM, GEORGE—Born in Norfolk, Eng., March 14th, 1830, third son of William Gooderham, sr. At an early age entered the employ of the firm of Gooderham & Worts, millers and distillers, and after the firm was made a joint stock company he became president. Elected president of the Bank of Toronto, 1882; also connected with various other financial concerns. An enthusiastic yachtsman; one of the owners of the "Canada," which won the international championship at Water color. Size 3 x 4. Head and shoulders.

1049—WORTS, JAMES G.—Born in England in 1818; came to Canada with his father in 1831, and from 1845 until his death was an active member of the firm of Gooderham & Worts, millers and distillers. For many years he was vestry clerk of Trinity (Anglican) Church, King street east. Served also as Harbor Commissioner for a time. Died, 1882. Water color. Size 3 x 4. Head and shoulders.

1050—BALDWIN, HON. ROBERT, 1804-58—"Father of Responsible Government" in Canada—Photogravure from a contemporary photograph. Size 5 x 6. Oval. See 269, 271, 461.

1051—FERGUS, U. C.—This view was made in 1835 from the large field, now owned by Mr. Robert Monro. The positions are not exact. For instance, St. Andrew street runs along the front of the building marked 4, while St. Patrick street is above the figure 8. The key, kindly made by Mr. J. C. Templin, Fergus, gives the principal buildings at the period: 1, Mill; 2, Distillery; 3, Dry kiln; 4, Storehouse and granary; 5, Webster's home; 6, Peter McLaren's; 7, Hedley and Dryden's houses; 8, Mathews' house; 9, Morrison's (tailor) house; 10, Archie Patterson's; 11, Baker Walker's; 12, Watts', Grant's and school close to church; 13, St. Andrew's Church; 14, James Edwards' and Sergt. Matthew's; 15, St. Andrew's Manse; 16, Provost Buist's farm. From a drawing by Miss J. D. Fordyce. Lithographed by Forrester & Nichol, Edinburgh. In color. Size 8 x 13.

1052—SOUVENIR BADGE—Designed for the occasion of the laying of the corner-stone of the Municipal Buildings, Toronto, Nov. 21st, 1891— The present (1917) Municipal Buildings on Queen street, at the head of Bay, were erected between 1891 and 1900, E. J. Lennox being the architect. The corner-stone was laid by Edward F. Clarke, M.P., then Mayor. On Sept. 18th, 1899, the building was formally opened, and in 1901 the old City Hall on Front street was vacated.

1053—FERGUS, U.C., 1837—From "Belsyde," Union street—"Belsyde," the point from which the picture was made, was formerly the property of the late A. D. Ferrier and John Beattie, and now owned by E. C. Robarts, manager Imperial Bank, Fergus. The village of Fergus is situated on the Grand River, in Wellington County, sixteen miles north of Guelph. A key to the picture gives the principal points, as follows:—1, Farm barn; 2, St. Andrew's Hotel; 3, Mill on Grand River; 4, Watt's house; 5, Granary, St. Andrew street; 6, Schoolhouse; 7, Houston's; 8, James Morrison's (tailor); 9, St. Andrew's Church on George street; 10, Frame of barn; 11, Cooper's shop, St. Andrew street; 12, Grant's house; 13, Walker's (baker) house in Provost lane; 14, Mennie's house; 15, Home of James Edwards; 16, Brewery; 17, Provost Buist's; 18, Owen Sound road; 19, A. D. Ferrier's. Water color. Size 6 x 11.

1054—NORTH-WEST MOUNTED POLICE, 1880—In the summer of 1872 Col. Robertson-Ross, adjutant-general, was despatched by the Canadian Government to make "a reconnaissance of the North-west provinces and Indian territories of the Dominion," and in the following year a bill was introduced in the Dominion Parliament by Sir John A. Macdonald, respecting "the administration of justice and the establishment of a police force in the North-West Territories." Recruiting for the North-West Mounted Police was begun in the autumn of 1873, and in 1874, with Lieut.-Col. George A. French commanding, the force commenced operations. A wholesome respect for these "riders of the plains" was speedily instilled in the minds of Indian and white man, and the force became a power for law and order in the prairie lands. In 1904 the title "Royal" was conferred upon the N.W.M.P. Water color from original drawing by Schell and Hogan, for "Picturesque Canada." Size 5 x 7.

1055—TORONTO LACROSSE CLUB—With key—"The Toronto Lacrosse Club. Champions of Canada. General view of the Lacrosse Grounds, Canadian Illustrated News, 25th March, 1876." It was founded in June, 1867, by Mr. George Massey, the first meeting being held in the old Victoria Rink at the south-west corner of Sherbourne and Gerrard streets. Mr. (Sir) William D. Otter was the first president. The old club was a strictly amateur one, all the members paying their own expenses while travelling. They originally played in Queen's Park, where the present (1917) Parliament Buildings stand, afterwards using the Toronto Cricket Grounds, on College street, which ran from Beverley to McCaul. Later they played on the Jarvis Street Lacrosse Grounds (shown in the picture). They then removed to South Rosedale, and eventually purchased the present Rosedale grounds. The team was afterwards a professional one, known as the Toronto Lacrosse and Athletic Association. Pen drawing, colored. Size 9 x 13. See 1056.

1056—TORONTO LACROSSE CLUB—Key to:—1, Col. W. D. Otter, C.M.G.; 2, Geo. Massey (father and founder of the T.L.C.); 3, C. E. Robinson; 4, C. H. Nelson; 5, J. Massey; 6, J. B. Henderson; 7, Col. J. L. Hughes; 8, Col. R. B. Hamilton; 9, T. Mitchell; 10, W. O. Ross; 11, H. E. Suckling; 12, C. McVittie; 13, T. Hodgetts; 14, J. McEachren; 15, Henry Langlois; 16, F. B. Ross; 17, H. Ross; 18, F. Peters; 19, R. H. Mitchell; 20, Henry Alexander; 21, H. Larmie; 22, E. Brown; 23, R. Wells; 24, K. Edwards; 25, "Tiny" Ellis; 26, R. Conron; 27, J. B. Boustead; 28, Geo. Wheeler; 29, J. L. Blaikie; 30, J. Crowther; 31, T. Lownsborough; 32, A. Muirhead; 33, George Milligan; 34, J. Pearson; 35, R. Pearson; 36, R. H. Bowes; 37, R. McKinley; 38, Major Foster; 39, J. Earskin; 40, J. Kniften; 41, R. Patton; 42, R. Duff; 43, Geo. Suckling; 44, R. Steele; 45, Prof. Torrington; 46, J. Davis; 47, Michael Sutherland; 48, D. Ross; 49, W. Bonnell; 50, R. W. Sutherland; 51, D. Hogg; 52, C. Cobban; 53, T. Rolph; 54, A. Boyd; 55, Nicholson Henderson; 56, Colonel Sherwood; 57, E. Butler; 58, James Boomer; 59, H. Leech; 60, F. Lord; 61, George Boyd; 62, R. Inglis; 63, W. J. Suckling, president 1889-93, 1895-7; 64, W. H. Lowe; 65, D. Denison; 66, A. Nordheimer; 67, E. S. Cox; 68, F. Stewart; 69, J. Longley; 70, J. Leask; 72, Fred. Menette; 73, Deputy Chief Stewart. See 1055.

1057—WINTER PASTIMES AT RIDEAU HALL, OTTAWA, 1876—Showing Earl Dufferin, Governor-General of Canada, 1872-8, and his house party engaged in a curling match. The following people are shown:— 1, Archibald J. L. Temple, Viscount Clandeboye, eldest son of Lord and Lady Dufferin. 2, Mrs. Stephenson, sister of Lady Dufferin. 3, Lady Helen Blackwood, eldest daughter of Lord and Lady Dufferin. Her husband, the Rt. Hon. Munro Ferguson, was appointed Governor-General of Australia in 1913. 4, Lady Dufferin. 4a, Lady Victoria Alexandrina Blackwood, youngest daughter of Lord and Lady Dufferin. She married Lord Plunkett, Governor-General of New Zealand, 1904-10, and is now (1917) residing in Ireland. 5, Mrs. Littleton, wife of Col. Littleton. 6, Major Hamilton, brother of Lady Dufferin. 7, Lord Dufferin, Governor-General of Canada, 1872-78. 8, Col. Littleton, Military Secretary, who succeeded Col. Fletcher. 9, Col. Stephenson, who spent a good deal of time at Rideau Hall as A.D.C. 10, Fred Knowles, personal attendant. 11, W. R. Baker. 12, Capt. Hamilton, A.D.C., brother of Lady Dufferin. 13, F. A. Dixon, tutor to the children of Lord Dufferin. He is at present (1917) in the Railway Department, Ottawa. 14, Capt. Ward, A.D.C. Photograph, colored. Size 7 x 15.

1058—**TORONTO ROLLING MILLS, 1863-9**—Between East (Cherry) street and Water street, prolonged, at intersection on the south side of Mill street. Photograph of pastel by William Armstrong, C.E., 1864. Size 6 x 9. See 1059.

1059—**TORONTO ROLLING MILLS, 1863-9**—Between East (Cherry) street and Water street, prolonged, at intersection on the south side of Mill street. They were built and managed by. C. S. (afterwards Sir Casimir Gzowski in the interests of his partners, D. L. (late Sir David) Macpherson, R. C. Pomeroy, of Pittsfield, Mass., and Montreal capitalists. The mills were the largest manufacturing industry in Toronto in their day, and the largest iron mills in Canada. Iron rails were manufactured here for the Grand Trunk Railway, but in 1869, when steel rails were being imported from England, the company concluded that they could not compete, and, rather than make the changes in the plant necessary for the production of steel rails, the place was dismantled. The Rolling Mills wharf stood on the south side of the present (1917) Esplanade at the foot of the then East street, bordering on the north bank of the Don River (previous to its deviation by the Corporation). The property is now occupied by the Grand Trunk Railway and the Standard Fuel Company, a tenant of the railway. Pastel, made in 1864 by William Armstrong, C.E., Toronto, and presented in 1914 to J. Ross Robertson by Mr. C. S. Gzowski, eldest son of the late Sir Casimir Gzowski. Size 27 x 40. See 1058.

1060—**"HOUSES OF PARLIAMENT AND GOVERNMENT OFFICES, FRONT STREET WEST, TORONTO, U.C.** 1835—To his Excellency Major-General Sir John Colborne, K.C.B., etc., etc., etc., Governor of Upper Canada. This plate is by permission inscribed by his obt. hble. servant, Thomas Young. Thomas Young, Archt. Delt., Toronto, U.C., 1835. W. K. Hewitt, Delt., on stone. N. Currier's Lith., No. 1 Wall St., N.Y." No. 1 shows the West Wing Departmental Offices. 2. Legislative Council Chamber, west of portico. 3, Main Entrance, Front street portico, with columns, which were never erected. 4, Legislative Assembly Chamber, east of portico. 5, East Wing Departmental Offices. 6, Spire of St. Andrew's Presbyterian church (first), corner Church and Adelaide streets. 7, Residence of Bishop Strachan, Front street, between Simcoe and York. 8, The Baldwin Residence, north-east corner Front and Bay streets. 9, Daily Guard of 66th Regiment of Infantry, serving in York, proceeding to Government House. 10, Green sward in front of Parliament Buildings on bay shore, now (1917) Esplanade property. The buildings were demolished in 1902. In 1903 the south sheds of the G.T.R. were erected, and in the following year those to the north. Lithograph in color. Size 9 x 18. See 292.

1061—**RED JACKETS AND CALEDONIAN CURLING MATCH**— Played on the Don River, Toronto, 1870. The players were: 1, Mr. Garvey; 2, Duncan Forbes, roofer; 3, Capt. J. T. Douglas, marine inspector; 4, Capt. Chas. Perry, commission merchant; 5, Charles G. Fortier, marine insurance inspector; 6, Major Gray, of No. 1 Rifle Co., Hamilton, subsequently in Customs Department, Toronto; 7, David Walker, of the American Hotel, later of the Walker House, Toronto; 8, T. McGaw, of the Queen's Hotel; 9, J. Pringle, insurance agent; 10, John O. Heward, who resided on Bloor street, opposite Church; 11, R. H. Ramsay, produce dealer. An expert curler in looking at the picture said: "It appears like a good end, for the stones are all in the house." Photograph, colored. Size 9 x 12.

1062—**ONTARIO LACROSSE CLUB, 1871**—With the City Championship Medal—In 1867 the Ontario Lacrosse Club came into being, but it was not destined to be very long lived, for it went out of existence in 1876. The medal shown was won in 1871 by the team, which for a number of years was Toronto's keen local opposition. The key to the picture is as follows: Top Row—W. Pearson, Jas. Carruthers, Thos. Brown, J. Sullivan,

A. Patterson. Centre Row—Chas. H. Varcoe, W. K. McNaught, Col. Arthurs, Q.O.R. (vice-president), Jas. Michie (president), Chas. Pearson, John Innes. Bottom Row—Col. Bruce, Fred. Walker, White Miller, John F. Scholes, W. Witeman. Photograph, colored. Size 9 x 12.

1063-68—Directors of Toronto Magnetic and Meteorological Observatory, 1840-1917.

1063—RIDDELL, LIEUT. (MAJOR-GENERAL) C. J. BUCHANAN, R.A. —Director Toronto Observatory, 1840-1—He was born at Riddell, Roxburghshire, 19th Nov., 1817, third son of Sir John B. Riddell, Bart. Entered Royal Military Academy at Woolwich, 1832; appointed to his first station abroad at Quebec, 1835, and in 1837 was promoted to first liuetenant. Subsequently Lieut. Riddell was selected for the post of Superintendent of the Observatory at Toronto, where he directed the erection of the first building. Owing to ill-health he was compelled to resign in 1841 and returned to England. Later he obtained the position of Assistant Superintendent of Ordnance Magnetic Observatories at the Royal Military Repository at Woolwich, and while there compiled a "Magnetical Instruction for the Use of Portable Instruments." He retired from active service with the rank of major-general. On 25th Jan., 1903, his death took place at Chudleigh, Devonshire. Water color from a portrait in possession of Capt. E. W. Creak, F.R.S., England. Size 4 x 5. Head and shoulders.

1064—LEFROY, CAPT. (GENERAL SIR) HENRY—Director Toronto Magnetic Observatory, 1842-53—He was an English soldier and scientist; born 28th Jan., 1817, at Ashe, Hampshire, Eng. From 1840-2 he was occupied in taking magnetic observations at St. Helena. From there Lefroy was transferred to Toronto for the purpose of making a magnetic survey of British North America. In 1843-4 he travelled to Hudson's Bay in order to observe magnetic phenomena, obtaining valuable results. Capt. Lefroy returned to England in 1853, and four years later was made inspector-general of army schools there, and director-general of ordnance in 1868. He wrote extensively on military affairs and scientific matters. He died at Lewarne. Water color from a portrait in the Royal Canadian Institute, Toronto. Size 4 x 5. Head and shoulders.

1065—CHERRIMAN, PROF. JOHN BRADFORD—Director Toronto Magnetic Observatory, 1853-5—Born in Yorkshire, Eng., 1826, was Sixth Wrangler and Fellow of St. John's College, Cambridge. He became Professor of Mathematics and Natural Philosophy in the University of Toronto, 1855, holding the position until 1875. In the latter year he resigned to accept appointment of Inspector of Insurance at Ottawa. He was major of the University Company, Q.O.R., and served at Ridgeway. Prof. Cherriman wrote several books on mathematical subjects. He returned to England in 1885, and died there in 1908. Photograph, 1901, colored. Size 4 x 5. Head and shoulders.

1066—KINGSTON, PROF. GEORGE TEMPLEMAN—Director Toronto Magnetic Observatory and Dominion Meteorological Service, 1855-80—He entered the navy as a midshipman, but on account of ill-health was compelled to give up the life. He then went to Caius College, Cambridge, and was M.A., and Tenth Wrangler about 1848. Became head of Naval College, Quebec, in 1853, two years later receiving appointment as Professor of Mathematics and Natural Science at Toronto University. He, however, exchanged with Prof. Cherriman, then Director of the Magnetic Observatory, who became Professor of Mathematics, Mr. Kingston becoming Director of the Observatory. Through his efforts a meteorological service was established in Canada, with headquarters at Toronto. On 31st Jan., 1880, Prof. Kingston resigned, leaving the service thoroughly organized. He was born in Portugal, 1816, and died at Toronto, 1886. Photograph, colored. Size 4 x 5. Head and shoulders.

1067—CARPMAEL, CHARLES, F.R.C.S.—Director Toronto Magnetic Observatory and Dominion Meteorological Service, 1880-94—Born Sept. 19, 1846, at Streatham Hill, Surrey, Eng. In 1865 he obtained a scholarship at St. John's College, Cambridge, devoting his attention almost entirely to the study of mathematics and natural and experimental sciences. Entered for the mathematical tripos and classed sixth in the list of wranglers, 1869. In 1870, Mr. Carpmael was elected Fellow of St. John's College, and the same year became a member of the British Eclipse Expedition to Spain. He was on the first council of the Royal Society of Canada, and in 1888 appointed president of the Canadian Institute. His death took place in 1894. While in charge of the metorological service he increased its efficiency, and also added to the number of storm signal display stations. Photograph, colored. Size 4 x 5. Head and shoulders.

1068—STUPART, SIR ROBERT FREDERIC, K.B.—Director Toronto Magnetic Observatory and Dominion Meteorological Service, 1894-1917. Son of the late Capt. R. D. Stupart, R.N., born near Toronto, 24th Oct., 1857; educated at Upper Canada College. He entered the Canadian Meteorological Service in 1872; had charge of the chief station in Hudson's Straits in connection with the Canadian Expedition for reporting on navigation of the Straits, 1884-5. He was president of the Royal Astronomical Society of Canada, 1902-3, and of the Canadian Institute, 1906-7; elected a member of the International Meteorological Committee, 1907. Knighted June, 1916. Photograph, colored. Size 4 x 5. Head and shoulders.

1069 to 1076—Magnetical and Meteorological Observatory, University Grounds, Toronto, 1840-1917—In 1839 magnetical observatories were established by the Imperial Government at St. Helena, Cape Town and Toronto. As superintendent of the observatory at Toronto, Lieut. C. J. B. Riddell was chosen. The Council of the University of King's College (Toronto University) offered the Government a grant of two and a half acres of ground, on condition that the buildings erected should be used for no other purpose than that of an observatory, and revert to the college when the observatory should be discontinued. The sanction of the Governor-General was received in 1840, and the building, erected under the direction of Lieut. Riddell, was completed in September of that year.

1069—FIRST OBSERVATORY BUILDING, TORONTO—Erected 1840—It was built of twelve-inch logs, roughcast on the outside and plastered on the inside, the laths being attached to battens projecting two inches from the logs so as to leave a stratum of air between the logs and plaster. No iron was used, the nails being copper and locks of brass. The establishment consisted of: 1, Observatory; 2, The anemometer house; 3, Detached building for experimental determination; 4, Small shed, behind fence, for inclination circle; 5, Barracks for officers. The latter building stands (1917) west of the Physics building, University crescent, and was used as a printing office by the University. Water color. Size 5 x 7.

1070—SECOND OBSERVATORY BUILDING, TORONTO, ERECTED 1855—The picture shows: 1, Observatory on site of first building. 2, Weather or meteorological office. These were both removed to make room for the Physics building and Convocation Hall. 3, Self-recording magnetic instruments. 4, Stone Transit building, covering the pillar standing near present (1917) Physics building. The dome to main building was added in 1882. Water color. Size 5 x 7.

1071—SECOND OBSERVATORY BUILDING, RECONSTRUCTED—It stands at the east end of the main building of the University; was reconstructed with the same stone and restored to its original elevation as nearly as possible. The tower, however. in the reconstruction was placed at the south instead of the north end of the Observatory of 1855, otherwise all the old building, except the wooden addition, which contained the instruments, is in the present structure, and is now (1917) the astronomical observatory in connection with the University. Photograph, colored. Size 5 x 7.

1072—HISTORIC SECTION OF TORONTO UNIVERSITY GROUNDS —To right of picture is the Physics building (1), and to the left the Faculty of Applied Science building (2). Bordering the roadway is a pillar (3), which from 1854-1902 served as the support, in one of the Observatory buildings, for the transit instrument used in the time service of the Observatory. 4, Bronze tablet stone marking the site upon which stood one of the three magnetic observatories erected by the Imperial Government in 1840. 5, College street. 6, University crescent. Photograph, colored. Size 5 x 7.

1073—HEADQUARTERS METEOROLOGICAL SERVICE, BLOOR ST., TORONTO—Erected 1909—Owing to the expansion of the University of Toronto, it was decided in 1907 to remove the Meteorological Office. Temporary quarters were occupied until September, 1909, when the new premises at the south-west corner of Bloor street and Devonshire place were ready. In the new building provision has been made for a library, also for a laboratory, to be used in research work in connection with atmospheric physics. Water color by J. W. Cotton. Size 6 x 7.

1074—BARRACKS FOR OFFICER AND DETACHMENT, TORONTO OBSERVATORY—Situated at the western end of the Observatory, the buildings of which were originally enclosed by a picketing. It now (1917) stands west of the Physics building, and was used as a printing office by the University. Photograph, colored. Size 5 x 7.

1075—TRANSIT PILLAR, TORONTO UNIVERSITY GROUNDS— Formerly in one of the Observatory buildings. It stands east of the Physics building; was in 1854 placed in one of the buildings of the Magnetic Observatory, built 1840. Until 1908 it served as the support for the transit instrument used in the time service of the Observatory, but was no longer required when the present headquarters of the Meteorological Service were erected. Photograph, colored. Size 5 x 7.

1076—SITE OF FIRST OBSERVATORY, TORONTO, 1840—Where meteorological observations were recorded for many years—The first Observatory, of logs, roughcast on the outside, was erected under the direction of Lieut. (Major-General) Riddell, R.A. Here meteorological observations were recorded continuously for sixty-eight years. Later the old building was succeeded by one of stone, which in turn was torn down and re-erected, 1908, at the east end of the main building of Toronto University. On its re-erection, however, it was no longer used for meteorological purposes. The site of the building of 1840 is marked by a stone upon which an inscribed plate recording the fact was placed in 1910. Photograph, colored. Size 5½ x 6.

1077—BETHUNE, DONALD—One of the owners of the Royal Mail Line. Born at Charlottenburg, near Cornwall, U.C., July 4th, 1802, the youngest son of a U. E. Loyalist, Rev. John Bethune, who held the first Presbyterian service in Montreal in 1786, settling in Williamstown the following year, and founding a Presbyterian congregation there. Donald Bethune was a lawyer by profession. For a time was interested in the steamboat business, being owner of the Royal Mail Line in conjunction with Andrew Heron and Capt. Thomas Dick. He retired, however, in 1864, removing to Port Hope, where he resumed the practice of law. In 1868 came to Toronto. Died here June 29th, 1869, at the residence of his brother, the second Anglican Bishop of Toronto. Water color from oil in possession of his grandniece, Miss M. L. Bethune, Toronto. Size 6 x 8. Three-quarter length.

1078—HARVIE, JOHN—First passenger conductor on Ontario, Simcoe and Huron Railway—He was born at Campbelltown, Argyllshire, Scotland, 12th April, 1833, educated at the Grammar School there, and in 1851 emigrated to New York, later settling at Toledo, Ohio, where he became connected with the Michigan Southern and Northern Indiana Railway. He came to Toronto and was engaged by Superintendent Alfred Brunel as conductor in charge of the first passenger train of the Ontario, Simcoe and Huron Railway, 16th May, 1853, running from Toronto to Machell's Corners, now Aurora, Ont. He was appointed to fill vacancies at way stations, and was agent at Collingwood during 1865. Later he became traffic manager, acting as such for many years. In 1881 he retired from railway work, and resided in Toronto until a short time before his death, Sept. 6th, 1917. Mr. Harvie was a director of the Upper Canada Bible Society and of the Toronto General Burying Grounds Trust. Photograph, colored. Size 4 x 5. Head and shoulders.

1079-1106—Presidents Toronto Stock Exchange—In 1852 a number of Toronto business men held a meeting, with Mr. George Barrow presiding, and Mr. James Fraser as secretary, to discuss the question of forming an association of brokers. The outcome of the meeting was the passing of a resolution to proceed with the organization which has now developed into the second most important Exchange in the Dominion, the one in Montreal ranking as leader. For some nine years after its organization the Exchange held no regular sessions, the members going to each other's offices for the transaction of business. In Oct., 1865, a reorganization was effected, and an arrangement made whereby the daily meetings were regularly held in the office of the late Humphrey L. Hime, president of the Stock Exchange, 1868-70, 1888-9. In 1878 an act was passed by the Ontario Legislature incorporating the Exchange. On Jan. 2nd, 1914, it removed to a modern building, 82-6 Bay street.

1079—MORTIMER, HERBERT—President Toronto Stock Exchange, 1861-3 and 1867—He was a son of Rev. G. Mortimer, of Vicarage Madeley, Shropshire, Eng. Came to Canada in 1832, completing his education here under his father, who was at that time rector of Thornhill. Mr. Herbert Mortimer engaged in farming for some years near Bond Head. He removed to Toronto in 1851, where he became a broker. His death took place in Toronto, 19th April, 1893. Water color. Size 3 x 4. Head and shoulders.

1080—ALEXANDER, WILLIAM—President Toronto Stock Exchange, 1864—A Scotsman, born September, 1826, in Montrose, Forfarshire, and educated at Montrose Academy. He came to Toronto in 1857, the firm of Blaikie and Alexander being formed the following year. In 1884 he removed to Santa Barbara, Cal., where his death occurred, 6th Jan., 1910. Water color. Size 3 x 4. Head and shoulders.

1081—STIKEMAN, JOHN C.—President Toronto Stock Exchange, 1865 —He was for many years travelling agent of the Canada Life Assurance Co. of Hamilton, Ont., and later became manager of the North British Insurance Company, Toronto. Mr. Stikeman was born in 1822, and died at Carillon, on the Ottawa, in 1868. A son, F. H. Stikeman, now (1917) resides in Santa Cruz, Cal. Water color. Size 3 x 4. Head and shoulders.

1082—BRADBURNE, EDMUND—President Toronto Stock Exchange, 1866—He was born in England, 1817; came to Toronto about 1845, and acted as agent of the Canada Life Assurance Company from 1848-68. In the latter year he was manager in Toronto of the Provincial Permanent Building Society. Mr. Bradburne, who was well known in cricket circles, was a member of the original Toronto Club. He married Miss Anne Campbell, daughter of T. D. Campbell, clerk of the County Court and deputy clerk of the Crown in Brockville for the counties of Leeds and Grenville. In 1874 Mr. Bradburne returned to England, where his death took place a year later. Water color. Size 3 x 4. Head and shoulders.

1083—HIME, HUMPHREY L.—President Toronto Stock Exchange, 1868-70, 1888-9—Born in 1834 at Newtown Mount Kennedy, Ireland. In 1855 he came to Canada, and for a time was engaged in survey work in the Northwest. From 1860 carried on a brokerage, estate and insurance business. In partnership with Christopher C. Baines, 1866-72, previously and subsequently carrying on business under the firm name of H. L. Hime & Co. Alderman for St. Patrick's Ward in the City Council, 1873. He was one of the founders of the Toronto Stock Exchange, and for a time the meetings of the organization were held in his office. Mr. Hime died in Toronto, 1903. Sir Albert Hime is a brother. Water color. Size 3 x 4. Head and shoulders.

1084—CASSELS, W. G.—President Toronto Stock Exchange, 1871-2— Came to Canada in 1845; joined the staff of the Bank of British North America, later becoming general manager of the Gore Bank of Hamilton. In 1866 he entered into partnership as a stock broker with the late C. J. Campbell, and was a charter member of the Stock Exchange. Mr. Cassels, who died in 1890, was born in Leith, Scotland, 30th March, 1811. Water color. Size 3 x 4. Head and shoulders.

1085—BROWNE, JAMES—President Toronto Stock Exchange, 1873-5— Mr. Browne, was born at Lambeth, Surrey, Eng., Nov. 12th, 1819. Came to Canada about 1860, and for some years was a member of the firm of Philip Browne & Co., bankers and stock brokers, 67 Yonge street, Toronto. Prior to this connection, both brothers were with the Bank of Upper Canada. James Browne's death took place in Toronto, March 18th, 1887. In St. Philip's (Anglican) Church, Toronto, is a tablet erected to the brothers, James and Philip, "by their friends of the Toronto Stock Exchange," both having been founders of that body. Water color. Size 3 x 4. Head and shoulders.

1086—PELLATT, HENRY, SR.—President Toronto Stock Exchange, 1876-80—He was born in Glasgow, Scotland, 25th Feb., 1830; educated in England; came to Canada in 1852, settling first in Kingston. In 1859 he came to Toronto, and the following year commenced the brokerage business. For a time he conducted his business alone, but afterwards became connected with Sir E. B. Osler, and later with his son, Sir Henry Pellatt. Mr. Pellatt's death took place in Orillia, Ont., 23rd July, 1909. Water color. Size 3 x 4. Head and shoulders.

1087—HOPE, WILLIAM—President Stock Exchange, 1881—Son of the Rev. Henry Hope, at one time editor of the Old Countryman. For a number of years Mr. William Hope was in the land agency business, but subsequently became a partner in the firm of Hope & Temple, stock brokers, 18 King street east. He was born in Thorford, Eng., 14th Dec., 1839; died in Toronto, 8th May, 1894. Water color. Size 3 x 4. Head and shoulders.

1088—BEATY, ROBERT—President Toronto Stock Exchange, 1882-3— Born near Milton, County of Halton, 28th July, 1824. He was educated at Upper Canada College. Mr. Beaty followed the profession of banker and broker in Toronto, being head of the firm of Robert Beaty & Co. Water color. Size 3 x 4. Head and shoulders.

1089—FORBES, HARRISON R.—President Toronto Stock Exchange, 1884—He was an American, born in 1835; came to Toronto about 1859, and for a time carried on business as a broker under style of H. R. Forbes & Co. Later he was a partner in the firm of Forbes & King and the firm of Forbes & Lownsbrough. The latter was dissolved in the eighties, and Mr. Forbes returned to the States. He died at San Angelo, Texas, September 20th, 1913. Water color. Size 3 x 4. Head and shoulders.

1090—STARK, JOHN—President Toronto Stock Exchange, 1885 and 1893-4—Born in Bridgewater, Eng., 1837. Educated there, and came to Canada in 1857, becoming in due course the head of the stock-broking firm

14

of John Stark & Co. In 1881 he was elected a member of the Toronto Stock Exchange, and later elected president. He was a director of the Canada Landed and National Investment Co. Died in Toronto, June, 1912. Water color. Size 3 x 4. Head and shoulders.

1091—BAINES, W. J.—President Toronto Stock Exchange, 1886— Eldest son of Mr. Thomas Baines, at one time Crown Lands Agent for Upper Canada; born in Toronto, 1838; educated at U. C. College. For years he was engaged in the stock brokerage business. Died in Toronto, 1895. Dr. Allen Baines, of Toronto, is (1917) the only brother living. Water color. Size 3 x 4. Head and shoulders.

1092—HAMMOND, H. C.—President Toronto Stock Exchange, 1887— His birthplace was Grafton, Ont., 19th Oct., 1844. He was educated at Cobourg Grammar School and Upper Canada College, and on leaving school entered the Bank of Montreal in Cobourg. He later joined the staff of the Quebec Bank; on the organization of the Bank of Hamilton, was appointed cashier. Subsequently he became a partner of E. B. (Sir Edmund) Osler, remaining a member of the firm until his death in January, 1909. Water color. Size 3 x 4. Head and shoulders.

1093—CASSELS, W. GIBSON—President Toronto Stock Exchange, 1890-91—He was born at Ottawa, 28th Sept., 1852, and educated at the Quebec High School and Morin College. After having been engaged in business in Montreal for some years, he joined his father in 1877 in Toronto. The firm is known (1917) as Cassels, Son & Co. Water color. Size 3 x 4. Head and shoulders.

1094—GZOWSKI, C. S.—President Toronto Stock Exchange, 1892—He was born in Toronto, 2nd Dec., 1847, eldest son of Sir Casimir Gzowski. Educated at Leamington College, Warwickshire, Eng. Engaged in banking; joined the Toronto Stock Exchange in 1871. Water color. Size 3 x 4. Head and shoulders.

1095—BEATY, JOHN W.—President Toronto Stock Exchange, 1895— Son of the late Robert Beaty, broker; born at Toronto, 7th Dec., 1853, and educated at Upper Canada College. After leaving school he entered the banking and brokerage firm of his father, later becoming a member. In 1901 Mr. Robert Beaty died, his son continuing in business until 1904. He has since lived retired. Water color. Size 3 x 4. Head and shoulders.

1096—AMES. A. E.—President Toronto Stock Exchange, 1896-7—Well known in Canadian financial circles. In 1889 established the firm of A. E. Ames & Co., investment bankers, 53 King street west, Toronto. He was born at Lambeth, Ont., in 1866, and educated in the public schools and Brantford Collegiate. In 1881 entered the Owen Sound branch of the Merchants' Bank of Canada, and afterwards entered the service of the Imperial Bank of Canada. Acting accountant, Ontario Bank, Peterboro, 1885, and later manager of the Mount Forest and Lindsay branches of that institution. President Toronto Board of Trade, 1901-2. First chairman Timiskaming and Northern Ontario Railway Commission, 1902-4. Water color. Size 3 x 4. Head and shoulders.

1097—FERGUSSON, G. TOWER—President Toronto Stock Exchange, 1898-9 and 1915—Son of the late Geo. D. Fergusson, of Fergus, Ont., and a grandson of the Hon. Adam Fergusson, of Woodhill. Born at Fergus, Sept., 1856, he was educated at the Galt Grammar School, under the late Dr. William Tassie, and commenced business in Toronto as a stock broker and investment agent. He has taken a prominent part in connection with the Christian Endeavor movement. Water color. Size 3 x 4. Head and shoulders.

1098—**CAMPBELL, J. LORNE**—President Toronto Stock Exchange, 1900-1—Born in Simcoe, Ont., 22nd April, 1857, and educated at Upper Canada College. Entered the Canadian Bank of Commerce, where he was a member of the staff for some years. In 1892 became a member of the Stock Exchange. Died in 1917. Water color. Size 3 x 4. Head and shoulders.

1099—**SMITH, ROBERT A.**—President Toronto Stock Exchange, 1902-3 —Born in Scotland, 1859, and educated there. He was elected to Toronto Stock Exchange in 1896, and joined the firm of Osler & Hammond. Became a director of the Commercial Cable Board, also of the Mackay Company. He was secretary-treasurer of the Toronto Ferry Company, and a promoter of Toronto Hunt Club. His death took place, 17th July, 1912. Water color. Size 3 x 4. Head and shoulders.

1100—**TEMPLE, ROBERT H.**—President Toronto Stock Exchange, 1904-5—Born at Quebec, 16th Feb., 1841; entered the civil service in the Department of Crown Lands at Quebec, 1862, and at the time of Confederation removed to Ottawa, where he continued that employment. Shortly afterwards he came to Toronto, and entered the brokerage business. Water color. Size 3 x 4. Head and shoulders.

1101—**BURRITT, AUGUSTUS P.**—President Toronto Stock Exchange, 1906-7—Son of H. O. Burritt, of Ottawa, Ont.; born there January, 1867; educated in Ottawa and Galt. He is head of the firm of A. P. Burritt & Co., stock brokers, founded by him in 1892. Has been treasurer and vice-president of the Toronto Stock Exchange, and for years has taken a deep interest in aquatic sports. Water color. Size 3 x 4. Head and shoulders.

1102—**BUCHANAN, J. O.**—President Toronto Stock Exchange, 1908-9— Educated at McGill University, Montreal, whence he entered the service of the Bank of Montreal. In 1888 he became a stock broker, commencing business on his own account. Mr. Buchanan was born at Drummondville, Ont., 29th Nov., 1849. Water color. Size 3 x 4. Head and shoulders.

1103—**BROUSE, WILLIAM H.**—President Toronto Stock Exchange, 1910-11—His birthplace was Prescott, Ont., 26th May, 1859. Called to the Ontario Bar in 1882, he successfully practised his profession as a member of the firm Beatty, Blackstock & Co., Toronto, until 1887. He is head of the firm Brouse, Mitchell & Co., bond and investment brokers, Toronto. Water color. Size 3 x 4. Head and shoulders.

1104—**OSLER, F. GORDON**—President Toronto Stock Exchange, 1912-13—He was born in Toronto, educated at Trinity College School, Port Hope, and at Trinity University. In 1895 he entered the office of Messrs. Osler & Hammond, becoming a member of the firm four years later, and of the Stock Exchange in 1901. Water color. Size 3 x 4. Head and shoulders.

1105—**FREELAND, EDWARD B.**—President Toronto Stock Exchange, 1914—Born in Toronto, 13th Nov., 1860. He received his education at Upper Canada College. For some years he was with the Scottish Commercial Insurance Company and the Federal Bank, later becoming accountant with John Stark & Co. Since 1893 he has been a partner in the firm. Mr. Freeland was selected for service in North-west Rebellion, 1885. Water color. Size 3 x 4. Head and shoulders.

1106—**TUDHOPE, H. R.**—President Toronto Stock Exchange, 1917— Born at Orillia, Ont., Aug. 3rd, 1877. Three years later removed, with his parents, to Gravenhurst and was educated in the Public and High schools there. In 1894 came to Toronto; entered the employ of the Ontario Accident Insurance Company, remaining there for about two years, and then joining the staff of A. E. Ames Company; became a partner in 1898. Water color. Size 3 x 4. Head and shoulders.

1107—MACE OF THE LEGISLATIVE ASSEMBLY—Taken by Americans at York, April 27th, 1813—The mace, removed from the old Parliament Buildings west of the Don, on site of part of present (1917) gas works, is preserved in the library of the Naval Academy, Annapolis, Md., and is in much the same condition as at the time of its seizure. The head, or crown, has been cleaned and the gilding on the shaft is fairly well preserved. From crown to head of shaft it measures 10¼ inches; from head of shaft to end, 2 feet 11 inches, and from the lower end of the shaft to the turned and pointed end is 9¼ inches, bringing the entire length to 4 feet 6½ inches. It is similar in size to the mace used in the House at Ottawa and destroyed when the Administrative Buildings were burned in 1916. The Ottawa mace was, of course, much more elaborate. Water color. Size 6 x 30.

1108—PIONEER GATE HOUSE—A landmark of Parliament street, 1818-1914—About 1795 a land grant of considerable acreage in York township, comprising township lot No. 20, second concession, east side of Yonge and north of Bloor, was made to Captain George Playter. The pretty cottage at the entrance to the grounds, at the head of Parliament street, was erected by Captain Playter about 1818, for his gatekeeper. In 1831 Mr. John Cayley, brother of Hon. William Cayley, purchased the property, and in 1874 a portion of the land, about 34 acres, was bought by Mr. M. B. Jackson, Clerk of the Crown at Osgoode Hall. The cottage, a picturesque little building, was for years used as a studio by Mr. Frank Cayley, an artist, and brother of the owner. It was demolished in 1914. Water color. Size 10 x 14.

1109—OGDEN, LYNDHURST—Secretary Toronto Stock Exchange, 1881-1914—Born 12th March, 1847, at Kirby, Douglas, Isle of Man; educated at the Charterhouse, London, and Trinity College, Cambridge. He lived in Chili and Peru from 1869 to 1876. In the latter year Mr. Ogden came to Toronto. He was secretary of the Toronto Club for a time, and in 1881 became secretary of Toronto Stock Exchange, which position he held for thirty-three years. Died at Toronto, 26th April, 1915. Water color. Size 3 x 4. Head and shoulders.

1110—MORGAN, PETER—A well-known citizen of Toronto from 1846-60, and a prominent member of St. Andrew's Presbyterian Church, Church and Adelaide sts. He was born in Edinburgh in 1807, came to Canada in 1832, and was Cornet in the Queen's Light Dragoons of Montreal, retiring with the rank of Lieutenant. In 1846 he moved to Toronto, and was, with James McDonell and John Rose, a Government revenue inspector. Mr. Morgan's eldest son, Charles, is in the Merchants' Bank of Canada at Montreal. Water color. Size 3 x 4. Head and shoulders.

1111—"THE LADY ELGIN"—The first locomotive in Ontario as it appeared in 1881, in the Northern Railway yard at the foot of Brock street, Toronto. Built in Portland, Me., in 1851-2, for the Ontario, Simcoe and Huron Railroad Union Company, incorporated in 1849, became the Northern in 1859, and in 1884 amalgamated with the Hamilton and North-Western Railway. In 1888 the two latter, with the Northern, were merged into the Grand Trunk system. This engine was used in the construction of the railway and occasionally handled passenger trains, and later freight trains. Finally it was used for shunting purposes, and was broken up in 1881. On the left, near the fender, is John Harvie, the first passenger conductor on the road, and, on the right, sitting on the step of the tender, W. H. Adamson, secretary to F. W. Cumberland, managing director of the railway. Carlos McColl was the driver of the first train, and Joseph Lopez was the fireman. Water color from photograph. Size 7 x 13.

1112—VISIT OF THEIR ROYAL HIGHNESSES, THE DUKE AND DUCHESS OF CORNWALL AND YORK (King George and Queen Mary), to Canada—Royal party at Government House, Toronto. During their tour of Canada Their Royal Highnesses spent a few days in Toronto, and while here were the guests of his Honor Sir Oliver Mowat, the Lieut.-Governor, at old Government House, southwest corner King and Simcoe streets. Photo taken 11th Oct., 1901. With key. Size 11 x 14.

1113—CAPREOL, FREDERICK CHASE, 1803-86—Second son of Thomas Capreol, Hertfordshire, Eng. In 1828 he came to Canada to assist in settling the affairs of the old North-West Fur Company, returning to England on the conclusion of his business in 1830. Three years later, however, he returned, settling in York (Toronto), and buying a large tract of land at the Credit, where he lived for a time. Mr. Capreol was the projector and promoter of the Ontario, Simcoe and Huron Railway, afterwards the Northern, and was presented with a handsome service of plate of seventeen pieces, by the citizens of Toronto, in recognition of his services. He afterwards received authority from the Legislature to sell his lands at the Credit by lottery, and, with the money obtained, to erect a large cotton factory. This idea was abandoned, however, and Mr. Capreol turned his attention to the construction of a canal between Lakes Huron and Ontario. Ground was broken for the canal, Sept. 17th, 1866, but the project was never carried to completion. Mr. Capreol died in Toronto. Water color. Size 3 x 4. Head and shoulders.

1114—McMASTER, CAPTAIN WILLIAM FENTON—Born at Omagh, County Tyrone, Ireland, Sept. 1st, 1822. Came to Canada about 1838. Was employed in the wholesale dry goods business of his uncle (Hon.) Wm. McMaster, and subsequently a partner, with his brother, in the firm of A. R. McMaster & Bro., successors to the old business of Wm. McMaster. In 1886 entered the civil service, where he remained until his death in January, 1907. President of the Board of Trade, 1876. He was in 1866 Captain of the Naval Brigade. Water color from portrait in possession of his daughter, Mrs. Hertzberg, Toronto. Size 3 x 4. Head and shoulders.

1115—"THE TORONTO"—The second locomotive in Ontario and the first passenger engine of the Ontario, Simcoe and Huron Railroad Union Company. Built by James Good, Toronto, in 1852-3. It hauled the first passenger train from the shed station, south side of Front street, a few hundred feet east of the Queen's Hotel, 16th May, 1853, with the late William Huckett, master mechanic of the company, as engineer for the trip, and John Harvie as conductor. The first trip was to Machell's Corners, now Aurora, Ont. The picture, which was made in the railway yards, foot of Brock street, west of the bridge, shows: 1, W. H. Adamson, secretary to F. W. Cumberland, managing director. 2, John Broughton, machinist. 3, Joseph Benson, caretaker of the yards. 4, Daniel Sheehy, an engineer. 5, James Armitage, foreman mechanical department. 6, Joshua Metzler, in cab window. 7, James Phillips, standing on tender. 8, John Harvie. 9, Charles Storey, conductor. 10, Thomas Peters, who ran the stationary engine in the machine shop. Water color from photograph. Size 7 x 13.

1116—ARMSTRONG, WILLIAM, C.E., 1821-1914—Tinted photograph made in 1863. Presented to J. Ross Robertson by S. H. Fleming, Ottawa. Size 3 x 4. See 649.

1117—BURNING OF THE ROSSIN HOUSE, TORONTO—A well-known hostelry—Erected in 1856-7 on the south-east corner of King and York streets by Messrs. Marcus and Samuel Rossin; William Kaufmann, architect, and A. C. Joslin, lessee. The principal entrance faced on York street. In November, 1862, the hotel was burned and rebuilt the following year. The buildings to the south, on the east side of York, (1) the Club Chambers, kept by Henry Beverley, and (2) the Toronto Club, were saved. The Rossin is now (1917) the Prince George Hotel. Water color from old print. Size 5 x 6.

1118—THE "GREAT EASTERN" IN CANADA, 1861—An excursion to Quebec—When the "Great Eastern" steamship was at Quebec in the summer of 1861, excursions by rail and water were held from all parts of Canada to the ancient city. The late Capt. Charles Perry, of Toronto, was in command of the "Bowmanville," which carried an excursion party of some hundreds to Quebec. At the conclusion of the trip the passengers presented the captain with a handsome solid silver cup and salver, inscribed as follows: "Presented to Captn. Chas. Perry, of the steamer 'Bowmanville' by the passengers on the excursion trip to visit the 'Great Eastern,' as a token of acknowledgment for his kindness and attention, July, 1861." This once-famed steamship was launched in 1858. She was 679 feet long, 83 feet broad, 48 feet depe and 18,915 tons. Commercially she was never a success and underwent sales periodically, the last time being purchased by a firm of ship breakers and broken up at New Ferry, on the banks of the Mersey, in 1890. Photograph, colored, of the testimonials, which are in possession of Capt. Perry's daughter, Mrs. John A. Murray, of Toronto. Size 6 x 6.

1119—HOLY TRINITY CHURCH, TORONTO—Interior view, 1913— The "Church of the Holy Trinity," situated in the court formerly known as "The Fields," now called Trinity Square, was built in 1846, and opened and consecrated by the Right Rev. John Strachan, Bishop of Toronto, 27th Oct., 1847. The view shows the nave and chancel. At the north-west corner of the latter is seen the organ, and above the altar a large, variegated stained glass window, representing the four evangelists and four major prophets. The ceiling is buttressed directly from the walls, so that no pillars obstruct the view. Photograph, colored. Size 8 x 10.

1120—PRINCE OF WALES' LEINSTER REGIMENT—Formed 1st July,, 1881, from the 100th or Prince of Wales' Royal Canadians, and the 109th, originally the Hon. East India Company's 3rd Bombay European Infantry, the former becoming the first battalion and the latter the second. Major-General Sir Alexander Hamilton Gordon, K.C.B., was colonel-in-chief of the new regiment in 1881, and Lieut.-Col. Richard Doyle commanded it. Original lithograph in color by R. Simpkin. Published by George Berridge & Co., 179 and 180 Upper Thames st., London, E.C., Eng. Size 9 x 10.

1121—NICKINSON, JOHN—In "The Old Guard"—Mr. Nickinson was the pioneer in theatrical management in Toronto, and was the manager of the Royal Lyceum, Toronto, from 1853-8. He was an actor of high reputation. The picture shows him as "Havresack" in the play of "The Old Guard." Mr. Nickinson acted the part in 1848-52 in the Olympic Theatre, New York, and at various times between 1853-8, when manager of the Lyceum, Toronto. Miss Charlotte Nickinson (Mrs. Daniel Morrison), his eldest daughter, an accomplished actress, acted the part of "Melanie" in the piece. Mr. Nickinson's death took place in Cincinnati, Ohio, 1864. "The Old Guard" was produced at the Princess', London, in 1844, and was first performed in America at the Chatham Theatre, 1845. Water color by John Fraser, presented to J. Ross Robertson by Mr. Nickinson's granddaughter, Mrs. Raynald Gamble, Toronto. Size 11 x 14. Full length, sitting. See 585.

1122—SECTION OF THE NORTH SIDE OF KING ST. EAST, TORONTO, 1846—From one door east of n.e. corner of Yonge and King to the east side of the grounds of St. James' church at the north-east corner of King and Church. With key. Water color from a drawing made originally for Mr. F. C. Capreol, and which appeared in the "Illustrated London News" in 1847. Size 11 x 18.

1123—"PINEHURST," GRANGE ROAD, TORONTO—Mrs. Forster's School, a popular ladies' seminary, 1853-66—Situated on Grange road, just east of "The Grange," stood for many years a commodious building known as "Pinehurst." It was originally the residence of Mr. Clarke Gamble, who built it in 1840. In 1850 he rented it to M. and Mme. Des Landes as a ladies' school. Three years later they were succeeded by Mrs. Forster, an accomplished schoolmistress and charming woman. She had been the wife of an English army officer. From 1853-66 the school continued as a fashionable seminary, the daughters of many prominent Canadians having been educated there. On the retirement of Mrs. Forster in 1866, the Bishop Strachan School for Girls occupied "Pinehurst," for a year. The building was pulled down in the eighties to make way for the extension of McCaul street to College street. The picture, with key, shows a number of the pupils with Mrs. Forster and some of the teachers, in the summer of 1864. Photograph, colored. Size 9 x 12. See 1125.

1124—FORSTER, MRS. AUGUSTA A.—Mistress of "Pinehurst," Grange road, Toronto—In 1853 Mrs. Forster, widow of an English army officer and a cousin of Rev. Thomas Smith Kennedy, at one time secretary of the Toronto Church Society, succeeded M. and Mme. Des Landes at "Pinehurst," The seminary continued until 1866 under Mrs. Forster, an accomplished schoolmistress and charming woman, well liked and respected by her pupils. In that year, owing to ill-health, she was compelled to give up her duties, and on May 20th, 1886, died in Toronto. The picture shows Mrs. Forster in 1863. Photograph, colored. Size 4 x 7. Half length. See 1139.

1125—"PINEHURST," GRANGE ROAD, TORONTO—Mrs. Forster's school, a popular ladies' seminary, 1853-66. Photograph, colored. Size 9 x 12. See 1123.

1126—SIDE-LAUNCH OF S. S. "CORONA," TORONTO, 23RD MAY, 1896—With key. Designed by A. Angstrom and built by Bertram Engine Works Co. for the Niagara Navigation Company, Toronto, to replace the "Cibola," which had been burned at Lewiston Dock, N.Y., 15th July, 1895. The "Corona" is still (1917) in commission. Wash drawing. Size 12 x 30.

1127—100TH REGIMENT—"Her Majesty's 100th Regiment (Prince of Wales' Royal Canadian). W. Sharpe, del. et lith. M. and N. Hanhart, lith. impt. London: Publish'd June 1st, 1859, by E. Gambart & Co., 25 Berners St., Oxford St., and 8 Rue de Bruxelles, Paris."—With key, indicating the various uniforms. Raised during the Indian Mutiny by a number of officers of the Canadian volunteers for service in India. Baron de Rottenburg, son of Gen. de Rottenburg, Administrator of Upper Canada, and Alexander Roberts Dunn, of Toronto, son of Receiver-General Dunn, were appointed lieutenant-colonel and major, respectively. Recruiting began in April, 1858, and at the end of May the regiment was quartered in the citadel of Quebec, preparatory to embarkation for England. While they were stationed at Shorncliffe, Eng., the Mutiny ended and the Royal Canadians were ordered to Gibraltar. As the 100th (Prince Regent's County of Dublin) the regiment had done good work on the Niagara frontier, 1812-14, and in commemoration of this, H.R.H. presented them, before leaving Shorncliffe, with colors inscribed "Niagara." With the 109th, which originally was the Hon. East India Company's 3rd Bombay European Infantry, the 100th Prince of Wales' Royal Canadians became the Royal Leinster Regiment, 1st July, 1881. The 100th composed the first battalion and the second battalion was made up of the 109th Foot. Chromo lithograph. Size 11 x 18.

1128—MUSKOKA CLUB, 1866—With key—In 1860 three young Toronto men in Orillia, having heard of Muskoka, resolved to investigate, going as far as Muskoka Bay. The following summer a party of six set out to explore the new land, and for a time camped on the present (1916) site of Port Sandfield. For several years an island at the head of Lake Joseph was the camping spot. In time a group of islands was purchased by five of those who had visited Muskoka Lakes, viz., Prof. Geo. Paxton Young, William H. Howland, Montgomery Cumning, John Campbell, and James Bain. The largest island was called Yohocucabah, from the first two letters of the surnames, the "h" being added to give an Indian pronunciation.

Proving rather cumbersome, the name soon became shortened to Yoho. Subsequently the islands were purchased by Prof. Campbell, whose hospitality was unbounded and is remembered by many who had the privilege of being his guests. Two of the five islands were afterwards sold by Prof. Campbell to W. B. McMurrich. Photograph, colored. Size 6 x 6.

1129—**NEW REGISTRY OFFICE, TORONTO**—Corner Albert and Elizabeth streets—The corner-stone was laid April 14th, 1915, by his Worship Mayor Thos. L. Church, who, when he had performed the ceremony and given an address, called upon Mr. J. Ross Robertson to say a few words about the history of the city and county registry offices. The gentlemen shown in the front row are: 1, W. H. Bennett; 2, The Mayor; 3, John T. Scott; 4, J. Ross Robertson; 5, Alderman John Dunn Photograph, colored. Size 5 x 7.

1130—**TORONTO FROM THE ISLAND**—This view was made in the summer of 1880, near Hanlan's Point, in early days known as Gibraltar Point. The bay, especially near the Island, presents a gala appearance with sailing and rowing craft. To the left of picture, in background, is seen the Northern elevators at foot of Brock street (Spadina avenue). Towards the centre and also to the right are the tower of the old Union Station, the spires of the Metropolitan Church, St. Michael's Cathedral and St. James' Church. Water color from original drawing by Schell and Hogan, for "Picturesque Canada." Size 5 x 7.

1131—**TORONTO, 1834**—With key—The picture was made from two original sketches, one of which gave the city east as far as Parliament street, the other showing the waterfront west of Parliament. It is the first picture of Toronto which gives the Worts and Gooderham windmill. For a more detailed key and comprehensive description, see Robertson's Landmarks of Toronto, Vol. V., pp. 583-5. Water color. Size 12 x 30.

1132—**A SECTION OF THE SOUTH SIDE OF KING ST. EAST, TORONTO, 1846**—From No. 38, just east of the King Edward Hotel, to No. 104, south-west corner of King and West Market streets. With key. Water color from a drawing made originally for Mr. F. C. Capreol, and which appeared in the "Illustrated London News" in 1847. Size 10 x 18.

1133—**QUEEN'S OWN REGIMENTAL MACE OR BATON**—Presented on 25th May, 1863, by the ladies of Toronto—It is fifty-eight inches long, with a massive silver circular head, which joins the staff eight inches below the head. The staff is of Canadian oak. The head is topped with a Victorian crown, and on the plate which surrounds the crown are the words "Presented to the 2nd Battalion Vol. Mil. of Canada, the Queen's Own Rifles of Toronto, by the ladies, the friends and relatives of the officers of the corps, in testimony of their warm interest in the welfare of the battalion, 24th May, 1863." Just above where the staff joins the headpiece on one side of the plate, is an oval shield with the worlds, "Queen's Own Rifles" around a figure "2" denoting the official number of the corps, and on the other side a maple leaf in silver and the initials "V.R." spread thereon. Two bands of silver encircle the staff, one a few inches below the head, and another about midway. From the centre band to within 14 inches of the staff is twined with silver cord, and the fourteen inches has a covering of brass which reaches down to the end of the ferule. The mace is now (1917) in the Queen's Own Armory, Toronto. Water color from old drawing. Size 3 x 6. See 1134.

1134—**SCENE AT PRESENTATION OF MACE TO QUEEN'S OWN RIFLES, TORONTO**—On the morning of 25th May, 1863, the Queen's birthday falling on Sunday, the Queen's Own paraded on the lawn on the west, or Victoria street side of the Normal School building, St. James' Square, when Mrs. Draper, wife of Hon. Wm. H. Draper, Chief Justice of the Court of Common Pleas, in presence of a large concourse of citizens, presented the battalion with a handsome silver mace for the use of the band. On behalf of the battalion, Lieut.-Col. Durie, who was the first officer in command of the Rifles, gracefully accepted the mace, which is fittingly inscribed. Water color from old drawing. Size 5 x 6. See 1133.

1135—YORK PIONEERS' SOCIETY, 1880—Richard H. Oates was the founder of the society, the oldest of its kind in Canada, and in 1868 frequent meetings were held at his home in Isabella street, and also in the office of Alexander Hamilton, King street, to discuss the formation of a York Pioneers' Society. The first meeting was held, 17th April, 1869, in the Mechanics' Institute, later the Toronto Public Library, corner Church and Adelaide streets, Toronto, with Col. R. L. Denison, president; R. W. Phipps, treasurer, and Alexander Hamilton, secretary. In 1891 the society was incorporated under the name of "York Pioneer and Historical Society." From 1870 until 1905 meetings were held in the Canadian Institute building, Richmond street, but the institute, having sold this property, and bought 198 College street, the Pioneers also moved, and on 5th Dec., 1905, held their first meeting in the new quarters. Photo, with key. Size 12 x 20. See 99, 1141, 1145.

1136—CHAMPION, THOMAS, 1809-54—First rector's warden, Holy Trinity Church, Toronto—He was born in Sheffield, Eng., and came to Toronto in 1836, where he established the hardware firm of Champion Bros., north-east corner Yonge and Adelaide streets. "Champions' Axes" were noted. In 1843 Mr. Champion retired from business, and the following year became assistant secretary of the Church Society. Edited the "Church" newspaper, 1845-52. He was also connected with the Toronto Leader and Patriot. The late Thomas E. Champion, Toronto, was a son. Photograph from painting. Size 4 x 6. Head and shoulders.

1137—HARRIS, MRS. JAMES (FIDELIA KETCHUM), 1808-74—She was the second daughter of Jesse Ketchum, so well known as "The Children's Friend"; married Rev. James Harris, first pastor of Knox church, York (Toronto), and for several years lived at the Manse on Bay street. After the retirement of Mr. Harris, in 1844, they resided at Eglinton, Ont., the birthplace of Mrs. Harris. Water color. Size 3 x 3. Head and shoulders.

1138—ST. ANDREW'S PRESBYTERIAN CHURCH, YORK AND TORONTO—South-west corner Church and Adelaide streets—It was the second Presbyterian church in York, the first congregation of the denomination, Knox, having been formed in 1820, although not receiving the name of Knox until 1844, when some members of St. Andrew's united with it. In 1830-1 St. Andrew's was built. The tower and spire were added in 1850, and the church demolished in 1877. This church was the predecessor of St. Andrew's, corner King and Simcoe streets, and St. Andrew's, corner Carlton and Jarvis streets, two congregations having been formed out of the original one about 1875. St. Andrew's was the first Presbyterian church to introduce instrumental music in its service, not only in Toronto, but in Canada. In 1852 the band of the 71st Highland Light Infantry furnished music at the morning service, and the following year a choir was formed and a melodeon purchased. This drawing in water color by J. G. Howard, architect, was made in 1840, ten years before the addition of tower and spire. Size 10 x 14.

1139—FORSTER, MRS. AUGUSTA A.—Mistress of "Pinehurst," Grange road, Toronto. Photograph, colored. Size 4 x 5. Head and shoulders. See 1124.

1140—WALKER, ROBERT, 1809-85—A prominent dry goods merchant in Toronto—He was born in Carlisle, Eng.; came to York (Toronto) in 1828. Entered business as manager and then as partner with Thomas Lawson, a well-known clothier, on the south side of King street east. In 1846 became a partner of Thomas Hutchinson (Walker & Hutchinson),

10 King street east, and this firm continued for about eight years, when Mr. Hutchinson withdrew and Mr. Walker carried on the business in his own name. Mr. Hutchinson also had a dry goods shop on King street. About 1859 the firm of Robert Walker & Son was formed, and later his other sons were partners. The Walker store was known as the "Golden Lion" from about 1850, and the Hutchinson store as "Pantechnetheca"—later the site of China Hall. Mr. Walker was a Primitive Methodist, and his marble bust is in Carlton Street Methodist church, Toronto. Water color. Size 3 x 4. Head and shoulders.

1141—YORK PIONEER AND HISTORICAL SOCIETY, 1905—Photo, with key. Size 11 x 18. See 99, 1135, 1145.

1142—BERTHON, GEORGE THEODORE, 1806-92—A distinguished portrait painter in Canada. He was born of French parents in Vienna, Austria, May 3rd, 1806. His father, Rene Berthon, was Court painter during the Napoleon regime. In 1844 the son, a true master of his art, settled in Toronto. The finest portraits of the public men of his time are from his brush, and are to be found in the Senate Chamber, Ottawa, Osgoode Hall, and Government House, Toronto, and the City Halls of Toronto and Kingston. Mr. Berthon was a member of the Ontario and the Royal Canadian Society of Artists. His death took place, January 18th, 1892. Water color from a portrait by himself in possession of Miss Claire Berthon, his eldest daughter. Size 3 x 4. Head and shoulders.

1143—BROWNE, JAMES, 1802-52—A well-known pioneer wharfinger—He was an Irishman, having been born in Abington, Co. Limerick. In 1835 he emigrated to Canada, settling in Toronto. The wharf at the foot of Scott street, well-known for many years as Browne's Wharf, now the Toronto Electric Light property, was built by Mr. Browne, and relatives of his in Hamilton were owners of some of the principal wharves of that city. His death occurred in Toronto. Water color from miniature in possession of his grandson, Roden Kingsmill, Toronto. Size 4 x 5. Half length, sitting.

1144—YORK (TORONTO), 1820—Showing the peninsula which joined the mainland at the foot of Woodbine avenue, Toronto, and through which the waters of Lake Ontario broke in 1854, creating the present Island. In the picture are also shown the second Parliament Buildings in York, erected on Palace (Front) street, in 1818, at foot of Berkeley. The buildings were two in number, two storeys in height, the north one being used for Government offices and the south building as the Legislative Chambers. On 20th December, 1824, the latter was destroyed by fire. Water color from original oil in possession of the late Mrs. Stephen Heward, Toronto, painted by Mr. Irvine, a Scotch artist, who, prior to 1821, was a visitor in York. He was a cousin of Hon. George Cruickshank. Water color. Size 18 x 34.

1145—YORK PIONEERS' SOCIETY, 1893—Photo, with key. Size 12 x 18. See 99, 1135, 1141.

1146—ZION CONGREGATIONAL CHURCH (FIRST)—North-east corner of Bay and Newgate (Adelaide) streets, Toronto—Built in 1839 and opened for worship, January 1st, 1840. Rev. John Roaf was pastor until 15th June, 1855. On 26th February, of that year, the church was destroyed by fire and re-erected on the same site. The first house north of Zion church was the residence of Thomas Harding, and next building, the Fire Hall of No. 6 "Provincial" (south door), and No. 3 "British America" (centre door), and station of hose company (north door). The church with square tower, south-east corner of Bay and Richmond, was the United Presbyterian church, of which Rev. John Jennings was pastor. Lithograph, in color. H. Martin, del. Size 10 x 14. See 761, 797.

1147—CHAUNCEY, COMMODORE—"Isaac Chauncey, Esqr. of the United States Navy. J. Wood, pinxt. D. Edwin, sc." Born in Connecticut about 1772. In 1806 obtained the rank of captain in the American navy, and in 1812 was appointed commander of the U.S. naval forces on the northern Great Lakes. His squadron, with land forces, captured York (Toronto), April 27th, 1813. An interesting incident in connection with Chauncey is related by Mr. C. H. J. Snider in his book, "In the Wake of the Eighteen-Twelvers." The British brig-of-war "Earl of Moira" was intercepted by Chauncey's flagship, the "Oneida," while convoying the effects of General Sir Isaac Brock, who had shortly before lost his life at Queenston Heights. On learning of the "Moira's" task, the "Oneida" gave the reply: "The Commodore's compliments, and if you are convoying the effects of the late General, pass on. We'll meet again." Stipple engraving. Size 3 x 4. Head and shoulders.

1148—PIKE, GENERAL ZEBULON MONTGOMERY, 1779-1813— "General Pike. T. Gimbrede, Sc., N.Y." An American officer and traveller, born in New Jersey. In 1805 he set out to explore the sources of the Mississippi. Rose to rank of brigadier-general in War of 1812. Commanded the land forces that captured York (Toronto), 27th April, 1813, and was killed in that action by the explosion of a magazine. Stipple engraving. Size 4½ x 5. Head and shoulders.

1149—CAPTURE OF THE UNITED STATES' SCHOONERS "JULIA" AND "GROWLER"—Six British vessels of Sir James Lucas Yeo's squadron on the 10th of August, 1813, encountered the American fleet of eleven off Niagara, and, after a running fight, captured the "Julia," the first schooner the Americans had armed for the war, and the "Growler," each of 80 tons, and armed with four guns. They had been separated from their main body. As prize ships the schooners became the British transports "Confiance" and "Hamilton." They were, however, recaptured off the Ducks, Lake Ontario, by Commodore Isaac Chauncey, October 6th, 1813, but the "Growler" was again taken by the British at Oswego, May 6th, 1814. Water color on pen drawing by C. H. J. Snider. Size 6 x 20.

1150—THE "DISCOVERIE," 1611—Captain Henry Hudson's last ship. In the summer of 1610, while searching for the North-west Passage to India, Hudson discovered the bay which bears his name. Provisions ran short, and his crew, fearing that he would persist in his search until they all perished, mutinied in 1611, casting him and eight others adrift, with hardly any arms or provisions, in the shallop towing astern. They were never found. This picture is based on details supplied by the replica of Hudson's preceding ship, the "Half Moon," in which he discovered the Hudson River, 1609. Water color on pencil sketch by C. H. J. Snider. Size 11 x 14.

1151—THE "TORONTO" YACHT—This was a small, fast-sailing vessel, built in 1799, for Government service, by John Dennis, master builder, at the Humber River mouth, on Lake Ontario. She was used for carrying passengers, despatches, and a limited amount of freight. Lieut.-Governor Peter Hunter and his suite used her frequently between York (Toronto), Niagara and Kingston. The "Toronto" was wrecked on the shore of Toronto Island early in 1812, and for many years her ribs bleached on the sandbar. The picture shows her outward bound, off the lighthouse built on Toronto Island, 1809. Water color on pencil sketch by C. H. J. Snider. Size 8 x 10.

1152—HIS MAJESTY'S SLOOP OF WAR "SIR ISAAC BROCK"—On the stocks at York (Toronto), April, 1813. Built during the winter of 1812-13 at the Government shipyard in York (Toronto), probably at the foot of Yonge street, but burned before her completion, by General Sheaffe, the British commander, to prevent her capture by the Americans at the taking of York, April 27th, 1813. She was to have had at least 30 guns, but her armament was frozen in the shipyard mud at the time of the capture, and so useless. The dismantled schooner, "Duke of Gloucester," in the background, was captured by the Americans. The masts showing beyond her were those of the schooner "Prince Regent," which had sailed for Kingston just before the Americans arrived. Water color on pencil sketch by C. H. J. Snider. Size 8 x 10.

1153—PRIZE BRIG "PRESIDENT ADAMS"—An American vessel captured by Brock at Detroit, August 16th, 1812. She was re-named the "Detroit," in honor of the taking of that place, armed with six guns and sent to Fort Erie, opposite Buffalo. Subsequently recaptured by the Americans and burned by them Oct. 9th, 1812, to prevent the British from regaining her. The picture shows the vessel in the act of weighing anchor for her last voyage under British colors to Fort Erie. Water color on pencil sketch by C. H. J. Snider. Size 8 x 10.

1154—FRENCH FLEET ON LAKE ONTARIO, 1757—With vessels beating off the Niagara River—At this time Fort Niagara, built 1725-6, was in possession of the French. At the left of the fleet is a topsail schooner, "La Marquise de Vaudreuil," flagship. Her side shows seven gunports, A smaller schooner, "La Huzalt," of similar rig, showing six gunports, appears to her right, and a still smaller schooner, with four ports in her side and without topsails, is next. She is "La Louise." At the extreme right is "Le Victort." She had six guns, three to a side. The craft ranged in size from 40 to 70 feet in length on deck. This picture and that of the British fleet (No. 1158) are the first known of vessels on Lake Ontario. Wash drawing from original in the Royal Library, British Museum, made by Labroquerie, a French engineer at Fort Frontenac (Kingston, U.C.), 4th October, 1757. Size 10 x 27.

1155—SLOOP OF WAR "BONETTA"—She was in the attack on Fort Baccurano, near Havana, when, on Aug. 14th, 1762, that fort was captured from the Spaniards and nine ships taken by Lord Albemarle. Sir George Pocock and Hon. Augustine Keppel, Lieutenant-Colonel John Graves Simcoe, of the Queen's Rangers, and subsequently first Lieutenant-Governor of Upper Canada, 1792-6, sailed for New York in the "Bonetta" after the surrender of Yorktown, Va., by Lord Cornwallis, Oct. 19th, 1781. The vessel carried fourteen guns. Water color on pen drawing by C. H. J. Snider. Size 11 x 14.

1156—THE "MATTHEW" OF BRISTOL, ENG., 1497—John Cabot's ship on his first voyage of discovery. With his son, Sebastian, and a crew of eighteen men, Cabot set sail in the "Matthew" from Bristol, May 2nd, 1497. On June 24th he sighted Newfoundland, probably at Cape Bonavista, thereby establishing a claim to the discovery of the northern half of the American continent. Returned to Bristol, August 6th, 1497, and the following year, having interested Henry VII. in his expedition, again set sail for the "New Found Land," this time with a fleet of five vessels. Water color on pencil sketch by C. H. J. Snider. Size 8 x 10.

1157—BRITISH NAVAL ESTABLISHMENT ON LAKE ONTARIO, 1792—The naval service on Lake Ontario in 1792 consisted of the gunboats "Beaver" and "Buffalo," the schooners "Onondaga" and "Mississaga," and sloop "Caldwell." The gunboats carried one cannon and the schooners six guns each, although the latter were pierced for twelve. All of these vessels transported troops and provisions from Kingston to York and Niagara, and supplies for Fort Erie and Detroit were portaged from the Niagara River at Queenston to Fort Chippawa, three miles above the Falls, and then by boats and batteaux eighteen miles to Fort Erie, and then to Detroit. Water color from the original drawings in the J. Ross Robertson "Simcoe" collection. Size 10 x 16.

1158—**BRITISH FLEET ON LAKE ONTARIO,** 1757—Showing vessels, schooners and brigs of the early days—In the foreground are two small, unarmed schooners, probably used as tenders. Labroquerie gives them one name, the two "Livelies." In the centre of the picture is the "Montcalm," a brig pierced for nine guns on each side. To her right is a brigantine or ketch, the "George," showing eight guns to a side. To the extreme left is a schooner, the "Lactraguence." Her side shows five gunports. At the extreme right is a sloop, with four gunports, called the "Ontario." In the background is a large sloop of similar rig, but with five guns to a side, called the "Vigilant." The high sterns of all the vessels and antiquated watersails hanging from the bowsprits of the two brigs mark a vanished type of ship. Wash drawing from original in the Royal Library, British Museum, made by Labroquerie, a French engineer at Fort Frontenac (Kingston, U.C.), 4th October, 1757. Size 10 x 27.

1159—**THE "DUKE OF GLOUCESTER"**—British armed vessel on Lake Ontario, captured by the Americans at York (Toronto), April 27th, 1813; taken to Sackett's Harbour as a prize, and refitted for the American fleet as the "York." She was twice set on fire, once at York, to prevent her falling into the hands of the enemy, and again at Sackett's Harbour, May 29th, 1813, when the British attacked that place. She was originally armed with six guns, and early in the War of 1812 served as a prison ship. When captured by the Americans she was a sheer hulk, stripped of guns and spars, and being rebuilt for transport service. The "Prince Regent" had been stripped of her guns to fit out the "Brock" and the "Gloucester's" armament was being used to replace them. Her rig has been variously described. Commodore Chauncey says she was a schooner, intended for sixteen guns, and she is so shown in this picture. Water color on pencil drawing by C. H. J. Snider. Size 8 x 10.

1160—**HIS MAJESTY'S SCHOONER "PRINCE REGENT"**—A member of Sir James Yeo's fleet. She was built at York (Toronto), and launched early in July, 1812. The following year she became the "General Beresford," and again in 1814 re-named "Netley." Her armament consisted of twelve guns, and as one of the vessels in Sir James Lucas Yeo's fleet, took part in many of the engagements on Lake Ontario, including the attack on Sackett's Harbour, the American camp at Stoney Creek and the so-called "Burlington Races." Water color on pencil drawing by C. H. J. Snider. Size 8 x 10.

1161—**LE "DON DE DIEU" (GIFT OF GOD)**—The vessel in which Samuel de Champlain, with his courageous band of twenty-eight, crossed the Atlantic in 1608, ascending the St. Lawrence and founding the City of Quebec (Stadacona), July 3rd of that year. The picture is from the reproduction of the original vessel, built for the Champlain Tercentenary at Quebec, 1908. Water color on pencil drawing by C. H. J. Snider. Size 8 x 10. See 84.

1162—**THE BARQUE "GRIFFIN" OF LA SALLE**—Lake Erie's first vessel. Built in 1678 by La Salle (the first white man to explore the Niagara River), at Cayuga Creek, above the Falls on the American side of the Niagara River. She was a high-ended craft of forty-five tons, rigged as a galliot or brigantine, with an armament of five small cannon. La Salle, accompanied by Father Hennepin, of the Recollets, ascended the waterways of the Great Lakes and reached Green Bay, Lake Michigan, in her, in 1679, after having encountered many trials and storms. From Green Bay she was sent back with a cargo of furs, and was never heard of again. On the quarter deck in the picture may be seen Father Hennepin. The more common modern mode of spelling the name of the historic vessel is "Griffon," but Hennepin spelled it "Griffin," as did Parkman, the historian. Water color on pencil drawing by C. H. J. Snider. Size 10 x 14.

1163—"CUTTING-OUT" EXPLOIT, 1814—One of the brilliant events of the War of 1812-14 was the British capture of two out of three American schooners anchored under the batteries of Fort Erie, in the Niagara River, on the night of August 12th, 1814. Lieuts. Alex. Dobbs, of the "Charwell," and Copleston Radcliffe, of the "Netley," had a ship's boat carried all the way from Queenston—seventeen miles—there being no British vessels at the time above the Falls of Niagara. With this gig and some flat boats they found, they carried the American vessels by boarding, after a fierce conflict, in which Lieut. Radcliffe was slain. A third American vessel, the "Porcupine," shown to the left of the picture, escaped in the dark. In the foreground is the captured "Somers," and to the right is the "Ohio," also captured. Water color on pen drawing by C. H. J. Snider. Size 6 x 20.

1164—"CHESAPEAKE" AND "SHANNON" NAVAL BATTLE—"To Captain Sir Philip Bowes Vere Broke, Bart. and K.C.B., this representation of H.M.S. 'Shannon' commencing battle with the American frigate 'Chesapeake,' on the 1st June, 1813, is dedicated by his obliged and most grateful servant, R. H. King. Painted by J. C. Schetky, Esqre., and on stone by L. Haghe. Designed by Captn. R. H. King, R.N, London: Pubd. by Smith, Elder & Co., 65 Cornhill." On March 21st, 1813, the British ships "Shannon" and "Tenedos" sailed from Halifax to blockade the Port of Boston. The blockade continued until June 1st, when the "Shannon" and "Chesapeake" engaged in action, resulting in the capture of the latter. She was taken to Halifax and later to England, but in 1820 was sold to a ship broker. India proof. Size 12 x 17. See 1169, 1176, 1177.

1165—BRITISH SCHOONER "NELSON"—An innocent accessory of the War of 1812. The "Lord Nelson" was built at Niagara in 1811, and was owned by Messrs. James and William Crooks. The seizure of her was made under the Embargo Act, by the American brig-of-war "Oneida," on Lake Ontario, June 5th, 1812, just two weeks before the War of 1812 was declared, the "Nelson" being a British ship in American waters, off Niagara. The seizure was ultimately declared illegal, but, in the meantime, the "Nelson" had been condemned, sold as a prize, and, after being fitted as an American war schooner, renamed the "Scourge." She foundered in a squall off Niagara, August 8th, 1813. The award of $5,000, made to her owners in 1817 for her illegal seizure, was never paid, a clerk absconding with the funds. One hundred and one years after the seizure the claim of the heirs of the owners for damages came up at the Arbitration Court, at Washington, and they were awarded $33,000. The picture, drawn from a careful study of the records of the vessel, both as the "Lord Nelson" and the "Scourge," shows the schooner at the moment of her capture by the "Oneida." Water color on pen drawing by C. H. J. Snider. Size 11 x 14.

1166—PARRY SOUND, EAST COAST OF GEORGIAN BAY, 1880—The place received its name from Parry Sound (known also as Melville Sound), in the polar regions of the north. The Arctic Parry Sound was called after Capt. Parry (Sir William Edward Parry), who made several voyages in search of the North-west Passage. The view shows: 1, Conger Lumber Co.'s stables; 2, Parry Sound Lumber Co.'s lumber piles; 3, Pond, since filled in, and now (1917) a lumber yard; 4, Government Signal removed subsequently to another site; 5, Methodist Church, demolished long since; 6, Parry Sound Lumber Co.'s burners; 7, J. C. Miller residence, now General Hospital; 8, Road between Parry Sound and Parry Harbor; 9, Belvidere Hotel; 10, Conger Mill, replaced by a new building. The town is capital of Parry Sound District, and an extensive lumber centre. Water color from original drawing by Schell and Hogan for "Picturesque Canada." Size 3 x 7.

1167—"SACKETT'S HARBOUR—On Lake Ontario. Pub. 31 Oct., 1818, by J. Gold, 103 Shoe Lane, Juvenal. Pl. 519. Baily, Sc." Sackett's Harbour, in Jefferson County, N.Y., directly over against Kingston, was, during the War of 1812-14, to the Americans the most vital point on Lake Ontario, as

Kingston was to the British. In May, 1813, the British forces, accompanied by Sir George Prevost, but under the immediate command of Colonel Baynes, his adjutant-general, made an attack upon it, but were repulsed by a superior force, commanded by Major-General Brown. Size 6 x 10.

1168—"STORMING FORT OSWEGO, ON LAKE ONTARIO, NORTH AMERICA, MAY 6TH, 1814—Drawn by Captn. Steele. Engraved by R. Havell, etc." Engraved in aquatint and printed in color. Size 11 x 16. See 1171, 1174, 1175.

1169—"CHESAPEAKE" AND "SHANNON" NAVAL BATTLE—"To Captain Sir Philip Bowes Vere Broke, Bart. and K.C.B., this representation of the American frigate 'Chesapeake,' crippled and thrown into utter disorder by the two first broadsides fired by H.M.S. 'Shannon,' is dedicated by his obliged and most grateful servant, R. H. King. Painted by J. C. Schetky, Esqre., and on stone by L. Haghe. Designed by Capt. R. H. King, R. N. London: Pubd. by Smith, Elder & Co., 65 Cornhill." India proof. Size 12 x 17.

1170—BROKE, SIR PHILIP BOWES VERE, 1776-1841—Commander H.M.S. "Shannon"—Sir Philip, who eventually became a British rear-admiral, was educated at the Royal Naval Academy, Portsmouth, Eng. In August, 1811, after a five years' cruise in the Arctic, sailed for Halifax with his third command, H.M.S. "Shannon." Blockaded the Port of Boston, 1813, and on June 1st of that year engaged in combat with the American frigate "Chesapeake, commanded by Lawrence. After an engagement extending over a period of only fifteen minutes, the "Chesapeake" was captured by Broke, taken to Halifax, and eventually to England. Sir Philip was made a K.C.B. in 1815 and died in 1841. Engraved by W. Greatbatch. London: Richard Bentley, 1836. Size 3 x 4. Half length.

1171—"STORMING FORT OSWEGO BY 2ND BATTALION ROYAL MARINES AND A PARTY OF SEAMEN; 15 M. PAST TWELVE AT NOON—Dedicated to his Majesty's Royal Marine Forces and those employed on the Expedition. Drawn by J. Hewett, Lieut., Royal Marines. Engraved by R. Havell." With key. In the summer of 1813 the De Watteville Regiment arrived in Canada, and was immediately sent to the front. On 4th May, 1814, an expedition under command of Sir Gordon Drummond left Kingston, the fleet which formed a part of it arriving before Oswego the next day. On the morning of the 6th, part of the land forces and seamen, under command of Lieut.-Col. Fischer, of the De Wattevilles, embarked in boats. The "Montreal" and "Niagara," shown in the picture, cannonaded the battery, a landing was effected, and the fort, which the Americans abandoned, occupied by the British. Lieut. Hewett, of the Royal Marines, by whom the picture was drawn, climbed up the flagstaff, under fire of the retreating force, and tore down the colors, which had been nailed to it. Engraved in aquatint and printed in color. Size 14 x 21. See 1168, 1174-5.

1172—"BOARDING AND TAKING THE AMERICAN SHIP 'CHESAPEAKE' by the officers and crew of H.M. ship 'Shannon," commanded by Capt. Broke, June, 1813. Heath, delt. M. Dubourg, sculpt. Published and sold July 1, 1816, by Edwd. Orme, Publisher to His Majesty and the Prince Regent, Bond Street, corner of Brook Street, London." Lithograph in color. Size 8 x 11. See 1176.

1173—THOROLD, ONT., 1880—On the Welland Canal—Three canals have been built, and a fourth, the Welland Ship Canal, is (1917) under construction. The view shows. 1, Oddfellows' Hall; 2, Masonic Hall; 3, Fire Hall; 4, Grist mill, built 1827 by George Keefer. "So long as grass grows and water runs" it has free water for power. To-day (1917) the Foley-Riger Co., Ltd., operate it as a pulp mill. 5, Entrance first Welland Canal. When the Government took over the holdings of the original company Mr.

George Keefer gave the proceeds of his shares to King's College, Toronto, thus forming a fund for the Wellington (the Duke of Wellington was a shareholder in the company), scholarship at Toronto University. 6, Canal of 1845; 7, Vessel in lock 24. Water color from original drawing by Schell and Hogan, for "Picturesque Canada." Size 4 x 7.

1174—ATTACK ON FORT ONTARIO (OSWEGO), 1814—The attack on Fort Ontario, the fortification built on the north side of the River Oswegatchie for the protection of the village of Oswego, was one of the minor affairs of the War of 1812-15. The fort was on a bluff overlooking the village, and was partly built on colonial lines, spacious, but not strong. The attack was made on 6th May. The British fleet was under the command of Sir James Yeo with a force of 1,200. They landed near where the City Hospital now (1917) stands, and the battle took place in rear of it. The British ascended the long, steep hill, and by their attack compelled the Americans to evacuate. Mitchell, the American commander, retreated up the river. Water color from old print. Size 4 x 7. See 1168, 1171, 1175.

1175—"STORMING FORT OSWEGO, ON LAKE ONTARIO, NORTH AMERICA, MAY 6TH, 1814—Drawn by Captn. Steele. Engraved by R. Havell, etc." Engraved in aquatint and printed in color. Size 11 x 16. See 1168, 1171, 1174.

1176—"CHESAPEAKE" AND "SHANNON" NAVAL BATTLE—"To Captain Sir Philip Bowes Vere Broke, Bart. and K.C.B., this representation of H.M.S. 'Shannon' carrying by boarding the American frigate 'Chesapeake' after a cannonade of five minutes on the 1st of June, 1813, is dedicated by his obliged and most grateful servant, R. H. King. Painted by J. C. Schetky, Esqre., and on stone by L. Haghe. Designed by Capt. R. H. King, R.N., London: Pubd. by Smith, Elder & Co., 65 Cornhill." India proof. Size 13 x 17. See 1172.

1177—"CHESAPEAKE" AND "SHANNON" NAVAL BATTLE—"To Captain Sir Philip Bowes Vere Broke, Bart. and K.C.B., this representation of H.M.S. 'Shannon' leading her prize, the American frigate 'Chesapeake,' into Halifax harbour on the 6th June, 1813, is dedicated by his obliged and most grateful servant, R. H. King. Painted by J. C. Schetky, Esqre., and on stone by L. Haghe. Designed by Captn. R. H. King, R.N. London: Pubd. by Smith, Elder & Co., 65 Cornhill." India proof. Size 12 x 17.

1178—H.M. SCHOONERS "CONFIANCE" AND "SURPRISE," SEPT. 5TH, 1814—The two vessels are shown beating up for Michillimackinac, after their capture by Lieut. Miller Worsley. Originally the U.S. schooners "Scorpion" and "Tigress." They destroyed Lieut. Worsley's schooner, the "Nancy," in the Nottawasaga River, Aug. 14th, 1814. Worsley, escaping, secured boats at Fort Michillimackinac, boarded the "Tigress" as she lay at anchor in the Detour Passage in the night of Sept. 3rd, and captured her after a gallant struggle. At dawn on Sept. 6th he sailed up to her consort, the "Scorpion," and carried her by boarding, her crew being entirely ignorant of the fate which had befallen their comrades. Both vessels had been in the Battle of Put-in-Bay, Lake Erie, the year before, where the "Scorpion" fired the first and last gun in the contest. They formed part of the American expedition against Michillimackinac in 1814, when they destroyed the schooner "Perseverance," captured the "Mink," and blockaded and burned the "Nancy." The schooners were left to blockade the Nottawasaga River, so that no supplies might reach the British garrison at Michillimackinac. Worsley renamed the pair "Surprise" and "Confiance," carried their crews prisoners in them to the Nottawasaga, and sailed back to Michillimackinac. The vessels became the nucleus of a new British navy for the Upper Lakes. The pen drawing by Mr. C. H. J. Snider, in which the "Confiance" is to the left and the "Surprise" to the right, is

based upon the details shown in a naval officer's painting of Penetanguishene, about 1819, a water color found in London by the late James Bain
when head of the Toronto Public Library; descriptions of both vessels
given by Lieut. Worsley in his despatches; and careful examination and
measurements of the hull of the "Confiance," sunk in Penetanguishene
Harbor. Size 9 x 10.

1179—**ENTRANCE TO WELLAND CANAL**—View at Port Colborne,
1880—On 30th Nov., 1829, the first Welland Canal, which then was only
built to Port Robinson and thence via Chippawa, was formally opened. In
1842 the shareholders were bought out by the Government, which assumed
entire control. The channel was enlarged and a new waterway made from
Welland Junction to Port Colborne, the latter place being bisected by the
canal, which formed the first direct all-canal connection between Lakes
Erie and Ontario. To the left of picture, in background, is the old G.T.R.
elevator for lightering vessels of grain coming from the Upper Lakes, and
on the right is the business part of Port Colborne. Water color from
original drawing by Schell and Hogan for "Picturesque Canada." Size 4 x 7.

1180—**LOCK 23, THOROLD, ONT., 1880**—The Welland Canal in picture
was that commenced in 1870 and completed 1884. It lies about a hundred
yards east of the 1829 and 1845 waterways. 1, Lock 23; 2, Anglican Church,
built by the Rev. T. Fuller (afterwards Bishop of Niagara), when rector of
Thorold; 3, Bank cut away in 1915 for canal under construction. Single
lock No. 7 and triple locks Nos. 6 and 5, in flight, have been excavated in
the rock under this embankment. These locks have thirty feet of water
on the sill. They are 800 feet long and 80 feet wide and are
the first locks to have the single gates—not double as the Soo or
Panama Canals. Water color from original drawing by Schell and Hogan,
for "Picturesque Canada." Size 5 x 6.

1181—**"BURLINGTON RACES," LAKE ONTARIO, SEPT. 28TH, 1813**
—With key. This four-hour running fight, from York (Toronto) to
Burlington (near Hamilton), was a drawn battle between Sir James Yeo's
British squadron of six vessels, and the American Commodore Chauncey's
squadron of eight. The American sought shelter from the rising gale in
Niagara River, and the British rode it out in Burlington Bay. Water color
on pen drawing by C. H. J. Snider. Size 6 x 20.

1182—**NAVAL ENGAGEMENT OFF KINGSTON, C.W.**—Commodore
Chauncey in pursuit of the British, Nov. 9th, 1812—The British sloop of war,
"Royal George," was pursued into Kingston harbor by Chauncey in the
American brig "Oneida" and several schooners. These used sweeps and
fired repeatedly on the British ship at long range, finally coming into close
action, when she anchored under the shelter of the batteries. In the evening the Americans, who had kept up the bombardment for hours, were
forced to withdraw to Four-Mile Point, opposite Kingston. Water color on
pen drawing by C. H. J. Snider. Size 8 x 10.

1183—**HIS MAJESTY'S BRIG "MAGNET"**—Originally the schooner
"Sir Sydney Smith," armed with twelve guns, but in 1814 altered to a brig,
given fourteen guns and re-named the "Magnet." As one of Sir James
Yeo's squadron, she took part in most of the naval engagements of the
War of 1812-14. Was at the storming of Oswego, May 6th, 1814. In the
August of that year ran ashore at Ten-Mile Creek, west of Niagara, and
was burned to avoid capture by the Americans. Water color on pencil
drawing by C. H. J. Snider. Size 10 x 10.

1184—**YEO**—"Captn. Sir James Lucas Yeo, Knt. A. Buck, pinxt. H.
R. Cook, Sculp. Published Nov., 1810, by J. Gold, No. 103 Shoe Lane,
Fleet St." Born in 1782, entered the navy, 1793. Took part in the siege of

15

Genoa, 1800; captured Cayenne nine years later. Served in the West Indies, 1811, and arrived at Quebec from England, May, 1813, to take command on the Great Lakes. In command at the "Burlington Races" and the "Niagara Sweepstakes." Blockaded Sackett's Harbour; took Oswego, 1814. Commander-in-chief at Jamaica, 1817. His death occurred the following year while he was on a voyage from the coast of Africa. Line engraving. Size 3 x 4. Head and shoulders.

1185—**CAPT. R. H. BARCLAY'S FLAGSHIP "DETROIT,"** 1813—The second unlucky British ship of that name. Built at Malden, near Amherstburg, N.C., and named in honor of Brock's victory at Detroit. In order to supply her with guns Barclay dismantled Fort Malden and gathered up the field guns and battery artillery which had been used at the attack in Fort Meigs, mustering in all nineteen cannon, of six different calibres. Some pieces of the armament could only be discharged by flashing pistols at their touch-holes. The "Detroit" was in the disastrous Battle of Lake Erie, Sept. 10th, 1813, and was afterwards dismantled by her American captors and sent over the Falls of Niagara. Water color on pencil drawing by C. H. J. Snider. Size 11 x 14.

1186—**SIR JAMES LUCAS YEO'S FLAGSHIP "ST. LAWRENCE," LAKE ONTARIO,** 1814—The "St. Lawrence" was the largest warship ever floated on the Great Lakes. Built at Kingston and launched in September, 1814. She was alone more powerful than the combined American fleet, and Commodore Chauncey withdrew his vessels to Sackett's Harbour and began building a ship to match her. Ere this vessel was launched peace was declared. The "St. Lawrence," manned by 1,000 men, carried 102 guns, arranged in two tiers. Her main dimensions were, approximately, 190 feet length of keel, 60 feet beam, and 23 feet draught. She made two voyages to Niagara with troops and stores in the autumn of 1814, and after peace was declared, was used as a floating barracks at Kingston, but was eventually sunk in Kingston Harbor. To the left of the picture is shown one of the lugger-rigged gunboats, stationed at Kingston in 1814, the "Buffalo," and to the right, the tender-schooner "Vincent." Water color on pencil drawing by C. H. J. Snider. Size 9 x 10.

1187—**REPRODUCTIONS OF CARAVELS OF COLUMBUS**—Vessels under full sail. They were reproduced in Spain with great accuracy of detail for the Chicago World's Fair in 1893. In the centre is shown Columbus' own ship, the "Santa Maria," which was ninety feet long and drew eight feet of water. To the left of the picture is the "Nina," a smaller caravel, rigged like a felucca, and to the right is the "Pinta," which is sometimes credited with being the first to sight the new world—the Island of San Salvador, in the Bahamas, 12th October, 1492. The reproductions of the caravels were towed across the Atlantic and up the Great Lakes in 1893, and in 1913 made an exhibition voyage from Chicago to Detroit. Water color on pencil drawing by C. H. J. Snider. Size 10 x 14.

1188—**COMMODORE PERRY'S FLAGSHIP "NIAGARA"**—At Perry's Lookout, the "Needle's Eye," Put-in-Bay, Lake Erie. Commodore Perry's second flagship in the famous Battle of Put-in-Bay, Sept. 10th, 1813. After the peace of 1815 she was dismantled, and in 1825 sunk at her moorings at Erie, Pa. In March, 1913, she was raised, completely refitted, and taken on a triumphal tour of the Great Lakes during the summer of 1913. The picture, drawn on the spot, shows her at anchor in the very anchorage where she "put in" among the Bass Islands, a hundred years before, after the great Battle of Lake Erie, usually called the Battle of Put-in-Bay. Water color on pen drawing by C. H. J. Snider. Size 11 x 14.

1189—**"COLONEL MYERS"**—This vessel, a British schooner-rigged gunboat, was used in the spring of 1813 at the siege of Fort Meigs, built by General Harrison at the foot of the rapids some twelve miles from the mouth of the Maumee. The British, under Proctor, abandoned the siege, however, and in the autumn of 1813 the Myers was burned and sunk in the Thames, near Chatham, to avoid capture. In the summer of 1900 it was accidentally found, the presence of cannon balls determining the nature of its timbers, and the sunken hull raised the following year, through the efforts of Lieut.-Col. J. S. Black. It was taken to Chatham, where it remained high and dry in Tecumseh Park until 1912, when the old warrior gunboat was broken up as souvenirs. The vessel was named after Col. Christopher Myers, quartermaster-general of the British Forces in Canada in 1812. Water color on pen drawing by C. H. J. Snider. Size 8 x 12.

1190—TRANSPORT "BECKWITH" AND BATTEAUX, LAKE ONTARIO, 1816—The "Beckwith" was launched from Kingston Navy Yard, July 8th, 1816, and was used for carrying troops and military stores. These were transferred from the ship to the shore in flat-bottomed boats called batteaux. Both the ship and the boats are drawn from their original designer's lines. Water color on pen drawing by C. H. J. Snider. Size 10 x 13.

1191—THE "GOVERNOR SIMCOE" RUNNING THE GAUNTLET— While endeavoring to make Kingston in a strong breeze, Capt. James Richardson (father of the Capt. Jas. Richardson who commanded the "Moira," and afterwards served in the Rebellion of 1837), in command of the British Government schooner "Governor Simcoe," when intercepted by the American fleet, Nov. 10th, 1812, drove his vessel over Seven-Acre Shoal at the entrance to the harbor. The Americans were unable to cross the shallows, but just as the "Simcoe" had cleared the reef and was gaining the deep water inside, the foe fired a broadside which passed through the "Simcoe's" starboard quarter and came out under her bows. She sank with colors flying, settling in four fathoms of water. Boats from the garrison rescued the crew. The "Governor Simcoe," the first vessel built for trade on Lake Ontario, was subsequently raised and for many years sailed the Great Lakes. Water color on pen drawing by C. H. J. Snider. Size 8 x 11.

1192-7—UNIFORMS WORN BY OFFICERS AND SEAMEN OF THE BRITISH NAVY FROM 1768-86—The only set of these drawings known was bequeathed in May, 1913, to the Trustees of Greenwich Hospital, under the will of the late Henry Cooper Henderson, of Ramsgate. They were, by special permission of the Secretary of the Navy, copied for J. Ross Robertson, in September, 1913, by an artist whose specialty is British naval and military uniforms. The drawings are of interest on this continent, showing as they do the uniform worn by officers of the fleet under such men as Howe, Boscawen, Saunders, Byron, Parker, Rodney and others. Water color reproductions of drawings by Dominic Serres, who in 1790 became marine painter to George III., and later librarian to the Royal Academy. His prints are inscribed: "Published as the Act directs by D. Serres, in Warwick street, Golden Square, 1777." Size of each picture (six in set) 7 x 10. See 162-8.

1198—CRISIS IN THE BATTLE OF LAKE ERIE—Off Put-in-Bay, Ohio, Sept. 10th, 1813—In this battle, between Commander Perry's American fleet of nine vessels and six British vessels, under Commander Robert H. Barclay, R.N., "the superiority of the Americans in long gun metal," says Theodore Roosevelt, "was as 3 is to 2, and in carronade metal greater than 2 is to 1." Barclay had but 55 man-o'-warsmen in his fleet; nevertheless he fought with such desperate valor that Capt. Perry was beaten out of his flagship, the "Lawrence." Perry won the day by bringing up a fresh flagship, the "Niagara." The entire British fleet, helpless through lack of sailors, was captured. The picture shows the "Niagara" coming into action. Water color on pen drawing by C. H. J. Snider. Size 6 x 19.

1199—HIS BRITANNIC MAJESTY'S SCHOONER "SPEEDY"—Lost off Presqu' Isle, Lake Ontario, Oct. 8th, 1804. The "Speedy" left York (Toronto) on Sunday, Oct. 7th, bound for Presqu' Isle, with distinguished passengers, including Mr. Justice Cochrane, Solicitor-General Gray, High Constable Fisk, Angus Macdonald, member of the House of Assembly; George Cowan, Indian interpreter, and a Chippewa Indian who was to be tried for murder at Presqu' Isle. She was sighted off that port the following evening, but foundered in a heavy snowstorm which set in ere she could enter the harbor. All on board, thirty or forty persons, perished. Water color on pencil drawing by C. H. J. Snider. Size 9 x 12.

1200—ARMED BRITISH SCHOONER "NANCY"—Commanded by Lieutenant Miller Worsley, 1814—She was built in 1789 by Forsyth Richardson & Co., at Detroit, for a Montreal trading firm, and later taken over for service in the War of 1812-14. After their repulse at Michillimackinac the Americans chased the vessel into the Nottawasaga River, and there destroyed her, August 14th, 1814. Lieutenant Worsley, however, captured within twenty days the "Tigress" and "Scorpion" (afterwards the British vessels "Surprise" and "Confiance"), which had destroyed the "Nancy," and sent them back to the mouth of the Nottawasaga, with their original crews in their holds as prisoners of war. The prisoners were then transported to Quebec. Water color on pen drawing by C. H. J. Snider. Size 6 x 9.

1201—BARCLAY, LIEUT. ROBERT H., 1805—In undress uniform of the period. Water color. Size 5 x 6. Half length. See 1202-3.

1202—BARCLAY, CAPTAIN ROBERT H., 1814—In uniform of period. Water color. Size 4 x 6. Head and shoulders. See 1201, 1203.

1203—BARCLAY, LIEUT. ROBERT H., 1809—In full uniform of period. Born at Kettle, Fifeshire, Scotland, 1785. Entered naval service in 1798, and shortly afterwards was rated as midshipman in the "Anson"; became lieutenant, and as such served at Trafalgar in the "Swiftsure." Commanded British flotilla on Great Lakes in the War of 1812. On Sept. 10th, 1813, was defeated in action with a superior American squadron under Commodore Perry on Lake Erie, and severely wounded in the thigh and only remaining arm. It has been stated that he lost his left arm at Trafalgar; but this was not the case. His loss occurred several years later at Moir Montier Roads. Tried by court-martial for the loss of his flotilla, but fully and honorably acquitted. In 1814 was promoted to a captaincy. His death occurred at Edinburgh, 1837. Water color. Size 5 x 6.. Half length. See 1201-02.

1204—BARCLAY, REV. JOHN—First pastor of St. Andrew's Presbyterian church, Kingston, U.C. He was a native of Kettle, Scotland, and a brother of Capt. Robert H. Barclay, who took a prominent part in the naval engagements during the War of 1812-14. The Rev. Mr. Barclay was educated at Edinburgh University, afterwards becoming assistant at Collessie, where he remained for two years. Ordained to the charge of St. Andrew's, Kingston, Sept. 26th, 1821, arriving there in 1822. He died five years later, and a memorial was erected in the old Presbyterian burying ground at Kingston. Mr. Barclay was highly esteemed by his people, "as a pious and devoted minister." Water color. Size 3 x 4. Head and shoulders.

1205—BARCLAY, REV. PETER, D.D.—Father of Captain Robert H. Barclay and Rev. John Barclay, of Kingston. He was twentieth in descent from John, second son of the first Earl of Berkeley, the family later being known as Barclay. Became minister of Kettle parish church, Scotland, and remained there for seventy-two years. He was a personal friend of John Strachan, teacher in the parish school at Kettle, from 1797-9, and afterwards first Anglican Bishop of Toronto. Rev. Mr. Barclay died in the parish where he so long ministered, at the age of ninety-three. Water color. Size 3 x 4. Head and shoulders.

1206—WICKHAM, MRS. BENJAMIN (MARGARET ANN BARCLAY)
—Eldest daughter of Capt. Robert H. Barclay, R.N., and granddaughter of Rev. Peter Barclay, of Kettle, Scotland. She married Benjamin Wickham, R.N.. Governor of the Ascension Isles for five years, and then Purser in the Navy. Mrs. Wickham died when over eighty years of age at Dawlish, Devonshire, Eng. Photograph, colored. Size 3 x 4. Head and shoulders.

1207—STOREHOUSE IN FORT GEORGE GROUNDS. NIAGARA—
The centre part, with chimney. was standing after the War of 1812-15. It was occupied by the Military Guard during and after the war. Near this spot Sir Isaac Brock and his aide, Col. John Macdonell, were buried, October 16th, 1812. Water color by Owen Staples. Size 20 x 26.

1208—FOOT OF KING STREET, NIAGARA—From the river, 1839. Showing Mrs. Elliott's house. built 1838, and the guard-house, Gleaner office. Oates' tavern. Dugdale's soap factory, and Fort Mississaga. Water color by Owen Staples from a pencil sketch by F. H. Granger. Size 15 x 21.

1209—BISHOP HOUSE, NIAGARA—One of the oldest buildings at Niagara; built about 1800, and now in a dilapidated condition. It is constructed of logs and covered with clapboard, with a wing built partly of stone. The house, which was formerly occupied by Mr. McMullen. is now owned by the Bishop family. Water color by Owen Staples, Toronto. Size 19 x 25.

1210—HORSESHOE FALLS, NIAGARA. 1882—Water color by H.R.H. Princess Louise (wife of the late Marquis of Lorne) during her residence in Canada, 1878-1883. Size 18 x 26.

1211—POWDER MAGAZINE. NIAGARA—Built near Fort George by Governor Simcoe, 1796. Water color by Owen Staples, Toronto. Size 19 x 25.

1212—FOOT OF KING STREET. NIAGARA—Looking towards Old Fort Niagara, 1839—Showing Dugdale's soap factory, the Gleaner office. Oates' tavern, the Guard House, Mrs. Elliott's house, built in 1838. and Andrew Heron's house. Fort Niagara. N.Y., is seen in the distance. Water color by Owen Staples from a pencil sketch by F. H. Granger. Size 15 x 21. See 1208.

1213—FORT GEORGE. U.C.—View from Old Fort Niagara, N.Y., 1800 —The original is said to have been made by an officer of the 49th Regiment. Water color. Size 14 x 19.

1214—PUISAYE, COMTE JOSEPH DE—Born at Montagne. 1755, the youngest son of a noble family. He was intended for the church. but entered the army and was raised to the rank of major-general in 1791. In 1797 he applied to the British Government to found a Royalist settlement in Canada, having previously failed in his efforts in the Royalist cause in France. and generally blamed for the disastrous result of the Quiberon expedition. He and his party arrived in Canada in the autumn of 1798; a settlement was founded on Yonge street, near Markham, and the following year the Count settled at Niagara, where he lived for some years. He was never allowed to return to France. and died in England, near Hammersmith. Middlesex. in 1827. Chalk drawing by Owen Staples from a portrait in Niagara Historical Museum. Size 5 x 7. Half length.

1215—PUISAYE. COMTESSE DE (SUSANNE SMITHERS)—It is not supposed that she ever came to Canada, but died previous to 1798. Her mother, however. resided at Niagara with Comte de Puisaye. Chalk drawing by Owen Staples, from a portrait in the Niagara Historical Museum. Size 5 x 7. Head and shoulders.

1216—ROBINSON, JOEL R., 1809-63—One of the best-known men on the Niagara River—He was born in Boston, Mass., and about 1847 came to Niagara Falls, N.Y. By trade he was an expert machinist and engineer, and held that position on both the first and second "Maid of the Mist," the river ferry boats so well known to tourists. In the summer of 1860 Robinson, in a spirit of daring, walked out in the water about 150 feet from the shore of Luna Island, at the south end of the American Falls. It was he who, in June, 1861, had the courage to run the second "Maid of the Mist" through the rapids and the whirlpool to save her from seizure by the sheriff at Niagara Falls, N.Y. During his residence at Niagara Falls, Robinson made several rescues of persons caught in the upper rapids, who otherwise would have perished. He died at Niagara Falls, N.Y., 30th June, 1863. Water color. Size 3 x 4. Head and shoulders. See 1218.

1217—FITZGIBBON, COLONEL JAMES—A veteran of the War of 1812-15—At age of seventeen he enlisted in 49th Regiment, and almost immediately fought under Brock at Egmont-op-Zee. Appointed sergeant-major, 1801; saw service in Canada at Stoney Creek, Fort George, Fort Erie and Beaver Dams, and, on the conclusion of the war, settled in this country. In 1820 he was appointed one of the Justices of the Peace in the Home District; became assistant adjutant-general, 1826, and later adjutant-general. Took an active part in the Rebellion of 1837, in Toronto. Col. Fitzgibbon was born in Ireland, 1780. Died in London, 1863. Photograph, colored. Size 3 x 4. Head and shoulders. See 3406.

1218—DARING ACT AT NIAGARA FALLS, N.Y.—Joel Robinson, in the summer of 1860, walked out into the water about 150 feet from the shore of Luna Island, at the south end of the American Falls, and stood looking over the edge of the Falls, 100 feet from the brink. He wore felt shoes, such as are worn by visitors to the Cave of the Winds, and used a wooden staff with a sharp iron point to steady himself. As soon as he was photographed he returned to shore. The following summer he took the second "Maid of the Mist" through the rapids and whirlpool, landing at Queenston. Robinson was born at Boston, and died at Niagara Falls, N.Y. Water color from a photograph in possession of the Hon. Peter A. Porter, Niagara Falls, N.Y. Size 4 x 5. See 1216.

1219—SECOND "MAID OF THE MIST," NIAGARA FALLS—The first "Maid of the Mist" was built in 1846, and the second, 1854. In 1861 the owners of the latter, who were in financial trouble, determined to run down the river in order to avoid seizure by the sheriff of Niagara Falls, N.Y. On June 6th, the boat, in command of Captain Joel Robinson, commenced the terrifying journey through the rapids and whirlpool, shortly afterwards landing at Queenston, where the Collector of Customs insisted on fees for landing and clearing to Lake Ontario. The vessel then sailed to Port Dalhousie, where she was placed in dry dock and repaired. Subsequently she was re-named the "Maid of Orleans," and for several years did service as a ferry boat between Quebec and the Island of Orleans, on the St. Lawrence. The picture shows the "Maid" making her perilous descent down the Niagara River. Water color from an old print. Size 4 x 7.

1220—FORT GEORGE, U.C.—A view from Old Fort Niagara, N.Y., 1812—Fort George stood on the heights above Navy Hall, at the entrance to the Niagara River. It partly commanded Fort Niagara, but was in turn commanded by the elevation near Youngstown. As a port of defence, it was very effective. On 27th May, 1813, it was attacked by the Americans. A close fight ensued, but General Vincent, feeling the Fort could not be saved, ordered its destruction. This, however, was not entirely completed before the arrival of Colonel Winfield Scott. Although the Battle of Fort George may be said to have resulted in a victory for the Americans, yet their success was incomplete. Aquatint, printed in color, by Ackermann. Size 5 x 8. See 1221.

1221—"BRITISH FORT AT NIAGARA—Taken from the East Bank of the St. Lawrence (Niagara). G. Heriot, Esqr., pinxt. F. C. Lewis, sculp. Printed for Richard Phillips, 6 New Bridge Street, London, 1807." Aquatint, printed in color. Size 6 x 8. See 1220, 1236.

1222—CARNOCHAN, MISS JANET—Historian of Niagara—Born at Stamford, Ont., Nov. 14th, 1839, of Scottish Covenanting stock. Educated at Niagara. Taught in Brantford, Kingston and Peterboro, and for twenty-three years in Niagara High School. Since her retirement from professional life has devoted herself to historical research work, chiefly in connection with Niagara. Her "History of Niagara" is the authoritative work on all pertaining to the early days of the town, and she has also written many pamphlets and articles throwing fresh and important light on its history. Miss Carnochan is the president of the Niagara Historical Society, and it was through her indefatigable efforts that the Niagara Memorial Hall, opened to the public in 1907, and containing an invaluable collection of manuscripts, books, pamphlets portraits and other relics, was erected. Since its opening she has acted as curator of the museum without remuneration. Miss Carnochan is also secretary of the Niagara Public Library. Water color. Size 4 x 5. Half length.

1223—"THE WHIRLPOOL OF THE ST. LAWRENCE (NIAGARA RIVER)—G. Heriot, Esqr., pinxt. F. C. Lewis, sculp. Printed for Richard Phillips, 6 New Bridge Street, London, 1807." The Whirlpool is situated at the southern extremity of the first rapids, two miles below Niagara Falls. Aquatint, printed in color. Size 6 x 8. .

1224—BAYNES, COLONEL (MAJOR-GENERAL) EDWARD—Military secretary to General Sir Isaac Brock—He entered the army in May, 1783, was made lieutenant in 32nd, August, 1790, and four years later became aide-de-camp to Sir James Craig. In 1807 he was appointed Adjutant-General North America, and Colonel Nova Scotia Fencibles from the 4th Garrison Battalion. Became Colonel of Glengarry Light Infantry in 1812. Col. Baynes died at Sidmouth, Eng., March, 1829. Water color from a miniature in possession of his grandson O'Hara Baynes, B.C.L., Montreal. Size 4 x 5. Head and shoulders.

1225—BROCK, MAJOR-GENERAL SIR ISAAC—Water color from a portrait, artist, unknown, in possession of his great-grandniece, Miss May Carey, Guernsey, Channel Islands. Size 5 x 7. Head and shoulders. See 410, 1690.

1226—COCKED HAT OF MAJOR-GENERAL SIR ISAAC BROCK—It was sent to Canada by his brother, Irving, but did not arrive until shortly after the General's death. The hat measures twenty-four inches inside, and was used at the re-interments of Brock at Queenston Heights in 1824 and 1853, when many old soldiers were allowed to try it on. It is amongst the relics of the War of 1812 in the Niagara Historical Society Museum. Water color. Size 4 x 6.

1227—COAT WORN BY MAJOR-GENERAL SIR ISAAC BROCK AT QUEENSTON HEIGHTS—It shows on the breast the hole made by the entry of the bullet, when Brock, on the morning of the 13th Oct., 1812, was shot by, it is supposed, an Ohio scout named Wilklow, one of Moseley's riflemen. The coat is in the Dominion Archives. Water color. Size 3 x 6.

1228—BUTLER, COLONEL JOHN—Born in New London, Conn., in 1725, his father, an Irish officer, having come to the North American colonies with his regiment about 1711. Butler's first service was as a captain in the Indian Department in the expedition against Crown Point under Sir William Johnson, where he greatly distinguished himself. He also served under Abercrombie at Ticonderoga, and with Bradstreet at the capture of Fort Frontenac. He accompanied Johnson against Fort Niagara as second in command of the Indians, and after Gen. Prideaux's death followed him in the command. He afterwards served through the revolutionary war at the head of the famous corps of "Rangers" bearing his name. This corps was disbanded June, 1784. Butler, after the war, was appointed Deputy Superintendent of the Indians. He was Senior Grand Warden of the Grand (Masonic) Lodge, Niagara, 1791. Died at Niagara, 1796. Water color from original in Dominion Archives. Size 9 x 12. Head and shoulders.

1229—KIRBY, WILLIAM, F.R.S.C., 1817-1906—Author of "Le Chien d'Or" ("The Golden Dog")—Photogravure from painting by J. W. L. Forster. Size 5 x 6. Half length, sitting. See 1232.

1230—INGLIS FALLS, 1880—Showing the old-time mill. Water color from original drawing by L. R. O'Brien, for "Picturesque Canada." Size 5 x 7.

1231—BURNING OF THE "CAROLINE"—"From a Sketch by W. R. Callington, Engineer, Boston. The American Steam Packet 'Caroline,' descending the Great Falls of Niagara after being set on fire by the British, Decr. 29th, 1837, with a distant view of Navy Island, Chippewa and Schlosser. J. Grieve, litho., 33 Nicholas Lane, Lombard St. Published by J. Robins, Bride Court, Fleet Street." The "Caroline" had been engaged by the rebels in 1837, to carry men and stores to Navy Island, where William Lyon Mackenzie's followers were ensconced. Lieutenant Drew (afterwards admiral), of the Royal Navy, was ordered by Col. McNab to "cut the vessel out," and, accordingly, set out secretly with seven boats, each containing four men to row and three or four to be available for the attack. The "Caroline" was boarded, fired in four places and set adrift in the rapids above the Falls. Drew's undertaking was extremely hazardous and its successful completion exceeded McNab's most sanguine hopes. This capture opened the eyes of the people of the United States to the real sentiment of Canada, which had been represented by the instigators of the rebellion as one of seething dissatisfaction towards the existing form of government. Lithograph in color. Size 9 x 15.

1232—KIRBY, WILLIAM, F.R.S.C.—Born in Hull, Yorkshire, Eng., in 1817, but when a lad emigrated to the United States; educated at the Cincinnati Academy. In 1838 young Kirby removed to Canada, and in 1850 settled at Niagara, having previously lived at St. David's. Became editor of the Niagara Mail, and from 1871-95 was Collector of Customs. He was one of the first members of the Royal Society of Canada, and an author of considerable repute, his chief work "Le Chien d'Or" ("The Golden Dog") being considered one of the greatest of Canadian historical novels. Mr. Kirby's death occurred at Niagara-on-the-Lake, Ont., in 1906. Photograph, colored. Size 3 x 4. Head and shoulders. See 1229.

1233—HOME OF WILLIAM KIRBY, F.R.S.C., NIAGARA-ON-THE-LAKE, ONT.—The house, built 1849-50, is on lot 11, Front street, opposite the Queen's Royal. Mr. Kirby, who is widely known as the author of the historical novel, 'Le Chien d'Or" ("The Golden Dog") and "Canadian Idylls," giving many events in Canadian history, lived here from 1850 until his death in 1906. Water color. Size 5 x 6.

1234—CROOKS, HON. JAMES, 1778-1860—Came to Niagara about 1791, residing there until after the War of 1812. Served in the 1st Regiment of Lincoln Militia, becoming lieutenant in 1797 and captain, 1807. Was present at Queenston; taken prisoner in 1813, and detained at Burlington, Vermont. After the cessation of hostilities, Mr. Crooks settled in West Flamboro', where he operated paper and grist mills. The paper mill, like that on the Don River, claimed the honor of making the first sheet of paper in

Upper Canada. The race was such a close one that the prize offered by the Provincial Government was divided between the two mills. Mr. Crooks shipped the first load of flour and wheat from Upper Canada to Montreal. He was a member of the Legislative Assembly in 1820, and afterwards a Legislative Councillor. His death occurred at West Flamboro', 2nd March, 1860. Photograph, colored. Size 4 x 5. Head and shoulders.

1235—NIAGARA FALLS—"View of the Falls of Niagara from beneath the bank on the Fort Slausser (Schlosser) side. G. Heriot, Esqr., delint. F. C. Lewis, sculp. Printed for Richard Phillips, 6 New Bridge Street, London, 1807." On the American shore, almost opposite Chippawa. Fort Schlosser was built in 1760 by a British army colonel of that name, to replace the second Fort Little Niagara, which had been burned by General Pouchot, commander of Fort Niagara, in 1759. Fort Schlosser was never a strong fort, and nothing whatever now remains of it. A stone chimney, however, which stood a short distance away, is still in existence. It was attached to the barracks which the French built for Fort Little Niagara, and later to the mess house which the British constructed in connection with Fort Schlosser. Aquatint, printed in color. Size 6 x 8.

1236—FORT GEORGE, NIAGARA, 1805—This picture is enlarged from one by Heriot, published in his "Travels in Canada," 1807, and from Ackermann's (London) picture of Fort George, taken about 1800. The combination gives an excellent picture of Fort George and Niagara, before the War of 1812-15. Water color by E. Wyly Grier. Size 12 x 18.

1237—QUEENSTON HEIGHTS—The battle ground as it appeared in July, 1897. After the capture in August, 1812, of Detroit by Brock, the Americans began preparations for a second attack on Canada. This was made in October, and on the 13th the famous Battle of Queenston Heights was fought. Colonel Winfield Scott, an able officer, and General Brock commanding the respective forces. Several attempts by the British to storm the heights were unsuccessful, but they eventually, through Sheaffe's movement, along what is now the Queenston and Grimsby Stone road, gained the summit. The encounter was sharp while it lasted, and soon one more victory was added to the British list. Gen. Brock was killed during the morning, and his aide, Col. Macdonell, received a wound from which he died next day. Water color by E. Wyly Grier. Size 14 x 18.

1238—THIRD SERVOS GRIST MILL—Palatine Hill, Four-Mile Creek, Niagara Township—The first mill did service as a saw and grist mill in connection with which Government records show that the Home Government sent machinery to help, and that early settlers in the district came for miles with their grain. An old account book, bearing date 1779, is exceedingly interesting in its curious particulars. The second mill was burnt during the bombardment of Niagara, 1813, and a third, built in 1820 by the late Col. John D. Servos. Some of the timbers, blackened with smoke, were used in the present building. Water color by Owen Staples, Toronto. Size 18 x 22. See 1244.

1239—AMERICAN FORT—Niagara River (N.Y.)—Lithograph in color by Coke Smyth. Size 11 x 15.

1240—SEXTON'S HOUSE, ST. ANDREW'S PRESBYTERIAN CHURCH, NIAGARA—This house was, before the War of 1812-14, a schoolhouse for the church. In 1818 it was repaired, as part had been left unburned, and was used till 1831 for church services. Here the first Sunday school in the town was held, a union Sunday school, with John Crooks as superintendent. The building was subsequently used as a school, under the charge of St. Andrew's church, and upstairs a school for colored children was kept. Pen drawing, colored, by Owen Staples. Size 10 x 12.

1241—"UPPER BRIDGE," NIAGARA FALLS—Near the Clifton Hotel. It was a suspension bridge, erected 1867-8, by Samuel Keefer, C.E. From centre to centre it measured 1,260 feet. In 1888 the structure was rebuilt and widened, but on January 5th, of the following year, was blown down. Work was immediately commenced on a new suspension bridge, with steel cables, towers and stiffening trusses. This, in turn, was in 1899 superseded by the present steel arch. Water color. Size 7 x 9.

1242—PLUMB HOUSE, NIAGARA, 1911—This house was built prior to 1830 by Judge Campbell, son of Fort Major Duncan Campbell, who was with Cornwallis in 1781 at Yorktown, and subsequently fort major at Fort George. Since Judge Campbell's death, in 1860, the property has been owned by several people—Mr. Allan, Senator Plumb (who enlarged and altered the house), Mr. Sayer, Mr. Carnochan and Mr. Hewitt, the present owner. Pen drawing, colored, by Owen Staples. Size 10 x 13.

1243—HOMESTEAD OF MAJOR DANIEL SERVOS—Palatine Hill, Niagara Township—This house, probably the oldest in the township, is built on an eminence commanding a view of the Four-Mile Creek, now Virgil, Ont. The house has been altered, but the principal room, with its heavy rafters, dates back to 1783. It was used at one time as a Government store. The Servos family were of Prussian origin. Some of the sons were present at the Siege of Niagara, 1759, while grandsons served in Butler's Rangers. Four generations of the Servos family have served in capacities as ensign, lieutenant, captain and colonel. In 1779, Governor Haldimand gave Daniel Servos a commission as lieutenant in Colonel Johnson's company of North American Indians, and in 1788 he received a commission from Lord Dorchester to be captain of the first regiment of militia in the district of Nassau. Mrs. Jarvis, wife of William Jarvis, Provincial Secretary, 1792-1817, writes of the Four-Mile Creek: "There is a great mill upon it, and the family that it belongs to are Dutch." The house is now (1917) occupied by Miss Mary Servos, great-granddaughter of Major Daniel Servos. Water color by Owen Staples. Size 22 x 28. See 1271.

1244—THIRD SERVOS GRIST MILL—Palatine Hill, Niagara Township. Water color by Owen Staples. Size 17 x 24. See 1238.

1245—FALLS OF NIAGARA—Moonlight scene. Lithograph in color by Coke Smyth. Size 11 x 15.

1246—BUTLER HOUSE, NIAGARA—Now occupied by Mr. Nelson Bissell; was the property of Col. John Butler, of Butler's Rangers; then Andrew Butler, his son, 1802; then Joseph Butler, 1821. Sheriff Mercer subsequently owned the property. Mr. Bissell, an uncle of Mr. Nelson Bissell, who lived to be almost a hundred years of age, said that he remembered the house before the Battle of Queenston Heights. The dwelling contains some interesting colonial woodwork. Water color by Owen Staples. Size 11 x 15.

1247—CHAPMAN HOUSE, NIAGARA—Interior view, showing old fireplace and oven. Pen drawing, colored, by Owen Staples. Size 10 x 14. See 1259.

1248—DICKSON. HON. WM., NIAGARA—Born in Dumfries, Scotland, 1769; came to Canada, 1792, settling in Niagara, and began the practice of law there. He took an active part in the War of 1812, was taken prisoner and sent to Greenbush, N.Y., but was subsequently released. In 1816 Mr. Dickson founded the Township of Dumfries, Ont., and in that year became a member of the Legislative Council of Upper Canada. He lived for a time in Galt, but in 1836 returned to Niagara, where he died ten years later. Facsimile water color from original by Hoppner Meyer. Size 8 x 10. Half length.

1249—CLEMENT, MRS. JOHN (MARY BALL)—Daughter of Jacob Ball, who, in 1780, was a member of Butler's Rangers. She married Captain John Clement, of Niagara, an active leader of the Northern Confederate Indians, 1812-15, popularly known as "Ranger John." Facsimile water color from original by Hoppner Meyer. Size 8 x 10. Half length.

1250—CLIFTON HOUSE, NIAGARA FALLS, C.W.—Rear view in December, 1850. Water color, made on the spot, by Gen. A. R. V. Crease, R.E. Size 7 x 10. See 1251-2, 1276.

1251—CLIFTON HOUSE, NIAGARA FALLS, ONT.—Scene at the burning of the hotel, at 1.30 p.m., June 26th, 1898—The building was entirely destroyed. Water color from a photograph by Mr. Harry Brown, of Niagara Falls, now of St. Augustine, Fla. Size 6 x 8. See 1250, 1252, 1276.

1252—CLIFTON HOUSE, NIAGARA FALLS, C.W.—This hostelry, which stood on the west side of the Niagara River, opposite the Falls, was erected in 1835 by Harmanus Crysler. On June 26th, 1898, it was destroyed by fire, and rebuilt as the Clifton Hotel in 1905. Water color. Size 7 x 9. See 1250-1, 1276.

1253—ST. ANDREW'S—First Presbyterian Church at Niagara, U.C.— Built, 1794; burned during War of 1812-14; rebuilt, as shown in picture, 1831. Water color. Size 6 x 9. See 225, 1273.

1254—BURLINGTON CANAL RANGE LIGHTS—These lighthouses mark the entrance to Burlington Bay from Lake Ontario. The smaller is called the Pier Head Light, and the larger one the Main Light. Both are situated on the south side of the channel. The view is north-eastward toward Toronto, and the steamer is coming in from the lake en route to Hamilton. Water color from original drawing by F. B. Schell, for "Picturesque Canada," 1880. Size 4 x 7.

1255—RESIDENCE OF D. W. (SIR) SMITH, NIAGARA, U.C.—D. W. Smith, Surveyor-General, Upper Canada, owned what is now (1917) Court House Square, or Market Square, Niagara, his house being situated on the west side of King street, between Queen and Johnson. In 1798 it was offered for sale as a free Grammar School, with four acres as endowment, and again in 1800 at a reduced price. Governor Hunter, however, opposed the purchase, on the ground that position was too exposed, being opposite Fort Niagara. Miss Carnochan, historian of old Niagara, says it is not known what became of the house, but its site was occupied in 1812 by the Government House, which was burned in 1813. La Rochefoucauld, in his "Tour Through Upper Canada," in 1795, states that the dwelling "consists of joiners' work, but is constructed, embellished and painted in the best style; the yard, garden and court are surrounded with railings, made and painted as elegantly as they could be in England." Water color from a drawing by Mrs. Simcoe. Size 5 x 6.

1256—AN OLD MASONIC MEETING PLACE, ST. DAVID'S, NIAGARA TOWNSHIP—The meeting place, 1811-19, of Masonic Lodge No. 2 of the Provincial Grand Lodge. The minutes of the P.G.L., 1798, show that the lodge met at Niagara, in 1799 at Queenston, and in 1811 at St. David's, Niagara Township. The village of St. David's is built on lot No. 90 in the Township of Niagara, part of which lot is the north-west corner of Main street and the Queenston and Grimsby macadamized road, in St. David's. Water color by Mrs. E. Currie, St. Catharines, Ont. Size 8 x 12.

1257—ROYAL COAT-OF-ARMS, NIAGARA—A copy of the orginal oil painting of the Royal Coat-of-Arms, which from 1817-47 decorated the upper part of the north wall over the judge's seat in the old Court House, Niagara, Upper Canada. The original painting was removed to the new

Court House on Queen street, in 1847, and occupies the same position over the judge's seat as in the old Court House. Water color by Owen Staples, copied from original oil. Size 15 x 20.

1258—NIAGARA FALLS, FROM GOAT ISLAND, 1850—The picture shows the bridge joining Goat Island on the American side to the Terrapin Rock. On the brink of the Falls in 1833 the Terrapin Tower was erected by Judge Porter. For many years this tower was a point of interest at Niagara Falls, but in 1873 it was blown up by persons unknown, whom, it is said, were of opinion it might rival Prospect Point in attraction. Water color by Wm. Armstrong, C.E., Toronto. Size 10 x 14. See 1752.

1259—CHAPMAN HOUSE, NIAGARA—Built in 1815 by George Young, master builder, who in that year was employed by the Government in the construction of the forts. It was occupied by Jacob Putnam in 1825, and Mr. George Putnam, of Buffalo, was born here in 1830. Pen drawing, colored, by Owen Staples. Size 10 x 14. See 1247.

1260—OLD MILITARY HOSPITAL, NIAGARA—In a map of 1799 is given the position of the Indian Council House, which in a map of 1822 is the site of the hospital. The latter, however, was not the first hospital at Fort George; there was one there at an earlier date. The structure shown in the picture was burned in 1882. The sycamore tree to the left in the background, stood close to the ramparts of Fort George. Water color by J. W. Cotton from a sketch by F. H. Granger, 1864. Size 8 x 12.

1261—WESTERN HOME FOR GIRLS, NIAGARA—This building was used in 1817 as a jail and Court House, and discontinued as the latter in 1847, when the present Court House was built. Later, on the removal of the jail to St. Catharines, it was unoccupied for several years. Miss Rye purchased it in 1869, and the place was a home for orphan children. For the past twenty-five years it has been known as the Western Home for Girls. Pen drawing, colored, by Owen Staples. Size 11 x 14.

1262—"THE WATERFALL OF NIAGARA, IN NORTH AMERICA—This most surprizing Cataract of Nature is 137 feet high and its breadth about 360 yards. The Island in the middle is about 420 yards long and 40 yards broad at its lower end. The water, on its approaching the said Island, becomes so rapid as almost to exceed an arrow in swiftness, 'till it comes to the Fall; where it reascends into the air, foaming as white as milk, and all in motion like a boiling cauldron; its noise may be heard 15 leagues off, and in calm weather its vapours rise a great hight into the air, and may be seen like a thick smoak at 30 miles distance. R. Hancock, fecit." This view of the Falls was engraved for Middleton's (Charles Theodore) Complete System of Geography, two volumes, published in London, Eng., 1777. The picture appeared in Vol. II., the date of which is 1778. Engraving, colored. Size 10 x 15.

1263—FORT NIAGARA, N.Y., 1911—From the foot of King street, Niagara-on-the-Lake, Ont. Water color by Owen Staples. Size 10 x 14.

1264—BUTLER FAMILY GRAVEYARD, NIAGARA, U.C.—Situated about a mile from the town, at the west end, originally a part of the farm of Colonel John Butler, who, during the Revolutionary War, commanded the corps of Rangers bearing his name. The burial plot, consisting of half an acre, stands in the centre of the farm, which was divided and sold some years ago. The boundary line between the two sections runs exactly through the middle of the plot. No stone marks the spot where Colonel Butler lies, although an attempt was made to locate the grave and re-inter the remains in St. Mark's churchyard. The search was, however, abandoned. Water color. Size 3 x 7.

1265—**OLD RED MEETING HOUSE**—Township of Stamford—It was erected about 1800 on lot 130, at the west end of Lundy's Lane, and opposite the old Lundy's Lane House. Here the "Lodge of Friends," or No. 12 Stamford, met until 1818, when they removed to quarters on lot No. 95, Township of Stamford. The site is now (1917) occupied by the Lundy's Lane schoolhouse. Water color. Size 4 x 7.

1266—**TAVERN AT THE WHIRLPOOL, NEAR NIAGARA FALLS, ONT.**—Situated a mile west of the Whirlpool, on the west side of the bridge, on the road leading from Queenston Heights to Lundy's Lane. It was built about 1816 by Andrew Rosebank, and was a favorite resort in the early days for the Freemasons of the Niagara District. In 1914 the old-time tavern was converted into a double dwelling, without, however, any marked change in the exterior of the building. Water color. Size 4 x 7.

1267—**STAMFORD COTTAGE**—The residence of Sir Peregrine Maitland, Lieutenant-Governor of Upper Canada from 1819-28. It was situated in a large park at Stamford, three miles west of Niagara Falls. Here Sir Peregrine and Lady Maitland, during their stay in Canada, dispensed hospitality to many members of the English nobility and others of note from the Old Land. Stamford Cottage was destroyed by fire many years ago, and the grounds adjoining have been turned into a sand pit. Water color. Size 4 x 6.

1268—**GOVERNOR SIMCOE'S CHAIR**—A relic of Navy Hall, Niagara —Used by the first Lieutenant-Governor of Upper Canada during his stay at Navy Hall, 1792-6. It was subsequently brought to York (Toronto) by Lieutenant (Colonel) James Givins, Superintendent of Indian Affairs, and finally became the property of the York Pioneers. For years it has stood in the old log cabin at the Exhibition Grounds, Toronto. Water color. Size 4½ x 5.

1269—**"NAVY HALL," NIAGARA**—It is claimed by local historians that the building shown in picture was one of a group of three or four buildings on the bank of the Niagara River, occupied by Gov. Simcoe and his suite from 1792-6. It is asserted, however, by others, that the buildings of the Simcoe group were burnt by the Americans in May, 1813. An examination of the records and plans of the original Navy Hall buildings fails to show any of the same dimensions as that in picture, and for that reason doubt is expressed as to the date of its erection. A further claim, and one that has the support of documentary evidence, is made that the building was not erected until 1815-17. Its exact location is shown in a map of 2nd May, 1817, signed by Lieut. Willson, R.E., and used in a plan by Lieut.-Col. Durnford in 1823, showing the actual elevation of the building, described as "the Commissariat Store-house at Navy Hall." In 1862, when the terminus of the Southern Railway (now the Michigan Central) was to be changed, it was found that the tracks would go partly through the oak grove and this old structure and, to save the relic, the Government permitted the removal of the building to its present location. There is so far no documentary evidence in proof of the claim that any of the buildings at Navy Hall were used for legislative purposes. Indeed, the first meeting was held in Freemasons' Hall, and later meetings, beyond doubt, in Butler's Barracks, which had been enlarged to accommodate the Legislature. The building in picture, which for some time had been in a dilapidated condition, was in 1912 restored by the Dominion Government by petition of the Niagara Historical Society. Water color by Owen Staples. Size 19 x 25. See 3303.

1270—**ST. MARK'S ANGLICAN CHURCH, NIAGARA**—Pulpit and Chancel—Water color by Owen Staples. Size 20 x 28. See 1274.

1271—**INTERIOR OF SERVOS HOMESTEAD**—Home of Major Daniel Servos, of Palatine Hill, Four-Mile Creek, Niagara Township. Water color by Owen Staples. Size 18 x 22. See 1243.

1272—"THE WILDERNESS," KING STREET, NIAGARA—The property consisted primarily of lots 235, 236, 237, 238, Niagara, being conveyed to Ann Claus (daughter of Sir William Johnson), on 3rd December, 1799, she obtaining it from Robert Pilkington. It was also the home of Col. William Claus (son of Col. Daniel Claus and Ann Johnson), who served as an officer in the 60th Regiment, and was in 1796 Deputy Superintendent of Indian Affairs at Niagara. The house is now occupied by Major and Mrs. Evans. The latter is a great-granddaughter of Col. Daniel Claus. Water color by Owen Staples. Size 20 x 28.

1273—ST. ANDREW'S PRESBYTERIAN CHURCH, NIAGARA—In 1794 the erection of the first church at Niagara—subsequently known as St. Andrew's Presbyterian—was begun. An old record book of the church gives many interesting incidents in connection with its early history, of efforts for religious liberty, of encouragement and difficulties, of generous offerings, and of poverty in the struggle made by the handful of people who formed the congregation in its pioneer days. During the War of 1812-14 the church was burnt, and in 1831 the present structure built. Water color by Owen Staples. Size 15 x 21. See 225, 1253.

1274—ST. MARK'S ANGLICAN CHURCH, NIAGARA—Rev. Robert Addison, first incumbent of the church, was sent to Canada in 1792 by the Society for the Propagation of the Gospel. Before the erection of the church the congregation met in the Court House, near the site of the present one, Niagara, but in 1805 building was begun, and in August, 1809, service was held in the primitive place of worship. In a letter written by Mr. Addison in January, 1811, he stated that "The church is now very nearly finished, except some seats in the gallery, and the congregation, which is large, is well accommodated for public worship." In the winter of 1813, however, the church was destroyed by the Americans, only its stone walls remaining. The re-building took place between 1816-18, and an addition forming the transepts was made in 1843. The Hon. and Rt. Rev. Charles James Stewart, Lord Bishop of Quebec, consecrated the church on 3rd August, 1828. With its registers dating back to 1792, its tablets and tombstones, the place teems with the pioneer life, history and military occupation of old Niagara. Water color by Owen Staples, Toronto. Size 19 x 25. See 1270.

1275—NORTHWEST CORNER QUEEN AND GATE STREETS, NIAGARA, ONT., 1860—1, Gibson's furniture store, in upper storey of which Niagara Masons met for some time. It was burned 1860. 2, Residence of Dr. D. Campbell. 3, Residence of John Crooks. 4, House and barns of David Talbot. 5, Occupied by Mr. Savage and also Ralph Clench. 6, Home of F. H. Granger's brother. F. H. Granger made the original sketch of this picture. The property at the corner is now (1917) residential, owned by Mrs. Riggs. Water color. Size 4 x 7. See 1316.

1276—CLIFTON HOUSE, NIAGARA FALLS, C.W., 1835-98—Water color. Size 7 x 7. See 1250-1-2.

1277—MACDONELL, LIEUTENANT-COLONEL HON. JOHN—Killed at Queenston Heights—Son of Lieut.-Col. Alexander Macdonell, 1st Glengarry Militia, and nephew of Lieut.-Col. John Macdonell, Speaker of the first House of Assembly, Upper Canada; Provincial A.D.C., 15th April, 1812; was at the taking of Detroit the following August, and awarded a gold medal. At Queenston Heights, he, with Brock, was mortally wounded, and the two were subsequently buried side by side. Col. Macdonell was at the time of his death Attorney-General of Upper Canada. M.P. for Glengarry, 1812. From a silhouette in possession of his grand-nephew, J. A. Macdonell, K.C., Alexandria, Ont. Size 2 x 4.

1278—KEEFER, SAMUEL, C.E., 1811-90—A noted Canadian surveyor and engineer—In 1833 appointed secretary of the Board of Canal Commissioners for the improvement of the navigation of the St. Lawrence. Became assistant engineer on the Cornwall Canal, 1834; five years later made secretary of the Board of Works, then established for Lower Canada, and on the union of the provinces appointed chief engineer to the Department of Public Works, holding that position until 1853. Surveyed and established the line of the Beauharnois Canal, and was the engineer of the Suspension Bridge over the Chaudiere Falls at Ottawa, the first bridge of the kind in Canada. In 1853 accepted an appointment with the Grand Trunk Railway, and fixed the line of the Victoria Bridge, Montreal, where it now (1917) stands. From 1857-64 Mr. Keefer was Government Inspector of Railways. He was born at Thorold, Ont. Photograph, colored. Size 4 x 5. Head and shoulders.

1279—TIFFANY, GIDEON, 1774-1854—An early Upper Canada journalist—The Tiffanys, Silvester and Gideon, were direct descendants of Humphrey Tiffany, the founder of the American branch of the family, who emigrated to America about 1660, settling at Massachusetts Bay. Their father was Dr. Gideon Tiffany, of Attleboro, Mass. Subsequent to graduating from Dartmouth College, N.H., Gideon was associated with his brother in the publication of the first newspaper in Upper Canada, the Upper Canada Gazette, or American Oracle, at Niagara (Newark), 1793, in succession to Louis Roy. In 1800 the brothers published "The Canadian Constellation." The following year, however, Gideon decided to abandon journalism for agriculture, and settled in Middlesex County, Ont. Here he operated successfully until his death at Delaware, Middlesex County. The late Mr. E. H. Tiffany, K.C., of Alexandria, Ont., was a grand-nephew. Photograph, colored. Size 4 x 5. Head and shoulders.

1280—STREET, THOMAS CLARK—Son of Samuel Street, Niagara Falls—Born at Bridgewater, near Niagara Falls, in 1814. Studied law, and in 1838 was admitted to the bar. From 1851-4, and again from 1861-7, represented Welland in the United Parliament of Canada. He was also a lieutenant-colonel in the Militia. His death took place at Clark Hill, Ont. in 1872. Rev. Sutherland Macklem, of Toronto, is a nephew. Photograph, colored. Size 3 x 4. Head and shoulders.

1281—STREET, SAMUEL—An old-time resident of Niagara Falls, and a U.E. Loyalist. Born at Farmington, Connecticut, in 1775, the eldest son of Nehemiah Street, a fur-trader, who in 1787 was murdered near Lewiston, N.Y., and grandson of the Rev. Nicholas Street, who emigrated from England to America in 1630. During the War of 1812, Samuel served as a colonel of militia. He was for many years engaged in an extensive business as miller and general merchant at Niagara Falls. His death occurred at Port Robinson, Thorold Township, in 1844. Water color from a miniature in possession of his grandson, Rev. Sutherland Macklem, Toronto. Size 3 x 4. Head and shoulders.

1282—MASONIC HALL, NIAGARA, ONT.—Northwest corner of King and Prideaux streets, lot 33. As early as 1791 there was a Freemasons' Hall on this site, and in the Crown Lands Department, Ontario, lot No. 33. was marked in 1795 as Freemasons' Lodge. The present building, was erected about 1817-18, used at different times as a store, for the military, a school, called the "Stone Barracks," and, finally, bought by the Masons. Water color by J. W. Cotton. Size 5 x 7.

1283—SITE OF REDAN BATTERY—On the slope of the hill below Queenston Heights—It was near this spot that Lieut.-Col. John Macdonell, Provincial Aide-de-Camp to Brock, and Attorney-General of Upper Canada, was mortally wounded, October 13th, 1812. Lieut.-Col. Macdonell was a nephew of the Speaker of the first House of Assembly of Upper Canada.

Near this same redan battery, too, Sir Isaac Brock fell while leading his men up the Heights. The memorial on the site was erected in 1906 by the Lundy's Lane Historical Society. Water color. Size 6 x 7.

1284—RUINS OF WILLIAM LYON MACKENZIE'S PRINTING OFFICE, QUEENSTON—Water color. Size 6 x 9. See 1303.

1285—MONUMENT AT STONEY CREEK—Erected in 1908 through the united efforts of the Women's Wentworth Historical Society and the County of Wentworth Veterans' Association, as a memorial to those who died and were buried on this knoll. The engagement at Stoney Creek took place on the night of June 6th, 1813, between Col. Harvey, who acted as Dep. Adjt.-Gen. to Vincent's army, and the Americans under Generals Chandler and Winder. The latter were defeated. Water color. Size 5 x 7.

1286—BROCK'S MONUMENT IN ST. PAUL'S CATHEDRAL, LONDON, ENG.—"Erected at the Public Expense to the Memory of Major-General Sir Isaac Brock, Who Gloriously Fell on the 13th of October, MDCCCXII in Resisting an Attack on Queenston in Upper Canada." Photograph. Size 6 x 9.

1287—A GROUP OF HISTORIC THORN TREES—Near Fort George, Niagara. The tradition is that these interlaced, gnarled old trees were planted by French officers stationed at Fort Niagara, who had brought the slips from France. The fragrant blossoms now grow in profusion on the commons, near Fort George, an old-time military post on the heights above Navy Hall. Water color. Size 5 x 7.

1288—OLD COURT HOUSE, NIAGARA—Built in 1817 as a jail and court house. In this building many remarkable trials took place, notably that of Robert Gourlay. The present court house, Niagara, was erected in 1847, and the historic house of 1817 was used only as a jail until that in St. Catharines was erected, in 1864. In many books of travel in Canada from 1820-1830 the jail and court house, Niagara, is spoken of as the handsomest building in Upper Canada. Water color. Size 13 x 15. See 1294.

1289—FOG BELL, FORT MISSISSAGUA, 1880-9—This bell, which was erected about 1880, was used to warn steamers and other craft entering the Niagara River. It was situated on the rampart surrounding the tower known as Fort Mississagua, and was wound up by hand, the bell ringing until it ran down. It was blown down during a violent storm, January 10th, 1889, and never re-erected. In 1904 a foghorn was placed near the landing-place at Niagara, and at the same time two lighthouses were erected on the wharf. By this means vessels are now guided while coming in at night. Water color by Owen Staples. Size 6 x 10.

1290—STONEY CREEK BATTLEGROUND—Rear view from Hamilton and Niagara main road. Photograph, colored. Size 6 x 10. See 1301.

1291—EASTHAM HOUSE, QUEENSTON, 1817-35—North-east corner Queen and Highland streets. Thomas Eastham, a driver in H.M. Royal Artillery, was General Brock's trumpeter at the Battle of Queenston Heights. His hotel, in its day the best in the village, was kept for several years by Mrs. Eastham after her husband's death. It was built of frame and demolished many years ago. The sign shown portrayed the death of Brock. Water color. Size 7 x 9.

1292—SHEAFFE'S PASS—West of Queenston, near St. David's, U.C.—General Sheaffe's "path to victory," October 13th, 1812, is on the Queenston and Grimsby Stone road, between lots 44-9, and between concessions 2-3 of Niagara Township. Over this road Sheaffe's troops marched to victory, driving the American forces from the Heights into the river. Water color. Size 7 x 9.

1293—"THE 43RD LIGHT INFANTRY—As they turn out in their sleighs at the Falls of Niagara, 1839. R. G. A. Levinge, 43rd, 1839. Ackermann, dirext." With key—In 1741, what was known as the 54th Regiment of Foot, was formed in England. On the Treaty of Aix-la-Chapelle, October, 1748, several corps were disbanded and the title of the regiment changed to the 43rd. Sailed for Halifax in 1757; was at Quebec, 1759; took part in American Revolutionary War and in Peninsular War. In 1835 embarked again for Canada, being stationed in New Brunswick. The famous march across the portage of the Madawaska to Quebec took place in 1837, and in 1839 the 43rd was on the Niagara frontier. The regiment left Canada in 1846. The picture shows a number of the regiment in one of their winter pastimes on the Niagara River, near the Falls. It was drawn by Sir Richard George Augustus Levinge, who, in 1839, was lieutenant in the 43rd. Lithograph in color. Size 15 x 25.

1294—OLD COURT HOUSE, NIAGARA—View of the court room as in 1877. An old and historic building. When Niagara ceased to be the county town, the career of the old jail and Court House, as the former, ended, for since 1847 courts had been held in the new building. For several years the place was unoccupied, when in 1869 it was purchased by Miss Rye, altered and beautified. It is now known as the Western Home for Girls. Water color. Size 14 x 15. See 1288.

1295—TRINITY (ANGLICAN) CHURCH AND SUNDAY SCHOOL, BRIDGEWATER STREET, CHIPPAWA, ONT.—Erected in 1842, to replace the first church which was built in the early part of the nineteenth century and burned by rebel sympathizers in 1837. The graveyard about the church is evidently ancient also, as around the three sides may be seen the stumps of rows of great trees which from their weather-worn appearance, must have been cut down long ago. From the fact that this district was the site of a battle, it might be assumed that in this old-time cemetery would be found military graves, but such is not the case. The present edifice has had within its walls as worshippers, his Majesty King Edward VII., Jenny Lind, the Swedish singer, and Laura Secord, the heroine of Beaver Dams. Water color by J. W. Cotton. Size 5 x 6.

1296—RESIDENCE OF JAMES H. CUMMINGS, CHIPPAWA, ONT.— On Queen Victoria Park Boulevard. It was erected about 1845 for James H. Cummings by his father, James Cummings, who represented. Lincoln (S. R.) in the United Parliament of Canada in 1844. The younger Cummings, however, only occupied the residence for a year, and the property subsequently passed into the possession of Dr. T. C. Macklem, who resided there until 1859. Water color by J. W. Cotton. Size 5 x 7.

1297—PETER BALL'S HOUSE, NIAGARA—The dwelling of an old pioneer. It was built in 1816, and stood two and a half miles south-west of Niagara, on the south side of the Niagara and St. Catharines stone road. Peter Ball was a son of Jacob Ball, a captain in Butler's Rangers, who settled at Niagara in 1782, bringing with him some forty immigrants. About twenty years ago the old house was removed from its original site and used as a fruit-packing house. Water color by J. W. Cotton. Size 5 x 7.

1298—BATTLE GROUND AT LUNDY'S LANE—Township of Stamford—The picture gives the battlefield as it was in July, 1897, and shows interesting and historical spots, such as Brock's Monument, Lundy's Lane and Old Burial Ground. The battle, fought on 25th July, 1814, was one of the most stubbornly contested engagements fought during the war. It resulted in a victory for the British. Sometimes it is styled by American writers as that of Bridgewater, or Niagara Falls, but Canadians usually speak of it as "Lundy's Lane." Water color made on the spot for J. Ross Robertson by E. Wyly Grier. Size 7 x 40.

16

1299—**WHERE GENERAL BROCK FELL**—The cenotaph which marks the spot stands just below the escarpment or hill where the present monument stands, and was erected in 1860 by the Provincial Government. H.R.H. the Prince of Wales (King Edward VII.) laid the corner-stone during his visit here in September, 1860. The inscription reads: "Near this spot Major-General Sir Isaac Brock, K.C.B., Provisional Lieutenant-Governor of Upper Canada, fell on 13th October, 1812, while advancing to repel the invading enemy." Water color by Owen Staples. Size 6 x 10.

1300—**OLD CUMMINGS RESIDENCE, CHIPPAWA, ONT.**—It was erected in 1840 by James Cummings, a member of the United Parliament of Canada; elected in 1844. He resided in the house, which is at the north-east end of the village, on Water street, until his death in 1860. The property came into possession of James Francis Macklem about 1865, but the latter never lived in it. It has been leased since that date. Water color by Owen Staples. Size 5 x 7.

1301—**GAGE HOMESTEAD AND MONUMENT**—View looking from the north, showing the rear of the old dwelling and the monument on a hill, a few hundred feet to the southwest. The night of 5th June, 1813, was one of ill-omen for the American forces under Generals Chandler and Winder, who lay encamped west of Stoney Creek, with about 3,500 men. The British, about 700 strong, under Gen. Vincent and Col. Harvey, attacked the Americans, who were surprised and routed. The American generals were captured in the action, which lasted an hour and a half. Photograph, colored. Size 6 x 10. See 1290.

1302—**ALEXANDER HAMILTON HOUSE, QUEENSTON, 1834**—On the Niagara River road. The original Hamilton house was erected about 1789 by the Hon. Robert Hamilton, but on the day of the Battle of Queenston Heights, Oct. 13th, 1812, was destroyed by fire. Alexander Hamilton, a son of the Hon. Robert Hamilton, erected a colonial residence a little higher up and further from the river, about seven miles from Niagara. In 1831 Alexander Hamilton was postmaster of Queenston. Water color by Owen Staples. Size 7 x 10.

1303—**WILLIAM LYON MACKENZIE'S PRINTING OFFICE, QUEENSTON**—Corner of York and Clarence streets, lots 26-7-8. The noted building, which was of stone, stood below the Heights of Queenston, and was in 1824 the printing office of William Lyon Mackenzie. From May 18th to November 18th, 1824, the Colonial Advocate was printed there. Mackenzie then removed to York (Toronto). From 1848-55 the house was occupied by Charles Bradley. In the late thirties Mr. Wynne lived in the small dwelling to the left. Water color by Owen Staples. Size 6 x 9. See 1284.

1304—**HAMILTON'S HOTEL, QUEENSTON, 1830**—On Queen street, Niagara River road. The old building, which still (1917) stands, was erected about 1825 on the estate of the Hon. Robert Hamilton, and owned by his son, Alexander. The old-time gateway shown to the right is the entrance to the original Hamilton estate. Water color by Owen Staples. Size 6 x 8.

1305—**HOME OF COMPTE JOSEPH DE PUISAYE**—On Farm No. 19, Niagara and Queenston River road. The Count came to Canada for the purpose of founding a Royalist settlement. About 1798 he settled at Niagara, building for himself a long, low dwelling, with dormer windows and steep, sharply sloping roof, after the style of the Norman French houses. Here de Puisaye lived for many years. His closing days were spent in England, where he died in 1827. During the War of 1812 his chateau, which still (1917) stands, was used as a hospital, as were many other Niagara houses of the time. To the left may be seen an old powder magazine. Water color. Size 5 x 7.

1306—HAMILTON, HON. ROBERT—Prominent in mercantile and official life in Niagara District. Shortly after the close of the Revolutionary war, Mr. Hamilton removed to Queenstown (Queenston), U.C., from Carleton Island, where, in partnership with Richard (Hon.) Cartwright, he had carried on an extensive trade with the Indians. He built a brewery, wharves and warehouses at Queenston, and soon became prominent in that part of Upper Canada. He was a member of the Land Board, and was also first judge of the District of Nassau. Under William Jarvis he became Deputy Provincial Grand Master of the First Provincial Grand Lodge of Freemasons, and in 1797 was elected Grand Master in place of Jarvis. For some time he distinguished himself in connection with his former partner, Mr. Cartwright, by opposing Government measures, thereby incurring Governor Simcoe's displeasure. The latter received from Hon. Robert Hamilton much valuable information respecting the commerce of the country, and particularly the Indian trade. His death took place at Queenston, 8th March, 1809. Water color from a miniature in possession of his grandson, Clark Hamilton, Kingston, Ont. Size 3 x 4. Head and shoulders.

1307—RESIDENCE OF HON. ROBERT HAMILTON, QUEENSTOWN (QUEENSTON), U. C.—It was a substantial stone house on the Niagara River road, erected by Mr. Hamilton, who settled at Queenston at the close of the Revolutionary War. Mrs. Simcoe, wife of the first Lieut.-Governor of Upper Canada, during her stay at Niagara, frequently visited the Hamilton home, noted for its hospitality. In her diary she writes of it as " a very good stone house, the back rooms overlooking on the river. A gallery, the length of the house, is a delightful covered walk, both below and above, in all weather." Water color, from a drawing by Mrs. Simcoe, July, 1792. Size 5 x 6.

1308—BROCK'S SPRING, QUEENSTON HEIGHTS—Used by the British troops during the War of 1812-14. The spring is situated in the Brock Monument ground, Queenston Heights, on the edge of the escarpment, about three hundred yards west of the present Brock's Monument. The water is excellent, and is still (1917) used for drinking purposes. Water color. Size 6 x 7.

1309—FALL OF QUEENSTON SUSPENSION BRIDGE, 1864—The bridge, which crossed the Niagara River between Queenston and Lewiston, six miles lower down the river than the first Suspension Bridge, originally used by the old Great Western Railway of Canada, was 800 feet long, 20 feet wide and 200 feet above the water surface. During the January of 1864 the torrent brought down the floating ice, which wedged and piled into a barrier, 60 feet in height, from shore to shore, some distance above the bridge. The descending ice wedged the barrier higher and higher until on the morning of Feb. 1st the bridge was swept away, as shown in the picture, taken a week before the disaster. The bridge was rebuilt in 1899, partly from material the gale had left, and partly from that of the discarded "Upper Bridge." Water color from old print. Size 5 x 9. See 1342.

1310—RESIDENCE OF THE FIELD FAMILY—This century-old house stands on the west side of the Niagara River road, some four miles from the Town of Niagara, and was built by Gilbert Field, who died in 1815. The structure, which is of brick, originally had a high, sloping roof, but this was burned about fifty years ago and replaced by the present (1917) lower roof. In the War of 1812 a cannon ball, fired from the American side of the Niagara River, penetrated the wall of the house. For some time the old homestead was used as a hospital, as were many of the dwellings of the day. Water color by J. W. Cotton. Size 5 x 7.

1311—PARTITION STREET, QUEENSTON, ONT.—View looking towards the Niagara River—The old Forest Hotel, of which Joseph Wynn was proprietor in 1832, is shown in the picture, and adjoining, to the left, are buildings on the Chubbuck property. Prior to the opening of the first Queenston Bridge, in 1852, Job Chubbuck operated a horse ferry from Queenston to Lewiston. The scene is as it appeared in the autumn of 1913. Water color by Owen Staples. Size 6 x 9.

1312—QUEENSTON (THE LOWER LANDING), U.C., 1792—View from Vrooman's Point—The old log house in foreground was built in 1784 by Adam Vrooman, a sergeant in Butler's Rangers. At this point about half a mile from Queenston a battery operated by his son, Solomon, a militiaman during the War of 1812, supported the British garrison in discomfiting the crossing of the Americans at the Battle of Queenston Heights. Midway between Vrooman's and the Queen's Rangers' huts in the distance, may be seen the Hamilton wharf and warehouses. Water color. Size 7 x 10.

1313—VROOMAN, SOLOMON S., 1783-1874—Active in annoying the crossing of the Americans at Queenston—He was a militiaman during the War of 1812-14, and the son of Sergeant Adam Vrooman, of Butler's Rangers. When the original gunners abandoned the battery at Vrooman's Point, half a mile from Queenston, on October 13th, 1812, Vrooman took command with Lewis Clement and James Durham, and with two twenty-four-pounders sank the American rowboats in the Niagara River. The position of Vrooman's battery is still pointed out. Photograph, colored. Size 3 x 4. Head and shoulders.

1314—VROOMAN, SOLOMON A., 1829-1913—A lifelong resident of Queenston, Ont.—He was a son of Solomon S. Vrooman, who at the Battle of Queenston Heights, October 13th, 1812, took a prominent part in harassing the Americans crossing the river. In 1853 the younger Vrooman erected two hundred feet of scaffold for the present (1917) Brock's Monument. Died at Queenston. Photograph, colored. Size 3 x 4. Half length.

1315—OLD PRESBYTERIAN CHURCH, QUEENSTON—On lot 6, on the west side of the Niagara River road, Niagara Township—Chiefly through the efforts of Mrs. John Hamilton, daughter-in-law of the Hon. Robert Hamilton, this pioneer place of worship was erected on property belonging to the Hamilton family. It was subsequently used for some years by the Methodists, but in 1875 was turned into a residence by Jarvis Hamilton. In 1905 it was purchased by Major Shepherd, who had it demolished, and in 1906, built the house now (1917) standing on the site. Water color by J. W. Cotton from an old sketch. Size 5 x 7.

1316—NORTH-WEST CORNER QUEEN AND GATE STREETS, NIAGARA, U.C., 1832—The store of R. and J. Crysler, members of one of Niagara's pioneer families, is shown. It afterwards became Gibson's furniture wareroom. In the upper storey of the old building the Niagara Masons met at one time. When the structure was destroyed by fire in 1860 they lost their regalia and records. Water color. Size 5 x 7. See 1275.

1317—MEMORIAL HALL, NIAGARA HISTORICAL SOCIETY, NIAGARA-ON-THE-LAKE, ONT.—The society was founded in 1895, and in April, 1906, work was commenced on the present museum, which was formally opened, June 4th, 1907. It contains over five thousand articles, which have been labelled and catalogued. The president of the Niagara Historical Society is Miss Janet Carnochan, author of the "History of Niagara," who acts as curator and editor from love of the work. The society's anniversary is held on September 17th, to celebrate the meeting of the first Parliament of Upper Canada at Niagara (then Newark), 1792, and the annual meeting takes place on Oct. 13th, the anniversary of the Battle of Queenston Heights. Photograph, colored. Size 4 x 6.

1318—ANGLICAN CHURCH AT QUEENSTON, ONT.—This pioneer church, south side Queenston and St. Catharines stone road, erected in 1818, was the first Anglican place of worship in Queenston. The earliest record is of a communion service in 1820, held by Rev. B. B. Stevens, M.A., chaplain of H.M. Forces. The church stood on the slope of the hill, overlooking Queenston, below the heights, and west of the W. L. Mackenzie printing office. After the demolition of the church the congregation met in the Methodist church in 1875. The present St. Saviour's church was erected 1877-79. Part of the foundation of the old church is still (1916) standing. Water color by J. W. Cotton from an old drawing. Size 5 x 6.

1319—METHODIST CHURCH AT BEAVER DAMS—Exterior view— Situated on the south side of the Hamilton to the Falls Indian trail, lot 51, Thorold Township. In 1832 the Trustee Board of the Methodist Church for the Niagara District, purchased from Hiram Swayze an acre of land, and here the frame building shown in the picture was erected. It had a gallery at the two sides and north end, until 1868, when being no longer required for use, it was shut off by a ceiling. In 1879 repairs were made and the church re-dedicated by Rev. Wm. S. Griffin. Since 1890 no regular services have been held in the church, which for many years had had large congregations. Amongst prominent ministers who preached in the old church were Dr. Egerton Ryerson and Rev. Nathan Bangs, who was afterwards editor of a Methodist Episcopal journal in New York. Water color by J. W. Cotton from an old drawing. Size 5 x 6. See 1320.

1320—METHODIST CHURCH AT BEAVER DAMS—Interior view— Water color by J. W. Cotton, from an old drawing. Size 5 x 6. See 1319.

1321—HAMILTON WHARF AND LANDING, QUEENSTON, U.C., 1789 —Situated at what is now (1917) known as Deep Hollow, below the present steamboat landing, opposite Lewiston. The wharves and storehouses at Queenston were erected by Hon. Robert Hamilton, a member of the Legislative Council for the new Province of Upper Canada from 1792 until his death. Mr. Hamilton carried on extensive trading operations, and was one of the prominent men of the community. Water color by Owen Staples, from an old drawing. Size 6 x 9.

1322—OLD LOWER LANDING ROAD AT QUEENSTON—Leading from the Hamilton wharf and storehouses—It was used by the troops in the War of 1812-14; is at the north end of Queenston, opposite the Hamilton estate, and is now (1917) known as Deep Hollow. In the old days Queenston and Lewiston were called Lower Landings, and Chippawa and Schlosser the Upper Landings, on the Canadian and American sides, respectively. Water color. Size 7 x 9.

1323—STONEY CREEK MONUMENT—Unveiled by electricity, June 6th, 1913, by her Majesty Queen Mary from Buckingham Palace, and erected by the people of Canada through representations and under the direction of the Women's Wentworth Historical Society, to commemorate the Battle of Stoney Creek, June 6th, 1813. In 1899 the Women's Wentworth Historical Society purchased a portion of the battlefield of Stoney Creek, including the site presented to the Government for this monument, and on Oct. 17th the ground was declared open as a public park by the Countess of Aberdeen. In 1910 the society made an additional purchase; so that in all $17\frac{1}{2}$ acres of this historic ground have been preserved to the people of Canada. On May 26th, 1909, the Countess Grey turned the first sod on the site of this monument, and on May 28th, 1910, Lieut.-General Sir John D. P. French, K.C.B., K.C.M.G., laid the corner-stone. Photograph, colored. Size 5 x 9.

1324—SECORD, LAURA (INGERSOLL), 1775-1868—Heroine of the War of 1812, daughter of Thomas Ingersoll, founder of the town of that name, who removed to Canada at the close of the Revolutionary War. Her husband, James Secord, of Huguenot descent, was, like her father, a U.E. Loyalist. Secord had been severely wounded at Queenston Heights, and while home under parole, American soldiers domiciled themselves in his house. It was here that hints of the intended night surprise on Beaver Dams were dropped. To take this post would be to open up the whole peninsula. Lieut. Fitzgibbon, of the 49th, was stationed at the cross roads at Beaver Dams, in DeCew's house, and to warn him of the intended attack, Laura Secord, on 23rd June, 1813, walked twenty miles by a circuitous route from Queenston, through swamp and forest. Her trying experiences and Fitzgibbon's success owing to the timely warning he received, are well known in Canadian history. A monument to Mrs. Secord's memory has been erected in the cemetery at Lundy's Lane, and through the indefatigable efforts of the late Mrs. E. A. Currie, of St. Catharines, a fitting memorial was placed on Queenston Heights, June, 1911. Water color from the portrait in Niagara Historical Museum. Size 5 x 6. Head and shoulders.

1325—NIAGARA FALLS—"View of the Falls of Niagara from the bank near Birche's Mills. G. Heriot, Esqr., pinxt. F. C. Lewis, sculp. Printed for Richard Phillips, 6 New Bridge street, London, 1807." As far back as 1786 John Burch owned a saw and grist mill, about two miles above Niagara Falls, lot 174, Township No. 2. He was a prominent pioneer, being a member of the Land Board in 1791, and four years later acting as Justice of the Peace. His son, John Burch, Jr., was Grand Secretary of the Provincial Grand Lodge of Freemasons of Upper Canada, 1817-19. From the settlement known as Burch's Mills an excellent view of the rapids is obtained. Aquatint, printed in color. Size 5 x 8.

1326—QUEENSTON (LOWER LANDING), U.C., 1834—View looking north, and showing: 1, Old Brock Monument, built 1824, shattered 1840. 2a, Old Barracks, 1812, near spot where Macdonell fell. 2b, William Rees' house, 1832. 3, Government storehouse. 4, Barracks. 5, Storehouse. 6, Mr. Kitson's, cabinetmaker. 7, Loghouse and barn of Joseph Wynn, Sr. 8, Stone house belonging to Major Adam Brown. 9, Monument House. 10, Joseph Wynn's hotel (Forest House). 11, Zimmerman's Bank. 12, Ross' clothing and dry goods store. 13, Post office. 14, Stone barracks. 15, Old stone house and barn. 16, Eastham Hotel. 17, Chester Wadsworth's Hotel. 18, Old hotel on Hamilton property. 19, Alexander Hamilton's house. 20, Custom House, afterwards Customs and Post Office, on site of Hon. Robert Hamilton's house, now occupied by R. K. Noyes. 21, Below here, in what is called the deep hollow, Robert Hamilton erected storehouses and wharves in 1789. 22, Vrooman's Point, where battery of two 24-pounders was mounted in 1812. 23, Lewiston, N.Y. Oil. Size 10 x 13. See 1327.

1327— QUEENSTON (LOWER LANDING), U.C., 1834—View from the Hamilton estate, looking south—1, Shows old Brock Monument, built 1824; shattered 1840. 2a, Old Barracks, 1812, near spot where Macdonell fell. 2b, William Rees' house, 1832. 3, Government storehouse. 4, Barracks. 5, Storehouse. 6, Mr. Kitson's, cabinetmaker. 7, Log house and barn of Joseph Wynn, Sr. 8, Stone house belonging to Major Adam Brown. 9, Monument House. 10, Joseph Wynn's hotel (Forest House), 11, Zimmerman's Bank. 12, Ross' clothing and dry goods store. 13, Post office. 14, Fennimore, the ferryman's house. 15, Fort Porter battery. Oil. Size 10 x 13. See 1326.

1328—PLAN OF LAURA SECORD'S HEROIC WALK FROM QUEENSTON TO DECEW FALLS, 23RD JUNE, 1813—With Key—This map or plan is absolutely accurate and shows the exact path Mrs. Secord travelled from Queenston Heights to Beaver Dams, to warn Lieut. Fitzgibbon of the intended American attack. The artist walked over the route and verified, by the aid of notes and interviews with old inhabitants, every foot of the route. Size 12 x 16.

1329—STONE HOUSE AT QUEENSTON WHERE GEN. BROCK DIED—Southeast corner Queen and Partition streets, lot 4, Township of Niagara—As it appeared in 1812-15—It was occupied in 1813 by a woman who had a servant named Christine de Chambers. The latter stated to Major Sheppard, a resident of Queenston, that she remembered perfectly the day of battle, for she was in the house at the time the British officers carried in the body of Gen. Brock and laid it on a lounge in the front room. The body was later carried to Government House, Niagara, and buried under north-east bastion, Fort George, where it remained until re-interred under the first monument erected in 1824, destroyed in 1840, and the present monument built in 1853. Water color. Size 5 x 8.

1330—STONE HOUSE AT QUEENSTON, WHERE GEN. BROCK DIED—As it appeared in 1913—The old-time dwelling is now (1917) falling into decay. Water color. Size 5 x 8.

1331—DAVID SECORD'S HOUSE, ST. DAVID'S, U.C.—The only dwelling left in the town after its burning in 1813—It is of stone, plastered in roughcast and still (1917) standing. In 1813 it was occupied by the widow of Stephen Secord, and Laura Secord's brother, Charles Ingersoll, also resided there. The heroine of Beaver Dams wished this brother to warn Lieut. Fitzgibbon of the contemplated American attack, but he was ill, and she proceeded alone to the British encampment. After the war the house became the home of David Secord, brother of James Secord, who married Laura Ingersoll. Water color by Owen Staples. Size 7 x 9.

1332—MONUMENT AT LUNDY'S LANE—Erected to commemorate the victory of July 25th, 1814—The battle was one of the most stubbornly contested in the War of 1812. This spot, at one time a neglected graveyard, is now well and properly kept. The obelisk was erected in 1895 by the Dominion Government, through the persistent efforts of the Lundy's Lane Historical Society, with Rev. Canon Bull as President. It bears the following inscription: "Erected by the Canadian Parliament in honor of the victory gained on 25th July, 1814, by the British and Canadian forces, and in grateful remembrance of the brave men who died on the field of battle fighting for the unity of the British Empire." Water color by J. W. Cotton. Size 6 x 9.

1333—LAURA SECORD'S EVENTFUL WALK—Where the heroine crossed the Twelve-Mile Creek—In her wanderings on June 23rd, 1813, Mrs. Secord crossed the Twelve-Mile Creek at St. Catharines. Discovering that she had gone too far, she recrossed by means of a fallen tree, at the Boyle farm, near the junction of the present (1917) Pelham and Boyle roads, below De Cew Falls. Water color by J. W. Cotton. Size 5 x 6.

1334—HOMESTEAD OF JAMES McFARLAND, NIAGARA, U.C.—An historic house, situated on the banks of the Niagara River, about two miles south of Niagara—It was built in 1800, and was one of the largest and most comfortable houses in the district. During the War of 1812-14 it was used, as were many Niagara houses, for hospital by both British and Americans. A battery was built on the bank behind the house, and a little to the north is the ravine, in which were concealed the boats used in taking Fort Niagara, Dec. 10th, 1813. Water color. Size 5 x 6.

1335—LAURA SECORD'S DWELLING, QUEENSTON, 1800—Exterior view—It was in this house, which is on the north-west corner of Queen and Partition streets, lots 92-3, that Mrs. Secord overheard the American officers discussing the proposed attack on the British force under Lieut. Fitzgibbon at Beaver Dams. To warn the latter Mrs. Secord tramped twenty miles through bush and swamp. The result of her warning was that Col. Boerstler, the American commander, surrendered, accepting Lieut. (Col.) Fitzgibbon's story that, owing to the strength of the British force, attack was useless. This was the great event of Fitzgibbon's life. The Secord house is still (1917) standing on its original foundation. The exterior has been altered, but the interior—the sitting-room and bedroom occupied by Lieut. Fitzgibbon—are still unaltered. The historic house is now occupied by Mr. F. H. Sheppard. Water color by J. W. Cotton. Size 5 x 7. See 1336.

1336—LAURA SECORD'S DWELLING, QUEENSTON, 1800—Living-room. Water color by J. W. Cotton. Size 5 x 7. See 1335.

1337—CANAL BOAT ON EDGE OF HORSESHOE FALLS, 1850—In the last week of June, 1850, a canal boat, laden with pork and whiskey, but with no one on board, broke loose from the harbor of Chippawa, C.W., at the confluence of the Niagara and Welland Rivers, two and a half miles from the Falls, and was carried down the river and lodged on a rock at the verge of the Falls. She remained in that position for six weeks, and was eventually swept over. It was a great attraction for thousands of visitors from Canada and the United States. Water color from print in Illustrated London News. Size 4 x 6.

1338—MONUMENT HOUSE—South-west corner of Front and Partition streets, Queenston, Ont.—It was built in 1834 by Thomas Humphries, and subsequently run by Wm. Palmer, O. Hudson, Isaac Upper, and others. When local option came into force in that district, May, 1904, the hotel was closed, and afterwards used as a store and dwelling until its destruction by fire, August 19th, 1906. In this old hostelry was a beautifully carved stone mantel, showing the fruits grown in the district, and executed by the men who did the ornamentation on the present Brock Monument on Queenston Heights. Water color. Size 5 x 6.

1339—HOME AND GRIST MILL OF GEORGE BALL, TWENTY-MILE CREEK (JORDAN, ONT.)—George Ball, youngest son of Jacob Ball, who fought in Queen's and Butler's Rangers through the Revolutionary War, erected here in 1784, a house and three mills. In 1812 a portion of the 104th British Regiment was stationed there to protect the property, with Captains Brock (nephew of General Sir Isaac Brock) and Vavasour in command, and for many years a verse in red chalk was distinctly visible in the old Ball house:—

"The blessing of God attend this house
For kindness they have shown,
To the 104th when stationed here
The country to defend."

Brock's cocked hat, which came from England after the General's death, was presented by Captain Brock to George Ball. It is now in the Niagara Historical Society Museum. Mr. Mortimer Ball, barrister, County Clerk of Louth, resides in a handsome brick residence on the site of the old log homestead—Twenty-Mile Creek, lot 22, concession 5, Township of Louth, Lincoln County. Water color by J. W. Cotton, from an old sketch. Size 5 x 6.

1340—LAURA SECORD'S COTTAGE, CHIPPAWA—Corner Water and Adelaide streets, lots 108-9—In this quaint little cottage Mrs. Secord resided from 1830 until her death in October, 1868. She and her daughter, Mrs. Smith, for some years conducted a private school there. The house still (1917) stands. Water color. Size 5 x 6.

1341—MONUMENT ON THE GRAVE OF LAURA SECORD—Lundy's Lane Burying Ground, Niagara Falls South, Ont.—The inscription reads: "To perpetuate the name and fame of Laura Secord, who walked alone nearly 20 miles by a circuitous, difficult and perilous route, through woods and swamps and over miry roads, to warn a British outpost at De Cew's Falls of an intended attack, and thereby enabled Lieut. Fitzgibbon on the 24th June, 1813, with less than 50 men of H.M. 49th Regiment, about 15 militiamen, and a small force of Six Nation and other Indians, under Captains William Johnson Kerr and Domenique Ducharme, to surprise and attack the enemy at Beechwoods (or Beaver Dams), and after a short engagement to capture Col. Boerstler of the U.S. Army and his entire force of 542 men with two field pieces. This monument, erected by the Ontario Historical Society from contributions of schools, societies, Her Majesty's 49th Regiment, and other militia organizations and private individuals, was unveiled 22nd of June, 1901." Water color. Size 4 x 6.

1342—THE FIRST LEWISTON AND QUEENSTON SUSPENSION BRIDGE, 1850-64—The project of erecting a chain suspension bridge at Queenston had been set on foot in 1836; but building was not commenced until 1850. On March 19th, 1851, the structure, designed and built by Edward W. Serrell, C.E., was opened at Queenston, and a few days later at Lewiston. In 1864, for fear of an ice jam, the guys were taken down, and not being replaced, a storm wrecked the bridge on Feb. 1st. The cables and towers remained intact, but were never used again. The bridge was reconstructed in 1899, the material used being partly that which the gale had left and partly that of the discarded "Upper Bridge," replaced by the present upper steel arch structure. The total length of the cable in the first Queenston bridge was 1,245 feet, and the length of roadway 849 feet. Old engraving, colored. Size 6 x 12. See 1309.

1343—DE CEW HOUSE, LOT 40, THOROLD TOWNSHIP, 1809-1917—Here Lieut (Colonel) James Fitzgibbon had his headquarters while at Beaver Dams. Laura Secord, wife of Sergeant Secord, having heard that the Americans proposed attacking Fitzgibbon, walked from Queenston by a circuitous route for about twenty miles, through bush and swamp, to De Cew's and notified Fitzgibbon, who was stationed there with a detachment of the 49th and a party of Indians. He bluffed Lieut.-Col. Boerstler, the American commander, into the belief that the British force was so strong it would be useless bloodshed to fight, and demanded surrender. Consequently Boerstler surrendered his force of 519 men and 25 officers. This stone house, built by Capt. John De Cew, still (1917) stands, the same outwardly as a hundred years ago, though the interior has been somewhat modernized. Water color by J. W. Cotton. Size 5 x 6. See 1346.

1344—BEAVER DAMS BATTLEFIELD—Situated about a mile east of the present village, close to the Welland Canal—The monument stands near the Niagara Falls and St. Catharines trolley line steel bridge, over a grave which contains the remains of a number of American soldiers who fell during the War of 1812-14. The inscription on the stone reads simply "Beaver Dams, June 24th, 1813." Water color by J. W. Cotton. Size 5 x 7. See 1345.

1345—MONUMENT AT BEAVER DAMS—Thorold Township, Welland County, Ont.—Erected by the Wentworth Historical Society to commemorate the surrender of Lieut.-Col. Boerstler and the American troops to

Lieut. (Colonel) Fitzgibbon, of the 49th Regiment. It stands close to the east side of the present Welland Canal. There are no landmarks to show the precise spot of the surrender. Water color. Size 3 x 5. See 1344.

1346—ROOM IN OLD STONE HOUSE AT DE CEW'S—View showing the fireplace—It was in this house, which is situated on lot 40, about three miles west of the present Town of Thorold, Ont., that Lieut. (Colonel) James Fitzgibbon, with his band of scouts, had taken up headquarters before the memorable skirmish at the Beechwoods, more familiarly known as the Battle of Beaver Dams, June 24th, 1813. The old house was erected 1808-9 by Captain John De Cew, and is now occupied by Mr. Michael J. Griffiths. Water color by J. W. Cotton. Size 5 x 6. See 1343.

1347—OLD STONE MILL, KINGSTON MILLS, ONT.—Site of the first Government grist mill in Upper Canada, erected 1782-3 by Robert Clark, a well-known U.E. Loyalist. It was situated on the Cataraqui River, five miles from Kingston, where the first locks of the Rideau Canal now stand. Farmers brought their grist from Cornwall in the east and the settlements about the Bay of Quinte. Water color from picture in possession of Dr. C. K. Clarke, Toronto. Size 8 x 10.

1348—MURNEY MARTELLO TOWER, KINGSTON, U.C.—One of the four Martello towers, which in early days formed part of Kingston's fortifications. It was a loop-holed guardhouse, built 1837, situated on the lake shore at the west end of the town, south-west corner Macdonald Park. It was built by Contractor Murney, of Belleville, after whom it is named. Water color from picture in possession of Dr. C. K. Clarke, Toronto. Size 6 x 11.

1349—"KINGSTON, ON KING'S RIVER—Drawn from nature by Aug. Kollner. Lith. by Deroy. Printed by Jacomme & Co. in 1849." This picture is from the north-easterly end of Fort Henry, overlooking Navy Bay. The main features in the picture are: 1, The stone frigate in the Royal Navy Yard, now the site of the Royal Military College. 2, Tete du Pont Barracks. 3, Cataraqui Bridge. 4, St. Mary's Cathedral. 5, Regiopolis College. 6, Tower of St. Andrew's Church. 7, Martello tower in the harbor. 8, Murney tower, now in Macdonald Park. 9, City Hall. 10, Navy Bay. The term, "King's River," was in all probability a creation, as there is no historical foundation for the Cataraqui having ever been known as such. Chromo lithograph. See 7 x 11. See 1350, 1355, 1372, 1376.

1350—KINGSTON, U.C., 1827—View from Barriefield, showing: 1, H.M.S. "Grampus"; 2, Stone Frigate, now the site of the Royal Military College; 3, Fort Frederick; 4, Commodore Barry's residence; 5, Marine Cottages; 6, Marine Hospital; 7, St. George's (Anglican) Church; 8, Market house; 9, Dean's schoolhouse; 10, Ordnance Stores; 11, Cataraqui Bridge, connecting Kingston and Barriefield. Lithograph. Size 6 x 12. See 1349, 1355, 1372.

1351—FAIRFIELD MILL AT MILL CREEK, NOW FLOATING BRIDGE—Built by Harmon Fairfield, grandson of William Fairfield. Water color from picture in possession of Dr. C. K. Clarke, Toronto. Size 11 x 14.

1352—FIRST STONE HOUSE ERECTED IN KINGSTON, U.C.—It stands on the corner of Queen and Ontario streets, was built for a commissariat department, and used as such for many years while the British troops were stationed in Kingston. It was subsequently changed into an hotel, continuing as such until recently, when it became a bottling works. It is in excellent state of preservation. Photograph, colored. Size 7 x 9.

1353—**ONE OF KINGSTON'S OLD HOUSES**—Stone house, Rideau street, overlooking Cataraqui Bay, built about 1800; occupied for many years by Col. McLean, a retired English officer. The house, which is still standing, is near the Kingston & Pembroke Ry. Roundhouse, and is the property of the company. Water color from picture in possession of Dr. C. K. Clarke, Toronto. Size 9 x 10.

1354—**BUST OF SIR JOHN A. MACDONALD**—In the crypt of St. Paul's Cathedral, London, England. Photograph. Size 7 x 10. See 177.

1355—**CATARAQUI (KINGSTON)**—A south-east view, 1783, with key —This is the first picture of Cataraqui, showing what was left of Fort Frontenac in that year. The city of Kingston is situated at the head of the St. Lawrence, at the outlet of Lake Ontario. The harbor is an excellent one, and ships of any size can be accommodated in perfect safety. In 1671 the place was known as Cataraqui, and visited by De Courcelles, the Governor of New France. He was succeeded by Count Frontenac, and the fort was built by him, and named in his honor. The fort was held by the French until 1758, when it fell into the hands of the British under Colonel Bradstreet. In 1783 a number of Loyalist emigrants under Captain Michael Grass settled in what is now the township of Kingston. Water color by James Peachey, ensign, 60th Regiment. Taken by Louis Kotte, Size 11 x 21. See 1349, 1350, 1372.

1356—**KINGSTON, C.W.**, 1851—From Fort Henry Hill, north-east of Main Gate. The view shows: 1. Dockyards, now (1917) site of Royal Military College. 2. Sydenham Street Methodist Church. 3. St. George's Anglican Church (Cathedral). 4. City Hall. 5. Regiopolis (R. C.) College, founded about 1850. 6. St. Mary's (R.C.) Cathedral. 7. Tete du Pont Barracks. 8. St. Andrew's (Presbyterian) Church. 9. Cataraqui bridge. Water color. Size 5 x 7.

1357—**KINGSTON, ONT.**, 1880—View from Barriefield Common, East of city—The picture shows: 1. North-easterly end of Barriefield Common. 2. Wood scow coming down from Rideau Canal. 3. M. Strachan's sawmill. 4. Steamer "Firefly," a Rideau Canal-er. 5. Sydenham Street Methodist Church. 6. St. Mary's Cathedral. 7. Old St. Andrew's Church. Water color, from original drawing by Lucius Richard O'Brien, for "Picturesque Canada." Size 5 x 7.

1358—**PENETANGUISHENE, ON AN ARM OF GEORGIAN BAY**— View taken from the east wing (removed in 1892) of Georgian Bay Hotel, looking n.w. across Roberts and Peel streets and harbor. The main building of hotel is on n.e. cor. of Main and Roberts streets. Key: 1. Beck & Co.'s sawmill and lumber yards. 2. Penetanguishene or Main street. 3. Original Methodist Church, built 1833. 4. "Canada House," sheds and stables. 5. Post-office block. 6. Peel street. 7. All Saints' Church (Anglican), built 1874. 8. Church street. 9. Brick chimney for glass furnace and manufactory, erected 1879-80. 10. Buchanan's carriage shop, burned 1884, replaced by residence of Dr. A. P. McDonald. 11. W. F. H. Thompson's general store, frame skeleton, Main street. 12. Building of H. H. Thompson, general merchant. 13. Residence of Dr. Spohn, formerly home of A. A. Thompson—first brick building in Penetang, erected 1835. Water color, from original drawing by Schell & Hogan for "Picturesque Canada," 1880. Size 3 x 7.

1359—**GRAND TRUNK RY. VIADUCT, PORT HOPE**—It was known as the Albert Bridge, so named in honor of the Prince Consort. A coincidence in connection with the viaduct is that it was built in 1856, measured 1856 feet, and rested on 56 piers. The Grand Trunk, 1887-93, replaced it by a double track structure on large stone piers, and in 1906 put in new heavy girders. The view shows in addition to the viaduct: 1. Midland Railway elevator, since torn down. 2. Roman Catholic Church. 3. St. John's (Anglican) Church. 4. Baptist Church. 5. Chimney of car factory. 6. Town Hall, destroyed by fire and rebuilt. 7. St. Mark's (Anglican) Church. 8. Elevator, still (1916) in existence. 9. Dock. 10. Harbor. Water color, from original drawing by F. E. Lummis, for "Picturesque Canada," 1880. Size 5 x 7.

1360—"ROCKWOOD," KINGSTON, U.C.—View from the grounds. Photograph, colored, from picture in possession of Dr. C. K. Clarke, Toronto. Size 7 x 12. See 1363.

1361—FAIRFIELD HOUSE, KINGSTON, U.C.—This quaint U. E. L. dwelling on Bath road was built in 1793 by William Fairfield. It is still in a fine state of preservation, and has been occupied by four generations. Stephen Fairfield succeeded his father. Harmon Fairfield succeeded Stephen, and the present occupant, Thomas D., is the son of Harmon Fairfield. Wm. Fairfield, who was one of the pioneers of Ernestown, succeeded Christopher Robinson as a member of the Second Legislature for Addington and Ontario. Water color from picture in possession of Dr. C. K. Clarke, Toronto. Size 10 x 10.

1362—CARTWRIGHT STABLES, KINGSTON, U.C.—At Rockwood, afterwards first asylum in Upper Canada. Of these stables Dr. Sampson, a leading physician of the town, remarked on one occasion, in passing with a friend:—

> "Oh, much I wish that I were able
> To build a house like Cartwright's stable,
> For it doth cause me great remorse
> To be worse lodged than Cartwright's horse."

Water color from picture in possession of Dr. C. K. Clarke, Toronto. Size 8 x 9.

1363—"ROCKWOOD," THE CARTWRIGHT RESIDENCE, KINGSTON, U.C.—Built about 1837 by J. S. Cartwright, son of Hon. Richard Cartwright, a one-time member of the Legislative Council of Upper Canada, on his property at Rockwood. A few hundred feet south, on the right hand side, towards the lake, stood "Rockwood Cottage," the home of Sir Richard Cartwright, in his boyhood. "Rockwood" is now the residence of the Superintendent of the Hospital for Insane, Kingston. Photograph, colored, from picture in possession of Dr. C. K. Clarke, Toronto. Size 7 x 9. See 1360. 7 x 9. See 1360.

1364—AN OLD BLOCK HOUSE, KINGSTON, U.C.—Rooney Castle, at the north-easterly end of Sydenham street, overlooking the quarries between it and Montreal street. It was one of the five blockhouses built soon after the War of 1812 as a defence around the limits of the town. These blockhouses were originally connected by a high stockade, and Rooney Castle was the last to remain. For many years it was occupied, but was abandoned about 1900, and in 1909 was demolished. Water color from picture in possession of Dr. C. K. Clarke, Toronto. Size 6 x 10.

1365—"THE ADMIRALTY HOUSE, KINGSTON, CANADA WEST— Late residence of Captain Fowell, of H.M.S. Cherokee. J. Gillespie, del. Scobie & Balfour, lith., Toronto." Opposite the house is the man-of-war "Cherokee." The Admiralty House, also known as the Commodore House, was on the Royal Military College grounds in front of the present residence of the Commandant. It was torn down to make room for the new building. When the forces were removed to England the Admiralty House was abandoned as naval headquarters. The "Cherokee" was built at Kingston in

1843-4. She was of wood, schooner rigged, 800 tons burden, disarmed about 1860, and ran for years as a passenger steamer between Halifax and St. John. Lithograph. Size 10 x 14.

1366—**PORT HOPE, C.W.,** 1851—View taken from the south-west, with key. Water color. Size 5 x 7.

1367—**FALL OF TABLE ROCK**—On June 25th, 1850, the great overhanging mass known as Table Rock, on the Canadian side of Niagara Falls, crashed into the abyss below, leaving only a narrow bench along the bank. It fell at noon, when few people were in the vicinity, and no lives were lost. The driver of a local omnibus had just taken off his horses for their mid-day meal, and was washing his vehicle, when he felt a preliminary cracking. He was able to escape, but the omnibus was plunged into the gulf beneath. For miles around the sound of crashing rock was heard, the ledge being of immense proportions—two hundred feet long, sixty feet wide, and a hundred feet deep. This was not the first fall of rock here, fragments having broken off previous to 1750 and on several subsequent occasions. The name, "Table Rock," still adheres to the place. Water color. Size 4 x 7.

1368—**BLONDIN CROSSING THE NIAGARA RIVER ON A ROPE**—With a man on his back—Blondin, the noted tightrope walker (whose real name was Jean Francois Gravelet), was born in Hesden, France, 1824. On August 17th, 1859, he crossed the Niagara River on a rope two inches in diameter, just below the railway suspension bridge, carrying his agent, Henry Colcord, on his back. Five times in crossing they stopped to rest, Mr. Colcord dismounting each time. The perilous trip occupied forty-two minutes. Among Blondin's other feats were balancing on a cable, hanging from it by his hands and feet, standing on his head, and lowering himself to the surface of the water. He also trundled a loaded wheelbarrow across, and walked in a sack. In 1860 Blondin gave a special performance in honor of the Prince of Wales. His death occurred in 1897. Water color. Size 4 x 7.

1369—**BROCKVILLE, U.C.,** 1841—Sketch from above the town off what is now called Refugee Island. The "Three Sisters," below the town, are in the centre of picture; Morristown, in New York State, on the right. St. Peter's Church, Blockhouse Island, and the Jones Wharf, with vessels moored to it, are conspicuous. The buildings shown immediately to the left of the Blockhouse are "Colton's Foundry"; the warehouse of Sydney and Henry Jones, a building since incorporated in the C.P.R. freight shed; and Flint's Hotel. The commanding position of St. Peter's Church has often been noticed from the river, as shown in picture. Pencil drawing by Frederick Holloway. Size 7 x 11. The views of Brockvilyle, Nos. 1375, 1384, and that of Morristown, were a gift of Rev. H. Bedford-Jones, Brockville, to J. Ross Robertson.

1370—**ORANGE ARCH ERECTED ON PRINCESS STREET, KINGSTON, ONT.,** 1860—In honor of H. R. H. Prince of Wales—Because of the demonstrations and special preparations made by Orangemen in Kingston and Belleville, H.R.H. Prince of Wales (late King Edward), on the advice of the Duke of Newcastle, declined to land at these places in September, 1860. One of the Orange arches erected in Kingston was on Princess street, facing southerly and adjacent to King street. The picture shows: 1, The News office. 2, Dr. Sullivan's. 3, Arch. 4, McGuire's wharf. 5, The harbor. 6, Fern's building in 1860, occupied as a shoe store. The buildings have been slightly changed for business purposes. Water color. Size 6 x 8.

1371—**GRASS HOUSE**—Four miles from Kingston, on shore of Lake Ontario; built 1783-4 by Capt. Michael Grass, a U.E. Loyalist, who had owned a farm near New York; was a British prisoner of war with the French at Fort Frontenac for a time; refused a captaincy in Republican service during Revolutionary War. At the close of the war he commanded a party of Loyalists, who settled in the Township of Kingston. Water color from original in possession of Dr. C. K. Clarke, Superintendent Toronto General Hospital. Size 5 x 6.

1372—KINGSTON, C.W., IN 1862—The place was known in 1671 as Cataraqui, and visited by De Courcelles, Governor of New France. He was succeeded by Frontenac, who built the fort named in his honor, and which the French held until 1758. It then fell into the hands of the British under Col. Bradstreet. In 1783 a number of Loyalists, under Captain Michael Grass, settled in what afterwards became the Township of Kingston, and the town plot was laid out in that year. About 1788 Kingston was selected by the British Government as a military and naval station. The Legislature of the Province of Canada, after the Act of Union, held three sessions in Kingston, from 1841-44, when the seat of Government was removed to Montreal. The picture shows: 1, Ontario street, in front of City Hall; 2, City Hall tower; 3, Sydenham Street Methodist Church; 4, Swift's Wharf; 5, The harbor. Water color from a sketch by G. H. Andrews, of the London Illustrated News. Size 5 x 9. See 1349-50, 1355, 1376.

1373—CATARAQUI BRIDGE, KINGSTON, U.C., SHOWING TOLL HOUSE—The bridge, which was formally opened, August 5th, 1829, was erected to supersede the ferry established about 1789, and running from Fort Frontenac (Kingston) to the Pittsburg shore. It is still in a good state of repair. Water color by Miss E. Fraser, Kingston. Size 7 x 14.

1374—ENGAGEMENT AT DICKINSON'S LANDING, 10TH NOV., 1813—This engagement is identical with Hoople's Creek, a quarter of a mile west of where Dickinson's Landing is to-day (1917). The Americans came from Ogdensburg and were met by the Grenville and Dundas militia and by them defeated. Hoople's Creek was so called because Hoople got from the Government in 1797-8 a grant of land here. Lithograph in color by Coke Smyth. Size 11 x 15.

1375—BROCKVILLE, U.C., 1841—From a point in the river opposite— It shows St. Peter's Anglican Church to the right on the hill and the block-house on island in centre. On the extreme left of picture the house with trees behind was built probably about 1815-18 by a Mr. Fraser, Collector of Customs. In the centre is the old Court House, of brick, built 1824. To the immediate left of the Court House is the first Presbyterian Church building in Brockville, afterwards destroyed by fire, while the first Methodist Church building is seen to the right of the Court House. Pencil drawing by Frederick Holloway. Size 7 x 11.

1376—KINGSTON, U.C., 1819—The sketch, of which this picture is a copy, was made by Cadet Bayfield, R.N., afterwards Admiral Bayfield. It came into possession of Major-General Cameron, R.M.C. At the dockyard are shown several frigates which had been active in the War of 1812, one being the Princess Charlotte, 102 guns. The fortification shown to the left of picture is Fort Henry, successor to old Fort Frontenac. In 1820 barracks were added to the fort, and in 1832 the modern defence erected. The trees on the right of the foreground are on Barriefield Heights. Water color. Size 10 x 27. See 1349, 1350, 1355.

1377—MORRISTOWN VILLAGE, ST. LAWRENCE COUNTY, N.Y.— This sketch of Morristown is taken from one of the "Three Sisters," and shows the head of one of the other islands. The Protestant Episcopal Church is visible near the centre. The building more to the left, with tower, is the Methodist Chapel, and on the extreme left is the old windmill, used at times as a jail. On the right, near the well-known Ford family house, is shown an old mill which has disappeared. The view looks into the bay, into which the little creek shown flows. Pencil drawing by Frederick Holloway, 1841. Size 6 x 10.

1378—TURKEY POINT, REMAINS OF EARTHWORKS AT—From the site of the old town of Charlotteville, Norfolk County. Turkey Point was first settled in 1793, and was visited two years later by Governor Simcoe, who reserved near there the town-site of Charlotteville. It is said that the Governor purposed founding here the commercial and governmental metropolis of Upper Canada. From 1802-15 the District Courts were held at Charlotteville. After the war, however, they were removed to Vittoria, and the town relapsed once more into Turkey Point. When hostilities broke out in 1812, the Court House was used for barracks purposes, and a substantial fort erected, known as Fort Norfolk. The Americans, with three schooners, attempted to make a landing here, but were forced to retreat up the lake by the four hundred British and colonial troops defending the fort. No traces save the trenches now remain of the old-time judicial metropolis. Water color by W. Edgar Cantelon. Size 6 x 11.

1379—PRINCE OF WALES' EXCURSION DOWN THE RAPIDS OF THE ST. LAWRENCE RIVER, 1860—During the visit of the Prince of Wales to Canada he had many enjoyable outings, one of which was that of running the rapids. On the 28th of August the Royal party, with Sir Edmund Walker Head, Governor-General, the Commander-in-Chief of the Forces, and other distinguished Canadians, left Montreal at 11 a.m. by rail for Dickinson's Landing, where they embarked on the steamer Kingston of the Royal Mail Line and steamed down the rapids of the Long Sault, Coteau, Cedars, Cascades and Lachine, arriving at Montreal at 7 p.m. The Prince in after life frequently alluded to this trip. Water color from the original by George H. Andrews, of the Royal Water Color Society of Great Britain. Size 10 x 20.

1380—BROCKVILLE, C.W., 1851—From Old Man's Island, opposite town. With key. Water color. Size 5 x 7.

1381—OLD JESUIT MISSION, SANDWICH, U.C.—It was situated on part of lot 63, town of Sandwich, and formed a portion of the Assomption Church property. The Jesuit Fathers first landed at Sandwich in 1728, when Father Armand de la Richardie became a missionary to the Hurons. He labored with zeal and success, and in 1746 built a church and mission house. The remaining part of the latter, which stood on the church property on a splendid elevation overlooking the Detroit River, was destroyed by fire, 29th June, 1912. A wine cellar was erected on the site, and the property is now (1917) owned by Messrs. Gordon Wickett and W. C. Kennedy, of Windsor. Water color. Size 4 x 6.

1382—ENGAGEMENT IN THE THOUSAND ISLANDS, RIVER ST. LAWRENCE—The Americans went down the river in boats, the Canadians following, 11th November, 1813. The latter were victorious in the encounter, which took place near Ogden's and Touissaint's (All Saints') Island. The next day was fought the battle of Crysler's Farm. Lithograph in color by Coke Smyth. Size 11 x 15.

1383—BROCKVILLE, U.C., 1853—With key—From the west of Brockville, looking across the old Mill Pond, through which ran a creek, now much contracted by straightening. The road on which the houses in the centre front is King street, the chief business street in Brockville. Water color by Gen. A. R. V. Crease, R.E. Size 6 x 10.

1384—BROCKVILLE, U.C., 1841—Looking up the river from below King street—St. Peter's Church, the first ecclesiastical building to be erected in Brockville, 1826, is shown in its original, unenlarged condition. The first enlargement was made a few years later. To the left of the picture is shown the Island, with blockhouse on it, and a wharf, near which stood Flint's Hotel. Beyond them is a group of islands, a number of which have been sold. Others are leased by the town of Brockville as a park. The spire of what was the first Presbyterian Church is seen to the right about the trees. Pencil drawing by Frederick Holloway. Size 7 x 11.

1385—"THOUSAND ISLANDS (LAKE ONTARIO AND RIVER ST. LAWRENCE)—Drawn from nature by Aug. Kollner. Lith. by Deroy. Printed by Jacomme & Co. New York and Paris, published by Goupil & Co. Entered according to Act of Congress in the year 1851 by Wm. Schaus in the Clerk's Office of the District Court for the Southern District of New York." Lithograph. Size 9 x 12.

1386—FORT CARLETON, NEAR KINGSTON, U.C.—A fortification of pre-conquest days—Carleton Island, named after Sir Guy Carleton (Lord Dorchester), lies near Grand Island, opposite Kingston, nearest the south shore, where Lake Ontario descends into the St. Lawrence. It is not known when the first fortifications were erected, but probably by the French as the British found the place strongly fortified at the time of the conquest. As it commanded the main channel of the St. Lawrence, they greatly strengthened it. Sir John Johnson and Col. John Butler, of the "Rangers," encamped with the Indians from the Mohawk Valley, on Carleton Island, in 1775, when on their way to join the British in Montreal. Long, in his "Voyages," published in 1791, says it had an excellent harbor, with strong fortifications and well garrisoned. Before the War of 1812 the island was guarded by a military detachment from Kingston. After the war, however, it formed a part of Cape Vincent Township, Jefferson County, N.Y. The moat that surrounded the fort was dug in the rock, and so was the well in the north-western portion of the works. North of the fort lay the garrison cemetery, and beyond the ramparts an Indian burial ground. The view is from the n.n.e. point of the fort. Water color. Size 3 x 6.

1387—UNITED EMPIRE LOYALIST MONUMENT, ADOLPHUS-TOWN, COUNTY LENNOX, ONTARIO—It stands in what is known as the U.E. Loyalist Burying Ground, on the farm of Nicholas Hagerman. Here on their arrival from the United States in 1784, the Loyalists knelt in thanksgiving and celebrated their first communion on top of an over-turned canoe. On 16th June, 1884, to commemorate the centennial celebra-tion of the landing of the Loyalists, the corner-stone of the monument was laid with Masonic honors. Patriotic addresses were delivered, one of which was given by L. L. Bogart, then over eighty years of age, and the oldest living male representative of the U.E.L. band. The inscription on the monument reads: "In memory of the U.E. Loyalists, who, through loyalty to British institutions, left the United States and landed on these shores on the 16th of June, A.D. 1784." On a hill a short distance to the right of the steamboat landing in Adolphustown the St. Alban's Anglican Memorial church contains a brass tablet bearing the following inscription: "One hundred years after the landing of the United Empire Loyalists on these shores, this Church of St. Alban the Martyr is built in proud memory of those patriots who became the founders of the Province of Ontario, in Honor, Loyalty and Fear of God, 1884." Photograph, colored. Size 5 x 6.

1388—MACNAB, SIR ALLAN NAPIER, 1798-1862—Photograph from the painting in Senate corridor, Parliament Buildings, Ottawa. Size 6 x 7. Half length. See 26.

1389—MERRITT, HON. WM. HAMILTON—Projector of the Welland Canal—Born in Bedford, N.Y. At an early age came to Upper Canada with his parents, who settled at the Twelve-Mile Creek (St. Catharines). Served in the War of 1812-14. In 1816 purchased from the Hamilton estate a large portion of the land upon which the city of St. Catharines now stands. In 1818 assisted in making the first survey of the Welland Canal. He drew up a memorial to the Legislature, and the foundation for one of the greatest waterways in the world was laid. In 27th November, 1829, the first vessels passed through the canal. Mr. Merritt was elected member for Haldimand in 1833. Declined twice the office of Inspector-General. On 29th Sept., 1860, was elected by acclamation to the Legislative Council. Interested in the trade and navigation of the St. Lawrence, and had several interviews with the Government relative to deepening the river. His death took place 5th July, 1862. Water color from a portrait in possession of his granddaughter, Miss Catharine Welland Merritt, St. Catharines, Ont. Water color. Size 5 x 7. Head and shoulders.

1390—KEEFER, THOMAS COLTRIN, C.M.G., 1821-1915—A founder of the Canadian Society of Civil Engineers—Born at Thorold, Ont., and educated at Upper Canada College. In 1838 he began his career as an engineer, his first employment being on the Erie Canal. He was subsequently engaged on the Welland Canal, and then as chief engineer of the Ottawa River works. Victoria Bridge, Montreal, is the outcome of plans of Mr. Keefer. He also constructed waterworks at Montreal, Hamilton, Ottawa and other cities, and for a time was Chief Engineer of Railways in Upper and Lower Canada. In 1847 he commenced the advocacy of the Grand Trunk Railway, and in 1869, of the Canadian Pacific. Mr. Keefer was the author of a brilliant essay entitled "The Philosophy of Railroads," which attracted much attention. He was a brother of Samuel Keefer, C.E. Photograph, colored. Size 4 x 5. Head and shoulders.

1391—BY, LIEUT.-COL. JOHN, R.E., 1780-1853—The founder of Ottawa, known in the early days as Bytown—Came to Canada in 1800 as a lieutenant in the Royal Engineers, and shortly after his arrival was entrusted with the construction of the boat canal at the Cascades above Montreal. On successfully completing this undertaking he was removed to Quebec, where he superintended the building of the four martello towers outside the walls of that city. In 1811 went to England, but returned to Canada fifteen years later to construct the Rideau Canal. It was during the time that the canal was being built that the first huts were raised by Colonel By on the site of the present city of Ottawa. In 1832 the Colonel returned to England. Copy of silhouette in possession of Sir Frederick Williams-Taylor, Montreal. Size 3 x 4. Head and shoulders, in profile.

1392—BY, MRS. JOHN—Wife of Lieut.-Col. By, R.E., founder of the city of Ottawa and builder of the Rideau Canal. Copy of silhouette in possession of Sir Frederick Williams-Taylor, Montreal. Size 3 x 4. Head and shoulders, in profile.

1393—GILKISON, CAPTAIN WILLIAM—Born at Irvine, Ayrshire, Scotland, March 9th, 1777. In 1796 he emigrated to New York, and was given command of a schooner employed in the North-west Company's service on Lake Erie, by John Jacob Astor. Married at Amherstburg, in 1803, Isabella, daughter of Commodore the Hon. Alexander Grant. During the War of 1812 was appointed Field Quartermaster-General, with rank of captain, by Major-General Sir Isaac Brock. Captain Gilkison took part in the battle of Crysler's Farm, August, 1813, and on that occasion carried off the field the wounded Major Duncan Fraser. In 1815 returned to Scotland to edu cate his family. Came to Canada again in 1829, purchasing a large tract of land in Brantford, where he settled. Founded and named the town of Elora, 1832. Died near Onondaga, April 25th, 1833, and is buried in the old Mohawk Churchyard, Brantford. Water color from portrait in possession of his granddaughter, Miss A. I. Grant Gilkison, of Brantford. Size 3 x 3½. See 1394.

1394—GILKISON, CAPTAIN WILLIAM, 1777-1833—Silhouette. Size 3 x 4. See 1393.

17

1395—BIDWELL, MARSHALL SPRING—Member Legislative Assembly, U.C., 1824-36—He was born in Massachusetts, 1799; came to Canada with his father, Barnabas Bidwell, who became first master of the Bath Academy. The son studied law, practising in Kingston. Represented Lennox and Addington for thirteen consecutive sessions, during four of which he was Speaker. Bidwell, who was defeated in the general election of 1836, tried to secure the passing of an Act to abolish the law of primogeniture, and strongly championed Responsible Government. Although in sympathy with the Rebellion, he did not advise violence in any degree. Was, however, compelled to leave the country, going to New York, where he was admitted to the bar, and soon became recognized as a scholarly member of the profession. On his death in New York, 24th Dec., 1872, Judge Daniel P. Ingraham said, "A more learned lawyer never practised in our courts." Water color. Size 3 x 4. Head and shoulders.

1396—PULPIT AND PRECENTOR'S BOX, "OLD STONE CHURCH," BEAVERTON, ONT.—The rails of the square enclosure where the choir sat immediately behind the high pulpit with their backs to the congregation, the precentor's box and the pulpit balustrade, with its carved newel top carved from a solid block of oak, are now faded, like the pulpit upholstery, to the color of the pine pews. Drawing in water color by Owen Staples. Size 4 x 6. See 1397, 1403.

1397—PIONEER STOVES IN "OLD STONE CHURCH," BEAVERTON. ONT.—About 1855 the stoves shown were procured for the church. They are big cast iron box affairs, four and a half feet wide and five feet long. They stand yet (1917) in the rear of the building, with doors opening through a low bricked arch, furnace like, into the vestibule, from where they were fired with four-foot logs. Drawing in water color by Owen Staples. Size 4 x 6. See 1396, 1403.

1398—PERTH, U.C., 1853—Situated on the River Tay. The original picture was made from the brow of the hill near the residence of the late Dr. Thom, which at the time was the only residence in that part of the town, all the land being an extensive farm. The section is now well built. The principal buildings shown are still standing, as are also some of the old shacks in the foreground. In 1853 the portion of the town in the neighborhood given was the hub; now it has changed westward. Sixty years ago a great deal of timber floated down the River Tay, which later became the Tay Canal. The stone bridge crossing the river was torn down in order to build a swing bridge over the canal. The key gives main points in picture. From an oil painting by Mr. Field, of Perth. Size 7 x 14.

1399—ST. CATHARINES, U.C., 1850—View from the south bank of the Twelve-Mile Creek—The mills shown are the old Norris grist mills, now the Kinleith paper mills, and the green sward is the side of the hill leading down to the Twelve-Mile Creek, now part of the old, or first Welland Canal. To the left of the picture, the steep hill is part of the Merritt property, owned by Dr. W. H. Merritt. Between this incline and the bank where the Stephenson House stands, is part of the old Welland Canal. The greater part of the land on which the city of St. Catharines is built, was purchased in 1816 by the Hon. W. H. Merritt from the Hon. Robert Hamilton, of Queenston. The purchase consisted of about 400 acres, the larger portion being a level plateau, on the south of which is the ridge commonly known as "the mountain." A patent had been granted to Hon. Robert Hamilton, who, on the first survey of the place in 1809, named it in honor of his wife, Catharine Askin. "St. Catharines," however, was not universally used until after the purchase by Hon. W. H. Merritt in 1816, when, as a compliment to his wife, also called Catharine, the name was permanently established. Water color from a drawing in possession of Miss C. Welland Merritt, St. Catharines. With key. Size 11x15.

1400—BRIDGE OVER THE CHAUDIERE FALLS, OTTAWA—"Plan, Elevation and Section of the Truss Bridge, 212 feet Span, over the Chaudiere Falls, Ottawa River. Designed and executed under the direction of Lt. Coll. John By, Commanding Royal Engineer, Rideau Canal. Finished, 1828. C. Hullmandel's Lithography." The structure was commenced in 1827 and carried away by a windstorm the following year. A new bridge, erected 1829, met the same fate, and the third, destroyed by fire in 1900, was the next year replaced by a steel structure. Lithograph. Size 15 x 24. See 1794.

1401—"BARRIE—On Lake Simcoe, Canada West—View from the south-east—Drawn by Captn. W. H. Grubbe, Hone. East India Compy. Artilly., October, 1853. H. Scobie, Lith., Toronto. W. H. Grubbe." With key. Size 8 x 24.

1402—BEAVERTON, ONTARIO COUNTY, 1890—View from St. Andrew's Church: 1, Knox Church; 2, Planing Mills and Factory; 3, Public School; 4, Thorah Island and Lake Simcoe; 5, Phoenix Foundry; 6, John Proctor's Residence; 7, Harbor; 8, Dobson's Flour Mill; 9, Victoria Park; 10, Hamilton House; 11, Ethel Park; 12, Dr. A. Grant's Residence; 13, McMillan Bros.' Rink and Carriage Works; 14, A. P. Cockburn's Residence; 15, G. R. Proctor's Residence; 16, Old School Ground; 17, Telegraph Office; 18, Dr. A. McKay's Residence. The second building is to the north of No. 6. The building is not shown in this picture. The street north of No. 18 is Simcoe street. Drawing in water color. Size 7 x 18.

1403—"OLD STONE CHURCH" (ST. ANDREW'S PRESBYTERIAN), BEAVERTON, ONT.—Away back in 1832 a few Glengarry folk, who came to Canada from Islay, Scotland, settled on the eastern shores of Lake Simcoe. Soon the need of a place of worship was felt. St. Andrew's congregation was founded and the building of the old kirk commenced shortly afterwards. It was constructed of grey limestone, by heroic pioneers of the neighboring country, and in 1840 neared completion. For ten years the people worshipped in the unfinished church without floor or pew. The first minister, a graduate of Queen's University, was Rev. David Watson, A.M., D.D., who from 1853-98 carried on the work. The old and much-loved clergyman died in Beaverton, December, 1903, and to mark the fiftieth anniversary of his ordination, a memorial window was put in new St. Andrew's, Beaverton, and a brass tablet erected in the "Old Stone Church." Water color. Size 6 x 7. See 1396, 1397.

1404—SHICKLUNA'S (SHICALUNA'S) SHIPYARDS, ST. CATHARINES, U.C., 1860—At foot of old Welland Canal, showing sailing vessels. Water color from original in possession of Miss Catherine Welland Merritt, St. Catharines. Size 4½ x 5.

1405—"CHAUDIERE FALLS, OTTAWA RIVER, UPPER CANADA—From a sketch by an officer of the Royal Staff Corps prior to the erection of the bridges thrown over the Falls in 1827 by Lieut.-Colonel J. By, Comr. Royal Engrs. Rideau Canal, Upper Canada. Lithographed by C. Ingrey, 310 Strand, London." Lithograph in color. Size 9 x 15.

1406—RIDEAU RIFLE RANGES, OTTAWA, 1876—Picturesquely situated on the bank of the Rideau River, immediately south of what is now (1917) Laurier avenue, Ottawa. The ranges were abandoned as such in 1897, and the land has become Strathcona Park. Water color. Size 11 x 15.

1407—LAST RAFT OF SQUARE TIMBER FLOATED DOWN THE OTTAWA RIVER—The photograph from which this picture is made was taken in 1901, from Queen's Wharf, Ottawa. It shows Nepean Point, a rocky promontory overlooking the river, and one of the piers of the Inter-provincial Bridge, then in course of erection, finished in 1903. The raft is nearly completed. It was the last to float down the Ottawa River, over the slides at Ottawa and thence down the St. Lawrence to Quebec. The rafts-men slept in the small house, and the large caboose was used for cooking. Near at hand is seen the tug in readiness to tow the timber to Quebec for shipment to England. Water color. Size 6 x 9.

1408—**OTTAWA, C.W.,** 1855—Now the capital of Canada—On the Ottawa River, 87 miles from its confluence with the St. Lawrence, and at the mouth of the Rideau River. Founded by Col. By, of the Royal Engineers, commissioned in 1827 to construct the Rideau Canal. In 1854 Bytown, named after its founder, was created a city and its name changed to Ottawa. The canal divided the city into the Upper and Lower Towns. In 1857 it was selected by Queen Victoria as the capital of the Dominion of Canada. The corner-stone of the Parliament Buildings was laid by King Edward VII., then Prince of Wales, in 1860, and the first Parliament of the Dominion was held there in 1867. The picture is taken from the east side of the Military Barracks, which stood on the site of the present Parliament Buildings, and shows that part of the old town bounded on the north by the Ottawa River, on the east by Sussex street, on the south by Rideau street, and on the west by the Rideau Canal and Ottawa River. With key. Water color. Size 5 x 9.

1409—**NARROW ESCAPE AT THE CHAUDIERE FALLS**—Lives of nine men saved—The accident occurred at night, in the summer of 1853, at the Chaudiere Falls, where the crib or raft, missed the slide and was carried to the edge of the Fall, and held there on the point of a projecting rock. Early in the morning the perilous situation of the men was observed and nearly everyone in Ottawa was at the river side, at every point of vantage, watching the work of the rescuers. Mr. Charles B. Wright, father of Sheriff Wright, of Hull, managed the rescue. It was impossible to get a rocket to carry a light rope across, so Mr. Wright tied a light cord to a stone, and, after several attempts, landed the stone with the cord attached. A smaller rope was drawn over, and then a heavy rope or cable; this was made fast to a gin pole on the rock, and tightened by a crab or wrench. Then Wright and his fellow rescuers rigged up a sling similar to those used in rescuing people from vessels. The first man to come across was the heaviest of the nine on the raft, and to prove to his comrades that the arrangement was safe he went back to the crib and was the last man to be hauled across. Even food and utensils were saved. The rescuers are on a rock to the east of the Falls. This rock forms part of the mainland on the Hull side of the river, where the Eddy Mill now (1917) stands. The people in the foreground are standing on a small island near the Ottawa shore, and to the north of this are the slides through which the raft should have passed if properly guided. Water color. Size 7 x 10.

1410—**SAPPER'S BRIDGE, OTTAWA,** 1867—View looking south. The bridge, which connects Sparks and Rideau streets, was built in 1832 by the British Government in connection with the Rideau Canal, and rebuilt along with the Dufferin Bridge, 1873-4. Sapper's Bridge was demolished in 1912, and the space between it and Dufferin bridge converted into a wide plaza with the Post Office as the base. Water color by Henry Cotton. Size 7 x 10.

1411—**MACKAY'S WHARF AND WAREHOUSES, HAMILTON, C.W.,** 1864—For the accommodation of the merchants and marine trade of the city, Aeneas Donald Mackay, an enterprising pioneer citizen of Hamilton, who emigrated from Golspie, Sutherlandshire, Scotland, in 1849, built on Burlington Bay front, at the foot of James street, the wharf and warehouses shown in the picture. Since 1860 all the large lake steamers have used this wharf, which is now (1917) the property of the Canada Steamship Lines. Water color. Size 4 x 6.

1412—SMITH'S TAVERN, HAMILTON, C.W., 1850—An early Masonic meeting place—The original building in which Barton Lodge met from January, 1796, to November, 1797, was of log construction, situated in the Township of Barton, now the north-west corner of King and Wellington streets, Hamilton. As seen by the picture, this pioneer tavern was more extensive in 1850 than in 1797. The log house had practically disappeared; for it had been covered with a sheeting of clapboard about 1830 when the two-storey building to the left and the driving shed on the right of view, were erected. In 1840 the tavern and surrounding grounds were known as "Victoria Gardens." The front door of the original tavern was 80 feet west of Wellington street and the same distance north of King street, Hamilton. There are now three buildings on the old site, the east end branch of the Bank of Hamilton being on the corner. Drawing in color. Size 4 x 6.

1413—BUCHANAN, ISAAC, 1810-88—Member of the old-time dry goods firm of Buchanan, Harris & Co., Hamilton, Montreal and Liverpool. Photograph, colored. Size 3 x 3. Head and shoulders. See 942.

1414—HARRIS, ROBERT W., 1808-61—Born in County Antrim, Ireland. Came to Canada about 1830. He was a captain of militia in Toronto during the Rebellion of 1837, and early in the forties became a partner in Hamilton of the dry goods firm of Buchanan, Harris & Co., of Hamilton, Montreal and Liverpool. He was president of the Great Western Railway Co. from 1855 until shortly before his death, and the town of Harrisburg, Ont., on the line of that road is named after him. Water color. Size 3 x 3. Head and shoulders.

1415—ALTAR, ST. MARY'S CATHEDRAL (R.C.), HAMILTON, C.W., 1863—It was erected after the Gothic style of architecture by M. Zepher Perrault, of Montreal, with a height of 48 feet and width 20 feet, the front elaborately carved and finished in white, tipped with gold leaf. A statue of the Virgin Mary and Child was placed in the centre, and at the sides, finished in oak, were figures of the twelve Apostles. The Bishop's Throne, surmounted by a richly carved canopy, is shown to the left, and immediately opposite is a niche containing a beautiful group representing the Holy Family, and a scene of the crucifixion, which, however, is not shown in picture. Neither does the picture show the pulpit or the side altars in the wings, which were added later. The main altar, too, has been enlarged and the whole finished beautifully in white tipped with gold. St. Mary's Cathedral, which succeeded the old church built in 1838, faces north, on the corner of Park and Sheaffe streets. Water color. Size 4 x 6.

1416—ST. MARY'S CHURCH (R.C.), HAMILTON, C.W.—View of first church—The first St. Mary's, a frame structure, was opened in November, 1838, and destroyed by fire in 1859. The present cathedral, of red brick, erected in 1862, stands at the corner of Park and Sheaffe streets, facing north, a short distance west of its predecessor. Water color. Size 5 x 6. See 1415, 1417.

1417—ST. MARY'S (R.C.) CATHEDRAL, HAMILTON—Corner Park and Sheaffs streets. Water color. Size 5 x 6. See 1415, 1416.

1418—HAMILTON, ONT., 1857—View from foot of Mountain, head of James street—In the foreground is the road near the base of the Mountain, leading to (1) James street, (2) Macnab street. The entire wooded space is now (1917) occupied by residences; (3) Residence of T. C. Kerr, corner of James and Aberdeen streets (now occupied by Wm. J. Southam); (4) Residence of Peter Hamilton, on east side of James street, foot of the Mountain; (5) Burlington Bay; (6-7) Wentworth and Halton Counties; (8) Beach and Burlington Canal. Water color from original oil by Robert Whale, A.R.C.A., and presented to the city of Hamilton by John Brown, of Kerr, Brown & Co., merchants. Size 7 x 12.

1419—HAMILTON, C.W., 1855—From the south end of Upper John street—With key. Founded in 1813 by Hon. George Hamilton, son of Hon. Robert Hamilton, of Niagara. The former was for many years member of Parliament for Gore district. The city is attractively situated at the south-western extremity of Burlington Bay, on land which rises gradually from the bay to "The Mountain." This picture, one of the earliest views of the city, gives a fair idea of its area at the time. Water color from old print. Size 7 x 12.

1420—OLD CITY HALL, HAMILTON, ONT., 1839-88—This view shows the hall in 1872 and section of the west side of James street, south of Merrick street, as far as St. Paul's, formerly St. Andrew's Presbyterian church. On the south-west corner of Market Square is the Stuart store, and on the north-west corner the Murphy store. The hall, as shown, was built in 1839. In 1873 a high clock tower was erected in front of its centre, and the dome and the small tower removed. The present edifice was constructed after the demolition of the old building and clock tower in 1888. Water color. Size 6 x 8.

1421—GREAT WESTERN RAILWAY WORKS, HAMILTON, C.W., 1863—The buildings, the first large equipment of the kind in Canada West, were the property of the Great Western Railway of Canada. They are of stone, with slate roof, and stand on the Hamilton Bay front, at the west end of Stuart street, where it joins the old Station street, now Queen. The entrance on the south side is by a bridge from the foot of Locomotive street, which crossed Concession street, now Barton. A stairway led down to the shops. Key: 1, High level bridge for waggon traffic over the Desjardins Canal; 2, Desjardins Railway bridge; 3, Boiler shop; 4, Tender shop; 5, Erecting shop; 6, Machine shop; 7, Engine house; 8, Elevator, afterwards burned down; 9, Storehouse; 10, Roundhouse, with twelve stalls for engines; 11, Immigrant sheds; 12, Immigrant wharf. Water color from print. Size 3 x 10.

1422—CLINE'S SAWMILL, HAMILTON—This old-time sawmill was situated at the south-westerly limits of the city of Hamilton, on what is now known as Cline's Park, opposite Ainslie Wood—halfway to Dundas, and at the base of the mountain. It was demolished many years ago. The water color, of which this is a reproduction, was made by Captain Caddy, and was awarded the first prize at the Provincial Exhibition, Hamilton, in 1860, as the best water color shown there of Canadian scenery. Size 5 x 6.

1423—STEEL SUSPENSION AND SWING BRIDGES, BURLINGTON HEIGHTS, 1854—A steel suspension bridge (upper elevation in picture) joining the township of Barton and the city of Hamilton, was built in 1854, blown down in 1874 and replaced by a whipple truss bridge at the lower level highway. This whipple truss stood until 1897, when it was removed to make room for the present high level steel arch erected by the C.P.R. to connect Hamilton with the G.T.R. at this point. In 1896 the former railway had obtained running rights over the Toronto-Hamilton rails of the G.T.R. (the old G.W.R.), carrying its trains from the G.T.R., Toronto, to the C.P.R. station at the corner of James and Hunter streets, Hamilton. The Great Western in 1853 erected a swing bridge east of the high level bridge, but only at half the elevation above the water level. Here a serious railway accident took place in March, 1857, when the deck or flooring alone failed and the engines and cars left the rails. As the ties in those days were spaced four feet apart, the wheels would shove the ties ahead of them and thus cause everything to drop through to the river below. This bridge, reconstructed, was replaced by one of iron, which stood until 1886 and was then replaced by the steel structure at present in use. Water color from print. Size 5 x 8.

1424—HAMILTON, ONT., 1861-2—View from below Chedoke—The Chedoke is a small stream running down the mountain two miles from James st., west of Garth, now (1917) Dundurn st., Hamilton. (1) Farm of late Capt. Nicholls, Chief of Police. The land has been laid out in streets and built up with dwellings and factories, such as the Zimmerman Knitting Co. and Westinghouse Works. (2) Old Crystal Palace, Victoria Park, between King and York streets; building demolished, and the park used for public purposes. Water color from original by Miss Bourne. Size 7 x 12.

1425—BUSINESS CENTRE OF HAMILTON, C.W.—The Gore Park, 1863—With key—The open space, now known as the Gore Park, Hamilton, was nothing but a grass plot up to 1860. In that year it was enclosed with an iron fence. A drinking fountain was erected in the centre. Plots of flowers were laid out and seats placed throughout, so that this little park, in the midst of Hamilton's business section, is to-day not only a breathing spot, but a resting place for the enjoyment of the people of the "Ambitious City." The picture shows warehouses and business places on the surrounding streets. Water color from print. Size 7 x 19.

1426—ORIGINAL ENTRANCE TO BURLINGTON CANAL, HAMILTON, ONT.—On 30th Jan., 1826, an Act was passed by the Legislature of Upper Canada, incorporating a company with authority to build a canal from Burlington Bay to the village of Coote's Paradise (Dundas). The work afterwards became known as Desjardins Canal, called after Peter Desjardins, and extended from the head of Burlington Bay to the town of Dundas. On 16th Aug., 1837, the canal, nearly four miles in length, was opened for vessels drawing 7½ feet of water. The entrance was not where it is at the present time, but followed the old channel of the river as shown. In 1854 a new cut, that in use at the present time, was made. Map. Size 13 x 17.

1427—JAMES STREET, HAMILTON, C.W., 1855—A reproduction of a very rare picture, showing a part of James street, Hamilton, with the old City Hotel on the south-west corner of James and Merrick streets, of which Thomas Davidson was the proprietor. It was the popular hotel of the fifties and early sixties. MacQuesten & Co., on the north-west corner of these streets, were foundrymen, and carried on an extensive and profitable business. They retired many years ago. The site of this foundry is now the Royal Hotel. Photograph from a lithograph. Size 8 x 12.

1428—JAMES STREET, HAMILTON, 1860—THE GORE OR PUBLIC PARK—This is a view of the west side of James street, from the southwest corner of James and King, to the R. Juson & Co.'s hardware building. (1) The foreground shows the Gore or Public Park, which extended in 1861 from James street to Hughson, and now (1917) to John street. The stores on the south-east corner of James and King are those of (2) Brown, Gillespie & Co., and the former hardware store of Daniel Macnab (3). Water color. Size 5 x 8.

1429—AUCHMAR HOUSE, CLAIRMONT PARK, HAMILTON, C.W., 1863—Residence of Hon. Isaac Buchanan—This residence, one of the finest in Canada at the time of its erection, was built by the late Hon. Isaac Buchanan, of the firm Buchanan, Harris & Co., the most prominent dry goods house of its day in Western Canada. The residence was originally red brick, two storeys in height, but some years after it was roughcast with white lime, pebbles and cement. It was called "Auchmar," after the name of the ancient seat of the Buchanans in Stirlingshire, Scotland, and the part of 100 acres surrounding it was known as "Clairmont Park." A portion of the property was subsequently sold to the Ontario Government for use as an institution for inebriates, although instead the site became a Hospital for Insane. Miss Buchanan now (1917) resides at Auchmar.

The firm of Buchanan, Harris & Co., in Hamilton, was succeeded by Buchanan, Hope & Co., which went out of existence in 1867. The latter in turn became Buchanan & Co., and afterwards Buchanan, Binny & Mc-Kenzie. In Montreal the firm Buchanan, Harris & Co. also went out of existence on the death of Mr. Harris in 1861, successively becoming Isaac Buchanan & Co., Buchanan, Leckie & Co., and Leckie, Matthews & Company. Drawing in water color. Size 5 x 7.

1430—**LAUNCHING OF THE SCHOONER "HERCULES" AT HAMIL-TON, C.W.**, 1863—The schooner, which was the property of Edward Zeeland, Jr., was launched from Zeeland's Wharf, on the Burlington Bay front, August 6th, 1863, in the presence of a large concourse of citizens. It was an excellent specimen of marine architecture, measuring 111 feet in length, beam 25 feet 10 inches, and depth of hold at fore of hatch, 12 feet. For many years the vessel carried freight between Hamilton and other Lake Ontario ports. She was lost in the St. Clair River. Water color. Size 4 x 7.

1431—**WESLEYAN LADIES' COLLEGE, HAMILTON, C.W.**, 1863—In 1860 the Anglo-American Hotel, a fine structure, with 170 apartments, was erected at a cost of $100,000 on the south side of King street east, Nos. 100-10, between John and Catherine streets, Hamilton. It became vacant and was sold to the Wesleyans for $24,000. The college was opened in 1861 as the Hamilton Wesleyan Female College, and closed in 1898 after the death of Rev. Dr. Burns, of Hamilton. The following year it was again hotel property, known as the "Waldorf." This hotel in 1914 went out of business. The building was subsequently demolished and the property sold to the proprietor of a new hotel which in 1915-16 is in process of erection on the site. Drawing in water color. Size 6 x 6.

1432—**SECTION OF WEST SIDE OF JAMES ST., HAMILTON, 1860**—From near south-west corner of King street. With key. Water color. Size 5 x 7.

1433—**HAMILTON, WENTWORTH CO., ONT.**, 1878—View from the head of Macnab street. With key. Water color. Size 6 x 12.

1434—**HAMILTON, ONT.**, 1860—North side of King street, looking west from the Gore—The view was taken shortly after the opening of the Gore or Public Park, which then extended on King street from James to Hughson. About 1904 it was extended to John street. To the west is row of stores (1) China Bazaar, north of James street, at corner of King, and south (2) Osborne's and other stores. On north-west corner of King and James (3) Hamilton's Medical Laboratory, and the north-east corner of King (4) Lawson's clothing store; (5) McCrea, dry goods; (6) Bickle & Son, druggists; (7) A. Murray & Co. The Gore at this time had an iron fence around it, and gates at four corners, but later the fence and gates were removed. Water color. Size 7 x 12.

1435—**CENTRAL SCHOOL, HAMILTON, 1853 and 1903**—Erected on an elevated site, covering two acres, bounded on the north by Bold street, on the south by Hunter, on the east by Park, and on the west by Queen street. At the time of its opening, May 2nd, 1853, this was the central portion of Hamilton—hence the appellation, "Central," which is still (1917) retained Some years ago it was suggested that the building be transformed into a modern collegiate, but to this there was strong opposition, especially from those who formerly attended the school. Finally it was decided that it be remodelled and made into a first-class school. This was done, and Central School is now, as it always has been, the great Public school of Hamilton. Here many of Canada's prominent men received their early education. Dr. John Herbert Sangster was the first principal. Photograph, colored. Size (each) 5 x 7.

1436—DUNDURN CASTLE, HAMILTON, ONT.—Richard Beasley, one of the earliest settlers at the "head of the lake," was original owner of what is now (1917) Dundurn Park. He built, about 1800, a part of the "Castle," at that time the only brick house in Wentworth County, and around this dwelling Allan (Sir) Macnab erected his mansion thirty years later. After his death it was used as an institute for the Deaf, Dumb and Blind. Subsequently Dundurn Castle became the property of Senator McInnes, who made some additions, and in 1899 the city of Hamilton acquired it. In the historic pile at Dundurn, surrounded by a park of thirty-one acres, an historical museum was opened in 1902. Water color. Size 5 x 7.

1437—HAMILTON, ONT., 1845—Head of John street, east of Mountain View Hotel—The picture is not carefully drawn. Christ Church spire (James street) is shown far east of its location. In 1845 the church had a spire, but it was later removed. Burlington Bay, with sailing craft and steamers, is in evidence, and in the background are Wentworth and Halton counties. There is too much sameness in all the buildings shown to make it possible for old inhabitants (in 1917) to identify them. Water color. Size 6 x 12.

1438—FIRST LOCOMOTIVE BUILT IN HAMILTON, C.W., 1860—The "George Stephenson," built by the Great Western Railway at their works in Hamilton—It was named after the "father of railways," and was on the road in September, 1860. 1, Standing on the front part of the fender may be seen F. W. Gates, a director of the road; 2, Thomas Reynolds, financial director; 3, C. J. Brydges, managing director; 4, G. H. Mingate, paymaster; 5, R. Eaton, locomotive superintendent, formerly of the London and South-western Railway, standing on the foot plate of the engine; 6, A. Ayres, mechanical draughtsman; 7, W. G. Stephens; 8, G. F. Forsyth, foreman of the machine shops. He is in front, with his hands in the pockets of his velveteen jacket. Drawing in water color. Size 4 x 8.

1439—POLICE OFFICE, HAMILTON, C.W., 1841—The police office, a pioneer building in Hamilton, was a two-storey structure of red brick, on the north side of King William street, between Hughson and John streets, the present site of the central fire station, of which it forms a part. It was originally built for a market house and remodelled. The engine station was on the ground floor, the police office on the second, and the market in the basement. Barton Masonic Lodge held meetings in the police office on the 8th and 24th November, 1841. At the last meeting it was resolved that the thanks of this meeting (lodge) be given to Bro. R. O. Duggan and the members of the Board of Police for their kindness in offering us the temporary use of their room." Drawing in water color. Size 5 x 6.

1440—WHITE'S BLOCK, HAMILTON, C.W., 1863—An old-time business centre—This block of stores, built of fine cut Hamilton Mountain stone, by the late John White, M.P., of Halton County, in 1853-4, stands on the north side of King street midway between James and Hughson streets, in front of the Gore. Some of Hamilton's well-known merchants were tenants. To the right or west was the store of Alexander Murray & Co., dry goods, brother of W. A. Murray, of Toronto. East of this the store of John Eastwood, the pioneer bookseller, D. B. McDonald & Co., drugs, and Taylor and Grannis, fruit store. There were originally four stores in the block, but these were reduced to three, as a staircase was erected in the middle of the block for the use of the upper tenants. The property is now part of the White estate. Drawing in water color. Size 4 x 6.

1441—LONDON, C.W., 1857—View from the north-west looking southeast—1, House of George Murray, miller for Dennis O'Brien. O'Brien had a flour mill on west side of Ridout street. During the Rebellion of 1837 he held lucrative contracts for conveying goods and material for the military authorities. 2, The toll gate, east side of Blackfriars' Bridge. 3, Blackfriars' Bridge, Ridout street. The old bridge was replaced by an iron bridge in 1875 on same site. The district to the south-west, that is to right of picture, is (1917) occupied by dwellings and factories. To the east (left of picture), on the flats, is the Harris property. Water color from original painting by the late James Hamilton. Size 7 x 10.

1442—**LONDON, ONT.**, 1870—Richmond street, looking north from the corner of Dundas street—1, John Siddons' Prototype office, s.w. corner Dundas and Richmond, now (1917) C.P.R. office—building altered. 2, Palmer block, n.w. corner Dundas and Richmond. 3, J. Barkie, fruit store. 4, W. L. Carrie, stationery. 5, Hugh S. Murray, jeweller. 6, Harry Beeton, hatter. 7, J. Peacock, fancy goods. 8, E. A. Taylor, books. 9, Carling street. 10, Carling block, n.w. corner Richmond. 11, Post office. 12, Queen's avenue. 13, Part of tower of St. Paul's Cathedral. 14, F. Rowland, hardware. 15, Rowland & Jewell, grocers. 16, E. Rowland, Montreal store. 17, Whycoff, jeweller, Dundas street, opposite E. Rowland. 18, south-east corner Richmond and Dundas streets, fruit and oyster depot; John Cruikshank, cigars. The Grand Trunk Railway ticket office has been built on this site. Water color from an old view. Size 5 x 8.

1443—**LONDON, C.W.**, 1837—North branch of the Thames River, looking south from Blackfriars' Bridge—1, Wooden bridge leading from Ridout street over the head race of Dennis O'Brien's grist mill to John Jennings' distillery. 2, Fowler's house, Ridout street. 3, Eldon House, built 1835, by John P. Harris. 4, Distillery of John Jennings, on the flats, built 1836, later destroyed by lightning. 5, North branch Thames River. From a water color sketch in possession of Mr. George B. Harris, London, Ont. Size 6 x 9.

1444—**LONDON, ONT.**, 1870—Free Press office, on Carling street— The journal was founded by William Sutherland in 1849 as a weekly, and for seven years was run as such. In 1852 Mr. Sutherland sold out to Josiah Blackburn. Four years later Stephen Blackburn arrived at London and was taken into partnership, the firm then being known as J. & S. Blackburn. The first office of the Free Press was on Talbot street, the second (shown in the picture) on the site of the present Queen's Hotel, Carling street, the original North street. The old barn and property to the right was destroyed by fire in 1878. The building now standing on the site is occupied by Messrs. Blackburn & Weeks, barristers. Water color from photograph. Size 5 x 8.

1445—**LONDON, C.W.**, 1842—North branch of the Thames River, looking north—1, John Jennings' distillery, built 1836, on the flats south of Blackfriars' Bridge, later destroyed by lightning. 2, John Plummer's residence, Ridout street. 3, John Pacey, waggonmaker, Ridout street. 4, Eldon House, built 1835, by John P. Harris, now (1917) occupied by his son, George B. Harris. It was a social centre in London in the early days. The flats below are the property of Geo. B. Harris. Water color from original painting by the late James Hamilton, of London. Size 6 x 9.

1446—**LONDON, C.W.**, 1854—From the hill near Wortley road, looking north-east on the south branch of the River Thames—To right is southern part of town, a district now (1917) devoted to manufacturing establishments. The original picture was made during the grading of the Great Western Railway. Points of interest shown are: 1, Court House, Dundas and Ridout street. 2, St. Paul's Cathedral, east side Richmond st., north of Queen's ave., built 1846. 3, Old Grammar School, King st., s.w. cor. Court House Square. 4, York st., south side of which is the London Electric Power Company. 5, The present Grand Trunk Railway bridge crosses river at this point, completely changing the view. Water color from original painting by the late James Hamilton, of London. Size 5 x 10.

1447—**WRECK OF THE STEAMER "VICTORIA"**—On the Thames River, near London, Ont.—The "Victoria" was one of three craft plying between London and Springbank, a charming natural park, five miles from London, and was simply a flat-bottomed scow, some sixty feet long with upper and lower decks, the latter having a canopy. On May 24th, 1881, while returning overladen with passengers from Springbank, the boat suddenly listed to one side and sank in ten feet of water, near Cove Bridge, a mile below London. The portable engine broke from its moorings, and rolled off the craft, carrying away the supports of the upper deck. The canopy top of the latter came down upon the crowd and held them in the water, with the result that one hundred and eighty-two people were drowned in the catastrophe. Water color from old print. Size 6 x 10.

1448—**STEAMER "PRINCESS LOUISE"**—The picture shows the "Princess Louise," sister steamer of the "Victoria," at the accident to the latter near London, Ont., 24th May, 1881. The "Louise" hurried down the river and took on board those who had been rescued and about a hundred bodies. The railway bridge to the right is that of the Sarnia branch of the Grand Trunk. Water color from old print. Size 6 x 10.

1449—**OPENING OF CENTRAL SECTION OF GREAT WESTERN RAILWAY**—London, C.W. (Ontario), 15th Dec., 1853—The view shows the train passing the old freight sheds on her approach to the station. Drawing in color. Size 4 x 9. See 1456.

1450—**LONDON, C.W.**, 1843—From the north-east, looking south-west, and showing an old-time hostelry—1, Clark's Bridge, built of wood, so called after a farmer named Clark who owned a farm on Wellington road, outside of London. 2, Forest to the south-east of the bridge is site of W. T. Parsons' dwelling and shoe shop, built 1876. 3, The Junction of Wellington road (Wellington street) and High street. 4, Westminster Abbey Hotel, kept in the early days by a man named Dawson. The building still stands, used as a private dwelling. Water color from the original painting by the late James Hamilton, of London. Size 7 x 10.

1451—**LONDON, C.W.**, 1843—Waters' Mill—View from Blackfriars' Bridge, north branch of the Thames River—1, Property of Samuel Peters, west side of the river, called Petersville, after him. He was a butcher, ran a distillery, and later became a magistrate. 2, Waters' Mill, Carling's Creek. Building removed years ago. Thomas Waters, a U.E.L. from New Brunswick, came to Westminster, 1820, and was first owner of the pond mills, subsequently taking up land along Carling's Creek. 3, Where the Carling Malting and Brewing Co. now (1917) stands, covering west side of Talbot street, north of the creek. 4, Cribwork of old Blackfriars' Bridge (first). Water color from the original by the late James Hamilton in possession of Mr. Geo. B. Harris, London, Ont. Size 6 x 10.

1452—**LONDON, ONT.**, 1870—View looking south, showing Covent Garden Market—1, Hotel kept by Bartholomew Drake, and old market stores. Removed about 1884. 2, Old fish market, also removed. 3, Coomb's furniture factory. 4, Tecumseh House, erected 1858, south-west corner York and Richmond streets. 5, Fish store of F. S. Onn. 6, F. W. Silverwoods, poultry. 7, R. Hookway, flour and feed. 8, Chas. Rudd, veterinary establishment. 9, Benjamin Shaw, wool. 10, Ontario House, Edward Hodgins, proprietor. 11, Old Market House (still in existence). Old buildings to left of picture have been removed to enlarge the market space. Water color from an old view. Size 7 x 10.

1453—**LONDON, C.W.**, 1844—View looking towards the south-west— 1, First brick block in London. 2, A corner of the Court House shows behind the wooden building. 3, The residence on Wortley road of Judge

John Wilson, a Scotsman who settled in London in 1834. 4, Second Westminster Bridge over the Thames at York street. 5, Burwell Park, named after Mahlon Burwell, who settled in Middlesex County in 1809. 6, Residence on York street of the late Judge Givins. House still stands and is used as a dwelling. 7, Thames street, which runs parallel with the river, and with Wortley road. The old buildings in the foreground are east of the Court House and west of Ridout street, on Dundas street, at present the Court House Square. Original water color by the late James Hamilton, of London. Size 12 x 20.

1454—LONDON, C.W., 1842—View looking west, with the old Westminster Bridge in the foreground—1, The Jail. 2, Court House. 3, Old Grammar School, built of frame, and still standing. 4, King street. Runs east and west. Eastern end has business houses and the western, residences. 5, Residence of the late Rev. Benjamin Cronyn. 6, Soap Works of J. D. Dalton, York street and Thames street. Moved years ago. 7, York street. 8, Thames street runs north and south at right angles to the river. 9, Residence on Bathurst street of Hon. George Jarvis Goodhue. Destroyed by fire. 10, Westminster bridge. The railway crosses the river a few hundred yards south of the old bridge. 11, Right foreground—site occupied by residence of the late C. H. Hutchinson, County Crown Attorney. Original water color by Capt. F. H. Caddy, of the Royal Artillery, and of London. Size 10 x 16.

1455—LONDON, C.W., 1840—Looking east, from the main branch of the River Thames—1, Bank of Upper Canada (second), Ridout street, now (1917) No. 445. A branch of this bank was first opened in 1835 at King and Ridout streets, with Richard Richardson as manager. Later, while James Hamilton was manager, it was moved to Ridout street, north of Dundas. Mr. Hamilton lived in the building, which is at present occupied by Mr. Rowland Harris, son of George B. Harris. Ridout street runs along the crest of the bank of the north fork of the river, and continues southerly. Original oil by the late James Hamilton, of London, Ont. Size 10 x 14.

1456—OLD GREAT WESTERN RAILWAY STATION, LONDON, C.W., 1858—In 1845 an Act was passed reviving that of the Canadian Legislature in 1834 with amendments to incorporate the London and Gore Railroad Company. One amendment was to change the name to "The Great Western Railway Company." The central section of the latter was opened at London, 15th December, 1853, and the Toronto and Hamilton branch was opened for traffic 3rd December, 1855. The picture shows the old station at London in the summer of 1858, and in the distance is given the Tecumseh Hotel, erected in that year. It stands on the south-west corner of York and Richmond streets, opposite the Grand Trunk Railway station. The engine house in connection with the old Great Western station was only pulled down in 1905, after half a century of service. Water color from an oil in possession of C. H. Peacock, London, Ont. Size 7 x 10. See 1449.

1457—LONDON, C.W., 1840—Looking south-east across the river, and showing some of the principal buildings of the period—1, First red brick block of three stores in London. 2, Court House, s.w. cor. Dundas and Ridout streets, completed 1829. 3, Magazine used by the military, 1840. 4, Wilson & Hughes' law office. 5, Mechanics' Institute, Court House Square. Burned 1845. 6, Residence about 1833 of Rev. Benjamin Cronyn, D.D. 7, Residence of John Jennings, first town warden of London. 8, J. D. Dalton's soap factory, Thames street. 9, York street, Westminster Bridge, first bridge over the river at that point, built by Levi Merrick in 1826. 10, House of Rev. Francis Wright, Thames street, first principal of the Grammar School. Water color from the original by the late James Hamilton, of London. Size 5 x 10.

1458—**LONDON, C.W.**, 1874—Great Western Railway Cove Bridge—View looking south-west—1, Bridge over Thames River, where the railway crosses, south-west of London, near what is now (1917) Railway street. The bridge was altered and raised eighteen feet in 1906. 2, Overhead bridge for traffic, on the river road. The opening of the central section of the Great Western Railway of Canada took place at London on 15th Dec., 1854. Original water color by the late James Hamilton, of London. Size 7 x 12.

1459—**LONDON, ONT.**, 1872—Looking east from the main branch of the Thames, west of the Forks—1, St. Paul's Anglican Cathedral, Richmond st. and Queen's ave. 2, Eldon House, Ridout st. 3, Bank of Upper Canada, Ridout st. 4, Dundas st. bridge. 5, Royal Exchange, n.w. cor. Ridout and Dundas sts. 6, Robinson Hall, named after Chief Justice Robinson. It was the principal hotel in London in 1845, the year of the great fire, which started in this building. It still stands as an office and tenement building. 7, Court House and Jail. At first there was no separate jail, and criminals were locked in a cell underground. 8, Old Grammar School, which in 1827 was used as a Court House. 9, Sulphur Springs, at present the London Mineral Baths. Original water color by the late James Hamilton, of London. Size 8 x 15.

1460—**LONDON, C.W.**, 1846—View west of the Forks, looking east from the main branch of the River Thames—1, St. Paul's Cathedral (second building), Richmond street, just north of Queen's Avenue. 2, Eldon House, built 1835, by Mr. John Harris. 3, Bank of Upper Canada, where late James Hamilton was manager. 4, Dennis O'Brien block, built 1837; first brick block in London. It comprised three stores. 5, Robinson Hall, the principal hotel in London in 1845. It still (1917) stands as an office and tenement building. 6, Court House, south-west cor. Dundas and Ridout sts. Original water color by the late James Hamilton, of London. Size 6 x 11.

1461—**LONDON, C.W.**, 1840—With detailed key—Dundas street—View looking west from Wellington to Ridout sts.—The stumps to the left of the picture are on the site of what is now Federal Square, where the Municipal Buildings are to be erected. The McCormack biscuit factory was torn down and the land taken over by the city for a new City Hall and square. Dundas st. is one of the pioneer thoroughfares of London. Water color from original by James Hamilton, London. Size 5 x 10.

1462—**LONDON, C.W.**, 1851—From the south-west, showing branches or forks of the River Thames—1, Dundas street bridge—a temporary bridge of the north branch. 2, The jail on Dundas st. 3, Court House. 4, Grammar School. A temporary frame building was erected on the north-east corner of Court House Square, and the first Court of Quarter Sessions was held Jan. 9th, 1827, Col. Ryerse as chairman. 5, Thames st. 6, The branches of forks of the river, with the present (1917) bowling green to the west. Water color from original painting by the late James Hamilton. Size 4 x 10.

1463—**PORT STANLEY EAST, ONT.**, 1876—View from the mill cutting—With key—Port Stanley, on Lake Erie, twenty-four miles south of London, is the terminus of the London and Port Stanley Division of the Pere Marquette Railway. Original water color by the late James Hamilton, of London. Size 7 x 12.

1464—**THE 1ST OR ROYAL REGIMENT OF FOOT (ROYAL SCOTS)**—Captain and private, Canada, 1757-60, 1812 and 1837—Formed during the reign of James VI. of Scotland, and in 1633 was constituted a regiment under Sir John Hepburn. From 11th Feb., 1812, it was known as "The First Regiment of Foot, or Royal Scots." They were at Louisburg, Ticonderoga, and in 1760 at the conquest of Montreal. On 7th Dec., 1812, the Grenadier and one battalion company marched towards Niagara from Burlington, the Grenadiers assisting at the capture of Fort Niagara. On 29th Dec. five companies of the first battalion, under Lieut.-Col. John Gordon, were employed in storming the American batteries at Black Rock and Buffalo. The regiment also saw service at Chippawa, Lundy's Lane and Fort Erie. In 1836 the second battalion was divided into six service and four depot companies, the former leaving for Canada in July. They took part in different actions under Lieut.-Col. Wetherall in Lower Canada, 1837. Water color. Size (each) 5 x 9.

1465—THE 1ST OR GRENADIER REGIMENT OF FOOT GUARDS— Captain and private, Canada, 1838—Raised in Flanders, 1656, by Charles II., with Lord Wentworth as colonel. A Grenadier company was first added in April, 1678, and in 1815 H.R.H. the Prince Regent was pleased to have the regiment known as the "First, or Grenadier Regiment of Foot Guards," in commemoration of its services at Waterloo. The second battalion was ordered to Canada at the time of the Rebellion, and landed at Quebec, 9th May, 1838. In the autumn of the same year it took part at St. Ours, La Prairie, and St. Charles; was at Montreal, April, 1840. The battalion left Canada in 1842. Water color. Size (each) 5 x 9.

1466—THE 3RD (THE BUFFS) REGIMENT OF FOOT—Captain and private, Canada, 1813-14—In the spring of 1572 the third (the Buffs) was formed by the London Guilds, under command of Capt. Thomas Morgan. In 1814 the first battalion proceeded to America. Arrived in Lower Canada in May, being formed in brigade with the 5th, 27th and 58th, commanded by Major-General Sir Manley Power. The forces of which the Buffs were a part assembled, and in September, 1814, took part in the attack on Plattsburg. The battalion remained in Lower Canada during the succeeding winter, embarking from Quebec for Europe, 4th June, 1815. On the restoration of peace the second battalion, which had been in England since 1807, transferred the whole of its men who were fit for active service to the first, and was disbanded at Hythe, 24th Dec., 1815. Water color. Size (each) 5 x 9.

1467—THE 4TH (KING'S OWN) REGIMENT OF FOOT—Captain and private, Canada, 1787-93—The old "Fourth King's Own" was raised chiefly in West of England under royal authority to Charles Fitzcharles, Earl of Plymouth, dated 13th July, 1680. It ceased in 1710 to be a marine corps, but before as well as after that date it saw service on coast of France, in Nova Scotia, and in the fruitless attempt on Quebec, 1711. The regiment received from George I. in 1715 the title "King's Own." It was in Halifax, 1776, and during the first three years of the American Revolutionary War took part in the principal actions; returned home and from 1787-93 was in Canada and Newfoundland. Water color. Size (each) 5 x 9.

1468—THE 5TH (NORTHUMBERLAND FUSILIERS) REGIMENT OF FOOT—Captain and private, Canada, 1787-97—This regiment, formed in 1674, was in 1782 given its county title. From 1792-6 it was at Niagara, and in August, 1792, was reviewed by Prince Edward (Duke of Kent), who reported it as "most fit for actual service." After its return to England a second battalion was raised. The first battalion came to Canada in 1814; served at Plattsburg, and later stationed at La Prairie and Coteau-du-Lac. Embarked for Europe, June, 1815. William IV. commanded that the regiment should be made fusiliers, and thenceforward known as the Fifth (Northumberland) Regiment of Foot. Water color. Size (each) 5 x 9.

1469—THE 6TH ROYAL WARWICKSHIRE REGIMENT OF FOOT— Captain and private, Canada, 1813-14—Founded 1673; in Nova Scotia, 1786, and in 1793 left for the West Indies. The regiment returned to Canada in

1799, and was stationed at Quebec, Montreal and Kingston. The first battalion returned to England in 1806. After having served with distinction in Peninsular War the regiment embarked from Bordeaux, 5th May, 1814. With the 82nd it formed General Brisbane's brigade and took part in the sortie, Fort Erie. For their gallantry they had permission to use "Niagara" on their colors. Left Canada, July, 1815. A second, or "reserve," battalion was sent to the Red River during the dispute with the States respecting the Oregon territory in 1846, to defend the British settlements in what was at that time known as Rupert's Land, in event of hostilities. Water color. Size (each) 5 x 9.

1470—THE 7TH, OR QUEEN'S OWN HUZZARS—Captain and sergeant, Canada, 1837-42—The regiment was originally a corps of heavy cavalry, raised in Scotland, 1688. In the spring of 1838 orders were received for the regiment to transfer its services to Canada, and it was divided into four service and two depot troops. The former embarked at Cork, 1st May, 1838, arrived in Montreal in June, and in November were employed against insurgents in Lower Canada. One troop was similarly employed in January, 1839. From 1839-41 the service troops were stationed at Montreal and Laprairie. Returned to England the following year. Water color. Size (each) 6 x 9.

1471—THE 7TH (ROYAL FUSILIERS) REGIMENT OF FOOT—Captain and private, Canada, 1775 and 1791-1801—Raised in 1685 by James II., and known as the Ordnance Regiment, whose men carried a long musket called a "fusil." In patronizing this regiment the King styled them the Royal Fusiliers. Proceeded to Canada in April, 1773, and were stationed at Quebec, Montreal and St. John's; fought during the War of the Revolution. In 1791 the regiment was again in Canada, under command, until 1801, of Prince Edward (Duke of Kent). Embarked for England, 1810, from the West Indies. A second battalion, raised 1858, served some time at Gibraltar, Malta, and in Canada, whence it returned home, 1867. Water color. Size (each) 5 x 9.

1472—THE 8TH (KING'S) REGIMENT OF FOOT—Captain, sergeant, private and drummer, Canada, 1812-15—Formed in England, 1685, under title of "The Princess Anne of Denmark's Regiment of Foot." In 1751 it was designated "the 8th," or "King's Regiment," and embarked for America in 1768. Took active part in Revolutionary War, returning to England in 1785. In 1803 the regiment, which at that time consisted of one battalion, again landed at Halifax, and the following year a second battalion was formed. In nearly all the battles of the Niagara frontier the 8th was engaged during the War of 1812-15. For its gallantry it was allowed to use the word "Niagara" on its colors. The first record of Masonry in Upper Canada is the original Mss. certificate, dated 1780, issued by Lodge No. 156, E.R., in the King's or 8th Regiment of Foot. The lodge met in the old stone building or castle which still (1917) stands within the precincts of Fort Niagara, N.Y. Both battalions embarked for England in June, 1815. Water color. Size (each) 5 x 9.

1473—THE 8TH (KING'S) REGIMENT OF FOOT—Captain and private, Canada, 1768-85—In May, 1768, the regiment embarked for North America to relieve the 15th. After passing several years at Quebec, Montreal and Chambly, it was in 1773 ordered to Upper Canada. One division landed at Fort Niagara, occupying the fort on the east side of the river and the town on the west side. Different detachments were in the expedition against Fort Stanwix, Cherry Valley, and in the raid down the Mohawk Valley. After the winter of 1776 a part of the regiment was sent to Lower Canada, and in 1785 the 8th, on the arrival of the 65th, returned to England. Water color. Size (each) 5 x 9.

1474—THE 9TH (EAST NORFOLK) REGIMENT OF FOOT—Captain and private, Canada, 1814-15—The Norfolk Regiment was raised in Gloucestershire, Eng., by Capt. Henry Cornwall, in 1685. At outbreak of American War it embarked for Canada, and was with Gen. Burgoyne at Saratoga. In 1782, after its return to England, the regiment was directed to style itself the 9th, or East Norfolk Regiment of Foot. From the South of France the 2nd battalion arrived in Canada, August, 1814. In September it was stationed near Fort Wellington (Prescott, U.C.), and in October at Kingston, where it remained until June, 1815. The 9th proceeded to the Crimea in 1854, and afterwards to Canada, returning to England in 1857. Water color. Size (each) 5 x 9.

1475—THE 10TH (NORTH LINCOLN) REGIMENT OF FOOT—Captain and private, Canada, 1776—The origin of this regiment is traced to an Independent Company of Foot, garrisoned at Plymouth for some time, and which was expanded into a regiment of ten companies in 1685. It came to America in 1767, was in Halifax, and at Boston on the outbreak of the Revolutionary War; took part in engagements at Bunker's Hill, Brandywine and Germantown. The tenth fought in the Peninsular War and the first Sikh War, and has been stationed in various parts of the world. Water color. Size (each) 5 x 9.

1476—THE 11TH (NORTH DEVONSHIRE) REGIMENT OF FOOT—Captain and private, Canada, 1837-8—Formed at Bristol, Eng.; sailed for Canada with the troops that took part in disastrous attempt upon Quebec, 1711. In 1838, on arrival of the regiment at Gibraltar, orders were received to proceed to North America. It landed at Halifax, was at Quebec, Sorel and St. John's, L.C., and in the Madawaska territory during negotiations for settlement of the international boundary question, which was decided by the Ashburton Treaty, 1842. Water color. Size (each) 5 x 9.

1477—THE 13TH (1ST SOMERSETSHIRE) REGIMENT OF FOOT—Captain and private, Canada, 1813-14—The old Thirteenth Foot, like the other regiments standing immediately before it on the rolls, dates its existence from 1685. It received the appellation "1st Somersetshire" in 1782. In June, 1813, the regiment, under Lieut.-Colonel William Williams, arrived at Quebec from Port Royal, Martinique, returning to Portsmouth 15th July, 1815. It served entirely in Lower Canada, taking part at Plattsburg, Odelltown and La Colle. A second battalion, the first the regiment ever had, was formed in 1858. Water color. Size (each) 5 x 9.

1478—THE 14TH (BUCKINGHAMSHIRE) REGIMENT OF FOOT—Captain and private, Canada, 1841-8—The "Old Fourteenth" was in 1685 formed at Canterbury by Sir Edward Hales, of Woodcot, from companies raised in different parts of Kent. In 1766 the regiment went to America and served there till 1771. As a single battalion, like many other line regiments, after the Peninsular War, the 14th served in West Indies from 1836-41, and in Canada and Nova Scotia, 1841-8. In 1876 her Majesty's command was that the 14th (Buckinghamshire) Regiment should hereafter be known as 14th (Prince of Wales) Own Buckinghamshire Regiment of Foot. Water color. Size (each) 5 x 9.

1479—THE 15TH, OR YORKSHIRE (EAST RIDING) REGIMENT OF FOOT—Captain and private, Canada, 1758-60—This corps was raised in Nottinghamshire, Eng., and surrounding counties, 1685, by Sir Wm. Clifton and others. The King (James II.) fixed its establishment by warrant, 1st Jan., 1685-6. In 1757 the Fifteenth sailed for America, and took part in the siege of Louisburg. From there the regiment joined the expedition against Quebec, and fought on the Heights of Abraham. In 1760 it was sent against Montreal under Gen. Murray, and was stationed there until April, 1761. Served in Cuba; was at Quebec and Montreal, 1827. Returned to England in 1838, after having served in the War of Insurrection. Water color. Size (each) 5 x 9.

239

1480—THE 16TH (BEDFORDSHIRE) REGIMENT OF FOOT—Captain and private, Canada, 1814-15—Raised in 1688 in southern counties of England. The Sixteenth went to Nova Scotia in 1790, where it remained until the following year. In May, 1814, it embarked in Ireland for Quebec, and was stationed there as well as at Chambly, Montreal and Fort Wellington (near Prescott, U.C.) Again, at the "Trent" difficulty, 1861, the regiment was sent to Canada, serving in North America and Bermuda until 1870, when it returned to England from Nova Scotia. Water color. Size (each) 5 x 9.

1481—THE 17TH LIGHT DRAGOONS, "DEATH OR GLORY"—Captain and private, Canada, 1776—Under warrant 7th Nov., 1759, by Lieut.-Col. Hale, who brought home the despatches announcing the capture of Quebec, the 17th, originally called the 18th Light Dragoons, was raised. On the breaking out of hostilities in America the 17th was the first cavalry corps to cross the Atlantic, and was at Bunker's Hill. The regiment, on the evacuation of Boston, proceeded to Halifax, whence in June, 1776, it joined the British force in Staten Island. It was in several engagements during the Revolutionary War. Water color. Size (each) 10 x 10.

1482—THE 17TH (LEICESTERSHIRE) REGIMENT OF FOOT—Captain and private, Canada, 1757-60 and 1861—In 1688 the regiment was formed in vicinity of London. Sailed to Halifax, June, 1757. Was with Amherst in expedition against Cape Breton, and engaged in Siege of Louisburg. In 1759 was at Siege of Ticonderoga and proceeded to Crown Point. Advanced upon Montreal, 1760. Returned to England, 1767, and came back to America, 1775, to take part in Revolutionary War. From 1783-88 the Seventeenth was stationed in Nova Scotia and Newfoundland. Her Majesty Queen Victoria conferred the Colonelcy of the regiment on Lieut.-General Sir Peregrine Maitland, at one time Lieutenant-Governor of Upper Canada. The Second Battalion was disbanded after Peace of Amiens, and the single battalion served in Canada from 1855-65. A second battalion was again added in 1858 and stationed in Quebec, Montreal and Toronto, returning to England in 1868. Water color. Size (each) 5 x 9.

1483—THE 18TH (ROYAL IRISH) REGIMENT OF FOOT—Captain and private, Canada, 1776—The regiment fought for King William at the Battle of the Boyne and throughout the Irish campaigns down to the fall of Limerick. It was at home during the Seven Years' War; went to America in 1767, and was at Boston at the outbreak of the War of Independence. The 18th was present at the Battle of Bunker's Hill, but left Boston for Nova Scotia, and returned to England in July, 1776. Water color. Size (each) 5 x 9.

1484—THE 19TH (DROGHEDA LIGHT HORSE) LIGHT DRAGOONS—Captain and private, Canada, 1813-14—Four British cavalry regiments have in succession been numbered the Nineteenth. The Drogheda Light Horse, as it was popularly called, was raised in Ireland, 1759-60 as the 19th Light Dragoons. Under Lieut.-Col. the Honble. J. B. R. O'Neill it served in Canada, taking part at the capture of Fort Niagara by assault, the Battles of Chippawa and Lundy's Lane. It was granted the badge "Niagara" for its distinguished conduct. The regiment was also represented at Plattsburg. In 1821 this 19th was disbanded in England. Water color. Size (each) 10 x 10.

1485—THE 20TH (EAST DEVON) REGIMENT OF FOOT—Captain and private, Canada, 1789-92—At the beginning of the Seven Years' War the regiment which distinguished itself at the Boyne, raised a second battalion, known as the 67th Foot, with Wolfe as its first Colonel. The regiment was among the troops sent to the relief of Quebec at the outbreak of the American War; served under Burgoyne, and after being "interned" in America for some time, returned to England in 1781. From 1789-92 it was at Halifax, N.S. Water color. Size (each) 5 x 9.

18

1486—THE 21ST (ROYAL SCOTS FUSILIERS) REGIMENT OF FOOT—Captain and private, Canada, 1776-81—Raised for the King's service in Scotland, during the reign of Charles II. It served at the Siege of Belle Isle in 1761, was sent to the relief of Quebec in 1776, and took part in the campaigns under Burgoyne down to the disaster at Saratoga, 1777. From 1789-93 it was in Nova Scotia, went through some hard fighting in West Indies, for which it was commended by General Prescott. Water color. Size (each) 5 x 9.

1487—THE 22ND, OR CHESHIRE REGIMENT OF FOOT—Captain and private, Canada, 1757-60—Formed in 1689 by the Duke of Norfolk. Served at the Battle of the Boyne and Siege of Limerick. In 1756 the regiment embarked for America from Ireland, was engaged at the Siege of Louisburg and Capture of Cape Breton, and in 1759 took part at Quebec. The following spring it advanced to Montreal. In 1765 returned to England, and ten years later embarked again for America; saw active service in War of Revolution. Major-General John Graves Simcoe (first Lieut.-Gov. Upper Canada) succeeded Major-General Crosbie in command in 1798. The regiment went abroad again in 1860 and served in Malta and North America until 1869, when it returned home from New Brunswick. Water color. Size (each) 5 x 9.

1488—THE 23RD (ROYAL WELSH FUSILIERS) REGIMENT OF FOOT—Captain and private, Canada, 1838-48—This renowned regiment formed in 1689, fought and lost heavily at Bunker's Hill. It served under Howe, Clinton and Cornwallis, being, in the words of an American writer, everywhere distinguished "by its gallantry and heavy losses." The first battalion of the Royal Welsh Fusiliers was in Nova Scotia, 1808, and again in 1810. From 1838-48 the regiment served on this continent, and, subsequently, a battalion, raised at Cardiff in 1858, came to Canada. Note "the flash," a bow of black silk ribbon, with long ends, attached to the back of the tunic collar of officers and sergeants. There is no authentic explanation of the origin of "the flash." Water color. Size (each) 5 x 9.

1489—THE 24TH (2ND WARWICKSHIRE) REGIMENT OF FOOT—Captain and private, Canada, 1776-7—In 1776 the regiment was among the reinforcements sent to Canada, serving under Gen. Burgoyne down to the surrender of Saratoga. It was then "interned" until the peace. The 2nd Warwickshire again proceeded to Nova Scotia and Canada in 1789, and it is said that a part of the regiment left Halifax, N.S., to assist in quelling an uprising of the blacks in Sierra Leone. The first battalion—a second had been formed after the Peace of Amiens—was stationed in Canada during the Rebellion of 1837-8. Water color. Size (each) 5 x 9.

1490—THE 26TH (CAMERONIANS) REGIMENT OF FOOT—Captain and private, Canada, 1767-76—The regiment was at home during the Seven Years' War. In 1767 it embarked for Canada, and on outbreak of American War was sent from Montreal, where it had been stationed, and took part in the defence of Quebec. It also was active along the frontier, then went to New York, serving under Clinton until 1780. The title of "Cameronians," by which the regiment was originally known, became obsolete. From 1787-1800 the 26th was stationed in Canada and Nova Scotia. The staunch old corps which afterwards formed the first battalion of the Cameronians, was embodied at Douglas, Scotland, 1689, and first fought at Dunkeld. Water color. Size (each) 5 x 9.

1491—THE 27TH (INNISKILLING) REGIMENT OF FOOT—Captain and private, Canada, 1757-60—Formed from three regiments of the Inniskilling Forces, 1689. Col. Tiffen's, as the regiment was first called, fought with bravery throughout King William's Irish campaign, from the passage of the Boyne to the fall of Limerick. At beginning of Seven Years' War the 27th came to Canada, served in the operations at Ticonderoga and Crown Point, and subsequently in expedition to Montreal. Removed to Nova Scotia, 1761; was at siege and conquest of Havana. Returned to England, 1767. Again in America during Revolutionary War. In the War of 1812-14 the first and third battalions were in expedition to Lake Champlain. Water color. Size (each) 5 x 9.

1492—THE 28TH (NORTH GLOUCESTERSHIRE) REGIMENT OF FOOT—Captain and private, Canada, 1757-60—Formed 1694. Little can be gleaned of its early history, but it was employed in the West Indies and Newfoundland. Ordered by Pitt to Canada, 1757; was at Louisburg, Quebec, Sillery and Martinique. Wolfe received his mortal wound at the head of the 28th (Bragg's, so named from the Colonel, 1734-51), and a provisional battalion formed of the Grenadier companies of various regiments. Afterwards the regiment took part in the defence of Quebec, expedition against Montreal, and in siege and conquest of Havana. In America during Revolutionary War. The second battalion, 61st (South Gloucestershire) served in Bermuda and Nova Scotia, 1866-72. Water color. Size (each) 5 x 9.

1493—THE 29TH (WORCESTERSHIRE) REGIMENT OF FOOT— Captain and private, Canada, 1814-15—Raised in 1694 by Col. Thomas Farrington. From Gibraltar in 1745 the regiment sailed for Louisburg, where it remained until 1749. In the latter year it left for Chebucto Harbor, N.S., and was employed in clearing the site of the present City of Halifax. It returned to England in 1773 from Florida, but three years later embarked for Quebec, which was at that time besieged by the Americans. "The Worcestershire Regiment" was given the title 29th Foot in 1782. From 1802-07 the regiment was in Halifax, and also in 1814, when it joined the expedition up the Penobscot River. Water color. Size (each) 5 x 9.

1494—THE 30TH (CAMBRIDGESHIRE) REGIMENT OF FOOT— Captain and private, Canada, 1860-70—The first battalion of this regiment was chiefly recruited in Lincolnshire, and on the Tyne, England, and a second battalion formed from men enrolled under the Defence Acts, was raised in Huntingdonshire. Both battalions saw service in different parts of the world, and as a single battalion corps the 30th served in the Mediterranean, Bermuda and Canada from 1834-45. Again from 1860-70 it was stationed in Canada and Nova Scotia. Water color. Size (each) 5 x 9.

1495—THE 31ST (HUNTINGDONSHIRE) REGIMENT OF FOOT— Captain and private, Canada, 1776-87—The regiment, long known as the 31st, was originally a marine corps. At the peace of 1715 it was disbanded, but afterwards restored as a regiment of Foot. It served in various parts of the world, and in 1776 arrived in Canada, where it helped to garrison Quebec during the Revolutionary War. The flank companies, with Burgoyne, surrendered at Saratoga. After eleven years' service in Canada, receiving in the interval the title of "Huntingdonshire," the regiment returned to England. The second battalion (the 70th) was in Nova Scotia, 1778-82, and during the War of 1812 saw service in Upper Canada. Water color. Size (each) 5 x 9.

1496—THE 34TH (CUMBERLAND) REGIMENT OF FOOT—Captain and private, Canada, 1757-60—The old 34th Foot was recruited from the eastern counties of England, 1702. The second battalion was in Canada during the Seven Years' War, at the capture of Montreal, and the final conquest of the Canadas, 1760. In the War of Independence the first battalion saw hard service in the backwoods, and the flank companies were with Burgoyne at Saratoga. After spending some years at home the 34th served in North America from 1830-40, and in the disturbances in Lower Canada was one of the regiments despatched on horse sleighs from New Brunswick. Water color. Size (each) 5 x 9.

1497—THE 35TH (ROYAL SUSSEX) REGIMENT OF FOOT—Captain and private, Canada, 1757-60—The old 35th Regiment was raised in Belfast, by Arthur Chichester, third Earl of Donegal, in 1701, and received their orange facings as a special favor from William of Orange. The "Orange Lilies," as they were then facetiously styled, were among the troops sent out to Nova Scotia in 1756 under General Hopson, and took part in the capture of Louisburg, C.B., and afterwards were with Wolfe at Quebec and Murray at defence of Quebec and capture of Montreal, leaving Canada in 1760. Water color. Size (each) 5 x 9.

1498—THE 36TH (HEREFORDSHIRE) REGIMENT OF FOOT—Captain and private, Canada, 1838-42—This brave old corps was raised in Ireland by Viscount Charlemont in 1701. In 1705 it went to Spain, and, having re-formed in England, left for Nova Scotia, and was engaged against Quebec, 1711. During the American War the 36th received the county title "Herefordshire." For some years the regiment served in the West Indies and North America. The 1st battalion, 29th (Worcestershire) was previously at Louisburg and at Halifax. Water color. Size (each) 5 x 9.

1499—THE 37TH (NORTH HAMPSHIRE) REGIMENT OF FOOT—Captain and private, Canada, 1814-26—Raised in Ireland, 1792, by Colonel Thomas Meredith. At the commencement of the Seven Years' War a second battalion was formed. The 37th was sent to Amerrca at the beginning of the Revolutionary War, and was at Charleston and the expedition to Philadelphia. The first battalion left Bordeaux for Pouliac in 1814, embarking with reinforcements for Upper Canada, serving there until 1826. As a single battalion corps the regiment was in North America from 1830-42, returning to England from Nova Scotia in the latter year. Water color. Size (each) 5 x 9.

1500—THE 38TH (1ST STAFFORDSHIRE) REGIMENT OF FOOT—Captain and private, Canada, 1842-50—At the commencement of the Revolutionary War the 38th was one of the first corps to be despatched from Ireland to America. It was at Bunker's Hill, and afterwards stationed at New York, where in 1782 it received the county title of the "1st Staffordshire." After peace was declared the regiment remained in Nova Scotia for some years. It served under Sir Ralph Abercromby, in 1796; and did duty in the Ionian Islands, at Gibraltar, in Jamaica and Nova Scotia. Water color. Size (each) 5 x 9.

1501—THE 39TH (DORSETSHIRE) REGIMENT OF FOOT—Captain and private, Canada, 1814-15—Col. Richard Coote, under warrant dated 13th February, 1702, raised the old 39th in Ireland. It served in Portugal, Spain, India and Gibraltar, and whilst at the latter place received its first county title of the "East Middlesex Regiment." On the renewal of the French Revolutionary War it was called "Dorsetshire." From the south of France the regiment went to Canada and served in the unsuccessful expedition against Plattsburg. Subsequently it was stationed in Canada and Bermuda, returning to England from the latter station in 1864. In the early fifties the second battalion (54th) was in Canada. Water color. Size (each) 5 x 9.

1502—THE 40TH REGIMENT OF FOOT, OR SECOND SOMERSETSHIRE—Captain and private, Canada, 1757-60—Formed August 25th, 1717, from Col. Richard Philipps' four independent companies of foot serving at Annapolis Royal, N.S., and four independent companies at Placentia, Newfoundland. In 1751 the regiment was given its number. Concentrated at Halifax, 1758, and despatched to Louisburg with other troops. Took part in the expedition against Quebec under Wolfe, 1759. Participated in attack on Montreal, 1760. Later saw service in Barbadoes, in operations against Havana. Returned to Nova Scotia in 1763, and transferred to Ireland the following year. Water color. Size (each) 5 x 9.

1503—**THE 41ST (THE WELSH) REGIMENT OF FOOT**—Captain and private, Canada, 1812-14—Founded by royal warrant in 1719 and recruited from old soldiers of the Guards, horse and foot, at Chelsea Hospital, near London, at which time it was known as the Regiment of Invalids. In 1798 the regiment was in Ireland, and in 1800 embarked for Upper Canada. It saw service at Detroit, Queenston, Miami, Fort George and other places, and has the honor of bearing "Fort Detroit, Queenston, Miami and Niagara" on its colors. Leaving Quebec in 1815, the 41st arrived at Ostend a month after the Battle of Waterloo. A second battalion, formed in England during the war, was reduced after peace. Water color. Size (each) 5 x 9.

1504—**THE 42ND (ROYAL HIGHLAND) REGIMENT OF FOOT**—Captain and private, Canada, 1759-60—This corps traces its origin to six independent companies of Highlanders raised for service in Scotland, 1725-29. The name "Black Watch" was given to them. At the beginning of the Seven Years' War, the 42nd, as the regiment had become, embarked for America, and distinguished itself at Ticonderoga, July, 1758. A second battalion (subsequently the 73rd) was formed at this time and joined the forces on Lake Ontario in 1759. The two battalions were employed in operations which ended with the capture of Montreal and final conquest of the Canadas in 1760. In 1787 the regiment returned to England from Cape Breton. Water color. Size (each) 5 x 9.

1505—**THE 43RD (MONMOUTHSHIRE) REGIMENT OF FOOT**—Captain and private, Canada, 1757-60 and 1835-46—Under a Letter of Service, dated 3rd Jan., 1741, this regiment was raised by Colonel (afterwards General) Fowke, who had for some years commanded the 7th Dragoons. At the outbreak of the Seven Years' War the 43rd embarked for North America. It was employed in Nova Scotia in 1757-8, and the following year fought under Wolfe at Quebec, subsequently serving under Murray at the defence of that place. It returned home in 1764, came to America on the outbreak of the Revolutionary War, and again after a term of home service embarked for New Brunswick in 1835. On the occasion of the insurrection in Lower Canada it was one of the regiments despatched from New Brunswick to Quebec on horse-sleighs in the depth of winter. It removed to Nova Scotia, remaining there for two years. A second battalion was raised as the 54th Foot in 1755, by Colonel Hedworth Lambton. Water color. Size (each) 5 x 9.

1506—**THE 44TH (EAST ESSEX) REGIMENT OF FOOT**—Captain and private, Canada, 1755-65—The 55th, as the regiment then was, served with Sir John Cope in 1745. Ten years later, as the 44th, it came with reinforcements to North America, was at Fort du Quesne, Ticonderoga, and Fort Niagara, and in the expedition against Montreal. It returned to England from Canada in 1765. When the Revolutionary War broke out the 44th embarked for Boston, arriving just after the Battle of Bunker's Hill. It took part in other engagements during the campaign, coming to Canada in 1780, where it remained until 1786. Water color. Size (each) 5 x 9.

1507—**THE 45TH (NOTTINGHAMSHIRE) REGIMENT OF FOOT**—Captain and private, Canada, 1757-66—The position of the 45th Regiment of British Foot was from 1741-8 held by Frazer's, or the 2nd Marines, called the "Green Marines," from the color of their facings and caps. They were, like other marine regiments, disbanded in 1748, when their place was taken by the 1st Sherwood Foresters, raised in 1741 by Col. D. Houghton. The regiment was sent to Gibraltar, and afterwards to America in 1746, to assist the New Englanders against Cape Breton. It was withdrawn from Louisburg to Nova Scotia, and was there on the outbreak of the Seven Years' War. After the capture of Louisburg it remained stationed in Cape Breton and Nova Scotia until 1766, when it returned home. Water color. Size (each) 5 x 9.

1508—THE 46TH (SOUTH DEVONSHIRE) REGIMENT OF FOOT— Captain and private, Canada, 1757-60—Under a Royal Warrant, dated 13th January, 1741, this regiment was raised by Colonel John Price. After fourteen years' home service it went to America, suffering heavy loss in the attempt on Ticonderoga, at that time headquarters of the French under Montcalm. It was in the expedition against Fort Niagara and other engagements ending in the conquest of the Canadas. The 46th saw hard service during the early part of the War of Independence. It was not until 1782 that the county title of "South Devonshire" was conferred. Water color. Size (each) 5 x 9.

1509—THE 47TH (LANCASHIRE) REGIMENT OF FOOT—Captain and private, Canada, 1757-60 and 1858-67—Took part in siege and capture of Louisburg, June, 1758, and went with Wolfe to Quebec the following year, forming with the 43rd the centre of the front line on the Plains of Abraham. It served at the winter defence of Quebec under Murray, as well as in the expedition against Montreal, 1760. It was in America during the Revolutionary War, and, upon returning to England, received the county title of the Lancashire Regiment. In April, 1861, the regiment re-embarked to Canada. Up to 1865 it was stationed in Montreal, London, Hamilton, and in the spring of that year moved to Toronto, with headquarters in the Old Parliament Buildings and Old Fort. During the Fenian Raid the 47th was on the Niagara frontier, where it did good service. Water color. Size (each) 5 x 9.

1510—THE 49TH (HERTFORDSHIRE) REGIMENT OF FOOT— Captain and private, Canada, 1803-15—In army lists of 1742-8 the place of the 49th Foot is filled by the 6th or Cotterill's Marines. On the disbandment of marines and other corps at peace of 1748 the companies regimented in 1744 by Gov. Trelawney, of Jamaica, became the 49th Foot. It was sent to America under Howe in 1776, and fought in various engagements. When county titles were bestowed in 1782 the 49th became the "Hertfordshire" Regiment of Foot. It was Brock's regiment, commanded successively by him, Sheaffe and Vincent. The 49th was actively engaged in Canada during the War of 1812, including the Battle of Queenston Heights (it bears the name "Queenston" on its flag) and Beaver Dams. Other actions in which it took part are York, Fort George, Black Rock and Crysler's Farm. Water color. Size (each) 5 x 9.

1511—THE 53RD (SHROPSHIRE) REGIMENT OF FOOT—Captain and private, Canada, 1776-7 and 1866-9—This regiment (1st battalion), raised in 1755, was sent to Gibraltar soon after its formation, remaining in that fortress until the end of the war. In 1776 the 53rd came to America. Its flank companies were with Burgoyne at Saratoga, but the rest of the regiment remained in Canada, where it stayed until 1787. It saw service in various parts of the world until 1866, when it came again to Canada, stationed at London, C.W., and Quebec, and was here until the withdrawal of the line regiments from the Dominion. Water color. Size (each) 5 x 9.

1512—THE 55TH (WESTMORELAND) REGIMENT OF FOOT—Captain and private, Canada, 1757-60—The original warrant was dated December, 1755. Shortly after, the regiment left Cork under General Hopson for an attack upon Cape Breton. The enterprise, however, was abandoned for the time being and the regiment wintered in Nova Scotia. Next year it served in the attack on Ticonderoga, then went to Niagara with Gen. Prideaux, and was employed subsequently in various operations in connection with the conquest of the Canadas. Returned to England, but was again in America during early part of the Revolutionary War, during which it received its county title of the "Westmoreland" Regiment. Water color. Size (each) 5 x 9.

1513—THE 57TH (WEST MIDDLESEX) REGIMENT OF FOOT— Captain and private, Canada, 1783-91—This regiment, which became the 57th in 1757, was raised as the 59th Foot by Lieut.-Colonel John Arabin in Somersetshire and Gloucestershire, Eng. It became the West Middlesex in 1783, embarked for Nova Scotia the following year, being quartered at Annapolis Royal and Fort Howe. Two companies assisted in building Frederick Town (Fredericton). The regiment returned to England in 1791. Again it came to Canada. During the expedition against Plattsburg it was at Montreal, and was afterwards stationed at Brockville and Johnstown, U.C. Under direction of Col. Arbuthnot a substantial stockade and blockhouse were erected at the former place. In the summer of 1815 the 57th returned to England. The second battalion, 77th (East Middlesex), from 1837-48, served in the Mediterranean, West Indies and North America. Water color. Size (each) 5 x 9.

1514—THE 58TH (RUTLANDSHIRE) REGIMENT OF FOOT— Captain and private, Canada, 1757-60—The first battalion served in expedition against Fort Duquesne, under Braddock, and later at Louisburg and Quebec. Returned to England on peace of 1763; was in America during Revolutionary War, when it received title of Northamptonshire Regiment, and in 1814 took part in expedition to Plattsburg. The second battalion (Rutlandshire), raised as the 60th in 1755, was also at Louisburg and Quebec, and in advance on Montreal. It was stationed for a time on the lakes, subsequently assisting in Havana Expedition. After Cuba was restored to Spain the regiment returned to Ireland. Water color. Size (each) 5 x 9.

1515—THE ROYAL AMERICAN REGIMENT OF FOOT—60th King's Royal Rifle Corps— Captain and private, Canada, 1757-60—Raised in 1755-6 in Pennsylvania, with Lord Loudoun as Colonel-in-Chief. In 1758 Col. Jeffery Amherst had charge of the siege of Louisburg, in which the 2nd and 3rd battalions of the 60th took part. They were with Wolfe at Quebec, 1759, and present when the British ensign was hoisted over the captured city by an officer of the Royal Artillery; and in November, 1871, a detachment of the 1st battalion of the 60th, consigned the Imperial flag to the keeping of another artillery officer, whilst the flag of the Dominion of Canada was hoisted in its stead. Part of the regiment fought in the Revolutionary War. The 1st battalion was in Toronto in 1869, and from May till October, 1870, was with Wolseley in the Red River Expedition. Water color. Size (each) 5 x 9.

1516—THE 70TH (SURREY) REGIMENT OF FOOT— Captain and private, Canada, 1813-14—At the beginning of the Seven Years' War, the 31st (Huntingdonshire) Foot raised a second battalion, which in 1758 became the 70th. It was recruited chiefly in Glasgow. In 1813 the regiment was styled "The Glasgow Lowland Regiment," and in August of that year left Ireland for Canada, where it was stationed during the war. Returned home in 1828. It was again in Canada from 1841 to 1843. Water color. Size (each) 5 x 9.

1517—THE 71ST HIGHLAND LIGHT INFANTRY— Captain and private, Canada, 1842-54—Embarked for North America in May, 1824. Detachments were stationed during the summer of 1826 at Sorel and Three Rivers. In 1827 the headquarters division of the 71st was at Montreal, and subsequently at Kingston and York (Toronto), one company from the latter place being detached to Niagara, Amherstburg and Penetanguishene for two years. In 1842 a "reserve" battalion landed at Montreal, where the 1st battalion was stationed, and from there marched to Chambly in 1843, going to Kingston in 1845. The headquarters and two companies of the reserve battalion arrived in Toronto, 23rd May, 1850, from St. John's and Chambly, and during 1851 the reserve continued at Toronto, where Lieut.-Col. Sir Hew Dalrymple was very popular. In 1854 the regiment left Canada. Water color. Size (each) 5 x 9.

1518—THE 74TH REGIMENT OF FOOT, OR "ARGYLE" HIGH-LANDERS—Captain and private, Canada, 1777-83—As the 74th Foot this battalion stood third in a series of regiments so numbered. It was raised by Col. John Campbell, a veteran of the old 78th, or Fraser Highlanders, of 1756-63, and was distinguished by its defence of Penobscot against an American squadron under Commodore Saltanstat. The flank companies were employed in Carolina. The regiment was disbanded at Stirling in 1783. Water color. Size (each) 5 x 9.

1519—THE 76TH (HINDOSTAN) REGIMENT OF FOOT—Captain and private, Canada, 1814-27—This is the third regiment in succession which has ranked as the 76th of the British Line. Raised at expense of the East India Company, 1787. Left India in 1807. From the South of France it came to Canada, 1814, and was employed in the unsuccessful expedition to Plattsburg, on Lake Champlain, after which it remained in the country for thirteen years. It afterwards served in Canada, from 1834-73, and in North America, from 1848-57. Water color. Size (each) 5 x 9.

1520—THE OLD 78TH REGIMENT OF FOOT, OR "FRASER" HIGH-LANDERS—Captain and private, Canada, 1758-9—This famous corps was raised by Simon Fraser, Master of Lovat. It was first known as the 2nd Highland Battalion. It won fame (as 78th) at Louisburg, Montmorenci and Quebec, and was highly praised by Wolfe. Subsequently the regiment was at the defence of Quebec and in the expedition against Montreal. It was sent in 1762 to re-take St. John's, Newfoundland, which had been captured by the French. At the peace of 1763 it was disbanded, large numbers of the officers and men receiving grants of land in America. Water color. Size (each) 5 x 9.

1521—THE 79TH (CAMERON HIGHLANDERS) REGIMENT OF FOOT—Captain and private, Canada, 1825-36—This regiment, the junior of three which in succession have ranked as the 79th Regiment of British Foot, was raised by Alan Cameron, of Erracht, in 1793. In April, 1825, it was augmented from eight to ten companies, and in August the six service companies embarked for Canada. On the anniversary of Waterloo, 18th June, 1828, the 79th, which had been removed to Montreal, was presented with new colors; embarked for England 1836. Again the Camerons were in Canada, coming from Gibraltar in 1848, and leaving for home in 1852. Col. Duncan B. Cameron, C.B., of York Mills, near Toronto, was its Colonel during part of Peninsular War. Water color. Size (each) 5 x 9.

1522—THE 83RD (COUNTY OF DUBLIN) REGIMENT OF FOOT—Captain and private, Canada, 1838-9—This corps, the third regiment in succession which has ranked as the 83rd Foot, was embodied in Dublin, 1793, by Col. William Fitch. Popularly it was known as "Fitch's Grenadiers" from the diminutive stature of the men. In 1831-4 it (the first battalion) was stationed in Scotland, whence it proceeded to Halifax, N.S., remaining until June, 1837, then moving to Lower Canada, where it served during the operations under Sir John Colborne, and also at Prescott, U.C. Returned to England, July, 1843. In 1881 the 83rd became 1st Battalion Royal Irish Rifles. Water color. Size (each) 5 x 9.

1523—THE 84TH ROYAL HIGHLAND EMIGRANT CORPS—Captain and private, Canada, 1763-84—Three regiments have ranked as the 84th Foot. The picture shows the second raised at outbreak of War of Independence, and which was known first as the Royal Highland Emigrant Corps, and later as the 84th (Royal Highland Emigrants) Regiment of Foot. The first battalion was raised in Canada by Col. Allan Maclean, of the old 114th Royal Highland Volunteers of 1763, from families of soldiers of the 42nd, 77th and 78th Highlanders, who at the peace of 1763 had settled in Canada. It defended Quebec against the Americans under Arnold, and was afterwards on the frontier. The second battalion, raised from settlers in Nova Scotia, served there and in Carolina and Virginia. These battalions were disbanded in Canada, 1784. Water color. Size (each) 5 x 9.

1524—THE 85TH (KING'S LIGHT INFANTRY) REGIMENT OF FOOT —Captain and private, Canada, 1835-42—The old 85th Light Infantry, the 2nd battalion of the 53rd (Shropshire), was the first light infantry regiment formed in the British Army. The present regiment was raised in 1794. It served in Malta and at Gibraltar from 1821-32, and in North America from 1835-42, during which time it was one of the regiments despatched on horse-sleighs from New Brunswick to Quebec in the Rebellion of 1837. Water color. Size (each) 5 x 9.

1525—THE 88TH (CONNAUGHT RANGERS) REGIMENT OF FOOT —Captain and private, Canada, 1814-15—This corps was raised by Colonel the Hon. Thomas De Burgh, subsequently Earl of Clanicarde, under an order dated 25th Sept., 1793. As it was recruited chiefly in Connaught, it was styled the Connaught Rangers, and shortly afterwards took rank as the 88th Foot. It disembarked at Quebec, 3rd Aug., 1814, having sailed from France. Was at Plattsburg; stationed on the banks of the Richelieu. Served eleven months, during which period not one man deserted Returned to Europe, landing at Ostend a month after the Battle of Waterloo, and marched to join the army at Paris. Water color. Size (each) 5 x 9.

1526—THE 89TH (ROYAL IRISH FUSILIERS) REGIMENT OF FOOT —Captain and private, Canada, 1814—The uniform depicted is that of the third 89th Regiment, raised in 1793-4 by Colonel (afterwards Lieutenant-General) Crosbie. It was in Ireland 1798, and later in Malta. A second battalion subsequently raised in Ireland, arrived at Quebec 7th Aug., 1814; took part at Lundy's Lane, Crysler's Farm, Fort Erie (assault). Returned home after peace was declared. Disbanded 24th Nov., 1816. It is authorized to carry "Niagara" on its colors. Water color. Size (each) 5 x 9.

1527—THE 90TH (PERTHSHIRE VOLUNTEERS) REGIMENT OF FOOT—Captain and private, Canada, 1814-15—This, the third regiment bearing the number 90, was raised in 1794, as the "Perthshire Volunteers," and formed into a "Light Infantry" corps. In 1804 the 90th, then in Ireland, raised a second battalion from men enrolled in Scotland under the Defence Acts. The first battalion embarked for West Indies, and in 1814 was removed from there to Canada. It was sent to Montreal, and after the declaration of peace embarked for Ostend. Some of its companies were quartered at Coteau du Lac. Water color. Size (each) 5 x 9.

1528—THE 93RD (SUTHERLAND HIGHLANDERS) REGIMENT OF FOOT—Captain and private, Canada, 1838-48—Four regiments in succession have ranked as the 93rd Foot. Amongst the regiments of Fencible Infantry, raised in 1793, was a Sutherland Regiment, commanded by Col. Wemys. In 1814 it sailed with the expedition against New Orleans, and a second battalion, which had been raised for the regiment the same year, was on duty in Newfoundland for sixteen months. It was then brought home and disbanded. During the insurrection of 1838 the 93rd was in Canada, and served in North America until 1848. Water color. Size (each) 5 x 9.

1529—THE 100TH (THE PRINCE REGENT'S) REGIMENT OF FOOT —Captain and private, Canada, 1813—No fewer than six different regiments have borne the number 100; this is the fourth, raised in 1805. It was recruited chiefly in the North of Ireland. A wing of the regiment perished on the coast of Newfoundland, 21st Oct., 1805, en route to Quebec. During War of 1812-14 the 100th did good service on Niagara frontier; was at Sackett's Harbour, Plattsburg, Chippawa, and acted as marines on the "Wolfe" and "Melville." It was re-numbered the "99th," and as such was disbanded at Chatham in 1818. Its successor was the Prince of Wales' Royal Canadian Regiment, formed after the outbreak of the Indian Mutiny. Water color. Size (each) 5 x 9.

1530—THE 101ST (DUKE OF YORK'S IRISH) REGIMENT OF FOOT —Captain and private, Canada, 1813-14—In 1761 a 101st Regiment of Foot first appeared on the rolls of the British army. Another 101st appeared in 1791, but was speedily "drafted." In 1806, the number having then been vacant about ten years, this corps was raised. It served in the West Indies and on the Canadian frontier during 1813-14, and was disbanded at Haslar, 1st January, 1817. Water color. Size (each) 5 x 9.

1531—THE 103RD REGIMENT OF FOOT—Captain and private, Canada, 1813-14—The number 103 has been borne by several corps, the earliest bearing date 1761. The regiment represented was raised in 1805, and in 1812 a General Order gave Col. Scott authority to add two militia companies to its strength. A bounty of $17 was offered to recruits, the length of service to be for a period of eighteen months, restricted to Canada. The 103rd fought at Sackett's Harbour, Plattsburg, Lundy's Lane and Fort Erie (assault). It was authorized to bear "Niagara" on its colors. After giving volunteers to other corps, the six surviving companies of this regiment were disbanded in 1817. Water color. Size (each) 5 x 9.

1532—THE 104TH REGIMENT OF FOOT (NEW BRUNSWICK FENCIBLE INFANTRY)—Captain and private, Canada, 1812-17—Various regiments have been numbered as the 104th, from 1761. This one was raised by Gen. M. Hunter in New Brunswick and Nova Scotia, in 1803. In 1810 it was taken into the line as the 104th, and during the winter of 1812-13 performed a memorable forced march on snowshoes, through the backwoods, from St. John, N.B., to Quebec, arriving there on 15th March. The 104th was at Sackett's Harbour, Fort George, Lundy's Lane and Fort Erie (assault), and for its services had the honor of bearing "Niagara" on its colors. Disbanded at Montreal, 1817. Water color. Size (each) 5 x 9.

1533—REGIMENT OF COLDSTREAM GUARDS—Captain and private, Canada, 1838—Before marching from Scotland into England to restore Charles II., Gen. Monk (Monck) raised this regiment, at Coldstream, Berwickshire, Scotland, 1660. For its services in suppressing Venner's insurrection in 1661 it was not disbanded, but constituted the Second Regiment of Foot Guards. The Coldstreams embarked for Canada on 17th April, 1838, served in the campaign along the Richelieu, and returned to England in 1842, with the First or Grenadier Regiment of Foot Guards. Water color. Size (each) 5 x 9.

1534—THE SCOTS FUSILIER GUARDS (SCOTS GUARDS)—Captain and private, Canada, 1862-4—The Scots Guards were raised in 1660. With James Earl Douglas as Colonel, they declared for William of Orange, and fought in the campaign in Flanders. The first and second companies were at Brooklyn, Brandywine and Germantown in American Revolutionary War. On 22nd April, 1831, the regiment received from William IV. the title of "Scots Fusilier Guards." The 2nd battalion was sent to Canada in 1861, remaining until 1864. The regiment, which since its inception had borne various names, was in 1877 again given its ancient title "Scots Guards." Water color. Size (each) 5 x 9.

1535—QUEBEC ROYAL ENGINEER RIFLES, 1ST AND 2ND COMPANIES, 1839—Formed 1837—The corps consisted of two companies, which in 1837 were placed under the command (as Major) of Lieut. George H. Vincent Whitmore, of the Royal Engineers. The picture shows the uniform, white blanket frock coat, red shoulder straps, blue collar and cuffs, blue cap with red band and blue breeches with red stripe. Lithograph in color. Size 8 x 10.

1536—"THE QUEBEC VOLUNTEERS—Quebec. Printed and published by Peregrine Pouchbelt and Roderick Ramrod, No. 32 Carronade Square, 1839." Title page of publication containing set of nine representatives of volunteer corps of Quebec, 1839. The pictures, said to be from life, are by an artist, Rollo, clerk in the office of the late Hon. Matthew Bell, of Three Rivers and Quebec. Names of printer and publisher are noms de plume. The Palace Gate, Quebec, through which a corps is marching, was so called because the highway led to the residence of the Intendants. It was built during French regime, razed 1791, and a new structure erected 1830, which, in turn, was demolished, 1874. In Dec., 1837, the garrison of Quebec having been reduced to one company of the Royal Artillery, in consequence of the hurried drafting away of the Imperial troops to the various scenes of disorder, created by the rebels of the period, the volunteers of Quebec were employed to garrison the citadel and other portions of the fortress. Size 8 x 10.

1537—QUEBEC VOLUNTEER CAVALRY, 1839—Organized in 1812 by Hon. Matthew Bell, of Three Rivers and Quebec, who was also their first commander. Newspapers of 1837 show that the Quebec Volunteer Cavalry then consisted of sixty troopers. Its name was changed some years ago to the Queen's Own Canadian Hussars, Col. Turner, V.C., D.S.O., of Quebec, was connected with the corps for over half a century, and on retirement from its active command was authorized to raise the Royal Canadian Dragoons. This picture portrays Alexander Bell, son of Hon. Matthew Bell, he having been a member of the volunteers in 1839. Lithograph in color. Size 8 x 10.

1538—QUEEN'S VOLUNTEERS, QUEBEC, 1839—This was apparently a local appellation given to one of the companies of the Royal Quebec Volunteers, six companies of which wore the following picturesque uniform —blue loose coat with red collar, blue breeches, high fur cap with long ears. Lithograph in color. Size 8 x 10.

1539—RIFLEMAN OF THE QUEEN'S RANGERS, 1780—Exact reproduction in water color from original from life by Capt. Murray, of the regiment. This is the first copy made of original at Wolford, Devon. Size 6½ x 7.

1540—LIGHT INFANTRYMAN AND A HUZZAR OF THE QUEEN'S RANGERS, 1780—Exact reproduction in water color from original made from life by Capt. Murray, of the regiment. This is the first copy made of the original at Wolford, Devon. Size 8 x 9.

1541—GRENADIER OF THE QUEEN'S RANGERS, 1780—The original corps known as "Roger's Rangers" was raised in Connecticut and the vicinity of New York by Col. Robert Rogers. In 1776 Rogers was appointed Governor of Michillimackinac. He was succeeded in his command by Col. French and afterwards Major Wemys, whom Major Simcoe (first Lieut.-Governor of Upper Canada, 1792-6), succeeded. The latter reorganized the corps as the Queen's Rangers, and it fought under him in the American Revolution. It was disbanded, 1782, and a new regiment formed subsequently for service in Canada. This, however, was finally disbanded in 1820. Exact reproduction in water color from original made from life by Capt. Murray, of the regiment. This is the first copy made of original at Wolford, Devon. Size 6 x 7.

1542—QUEBEC LIGHT INFANTRY, 1ST COMPANY, 1839—On 24th Nov., 1837, a number of leading merchants and others of Quebec offered their services to the Crown in the following communication to his Excellency the Governor-in-Chief: "May it please your Excellency. In the present state of the Province we beg to tender our services as volunteers in and of her Majesty's Government, to be enrolled as a corps of light infantry or in any way his Excellency may appoint. We neither want pay nor allowance, and will serve under any officers his Excellency may appoint." An order was issued 27th Nov. accepting the offer and authorizing formation of four companies of volunteers, two of which were to be rifle companies; the whole to be known as the "Quebec Light Infantry Corps." The uniform represented is that of No. 1 Company. Lithograph in color. Size 8 x 10.

1543—THE RIFLE BRIGADE (THE PRINCE CONSORT'S OWN)— Captain and private, Canada, 1861-70—The original "Corps of Riflemen" was formed in 1800. It had four battalions at different periods, the first of which saw service in Canada. It sailed for Canada in 1861, and in the winter of that year was at St. John, N.B., Montreal and Hamilton, remaining at the latter place till 1864. In 1866, while at Quebec, the Riflemen took an active part in endeavoring to suppress the great fire there, and two companies were at St. John and Chambly during the Fenian Raid. The following year one company was employed in the construction of fortifications of Point Levis. The headquarters of the 1st battalion was at Ottawa in 1868-9. By order, dated Horse Guards, Jan. 22nd, 1862, it was intimated that the Queen, "desiring to perpetuate the remembrance of her beloved husband's connection with the Rifle Brigade, had been pleased to command that it should in future bear the designation 'The Prince Consort's Own Rifle Brigade.'" Water color. Size 10 x 10.

1544—MONTREAL RIFLE RANGERS—"To Captain Lyman, the officers and gentlemen of the first Volunteer Militia Rifle Company, of Montreal, by Henry Prince. Entered according to Act of Congress in the year 1856 by S. T. Gordon in the Clerk's Office of the District Court of the Southern District of N.Y." The corps of the Montreal Rifle Rangers originated from the visit of several New York volunteer companies to Montreal during the mayoralty of Dr. Wolfred Nelson. A number of young men in Montreal enrolled their names at this time, with a view of forming a military company, and as soon as the new Volunteer Militia Bill was reported, Capt. (Lieut.-Col.) Lyman secured an interview with Sir Edmund Head, the new Governor, to obtain official recognition. The Rangers being the first to apply for admission under the Act were on 31st Aug., 1855, gazetted as the "First Volunteer Militia Rifle Company of Montreal." On the formation of the Prince of Wales' Regiment of ten companies the Rangers were merged into the new corps, becoming No. 1 Company. Capt. Theodore Lyman, who raised the Rangers, was of the firm of Savage & Lyman, jewellers, Montreal. It is noteworthy that the organization of the Rangers as a volunteer company, not only antedates the general volunteer movement in Canada, but also that of England. Lithograph in color. Size 8 x 10.

1545—THE HIGHLAND COMPANY, QUEBEC, 1839—It ranked as No. 6 Company of the Royal Quebec Volunteers, and was raised chiefly in the County of Megantic, through the instrumentality of the then representative of the country in Parliament, the late J. Greaves Clapham, of Quebec. The following officers were gazetted in 1837: Capt. A. McKillop, Lieut. P. McKillop, Ensign J. G. Clapham. The uniform worn was Rob Roy Tartan trews, Scotch bonnet and dark frock coat. Lithograph in color. Size 8 x 10.

1546—QUEBEC LOYAL ARTIFICERS, OR FAUGH-A-BALLAGH, 1839— Raised in the Rebellion of 1837. The company at that time was in command of Capt. John C. Nixon. The uniform was white blanket coat, red sash, green buttons, green facings and green seams. High cap with green top falling over, blue breeches, red stripe. Lithograph in color. Size 8 x 10.

1547—QUEEN'S OWN LIGHT INFANTRY, QUEBEC, 1839—Major Henry Temple commanded this company in 1837, with Frederick Wyse as lieutenant and William Clarke as ensign. The uniform, like all others of the Quebec Volunteer Corps, was unique—white blanket coat with band of blue, red facings, blue breeches, red stripe, high cap. Lithograph in color. Size 8 x 10.

1548—OFFICERS OF QUEEN'S OWN RIFLES—At inauguration of Ridgeway Monument, Queen's Park, 1st July, 1870—With key—The monument, situated just west of the Parliament Buildings, was erected by the Canadian Volunteer Movement Campaign of 1866 in memory of the men who fell in defence of the Canadian frontier in June, 1866. It was unveiled in 1870 by the Governor-General, Sir John Young, restored in 1913, and re-unveiled 8th Sept. of that year. Tablets on the various faces of the monument are suitably inscribed. Photograph, colored. Size 10 x 14.

1549—ROYAL QUEBEC VOLUNTEER ARTILLERY, 1839—This corps was composed of three companies, with William Burns Lindsay, Edward H. Bowen and W. K. McCord as first captains. Many members of the Artillery were leading commercial and professional men in the ancient capital, such as W. B. Lindsay, H. H. Wickstead, H. Lemesurier, W. K. McCord and Andrew Stuart. The uniform was identical with that of the Royal Artillery. Lithograph in color. Size 8 x 10.

1550—THE SAILORS' COMPANY, OR "QUEEN'S PETS," QUEBEC, 1839—This was No. 8 Company of the Royal Quebec Volunteers. It was composed chiefly of seamen and seafaring men who happened to be in the port of Quebec and were enrolled under command of Capt. Rayside, a veteran naval officer, subsequently harbormaster of the port. The services of the sailors' company were often called into requisition during the Rebellion of 1837-8 to hunt up concealed arms, ammunition and disaffected parties. The Queen's Pets wore long blue pea jackets, blue breeches, a round fur cap with long ears and red woollen cravat. Their arms were horse pistols, broad cutlasses and a carronade. Lithograph in color. Size 8 x 10.

1551—OFFICERS OF THE 30TH IMPERIAL REGIMENT, TORONTO, 1861—As a single battalion corps the 30th served in the Mediterranean, Bermuda and Canada from 1834-45, and from 1860-70 it was again in Canada. While in Toronto in the early sixties the headquarters of the regiment were the old Parliament Buildings, Front street. This group was taken on the steps of the main entrance. Key: Left to right. Front row—1, Capt. Singleton. 2, Major Dillon. 3, Capt. Smith. 4, Capt. Fleming. 5, Capt. L'Estrange Herring. Second row—6, Capt. Brook. 7, Lieut. Williamson. 8, Capt. Clarkson. Third row—9, Lieut.-Col. Atcherley. 10, Lieut. Sharp. 11, Major Eden. Fourth row—12, ————. 13, Capt. C. Moorson. 14, Capt. Macpherson. 15, Lieut. Cook. 16, Lieut. ————. On pillar—17, Capt. Stevenson. 18, Capt. Hobbs. The sentry, in his old-fashioned accoutrements, is seen at the front of the picture. From a photograph in possession of the late Col. J. Vance Graveley, O.S.C., Old Fort, Toronto. Size 7 x 10.

1552—"LAKE MASSAUWIPPI—From a point on the road leading from West to East Hatley, Eastern Townships, C.E.—(corner vignettes) On Massauwippi Lake; North End of Massauwippi Lake; View on Road leading from Ayer's flat to Outlet; View of Lake Massauwippi. W. S. Hunter, Jr., del. Boston, J. H. Bufford's Lith." Colored. Size 8 x 12.

1553—"MOUNTAIN SCENERY, EASTERN TOWNSHIPS, C.E.— From a point looking north-west from Owl's Head Mountain—(corner vignettes) Orford Lake; Orford Mountain; Mountain Pass; Trout Brook among the mountains. W. S. Hunter, Jr., del. Boston, J. H. Bufford's Lith." Colored. Size 8 x 12.

1554—"VIEW ON THE RIVER ST. FRANCIS, C.E.—Looking North from the Residence of G. F. Bowen, Esq., Sherbrooke, Eastern Townships —(corner vignettes) Near Sherbrooke; St. Francis, near Sherbrooke; Near Sherbrooke; Near Sherbrooke. W. S. Hunter, Jr., del. Boston, J. H. Bufford's Lith." Colored. Size 8 x 12. See 1558, 1575.

1555—"VIEW FROM THE ARTIST'S RESIDENCE, STANSTEAD, EASTERN TOWNSHIPS, C.E.—(corner vignettes) Rustic Bridge, Line River; Bridge over the Line River at Rock Island, C.E.; View near Stanstead; The old Elm Tree, Stanstead. W. S. Hunter, Jr., del. J. H. Bufford's Lith." Colored. Size 8 x 12.

1556—"VIEW OF THE LOCKS—Looking up the Ottawa River, Ottawa City, Canada. W. S. Hunter, Jr., del. J. H. Bufford's Lith., Boston." Colored. Size 8 x 12.

1557—"VIEW OF OWL'S HEAD FROM SUGAR LOAF MOUNTAIN, LOOKING SOUTH, LAKE MEMPHREMAGOG, C.E.—(corner vignettes) Shetter Rock, Owl's Head; Near Perkins' Landing; Mount Elephants, Memphremagog; Trout Pond on Sugar Loaf Mountain. W. S. Hunter, Jr., del. J. H. Bufford's Lith." Colored. Size 8 x 12. See 1597, 1784.

1558—"RIVER ST. FRANCIS—Near Richmond and Melbourne, College in the distance, Eastern Townships, C.E.—(corner vignettes) View from Rail Road Bridge looking down the St. Francis; View looking South from Melbourne; View near Richmond Junction; Rail Road bridge across the St. Francis near Richmond. W. S. Hunter, Jr., del. J. H. Bufford's Lith." Colored. Size 8 x 12. See 1554, 1575.

1559—"THE BIG KETTLE—Chaudiere Falls, Ottawa River, Canada. Wm. S. Hunter, Jr., del. J. H. Bufford's Lith., Boston." Colored. Size 8 x 12.

1560—"FALLS ON THE COATICOOK RIVER—Near Coaticook Village, Eastern Townships, C.E.—(corner vignettes) Bridge near Compton over the Coaticook, C.E. View on the Coaticook Road looking from Coaticook to Compton, C.E.; Falls on the Coaticook, near the Village of Coaticook, C.E.; Falls on the Coaticook, near Coaticook Village, C.E. W. S. Hunter, Jr., del. J. H. Bufford's Lith., Boston." Colored. Size 8 x 12.

1561—"RIDEAU FALLS, FALLING INTO THE OTTAWA RIVER, OTTAWA CITY, CANADA—Wm. S. Hunter, del. J. H. Bufford's Lith., Boston." Colored. Size 8 x 12.

1562—"NATURAL CURIOSITY. OTTAWA RIVER, CANADA—Two miles above Chaudiere Falls, on the Hull side. Wm. S. Hunter, Jr., del. J. H. Bufford's Lith., Boston. Colored. Size 8 x 12.

1563—"THE APPROACH TO SUSPENSION BRIDGE, OTTAWA CITY, CANADA—Wm. S. Hunter, Jr., del. J. H. Bufford's Lith. Boston. Original Sketch, by J. P. Newel." Colored. Size 8 x 12.

1564—"SUSPENSION BRIDGE OVER CHAUDIERE FALLS—From Harris's Mill, Victoria Island, Ottawa River, Canada. Wm. S. Hunter, Jr., del. J. H. Bufford's Lith., Boston." Colored. Size 8 x 12.

1565—"VIEW FROM BARRACK HILL—Looking down the Ottawa, Ottawa City, Canada. Wm. S. Hunter, Jr., del. J. H. Bufford's Lith., Boston." Colored. Size 8 x 12. See 1570.

1566—"TIMBER SLIDE ON HULL SIDE, OTTAWA CITY, CANADA— Wm. S. Hunter, Jr., del. J. H. Bufford's Lith., Boston." Colored. Size 8 x 12.

1567—"BIRD'S EYE VIEW OF THE CHAUDIERE FALLS, OTTAWA RIVER, CANADA—W. S. Hunter, Jr., del. J. H. Bufford's Lith., Boston." Colored. Size 8 x 12.

1568—"VIEW FROM THE INTERIOR OF CHASM—Chaudiere Falls, Ottawa River, Canada. Wm. S. Hunter, Jr., del. J. H. Bufford's Lith., Boston." Colored. Size 8 x 12. See 1573.

1569—"JUNCTION OF THE GATINEAU WITH THE OTTAWA RIVER, CANADA—Wm. S. Hunter, Jr., del. J. H. Bufford's Lith., Boston." Colored. Size 8 x 12.

1570—"VIEW FROM BARRACK HILL—Looking down the Ottawa River, Ottawa, City, Canada. W. S. Hunter, Jr., del. J. H. Bufford's Lith., Boston." Colored. Size 8 x 12. See 1565.

1571—"CONFLUENCE OF THE MASSAUWIPPI WITH RIVER SAINT FRANCIS, AND BISHOP'S COLLEGE, LENNOXVILLE, EASTERN TOWNSHIPS, C.E.—(corner vignettes) Near Lennoxville; on the Massauwippi River; Bridge St. Francis River; Near Lennoxville. W. S. Hunter, Jr., del. Boston, J. H. Bufford's Lith." Colored. Size 8 x 12.

1572—"THE PINNACLE—Looking North from the Little Lake, Barnston, C.E.—(corner vignettes) Pinnacle from Baldwin's Lake; View near Baldwin's Lake; Base of the Pinnacle, Baldwin's Lake; Fishing Ground, Baldwin's Lake. W. S. Hunter, Jr., del. J. H. Bufford's Lith." Colored. Size 8 x 12.

1573—"THE CHASM—Chaudiere Falls, Ottawa River, Canada Wm. S. Hunter, Jr., del. J. H. Bufford's Lith. Boston." Colored. Size 8 x 12. See 1568.

1574—"LAKE MEMPHREMAGOG, C.E.—Looking South from the residence of M. W. Copp, Esq., Mt. Pleasant, Magog, E.T.—(corner vignettes) Steamboat Landing Outlet, Magog; Trout Fishing Rapids, Magog; View of Orford Mountain from the Outlet; View of the Road from Outlet to Sherbrooke. W. S. Hunter, Jr., del. J. H. Bufford's Lith." Colored. Size 8 x 12.

1575—VIEW ON THE ST. FRANCIS RIVER—Near Sherbrooke, Eastern Townships, C.E.—With corner vignette—View in the vicinity of Sherbrooke. W. S. Hunter, Jr., del. J. H. Bufford's Lith." Colored. Size 8 x 12. See 1554, 1558.

1576—GASPE BASIN, C.E., 1834—South side of the entrance to Gaspe Bay—Gaspe Bay, which is twenty miles in length, ends in a basin large enough to shelter hundreds of ships. The town fronts on the southwest arm of the basin, and is noted for its extensive fisheries, and every summer is visited by many tourists. On the high ground to the rear of the town is Fort Ramsay. Thomas Pye, delineator. Roberts & Reinhold, lith, Place d'Armes, Mtl., Pl. 2. Colored. Size 8 x 12. See 1587.

1577—GRAND RIVER, C.E., 1834—Near the mouth of the Grand River —The view is taken from a point looking north-east. The place, which clusters about the fishing establishment of Robin & Co., is the largest in the County of Gaspe, having stores, churches and public wharf. It is a railway terminal and a centre of the fishing industry. The Grand River falls into the Gulf of St. Lawrence east of the Baie des Chaleurs, sixteen miles from Perce. Thomas Pye, delineator. Roberts & Reinhold, lith., Place d'Armes, Mtl. Colored. Size 8 x 12.

1578—**HOUSE HARBOUR, MAGDALEN ISLANDS, C.E., 1834**—A post settlement in the Gulf of St. Lawrence—The Magdalen Islands, formerly attached to Newfoundland, now (1917) in the County of Gaspe, Que., are situated at the entrance to the Gulf of St. Lawrence. The inhabitants are mostly Acadian fishermen. On account of abundant fishing returns these Islands have been called "The Kingdom of Fish." House Harbour is fifty miles from Souris, P.E.I. Thomas Pye, delineator. Roberts & Reinhold, lith., Place d'Armes, Mtl. Colored. Size 8 x 12.

1579—**PASPEBIAC, BONAVENTURE CO., QUE., 1834**—On the north shore of Baie des Chaleurs—The harbor is formed by a fine beach of sand curving to the south and forming a natural breakwater. The village, the meaning of whose name is "broken banks," has an extensive trade in the fisheries. The inhabitants are nicknamed Paspy Jacks, and live in dwellings built above the red cliffs of the shore. Thomas Pye, delineator. Roberts & Reinhold, lith., Place d'Armes, Mtl. Pl. 1. Colored. Size 8 x 12.

1580—**DALHOUSIE, N.B., 1834**—Situated at the point where the estuary of the Restigouche merges into the Baie des Chaleurs—The site of this port, which faces the harbor on three sides, was called by the Indians Sickadomec. Excellent facilities are afforded for the exportation of lumber, and the salmon and lobster fisheries in the vicinity are most productive. Mount Tracadiegash, one of the highest of the Gaspe Mountains, juts forward into the water opposite Dalhousie, while directly back of the town is Mount Dalhousie. Thomas Pye, delineator. Roberts & Reinhold, lith., Place d'Armes, Mtl. Colored. Size 8 x 11.

1581—**BATHURST, N.B.**—Thomas Pye, delineator. Roberts & Reinhold, lith., Place d'Armes, Mtl. Colored. Size 8 x 11.

1582—**VIEW OF PERCE, C.E., 1834**—As seen from the harbor—The harbor of Perce is very insecure and is open to north-east winds. In earlier times this port was called La Terre des Tempetes, so frequent and disastrous were the storms. Many of the villagers are fisher folk. In the background is shown Mount St. Anne, which rises 1,400 feet above the sea, and is visible for a distance of seventy miles over the water. On its summit is a shrine to St. Anne. Thomas Pye, delineator. Roberts & Reinhold, lith., Place d'Armes, Mtl. Pl. 2. Colored. Size 8 x 12. See 1586.

1583—**CAPE COVE, C.E., 1834**—A post village in Gaspe Co., Que.—Just beyond Cape Despair is situated the prosperous fishing station of Cape Cove, nine miles from Perce, where the Grand River enters the Gulf of St. Lawrence. Besides fishing, farming is carried on, as the land throughout this section of the country is well adapted for agricultural purposes, being comparatively level and well watered. Thomas Pye, delineator. Roberts & Reinhold, lith., Place d'Armes, Mtl. Colored. Size 8 x 12.

1584—**POINT ST. PETER, C.E., 1834**—At the western entrance of Gaspe Bay—The chief industry of the village, which is fifteen miles from Perce, is cod fishing, scores of boats being engaged in the pursuit. In recent years a breakwater and pier have been completed, thus enabling steamers to call at the port. Thomas Pye, delineator. Roberts & Reinhold, lith., Place d'Armes, Mtl. Colored. Size 8 x 12.

1585—**NEW CARLISLE, C.E., 1834**—Established near the mouth of the Grand Bonaventure River in 1785 by American Loyalists. The town is the most important fishery station on the north side of the Baie des Chaleurs, and is the capital of Bonaventure County; also a port of entry of Quebec. Thomas Pye, delineator. Roberts & Reinhold, lith., Place d'Armes, Mtl. Colored. Size 8 x 12.

1586—**PERCE, C.E.,** 1834—Perce, on a promontory of the St. Lawrence, is divided into North and South Beach, the principal part of the inhabitants residing at the former. The latter is devoted almost entirely to fisheries. The place was visited by Cartier in 1534. In 1690 is was taken by the British, and in 1711 another naval attack made by them. Perce Rock is seen opposite the village, and Bonaventure Island in the distance, three miles s.e. of the village. Thomas Pye, delineator. Roberts & Reinhold, lith., Place d'Armes, Mtl. Colored. Size 8 x 12. See 1582.

1587—**GASPE BASIN, C.E.,** 1834—South side of entrance to Gaspe Bay——Jacques Cartier entered the Baie des Chaleurs, July 9th, 1834, and landed at Gaspe, taking possession of the country in the name of the Church and the King of France. On the hill to the south of the town, which has grown to be of considerable importance, is Fort Ramsay. The York and Dartmouth Rivers empty into the basin, and are famous for their game and fish. Thomas Pye, delineator. Roberts & Reinhold, lith., Place d'Armes, Mtl. Pl. 1. Size 8 x 12. See 1576.

1588—**THOS. PYE'S MAP OF GASPE**—"Map of Gaspe, Magdalen Islands, Pr. Ed. Island, and part of New Brunswick and Cape Breton, compiled for Thos. Pye's Views of Gaspe. P. Murison, Land Surveyor. Roberts & Reinhold, lith., Montreal." Size 9 x 12.

1589—**FOX RIVER (CLORIDORME), C.E.,** 1834—At the mouth of the Great Fox River—The inhabitants, nearly all of whom are French, are largely engaged in the cod and mackerel fisheries. Its harbor is well sheltered and affords good accommodation for vessels of light draught. The great Fox River falls into the south shore of the Gulf of St. Lawrence, between Griffin Cove and Petit Cap. Thomas Pye, delineator. Roberts & Reinhold, lith., Place d'Armes, Mtl. Colored. Size 8 x 12.

1590—**GRAND GREVE, C.E.,** 1834—A post village, originally settled about 1770—It is situated in Gaspe Co., Que., on the north side of Gaspe Bay, eighteen miles from the basin of the same name. There is a large fishery station in the village, and also a lead mine in the neighborhood, but the latter is not now in operation. Thomas Pye, delineator. Roberts & Reinhold, lith., Place d'Armes, Mtl. Colored. Size 8 x 12.

1591—**PERCE ROCK,** 1834—On the Gaspe Coast, Que.—Its name is not derived from the hole now seen, but from that which formerly existed, forming the space between the rock and its outward watch tower. The arch gave way in 1846, and this is now called the split. The present "Hole in the Wall" forms an arch 60 feet in height. Perce is about 300 feet high and 1,200 feet long. It is one of the most remarkable sights along the Canadian seaboard. Thomas Pye, delineator. Roberts & Reinhold, lith., Place d'Armes, Mtl. Colored. Size 8 x 12.

1592—**AMHERST HARBOR, MAGDALEN ISLANDS, C.E.,** 1834—Near the centre of the Gulf of St. Lawrence—Amherst Island, nearly six miles in length, has the best harbor in the chain of thirteen Magdalen Islands. They were formerly attached to the Government of Newfoundland, but are now (1917) under the jurisdiction of the Canadian Government. The inhabitants of Amherst, who are chiefly of Acadian origin, depend largely upon the cod fisheries. Gypsum, an important article of export, is found in the hollows and basins of the island. Thomas Pye, delineator. Roberts & Reinhold, lith., Place d'Armes, Mtl. Colored. Size 8 x 12.

1593—**CARLETON, C.E.,** 1834—The village, which is situated on the north shore of the Baie des Chaleurs, was first settled by Acadians. The mountains rise almost perpendicularly about a mile from shore, to a height of 1,400 feet. Excellent shelter from easterly and northerly winds

19

is afforded by the bay. Herring fisheries are carried on extensively in the vicinity. Carleton is one of the most attractive settlements on the coast. Thomas Pye, delineator. Roberts & Reinhold, lith., Place d'Armes, Mtl. Colored. Size 8 x 12.

1594—"VIEW FROM SUGAR LOAF, LOOKING NORTH—Lake Memphremagog, Townships of Stanstead, Hatley and Magog in the distance, and village of Georgeville, Eastern Townships, C.E.—(corner vignettes) Trout fishing on Sugar Loaf Mountain; Preparing for Lunch; Party at the Crossing; Party and Guide at the top of Owl's Head. W. S. Hunter, Jr., del. J. H. Bufford's Lith." Colored. Size 8 x 12.

1595—LE BOUTILLIER BROS.' ESTABLISHMENT, PASPEBIAC, 1834—On the north shore of Baie des Chaleurs—the firm, originally from Jersey, off the coast of France, are exporters of fish and oil. They still exist at Paspebiac, though only in name. The owners are now Whitehead, Turner & Co., of Quebec. In the winter season it is very cold in the vicinity of Paspebiac, and the bay is overhung by masses of "frost smoke." The Aurora Borealis is then seen illuminating the whole northern horizon. Thomas Pye, delineator. Roberts & Reinhold. lith., Place d'Armes, Mtl. Size 5 x 8.

1596—"SOUTH VIEW OF THE DISTRICT SCHOOL-HOUSE, CORN-WALL—Where the Hon. Chief Justice Robinson, Hon. J. B. Macaulay, Hon. Jonas Jones, Hon. Archibald M'Lean, and other influential gentlemen of the Province were educated. Dedicated, by permission, to the Lord Bishop of Toronto, by his Obedient Humble Servant, John G. Howard. John G. Howard, Arc't., Delt. Toronto, 1845. Drawn on stone by J. Gillespie. Lith'r., Hugh Scobie, Toronto." John Strachan (Bishop) was ordained 22nd May, 1803, and on the same day appointed to Cornwall, where, in addition to his parochial work, he commenced taking pupils, gradually forming the school afterwards so well known—"The Cornwall Grammar School." Lithograph, colored. Size 6 x 10.

1597—"OWL'S HEAD, ROUND ISLAND, WHET STONE ISLAND AND MAGOON POINT, LAKE MEMPHREMAGOG, C.E.—(corner vignettes) Round Island; Balance Rock; View near Mountain House on Harvey's Landing. W. S. Hunter, Jr., del. J. H. Bufford's lith." Colored. Size 8 x 12. See 1557, 1784.

1598—OIL WELLS AT GASPE, C.E., 1834—Situated on the York River and Gaspe Bay—For several years in the long ago borings were made for oil at Gaspe, and more recently by an English syndicate. Small quantities were found, but not sufficient to warrant further development. The place has been for some time, and is still (1917) the seat of extensive fisheries. Thomas Pye, delineator. Roberts & Reinhold, lith., Place d'Armes, Mtl. Colored. Size 8 x 12.

1599—ROBIN & CO.'S FISHING ESTABLISHMENT, PASPEBIAC, 1834—North shore of Baie des Chaleurs.—Paspebiac was settled in 1766 by Charles Robin, who established there a large fishing station with inhabitants from the Isle of Jersey, off the coast of France. In June, 1778, the place was taken by two American privateers. Robin left for some years, but returned in 1783. At the present time (1917) the concern, which in 1910 became Robin, Jones & Whitman, Ltd., has branches all around the Gulf Coast. Thos. Pye, delineator. Roberts & Reinhold, lith., Place d'Armes, Mtl. Colored. Size 8 x 12.

1600—ELGIN, RIGHT HON. JAMES BRUCE, EARL OF—Governor-General of Canada, Jan. 30th, 1847—Dec. 18th, 1854. Water color from a painting by Berthon. Size 6 x 8. Half length. See 172.

1601—FORTIFICATION AND DEFENCE OF CANADA, 1862—Commissioners Appointed to Report on Subject—In February, 1862, Viscount Monck, Governor-General of Canada, appointed Col. William Gordon, R.E., C.B., who in 1861 came to Canada to command the engineers on the occasion of the Trent affair; Lieut.-Col. Henry Lynedoch Gardiner, R.A.; Hon. Hamilton H. Killaly, Chairman Board of Public Works, 1841-6, commissioners for consideration of the fortification and defence of Canada. Capt. Wm. Crossman, R.E., was nominated secretary. On 31st March, Col. Edward R. Wetherall, as chief of the staff, and Capt. T. Bythesia, R.N., were added to the commission. The following September a report was submitted, but never published, although a copy is in the Privy Council. The picture shows from left to right: Hon. H. H. Killaly, Capt. T. Bythesia, Col. Lynedoch Gardiner, Col. Edward R. Wetherall, Col. Gordon and Capt. W. Crossman. Photograph, colored. Size 5 x 8.

1602—GOVERNORS-GENERAL OF THE DOMINION OF CANADA— (1) Monck, Charles Stanley, Viscount—1861-8—(See 1616.) (2) Lisgar, Sir John Young, Baron—1868-72—Born at Bombay, 1807. In addition to Governor-Generalship, was Governor of Prince Edward Island, which was not annexed to the Dominion until 1873. Died, 1876. (3) Dufferin and Ava, Frederick Temple Hamilton Blackwood, Marquis of—1872-8—Visited British Columbia in connection with difficulties arising from Confederation. Mission partially successful. Born, 1826. Died, 1902. (4) Argyle, John Douglas Sutherland, Marquis of Lorne, Duke of—1878-83—(See 155). (5) Lansdowne, Henry Charles Keith Petty-Fitzmaurice, Marquis of— 1883-8—Born in 1845. Viceroy of India, 1888-93. Secretary for War, 1895-1900, and Foreign Secretary, 1900-1905. (6) Derby, Frederick Arthur, Baron Stanley of Preston, Earl of—1888-93—Secretary of State for War, 1878-80. Secretary of State for the Colonies, 1885-6. President Board of Trade, 1886-8. Born, 1841. Died, 1908. (7) Aberdeen, Sir John Campbell Hamilton Gordon, Earl of—1893-8—Appointed Viceroy of Ireland, 1886, and again in 1905. Born in Scotland, 1847. (8) Minto, Gilbert John Murray Kynynmond Elliot, Earl—1898-1904—In 1885 served through Riel Rebellion as chief of staff to General Middleton. Viceroy of India, 1905-10. Born, 1847. (9) Grey, Albert Henry George, Earl—1904-11—(See 149). (10) Connaught and Strathearn, H.R.H. Duke of — 1911-17—(See 169). Photogravure from photographs by Topley, Ottawa.

1603—VICE-REGAL CONSORTS IN CANADA—(1) Monck, Viscountess—Came to Canada with her husband, but did not remain throughout his term of office. (2) Lisgar, Lady—A talented artist, and during her stay in Canada sketched many bits of Canadian scenery. (3) Dufferin and Ava, Marchioness of—Author of several literary works, notably her "Canadian Journal," "Our Vice-Regal Life in India," and "The Record of Three Years' Work of the National Association for Supplying Female Aid to the Women of India." (4) H.R.H. Princess Louise, Duchess of Argyle—Fourth daughter of Queen Victoria. In 1871 married the Marquis of Lorne, afterwards Duke of Argyle, and on his appointment as Gov.-General accompanied him to Canada. The statue of Queen Victoria in front of the Royal Victoria College, Montreal, was executed by her. (5) Lansdowne, Marchioness of—One of group of sisters immortalized by Lord Beaconsfield in "Lothair." (6) Derby, Lady Stanley, Countess of— Eldest daughter of fourth Earl of Clarendon. Instrumental in securing foundation of the Lady Stanley Institute for Trained Nurses, Ottawa. (7) Aberdeen, Countess of—Foundress of National Council of Women in Canada, and first President of that organization; also founded Victorian Order of Nurses, in commemoration of Queen Victoria's Diamond Jubilee. (8) Minto, Countess of—Interested in hospital work. Instituted a fund for the location, protection and decoration of the graves of Canadians who fell in South Africa. (9) Grey, Countess of—Carried on work, inaugurated by the Countess of Minto, of bestowing prizes for well-kept gardens in Ottawa. Turned the first sod for the monument commemorating the Battle of Stoney Creek, 1909. (10) H.R. H. Duchess of Connaught—Indefatigable up to the time of her death in 1917, in her efforts to promote the welfare of the soldiers engaged in the great world struggle. Photogravure from photographs by Topley, Ottawa.

1604—MURRAY, GENERAL JAMES, 1719-94—Fifth son of Alexander, fourth Lord Elibank. He became major in the 15th in Ireland, 1749; was in command of the regiment in the Rochefort Expedition of 1757, and at the Siege of Louisburg the following year commanded a brigade. Murray was one of the three brigadiers (Monckton and Townshend, the others) under Wolfe at Quebec. On the city surrendering, he was left there with 4,000 troops. He attacked the French at Sillery, and in turn was besieged by them. He was at the Conquest of Montreal, 1760, and in that year appointed by Amherst, Governor of the District of Quebec. In 1762 he became Major-General. When Canada was ceded to the British by the Treaty of Paris he was made Governor of Canada, holding the position until 1766. Subsequently he was Governor of Minorca and of Hull. Died at his residence, Beauport House, near Battle, Sussex. Photogravure from painting in Dominion Archives, Ottawa. Size 4 x 5. Half length.

1605—CRAIG, SIR JAMES HENRY, 1748-1812—Son of Hew Craig, for many years Civil Judge at Gibraltar, and Judge-Advocate-General of the forces stationed there. Gazetted ensign at Gibraltar, 1763, but allowed leave to complete military education. On returning to Gibraltar, appointed Aide-de-Camp to Gen. Sir Robert Boyd, K.B., Lieut.-Governor of the fortress. Served in America, 1774; wounded at Bunker's Hill. Transferred to Canada, 1776. At Capture of Ticonderoga. So distinguished himself in early part of Burgoyne's advance on Saratoga that the General sent him home with despatches. Made Major without purchase in newly organized 82nd, with which he came to Nova Scotia. In conjunction with Major-Gen. Alured Clarke, took Dutch colony of Cape of Good Hope, 1795. Took over civil government and military command of Cape until arrival of Lord Macartney in 1797. Invested with Order of the Bath by special permission from King. Appointed Captain-General and Governor-General of Canada, Aug. 29th, 1807, proving an able administrator. Resigned, Oct., 1811, and on return to England promoted General. Died in London. Photogravure from a portrait in the Dominion Archives, Ottawa. Size 4 x 6. Head and shoulders, oval.

1606—CATHCART, CHARLES MURRAY—Second Earl, Governor-General of Canada, 1846-7—Born at Walton, Essex, Eng., 1783. Entered the army as a cornet in 2nd Life Guards and served on the staff of Sir James Craig in Naples and Sicily during 1805-6. He was made lieut.-colonel in August, 1810, was present at Barossa, Salamanca and Vittoria, distinguishing himself at Waterloo. He became lieut.-colonel of a scientific corps at Hythe. Leaving there in 1830 he took up residence in Edinburgh, occupying himself for some years in scientific pursuits; discovered a new mineral in 1841; held appointment of Commander of the Forces in Scotland and Governor of Edinburgh Castle, 1837-42. In June of the following year succeeded his father as second Earl and eleventh Baron Cathcart. His sojourn in Canada was during a difficult period, and for a time he combined military command with civil government. Died in 1859. Water color. Size 3 x 5. Head and shoulders.

1607—PREVOST, GENERAL SIR GEORGE, BART.—Eldest son of Major-General Prevost, who had served under Wolfe. Born at New York, 10th May, 1767; made a baronet in 1805. He arrived at Halifax, April, 1808, as Lieut.-Governor of Nova Scotia, and served with distinction in the West Indies. Upon the resignation of Sir James Craig, became Governor-in-Chief and Commander of the Forces in British North America. He was active in the War of 1812, and was severely censured in connection with his action at Sackett's Harbour, May, 1813, and Plattsburg, Sept., 1814. In the latter engagement he is said to have hurried Capt. Downie into action, unprepared and against his judgment. Returned to England to answer charges against him. Died in 1816 before the date set for the court-martial. Water color from painting by Berthon. Size 6 x 8. Three-quarter length. See 1623.

1608—HARDY—"Sir Charles Hardy, Admiral of the White, and Commander-in-Chief of His Majesty's Fleet in the Channel—Thos. Hudson, pinxt. P. Dawe, fecit. London. Publish'd as the Act directs, 23d of Septr., 1779, by Robert Wilkinson at 58 Cornhill." Son of Vice-Admiral Sir Charles Hardy. Entered the navy as a volunteer on board the "Salisbury," 1730. In 1745 he commanded the "Jersey" on the coast of Portugal, and in 1755 received appointment as Governor of New York, being knighted before his departure from England. A commission as Rear-Admiral of the Blue was sent out to him the following year. Hardy returned to England in 1758. He, however, was sent out in the "Captain" to arrange the transport of colonial forces to Louisburg, where he joined Boscawen and took an active part in the siege and reduction of the town. Became Vice-Admiral in 1762, and in 1770 made Admiral of the Blue. On Keppel's resigning command of the Channel Fleet in 1779, Hardy was chosen to fill the post. Died at Portsmouth, Eng., 18th May, 1780. Line engraving. Size 10 x 12. Three-quarter length.

1609—HER MAJESTY QUEEN VICTORIA INVITED TO VISIT CANADA—Deputation that Presented Memorial—In the Provincial Parliament of 1859, Hon. P. M. Vankoughnet, Commissioner of Crown Lands, presented an address petitioning her Majesty Queen Victoria to visit Canada. The address was moved in the Assembly by Hon. Mr. Cartier, the Premier, seconded by Hon. Mr. Foley, and carried in both Houses. The Speaker of the Assembly, the Hon. (Sir) Henry Smith, was deputed to present the same to her Majesty. She was, however, compelled to decline, but in appreciation of the loyalty of her Canadian subjects consented to allow his Royal Highness, the Prince of Wales, afterwards King Edward VII., to visit the Dominion. The picture shows (1) Sir Hector Langevin, K.C.M.G., C.B. (2) Colonel George Herman Ryland, son of Herman Witsius Ryland, Civil Secretary to Lord Dorchester. (3) Hon. (Sir) Henry Smith, K.B., Q.C. (4) Hon. (Sir) L. N. Casault, member of Legislature, later judge Superior Court of Quebec. (5) Col. Wm. Botsford Jarvis, Sheriff Home District, 1826-57. Messrs. Langevin, Casault, Ryland and Jarvis had at this time to go to England on other business, and the Canadian Government gave them authority to accompany Hon. Henry Smith, thus forming a Canadian deputation when the latter presented the address to her Majesty. From original water color in possession of Col. Henry Smith, Kingston, Ont. Size 4 x 6.

1610—BORDEN, RT. HON. SIR ROBERT LAIRD, G.C.M.G., K.C.—Descended from Samuel Borden, a surveyor, who came from the American colonies in 1760, settling at Falmouth, N.S. Premier Borden was born at Grand Pre, N.S., June 26th, 1854, and educated at Acacia Villa Academy, Horton. Studied law and was called to the bar, 1878, practising successfully, first at Kentville, N.S., and afterwards at Halifax. Represented Halifax in the House of Commons, 1896-1904, and Carleton, 1905-8. In the general election of 1908 he was returned for both Carleton and Halifax, electing to sit for the latter seat. Leader of the Opposition, 1905-11. In the general election of 1911 returned for Halifax, and called upon to form new Administration. Created Privy Councillor, Jan. 1st, 1912. Knighted, 1914. Still (1917) holds the Premiership of the Dominion. Photogravure from photograph. Size 4 x 6. Head and shoulders.

1611—PREMIERS OF ONTARIO, 1867-1914—(1) Macdonald, John Sandfield, 1867-71, Solicitor-General in LaFontaine-Baldwin Government, Attorney-General in Brown-Dorion Ministry; born at St. Raphael's, Glengarry, 1812; died, 1872. (2) Blake, Hon. Edward, 1871-2, eminent lawyer and statesman; born in Ontario, 1833; died, 1912. (3) Mowat, Sir Oliver, 1872-1896. (See 428, 468.) (4) Hardy, Hon. Arthur Sturgis, 1896-99; called to bar of Upper Canada, 1865; elected to Ontario Legislature, 1873; Commissioner of Crown Lands, 1889; born, 1837, and died in 1899. (5) Ross, Sir George, 1899-1905; Minister of Education, 1883-99; appointed to Senate, 1906; born, 1841; died, 1914. (6) Whitney, Sir James Pliny, 1905-14; one of the leaders of the bar in Eastern Ontario; declined a seat in Borden Cabinet on its formation; born at Williamsburg, Ont., 1843; died, 1914. Photogravure.

1612—DURHAM, RT. HON. JOHN GEORGE, EARL OF—Born at Lambton Castle, Durham, 1792. In 1813 was returned to Parliament, where he acted with the Whig party; raised to peerage as Baron Durham in 1828; was one of the four persons who prepared the Reform Bill. In 1838 he became Governor-General of Canada, being vested with extraordinary powers to restore peace in the province then in throes of rebellion. Returned suddenly to England in December, 1839, in consequence of disagreement with home Ministry. Died the following year. Photogravure from drawing by J. Stewart. Size 4 x 5. Half length.

1613—LAURIER, RT. HON. SIR WILFRID, G.C.M.G.—Born at St. Lin, Que., Nov. 20th, 1841. Educated at L'Assomption College and McGill University (B.C.L., 1864). Practised profession of law in Montreal, and afterwards at Arthabaskaville. Served as ensign in volunteer militia in the Arthabaskaville Infantry Co., and saw service in the last Fenian Raid. Entered local Parliament, 1871, as member for Drummond and Arthabaskaville, afterwards entering Dominion House. Minister of Inland Revenue in Mackenzie Administration, 1877-8. One of those who signed the address from the Liberal party to the Pope, 1896, resulting in the appointment of a Papal Ablegate for Canada. Succeeded Hon. Edward Blake as leader of the Opposition, 1887, Premier, 1896-1911, when his Government was defeated. Still (1917) leader of the Opposition. Represented Canada at Queen Victoria's Diamond Jubilee, 1897. Member Privy Council. Received gold medal from Cobden Club in recognition of his services in cause of international free exchange. Photogravure from photograph by Pittaway, Ottawa. Size 4 x 6. Head and shoulders.

1614—SIGNATURE OF THE TREATY OF GHENT BETWEEN GREAT BRITAIN AND THE UNITED STATES OF AMERICA, DEC. 24TH, 1814—(With key)—Owing to its convenient situation Ghent was chosen as the meeting place of the plenipotentiaries of Britain and the States, and also because an English garrison was stationed there, thus affording security to the negotiators. The treaty, which was the means of building up the cordial relations existing to-day between the world's two great English-speaking nations, was signed in the old Carthusian Monastery in Ghent, Belgium. It is to be noted in the picture that the Chief British Plenipotentiary, Admiral Lord Gambier, holds in his hand an actual copy of the original treaty. Mezzogravure from a painting by A. Forestier, 1914. Size 16 x 24. See 1615.

1615—SIGNATURE OF THE TREATY OF GHENT—Key to picture. See 1614.

1616—MONCK, RT. HON. VISCOUNT CHARLES STANLEY—Governor-General of Canada, Nov. 28th, 1861-Nov. 13th, 1868—Son of the third Viscount; born at Templemore, Co. Tipperary, Ireland, 1819. Educated at Trinity College, Dublin, and called to the Irish bar, 1841. Succeeded his father as Viscount eight years later. Entered Parliament, 1852, as member for Portsmouth, and from March, 1855, until the general election of 1857 was a Lord of the Treasury. In October, 1861, he was appointed to succeed Sir Edmund Walker Head as Governor-General of Canada, and arrived at Quebec in the same month. Owing to the absence of Court at Balmoral on his leaving England, his commission was not made out until November. In the interval he was designated as Administrator. Died, 1894. Water color. Size 4 x 5. Head and shoulders.

1617—McBRIDE, SIR RICHARD, K.C.M.G.—Premier British Columbia, 1903-15—Born at New Westminster, B.C., 15th Dec., 1870. Educated at Public and High schools of New Westminster, and at Dalhousie University, Halifax, N.S. (LL.B., 1890). Called to the bar of British Columbia, 1892. K.C., 1905. Returned member for Dewdney, B.C., in local elections, 1898, 1900 and 1903. Represented Victoria City, 1907; Victoria City and Yale, 1909, and Victoria, 1912. Minister of Mines in Dunsmuir Administration. Died Aug. 6th, 1917, in London, Eng. Photogravure from photograph by Savannah. Size 4 x 6. Head and shoulders.

1618—PREMIERS OF BRITISH COLUMBIA, 1871-1915—(1) McCreight, Hon. John Foster—1871-2—Attorney-General during last days of Governor Musgrave's regime. (2) DeCosmos, Hon. Amor—1872-4—One of the pioneer journalists of British Columbia. Founder of "British Colonist," 1858, and "Victoria Standard," 1872. One of the earliest and most energetic supporters of Confederation. (3) Walkem, Hon. G. A.—1874-6, 1878-82—Made trip to London to urge upon Home Government the claims of British Columbia in regard to railway development. (4) Elliott, Hon. A. C.—1876-8 —One of the first acts of the Elliott Government was to improve the existing voting laws. (5) Beaven, Hon. Robert—1882-3. (6) Smithe, Hon. William—1883-7. (7) Davie, Hon. A. E. B.—1887-9. (8) Robson, Hon. John—1889-92. (9) Davie, Hon. Theodore—1892-5. (10) Turner, Hon. J. H.—1895-8—Took an active part in formation of first Rifle Company enrolled in Prince Edward Island, where prior to settling in British Columbia he had engaged in business. (11) Semlin, Hon. C. A.—1898-1900—Entered British Columbia Legislature, 1871. Chief Commissioner Lands and Works. Provincial Secretary and Minister of Education. (12) Martin, Hon. Joseph—1900—Attorney-General of Manitoba, 1888-91, and appointed to same office in British Columbia, 1898. Since 1902 has sat in the English Parliament. (13) Dunsmuir, Hon. James—1900-2—Lieut.-Governor of British Columbia, 1906-9. Built magnificent railway and traffic bridge over Fraser River during his administration. Contributed largely to endowment of McGill University, B.C. (14) Prior, Hon. E. G.—1902-3—Came to Vancouver Island, 1873, as mining engineer and surveyor for the Vancouver Coal Mining and Land Company. Govt. Inspector of Mines, 1878-80. Took part in military display in connection with Queen Victoria's Diamond Jubilee, London, 1897. on invitation. (15) McBride, Hon. Richard—1903-15—(See 1617). Photogravure from photographs by Savannah.

1619—SMYTH—"Major-General Sir James Carmichael Smyth, Bart, C.B., K.C.H. K.M.T., and K.S.W. E. H. Latilla Pinxit, Post Mortem. Thos. Hodgetts, sculpsit, London, July 19th, 1841. Published for private circulation by Messrs. Colnaghi and Puckle, No. 23 Cockspur Street." Sir James Carmichael Smyth, military engineer, eldest son of James Carmichael Smyth, was born 22nd Feb., 1779, in London, Eng., and died at Georgetown, Demerara, B.W.I., 4th March, 1838. He received a commission as second lieutenant of the Royal Artillery, 20th Nov., 1794, and was transferred to the Royal Engineers the following year. At the Battles of Quatre Bras and Waterloo he served on Wellington's staff and entered Paris with him. As Governor of the Bahamas, he abolished the flogging of female slaves. The Duke of Wellington was so highly satisfied with

Smyth's report regarding the defence of the West Indies that he selected him to proceed to Canada on a similar service in 1826. In December of that year Sir Peregrine Maitland, Lieut.-Governor U.C., in his speech from the throne, spoke in complimentary terms of the report in connection with military defence of Canada. Line engraving. Size 9 x 11. Head and shoulders.

1620—MASERES, FRANCIS—Attorney-General of Quebec, 1766-9— He was born in London, Eng., 15th Dec., 1731, descended from a family originally French, which came to England after the revocation of the edict of Nantes. Entered Clare College, Cambridge, 4th July, 1748, and won the first Chancellor's Classical Medal, 1752. In 1758 Maseres was called to the Bar from the Inner Temple, becoming in turn a bencher, reader and treasurer. He filled the post as Attorney-General of Quebec with such zeal and dignity that on his return to England he was requested by the Protestant settlers in that city to act as their agent. He was Cursitor Baron of the Exchequer, 1773-1824. His death took place in the latter year. Amongst many other works he wrote "Considerations on the Expediency of Admitting Representatives from the American Colonies to the House of Commons," and "Collection of Commissions and other Public Instruments Relating to Quebec Since 1760." Mezzotint by Sayers, private plate. Proof before All Letters. Size 7½ x 8. Head and shoulders, with hand, in circle.

1621—CARTWRIGHT, RT. HON. SIR RICHARD JOHN—Grandson of Hon. Richard Cartwright, a Judge of the Common Pleas, District of Mecklenburgh. Born in Kingston, 1835; educated at Trinity College, Dublin, and entered public life in 1863 as member for Lennox and Addington. He was Minister of Finance in the Mackenzie Administration, 1873-8. He had a high reputation as an orator, some of his speeches being still regarded as masterpieces of Parliamentary eloquence. In 1879 was created a K.C.M.G., and in 1904 called to the Senate by Earl Grey. On several occasions Sir Richard acted as Premier of Canada in the absence of Sir Wilfrid Laurier. He went to Washington as a delegate to promote better relations between Canada and the States. The Lieut.-Governorship of Ontario was declined by him in 1908. Died at Kingston, 24th Sept., 1912. Photogravure from a photograph. Size 4 x 6. Three-quarter length, sitting.

1622—GARNEAU, FRANCOIS XAVIER, 1809-66—A native of Quebec Province; received his education at the Quebec Seminary, and studied for the bar. For a time served as clerk in the Legislative Assembly. Afterwards became City Clerk of Quebec. M. Garneau was a member of the Council of Public Instruction of Lower Canada, and for several years held the presidency of the Institut Canadien, Quebec. Author of a valuable history of Canada. Photogravure from a painting by Albert Ferland. Size 5 x 7. Head and shoulders.

1623—PREVOST—"Lieut.-Genl. Sir George Prevost, Governor of Canada. Pub'd. by Dighton, Spring Gardens, Novr., 1812." Xylograph in color. (caricature). Size 9 x 11. See 1607.

1624—TUPPER, RT. HON. SIR CHARLES, BART., G.C.M.G., C.B.—He was born at Amherst, N.S., in 1821; educated at Wolfeville, later taking a medical course at Edinburgh, where he graduated M.D. in 1843. He became a member of the Royal College of Surgeons, practised his profession in Amherst for some years, commencing his political career in 1855. From 1864-7 he was Prime Minister of Nova Scotia; advocated Confederation; opposed Howe's petition to Home Government for repeal of British North America Act. Filled the offices of Minister of Customs, of Public Works, and of Railways and Canals. He held the position of High Commissioner for Canada in England, 1883-7, and 1888-96. Sir Charles was leader of the House of Commons in the Bowell Administration. Retired from active political life in 1906. It has been said of Sir Charles, who passed away in England, Oct., 1915, that "the two aims he always kept in view, have been the strengthening of the golden link which connects Great Britain with the first and greatest of her colonies, and the holding aloft of the standard of the right of the nation, so that she may prove herself worthy of the proud position she has made her own." His grandson, Charles Stewart Tupper, son of J. Stewart Tupper, K.C., succeeded to the title. Photogravure from a photograph. Size 4 x 6. Head and shoulders.

1625—HOWE, JOSEPH—A Nova Scotian poet, journalist and statesman—Born at Halifax, 13th Dec., 1804, son of John Howe, a U.E.L., who for many years was King's Printer there. The younger Howe was taught the trade of printer in the "Gazette" office, and in 1827, in partnership with James Spike, purchased the "Halifax Weekly Chronicle," changing its its name to "Acadian." Sold his share and bought the "Nova Scotian," in which were reported debates in the Assembly. In 1832 he opened a Mechanics' Institute in Halifax, which, through his influence, became a permanent and useful institution. Elected for County of Halifax, 1836; agitated strongly for responsible government in Nova Scotia. In 1840 he was appointed a member of the Executive Council and elected Speaker of the House of Assembly. As a delegate from Nova Scotia, Howe was in England, 1850-1. His essay on the organization of the Empire appeared in 1866. He became Secretary of State for the Lower Provinces, 1870, and three years later nominated Governor of Nova Scotia. The death of "the greatest Nova Scotian" took place 1st June, 1873. Photogravure from engraving. Size 4 x 5. Head and shoulders (oval).

1626—THOMSON, RT. HON. C. E. POULETT (BARON SYDENHAM), 1799-1841—"From a painting by George Hayter, Esq., M.A.S.L., etc. Engraved by W. H. Mote, London, John Saunders, Junr., 7 Dyers Buildings, Holborn Bars." Entered political life, 1826; appointed Governor-General of Canada in 1839; acted as Lieutenant-Governor Upper Canada, 22nd November, 1839, to 18th Feb., 1840; resigned 1841. He opened the first Parliament of the United Canadas. Line engraving. Size 4 x 5. Half length. See 419.

1627—GOSFORD, RT. HON. ARCHIBALD, G.C.B., EARL OF—"Archibald, Earl of Gosford. Painted by T. Phillips, R.A., 1826. Drawn on stone by R. J. Lane, A.R.A., 1828. Printed by C. Hullmandel." Governor-General of Canada, July 1st, 1835-March 30th, 1838. Chief of a commission of inquiry and pacification, which it was hoped would lead to the adjustment of political differences and the establishment of the Provincial Government on a firm and liberal footing. Lord Gosford's efforts to form a Government by uniting the most moderate of the two factions in Canada were unavailing, however, and subsequent to the proceedings at the meeting of the six counties, held at St. Charles, October 23rd, 1837, which made it clear that Lower Canada could not be governed under the existing constitution, he asked to be relieved of his duties. Consent being received from the Home Government he returned to England where his death took place, March 29th, 1849. Lithograph. Size 3 x 4. Half length.

1628—HEAD, RIGHT HON. SIR EDMUND WALKER, K.C.B.— Governor-General of Canada, 19th Dec., 1854-25th Oct., 1861—Only son of Rev. Sir John Head, M.A. Born near Maidstone, Kent, Eng., and educated at Winchester and Oriel College, Oxford. He was Lieutenant-Governor of New Brunswick from 1847-54, and succeeded Lord Elgin as Governor-General of Canada in the latter year. In 1857 he was made a member of the Privy Council. Sir Edmund was a man of high literary attainments, amongst his works being a treatise on the use of "Shall and Will," and "A Handbook of Spanish Painting." His death took place in 1868. Water color from painting by G. T. Berthon. Size 6 x 8. Half length.

1629—METCALFE, SIR CHARLES THEOPHILUS—Governor-General United Canada, 30th March, 1843-26th November, 1845. Water color from painting by G. T. Berthon. Size 6 x 8. Half length, sitting. See 153.

1630—MORNAY, LOUIS FRANCOIS DUPLESSIS DE—"Le R. P. Francois de Mornay, Capucin Evesque et Coadiuteur de Quebec, Sacre par Monseigr. le Cardinal de Rhoan dans leur Eglise de la rue St. Honnore, 22 Avril, 1714. Abandonnant son Saint Azile Mornay paroit bien plus touche, de la gloire de l'Evangile que des honneurs de l'Eveche. Gacon." Rev. Brother Louis Francois Duplessis de Mornay, Capuchin, Bishop, and Coadjutor of Quebec, consecrated by the Cardinal Bishop of Rohan in their Church of St. Honore street, Paris. April 22nd, 1714. Leaving behind his Holy Refuge, Mornay seems much more impressed by the glorious diffusion of the Gospel than the honors of the Bishop's dignity. Bishop de Mornay, who succeeded Mgr. de St. Vallier, was recognized as third Bishop of Quebec at Paris, May 31, 1728. He sent Mgr. Dosquet as his Coadjutor in 1729, and resigned his seat in 1733. Owing to ill-health he never came to Canada, and died at Paris, 27th November, 1741. Line engraving. Size 4 x 5. Head and shoulders, oval.

1631—VAUDREUIL, PHILIPPE DE RIGAUD, MARQUIS DE—Governor of New France, 1703-25—Generally known as Vaudreuil the Elder. Lieut.-General in the French army; distinguished himself at Valenciennes. Sent to Canada, 1687, in command of 800 troops. In 1696 commanded a division of Frontenac's army against Iroquois and led a detachment to destroy the Oneida town. Appointed Governor of Montreal two years later. On the death of De Callieres in 1703, the Marquis was appointed Governor of the colony. Photogravure from the painting in the Chateau de Ramezay, Montreal. Size 4 x 6. Half length.

1632—TALON, JEAN BAPTISTE—Second Intendant of New France, 1663-8, and 1670-72—Born in Picardy, France, 1625. Held offices in the Intendancies of Bordeaux and Lyons, and Intendant of Hainant, 1661-3. Established an excellent judiciary system in Canada. Opened up trade between Canada and the West Indies. Established first brewery in North America, and developed cod fisheries along the St. Lawrence. In 1668 left for France, but returned to Canada, 1670, resuming the Intendancy. two years later finally returned to France, where for several years he held high positions in the King's Household. Died 1691. Photogravure after painting in Hotel Dieu, Quebec. Size 5 x 7. Head and shoulders.

1633—BREBOEUF, JEAN DE, 1593-1649—Scion of a noble family of Normandy. Studied at Rouen, and ordained to the priesthood, 1623. Came to Canada with De Caen, two years later, spending the winter of 1625-6 among the Algonquins. Visited the villages of the Hurons on Georgian Bay, where he established the first mission. Returned to College of Rouen, 1629, but again came to Canada with Champlain, 1633. In 1640 attempted, unsuccessfully, to establish a mission among the intractable Neutral Nation, north of Lake Erie. Returned to Huron Mission, where in 1649 he was captured, tortured, and burned at the stake by the Iroquois. His skull is preserved in the Hotel Dieu, Quebec. Photogravure from painting in the House of the Immaculate Conception, Montreal. Size 4 x 6. Head and shoulders.

1634—GALISSONNIERE, ROLAND MICHEL BARRIN, COMTE DE LA —Governor of New France, 1747-9. Photogravure from an engraving in the Chateau de Ramezay. Size 4 x 6. Head and shoulders. See 1644.

1635—LE JEUNE, FATHER PAUL, 1592-1664—Superior of Jesuits in Canada—In 1632 came to Canada; engaged in a mission to the Algonquins the following year. In 1639 was succeeded by Vimont as Superior. Appointed to Governor's Council, 1640, and returned to his native France in the same year. Offered Bishopric of Quebec. Published a descriptive work on Canada and its native tribes, in seven volumes, 1640. It was Father Le Jeune who preached Champlain's funeral sermon. Photogravure from painting in the House of the Immaculate Conception, Montreal. Size 4 x 6. Head and shoulders.

1636—VAUDREUIL-CAVAGNAL, PIERRE DE RIGAUD, MARQUIS DE—Governor of New France, 1755-60—Son of Vaudreuil the Elder, a former Governor of the colony, whose wife was a Canadian. Vaudreuil the Younger, the last Governor of New France, was born at Quebec in 1698. Entered the military service at an early age. In 1730 gained the coveted honor of Chevalier of the Order of St. Louis. Appointed Governor of Three Rivers, 1733, and of Louisiana, 1742. Photogravure from painting in the Chateau de Ramezay, Montreal. Size 4 x 6. Half length.

1637—YORK, JAMES, DUKE OF (KING OF ENGLAND)—"His Royall Highness, James Duke of Yorke and Albany, Kt. of the most noble order of the Garter, and sole brother to his sacred Maty. King Charles the 2d, etc." Son of Charles I., born at Saint James' Palace, London, 1633, and soon afterwards created Duke of York. After the death of Prince Rupert in the latter part of 1682 he was appointed to succeed him as Governor of the Hudson's Bay Company, retaining the office until his accession to the throne as James II., 1685. Lord Churchill, afterwards Duke of Marlborough, then became Governor of the Company. James died in September, 1701. Line engraving. Size 6 x 9. Full length, with coat-of-arms.

1638—D'AMVILLE—"Francois Christophle de Levy Vantadour, Duc d'Amville, Comte de Brion, Premier Esquier de Monseigneur le Duc d'Orleans. B. Moncornet, excudit cum Privilegio Regis."—Fifth Viceroy of New France, 1644-60. He was Lieutenant-General in all America. Died at Paris, 9th September, 1661, having resigned the previous year. Line engraving. Size 4 x 5. Head and shoulders, oval.

1639—BEGON, MICHEL, SIEUR DE LA PICARDIERE—Intendant of New France (Canada), 1710-26—"Michel Begon in supr. Provinciae curia senator Primarius alnetensis prov. Et rei marit. In Gallia occid. Praefect. J. Lubin sculpsit Rupellae." Although appointed in 1710, he did not arrive in Quebec until two years later. Shortly afterwards his palace was destroyed by fire and several lives lost. The foundation of the fortifications of Quebec were laid by Begon. He was born in 1674, and died in 1740. Begon was the eldest son of Michel Begon, who from 1683-5 was Governor of St. Domingo, and after whom the Begonia plant is named. Line engraving. Size 7 x 8. Head and shoulders, oval.

1640—COOK, CAPT. JAMES, 1728-80—Celebrated surveyor, explorer and navigator—It is stated by several writers that Cook was appointed master of the Mercury in 1759. From the Public Records, however, it has been ascertained that he was never on board in any capacity. In 1759 became master of the Pembroke, commanded by Capt. Simcoe, father of the first Lieut.-Governor of Upper Canada. The Pembroke sailed from Plymouth with Amherst to recapture Louisburg, arriving too late to take part in the landing there. Cook, by order of Admiral Saunders, went on board the Northumberland in September. He surveyed the channel of the St. Lawrence, was engaged in piloting vessels on the river, made observations and draughts of the coasts of Nova Scotia and Newfoundland. Between 1768 and 1775 he made two explorations of the Southern Pacific. Shortly after his return from the second voyage Cook was promoted to rank of captain, and received an appointment in Greenwich Hospital. The Admiralty gladly accepted his services in an expedition to discover a north-west passage between the Pacific and Atlantic Oceans. The Resolution and Discovery were fitted out, and Cook left Plymouth Sound, 12th

July, 1776. The visit to Nootka Sound marked the beginning of fur trade on the north-west coast, south of Alaska, and was also the first step in bringing that coast under British rule. Cook's geographical discoveries were numerous and important. A memorial has been erected near the spot where he met his death. February, 1780, Karakakoa Bay, Hawaii. Photogravure from original portrait by Dance in the Gallery of Greenwich Hospital, England. Size 4 x 6. Half length.

1641—CHAMPLAIN, SAMUEL DE—Governor of New France, 1612-29 and 1633-5—Born about 1567, at Brouage, in the Province of Saintonge, France. In 1598 made a voyage to Spain and the following year joined an expedition against the English to the West Indies. Set out for New France in March, 1603, with Pont-Grave, explored the St. Lawrence to Lake St. Louis and set sail for France in August of the same year. Returned as geographer and historian with De Mont's expedition in 1604, and from then on made many voyages between France and this country. Founded Quebec, July, 1608, and Montreal in the spring of 1611. In 1610 discovered the lake which bears his name. Defended Quebec successfully against Sir David Kirke in 1628, but on the latter's reappearance the following year was forced to capitulate on honorable terms. By the Treaty of St. Germain-en-Laye, March 29th, 1632, France's possessions in Canada were restored, and the next year Champlain returned to Quebec, where he died on Christmas Day, 1635. Published many interesting works relating to his discoveries. Photogravure after the painting by Th. Hamel. Size 4 x 6. Head and shoulders. See 82.

1642—MARBLE GROUP OF JOHN AND SEBASTIAN CABOT— Modelled by John Cassidy, R.B.S., R.C.A., sculptor, Governor of Royal Manchester Institution, and deposited in London, Eng., 1897. Amongst many examples of Mr. Cassidy's work are the statues of Queen Victoria, in Belfast, and of King Edward, in Manchester. John Cabot, a native of Genoa, took up his residence in London, Eng., about 1484. In May, 1497, with his son Sebastian, he set sail in the "Matthew" from Bristol, landing at Cape Breton on 24th June. He took possession of the land in the name of Henry VII. The following year further explorations were made, on east coast of Greenland, which Cabot named "Labrador Land," and along the coast of Nova Scotia and New England. Photogravure from the model by John Cassidy. Size 4 x 6.

1643—KEAN—"Edmund Kean, Esqr. In the dress presented to and worn by him on the occasion of his being chosen a Chief and Prince of the Huron Tribe of Indians by the name of Alanienouidet. To the patentee, committee and performers of the Theatre Royal, Drury Lane, in commemoration of the return of that distinguished actor to his native country and with the intention of presenting at one view a faithful portrait of Mr. Kean, and a correct delineation of the costume of that warlike tribe who unanimously elected him a chieftain and a Brother at Quebec on Saturday, October 7th, 1826. This print is most respectfully dedicated by their obliged and obdt. Sert., William Kenneth. Painted by Frederick Meyer, Junr., 3 Red Lion Square. Engraved by G. F. Storm. Printed by Bishop & Co., London. Published by William Kenneth at his Dramatic Repository, corner of Bow St., Covent Garden, May 14th, 1827. Proof." Kean was born in London, Eng., Nov. 4th, 1787, of Irish descent. About 1790 he made his debut on the stage, playing children's parts. Ran away to sea a few years later. He returned to the stage, however, and in 1814 appeared at Drury Lane, six years afterwards making his first appearance in New York. During his second stay in America, 1825-6, several Huron chiefs dined with him at Indian Lorette, Que. Admiration was evidently mutual, for shortly afterwards Mr. Kean was adopted into the tribe under the name Alanienouidet. The custom of adoption has always been prevalent among Indian nations, and the person chosen becomes by the ceremony a member of the tribe and of a particular family of the tribe. Kean died 15th May, 1833. Line engraving. Size 7 x 10. Full length.

1644—GALISSIONNIERE, ROLAND MICHEL BARRIN, COMTE DE LA—Governor New France, 1747-9—"M. de la Galissioniere, avec privilege du Roi. Dessine par Graincourt, 1780. Grave par Hubert." He was a distinguished naval officer, born at Rochefort, France, 11th Nov., 1693. Enterer the navy in 1710; commanded Le Tigre in 1741. During the captivity of La Jonquiere, who had been made prisoner by the English off Cape Finisterre, 3rd May, 1747, he administered the Government of Canada. In 1756 his fleet defeated Admiral Byng in the vicinity of Minorca. His death took place in October of that year. Line engraving. Size 5 x 7. Head and shoulders, oval. See 1634.

1645—D'ESTREES, JEAN, COMTE—Eighth Viceroy of New France, 1687-1707—As Lieutenant-General he was at Valenciennes in 1655, commanded the French fleet at Solebay, 1672; made a Marshal of France in 1681, being the first naval officer to obtain that rank. Died in 1707. N. Largilliere, pinx. J. Audran, scul. Line engraving. Size 8 x 12. Head and shoulders, oval.

1646—D'ESTRADES, GODFREY, COMTE—Seventh Viceroy of New France, 1662-86—"Ludovicus Godefroy comes D'Estrades eques torquatus, etc. Stephanus Picart Rous, fecit." Born at Agen, France, in 1607—one of the ablest negotiators of his time. As Lieutenant-General commanded at the Siege of Dunkirk. Having been sent to Holland as Ambassador, the Marquis de Tracy came to Canada as his lieutenant until 1667. Died 1688. Line engraving. Size 10 x 12. Half length, oval.

1647—LE CANADIEN—HABITANT OF THE OLDEN TIME—The habitant, on his little farm on the banks of the St. Lawrence or the Richelieu, enjoyed a life of peace and prosperity. From the outside world he required little; in its problems he had no vital interest, and a tranquil old age crowned a life of toil interspersed with the simple pleasures afforded by the community in which he lived. Photogravure from painting by Cornelius Krieghoff. Size 5 x 6.

1648—LA CANADIENNE—A French-Canadian woman of the olden time—The habitants were an independent people, requiring little which their own farms could not provide. Almost every house had its spinning wheel and metier, so that the women were able to weave the linen and homespun required to clothe the household. These simple folk were hospitable to a degree. Indeed De Gaspe tells us that it was a rule that the table should be almost as copiously covered at the end of the meal as when the guests sat down to it. Photogravure from painting by Cornelius Krieghoff. Size 5 x 6.

1649—TACHE, ALEXANDRE ANTONIN, D.D., 1823-94—Bishop of St. Boniface—A Canadian prelate (R. C.); born at Riviere du Loup, Que.; educated at St. Hyacinthe College. He volunteered as a missionary to the Indians on the Great Lakes; was ordained to the priesthood. He was most earnest in his visitation to northern missions, comforting and aiding his missionary priests. Bishop Tache founded a number of missions, colleges and convents in the North-west. In 1869 he journeyed to Ottawa to warn the Government of mischief and unrest in the North-west. His warning was, however, disregarded by Cartier. The Bishop proceeded to Rome, but was asked to return to Canada at once to appease the trouble. He did so, the result being that through his influence, the insurgent half-breeds laid down their arms. Photogravure from a photograph. Size 5 x 7. Head and shoulders.

1650—LAVAL, FRANCOIS DE LAVAL DE MONTMORENCY, 1622-1708—First Roman Catholic Bishop of Canada (Quebec). Photogravure from painting in Laval University, Quebec. Size 5 x 7. Head and shoulders. See 248.

1651—MONCKTON—"The Honble. Robert Monckton, Major-General, Governor of New York. T. Hudson, pinxt. Js. McArdell, fecit." Second son of the first Viscount Galway. Born in 1726. Served in Germany in 1743, and in Flanders two years later. Represented Pontefract in Parliament, 1751. Sent to Nova Scotia the following year, and in 1755 assisted in the expatriation of the Acadians. Served under Wolfe and severely wounded at the Battle of Abraham's Plains, 1759. After the conquest of Quebec became Governor of New York. In 1761 he led a successful expedition against Martinique. Returned two years later to England, where he died in 1782. Line engraving. Size 11 x 14. Half length.

1652—MONTMORENCY—Viceroy of New France, 1620-25—"Henri II., Duc de Montmorency et D'Amville, Pair, Amiral, et Premier Baron de France, Chevalier des ordres du Roi, Gouverneur et Lieutenant-General du Languedoc, Comte de Dammartin, etc., etc. Ne a Chantilly le 30 Avril, 1595; mort a Toulouse le 30 Octobre, 1632. A Paris chez Blin Imprimeur en Taille-Douce, Place Maubert, No. 17, Vis-a-vis la rue des Portes, A. P. D. R. Sergent del et sculp., 1778." He commanded for Louis XIII. in the Civil War against the Huguenots. For his victory over the Imperialists at Veillane in 1629 he was made a marshal. Resigned his office as Viceroy in favor of his nephew, Henri de Levis duc de Ventadour. Engraving, printed in color. Size 5 x 6. Head and shoulders, oval.

1653—CONDE—Second Viceroy of New France, 1612-20—"Prince de Conde, Henry de Bourbon, Aux Exploicts de ce Mars Hercul' ne peut atteindre ny moins encor, Cesar de trofees vetu; mieux que ces deux Heros ce Prince s'est fait peindre, dans le Temple Sacre d'Honneur et de vertu. Non volvisse sat est. L. Gaultier, sculpsit, 1612." He was born at Saint Jean d'Angely, 1588, and was the father of the great Conde. By letters patent, dated 13th Nov., 1612, he was appointed Viceroy of New France. Transferred his commission to his brother-in-law, Henri, Duc de Montmorency. Died, 1646. The translation of the stanza under the picture is:

> Hercules could not have equalled this son of Mars,
> And still less Caesar, with his crown of laurels.
> Higher than these two heroes this prince has been placed
> In the sacred temple of honor and virtue.

Line engraving. Size 4 x 7. Half length, oval.

1654—DE SOISSONS—First Viceroy of New France, 1612—"Charles de Burbon, Conte de Soissons, Grand Maistre de France. Un Dieu fut le parrain de ce coeur magnanime et le mit icy bas, pour son roy maintenir, et pour combatre ceux qui veullent enuahir un estat dont leur race en est legitime. Leonard Gaultier fecit, 1596. Jean Le Clerc, Escu." He was born in 1566, a son of Louis I., Prince of Conde. Fought for Henry IV. against the League; appointed Grand Master of France in 1589. Through exertions of Champlain was appointed Lieutenant-General in Canada, 8th October, 1612. Died the same year. The following is translation of the lines under picture:

> A Deity was godfather to this magnanimous hero,
> And placed him on earth to uphold his king
> And to fight against the intending invaders
> Of a kingdom which legitimately belongs to his race.

Line engraving. Size 4 x 5. Half length, oval.

1655—**YORK, DUKE OF**—"Field Marshal, H.R.H. the Duke of York, etc., etc., etc. Painted by Sir Thomas Lawrence, P.R.A., etc., etc. Engd. by Geo. T. Doo, Engraver to H.R.H. the Duke of York, London. Published Decr., 1824, by Hurst, Robinson & Co., 90 Cheapside, and 8 Pall Mall." Frederick, second son of George III. Was born 1763; served in Prussian army; created in 1784 Duke of York and Albany; commanded a British corps in French campaigns, 1793-4, and in commemoration of the success of his Majesty's arms under H.R.H., by which Holland was saved from French invasion, the name "Toronto" was changed to "York" by Governor Simcoe in August, 1793. Died, 1827. Line engraving. Size 9 x 11. Half length.

1656—**TASCHEREAU, MGR. ELZEAR ALEXANDRE, D.D., 1820-98**— Archbishop of Quebec and first Canadian Cardinal. Photogravure from a photograph. Size 5 x 7. Half length. See 326.

1657—**DE GASPE, PHILIPPE AUBERT**—Son of the Seigneur of Saint-Jean Port-Joli. He was born at Quebec in 1786, but although an imaginative and precocious child, it was not until 1863 that he entered the literary field—with "Les Anciens Canadiens," an historical novel, descriptive of life and manners during the days of the final struggle between England and France for possession of Canada. He afterwards published his memoirs, which make very interesting reading. His mother, he tells us, was a friend of Mrs. Simcoe, wife of Governor Simcoe, first Governor of Upper Canada. His uncle, Charles de Lanaudiere, was aide-de-camp to Lord Dorcester. M. de Gaspe died in 1871. Photogravure from portrait in the Chateau de Ramezay, Montreal. Size 5 x 7. Head and shoulders.

1658—**FROBISHER, SIR MARTIN, Kt., 1535-94**—Explorer and navigator. Born at Doncaster, Eng.; was the first of his countrymen who sought to discover the North-west Passage, making three voyages in search of it. He sailed from the Thames, 7th June, 1576, explored the coast of Greenland, and discovered the strait which bears his name. In 1577 and the following year explorations were renewed, the object of the second expedition being chiefly the search of gold. Frobisher in 1588 commanded the "Triumph" against the Spanish Armada, for his bravery receiving knighthood. He took part, as Vice-Admiral, in Sir John Hawkins' expedition, 1590; was wounded near Brest, 1549, his injuries resulting in death. M. V. Gucht, sculp. Line engraving. Size 3 x 6. Head and shoulders, oval.

1659—**INTERIOR OF A FRENCH-CANADIAN FARMHOUSE**—A friendly game of cards—Throughout practically the whole of the nineteenth century the habitant, on his little farm on the shores of the St. Lawrence or the Richelieu, enjoyed peace and prosperity. Desiring neither political power nor wealth, he pursued the even tenor of his way. From the outside world he required little—even his farm implements were mostly made by himself. Through the summer he worked early and late, but a bountiful harvest amply rewarded him for his arduous toil. The late Sir Georges E. Cartier once remarked that his father exported from the parish of St. Antoine alone, five hundred thousand bushels of wheat per year. The winter season, when the habitant enjoyed a period of cessation from toil, brought a prolonged series of entertainments and feasts, which terminated only with Lent, the ice-bound rivers providing a pleasant and easy means for the promotion of social intercourse. Photogravure from painting by Cornelius Krieghoff. Size 5 x 7.

1660—**VANSITTART**—"Rear-Admiral Henry Vansittart—C. R. Bone, pinxt. M. Gauci, Lithog. Printed by C. Hullmandel." A resident of Woodstock, 1834-43. Born in 1777, the youngest son of George Vansittart, of Bisham Abbey, Berkshire, Eng. Entered the navy in 1791. Severely wounded at the siege of Toulon, 1793; at the reduction of Calvi the following year. Present at the capture of the Cape of Good Hope and the Dutch

Squadron in Saldanha Bay. Promoted to the command of the Hermes sloop in 1798, and advanced to post-rank three years later. Became a Rear-Admiral and eventually Vice-Admiral. In 1834 he came to Canada, settling at Woodstock, and during his residence there was instrumental in building churches and schools in the district. Funds of his, prior to his arrival, had been used in the construction of the first hotel in the town. Lithograph. Size 8 x 11. Half length.

1661—PLESSIS, JOSEPH OCTAVE—Bishop (R.C.) of Quebec, 1806-25 —He was a scholar, prominent ecclesiastic, and organizer, born near Montreal, Que., 3rd March, 1762. M. Plessis was ordained priest, 1786. In 1797 became Grand Vicar and Coadjutor to Bishop Denault, upon whose death he was made Bishop of Quebec. By his efforts to rouse loyalty of the French-Canadians in War of 1812-14 he won the good-will of the Government, and on the suggestion of Sir John Sherbrooke, was given a seat in the Legislative Council, where he ardently championed the rights of the Roman Catholic population. He established missions along the St. Lawrence and in the Red River district. His visit to England in 1819 for the purpose of completing the organization of the Roman Catholic Church in Canada, met with success. Although named Archbishop of Quebec, he never assumed the title. Died at Quebec, 4th Dec., 1825. Photogravure from an engraving in the Dominion Archives, Ottawa. Size 5 x 7. Head and shoulders.

1662—MUSKETOE, JOSEPH—Last of the Tutula Indians in Canada. The Tutula tribe came to Canada after the American Revolutionary War, sharing with the Six Nation Indians a grant of land extending for six miles on each side of the Grand River, and given to them in recognition of their loyalty to the Crown. The Tutula Heights, situated on the Mount Pleasant road, near Brantford, Ont., were named after this band of Indians. Water color from photograph taken when Musketoe was in his 107th year. Size 4 x 7. Full length.

1663—GIVINS, LIEUTENANT (COLONEL) JAMES—Water color from an oil painting in possession of his grandson, the late Robert C. Givins, Chicago, Ill. Size 11 x 15. Head and shoulders. See 1671.

1664—ANDREWS, CAPT.—In command of one of the vessels of the Lake Ontario armed fleet during the War of 1812-15. One of his daughters became the wife of Lieut. (afterwards Colonel) James Givins, Superintendent of Indian Affairs, another married Walter Butler Sheehan, who in 1793 was Sheriff of the County of Lincoln. Water color silhouette from a miniature in possession of Miss M. A. A. Givins, Toronto. Size 3 x 5. Half length, in profile.

1665—RANSTON, DORSETSHIRE, ENG.—Near Blandford. The home of Sir Randolph Littlehales Baker, a grandson of Lieut.-Col. Littlehales (Sir Edward Baker Baker), Military Secretary of Governor Simcoe in Canada. Photograph. Size 4 x 6.

1666—BAYFIELD, ADMIRAL HENRY WOLSEY, R.N.—A descendant of the Bayfields, of Norfolk, Eng.—He was born in 1795, entered the navy, 1806, on H.M.S. "Pompey." In the "Duchess of Bedford" he received a wound in action in the Gut of Gibraltar; transferred to the "Beagle," taking part in attack of French fleet in Aix Roads, April, 1809. In 1814 Bayfield volunteered for service on the lakes of Canada; attained rank of lieutenant, March, 1815, and assisted Capt. W. F. W. Owen in the survey of Lake Ontario, the St. Lawrence from Kingston to Prescott, and the Niagara River. Became Admiralty Surveyor, 1817. Surveyed Lakes Erie, Huron and Superior, on his return to England in 1825 completing the charts. Between the years 1827-56 Captain Bayfield made exhaustive surveys of rivers, islands and coast lines in Eastern Canada. He was in

1856 made a Rear-Admiral. In 1854 he received the thanks of the Legislature for services rendered to Canada. Was one of the original members of the Literary and Historical Society of Quebec, and of the Canadian Institute, Toronto. The death of this noted maritime surveyor took place in 1885. Water color. Size 3 x 4. Head and shoulders.

1667—RANKIN, COL. ARTHUR, 1824-93—He was born at sea; joined the Queen's Light Infantry at Toronto, when it was sent to the Detroit frontier in 1838. In the Battle of Windsor, 4th Dec., 1838, he took part, capturing the flag of the "Patriots." He represented Essex in the United Parliament of Canada, 1854-61; obtained permission from the War Department to raise for the United States service a regiment of Lancers, which was mustered, but disbanded by order of the Department. When the Provinces were divided into military districts, Rankin was placed in command of the 9th U.C. District, with title of Colonel. Died at the Hotel Dieu, in Windsor. Water color. Size 3 x 4. Head and shoulders.

1668—MACAULAY—Hon. John Simcoe Macaulay, 1791-1855—Colonel Royal Engineers. Water color from a portrait in possession of the Misses Macaulay, Exmouth, Eng. Size 6 x 7. Half length. See 985, 3317.

1669—GORE—"Francis Gore, Lieut.-Governor, Upper Canada, 1806-11 and 1815-17. E. U. Eddis, delin. W. D. litho. London. Published June 26th, 1835, by Thos. McLean, 26 Haymarket. Printed by Laforce and Kohler, 52 Newman St." Lithograph. Size 4 x 5. Head and shoulders. See 362, 409.

1670—SHAW, MAJOR-GENERAL AENEAS—He was a member of the family of Tordorach, in Strathnairn, Scotland. Served in the Revolutionary War, at the close of which he settled in New Brunswick. In the winter of 1792 Shaw, at that time Captain in the Queen's Rangers, walked on snowshoes from Fredericton to Quebec. Mrs. Simcoe, in her Diary, gives an interesting account of the journey and arrival in Quebec. When Governor Simcoe selected Toronto as his capital, Capt. Shaw adopted the new settlement as his home, and for a time lived at the east side of Garrison Creek. Later he built in the midst of forest, what is now (1917) a short distance north-west of the site of Trinity College, a log cabin, where he took up residence with his family. Captain Shaw was a member of the Executive Council, became Lieutenant-Colonel in 1799, and later attained the rank of Major-General. On the occasion of Governor Hunter leaving York (the name Toronto had been changed to York in 1793) for a visit to Niagara, Aeneas Shaw was one of a committee of three left to administer the Government. A daughter of the Major-General's was the fiancee of Major-General Sir Isaac Brock. Water color from a portrait by J. W. L. Forster. Size 6 x 8. Three-quarter length.

1671—GIVINS, COL. JAMES—Came to Canada as a young man, spending some years among native tribes of the west, acquiring a knowledge of Indian dialects which in later years rendered his services valuable in the Indian Department. In 1791 he was appointed Lieutenant in the Queen's Rangers, from the 73rd, and accompanied Governor Simcoe on many of his journeys of exploration in Upper Canada. In 1803 he was Captain of the 5th Foot, and subsequently, on taking up his residence at York (Toronto), was appointed Superintendent in the Indian Department, an office which he held until 1842. On 14th August, 1812, appointed Provincial A.D.C., with rank of Major in U.C. Militia, and was with Brock at Detroit. At the attack upon York by the Americans in 1813 Givins commanded a company of Indians and part of the Glengarry Fencibles in opposing the landing of Major Forsyth. His death occurred in Toronto, 1846. Water color from a silhouette in possession of his grandson, the late Robert C. Givins, Chicago, Ill. Size 6 x 9. Half length, profile. See 1663.

20

1672—**LANAUDIERE, CHARLES TARIEU DE,** 1741-1811—A great-grandson of Claude de Ramezay, 11th Governor of Montreal, and builder of the Chateau de Ramezay. At sixteen years of age Lanaudiere was Aide Major in the Regiment of La Sarre in the Battle of Abraham's Plains. In 1775 he was Aide-de-Camp to Sir Guy Carleton, afterwards Lord Dorchester, and later served with General Burgoyne. Water color from an oil painting in the Chateau de Ramezay, Montreal. Size 6 x 7. Half length.

1673—**BRANT**—"Joseph Thayendaneken, commonly called the Brant, a Mohawk Chief. From an original drawing in the possession of James Boswell, Esqr." Engraving. Size 3 x 4. Half length, oval. See 158, 159.

1674—**BRANT, JOSEPH**—Thayendanegea—Captain of the Six Nations. Photogravure from an engraving in the Chateau de Ramezay, Montreal. Size 5 x 7. Head and shoulders.

1675—**PAPINEAU, LOUIS JOSEPH,** 1786-1870—Born in Montreal, son of Joseph Papineau, a member of first Legislative Assembly, L.C. In 1809 young Papineau was elected to represent Kent County in Assembly, subsequently sitting for West Ward of Montreal. Called to Bar, 1811. Opposed War of 1812, but when it became inevitable, served with militia through campaign of that year. Speaker Legislative Assembly, 1815-37. In 1820 accepted Dalhousie's offer of seat in Executive Council, but finding there was no chance of his advice being taken, immediately resigned. In 1827 became so hostile to Executive Government that Dalhousie refused to accept him as Speaker. Assembly insisted on their choice and Dalhousie resigned. In 1835 Papineau held conference with Wm. Lyon Mackenzie, and arranged for co-operation of advanced parties in both Provinces. In same year Commission sent out from England, presided over by Lord Gosford, new Governor of L.C., to examine grievances. Commissioners distrusted, and Assembly refused to grant supplies or discuss compromise. Charged with high treason, Papineau fled to U.S., where he remained during rebellion. Vainly tried to bring about American intervention. Went to Paris, 1839, remaining until 1847. Entered United Parliament, retiring from public life in 1854. During latter years advocated revival of old system of division into Upper and Lower Canada. Photogravure from a lithograph by Maurin, Paris. Size 5 x 7. Head and shoulders. See 78.

1676—**MURRAY**—"Major-General George Murray—Quarter-Master-General of the Army in Spain & Portugal. Sir Thomas Lawrence, P.R.A., Pinxt. Henry Meyer, sculpt. London, March 1st, 1841. Published by Welch and Gwynne, 24 St. James's St." Provisional Lieutenant-Governor Upper Canada, April-July, 1815. Line engraving. Size 10 x 12. Half length. See 413.

1677—**HOLLAND, SURVEYOR-GENERAL SAMUEL**—Born in England in 1717, receiving his military education there and in Holland. At an early age he entered the army as lieutenant of artillery, and served some time on the Continent. In 1756 promoted to a captaincy, and in the following year was appointed aide-de-camp to General Wolfe. Took part in the expedition against Louisbourg, and was engineer-in-chief with Wolfe and Saunders at Quebec. He stood near Wolfe when that officer fell. In 1763 Holland was appointed Surveyor-General of Quebec and Director of Surveys in British North America; also a member of the Council, Quebec. Many of the manuscript plans in the Dominion Archives are signed by him. Copy of original pastel, in possession of his grandson, A. E. C. Holland, Wallace Bridge, N.S. Size 8 x 10. Head and shoulders.

1678—**BRANT, CAPT. JOHN**—"Ahyouwaighs, Chief of the Six Nations —Published by F. W. Greenough, Philadelphia. Drawn, Printed & Coloured at J. T. Bowen's Lithographic Establishment, No. 94 Walnut St.

Entered according to Act of Congress in the year 1838 by F. W. Greenough in the Clerk's Office of the District Court of the Eastern District of Penn'a." Son of Joseph Brant (Thayendanegea), born at Mohawk Village, U.C., 1794; died there 1832. He was at the Battle of Queenston Heights, and in the engagements at Beaver Dams, Chippawa, Lundy's Lane and Fort Erie. He rose to the rank of Captain, and as Indian leader showed great bravery. In 1827 he was appointed Superintendent of the Six Nations, and in 1832 was returned a member of the Provincial Parliament for the County of Haldimand, but was, however, unseated on a technicality. Lithograph. Size 13 x 17. Half length.

1679—HOLLAND, AUGUSTUS, E.C.—A grandson of Surveyor-General Samuel Holland. He was born at Tryon, P.E.I., in 1827. In 1873 was elected to the Legislature, holding the fourth electoral district of the province for several years. He removed eventually to Wallace Bridge, N.S. Water color. Size 4 x 6. Head and shoulders.

1680—OSBORNE, CATHARINE ELIZABETH KERR—Born at Burlington, Ont.; only daughter of Col. Wm. Johnson Kerr and Elizabeth Brant, and granddaughter of Joseph Brant, Thayendanegea. She married John Osborne, a merchant of Hamilton and afterwards of Winnipeg and Morden, Man. Mrs. Osborne is said to have been a most beautiful and saintly woman. She is buried with her ancestors at the Mohawk Church, Brantford. Water color from a portrait in possession of her daughter, Mrs. Donald Kerby, Morden, Man. Size 4 x 6. Three-quarter length, sitting.

1681—BARRINGTON—"The Honble. Saml. Barrington, Adml. of the White Squadn. and General of Marines. J. S. Copley, R.A., pinx. Ridley, sc. Pubd. by Bunney & Gold, Shoe Lane, Oct. 1, 1800." Born in 1729, died, 1800; fifth son of John, first Viscount Barrington. Entered navy at eleven years of age; passed examination for lieutenant in 1745. In 1754-5 accompanied Commander Keppel to North America; commanded the "Achilles" under Sir Edward Hawke in expedition to Basque Roads. In 1760 the "Achilles" was one of a squadron sent out to destroy Louisburg. Barrington was in 1780 offered command of the Channel Fleet, which he declined. Line engraving. Size 5 x 7. Head and shoulders, oval.

1682—SCHANK—"John Schank, Esqr., R.N. Published by J. Asperne at the Bible, Crown & Constitution, Cornhill, 1 July, 1805." Line engraving. Size 4 x 5. Head and shoulders, oval. See 60.

1683—ROBINSON, SIR JOHN BEVERLEY, BART.—Chief Justice of Upper Canada, 1829-63. Photogravure from painting in the Department of Education, Toronto. Size 5 x 7. Head and shoulders. See 315.

1684—OSGOODE, WILLIAM—First Chief Justice, Upper Canada—At the early age of fifteen he entered Christ College as a commoner. He studied law, became M.A. in 1777, and was called to the Bar of Lincoln's Inn. He was appointed first Chief Justice of Upper Canada in 1792; was a Legislative Councillor of the Province, appointed to the Council in July, and in the following September became Speaker. In consequence of his charge to a grand jury that slavery ought not to exist in the colony of Canada, the Legislature of Upper Canada passed in July, 1793, an Act entitled "An Act to Prevent the Further Introduction of Slaves, and to Limit the Terms of Contracts for Service within this Province." In 1794 Osgoode became Chief Justice of Lower Canada, retaining the office until 1801, when he resigned and returned to England. He died in 1824, aged seventy. Photograph from original oil at Wolford, the Manor House of the Simcoe family in Devon. Size 8 x 9. Half length. See 300.

1685—**HOLLAND, MAJOR HENRY**—Of the 44th Regiment—Third son of Surveyor-General Samuel Holland. Previous to his death he had been serving with his regiment, stationed at Jamaica. Orders were received to sail for home, and while the ship was anchored near the Isle of Wight, Major Holland, with some other officers, anxious to get ashore, took a small boat and attempted to reach land through the surf. The boat was capsized and the Major drowned. Copy of original pastel, in possession of his grandson, A. E. C. Holland, Wallace Bridge, N.S. Size 8 x 10. Half length.

1686—**MACNAB, CAPT. ALEXANDER**—A Canadian U.E. Loyalist at Waterloo—Born in Virginia, second son of Dr. James Macnab. Some years after the doctor's death, which took place at Machiche, L.C., in 1780, his son came to Toronto, and in 1797 became confidential clerk to the Executive Council of Upper Canada. Gazetted as ensign in the Queen's Rangers, 1800; joined the 26th Foot, 1803; lieutenant in 30th Cambridgeshire Regiment, 1804, obtaining his captaincy five years later. Subsequently A.D.C. to Gen. Sir Thomas Picton, and with him was killed at Waterloo. The late Rev. Canon Macnab, rector of Darlington, Bowmanville, was a nephew of Capt. Macnab, and Rev. Canon A. W. Macnab, of St. Alban's Cathedral, Toronto, is a grandnephew. In the crypt of St. Paul's Cathedral, London, a tablet, bearing the following inscription, has been erected to the memory of Capt. Macnab: "Sacred to the memory of Captain Alexander Macnab, 30th Regt. Aide-de-camp to Lieutenant-General Sir Thos. Picton, who was with him slain at Waterloo. His body lies on the field of battle in the hope of a blessed resurrection. This tablet is erected by his nephews, the Rev. A. Macnab, D.D., and Rev. A. W. Macnab, both of Canada, September, 1876." Water color from the original miniature in possession of Rev. Canon A. W. Macnab, Toronto. Size 5 x 7. Half length.

1687—**HAMMOND, GEORGE, 1763-1853**—In 1783 he went to Paris as secretary to David Hartley, the younger, who was conducting peace negotiations between Great Britain and America. In 1791 he was sent to Philadelphia by Lord Grenville, Secretary for Foreign Affairs, to act as Minister Plenipotentiary to the United States, and was the first British Minister accredited to that nation. The conflicting claims of the two countries in giving effect to the Treaty of Versailles, 1783, involved Hammond and Thomas Jefferson, the American Secretary of State, in a serious controversy. Hammond left America in 1795 to become Under Secretary at Foreign Office, London. Oil painting from portrait in England. Size 6 x 8. Half length.

1688—**DE ROTTENBURG, COLONEL BARON**—Adjutant-General of the Militia of Upper Canada, 1855-8—He was a son of Major-General Francis de Rottenburg, Administrator of Upper Canada, 19th June-12th December, 1813. He entered the army in 1825, his first commission being in the 81st Regiment; later transferred to the 60th Rifles and then to the 49th Regiment. As captain de Rottenburg served in Canada during the Rebellion of 1837-8; was in Spain for a time, but returned to Canada, and while Adjutant-General of the Militia, the 100th Prince of Wales Royal Canadian Regiment was raised and he was given command. He went to England with the regiment, which was quartered first at Shorncliffe and afterwards at Aldershot. Colonel Baron de Rottenburg subsequently became a military Knight of Windsor, and as such passed the remainder of his life in the shadow of Windsor Castle. He was born near Kingston, U.C., 1807, and died in 1894. Water color from original oil in possession of Miss L. De Rottenburg Ridley, Hamilton, Ont. Size 4 x 5. Half length.

1689—**PRESCOTT, GENERAL ROBERT**—Governor of Canada, 1796-1807. Water color. Size 4 x 5. Head and shoulders. See 142.

1690—**BROCK, MAJOR-GENERAL SIR ISAAC**—From a miniature in possession of Miss Sara Mickle, Toronto, painted by J. Hudson in 1806, the year of Brock's last visit to England. Photogravure. Size 5 x 6. Head and shoulders, oval. See 410, 1225.

1691—**AMHERST, GENERAL JEFFERY**, 1717-97—First English Governor of Canada. He was born at Riverhead, Kent, Eng.; entered the army in 1731. Obtained the rank of major-general in 1758, and commanded at Cape Breton. Amherst performed an important part in the conquest of Canada. Although his name is usually placed first on the list of English Governors of Canada, it is well known that after the capitulation of Montreal he divided the Province into three districts, appointing a Governor for each during what is commonly called the period of military rule, 1760-64. He received the title of Baron Amherst in 1776, and in 1796 was made a field marshal. Aliamet, sculp. Engraving, printed in color. Size 5 x 6. Head and shoulders, oval. See 3389.

1692—**MONTRESOR, CAPTAIN (COLONEL) JOHN**—Chief Engineer of Expedition to North America, 1776. He was born at Gibraltar, 6th April, 1736, the eldest son of Col. Gabriel Montresor. Served as assistant-engineer under his father for four years, and on 28th October, 1754, was gazetted as ensign and chief engineer under Gen. Braddock for his expedition against Fort DuQuesne. From 1755-62 Montresor, then a lieutenant, acted as engineer and surveyor in Canada and Nova Scotia (Acadia). He was at the Siege of Louisburg, 1758, and the capitulation of Quebec. Ordered to construct a series of redoubts at Portage of Niagara before arrival of troops under Major-General Bradstreet on his way to treat with the Indians. Made extensive tour to the posts on the Northern Lakes, and returned to Boston, where he was actively engaged in professional duties until the evacuation of the town by the British, March, 1776. Obtained rank of colonel on his return to England, 1778. Died 26th June, 1799. Water color from a portrait in oil by Copley in possession of the late Col. E. H. Montresor (killed in action, 1914), 21st Royal Sussex Regt., great-grandson of Capt. John Montresor. Size 5 x 6. Half length.

1693—**SHANK, LIEUTENANT-GENERAL DAVID**—Was gazetted lieutenant in the Queen's Rangers, March, 1777. Served throughout the Revolutionary War; became brevet-major 1st March, 1794; in 1803 was appointed to the command of the Canadian Fencibles; became major-general 1811; lieutenant-general 1821, and died in Glasgow, 16th October, 1831. He acquired in York a large tract of land in what is now the north side of Queen street, Toronto, near Trinity College. Reproduction in oil of original portrait at Wolford, Devon. Size 6 x 7. Half length.

1694—**KERR, WILLIAM JOHN SIMCOE**—Youngest son of Col. Wm. Johnson Kerr (who commanded the Indians at Queenston and at Beaver Dams), and Bessie Brant, daughter of Joseph Brant. He was born in 1840 and died in 1875; was barrister-at-law, 1862, and chief of the Six Nations, 1866. Photograph, colored. Size 4 x 5. Head and shoulders.

1695—**JOHN, CATHERINE BRANT**—Second daughter of Joseph Brant (Thayendanagea) by his third wife. She married Peter, son of Captain John; died at Wellington Square (Burlington), 31st Jan., 1867, and is buried at the old Mohawk Church, Brantford, Ont. Water color from a portrait in possession of her grandniece, Mrs. Frank Dee, Toronto. Size 4 x 6. Half length.

1696—**SMITH, CHARLOTTE BRANT**—Daughter of Jacob Brant and granddaughter of Joseph Brant (Thayendanagea). She married Peter Smith, formerly interpreter at the Six Nations Reserve, near Brantford. Water color from a portrait in possession of her daughter, Mrs. Frank Dee, Toronto. Size 4 x 6. Three-quarter length, sitting.

1697—**STONE, COLONEL JOEL, 1749-1833**—Founder of Gananoque, Ont.—He was a U.E. Loyalist, born in Guilford, Conn., a descendant of William Stone, one of the emigrants who sailed from London, Eng., in May, 1639. He served under Sir William Howe in the Revolutionary War, and remained in New York until the evacuation of the British, 1783. In 1792 settled at Gananoque, on the St. Lawrence; became first collector of port; was appointed in 1809 Colonel of the 2nd Regiment of Militia, County of Leeds. Water color from an oil in possession of his grandson, Charles McDonald, Gananoque, Ont. Size 4 x 5. Head and shoulders.

1698—**VERRAZZANO, GIOVANNI DI**—"Giovanni Di Pier Andrea di Bernardo da Verrazzano patrizio fiorno. Gran capitno. Comandante in mare per il re cristianissimo Francesco primo, e discopritore della nuova Francia. Nato circa il MCDLXXXV; morto nel MDXXV. Dedicato al merito singre. Dell' Ill'mo; e Revmo. Sigre. Lodovico da Verrazzano patrizio, e canonico fiorentino agnato del medo. Preso dal quadro originale in tela Esistente presso la suda. Nobil famigia. G. Locchi del. F. Allegrini, inci., 1769." An Italian navigator, believed to have visited North America as early as 1508. Entered the French marine service, 1495, and in 1523 was sent by Francis I. to explore to the westward, and the following year arrived in La Dauphine, off the coast of North America, exploring Florida to New-foundland, and taking possession of the latter in the name of the King of France. Discoverer of the Bays of Narragansett and New York. Became a privateer, or pirate; was executed at Pico, Spain. Lithograph. Size 7 x 8. Half length.

1699—**COLBERT, JEAN BAPTISTE, 1619-83**—"Colbert, from the original by V. Mignard, in the Collection of the Institute at Paris. Engraved by W. Holl, under the Superintendence of the Society for the Diffusion of Useful Knowledge. London: Published by Charles Knight, Ludgate Street." Colbert, the eminent French statesman and financier, became Councillor of State when only twenty-nine years of age, and received the appointment of Controller-General of Finances in 1661. During his tenure of office taxes were reduced and economy in revenue and public expense established. In 1669 he was appointed Minister of Marine, and, as such, instituted many reforms. Line engraving. Size 4 x 5. Head and shoulders.

1700—**"LOUIS XV.**—Jones, fecit." King of France—Great-grandson of Louis XIV. Born at Fontainebleau, 1710, and in 1715 succeeded to the throne. Against the advice of his Prime Minister, Cardinal Fleury, joined in 1741 the Coalition against Maria Theresa of Austria, and sent an army into Bohemia. England then declared war against France. By the Treaty of Aix-la-Chapelle in 1748 hostilities were suspended, and about this time, Louis, who had, on the death of Fleury in 1743, dispensed with a Prime Minister, ceased to take an active part in the Government. In 1754 the rival claims of Britain and France in Canada were the pretext of a fresh outbreak of hostilities and Louis became engaged in the last of the series of wars between the two powers in North America, later becoming involved in the Seven Years' War as an ally of Maria Theresa. By the Treaty of Paris, Canada was ceded to England and the war ended. Louis died in 1774, leaving his kingdom in an impoverished and demoralized state. Line engraving. Size 4 x 5. Head in profile, oval.

1701—**ARMS OF SIR FREDERICK HALDIMAND, 1718-1791**—"Du Chevalier Frederick Haldimand, General et Colonel d'un Regiment d'Infanetrie au Service de sa Majeste; cy-devant General Commandant en chef dans l'Amerique, Septentrionale, Gouverneur de la Province de Quebec, Inspecteur-General des Troupes dans les Isles Occidentales; et Chevalier du tres honorable Ordre du Bain: Installe le 19me jour de May, MDCCLXXXVIII." Lieutenant-General, Colonel Commandant of the 60th

Foot. Appointed in 1778 to succeed Sir Guy Carleton as Governor and Commander-in-Chief in Canada, which post he held until 1784. Line engraving. Size 6½ x 7.

1702—LOUIS XIV., OF FRANCE, 1638-1715—Surnamed "Le Grand." —Eldest son of Louis XIII. Ascended throne 1643, under the regency of his mother. During his minority the Government was administered by Cardinal Mazarin, a foreigner, whose Ministry was very unpopular, and who became involved in a civil war with a faction known as La Fronde. On the death of Mazarin, 1661, Louis resolved to be his own Prime Minister. Ambitious to make France prosperous and the monarchy absolute, his policy was summed up in his famous saying, "L'Etat, c'est moi." The death of Philip IV. of Spain in 1665 furnished Louis with a pretext to extend his dominions toward the Rhine, and in lieu of the unpaid dowry of his queen, Maria Theresa, daughter of Philip IV., he claimed and successfully invaded Flanders and Franche-Comte. By the Treaty of Nymwegen, 1678, he retained the latter, and a large part of Flanders. In 1685 revoked Edict of Nantes, which had secured religious liberty of Protestants. Three years later engaged in war against Spain, Austria, England and Prince of Orange. Failed in attempt to restore James II. of England. Engaged subsequently in War of Spanish Succession. Photogravure from painting by Jean Garnier, in the Versailles Gallery. Size 5 x 6. Head and shoulders, oval.

1703—DEPARTURE OF THE CABOTS FROM BRISTOL—On their first voyage of discovery, 1497—John Cabot and his son, Sebastian, are represented as receiving the blessing of Abbot Newland, "Nailheart," and the farewell of the Mayor and friends, on the eve of departure from Bristol, on the 10th May, 1497. The ship "Matthew" in which the Cabots sailed, is shown drawn up against the quay. Sebastian is standing behind his father, holding the charter of Henry VII., while his mother is being reconciled by a nun to parting with her husband and son. The original picture, by Mr. Ernest Board, R.A., hangs in the Bristol Art Gallery. By kind permission of the artist this copy in oil was made for Mr. Robertson by Harvey Barton & Son, Bristol, who were complimented by Mr. Board on the excellent copy they made. Size 16 x 22.

1704—MONUMENT ON BRANDON HILL, BRISTOL, ENG.—In memory of Cabot's voyage of discovery, 1497—On June 24th, 1897, just four hundred years after the Cabots' discovery of the north-eastern seaboard of North America, the foundation stone of this tower was laid by the Marquis of Dufferin and Ava, and on Sept. 6th of the following year the tower was opened by the same nobleman. The Halifax National Memorial Tower stands not far from the spot where Cabot landed after his memorable voyage. Photograph, colored. Size 9 x 12.

1705—SECOND VISIT OF JACQUES CARTIER TO CANADA, 1535— His landing near Hochelaga (Montreal)—In the spring of 1534 Cartier, "with two ships of three-score tons apiece burthern and sixty-one well-appointed men in each," sailed from St. Malo. They reached Newfoundland, proceeded to Gaspe, and later returned to France. The following year Cartier again came to Canada, and after exploring the shores of the St. Lawrence, so called by him, he went on to Stadacona (Quebec), where he arrived in September. On 2nd October the party landed about six miles from Hochelaga (Montreal). Here they were cordially received by the natives. The next morning, with some of his company and three Indian guides, Cartier set out for Hochelaga. The picture shows one of the chiefs coming to meet the discoverer of Canada, who presented him with axes, knives and a cross, and all proceeded on their way through "lands tilled and fair large fields of corn." In the midst of the fields was situated

Hochelaga, near a mountain which the visitors called Mont Royal. A tablet on Metcalfe street, near Sherbrooke street, Montreal, bearing the following inscription, marks the site of the one-time village: "Site of a large Indian village, claimed to be the Town of Hochelaga, visited by Jacques Cartier in 1535." From original cartoon by Andrew Morris. Lith. of N. Sarony, New York. Drawing in water color. Size 8 x 12.

1706—**CARTIER**—"Jacques Cartier— Natif de St. Malo (France). Decouvre le Canada en 1534-5. L'Original existe a St. Malo. Lith. par F. Davignon. Imp. par L. Nagle, N.Y. Entered according to Act of Congress in the year 1848 by Theophile Hamel in the clerk's office of the District Court of the Southern Dist. of N.Y. Entered according to Act of the Provincial Legislature in the year 1848 by T. Hamel, in the office of the Registrar of the Province of Canada." The celebrated French navigator was born at St. Malo, 1484. Was first discoverer of the St. Lawrence River, 1534; returned to France, and the following year, in his second voyage, ascended the river as far as the site of Montreal. This is the commonly accepted portrait of Cartier, although there is no evidence that it is genuine. Lithograph in color. Size 14 x 17. Three-quarter length.

1707—**FACSIMILE OF FLAG PRESENTED BY HENRY VII. TO CABOT**—On the eve of John Cabot's departure for America from Bristol, May 10th, 1497, in the "Matthew," he was presented with a flag by Henry VII. of England. The flag was divided into four quarters, two red and two blue, with yellow fleur-de-lis on the diagonal blue grounds, and yellow running lions on the red. Above the flags on the dexter side (i.e., left facing the painting) are the Arms of the City of Bristol, and on the sinister side are the arms of the Society of Merchant Venturers. Oil by Harvey Barton & Son, Bristol. Size 15 x 20.

1708—**BOSCAWEN**, 1711-61—"The Honorable Edward Boscawen— Vice-Admiral of the Red Squadron of His Majesty's fleet, and one of the Lords Commissioners of the Admiralty. J. Reynolds, Pinxt. Js. McArdell, fecit." Son of Viscount Falmouth, and related on his mother's side to the Duke of Marlborough; fought against the French in India 1748; as Admiral of the Blue commanded expedition to America, 1758, and in that year was in command of fleet at taking of Louisbourg; subsequently general of the marines, and a member of the Privy Council. Line engraving. Size 14 x 19. Full length.

1709—**PRINCE RUPERT**—"The Most Illustrious and High Borne Prince Rupert, Prince Electour Palatine of ye Righne. Second Sonne to Fredericke King of Bohemia, Generall of ye Horse of His Ma'ties Army, Knight of ye Most Noble Order of the Garter, etc. Are to be sould by Robt. Peake at his shopp neere Holborne Conduitt, Ant. V. Dyck, Pinxit." The first Governor of the Hudson's Bay Company, 1670-82. He was born at Prague, 1609, and was the son of the King of Bohemia, who married Elizabeth, daughter of James I. of England. Served in the Thirty Years' War, and in the Royalist Army against Cromwell. After the Restoration of 1660 appointed Admiral against the Dutch. On May 2nd, 1670, he received from his cousin, Charles II., one of the most celebrated charters ever granted, that of the Hudson's Bay Company, under the name of "The Governor and Company of Merchants-Adventurers Trading in Hudson's Bay." In September, 1668, Sieur des Groseilliers had arrived at Rupert's River, where he established himself for trade with the Indians, forming the nucleus of the "Great Company." Line engraving. Size 7 x 8. Head and shoulders, oval.

1710—**VESPUCCI AMERIGO**—Born at Florence, 1451; was a famous navigator; gave his name to the New World, which was visited by him four times. The part of the continent discovered by him was near the equator. Had high reputation as an astronomer. Died in 1512 at Seville, Spain. He was a friend of Columbus. Engraved in lithography by Elevia. Size 5 x 5. Head and shoulders.

1711—BARRE, 1726-1802—"The Right Honorable Isaac Barre—Painted by C. G. Stuart, 1785. John Hall, sculpt., Engraver to his Majesty. Publish'd April 5th, 1787, as the Act directs, by J. Hall, 83 Berwick street, London. Printed by Wm. Richards." Adjutant-General in the campaign of 1759. Wolfe trusted him to the utmost, and by his will left Barre a hundred guineas with which to buy a sword and ring. Barre entered Parliament 1761; espoused the cause of the American Revolution; Privy Councillor 1766. Letters of Junius have been ascribed to him. Barre in Massachusetts, and Wilkes-Barre in Pennsylvania, preserve his name. Line engraving. Size 9 x 12. Half length, sitting.

1712—"A NORTH VIEW OF FORT FREDERIC, OR CROWN POINT —Proud, Sc." Fort Frederic, or Crown Point, now called Hammond's Corners, is a post village of Essex County, N.Y., situated on Lake Champlain. In 1755 the forces of Baron Dieskau and William Johnson (afterwards Sir William Johnson) had an encounter here resulting in the defeat of the former. Twenty years later Col. Ethan Allen surprised and took a British fort at Crown Point. Line engraving. Size 7 x 9.

1713—LIVIUS—"Peter Livius, now Chief Justice of Quebec—Bonus atque fidus, Judex honestum praetutit utile—et per obstantes catervas, Explicuit sua Victor arma."—These words are a direct quotation from Horace and translated read: "A good and faithful judge, he preferred honorable conduct to personal advantage and through opposing bands carried his arms unsullied to victory." He was born in Bedford, England, 1727; educated abroad. He came to America, and resided in Portsmouth, New Hampshire. Was a member of the Council under the Royal Government, and was proscribed as a Royalist in 1778. In May, 1777, received appointment as Chief Justice in Canada, acting as such until 1786, when he went to England. Harvard gave him the honorary degree of M.A. in 1767, and he also became a Fellow of the Royal Society. Died in England, 23rd July, 1795. Etching. Size 6 x 7. Half length, sitting, profile.

1714—MONTGOMERY—"General Richd. Montgomery—From the original picture of the publishers, Johnson, Foy & Co., New York. Entered according to Act of Congress, A.D. 1862, by Johnson, Foy & Co., in the Clerk's Office of the District Court of the Southern District of New York. Painted by Chappel. Engraved by G. R. Hall." Size 6 x 9. Full length, profile. See 1726.

1715—"DEATH OF GENERAL MONTCALM—Killed while defending Quebec in 1759, against the English. He asked that he be buried in a hole caused by the explosion of a shell. In the same engagement Gen. Wolfe, who commanded the English army, was also killed. The two generals succumbed to their wounds about the same instant. Valeau, delin. Engraved by G. Chevillet, engraver to His Majesty." The foregoing inscription (a translation from the French), under the picture, is incorrect regarding the time of Montcalm's death, which did not take place until early on the morning of 14th Sept., in the home of Surgeon Arnoux, St. Louis street, Quebec. Again, there is no proof that Montcalm asked to be buried in this excavation, although his burial did take place in the Chapel of the Ursuline Convent, under the floor, through which a shell had made a large excavation. Marquis Louis Joseph Montcalm was born in 1712, served in France and the Netherlands, and in 1756 was sent to defend the French colonies in North America. Line engraving. Size 17 x 24.

1716—JERVIS—"Right Honble. John Jervis, Earl St. Vincent, Baron Jervis of Meaford, in the County of Stafford, and K.B. Admiral of the White, etc. Publish'd Dec. 6, 1800, by J. Hinton, No. 44, top of Well street, Oxford street, London." He was the first Viscount, and was born at Meaford, Staffordshire, 1734. He entered the navy in his tenth year. Led the advanced squadron in charge of transports past Quebec, 1759. Became Admiral of the Blue, and commander of the naval forces in the Mediterranean in 1795. In consequence of his naval victory over the Spanish fleet off Cape St. Vincent in February, 1797, and previous valuable services, he was raised to the peerage. In 1821 became Admiral of the fleet. His death took place on 14th March, 1823. Photo from engraving in the Dominion Archives, Ottawa. Size 6 x 7. Three-quarter length.

1717—ARNOLD, COL. BENEDICT—"Colonel Arnold, who commanded the Provincial Troops sent against Quebec, through the Wilderness of Canada and was wounded in Storming that City under General Montgomery. London. Publish'd as the Act directs, 26 March, 1776, by Thos. Hart." Line engraving. Size 10 x 13. Three-quarter length. See 1719.

1718—CLARKE, SIR CHARLES ALURED, 1745-1832—Had a long and distinguished military career. When fourteen he entered the army as an ensign. Seventy-three years later, on the accession of William IV., he was made a field marshal. He was Governor of Jamaica from 1782-90, when he was transferred to the staff at Quebec. Appointed Lieutenant-Governor of Lower Canada, 1790, and remained in office until January 21st, 1796. During the two years' absence of Lord Dorchester, he acted as administrator of the Province. Subsequently became Governor-General of India, and later Commander-in-Chief of the Forces there. Photo from an engraving in the Public Library, Toronto. Size 13 x 16. Three-quarter length.

1719—ARNOLD—"General Arnold—Drawn from life at Philadelphia by Du Similier. Published Mar. 1st, 1783, by J. Fielding, Paternoster Row. J. Sewell, Cornhill, and J. Debrett, Piccadilly. European Magazine." Born at Norwich, Conn., 14th Jan., 1741; died at London, 3rd June, 1801. An American revolutionary general and traitor; commissioned colonel 1775; defeated British at Ridgefield, Conn., 1777, and was made major-general; appointed commander of Philadelphia, 1778; in command at West Point, and planned its surrender to the British. Plan was discovered, through capture of Andre, and Arnold escaped to the British, receiving rank of major-general in the British army. Andre was hanged by the Americans. Line engraving Size 4 x 5. Head and shoulders, oval. See 1717.

1720—PITT, WILLIAM, EARL OF CHATHAM—"Lord Chatham. Engraved by W. Holl from a print by Fisher, after a picture by Brompton." "The Great Commoner" and brilliant opponent of the Walpole Ministry, was born at Boconnoc, Cornwall, Eng., in 1708, and educated at Eton and Trinity College, Oxford. In 1735 chosen a member of Parliament for Old Sarum. Appointed paymaster of the forces, 1746. In 1755 became leader of the Opposition. On the outbreak of war between England and France soon afterwards, and the subsequent resignation of Newcastle as Premier, Pitt headed the Cabinet for five months. A Coalition was then formed between Pitt and Newcastle. in which the former became Secretary of State, with the supreme direction of the war and of foreign affairs, but in 1761 he resigned office. Condemned the Stamp Act, arguing that England had no right to tax the colonies. Prevailed upon in 1766 to form a new Administration, in which he took the office of the Privy Seal. At the same time accepted a peerage with the title of Earl of Chatham. Resigned from the Government in 1768, because of ill-health. Returned to public life, however, and in 1775 made a brilliant speech on the American War, in which he urged the repeal of the Boston Port Bill. His death occurred in 1778. Line engraving. Size 4 x 5. Head and shoulders.

1721—ASHBURTON, ALEXANDER BARING, FIRST BARON, 1774-1848—Financier and statesman—Entered Parliament in 1806. He was opposed to restrictions on commerce between nations, and, consequently, disapproved of the "system of hostility recommended and practised towards the commerce of America" by the English orders-in-Council. He was Master of Mint, 1834, and the following year raised to the peerage. In order to settle the dispute on the boundary between United States and British territories, Lord Ashburton was sent to Washington. Daniel Webster represented the States. The Ashburton Treaty resulted, in 1842, when the international boundary between Maine and Canada was settled, and the States received about seven-twelfths and Canada five-twelfths of the disputed territory. Photogravure from an engraving in the Dominion Archives, Ottawa. Size 5 x 7. Half length, sitting.

1722—LEVIS, GASTON FRANCOIS, CHEVALIER DE—A native of Languedoc; born August 23rd, 1720, at the Chateau of Azac, one of the oldest houses of France. Two members of this family had been Viceroys of New France in the seventeenth century—Henri de Levis, duc de Ventadour, and Francois Christophe de Levis, duc de Damville. At the age of fourteen Chevalier de Levis entered the army. Distinguished himself throughout his military career. Wounded at Siege of Prague. At Dettingen, 1743; afterwards joined the army of Haute-Alsace. Served under Prince of Conti, 1745, and was at the passage of the Rhine. Following year despatched upon Nice to defend frontiers of Provence. Received rank of Brigadier, under Montcalm, with troops in Canada. At defeat of British at Carillon and Montmorency. On death of Montcalm at Quebec, returned from Montreal to take command of French forces. Defeated British at St. Foy, 1760. After the capitulation returned to France, subsequently serving under Conde against Prince Ferdinand. As a reward for his services, created a Duke and Peer of France. Died, 1787. Photogravure from painting in the Versailles Gallery. Size 5 x 7. Head and shoulders.

1723—"THE DEATH OF MONTGOMERY AT QUEBEC—Painted by Jno. Trumbull, Esqr. Engraved by W. Ketterlinus, 1799. London. Published Sepr. 17, 1801, by A. C. de Poggi, No. 91 New Bond street." This picture is purely imaginary, for on the night of 31st Dec., 1775, there was a driving snowstorm, and Montgomery fell in the narrow pass below Cape Diamond, Quebec. Moreover, a note attached to the key (No. 1724) of the picture states that "Those that are marked with a star are the only real likenesses. The others are intended as memorandums of men who either were distinguished or killed or wounded in the action, and of whom no actual portrait could be obtained." Line engraving. Size 13 x 20.

1724—"DEATH OF MONTGOMERY"—Key to—*1, General Montgomery, of New York. *2, Major Cheesman, A.D.C. of Gen. Montgomery, of Philadelphia. *3, Major Macpherson, A.D.C. of Gen. Montgomery, of Philadelphia. 4, Col. Donald Campbell, Quartermaster-General and second in command, New York. 5. Col. Thompson, of Pennsylvania. 6. An Indian Chief known by the name of Col. Louis. 7. Major Meigs, of Connecticut. 8. Capt. Hendricks, Rifleman, of Virginia. 9. Capt. Ward. 10. Lieut. Humphries. 11. Cooper. 12. Ogden. P. Maverick, sculpt. Size 13 x 20.

1725—ROGERS—"Major Robt. Rogers, Commander-in-Chief of the Indians in the Back Settlements of America. Publish'd as the Act directs, Octr. 1, 1776, by Thos. Hart, London." Raised original corps of Rogers' Rangers, subsequently (under Simcoe) known as the Queen's Rangers. Appointed Governor of Michillimackinac, 1776. Line engraving. Size 9 x 12. Three-quarter length.

1726—**MONTGOMERY**—"Richard Montgomery. Engraved by R. Whitechurch at J. M. Butler's establishment, 84 Chestnut St. Born in Ireland, 1737. Served in Canada under Wolfe. He subsequently joined the American army, and in the winter of 1775, with Arnold, besieged Quebec. A united attack upon the city was planned for the last night in the year. It failed utterly, and in Champlain street, the narrow pass just below the citadel, Montgomery fell mortally wounded. Line engraving. Size 6 x 8. Head and shoulders. See 1714.

1727—**BRITISH SOLDIERS DRAWING WOOD FROM ST. FOY TO QUEBEC, 1760**—The British forces, under General Murray, spent the winter of 1759-60 in Quebec, the French having capitulated, September 18th, 1759. Photogravure from painting by J. H. Macnaughton, in the Chateau de Ramezay, Montreal. Size 5 x 7.

1728—**FRONTENAC**—"Henricaea Maria de Buade Frontenac—Tibi Henrico Ludouico Haberto de Montmor uxoris amantiss effigiem D.D. G. Mellan, 1641." Sister of Count de Frontenac, who was from 1672-1682, Governor of French Canada. The translation of the inscription is: "To thee, Henricus Ludovicus Habertus de Montmor (I present) the portrait (or likeness) of a loving wife." Engraving. Size 9 x 11. Head and shoulders, oval.

1729—**COFFIN**—"Sir Isaac Coffin, Bart., Rear Admiral of the White Squadron. Engraved by Ridley from an original miniature." Born at Boston in 1759. Entered the navy at the age of fourteen, and went to England as lieutenant in 1779. Took an active part in the Revolutionary War. Resident Commissioner of the Navy at Halifax, and afterwards at Sheerness, 1798-1804. Created baronet in 1804. Died in England, June 23rd, 1839. Line engraving. Size 3 x 4. Head and shoulders, oval.

1730—**TARLTON, 1754-1833**—"Lieut.-Col. Tarlton—In the possession of John Fielder, Esq. Sir Josh. Reynolds. S. W. Reynolds. London: Published, 1834, by Hodgson, Boys and Graves, 6 Pall Mall, and sold also by F. G. Moon, 20 Threadneedle street." Served under Cornwallis in American Revolution; gained several advantages over American troops, but was defeated at Battle of Cowpens, 1781. Returned to England; elected to Parliament for Liverpool; created a baronet and K.C.B. He wrote a "History of the Campaigns of 1780-81 in the Southern Provinces of North America." Line engraving. Size 4 x 6. Full length.

1731—**COBOURG, 1839-41**—On the north shore of Lake Ontario—A view from the harbor dock, showing: (1) Custom House; (2) Victoria College, University avenue; (3) St. Peter's Anglican Church, King street. Cobourg boasts of a safe and commodious harbor, and is a port of call for the Richelieu & Ontario Navigation Company's steamers. It was originally known as Amherst, after the famous general of that name; later it became Hamilton, and finally took the name of Cobourg. For a time also it was known locally as Buckville, after Elijah Buck, a pioneer settler, and in the early days the then struggling hamlet rejoiced in the nickname of "Hardscrabble," because of the difficulty in earning a living in the locality. Drawn by W. H. Bartlett. Engraved by R. Wallis. Size 5 x 7.

1732—**FALLS ON ST. JOHN RIVER, 1839-41**—About a mile above the city of St. John, N.B. Drawn by W. H. Bartlett. Engraved by C. Cousen. Size 5 x 7. See 40.

1733—**INDIAN TOWN, ST. JOHN'S COUNTY, N.B., 1839-41**—View of the St. John River where it empties into the harbor of St. John. Indian Town is now a suburb of the city. Drawn by W. H. Bartlett. Engraved by W. Mossman. Size 5 x 7.

1734—**ANNAPOLIS ROYAL, N.S., 1839-41**—Remains of the barracks and the old guns of the Fort—The quaint, old English barracks, with its steep roofs and huge chimneys, has since been demolished. Drawn by W. H. Bartlett. Engraved by J. Cousen. Size 5 x 7. See 2158.

1735—**CAPE SPLIT, 1839-41**—A prominent headland in King's County, N.S., extending into the Bay of Fundy. Drawn by W. H. Bartlett. Engraved by J. Cousen. Size 5 x 7.

1736—**HALIFAX, N.S., 1839-41**—View from Dartmouth on the opposite shore—On the right above the city is Citadel Hill, and to the right in harbor is the mooring ground of the British fleet. George's Island, well fortified, is in centre of harbor. Drawn by W. H. Bartlett. **Engraved.** Size 5 x 7.

1737—**KENTVILLE, N.S., 1839-41**—Kentville is the charming capital of King's County, and is situated some seventy miles from Halifax on the Cornwallis River. It received its name from H.R.H. the Duke of Kent. Drawn by W. H. Bartlett. Engraved by H. Adlard. Size 5 x 7.

1738—**SPLIT ROCK, ST. JOHN RIVER, N.B., 1839-41**—The rock is a portion of the falls on the St. John River, near the city of St. John. Drawn by W. H. Bartlett. Engraved by J. Cousen. Size 5 x 7.

1739—**EARLY DAYS IN NEW BRUNSWICK**—A first settlement by emigrants. The majority of these pioneer settlers hailed from the United States and engaged in the business of clearing land and then selling it to English and Scotch emigrants. Thousands of acres were cleared in this way. Drawn by W. H. Bartlett. Size 5 x 7.

1740—**LIGHT TOWER NEAR COBOURG**—View showing the lighthouse, and a Royal Mail Steamer coming west, up Lake Ontario. The "Gull" light is situated on a rock two miles from the mainland, midway between Cobourg and Port Hope. In 1840 the rock went by the name of Duck Island. Drawn by W. H. Bartlett. Engraved by C. Cousen. Size 5 x 7.

1741—**WELLINGTON, PRINCE EDWARD COUNTY, U.C., 1839-41**—Wellington is situated on an inlet of Lake Ontario, twenty miles from Brighton. In 1840, when the scene was depicted by the artist, the place was an important fishing station. Drawn by W. H. Bartlett. Engraved by R. Wallis. Size 5 x 7.

1742—**FREDERICTON, YORK COUNTY, N.B., 1839-41**—The city is prettily situated on a point of land on the west shore of the St. John River, and has been the capital of the Province of New Brunswick since 1787. The village at St. Anne's Point, opposite the site of Fort Nashwaak, was founded in 1740, and seventeen years later received many of the Acadian refugees. Subsequent to the cession of New Brunswick to the British, Governor Carleton changed the name of St. Anne to Fredericton, and ever since it has borne the name. Drawn by W. H. Bartlett. Engraved by J. B. Allen. Size 5 x 7. See 1749.

1743—**ST. JOHN, N.B., FROM SIGNAL HILL, 1839-41**—The view is taken from the west side of the river. The old Martello tower shown is now in the outskirts of West St. John, or Carleton. Drawn by W. H. Bartlett. Engraved by C. Cousen. Size 5 x 7. See 1750, 2268.

1744—**GENERAL'S BRIDGE NEAR ANNAPOLIS, 1839-41**—A favorite picnic ground near Annapolis. Drawn by W. H. Bartlett. Engraved by J. C. Bentley. Size 5 x 7.

1745—MONTREAL FROM THE MOUNTAIN—The island shown in the centre of the St. Lawrence, opposite the city, is St. Helen's. Drawn by W. H. Bartlett. Engraved by R. Wallis. Size 5 x 7.

1746—"NEW ROMAN CATHOLIC CHURCH, MONTREAL—Consecrated July, 1829. Calculated to hold upwards of 10,000 persons. Drawn by John Okill." Facing Place d'Armes, from Notre Dame street, stands the parish church of Notre Dame de Montreal. It was commenced in 1824 and opened 15th July, 1829, the style of architecture being Gothic composite. This structure replaced the second parish church of Ville Marie, which was built in 1672. Although sometimes called so, Notre Dame is not a cathedral. Line engraving. Size 12 x 19.

1747—CHRIST CHURCH CATHEDRAL, MONTREAL, CANADA EAST—Architectually this is said to be the most perfect church in Canada. It is an example of fourteenth century or decorated Gothic style of architecture, and was erected in 1859 under the guidance of the late Bishop Fulford. The material is rough grey limestone with facings of yellow caen sandstone carved in ornamented form. The spire is of stone 211 feet high, with clock. The original Christ Church, which was the predecessor of this one, stood in Notre Dame street, near St. Lambert Hill, where the site is marked by a tablet which reads, "Site of Christ church Cathedral, the first Anglican Church, 1814, burnt 1856." Published by Hill & Martin, Montreal, and Bosworth & Harrison, 215 Regent street, London. A. Newman. lith. Day & Son, lithrs. to the Queen. F. Wills and T. S. Scott, architects. Lithograph. Size 13 x 15.

1748—SHANTY ON LAKE CHAUDIERE, 1839-41—The shores of the lake were popular as summer camping grounds in the early days. Drawn by W. H. Bartlett. Engraved by R. Brandard. Size 5 x 7.

1749—FREDERICTON, N.B., 1839-41—A view of the city from the opposite or east side of the River St. John. Drawn by W. H. Bartlett. Engraved by W. Mossman. Size 5 x 7. See 1742.

1750—ST. JOHN AND PORTLAND, N.B., 1839-41—Portland, at the head of the harbor, is now a part of the city of St. John. Drawn by W. H. Bartlett. Engraved by R. Wallis. Size 5 x 7. See 1743.

1751—WINDSOR, N.S., 1839-41—The capital of Hants County and situated on the Avon River—Below the town the Avon and St. Croix unite in a wide estuary, which under the name, Avon, empties into the Basin of Minas. The oldest university in the British Empire, outside of the British Isles—King's College—is in Windsor, having received its charter from George III. in 1788. Pigiguit, or Pisiquid (as the Indians called the town), meaning "junction of the waters," was a thriving Acadian settlement before the expulsion of 1755. The view was taken from the residence of Judge Haliburton, or "Sam Slick," as he is known to the literary world. Drawn by W. H. Bartlett. Engraved by W. F. Topham. Size 5 x 7.

1752—HORSESHOE FALL, NIAGARA, 1839-41—From Table Rock, Canadian side, in front of the old Clifton House. The Terrapin Tower and Bridge, erected in 1833 by Judge Porter and blown up in 1873, is seen on the American side. Table Rock fell in June, 1850. Drawn by W. H. Bartlett. Engraved by J. Cousen. Size 5 x 7. See 1258.

1753—BARTLETT, WILLIAM HENRY—Topographical draughtsman, was born in Kentish Town, London, 26th March, 1800. In 1823 he was articled to John Britton, architect, who sent him to Essex, Kent, Bedfordshire, Wiltshire, and other parts of England, to sketch and study from nature. He was afterwards employed in making drawings at Bristol, Gloucester and Hereford for Britton's "Cathedral Antiquities of England," 1814-32, and his skill in landscape and scenic effects induced Britton to undertake his "Picturesque Antiquities of English Cities," which appeared in 1828-30, for which Bartlett made a number of elaborate drawings. Between 1836 and 1852 Bartlett made four voyages to the United States and Canada, the fruits of which appeared in "American Scenery," 1840, and "Canadian Scenery," 1842, with text by N. P. Willis. Bartlett died on board the French steamer "Egyptus" on his homeward voyage from the east between Malta and Marseilles, 13th Sept., 1854, and was buried at sea. H. Room. B. Holl. Engraving. Size 4 x 5. Half length.

1754—RESIDENCE OF JUDGE HALIBURTON ("SAM SLICK") WINDSOR, N.S.—The author-judge resided in an unpretentious wooden cottage on a hill overlooking the Avon River. Clifton, as the old Haliburton estate was known, no longer belongs to the Haliburton family; but is now (1917) the Clifton Hotel, or "Sam Slick" House. Drawn by W. H. Bartlett. Engraved by J. C. Armytage. Size 5 x 7.

1755—LILY LAKE, ST. JOHN, N.B., 1839-41—A pretty little lake about a mile from the King's Square, in the centre of St. John, and a favorite boating and skating resort. To the left of the picture Courtenay Bay is shown. Drawn by W. H. Bartlett. Engraved by R. Brandard. Size 5 x 7.

1756—THE GREEN—Fredericton, N.B., 1839-41—This green, which is situated in the centre of the city of Fredericton, near the barracks, was used as a parade ground when the New Brunswick capital was the headquarters of the British army in the Province. Drawn by W. H. Bartlett. Engraved by J. C. Armytage. Size 5 x 7.

1757—INDIAN SCENE ON THE ST. LAWRENCE, 1839-41—Among the islands on the beautiful Lake of the Thousand Islands. Drawn by W. H. Bartlett. Engraved by J. C. Armytage. Size 5 x 7.

1758—FRONTIER LINE BETWEEN CANADA AND THE UNITED STATES—A scene, 1839-41, in the Eastern Townships, near Stanstead Plains, Stanstead County, Que. Drawn by W. H. Bartlett. Engraved by W. Mossman. Size 5 x 7.

1759—GOVERNMENT HOUSE, FREDERICTON, N.B.—Drawn by W. H. Bartlett. Engraved by J. Cousen. Size 5 x 7.

1760—BAY OF ANNAPOLIS (ANNAPOLIS BASIN), N.S., 1839-41— View from Digby, at the south end of Annapolis Basin. The old town of Annapolis is situated at the mouth of the river of that name. Drawn by W. H. Bartlett. Engraved by C. Cousen. Size 5 x 7.

1761—CAPE BLOW-ME-DOWN (BLOMIDON), KING'S COUNTY, AND PARRSBORO, N.S., 1839-41—Blomidon is a lofty promontory, some five hundred and seventy feet in height, of red sandstone of the Triassic era, and bearing traces of volcanic action. A luxuriant growth of trees and shrubs clothes its side and its base is laved by the waters of the Basin of Minas. Parrsboro is a seaport town in Cumberland County, across the basin from Blomidon. It is shown in the distance at the right of the picture. Drawn by W. H. Bartlett. Engraved by R. Brandard. Size 5 x 7. See 2142.

1762—INDIAN WIGWAM IN THE FOREST—These once familiar conical habitations of the North American Indian were built of bark, mats or skins. Drawn by W. H. Bartlett. Engraved by J. Cousen. Size 5 x 7.

1763—CHAUDIERE BRIDGE, NEAR QUEBEC, 1839-41—This bridge, which spanned the mouth of the Chaudiere River, was replaced in 1890 by a handsome iron structure, now known as the Garneau Bridge. In the background are seen the cliffs on the north side of the St. Lawrence, below Cap Rouge, and just below the mouth of the Chaudiere is the site of the railway bridge over the St. Lawrence, where the original, uncompleted structure collapsed in 1907, killing seventy men. Drawn by W. H. Bartlett. Engraved by R. Brandard. Size 5 x 7.

1764—INTERIOR OF CHURCH OF NOTRE DAME, MONTREAL, QUE.—The Church of Notre Dame is said to have the finest and most impressive interior of any Roman Catholic Church in the Dominion of Canada. Drawn by W. H. Bartlett. Engraved by J. H. Lekeux. Size 5 x 7. See 1803.

1765—LOCKS ON RIDEAU CANAL, BYTOWN (OTTAWA), 1839-41 —View looking south between Parliament Hill and Major's Hill Park—The first locks where the canal empties into Ottawa River—Major's Hill Park is a pretty little spot east of Parliament Hill, and from which fine views of the river may be had. To the left, on the hill, is seen the small building which was occupied by members of the staff building the canal. At the end of the park, on Nepean Point, is the saluting battery (guns of 1797). The building below, near the steamer, is the old Sterling Brewery. The house to the left of the canal is the residence of Col. Coffin, of the Royal Engineers. On the right of the canal are the Military Stores, and on the top of the hill, to the right, is the mess of the R.E. officers. Drawn by W. H. Bartlett. Engraved by J. C. Armytage. Size 5 x 7.

1766—PASS OF BOLTON, EASTERN TOWNSHIPS, QUE., 1839-41— A path at the foot of Mount Orford, leading to Lake Orford, Brome County, near Knowlton, Que. Drawn by W. H. Bartlett. Engraved by Jno. Smith. Size 5 x 7. See 2018.

1767—LAKE MASSAWIPPI, EASTERN TOWNSHIPS, 1839-41—Massawippi is a beautiful sheet of water in Hatley Township, Stanstead County, Que., discharging its waters into the Massawippi River. This river, which never freezes, even in the coldest weather, is tributary to the St. Francis at Lennoxville, Sherbrooke, Que. Drawn by W. H. Bartlett. Engraved by S. Bradshaw. Size 5 x 7. See 1552.

1768—LAKE FARM ON THE FRONTIER, 1839-41—On the shore of an inlet on Lake Memphremagog, near Georgeville, Que. Drawn by W. H. Bartlett. Engraved by J. Cousen. Size 5 x 7.

1769—SCENE ON THE ST. FRANCIS, 1839-41—The River St. Francis takes its rise in the lake of the same name, in Wolfe County, and winds through some very picturesque country, finally, after a journey of about one hundred miles, giving up its waters to the St. Lawrence at Lake St. Peter. Falls, rapids and islands break the monotony of its lengthy course. Drawn by W. H. Bartlett. Engraved by R. Sands. Size 5 x 7. See 1554.

1770—MILL ON THE RIDEAU RIVER, NEAR BYTOWN (OTTAWA), 1839-41—The present site of the mills of Senator Edwards, in Ottawa. The falls are those of the Rideau emptying into the Ottawa at the suburbs of New Edinburgh. Drawn by W. H. Bartlett. Engraved by E. Benjamin. Size 5 x 7.

1771—TIMBER SLIDE AT LES CHATS, 1839-41—Twenty-five miles above the city of Ottawa, near Arnprior, is a magnificent expansion of the Ottawa River, fifteen miles in length, known as Lac des Chats. Below the lake the river falls over a long circular ridge of rock, forming what is known as the rapids of Les Chats, so named because of the number of raccoons (chats sauvages) found in the vicinity. The slides were constructed to overcome Chats Falls, Fitzroy Harbor, Ont., twelve miles from Arnprior. Drawn by W. H. Bartlett. Engraved by R. Wallis. Size 5 x 7.

1772—**CHAUDIERE FALLS, NEAR QUEBEC**—Drawn by W. H. Bartlett. Engraved by C. Cousen. Size 5 x 7.

1773—**RAFTS ON THE ST. LAWRENCE AT CAPE SANTE, 1839-41**— Cape Sante, or La Saint Famille as it was formerly known, is situated on the north shore of the St. Lawrence, some thirty miles from Quebec, in Portneuf County. In olden days large quantities of timber from the Upper Ottawa and elsewhere were floated down to Quebec on rafts, which were then broken up and the timber stowed on shipboard for foreign ports. Drawn by W. H. Bartlett. Engraved by R. Brandard. Size 5 x 7.

1774—**ALLUMETTE LAKE, 1839-41**—An expansion of the Ottawa River, opposite the Isle des Allumettes. In 1613 Champlain ascended the Ottawa Valley as far as the Isle des Allumettes, but discovering that his guide, Vignau, was an impostor, who had never been further up the river than this point, and also being unable to get assistance from the Algonquin (Ottawa) Indians in pushing on to Lake Nipissing, he had to return to Montreal without pursuing his explorations further. In 1615, however, he was able to return, exploring all the older parts of Ontario, with the exception of the Niagara Peninsula. Drawn by W. H. Bartlett. Engraved by J. T. Willmore. Size 5 x 7.

1775—**OTTAWA RIVER AT BYTOWN (OTTAWA), 1839-41**—A view taken from beach at the foot of Parliament Hill, and looking west—The bridge shown was first constructed in 1827, and has been rebuilt on three occasions since. It is, as will be observed, in two sections, with Victoria Island intervening. Drawn by W. H. Bartlett. Engraved by H. Adlard. Size 5 x 7.

1776—**ORFORD MOUNTAIN**—Overlooking Lake Memphremagog— Drawn by W. H. Bartlett. Engraved by W. Mossman. Size 5 x 7.

1777—**LAKE BENEATH OWL'S HEAD MOUNTAIN, 1839-41**—The mountain, which overlooks Lake Memphremagog, is about six miles from Georgeville, Stanstead Co., Que. On a clear day Montreal and the Green, White, and Adirondack Mountains may be seen from its summit. The water shown at the base is an inlet of the lake. Drawn by W. H. Bartlett. Engraved by J. T. Willmore. Size 5 x 7.

1778—**ORFORD LAKE, 1839-41**—A small lake at the foot of Orford Mountain, Sherbrooke County, Que., Surrounded by pine forests, which give it a dark and dreary appearance. In summer its shores afford a favorite camping ground for tourists. Drawn by W. H. Bartlett. Engraved by E. Benjamin. Size 5 x 7.

1779—**LAKE MEMPHREMAGOG, NEAR GEORGEVILLE, QUE.**—The lake, a beautiful sheet of water, known as "the Geneva of Canada," is situated partly in Brome and Stanstead Counties, Que., and partly in the State of Vermont. Mountains guard the western shore, while well cultivated farms and gentle slopes bound the eastern side. The waters of the lake empty into the Magog River. Drawn by W. H. Bartlett. Engraved by C. J. Armytage. Size 5 x 7. See 1574, 1787.

1780—**CHURCH OF ST. JOSEPH DE LEVIS AT POINT LEVIS, QUE.,** 1839-41—The sacred edifice was built by Sir John Caldwell (who in 1810 succeeded his father, Sir Henry Caldwell, as Receiver-General of Quebec) for the use of the English and French soldiers in the vicinity of Levis in 1818. Thirty-one years later it was demolished. Drawn by W. H. Bartlett. Engraved by J. T. Willmore. Size 5 x 7.

21

1781—JUNCTION OF THE OTTAWA AND ST. LAWRENCE RIVERS, 1839-41—At St. Anne's Rapids, twenty miles above the Island of Montreal, Que., the River Ottawa discharges its waters into the St. Lawrence. Drawn by W. H. Bartlett. Engraved by J. Cousen. Size 5 x 7.

1782—SCENE FROM THE SUMMIT OF THE FALL OF MONTMORENCY, 1839-41—View from the east side of the cataract. The Heights of Quebec, and also those of Levis on the opposite side of the river, are shown in the background. Drawn by W. H. Bartlett. Engraved by G. K. Richardson. Size 5 x 7.

1783—MONTMORENCY BRIDGE, NEAR QUEBEC, 1839-41—It was the first bridge over the Montmorency River, and was built with rough stone piers and roading of wood. A suspension bridge was later erected, a little below the elevation shown in the picture, and immediately over the brink of the precipice; but because of faulty construction it collapsed in the sixties and was hurled over the falls, carrying with it two or three people, who were crossing it at the time. The piers of the collapsed bridge still remain on either side of the cataract. Drawn by W. H. Bartlett. Engraved by S. Bradshaw. Size 5 x 7.

1784—OWL'S HEAD MOUNTAIN, LAKE MEMPHREMAGOG, 1839-41—A view taken about two miles from Knowlton, Que.—Owl's Head, which rises to a majestic height, is one of several mountains on the west shore of Lake Memphremagog. This island-studded lake was known to the Indians as "Memplowbowque," signifying "beautiful water." Drawn by W. H. Bartlett. Engraved by G. K. Richardson. Size 5 x 7. See 1557, 1597.

1785—THE CITADEL, QUEBEC, 1839-41—View of the King's Bastion at the Citadel, and of the residences facing what is now known as Dufferin Terrace. The monument seen is that erected to the memory of Wolfe and Montcalm in the Governor's garden. Some of the most distant houses shown below the Citadel were destroyed in the rockslide of September, 1889, in which from fifty to sixty people perished. In the foreground are the outbuildings of the Chateau St. Louis. Drawn by W. H. Bartlett. Engraved by E. Challis. Size 5 x 7.

1786—OUTLET OF LAKE MEMPHREMAGOG—The lake discharges its waters into the St. Francis by way of the River Magog. The St. Francis, in its turn, empties into the St. Lawrence at Lake St. Peter. Drawn by W. H. Bartlett. Engraved by H. Adlard. Size 5 x 7.

1787—LAKE MEMPHREMAGOG, 1839-41—A view over the lake from the Sugar Loaf Peak, overlooking not only the lake, but the surrounding country as well. Drawn by W. H. Bartlett. Engraved by G. K. Richardson. Size 5 x 7. See 1574, 1779.

1788—WORKING A CANOE UP A RAPID—Near the Cedars, below Coteau Junction—A once familiar scene on the St. Lawrence. Drawn by W. H. Bartlett. Engraved by S. Bradshaw. Size 5 x 7.

1789—SETTLER'S HUT ON THE FRONTIER—A view on the west shore of an inlet of Lake Memphremagog, on Canadian side of boundary line. Drawn by W. H. Bartlett. Engraved by R. Sands. Size 5 x 7.

1790—THE MARKET PLACE, QUEBEC, 1840—The site of the old market is the present Square between the Basilica (Cathedral) and the City Hall. Since the sketch was made, an additional tower has been added to the front of the Basilica, and the old building in front, formerly containing butchers' stalls, has been demolished. Some of the most modern shops in Quebec now occupy the sites of the old buildings, shown on Buade street —parallel to the Cathedral, on the right of the picture, and of those in Fabrique street, at the extreme left. Drawn by W. H. Bartlett. Engraved by F. W. Topham. Size 5 x 7.

1791—**PORTAGE DES CHATS, 1839-41**—The portage is from the west end of Lake Des Chenes, and avoids the Falls of Les Chats, on the Ottawa River, at Fitzroy Harbor, Carleton County, Ont. Drawn by W. H. Bartlett. Engraved by E. Benjamin. Size 5 x 7.

1792—**PRESCOTT GATE, QUEBEC, 1839-41**—At the head of Mountain Hill—Erected by Governor Prescott in 1797. The building on the right was the Roman Catholic Bishop's Palace. On its site was built the old Parliament House. Drawn by W. H. Bartlett. Engraved by J. Tingle. Size 5 x 7. See 2068.

1793—**QUEBEC**—From the Citadel, 1839—In the foreground is shown the King's Bastion, and the deep moat of masonry just outside the walls of the Citadel. Then come the Glacis, or grassy inclines sloping down to the Upper Town, and especially to the houses on the Cape. The Governor's residence, or Chateau St. Louis, is distinguished by the flag flying from it, and near by is the Bishop's Palace. Through the trees in the Governor's garden one gets a glimpse of the obelisk of the Wolfe and Montcalm monument, and to the extreme left of the picture are shown portions of the Roman Catholic Cathedral and Seminary buildings. In the background are the Laurentians, running behind Beauport and St. Anne de Beaupre. The straggling village of Beauport on the foothills to the left is plainly discernible, as are the Isle of Orleans, beyond the line of ships in the distance, and the point of St. Joseph de Levis on the other side of the ship channel. Drawn by W. H. Bartlett. Engraved by R. Wallis. Size 5 x 7.

1794—**BRIDGE AT BYTOWN (OTTAWA), U.C.**—The first bridge built across the Ottawa River, at the foot of the Chaudiere Falls, and between Ottawa and Hull, near Eddy's and Booth's mills. It was built in 1827, but was carried away in a gale the following summer, and then rebuilt. Bytown became Ottawa in 1854. The drawing was made a few weeks before the bridge fell down. Drawn by W. H. Bartlett. Engraved by J. Smith. Size 5 x 7. See 1400.

1795—**TIMBER DEPOT NEAR QUEBEC, 1839-41**—The timber depot shown here is in the neighborhood of Wolfe's Cove. On the left of the picture are seen the Heights of Quebec, with the Citadel in the distance, and on the right are the far-off Heights of Levis, with a portion of the village. Drawn by W. H. Bartlett. Engraved by H. Adlard. Size 5 x 7.

1796—**DAVIS' CLEARING, EASTERN TOWNSHIPS, QUE., 1839-41**— A picturesque spot, showing part of Lake Memphremagog in the distance. Drawn by W. H. Bartlett. Engraved by R. Wallis. Size 5 x 7.

1797—**NORTH SHORE OF THE ST. LAWRENCE, 1839-41**—View at Longue Pointe, Hochelaga County, Que., six miles east of Montreal. On the right is shown the Roman Catholic church, and Montreal and Mount Royal appear in the background. Drawn by W. H. Bartlett. Engraved by R. Wallis. Size 5 x 7.

1798—**BROCKVILLE, U.C., 1839-41**—At the foot of the Lake of the Thousand Islands, an expansion of the River St. Lawrence. St. Peter's Anglican Church, built in 1818, is seen on the right. Drawn by W. H. Bartlett. Engraved by R. Wallis. Size 5 x 7.

1799—**FITZROY HARBOR,** 1839-41—View from the Shirreff residence. Fitzroy Harbor is a village in Carleton County, Ont., situated on the Parry Sound River. Mr. Robert Shirreff, the owner of the pioneer abode of the picture, was an old army officer, lumberman and miller. Drawn by W. H. Bartlett. Engraved by J. T. Willmore. Size 5 x 7.

1800—**MILLS AT SHERBROOKE, QUE.,** 1839-41—The town of Sherbrooke is prettily situated at the confluence of the St. Francis and Magog Rivers, in the Eastern Townships, and is a thriving manufacturing town, within whose precincts are to be seen the picturesque rapids of the Magog. The Eastern Townships were originally settled by United Empire Loyalists, and from the English portion of Quebec Province. Drawn by W. H. Bartlett. Engraved by J. C. Armytage. Size 5 x 7.

1801—**FALLS OF THE OTTAWA AT LES CHATS,** 1839-41—Thirty miles from Ottawa, and at the east end of the Lake of the Chats, alongside of the village of Fitzroy Harbor. Drawn by W. H. Bartlett. Engraved by F. W. Topham. Size 5 x 7. See 1771, 1892.

1802—**WOLFE'S COVE, QUEBEC**—From near the spot at which the ascent of the cliff was made by the advance guard of Wolfe's army in 1759. It looks towards the west, and the point at the farther corner of the bay is the property of Spencer Wood, the picturesque residence of the Lieutenant-Governor of the Province of Quebec. Drawn by W. H. Bartlett. Engraved by J. Cousen. Size 5 x 7.

1803—**PARISH CHURCH OF NOTRE DAME, MONTREAL,** 1839-41— View facing Notre Dame street—On the right is seen the Seminary of St. Sulpice. The church is built in perpendicular Gothic style. Drawn by W. H. Bartlett. Engraved by J. Carter. Size 5 x 7. See 1764.

1804—**RIDEAU CANAL, BYTOWN (OTTAWA),** 1839-41—View looking north to the Ottawa River and showing the outlet of the Rideau Canal, as seen from a higher level. When the War of 1812 came to a close the British Government thought it unwise to leave Upper Canada connected with Montreal and Quebec by a frontier route along the St. Lawrence only, and so in 1826 Colonel By, of the Royal Engineers, began the work of constructing the Rideau Canal, which connects the fortified harbor of Kingston with the Ottawa River, below the Chaudiere Falls. Near Montreal the Ottawa, in turn, flows into the St. Lawrence. This canal system is partially formed by the Cataraqui River, which flows from Lake Rideau to Kingston. On the right of the picture is seen Nepean Point, while Parliament Hill is on the left. Drawn by W. H. Bartlett. Engraved by R. Sands. Size 5 x 7.

1805—**BRIDGE AT SHERBROOKE, QUE.,** 1839-41—This bridge, which crosses the River Magog at Sherbrooke, has since been replaced by a modern structure. Drawn by W. H. Bartlett. Engraved by C. Cousen. Size 5 x 7.

1806—**TIMBER SLIDE AND BRIDGE ON OTTAWA RIVER**—Beside the south section of the old bridge, near J. R. Booth's mills, Bridge street, Ottawa. Drawn by W. H. Bartlett. Engraved by J. Sands. Size 5 x 7.

1807—**CITADEL OF KINGSTON**—Kingston, Frontenac County, is situated at the outlet of Lake Ontario into the St. Lawrence River. This view is from Barriefield, and shows Fort Henry on Point Frederick to the left, and also the Cataraqui bridge. The buildings in the centre are on the site of the present (1917) Royal Military College. Drawn by W. H. Bartlett. Engraved by H. Griffiths. Size 5 x 7.

1808—**GEORGEVILLE, QUE., 1839-41**—A village in Stanstead County, two miles from Knowlton and ten miles east of Lake Memphremagog. It is noted for its beautiful scenery. Drawn by W. H. Bartlett. Engraved by H. Adlard. Size 5 x 7.

1809—**QUEBEC**—View from the Heights of Levis, west of the Grand Trunk terminals, facing that part of the Plains of Abraham known as the Cove Fields, just beyond the western limits of the Citadel. Both points of Cape Diamond, on which the Citadel is built, are shown. Portions of both the Upper and Lower Town are seen, but other parts are obscured by the eastern promontory of Cape Diamond. The long row of houses stretching out on the rising land above the river from the city towards the extreme right (facing the picture) is the village of Beauport. Drawn by W. H. Bartlett. Engraved by J. Cousen. Size 5 x 7.

1810—**COPP'S FERRY**—Near Georgeville, Stanstead County, Quebec, 1839-41—The ferry ran from the east side of Lake Memphremagog to various points along the lake. Drawn by W. H. Bartlett. Engraved by J. C. Armytage. Size 5 x 7.

1811—**BANKS OF THE NIAGARA RIVER, 1839-41**—A view of the river below the Falls, a short distance above the Whirlpool. Drawn by W. H. Bartlett. Engraved by R. Brandard. Size 5 x 7.

1812—**CEDAR RAPIDS, 1839-41**—The rapids are almost opposite the village of Cedars, Soulanges County, Que., and their descent is considered a very exciting experience. Drawn by W. H. Bartlett. Engraved by J. C. Bentley. Size 5 x 7.

1813—**PRESCOTT, U.C., 1839-41**—From Ogdensburg Harbor—The town of Prescott, Grenville County, is situated at the mouth of the Oswegatchie, or Blackwater River, opposite Ogdensburg, N.Y. Drawn by W. H. Bartlett. Engraved by J. C. Bentley. Size 5 x 7.

1814—**QUEBEC, 1839-41**—View from the vicinity of the present (1917) ferry wharf adjoining the Intercolonial Railway station at Levis. Immediately opposite the group of people on the wharf, who are apparently waiting to cross the river, is seen on the north or Quebec side the line of houses bordering the ascent of Mountain Hill to the Upper Town. Cape Diamond, surmounted by the Citadel, is shown toward the left (facing the picture). Behind the largest ship and between two of its masts, the Wolfe and Montcalm monument on the Heights of Quebec may be seen. On the east (right of the picture) the castle of St. Louis is visible behind the mizzenmast of the big ship, and then in order, the spires of the English and French cathedrals, the Bishop's Palace and the Seminary. Drawn by W. H. Bartlett. Engraved by H. Griffiths. Size 5 x 7.

1815—**MARCH TOWNSHIP, ONT.**—A view of March Township, on what is now called Lake Des Chenes. It is opposite Aylmer, and near the site of the ranges of the Dominion Rifle Association. Drawn by W. H. Bartlett. Engraved by F. W. Topham. Size 5 x 7.

1816—**MONTGOMERY COVE, 1839-41**—Near Quebec—Showing Montmorency Falls. Drawn by W. H. Bartlett. Engraved by E. Benjamin. Size 5 x 7.

1817—**INDIAN ENCAMPMENT**—In the forest near Georgeville, Stanstead County, Que., in the summer time. Drawn by W. H. Bartlett. Engraved by J. C. Bentley. Size 5 x 7.

1818—CANOE BUILDING AT PAPPER'S ISLAND, 1839-41—Indians constructing their craft at what is now one of the Chaudiere Islands, near Ottawa. The redskins built canoes for the people of the lake and river district as well as for their own use. Drawn by W. H. Bartlett. Engraved by H. Griffiths. Size 5 x 7.

1819—MONUMENT TO MEMORY OF WOLFE AND MONTCALM, IN GOVERNOR'S GARDEN, QUEBEC—The old Presbyterian Church at Levis is shown immediately across the river from the monument, and the Roman Catholic Church of St. Joseph de Levis is seen in the distance, near the point of land where the south channel of the St. Lawrence separates the south shore from the Isle of Orleans, near the extreme left of the picture. Drawn by W. H. Bartlett. Engraved by R. Wallis. Size 5 x 7.

1820—PICTURESQUE VIEW OF CHAUDIERE FALLS, NEAR BYTOWN (OTTAWA)—Drawn by W. H. Bartlett. Engraved by F. W. Topham. Size 5 x 7.

1821—VILLAGE AND FALLS OF LORETTE—The falls seen in this picture are those of the St. Charles River in the heart of the village, which, after a drop of over eighty feet, have cut a passage for a considerable distance through a tortuous and picturesque chasm. The small church shown across the river is the Huron Chapel, the Church of the Annunciation. Drawn by W. H. Bartlett. Engraved by W. Mossman. Size 5 x 7. See 2047, 2055.

1822—CEDARS VILLAGE—On the banks of the St. Lawrence, in Soulanges County, Que., twenty-nine miles south-west of Montreal. Drawn by W. H. Bartlett. Engraved by R. Brandard. Size 5 x 7.

1823—NELSON'S COLUMN, MONTREAL—The memorial, which is at the upper end of Jacques Cartier Square, near the Chateau de Ramezay, was erected in 1809 by subscriptions from English and French citizens of Montreal. It is of grey, compact limestone, and has a square base, about ten and a half feet high, supporting a Doric pillar rising to a height of fifty feet. The whole is surmounted by a figure of Nelson in the attitude in which he stood at the moment of receiving his death wound. His left and only remaining arm is resting upon the stump of a broken mast, surrounded by tackles, blocks, etc., as they appear to have fallen from the rigging. On the four sides of the pedestal are panels depicting incidents in the career of Nelson. Drawn by W. H. Bartlett. Engraved by E. J. Roberts. Size 5 x 7.

1824—JUNCTION OF ST. FRANCIS AND MAGOG RIVERS—The St. Francis rises in Lake St. Francis, Wolfe County, Que.; and at Sherbrooke is joined by the Magog, the town of Sherbrooke lying on both sides of the latter river. The united streams, after winding through a picturesque country, empty into the St. Lawrence at Lake St. Peter. Drawn by W. H. Bartlett. Engraved by J. Smith. Size 5 x 7.

1825—LAKE OF THE TWO MOUNTAINS, 1839-41—A beautiful expansion of the Ottawa River, near its mouth. Drawn by W. H. Bartlett. Engraved by F. W. Topham. Size 5 x 7.

1826—PLAINS OF ABRAHAM, QUEBEC, 1839-41—View looking towards the west. The artist errs in calling it "The spot where General Wolfe fell." The present monument more correctly has it, "Here died Wolfe victorious." He fell at the head of his army a few hundred paces nearer the city than the site of the memorial, and was carried to the rear after receiving his fatal wound. Drawn by W. H. Bartlett. Engraved by R. Wallis. Size 5 x 7. See 2821.

1827—VIEW ACROSS THE BOUNDARY LINE BETWEEN CANADA AND THE UNITED STATES—Sketched from a point on Sugar Loaf Mountain, overlooking Lake Memphremagog, Que.—Drawn by W. H. Bartlett. Engraved by S. Bradshaw. Size 5 x 7.

1828—SQUAW'S GRAVE OF THE EARLY DAYS—On Lake Deschenes, near Aylmer. Bartlett, in his "Canadian Scenery," says that as a rule the graves of the Indians were of a long, narrow shape, protected from attack on the part of wild animals by an outer covering of split wood, bound together with branches, and within this was a covering of birch bark, beneath which was placed the body, covered with sand. Blueberry Point is seen in the distance in the picture. Drawn by W. H. Bartlett. Engraved by J. C. Bentley. Size 5 x 7.

1829—LES MARCHES NATURELLES, OR NATURAL STEPS, MONTMORENCY RIVER—A mile above the falls. Drawn by W. H. Bartlett. Engraved by F. W. Topham. Size 5 x 7.

1830—ST. JOHN'S—On the Richelieu River, 1839-41—St. John's, formerly Dorchester, a quaint, French-looking little town in the Seigniory of Longeuil, is the capital of St. John's County, Que. It was at one time of considerable importance as a fortified post, commanding the line of approach by the Champlain Valley. In the campaigns of 1776-7 St. John's was one of the chief bases of supply for the troops of Burgoyne and Carleton. The bridge connects the town with St. Athanase on the opposite shore of the river. Drawn by W. H. Bartlett. Engraved by J. Carter. Size 5 x 7.

1831—HALLOWELL, U.C. (PICTON), 1839-41—The present town of Picton, on the Bay of Quinte, in Prince Edward County, was formerly known as Hallowell, west of the bridge. East of the bridge only was known as Picton, after the distinguished general of that name, who lost his life at Waterloo. Following considerable discussion as to which name should be retained, Picton was selected and the town so incorporated about 1847. Hallowell Township was the centre of a U.E. Loyalist settlement. Drawn by W. H. Bartlett. Engraved by J. C. Armytage. Size 5 x 7.

1832—MONTREAL—From the St. Lawrence, 1839-41—A picturesque river view—Mount Royal is shown overlooking the city in the background. The edifice in the centre is the Church of Notre Dame. Drawn by W. H. Bartlett. Engraved by C. Cousen. Size 5 x 7.

1833—ST. LAWRENCE, AT MONTREAL, 1839-41—With key. Drawn by W. H. Bartlett. Engraved by H. Griffiths. Size 5 x 7.

1834—SCENE ON THE BAY OF QUINTE, 1839-41—A large inlet to the west of Kingston, Ont., very singularly formed between Hastings County on the mainland to the north, and the irregular peninsula of Prince Edward to the south. The bay, which is about fifty miles in length, affords a safe harbor from the heavy gales of Lake Ontario. Drawn by W. H. Bartlett. Engraved by C. Cousen. Size 5 x 7.

1835—FORT CHAMBLY, 1839-41—On the west side of the Richelieu River, between the St. John's Canal and the Montreal River. Drawn by W. H. Bartlett. Engraved by J. T. Willmore. Size 5 x 7. See 1942-5, 1965.

1836—QUEENSTON—On the Niagara River, five miles north of Niagara Falls and seven above the town of Niagara. Drawn by W. H. Bartlett. Engraved by J. C. Armytage. Size 5 x 7.

1837—PORT HOPE, U.C., 1839-41—A port of entry on the north shore of Lake Ontario. Drawn by W. H. Bartlett. Engraved by E. Benjamin. Size 5 x 7.

1838—WHIRLPOOL RAPIDS, NIAGARA RIVER, 1839-41—At the south extremity of the first rapids, below the old town of Clifton (now Niagara Falls, Ont.) A reflex in the current, caused by an angle in the river, forms what is known as the "Whirlpool." Drawn by W. H. Bartlett. Engraved by E. Radclyffe. Size 5 x 7.

1839—BROCK'S MONUMENT, QUEENSTON HEIGHTS, 1839-41— Erected in memory of Major-General Sir Isaac Brock, who fell at Queenston Heights, October 13th, 1812. Drawn by W. H. Bartlett. Engraved by R. Wallis. Size 5 x 7.

1840—MAITLAND'S WHARF AND THE ONTARIO HOUSE, TORONTO, U.C., 1839-41—It was from Maitland's Wharf, at the foot of Church street, that the old horse boat and the first steam ferry ran to Privat's Hotel, which stood where the eastern channel now runs through Toronto Island. The Ontario House was at one time the principal hotel of Toronto, and stood on the north-west corner of Market (Wellington) and Church streets. It later became known as the Wellington Hotel. Drawn by W. H. Bartlett. Engraved by E. J. Roberts. Size 5 x 7.

1841—ST. REGIS, 1839-41—An Indian village in Huntingdon County, six miles from Cornwall, on the St. Lawrence and St. Regis Rivers. The Indians shown are Iroquois, who reside here on the reserve. Drawn by W. H. Bartlett. Engraved by H. Griffiths. Size 5 x 7.

1842—RAFT IN A SQUALL ON LAKE ST. PETER—The lake is a shallow expansion of the St. Lawrence, above Three Rivers, and forms the south-east boundary of Maskinonge County, Que. A deep channel has been dredged through the expansion, so that it has been made navigable for large ocean vessls. Numerous islands dot the southern portion of the lake. Drawn by W. H. Bartlett. Engraved by J. Cousen. Size 5 x 7.

1843—THREE RIVERS, QUE., 1839-41—Looking towards the east— Three Rivers, the capital of St. Maurice County, is situated at the mouth of the St. Maurice River—where it flows into the St. Lawrence. Trois Rivieres, as the French have it, early became an important fur trading centre, but it was not until 1634 that a permanent settlement was founded. Drawn by W. H. Bartlett. Engraved by R. Wallis. Size 5 x 7. See 1962, 2015.

1844—BURIAL PLACE OF THE VOYAGEURS—View on the banks of the Ottawa River, above Hull, showing Green Island—The Voyageurs, river boatmen of frontier days, in Quebec Province, were wont to select pretty spots on banks of rivers or shores of lakes for the burial of their dead, marking the location with a cross. Drawn by W. H. Bartlett. Engraved by S. Bradshaw. Size 5 x 7.

1845—FISH MARKET, TORONTO, U.C., 1839-41—The market was in a little bay just east of the old City Hall, on the bay shore on the south side of Palace (Front) street, and in the forties was frequented by Indians as well as citizens. Opposite this market was the City Hotel, formerly the Steamboat Hotel, long known as Ulick Howard's. At the junction of Front and Market (Wellington) streets is seen the Coffin Block, so named because of its striking resemblance at one end to a coffin. Drawn by W. H. Bartlett. Engraved by J. C. Bentley. Size 5 x 7.

1846—KINGSTON, U.C., 1839-41—A view from Fort Henry, on the mainland, above Point Frederick, or Navy Point. Drawn by W. H. Bartlett. Engraved by R. Brandard. Size 5 x 7. See 1849.

1847—**WINTER SCENE IN AYLMER, QUE., 1839-41**—The town of Aylmer is not in Upper Canada, as stated on the engraving in "Canadian Scenery," but in Wright County, Que., on Lake Deschenes, an expansion of the Ottawa River in Wright County. The building seen to the right of the picture is the original Holt's Hotel. Drawn by W. H. Bartlett. Engraved by J. C. Armytage. Size 5 x 7.

1848—**LONG SAULT RAPIDS**—On the St. Lawrence River, near Cornwall, between the Canadian shore and Long Sault Island. The rapids, nine miles in length, are avoided in ascending by the Cornwall Canal. Drawn by W. H. Bartlett. Engraved by C. Cousen. Size 5 x 7.

1849—**VIEW OF KINGSTON, U.C.**—Taken from Fort Henry, Barriefield, looking down the river—Cedars Island is shown in the centre. To the left is Deadman's Bay, and Milton Island is in the background. Drawn by W. H. Bartlett. Engraved by R. Wallis. Size 5 x 7. See 1846.

1850—**NAVY ISLAND, NIAGARA RIVER, 1839-41**—A view from the Canadian side above Niagara Falls, between Goat Island and the Canadian shore. Drawn by W. H. Bartlett. Engraved by C. Cousen. Size 5 x 7.

1851—**SCENE AMONG THE THOUSAND ISLANDS**—Drawn by W. H. Bartlett. Engraved by R. Brandard. Size 5 x 7.

1852—**BRIDGE NEAR QUEBEC**—The engraving is thought to represent a bridge that formerly crossed the River Gouffre, near St. Paul's Bay, opposite Isle Aux Coudres. The Gouffre, which rises in Charlevoix County, Que., pursues a very circuitous course, and is difficult to ascend because of its many rapids. Drawn by W. H. Bartlett. Engraved by F. W. Topham. Size 5 x 7.

1853—**LOOKING UP FROM THE WHARVES, QUEBEC**—With key, showing: 1, Houses in Little Champlain street, immediately under Dufferin Terrace. 2, Building formerly occupied by Thibaudeau Bros., wholesale dry goods merchants, now (1917) shops and boarding houses; it faces the old Champlain Market Place on east side. 3, Houses facing old Champlain Market Place on north side; site now occupied by station of National Transcontinental Railway. 4. Stairway leading to river boats; replaced by pontoon and shorter stairs. 5. Dufferin Terrace. Water color from original drawing by F. B. Schell, for "Picturesque Canada," 1880. Size 4 x 7.

1854—**"BIEN COMFORTABLE" (VERY COMFORTABLE)**—The aged habitant appreciates to the full his solacing pipe. Copy of oil by Henri Julien, in possession of O. S. Perrault, Montreal. Size 8 x 10.

1855—**"AVEC MA PETITE FILLE" (WITH MY LITTLE GIRL)**— Plodding through the snow drifts on a Quebec road. Copy of oil by Henri Julien, in possession of O. S. Perrault, Montreal. Size 7 x 9.

1856—**MONTREAL AND ST. HELEN'S ISLAND**—From a point in the centre of the River St. Lawrence, Oct. 1849—To the left of picture is a distant view of the city. Water color by Gen. A. R. V. Crease, R.E. Size 9 x 13. See 1864.

1857—**"SLEDGE RACE NEAR MONTREAL**—Published under the patronage of the Right Hon. the Earl of Elgin and Kincardine, Governor-General of British North America. Painted by C. Krieghoff. Lith. by A. Borum in Munic." The view is taken just below Longueuil Point, on the winter road between Longueuil and Montreal. No. 1 is Longueuil Point; No. 2, the City of Montreal; 3, the mountain; 4, Lord Elgin's turnout. The artist introduced Lord Elgin, who was his patron, in other views also; e.g., the Fall of Montmorency. Lithograph. Size 13 x 19.

1858—RAILWAY BRIDGE OVER ST. ANNE'S RAPIDS—On the St. Lawrence, near Montreal. The Montreal and Lachine Railway was built in 1847 and later taken over by the Grand Trunk, which built the bridge connecting on the left, or south side of the river, the Island of Montreal with Isle Perrot. The Rapids of St. Anne are those mentioned by Tom Moore in his "Canadian Boat Song." This picture was not made on the spot, but from the engineer's drawing, and is not quite correct; the two mountains should be the same height as the one on the left; also the bridge, the first erected at this point, is much shorter than it appears in the view. The latter was removed about thirty years ago and replaced by a modern steel double-track structure. Lithograph. Published by John Weale, London, 1860. Kell Bros., Lithrs., Castle St., Holborn. Size 8 x 12.

1859—"SHOVING OF ICE UPON WHARVES IN FRONT OF MONT-REAL—Kell Bros., lithrs., Castle street, Holborn. Published by John Weale, London, 1860." No. 1 is the dome of Bonsecours Market, in centre of building, which is situated near Jacques Cartier square. 2, Eastern end of market. 3, The old Church of Notre Dame de Bonsecours, completed, 1675; burned, 1754, and rebuilt, 1771. 4, Buildings in rear belonging to the church. 5, Houses in St. Paul street. Many houses of the French period exist in this neighborhood. The street fronting the harbor is Commissioners street. Lithograph. Size 7 x 9.

1860—"DESTRUCTION OF THE PARLIAMENT HOUSE, MONTREAL, APRIL 25TH, 1849—Sketched on the spot and drawn on stone by E. Hides. Matthews, Lith." On the afternoon of 25th April, 1849, Lord Elgin, Governor-General, sanctioned a number of bills that Parliament had just passed, amongst them the Rebellion Bill, providing for the payment of losses sustained during the Rebellion. As soon as it was known that this bill had become law, excitement prevailed in Montreal, a riot ensued, and some of the mob set fire to the Parliament Buildings. They were entirely destroyed, the only article saved being the mace belonging to the Lower House. Lithograph. Size 9 x 16. See 1939.

1861—"A VIEW OF THE CITY OF MONTREAL AND THE RIVER ST. LAURENCE FROM THE MOUNTAIN—E. Walsh, 49th Regt., delint. Engraved by John Black, London. Publish'd Jany. 1, 1811, at R. Ackermann's Repository of Arts, 101 Strand." With key. Line engraving. Size 14 x 21. See 1881, 2035.

1862—"THE DORCHESTER"—First train to run from La Prairie to St. John's, Que., 1836—It was built and equipped by the St. Lawrence and Champlain Railroad Co., no longer in existence. Twelve miles of the original line, however, from St. John's to the Junction is now (1917) owned and operated by the Grand Trunk. Photograph. Size 4 x 10.

1863—HOME OF DOWAGER BARONESS DE LONGUEUIL—Barony House of Le Moynes, St. Helen's Island, Montreal—Shortly after her marriage to Hon. Wm. Grant, in 1770, the Dowager Baroness de Longueuil (widow of the third Baron, Charles Jacques le Moyne) built on the picturesque family property of the Le Moynes on St. Helen's Island the house shown. In June, 1792, Mrs. Simcoe visited La Baronne "at a pretty house she and Mr. Grant have built on the north shore of her island of St. Helen's," and says, further, that "La Baronne has the only hothouse I have seen in Canada." The artist, in making his sketch, had his back to Montreal. The house could not be seen from Montreal, as high ground intervenes. The river and shore line is that of the Longueuil side. Water color by Gen. A. R. V. Crease, R.E., 1849. Size 6 x 10.

1864—ST. HELEN'S ISLAND, MONTREAL, 1849—This view of the island, opposite the east end of Montreal, is seen from the centre of the River St. Lawrence. Water color by Gen. A. R. V. Crease, R.E. Size 9 x 13. See 1856.

1865—"A VIEW OF MONTREAL, WITH THE PARISH OF LONGUIL IN CANADA—Taken near Longuil Point, by W. Peachy, 19th Octr., 1784. Aquatd. by J. Wells. Publish'd by J. Wells, No. 22 Charing Cross." The view shows (from left to right): 1, Longueuil; 2, St. Helen's Island; 3, Montreal; 4, The Mountain. Size 12 x 19.

1866—VICTORIA BRIDGE, MONTREAL—View from tower of Notre Dame looking south from north side of harbor, 1860—1, Land beyond the bridge, in background, is St. Lambert. The land joined by bridge is Point St. Charles on the city side and St. Lambert on the south shore. 2, First Custom House, built, 1833, on Place Royale, the first public square and market in Montreal. The building is now used by the Inland Revenue. 3, Montreal House, a prominent hotel in its day, now used as the Sailors' Institute. 4, At this point a building was erected in 1860 by the Royal Insurance Co.; it was bought by the Government for a Custom House and is used as such up to the present. The first Victoria Bridge which crossed the St. Lawrence at Montreal was designed by Robert Stephenson, celebrated English engineer, and was constructed for the Grand Trunk Railway. It was begun in the summer of 1854, finished in 1859, and opened by the Prince of Wales a year later. Reconstructed in 1897. The new structure is known as the Victoria Jubilee Bridge, in commemoration of the jubilee year of the late Queen Victoria, and was designed by Joseph Hobson, a distinguished Canadian engineer, who was chief engineer of the railway company. Photographed by Notman, Montreal. Published by John Weale, London, 1860. Kell Bros., Lithrs., Castle street, Holborn. Size 7 x 11. See 104, 115, 1867.

1867—FIRST VICTORIA BRIDGE, MONTREAL—The staging for the centre tube—This picture is taken from the Laprairie side of the River St. Lawrence, looking towards Mount Royal. Note that under the span to the right end of the bridge the towers of Notre Dame may be seen. The timber false work, or staging for the centre tubular span as shown in the picture, is erected on two intermediate cribs, with travelling gantries or derricks for the erection and rivetting of the iron tubes. All the timber work and the cribs are removed as soon as the tube is completed. The false work is for the same purpose in erecting a tubular bridge as a scaffold is in erecting a house. Lithograph. Published by John Weale, London, 1860. Kell Bros., Lithrs., Castle street, Holborn. Size 8 x 11. See 104, 115, 1866.

1868—"ELLE QUI AIME S'ASSEOIR DANS LE SOLEIL"—(SHE WHO LOVES TO SIT IN THE SUN)—The artist here portrays a typical old habitant woman, placidly enjoying the summer sun. Copy of oil by Henri Julien, in possession of O. S. Perrault, Montreal. Size 6 x 9.

1869—QUEBEC IN 1836—Reproduction of a drawing in water color by A. Steele. Size 4 x 6.

1870—A LA MARCHE (GOING TO MARKET)—A typical habitant jogging to market in his box sleigh. The artist, Henri Julien, a French-Canadian himself, was, perhaps, at his best when portraying scenes from habitant life such as this. Although a painter of note, Julien is remembered chiefly as an illustrator, and, as such, for twenty-two years, until his death in 1908, was chief illustrator for the Montreal Star. He was born in the city of Quebec in 1846, but at the age of sixteen removed to the Montreal district. Copy of oil by Henri Julien, in possession of O. S. Perrault, Montreal. Size 7 x 10.

1871—"THE GREAT BELL OF MONTREAL, CATHEDRAL OF NOTRE DAME—Cast by Thomas Mears, Whitechapel Bell Foundry, London, 13th May, 1843; weight, 7 tons, 6 cwt.; diameter at mouth, 7 feet 4 inches; height to top of crown, 7 feet 2 inches. Key G. Inscriptions—Negotiamini dum venio omnis spiritus laudet Dominum Anno Domini, 1843, fundatae Marianapolis 202 Greg. P.P. XVI. Pontificatus 13 Regni Victoriae Britanniarum 6 Ex piissimo mercatorum agricolarum artificumque Marianapolitanensium dono. Thomas Mears, Londini, fecit, 1843. Sketched and drawn on zinc by A. R. Grieve. Printed from zinc by J. Grieve, 33 Nicholas Lane, London." The translation is: "From the most dutiful gift of the merchants, farmers and workmen of the City of Mary. Trade ye until I come. Let everything that hath breath praise the Lord, 1843, in the 202nd year since the foundation of the City of Mary, in the 13th year of the Pontificate of Pope Gregory XVI., in the 6th year of the reign of Victoria of the Britains." The "foundation of the City of Mary" means "Ville Marie," where Maisonneuve and his party arrived 17th May, 1642, and had the spot destined for the future city of Montreal consecrated. The picture shows the first great bell of Notre Dame, which was heard for the first time on Sunday, 24th December, 1843, at noon. In 1845 it became cracked and was sent to London to be recast at the Mears Foundry, Whitechapel, London. Lithograph. Size 11 x 11. See 1883.

1872—"ATTACK ON ST. CHARLES, 25TH NOVR., 1837—Lithographed by N. Hartnell from a sketch by Lord Charles Beauclerk. London. Published March, 1840, by A. Flint, 4 Piccadilly." Rebellion in Lower Canada—About a quarter of a mile from St. Charles the light company of the Royals whilst skirmishing in advance of the main body received a brisk fire from outposts of the rebels. The place was then attacked by Col. Wetherall, the light company being extended on each flank under Major Warde, and the artillery in command of Capt. Glasgow. The encounter was sharp and losses were sustained by both forces. The insurgents were routed, one hundred stand of arms taken and destroyed, and two French six-pounders which were found mounted in the entrenchments, spiked and thrown into the Richelieu. Lithograph in color. Size 7 x 11.

1873—"EXPLANATORY SKETCH OF COLL. GORE'S OPERATIONS AT ST. DENIS—(With a chart), 23rd Nov., 1837. London. Published March, 1840, by A. Flint, 4 Piccadilly"—The Rebellion in Lower Canada—This expedition against the insurgents under Dr. Nelson at St. Denis resulted in defeat for Col. Gore with the loss of a field piece and several killed and wounded. Size 7 x 10.

1874—MONTREAL—View in 1851—From what is now the head of Drummond street, well up the slope of Mount Royal, showing: 1, St. Helen's Island. 2, Bonsecours Church, first built in 1658, burnt, 1754, and rebuilt, 1771. 3, Bonsecours Market. 4, Christ Church Cathedral, built 1805, destroyed by fire 1856. 5, Notre Dame Church, begun in 1824, completed in 1830. 6, St. Patrick's Church, built in 1846. 7, Zion Congregational Church, Beaver Hill. 8, The Hall House. 9, The Dougall Homestead. 10, The Grey Nunnery, lower end of McGill street. Drawn from nature by A. Kollner; lith. by Deroy. Printed by Jacomme & Co., New York and Paris. Published by Goupil & Co. Lithograph. Size 8 x 11. See 1881.

1875—"COLONEL WETHERALL'S BIVOUACK AT ST. HILAIRE DE ROUVILLE, 23RD AND 24TH NOVR., 1837—Lithographed by N. Hartnell from a sketch by Lord Charles Beauclerk. London. Published March, 1840, by A. Flint, 4 Piccadilly." The Rebellion in Lower Canada—En route to St. Charles, Col. Wetherall halted at Pointe Oliviere and then pushed forward to St. Hilaire de Rouville. Here a pleasant reception awaited the force "at the house of a Canadian gentleman, a colonel of militia, who entertained the officers; and in his outhouses and in the adjoining village our men were quartered." The picture shows the house in front of which the forces bivouacked. From Beloeil Mountain the rebels watched closely the movements of the brigade, and more than once an attack was threatened. Lithograph in color. Size 7 x 11.

1876—MONTREAL, QUE.—Lithograph in color, by Coke Smyth. Size 10 x 15.

1877—"A FORTIFIED PASS—Colonel Wetherall advancing to the capture of St. Charles, 25th Novr., 1837—Lithographed by N. Hartnell from a sketch by Lord Charles Beauclerk. London. Published March, 1840, by A. Flint, 4 l'iccadilly." The Rebellion of Lower Canada—On the morning of 25th November, Col. Wetherall began his march against St. Charles. Bridges across small streams which flowed into the Richelieu were destroyed. The last, near St. Charles, being not only destroyed, but the pass fortified. It was near this spot that the insurgents intended to make an active defence had the military attempted to pass by night. Lithograph in color. Size 7 x 11.

1878—"PLACE D'ARMES, MONTREAL—Published under the patronage of the Right Hon. the Earl of Elgin and Kincardine, Governor-General of British North America. Painted by C. Krieghoff. Lith. by A. Borum in Munic." 1, Building owned, 1650, by Jean Saint Pere; site occupied by Liverpool, London and Globe Insurance Co. 2, Bank of Montreal, now site of the City Post Office. 3, Mortuary Chapel of an old cemetery stood here at one time; demolished, 1816. 4, This lot was part of cemetery of 1674. In 1841 the Bank of Montreal purchased the property, erecting a building thereon. 5, Second lot granted on the Island of Montreal. The City Bank purchased it in 1841. Their building was demolished in 1912 and replaced by the Royal Trust Company. 6, St. James street. 7, Place d'Armes. 8, Lord Elgin's turnout. Lithograph. Size 14 x 19.

1879—"PASSAGE OF THE RICHLIEU BY NIGHT, 22ND NOVR., 1837—Lithographed by N. Hartnell, from a sketch by Lord Charles Beauclerk. London. Published March, 1840, by A. Flint, 4 Piccadilly." The Rebellion in Lower Canada—Two brigades, one under command of Colonel Hon. Charles Gore, and the other under Colonel Wetherall, were formed for the purpose of dislodging the rebels from St. Charles and St. Denis on the Richelieu. On 18th November, Col. Wetherall marched for Chambly, arriving at sunset. There he strengthened his force with two companies of the 66th under Capt. Dames. The brigade under Col. Wetherall remained at Chambly until Nov. 22nd, when, with the exception of the grenadiers of the Royals and one company of the 66th, the forces commenced a secret march to St. Charles. The landing of guns and horses on the east side of the Richelieu, which Col. Wetherall crossed in batteaux at the rapid of Chambly, caused delay. Blue lights were fired by the rebels while the landing was being effected, in order to ascertain the numbers against them, and also to make known to their associates the whereabouts of these troops. The picture shows the effect produced by the lights. Lithograph in color. Size 7 x 11.

1880—"BACK VIEW OF THE CHURCH OF ST. EUSTACHE AND DISPERSION OF THE INSURGENTS, 14TH DECR., 1837—Lithographed by N. Hartnell from a sketch by Lord Charles Beauclerk. London. Published March, 1840, by A. Flint, 4 Piccadilly." Rebellion in Lower Canada —On the burning of the church, the people tried to escape in every direction. Few, however, were successful. Many were made prisoners and the loss in killed and wounded was great. Col. Gugy, of the volunteers, a British subject of foreign extraction, was the first to enter the church, and, in doing so, was severely wounded. Besides the church, the nunnery and presbytery, many houses were destroyed. Lithograph in color. Size 7 x 11.

1881—"MONTREAL FROM THE MOUNT, LOWER CANADA, NORTH AMERICA—Drawn from nature by Lt. Hornbrook, R.M. On stone by T. M. Baynes. Printed by C. Hullmandel." Lithograph in color. Size 8 x 14. See 1874, 2035.

1882—RAPIDS OF THE ST. LAWRENCE—Lithograph in color by Coke Smyth. Size 11 x 15.

1883—"THE GREAT BELL OF MONTREAL (SECOND)—Cast by Chas. and Geo. Mears, Bell Foundry, Whitechapel, London, on the 20th Feby., 1847. Ex piissimo mercatorum agricolarum artificumque Marianapolitanensium dono. Weight, 13 tons 15 cwt.; dimensions—diameter at mouth, 8 ft. 7 in.; height to top of crown, 8 ft. 1 in.; thickness of sound bow, 8 in. Inscriptions—Negotiamini dum venio omnis spiritus laudet Dominum Anno Domini, 1847. Fundatae Marianapolis 206 Pii P.P. 9 Pontificatus 1 Regni Victoriae Britanniarium 1. Thos. Turner, delt. et litho., Crane Court, Fleet street. Printed by T. Turner, London." This bell arrived in Montreal, 19th Sept., 1847. It was landed on the 23rd, and taken to the church, when the ten bells in the tower pealed forth a welcome. On 21st June, 1848, it was hoisted to the southeast tower of the Church of Notre Dame, where it is suspended to-day, being, as a rule, rung on Sundays and on special occasions. The bell is ornamented with the images of the Holy Virgin and St. John the Baptist; between, a medal representing agriculture, manufacture and commerce, while around the edge are the makers' names. The translation of the inscription is the same as that on the first bell, with the exception of the dates and the name of the then Pope. Lithograph. Size 12 x 12. See 1871.

1884—"FRONT VIEW OF THE CHURCH OF ST. EUSTACHE, OCCUPIED BY THE INSURGENTS—The Artillery facing an entrance, 14th Decr., 1837—Lithographed by N. Hartnell from a sketch by Lord Charles Beauclerk. London. Published March, 1840, by A. Flint, 4 Piccadilly." Rebellion in Lower Canada—Sir John Colborne, with his force, left Montreal on 13th December to attack St. Eustache on the Du Chene River. On arrival at the village the artillery opened fire and bombarded the church, the fortress of the insurgents. Colonel Wetherall, after a tedious detour through fields three feet deep in snow, held a position in front of the church. Shortly afterwards it was deemed necessary to storm the building. This was done. The rebels were found in the gallery defending themselves, but as they had cut away the staircase, every attempt to dislodge them proved for a time fruitless. Suddenly the church appeared in flames, and all was lost for the rebels. Lithograph in color. Size 7 x 11.

1885—FIRE IN MONTREAL, JULY, 1852—Destruction of the "Hay's Hotel"—During the summer of 1852 two disastrous fires occurred in Montreal, which destroyed about eleven hundred houses and rendered eight thousand people homeless. The first conflagration broke out on 7th June and the second on 8th July. In the course of the latter "Hay's Hotel" in Dalhousie Square, an immense block of stone buildings, four storeys high, with a theatre at the back, caught fire. The flames shortly afterward leaped to the houses directly opposite on Notre Dame street, and in a few hours all the buildings on the square were destroyed. The fire was not checked until the following morning. Water color. Size 6 x 9.

1886—MONTREAL—From the towers of Notre Dame, overlooking the Place d'Armes—With key. Water color from original drawing by F. B. Schell, for "Picturesque Canada," 1880. Size 5 x 7.

1887—PULPIT OF NOTRE DAME, MONTREAL—The Parish Church of Ville Marie, called the Cathedral of Notre Dame, Montreal, was opened for worship on 15th July, 1829, when high mass was performed by the Bishop of Telmesse. The architecture of the church is composite Gothic.

From the entrance to the chancel the floor is gently inclined, and in its ampleness and decoration the interior is impressive. The pulpit and canopy shown in picture are attached to one of the pillars; in form the pulpit is said to resemble that in the Gothic Cathedral at Strasburg, Germany. Water color from original drawing by W. T. Smedley, for "Picturesque Canada," 1880. Size 5 x 7.

1888—CITY HALL AND NELSON'S MONUMENT, MONTREAL, 1880 —Fronting on Notre Dame street and overlooking the Champs de Mars in the rear, is the City Hall, a large and handsome building of modern French architecture, with mansard roofs. In the foreground is the grey limestone column erected, in 1809, to the memory of Nelson, by the English and French citizens of Montreal. Water color from original drawing by F. B. Schell, for "Picturesque Canada." Size 5 x 7.

1889—MONTREAL HARBOR, 1880—A good view of the harbor, with its wharves and shipping, may be had from Commissioners street, on which is shown, to the left in picture, the Customs House. On this spot Maisonneuve made his first settlement in 1642. In the distance are the towers of Notre Dame. The harbor of Montreal, open for the greater part of the year, is the chief port of entry of Canada. The river front is protected by a solid stone embankment, and the wharves, built of limestone, present for miles a display of masonry said to be unsurpassed in America. Water color from original drawing by Schell and Hogan, for "Picturesque Canada." Size 5 x 7.

1890—GOVERNMENT HOUSE, OTTAWA—From the skating pond— About two miles down the river from the Dominion Houses of Parliament, in the midst of well-wooded grounds and beautiful gardens, stands Rideau Hall,, a large, rambling, greystone structure—comfortable, though not at all pretentious—built in 1830 by Hon. Thomas MacKay, but since enlarged several times. In 1868 it was purchased from the Mackay estate by the Government, and to the present day (1917) is occupied by the Governor-General of the Dominion. It has twice been the home of Royalty. From 1878 to 1883 H.R.H. Princess Louise, wife of the Marquis of Lorne (Duke of Argyle), was its chatelaine, and from 1911 to 1916 T.R.H. the Duke and Duchess of Connaught dispensed gracious hospitality here. Northwest of the hall is the skating pond, or rather rink, the scene of many a festive winter gathering. Water color from original drawing by Schell and Hogan, for "Picturesque Canada," 1880. Size 5 x 7. See 3499.

1891—LUMBERMEN'S CAMP—In the Ottawa district, 1880—"Picturesque Canada" describes the construction of a shanty thus: "Logs are cut, notched at the ends, and dove-tailed together, so as to form a quadrangular enclosure. On the top of this, from end to end, two large timbers are laid, each several feet from the centre. On these and on the walls the roof rests. . . . All chinks and openings are filled up with moss or hay, and the rude building is made quite warm and weather-tight. In the end wall is a large doorway with door of roughly hewn timber; the floor consists of logs hewn flat; and the huge girders of the roof are each supported midway by two large posts, some four or five yards apart. The space between these four posts, in the genuine, old-fashioned shanty, is occupied by the 'caboose,' or fireplace, substantially built up with stones and earth. Within the shanty there is no chimney, but an opening in the roof has a wooden frame-work round it which does duty for chimney." Water color from original drawing by Schell and Hogan, for "Picturesque Canada." Size 5 x 6.

1892—THE CHATS—From Pontiac, 1880—From the hamlet, in the distance, may be seen the white smoke-like spray of the Chats Falls—"a pillar of mist," says "Picturesque Canada," "which, but for its purer whiteness, might be mistaken for one of the columns of bush-fire smoke in the country." Water color from original drawing by Schell and Hogan, for "Picturesque Canada." Size 5 x 7. See 1771, 1801.

1893—**VICE-REGAL CHAIR**—Senate Chamber, House of Parliament, Ottawa—This chair was saved from the fire in the Parliament Buildings, February, 1916. It is of oak, handsomely carved, and upholstered in crimson, On either corner it is surmounted by the lion and the unicorn, with the royal coat-of-arms, appropriately colored, as the top centrepiece. Water color from original drawing by J. W. H. Watts, for "Picturesque Canada," 1880. Size 4 x 6.

1894—**MASS IN A LUMBER SHANTY**—In the Ottawa district, 1880— Many of the lumbermen are French or half-breeds, and of the Roman Catholic persuasion. At least once during the season the men are visited by a priest of the Church, who drives from camp to camp, carrying his small portable altar along with him, and, in the rude shanty, after the men have had their supper, a short vesper service is held; then the priest hears confessions, sometimes until far on in the night. In the morning, before the day's work is begun, Mass is celebrated, and with a final benediction, the reverend father goes on his way. Water color from original drawing by W. T. Smedley, for "Picturesque Canada." Size 5 x 6.

1895—**WELLINGTON ST., OTTAWA, 1880**—From the junction of Wellington and Bank streets—What is still a typical winter scene in the Canadian capital is here depicted. The large building is western elevation of the western block of the Departmental Buildings, showing the Mackenzie tower and the western entrance to the Parliament grounds. To the right is the Bank of Montreal, and on the opposite corner, the Victoria Chambers, built for the accommodation of the Prince of Wales during his visit to Ottawa in 1860; the building is still largely patronized by parliamentarians and members of the Rideau Club. Water color from original drawing by Schell and Hogan, for "Picturesque Canada." Size 5 x 7.

1896—**TOWER OF EASTERN BLOCK, DEPARTMENTAL BUILD-INGS, OTTAWA**—The Eastern Block of the Departmental Buildings stands on Parliament Square, east of the Central Block, which was destroyed by fire in February, 1916. The tower, overlooking the square and Wellington street, at the corner of Elgin street, is, in its architectural lines, in keeping with the other original buildings erected after the choice of Ottawa as the capital. It was begun in 1859, the contractors being Messrs. Edward Haycock and Thomas C. Clarke. Water color from original drawing by C. E. H. Bonwill, for "Picturesque Canada," 1880. Size 5 x 7.

1897—**GUELPH, ONT.**—View from hill near Grove street, overlooking Duke street—With key. Water color from original drawing by F. B. Schell, for "Picturesque Canada," 1880. Size 5 x 7.

1898—**TIMBER SLIDE AT CALUMET FALLS, 1880**—On the Ottawa River—In order that timber may not receive injury through dashing against the rocks where cataracts occur, the Government has built "slides" at different points. These slides consist of artificial channels, the side walls and floors of which are lined with smooth, strong timber work, and at the upper end of the channel are gates through which pent-up water can be admitted or shut off. Near the Island of the Grand Calumet, about seventy miles up the river from Ottawa, it is said the brave French voyageur, Cadieux, is buried. His "Lament," composed just before his death, and which tells the story of his last deeds and thoughts, is still sung by Canadian voyageurs. Water color from original drawing by Schell and Hogan, for "Picturesque Canada." Size 5 x 7.

1899—BOWMANVILLE, ONT., 1880—From Vanstone's Hill, west of town—Bowmanville, called after Charles Bowman, a Scot from Arbroath, was at one time known as Darlington Mills; grist and saw mills were built there by John Burke. About 1820 the first store was opened in Darlington, although some years previously a post-offce had been established, the mail arriving once a week. The present town lies to the north and south of King street, the business quarter, the principal residential portion being situated to the north of that street. 1. St. Paul's Presbyterian Church. 2. Old fire hall, replaced by present municipal buildings. 3. Methodist Church. 4. Kingston road, of which King street is a continuation. 5. Block of stores. 6. St. John's Church (Anglican). 7. Vanstone's Mill. 8. Roadway deviating from and rejoining Kingston road. 9. Hill sloping to ravine, through which Barber's Creek runs. 10. Scugog road to Caesarea. Water color from original drawing by W. C. Fitler, for "Picturesque Canada." Size 5 x 7.

1900—GLIMPSES OF THE LOWER OTTAWA, 1880—The lumber trade—With key marking points of interest: 1. Tow boats on the Ottawa, opposite Rockliffe Park. 2. Timber raft in foreground, with a landing near Battson and Currier's mill, opposite Ottawa. 3. Nepean Point and Rockliffe Park, on right—Currier mill and Gilmour's mill, on left, and the church and village of Gatineau in the distance. Water color from original drawing by Schell and Hogan, for "Picturesque Canada." Size 6 x 8.

1901—PARLIAMENT BUILDINGS FROM MAJOR'S HILL, OTTAWA, 1880—Facing the river may be seen the Library of Parliament, a beautiful polygonal structure, its dome supported by graceful flying buttresses. The interior, with its bookcases and panelling of Canadian pine, contains some very fine carving and houses 250,000 volumes, including many on Canadiana. When the Houses of Parliament were swept by fire in February, 1916, the Library Building was preserved intact, although many rare volumes were destroyed by water and a passage burned from the reading-room to the walls. Major's Hill Park, to the east of Parliament Hill, commands an excellent view of the river. On Nepean Point, at the end of the park, is the saluting battery, with guns of 1797. Water color from original drawing by F. B. Schell, for "Picturesque Canada." Size 5 x 7.

1902—POST-OFFICE AND SAPPER'S BRIDGE, OTTAWA, 1880—In the centre of the picture is shown the post-office, on Wellington and Sparks streets. It was begun in December, 1872, and occupied, July, 1876. To the left is Sapper's Bridge (erected 1832, and rebuilt, along with Dufferin Bridge, 1873-4), connecting Sparks and Rideau street, and to right of picture is Dufferin Bridge, connecting Wellington and Rideau streets, with the Eastern Block in the distance. In 1912 the bridges were demolished to make way for a wide plaza, with the post-office as base. To the extreme left is the Russell House, commenced 1863, enlarged 1874, and again in 1880. It is still (1917) one of the prominent hostelries of Ottawa. Water color from original drawing by W. C. Fitler, for "Picturesque Canada." Size 5 x 7.

1903—CHAUDIERE FALLS, 1880—Near Ottawa, Ont.—So named from early times, for Champlain three hundred years ago wrote that these falls were called by the Indians "Asticou," which means "cauldron" (Chaudiere). The tumultuous waters dash over ragged, rocky ledges, sixty feet high and two hundred feet wide. Nearby are the timber slides, by which timber from the Upper Ottawa descends to navigable waters below. Water color from original drawing by F. B. Schell, for "Picturesque Canada." Size 5 x 6.

1904—SUSPENSION BRIDGE AT CHAUDIERE FALLS, 1880—It was the third bridge built at this point to connect Ottawa with Hull; erected in 1843 to succeed the bridge of 1829, destroyed by fire in 1900 and replaced the following year by the present steel structure Water color from original drawing by F. B. Schell, for "Picturesque Canada." Size 3 x 7.

22

1905—WESTERN BLOCK, DEPARTMENTAL BUILDINGS, OTTAWA
—These buildings at present (1917) house the Public Works, Railways, Trade and Commerce and Inland Revenue Departments. Built in 1859; enlarged during the time of Alexander Mackenzie and surmounted by the Mackenzie tower, the highest pinnacle of any structure in Ottawa. This view is taken looking west, the block facing Parliament Square on one side and Wellington street on the left or south side. The contractors for the original structure were Messrs. Edward Haycock and Thomas C. Clarke. Water color from original drawing by C. E. H. Bonwill, for "Picturesque Canada," 1880. Size 5 x 7.

1906—HOUSES OF PARLIAMENT, OTTAWA—From main entrance under Central Tower—The stately entrance to the buildings is here depicted. Looking south-east are shown the Eastern Block, and across Wellington street, on the left, the Bodega Hotel, with the Russell House and the tower of the City Hall further down. On the right is the old office of the Ottawa Free Press, now part of the Langevin Block site, and, in the rear the tower of the Grand Union Hotel. Water color from original drawing by C. E. H. Bonwill, for "Picturesque Canada," 1880. Size 5 x 7.

1907—MAIN BUILDING, HOUSES OF PARLIAMENT, OTTAWA, 1880
—In 1860 the Prince of Wales (King Edward VII.) laid the foundation stone of the Main Building, which, although still unfinished, was occupied in 1865. From the Victoria tower, which rose to a height of 220 feet over the entrance, a magnificent view of the Ottawa River and Chaudiere Falls was obtainable. To the left of the main entrance was the House of Commons—the "Green Chamber"—and to the right, the Senate—the "Red Chamber." Built in 12th century Gothic style, of cream-colored sandstone, with dressings of red sandstone and Ohio freestone, the Houses of Parliament, which covered an area of four acres, presented an imposing appearance, crowning as they did a bluff commanding the Ottawa River. Water color from original drawing by Schell and Hogan, for "Picturesque Canada." Size 5 x 7.

1908—"BREAKING A JAM"—On the Upper Reaches of the Ottawa— Although the square timber cribs are no longer on the Ottawa, the picture shows what is still a daily scene during the spring drive. The comparative ease with which these experienced lumber jacks or river drivers maintain their equilibrium, even in swift and treacherous currents and rapids, is one of the marvels of the industry. Water color from original by M. J. Burns, for "Picturesque Canada," 1880. Size 5 x 7.

1909—HABITANT OVEN—Method of bread-making in Province of Quebec. Water color from original drawing, for "Picturesque Canada," 1880. Size 5 x 6. See 79.

1910—TADOUSAC—Below the confluence of the St. Lawrence and Saguenay—It is a quaint old village, the oldest continuously occupied European settlement in Canada, receiving its name from the round hills or "mamelons" surrounding it. In 1535 Jacques Cartier visited the place, and in 1599 a trading post was established. Tadousac has a history. It was a market of the French fur-traders, occupied by Sir David Kirke in 1628, attacked by the Iroquois, and an early missionary centre. In 1615 the Recollets established a mission here. They were followed by the Jesuits, the last of whom was Father La Brosse. A point of interest in the village to-day is the quaint "Chapel of the Jesuit Mission," built 1747-50, on the site of the bark-covered hut which served as a mission chapel until the first church was built in 1648. Tadousac is now (1917) a popular summer resort. Water color from original drawing by F. B. Schell, for "Picturesque Canada," 1880. Size 5 x 7.

1911—OLD MOHAWK CHURCH, BRANTFORD, U.C.—Water color from original drawing by L. R. O'Brien, for "Picturesque Canada," 1880. Size 5 x 6.

1912—KILLARNEY, ONT., AUGUST, 1880—A fishing village on the north shore of Georgian Bay, and during the summer months a port of call for steamers. The houses of the hamlet cluster on the edge of a plain extending to the base of the mountains. To the west of Killarney are the wooded bluffs of Manitoulin Island, and on the east and north the Laurentian Hills. Water color from original drawing by L. R. O'Brien, for "Picturesque Canada." Size 3 x 6.

1913—CHATEAU DE RAMEZAY, 1705-1917—Notre Dame street, Montreal—Claude de Ramezay, eleventh Governor of Montreal, occupied this unembellished structure from its erection to the time of his death in 1724. During his regime it was the centre of gaiety, entertainment and hospitality. Its doors were open to all classes. In 1745 the chateau was sold to the Compagnie des Indes, which company made it the headquarters of the fur trade in Canada, and so it remained until the Conquest. It was then bought by William Grant, who in 1778 sold it to the English Government. Thus the building again became the residence of the Governors. Lord Metcalfe was the last resident Governor. Since that time Chateau de Ramezay served several purposes until 1894, when it was purchased by the Corporation of the City of Montreal, and in 1895 acquired by the Numismatic and Antiquarian Society as an Historical Portrait Gallery and Museum. In 1775 the chateau was the headquarters of the American army. Here Franklin set up his printing press and printed "The Gazette," and in the council room of this venerable edifice Lord Elgin signed the Rebellion Losses Bill after the Rebellion of 1837. Water color. Size 5 x 6.

1914—THUNDER CAPE—At entrance to Thunder Bay, Lake Superior —It is a basaltic cliff, the extremity of a long, rocky peninsula, one of the grandest sights on the continent in its towering height of over 1,300 feet. From the north-west the cape resembles a couchant lion, and from the north or south looks like a sleeping giant, of whom many legends are told. He is said to be Ninnabijou, an Ojibway Hercules, who performed many feats of prowess. It is not related, though, how he came to make Thunder Cape his last resting place. Near by is Silver Islet, at one time a noted mining settlement. Water color from original drawing by L. R. O'Brien, for "Picturesque Canada," 1880. Size 5 x 7.

1915—LINDSAY, ONT., 1880—From the bank of the River Scugog looking south-west—The view shows: 1. St. Joseph's Convent. 2. St. Mary's R.C. Church. 3. Kent street east. 4. Bible Christian Church, now (1917) Baptist Church. 5. Residence of James Growden. 6. Port Hope, Lindsay and Beaverton train (G.T.R.) The town site of Lindsay was surveyed as early as 1833, but because of bad roads and the distance from the seaboard, the early progress of the now flourishing town was slow. Water color from original drawing by W. C. Fitler, for "Picturesque Canada. Size 5 x 7.

1916—PETERBORO', ONT.—From Kirkpatrick residence, now (1917) owned by R. A. Morrow, looking east: 1. St. Peter's (R.C.) Cathedral. 2. Central Public School. 3. County Buildings, Court House and Jail. 4. St. John's (Anglican) Church. 5. Town Hall (larger than in reality). 6. South Ward Central School. 7. Group of dwellings at crossing of Sherbrooke and Park streets. 8. Dwellings on Charlotte street. Water color from original drawing by W. C. Fitler. for "Picturesque Canada," 1880. Size 5 x 6.

1917—NOTRE DAME DES VICTOIRES, QUEBEC, 1688-1917—The Little Lower Town Chapel, as it is often called, was erected under the auspices of Bishop St. Vallier, the funds being provided by the Lower Town ladies. Its erection, however, had been projected by Bishop Laval. The modest little structure at first bore the name L'enfant Jesus, but on the repulse of Phipps' attack on Quebec in 1690, was called Notre Dame de Victoire. In 1711, when Walker's invading fleet was wrecked in the Gulf of St. Lawrence, the name became Notre Dame des Victoires. During Wolfe's siege of Quebec the church was partially destroyed, rebuilt subsequently, and in 1888 the interior neatly frescoed. To-day it stands as an interesting historic relic of the troublous past. The square in front of the church was used as the market place of Quebec during French regime, and around it were the residences of the principal merchants of the town. Water color from original drawing by W. T. Smedley, for "Picturesque Canada," 1880. Size 5 x 7.

1918—GARDENS OF THE URSULINE CONVENT, QUEBEC—On 1st July, 1639, Madame de la Peltrie arrived in Quebec. Here she founded the Ursuline Convent. The first building was erected in 1641, destroyed by fire in 1650, again rebuilt, only to meet a similar fate later. Various buildings occupy the spacious grounds of the convent, which is situated in the heart of Quebec, and which, as an educational institution is well known. In the chapel of the convent Montcalm was buried, 14th Sept., 1759, his tomb most appropriately having been formed by the explosion of a shell. Many beautiful oil paintings and some fine carvings in ivory are to be found in the little chapel. Water color from original drawing by F. B. Schell, for "Picturesque Canada," 1880. Size 4 x 7.

1919—AT THE GATE OF LAVAL UNIVERSITY, QUEBEC—The original seminary was founded in 1663 by Mgr. de Montmorency Laval, first Bishop of Quebec, and in 1852 a university was attached by Royal Charter. Viewed from the river, Laval is one of the most prominent buildings in Quebec, and from its roof promenade one obtains a magnificent view of the valley of the St. Charles and down the St. Lawrence. Water color from original drawing by W. T. Smedley, for "Picturesque Canada," 1880. Size 5 x 7. See 2971.

1920—SOUS LE CAP STREET, QUEBEC—Ruelles de Chien (Dog Lane)—It is so narrow that at certain angles two carts going in opposite directions would be blocked. Prior to 1816 there was no other outlet in this direction at high water mark to reach St. Roch. In early times doubtless a watchman stood at either extremity of the street to give notice of any obstruction and so prevent collisions. To-day the locality is an interesting one to tourists, and apparently always has been, for Dickens, in his American notes, describes some of the characters who frequented Dog Lane in 1842. Water color from original drawing by F. B. Schell, for "Picturesque Canada," 1880. Size 5 x 7.

1921—LOOKING ACROSS THE ESPLANADE, QUEBEC, TO BEAUPORT—The Esplanade, at the foot of the green slope crowned by the fortifications of Quebec, was, until their withdrawal in 1871, a parade ground for the Imperial troops. A few dismounted cannon are, however, the only reminders of military glories of other days. 1. Part of promenade on summit of fortification wall, Quebec. 2. Laurentian Mountains in rear of Beauport. 3. Beauport Parish Church, of which Father Chiniquy was for many years parish priest. 4. Loyola Hall, property of the Jesuit Fathers, formerly the National School Hall. 5. Church of the Congregation of Men of Upper Town (served by Jesuit Fathers), built 1817. 6. Part of Quebec Harbor—the bay outside the mouth of the St. Charles River. Water color from original drawing by Lucius R. O'Brien, for "Picturesque Canada," 1880. Size 6 x 8.

1922—STREET IN CHATEAU RICHER—Montmorency Co., Que., 1880 —Nestling in the midst of orchards lies the village of Chateau Richer, fifteen miles below Quebec. An abundance of partridge, wild duck, snipe and trout make the vicinity a sportsman's paradise, while the lover of romantic scenery may revel in the Falls of La Puce, not far distant. There is a charm about the old French houses, with their high-pitched roofs, depicted by the artist, which is lacking in the more pretentious modern village house. Long, one-storey cottages, of wood or stone, are those of an older day, each with its gay little garden lot—for the habitant loves flowers. Water color from original drawing by Lucius Richard O'Brien, for "Picturesque Canada." Size 5 x 7.

1923—FALLS OF STE. ANNE—On the Grande Riviere Ste. Anne— Two miles above the village of Ste. Anne de Beaupre is a rocky vale— almost a natural grotto—through the centre of which the river rushes, escaping by a narrow channel between the rocks and forming a series of falls, one of which is 130 feet in height. Viewed from below the cataract the scene is one of inspiring grandeur. Water color by F. B. Schell, for "Picturesque Canada," 1880. Size 5 x 7.

1924—TOM MOORE'S HOUSE AT STE ANNE—Where the Ottawa River empties into the St. Lawrence, near Montreal, stands the picturesque old French house in which Tom Moore, the Irish minstrel, resided in 1805. It was here that he wrote the "Canadian Boat Song," known to all Canadians. Before the advent of the more prosaic railway and steamboat the batteau was a familiar sight on the mighty Ottawa, guided by skilful oarsmen to the lilt of their French chansons, and the strains of "A La Claire Fontaine" and other old-time favorites must often have been wafted to the ears of the poet. Water color. Size 5 x 6.

1925—FALLS OF LORETTE, QUEBEC, 1880—At the quaint old village of Indian, or Jeune Lorette, nine miles from Quebec, are the foaming waters of these falls, tumbling through a rocky gorge. Their height is about a hundred feet, and although differing greatly from Montmorency Falls, are quite as striking in their way. Water color from original drawing by L. R. O'Brien, for "Picturesque Canada." Size 4 x 6.

1926—CHURCH OF NOTRE DAME DE BONSECOURS—St. Paul St., Montreal—In 1657 a wooden chapel on a stone foundation was erected by order of Sister Marguerite Bourgeois, foundress of the Nunnery of the Congregation. The site of the chapel was upon land owned by Maisonneuve, a short distance from the town. In 1675 a second building, the first church of stone in the Island of Montreal, was erected, destroyed by fire, 1754, and the present church constructed on its foundation, 1771. The name "Bonsecours" (good help) was given on account of the escapes of the colony from the Iroquois. Although the quaint old church has been shorn of much of its beauty and uniqueness through alterations, it still retains the inward sloping walls, the altars and some paintings. A small statue was brought to Montreal from France by Marguerite Bourgeois in 1671, and remained in the church for many years, the patron of French sailors for over two centuries. It was reputed to be endowed with miraculous virtue. The statue of the Virgin Mary on the rear peak of the roof is quite a modern one. Water color from original drawing by F. B. Schell, for "Picturesque Canada," 1880. Size 5 x 7.

1927—CHAMP DE MARS, MONTREAL—The first parade ground of the French troops was on the Place Royale, or Custom House Square. This became too small and trouble arose also between the soldiers and farmers who used the "Place" as a market. The Place d'Armes was then used by the military and continued as a parade ground until the fortifications were removed, when the present (1917) Champ de Mars was formed. Water color from original by F. B. Schell, for "Picturesque Canada," 1880. Size 5 x 6.

1928—PART OF McGILL STREET, MONTREAL, 1880—The picture shows: 1. Victoria Square, so named in 1860, formerly known as the Hay Market. 2. Statue of Queen Victoria. 3. Y.M.C.A. Building—the first erected by the association in Montreal; all the upper storeys have been removed, the ground floor only now (1917) remaining. 4, St. Andrew's Church, Beaver Hall Hill, erected 1851. 5. Unitarian Church, built 1845 (Church of the Messiah); the tower has since been removed and the building is now used for commercial purposes. 6. Mount Royal. 7. Corner McGill and Notre Dame streets. 8, Albert Buildings. Water color from original drawing by W. T. Smedley, for "Picturesque Canada." Size 5 x 7.

1929—ST. FOYE MONUMENT, QUEBEC—The discovery of numerous bones near St. Foye Road, Quebec, suggested to the St. Jean Baptiste Society the idea of raising a column to the memory of De Levis and Murray, and to that of the brave soldiers who fought under them, 1760. The first stone was laid, 18th July, 1855, Sir Edmund Walker Head, Governor-General of Canada, presiding at the ceremony. On 19th Oct., 1862, the monument was inaugurated by Lord Monck, then Governor-General. It is of cast iron on a stone base, and is surmounted by a statue of Bellona, the Goddess of War, carrying the mythological lance and shield, and facing that part of the battlefield occupied by the French. The statue was given by Prince Napoleon, who visited Quebec in 1863. On the right side "Murray" is read above the arms and emblems of England, and on the left, "Levis" is inscribed above the arms and emblems of old France. The height of the monument, which was designed by M. Chas. Baillairge, engineer, of Quebec, is 75 feet, including the statue. Photograph, colored. Size 4 x 8.

1930—MANOR HOUSE AT SILLERY, QUE.—Home of Jesuit Missionaries—In 1632 Commandeur Noel Brulart de Sillery sold his property in Paris, and entered Holy Orders, 1634. He gave to Father Lalement, a zealous Jesuit, a large sum of money, with which the Mission of Sillery was founded in 1637, and named in honor of its founder. Prior to 1700 the "Manor House," as it is called, was built, facing the St. Lawrence at Sillery Cove, massive and heavy in construction, with walls three feet thick, pointed gable and steep roof. Alterations have been made in the old structure, which has stood the ravages of time, and to-day (1917) is used as a boarding house. It is said that the hospital and monastery of the mission were standing as late as 1825. Water color. Size 5 x 6.

1931—MARTELLO TOWER AT QUEBEC—Example of outer line of fortification—The Martello towers at Quebec were erected in 1812 as outposts of the scheme of fortifications on the western or land side of Quebec. Originally there were four, stretching across the upper level, formerly known as the Heights of Abraham, between the valleys of the St. Lawrence and the St. Charles. Their construction was weak towards the city, so as to be easily destroyed in event of capture, and strong on the outer sides, with mounted cannon. There are now (1917) three of these tower structures in existence: (1) Overlooking the St. Lawrence, close to the Ross Rifle Factory. (2) Near the Grande Allee, and (4) Overlooking St. Rochs and the valley of the St. Charles. The tower known as No. 3, on the western side of the Jeffrey Hale Hospital, was demolished some years ago by the hospital authorities. Water color. Size 4 x 7.

1932—"BREAK-NECK STEPS"—Leading from Mountain Hill to Little Champlain street—For long the quaint, narrow wooden stairway was a noted landmark, but modern local traffic has necessitated its being replaced by a broad, iron stairway. At the foot is an electric elevator which takes the visitor over the face of the cliff, on to Dufferin Terrace. Water color. Size 5 x 7.

1933—LITTLE CHAMPLAIN ST., QUEBEC—From head of Break-neck Stairs—This single narrow street, named after Samuel de Champlain, founder of Quebec, skirts the foot of Cape Diamond. Through the pass, on 31st Dec., 1775, Montgomery tried to lead an attack upon Quebec, which, however, failed utterly. Water color from original drawing by F. B. Schell, for "Picturesque Canada," 1880. Size 5 x 7. See 2835.

1934—MANOR HOUSE OF LACOLLE, SEIGNEURY DE BEAUJEAU, QUE.—Situated on the New York State border-line, about four miles southwest of Lacolle village, Que. The manor house is large, constructed of wood, and has an extensive stone gable wing. The main part of the house was built by Mrs. Henry Hoyle, formerly Mrs. Major Schuyler, of Troy, N.Y. In 1816, Henry Hoyle married Mrs. Schuyler for her fortune. They moved to Lacolle, where he used a part of the fortune of which he had obtained control, in making the property a prize stock farm, probably the first of the kind in Canada. At various points water powers were bought and developed, and mills erected, including those at Lacolle, Huntington and Athelstan. Mr. Hoyle died in 1849, and his widow in 1851. The old manor house was a treasure store of relics of the sixteenth and seventeenth centuries, as well as of the early Victorian age and modern days. Mrs. Mary Averill Hoyle, co-Seigneuresse, died at Lacolle in 1914. Water color. Size 4 x 6.

1935—CHIEN D'OR (GOLDEN DOG), QUEBEC—When the post office, Quebec, was erected in 1872, the stone, represented in picture, was placed on the northern facade of the building. It had been over the door of an ancient residence on the same site, occupied by Nicholas Philibert, who had many grievances against Intendant Bigot. Amongst other things Bigot organized a trade monopoly known as La Friponne, the transactions of which were most oppressive, and had also quartered troops upon le Chien d'Or. In order to have revenge Philibert placed above his door a gilt dog, with the following words: "I am a dog gnawing a bone. While I gnaw I take my repose. The time will come, though not yet, when I will bite him who bites me." In course of time a quarrel took place between Philibert and M. de la Repentigny, a companion of the Intendant's, which resulted in the death of Philibert, 21st Jan., 1748. His murderer was subsequently pardoned by Louis XIV. Water color. Size 3 x 6.

1936—MONTCALM MONUMENT, QUEBEC—Erected in Lansdowne Park, near the spot where the gallant French General fell mortally wounded in September, 1759. The Angel of Renown is shown supporting him as he fell. Many connoisseurs consider the Montcalm monument the most beautiful in Quebec. It is twenty-two feet high, an exact reproduction of the memorial at Vestric-Candiac; for Louis Joseph de Montcalm was born at the Chateau de Candiac, near Nimes, France. The statue in picture is by Leopold Morice and the pedestal, on which is engraved a short but eloquent inscription: "To Montcalm, France, Canada," is by Paul Chabert. Sir Francois Langelier, Lieutenant-Governor of Quebec, unveiled the statue, 16th Oct., 1911. Photograph, colored. Size 4 x 8.

1937—LA COLLE MILL AND BLOCKHOUSE—The village of La Colle, in St. John's County, Quebec, was the scene on 30th March, 1814, of a short but eventful fight between the Americans under General Wilkinson, with 4,000 men, and the British under Major Hancock, of the 30th Regiment, with 1,000 men, including two companies of the regiment and a force of Canadian Grenadiers and Voltigeurs. The fight, which only lasted two hours, was a desperate one, and the British were often repulsed. Finally the American force was driven back notwithstanding the fierce efforts of Wilkinson to capture the mill and blockhouse. Wilkinson withdrew his forces and retreated. The affair ended the military career of the American general, and he was relieved of his command of the Department of the Army of the North. Water color. Size 4 x 7.

1938—CHAMPLAIN MONUMENT, QUEBEC—It stanas on Dufferin Terrace, near the Chateau Frontenac, and was erected by subscriptions of the citizens of Quebec, the Municipal Council and the Governments of Quebec and Ontario. On 21st Sept., 1898, Lord Aberdeen, Governor-General of Canada, unveiled the statue, which is 14 feet 9 inches in height, and weighs over three tons. Champlain is represented saluting the Canadian soil as he lands, and holding his titles as founder of Quebec. A woman, personifying the city, is seated at the foot of the monument, and at her right a child, the genius of navigation, recalls the fact that Champlain was a great navigator and explorer. Above these is seen an Angel of Renown, proclaiming the glory of Champlain. On the upper part are the arms of Brouage, Quebec and Canada. The lateral faces are inscribed in English and French. The entire monument is about fifty feet high. The steps are of Vosges granite, and the pedestal of Chateau Landon stone. Photograph, colored. Size 6 x 9.

1939—RUINS OF THE HOUSES OF ASSEMBLY, MONTREAL, 1849 —Destroyed by fire, April 25th, on the Rebellion Losses Bill becoming law. The only article saved was the mace belonging to the Lower House. In 1849 the Houses of Assembly were bounded by Foundling, St. Peter, Commissioners' and McGill. The site is now (1917) Youville Square, Montreal. Water color from old print. Size 4 x 9. See 1860.

1940—HOUSE TO WHICH MONTGOMERY WAS CARRIED—St. Louis street, Quebec—On 31st December, 1775, under cover of a blinding snowstorm, Montgomery advanced from Wolfe's Cove, along the narrow pathway, now Champlain street, intending to meet Arnold at the foot of Mountain Hill. At the pres-de-ville barricade a sharp fusillade from the fifty defenders of the pass met him. The encounter was short, but it sufficed to defeat the invader, and several hours later Montgomery's body was found lying in the snow. It was taken to the little log house of the cooper Gaubert (shown in the picture) and there prepared for burial. The old building, which stood until 1889, was at the time of its demolition one of the oldest buildings in Quebec. Its rafters were simply rough poles from which the bark had never been entirely removed. A modern residence (No. 72 St. Louis street now (1917) occupies the site. Water color from original drawing by G. Gibson, for "Picturesque Canada," 1880. Size 5 x 7.

1941—MONTREAL FROM THE MOUNTAIN—View from Cote de Neiges, 1849—With key. Drawn by J. Duncan. Engraved by Matthews. Printed in color. Size 13 x 24.

1942—FORT CHAMBLY, L.C.—South-east view—Fort Chambly, or Portchartrain, was built of wood in 1665. Falling into ruin it was re-erected in 1711 in the form of a very large square, flanked by four bastions corresponding to the four cardinal points of the compass. In 1760 it fell into the hands of the British, and in 1775 was in possession of the Americans. Later it formed one of the chief bases for the troops of Carleton and Burgoyne, and during the War of 1812 a large force was stationed there. In 1838 the fort was finally abandoned, subsequently being taken charge of by the Canadian Government. Fort Chambly was named in honor of Captain Jacques de Chambly, a captain in the Carignan Salieres, the first regiment of regular troops ever sent to America by the French Government. Photograph, colored. Size 6 x 7. See 1835, 1943-5, 1965.

1943—FORT CHAMBLY, L.C.—View of South-east angle, inside. Photograph, colored. Size 5 x 9.

1944—FORT CHAMBLY, L.C.—View north-west front, inside. Photograph, colored. Size 5 x 9.

1945—FORT CHAMBLY, L.C.—View of the south-west angle. Photograph, colored. Size 5 x 9.

1946—JUNCTION OF THE ST. CHARLES AND LAIRET RIVERS—Where Jacques Cartier wintered, 1535-6—The St. Charles receives the Lairet about half a mile from the heart of St. Roch's, but owing to recent annexations it is now (1917) actually within the limits of Quebec. A cross and monument have been erected on the spot, where on 3rd May, 1536, Cartier planted the cross and fleur-de-lis before returning to France. Within the last few years the scene has changed greatly and the buildings shown in the picture have disappeared. On 23rd Sept., 1825, Fathers Jean de Breboeuf, Ennemond Masse and Charles Lalement took solemn possession of the land called Fort Jacques Cartier, situated at the confluence of the Rivers St. Charles and Lairet, to erect there the first residence of the Jesuit missionaries at Quebec. Near by, on the grounds of the late Mr. G. H. Parke, is Ringfield, site of one of Montcalm's fortified camps, the lines of which may still be distinguished. Water color from old print. Size 5 x 7.

1947—INTERCOLONIAL RAILWAY BRIDGE, METAPEDIA, QUE.—A winter scene during its construction—Built on the Restigouche River at Metapedia, Bonaventure County, Que., in 1875. It consisted of five skew spans through truss, 209 feet long. In 1903 it was replaced by a steel bridge the same length, built by the Canadian Bridge Co., of Walkerville, Ont. The original bridge, which was moved further up the stream, and alongside the new structure, is now (1917) used as a highway bridge. Water color by W. G. R. Hind. Size 6 x 13.

1948—SPENCER WOOD—The residence of the Lieut.-Governors of Quebec—It is about two miles from Quebec by the Grand Allee, and is approached by a forest drive through a noble avenue of trees, reminding one of the estate of an English nobleman. The original mansion was first known as Powell Place, the owner then being General Henry Watson Powell. Early in the nineteenth century it was purchased by Hon. Michael Henry Perceval, Collector of Imperial Customs at Quebec, who named it after his distinguished kinsman, Right Hon. Spencer Perceval, Chancellor of the Exchequer of Great Britain, who was assassinated by Bellingham in the lobby of the House of Commons in 1812. In 1860 Spencer Wood was destroyed by fire, which broke out just as a number of distinguished guests, including Cabinet Ministers, had assembled for a State dinner. The present (1917) residence, erected 1862-3, and altered in 1901, stands on the site, which in 1860 was visited by the Prince of Wales, afterwards King Edward VII. Water color from old print. Size 4 x 7. See 3591.

1949—TEMPERANCE MONUMENT NEAR LEVIS, QUE.—The monument was erected in 1842 by the Rev. Charles E. Poire, Cure of St. Joseph de Levis, and later Mgr. Poire, to commemorate the close of a great temperance campaign conducted by Grand Vicar Mailloux. It stood 50 or 60 feet back from the main road leading from the Quebec and Levis ferry to the Church of St. Joseph. At the elevated point on which the monument stood the street wound partly around it, and a stairway was erected to it from the street. The site still belongs to the parochial authorities of St. Joseph, but no trace of the structure remains. Where the former stairway stood is a house, No. 33, on the main street of the village of

Lauzon, belonging to a Mr. Corriveau. After an existence of 32 years the monument, which was by this time in ruins, was removed by Cure Fafard, of St. Joseph de Levis. There is no record of an inscription, although it is supposed that there was one. In the background of the picture is seen No. 1 Fort of the south shore, and the houses on the road leading to it. Water color from an old print. Size 4 x 6.

1950—**WHERE MONTGOMERY FELL, 31ST DEC.,** 1775—From Dufferin Terrace, Quebec, can be seen the narrow pass in Champlain street just below the Citadel, where General Richard Montgomery, his two aides, Majors Cheeseman and McPherson, and several of his soldiers were killed in the futile attempt to force a passage around the base of the Citadel. High up on the face of the rock, immediately overhanging the scene of Montgomery's death, is a large signboard painted black, and bearing in raised gilt letters the inscription, "Here Montgomery Fell, December 31st, 1775." Lower down on the face of the rock, under Cape Diamond, but not shown in picture, is a bronze tablet inscribed, "Here stood the undaunted fifty, safeguarding Canada, defeating Montgomery at the Pres-de-ville barricade, on the last day of 1775, Guy Carleton commanding at Quebec." Montgomery was buried in the yard of the old British military prison. Forty-three years later his remains, with consent of the British Government, were taken to New York and interred in St. Paul's Church. Photograph, colored. Size 5 x 7.

1951—**DONEGANA'S HOTEL, MONTREAL,** 1837-52—Built by a Mr. Bingham in 1837-8, and later fitted up in a splendid manner for the residence of the Governor-General, Lord Seaton. It was on the corner, facing Notre Dame and Bonsecours streets. Donegana bought the building and converted it into a hotel, having suites of luxurious apartments. On 16th Aug., 1849, the building was burned, but afterwards rebuilt. In 1866 about fifteen feet in depth was taken off the building to widen Notre Dame street. The remainder still stands, as well as the coachhouse and stables. After the fire Donegana built a hotel further east, corner of Dalhousie Square, which is now (1917) the Notre Dame Hospital. Drawing in water color. Size 5 x 6.

1952—**MONTCALM HOUSE, QUEBEC**—Situated at the corner of St. Louis and Garden streets—Called the Montcalm House, because it is supposed to have been the personal headquarters of the celebrated French General in Quebec. On St. Louis street, upon which the railway track is shown, it faces the St. Louis Hotel. The old dwelling is still (1917) in existence, occupied by a barber. It is the oldest building extant in Quebec regarding which reliable record exists. The next house on St. Louis street, to the west, adjoining the little porch, is a fancy goods and tobacco store, and the tall building next to it is a lodging house. Water color. Size 5 x 7.

1953—**MODERN CALECHE, QUEBEC**—The original type was found in the mountainous districts of France and Spain, and is still in use in the hilly parts of the latter country. On account of the hilly character of Quebec streets the caleche was introduced in early days. Reference is made to it in the first Canadian novel, "Emily Montague," by Mrs. Brooke. the old-time vehicle was much lighter than those now (1917) in Quebec, as they were for the use of the habitants owning them. Their use being at present almost entirely confined to a few cabmen who cater for the tourist trade, they have been strongly and more heavily built in order to stand heavier usage. Water color. Size 4 x 6.

1954—**BURIAL PLACE OF MAJOR THOMAS SCOTT**—Cemetery of St. Matthew's Church, St. John street, Quebec—In this old churchyard were interred the Protestant military under the British regime. At the right of the small gate opening on the pathway leading to the vestry of the church, is the grave of Major Thomas Scott, paymaster of H.M. 70th Regiment, which was stationed in Lower Canada, 1813-28. He was a brother of Sir Walter Scott, and for a time reputed to have written "Rob Roy" himself. The inscription on the stone reads: "Sacred to the memory of Thomas Scott, Esquire, late Paymaster of the 70th Regiment, who departed this life 10th February, 1823, and his daughter, Barbara Scott, who died on the 5th October, 1821, in the eighth year of her age." Water color. Size 4 x 6.

1955—MEMORIAL TO JOHN WILSON—In Mount Hermon Cemetery, Quebec—John Wilson, a celebrated Scottish vocalist, was born in Edinburgh, 1800. He was a printer in early life; helped set up the Waverley Novels, with the Ballantynes. Studied music under John Mather and Benjamin Gleadhill, of Edinburgh, and in March, 1830, appeared as Harry Bertram in "Guy Mannering"; subsequently engaged in other operas. In 1842 Mr. Wilson sang before the Queen. Later he toured the States and Canada, and in Quebec fell victim to cholera, July, 1849. The following inscription is on his monument: "Sacred to the memory of John Wilson, the Scottish vocalist, celebrated for the excellent taste, feeling and execution with which he sang the airs of his native Caledonia. He was an amiable and unassuming man. Died at Quebec, July, 1849. Erected by some of his friends and admirers in Canada, 1852." David Kennedy, Scottish vocalist, restored his tomb and made a bequest for its permanent preservation. Photograph, colored. Size 6 x 10.

1956—PRINCE OF WALES' CANOE—In 1860, when H. R. H. the Prince of Wales visited Canada, he attended on 1st August an Indian regatta given by the Hudson's Bay Company near Isle Dorval, about three miles above Lachine. Here Sir George Simpson, General Superintendent of the company's affairs in North America, had a beautiful residence. Nine birch bark canoes took part in the regatta, with crews composed of 100 Iroquois Indians from Caughnawaga and the Lake of Two Mountains. The Prince and suite occupied the canoe shown in picture. It was an excellent specimen of the North American canoe, 40 ft. long, 6 ft. broad and propelled by fourteen paddles. It was subsequently presented to her Majesty Queen Victoria as a memento of the Prince's visit to Canada, and for years was stationed at Virginia Water, near Windsor Castle. Water color from an old print. Size 4 x 7.

1957—HALDIMAND HOUSE, MONTMORENCY FALLS, QUE.— Built, 1782, near the brink of the Falls, by General Haldimand, Governor and Commander-in-Chief in Canada, 1778-84. During his stay in Quebec, 1791-4, Prince Edward (Duke of Kent) made this house his summer residence. Early in the last century it was purchased, together with all the Montmorency Falls property, by the large lumbering firm of Usborne & Co. Later it was owned by Mr. Peter Patterson, a member of that firm, and, subsequently, came into possession of his son-in-law, the late G. B. Hall. From the Hall estate the old manor house passed into the hands of the present owners, the Quebec Railway, Light, Heat & Power Company. Water color. Size 4 x 6.

1958—KENT HOUSE, MONTMORENCY FALLS, QUE.—The Quebec Railway, Light, Heat & Power Company operate the old-time manor house of Governor Haldimand as an hotel, and since becoming such it has been called Kent House. It has undergone a complete renovation, and while the walls and divisions of the house are intact, the interior has been greatly changed. Many a tourist who visits Montmorency Falls makes his abode at Kent House. Amongst the attractions in the extensive grounds is a splendid menagerie of Canadian big game, including buffalo, bear, moose and deer. Water color. Size 4 x 6.

1959—VIEW LOOKING EASTERLY FROM RAILWAY BRIDGE AT METAPEDIA, QUE.—The picture, made in the early seventies, shows: (1) Where Intercolonial Railway is built. (2) St. Lawrence Chapel (R.C.), burned in fire of 1902. The Restigouche Hotel stands almost on site. (3) House built for engineers at time railway was being constructed. It was first occupied by Peter Grant, engineer, later bought by Lord Strathcona, and now held by his heirs. (4) House occupied by James Harvey and used as a carpenter shop. (5) Part of present Restigouche Salmon Club. The building was formerly owned by a Mr. Webber. (6) Store belonging to Daniel Fraser. It was demolished several years ago. Water color by William G. R. Hind. Size 6 x 15.

1960—POSTING ON THE ST. LAWRENCE RIVER DURING THE WINTER MONTHS—Lithograph in color by Coke Smyth. Size 11 x 15.

1961—MONTMORENCY FALLS, QUE.—Lithograph in color by Coke Smyth. Size 11 x 14. See 93.

1962—AN OLD VIEW OF TROIS RIVIERES—From the St. Lawrence River. Engraving. Size 8 x 11. See 1843, 2015.

1963—"DORF ST. HYACINTH IN CANADA"—St. Hyacinthe is prettily situated on the Yamaska River, Quebec. Lithograph in color. Size 4 x 5. See 2029.

1964—"CASERNE UND MARKTPLATZ IN FREDERICK-TOWN"— Barracks and Market Place, Fredericton, N.B.—The view was taken from the St. John River, at an angle above the soldiers' barracks. The building with tower, to the left of picture, was the City Hall, destroyed by fire. The Court House stands near the site to-day. Towards the right are the soldiers' barracks, built 1827. Lithograph in color. Size 5 x 5. See 2225.

1965—"FORT CHAMBLY, UNTER CANADA" (LOWER CANADA)— On the Richelieu River, Quebec. Lithograph in color. Size 4 x 5. See 1835, 1942-5.

1966—"ANSICHT AUF DEM XENIBECASSIS BEI ST. JOHN"—View on the Kennebacasis River, near St. John, N. B.—The Kennebacasis is a picturesque river, rising near the sources of the Petitcodiac and flowing southwesterly. It enters the St. John River at Kennebecasis Bay. Lithograph in color. Size 4 x 5. See 2263.

1967—OLD ROMAN CATHOLIC CHURCH AT BEAUHARNOIS, QUE. —Beauharnois is the chief town of the county of that name, and is situated on Lake St. Louis, formed by the St. Lawrence. Lithograph in color by Coke Smyth. Size 11 x 15.

1968—QUEBEC FROM THE ST. LAWRENCE—Lithograph in color by Coke Smyth. Size 11 x 15.

1969—"SKETCHES IN THE CANADAS—By Coke Smyth. London. Published by Thos. McLean, 26 Haymarket. Printed at A. Ducote's Lithographic establishment, 70 St. Martin's Lane." Size 8 x 10.

1970—QUEBEC, 1854—From below the Citadel and looking towards the St. Charles River, showing: 1. Laurentian Mountains. 2. St. Charles River, near mouth. 3. Row of houses facing esplanade. 4. Old office of Royal Engineers (now Garrison Club). 5. Officers' quarters R.E., R.I., formerly residence of Chief Justice Sewell, later Government House, facing esplanade. 6. House at corner of Esplanade and St. Louis street, occupied as residence by Lord Monk when Governor-General. 7. Old chapel of Ursuline Convent. 8. Tower of Basilica. 9. Spire of English Cathedral. 10. Spire of Chalmers Church. 11. Road leading to Citadel. Water color by Gen. A. R. V. Crease, R.E. Size 7 x 10.

1971—**QUEBEC, 1850**—View from the Levis or south shore of the St. Lawrence—With key—Original wash drawing by Henry Cotton, Chief Clerk in Governor-General's office during the Administration of Lord Monk. Size 10 x 35.

1972—**"A VIEW OF ST. JOHN'S**—Upon the River Sorell in Canada with the redoubts, works, etc. Taken in the year 1776 during the late war in America. Publish'd as the Acts direct, Jany. 1st, 1789, by William Lane, Leadenhall St., London." In September, 1775, Montgomery besieged the fort at St. John's, which surrendered 3rd November, remaining in possession of the Americans until the latter part of May, 1776. This view, by an officer in the 29th Regiment of Foot, was made in the autumn of 1776, from "the blockhouse erected on the opposite side of the River Sorell." The barracks of the Royal Canadian Dragoons now occupy the site of the old fort, of which nothing remains except some entrenchments. 1. Shows the fort at St. John's and barracks. 2. Ship on stocks. 3. Rope walk. 4. Redoubt. 5. Vessels at anchor. 6. Sorell or Richelieu. 7. East side of river, now (1917) site of town of St. Athanase, or Iberville, Que. Line engraving by Thomas Anbury. Size 8 x 15.

1973—**QUEBEC**—From the Chateau—Considerable artistic license seems to have been taken with the topography of this picture. The Beauport Hills, the bay formed by the mouth of the St. Charles, and the general view of the Lower Town, are the most realistic points. The battery in the foreground did at one time exist, near what is now the Citadel end of Dufferin Terrace, and almost under the present King's Bastion. But the Chateau St. Louis is poorly represented in the foreground of the Heights, and no such tower as indicated in the centre of the picture ever crowned the Basilica, and it is altogether too high for a dome of that shape, or something very like it, which topped a market building in the square in front of the Basilica, early in the nineteenth century, and shown in the Model of Quebec in the Dominion Archives. Lithograph in color by Coke Smyth. Size 10 x 15.

1974—**CAP TOURMENTE**—From Chateau Richer—Both are on the north shore of the River St. Lawrence. Cap Tourmente, an abrupt and lofty promontory jutting into the river, thirty miles east of Quebec, and a little below the Isle of Orleans, lends a rugged aspect to the neighboring scenery. Lithograph in color by Coke Smyth. Size 11 x 15. See 2043.

1975—**FALLS OF MONTMORENCY**—From St. Joseph's. Lithograph in color by Coke Smyth. Size 11 x 15.

1976—**PRIVATE CHAPEL OF THE URSULINE CONVENT, QUEBEC** —The convent was built in 1641; destroyed by fire in 1650. It was rebuilt and fire again destroyed it in 1686, after which the present structure was erected. During the winter following the capture of Quebec the Fraser Highlanders were stationed in the convent. Lithograph in color by Coke Smyth. Size 11 x 15.

1977—**CUSTOM HOUSE, QUEBEC, 1880**—Situated on the point of land at the junction of the St. Lawrence and St. Charles—A handsome, dome-surmounted structure, with facade of Doric columns, approached from the water by a long, broad flight of steps. In the background may be seen Laval University. North of the Customs House is now (1917) the capacious Louise Basin, with a wet dock, 40 acres in area, and a tidal dock of half that size. On the Louise Embankment, which forms the outer wall of the dock, is the Immigration Office, with barracks in which immigrants are cared for until they can be sent on to their ultimate destinations. Water color from original drawing by F. B. Schell, for "Picturesque Canada." Size 5 x 7.

1978-80 and 1989-91—"**Depicting the Adventures of Captain Buzbie and Miss Muffin on a Picnic to Montmorency,**" were published by George E. Desbarats, Ottawa, and chromo-lithographed by Roberts and Reinhold, Montreal. "Entered according to Act of the Provincial Legislature in the year 1868, by George E. Desbarats in the office of the Registrar of the Dominion of Canada."

1978—**PICNIC TO MONTMORENCY**—Capt. Buzbie drives Miss Muffin. Size 8 x 12.

1979—**PICNIC TO MONTMORENCY**—How they climb up the cone. Size 9 x 12.

1980—**PICNIC TO MONTMORENCY**—Coming down is easier but more dangerous. Size 9 x 12.

1981—**FLOATING DAM USED IN ERECTING FIRST VICTORIA BRIDGE, MONTREAL,** 1854—This floating dam, or caisson, for one of the piers of the first Victoria Bridge, shows the dam anchored in position and sunk to a bearing on the river bottom, while the masonry for the pier was being built inside, and with the staging for the upper part of the pier masonry partly in place. A floating dam was used for each pier. Colored lithograph. S. Russel, delt. Published by John Weale, London, 1860. Kell Bros., lithrs., Castle street, Holborn. Size 14 x 20. See 1866-7.

1982—**THE CITADEL AND RIVER FRONT, QUEBEC**—Lithograph in color by Coke Smyth. Size 11 x 15.

1983—"**VIEW OF QUEBEC, CANADA**—From the River St. Charles, shewing the conflagration of June 28th, 1845, and the ruins of the fire of May 28th, 1845. On stone by C. T. Sanford, from a sketch by J. Murray and C. Crehen. Lith. and printed in colors by G. and W. Endicott, New York." The year 1845 is remembered in the history of the city of Quebec, as one of disastrous fires. On May 28th the entire suburb of St. Roch's was destroyed. Many lives were lost and some 1,600 houses, occupying the site of former pasture grounds and styled by the early French, La Vacherie, were burned. A month later St. John's suburbs, near the Upper Town, met the same fate. Lithograph in color. Size 13 x 20.

1984—**INDIANS OF LORETHE OR LORETTE**—At Jeune or Indian Lorette, about eight miles from Quebec, were of the Huron tribe. After the Indian massacres of 1648-9, parties of the tribe sought refuge in different places, one section seeking refuge on the Island of Orleans. In 1697 they settled at Lorette. Lithograph in color by Coke Smyth. Size 11 x 15.

1985—"**VIEW OF QUEBEC**—Taken from Point Levi—G. Heriot, Esqr., pinxt. J. C. Stadler, sculp. Printed for Richard Phillips, 6 New Bridge street, London." 1, The cliff bordering the Plains of Abraham towards the St. Lawrence. 2, Cape Diamond. 3, The Citadel. 4, Houses on present (1917) line of Des Carrieres street. 5, The old windmill on what was called Mount Carmel. 6, Chateau St. Louis. 7, English Cathedral (consecrated 1804). 8, Basilica, Seminary and Palace of R.C. Bishop. 9, Hotel Dieu. 10, Grand Battery. 11, The bay at junction of St. Charles and St. Lawrence, and in the distance the faint outline of the Laurentian Mountains. Aquatint in color. Size 10 x 20. See 1992.

1986—**CANADIAN TRAPPER NEAR QUEBEC**—In his summer garb— From a painting by Cornelius Krieghoff (1812-72), a celebrated artist who made his home in Canada for many years. He depicted scenes from habitant life very successfully. Chromo lithograph. Size 9 x 11.

1987—CANADIAN TRAPPER NEAR QUEBEC—A typical trapper is portrayed, starting off on a winter's day in search of fur-yielding animals in the woods of Quebec Province, and for which he had previously laid snares. Chromo lithograph from a painting by Cornelius Krieghoff. Size 9 x 11.

1988—" 'THE COLUMBUS'—Captn. Wm. McKellar; was built at Quebec, 1824, by Charles Wood, of Port Glasgow, and launched with about 4,000 tons of her cargo on board. The dimensions of this immense ship, which was only nine months on the stocks, are as follows: Length of keel, 300 feet; breadth of beam, 50 feet; depth of hold, 30 feet; and measures 3,800 register tons. She is more than a third longer than the 'Prince Regent', the largest ship in the British navy, which measures 2,620 tons, and was several years upon the stocks. Drawn on stone by Josh. Harwood. S. Vowles, Lithog., 3 St. Michael's Alley, Cornhill, London." Size 9 x 17.

1989—PICNIC TO MONTMORENCY—On the Way Home—Off the track. Capt. Buzbie would like very much to know where they are. Size 9 x 13.

1990—PICNIC TO MONTMORENCY—Assisted by some obliging habitants, Capt. Buzbie and Miss Muffin regain the road. Size 9 x 13.

1991—PICNIC TO MONTMORENCY—Captain Buzbie and Miss Muffin get home at last. Size 9 x 13.

1992—"QUEBEC, LOWER CANADA—View of Quebec from Point Levy—Drawn on stone by W. Walton from a sketch by R. A. Sproule. Printed by C. Hullmandel, London. Published by A. Bourne, February, 1832, and sold by A. Bourne, Engraver, Montreal. Proof." In color. Size 11 x 15. See 1971.

1993—"QUEBEC, LOWER CANADA—View of the Market-place and Catholic Church, taken from the barracks, Fabrique street. Drawn on stone by W. Walton, from a sketch by R. A. Sproule. Printed by C. Hullmandel, London; published by A. Bourne. 1832, and sold by A. Bourne, Engraver, Montreal. Proof." In color. Size 11 x 15.

1994—TIMBER COVES AT QUEBEC, 1862—In the small bays and coves on the north shore of the St. Lawrence, merchants made their timber depots by booming across the entrances. From here square timber was shipped to all parts of the world. The rock in the background is the westerly part of Cape Diamond, bordering that part of the Heights of Abraham known as the Cove Fields, upon which the Ross Rifle factory now stands. In 1863 the timber coves, such as shown in the picture, extended from the Pres-de-ville to Cap Rouge, a distance of eight miles. Five millions of dollars' worth of square timber were shipped from these coves annually. This trade has now entirely disappeared, and sawn lumber, which is shipped from schooners, batteaux or railway cars on to steamships has taken its place. Water color. Size 7 x 10.

1995—DESTRUCTION BY FIRE OF THEATRE ROYAL ST. LOUIS, QUEBEC, 1846—At the close of a Diorama exhibition on the evening of the 12th June, 1846, a camphine lamp exploded, the scenery took fire and the flames spread to the interior woodwork. Those of the audience who had not left immediately on the dropping of the curtain, in their efforts to escape, became panic-stricken, and forty-five were crushed to death. The theatre, which at one time was a racquet court and later a riding school, stood near the site of the famous Castle of St. Louis, destroyed by fire in 1835. The view is taken from the Place d'Armes. Accompanying the picture is a key. Drawing in water color from print. Size 6 x 8.

1996—GENERAL ARNOLD'S HEADQUARTERS AT QUEBEC, 1775-6 —This house was used by the American general, Benedict Arnold, during his memorable siege of the Ancient Capital. After Montgomery's death on 31st Dec., 1775, when he and Arnold made an assault upon the city, the latter took command of the American force. The dwelling is pleasantly situated on the banks of the St. Charles River, near Scott's Bridge, built subsequent to the siege, and which is shown in background of picture. It was at one time occupied by Hon. Justice Kerr, but is now (1917) owned and occupied by Mr. Bell. Water color. Size 5 x 6.

1997—STRUTT, WILLIAM GOODAY, 1762-1848—Honorary Governor of Quebec, 1800—He was a son of John Strutt, of Terling Place, Essex, Eng.; captain 61st Regiment, 1778, later 91st, and in 1782 exchanged to the 97th. Served at the Siege of Gibraltar. He purchased a majority in the 60th Regiment, succeeded to a lieut-colonelcy, removed to the 54th and went to Flanders. Subsequently he received the rank of brigadier-general, and in 1798 was made a major-general. Governor Strutt's death took place in England. Water color from a miniature in possession of the late Hon. Frederick Strutt, J.P., Derby, Eng. Size 3 x 4. Head and shoulders.

1998—"THE ICE CONE AT THE FALLS OF MONTMORENCY, NEAR QUEBEC, LOWER CANADA, IN 1853—C. Krieghoff, del. W. Simpson, lith., London. Pub'd. for the artist by Ackermann & Co., 96 Strand, Dec., 1853. Day & Son, Lithrs. to the Queen." Lithograph in color. Size 15 x 23. See 92.

1999—"VIEW OF THE VILLAGE OF CHAMBLY—Seignory of Chambly. Bourne." Made in 1836 from the east side of the Richelieu River. With key. Lithograph in color. Size 10 x 14.

2000—CARTIER-BREBOEUF MONUMENT, QUEBEC—Inaugurated 24th June, 1889, on the historic spot where Cartier and his companions spent the winter of 1535-6—On 3rd May, 1536, just before his return to France, Cartier erected a large cross, bearing a shield having thereon the fleurs-de-lis and the inscription: "Franciscus Primus, Dei Gratia Francorum Rex, Regnat." In 1888 a substantial cross of iron and copper, bearing a similar inscription, was erected on the same site by the Catholic Circle of Quebec. The monument, inaugurated the following year, is a memorial, not only to Cartier, but also to the Jesuit missionaries, who on 23rd Sept., 1625, took solemn possession of the land called Fort Jacques Cartier, at the confluence of the St. Charles and Lairet Rivers. The material used is granite, part polished and part dull, from the quarries of Migwick on the Lake St. John road. The shields and cornices are of Deschambault stone. At the summit may be seen the three ships of Jacques Cartier—"La Grande Hermine," "La Petite Hermine" and "L'Emerillon"—above them soars the royal crown of France. Facing the Lairet, on the west face of the monument, appears a martyr's palm, with the name of the principal martyrs of the Jesuit Society in Canada: Breboeuf, Lalement, Jogues, Garnier, Buteux, Masse, Daniel and Denoue. An iron fence surrounds a space of 140 x 50 feet, enclosing the cross and monument. The plan and design of the latter were made by the late M. Tache, Deputy Minister of Crown Lands, Quebec. Photograph, colored. Size 4 x 7.

2001—RUINS OF THE CHATEAU BIGOT, NEAR QUEBEC—This antique ruin stands in solitary loneliness in the centre of a clearing at the foot of the Charlesbourg Mountain, five miles from Quebec. The English call it "The Hermitage," while to the French it is "Chateau Bigot," or "Beaumanoir." It was built over two hundred years ago, supposedly by Intendant Talon, and afterwards improved and enlarged as a country home by Francois Bigot, thirteenth and last Intendant of the Kings of France in Canada. Bigot squandered the public funds of Canada, and was sent to the Bastile and his property confiscated. The chateau was two storeys high, with a deep cellar. The west cellar contained a vaulted apartment, eight feet square, probably for plate and treasure. Kirby, in his "Chien d'Or," places the scene of the murder of Caroline, the unhappy Algonquin maid, at the Chateau Bigot, which is not to be confounded with Bigot's town palace, upon the ruins of which a brewery now stands. Water color. Size 5 x 7.

2002—GENERAL HOSPITAL, QUEBEC—Mgr. de Saint Vallier, second Bishop of Quebec, bought in 1692 the Convent of the Recollets, on the bank of the River St. Charles, and later gave it to the Nuns of the Hotel Dieu to found a General Hospital. Two wings were added in 1710 and 1711, and in 1736 an additional wing was built for the reception of discharged soldiers unfit for service. To the west of this wing a new building was begun in 1743. Historically speaking, the General Hospital, Quebec, is interesting. After the Siege of Quebec, English soldiers received the same care and attention within its walls as the French, and the wounded in Arnold's and Montgomery's force were also attended. As well as caring for the sick, this hospital took charge of the insane until 1845. Water color. Size 5 x 6.

2003—ST. REGIS INDIAN CHURCH—During the period prior to 1750, when the northern frontiers of New England were harassed by savages, three children, two boys and a girl, named Tarbell, were carried by them from Groton, Mass. The girl escaped, but the boys were taken to Canada and adopted by Caughnawaga Indians, near Montreal. In time they married daughters of chiefs, but did not enjoy savage life, so, on the advice of the village priest, they, with their wives and the parents of the latter (four families), went up the St. Lawrence and landed where St. Regis stands. To the Indians the spot was "Ak-wis-sas-ne," the place "where the partridge drums." In 1760 Father Anthony Gordon, a Jesuit, joined the colony and named the settlement St. Regis. He erected a little log church, which, however, was burned and a wooden building put up, in the tower of which the bell ever heard in St. Regis was hung. It is said that this bell was that taken from Deerfield by the Indians after the destruction of the village by fire in 1704. The present church was built in 1792, of massive stone, its walls five feet thick. The belfry has four bells, the upper ones having been recast from the first bell heard in St. Regis. The full liturgy of the Roman Catholic Church is used, and for many years the preaching was in the Mohawk language. Water color from a drawing made in 1868. Size 4 x 5.

2004—HOPE, COL. HENRY—Commandant of the Forces and Administrator of Quebec—He was sworn in, 2nd Nov., 1785, and acted as Lieut.-Governor until the arrival of Dorchester on 23rd Oct., 1786. The first of the two purely British gates of Quebec was erected by Hope, from whom it took its name; it was demolished in 1874, for no apparent reason. In 1788, Hope, then brigadier-general, obtained leave of absence. He went to England, returning to Canada in autumn of the same year. Died at Quebec, 13th Jan., 1789. Water color. Size 4 x 5. Head and shoulders.

2005—"QUEBEC, LOWER CANADA—View of the Esplanade and Fortifications of Quebec, with part of the surrounding country. Drawn on stone by W. Walton, from a sketch by R. A. Sproule. Printed by C. Hullmandel, London. Published by A. Bourne, February, 1832, and sold by A. Bourne, Engraver, Montreal. Proof." In color. Size 11 x 15.

2006—"QUEBEC, LOWER CANADA—View of the Place d'Armes and of the Church of England, from the garden of the Governor. Drawn on stone by W. Walton, from a sketch by R. A. Sproule. Printed by C. Hullmandel. London. Published by A. Bourne, February, 1832, and sold by A. Bourne, Engraver, Montreal. Proof." In color. Size 10 x 15.

23

2007—"A VIEW OF THE CITY OF QUEBEC, THE CAPITAL OF CANADA—Taken from the Rock on Point Levis, Oct. 23rd, 1784." The height of Point Levis lies just opposite Quebec. What was in 1784 an unpopulated wilderness is to-day in the midst of a prosperous community in a most picturesque part of Quebec. Original water color by James Peachey, ensign, 60th Regiment. Size 13 x 19.

2008—HER MAJESTY THE QUEEN—Photograph of her Majesty Queen Mary, from the original in the Dominion Archives, Ottawa. Size 4 x 6. Three-quarter length.

2009—HIS MAJESTY KING GEORGE V.—From the signed photograph sent by his Majesty for the King's Book, published at Ottawa. Size 4 x 5. Three-quarter length.

2010—CITADEL OF QUEBEC FROM PRESCOTT GATE, 1860—An interesting part of the Ancient City. With key. Water color from drawing in the Illustrated London News, 1860. Size 7 x 10.

2011—BAGATELLE—The lodge at Spencer Wood, facing the Holland road, two miles from the city of Quebec. The long, straggling, picturesque cottage, built in the Italian style, was occupied by Mr. Denis Godley, private secretary to Lord Monk, Governor-General of Canada from 1861-8. It was situated on the Spencer Wood property on the portion now known as Spencer Grange, and belonging to the estate of the late Sir James MacPherson Lemoine. Photograph, colored. Size 5 x 7.

2012—FACSIMILE OF SIGNATURES OF H. M. GEORGE V. AND HIS ELDER BROTHER, THE LATE DUKE OF CLARENCE—These signatures were written when the royal brothers were boys together on the training ship "Britannia," they being at the time about thirteen and fourteen years of age, respectively.

2013—VIEW OF QUEBEC, 1760—Half-tone reproduction. Size 4 x 6.

2014—"VIEW OF QUEBEC—Dedicated by permission to Lt.-General Lord Seaton, G.C.B. and G.C.H., late Governor-General and Commander-in-Chief of the Forces in British North America. Drawing by Captain B. Beaufoy, unattached. T. Picken, lith. Day and Haghe, Lithrs. to the Queen." Lithograph. Size 15 x 20.

2015—"A VIEW OF THREE RIVERS IN CANADA—Taken from the road leading to Pointe du Lac by J. Peachey, Ensn., 60 Regt. (a) The Convent. (b) Cap Madelaine." Three Rivers is so called from its situation at the triple outlet of the St. Maurice River. To strengthen what had already become a trading post, a mission was founded at Three Rivers in 1617, and in 1634 Champlain had a fort erected here. In later years Three Rivers grew in importance, but, despite many natural advantages, her site was deserted by settlers, who were drawn towards Montreal. It is, however, a thriving city, most picturesquely situated. Original water color. Size 13 x 23. See 1843, 1962.

2016—ENCAMPMENT OF THE LOYALISTS AT JOHNSTOWN—On the banks of the River St. Lawrence, in Canada, taken July 6th, 1784, just east of the present town of Prescott, Ont.—During and after the Revolutionary War thousands who had remained loyal to the mother country sought refuge in Canada, many of them settling on the banks of the St. Lawrence, as well as in Nova Scotia and New Brunswick. Water color copy by E. Wyly Grier from original by James Peachey, ensign, 60th Regiment. Size 13 x 19.

2017—"QUEBEC, TAKEN FROM BEAUPORT—Entered according to Act of the Provincial Legislature in the year of our Lord Eighteen Hundred and Fifty-four, by P. L. Morin, in the office of the Registrar of the Province of Canada. Hub. Clerget, lith. Imp. Villain rue de Sevres, 19 Paris, Paris Massard Editeur, 53 rue de Seine J. and O. Cremazie, Editeurs, rue de Fabrique." Lithograph in color. With key. Size 17 x 28.

2018—PASS OF BOLTON, EASTERN TOWNSHIPS, QUE., 1841—A view near Knowlton, which is pleasantly situated near the head of Brome Lake. Mount Orford may be seen in the background of picture. Water color. Size 5 x 7. See 1766.

2019—"VIEW ON THE RIVER ETCHEMIN, NEAR QUEBEC—G. Heriot, Esqr., pinxt. F. C. Lewis, sculp. Printed for Richard Phillips, 6 New Bridge street, London, 1807." Aquatint in color. Size 5 x 7. The Heriot pictures in this collection were sketched by George Heriot, who, in the course of his duties as Deputy Postmaster-General for the Canadas, and also for the Provinces of Nova Scotia and New Brunswick, travelled extensively in British North America. These pictures were used to illustrate a comprehensive volume, "Heriot's Travels," "containing a description of the picturesque scenery on some of the rivers and lakes; with an account of the productions, commerce and inhabitants of those provinces (the Canadas), to which is subjoined a comparative view of the manners and customs of several of the Indian nations of North and South America." It was in 1800 that Heriot succeeded Hugh Finlay in office, and he continued to hold the position of Deputy Postmaster-General until 1816, when he was followed by David Sutherland.

2020—"HARROWER'S DISTILLERY AND MILL, RIVER TROIS SAUMONS—Drawn by Col. Bouchette. J. and C. Walker, sculpt." The village of Trois Saumons is situated at the mouth of the river of the name, fifty-four miles below Quebec, on the south shore of the St. Lawrence. The mills and distillery at Trois Saumons were erected in the latter part of the eighteenth century by Thos. Ainslie Young, who for many years carried on business there as a grain exporter. He failed, however, about 1800, the property passing into the hands of David and Robert Harrower. The buildings shown in the picture were demolished about fifty years ago to make way for lumber and saw mills. Aquatint in color. Size 4 x 7.

2021—"VIEW OF THE LOWER FALL OF LA PUCE—G. Heriot, Esqr., pinxt. Hassel, sculp. Printed for Richard Phillips, 6 New Bridge street, London, 1807." Descending from highlands near Chateau Richer, La Puce River winds picturesquely through mountain and woodland, and finally enters the noble St. Lawrence. The view shows the waters dashing tempestuously over the Lower Fall, a distance of over one hundred feet. Aquatint in color. Size 5 x 7. See 2023.

2022—"ENCAMPMENT OF DOMICILIATED INDIANS—G. Heriot, Esqr., pinxt. F. C. Lewis, sculp. Printed for Richard Phillips, 6 New Bridge street, London." Heriot, in his "Travels Through the Canadas," gives no indication as to the scene of the picture, nor does he mention the tribe to which the Indians represented belong. It is, however, the opinion of Mr. E. T. D. Chambers, of Quebec, a well-known authority on Quebec pictures, that the scene was painted from Indian Cove, on the south shore of the St. Lawrence, nearly opposite the mouth of the St. Charles River, at Quebec. Here, in the early days of the British regime, both the Micmacs and the Algonquins were in the habit of encamping for the purpose of trading their furs and of receiving aid from the Government. The wigwams and canoes, which are evidently of birch bark, are similar to those used by the Montagnais, Micmacs and Hurons. The last-named tribe, however, were, in the artist's time, comfortably housed at the village of Lorette, nine miles west of Quebec. Aquatint in color. Size 9 x 15.

2023—"VIEW OF THE FALL OF LA PUCE—G. Heriot, Esqr., pinxt. Hassel, sculp. Printed for Richard Phillips, 6 New Bridge street, London, 1807." Aquatint in color. Size 5 x 7. See 2021.

2024—"FALL OF THE GRANDE CHAUDIERE, ON THE OUTAOUAIS RIVER—G. Heriot, Esqr., pinxt. F. C. Lewis, sculp. Printed for Richard Phillips, 6 New Bridge street, London, 1807." Some six miles above the capital begin the rapids which terminate in the Chaudiere Falls, the waters of which disappear in the Lost Chaudiere by a subterranean passage whose outlet is unknown. Heriot, in his book, "Travels Through the Canadas," habitually uses the spelling "Outaouais" for Ottawa. Aquatint in color. Size 5 x 8.

2025—"VIEW OF THE FALLS OF CHAUDIERE—Nine miles west of Quebec—G. Heriot, Esqr., Pinxt. F. C. Lewis, sculp. Printed for Richard Phillips, 6 New Bridge street, London, 1807." The view is taken from near the mouth of the Chaudiere River. Aquatint in color. Size 5 x 7.

2026—"MINUETS OF THE CANADIANS—Drawn by G. Heriot, Esqr. Engrav'd by J. C. Stadler. Printed for Richard Phillips, 6 New Bridge street, London, 1807." The stately minuet came originally from Poitou, France, and was danced in 1653 by Louis XVI. at Versailles. It was introduced into Canada by some of the 17th century French Governors and their staffs, and became the fashion at the Vice-Regal festivities at old Chateau St. Louis. Naturally it was copied in the homes of the old French families who had the entree of the gubernatorial mansion. At these dances quaint costumes were worn. The Beau Brummel of the times depicted by the artist was wont to affect curled and powdered hair, sometimes worn in a queue, and surmounted by a low-crowned hat with caught-up brim. On ceremonial occasions this headdress was superseded by the stately three-cornered hat. The women, however, dressed more simply. In painting this picture it is unlikely that the artist had any particular interior in mind. Aquatint in color. Size 9 x 14.

2027—"QUEBEC FROM CAPE DIAMOND—G. Heriot, Esqr., pinxt. F. C. Lewis, sculp. Printed for Richard Phillips, 6 New Bridge street, London, 1807." The Canadian Gibraltar, Cape Diamond, on which stands the Citadel of Quebec, is situated at the junction of the Rivers St. Lawrence and St. Charles. To the west, and almost on a level with the ramparts, lie the Plains of Abraham, and at the eastern side of Cape Diamond is the spot on which Montgomery was killed, in 1775, while endeavoring to rush a barricade, in order to join Benedict Arnold. Aquatint in color. Size 5 x 7.

2028—"VIEW OF ST. PAUL'S BAY—On the River St. Lawrence—G. Heriot, Esqr., pinxt. F. C. Lewis, sculp. Printed for Richard Phillips, 6 New Bridge street, London, 1807." St. Paul's Bay, at the entrance of Riviere du Gouffre, was settled in the early part of the 17th century and has always been noted for its earthquakes and volcanic disturbances. It is in the form of an amphitheatre, surrounded by high hills, which lend a rugged and picturesque aspect to the scene. Aquatint in color. Size 5 x 7.

2029—"VILLAGE OF ST. HYACINTHE—Co. of St. Hyacinthe—R. S. M. Bouchette, delt. Day and Haghe, Lithrs. to the King, 17 Gate St., Linc. Inn Fs." The picturesque, old-time French-Canadian village, about thirty-five miles north-east of Montreal, is shown as it appeared in the first half of the nineteenth century. It is now (1917) a prosperous little city. In 1903 St. Hyacinthe was devastated by fire, but has since been rebuilt. Yamaska, the name of the stream on which St. Hyacinthe is situated, is the Indian equivalent for "rushfloored river." Lithograph in color. Size 6 x 8. See 1963.

2030—"NEW BRIDGE ON THE RIVER JACQUES CARTIER—G. Heriot, Esqr., pinxt. F. C. Lewis, sculp. Printed for Richard Phillips, 6 New Bridge street, London, 1807." The Jacques Cartier River, named after the great explorer, takes its rise sixty miles north of Quebec, flowing out of the lake of the same name and emptying into the St. Lawrence. The bridge shown crossed the river about six miles from its mouth, but has since been replaced by a more modern structure. It was long known as Dery's bridge, from the name of the occupant of the house nearby. Aquatint in color. Size 5 x 7.

2031—OLD WINDMILL ON LACHINE ROAD—On the shore of the St. Lawrence, near the village of Lachine—The history of the weather-beaten old mill is an interesting one. It is said that at one time a dispute arose between its owner and the Fathers of St. Sulpice, who claimed the sole right of milling on the Island of Montreal. The case was decided in favor of the miller, who, however, was forbidden to rebuild his mill, were it by any chance destroyed. It was then that he built around the wooden structure the substantial stone wall which gave it a fortress-like appearance. Water color from original drawing by F. B. Schell, for "Picturesque Canada," 1880. Size 5 x 7.

2032—"CASCADES OF THE ST. LAWRENCE—G. Heriot, Esqr., pinxt. F. C. Lewis, sculp. Printed for Richard Phillips, 6 New Bridge street, London. 1807." Passing down the St. Lawrence, a little below Lake St. Francis, one comes upon an effective series of rapids. These rapids, four in number, Couteau, Cedars, Split Rock and the Cascades, come so closely upon one another that they practically form one long, flashing cascade, delighting the eye of the beauty-loving traveller. Aquatint in color. Size 5 x 7.

2033—CHIEFS OF IROQUOIS NEAR CAUGHNAWAGA—A woodland scene in the autumn of 1860—The Indians at the Caughnawaga reservation, on the south shore of the River St. Lawrence, opposite Lachine, are remnants of the Iroquois tribe. They are famous as lacrosse players and boatsmen. In the latter capacity a band of fifty did splendid service for England in the Nile Expedition of 1884. Lithographed. C. Krieghoff, del. Kell Bros., lithrs., Castle street, Holborn. Published by John Weale, London, 1860. In color. Size 8 x 11.

2034—"MOOSE DEER OF NORTH AMERICA (17 HANDS HIGH)—G. Heriot, Esqr., pinxt. F. C. Lewis, sculp. Printed for Richard Phillips, 6 New Bridge street, London, 1807." The moose, the largest animal of its kind on the continent, presents a rather ungainly appearance. It corresponds to the elk of Europe, although very different from the American elk or wapiti. Its hair is of a reddish brown, variable shade, becoming more hollow with the advance of age, but never losing its elastic property. The animal is native to various parts of Canada, chiefly New Brunswick and the Far West. It is also to be found in the northern part of the United States. Aquatint in color. Size 8 x 10.

2035—"CITY OF MONTREAL (TAKEN FROM THE MOUNTAIN)— Drawn on the spot by G. Heriot, Esqr. Engrav'd by Cartwright. Printed for Richard Phillips, 6 New Bridge street, London, 1807." Aquatint in color. Size 6 x 8. See 1881.

2036—"VIEW ON THE UPPER LAKE ST. CHARLES, NEAR QUEBEC —G. Heriot, Esqr., pinxt. F. C. Lewis, sculp. Printed for Richard Phillips,

6 New Bridge street, London, 1807." A beautiful sheet of water, north-north-west of the city, the St. Charles is noted for its echo, which differs from other echoes in that it tarries before repeating the sound uttered. Aquatint in color. Size 5 x 7.

2037—"LA DANSE RONDE—Circular dance of the Canadians—Drawn by G. Heriot, Esqr. Engrav'd by J. C. Stadler. Printed for Richard Phillips, 6 New Bridge street, London, 1807." The danse ronde, or circular dance of the old-time Canadian families, was similar to some of the English "country dances," except that the Canadians did not follow a set figure, but rather indulged in a general frolic after the manner of children at play. The background is, in all probability, fanciful, the artist's aim being to portray the recreations of the country people of his day. Aquatint in color. Size 9 x 14.

2038—"FALL OF MONTMORENCI (246 FEET HIGH)—G. Heriot, Esqr., pinxt. F. C. Lewis, sculp. Printed for Richard Phillips, 6 New Bridge street, London, 1807." View taken at the mouth of the Montmorency River. Aquatint in color. Size 5 x 7. See 2044.

2039—"VIEW OF QUEBEC FROM THE DISTILLERY AT BEAUPORT —G. Heriot, Esqr., pinxt. F .C. Lewis, sculp. Printed for Richard Phillips, 6 New Bridge street, London, 1807." The view is taken on the line of road to Montmorency. The parish of Beauport was conceded to M. Giffard by the company of New France in 1635, and was one of the pioneer settlements in Quebec. When in 1759 the city of Quebec was under siege a portion of the French soldiery were stationed in Beauport. Aquatint in color. Size 5 x 7.

2040—"FALLS OF MONTMORENCI, WINTER—On stone by L. Haghe. Drawn by R. S. M. Bouchette, Esqr. Day and Haghe, lithrs. to the King, 17 Gate street." Lithograph in color. Size 6 x 8.

2041—"CITY OF QUEBEC—Taken from the Harbour—R. S. M. Bouchette, Delt. Day and Haghe, Lithrs. to the King, 17 Gate street, Lincoln's Inn Fds." The view shows portions of the Lower and Upper Towns on the cliff along the waterfront. To the left of the picture, at the highest point of the plateau, stands the Citadel, covering forty acres of ground, and dating in its present form from 1823. Lithograph in color. Size 6 x 8.

2042—"FORT CHAMBLY—Drawn by Col. Bouchette. J. and C. Walker, sculpt." In color. Size 5 x 8. See 1835, 1942-5, 1965.

2043—"RUINS OF CHATEAU RICHER, WITH CAPE TOURMENTE— G. Heriot, Esqr., pinxt. F. C. Lewis, sculp. Printed for Richard Phillips, 6 New Bridge street, London, 1807." The parish or settlement derived its name from a Franciscan Monastery, the ruins of which are situated on a rocky point in the St. Lawrence. In the distance Cap Tourmente is shown jutting into the river. Aquatint in color. Size 5 x 7. See 1974.

2044—"FALL OF MONTMORENCI (246 FEET HIGH)—G. Heriot, Esqr., pinxt. F. C. Lewis, sculp. Printed for Richard Phillips, 6 New Bridge street, London, 1807." Aquatint in color. Size 5 x 7. See 2038.

2045—"LONG'S FARM ON LAKE TEMISCOUATA, AT THE EXTREMITY OF THE PORTAGE, ON THE LINE OF THE TEMISCOUATA ROAD—Drawn by Col. Bouchette. J. and C. Walker, sculpt." The Temiscouata road formed a part of the road from Riviere-du-Loup to New Brunswick, and it is possible that Long was one of the early guardians who were located along the highway to assist in keeping it. However, even the name of Long is now forgotten by the people of the vicinity and no traces of the buildings on Long's farm remain, a portion of the site being covered by the parish of Notre Dame de Portage. From the farm a fine view of Lake Temiscouata ("winding water") was obtainable. In color. Size 4 x 7.

2046—"COSTUME OF DOMICILIATED INDIANS OF NORTH AMERICA—G. Heriot, Esqr., pinxt. Stadler, sculp. Printed for Richard Phillips, 6 New Bridge street, London, 1807." With this picture, as with the "Encampment of Domiciliated Indians," Heriot does not mention the tribe represented in his picture. It was evidently made for illustration purposes, as the costumes are partly European. The squaw, too, is not carrying the child in the usual way, laced on hide, or in a casing of birch bark. It is to be noted, also, that rifles are carried by the Indians. Aquatint in color. Size 7 x 12.

2047—"VIEW OF JEUNE LORETTE—The village of the Hurons, nine miles north of Quebec—G. Heriot, Esqr., pinxt. F. C. Lewis, sculp. Printed for Richard Phillips, 6 New Bridge street, London, 1807." Lorette, on the highlands rising toward the mountains, was settled by the Hurons about 1697, and several hundred of the tribe still (1917) live in the little village. In the distance, Lorette Chapel, dating back to 1731, is seen. Aquatint in color. Size 5 x 7. See 1821, 2055.

2048—"A GENERAL VIEW OF QUEBEC FROM POINT LEVY—To the Honble. Sr. Charles Saunders, Vice-Admiral of the Blue, and Knight of the Most Honourable Order of the Bath, these twelve views of the principal buildings in Quebec are most humbly inscribed by his most obedient servant, Richard Short. Engraved by P. Canot, Septr. 1st, 1761. Publish'd according to Act of Parliament by R. Short, and sold by T. Jefferys, the corner of St. Martin's Lane, Charing Cross." The foreground of this view is much more like the scene of the old Indian encampment at Indian Cove than like Point Levis, opposite Quebec. The I.C.R. station at present occupies the site immediately facing the centre of the picture. The following key gives the location of the buildings: 1. Redoubt on site of present Citadel, a prominent feature of the system of fortifications built by de Lery at the end of the 17th century. 2. Powder magazine. 3. Chateau St. Louis. 4. Church of Recollets. 5. Jesuits' Church. 6. Ruins of Bishop's Palace. 7. Ruins of Cathedral. 8. The Seminary. 9. Hotel Dieu. Line engraving. Size 13 x 20.

2049—"A VIEW OF THE NORTH-WEST PART OF THE CITY OF QUEBEC—Taken from St. Charles's River—Drawn on the spot by Richd. Short. Engraved by P. Benazech. London. Publish'd according to Act of Parliament, Sepr. 1, 1761, by Richd. Short, and sold by Thos. Jefferys, the corner of St. Martin's Lane." The mouth of the St. Charles has been so much changed since 1761, or else the artist has taken such liberties, that the foreground is unrecognizable. So are the buildings near the water front, when compared with old plans. Reading from left to right of picture the main points of interest are: 1. The Hotel Dieu, near corner of Heights. 2. The Basilica. 3. The Jesuits' Church. 4. Recollets' Church. 5. The long, low buildings at the edge of the cliff were barracks, and the site is now occupied by buildings of Grey Nuns. The western city wall (6) followed at that date very nearly the present line of Ste. Ursule street. Line engraving. Size 13 x 20.

2050—QUEBEC—"A View of the Bishop's House—With the ruins as they appear in going down the hill from the Upper to the Lower Town. Drawn on the spot by Richd. Short. Engraved by J. Fougeron. London. Publish'd according to Act of Parliament, Sepr. 1, 1761, by Richd. Short, and sold by Thos. Jefferys, the corner of St. Martin's Lane." Line engraving. Size 13 x 20. See 2061.

2051—QUEBEC—"A View of the Orphans' or Urseline Nunnery— Taken from the Ramparts. Drawn on the spot by R. Short. Engraved by James Mason, Sept. 1st, 1761. Published according to Act of Parliament by R. Short, and sold by T. Jefferys, the corner of St. Martin's Lane, Charing Cross." Many local authorities insist that the main building (3) shown, was the Convent of the Recollets, and not one of the Ursuline buildings. It somewhat resembles that convent as shown in Des Jardins' Churches and Chapels of Quebec. But a building connected with the Ursulines in the Model of Quebec in the Archives Department, Ottawa, corresponds exactly with that shown in the picture, even to the number of windows. To the left of the main block are seen the spires of the Jesuits' Church (1) and the Basilica (2), while on the right is the Recollet Chapel (4). Line engraving. Size 13 x 20.

2052—"VIEW OF THE CITY OF QUEBEC—Taken from the north bank of the Saint Charles—London. Published June 4th, 1805 (for the proprietor at Quebec), by E. Walker, No. 7 Cornhill. Geo. Heriot, D. Post Master General for British American, pinxt. J. C. Stadler, sculp." Aquatint in color. Size 13 x 19.

2053—"AN EAST VIEW OF MONTREAL IN CANADA—Drawn on the spot by Thomas Patten. Engraved by P. Canot. Publish'd according to Act of Parliament, Novr. 11, 1762, by Thos. Jefferys at Charing Cross." This view of Montreal, in 1760, was taken from St. Helen's Island, and shows several points of interest in the town at that period. Among these are the Chateau Callieres, built, 1690, by the Governor of that name; demolished, 1780; the Grey Nunnery, or Hospital, founded, 1692, by the freres Charron, and the first institution in America to take in foundlings; the Congregation Nuns (teachers), founded by Marguerite Bourgeois in 1659. The grounds are to-day (1917) occupied by convent buildings. The Jesuits' Church, Chapel and Monastery are also shown. After the conquest the church was used as an English Church, and the monastery as a prison. The chapel served for a time as a court house. With key. Line engraving. Size 12 x 20.

2054—OVERLOOKING THE ST. LAWRENCE AT QUEBEC—From a point on the Glacis outside the west fortifications of the Citadel—Wolfe's Cove lies in the rear of where the smoke is seen ascending from the beach, while near the old Martello tower (No. 1) has been erected the Ross Rifle Factory. The extreme point of land jutting into the St. Lawrence a short distance beyond, is Sillery Point. Water color. Size 8 x 11.

2055—VIEW OF INDIAN OR JEUNE LORETTE, 1765—Near the city of Quebec—Since 1697 this has been the home of the Huron Indians, who, after the massacres of 1648-9, wandered here and there, seeking refuge from their enemies, the Iroquois. They finally settled on the elevated plateau close to the rapids of St. Ambroise, now known as Indian, or Jeune Lorette. The chapel shown in the picture dates back to 1731, although in 1862 it suffered much by fire. The remnant of the once warlike Huron race still (1917) lives in the peaceful little village. Water color. Size 6 x 9. See 1821, 2047.

2056—ST. ANDREW'S PRESBYTERIAN CHURCH, ST. ANN STREET, QUEBEC, 1810-1916—The first congregation of the Church of Scotland in Quebec assembled in 1759 in a room in the Jesuits' Barracks, the original members being soldiers of the 78th Highlanders (Frasers), under their regimental chaplain, the Rev. Robert MacPherson. In 1802 a lot was granted on St. Ann street for the erection of a church, and on November 30th, 1810, the building was set apart for worship. The church still stands on the original site and its external appearance remains the same. About forty years ago the steeple was taken down, but in 1912 it was fully restored through the generosity of Col. Turnbull, and the old bell replaced in it. St. Andrew's contains a number of beautiful memorial stained glass windows. The Rev. Alexander Sparks was first pastor. Lithograph. Size 12 x 18.

2057—QUEBEC—"A View of the Inside of the Recollect Friars' Church —Drawn on the spot by Richd. Short. Engraved by C. Grignion, London. Publish'd according to Act of Parliament, Sep. 1, 1761, by Richd. Short, and sold by Thos. Jefferys, the corner of St. Martin's Lane, Charing Cross." It is said that the first ecclesiastics who came to New France, were Recollets, brought out by Champlain in 1615. After many trying experiences, vicissitudes and a return of the order to France, Father Germain Allard, Provincial of the Recollets, embarked in May, 1670, with M. Talon, three other ecclesiastics, and a deacon, named Brother Luke, a skilled painter, who later decorated the interior of the Recollet Church. They took up their abode on the bank of the St. Charles River, where the Recollets had previously lived. In 1690, however, they made a transfer of their property to Bishop de St. Vallier in return for land immediately opposite Fort St. Louis, where shortly afterwards the Recollet Church and Convent were built. Both buildings were destroyed by fire in 1796, and the Church of England Cathedral now occupies the site, which was appropriated by the British Government. The Recollet Fathers allowed Protestant services to be held in their old church before the erection of a Protestant Church in Quebec. Line engraving. Size 13 x 20.

2058—QUEBEC—"A View of the Church of Notre Dame de la Victoire —Built in commemoration of the raising the siege in 1695, and destroyed in 1759. Drawn on the spot by Richd. Short. Engraved by A. Bennoist, London; publish'd according to Act of Parliament, Sep. 1, 1761, by Richd. Short, and sold by Thos. Jefferys, the corner of St. Martin's Lane, Charing Cross." (1) Ruins of warehouse erected under French regime. (2) Ruins of Church of Notre Dame des Victoires after the bombardment of 1759. Bishop Laval planned the erection of this church in 1684, but it was built by his successor, Bishop St. Vallier, in 1688. After Frontenac's victory over Sir William Phipps in 1690, it was given the name of Notre Dame de la Victoire, which, after the dispersion of Admiral Walker's squadron by a storm in 1711, was changed to Notre Dame des Victoires. (3) Notre Dame street, the ruins in the distance, marking very closely the supposed site of Champlain's 'Abitation,' or first residence in Canada, (4) Ruins, after the siege of 1759, of residential buildings under the French regime. Line engraving. Size 13 x 20.

2059—QUEBEC—"A View of the Jesuits' College and Church—Drawn on the spot by Richd. Short. Engraved by C. Grignion, London. Publish'd according to Act of Parliament, Sep. 1, 1761, by Richd. Short, and sold by Thos. Jefferys, the corner of St. Martin's Lane, Charing Cross." (1) Old buildings, site of which is now occupied by a row of houses forming the south side of Buade street. Chapel of the Jesuits (2), served as a parish church prior to the erection of the Basilica (consecrated 1666). It was demolished many years before the razing of the old College, and in 1844, wooden stalls for the accommodation of butchers in the market square, were built. They were, however, torn down in 1877, when a new stone market building was erected near St. John's Gate. (3), Jesuits' Barracks, as they were called under British regime, originally the Jesuits' College, were erected in 1637, burned in 1640, and largely rebuilt in 1720. They were demolished about thirty years ago. The new City Hall now occupies the site of these buildings, and faces the Basilica. (4) Space used as a public market place from 1686 to 1877. Line engraving. Size 13 x 20.

2060—QUEBEC—"A View of the Inside of the Jesuits' Church—Drawn on the spot by Richard Short. Engraved by Anthony Walker. Publish'd according to Act of Parliament by Richd. Short, and sold by Thos. Jefferys, the corner of St. Martin's Lane, Charing Cross." As early as 1625 a Jesuit Mission was founded at Quebec; in 1635 the foundation of the Jesuits' College was laid, and in 1639 the Jesuits' Church served as the parish church of Quebec. It is described as being then a handsome building, of wood, with an arched roof and gallery and such appropriate decoration as gave it all the appearance of a church. On 14th June, 1640, the College and Church of the Jesuits were destroyed by fire. Line engraving. Size 13 x 22.

2061—QUEBEC—"A View of the Bishop's House—With the ruins as they appear in going up the hill from the Lower to the Upper Town. Drawn on the spot by Richard Short. Engraved by A. Benoist, Septr. 1st, 1761. Publish'd according to Act of Parliament by R. Short, and sold by T. Jefferys, the corner of St. Martin's Lane, Charing Cross." The ruins in the distance (1) above the top of the hill, conceal from view the Chien d'Or building, and those (2) shown prominently are of old French buildings near the head of Mountain Hill, directly below where the Prescott Gate was afterwards erected. The roadways, indicated by the figure "3," is the upper part of Mountain Hill. To the right of the picture is the Bishop's Palace (4) erected by Bishop St. Vallier, founder of the General Hospital, Quebec. The Palace commands an extensive view towards the north. Line engraving. Size 13 x 20. See 2050.

2062—QUEBEC—"A View of the Treasury and Jesuits' College— Drawn on the spot by Richd. Short. Engraved by C. Grignion. London. Publish'd according to Act of Parliament, Sepr. 1, 1761, by Richd. Short, and sold by Thos. Jefferys, the corner of St. Martin's Lane, Charing Cross." The ruins of the Treasury (1). The street upon which it stands (2) is the present Garneau street, and in the distance is seen the small steeple of the Quebec Seminary (3). The ruins (4) mark the then termination, towards the west, of the narrow block of buildings between Garneau and Fabrique streets. The block extends further west to-day, and ends in a very narrow building. (5) Ruins of the Cathedral (present Basilica). (6) Fabrique street. (7) Jesuits' Barracks. The two-storey building in the foreground, on the extreme right, was apparently a private house, which has, of course, long since disappeared. Line engraving. Size 13 x 20.

2063—QUEBEC—"A View of the Intendant's Palace—Drawn on the spot by Richd. Short. Engraved by William Elliott. Publish'd according to Act of Parliament, Septr. 1, 1761, by Richd. Short, and sold by Thos. Jefferys, the corner of St. Martin's Lane." With key. (1) Corner of old French Arsenal, near the present (1917) St. Vallier street. A brewery stands on the site. (2) One of the warehouses used for the King's stores during the French regime. (3) The Intendant's Palace. In the middle of the seventeenth century the Intendant Talon erected on this site a brewery. It was subsequently unoccupied for several years, and a later Intendant, de Meules, about 1684, induced the King to erect on the site a residence for the Intendant. The new structure was destroyed, however, in 1713, and the building shown in the picture erected to take its place. Some of the old vaults connected with it are still used by the proprietor of the adjoining brewery. After Canada came into the hands of the British, the palace was neglected, and in 1775, when Arnold's sharpshooters resorted to it for cover, it was demolished by the guns of the garrison. Line engraving. Size 13 x 20.

2064—QUEBEC—"A View of the Cathedral, Jesuits' College and Recollect Friars' Church—Taken from the gate of the Governor's House. Drawn on the spot by R. Short. Engraved by P. Canot. Publish'd according to Act of Parliament by R. Short, and sold by T. Jefferys. the corner of St. Martin's Lane, Charing Cross, London, Sepr. 1, 1761." (1) Church of the Recollets. The wing to right of church was the monastery, occasionally used as a State prison. (2) Steeple of Jesuit Church, built 1666; demolished 1807. (3) Old French house—now site of residence occupied for years by Hon. P. J. O. Chauveau. (4) Tresor Lane, one of the shortest and narrowest streets in Quebec; so called because under the French regime it led to the Treasury. (5) Old building replaced by a residence. (6) Ruins of French Cathedral, now Basilica. (7) Residence of Dr. Longmore, staff medical officer; now a business block. (8) Fort street, leading to the post office. (9) Place d'Armes, known under French regime as La Grand Place du Fort. Line engraving. Size 13 x 20.

2065—"ST. JOHN'S GATE, QUEBEC—On stone by Sproule, from an original by A. J. Russell, for Hawkins' Picture of Quebec. Bourne, Lithr." This view is taken from the outside of the fortification walls. The structure shown was the second of the three gates that have stood here and was built after the demolition of the original French structure in 1791 and replaced by the third gate in 1865. The latter was torn down in 1897. The French Congregational Church, beyond the fortification wall, still stands, and is served by the Jesuits, but it is not a parish church. To the right of it are some of the residences facing the Esplanade. To the left is the old National school building, sold to the Jesuit Order some years ago. Lithograph in color. Size 6 x 10. See 2076.

2066—"OFFICERS' BARRACKS, CAPE DIAMOND—On stone, by Sproule, from an original by Capt. Alderson, R.E., for Hawkins' Picture of Quebec. Bourne, Lithr." View of the interior of the Citadel at Quebec, looking towards the Officers' Quarters and the King's Bastion. The flag in the distance flies from the King's Bastion, and the adjacent building is used as a guard room. The officers' quarters were erected between 1825-30, and stand to-day exactly as shown, except that at the end near the King's Bastion there were erected, while H.R.H. Princess Louise was in Canada, additional accommodations for the Vice-Regal party, now known as the Governor-General's quarters. The men preparing stone for further buildings were members of the Royal Engineers, by whom the Citadel was built. Stones and other material for the work were brought up from the riverside by means of an incline railway up the face of Cape Diamond, upon the summit of which the Citadel stands. Lithograph in color. Size 6 x 10.

2067—"DALHOUSIE GATE, QUEBEC—On stone by Sproule, from an original by A. J. Russell, for Hawkins' Picture of Quebec. Bourne, Lithr." This massive structure, which forms the inner entrance to the Citadel of Quebec, after the passage of the outer or chain gate, was erected in 1827. Within the arch of the gate are the main guard rooms for a detachment and non-commissioned officer, and in front is the spacious area used as a parade ground, which is really an enlargement of the ditch formed by the retiring angles and face of the bastion. The gate was named after the Earl of Dalhousie, who succeeded the Duke of Richmond as Governor-General in 1820. In the face of the bastion are seen the loopholes for the fire of musketry from within, which also serve for the admission of air and light into the casemated barracks within, for the troops composing the garrison. When this picture was published, the Citadel was occupied by the 32nd Regiment of the line. Lithograph in color. Size 7 x 10.

2068—"PRESCOTT GATE, QUEBEC—On stone by Sproule, from an original by A. J. Russell, for Hawkins' Picture of Quebec. Bourne, Lithr." Erected in 1797 by General Robert Prescott, who succeeded Lord Dorchester as Governor-General of Canada. It formerly commanded the approach to the Upper Town from Mountain Hill, the summit of which it spanned, until its demolition in 1871. The building to the right of the gate was the palace of the Roman Catholic Bishop, where for several years in the early part of the nineteenth century the Provincial Legislature sat.

When this building was destroyed by fire the Government erected the Parliament House on its site. The houses shown on the other side of the street have long since been torn down. Overshadowing them is the gable wall of the old Chien d'Or building, on the site of which the post office now (1917) stands. Lithograph in color. Size 6 x 10.

2069—BELOW CAPE DIAMOND, QUEBEC—A portion of Champlain street, some distance "up the Coves," in local parlance, and a mile or so higher up the street than the spot where Montgomery fell, 31st December, 1775. Next the last low house on the extreme right is the old Norwegian chapel, and alongside of it is the long stairway leading up from Champlain street to the Cove Fields behind Grand Allee. The locality must not be confused with "Sous le Cap," properly so called, which is the exceptionally narrow street behind St. Paul and Sault-au-Matelot streets, and directly beneath the cliff supporting the Grand Battery. Pastel by Owen Staples, Toronto. Size 11 x 13.

2070—"ST. LOUIS GATE, QUEBEC—On stone by Sproule, from an original by A. J. Russell, for Hawkins' Picture of Quebec." The view is taken from the St. Louis Road, or "La Grande Allee," almost in front of where the Parliament Buildings now stand, and looking towards the city. It was protected by outworks of great strength and powerful combination. The erection of the original gate, which was intended as a defence against the Iroquois, dates from 1694. In 1791, after Quebec had fallen into British hands, the St. Louis Gate was pulled down and rebuilt. Between this date and 1823 it appears to have undergone several changes; but in the latter year, as part of the plan of defence, including the Citadel, adopted by the Duke of Wellington, was replaced by a structure retaining the same name. On the site of this gate, which was demolished in 1871, the present magnificent archway with Norman spires and castellated turrets was erected by Mr. H. J. Beemer, in accordance with Lord Dufferin's improved project. Lord and Lady Dufferin, before their departure from Canada in 1878, assisted at the laying of the foundation stone of this structure. Lithograph in color. Size 6 x 10.

2071—SHIELD ON A QUEBEC GATE—"This shield was taken from off one of the gates of the city of Quebec at the time that a conquest was made of that city by His Majesty's sea and land forces (in the memorable year, 1759), under the command of the Admirals Saunders and Holmes, and the Generals Wolfe, Monckton, Townsend and Murray, which latter being appointed the first British Governor thereof, made a present of this trophy of war to this corporation, whereof he then was one of the Jurats." Gen. (Sir James) Murray was British Governor of Canada, 1764-66, returning to England in the latter year. He purchased the estate of Beauport, near Hastings, Eng., and during his residence there presented this trophy of war to the Corporation of Hastings, of which he was a jurat. The shield, which is in a good state of preservation, now hangs in the Council Chamber of the Corporation of Hastings. Photograph, colored, by J. H. Blomfield, of Hastings, Eng., 1911. Size 13 x 15.

2072—CHAMPS DE MARS, QUEBEC—An historic spot—The entire scene has now (1917) changed. On the left may be seen a wing of Frontenac's old castle, demolished in 1891 to make way for the Chateau Frontenac, as were also the houses in centre of picture, so that extensions might be made to the same building. At the extreme right is the old Court House, burned, 1870, and since rebuilt. Water color. Size 5 x 10.

2073—"KILBORN'S MILLS, STANSTEAD, LR. CANADA, AND THE UNITED STATES SETTLEMENTS, VERMT.—South of Province Line, Lat. 45 N. On stone by C. Haghe. Sketched by Coln. Bouchette. W. Day, Lithr. to the King, 17 Gate St., Linc. Inn Fds." In 1800 Charles Kilborn, the owner of the mills shown in the picture, obtained a grant of land in the village of Stanstead, Que. The difference between the old and new province line (see margin of picture) is estimated from the topography at about sixty feet. Stanstead, being on the 45th parallel, is not affected by the Ashburton Treaty, passed in 1842. Lithograph in color. Size 6 x 8.

2074—FRENCH CATHEDRAL (BASILICA) AND MARKET SQUARE, QUEBEC—It appears to-day (1917) exactly as in the picture, except that there is now an iron railing on the foot of the steps. The centre of the square in front of the Basilica is now a parterre of grass, traversed by foot paths. To the right of the Basilica, facing the picture, is Buade street, leading to the post office and to the top of Mountain Hill. The high buildings near the Basilica are still to be seen. The lower ones also, for the most part, have the old sloping roofs and attic windows, but have been modernized with plate glass windows, etc., on the ground floor. This square was formerly the Upper Town Market Place. Facing the Basilica stands the new City Hall, on the site of what was the old Jesuit College of the early days. Between the round cornered building, now occupied by the Quebec Bank, to the left of the Basilica, and the Basilica itself is the entrance to the Seminary and Laval University. Between the bank building and the next house on the left is Ste. Famille street, which leads down to the ramparts overlooking the St. Charles valley. In front of the buildings on the left of the picture is Fabrique street. Lithograph from a drawing by Henry Cotton. Size 7 x 10. See 2075.

2075—THE BASILICA, QUEBEC—Facing upon the old Market Square stands the Basilica, the erection of which was begun in 1647, and first mass celebrated, Christmas, 1650. It superseded the chapel of the Jesuits' College, for some time used as the parochial church of Quebec. Although fires and sieges have partly destroyed the edifice, which in 1874 was raised to the dignity of a Basilica, still the foundations and portions of the walls are those in existence over two centuries ago. The building is 216 feet long and 108 feet wide, and accommodates 4,000 people. On the walls hang a rare collection of paintings, secured mostly by Canadian priests in France after the Reign of Terror. The building is not an example of architecture, but rather of solidity. Pastel by Owen Staples, Toronto. Size 11 x 14. See 2074.

2076—ST. JOHN'S GATE, QUEBEC—The second of the three successive gates erected at this point of Quebec's fortifications—the original structure was erected about 1694, and stood for nearly a century. It was demolished under British rule in 1791, because of its ruinous condition, and some years later replaced by that shown in the picture, and which was torn down in 1865. A more ornate and convenient substitute took its place, but it was altogether removed in 1897. The small building close to the flank of the gate, on its right, was a military laboratory, destroyed by an explosion that shook the whole city like an earthquake in 1864. The buildings shown on either side of the street no longer exist. Lithograph in color from a drawing by Henry Cotton. Size 7 x 10. See 2065.

2077—"PALACE GATE, QUEBEC—On stone by Sproule, from an original by A. J. Russell, for Hawkins' Picture of Quebec. Bourne, Lithr." The ornate structure depicted is said to have somewhat resembled one of the gates of Pompeii. It was erected in 1830-1, on the site of the old French gate, torn down in 1791, and was itself demolished in 1874. It took its name from that of the street which it spanned, and which was so called because it led to the palace of the Intendant, which stood near the foot of the hill and not far from the present C.P.R. station. The old French structure which formerly occupied the site of the gate shown in the picture had in 1775 gallantly withstood the assault made upon it by the American invaders under Benedict Arnold. Lithograph in color. Size 6 x 10.

2078—MONUMENT TO WOLFE AND MONTCALM, GOVERNOR'S GARDEN, QUEBEC—The idea of erecting a twin-faced monument to the victor and the vanquished on the Heights of Abraham, 13th September, 1759, was originated by Lord Dalhousie, and the corner-stone laid, 1827. In 1871 the column was taken down and rebuilt at the expense of some citizens of Quebec. On it is the following inscription: "Mortem, Virtus, Communem, Famam Historia, Monumentum Posteritas Dedit." Which may be translated: "Valor gave them a common death, history a common fame and posterity a common monument." The Governor's Garden is a small, but beautiful, park between Dufferin Terrace and the base of the glacis that leads to the Citadel. The houses beyond the Monument and the King's Bastion of the Citadel, in the distance, flying the flag, are depicted as they appear to-day (1917). Lithograph in color from a drawing by Henry Cotton. Size 7 x 9. See 1819, 2967.

2079—"HOPE GATE, QUEBEC—On stone by Sproule, from an original by A. J. Russell, for Hawkins' Picture of Quebec. Bourne, Lithr." It stood on the northern face of the Ramparts of Quebec, at the foot of St. Famille street, which leads down to the Ramparts from the Upper Town Market Place. The hill running down from it ends in St. Paul street, in Lower Town. Hope Gate was the first to be erected of the two purely British gates of Quebec. It was built in 1786 by Colonel Henry Hope, commandant of the forces and administrator of the Government, and named after him. In 1874 it was demolished. Lithograph in color. Size 7 x 10.

2080—QUEBEC—"A view of the City of Quebec, the Capital of Canada, taken partly from Pointe des Peres, and partly on board the 'Vanguard' man-of-war, by Captain Hervey Smyth. To the Right Honourable William Pitt, one of his Majesties most Honourable Privy Council & Principal Secretary of State. These six views of the most remarkable places in the Gulf and River of St. Laurence are most humbly inscribed, by his most Obedient humble servant, Hervey Smyth, Aid du Camp to the late Genl. Wolfe. London. Printed for John Bowles at No. 13 in Cornhill, Robert Sayer at No. 53 in Fleet street, Thos. Jefferys, the corner of St. Martin's Lane in the Strand, Carington Bowles at No. 69 in St. Paul's Church Yard, and Henry Parker at No. 82 in Cornhill. P. Benazech, Sculp. a.1." This view of the City of Quebec was sketched by Capt. Hervey Smyth, A.D.C. to Gen. Wolfe, in 1759, from the Levis side of the St. Lawrence. Capt. Smyth became later Sir Hervey Smyth, Bart., and died in 1811. With key. Line engraving. Size 12 x 20.

2081—"A VIEW OF THE PIERCED ISLAND—A remarkable rock in the Gulf of St. Laurence, two leagues to the southward of Gaspee Bay—Drawn on the spot by Capt. Hery. Smyth. Engraved by P. Canot. London. Printed for John Bowles at No. 13 in Cornhill, Robert Sayer at No. 53 in Fleet street, Thos. Jefferys, the corner of St. Martin's lane in the Strand, Carington Bowles at No. 69 in St. Paul's Church Yard, and Henry Parker at No. 82 in Cornhill." The view depicts the "Vanguard," 70 guns, passing the Pierced Island, better known as Perce Rock, situate some two leagues to the south of Gaspe Basin. From 1759-60 Capt. Hervey Smyth, an officer of the 15th Regiment of Foot, and one of Wolfe's aides, was on board the "Vanguard." Smyth made a number of excellent drawings, many of which have been engraved on copper, and were published in November, 1760. They are now so rare that the only complete set extant is in the British Museum. There was an English Masonic Lodge, warrant No. 254, issued in 1760 on the "Vanguard." Line engraving. Size 13 x 20.

2082—"A VIEW OF THE FALL OF MONTMORENCI—And the attack made by General Wolfe, on the French Intrenchments near Beauport, with the Grenadiers of the Army, July 31, 1759—Drawn on the spot by Capt.

Hervey Smyth. Engraved by Wm. Elliot. London. Published according to Act of Parliament, Nov. 5, 1760, by T. Jefferys the Corner of St. Martin's Lane. Printed for J. Bowles, R. Sayer, T. Jefferys, C. Bowles & H. Parker." H.M.S. "Centurion," shown in the foreground of picture, was a vessel of 60 guns, formerly the flagship of Lord Anson in his famous voyage around the world, and commanded at the siege of Quebec by Captain Mantle. With key. Line engraving. Size 13 x 21. See 65.

2083—"A VIEW OF QUEBEC FROM THE BASON—Painted from a drawing by Hery. Smyth, Esq., by Francis Swain. P. C. Canot, sculp. London. Printed for T. Bowles in St. Paul's Church Yard, E. Bakewell and H. Parker, opposite Birchin Lane in Cornhil, Robt. Sayer, at the Golden Buck in Fleet street." With key. Line engraving. Size 12 x 18.

2084—GASPE BAY—"A view of Gaspe Bay, in the Gulf of St. Lawrence. This French Settlement used to supply Quebec with Fish, till it was Destroyed by General Wolfe after the surrender of Louisburg in 1758. During the stay of the British Fleet in 1759, General Wolfe resided at the House on the Beach, (1); (2) 1,500 Quintals of Fish. Drawn on the spot by Capt. Hervey Smyth. Engraved by Peter Mazell. London. Publish'd according to Act of Parliament, Nov. 5, 1760, by T. Jefferys, the corner of St. Martin's Lane." This view of the Peninsula, the great three-cornered sandspit which lies just across the bay from Gaspe Basin, on the shores of the Gulf of St. Lawrence, is said to be the oldest picture of the Upper Bay. On the sands the French had established a "custom house" for the purpose of stopping smuggling. This building was the headquarters of Wolfe during his stay at Gaspe. In making his sketch Hervey Smyth considerably shortened the sandbar, fore and aft, at the same time contracting his whole sketch abeam in order to bring into the view the south side of the bay. The four small houses were doubtless homes of fishermen, as in those days cod and mackerel were within easy reach. The view was sketched in 1758 (not 1759 as given on engraving), during the artist's visit to Gaspe with General Wolfe. Line engraving. Size 13 x 20.

2085—CAPE ROUGE—"A view of Cape Rouge or Carouge, nine miles above the City of Quebec on the north shore of the River St. Laurence. From this place 1,500 chosen troops at the break of day fell down the river on the ebb of tide to the place of landing, 13th Sept., 1759. Drawn on the spot by Capt. Hervey Smyth. Engraved by Peter Mazell, London, printed for John Bowles at No. 13 in Cornhill, Robert Sayer, at No. 53 in Fleet street, Thos. Jefferys, the corner of St. Martin's Lane in the Strand, Carington Bowles at No. 69 in St. Paul's Church Yard, and Henry Parker at No. 82 Cornhill." The first detachment of Wolfe's army to land below the Heights of Abraham on 13th Sept., 1759, disembarked here from the fleet in small boats and floated silently down the river. The Cap Rouge is a small stream flowing into the St. Lawrence between the two headlands shown, one on either side of the picture. Its valley, forming the central portion of the picture, is now spanned by a viaduct three-quarters of a mile long, for the crossing of the G. T. Transcontinental Railway. With key. Line engraving. Size 13 x 20.

2086—"TRADING POST ON THE RIVER AUX RATS—Jos. Bouchette, Junr., Depy. Sur.-Genl., delt. Day and Haghe, Lithrs. to Her Majesty." La Riviere aux Rats, or Rat River, so named because of the number of muskrats found in the vicinity, is a broad stream flowing into the St. Maurice, eighty-one miles from its mouth, at Three Rivers. For many years a trading post of the Hudson's Bay Co. has been situated near the mouth of the river, on an alluvial flat between it and a smaller stream, the Little Batiscan, and at the foot of a high mountain bearing the Indian name of Sintamaskine. Lithograph in color. Size 3 x 6.

2087—"THE FORGES, RIVER ST. MAURICE—Jos. Bouchette, Junr., Depy. Sur.-Genl., delt. Day and Haghe, Lithrs. to Her Majesty." The St. Maurice Forges, about nine miles west of Three Rivers, are frequently referred to in the literature of Lower Canada. They ceased operations in 1883—the oldest active blast furnace on the American continent. The company first operating them, having exhausted its capital in erecting furnaces, smelting houses, etc., was forced to return its charter, and in 1743 the King of France took possession of the works, which were then operated for the benefit of the Crown. In 1746 the furnace turned out a great deal of work, nevertheless, because of extravagant management, the project did not pay under the French regime. After the conquest of Canada the forges passed through many hands before finally ending their usefulness. The large house in the picture, built in the time of the French, and occupied by successive managers of the property, was burnt in 1863 and rebuilt on the original site. Some of the other old buildings still remain. Lithograph in color. Size 3 x 6.

2088—"FALLS OF THE GRAND MERE ON THE ST. MAURICE—Jos. Bouchette, Junr., Depy. Sur.-Genl., delt. Day and Haghe, Lithrs. to Her Majesty." The Falls of Grand-Mere (Grandmother) take their name from the fancied resemblance of the side view of the rock dividing the falls, to the profile of an old woman's face. In 1899 the water power of the cataract, estimated at 65,000 h.p., was acquired by the Laurentide Pulp Co., and where, prior to that year, the falls were surrounded by wilderness, as shown in the picture, there is now a flourishing town. Lithograph in color. Size 3 x 6.

2089—"A VIEW OF THE LANDING PLACE ABOVE THE TOWN OF QUEBEC—Describing the assault of the enemy's post on the banks of the River St. Lawrence, with a distant view of the action between the British and French Armys on the Hauteurs d'Abraham, Sept. 13th, 1759. Inscribed to the Right Honble. Field Marshal Lord Viscount Ligonier, Commander-in-Chief of His Majesty's Forces, by His Lordship's most obedt. servant, Hery. Smyth, Aide-de-Camp to Gen. Wolfe. London. Printed for Robt. Sayer, map and printseller at the Golden Buck in Fleet St., T. Bowles in St. Paul's Church Yard. John Bowles & Son at the Black Horse in Cornhil. E. Bakewell and T. Parker opposite Birchin Lane in Cornhil. Capt. Hery. Smyth, delin.; Francis Swain, pinxit. P. C. Canot, sculpt." With copious key. Line engraving. Size 12 x 18.

2090—WOLFE—"Major-General James Wolfe—Commander-in-Chief of His Majesty's Forces on the Expedition Against Quebec. From an original picture in the possession of Her'y Smith, Esqr. Richd. Houston, Fecit." There are two mezzotints of General Wolfe by Richard Houston, one with the right hand extended and the other with the left hand extended. No explanation is given for the making of two pictures exactly similar, except in the position of the arms. This portrait shows the left hand extended. Mezzotint, colored. Size 10 x 13. Full length. See 2114.

2091—WESTERHAM, ENG., LOOKING EAST—In this quaint Kentish village, James Wolfe (Major-General) was born 2nd Jan., 1727. The picture shows to the left a portion of the green and to the right, old houses on the village street. Photograph, colored. Size 4 x 6.

2092—TABLET TO MEMORY OF WOLFE, ST. ALPHEGE CHURCH, GREENWICH, ENG.—On 20th Nov., 1908, Field Marshal Sir George White unveiled the memorial, upon which is the following inscription: "To the Glory of God and to the memory of James Wolfe, Major-General, born at Westerham, in Kent, 2 January, 1727; died victorious on the Heights above Quebec, 13 September, 1759, thereby adding Canada to the Empire. He was buried beneath this spot 20 November, 1759." Photograph of original. Size 5 x 7.

2093—SWORDS OF GENERAL WOLFE AND CAPT. JAMES COOK— View in profile—The military sword was one of those worn by General Wolfe between 1750-9, and the naval by Capt. James Cook, the explorer, between 1757-79. The various parts of the swords are numbered and described. (See inscription on picture.) Photograph, colored. Size 6 x 10.

2094—WOLFE—"General Woolfe—Engrav'd from Mr. Isaac Gosset's model by T. Miller." In color. Size 2½ x 3. Head and shoulders, oval.

2095—AUTOGRAPH LETTER FROM WOLFE TO AMHERST, 6TH SEPT., 1757—In this letter Wolfe presents his magnifying glass to Amherst (General Jeffery). The glass is in an oval rim, fixed on a swivel pin between tortoise shell covers, and measures about 2 x 3 inches. Half-tone.

2096—THE GREEN, WESTERHAM, ENG.—Situated midway in the ancient town—To the left may be seen the tower of the parish church, and in the foreground the Wolfe statue. Photograph, colored. Size 4 x 7.

2097—NATIONAL MONUMENT TO GENERAL WOLFE—North transept Westminster Abbey, London, Eng.—In November, 1759, the thanks of the House of Commons was given to the Admirals and Generals who had been employed against Quebec and it was resolved that a monument be erected to the memory of Wolfe. The memorial of white marble, was, however, not unveiled until 1773. It bears on a large oval tablet in the middle of the sarcophagus, the following inscription: "To the memory of James Wolfe, Major-General and Commander-in-Chief of the British land forces on an expedition against Quebec, who, after surmounting by ability and valor all obstacles of art and nature, was slain, in the moment of victory, on the XIII of September, MDCCLIX., the King and Parliament of Great Britain dedicate this monument." The sculptor was Joseph Wilton, one of the founders of the Royal Academy. Amongst his best works are the monument to Wolfe and busts of Newton, Bacon, Chatham and Swift. Photograph. Size 10 x 12.

2098—WOLFE MEMORIAL WINDOW, ST. ALPHEGE CHURCH, GREENWICH, ENG.—Designed in late Italian Renaissance. The sides form a rich framework for the figure of St. George, to the left and right of which are the names of the following battles, in all of which Wolfe was engaged, except Fontenoy: Dettingen, Fontenoy, Falkirk, Culloden, Maestricht, Rochefort. At Fontenoy, Wolfe's old regiment (Duroure's) was, however, present and suffered heavily. The glass is known as Chance's Antique, carefully carried out in the "stipple" method of painting. Although containing much interesting detail, the window cannot be regarded as a first-class example of the English School of Glass Painting. The window is, nevertheless, worthy of careful inspection, owing to its technical qualities. "The paths of glory lead but to the grave," from Gray's Elegy, is appropriately used, since Wolfe was a great admirer of the poem, and repeated it in nearing Quebec the evening before the battle of the Plains of Abraham. Below West's picture are the General's last words, "I thank God and die contented." Photographic reproduction in color by H. Richardson, Greenwich, Eng. Size 8 x 18.

2099—WOLFE MEMORIAL WINDOW, WESTERHAM CHURCH, WESTERHAM, ENG.—The design of this window has been adapted in part from the picture by Sir E. Burne-Jones, entitled "The Star of Bethlehem," in the Birmingham Art Gallery. The original is based on the text, St. Matt. 2:10-11, but in the window design, the makers have taken too free a liberty, inasmuch as the figure of Joseph and the Kings have been omitted and three angel figures bearing harps, which have no special significance, have been introduced, as have also two other figures in the semi-background. The latter are intended to represent the "Shepherds."

24

Although the window contains drawings by the late Sir E. Burne-Jones, it cannot be attributed to him, but rather to the work of the glass painters who have "churned" his figures from various sources into a group to fill the spaces. This was done without regard to the original composition, in itself a work of beauty. The window is composed of antique glass, richly arranged in subdued tones, relieved by various lighter shades verging into whites, and the whole is drawn together by enamel pigments, fused into the surface of the glass, and all strongly leaded and barried. Photographic reproduction in color, by H. Richardson, Greenwich, Eng. Size 10 x 19.

2100—BOLTON, HER GRACE THE DUCHESS OF, 1734-1809 (KATHERINE LOWTHER)—When Wolfe left England in 1759 he was engaged to Katherine Lowther, sister of the first Lord Lonsdale. She remained unmarried until 1765, when she became the second wife of Harry, the sixth and last Duke of Bolton. Water color from the miniature by Conway, in possession of Lord Barnard of Raby Costle, Darlington, Eng. Size 3 x 4. Head and profile.

2101—WOLFE, HENRIETTA (THOMPSON), 1703-64—Mother of General James Wolfe—She was a daughter of Edward Thompson, of Marsden, Yorkshire. After her marriage to Col. Edward Wolfe, in 1726, they took up their residence in Westerham. Water color from a portrait by Hudson, at Squerryes, Westerham, Eng. Size 4 x 6. Three-quarter length.

2102—WOLFE, MAJOR-GENERAL JAMES, COMMANDER OF EXPE-DITION AGAINST QUEBEC, 1759—This is said to be an excellent likeness of General Wolfe, made "in his camp at Montmorenci, near Quebec, 1st September, 1759," by Captain John Montresor, and afterwards mezzotinted and published by B. Killingbeck, Gt. Dover street, London. July 30th, 1785. It appears to be a rare print, as it is said there is not a copy in the British Museum. See Doughty's "Siege of Quebec," Vol. I., p. 266. Size 3 x 4. Head and shoulders.

2103—HEIGHTS OF ABRAHAM, QUEBEC—The old wooden stairway leads from that part of Champlain street known as Cap Blanc, to the Cove Field, between the outer works of the Citadel and the Ross Rifle Factory. For a time in a state of partial ruin, it has recently been put into good order. The church with the spire is the Roman Catholic Church of Cap Blanc. It was in Champlain street, but nearly half a mile nearer the city than the foot of the stairway, that General Montgomery was killed on 31st Dec., 1775. Water color from original drawing by F. B. Schell, for "Pic-turesque Canada," 1880. Size 5 x 7.

2104—DUFFERIN TERRACE, QUEBEC—With key. Water color from original drawing by C. E. H. Bonwill, for "Picturesque Canada," 1880. Size 5 x 7.

2105—DALHOUSIE GATE—Leading from the moat to the inner works of the Citadel, Quebec. Water color from original drawing by L. R. O'Brien, for "Picturesque Canada." Size 5 x 7. See 2067.

2106—ON THE ROAD TO SILLERY, 1880—On the north shore of the St. Lawrence, four miles from Quebec, is the historic village of Sillery Cove, or St. Colomb de Sillery, originally founded by the French as a pro-tection from the incursions of the Iroquois. Here in 1637 the Jesuit Mission of Sillery—so named after its benefactor—was established by Pere Lale-mant, with funds supplied by Commander Noel Brulart de Sillery, who a few years previous had entered Holy Orders. Water color from original drawing by L. R. O'Brien, for "Picturesque Canada." Size 5 x 7.

2107—**WOLFE**—"James Wolfe, Esq.—Commander-in-Chief of His Majesty's Forces in the expedition to Quebec. Printed for R. Baldwin at the Rose in Paternoster Row." Engraving, printed in color. Size 3 x 4. Head and shoulders, oval.

2108—**PARISH CHURCH OF ST. ALPHEGE, GREENWICH, ENG.**— At junction of London, Church and Stockwell streets—Built on the site of the Old Parish Church, whose roof had fallen in 29th November, 1710. It was completed 1718 and consecrated by Bishop Atterbury in September of that year. The architecture is entirely Roman, the body of the church being erected after the design of Nicholas Hawksmore and the tower from the design of John James. Both these architects were formerly in the employ of Sir Christopher Wren. The interior is spacious, planned in the form of a cross and richly fitted in dark oak, highly carved and polished. Photograph, colored. Size 6 x 8. See 2109.

2109—**PARISH CHURCH OF ST. ALPHEGE, GREENWICH, ENG.**— View of the chancel and altar—The galleries and pew fittings are of oak, darkly stained by time, and polished; the pulpit, hexagonal in shape, is also of dark oak, with a curiously inlaid sounding board. The altar, above which is a beautiful window portraying the Crucifixion, stands in an arched recess, ornamented with angle pilasters. In a screen of fluted oak columns, with carved Corinthian capitals, are placed the communion tables. The easternmost window on the north wall, over the gallery, was raised in April, 1896, by Mr. Frederic Fountain to the memory of Major-General Wolfe. Photograph, colored. Size 6 x 8. See 2108.

2110—**QUEBEC SQUARE, WESTERHAM, ENG.**—A picturesque spot in the old town, and so named in honor of Major-General Wolfe's victory at Quebec, 13th September, 1759. Photograph, colored. Size 4 x 6.

2111—**BAPTISMAL FONT, PARISH CHURCH OF ST. MARY, WESTERHAM, ENG.**—Where General Wolfe was baptized, 11th January 1727. Photograph, colored. Size 4 x 7.

2112—**WOLFE, LIEUT.-COL. EDWARD,** 1685-1759—Father of Major-General Wolfe—He was born at York, Eng., the son of Capt. Edward Wolfe, whose ancestors, it is said, emigrated to Ireland in the fifth century. At the age of sixteen, Edward Wolfe, Jr., received his first commission as second lieutenant of marines. Three years later he appears as captain in Temple's Regiment of Foot, and in 1708 served as brigade-major with Marlborough in Flanders. In 1726 he settled in Westerham, and here the future commander of the British army at Quebec, 1759, was born. Half-tone. Size 4 x 5. Half length.

2113—**BAPTISMAL REGISTER OF GEN. JAMES WOLFE, PARISH CHURCH OF ST. MARY, WESTERHAM, ENGLAND**—It shows the record of baptism of "James, son of Collonel Edward Wolfe," 11th January, 1727. Photograph. Size 6 x 7.

2114—**WOLFE**—"Major-General James Wolfe—Commander-in-Chief of His Majesty's Forces on the Expedition against Quebec—From an original picture in possession of Her'y Smith, Esq. Richd. Houston, Fecit." Portrait shows right hand extended. Mezzotint. Size 10 x 13. Full length. See 2090.

2115—**MACARTNEY HOUSE, GREENWICH, ENG.**—Home of Major-General Wolfe—This house, which is still (1917) standing, is situated at the top of Croom's Hill in Chesterfield Walk, Greenwich. In 1738, Wolfe's father removed to Greenwich from Westerham, residing at East lane, now called East street. From 1745-52 the family lived in Church Fields, behind the Parish Church of St. Alphege, and in the latter year made Macartney House their home. It was from here that General Wolfe went to Quebec. Photograph, colored. Size 6 x 8.

2116—PARISH CHURCH OF ST. ALPHEGE, GREENWICH, ENG.— Showing entrance to vaults, facing Stockwell street—Burial place of Major-General James Wolfe, whose remains were brought from Canada and interred here on 20th Nov., 1759, beside his father, the latter's death having taken place the previous spring. Wolfe's mother is also buried here. The entrance shown is on the south side of the church, the north door being now used. The entire space under the floor is taken up with vaults. Photograph, colored. Size 6 x 8.

2117—CHAPEL AND GROTTO AT STE. ANNE DE BEAUPRE, QUE. —Or La Bonne Ste. Anne—The bare little chapel marks the site of the church of 1676-1876, dedicated to the same saint—the mother of the Virgin Mary—and was built from the materials of the old church in 1876. At the roadside, close to the chapel, stands a rough grotto, surmounted by the image of Ste. Anne, set in a niche, over which is a cross. Over the stones bubbles the clear water of a spring, said to have miraculous healing powers. The Basilica at Ste. Anne de Beaupre was opened in 1876, enlarged ten years later, and raised to the dignity of a Basilica by Pope Pius IX. It is Corinthian in design and of immense proportions. Water color from original drawing by Lucius Richard O'Brien, for "Picturesque Canada," 1880. Size 5 x 7.

2118—VICARAGE, WESTERHAM, ENG.—Where James (Major-General) Wolfe, son of Col. Edward Wolfe, was born, 2nd January, 1727. Photograph, colored. Size 5 x 6.

2119—QUEBEC HOUSE, WESTERHAM, ENG.—Home of Col. Edward Wolfe—It is a gabled Tudor dwelling, picturesquely situated at the foot of a hill on Maidstone road. Formerly the house was known as "Spiers." Photograph, colored. Size 4 x 6.

2120—CENOTAPH TO GENERAL JAMES WOLFE—In Squerryes Park, Westerham, Eng.—Erected by the Warde family to mark the spot where Wolfe received his first commission. On the side of the cenotaph shown in picture is given "Gen'l. James Wolfe, born in this parish Jan. the 2nd, 1727. Planned, attempted and completed the reduction of Quebec the 13th September, 1759, at the expense of his life." Photograph, colored. Size 5 x 7.

2121—OLD HOUSES AT POINT LEVIS—The old buildings shown in the picture were demolished some years ago. The hill to the left is known as Davidson's Hill, and to the left is also seen Commercial street. Water color from original drawing by J. Weston, for "Picturesque Canada," 1880. Size 7 x 9.

2122—COFFIN PLATE OF MAJOR-GENERAL WOLFE—"Major-Genl. James Wolfe. Aged 32 years, 1759." On 20th Nov., 1759, the remains of the General were interred in a vault beneath the Parish Church of St. Alphege, Greenwich, Eng. Photograph reproduction of brass plate. Size 5 x 5.

2123—BUST OF MAJOR-GENERAL JAMES WOLFE—Presented to Captain (Colonel) Thomas Gwillim, one of the three majors of Brigade of Wolfe at Quebec, 1759. It is now in the saloon at Wolford, Devon, the Simcoe estate. Col. Gwillim was the father of Mrs. John Graves Simcoe. Photograph (two views). Size 4 x 6.

2124—FIELD CANTEEN OF MAJOR-GENERAL WOLFE—Showing utensils ready for service—From original in Royal United Service Museum, Whitehall, S.W. London, Eng. Presented to that institution in 1906 by Colonel the Viscount Galway, C.B., A.D.C., Sherwood Rangers (Nottinghamshire), Imperial Yeomanry. Photograph, colored. Size 10 x 12. See 2125.

2125—FIELD CANTEEN OF MAJOR-GENERAL WOLFE—Showing utensils in repose—The canteen used by Wolfe in Canada became the property of the Hon. Robert Monckton, second in command at Quebec, and who subsequently attained the rank of lieutenant-general. It remained in possession of his family until 1906, when it was presented to the Royal United Service Museum, Whitehall, S.W. London, Eng., by Col. the Viscount Galway, C.B., A.D.C., Sherwood Rangers (Nottinghamshire), Imperial Yeomanry. Photograph, colored, from original in the museum. Size 9 x 11. See 2124.

2126—WOLFE, MAJOR-GENERAL JAMES—In command of the British land forces against Quebec, 1759—Sent with rank of brigadier-general in expedition against Cape Breton, 1758. The operations of the Siege of Louisburg were mainly conducted by him. Shortly afterwards he returned to England, and the following year left for Canada. On 13th September he fell before Quebec in the memorable action which gained Canada for the British Empire. From an oil in Laval University, Quebec. Size 10 x 12. Half length. See 2127-8, 2132-3, 2138.

2127—WOLFE, MAJOR-GENERAL JAMES—Commander of British army at Quebec, 1759—From a portrait, No. 1111 (painter uncertain) in National Portrait Gallery, St. Martin's place, London, Eng. Size 8 x 10. Three-quarter length.

2128—WOLFE, MAJOR-GENERAL JAMES, 1727-59—Commander of the British army at Quebec—The original of this portrait is in possession of J. Vowler-Simcoe, Penheale, Cornwall, Eng. It is painted on wood and bears the following inscription, "Brigadier-General James Wolff's profil, taken during Siege of Louisburgh in the year 1758, by Captain Inch, of the 35th Grenadiers." This copy, the only one in existence, was made for Mr. Robertson by J. Barnard Davis, London, Eng., November, 1913. Size 9 x 12. Half length.

2129—DEATH OF WOLFE—"To the King's Most Excellent Majesty, this plate, The Death of General Wolfe, is with his gracious permission humbly dedicated by his Majesty's most dutiful subject and servant, William Woollett, from the original picture in the collection of Lord Grosvenor. Painted by B. West, Historical Painter to His Majesty. Engraved by Wm. Woollett, Engraver to His Majesty. Published as the Act directs, January 1st, 1776, by Messrs. Woollett, Boydell & Ryland, London." The central figure represents General Wolfe, while immediately to his right is Surgeon Adair, who joined the 53rd Regiment in 1756. To the left, by the side of the General, are Capt. Hervey Smyth, his A.D.C., and Col. Isaac Barre, adjutant-general in the campaign of 1759. Looking down upon the group are Col. Williamson, in command of the artillery at Quebec, 1759, and Hon. Arthur Browne. The first figure in the row to left of picture has not been identified. Next in order are the Master of Lovat, Lieut.-Col. (General) Simon Fraser, of the Fraser Highlanders; General Robert Monckton, second in command in Wolfe's expedition against Quebec; and Capt. Hugh Debbieg (afterward General), engineer in Newfoundland, 1765. Under the person unidentified is Lieut.-Col. Howe (Sir William), in command of the 58th. To the extreme right are the servant of General Wolfe and a grenadier of his regiment. Note—West's picture is absolutely valueless as a historical representation. The greater number of the men depicted were in different parts of the field at the time of Wolfe's death, and some were not even at Quebec. Line engraving. Size 17 x 23.

2130—DESIGN FOR MONUMENT OF GENERAL WOLFE, 1760 —A Caricature—It is entitled "The Vanity of Human Glory" and was intended as a satire on Lord George Sackville (Germain) contrasting the conduct of Wolfe at Quebec, 13th Sept., 1759, with that of Lord Sackville at Minden, 1st Aug., 1759. There the English and German forces, under Duke Ferdinand of Brunswick, defeated the French. Blunders were committed and it is said Sackville disobeyed orders. For that reason he was censured and dismissed from the army. He was a great friend and patron of Wolfe. Etching. Size 9 x 13.

2131—SHORT SWORD OR HANGER OF MAJOR-GENERAL JAMES WOLFE—Worn by him when he fell at Quebec, 13th September, 1759. It was given by his mother to his school fellow and lifelong friend, General the Hon. George Warde, Colonel of the 4th Dragoon Guards. It bears the inscription: "Heinrich Koll me fecit, Heinrich Koll Solingen." Above the sword is a leaden ball found on the spot where Wolfe received his mortal wound. Photograph, colored, from original in Royal United Service Museum, Whitehall, London, England. Size 7 x 12.

2132—WOLFE, MAJOR-GENERAL JAMES—Victorious at Quebec, 13th Sept., 1759—Born at Westerham, Eng., 1727; entered military service at an early age. Served with distinction in Germany during the early part of Seven Years' War. Joined Boscawen and Amherst in reduction of Louisburg in 1758, and the following year was entrusted with expedition against Quebec. He died in the moment of victory, and Montcalm's death took place the following day. From an oil (No. 48) by J. S. C. Schaak, in the National Portrait Gallery, London, Eng. Size 7 x 10. Head and shoulders.

2133—WOLFE, MAJOR-GENERAL JAMES—From a portrait drawn by William, Duke of Devonshire, K.G., in the National Portrait Gallery (No. 688), London, Eng. Size 7 x 10. Head and shoulders.

2134—WOLFE, MAJOR-GENERAL JAMES, SHORTLY BEFORE HIS DEATH AT QUEBEC—Facsimile tracing of a sketch taken at Quebec by Capt. Hervey Smyth, of the 15th Foot, from original sketch preserved in library of the Royal United Service Museum, Whitehall, London, Eng. This tracing was presented to the National Portrait Gallery, London, in 1884, by the Hon. Harold Dillon, F.S.A. Size 5 x 7. Head in profile.

2135—ROOM WHERE JAMES WOLFE WAS BORN—The Vicarage, Westerham, Kent, 2nd January, 1727—According to our reformed calendar the date 2nd January, 1727, was Christmas Eve, 1726. Water color. Size 6 x 8.

2136—STATUE OF GENERAL WOLFE—Erected on the Green, Westerham, Eng.—The following is inscribed on the pedestal: "Maj.-Gen. James Wolfe, born at Westerham, Jan. the 2nd, 1727, died at the Battle of Quebec, the 13th September, 1759." Photograph, colored. Size 5 x 6.

2137—PARISH CHURCH OF ST. MARY, WESTERHAM, ENG.— Where James Wolfe was baptized, 11th January, 1727. Photograph, colored. Size 4 x 6.

2138—WOLFE, MAJOR-GENERAL—Shortly before his death at Quebec—A replica of the sketch by Capt. Hervey Smyth, of the 15th Foot. It passed through the hands of Col. Gwillim, one of Wolfe's majors of brigade at Quebec, and others, to Major-General Darling, who presented the sketch to His Grace Hugh Percy, Duke of Northumberland, in January, 1832. From original in Royal United Service Museum, Whitehall, London, Eng. Size 9 x 12. Head and shoulders.

2139—"HALIFAX, N.S., FROM EASTERN PASSAGE—Drawn by Wm. Eagar, Halifax. Engd. by J. Gellatly, Edinr." The view is looking westward from near Fort Clarence on the Dartmouth shore. 1. Halifax Harbor; 2. Northern end George's Island; 3. Present St. Mary's Cathedral; 4. Citadel; 5. Town clock, erected 1802; 6. St. Paul's Anglican Church, erected, 1750; 7. Old St. Matthew's Presbyterian Church, erected 1751, destroyed by fire 1857; 8. Old Military Hospital, the site of which is occupied by the Glacis Barracks; 9. St. George's Anglican Church; 10. Admiralty House; 11. Fort Needham, where earthwork redoubt was erected during the Revolutionary War. Engraving, printed in color. Size 7 x 10.

2140—THE WESTERN CLIFFS OF CAPE DORE—(From the Atlantic Neptune). Cape Dore, N.S., given on ancient maps as Cap Dore, is situated near Advocate Harbor. It is an immense rocky peninsula, five hundred feet high, and almost cut off from the mainland by a deep ravine, in the bottom of which the salt tides flow. It received its name from the deposits of copper ore found there by early French explorers. These deposits are, however, not great enough to be profitably worked. Xylograph in color. Size 5 x 18.

2141—"THE ISLE HAUTE—Bearing W.N.W. distant 2 miles"—(From the Atlantic Neptune).—Isle Haute, also known as Hare Island, in the Bay of Fundy, eight miles south-west of Cape Chignecto, is a lofty, lonely rock, three hundred and fifty feet in height. Xylograph in color. Size 5 x 9. See 2145.

2142—"CAPE BLOWMEDOWN—Open with Cape Split, bearing E.N.E. 1 league distant"—(From the Atlantic Neptune).—Cape Blomidon (Blowmedown) is a lofty and striking promontory of red sandstone, about five hundred and seventy feet in height, and bearing strong marks of volcanic action. To the west of it lies the headland of Cape Split, extending into the Bay of Fundy, twisted into its present position, says the Micmac legend, by the demi-god, Glooscap, whose favorite haunt was the Basin of Minas. Xylograph in color. Size 5 x 9. See 1761.

2143—"VIEW OF DIGBY, NOVA SCOTIA—M. G. Hall, delt. Pendleton's Lithography, Boston." The Township of Digby was originally formed out of an extensive tract of land granted to a party of U.E. Loyalists in 1783. The town is situated on the slope of a hill on the south-west shore of the Annapolis Basin, of which it commands a beautiful view. Lithograph in color. Size 6 x 9. See 38.

2144—"WRECKERS' DEN, NEAR THE POND, ON THE ISLE OF SABLE"—(From the Atlantic Neptune)—This scene depicts a condition that existed prior to Confederation. After the Dominion Government assumed authority in 1867 the day of the wreckers was past. These men for years were found on different parts of the shore, looking for wreckage and ready to loot anything within their reach. The animals shown are wild horses, which are native to the island. Sable Island is in the Atlantic Ocean, about 110 miles south-east of Cape Canso. It is a barren expanse of sand, and since first sighted by Cabot in 1497 has been an object of terror to mariners. The island is now manned by lighthouses, foghorns and a life-saving station. Xylograph in color. Size 16 x 24. See 2167.

2145—"THE ISLE HAUTE—Bearing N.b.W. distant 4 miles; and Cape Chignecto, N.N.E. 3 leagues"—(From the Atlantic Neptune). To the left of the picture is seen Isle Haute, a rocky island, one and a half miles long and three hundred and fifty feet in height. To the right, at the head of the Bay of Fundy, is Cape Chignecto, a rocky headland running down sheer into deep water. Xylograph in color. Size 5 x 20. See 2141.

2146—HALIFAX, FROM DAVIS' MILL—On the Dartmouth shore, about a mile north-west of the town of Dartmouth—This view shows many points of interest in Halifax in the early days. 1, Halifax harbor. 2, George's Island (with Fort Charlotte). 3, McNab's Island. 4, Mouth of harbor. 5, The Citadel. 6, St. Matthew's Church. 7, St. Paul's Church. 8, St. George's (Round) Church. 9, Military Hospital, formerly town residence of Edward. Duke of Kent. 10, H. M. naval yard. 11, Commissioner's house. 12, Shears for taking out and replacing ships' masts. 13, North barracks. 14, Fort Needham. Aquatint and water color by G. I. Parkyns, 1801. Size 12 x 21.

2147—COWIE'S HILL, NEAR HALIFAX, N. S.—Looking in a north-easterly direction at Melville Island Cove—The western slope of the city, 350 feet high, and rising from the shore of Melville Island Cove, is here shown from Cowie's Hill, just on the west side of the north-west arm. 1, The Citadel. 2. Jubilee Road. 3, North-west Arm (near the head). 4, Melville Island Cove. 5, Melville Island. 6, Governor's (of prison) house, still (1917) in existence. 7, Military prison (still standing); French prisoners of war were kept here about the end of the eighteenth century, and American prisoners of war during the War of 1812. 8. Dead Man's Island. 9, Road from Halifax to Springfield. Aquatint and water color by G. I. Parkyns, 1801. Size 12 x 21.

2148—HALIFAX N. S., FROM GEORGE'S ISLAND—Looking north-west from semi-circular battery—1, Semi-circular battery at the north end of George's Island (part of Fort Charlotte). 2, Halifax Harbor. 3, The Citadel. 4, Grand Battery at H.M. lumber yard. 5, "Belle Vue," still the official residence of the commander-in-chief. 6, Government House, the corner-stone of which was laid September, 1800. 7, St. Mary's Chapel. 8, Military Hospital. 9, St. Paul's Church. 10, St. Matthew's Church, burned in 1857. 11, St. George's (Round) Church. 12, Dartmouth. Aquatint and water color by G. Isham Parkyns, 1801. Size 12 x 21.

2149—HALIFAX, N.S., FROM FORT NEEDHAM—Above Richmond, looking south-east—1, Earthen ramparts and ditch of Fort Needham, 235 feet high (now in ruins), erected to defend the naval yard from landward attack. 2, The Citadel. 3, Military hospital, now (1917) site of Glacis barracks. 4, St. George's (Round) Church, built under auspices of Duke of Kent. 5, H. M. naval yard. 6, Residence of Commissioner of H. M. naval yard (razed a few years ago). 7, Shears for taking out and replacing ships' masts. 8, Dartmouth. 9, Fort Clarence. 10, Halifax harbor. 11, George's Island. 12, Eastern passage. 13, McNab's Island. 14, Mouth of Halifax harbor. 15, Sandwich Point, near York Redoubt. Aquatint and water color by G. Isham Parkyns, 1801. Size 12 x 21.

2150—"CHEBUCTO HEAD—Bearing North 6° east, distance 2 miles" —(From the Atlantic Neptune). Chebucto Head, or Chebuctou, a Micmac word, signifying "Chief Haven," is a bold, rocky headland, upon which is a light visible for miles, at the eastern entrance to Halifax Harbor. Devil's Island, at the eastern entrance, also has a lighthouse. Xylograph in color. Size 4 x 26.

2151—"SAMBRO LIGHTHOUSE—South-east distant 1 mile"—(From the Atlantic Neptune). Cape Sambro is an island on the south-east coast of Nova Scotia, near Halifax. In 1606 it was named Sesambre by Champlain, from a small island near St. Malo, France. The island is still (1917) equipped with a lighthouse. Xylograph in color. Size 4 x 12. See 2157.

2152—"HALIFAX, N.S., FROM FORT NEEDHAM—Drawn by Wm. Eagar, Halifax. Engraved by J. Gellatly, Edinr." The view, looking in a south-easterly direction towards George's Island, from the eastern slope of Fort Needham, shows: 1, Black Rock Point at Dartmouth. 2, The south-eastern passage. 3, McNab's Island. 4, H.M. Naval Yard. 5, Halifax Harbor. 6, George's Island, with Fort Charlotte. 7, St. George's Church, somewhat misplaced for pictorial effect. 8, The Citadel. 9, Eastern slope of Fort Needham. Engraving, printed in color. Size 7 x 10.

2153—"VIEW OF THE CLIFFS OF TRAP ROCK, AT THE ENTRANCE OF ANNAPOLIS BASIN—(From the Atlantic Neptune). Pendleton's Lithogy., Boston." Annapolis Basin, N.S., gradually decreases in width from nearly five miles to one mile, and is hemmed in between ridges of the North and South Mountains. The North Mountain, composed of trap rock resting upon sandstone, is bold in its outline, and has a height of almost seven hundred feet. Lithograph in color. Size 5 x 16.

2154—"CORNWALLIS, GRAND PRIARE AND BASIN OF MINAS FROM NORTH MOUNTAIN—Drawn by Wm. Eagar, Halifax. Eng'd. by J. Gellatly, Edinr." View in vicinity of the Deep Hollow road, looking in an east, south-easterly direction. 1, Southern escarpment, North Mountain. 2, Cheverie. 3, Minas Basin and Avon River Estuary. 4, Boot Island (extremity of Grand Pre). 5, Kingsport. 6, Oak Island. 7, Mouth of Gaspereau River. 8, Cornwallis River. 9, Grand Pre, from which Acadian French were deported in 1756. 10, Starr's Point. 11, Road to Scott's Bay. 12, Habitant River. 13, Canning. Engraving, printed in color. Size 7 x 10.

2155—HALIFAX, N.S.—Looking down the harbor from the Citadel, September, 1849—Water color by Gen. A. R. V. Crease, R.E. Size 7 x 10. See 2156.

2156—HALIFAX—Looking up the harbor from Citadel, 1849—Halifax was founded by Hon. Edward Cornwallis in 1749. It lies along the shores of one of the finest harbors on the Atlantic coast, called by the Indians Chebucto, but re-named in honor of the Earl of Halifax. The Citadel, from which the artist made his water color, is high above the sea level, and covers the summit of the hill upon which Halifax slopes. The fortifications on Citadel Hill are said to date back to 1794. Water color by Gen. A. R. V. Crease, R.E., who in 1849 was stationed at Halifax. Size 7 x 10. See 2155.

2157—"SAMBRO LIGHTHOUSE—Bearing west 1½ miles distant"— (From the Atlantic Neptune). Xylograph. Size 3 x 22. See 2151.

2158—"ANNAPOLIS ROYAL, N.S.—Published by J. F. W. Des Barres, Esq., as the Act directs, Jan. 1st, 1781." Port Royal, as it was formerly called, received its new name in June, 1713, in honor of Queen Anne. About the time the picture was made the population of the place numbered 120, comprising eighteen families. A large part of the Maritime Provinces was surveyed by Des Barres, founder of Sydney, C.B. (Nova Scotia), and many of the best maps of the period were made by him. Xylograph in color. Size 15 x 22. See 1734.

2159—IN DOCKYARD, AT HALIFAX, N.S., 1850—The frigate "hove down," or careened, is an example of the process of repairing vessels in the early days. Water color. Size 4 x 7.

2160—HISTORIC WILLOW TREES—King's College Road, near Windsor, N.S.—These fine old trees, about three-quarters of a mile from the present town of Windsor, were planted by the French, who settled in the vicinity about the middle of the 17th century. The ancient name of Windsor was Piziquid, "The Junction of the Waters." Water color by W. G. R. Hind, 1880. Size 9 x 12.

2161—HALIFAX MEMORIAL TOWER—Erected to commemorate the gift of self-government to Nova Scotia—This tower stands on the western shore of the North-west Arm, adjacent to Halifax, in a park donated by Sir Sandford Fleming, and was erected under the auspices of the Canadian Club of Halifax. The corner-stone was laid 2nd October, 1908, the one hundred and fiftieth anniversary of the first meeting of the General Assembly in Nova Scotia, and formally opened and dedicated by H.R.H. the Duke of Connaught, 14th August, 1912. Water color. Size 5 x 7.

2162—HALIFAX HARBOR—(1) "A view from the south-eastward of Halifax Harbor. (a) The High-lands of Jeddore, bearing N.E. by E. 3 leagues distant." (2) "Appearance of the shore at three miles off, four or five leagues to the eastward of Halifax Harbor." (3) "A view taken 4 miles off shore, Halifax Harbor bearing north. (a) Sambro Lighthouse. (b) Halifax Harbor. (c) Rocky Bay." The approach to Halifax Harbor is between Chebucto Head and Devil's Island, which are seven and a half miles apart. The harbor proper, commencing at an imaginary line drawn from Sandwich Point to Maugher's Beach, opens from Chebucto Bay, and thence to the Narrows, gradually increasing in width from half a mile to one and a quarter miles; but at the entrance to Bedford Basin it decreases to a quarter of a mile. Jeddore is on the south-east coast of Nova Scotia, forty-two miles east-north-east of Halifax. Xylographs. Size (each) 3 x 26.

2163—"HALIFAX, NOVA SCOTIA—William Hickman, Esq., B.A., Del. Day and Son, Chromolithographers to the Queen. Published by John B. Strong, Bookseller and Librarian." The view is a comprehensive one of the city from the harbor. Lithograph in color. Size 12 x 24.

2164—"A VIEW OF CAPE BAPTISTE—In the entrance into the Bason of Mines, bearing W. b N. 2 Miles distant—(From the Atlantic Neptune). Pendleton's Lithogy., Boston." It was known in the early part of the eighteenth century as Cape St. Patrick, but from 1775 as Cape Sharp. It lies at the northern entrance to the Basin of Minas, and is almost opposite Cape Blomidon, the passage between them being about three miles wide. Xylograph in color. Size 7 x 15.

2165—"A VIEW OF THE ENTRANCE INTO THE BASON OF MINES bearing east distant 4 leagues."—The Basin or Bay of Minas (Mines) is an eastern arm of the Bay of Fundy, N.S., penetrating sixty miles inland. Its shores, which are most imposing, are lined with bluffs, and the tides rush here with great impetuosity. Xylograph in color. Size 3 x 15.

2166—HAMMOND, SIR ANDREW SNAPE—Governor of Nova Scotia and Commander-in-Chief, Halifax, 1780-83—Entered the navy in 1753, and in 1775 appointed to the "Roebuck." Served on the North American station under Lord Shuldham, and under Lord Howe, especially in the expedition to the Chesapeake in 1777, and in the defence of Sandy Hook, 1778. Also served under Vice-Admiral Arbuthnot, who hoisted his flag on board the "Roebuck" at the reduction of Charlestown, April, 1780, after which Hammond was sent home with despatches. Towards the end of the same year he was sent out as Governor of Nova Scotia and Commander-in-Chief at Halifax, where he remained until the conclusion of the war. During the Spanish armament, in 1790, Hammond commanded the "Vanguard," and three years later was appointed a commissioner of the navy; deputy-comptroller, 1794. Mezzotint. Size 9 x 10. Half length.

2167—"A VIEW FROM THE CAMP AT THE EAST END OF THE NAKED SAND HILLS—On the south-east shore of the Isle of Sable"—Sable Island, a small island in the Atlantic, is about 110 miles south-east of Cape Canso. It is a barren expanse of sand, constantly swept by storms, under whose powerful pressure the whole aspect of the land changes by the shifting of the low dunes Since it was first sighted by Cabot, in 1797, it has been feared by mariners; hundreds of vessels have met their doom on its shores; but two lighthouses, fog horns and a life-saving station now mitigate the terrors of the spot. By some Sable Island is supposed to be the "Markland" on which Leif Ericson landed in 994. Xylograph in color. Size 16 x 24. See 2144.

2168—FISHING WHARVES, FALKLAND, N. S.—The artist has here depicted some of the old fishing jetties or wharves at Falkland village, Ferguson's Cove, on the west side of the entrance to Halifax Harbor, just to the north of the York Redoubt. The hill in background is between Falkland and Purcell's Cove. Etching by F. Leo Hunter, Ossining, N.Y. Size 13 x 22.

2169—ENTRANCE TO HALIFAX HARBOR—From hill near "The Brae," First Dartmouth Lake—The view, looking south 10 degrees east, was made in 1838, and shows: 1, Dartmouth; 2, Dartmouth Cove; 3, Eastern passage; 4, Fort Clarence, which guards the eastern passage; 5, Ives' Point; 6, George's Island; 7, Halifax Harbor; 8, Halifax; 9, McNab's Island; 10, Entrance to Halifax Harbor; 11, Sandwich Point; 12, Point Pleasant; 13, Chebucto Head; 14, York Redoubt. Drawn from nature and on stone by Wm. Eagar. Size 7 x 10.

2170—PICTOU, N.S.—From Fort Hill—This view shows the town of Pictou, looking west-south-west from Fort Hill, which is at the eastern end of the town. No. 1 is Pictou (from Piktook, an Indian word meaning "Bubbling" or "Gas-exploding"); 2, Pictou Harbor; 3, Norway Point of recent maps, probably the "Mortimer's Point," from which another of Mr. Eagar's views of Pictou was taken. Drawn from nature on stone by William Eagar. Size 7 x 10. See 2181.

2171—HALIFAX, N.S., 1838—From McNab's Island—View looking north-west from at or near the old McNab house, near Ives' Point. The following is a key to the picture: 1, Ives' Point, McNab's Island; 2, Halifax Harbor; 3, Halifax, along the shore of the harbor; 4, The Citadel; 5, George's Island; 6, The Narrows, with Bedford Basin beyond; 7, Dartmouth, opposite the city of Halifax; 8, Fort Clarence on the Dartmouth shore; 9, Eastern passage, a narrow strait between McNab's Island and the mainland. Drawn from nature and on stone by William Eagar. Size 7 x 10.

2172—RUINS OF THE DUKE OF KENT'S LODGE—Looking west from the Windsor road—Situated on the western shore of Bedford Basin, some six or seven miles from Halifax. It was built as a summer home by Prince Edward, later Duke of Kent, during his residence at Halifax, on property belonging to Governor Sir John Wentworth. The lodge has long since disappeared, but the rotunda, or band-house, on the east side of the roads still stands. Drawn from nature and on stone by W. Eagar. Size 7 x 10.

2173—VIEW FROM THE HORTON MOUNTAINS—Looking over Grand Pre diked lands, Nova Scotia, 1838—This view of the Land of Evangeline was doubtless taken from the hill to the south of Grand Pre (King's County) formerly part of the Horton Mountains, towards Cape Blomidon: 1, The Grand Pre diked lands; 2, Cornwallis River; 3, Kingsport; 4, Cape Blomidon; 5, North Mountain; 6, Minas Basin; 7, Parrsboro shore. Drawn from nature and on stone by W. Eagar. Size 7 x 10.

2174—"HALIFAX FROM THE RED MILL, DARTMOUTH—Drawn from nature and on stone by Wm. Eagar. T. Moore's Lithogy., Boston." With key. The Red Mill, a grist mill, was on slightly elevated ground, a short distance north-westward of what was formerly Davis' Mill. Both were about a mile n.w. of Dartmouth. Size 6 x 10.

2175—"NOVA SCOTIA ILLUSTRATED IN A SERIES OF VIEWS— Taken on the spot and on stone by William Eagar. Published at Halifax for the proprietor by C. H. Belcher, Hollis St. Entered at Stationers' Hall. T. Moore's Lithogy., Boston." These views were drawn by William Eagar, an Irishman who went to Newfoundland in the early thirties, arriving at Halifax in 1834. In December, 1837, he advertised that he would publish, in numbers a series of landscape illustrations of British North America in two volumes, Nova Scotia and New Brunswick, after his own drawings. These were never completed, as he died at Halifax, 24th Nov., 1839.

2176—OLD BLOCKHOUSE OF FORT GEORGE, 1755—On what is now Citadel Hill, Halifax, N.S.—The original defence of Halifax, which was settled in 1749, consisted of five forts, with palisades connecting them. By this means the little settlement was completely surrounded. The central fort, known as Fort George, contained the blockhouse shown in the picture. It was demolished when new fortifications were begun there subsequent to 1762. These new fortifications also had a large blockhouse, entirely different, however, to this one. About 1765, when the five-acre lots were laid out on the outskirts of the original town, three blockhouses, the same as Fort George, were executed on a line extending from Bedford Basin to the head of the North-west Arm. The lines of the old palisaded forts are roughly indicated by Salter, Barrington and Jacob streets, Halifax. Water color. Size 5 x 6.

2177—"PICTOU FROM THE ROAD TO HALIFAX—Drawn from nature and on stone by Wm. Eagar." The view looks north-eastward from across Pictou Harbor, and shows the town of Pictou (1). Size 7 x 11.

2178—WINDSOR,N.S., FROM FORT HILL, 1838—View looking south-west from the blockhouse at Fort Edward, and showing: 1, Blockhouse on Fort Edward. This blockhouse, erected about 1749, is still (1917) standing and is the last surviving in Nova Scotia. 2, Town of Windsor; 3, Avon River; 4, Old Avon bridge, replaced by an iron bridge; 5, "Clifton," the residence of Judge Thomas Chandler Haliburton ("Sam Slick"); 6, Falmouth. Windsor lies on a point between the Avon and the St. Croix, which unite in a wide estuary below the town. Drawn from nature and on stone by Wm. Eagar. Size 7 x 10.

2179—HALIFAX, N.S.,—Old Wharf—The building with the sign over the door stood between the wharf of F. D. Corbett and that of the late Capt. John Taylor Wood, commander of the Confederate cruiser "Tallahasse." John Flemming, whose name is on the sign, started business here many year ago. His old place on the wharf has been demolished. Capt. Wood was agent for the ill-fated Cromwell line of steamers running between New York and Newfoundland. Two were lost in succession; they sailed from Halifax and were never heard of again. Corbett's Wharf is owned by G. S. Campbell & Co., agents for the Red Cross line of steamers plying between New York and Newfoundland. Etching by Leo Hunter, Ossining, N.Y., 1888. Size 15 x 22.

2180—OLD STREET SCENE, HALIFAX, N.S.—In the winter of 1888— View looking south-east—It is impossible to determine the exact locality of this picture, as the artist has exercised great artistic freedom with the view. Looking at it generally it appears to be from some of the hill streets leading westward from Lower Water street, which borders the harbor front. The land in the distance to the right is probably McNab's Island, with Mauger's Beach and Mauger's Beach lighthouse. The water is Halifax harbor. From a topographical standpoint, however, the drawing is not accurate. Etching by F. Leo Hunter, Ossining, N.Y. Size 13 x 21.

2181—**PICTOU, 1838**—View looking southward from Mortimer's Point —Pictou Harbor and the town are shown in the distance. Mortimer's Point is doubtless what is now known as Norway Point. This view is about in the opposite direction to that of "Pictou from Fort Hill." Drawn from nature and on stone by William Eagar. Size 7 x 10. See 2170.

2182—**HALIFAX, N.S.**—View on the North-west Arm—A narrow inlet on the west side of the city—The view shows the head of the Arm and looks west, probably from the late Sir Sandford Fleming's place, west of Oxford street, Halifax. 1, North-west Arm; 2, Deadman's Island; 3, Melville Island, with prison governor's house (small building), and military prison (larger building); 4, Hosterman's grist mill, since burnt; 5, Extreme head of Arm; 6, Geizer's Hill; 7, Western suburbs of Halifax. Drawn from nature and on stone by Wm. Eagar. Size 7 x 10.

2183—**BEDFORD BASIN, 1838**—View from the hills at Roach's Cove, near Bedford, looking south-east, directly opposite to the point of view of "View of Halifax from McNab's Island." 1, Bedford Basin; 2, Halifax; 3, The Dartmouth shore; 4, Halifax harbor; 5, George's Island and McNab's Island; 6, The Narrows. Drawn from nature and on stone by Wm. Eagar. Size 7 x 10.

2184—**VIEW FROM RETREAT FARM, WINDSOR, N.S., 1838**—Looking towards the north-west—Retreat Farm is about a mile east of Windsor, on the Wentworth road, and belonged to Major Thomas King, a retired army officer, who occupied it as a summer home. The house still (1917) stands. 1, The Avon River, below Windsor; 2, St. Croix River, a tributary of the Avon; 3, The Falmouth shore; 4, Avondale (Newport Landing), beyond the mouth of the St. Croix River; 5, Cape Blomidon, a towering precipice of red sandstone; 6, Minas Basin. Drawn from nature and on stone by Wm. Eagar. Size 7 x 10.

2185—**THE OLD PARISH CHURCH, WINDSOR, N.S.**—"Parish of Christ Church"—A front view facing on King street, and showing the stone wall which had become dilapidated. In order to secure funds for "reverently preserving from desecration" the churchyard, Prof. Henry Youle Hind issued in pamphlet form "The Old Parish Burying Ground at Windsor," thus raising sufficient funds to enable the necessary repairs to be made. Drawing in color by Miss Susan Haliburton (Mrs. Weldon), daughter of Judge Haliburton ("Sam Slick"). Size 5 x 6. See 2191.

2186—**NEW GLASGOW, N.S., 1876**—View from the west side of Pictou River, showing: 1, East River of Pictou; 2, St. Andrew's Presbyterian Church; 3, St. James' Presbyterian Church; 4, Coal train of the General Mining Association running down to the loading ground (Abercrombie); 5, Fraser's Mountain. The boats on the river are evidence that the view was made during the great shipbuilding activities, which at one time promised to eclipse the steel and coal trade of Pictou County, N.S. Water color by William G. R. Hind. Size 5 x 11. See 2206.

2187—**"INDIAN OF THE MICMAC TRIBE**—Drawn from nature and on stone by R. Petley, Lieut. 50th Regt. Printed by C. Hullmandel, London. Published by J. Dickinson, 114 New Bond Street." The Micmacs were once an important Algonquin tribe, occupying portions of Nova Scotia, Cape Breton, Prince Edward Island, New Brunswick and Newfoundland. They early became staunch friends of the French and their hostility to the English for a long time prevented any serious attempts at establishing British settlements on the northern coast of Nova Scotia and the southern and eastern coasts of New Brunswick, after the Treaty of Utrecht, 1713, by which Acadia was ceded to England. The dwellings of the tribe were usually the ordinary conical wigwams covered with bark, skins or matting. By the French the Micmacs were called Souriquois, imitating words meaning "good canoe men." Lithograph in color. Size 7 x 8.

2188—**GUT, OR STRAIT OF CANSO**, 1876—A picturesque passage separating Nova Scotia and Cape Breton—The word "Canso" is derived, it is said, from the Indian "Camsoke," signifying "facing the frowning cliffs." For many years the strait, a deep, narrow channel, much used by sailing craft as a short cut between the Atlantic and the Gulf of St. Lawrence, was called Campseau or Canseau. In background, to left of picture, is shown Cape Porcupine, contracting the strait to its narrowest part, and in background, to right, is Plaster Cove, or Port Hastings, a seaport village with a good harbor and shipping facilities. Water color by William G. R. Hind. Size 10 x 13.

2189—**SCOTT'S CORNER AT THE DELTA OF KING AND GERRISH STS., WINDSOR, N.S.**—So called because it belonged to a family named Scott who settled in Windsor in the early days. In the great fire of 1897 the house was destroyed and never rebuilt. Drawing in color by Miss Susan Haliburton (Mrs. Weldon), daughter of Judge Haliburton ("Sam Slick"). Size 5 x 6.

2190—**"INTERIOR OF A WIGWAM**—Drawn from nature and on stone by R. Petley, Lieut. 50th Regt. Day and Haghe, Lithrs. to the King. London. Published by J. Dickinson, 114 New Bond street." The view shows squaws of the Micmac tribe in their camp home, 1837. Lithograph in color. Size 7 x 11.

2191—**OLD PARISH CHURCH, WINDSOR, N.S.**, 1788-1890—"Parish of Christ Church." Built during incumbency of Rev. William Ellis upon land given by Hon. Michael Francklin "for the purpose of erecting thereon a church or place of public worship conformable to the Established Church of England." It received its designation as "The Parish Church" when the "Parish of Christ Church" was established, 26th May, 1805. Right Rev. John Inglis, D.D., third Bishop of Nova Scotia, consecrated Christ Church and the burying ground on 5th Nov., 1826. The church was burned in 1890, but was not rebuilt. Pencil drawing by William G. R. Hind. 1870. Size 7 x 14. See 2185.

2192—**DETACHED MASSES OF TRAP ROCK, SOUTH-WEST EXTREMITY OF PARTRIDGE ISLAND, N.S.**—Partridge Island, so called, though connected with the shore by a beach, is about six miles north of Blomidon, N.S., separated from it by the outlet of the Basin of Minas, called "The Gut." Celebrated for minerals abounding there, and for beautiful scenery. It is supposed to have derived its name from numerous broods of partridges, said to have frequented the place. The island itself presents a high cliff to the bay and slopes downward on the land side. On the west side the basaltic trap forms many cliffs, and at the south-east extremity there are small detached and grotesque rocks, beautifully crowned with low evergreens. Water color. Size 4 x 6.

2193—**CORNWALLIS, HON. (LIEUT.-GENERAL) EDWARD**, 1713-76 —Founder of Halifax, N.S.—He was born in London, Eng., sixth son of Charles, fourth Baron Cornwallis, and was twin brother of Frederick Cornwallis, who in 1768 became Archbishop of Canterbury. In 1731 was gazetted ensign in 47th Foot, made lieutenant three years later, and in 1737 transferred to the 20th Foot, of which he subsequently became major. Cornwallis joined his regiment in Flanders, fought at Fontenoy, and later was stationed at Edinburgh and Stirling. He resigned his command in the 20th Regiment, 1748, Wolfe succeeding him. He left England in May, 1749, as Governor and Captain-General of Nova Scotia, arriving at Chebucto (Halifax), 21st June. In the foundation of the colony he showed executive ability, tact and energy, and was ably assisted by his aides, Bulkeley and Gates. While resident in Halifax, Governor Cornwallis was W.M. of the Masonic Lodge there, the first meeting of which was held 19th July, 1750. He returned to London in 1752. Received rank as lieut.-gen., 1760, and col. of 24th Foot; in 1762 went to Gibraltar as Governor and Commander-in-Chief. Water color from photo said to be of an original oil at one time in Gibraltar, the existence of which has not been proven. The water color is, however, not unlike an oil of Cornwallis in London, Eng. Size 3 x 4. Head and shoulders.

2194—BRIDGE OVER THE AVON, WINDSOR, N. S., 1876—It was built by John Cameron, demolished in 1882, and replaced by an iron road bridge. About a hundred feet to the left of this iron bridge a railway bridge was erected by the Western Counties Railway, and is now (1917) owned by the C.P.R. To the left of picture Windsor is shown, and Falmouth to the right. Drawing in color by Miss Susan Haliburton (Mrs. Weldon), daughter of Judge Haliburton ("Sam Slick"). Size 5 x 6.

2195—"VIEW OF HALIFAX FROM DARTMOUTH COVE—On stone by L. Haghe. Day & Haghe, Lithrs. to the King, 17 Gate street, Linc. Inn Fds." Halifax and the town of Dartmouth, which was formed in 1750, are connected by ferry and railway. In the background is Citadel Hill, upon whose slopes the city of Halifax is built. Immediately opposite is Dartmouth Cove, near which is situated the town and chain of lakes of that name. Lithograph in color. Size 6 x 8.

2196—"ROCKING STONE, NEAR HALIFAX—Charpentier, printer, Portsmouth. Drawn on stone by R. Petley, Rifle Brigade, 1836." On the margin of Rockingstone (Kidston's) Lake, near Halifax—It is on property which at one time belonged to Colonel Spry, who commanded the Royal Engineers in Nova Scotia in the eighteenth century. The stone is a granite boulder and can be rocked by means of a wooden lever, although in the early days it could be rocked by force from the shoulder alone. Lithograph. Size 7 x 10.

2197—"VIEW OF THE COBAQUID MOUNTAINS—Drawn from nature and on stone by R. Petley, Lieut. 50th Regt. Printed by C. Hullmandel. Published by J. Dickinson, New Bond street." The succession of rounded hills, varying in height from four hundred to one thousand feet, runs almost due east and west from Truro and extends for about one hundred miles. Tall and luxuriant forests of beech and sugar maple picturesquely clothe the range. From Truro a road runs west between the Mountains and the Basin of Minas. Lithograph. Size 7 x 11.

2198—"WINDSOR, N.S.—From the Barracks—Drawn from nature and on stone by R. Petley, Lieut. 50th Regt. Printed by C. Hullmandel. London. Published by J. Dickinson, New Bond street." View looking s.w. from the blockhouse at Fort Edward. Windsor lies on a point between the Avon and the St. Croix, which unite in a wide estuary below the town. 1. Blockhouse on Fort Edward, erected about 1754, and still (1917) standing. 2. Town of Windsor. 3. Avon River. 4. "Clifton," the residence of Judge Thomas Chandler Haliburton ("Sam Slick"). 5. Falmouth. Lithograph. Size 7 x 10.

2199—CHURCH OF SAINT PAUL AND THE PARADE, HALIFAX, N.S.—"To the Right Honourable George Dunk, Earl of Halifax, His Majesty's Principal Secretary of State, etc., etc., etc., this plate representing the Church of Saint Paul and the Parade at Halifax, in Nova Scotia, is most humbly inscribed by His Lordship's most devoted servant, R. Short. Serres, pinx. R. Short, delint. Jno. Fougeron, sculp. Published Ap. 25th, 1777, by John Boydell, engraver in Cheapside, London. (1) St. Paul's Church, built 1750. (2) Jno. Bushell's Printing House. (3) Old Artillery Barracks. (4) Parade. (5) Barrington St. (6) Argyle St. (7) Prince St." Line engraving. Size 13 x 20.

2200—"A NIGHT ENCAMPMENT—Moose Hunting—Drawn from nature and on stone by R. Petley, Lieut., 50th Regt. Printed by C. Hull-mandel." The picture shows a hunting party of Micmacs preparing their evening meal in the woods of New Brunswick. Lithograph, colored. Size 7 x 10.

2201—SQUAWS OF THE MICMAC TRIBE, 1837—A nomad branch of the Algonquins—It was customary for the women to do manual work while the men followed the hunt and defended the tribe. In some tribes the women had a share in political matters, and it is noteworthy that among the Six Nations, if not others, a hereditary chieftainship rests with the senior woman of the deceased chief's family. The Micmacs are scattered throughout the Maritime Provinces. Drawn from nature and on stone by R. Petley, Lieut., 50th Regiment. Day & Haghe, Lithrs. to the King, London. Published by J. Dickinson, New Bond street. Lithograph in color. Size 6 x 9.

2202—"THE RETREAT," WINDSOR, N. S., 1876—Situated on Went-worth Road—It was a plain farm house owned by a Mr. Church, who sold it to Major King, a retired army officer. The latter for a time used it as a summer home, and subsequently transformed the dwelling into a hand-some residence. Again "The Retreat" underwent changes in the removal of wings and bow windows, and to-day only the original house is left. Drawing in color by Miss Susan Haliburton (Mrs. Weldon) daughter of Judge Haliburton ("Sam Slick"). Size 5 x 6.

2203—"HALIFAX, NOVA SCOTIA, FROM DARTMOUTH POINT—G. I. Parkyns, Esqr., delt., et sculpt. London. Published, June 1, 1817." View of the city's water front, showing to the left George's Island, with Martello tower and entrance to harbor. Towards the right, in the background, is seen Citadel Hill. Dartmouth lies opposite Halifax, on the harbor. This view is by the same artist as the four large pictures of Halifax (Nos. 2146-9 in the collection. Engraving in aquatint. Size 5 x 8.

2204—"STREAM NEAR THE GRAND SCHUBINACADIE LAKE—Drawn from nature and on stone by R. Petley, Lieut., 50th Regt. Printed by C. Hullmandel, London. Published by J. Dickinson, New Bond street." The artist was in error in giving the name Schubenacadie to his view, which shows a picturesque spot on the Grand Lake, about twenty-five miles north of Halifax, and which forms the chief volume of the waters of the Schubenacadie River. The date of the view is 1837. Lithograph. Size 8 x 9.

2205—"BEDFORD BASIN—From near the Three Mile House—Drawn from nature and on stone by R. Petley, Lieut. 50th Regt. Day & Haghe, Lithrs. to the King." Bedford Basin is a lake-like expansion of Halifax Harbor. On its south shore and on the Windsor road from Halifax to Bed-ford, stood the Three-Mile House, on old inn, removed in 1913 to make room for the new railway approach to Halifax. This view was made in 1837. Lithograph. Size 7 x 10.

2206—NEW GLASGOW, N. S., 1876—View from Norman McKay's Hill —The town of New Glasgow is situated on the East River, near its entrance into Pictou Harbor, and occupies both sides of the river. The picture shows: 1. St. Andrew's Presbyterian Church, behind which the view is taken. 2. Trestle bridge on the Albion Mines Railway. 3. The Old Middle River Road. 4. Carriage Road to Stellarton and Westville on the East and Middle Rivers, respectively. They are now (1917) connected by an electric railway. 5. Site of the Aberdeen Hospital. In 1893 the first steel steamer of Nova Scotia was constructed and equipped at New Glasgow. Water color by William Hind. Size 5 x 11. See 2186.

2207—RED HEAD MOUNTAIN, CAPE BRETON, 1872—From the hill behind the village of Baddeck—This view looks almost due east over

Baddeck Bay, showing on the right Kidston's Island, and between that and the shore line in the foreground, Baddeck Harbor. Beyond Kidston's Island is the Little Bras d'Or Lake (Arm of Gold). Practically the entire background is taken up by the estate of Prof. Alexander Graham Bell, of telephone and air machine fame. It is a cape of which Red Head is the point, so called from being made up of red conglomerate and sandstone. Water color by William G. R. Hind. Size 8 x 14.

2208—"VIEW OF HALIFAX—From the Indian encampment at Dartmouth—Drawn from nature and on stone by R. Petley, Lieut. 50th Regt. Day and Haghe, Lithrs. to the King." Halifax, the capital of Nova Scotia, occupies a commanding position on the south-east coast of the province, on one of the finest harbors of the Atlantic coast. It was founded in 1749 by Hon. Edward Cornwallis, Governor of Nova Scotia. In 1905-6 the military command of the city was taken over by the Dominion Government. Halifax is also the chief winter harbor of Canada. This picture was made in 1837. Lithograph. Size 9 x 12.

2209—"NEW GOVERNMENT HOUSE, FREDERICKTON, N.B.—Drawn by a Lady. On stone by L. Haghe. Day and Haghe, Lithrs. to the King, 17 Gate St., Lincoln's Inn Fields." Shortly after Fredericton became the capital of New Brunswick in 1787, the Governor, Sir Thomas Carleton, purchased a large tract of land on the right bank of the River St. John, at the western end of the town, and erected thereon a large wooden residence, which was designated as "Government House." In 1816 it was purchased as a gubernatorial mansion by the Provincial Government, but some nine years later destroyed by fire. On its site Sir Howard Douglas, the then Lieut.-Governor, erected a handsome colonial mansion of stone, now known as "Old Government House." As a residence for the Chief Executive of the province it has been unused since the eighties, Sir Leonard Tilley having been the last occupant. Lithograph. Size 5 x 8.

2210—OLD WINDSOR TOLL BRIDGE, CROSSING THE AVON RIVER, N.S.—Built, 1834, by John Cameron, cousin of Col. Duncan Cameron, of the 79th Highlanders. It was burned in 1887, and with it the last toll bridge in the Province of Nova Scotia passed out. The Government in the same year built a carriage bridge to the north of the old bridge. About 1869 a railway bridge was constructed over the Avon by the Windsor-Annapolis Railway, subsequently the Dominion Atlantic and now the C.P.R. When the latter took over the control of the Dominion-Atlantic it was decided that a new railway bridge should be constructed over the Avon at Windsor, and in the summer of 1912 work was commenced under the superintendence of Mr. A. F. Kennedy, of the Nova Scotia Construction Company. On 27th Nov., 1914, the bridge was completed, and on 1st Feb., 1915, the first train went over it. To the left of picture is the Windsor shore, and in the background to the right is the Falmouth district. Water color. Size 5 x 7.

2211—HALIBURTON, JUDGE THOMAS CHANDLER (SAM SLICK)— "The Honourable Mr. Justice Haliburton, M.P., etc., Sam Slick, etc. The Drawing Room Portrait Gallery of Eminent Personages. Presented with the Illustrated News of the World. The London Joint-Stock Newspaper Company, Limited, 199 Strand and Regent Street, London. Engraved by D. J. Pound from a photograph by Mayall." The well-known author and humorist, son of Hon. W. H. O. Haliburton, Chief Justice Court of Common Pleas, Nova Scotia, was born at Windsor, N.S., in 1796, his ancestors having settled in Nova Scotia after the removal of the Acadians. He was educated at the Grammar School, Windsor, and the University of King's College, graduating with honors from the latter in 1815. Studied law and called to the bar in 1820. Practised his profession at Annapolis Royal, N.S., and on the death of his father in 1828, became Chief Justice of the Court of

25

Common Pleas of Nova Scotia, holding that position until the abolition of the court in 1841, when he was transferred to the Supreme Court of the province. He resigned in 1856 and removed to England, where he died in 1865, at Islesworth, near London. For some years politics engaged Haliburton's attention, he having become a member of the House of Assembly in 1826, and his ability and oratorical powers rapidly gave him a prominent position in the Legislature. Amongst his writings are a series of sketches known as "The Clockmaker, or Sayings and Doings of Samuel Slick, of Slickville." Line engraving. Size 7 x 8. Three-quarter length, sitting. See 2746.

2212—ST. MATTHEW'S CHAPEL OF EASE, WINDSOR, N.S.—Facing west on Grace street; erected on land given by Judge Haliburton, better known, perhaps, as "Sam Slick," historian and satirist. On the Christmas Eve of 1881 the chapel was partially destroyed by fire. It was decided not to repair the damaged building, but to erect a new and larger church, and the old structure was later sold to provide funds for a new one, known as the New Christ Church. Drawing in color by Miss Susan Haliburton (Mrs. Weldon), daughter of Judge Haliburton. Size 5 x 6.

2213—KING'S COLLEGE, WINDSOR, N.S.—The oldest existing college in Canada—It is a plain wooden building, with Ionic porticoes, and a chapel and library of stone, and stands on a hill overlooking the valley of the Avon. Building was commenced in 1790, occupied, 1797, and chartered by George III. in 1802, as a Church of England institution. The picture shows the building before the porticos were added. Drawing in color by Miss Susan Haliburton (Mrs. Weldon). Size 5 x 6.

2214-16, 2219, 2226 and 2228-30—The Series Comprises Eight "Sketches on the Nipisaguit, a river of New Brunswick, B. N. America, by William Hickman, B.A., Halifax, N.S. Published by John B. Strong, Bookseller and Librarian, London. Day & Son, Lithographers to the Queen, Gate Street, Lincoln's Inn Fields, 1860. To His Excellency the Right Honorable the Earl of Mulgrave, Lieutenant-Governor of Nova Scotia, etc., etc. This work is respectfully dedicated, by His Obedient Humble Servant, The Author."

2214—"THE TOWN OF BATHURST—W. Hickman, del. F. Jones. lith. Day and Son, Lithrs. to the Queen." The picture shows a fishing party's return to Bathurst in 1860, after a successful six weeks' trip on the Nepisiguit River. The four canoes are lashed together and gaily decorated. Bathurst, the capital of Gloucester Co., N.B., is on Bathurst Bay, which opens into Baie des Chaleurs. In the early days the basin was known to the Indians as Winkapiguwick, or Nepisiguit, meaning the "Foaming Waters." The district was an old battle ground of the Mohawks and Micmacs. It was settled in 1638 by Jean Jacques Enaud, a wealthy Basque, and his retainers. Mills were erected and an extensive fur trade established; but difficulties acrose between the French and Indians, and the latter at length destroyed the settlement. At different times colonies were begun on the harbor, only to be destroyed by the Indians or by American privateers. The present town was founded in 1818 by Sir Howard Douglas and named in honor of the Earl of Bathurst. Lithograph in color. Size 8 x 11.

2215—"THE CAMP, GRAND FALLS—W. Hickman, del. F. Jones, Lith. Day & Son, Lithrs. to the Queen." The picture, taken in 1860, shows a fisherman's wooden camp on the side of a steep hill overlooking the Nepisiguit River, N.B. It is raised upon a platform of logs and is dry in all weather. To the right is the sleeping apartment, and the little bark hut to the left is the curing-house for salmon. The Nepisiguit, which has been called the "fisherman's elysium," is noted for its large salmon. Lithograph in color. Size 8 x 11.

2216—"ABOVE THE GRAND FALLS—W. Hickman, del. F. Jones, Lith. Day & Son, Lithrs. to the Queen." The view represented is that part of the Nepisiguit River, N.B., immediately above the Grand Falls, twenty miles from Bathurst, as it was in 1860. The banks are formed of rocks and crevices in this locality and for miles above and below the cataract the river is very much contracted. As early as 1620 the Recollets had a mission station at Nepisiguit. Lithograph in color. Size 8 x 11.

2217—SHEDIAC, N.B., 1860—View looking towards the Bay—This marine village, now a town, sixteen miles north-east of Moncton, is an attractive summer resort, quite popular on account of its fishing and bathing. As early as 1750 the place was occupied by a French garrison to protect the borders of Acadia. Near Shediac is Point du Chene, a terminus of the branch line of the Intercolonial Railway. To the left of picture, in the distance, is the old schoolhouse. Oil painting by W. G. R. Hind, brother of Prof. Henry Youle Hind. Size 6 x 14. See 2222.

2218—"NEW BRUNSWICK FASHIONABLES!!! FREDERICTON, JANY., 1834—From the original sketch made on the spot. Drawn on stone by J. W. Giles. Printed by Graf and Soret." 1. Shows the River St. John in the distance. 2. Old Market House, the upper part of which was converted into a temperance hall and the lower floor used as saloon. 3. Road leading to the ferry behind the Market House. 4. Queen street, the main thoroughfare in Fredericton. 5. Queen street, leading towards Government House. Lithograph. Size 10 x 18.

2219—"PORTAGE BELOW THE LITTLE FALLS—W. Hickman, del. F. Jones, Lith. Day & Son, Lithrs. to the Queen." Although these falls, on the Nepisiguit River, N.B., are only three miles from the Grand Falls, the scenery is entirely different. The river is rapid and shallow, and the falls are little more than strong rapids, which render a portage necessary. The waters in this vicinity are a favorite haunt of numbers of grilse. The view was taken in 1860. Lithograph in color. Size 8 x 11.

2220—"VIEW OF THE TOWN AND HARBOUR OF ST. ANDREW'S, N.B., AMERICA—Taken from Navy Island, W. M. Buck, Delt. Lithd. by John Kelly, 45 Upr. Gloucester St., Dublin. On stone by J. T. Ashenhurst." 1, Shows "Watts" Wharf; 2, "Raits" Wharf; 3, Roman Catholic Church; 4, Wilson's Wharf; 5, Fort Tipperary; 6, Greenock Presbyterian Church; 7, Church of England; 8, Market Wharf; 9, Chamook Mountains; 10, Market Square and Town Hall; 11, Steamboat Wharf; 12, Old Steam Saw Mill. St. Andrew's is beautifully situated on a peninsula between Passamaquoddy Bay, an inlet of the Bay of Fundy, and the St. Croix River, and is the chief town of Charlotte Co., N.B. Lithograph in color. Size 11 x 28. See 2267.

2221—"A VIEW OF MIRAMICHI—A French Settlement in the Gulf of St. Laurence, destroyed by Brigadier Murray, detached by General Wolfe for that purpose from the Bay of Gaspe. Drawn on the spot by Capt. Hervey Smyth. Etch'd by Paul Sandby. Retouch'd by J. Benazech. London. Publish'd according to Act of Parliament, Nov. 5, 1760, by T. Jefferys, the corner of St. Martin's Lane." The land on either side of picture is now part of the "Indian Reserve," extending along the northerly side of the Miramichi River for a distance of about a mile and a half. The front of the reserve is settled and under cultivation by Micmacs. A new R. C. Indian Chapel is situated a little further back than the site occupied by the chapel in picture, and a passenger bridge crosses the mouth of the Church River about 200 yards from point on which cross is shown. Clearing has changed the appearance of the land, and the different points, prominent when the sketch was made are now mere sand juttings. In 1759 a boat's crew from a British war vessel entered the bay, and was attacked by Indians. In turn the frigate bombarded, annihilated the town at Canadian Point and burned the first Roman Catholic Church at Neguak, since which time the place has been known as Burnt Church. It formerly included the front of the Indian Reserve and the settlement above it. The settlement extending some four miles below the Church River (which at one time comprised a part of Neguac) has for many years been known and distinguished as Riviere des Caches, and the part now known as Neguac (and so spelled) extends easterly about five miles below Riviere des Caches Settlement. Line engraving. Size 13 x 20.

2222—MAIN ST., SHEDIAC, N.B.—In the winter of 1878—Shediac, an attractive town in New Brunswick, is situated on Shediac Bay, Westmoreland County. The picture shows Main street, which runs east and west. Just east of the semaphore is the station of the Intercolonial Railway. In 1879 fire swept the street, destroying all the buildings except the two on the extreme right, at the west end. The street was rebuilt, destroyed again in 1902 and once more rebuilt, the buildings now standing being erected shortly after that date. Where the tree is shown in picture the handsome office of the Bank of Montreal stands (1917). Water color by William G. R. Hind. Size 5 x 9. See 2217.

2223—GORDON, SIR ARTHUR HAMILTON—Lieutenant-Governor of New Brunswick, 1861-6—Member of Parliament for Beverley, 1854-7. Appointed secretary of a commission to the Ionian Islands, 1858, and three years later was sent to New Brunswick. Sir Arthur, who was opposed to Confederation, was called to England to state his views in the matter. Became Governor of the Fiji Islands, 1874. Governor of New Zealand, 1880, and of Ceylon, 1883. Water color. Size 4 x 5. Head and shoulders.

2224—"WINTER TRAVELLING ON THE KENEBEKACIS (KENNE-BACCASIS), NEW BRUNSWICK—Mary Hall, delt. Pendleton's Lithogy., Boston." The Kennebacasis is a beautiful river in New Brunswick, rising near the sources of the Petitcodiac, and entering Kennebacasis Bay. The scenery in the vicinity is magnificent. This view is intended to illustrate the mode of winter travelling in New Brunswick at that time. The rivers were converted into public roads, and were covered with sleighs and sleds traversing the country in all directions. Lithograph in color. Size 6 x 9.

2225—"BARRACKS AND MARKET HOUSE, FREDERICKSTON, N.B.,—By a Lady. Day and Haghe, Lithrs. to the King, 17 Gate St., Linc. Inn Fds." To right are shown officers' and soldiers' barracks. The former has since been replaced in part by a stone building, while the soldiers' quarters, probably erected about 1827, of stone, are still (1917) standing. The City Hall (building shown with tower) was long ago destroyed by fire. The present Court House stands in the vicinity of the site, and the land between the old-time structures and the river is now covered with buildings. Evidently this sketch was made from the river, and at an angle above the soldiers' barracks. Lithograph in color. Size 5 x 7. See 1964.

2226—"THE PABINEAU FALLS—W. Hickman, del. F. Jones, lith. Day & Son, Lithrs. to the Queen." The falls are known also as the Cranberry Falls, and are seven miles from Bathurst, on the Nepisiguit River. They consist of a series of chutes and small falls. The picture represents a salmon pool in 1860, at low water, surrounded by brilliantly colored water-stained rocks. Trout fishing is better in this locality than salmon, and the trout run to a large size. Lithograph in color. Size 7 x 11.

2227—MOOSE HUNTERS—The Micmac Indians of New Brunswick—Lithograph in color by Coke Smyth. Size 11 x 15.

2228—"THE GRAND FALLS—W. Hickman, del. F. Jones, Lith. Day & Son, Lithrs. to the Queen." These falls, on the Nepisiguit River, N.B., descend from a height of over one hundred feet, and are about twenty miles above Bathurst. They consist of four distinct and steplike cliffs, and are at the head of the Narrows, where the river flows through a canyon between cliffs of slatey rock. At the foot of the falls the Nepisiguit whirls away in a dark-foam course for two miles. Lithograph in color. Size 8 x 11.

2229—"MORNING AT THE MID-LANDING—W. Hickman, del. F. Jones, Lith. Day & Son, Lithrs. to the Queen." View in 1860. The Nepisiguit River is here contracted within a rocky channel of about twenty yards, through which the waters pour in a long rapid. The high rock in centre of picture forms a good camping ground. In the neighborhood of Mid-Landing the scenery is most picturesque. Lithograph in color. Size 8 x 11.

2230—"SHOOTING A RAPID—W. Hickman, del. F. Jones, lith. Day and Son, Lithrs. to the Queen." On the Nepisiguit River 1860. The canoeists are having the exciting experience of shooting "Willis Pitch," one of the best rapids on the Rough Waters, near Bathurst, N.B. They are broken water, roaring and foaming over masses of rock. Although the proceeding is attended with danger, accidents are of rare occurrence. Lithograph in color. Size 7 x 11.

2231—"THE MILL DAM AT STANLEY, OCTR., 1834—W. P. Kay, del. S. Russell, lith. London. Published March 1st, 1836, by Ackermann and Co., Strand. Day and Haghe, Lithrs. to the King."—This view shows the dam when completed and the waters of the Nashwaak flowing over it. The frame of the mill had not then been placed in its position in front of the flume. In the foreground are the log canoes which, towed by horses. conveyed provisions to the parties engaged in the several works in operation. Some of these canoes were thirty-six feet in length, by three in breadth, hewn out of single pine trees. Their navigation required great skill and hardihood, both in the management of th ecanoe and the riding of the horse over the uneven and rocky bed of the impetuous river. Lithograph in color. Size 8 x 11. See 2242-43.

2232—"GENERAL VIEW OF STANLEY, FROM THE ROAD, AUGUST, 1835—P. Harry, delt. S. Russell, Lith., London. Pub'd. March 1st, 1836, by Ackermann and Co., Strand. Day and Haghe, Lithrs. to the King." Looking towards the north-east—At the time this view was taken the hill on the opposite side, comprising thirty-four acres, was cleared and cropped. On a part is now a Government demonstration orchard. On the right are shown men engaged in shingling the roof of a pioneer house. Workmen's dwellings are shown in the centre of the picture; also the tavern. Lithograph in color. Size 7 x 11.

2233—"VIEW OF KING'S COLLEGE, PROVINCE OF NEW BRUNSWICK, NORTH AMERICA—Dedicated to His Excellency Major-General Sir Howard Douglas, Bart., K.C.B., Chancellor to the President of Council, etc., etc. Drawn by the Revd. Abm. Wood. Drawn on stone by W. Gauci. Printed by Engelmann & Graf, Coindet & Co., London. Published by Colnaghi, Son & Co., Pall Mall East, Jany. 1, 1829." The University of New Brunswick, which had its origin in Fredericton Academy, was established by provincial charter as the College of New Brunswick, in 1800; founded and incorporated by Royal Charter in 1828, under the name of King's College, Fredericton, with the style and privileges of a University. It was reorganized by an amended charter in 1860 and denominated "The University of New Brunswick." Lithograph. Size 9 x 14.

2234—"A WINTER SCENE IN FREDERICTON—W. P. Kay, delt. R. T. Bone, lithog. London. Published, April, 1836, by Ackermann & Co., Strand." The years have brought so many changes to the locality that it is almost impossible to identify it. An old resident of Fredericton, Mr.

George Barrett, is of the opinion, however, that the house is one which stood, when he was a boy, on the site of the wholesale grocery of Mr. George W. Hodge, 335-9 Queen street, and was occupied by an old soldier. Lithograph. Size 9 x 12.

2235—"THE COMMISSIONER'S CAMP AT STANLEY, 1835—W. P. Kay, del. S. Russell, lith. Pub'd. March 1st, 1836, by Ackermann and Co., Strand, London. Day and Haghe, Lithrs. to the King." Before any houses could be erected this temporary camp or wigwam was built and occupied by Mr. Kendall, during his superintendence of the operations going forward at Stanley, for the first season. It was made by arranging a number of twenty-foot poles so as to meet in a point in the centre, where they were firmly secured. A quantity of spruce bark was then laid on and fastened to the poles, and a flooring of spruce boughs and a buffalo skin completed the furniture. The following year a house was built on the site and occupied by Col. Hayne. It is still standing in a good state of preservation, and is owned and occupied by Mr. Frederick Brown. Lithograph in color. Size 7 x 11.

2236—"WINTER VIEW FROM THE COMPANY'S OFFICE, ST. MARY'S—Opposite Fredericton, looking up the River St. John—Kay, delt. S. Russel, Lith. London. Pub'd. March 1st, 1836, by Ackermann and Co., Strand. Day and Haghe, Lithrs. to the King." The Nova Scotia and New Brunswick Land Company first established their office at St. Mary's, opposite Fredericton on the left bank of the River St. John, but it was afterwards transferred to Stanley. This view, looking south-westerly, shows vehicles of various kinds for winter travel. Lithograph in color. Size 8 x 11.

2237—"PROCESS OF CLEARING THE TOWN PLOT AT STANLEY, OCTR., 1834—W. P. Kay, delt. S. Russell, Lith. London. Pub'd. March 1st, 1836, by Ackermann and Co., Strand. Day and Haghe, Lithrs. to the King." View looking south-easterly. The fire has run over the ground once, and the men are depicted piling and burning the limbs left unconsumed. The surveying party on the right is represented as about to start on an exploring expedition, and the provisions are being brought by oxen for the supply of the different parties. To the left is a glimpse of the Nashwaak River. The mill (1) and the tavern (2) are shown in the course of erection; the other buildings are workingmen's dwellings. The town of Stanley is situated twenty-five miles north of Fredericton, N.B. Lithograph in color. Size 8 x 15.

2238—"BRITISH TROOPS ON THE MARCH—CANADA"—March of 43rd Light Infantry from Fredericton, N.B., to Quebec, Dec., 1837—The regiment was ordered from New Brunswick to Lower Canada in December, 1837, owing to the rebellions in Lower and Upper Canada. It left Fredericton, 11th Dec., 1837, and marched due west along the road of the St. John River, north through Woodstock, Tobique and part of the Grand Falls of the St. John River, through Edmundston to the French Madawaska Settlement, crossing Lake Temiscouata along the north side, and its surface, then across the famous 36-mile portage, and back across the mountains to south bank of the St. Lawrence near Riviere du Loup, thence along the river side to Point Levis and across to Quebec. The march of 370 miles occupied eighteen days, and the thermometer ranged from twenty to thirty degrees below zero. Xylograph in color. Size 14 x 18.

2239—WINDSOR, N.S.—Looking west from Ferry Hill, 1868—At intersection of Avon and St. Croix Rivers, showing: 1. Falmouth. 2. Avon River, which forms the harbor of Windsor. 3. St. Croix River. 4. Ferry Hill, one of the rounded hills on which the town is built. 5. Nisbet Island. Lithograph in color. Size 10 x 17.

2240—"A SLEIGH LEAVING WINDSOR, N.S.—Drawn from nature and on stone by R. Petley, Lieut. 50th Regt. Day and Haghe, lithrs. to the King." Lithograph. Size 8 x 13.

2241—"TAVERN AT STANLEY, BUILT OF LOGS, JUNE, 1835—P. Harry, Delt. S. Russell, Lith. London. Pub'd. March 1st, 1836, by Ackermann, Strand. Day and Haghe, Lithrs. to the King." The building was almost cruciform in shape, the angles being dove-tailed together, and each course of timber being firmly connected by treenails of hardwood to the one beneath it. The interior square was continued one storey higher than the others so as to allow their roofs to abut against it; by this means a very strong and commodious building was constructed. It is still (1917) standing, and is owned and occupied by James Malone. The buildings to the right are workmen's houses. The machine drawn by oxen was made of solid birch wheels bound with iron, with a strong axle and pole, used for conveyance over the rough and uneven ground, previous to the formation of roads. Lithograph in color. Size 7 x 11.

2242—"THE MILL AT STANLEY, AUGT., 1835—P. Harry, delt. S. Russell, lith. Day and Haghe, Lithrs. to the King. London. Published March 1st, 1836, by Ackermann & Co., Strand." The sawmill is here shown completed and in operation, as seen from the mill pond above the dam. The logs are cut on the borders of the river and floated down to the mill pond to be sawn. The deals are thrown out at the lower side of the mill ready to be collected in rafts and conveyed to market. On the right is seen one of a series of pier-frames, built of logs, filled with stones, for the purpose of breaking the force of the ice in the spring freshet, and to conduct the logs to the mill by means of a boom, connected by chains from pier to pier. A steam mill now occupies this site, and lumber is shipped by train. Lithograph in color. Size 7 x 11. See 2231, 2243.

2243—"ERECTING THE MILL DAM, AUGUST, 1834—E. N. Kendall, R.N., delt. London. Published March 1st, 1836, by Ackermann & Co., Strand. Day & Haghe, Lithrs. to the King." In laying out the site of Stanley, a sawmill was found necessary, and advantage was therefore taken of a slight natural fall in the Nashwaak River, to throw across a dam 150 feet in length. The picture shows how it was done. A number of the largest trunks of elm and pine trees were placed "up and down" the stream, in the direction of the current; these were crossed by others of great length, notched on to them transversely, and well loaded with stones. A second series of trees, very much longer than the first, was then crossed on the transverse logs, and in like manner well loaded with rocks; and so on, until the structure attained a sufficient height. The birch timber framework on the left is called the flume, and through this the water, acting on the wheel in the mill, is designed to be conveyed. The dam was finished off by a covering on the back, of stout planking, closely fitted. The joints were then rendered tight with hay and gravel to prevent the escape of water. On the completion of the mill the flume was planked and the water suffered to accumulate behind the dam to a required head. In the centre of the picture is seen the first log house built on the surveying party's first encampment, while on the left is a shed, covered by spruce bark, forming a sort of shop for the carpenters until something more substantial could be made for their use. The view looks toward the west. Lithograph in color. Size 8 x 11. See 2231, 2242.

2244—"ENCAMPMENT OF SURVEYING PARTY AT THE SITE OF STANLEY, JULY, 1834—P. Harry, delt. S. Russell, lith. London. Pub'd March 1st, 1836, by Ackermann & Co., Strand. Day & Haghe, lithrs. to the King." View looking westerly. The surveying party of the New Brunswick and Nova Scotia Land Company appointed to explore the line of road to be opened through the forest started from Fredericton, N.B., July, 1834. After tracing out a practicable line, nearly straight, they struck the Nashwaak River at the spot here delineated, north of Fredericton. This view was taken on the evening of their arrival and shows the party felling the first trees, and forming their encampment. The location was found suitable for a town and was subsequently laid out as such. The name, Stanley, was given in compliment to Lord Stanley, Secretary of State for the Colonial Department, 1833-4. Lithograph in color. Size 7 x 11.

2245—SHERBROOKE, EASTERN TOWNSHIPS, LOWER CANADA— Principal station of the British American Land Company—Printed by W. Day, 17 Gate St. The view looks south-east and was taken in 1836. With key. Lithograph. Size 8 x 10.

2246—SAILING FLEET AT POINTE DU CHENE—Near Shediac, N.B., 1870—At the entrance of Shediac Harbor, or Bay, lies Pointe du Chene, about whose wharves clusters a village. The view, which shows a large number of sailing vessels, was made in the days of flourishing lumber trade and at a time when some schooners had come into the harbor for shelter. As early as 1750 Shediac was occupied by a French garrison to protect the borders of Acadia, and in 1757 French and Acadian troops were settled there. Water color by W. G. R. Hind. Size 8 x 11.

2247—FRENCHMEN RAKING OYSTERS IN THE HARBOR—Shediac, N.B., 1870—Oysters are still found in some parts of the harbor and are raked from boats in the summer and through holes in the ice in winter. The raker puts his leg on the handle of the rake and works the long teeth under the oysters to loosen them, and then they are carefully drawn to the surface. The law fixes a minimum size, but in many cases small oysters, instead of being thrown back, were left upon the ice to freeze, and in this way the beds were exhausted. Water color by W. G. R. Hind. Size 8 x 11.

2248—DIGGING OF OYSTER MUD THROUGH THE ICE—Shediac, N.B., 1870—The beds grow up towards the surface until they come within reach of the frost, when they die out. They are dredged with a long iron scoop worked by horse power and regulated by its long wooden handle. The mud is loaded on sleds and taken right to the fields and spread on the snow. The shells gradually disintegrate and the lime passes into the soil, as does also the nitrogenous matter from the decayed oysters. Water color by W. G. R. Hind. Size 8 x 12.

2249—NAGLE—"Admiral Sir Edmund Nagle, K.C.B., etc., etc. Dedicated by special permission to His Most Gracious Majesty George 4th, by His Majesty's humble and devoted servant, William Sams. Painted by Wm. Corden. Engraved by Wm. Ward, Engraver to' H.R.H. the Duke of Clarence. London. Published, 1830, by W. Sams, book and printseller to the Royal Family, 1 St. James St. Proof." Born in 1757. Said to have been a nephew of Edmund Burke. Entered the navy in 1770 and seven years later was promoted to be lieutenant of the Greenwich storeship on the North American station. Became rear-admiral Nov. 9th, 1805, and vice-admiral, July 31st, 1810. Appointed Governor of Newfoundland in 1813, in the interval between Duckworth and Keats, and the following year, when the allied monarchs reviewed the fleet at Spithead, he was nominated aide-de-camp to the Prince Regent. Made a K.C.B. in 1815. Raised to the rank of admiral, 1819. Died at East Molesly, Surrey, Eng., March 14th, 1830. Line engraving. Size 6 x 7. Half length.

2250—POLE—"Admiral Sir Charles M. Pole, Bart., K.G.C.B. Engraved by Turner from a picture by Sir Will'm Beechey, R.A., for Capt. Brenton's Naval History, London. Published Nov. 1, 1823, by C. Turner, 50 Warren Street, Fitzroy Square." Governor of Newfoundland, 1800. Commander-in-chief of the Baltic, 1801. G.C.B., 1818. Represented Newark, Notts., and Plymouth in the English Parliament. He was born in 1757 and died in 1830. Line engraving. Size 4 x 5. Half length.

2251—PALLISER—"Sir Hugh Palliser, Bart. D. Orme, del. Ed. Orme, sculp. Published, 1796, by J. Sewell, 32 Cornhill. European Magazine." Directed a survey, which was carried out by Cook, of the coasts of Newfoundland; from 1764-6 was Governor of Newfoundland; Lord of the Admiralty in 1775; second in command under Keppel at the battle off Ushant, July 27th, 1778. Born in 1723 and died in 1796. Line engraving. Size 3 x 4. Head and shoulders, oval.

2252—"NEWFOUNDLAND, 1610-1910—Issue of stamps to commemorate the 300th anniversary of the earliest settlement in the British Empire, made in Conception Bay, Newfoundland, in June, 1610. With the compliments of the Government of Newfoundland. R. Watson, Colonial Secretary." Chromo lithograph with original stamps.

2253—"NEWFOUNDLAND, CORONATION YEAR, 1911—Issue of Newfoundland stamps to commemorate the coronation of Their Majesties King George the Fifth and Queen Mary, June 22nd, 1911. With the compliments of the Government of Newfoundland. R. Watson, Colonial Secretary." Chromo lithograph with original stamps.

2254—EDWARDS—"Richard Edwards, Esqr., Rear Admiral of the Red, Governor and Commander-in-Chief of His Majesty's Squadron at Newfoundland. Painted by N. Dance, Esq., R.A. Engraved by W. Dickinson, London. Publish'd Feby. 20th, 1781, by Dickinson and Watson, No. 158, New Bond street." Appointed commander in 1747, and in 1777 was captain of H.M.S. "Sandwich" at Ushant, under Admiral Keppel. Became Admiral of the Blue, March, 1779, and in that year was sent to Newfoundland as Governor, remaining there until 1782. His death took place in 1794. Line engraving. Size 13 x 16. Three-quarter length.

2255—DISEMBARKATION OF THE FRENCH AT ST. JOHN'S— Translation of inscription on picture: "Perspective view of the French disembarkation at St. John's on the west shore of Newfoundland, in charge of the Chevalier de Ternay, captain of the fleet of His Most Christian Majesty, who had under his command the men-of-war le Robuste, l'Eveille, la Fregate, la Licorne and la Flute. La Garonne, with some troops of the disembarkment, made a descent on the St. John's side of the Island of Newfoundland, where it seized upon an English man-of-war as well as several ships and fishing boats it had destroyed. At Basset's, Rue St. Jacques, Paris. Also Geneva." In the opinion of Mr. W. G. Gosling, of St. John's, Nfld., this view is a fake. In no way does it resemble any of the coast of Newfoundland. When news of the engagement at St. John's in June, 1762, between the French and English reached Paris, it is supposed that a French artist, of a very imaginative turn of mind, proceeded to put his impressions on paper, with the result shown. Presumably the view looks east. Engraving, colored. Size 10 x 14.

2256—"ST. JOHN'S, NEWFOUNDLAND—From the domain of Government House, looking west—To His Excellency Sir John Gaspard Le Marchant, Knt., K.C.S.F., C.T.S., Governor of Newfoundland, etc., this print is by permission respectfully inscribed by the publishers. W. R. Best, delt. W. Spreat, lith. Printed at W. Spreat's Litho. Establishment, High St., Exeter." On extreme right is the House of Legislature, erected 1847-8. In centre of the picture may be seen a tower which was never completed, the fire of 1846 having swept away the building. The Mercy Convent, built 1850, now occupies site. The large structure in background is the Roman Catholic Cathedral, built 1841, overlooking the harbor. The roadway leading into the distance is the Military Road, running in a semi-circle, built to connect Fort William in east end of Fort Townsend with west of St. John's. A little to the left of the roadway is the spire of the Established Church of Scotland. Lithograph in color. Size 8 x 14.

2257—ST. JOHN'S, NEWFOUNDLAND—"St. Thomas's Church, the Narrows, etc., from Government House. To His Excellency Sir John Gaspard Le Marchant, Knt., K.C.S.F., C.T.S., Governor of Newfoundland, etc., this print is by permission respectfully inscribed by the publishers. W. R. Best, delt. W. Spreat, lith. Printed at W. Spreat's litho. establishment, High st., Exeter." The view shows Signal Hill, which in 1762 was the scene of a sharp struggle between French and English; St. Thomas' Anglican Church, built 1834, still in existence, but enlarged; the Narrows, directly commanded at that time by Fort William, now dismantled, and other points of interest. Lithograph in color. Size 9 x 14.

2258—ST. JOHN'S—"This drawing taken 16th March, 1838, during a severe frost, contains a south view of St. John's Harbour, Newfoundland, together with the vessels of that port, bound to the seal fishery, preparing to depart by means of ice channels. Dedicated by permission to His Excellency, Capt. Henry Prescott, C.B., Governor and Commander-in-Chief." Lithograph. Size 8 x 23.

2259—GREENSPOND, NEWFOUNDLAND, 1846—View from the south, showing the outer harbor on the left, and part of Bonavista Bay, on the north side of which Greenspond is situated. The harbor is formed by the Island of Greenspond on the one side and Newell's and Ship Island on the other. Puffin Island is at the entrance to the harbor. Although a barren island, considerable business has been done and is done at Greenspond. T. Whitaker, litho. B. Smith, delt. Lithograph in color. Size 7 x 15.

2260—ST. JOHN'S, NEWFOUNDLAND—"Free St. Andrew's Church, Bank B.N.A., etc., etc., Duckworth street. W. R. Best, delt. W. Spreat, lith. Printed at W. Spreat's Litho. Establishment, High St., Exeter." A view of Duckworth street facing on which were, at the time the picture was made, Free St. Andrew's Church, Bank of British North America, and homes of some of St. John's prominent citizens. The sites are now differently occupied, as nearly all the buildings shown were destroyed by fire. Lithograph in color. Size 9 x 14.

2261—"ST. JOHN'S, NEWFOUNDLAND—From the Freshwater Road, looking east—To His Excellency Sir John Gaspard Le Marchant, Knt., K.C.S.F., C.T.S., Governor of Newfoundland, etc., this print is by permission respectfully inscribed by the publishers. W. R. Best, delt. W. Spreat, lith. Printed at W. Spreat's litho. establishment, High Street, Exeter." To the left is seen the Established Church of Scotland, built 1842; destroyed by fire, 1876. It then united with Free St. Andrew's and was opened in 1880 under the latter name. The Church of England Cathedral, of Gothic architecture, is also shown, and to the right of the picture are Signal Hill and Signal Station, 520 feet high. Lithograph in color. Size 8 x 13.

2262—TELEGRAPH HOUSE, TRINITY BAY, NEWFOUNDLAND, IN 1857-8—The first Atlantic cable was landed at Bay of Bull's Arm, head of Trinity Bay, in 1858. Its life was short, however, and precarious, and in 1866 cable communication was established between Heart's Content, on the east shore of the bay, and Valentia Island, off the west coast of Ireland. The existing cables of the Anglo-American Company have their western terminus at Heart's Content, after traversing the great submarine plain of 1,500 miles between Newfoundland and Ireland. It is said that from Newfoundland to Ireland "the bottom of the sea is a plateau, which seems to have been placed there especially for the purpose of holding the wires of a submarine telegraph and of keeping them out of harm's way. The depth of this plateau is quite regular, gradually increasing from the shores of Newfoundland to the depth of from 1,500 to 2,000 fathoms as you approach the other side." London. Published by Day & Son, Limited, Gate St., Lincoln's Inn Fields, W.C. Lithograph in color. Size 6 x 9.

2263—"ON THE KENIBECKASIS—Near St. John—Day & Haghe, Lithrs. to the King, 17 Gate Street, Linc. Inn Fds." The beautiful New Brunswick river takes its rise near the sources of the Petitcodiac, and, after flowing for about twenty miles in a south-westerly direction, opens into a deep and wide estuary of the River St. John, Kennebecasis Bay. Lithograph in color. Size 5 x 8. See 1966.

2264—NEW BRUNSWICK AND U.S. BOUNDARY MONUMENT, 1817 —Erected at the source of the St. Croix, 31st July, 1817, by Col. Joseph Bouchette and John Johnson, in connection with the boundary line between Canada and United States. Col. Joseph Bouchette had in 1814 been nominated Surveyor-General under the Treaty of Ghent for establishing the boundary line between Canada and the States. In the summer of 1817 he, with John Johnson, erected a new monument (the former one being but an iron hoop on a beech tree) at the source of the St. Croix River, N.B., made explorations, sketched the face of the country, and prepared plans and reports in connection with the question. Although the Ashburton Treaty has made the boundary line much further north, it is generally admitted that the line indicated by Bouchette is the one which should have obtained. Drawn on stone by L. Haghe. Sketched by Col. Bouchette, 31st July, 1817. Lithograph in color. Size 5 x 8.

2265—KEATS, ADMIRAL SIR RICHARD GOODWIN—Governor of Newfoundland, 1813-15—He was born in Hampshire, Eng., 1757. Entered the navy, and in 1778 was promoted to a lieutenancy; at the relief of Gibraltar, 1780-1; served with distinction against the Americans and French. Received a commander's commission, 1782. With Nelson off Toulon, and in the West Indies, 1803-5. Present at St. Domingo. Convoyed Sir John Moore's troops to Gottenburg, 1807, and made K.B. and rear-admiral in the same year. Received his commission as Governor of Newfoundland 6th April, 1813, and arrived at St. John's 31st May. Governor of Greenwich, 1821. Died in 1834. Mezzotint. Size 8 x 9. Head and shoulders, oval.

2266—"FREDERICTON, N.B.—From the Oromocto Road—Drawn from nature and on stone by R. Petley, Lieut. 50th Regt. Printed by C. Hullmandel. London. Published by J. Dickinson, New Bond street." View looking westward in 1837. The town of Fredericton, in the distance, is on a point of land on the west side of the River St. John. It was originally called St. Anne's, but in 1785 the name was changed to Fredericton by Governor Carleton, and two years later it was made the capital of the province. Oromocto, situated ten miles away, was in the early days a favorite resort of the Indians. Lithograph. Size 7 x 10.

2267—VIEW OF THE HARBOR AND BAY, ST. ANDREW'S, N.B., 1862—A seaport town on the peninsula between Passamaquoddy Bay and St. Croix River, about three miles from the Maine (U.S.) boundary. It lies on a gentle slope, and is popular as a summer resort. The port, which is open all the year round, has two harbors, a large outer, or head one, and a commodious inner one. St. Andrew's was founded in 1783 by the Loyalists. Water color. Size 7 x 10. See 2220.

2268—"THE CITY OF ST. JOHN, NEW BRUNSWICK—M. G. Hall. del. Pendleton's Lithography, Boston." The site of St. John was discovered by Champlain and De Monts on St. John's Day (June 24), 1604, but was unoccupied for some thirty years; in 1785 created a town by royal charter. It is picturesquely situated at the mouth of a river of its own name, on a rocky peninsula projecting into the harbor. The entrance of the river into the harbor, about a mile and a half above the city, is through a rocky gorge, which occasions some falls, while spanning this gorge, about a hundred feet above low water, is a suspension bridge. Lithograph in color. Size 6 x 9.

2269—"ELM TREE ON THE ROYAL ROAD, NEW BRUNSWICK— W. P. Kay, delt. S. Russell, Lith. London. Pub'd. March 1st, 1836, by Ackermann and Co., Strand." This remarkable tree standing by the roadside six miles from Fredericton rejoices in the dignified name of "Sir Archibald's Walking-stick," in compliment to His Excellency Sir Archibald Campbell, Lieutenant-Governor of New Brunswick from 1831-7. Lithograph in color. Size 7 x 11.

2270—STARVE HARBOR, NEWFOUNDLAND, 1857—On the Bay of Exploits—Although an ill-omened name, no prettier spot can be found in Newfoundland than this harbor, situated on New World Island, in one of the most northern of the fine bays on the eastern coast of Newfoundland. The innumerable islands which dot the bay offer calm channels for picturesque and pleasurable boating. Drawn by Rev. William Grey, of Portugal Cove, Nfld. Printed and published by S. D. Cowell, Anastatic Press, Ipswich. Lithograph, colored by hand. Size 9 x 13. The views of the coasts of Newfoundland and Labrador by Rev. William Grey, in this collection, are from sketches made in the summer of 1857. The Rev. William Grey was from 1849-51 principal of Queen's College (theological), St. John's, and incumbent of Portugal Cove, a fishing village about nine miles from St. John's. His son, William Grey, born at Portugal Cove in 1850, succeeded to the Earldom of Stamford in 1890 and is now (1917) the 9th Earl of Stamford.

2271—CATHEDRAL CHURCH (ANGLICAN) OF ST. JOHN THE BAPTIST, ST. JOHN'S, NEWFOUNDLAND, 1857—The edifice, the cornerstone of which was laid on September 29th, 1847, was erected in pure Gothic, after the design of Sir Gilbert Scott, and considered his masterpiece. Looking east, the view shows: 1, West end of nave. 2, West porch and steps, of Irish limestone. 3, Church Hill. 4, Sexton's house. 5, Henry street. On 21st Sept., 1850, the nave was consecrated, and the choir and transepts, built later, were dedicated in 1885. The building, which was destroyed by fire in 1892, has since been restored. Drawn by Rev. William Grey, of Portugal Cove, Nfld. Printed and published by S. D. Cowell. Anastatic Press, Ipswich. Lithograph, colored by hand. Size 5 x 8.

2272—"COLONIAL BUILDING, ST. JOHN'S, NEWFOUNDLAND— Opened, Jany. 28th, 1850—To His Excellency Sir John Gaspard Le Marchant, Knt., K.C.S.F., C.T.S., Governor of Newfoundland, etc., this print is by permission respectfully inscribed by the publishers. Drawn by W. R. Best. On stone by W. Spreat. Printed at W. Spreat's litho. establishment, High St., Exeter." Erected of Irish limestone in 1847-50, on the Military road. In it are chambers for both branches of the Legislature— i.e., the House of Assembly and the Legislative Council, and also the Legislative Library. The corner-stone was laid by his Excellency Sir John Gaspard Le Marchant, Governor of Newfoundland, 1847-52. Lithograph in color. Size 8 x 12.

2273—"GOVERNMENT HOUSE, ST. JOHN'S, NEWFOUNDLAND— To His Excellency Sir John Gaspard Le Marchant, Knt., K.C.S.F., C.T.S., Governor of Newfoundland, etc., this print is by permission inscribed by the Publisher. Drawn by W. R. Best. On stone by W. Spreat. Printed at W. Spreat's litho. establishment, High St., Exeter." Erected by the Imperial Government in 1828 from the plans of the Admiralty House, Portsmouth, England. It is a plain, substantial residence of stone, standing in the centre of well-kept grounds and surrounded by a moat. On the vote for its completion in the House of Commons, England, the Marlborough Government was only sustained by a majority of one vote. Lithograph in color. Size 8 x 12.

2274—VIEW OUTSIDE ST. JOHN'S, NEWFOUNDLAND, 1857—From the sea, north-north-east from Cape Spear—1, Cape Spear. 2, Entrance to St. John's harbor. 3, Northern Head at entrance to St. John's. 4, Signal Hill. 4a, Signal station erected here 1897. 5, Entrance to Cuckold's Cove and Quidi Vidi. 6, Sugar Loaf. 7, Entrance to Outer Cove—fishing village. 8, Entrance to Middle Cove—fishing village. 9, Entrance to Torbay—fishing village. 10, Fishing boat. 11, Topsail schooner. 12, Brigantine, like No. 11, engaged in carrying dry fish to market. (Note—Dry fish is now mostly sent to market by steamer.) Drawn by Rev. William Grey, of Portugal Cove, Nfld. Printed and published by S. D. Cowell, Anastatic Press, Ipswich. Lithograph, colored by hand. Size 6 x 12.

2275—PETTY HARBOR, NEWFOUNDLAND, 1857—About nine miles from St. John's—A pretty little town at the mouth of a deep ravine through which flows a crystal stream, emptying into the fish-flake fringed harbor to the left. Some years ago a steam factory for the manufacture of cod liver oil on the improved Norwegian principle was erected here, but it has long since been destroyed. Drawn by Rev. William Grey, of Portugal Cove, Nfld. Printed and published by S. D. Cowell, Anastatic Press, Ipswich. Lithograph, colored by hand. Size 10 x 13.

2276—SOUTH SIDE OF WEST END OF ST. JOHN'S, NEWFOUNDLAND, 1857—Looking north-east—1, Site is now (1917) occupied by a wooden dry-dock, built 1884, 600 ft. long, 130 ft. wide, with a depth of 25 ft. on its sill at low water. 2, Long Bridge, connecting north with south side. Built about 1842, previous to which communication was by ferry. 3, Store owned by Mudge's, on ground leased from Admiralty. The land is now leased by Bowring Bros., Ltd., who have added large stores and wharves. 4, Residence of R. Allsop, merchant. Site occupied by St. Mary's Church and Rectory (Anglican). 5, Residential section. Some of the houses are still standing. 6, Southside road. 7, The water above bridge, west, is not navigable. Drawn by Rev. William Grey, of Portugal Cove, Nfld. Printed and published by S. D. Cowell, Anastatic Press, Ipswich. Lithograph, colored by hand. Size 8 x 13.

2277—ST. JOHN'S, NEWFOUNDLAND, 1857—Looking to the sea from the west-north-west—1, Presbyterian school. 2, Church of England rectory, 3, Cathedral Church of St. John the Baptist. 4, Old factory, used as the Supreme Court, 1846. 5, Premises of W. H. Thomas & Co. 6, Old Commercial Rooms, Duckworth street. 7, Wesleyan Chapel. 8, School of Colonial and Continental Society. 9, Queen's road. 10, Forts on Signal Hill. 11, Signal station, destroyed by fire, 1894. site now (1917) occupied by the Cabot Memorial Tower. 12, Signal Hill. 13, Northern Head. 14, The Narrows. 15, South Battery. Drawn by Rev. William Grey, of Portugal Cove, Nfld. Printed and published by S. D. Cowell. Anastatic Press, Ipswich. Lithograph, colored by hand. Size 9 x 10.

2278—ST. JOHN'S NEWFOUNDLAND, 1750—View looking south-south-east. With key. Sepia. Size 13 x 21.

2279—QUIDI VIDI LAKE, NEWFOUNDLAND, 1857—A small sheet of water, a little over three-quarters of a mile in length, north of the city of St. John. A small river flowing through the lake forms a charming cascade, as it tumbles over the rocks into the harbor, which is connected with the ocean by a narrow gut. All around are strangely shaped cliffs. Below the lake is the village of Quidi Vidi, a typical fishing hamlet. The name is the old Spanish equivalent for "What do I see." Drawn by Rev. William Grey, of Portugal Cove, Nfld. Printed and published by S. D. Cowell, Anastatic Press, Ipswich. Lithograph, colored by hand. Size 8 x 13.

2280—CHURCH AT PORTUGAL COVE, NEWFOUNDLAND, 1857— From the St. John's Road—The Cove is situated on the south shore of Conception Bay, and is picturesquely situated on the ledges near the foot of a range of lofty hills. It was through Gaspar Corte-Real, who explored this coast of 1500 and named Conception Bay, that Portuguese settlers were induced to form a colony on the seaboard, fifty ships being sent out to the fisheries. The Anglican Church of St. Peter, shown in the picture, was designed and built by the Rev. William Grey and is still (1917) standing. Drawn by Rev. William Grey, of Portugal Cove, Nfld. Printed and published by S. D. Cowell, Anastatic Press, Ipswich. Lithograph, colored by hand. Size 8 x 10.

2281—CREMAILLIERE HARBOR, NEWFOUNDLAND, 1857—A romantically situated harbor in the St. Barbe district, near the extreme north point of Newfoundland, on what is known as the French Shore. By the Treaty of Utrecht, 1713, and several subsequent treaties the French had the privilege of taking and drying fish on that portion of the coast extending from Cape Ray round the west and north to Cape St. John, on the northeast shore. They, however, had no right to occupy permanently any portion of the coast, nor to erect any buildings save such huts and scaffolds as might be necessary for drying their fish, nor could the French fishermen winter on the island. By the Anglo-French Treaty of 1904 the French formally resigned their former rights in return for monetary and other considerations. Drawn by Rev. William Grey, of Portugal Cove, Nfld. Printed and published by S. D. Cowell, Anastatic Press, Ipswich. Lithograph, colored by hand. Size 9 x 13.

2282—BELL ISLAND BEACH, NEWFOUNDLAND, 1857—On Bell Island, Conception Bay, are located the valuable mines of the Nova Scotia Steel and the Dominion Iron and Steel Companies, iron ore having been discovered on it some years ago. In 1913, 1,245,797 tons were exported from the two mines. The Beach, which is now known as Wabana, is situated on the southern part of the island, which lies three miles off shore from Portugal Cove, and is divided into two villages, one known as Lance Cove, and the other as Wabana. Fronting on the sea are bold cliffs, in some cases carved into fantastic shapes by the action of the waves. Drawn by Rev. William Grey, of Portugal Cove, Nfld. Printed and published by S. D. Cowell, Anastatic Press, Ipswich. Lithograph, colored by hand. Size 11 x 11.

2283—"CUSTOM HOUSE—Erected, 1848—St. John's, Newfoundland— To His Excellency Sir John Gaspard Le Marchant, Knt. K.C.S.F., C.T.S., Governor of Newfoundland, etc., this print is by permission respectfully inscribed by the Publisher. Drawn by W. R. Best. On stone by W. Spreat. Printed at W. Spreat's litho. establishment, High St., Exeter." Built of brick with freestone facings, on the King's Beach. In the great conflagration of July 8th, 1892, when fully half the city was swept away, the Custom House was destroyed. It was rebuilt, however, at the east end of East Water street. Lithograph in color. Size 8 x 12.

2284—"COURT HOUSE AND MARKET—Erected, 1849—St. John's, Newfoundland—To His Excellency Sir John Gaspard Le Marchant, Knt., K.C.S.F., C.T.S., Governor of Newfoundland, etc., this print is by permission respectfully inscribed by the Publisher. Drawn by W. R. Best. On stone by W. Spreat. Printed at W. Spreat's litho. establishment, High St., Exeter." This building was erected in 1849, on Water street. The lower part served as a market place, while the upper portions were used as court rooms. Until 1885 the post-office was also located there. The structure was destroyed in the fire of 1892 and a new and larger one of native granite erected on the site. His Majesty King George V. when he visited Newfoundland as Duke of Cornwall and York, in 1901, laid the corner-stone of the new building, in which are located the court rooms, Law Society and departments of the Prime Minister, Colonial Secretary and Government Engineer. Lithograph in color. Size 9 x 13.

2285—AQUAFORTE, NEWFOUNDLAND, 1857—A hamlet in the Ferryland district, about fifty miles from St. John's. It is situated on a long, deep and narrow harbor surrounded by lofty hills. Good fishing may be had in the vicinity, and the harbor (to the left of the picture) is excellent. The road leading from St. John's to Aquaforte passes through some very beautiful scenery. Drawn by Rev. William Grey, of Portugal Cove, Nfld. Printed and published by S. D. Cowell, Anastatic Press, Ipswich. Lithograph, colored by hand. Size 9 x 11.

2286—TOAD'S COVE, NEWFOUNDLAND, 1857—A rock-bound fishing hamlet and harbor on the Atlantic coast, in Ferryland district, Eastern Newfoundland, some twenty miles south of the city of St. John's, and very popular as a summer resort for the people of the latter. The winding road on the steep hillside is crossed by a tempestuous stream, which falls precipitously into the lake beneath, thence proceeding to the sea, the whole presenting a scene of rugged beauty. Toad's Cove is now (1917) known as Tor's Cove. Drawn by Rev. William Grey, of Portugal Cove, Nfld. Printed and published by S. D. Cowell, Anastatic Press, Ipswich. Lithograph, colored by hand. Size 10 x 12.

2287—OLD CHURCH OF HOLY TRINITY AT NEW WESTMINSTER, B.C.—Built in 1860 on the site occupied by Holy Trinity Cathedral, head of Church street, a short street running at right angles to Columbia street between Sixth and Fourth streets. It was destroyed by fire in 1865 while the clergyman of the parish, Rev. John Sheepshanks, was in England. He at once set about raising money for the erection of a new church, securing $6,000 on condition that the church be built of stone, which was done. Mr. Sheepshanks was afterwards Bishop of Norwich, Eng. The bridge in the middle distance, towards right of picture, is where Columbia street, the main street of New Westminster, is situated. That part of the ravine occupied by the street has been filled in, but to the north of the street there is still a large ravine. The church appears to be but a few steps from Columbia street, but in reality it is about 200 feet, the picture being somewhat foreshortened. Water color. Size 4 x 6.

2288—BOUNDARY CAIRN BETWEEN CANADA AND U.S.—In 1856 commissions appointed by the United States and Great Britain were authorized to survey the boundary between the States and Canada along the 49th parallel west of the Rockies. In 1861 the survey was completed, though not until 1869 were the final joint reports signed at Washington by the commissioners and transmitted to their respective Governments. The picture shows a cairn erected at East Kootenay, B.C., during the survey. For many years the report was lost, and, although sought for everywhere, could not be found. In 1898, however, it was fortunately discovered by Mr. Otto Klotz, Assistant Chief Astronomer, Canada, in the Royal Observatory, Greenwich. It was decided in 1900 to re-mark the boundary, and a survey was carried out 1901-07. However, the line as now marked is based on monuments and positions established in 1857-61. Water color. Size 4 x 5.

2289—OLD MILL AND FARM AT FORT DOUGLAS—Red River Settlement, 1861—Typical view of a farm near the spot where the Earl of Selkirk. founder of the Red River Settlement, planted his colony in 1813. The site of Fort Douglas is now (1917) at the foot of George street, Winnipeg, Man. Water color by J. W. Cotton. Size 5 x 7.

2290—"POLING UP"—The picture gives a scene on the Kaministiquia River, which has a regular and rapid current, with cataracts at intervals. The canoeists shown are "poling up" above Fort William, in Thunder Bay district. Water color by W. H. E. Napier, engineer Canadian Red River Expedition, 1857. Size 6 x 10.

2291—FORT PEMBINA, 1860—On the banks of the Red River—This view shows the Hudson's Bay post re-established on what was supposed to be British territory. It was, however, again found to be within the United States by about half a mile. On the post finally established on the Canadian side, a Fenian Raid, under O'Neil and O'Donoghue, was made in the fall of 1871. A year or two after, the establishment became the Hudson's Bay shop in the town of West Lynne, Man., which arose about it. This town on the west or left bank of the Red River is now (1917) known as Emerson Junction, Man., and is separated from Pembina, North Dakota, by only a street. Water color by J. W. Cotton. Size 5 x 7. See 2309, 2339, 2390.

2292—NEAR FORT GARRY—Red River Settlement, 1860—This scene, which is characteristic of the dwelling and surroundings of settlers near Fort Garry (Winnipeg) fifty years ago, shows to the left a windmill of the time. There were then in the settlement sixteen windmills and eight water-mills, the former used by the settlers to grind their wheat. There was, in addition, but one steam (saw and grist) mill, with two run of stones and a set of saws. The steam mill was burned in June, 1860. Water color by J. W. Cotton. Size 5 x 6.

2293—"BANK OF BRITISH NORTH AMERICA, ST. JOHN'S, NEW-FOUNDLAND—Erected, 1848—To His Excellency Sir John Gaspard Le Marchant, Knt., K.C.S.F., C.T.S., Governor of Newfoundland, etc., this print is by permission inscribed by the Publisher. Drawn by W. R. Best. On stone by W. Spreat. Printed at W. Spreat's litho. establishment, High St., Exeter." The building was erected for this bank and afterwards acquired by the Commercial Bank of Newfoundland. It was gutted in the fire of 1892, but the walls, which are of freestone, were left standing, and the bank was re-erected practically as before, except that the fence in front has been removed and the roof is mansard instead of flat. After the failure of the Commercial Bank the building was occupied for a time by the Bank of Montreal, later bought by the late Rt. Hon. Sir W. V. Whiteway, who subsequently sold it to the Bank of Montreal. The ground floor is leased to the Government and occupied by the Savings Bank, and the upper portion is the residence of the manager of the Bank of Montreal. Lithograph in color. Size 9 x 12.

2294—WINNIPEG, MAN., 1872—Looking west from the bridge on Main Street—In the foreground is J. H. McTavish, Hudson's Bay Company's accountant at Fort Garry, 1869-70, and later chief factor, driving to Port Garry on the trail between the fort and the Hudson's Bay Company "town" store. The latter was erected by an American named Burdock, who had a freighting contract between St. Paul and Fort Garry for the company. The picture shows: 1, Hudson's Bay Company store. It was rented to the Canadian Government for offices after the company opened their new shop inside Fort Garry. The old "town" shop stands nearly on its original site, moved merely to conform to the street line, No. 299 Fort street, and used as a blacksmith's shop. 2, William Drever's. 3, Red River Hall, used for public meetings, entertainments and worship. 4, Bryan Devlin's hotel. 5, Rev. George Young's church, east side Main street. This was the first Methodist church in the North-west for work among the whites, erected in 1871, with Rev. George Young as first missionary. Oil painting by William G. R. Hind. Size 4 x 12. See 2342.

2295—BISHOP OF MONTREAL'S CANOE—The Rev. George J. Mountain, D.D., who for many years administered the bishoprics of Quebec and

Montreal, Western Canada and the North-West as far as the Red River Settlement, in 1844 paid a visit to the latter district. He left Quebec by steamer on 13th May, and on the 16th embarked at Lachine in a Hudson's Bay canoe, provided by the company. The craft, 36 feet in length, was of the largest class called a "canot de maitre," having fourteen paddles, and a crew of picked men. The route was by the Ottawa River, Mattawan River, Lakes Huron and Superior, Rainy Lake and River, Lake of the Woods, Winnipeg River and Lake. At Fort William the large canoe was exchanged for two smaller ones, more adapted to the travelling from that point. The party arrived at the Red River Settlement on Sunday, 23rd June; the return journey was commenced on 10th July, and Lachine reached on 14th August. Water color from old print. Size 3 x 7.

2296—GAMBIER—"James. Lord Gambier, Admiral of the Blue. From an original picture by Sir William Beechey, R.A., in his own possession. Drawn by W. Evans. Engraved by F. Bartolozzi. Published, Feb. 12, by T. Cadell & W. Davies, Strand, London." He was born in one of the Bahama Islands, 1756. Served in the American War at the capture of Charlestown. In the "defence" was first to break the enemy's line in Howe's victory of June 1st, 1794. Made rear-admiral, 1795, and vice-admiral in 1799. Governor of Newfoundland, 1802-4. Led the fleet at Copenhagen, 1807. Blockaded the French fleet in Basque Roads, and was one of the commissioners who negotiated the treaty of peace between England and the United States at Ghent, 1814. Made a G.C.B. in 1815, and received the rank of admiral of fleet in 1830. Died three years later. Line engraving. Size 8 x 10. Half length.

2297—BOUNDARY BETWEEN CANADA AND U. S.—Along the 49th parallel, B.C.—The cutting and camp shown is merely typical and might be at different places. The line of boundary, as determined in 1846, was not opened out in the original survey, but only in patches. It is now opened from end to end. Water color. Size 5 x 6.

2298—NANAIMO (NANYMO), B.C., 1862—View from the Anchorage, showing Fort and Coal Works, with key—From time immemorial the locality of Nanaimo was the home of five bands of Indians formed into a sort of confederacy known as "Sne-ny-mo," meaning the whole. This view was made about five years after the officers of the Hudson's Bay Company surveyed the harbor of Nanaimo and Departure Bay. Water color. Size 6 x 9.

2299—YATES STREET, VICTORIA, B.C., 1862—From the corner of Government to Wharf street, with key—The picture is in part a fancy sketch; so that on account of embellishment, it has been impossible to identify all the buildings. Water color. Size 6 x 9.

2300—"HARBOUR, TOWN AND NARROWS OF ST. JOHN'S, NEW-FOUNDLAND—This print is by kind permission dedicated to His Excellency Major General Sir John Harvey, K.C.B. and K.C.H.. Governor General of Newfoundland, by his most obedient humble servant, William Pardoe Clarke. Wm. P. Clarke, Pinxt. T. Picken, lith. Day and Haghe, Lithrs. to the Queen." Proof. In color. Size 13 x 20.

2301—RED RIVER ACADEMY, 1844—Afterwards first residence of the Bishop of Rupert's Land—Rev. D. T. Jones conducted the school, assisted from 1833-8 by Mr. John Macallum, M.A., of King's College, Aberdeen. Upon the former leaving the country in 1838, Mr. Macallum took full charge. He was ordained a priest of the Church of England in 1844. Before his death he appears to have become owner of the property, which he desired by his will to be sold to the Church of England authorities in order to continue the work. Bishop Anderson, who arrived at the Red River Settlement on the day of Mr. Macallum's death, acquired the establishment and renamed it St. John's College. Part of it—St. John's—was the bishop's

26

residence from 1849-54. In the left background of the picture is seen St. John's Church. The left wing of the academy was occupied by girls and the right wing by the master, and afterwards by the bishop, the connecting hall being used as the dining hall. The separate building on the right was used as school and dormitory for the boys. The buildings, which stood on the bank of the Red River in front of St. John's Churchyard, were badly damaged by the flood of 1852. Water color from a drawing by Peter Jacobs, an Indian scholar, who attended the school under Rev. John Macallum, and who subsequently became an ordained missionary. Water color from old print. Size 4 x 6.

2302—BISHOP'S COURT, RED RIVER, 1857—Second residence of the Bishop of Rupert's Land—It was close to the river bank, about two miles below, or north of Fort Garry, and was built by Chief Factor John Charles on his retirement from the Hudson's Bay service. On leaving for Scotland about 1850, he sold it to Mr. Adam Thom, recorder of Rupert's Land, by whom, on his leaving the country in 1854, it was sold to Bishop Anderson. The property then became known as "Bishop's Court," a name which had also been given to Bishop Anderson's residence in the "Red River Academy," on the bank of the Red River, in front of St. John's Churchyard. The fine modern home of Archbishop Matheson, Primate of All Canada, corner Machray and St. Cross streets, Winnipeg, now (1917) occupies the site of the old Bishop's Court. Water color from a photo by Prof. Henry Youle Hind, Canadian Red River Expedition. Size 5 x 7.

2303—INDIAN SETTLEMENT AT THE RED RIVER—This settlement, or St. Peter's Parish, begins twenty-five miles below Fort Garry, and was founded in 1832 by the Rev. William Cochran, of the Church Missionary Society, and some houses erected; but in 1833 a better location, three miles further up the river and twelve miles from "Grand" Rapids of the Red River, was selected. It was the chief Anglican Mission for Indians in the Hudson's Bay Territory, or Prince Rupert's Land. Rev. Dr. Mountain, Bishop of Montreal, visited the settlement in 1844, arriving there on Sunday, 23rd June. At that time the church, finished in 1834, had been built, also a parsonage or mission house and a school house. Rev. John Smethurst became the missionary in charge in 1839. He left the settlement in 1850, and Mr. Cochran went there to reside. The wooden church the latter had built while residing at St. Andrew's, was succeeded by a substantial structure, erected by him in 1854, and which still (1917) exists. Unlike any of the other Red River Protestant churches, it stands on the east instead of the west side of the river. The present town of Selkirk is just within the former southerly boundary of St. Peter's Parish. In the centre of the picture is the home of the missionary, and to the right, the church, with the schoolhouse behind it. Water color. Size 4 x 6.

2304—HUDSON'S BAY COMPANY'S PADDLE STEAMER "BEAVER" —Pioneer on the Pacific coast. Built in London, Eng., by Green, Wigram & Green, launched 2nd May, 1835, and the following August left London in charge of Capt. David Home. The company's barque, "Columbia," built at the same time, commanded by Capt. Darby, acted as her consort. For the passage out she was rigged as a brig, paddles unshipped. She arrived off the Columbia River, 18th March, 1836, and anchored off Fort Vancouver, on 10th April. Here the paddles were shipped and boilers and engines connected. The "Beaver" had a long and successful career in collecting furs for the company, and during her service was from 1863-70 employed by the British Government, under command of Daniel Pender, R.N., in surveying Western waters. She was sold in 1874, and used as a general freight and tow boat.. On 26th July, 1888, this little historic vessel was carried by the tidal current on the rocks at Prospect Point, entrance to Vancouver Harbor. Here she remained for some years, until piece by piece she was raised from her resting place by relic seekers from far and near. Photograph. Size 6 x 8.

2305—**DUCKWORTH**—"Admiral Sir John Thomas Duckworth, K.B., from an original picture by Sir William Beechey, R.A., in the possession of the Earl of St. Vincent. Drawn by W. Evans. Engraved by J. Vendramini. Published Dec. 4, 1809, by T. Cadell and W. Davies, Strand, London." Born at Leatherhead, Surrey, Eng., in 1748; educated at Eton, and in 1759 joined the navy. Served at Lagos Bay and Quiberon Bay. Became post-captain in 1780. Won distinction by his skill and courage in Lord Howe's victory over the French, June, 1794. Promoted to be rear-admiral, and in 1802 was appointed commander-in-chief at Jamaica. Four years later defeated the French near St. Domingo, for which Parliament voted him thanks and a large pension. As vice-admiral he performed a daring exploit by entering the Dardanelles in 1807. Governor of Newfoundland, 1810-13. Received a knighthood in 1813. Died, 1817. Line engraving. Size 8 x 10. Half length.

2306—**VICTORIA, VANCOUVER ISLAND**, 1858—View from James Bay. 1, South-west Bastion. 2, Hudson's Bay Co. group of buildings. 3, Old H. B. Co. cooperage. 4, Spire of Christ Church. 5, Residence of ex-Senator W. J. MacDonald, previously in employ of H. B. Co. 6, Residence of A. G. Dallas, Commissioner of H. B. Co., afterwards Governor. This house was subsequently turned into the Seamen's Institute. 7, Church of England Rectory, occupied by the late Rev. Edward Cridge, later Bishop of Reformed Episcopal Church. 8, James Bay. 9, Approximate position of James Bay Causeway, following the line of the old bridge, to the right of which now stands, on reclaimed ground, the Empress Hotel. 10, Approximate site of present Parliament Buildings. The perspective in this view is very poor, so that it is difficult to locate even prominent points of interest. Water color from print. Size 4 x 9. See 34, 2338.

2307—**OBELISK AT POINT ROBERTS, WASHINGTON**—Marking boundary between U. S. and British Columbia. This monument, erected at the western extremity of the 49th parallel of latitude, is 150 feet above the water, and faces the Gulf of Georgia. By the treaty signed at Washington, 15th June, 1846, dealing with the Oregon boundary, the 49th parallel was continued westward from the Rocky Mountains "to the middle of the channel which separates the continent from Vancouver's Island; and thence southerly through the middle of said channel, and of Fuca's Straits, to the Pacific Ocean." Former treaties and conventions had left this part of the boundary unsettled. Water color. Size 6 x 7.

2308—**FORT QU'APPELLE**, 1877—Between the Second and Third Fishing Lakes, Qu'Appelle River—This picture does not show all the buildings as they appeared in the 1867 view, a number having been demolished in the interval. The centre house at the back facing the river in the 1867 picture was that of Archibald McDonald, then Chief Clerk. He retired in May, 1911, and on his death in January, 1915, was the last of the chief factors of the Hudson's Bay Co. This house is still (1917) standing. From a water color, the oldest picture in existence of Fort Qu'Appelle, by Neison, in possession of Mr. Donald H. McDonald, Fort Qu'Appelle, Sask. Size 8 x 11. See 2334.

2309—**VILLAGE OF PEMBINA**, 1860—At the mouth of the Pembina River. Water color by J. W. Cotton. Size 5 x 7. See 2291, 2339, 2390.

2310—**LANDING OF FIRST LOCOMOTIVE IN MANITOBA**—Scene at Winnipeg, 9th Oct., 1877—On 3rd Oct. the "Selkirk" left Fisher's Landing, Minn., with the barge "Freighter" loaded with the first locomotive, six flat cars and a caboose for the Canadian Pacific Railway. They arrived at Winnipeg on 9th October, first putting ashore at No. 6 warehouse (foot of present Lombard street). Thence the boats dropped down and crossed the Red River to the mouth of the Seine, on the right bank of which the cars were landed. Shortly after landing the engine was examined by the crowds which swarmed aboard, and later in the day taken a short distance below Point Douglas, near the mouth of the Seine. Subsequently the engine was employed in laying rails to Emerson on the international boundary, where connection was made with the American road. It is a coincidence that Mr. Joseph Whitehead, who introduced the first locomotive into Manitoba, should have operated as fireman on the engine which drew the train on the first railway in England, between Stockton-on-Tees and Darlington. This old "iron horse" now (1917) has a place of honor across the street from the main entrance of the C.P.R. station, Winnipeg. Water color from a photograph taken on arrival of locomotive at Winnipeg, Man. Size 6 x 11. See 2347.

2311—FORT GEORGE, OR ASTORIA—On south side of the Columbia River, where it runs into the Pacific—Founded in 1810 by John Jacob Astor, a fur monopolist of New York, the Pacific Fur Company then becoming formally organized. In the War of 1812, Astoria changed hands and was re-named Fort George. By the Treaty of Ghent it was ceded back to the States, but without prejudice to the rights of Britain to the territory in which the fort was situated. However, the Pacific Fur Company did not attempt to again take up the work, so that the North-West, followed by the Hudson's Bay Company, continued to occupy the post until 1846, when Astoria became a part of the State of Oregon. The houses shown in the picture were those left during the last year of the company's possession— eight or nine houses and a long pine stick that upheld the British flag. Water color. Size 5 x 6.

2312—GROUP OF INDIAN GRAVES, RED RIVER SETTLEMENT, 1858—Water color by J. W. Cotton. Size 5 x 7. See 2374.

2313—ROLETTE, JOE, PEMBINA, DAKOTA, 1860—"The King of the Border"—He was a noted character in the West from 1850-70, well-known for his hospitality to passing travellers. By a writer who sojourned with Rolette for a time he is described as "muscular, a bullety head, the neck and chest of a young buffalo bull, a man of character, educated in New York, hospitable and generous." As chairman of the Capitol Bill he was prominent. It is a coincidence that Rolette was the guide of J. Ross Robertson, of The Toronto Daily Telegraph, now (1917) proprietor of The Toronto Evening Telegram, and Robert Cunningham, of The Toronto Globe, in their perilous journey to Fort Garry in December. 1869. Water color. Size 2½ x 3. Head and shoulders, profile.

2314—BLOCK HOUSE FORT OF HUDSON'S BAY COMPANY, KAM-LOOPS, B.C., 1862—These old-time posts of the Hudson's Bay Company were usually constructed in the form of a hundred-yard square, enclosed by a picket of logs rising from fifteen to twenty feet above it. Wooden bastions were built at two of the corners, and constructed of sufficient height to enable the garrison to obtain a good view of the surrounding country. In the gallery of the bastions stood a number of guns, covered in and used with regular ports like those of a ship. The ground floor served as a magazine. Inside the pickets were several buildings, including quarters for the officers and staff, and for trappers, voyageurs, trading store, etc. At this time Mr. McLean was the officer in charge of the fort at Kamloops. Water color. Size 4 x 6.

2315—WINNIPEG (FORT GARRY), 1872—From east bank of Red River, opposite the Forks of the Assiniboine and Red Rivers—The banks have fallen away to such an extent in recent years that the land at the Forks in 1872 would be about a quarter mid-stream. 1, The C.N.R. passes this point. 2, Site of Fort Rouge. 3. Pontoon bridge, east of present (1917) bridge spanning the Assiniboine. 4, South-east bastion, Fort Garry. 5, Hudson's Bay warehouse. 6, Government House. 7, Court House and Jail for Assiniboine. 8, C.N.R. tracks. 9, Grey Nuns, in charge of convent in St. Boniface. 10, Ferry between the Assiniboine and Pembina road. 11, French half-breeds with oxcarts. 12, Site of Fort Gibraltar. Water color from a picture in possession of Dr. Bryce, Winnipeg. Size 5 x 10.

2316—NORWAY HOUSE—On Little Playgreen Lake, near the mouth of the Jack River, and about twenty miles from Warren's Landing, Man. The post was first known as "Jack River." Subsequently, as it grew to be an important inland depot, it assumed the official name of Norway House, which is said to have been in honor of a large number of Norwegian recruits for the company's service for some time stationed there. The fishery of the first fort was at Jack River, but as it was found more convenient for the fort to move to the fishery than for the fish, the staple food, to be moved to the fort, Norway House was established on its present (1917) site. In 1831 the place became the depot for Athabasca as well as the Mackenzie River, and boats were built here for other districts also. The annual council of Hudson's Bay officers, who travelled such immense distances as Fort Vancouver, at the mouth of the Columbia River, New Caledonia and Mackenzie River, usually met here after York Factory had ceased to be the regular rendezvous. Water color from picture in "The Company of Adventurers," by Isaac Cowie. Size 5 x 7.

2317—THE STONE FORT, OR LOWER FORT GARRY—A Hudson's Bay post, built 1831-5, on the banks of the Red River, twenty miles north of Winnipeg. It was established by Governor (Sir George) Simpson, and named after Deputy-Governor Nicholas Garry, who came to the Red River in order to complete coalition arrangements of the Hudson's Bay and North-west Companies. It was occupied by the 2nd, or Quebec Battalion, Wolseley's Red River Expedition, 1870-1, and in the latter year Indian Treaty No. 1 was made there. The fort covered an area of about four acres and enclosed within its walls numerous buildings. It is (1917) a recognized place of itself and has a station on the Winnipeg-Selkirk Electric Railway. Water color from a photo by Prof. Henry Youle Hind, Canadian Red River Expedition, 1857-8. Size 5 x 9. See 2332-3.

2318—ST. ANDREW'S (ANGLICAN) PARSONAGE, RED RIVER— Sixteen miles below Fort Garry (Winnipeg)—The parsonage, which is situated near St. Andrew's Church, was erected in 1852-3 by the Church Missionary Society for the Rev. William Cochran. "It is," writes Prof. Henry Youle Hind in his narrative of the Red River Expedition of 1857, "in every respect fitted for the severities of the winter climate of the country. The walls, of limestone, are 2 feet 8 inches thick, the rooms lofty and capacious. This old rectory is still in an excellent state of preservation. The parish is now included in Selkirk County, Man. Water color from a photo by Prof. Henry Youle Hind, of the Canadian Red River Expedition, 1857-8. Size 5 x 8.

2319—VIEW OF FORT WILLIAM—Looking up the Kaministiquia River—On the right side are the fort and observatory, established 1803 by the North-west Company, which in 1821 amalgamated with the Hudson's Bay, the latter name prevailing since that time. The tents to the left and across the river are those of the Ojibway tribe, where a mission was subsequently founded by the Roman Catholic Church. Mount Mackay is immediately across the river, within a mile and a half of the city limits. Sepia by John Fleming, assistant surveyor, Canadian Red River Expedition, 1857-8. Size 6 x 11. See 2364, 2369.

2320—**FORT FRANCES**—Below Alberton Falls, on the north bank of Rainy River—Fort Frances was established by the Hudson's Bay Company in 1822. The original site of the fort is about a mile from the town; but the old buildings were burned about 1830 and the storehouses rebuilt on the present (1917) Central avenue, along the north bank of the river, just below Alberton Falls. Some years ago they were destroyed by fire. The Hudson's Bay Company has no stores or storehouses in the town at the present day. At Fort Frances were frequently held the grand medicine ceremonies of the Lac La Pluie Indians, who were very numerous, although diminishing in numbers at the time of the Hind party's visit to the locality in 1857. Water color by John Fleming, assistant surveyor, Canadian Red River Expedition, 1857-8. Size 5 x 9.

2321—**CATHEDRAL OF ST. BONIFACE (R. C.) AND NUNNERY**—On the banks of the Red River, opposite Fort Garry (Winnipeg, Man.)—The buildings were erected by Bishop Tache, who succeeded Bishop Provencher in 1854, establishing his throne at St. Boniface. The cathedral was destroyed by fire, December 14th, 1860, rebuilt 1864-6, and demolished some years ago to make way for the present (1917) edifice. The nunnery is still standing. A trolley line connects the city of St. Boniface with Winnipeg. Water color from a photo by Prof. Henry Youle Hind, Canadian Red River Expedition, 1857-8. Size 5 x 9.

2322—**ST. ANDREW'S CHURCH (RAPIDS CHURCH)**—Sixteen miles below, or north of Fort Garry—The commencement of the Anglican mission of St. Andrew dates as far back as 1824, when a small group of retired servants of the Hudson's Bay Company, with their native wives, first sought a permanent home at "the Grand Rapids." In 1829 the Rev. William Cochran, after Ven. Archdeacon, was placed in charge, and in 1831 built a church there. This building was succeeded by a more commodious one, consecrated by the Bishop of Rupert's Land in the autumn of 1849. Concerning it Prof. Hind said: "St. Andrew's Church, called also the Rapid's Church, is a new and very substantial structure of stone, well buttressed and very conveniently and neatly furnished. All its interior arrangements are attractive and substantial." The old building is still (1917) in a good state of preservation. Water color from a photo by Prof. Henry Youle Hind, of the Canadian Red River Expedition, 1857-8. Size 5 x 7.

2323—**STEAMER "COLLINGWOOD" (KALOOLAH)**—On a rock near Michipicoten Island, July, 1857—While en route to Fort William, with the Canadian Red River Expedition on board, the steamer in a fog ran on a low, rocky island, two miles from the harbor of Michipicoten, as shown in the picture. In 1860 she was wrecked off Southampton. Water color by John Fleming, assistant surveyor, Canadian Red River Expedition. Size 4 x 6. See 2595.

2324—**ANDREW McDERMOT'S STORE**, 1857—Near Fort Garry, on what is now (1916) Lombard street, near Victoria street, Winnipeg, immediately adjacent to the Kemp Manufacturing Company (Hon. A. E. Kemp, of Toronto). The old-time wooden building, one of the first erected at Red River, went out of existence about 1880. According to Prof. Henry Youle Hind, McDermot was in 1857 "the most enterprising and wealthy merchant and freighter in the settlements." Water color from photo by Prof. Henry Youle Hind, Canadian Red River Expedition. Size 5 x 7.

2325—**NOTED FUR STOREHOUSE**—The Hudson's Bay depot at Lower Fort Garry—The building was of stone and was one of the most commodious storehouses of the Hudson's Bay Company in the North-west. It has been in continuous use since its erection in 1831. Water color from a photo by Prof. Henry Youle Hind, Canadian Red River Expedition, 1857-8. Size 5 x 8.

2326—FREIGHTER'S BOAT ON THE BANKS OF THE RED RIVER— Close to St. Paul's Parish and below Kildonan—The regular "York" boat of the Red River Settlement is here portrayed, laid up for the winter. The design was after the model of the ancient Norse galley; used principally for freighting between York Factory and Red River Settlement, also on the Saskatchewan. They were portaged in the usual manner. All kinds of goods were carried, generally in "pieces" of ninety pounds each. Water color from photo by Henry Youle Hind, Canadian Red River Expedition, 1857-8. Size 5 x 7.

2327—RESIDENCE OF A. G. B. BANNATYNE, a leading merchant of the "Town" of Fort Garry, and famed for his hospitality to travellers passing through the Red River district. The house stood in the vicinity of the present (1917) Bannatyne, Rorie and McDermot streets, in the city of Winnipeg. Many years ago the original dwelling was replaced by a much better one, but the second also disappeared, some time in the eighties. Transfer railway tracks and delivery yards now occupy the site, which is in the rear of the Dominion Government Customs Examining warehouse. Water color from a photo by Prof. Henry Youle Hind, Canadian Red River Expedition, 1857-8. Size 5 x 7.

2328—TYPICAL GROUP OF OJIBWAY INDIANS AT FORT FRANCES, ONT., AUG., 1857—These Indians, known also as the Chippawas, or Saulteaux, were accustomed to visit Fort Frances for the purpose of trade, and frequently held their grand medicine ceremonies in the neighborhood. The original fort was established here in 1822 by the Hudson's Bay Company, and subsequently named in honor of Lady Frances Simpson, whose husband, Sir George Simpson, was for many years governor of the company. Water color from photo by Prof. Henry Youle Hind, Canadian Red River Expedition. Size 5 x 7.

2329—FORT YORK, OR YORK FACTORY—On the north bank of the Hayes River, five miles from its mouth—A great emporium, which for many years was a distributing centre of commerce of the Hudson's Bay Company. In August, 1782, the French, under La Perouse, attacked the fort, which surrendered without defence. As Fort Garry grew in importance, Fort York diminished, until it became merely a depot for posts nearer the coast than to Lake Winnipeg. Water color. Size 4 x 7.

2330—KA-KA-BE-KA FALLS, KAMINISTIQUIA (KAMINISTIQUE) RIVER, 1856—These falls are about thirty miles west of Fort William, Ont. They are now being used to develop power for running mills in Fort William and Port Arthur, especially the former place. Ka-ka-be-ka means water falling over a rock, while Kaministique is a corruption of the word Cah-mah-na-te-gwa-yaug, a river with several branches. Water color by Wm. Armstrong, C.E., Toronto. Size 9 x 13.

2331—ISLINGTON MISSION, OR CHIEN BLANC—On the Winnipeg River, fifty miles from Fort Alexander—It was formerly held by the Roman Catholics; left vacant for six years, and in 1850 Mr. Philip Kennedy was appointed catechist. In 1853 Rev. Robert Macdonald revived the mission, which in 1857 consisted of five houses and a schoolhouse, used as a chapel. There is still (1917) an Anglican mission at Islington, on east side of Winnipeg River, just beside Yellow Earth Falls. Water color by John Fleming, assistant surveyor, Canadian Red River Expedition, 1857-8. Size 8 x 11.

2332—LOWER FORT GARRY, OR STONE FORT—View of the Red River and the exterior of the fort. Water color by John Fleming, assistant surveyor, Canadian Red River Expedition, 1857-8. Size 7 x 13. See 2317, 2333.

2333—**LOWER FORT GARRY, OR STONE FORT**—Interior view—The building to the left is the Governor's house, the first stone house west of Lake Superior (1857), and now (1917) the Winnipeg Motor Club. The centre building is the Hudson's Bay fur store, also built of stone. Water color by John Fleming, assistant surveyor, Canadian Red River Expedition, 1857-8. Size 5 x 7. See 2317, 2332.

2334—**FORT QU'APPELLE,** 1867—Bird's-eye view, between the Second and Third Fishing Lakes, Qu'Appelle River—In 1858 a mission was established here, and Rev. James Settee, of Swampy Cree origin, sent as missionary to the Plain Crees. Facing the gate of the fort was the master's house. To the west stood a row of five dwelling houses, and directly opposite, on the east, or right, was a similar row used as fur and provision stores. To right of front gate is seen the flagstaff, with British ensign, and letters H.B.C. hoisted on Sundays and holidays. Fort Qu'Appelle is (1917) in Saskatchewan, near Lipton. Drawing in water color from "The Company of Adventurers," by Isaac Cowie. Size 6 x 9. See 2308.

2335—**ST. PAUL'S CHURCH (ANGLICAN) AND PARSONAGE, RED RIVER**—Eight miles north of Fort Garry (Winnipeg)—In 1824 in the parish of St. Paul, which adjoined that of St. John, the Rev. David T. Jones erected a temporary place of worship. In 1844 a second church was erected to succeed the old one, but a regular clergyman was not appointed until five years later, when the Rev. John Chapman began his labors there. In his account of the Canadian Red River Expedition in 1857 Prof. Hind says: "St. Paul's Church parsonage and schoolhouse are substantial and serviceable buildings, with no pretension to architectural display, but well fitted for the object of their construction." The church is still (1917) standing. To the right of the picture may be seen the old schoolhouse. Water color from a photo by Prof. Henry Youle Hind, of the Canadian Red River Expedition, 1857-8. Size 5 x 8.

2336—**JOHN INKSTER'S HOME AND FARM BUILDINGS**—At Seven Oaks, now (1917) in North Winnipeg, on the main street or road to Selkirk —Mr. Inkster was a Hudson's Bay Company official and the father of Sheriff Inkster, of the Manitoba Courts at Winnipeg. The old property has always been known as "Seven Oaks," and is the exact site of the battle on 19th June, 1816, between the French Metis (Halfbreeds) of the North-west Company, and the Hudson's Bay Company and Selkirk settlers under Governor Semple, who was killed in the fight. The historic property is now largely built upon. Water color from photo by Prof. Henry Youle Hind, Canadian Red River Expedition, 1857-8. Size 5 x 7.

2337—**HOME OF THE CHIEF FACTOR OF THE MIDDLE SETTLEMENT, RED RIVER**—At the time the picture was made, the large and comfortable house shown was occupied by Mrs. Bird, widow of a Hudson's Bay Company official, who had served in different districts of Rupert's Land. It still (1917) stands, above the new Dominion Government St. Andrew's Locks. Water color from a photo. by Prof. Henry Youle Hind, Canadian Red River Expedition, 1857-8. Size 5 x 7.

2338—**VICTORIA, B.C.,** 1862—At the south-east end of Vancouver Island—View from James' Bay—The fort, which became the future city of Victoria, was established in 1842 by the Hudson's Bay Company, and named in honor of Her Late Majesty Queen Victoria. Since the union with Canada in 1871 it has been the capital of British Columbia. With key. Water color. Size 6 x 9. See 34, 2306, 2345.

2339—**FORTS DAER AND PEMBINA,** 1822—At the junction of the Red and Pembina Rivers. The larger fort is the Hudson's Bay establishment, and the smaller (left of picture) the refuge of Lord Selkirk's colonists,

1812-13. These forts were found to be south of the international boundary when determined, so that the Hudson's Bay post was moved a little north of the line. The American military post, now (1917) capital of Pembina County, North Dakota, was subsequently established in the vicinity. Later the H. B. post of Pembina was again found to be in U.S. territory, and a Hudson's Bay shop was established in West Lynne, now known as Emerson Junction, Man. Drawing in water color from picture in Dominion Archives, Ottawa. Size 7 x 9. See 2291, 2309, 2390.

2340—VAST OCEAN OF PRAIRIE LEVEL—It is impossible to assign any locality to this view, which was evidently taken simply to show the flat character of the land. Prof. Hind writes of the prairies having "unrelieved immensity which belongs to them in common with the ocean, but which, unlike the ever-changing and unstable sea, seem to promise a bountiful recompence to millions of our fellow-men." Water color from a photo by Prof. Henry Youle Hind, Canadian Red River Expedition, 1857-8. Size 5 x 7.

2341—RED RIVER FROM THE STONE FORT—Twenty miles north of Winnipeg, Man.—The Red River, which takes its rise in Ottertail Lake, Minnesota, has within British territory a length of about 140 miles, and at last enters into Lake Winnipeg by six distinct channels. With regard to the stretch of river shown in the picture, Professor Henry Youle Hind says: "At the Stone Fort, massive layers of limestone crop out, which have been extensively quarried and their application is seen in the walls and bastions of the fort built upon the bank, here about forty feet in altitude." Water color from a photo by Prof. Henry Youle Hind, Canadian Red River Expedition, 1857-8. Size 5 x 8.

2342—WINNIPEG, MAN., 1870—View from the north-eastern part of Main street—The entire site of the picture takes in Rupert street to Assiniboine avenue. It also shows part of Portage road, now (1917) Portage avenue. 1, Bannatyne house, the old post-office. 2, Bannatyne's store, Merchants' Bank. 3, Red River Hall. 4, Hudson's Bay liquor store. 5, Lyon's, or Couture's store, Ashdown hardware. 6, 6, 6, Several banks, stores and hotels occupy this locality, between Rupert and Market street east. Drawing in water color. Size 6 x 9. See 2294.

2343—KILDONAN PRESBYTERIAN CHURCH—Seven miles below Fort Garry (Winnipeg)—Lord Selkirk had promised his Scottish Presbyterian settlers in the Red River district a clergyman of their own faith, but notwithstanding their repeated representations to those in authority, it was not until 1851 that the first Presbyterian minister, in the person of the Rev. John Black, arrived at the colony. The old stone church in which Mr. Black preached for many years is still (1917) standing, in Kildonan municipality. The name "Kildonan" was given to that part of the Red River Settlement which Lord Selkirk colonized with emigrants from the parish of the name in Sutherlandshire, Scotland. Water color from a photo by Prof. Henry Youle Hind, of the Canadian Red River Expedition, 1857-8. Size 5 x 8.

2344—GOVERNOR'S HOUSE, HUDSON'S BAY COMPANY, RED RIVER, 1857—At the Stone Fort, or Lower Fort Garry—The old-time building, which was the first stone house to be erected west of Lake Superior, has been improved and is now (1917) the home of the Winnipeg Motor Club. Large trees enhance the beauty of the lawn in front. Water color from a photo by Prof. Henry Youle Hind, Canadian Red River Expedition, 1857-8. Size 5 x 8.

2345—HUDSON'S BAY COMPANY ESTABLISHMENT AT VICTORIA, VANCOUVER ISLAND, B.C., 1846—The view shows: 1, "Hospital Point," in the old days the beginning of the Songhees Reserve. 2, Indian houses. 3, Barracks for new arrivals. 4, Palisade by which Hudson's Bay Co. buildings were surrounded. 5, Needle Gateway. 6, H. B. Co. slip (wharf). 7, S. W. bastion. 8, Farm building. 9, Old steamer "Labouchere." 10, Laurel Point, now (1917) known as Sehl's Point. Water color from old print. Size 4 x 6. See 34, 2306.

2346—CUMBERLAND HOUSE, 1858—A pioneer post of the Hudson's Bay Company. Water color by John Fleming, assistant surveyor, Canadian Red River Expedition, 1857-8. Size 4 x 9. See 2387.

2347—CANADIAN PACIFIC RAILWAY STATION, WINNIPEG, MAN., AND "COUNTESS OF DUFFERIN"—The station of the C.P.R. in Winnipeg was opened to the public in August, 1905. It is an imposing structure of buff brick with stone dressings over the entire front, and faces south on Higgins avenue. To the east, or right, is situated the Immigration Hall, and to the left or west the Royal Alexandra Hotel. An attractive feature in the view is the "Countess of Dufferin," the first locomotive in Manitoba, landed at Winnipeg on 9th Oct., 1877. As a memorial of the event, the engine, instead of being consigned to the scrap heap, was put in good order, and now (1917) rests from its labors across the street from the main entrance of the station. Photograph, colored. Size 4 x 7.

2348-2353—"Views in Hudson's Bay, Taken by a Gentleman on the Spot, In the years 1823 and 1824. Illustrative of the Customs, Manners and Costumes of those Tribes of North American Indians amongst whom Capt'n. Franklin has passed in his present and former arduous undertaking. To be continued in numbers." Further numbers, however, were never issued.

2348—"THE RED LAKE CHIEF—Making a Speech to the Governor of Red River at Fort Douglas in 1825—H. Jones, Del. W. Day, Lithog., 59 Gt. Queen Street." Fort Douglas, so named in honor of the family name of the Earl of Selkirk, founder of the Red River Settlement, stood about a mile below the confluence of the Assiniboine and Red River, upon the south side of Point Douglas. This picture relates to a visit of the Red Lake Indians to the settlement at that place, which was not an uncommon practice. Peguis, the Red Lake chief, is making a speech to Governor Pelly, who is seated to the right. Lithograph in color. Size 8 x 12.

2349—"THE GOVERNOR OF RED RIVER—Driving his family on the river in a horse cariole—H. Jones. Printed by W. Day, 59 Gt. Queen St." This view shows the mode of pleasure travel in winter, at the Red River Settlement, Western Canada. The driver of the carriole is Captain Robert P. Pelly, who from 1823-5 was Colony Governor. In the distance is Fort Douglas, constructed in 1813 by Lord Selkirk, and which in 1816 capitulated, after the massacre at Seven Oaks, the colonists leaving for Jackfish House at the north end of Lake Winnipeg. Lithograph in color. Size 7 x 12.

2350—"A SOUTEAUX INDIAN—Travelling with his family in winter near Lake Winnipeg—H. Jones, Del., 59 Gt. Queen Street." The party is travelling in the ordinary way with a baggage sledge, a thin board ten or twelve feet long, twelve inches broad, and turned up at one end. The baggage is attached by means of buffalo thongs, and two or three dogs are harnessed to the vehicle with the same materials. A winter road rarely exceeds fifteen inches, and is of a depth proportioned to the quantity of snow which has fallen. To make the new road is regarded as the chief difficulty in travelling with dogs. Lithograph in color. Size 7 x 12.

2351—"A GENTLEMAN TRAVELLING IN A DOG CARIOLE—In Hudson's Bay with an Indian Guide—H. Jones, del. W. Day, Lithog., 59

Gt. Queen Strt." This primitive vehicle is constructed of a very thin board, ten feet long and twelve or fourteen inches broad, turned up at one end in the form of a half-circle, like the bow of an Ojibway canoe. To this board a high cradle, like the body of a small carriage, is attached, about eighteen inches from the end of the board or floor. The framework is covered with buffalo skin parchment, and painted or decorated according to taste. The inside is lined with a blanket or buffalo robe, and when the traveller is seated he is separated from the snow only by the thin plank which forms the floor. The traveller is Capt. Pelly, Colony Governor of the Red River Settlement. Lithograph in color. Size 7 x 12.

2352—"THE GOVERNOR OF RED RIVER, HUDSON'S BAY—Voyaging in a light canoe, 1824—H. Jones, Del. W. Day's Lithogy., 59 Gt. Queen St." Capt. Robert J. Pelly, a brother of Sir John Pelly, Governor of the Hudson's Bay Company, was Colony Governor from June, 1823-June, 1825. It has been said of him that he "lacked nerve and decision." The picture shows him with his party, voyaging in what was known as a light canoe of birch rind, with a round bottom. Lithograph in color. Size 7 x 12.

2353—"RED LAKE CHIEF—With some of his followers arriving at the Red River and visiting the Governor—H. Jones, del. W. Day's Lithog'r., 69 Gt. Queen Street." The Red Lake Indians were and are a small branch of the Ojibways (Saulteurs or Chippawas). These Indians were evidently always in touch with their fellow tribesmen who remained on the Canadian side of the international boundary. The Colony Governor of the Red River at this time was Capt. R. P. Pelly, who succeeded Bulger in 1823. He is seen to the right of picture, shaking hands with Peguis, chief of the settlement at Red River. Lithograph in color. Size 8 x 12.

2354—SELKIRK, THOMAS DOUGLAS, FIFTH EARL, AND BARON DAER AND SHORTCLEUGH, 1771-1820—Founder of the Red River Settlement, Western Canada. From marble bust by Chantry at St. Mary's Isle, Kirkcudbrightshire, Scotland, and showing three aspects. Photographs. Size 4 x 5. See 2365-6-7.

2355—ST. BONIFACE NUNNERY—Opposite the city of Winnipeg (Fort Garry)—This building, which to-day (1917) stands on Tache avenue, St. Boniface, was, with the Cathedral of St. Boniface, erected by Bishop Tache. The cathedral, burned 14th Dec., 1860, was rebuilt, and three or four years ago demolished to make room for a new structure. Pencil drawing by John Fleming, assistant surveyor, Canadian Red River Expedition, 1857-8. Size 5 x 7.

2356—CLOTHING OF THE SIOUX INDIANS—The Sioux coat, leggings and moccasins are characteristic of the dress of Western tribes in early days. The painting on the tanned buckskin is well done. The ornamentation on the sleeves and leggings is probably ermine or some other fur used by Western tribes. Drawing in water color by John Fleming, assistant surveyor, Canadian Red River Expedition, 1857-8. Size 4 x 6.

2357—FALLS AT RAT PORTAGE (KENORA), ONT., RAINY RIVER DISTRICT, NORTH-WEST ONTARIO—This spot is now (1917) the site of the Kenora Hydro-Electric Development, on the east branch of the Winnipeg River, within half a mile of the business section of Rat Portage, the name of which was changed to Kenora, May 17th, 1905. The latter name is derived from Keewatin, a neighboring town, from Norman, now a suburb of Kenora, and from the town of Rat Portage, the first syllable of each name being used. Pencil drawing on toned paper by John Fleming, assistant surveyor, Canadian Red River Expedition, 1857-8. Size 5 x 5.

2358—INDIAN PIPE OF WESTERN TRIBE—This dark green stone totem pipe is strictly characteristic of British Columbian work; and also rare at the present time. The figures are purely Indian, except the central one with the wheel underneath. The figures from right to left represent: First, a man with a mastodon head; second, probably an eagle with the feathering well marked thereon; third, a rabbit; fourth and fifth, two indefinite and typical figures found on totem poles in British Columbia. Pencil drawing on toned paper by John Fleming, assistant surveyor, Canadian Red River Expedition, 1857-8. Size 5 x 11.

2359—INDIAN PIPE OF WESTERN TRIBE—This pipe, coming from the Red River District, is somewhat of a mixture between a Dacotah catlanite pipe and some of those from British Columbia. It is evidently of modern origin, as the human figure sitting, probably on a dog, has braces; and the central structure is evidently a house with windows; something unknown to the Western Indians. The bowls in these pipes are very small, as the Indians always powdered their tobacco before using. Pencil drawing on toned paper by John Fleming, assistant surveyor, Canadian Red River Expedition, 1857-8. Size 5 x 11.

2360—"THE FOX," CHIEF OF THE PLAIN CREES—Near Elbow, South Branch of the Saskatchewan—Hind says: "The great chief of the Plain Crees is styled 'The Fox'; he is held in high estimation by all the Plain Indians with whom he comes in contact, either in peace or war. He is dreaded by the Sioux, the Blackfeet, the Bloodies, the Fall Indians, the Assiniboines and the tribes who occasionally hunt on the Grand Coteau de Missouri and the South Branch of the Saskatchewan." In the background is a Plain Cree tent, decorated, as the custom was, with emblems representing incidents, such as battles, horse stealing, etc. Chromoxylograph from a drawing by John Fleming, assistant surveyor, Canadian Red River Expedition, 1857-8. Size 4 x 6.

2361—OJIBWAY SQUAW WITH PAPOOSE—The picture was made at the time of the annual spring assemblage of the Crees, Ojibways and Swampys. It was the custom of these Indians to celebrate their medicine feasts at the time when the migratory birds began to arrive or the sturgeon commenced to ascend the rivers. Chromoxylograph by Prof. Henry Youle Hind, Canadian Red River Expedition, 1857-8. Size 4 x 6.

2362—"WIGWAM," AN OJIBWAY HALF-BREED—With the Hind party in October, 1858. The expedition took the "pitching track," an Indian trail from one part of the country to another, in order to reach Riding Mountain, which they had decided to ascend. "Wigwam" was most useful in carrying articles, in addition to his pack, over quaking bogs and marshes. He belonged to the tribe whose totem was the "Bear." Chromoxylograph from a drawing by Prof. Henry Youle Hind. Canadian Red River Expedition, 1857-8. Size 4 x 6.

2363—SUSAN, A SWAMPY CREE HALF-BREED—Near camp at the mouth of the Saskatchewan River—On the evening of the 25th September, 1858, Prof. Hind and his party arrived at a camp of Swampys, on the edge of a cranberry marsh, on banks of the river. They remained near the Indians all night, and the following morning both parties proceeded towards St. Martin's Lake. Chromoxylograph from a drawing by John Fleming, assistant surveyor, Canadian Red River Expedition, 1857-8. Size 4 x 6.

2364—FORT WILLIAM—From the south side of the Kaministiquia River, showing the Hudson's Bay post and the Observatory—The fort, named in honor of Hon. William McGillivray, was commenced in 1800 by the North-west Company, and completed three years later, on the site of Fort Caministigoyon, which was built in 1678 by Sieur Duluth. In 1821 it became a Hudson's Bay post. The picture shows the fort, near the river's edge, and the observatory (towards the centre) above the gateway of the middle entrance into the fort, on the river side. It was used to watch the incoming fur traders' boats and canoes. The store and storehouses of the Hudson's Bay Company were located about half a mile from the river's mouth, where the present (1917) McTavish street is. The site is now occupied by the C.P.R. roundhouse, railway tracks and workingmen's homes. Situated near the centre of the continent, the city of Fort William has exceptional harbor advantages as the head of navigation to the Atlantic, and the shipping facilities in connection with the Canadian Pacific and Canadian Northern Railways. Sepia by John Fleming, assistant surveyor, Canadian Red River Expedition. Size 8 x 24. See 2319, 2369.

2365—SELKIRK, THOMAS DOUGLAS, FIFTH EARL OF—The founder of the Red River Settlement, Western Canada. Lord Selkirk, Baron Daer and Shortcleugh, was born at the family seat in Kirkcudbright-shire, Scotland, 1771; died at Pau, France, 1820. He was educated at Edinburgh University, associating there with Sir Walter Scott. In 1792 Selkirk became interested in the Highland peasantry, who at that time were being frequently evicted from their homes, and in 1803 formed a Scottish colony in the Island of St. John (Prince Edward Island). He later founded the Red River Settlement, the first party leaving the Highlands of Scotland, the Orkneys and Ireland, for York Factory, Hudson's Bay, July 26, 1811. The fourth contingent went out to Hudson Bay in the summer of 1815. The Earl met with many discouragements, but success finally crowned his efforts. His treatise on emigration, an exhaustive treatment of the subject, was long considered a standard work. In default of a lineal descendant on the death of the Sixth Earl, the Selkirk title was merged with the Dukedom of Hamilton. Water color from a portrait by Raeburn, at St. Mary's Isle, Kirkcudbrightshire, Scotland. Size 10 x 12. Half length. See 2354, 2366-7.

2366—SELKIRK, THOMAS DOUGLAS, FIFTH EARL, 1771-1820. Water color. Size 4 x 5. Head and shoulders. See 2365.

2367—SELKIRK, THOMAS DOUGLAS, FIFTH EARL OF SELKIRK, 1771-1820. From marble bust by Chantry, at St. Mary's Isle, Kirkcudbright-shire, Scotland. Size 4 x 6. See 2354, 2365.

2368—"NORTH-WEST VIEW OF PRINCE OF WALES'S FORT IN HUDSON'S BAY, NORTH AMERICA—By Saml. Hearne, 1777." At the mouth of the Churchill River—In 1718 a wooden fort was constructed five miles up the river, the site of which had been occupied since 1688. The Hudson's Bay Co., in 1734, built the stronghold shown in picture, and in 1746 stone parapets instead of wooden ones were erected. The fort was attacked 8th Aug., 1782, by La Perouse, surrendered immediately by Gov. Hearne, and attempts made by the French to destroy it. The parts displaced, for the fort was almost impregnable, were never rebuilt. Engraving in color. Size 5 x 8. See 2384, 3252.

2369—FORT WILLIAM (FORT CAMINISTIGOYON)—A view from the Observatory looking east—The Observatory, established on the completion of the fort in 1803, was situated on the river side, above the gateway of the middle entrance into the fort, and was used to watch incoming fur traders' boats and canoes. To facilitate this, an avenue of from two to three hundred yards wide was cut across "Island Number One," exposing a clear view out to the Welcome Islands. Sepia by John Fleming, assistant surveyor, Canadian Red River Expedition, 1857-8. Size 7 x 11. See 2319, 2364.

2370—HUDSON'S BAY POST AT RAT PORTAGE (KENORA), ONT. —The first post of the Hudson's Bay Company at this point. Situated on

Fort Island, about half a mile from Rat Portage. In 1866 the company erected a frame building on Main street. This structure, however, was burned June 9th, 1885, and was succeeded by one of stone, at the corner of Main and First streets. The later building, with an addition, is still (1917) in use. In 1892 Rat Portage was incorporated as a town, and on May 17th, 1905, the name became Kenora. Water color by John Fleming, assistant surveyor, Canadian Red River Expedition. Size 8 x 11.

2371—CASCADES AT COUTEAU PORTAGE, KAMINISTIQUIA RIVER—Thirty miles from its mouth—Known (1917) as Mokoman Portage. The cascades are five chains long, and there is a drop of nineteen feet in the river in that distance. Couteau is the French for "knife," and Mokoman is Ojibway for the same word. The Indians used to call the place "Michi-Mokoman," on account of some association with the "Big Sword of the Americans," but it is now universally called Mokoman. Sepia by John Fleming, assistant surveyor, Canadian Red River Expedition. Size 6 x 10.

2372—FORT DOUGLAS—Built in 1813 by Earl Selkirk, founder of the Red River Settlement. It stood about a mile below the confluence of the Assiniboine and Red Rivers, on the south side of Point Douglas, and received its name from the patronymic of the Selkirks. The site of the old fort is now (1917) in the city of Winnipeg, at the foot of George street. Water color from a pencil sketch by Lord Selkirk at St. Mary's Isle, Kirkcudbrightshire, Scotland, the seat of the Selkirk family. Size 5 x 9.

2373—ST. JOHN'S CHURCH (ANGLICAN) AND COLLEGE, RED RIVER—Two miles below or north of Fort Garry. In 1834 the second church here, which was of stone, was opened under the Rev. David T. Jones, who succeeded the Rev. John West as chaplain for the Hudson's Bay Company. It was not, however, until October, 1853, that it was consecrated by the name of St. John's. At the time of the taking of the picture the sacred edifice was in a very unstable condition, the walls being supported with wooden props. The school, founded 1833 for boys and girls, was at this time under supervision of the Bishop of Rupert's Land, and was attended only by boys. In 1862 St. John's Cathedral was erected on the site, and in 1914 the old cathedral building was demolished to make way for a large, new structure. Pencil drawing by John Fleming, assistant surveyor, Canadian Red River Expedition, 1857-8. Size 5 x 9.

2374—MODE OF INDIAN BURIAL—Graves covered with split sticks— The picture shows an old-time burial ground, called by the Hurons, Oi-go-sa-ye. If death had been due to natural causes, the remains were encased in birch bark and elevated on four poles, remaining there until the celebration of the "Feast of the Dead," which took place every eight or ten years. The dead were then placed with much solemnity in a large excavation richly decorated with furs. As often as the sticks and boards decayed they were replaced by others. Before the dispersion of the Hurons, about 1850, these customs were religiously observed among this tribe. Chromoxylograph from a drawing by John Fleming, assistant surveyor, Canadian Red River Expedition. Size 4 x 7. See 2312.

2375—"ANSON NORTHRUP," 1859—First steamer to arrive at Fort Garry (Winnipeg)—In the autumn of 1858 Mr. Anson Northrup ran his boat up the Crow Wing River, a tributary of the Mississippi, took it to pieces, packed the machinery and timber for building the hull on sleighs, which in the winter of 1859 were with great difficulty drawn by horses and oxen to Otter Tail Lake, and thence westward to the mouth of the Cheyenne, on the Red River. Assisted by the St. Paul Chamber of Commerce, but mainly depending on his own private resources, and by hard work and perseverance, the boat was rebuilt on the banks of the Red River, launched on 19th May and christened the "Anson Northrup." In the high water of early spring she made her trial trip down to Fort Garry and back. She had to lie by every night, of course, and must have been greatly delayed by the necessity of stopping to cut timber for the fire. In spite of these delays she made the return trip in eight days. The "Anson Northrup," later known as "The Pioneer," was a steam-propelled craft of the flat-bottomed build, similar to those running on the Mississippi, U.S. Water color. Size 5 x 7.

2376—FORT GARRY (WINNIPEG), 1840—The south and east faces of the Western stronghold. Water color from a sketch by the wife of Governor Finlayson, of the Hudson's Bay Company. Size 5 x 7. See 2377.

2377—FORT GARRY IN WINTER OF 1882—The east face of the fort, just before it was dismantled—The first fort, said to have been on the south bank of the Assiniboine, immediately above its confluence with the Red River, was a temporary post, Fort Rouge, built by one of Verandrye's men, 1738. In 1806, on north bank of Assiniboine, was built by the Northwest Co., Fort Gibraltar, destroyed 1816, rebuilt the following year, and renamed Fort Garry, 1822. A new Fort Garry, close by on the west, was built by Gov. Pelly in 1826. Destroyed by great flood of that year, and at once rebuilt. The structure shown, the third Fort Garry, was built by Governor Christie, 1835-6, reconstructed and extended to the north in 1850-1, by a wall of heavy oak logs, with stone, arched gateway. The fort was dismantled in 1882, and the gateway, which stands in a small city park at the rear of the Manitoba Club, is the only part remaining to-day (1917). The cross shows where Thomas Scott, a young Ontario Orangeman, was executed by order of Louis Riel, March 4th, 1870. Main street, Winnipeg, now runs through an angle of the old stronghold, ending on Main street bridge, about in front of where the large gate or entrance is given. Water color. Size 4 x 7. See 2376.

2378—VALLEY OF THE SOURIS—Looking towards the Blue Hills— Next to the valley of the Qu'Appelle, the old course of the Little Souris (Mouse) through the depression occupied by the Backfat Lakes, is the most curious and imposing. Standing on one of the most prominent of the Blue Hills of the Souris, near their southern extremity, the ancient valley can be traced as far as the first lake, which is visible with the unassisted eye, and with a good marine telescope is distinctly seen. The Little Souris here pursues a course at right angles to its former valley, and has excavated a channel from 300 to 400 feet deep through the loose drift of the Blue Hills and the cretaceous rock underlying it. Drawing in water color by John Fleming, assistant surveyor, Canadian Red River Expedition, 1857-8. Size 4 x 6. See 2379-80, 2407.

2379—VALLEY OF THE SOURIS (MOUSE)—View near the Blue Hills. Drawing in water color by John Fleming, assistant surveyor, Canadian Red River Expedition, 1857-8. Size 4 x 6. See 2378, 2407.

2380—VALLEY OF THE SOURIS—Opposite the valley of the Backfat Lakes—The Backfat Lakes, now (1917) known as the Chain Lakes, lie to the south of the Souris River, and seem to be continuations. They come in longtitude 100, latitude 50. Drawing in water color by John Fleming, assistant surveyor, Canadian Red River Expedition. Size 4 x 6.

2381—INDIAN HUNTERS' TENTS—Scene in the rear of Fort Garry— The tepees, or leather tents of the Plain Crees who have camped in readiness to trade at this well-known Hudson's Bay post, are here shown and also the typical Red River carts. These strong conveyances used by the early settlers to carry their effects, were fashioned entirely of wood, wooden pegs even being used instead of nails. They were easily mended if a breakdown occurred, by the use of green hide, cut in strips and bound around the break. When the hide dried it fastened the broken part with iron pressure, making it as strong as ever. The body of the cart consisted of a rude box with willow hoops over which sail cloth or strong cotton was stretched for protection from the sun. Water color by John Fleming, assistant surveyor, Canadian Red River Expedition, 1857-8. Size 4 x 7.

2382—FAIRFORD, OR PARTRIDGE CROP, SEPTEMBER, 1858—On the north arm of Lake Manitoba—The "Crop" was so called by the Indians on account of the resemblance to the crop of a partridge, of a narrow passage in the Partridge Crop River between beds of rushes, covering many square miles. Fairford, originally a Hudson's Bay post and an Indian mission (Anglican), established by the Rev. Mr. Cowley in 1840, shortly after the Cumberland Mission was founded, is now a settlement about 120 miles from Winnipeg. Drawing in water color by John Fleming, assistant surveyor, Canadian Red River Expedition, 1857-8. Size 4 x 6.

2383—FALLS ON THE RAINY RIVER, AUGUST, 1857—In the distance, to the left, is Fort Frances, Ont., established by the Hudson's Bay Company in 1822, and in the foreground is shown an encampment and fishing place of Lac La Pluie Indians. Prof. Hind in 1857 writes of the falls as "magnificent cascades" which let the river down 22.88 feet. At Fort Frances were frequently held the grand medicine ceremonies of the Lac La Pluie Indians, who were very numerous, although diminishing in numbers when the Hind party visited the locality. Wood cut from drawing by John Fleming, assistant surveyor, Canadian Red River Expedition, 1857-8. Size 4 x 7.

2384—"A SOUTH-WEST VIEW OF PRINCE OF WALES'S FORT, HUDSON'S BAY—Published by J. Sewell, Cornhill, March 1st, 1797. Saml. Hearne, del. Wise, sculp." Showing the fort, at the mouth of the Churchill River, surrounded by parapets of wood supplied by denuding the old Prince of Wales fort, built in 1718, five miles up the Churchill River. These parapets were replaced by stone erections in 1746. Although not published until 1797, this picture gives the fort in its early days, while that published in 1777 shows the stronghold at a later period. Engraving printed in color. Size 5 x 7. See 2368, 3252.

2385—McDERMOT, ANDREW, 1791-1881—Born of Irish parentage; went to Rupert's Land in 1812 as a clerk in the Hudson's Bay Company. Resigning from the employ of the company, he made his initial trip as a free trader in 1824, and for ten years followed the wild, free life of an Indian trapper. Success attended him in all his ventures and he soon became a power in the community and one of the wealthiest merchants in Manitoba. No one knew the Indian better than McDermot, and no one knew better how to trade and dicker with him. His death occurred in Winnipeg in 1881. Water color. Size 4 x 5. Head and shoulders.

2386—THE PAS, OR CUMBERLAND STATION—An Anglican missionary post, at the confluence of the Saskatchewan and Basquia Rivers. The Red River Expedition arrived here at sunset, 17th August, 1858. In the sketch may be seen Christ Church on the right or south bank of river, and near it the parsonage, occupied at that time by Rev. E. A. Watkins. Adjoining the church is a schoolhouse. On the opposite side of the river are some Indian dwellings in a dilapidated condition. The mission is still (1917) in existence. Water color by John Fleming, assistant surveyor, Canadian Red River Expedition, 1857-8. Size 4 x 6.

2387—CUMBERLAND HOUSE—A Hudson's Bay post, established in 1774 by Samuel Hearne, discoverer of the Coppermine River to the Arctic Ocean. As many of the rival North-west Company's officials were Jacobites, the name, "Cumberland," was a detested one with them. In 1776 the dimensions of the settlement were 26 feet broad, 38 feet long and 21½ feet high. On Prof. Hind's visit in 1858 there were about ten acres of ground enclosed and under cultivation at Cumberland, which at one time was the chief depot or fort of the Cumberland district of the Hudson's Bay Co. It was situated on the west shore of Cumberland, or Pine Island Lake, about two miles in an air line north of the Saskatchewan, and at the junction of two great lines of water communication, one leading from the Pacific, and the other from the Arctic seas to the Winnipeg basin. The post still bears the name of Cumberland House. Water color by John Fleming, assistant surveyor, Canadian Red River Expedition, 1857-8. Size 4 x 6. See 2346.

2388—FORT GARRY (WINNIPEG), SEPTEMBER, 1857—A rear view of the fort—The stone gateway shown on the north was erected 1850-1, when the fort was extended. Water color by John Fleming, assistant surveyor, Canadian Red River Expedition, 1857-8. Size 8 x 11.

2389—VILLAGE OF PEMBINA—In Dakota, at the mouth of the Pembina River—Situated nearer the forks of the Pembina and Red Rivers than the old Hudson's Bay post, Fort Pembina. In October, 1857, Prof. Hind was at the American village, at that time "only a small and scattered collection of log houses," although "the ruins of several good houses formerly occupied by a Roman Catholic Mission are still to be seen." Formerly a frontier post, it is now (1917) the capital of Pembina County, North Dakota, and is divided from the Canadian town of Pembina, now Emerson Junction, Man., by only a street. Water color by John Fleming, assistant surveyor, Canadian Red River Expedition, 1857-8. Size 4 x 8.

2390—PEMBINA, 1857—A post of the Hudson's Bay Company, on the west bank of the Red River—opposite Fort Daer, and with it abandoned some time after the 49th parallel was fixed as the international boundary. Fort Pembina, however, was re-established on supposed British territory, moved again, and is now (1917) known as Emerson Junction, Man., separated from the American town of Pembina, North Dakota, by merely a street. Water color by John Fleming, assistant surveyor, Canadian Red River Expedition, 1857-8. Size 4 x 8. See 2291, 2309, 2339.

2391—RUNNING TANNER'S RAPID, RIVIERE MALIGNE—An interesting incident—Chief Trader John Bell, of the Hudson's Bay Company, a notable explorer, on furlough for two years, accompanied by his twelve-year-old daughter, Flora, and guides, was the occupant of this canoe. They had been travelling since May (it was now August) from the Mackenzie River, en route to Montreal, through a trackless wilderness. As they journeyed towards Fort Garry (Winnipeg) they were sighted with delight by the voyageurs of the Red River Expedition. Maigne, or Sturgeon River, lies in longtitude 93, latitude 49. Water color by W. H. E. Napier, engineer, Canadian Red River Expedition, 1857-8. Size 8 x 11.

2392—GREAT FALLS ON THE LITTLE DOG RIVER—District of Thunder Bay, North-west Ontario. The Dog River, on which these falls are located, is in reality a continuation of the Kaministiquia. This view, made in the summer of 1857, is described by Prof. Hind as extraordinary in height, while the "broken surface they present imparts to them singular and beautiful peculiarities." Chromoxylograph from drawing by John Fleming, assistant surveyor, Canadian Red River Expedition. Size 4 x 7.

2393—RED RIVER, 1857—From St. Andrew's Anglican Church, sixteen miles north of Fort Garry and four miles above the Stone Fort—This view, made in the early autumn of 1857, shows a bend in the Red River, and the parish at the "Grand Rapids." St. Andrew's Church, which as a mission dates back to 1824, is still (1917) to the fore in Selkirk County, Man. Chromoxylograph from drawing by John Fleming, assistant surveyor, Canadian Red River Expedition. Size 4 x 7.

27

2394—ENTRANCE TO LITTLE DOG LAKE—Little Dog and Great Dog Lake are connected by a portage a mile and three-quarters long, a rise of 500 feet. The Dog River, entering the west side of Dog Lake, from the south, is really the continuation of the Kaministiquia. All other feeders of the lake are of little moment. Water color by John Fleming, assistant surveyor, Canadian Red River Expedition, 1857-8. Size 6 x 6.

2395—SOUTH END OF GREAT DOG PORTAGE—The portage is from Little Dog Lake to Great Dog Lake, or as it is now (1917) called, Dog Lake, twenty miles air line from Port Arthur. In the early days Port Arthur was known as "The Landing," and later as Prince Arthur's Landing, in honor of H.R.H. the Duke of Connaught, now Governor-General of Canada. The nearest settlement is Kaministiquia Station, on the Canadian Pacific Railway, about nine miles south. Water color by John Fleming, assistant surveyor, Canadian Red River Expedition, 1857-8. Size 6 x 9.

2396—FALLS AT THE LITTLE DOG PORTAGE—A picturesque view on the Kaministiquia River—The falls are situated about two miles south of Little Dog Lake, and were recently embraced in Concession VI, Ware Township. They are now more familiarly known as the Crooked Rapids. The nearest village is Kaministiquia Station, six miles south. The scenery in this locality is singularly beautiful. Water color by John Fleming, assistant surveyor, Canadian Red River Expedition, 1857-8. Size 6 x 6.

2397—PORTAGE AT THE SECOND FALLS, KAMINISTIQUIA RIVER —Situated about twenty-one miles from Fort William and half a mile above the Kakabeka Falls. The picture shows the falls and Rocky Portage as they appeared when the Canadian Red River Expedition passed that way. Birch trees lined the banks, while the underbrush consisted principally of hazel nut trees. The course of the river from Fort William to Dog Lake is broken by falls and rapids. Water color by John Fleming, assistant surveyor, Canadian Red River Expedition, 1857-8. Size 6 x 9.

2398—FALLS OF KAKABEKA (CLEFT ROCK), KAMINISTIQUIA RIVER—The scenery is of a very beautiful and wild character. Here, twenty miles from Fort William, and thirty miles from the river's mouth, the Kaministiquia precipitates its waters over a sharp ledge into a narrow chasm, and then sweeps through a narrowed bed to its outlet in Thunder Bay, Lake Superior. Near the falls are situated the upper works of the Kaministiquia Power Company. Water color by John Fleming, assistant surveyor, Canadian Red River Expedition, 1857-8. Size 4 x 6.

2399—DECHARGES DES PARESSEUX—On the Kaministiquia River— Prof. Hind says in his narrative of the Red River Expedition: "The current begins to be rapid about nine miles from Fort William and continues so in the ascending course of the stream, to the foot of the first demi-portage called the Decharges des Paresseux, where an exposure of shale creates the rapids which occasion the portage. The fall here is five feet one inch in a space of 924 feet." The distance of this portage from Lake Superior, by the windings of the river, is about twenty-two miles, and the total rise probably reaches 35 feet. The country in the vicinity of the Paresseux Rapids and portage is farm land. The nearest village (1917) is that of Stanley. Water color by John Fleming, assistant surveyor, Canadian Red River Expedition, 1857-8. Size 6 x 9.

2400—FALL AT THE THIRD PORTAGE ABOVE KAKABEKA. KAMINISTIQUIA RIVER—These falls form one of the most magnificent cascades to be found in any country. Between Kakabeka and the Dog the course of the river is broken by numerous falls and portages. Prof. Hind. in the narrative of his great exploring expedition, remarks: "The shoals, rapids, and falls on the Kaministiquia will always prevent that river from being used as a means of communication with the interior for commercial purposes." The Canadian Pacific Railway station at Kaministiquia is the nearest place to what sixty years ago might have been known as "The Third Portage about Kakabeka." Water color by John Fleming, assistant surveyor, Canadian Red River Expedition, 1857-8. Size 6 x 9.

2401—FORT GARRY (WINNIPEG)—At the confluence of the Red and Assiniboine Rivers. Water color by John Fleming, assistant surveyor, Canadian Red River Expedition, 1857-8. Size 8 x 11.

2402—GRAND FALLS OF THE NAMEUKEN RIVER—Rainy River District, west of the head of Lake Superior—The picturesque cascade of the view is at Grand Falls Portage, on the old "Dawson route," this side of Rainy River. "After leaving Rattlesnake Portage," says Hind, "rapids and falls follow one another in quick succession. The most important are Crow Portage, with 9.88 feet fall, the Grand Falls Portage, 16 feet, and the great and dangerous Nameaukan (Nameuken) Rapids, letting the river down in steps between fifteen and sixteen feet." Mine Centre is the nearest village in the vicinity. (1917). Drawing in water color by John Fleming, assistant surveyor Canadian Red River Expedition, 1857-8. Size 9 x 9.

2403—FISHING LAKES (IN CREE, PAKITAWIWIN)—Two miles from Fort Qu'Appelle, looking north—The Qu'Appelle or "Who Calls" River takes its rise within a few miles of the Southern or Lower Saskatchewan, and forms one of the chief tributaries of the Assiniboine, sweeping through a charming valley, and expanding during its course of 270 miles into eight lakes, which abound in fish. It the background are glimpses of the Squirrel, File and Pheasant Hills. In the immediate foreground are Red River carts, used by early travellers and settlers. Water color by John Fleming, assistant surveyor, Canadian Red River Expedition, 1857-8. Size 8 x 11.

2404—FORT ALEXANDER—At the mouth of the Winnipeg River— Fort Maurepas, one of the forts successively established between 1731-48 by Verandrye and his sons, subsequently became Fort Alexander. It is now (1917) a post settlement in Selkirk Co., Manitoba, on the Winnipeg River, on an inlet near the south-east shore of Lake Winnipeg. Water color by John Fleming, assistant surveyor, Canadian Red River Expedition, 1857-8. Size 5 x 8.

2405—SLAVE FALLS, WINNIPEG RIVER—Twenty-five miles from Fort Alexander—Their name is derived from a tragic story of a slave, who, maddened by the cruelty of a ferocious master, stepped into a canoe above the falls in presence of the tribe, wrapped her deerskin around her face, and glided over the crest of the cataract, to find rest in the surging waters below. Water color by John Fleming, assistant surveyor, Canadian Red River Expedition, 1857-8. Size 5 x 7.

2406—WHERE THE KAMINISTIQUIA RIVER EMPTIES INTO LAKE SUPERIOR—Fort William is seen in the distance—On the left is Mount Mackay, and also in the distance, to right, on the north or left bank of river (A) is the Hudson's Bay post, of which, from 1855-78, Mr. John McIntyre was agent. The Fort William of to-day has excellent harbor facilities, being the head of navigation of the rivers and inland seas which begin with Lake Superior and find an outlet to the Atlantic, and on the west is directly in connection with the Canadian Pacific and the Canadian Northern Railways. Pencil drawing by John Fleming, assistant surveyor, Canadian Red River Expedition, 1857-8. Size 8 x 12.

2407—VALLEY OF THE SOURIS—From the last ridge of the Blue Hills—The Souris River rises in Saskatchewan and flows through the south-west section of Manitoba. Its valley is most picturesque and imposing, excavating in places a channel from three to four hundred feet through the loose drift of the Blue Hills. Chromoxylograph from drawing by John Fleming, assistant surveyor, Canadian Red River Expedition, 1857-8. Size 4 x 7. See 2378-9.

2408—FROBISHER, JOSEPH—One of the founders of the North-west Company—In the winter of 1783-4, Frobisher, with Simon McTavish and others, of Montreal, formed the North-west Company, which in 1821 amalgamated with the Hudson's Bay Company. Previously Frobisher had been as far as the Churchill River, and had established a firm trade with the Indians of that region, who were accustomed to carry their furs to the Hudson's Bay. In 1792-6 he, with John Richardson, represented the East Ward of Montreal in the first Parliament of the Province of Lower Canada. His retirement from commercial life took place in 1798. In 1801 Frobisher and several others formed the first company to construct water works for the city of Montreal. His fine, large residence, which he called "Beaver Hall," as a reminder of his fur trading days, was burned in 1847. The name is perpetuated to the present day in that part of Montreal, "Beaver Hall Hill." Water color. Size 4 x 5. Head and shoulders.

2409—CONFLUENCE OF THE LITTLE SOURIS AND ASSINIBOINE RIVERS—Fifty-five miles east of Souris, Brandon County, Manitoba—En route from Prairie Portage to Fort Ellice, the Red River Expedition reached the mouth of the Little Souris on 24th June, 1858, and made preparations to cross the Assiniboine at that point, having travelled through the Sandy Hills along the northern bank of the Assiniboine, which at this junction was found to be 230 feet wide, and the Little Souris, 121 feet in width. Water color by John Fleming, assistant surveyor, Canadian Red River Expedition, 1857-8. Size 4 x 6.

2410—HALF-WAY BANK, ASSINIBOINE RIVER—Showing the great wooded valley through which the river meanders—On June 19th, 1858, the Red River Expedition (second) left Prairie Portage (Portage La Prairie), sixty-six miles west of Winnipeg. The route was through the Bad Woods, Sandy Hills to Pine Creek, Plum Creek, Odd Lake, and across the great prairie from Red Deer's Head River to the Hudson's Bay post of Fort Ellice, at Beaver Creek, which they reached July 10th. In the distance is Pembina Mountain, with the partially wooded country intervening. Water color by John Fleming, assistant surveyor, Canadian Red River Expedition, 1857-8. Size 4 x 6.

2411—FORT ELLICE, OR ST. LAZARE—On the forks of the Qu'Appelle and Assiniboine Rivers—Situated on the prairie, where the picturesque valley of the Beaver Creek joined that of the Assiniboine River. The Hudson's Bay post, founded in 1832, "to protect the trade of the Assiniboines and Crees of the Upper Red River district from American opposition on the Missouri," may be seen in background of picture. The post settlement of Fort Ellice is now (1917) eight miles from Foxwarren Station, Man. Water color by John Fleming, assistant surveyor, Canadian Red River Expedition, 1857-8. Size 8 x 11.

2412—CAMP ON THE PRAIRIE—Homes of the Plain Crees and Ojibways—The Plain Cree tents were of leather, the chief and head men having theirs decorated with emblems representing incidents in their lives, such as battles, horse stealing, etc. The Ojibways had a plain stretch of birch bark sewn with roots of the tamarac, which they rolled and carried in their canoes. As a rule the tents were commodious and clean. Water color by John Fleming, assistant surveyor, Canadian Red River Expedition, 1857-8. Size 4 x 6.

2413—PLAIN CREES DRIVING BUFFALO INTO A POUND—Near the Elbow of the South Branch of the Saskatchewan—This picture was made in July, 1858, when the Red River Expedition visited the Plain Crees at Sandy Hills, about two miles west of Sand Hill Lake. Mis-tick-oos, or "Short-stick," the chief, wished the party to see the buffalo entrapped in the pound. There is one in the background, a circular fence, 120 feet broad, constructed of the trunks of trees, laced with withes, and braced by outside supports. Water color by John Fleming, assistant surveyor, Canadian Red River Expedition, 1857-8. Size 4 x 7.

2414—GRAND RAPID OF THE SASKATCHEWAN—Portage between Cross Lake and Lake Winnipeg—North-west of the latter, at the mouth of the Saskatchewan, where it empties into Lake Winnipeg. It is a portage of several miles' length. The Cross Lake portage between Cedar Lake and Cross Lake may be called the "Upper," and Grand Rapids the "Lower," between the latter lake and Lake Winnipeg. Water color by John Fleming, assistant surveyor, Canadian Red River Expedition, 1857-8. Size 4 x 6.

2415—PRAIRIE PORTAGE (PORTAGE LA PRAIRIE), SEPT., 1857— On the Assiniboine, 66 miles west of Winnipeg—Portage La Prairie is on the site of Fort la Reine, built by La Verandrye in 1737. The name was derived from the existence of a nine-mile portage between this part of the Assiniboine and Lac du Prairie (Lake Manitoba). In 1853, Ven. Archdeacon Cochrane founded an Anglican mission here. The old Church of St. Mary, to the left of the picture, still stands, and the adjoining ground is used as a cemetery. Water color by John Fleming, assistant surveyor, Canadian Red River Expedition, 1857-8. Size 2 x 6.

2416—NEPOWEWIN MISSION AND FORT A LA CORNE—"The name Nepowewin," writes Prof. Hind, "is derived from an Indian expression, signifying 'the standing place,' where the natives were accustomed to await the arrival of the Hudson's Bay Company's boats tracked up the north side of the river. It is said by some, however, that the name means 'wet place.'" The mission (Anglican), on the north side of the Saskatchewan River, facing Fort a la Corne, was founded in 1852, the Rev. Henry Budd commencing his labors there in September of that year. Nepowewin is (1917) about 40 miles east of Prince Albert, Sask. Water color by John Fleming, assistant surveyor, Canadian Red River Expedition, 1857-8. Size 4 x 6.

2417—OLD FORT MACLEOD, ALTA.—Founded in 1874 on the banks of Old Man's River—Col. Macleod, coming in overland from Fort Assiniboine on the Mississippi, selected as the site of his fort a level strip of land down the river on an island about two miles from the present town. It was in the approved form of a square, the buildings including living quarters, stables, workshops, etc. Subsequently the site was moved and strung along what is now (1917) Twenty-fourth street, Macleod, between First and Third avenue. In the right-hand corner of picture is an old shoe shop occupied by Dan Horan, who in 1885 also moved to 24th street. Water color. Size 5 x 7.

2418—SHEBANWANNING, NOW KILLARNEY, ONT.—On the north channel of Georgian Bay, just east of Manitoulin Island—The picture is taken at an angle looking towards the north-east. The high hills and rocks in the background are the mainland. The steamer in the distance is going through the north channel, heading for Manitoulin Island, while the island to the left of the picture is known as George Island. The present village of Killarney occupies the same site as old Shebanwanning, though much improved since the making of this picture. The water front is now covered with fish docks. Water color by Wm. Armstrong, C.E., Toronto, 1856. Size 9 x 13.

2419—FORT WILLIAM, C.W., 1861—Hudson's Bay Post, established 1803, on the site of the present town of Fort William, on the Kaministiquia River, a mile from its discharge into Thunder Bay. To the east are shown the houses of Mr. John McIntyre, Chief Factor, and other officials. To the left, across the river, is Mackay Mountain. Water color by William Armstrong, C.E. Size 9 x 13.

2420—"HOLY CROSS" CHURCH, (R.C.), MACLEOD, ALTA.—View from the south—The little log shack church at the old townsite was moved up to the present Macleod and used until the erection in 1899 of the church shown in the picture. The older church was moved by Father Vantigen, a Belgian priest, who did nearly all the work of reconstruction with his own hands. The structure in the picture is situated on Third avenue, east side, between 26th and 27th streets. The old log house just this side of the church is that of Dr. Girard, the Indian doctor at the time. Water color by Wm. Armstrong, C.E. Size 7 x 11.

2421—CAMP OF ONTARIO RIFLES AT SAULT STE. MARIE—Wolseley Expedition, 1870—Immediately on his arrival at the Sault, Lieut.-Col. Bolton set to work to complete the road across the portage. The picture shows his camp of the 1st Ontario Rifles, about half way across the portage, fronting the river. The Hudson's Bay Company's post was at the end of the road to the left. Water color by William Armstrong, C.E., Toronto. Size 8 x 12.

2422—NUMBERING AND NAMING THE INDIANS AT WEQUAMI-KOONG (WIKEMIKONG), OR BEAVER BAY, 16TH AUGUST, 1856—At eastern end of Manitoulin Island—In dealing with the Indians from the treaty standpoint, they were entitled to so many dollars for the head of the family and so many for each child, the amount to be paid half-yearly. This census was taken in order to ascertain the number on the reserve. Chief Assigenack (deserving chief) is shown naming the Indians to Capt. Ironsides, the Indian Superintendent, whose office was in the front room of the frame building to the right of the picture. The chief was provided by the Dominion Government with an undress uniform in blue, which made him feel quite an official. Hudson Bay voyageurs are represented in the centre of the picture. There is a considerable Indian village on the site of Wequamikoong (1917), while a township immediately adjoining is called Assigenack. Water color by Wm. Armstrong, C.E., Toronto. Size 10 x 14.

2423—LANDING AT SAULT STE. MARIE—Wolseley Expedition, 1870—On commencement of difficulties the Americans closed the canal at the Sault. In consequence Lieut.-Col. Bolton, with two companies of the Ontario Rifles, left Toronto on 14th May to superintend the passage of troops and the transport of stores across the "portage" road around the rapids. Unloading was done at the lower end of the rapids, and re-embarkation took place at the upper end. The order to close the canal was later rescinded. Water color by William Armstrong, C.E., Toronto. Size 8 x 13.

2424—INDIANS NEAR FORT WILLIAM, C.W., 1861—The picture shows Indians of the Chippawa tribe camping at the Birch Tree, between Mackay Mountain and the Kaministiquia River, two miles from the Hudson's Bay post. Water color by William Armstrong, C.E. Size 10 x 15.

2425—STEAMER "PLOUGHBOY," 1ST JULY, 1859—Off Lonely Island, Georgian Bay—Mr. Macdonald (Sir John A.) and a party of his colleagues left Toronto, 1st July, 1859, on an excursion to Sault Ste. Marie. They took the steamer "Ploughboy" at Collingwood, and shortly before arrival at Lonely Island an accident happened, making it necessary to shut off steam. The vessel, in a heavy gale, drifted towards the coast until Sunday at midnight (3rd July), when the "Canada," from Owen Sound, which had been sent to the rescue, took the "Ploughboy" in tow and landed her passengers at Collingwood. Water color by William Armstrong, C.E., Toronto. Size 9 x 13.

2426—HUDSON'S BAY POST, SAULT STE. MARIE, CANADA, 1853—The buildings shown in picture have been demolished; site now occupied by pulp mills and water-power buildings. Just west of the house to the left is a miniature lock erected by Mr. Clergue as a memorial of the old lock the Hudson's Bay people used, and which was the first lock ever constructed on the Canadian side. Water color by Wm. Armstrong, C.E., Toronto. Size 7 x 12.

2427—ISLAND NO. 1, KAMINISTIQUIA RIVER—Opposite Fort William, 1871—In the early days this island was the camp ground of Indians, who came every spring with their furs for the Hudson's Bay Company, and pitched their tents opposite the old fort. The point of land shown in the left-hand corner is the site of the Hudson's Bay burying ground, and as it is located on the same side of the river as Fort William, there is therefore nothing of the city of to-day shown in the painting. Water color by Wm. Armstrong, C.E., Toronto. Size 8 x 12.

2428—FORT GARRY (WINNIPEG), 1857-8—The picture is a somewhat fanciful one as to the surroundings of the fort. In his artistic license the artist shows the fort with its west side parallel to the Assiniboine River, instead of having its south front facing the bank. There was only about 150 feet space between the gate and the first break of the river bank. The key shows: 1, Stone bastion, n.w. corner original fort. 2, South-west bastion, where body of Scott, shot by Riel, March, 1870, was placed. 3, One of a line of warehouses which extended inside the fort along its west walls. 4, Official residence of chief factor, occupied by Riel as president of his provisional government. 5, Back, or main, gate of fort. 6, Trading store, with entrance from east. 7, Liquor store. 8, Bastion at southern corner on east side of Main street, near Main street bridge, leading to Fort Rouge. 9, Group of log buildings, n.w. corner of fort, outside. 10, Assiniboine shore. 11, Collection of dog teams. Water color by Wm. Armstrong, C.E., from a sketch by W. H. E. Napier, engineer, Canadian Red River Expedition. Size 9 x 14. See 2376-7.

2429—CAMP AT McVICAR'S CREEK—Wolseley Expedition, 1870— On 21st May, 1870, Col. Wolseley and staff, with the advance guard of the expeditionary force, left Toronto. They arrived at "Prince Arthur's Landing" (Port Arthur) on the 25th. The picture gives the site of the camp, near Prince Arthur's Landing, on what was known as Mr. Dawson's road. On top of the flour barrel to the left was a sun dial, made by the doctor of the 60th Rifles. The camp of the 2nd Battalion (Quebec) was at the north-west side of McVicar's Creek, to right of picture, Colonel Cassault commanding. Water color by William Armstrong, C.E., Toronto. Size 8 x 11.

2430—SAULT STE. MARIE, U.S., 1871—To the left or west of the picture the house marked "1" was the power house belonging to the first American lock. 2, Steamer going through. 3, Buildings in connection with the lock and squatters' houses. 4, Two new locks which have taken the place of the old ones. 5, An island in the rapids. 6, Indians poling their boats in the swift water and catching fish with dip nets, which is a common practice. St. Mary's River is towards the north, which is the background of the picture. Water color by Wm. Armstrong, C.E., Toronto. Size 7 x 13.

2431—**ON THE KAMINISTIQUIA RIVER**—Wolseley Expedition, 1870 —On 6th June, Col. Wolseley, accompanied by Assistant Controller Irvine, made a second inspection of Dawson's road, penetrating to the end of it. Returning he descended the rapids of the Kaministiquia River. The portage around the Kakabeka Falls was reported by Capt. Young to be a mile in length, and the labor great, as the boats had to be "tracked" against the rapids. However, batches of boats, such as portrayed in picture, were sent up almost every day, or as often as Indians would take them. Water color by Wm. Armstrong, C.E., Toronto. Size 9 x 12.

2432—**DIFFICULTIES OF A MILITARY PORTAGE**—Wolseley Expedition, 1870—The labor of portaging in the expedition was very severe, especially on steep ground, where it was necessary to keep the skids in place by driving strong wooden pegs into the ground alongside of them. A boat was usually taken over first, and provisions afterwards. The scene shows the Ontario Battalion crossing three rivers by the old Indian portage, en route from Prince Arthur's Landing (Port Arthur) to Fort Garry. Water color by Wm. Armstrong, C.E., Toronto. Size 8 x 12.

2433—**"A VIEW OF LOUISBURG IN NORTH AMERICA**—Taken near the Light House, when that city was besieged in 1758. Drawn on the spot by Capt. Ince, of the 35t Regt. Engraved by P. Canot. Publish'd according to Act of Parliament, Novr. 11, 1762, by Thos. Jefferys at Charing Cross. 1, The City; 2, Gabarus Bay; 3, English Camp; 4, French Fleet; 5, Island Battery; 6, The Light House." Engraving in aquatint. Size 12 x 20.

2434—**"VIEW OF LOUISBOURG IN 1731**—From a sketch in the Paris Archives. By Verrier. Copyrighted in Canada and the United States by Albert Almon." With key. This view represents Louisburg, the "Dunkirk of America," when about half completed. At the extreme end of Rochefort Point (15) may be seen the place where hundreds of New England soldiers lie buried. More inland, on the same point, are buried French soldiers, and on the right of Black Rock Point (19) may be seen the grave of Lord Dundonald and the Highlanders who fell there in 1758. At the further end of the Citadel grounds the Society of Colonial Wars of Boston and New York, 1895, erected a granite shaft as a monument to commemorate the capture of Louisburg, 1745. Size 6 x 19.

2435—**INDIANS BARTERING**—The Indians in disposing of their furs bartered with the white men, receiving in exchange clothes, trinkets, etc. Lithograph in color by Coke Smyth. Size 11 x 15.

2436—**BUFFALO HUNTING**—A scene in the North-west of Canada in the days of the Hudson's Bay Company regime. Lithograph in color by Coke Smyth. Size 11 x 15.

2437—**"A VIEW OF THE LANDING THE NEW ENGLAND FORCES IN YE EXPEDITION AGAINST CAPE BRETON, 1745**—When after a siege of forty days the town and fortress of Louisbourg and the important territories thereto belonging, were recover'd to the British Empire. The brave and active Commodore Warren, since made Knight of the Bath and Vice Admiral of ye White, commanded the British Squadron in this glorious expedition. The Hon. Willm. Pepperell, Esqr. (since knighted) went a Volunteeer, and commanded the New England men who bravely offer'd their service and went as private soldiers in this hazardous but very glorious enterprize. J. Stevens, pinxt. Brooks, sculp. London. Printed by R. Wilkinson, No. 38 Cornhill." Colored. Size 9 x 13.

2438—**GOOSE AND GRIDIRON TAVERN—View in 1896**—No. 8 London House Yard, St. Paul's Churchyard, London, Eng.—The old-time hostelry, a four-storey structure, was erected in 1670, on the site of the Mitre public house, the first music house in the city, destroyed in the great fire of London, 1666. East of the doorway shown in the picture was a five-storey extension of the original building, erected in 1786 on part of Mitre Court. The date of the erection of the addition was marked by a carving in stone, over the second-storey window, bearing the date, 1786. The view does not show the entire front, the portion to the west, which included one-half the original structure, being hidden by the buildings on the left. Directly over the doorway was the quaint sign of the "Goose and Gridiron." In this inn, the festival of St. John the Baptist was celebrated in 1717 by the original Grand Lodge of England. The structure was demolished in 1896. Water color by E. Wyly Grier from a sketch in the London Graphic. Size 6 x 10.

2439—BAR ROOM, GOOSE AND GRIDIRON TAVERN, LONDON, ENG.—As in 1820—Into this room the staircase (No. 2441) descended. An interesting feature of the bar was the quaint panelled counter of ancient date. The place was patronized by many curious tourists, who, puzzled at the unique sign of the "Goose and Gridiron," entered the inn, not so much to satisfy their thirst, as to ascertain the origin of the sign. There are various explanations, the one in Chambers' "Book of Days" being that the inn originally on the site was the headquarters of a musical society whose arms were the lyre of Apollo, with a swan as the crest; that this device was appropriated as the new sign when the house was rebuilt after the fire, and that it was nicknamed the "Goose and Gridiron," by which name it was always known. Water color by E. Wyly Grier, Toronto, from original sketch. Size 7 x 9. See 2441.

2440—INTERIOR OF FIRST FLOOR OF THE GOOSE AND GRIDIRON TAVERN, LONDON, ENG.—Where the original Grand Lodge met in 1717, on the festival of St. John the Baptist, and "Mr. Anthony Sayer, Gentleman," was placed at the head of the Craft as Grand Master. The picture was made in 1895. In the previous fifty years very few changes had been made in the room. The paper on the walls was yellowed with age, and was of an old-time French pattern that reminded one of the faded brocade of the days of Louis XV. Water color by E. Wyly Grier from original sketch. Size 6 x 9.

2441—STAIRCASE, GOOSE AND GRIDIRON TAVERN, LONDON, ENG., 1670-1895—This staircase led up to the unpretentious landing, off which was the pine-sheeted vestibule, outside the room where the festival of St. John was held in 1717, by the original Grand Lodge of England. The treads of the old stairway were made of dark wood, and each balustrade consisted of a carefully turned stick of pine, while at the fourth step a square piece of hardwood gave support to the landing before mentioned. Water color by E. Wyly Grier from original sketch. Size 5 x 9.

2442—"LOUISBOURGH—London. Printed for R. Sayer and J. Bennett, No. 53 Fleet Street." View of Louisburg in 1760, looking from the south to the north, opposite the entrance and approach to the harbor. No. 1 shows the lighthouse, erected during the French regime, and still standing; 2, Channel leading to the harbor; 3, Government Buildings of the French regime; 4, Square rigged British frigate; 5, Reefs and fort; 6, Man-of-war rowboat; 7, Ships of war at anchor in the bay; 8, Eastern end of the original walls; 9 and 10, Roman Catholic churches. Mezzotint, colored Size 9 x 14.

2443—"A VIEW OF LOUISBURG—Publish'd according to Act of Parliament, Octr, 4, 1777, by J. F. W. Des Barres, Esqr." The port of Louisburg was in early times called Havre aux Anglois, but until after the Treaty of Utrecht, 1713, no important settlements were made there. Then French troops and inhabitants came from Newfoundland to Louisburg, which subsequently became a stronghold of France. By the Treaty of Paris, 1763, Cape Breton finally, however, became a possession of Great Britain. This view of the old town opposite the entrance and approach to the harbor was made in 1777 by J. F. W. des Barres, who from 1784-87 was Lieut.-Governor of Cape Breton. Xylograph in color. Size 13 x 20.

2444—"BRITISH RESENTMENT, OR, THE FRENCH FAIRLY COOPT AT LOUISBOURG—L. Boilard, invt. et delin. J. June, sculp. Printed for J. Bowles, in St. Paul's Churchyard, and Jno. Bowles & Son, in Cornhil. Publish'd according to Act of Parliament, 25 Septr., 1755." This cartoon is a satire on hostilities between the French and English before the declaration of the Seven Years' War. During the summer of 1754 France endeavored to gain time by deceiving the English Government. The latter, however, knew their intentions, and applied to Parliament for money to strengthen and enlarge the army and navy. A powerful armament was ordered by the French Ministry to be fitted out for America. Boscawen was despatched from England in April, 1855, with eleven ships of the line, one frigate and two infantry regiments. Vice-Admiral Holborne followed on 11th May. The squadrons joined company on the passage. Two of the British fleet and two of the French ships became separated in a fog, had an encounter, resulting in capture of the French vessels. They were sent to Halifax. Boscawen and Holborne sailed to Louisburg, which they blockaded, thus preventing aid being sent to Beausejour, where M. du Chambon de Vergar had been sent as commandant, recommended by Bigot. It will be seen that the artist, to a certain extent, anticipated events. With key. Engraving. Size 8 x 13.

2445—WARREN—"Sir Peter Warren, Vice Admiral of the Red—Sold by J. Fuller. Engraved for the Naval Chronicle." An Irishman, born in 1703. Served on the American Naval Station, 1735-41; commanded at the taking of Louisburg from the French, 1745. Two years later assisted Anson in defeating a French squadron. M.P. for Westminster, 1747-52. Died 1752, and a monument to him by Roubiliac was placed in Westminster Abbey. Line engraving. Size 4 x 6. Half length.

2446—KNOWLES—"Sir Charles Knowles, Bart., Admiral of the White Squadron—Engraved by W. Ridley. Pubd. by J. Gold, 103 Shoe Lane, June 30, 1803." Governor of Louisburg, 1746. Surveyor and engineer of the fleet against Cartagena, 1741. Afterwards at Jamaica, first as Commander-in-Chief and from 1752-6 as Governor. Took command of the Russian navy in 1770. His death occurred seven years later. Line engraving. Size 3 x 4. Head and shoulders, oval.

2447—HURON INDIAN—The northern part of the present county of Simcoe, Ont.—Matchadash Bay and Penetanguishene—contained the chief settlements of the Huron tribe. Under Champlain, 2,000 warriors came east and fought the Iroquois, but were defeated. Champlain returned to Quebec. About 1650 the Hurons, pursued by the Five Nations, divided into five detachments, one going to Manitoulin Island, another to Quebec, at Beauport. In 1651 the latter section settled on the island of Orleans, but were driven from there by the Iroquois. They then encamped under the guns of Quebec, and in 1693 shifted to Ancienne Lorette, whence they went to Jeune or Indian Lorette, where a remnant of the tribe still lives. Lithograph in color by Coke Smyth. Size 11 x 15.

2448—ZITYA—A Huron Indian. Lithograph in color by Coke Smyth. Size 11 x 14.

2449—PEPPERELL—"Lieutenant-General Sir Wm. Pepperell, Bart.— From an original full length life size portrait in the Gallery of the Essex Institute, Salem, Masstts., deposited by Mr. Geo. A. Ward, A.D. 1821. Born at Kittery, Maine, June 27, 1696. Died there June 6th, 1759. The only native American ennobled by the British Government for services rendered America. Engraved by J. C. Buttre." An active officer in Maine militia, of which he was colonel, 1722. The New England colonies were constantly annoyed by depredations of the French, from Louisburg, and in 1745 Pepperell was appointed to command an expedition against them. On 16th June, the fortress capitulated. He afterwards projected the conquest of Canada, but was never called upon to carry out any important operations. For his services Pepperell was created a baronet, with title, "Pepperell of Massachusetts." He built in 1747 a frigate and two other vessels for the British navy. When he visited England in 1749 he was cordially received by George II. and presented by the City of London with a service of plate. Line engraving. Size 8 x 10. Half length.

2450—SHAWUNDAIS (SULTRY HEAT)—Rev. John Sunday—About 1796 he was born in the State of New York, and belonged to the Mississagas, a sub-tribe of the Ojibways. His boyhood days were spent with a band who wandered from the County of Northumberland to Leeds, making Kingston, Bath and Brockville their chief places of resort. In 1826 he became a Christian, and, subsequently, a missionary. The temporal welfare of his people interested him, too, and he, with a deputation of chiefs, interviewed the Government on matters relating to timber and land. He visited New York and other places in the States in 1828 in the interests of missionary work among the natives of Canada. Became an eloquent preacher to his own people, several times visiting the Indians at Penetanguishene and Sault Ste. Marie. In 1832 he was appointed, by the Conference, missionary to Sault Ste. Marie and other bodies of natives. Owing to ill-health he visited England and was in 1837 presented to Queen Victoria. He labored untiringly among all classes of Indians until 1867, when he was superannuated, spending the remaining years of his life at Alderville, Ont. He died there 14th Dec., 1875. Painted by W. Gush. Engraved by J. Thomson. Size 4 x 5. Half length.

2451—SECOND STEAMER TO APPEAR IN NEWFOUNDLAND—The "John McAdam," of 100 h.p., arrived at St. John's, Nfld., on the morning of 4th August, 1842, whence she took an excursion party to Trinity Bay. She had been previously engaged in running between Cork and Liverpool, and was sent across the Atlantic to be sold. The first steamer in a port of Newfoundland was H.M. "Spitfire," which brought from Halifax a detachment for the Royal Veteran Companies, arriving at St. John's, 5th Nov., 1840. The first Royal Mail steamer employed in Newfoundland was the "North America." She entered St. John's harbor, 22nd April, 1844. Water color. Size 4 x 6.

2452—HUDSON'S BAY POST, MINGAN—On the Labrador Peninsula, 1861—In this picture a number of Nasquapee Indians are shown trading at the Hudson's Bay post, Mingan, near the mouth of the Mingan River, where Henry Youle Hind visited in the summer of 1861. He states, in writing of their visit, that "we were very cordially received by Mr. Anderson, chief factor, for whose kind attention and valuable assistance in many different ways I am glad to have an opportunity of recording my warm acknowledgments." The Seigneury of Mingan was granted in 1661 to Francois Bissot, and the Mingan Islands were in 1676 granted for purposes of fishing and peltry to Louis de Lalande and Louis Jolliet. In 1807 the Seigneury was purchased by a company, who for a few years carried on a seal fishery. It was then given up, the best stations sold and the Seigneury later leased to the Hudson's Bay Company. Mingan is still (1917) a Hudson's Bay post, situated about 400 miles below Quebec, on the north side of the Gulf of St. Lawrence. From a water color sketch by William G. R. Hind, artist, Canadian Government expedition to Labrador. Size 3 x 5.

2453—MEMORIAL TABLET ERECTED BY THUNDER BAY HIS-TORICAL SOCIETY, 1914—It is of polished red granite, about eight feet high, and commemorates the locality made famous by the pioneer fur traders of the great North-west. The site is the nearest available spot—intersection of McTavish and McIntyre streets, Fort William—on which stood the old Hudson's Bay Company's fort, and also quite close to the supposed landing-place of Duluth. The C.P.R. roundhouse now (1917) occupies the site of the old fort. Water color. Size 4 x 7.

2454—HEALEY, JOE—Potina—A Blood Indian—The Bloods (Kainah) are a tribe of the Blackfoot Confederacy, which until comparatively recently inhabited the foothills of the Rocky Mountains, on the upper waters of the Saskatchewan. They now (1917) occupy reservations in Alberta. The subject of this picture, Joe Healey, a son of an old Indian who was a friend of Mr. Healey, a Yukon trader at Fort Benton, was educated by the latter. He had, so states the artist, "the cunning of both the white and red races, and, unlike the other older Indians, speaks English." Photogravure from painting by Edmund Morris, A.R.C.A., who in 1907 was commissioned by the Government of Ontario to make portraits of chiefs of North-west Indian tribes. Size 5 x 7. Head and shoulders.

2455—BLACKFOOT CHIEF AND HIS SUBORDINATES—In "Wanderings of an Artist in North America," published 1859, Paul Kane tells us that shortly after leaving Fort Pitt his party encountered a band of Indians of various tribes, intent on the annihilation of the Crees and Assiniboines. Mr. Kane and his party accepted the warriors' invitation to camp with them for the night, and thus the artist was enabled to make several sketches. In the picture here given, reading from left to right, in the foreground, are:—Little Horn, Wah-nis-stow, or "The White Buffalo," principal chief of the Sur-cee tribe. The central figure is Omoxesisxany, Big Snake, Blackfoot chief. Mis-ke-me-kin, "The Iron Collar," a Blood Indian chief. The two in the background are inferior chiefs. The Blackfeet were a Western confederacy of Siksika stock, considered the best looking of all the North American tribes. Until comparatively recent times they inhabited the foothills of the Rockies and the country along the upper waters of the Saskatchewan. They are now for the most part in reservations in Alberta. Photogravure from painting by Paul Kane, in the Dominion Archives, Ottawa. Size 5 x 7.

2456—HIS MAJESTY'S CAREENING YARD, HALIFAX, N.S., 1786—From the harbor, looking south-west—With detailed key—The right of this view joins the left of that of "The Hospital and Entrance of Bedford Bason." Exact reproduction of the water color sketch by the Duke of Clarence, afterwards William IV., in the private log book of H.M.S. "Pegasus." when commanded by him in 1786. Size 6 x 15.

2457—PLACENTIA HARBOR, NEWFOUNDLAND, 1786—From Point Verde Signal Station, looking north-east—1, Creve Coeur Point. 2, Castle Hill, on which are still (1917) remains of old French fortifications. 3, Mount Pleasant. 4, Blockhouse Hill. 5, Roadstead. 6, Point Verde Beach and Barrisway. 7, Fishing establishments. 8, Flagstaff at signal station, Point Verde, three miles from Placentia. 9, 10, 11, Fishing establishments. In early days the British dreaded the batteries of Placentia to such an extent that Admiral Walker anchored at Sydney instead of trying to reduce the little French fortress. In 1713, however, when France surrendered Newfoundland, the soldiers and citizens of Placentia migrated to Cape Breton. Exact reproduction of the water color sketch by the Duke of Clarence, afterwards William IV., in the private log book of H.M.S. "Pegasus," when commanded by him in 1786. Size 5 x 15.

2458—**ENTRANCE OF HALIFAX HARBOR, N.S.,** 1786—From the King's Lime Kiln Yard Wharf—This view, looking S.S.E. out towards the Atlantic Ocean, is taken from H.M. Lumber Yard, until lately the head-quarters of the Royal Engineers and the site of the old Grand Battery. The Lumber Yard is at the southern end of Halifax—With key—Exact reproduction of the water color sketch by the Duke of Clarence, afterwards William IV., in the private log book of H.M.S. "Pegasus," when commanded by him in 1786. Size 6 x 12.

2459—**ENTRANCE TO ST. JOHN'S HARBOUR, NEWFOUNDLAND,** 1786—From Gunner's Cove. Looking to sea S.S.E. 1, Northern Head. 2, Buoys used to warn vessels in the Narrows. The buoy shown in picture should be at "X." When a vessel reached this point all sails were furled and the ship was towed in. 3, H.M.S. "Pegasus." 4, Cape Spear, the most easterly point of North America. 5, Village of Blackhead. 6, Southern Head. 7, Fort Amherst. A lighthouse is now erected there, and a battery used for practice by the Royal Naval Reserve. 8, Boat going to buoy. 9, The Narrows. 10, English schooner used in the fish-carrying trade. 11, Naval yacht. Exact reproduction of the water color sketch by the Duke of Clarence, afterwards William IV., in the private log book of H.M.S. "Pegasus," when commanded by him in 1786. Size 6 x 12.

2460—**HOSPITAL AND ENTRANCE OF BEDFORD BASIN, N. S.,** 1786 —From the Anchorage off the Naval Yard, Halifax. Looking northward— Bedford Basin is entered by way of the Narrows, leading from Halifax harbor. Along the shores of the basin were the hospitals and camps of the French Armada which sailed from Brest in 1746 to conquer the British North American coast, from Virginia to Newfoundland. The following is a key to the picture: 1, Grounds of Naval Hospital. 2, Naval Hospital, built about 1783, burnt 1819, and subsequently rebuilt. The Naval College of Canada now occupies the hospital building. 3, Fort Needham. An old earthen redoubt was here, having been erected several years before the date of this picture. 4, West side of the Narrows. 5, Norris' Cove and Point. 6, Tufts' Cove. 7, Vicinity of Black Rock Point, north end of Dartmouth. 8, Halifax Harbor. 9, Bedford, then called Sackville. 10, Dartmouth shore, extending from 10-7. Exact reproduction of the water color sketch by the Duke of Clarence, afterwards William IV., in the private log book of H.M.S. "Pegasus," when commanded by him in 1786. Size 5 x 12.

2461—**GREAT AND LITTLE ST. LAWRENCE HARBORS, NEW-FOUNDLAND,** 1786—West side of Placentia Bay—(a) This view of the upper part of the harbor, from the sea, looking north-west, shows: 1, The Mountain. 2, Fisherman's house. 3, Beach. 4-5, Vessels on beach for repairs. 6, Harbor Great St. Lawrence. 7, 8, 9, Fishermen's stages. (b) Taken from the land, looking south-east: 1, Road to Great St. Lawrence. 2, Channel between island and mainland. 3, 4, 5, Jersey fishing rooms on Little St. Lawrence Island, owned by Nicholls & Co. 6, Entrance to harbor. 7, Cape Chapeau Rouge Hill, a huge rock several hundred feet high, and resembling in shape the crown of a hat. 8, Land-wash. 9, H.M.S. "Pegasus." 10, Harbor of Little St. Lawrence. Exact reproduction of the water color sketch by the Duke of Clarence, afterwards William IV., in the private log book of H.M.S. "Pegasus," when commanded by him in 1786. Size (a) 3 x 12. (b) 4 x 12.

2462—**POSTMAN OF THE NORTH**—Delivery of the Mackenzie River mail—Factor Gairdner, in charge of the Hudson's Bay Company's post at Lac la Biche, Alberta, welcoming the arrival of the Mackenzie River mail from Fort Macpherson at the mouth of the Mackenzie River, after having travelled by dog train 2,012 miles. He is seen shaking hands with

James Spencer, H.B.C. trader, who accompanied the mail from Fort Mc-Murray. Arthur Hemming, the Canadian artist, is standing beside the factor. The mail arrived Jan. 30th, 1895, after having averaged 27½ miles a day. Drawn from life by Arthur Hemming. Photogravure from original. Size 5 x 7.

2463—CALLICUM AND MAQUILLA (MAQUINNA), CHIEFS OF NOOTKA SOUND—On 13th May, 1788, Capt. Meares and Capt. William Douglas, commanding the "Felice" and "Iphigenia Nubiania," arrived at Nootka Sound, on the west coast of Vancouver Island. They were cordially welcomed by the Indians, whose most notable chiefs were Maquinna, called by Meares, Maquilla, and Callicum. Capt. Meares intended to establish a post at Nootka, and bought from Maquinna some land on the shore of Friendly Cove, a harbor at the entrance to the sound. Here a substantial structure was built. Photogravure. Size 5 x 7.

2464—H. R. H. PRINCE EDWARD (DUKE OF KENT)—As colonel of the 7th Fusiliers, 1790. Water color. Size 7 x 10. Full length.

2465—H. R. H. PRINCE EDWARD (DUKE OF KENT), 1767-1820—The fourth son of George III., and father of Queen Victoria. Gazetted colonel of the 7th Fusiliers, stationed at Gibraltar, 1790; transferred to Canada, 1791, and, having previously been made a Mason, was the following year appointed Provincial Grand Master, Lower Canada; in 1793 became major-general; served at Martinique and St. Lucia; on the close of operations returned to Canada. In 1796 was promoted to the rank of lieutenant-general, and three years later raised to the peerage as Duke of Kent and Strathearn and Earl of Dublin. In the same year became commander-in-chief of the forces in British North America; Governor of Gibraltar, 1802, and field marshal, 1805. Some time afterwards the Duke married Victoria Mary Louisa, widow of Enrich Charles, Prince of Leiningen. His death occurred in England, January 23rd, 1820. Miniature water color by James Gillray (1757-1815), the celebrated British artist. Size 6 x 8. Head and shoulders, oval. See 152, 2464, 2472-5, 3630.

2466—ST. JOHN'S, NEWFOUNDLAND, 1786—From the south side, looking north—In this view are following points of interest: 1, Pokeham Path. 2, What is now (1917) Barter's Hill. 3, Fort Townshend, built about 1748, enlarged and at present used as barracks for Mounted Police. 4, King's road, along the crest of the ridge. 5, Cochrane street. 6, The nunnery. 7, 8, 9, 10, 15, Mercantile premises. 11, Church of England. 12, Court House. 13, The London Tavern. 14, 16, Vessels engaged in fish-carrying trade. 17, Government House, built 1828, by the Imperial Government. Exact reproduction of the water color sketch by the Duke of Clarence, afterwards William IV., in the private log book of H.M.S. "Pegasus," when commanded by him in 1786. Size 4 x 12.

2467—DARTMOUTH SHORE, N.S., 1786—From the anchorage off the Naval Yard, Halifax, looking eastward. A general view of the town of Dartmouth as it appeared at this period is here given. It is impossible, however, to identify most of the buildings, which were merely whalers' dwellings. Dartmouth was first settled in 1750. On 2nd March, 1786, the old town lots were escheated, the town re-planned and granted to twenty families of Quaker whalers from Nantucket. They resided there until about 1792, when most of them moved to Milford. 1, Main centre of present town. 2, Old grist mill in Dartmouth Cove. Lawrence Hartshorne and Jonathan Tremaine worked a grist mill there about 1820. Of late years it was destroyed by fire. 3, Halifax Harbor. 4, This elevation is now known as Prince Arthur's Park, a recent name. Exact reproduction of the water color sketch by the Duke of Clarence, afterwards William IV., in the private log book of H.M.S. "Pegasus," when commanded by him in 1786. Size 7 x 12.

2468—VIEW OF PLACENTIA, NEWFOUNDLAND, 1786—From the North-east Arm, looking south-west—Placentia Bay, the largest bay of Newfoundland, and upon which the town is picturesquely situated, is ninety miles long and fifty wide at its mouth. 1, Meadow Point. 2, Town Side, Placentia. 3, Military Barracks. 4, Fort Frederick. 5, Blockhouse Hill. 6, Point Verde. 7, Castle Hill, upon which may still be seen remains of the old French fortifications. 8, Fort Louis. 9, North-east Arm. 10, Main Gut, which was larger and deeper at the time the picture was made than at present. Exact reproduction of the water color sketch by the Duke of Clarence, afterwards William IV., in the private log book of H. M. S. "Pegasus," when commanded by him in 1786. Size 6 x 12.

2469—ST. JOHN'S HARBOR, NEWFOUNDLAND, 1786—View of the upper part of the harbor from the centre, looking west, showing: 1, 3, 5, Fish flakes for drying fish. 2, 4, 6, Waterside premises with fish stage shown in No. 6. 7, Waterford Valley. 8, Hospital. 9, H.M.S. "Pegasus." 10, North side of St. John's Harbor. 11, Southside Hills. Vessels of the largest tonnage can enter St. John's Harbor at all periods of the tide, the rise of which does not exceed 4 feet. Exact reproduction of the water color sketch by the Duke of Clarence, afterwards William IV., in the private log book of H.M.S. "Pegasus," when commanded by him in 1786. Size 6 x 12.

2470—SIR GEORGE SIMPSON ON A TOUR OF INSPECTION—Sir George, known to his contemporaries as the "King of the Fur Trade," is here shown with his party, travelling by canoe. He came to Canada in 1820, in the service of the Hudson's Bay Company, and on the coalition of the Hudson's Bay and North-west Companies, was made Governor of the northern department (afterwards known as Rupert's Land) and general superintendent of the Hudson's Bay Company's affairs in North America. Photogravure, colored. Size 4 x 5. See 35.

2471—ROUNDING UP CARIBOU IN LABRADOR—Factor John McLean rounding up the herd for the Hudson's Bay Company—The caribou still muster in large numbers through Labrador, and afford excellent sport for the hunter in the wilds. McLean, author of "Notes of a Twenty-five Years' Service in the Hudson's Bay Territories," was the first discoverer of the Grand Falls of the Hamilton River, Labrador. Photogravure, colored. Size 5 x 6.

2472—"EDWARD, DUKE OF KENT AND STRATHEARN, K.G., K.T., K.S.T.P., ETC., ETC.—Painted by Sir Wm. Beechey, R.A. Engraved by E. Scriven. Fisher, Son & Co., London, 1841"—At forty years of age. Size 4 x 5. Half length.

2473—KENT—"Prince Edward—Published Septr. 1, 1792. Messrs. Robinson's, Paternoster Row"—At twenty-five years of age. Line engraving. Size 3 x 4. Head and shoulders, profile, oval.

2474—KENT—"His Royal Highness Prince Edward—London Mag'e, Jany., 1782"—At fourteen years of age. Line engraving. Size 3 x 4. Head and shoulders.

2475—KENT—"His Royal Highness, Edward, Duke of Kent, etc., etc. From a picture by G. Dawe, R.A., in the possession of H.R.H. the Duchess of Kent. Jos. Brown, Sc. London. Richard Bentley, 1850"—At forty-five years of age. Line engraving. Size 3 x 4. Half length, sitting. See 152, 2464-5, 2472-4.

2476—TOWN AND HARBOR OF PLACENTIA, NEWFOUNDLAND, 1786—From Castle Hill, looking east—Placentia, a quaint little town on the bay of its own name, was founded and fortified by the French in 1660, and held by them until 1713. It lies on a shingly beach, overshadowed by hills, and surrounded by beautiful scenery. The view shows: 1, Dunephy's Point. 2, Mount Pleasant. 3, Dixon's Hill. 4, South-east Arm. 5, North-east Arm. These channels extend from the harbor in among the mountains. 6, Meadow Point. 7, Fort Louis. 8, Fort Frederick. 9, South-east Arm. 10, Roadstead. 11, Castle Hill, from which a fine view of the bay is obtained. 12, The Castle. 13, Main Gut. Here the tide runs at six knots an hour. Exact reproduction of the water color sketch by the Duke of Clarence, afterwards William IV., in the private log book of H. M. S. "Pegasus," when commanded by him in 1786. Size 6 x 20.

2477—NAVAL STATION, FOOT OF BLOCKHOUSE HILL, PLACENTIA, NEWFOUNDLAND, 1786—1, Blockhouse Hill. 2, 3, 4, Houses for accommodation of commandant and crew. 5, Beach. Exact reproduction of the water color sketch by the Duke of Clarence, afterwards William IV., in the private log book of H.M.S. "Pegasus," when commanded by him in 1786. Size 8 x 10.

2478—TRINITY, NEWFOUNDLAND, 1840—Looking east—Part of the North-west Arm—Trinity Harbor, so called because an early navigator entered it on Trinity Sunday, is one of the best harbors in the world. The picture is a representation of part of the North-west Arm, which runs in various directions for a distance of three miles. The South-west Arm also flows in different branches to about the same distance, and both arms nearly meet, forming Rider's Hill (which is situated in the centre of the harbor and at the foot of which stands the town) into a peninsula. Heart's Content, at the head of Trinity Bay, is the station of the Anglo-American Cable Company. Water color from a print. Size 3 x 6.

2479—NIGHT VIEW OF ST. JOHN'S HARBOR, NEWFOUNDLAND, 1786—From the north side looking due east—This harbor, which is completely landlocked and sheltered from the waves of the Atlantic, is a mile long and about half a mile wide. This view, which is said to be an excellent one, gives: 1, Gibbet Hill. 2, Signal Hill on the north side of the Narrows, entrance to the harbor. 3, Harbor of St. John's. 4, H.M.S. "Pegasus." 5, Cahill's Point. 6, The Southside Hills. Exact reproduction of the water color sketch by the Duke of Clarence, afterwards William IV., in the private log book of H.M.S. "Pegasus," when commanded by him in 1786. Size 6 x 12.

2480—ST. JOHN'S HARBOR, NEWFOUNDLAND—A south view —St. John's, the most eastern seaport and city of North America, and capital of Newfoundland, is 1,076 miles north-east of Montreal. It has a fine harbor. This picture was sketched by Mr. Gosse on 16th March, 1838, and presented to his Excellency Sir John Harvey, then Governor. It shows a line of vessels, bound to the seal fishery, preparing to depart by means of ice channels. Key: 1, Wood's docks. 2, Fish flakes. 3, Bowden's premises. 4, The Narrows. 5, Signal Hill. 6, Southside Mills. 7, St. John's Harbor. 8, Vessels leaving for seal fishing. 9, Temperance street. 10, Stone houses still standing. Water color. Size 4 x 6.

2481—HENLEY ISLAND, LABRADOR, 1857—One of the natural features of the coast—Passing up the Straits of Belle Isle to the north, and just clear of them, is found a large group of rocks of basaltic formation, 200 feet high, the most striking feature of which is Henley Island. The hexagonal columns surmounting the group are about two feet in diameter. Around the island is a favorite fishing ground. Drawn by Rev. William Grey, of Portugal Cove, Nfld. Printed and published by S. D. Cowell, Anastatic Press, Ipswich. Lithograph, colored by hand. Size 10 x 13.

2482—**EAGLE RIVER FISHERY, LABRADOR,** 1857—View about two miles from the mouth of the river. On the west side of Sandwich Bay are the Eagle and West Rivers, noted for their salmon. At this point is seen the fishery or cannery which at one time belonged to Messrs. Hunt, where salmon from the different "posts" were cleaned and packed. The Hudson's Bay Company took over the Hunt premises, subsequently abandoning them, however, for want of a sufficient quantity of fish to maintain business in competition with the British Columbia fisheries. Drawn by Rev. William Grey, of Portugal Cove, Nfld. Printed and published by S. D. Cowell, Anastatic Press, Ipswich. Lithograph, colored by hand. Size 9 x 12.

2483—**VIEW OF SEVEN ISLANDS IN HARBOR OF PLACENTIA, NEWFOUNDLAND,** 1786—From the North-east Arm, looking south-west. 1-7, The Seven Islands in harbor. 8, The Narrows. 9, North-east Arm. 10, Dunville, four miles east of Placentia. 11, Jersey Side, a settlement in the district of Placentia. 12, Roadstead. 13, Main Gut, where the tide runs at the rate of six knots an hour. Exact reproduction of the water color sketch by the Duke of Clarence, afterwards William IV., in the private log book of H.M.S. "Pegasus," when commanded by him in 1786. Size 6 x 12.

2484—**NOR'WESTER OFFICE, FORT GARRY (WINNIPEG, MAN.),** 1860—The publication of the Nor'Wester was begun 28th Dec., 1859, by Messrs. Buckingham & Coldwell, in a log building in rear of Sheriff Ross' residence, "Colony Gardens," the site of which is now included in Victoria Park, Winnipeg. The building in picture, on the left bank of the Red River, lower down, was the first permanent office of the paper. On Mr. Buckingham leaving the Red River in 1860, Coldwell continued the Nor'Wester for a time in partnership with James Ross (son of Sheriff Ross). Later the property was acquired by Mr. Edward L. Drewry, and now (1917) stands on the grounds surrounding his brewery establishment. The old building, however, situated near the river bank, on the north side of Redwood avenue, Winnipeg, has been transformed by raising it a half-storey, substituting clapboards for the rough-casting and a shingle for the thatched roof. Water color on print. Size 4 x 6.

2485—**HERD OF BUFFALO GRAZING**—At the foot-hills of the Rocky Mountains—The days when the buffalo roamed at will over the western plains are long since past and the only herds now (1917) to be seen are found in the Government parks. At Wainwright Buffalo Park, Alberta, there are 2,077 head—this being the largest herd in the world. By 1870, following the completion of the Union Pacific Railway, the great herd was broken into two portions—the northern keeping to the north-west, and the southern, to Texas and other States in the American West. Division again occurred in the northern herd, one portion ranging along the foot-hills of the Rockies and as far south as the grass lands of Montana, always, however, returning to the hills near Calgary in winter. The construction of the C.P.R. made the bison accessible from all quarters, and the doom of the monarch of the plains was sealed; were it not for the care of the Government he would now be extinct. Water color from original drawing by Schell and Hogan, for "Picturesque Canada," 1880. Size 5 x 7.

2486—**HAWK ISLAND, LABRADOR,** 1857—A singular outline from Boulter's Rock, Hawk Island, a solid mass of granite, is situated on the Atlantic seaboard of Labrador. Somewhat extensive fishing operations are carried on in the neighborhood. When Gaspar Corte-Real explored the Labrador coast in 1500 he seems to have visited Hawk Island, and now tourist steamers make this coast part of their summer route, leaving, amongst other places, Boulter's Rock, shown in the foreground of the picture, for the bays and inlets reaching into the interior. Drawn by Rev. William Grey, of Portugal Cove, Nfld. Printed and published by S. D. Cowell, Anastatic Press, Ipswich. Lithograph, colored by hand. Size 10 x 12.

28

2487—**BATTLE HARBOR, LABRADOR, 1857**—Where the Straits of Belle Isle meet the Atlantic—A narrow gulf of deep water, forming a sheltered roadstead on the coast of Labrador between Battle and Great Caribou Islands. It is a great fishing centre, and during the fishing season is crowded with boats, presenting an exceedingly lively scene. Drawn by Rev. William Grey, of Portugal Cove, Nfld. Printed and published by S. D. Cowell, Anastatic Press, Ipswich. Lithograph, colored by hand. Size 9 x 12.

2488—**ST. FRANCIS' HARBOR, LABRADOR, 1857**—A sequestered port on Granby Island, about half a mile west of Cape St. Francis, in the estuary of the Alexis River. Several precipitous rocks rise from the sea in the vicinity. In the background is depicted the Anglican Church, said to have been one of the earliest on the coast, and consecrated in 1853 by Bishop Field, of Newfoundland. In 1914 it was torn down to be re-erected at Cape Charles. Drawn by Rev. William Grey, of Portugal Cove, Nfld. Printed and published by S. D. Cowell, Anastatic Press, Ipswich. Lithograph, colored by hand. Size 10 x 12.

2489—**TAYLOR'S GULCH, NEAR FORTEAU, LABRADOR, 1857**—A romantic chasm and cliff of sandstone—The gulch, a mile and a half in length, lies about two miles north of Forteau Church, at the head of Forteau Bay. Through it rushes a roaring stream, forming a grand and continuous cascade. This charming spot is a favorite resort of Newfoundlanders and tourists during the summer months. Drawn by Rev. William Grey, of Portugal Cove, Nfld. Printed and published by S. D. Cowell, Anastatic Press, Ipswich. Lithograph, colored by hand. Size 10 x 12.

2490—**FALLS OF THE EAGLE RIVER, LABRADOR, 1857**—A mass of water on the west side of the river—This is one of the impressive scenes on the Atlantic coast of Labrador. The Eagle River is on the west coast of the Sandwich Bay, wherein are found many picturesque islands. The peaks of the Mealy Mountains, in some places reaching an altitude of nearly 1,500 feet, in the background, may be seen. Drawn by Rev. William Grey, of Portugal Cove, Nfld. Printed and published by S. D. Cowell, Anastatic Press, Ipswich. Lithograph, colored by hand. Size 10 x 12.

2491—**YALE (FORT YALE), B.C., 1880**—A Hudson's Bay post on the Lower Fraser—Founded in the spring of 1848 near a village of the Sachinos, and named in honor of Chief Factor James Murray Yale, at that time in charge of Fort Langley. The town site was surveyed in 1858, and the following year government established. The place was an outfitting point for miners and ranchmen northward. At Yale extensive mining operations were carried on in the fifties, miners being with difficulty restrained from digging away the town. The buildings were constructed of wood, so that the fires of 1880 and 1881 were disastrous. To-day (1917) Yale is a station on the main line of the C.P.R. about a hundred miles east of Vancouver. Water color from original drawing by Lucius O'Brien, R.C.A., for "Picturesque Canada," 1880. Size 6 x 7.

2492—**ON THE EAGLE RIVER, LABRADOR, 1857**—A view at Sandwich Bay, showing the narrow pass of the stream, where its waters are lashed into an angry rapid by rocky heights on either side. Salmon are abundant in the Eagle, affording excellent sport. Numerous picturesque islands dot Sandwich Bay, and on the north shore are the Mealy Mountains, nearly 1,500 feet in height, and forming part of the Labrador coast dependency of Newfoundland. Drawn by Rev. William Grey, of Portugal Cove, Nfld. Printed and published by S. D. Cowell, Anastatic Press, Ipswich. Lithograph, colored by hand. Size 10 x 11.

2493—ST. MICHAEL'S BAY, LABRADOR, 1857—On the picturesquely indented coast line of the east shore of Labrador, a little to the north of the Straits of Belle Isle, lies beautiful St. Michael's Bay. This view is from the lofty eminence behind Square Island harbor. Square Island is situated in the mouth of the Bay. Drawn by Rev. William Grey, of Portugal Cove, Nfld. Printed and published by S. D. Cowell, Anastatic Press, Ipswich. Lithograph, colored by hand. Size 10 x 12.

2494—ST. LEWIS' BAY, LABRADOR, 1857—An inlet on the Atlantic coast of the Peninsula—Deep Water Creek, on St. Lewis' Bay, is situated at the western end of St. Lewis' Sound. The sound, which is quite deep, is some four miles wide. Fishing is carried on extensively during the summer season, but very few people live at this point. Drawn by Rev. William Grey, of Portugal Cove, Nfld. Printed and published by S. D. Cowell, Anastatic Press, Ipswich. Lithograph, colored by hand. Size 10 x 12.

2495—CHURCH AT FORTEAU BAY, LABRADOR, 1857—The prosperous fishing village of Forteau is situated on the west shore of Forteau Bay, near the south-west extremity of the Straits of Belle Isle. At the head of the inlet stood the Anglican Church of St. Peter, consecrated by Bishop Field, August 9th, 1857. It was replaced by a new edifice of the same name, consecrated in 1911 by Bishop Jones. A few miles to the north-west are the Bradore Hills, several rounded summits, of which the chief is 1,264 feet high. Drawn by Rev. William Grey, of Portugal Cove, Nfld. Printed and published by S. D. Cowell. Anastatic Press, Ipswich. Lithograph, colored by hand. Size 11 x 11.

2496—YORK FACTORY ON THE HAYES RIVER—Arrival of Hudson's Bay Company's ship in autumn of 1880—The site of this important establishment was several acres on the northern bank of the river, five miles from its mouth. Pickets enclosed the space occupied by the factory, which comprised stores, dwellings, offices and workshops, constructed of logs clapboarded and painted. York was a factory in the real sense of the term, for such articles as axes, nails, earthenware cups and bowls, wooden kegs and firkins were manufactured there. Until the early seventies the post retained its importance as a seaport and storehouse for imports and exports of the north. Many of the old buildings have been demolished or have fallen into ruin. To-day (1917) York Factory is merely a settlement near Fort Nelson. The picture shows the arrival of the Hudson's Bay Company's ship in the autumn of 1880, with supplies from England. Water color from original drawing by Schell and Hogan, for "Picturesque Canada." Size 5 x 7.

2497—MARGAREE HARBOR, 1876—A seaport on the Gulf of St. Lawrence. Situated at the mouth of the Margaree River, which is noted for its trout and salmon fishing. The harbor also is famous for its salmon fishing, as well as its scenery. In 1876 Margaree Harbor was simply a hamlet, but now (1917) it has grown to be a thriving post town. Water color by William G. R. Hind. Size 8 x 13.

2498—BATTLE HARBOR, LABRADOR, 1857—View of the church and parsonage—During the summer and autumn months of 1857, Right Rev. Bishop Field made one of his voyages of visitation along the Newfoundland coast and to the missions of Labrador. At Battle Harbor he consecrated the church shown in the picture, and also confirmed a number of candidates, amongst them five Esquimaux, the first of that race, it is supposed, ever confirmed on the Labrador coast. To the left of the church is the parsonage. A Deep Sea Mission, including a hospital, has been supported by the Anglican Church at Battle Harbor for many years. Drawn by Rev. William Grey, of Portugal Cove, Nfld. Printed and published by S. D. Cowell, Anastatic Press, Ipswich. Lithograph, colored by hand. Size 9 x 12.

2499—CARTWRIGHT, ON SANDWICH BAY, LABRADOR, 1857—View of the trading post and harbor. Cartwright, which is situated on a narrow channel running from Sandwich Bay to the sea, is one of a series of trading posts established at intervals along the Labrador coast from Cape Charles to Sandwich Bay by Major George Cartwright, an aide-de-camp to the Marquis of Granby during the Seven Years' War. Failing to obtain promotion, Major Cartwright resigned his commission and emigrated to Labrador, cultivating trade with the Indians and Eskimos. He met with many reverses, and in 1786 decided to return to England. The Hudson's Bay Company and Revillon Freres now operate stations at the post bearing the name of the early trader. Drawn by Rev. William Grey, of Portugal Cove, Nfld. Printed and published by S. D. Cowell, Anastatic Press, Ipswich. Lithograph, colored by hand. Size 7 x 13.

2500—MOUNTAIN, RT. REV. JACOB, D.D., 1749-1825—First Anglican Bishop of Quebec—He belonged to a French Protestant family (the name was originally Montaigne) who settled in England upon the revocation of the Edict of Nantes. He was a graduate of Caius College, Cambridge. B.A., 1774; M.A., 1777, and D.D., 1793. At the time of his selection for the See of Quebec he was examining chaplain to the Bishop of Lincoln. In 1793 George III. erected the Canadas into a diocese, and Dr. Mountain was appointed to take charge. At that time there were nine clergymen of the Church of England in Canada, and at his death there were sixty-one. He promoted missions and erection of churches. These he visited regularly. Through his efforts the Cathedral at Quebec was erected in 1804. He advocated a plan of superior education for the entire country and obtained a royal charter for McGill College. Bishop Mountain, who labored here for thirty-two years, has been called "the father and founder of the Anglican Church in Canada." Photogravure from an engraving in the Dominion Archives, Ottawa. Size 5 x 7. Three-quarter length, sitting.

2501—INGLIS—"The Right Reverend John Inglis, D.D., Lord Bishop of Nova Scotia, consecrated 1825. W. C. Ross, pinxt. M. Gauci, Delt. C. Mottes, Lithogy, 70 St. Martin's Lane." He was born in New York, 1777, a son of Rev. Charles Inglis, D.D., and educated at the Academy, Windsor, N.S., and King's College, having been the first boy to enter the former institution. In 1801 he was ordained by his father, and later appointed second missionary at Aylesford. Third rector of St. Paul's Church, Halifax, and ecclesiastical commissary of the diocese. During the first year of his episcopate Bishop Inglis consecrated forty-four churches. In 1826 in a man-of-war he visited Bermuda, being probably the first bishop who had ever been there. For twenty-five years the "good bishop" continud his indefatigable labors in Nova Scotia. He died in London, Eng., 27th October, 1850. Lithograph. Size 5 x 6. Half length, sitting.

2502—INGLIS—"The Right Reverend Charles Inglis, D.D., the first Protestant Bishop in the British Colonies. Consecrated for the See of Nova Scotia, 1787. M. Gauci, Lithog." At Lambeth, Eng., Dr. Inglis was consecrated first Bishop of the Church of England in British America. He was in title Bishop of Nova Scotia, although his jurisdiction practically included the whole of British North America. At the breaking out of the Revolutionary War he was rector at Trinity Church, New York, where his loyalty to the Royalist cause involved him in trouble. Upon the evacuation of New York he proceeded to Halifax. Bishop Inglis, who was a member of the Executive Council, and the founder of the University of King's College, Windsor, N.S., died in 1816. He was born in Ireland, 1734, and came to America when a youth. Lithograph. Size 5 x 6. Half length, sitting.

2503—ROAF—"Revd. John Roaf—J. W. Cook, sc. Thomas Ward & Co., Paternoster Row." He was born at Margate, Kent, in 1801. Came to Canada from Wolverhampton, Eng., and in 1838 was appointed the second

Congregational minister in Toronto, succeeding the Rev. Mr. Merryfield as pastor of Zion Church—the Mother of Toronto Congregationalism—then on George street, and latter on the north-east corner of Bay and Adelaide streets. Mr. Roaf continued to hold this pastorate for seventeen years, resigning in 1855. His death occurred in Toronto seven years later. Engraving. J. R. Roaf, barrister, of Toronto, is a grandson. Size 4 x 4. Head and shoulders.

2504—STEWART, HON, AND RIGHT REV. CHARLES JAMES, D.D.— Second Anglican Bishop of Quebec—He was fifth son of the Earl of Galloway, born 13th April, 1775, came to Canada as a missionary in 1807, and in his work is said to have commenced twenty-four churches, nearly all on the model of that at Freligsburg, Que., which he built at his own expense. In 1817 on his return from England he took up work in a neglected district named Hatley. Two years later he became a travelling missionary. On the death of Bishop Mountain he was appointed second Bishop of Quebec, his consecration taking place in England on 21st Jan., 1826. As Bishop, he was watchful, steady and untiring in his labors, which were arduous and severe. In 1836 Archdeacon G. J. Mountain was selected as coadjutor to Bishop Stewart, whose health had failed. He returned to England, where he died 13th July, 1837. Water color. Size 3 x 5. Half length.

2505—CAUGHEY—"The Revd. James Caughey, of the M.E. Church, U.S.—Dedicated to the Wesleyan Methodist Society in Toronto by the publisher, J. E. Pell, Carver and Gilder, 30 King St. W., Toronto. Drawn on stone by W. Hunt. H. Scobie, Lith., Toronto." A well-known Methodist evangelist; born in Ireland, 1811. He emigrated to America in his youth and was ordained a deacon of the Methodist Episcopal Church in 1834. In 1839 he was appointed to Whitehall, N.Y., and the following year commenced his evangelistic labors in Montreal and Quebec. He then went to England and Ireland, where he preached with great success, remaining for seven years. In 1851-2 he conducted revival services in the Richmond, Adelaide and Queen Street Methodist Churches, Toronto, and in 1853-4 conducted a series of meetings at Hamilton and London, revisiting Toronto in 1868. He was the author of several works, amongst them "Revival Miscellanies" and "Showers of Blessing." Died at New Brunswick, N.J., 30th Jan., 1891. Lithograph. Size 9 x 12. Half length, sitting.

2506—MACDONELL—"The Rt. Revd. Alexr. Macdonell, Catholic Bishop of Upper Canada. Painted by M. A. Shee, Esqr., R.A. Engraved by C. Turner, Mezzotinto Engraver in Ordinary to His Majesty, London. Pubd., Augt. 1, 1825, by C. Turner, 50 Warren St., Fitzroy Square." Born in Glen Urquhart, Inverness-shire, Scotland, 17th July, 1762; educated at Scots' College, Valladolid, Spain, where he was ordained priest, 16th Feb., 1787. In 1794 he raised in Scotland the Glengarry Fencible Regiment, a Catholic corps, the first raised as such since the Reformation. During the Rebellion in Ireland, 1798, this regiment rendered efficient service. In 1804 Father Macdonell embarked for Canada, and shortly after his arrival was appointed to the Mission of St. Raphael's, in Glengarry, which for twenty-five years remained his headquarters. He was instrumental in raising a band of Highland loyalists who had made their home in Glengarry, Canada, organizing what was known as the Glengarry Light Infantry Regiment, which fought during the War of 1812-14; he was consecrated Vicar Apostolic of Upper Canada in 1820, and in February, 1826, became first Roman Catholic Bishop of Upper Canada under the title of Regiopolis or Kingston. Resided in Kingston from 1836-39. Died in Dumfries, Scotland, 14th Jan., 1840. Mezzotint. Size 9 x 12. Half length, sitting.

2507—DARLING, REV. WM. STEWART—Second rector Holy Trinity Church, Toronto, 1875-86—Born in Edinburgh, Scotland, 1818. Came to Canada and was incumbent of Scarboro, 1843-53. It was through his efforts that Christ Church was built there. From 1868-75 he was rector's assistant at Holy Trinity Church, Toronto, and in 1875 succeeded Rev. Dr. Scadding as rector. Mr. Darling's death took place in Alassio, Italy, in 1886. Photograph, colored. Size 3 x 4. Head and shoulders.

2508—CRONYN, RIGHT REV. BENJAMIN, LL.D.—First Bishop of Huron, 1857-71—In 1833 the Rev. Benjamin Cronyn came from Ireland, where he was born in 1802, and settled in London, C.W., being appointed to the rectories of London and St. John's, London Township. On the erection of St. Paul's Church (Cathedral), London, in 1835, on the corner where the Customs House now stands, Mr. Cronyn became first rector. This building was burned in 1844. Its successor, the corner-stone of which was laid in June, 1844, by Bishop Strachan, was completed in 1846. Dr. Cronyn was consecrated first Bishop of Huron, October 28th, 1857. Died at London, 1871. Photograph, colored. Size 3 x 5. Half length.

2509—SCADDING, REV. HENRY, D.D.—At fifty-six—Dr. Scadding's "Toronto of Old" still remains an authoritative work on the early history of Toronto. Water color, from portrait in possession of his daughter, Mrs. Robert Sullivan, Toronto. Size 4 x 5. Three-quarter length, sitting. See 314, 2511, 3698.

2510—LEACH, REV. WM. TURNBULL—Second minister St. Andrew's Presbyterian Church (Church and Adelaide streets), Toronto. He was born at Berwick-on-Tweed, 1805; educated at Stirling and at University of Edinburgh, where he received degree of M.A., in 1827. Sent to Canada by the Glasgow Colonial Society, and in 1835 succeeded Rev. Mr. Rintoul as minister of St. Andrew's. In 1837-8 served as chaplain to the 93rd Highlanders then in Toronto. He joined the Church of England in 1842, removed to Montreal, where he became first rector of St. George's Church. In 1865 appointed Archdeacon of Montreal. In the meantime he had been elected Professor of Classical Literature in McGill College. Mr. Leach took a deep interest in educational matters. In recognition of his literary qualities he received degrees of D.D., D.C.L., and LL.D. His death took place 13th October, 1886, in Montreal. Water color. Size 4 x 5. Head and shoulders, profile. See 3532.

2511—SCADDING, REV. HENRY, D.D.—At twenty-eight—First rector Holy Trinity Church, Toronto, 1847-75. Dr. Scadding, on the day after his arrival in Canada (for the second time), in 1837, was ordained deacon at Quebec, by Bishop Stewart. Water color from portrait by Hoppner Meyer. in possession of his daughter, Mrs. Robt. Sullivan, Toronto. Size 4 x 5. Head and shoulders. See 314, 2509, 3698.

2512—BARCLAY, REV. JOHN, D.D.—Third minister St. Andrew's Church (Church and Adelaide streets), Toronto, 1842-70—Born in Ayrshire, Scotland; came to Canada, 1842. Shortly after his arrival he succeeded Rev. W. T. Leach as pastor of St. Andrew's Church. He was appointed to the Board of Trustees of the Home District Grammar School in July, 1843. For many years Dr. Barclay was chaplain to St. Andrew's Society, and a trustee of Queen's College. Few men ever held a congregation together better than he did, especially in 1843, when the celebrated "Disruption" occurred in the mother Church of Scotland. Although a secession took place in St. Andrew's, resulting in the formation of Knox Church, yet the utmost good feeling prevailed. Dr. Barclay died in Toronto, 27th Sept., 1887. Water color. Size 4 x 6. Head and shoulders. See 3533.

2513—STUART, REV. GEORGE O'KILL, 1776-1862—A son of Rev. John Stuart, D.D., first incumbent of the Protestant Church, afterwards known as St. George's, Kingston, Ont. He was born at Fort Hunter on the Mohawk River, where his father was a missionary to the Indians. Ordained in 1800, and the following year sent as a missionary to York (Toronto), where he became first rector of the Anglican Church, now St. James'.

Appointed rector of Kingston in 1812; was the Bishop of Quebec's "official" in Upper Canada; later Archdeacon of York, and the first Dean of the See of Ontario. Water color. Size 5 x 6. Head and shoulders. See 2804, 3198.

2514—BURNS—"Revd. Robert Burns, D.D. Principal of the Theological Institute, Presbyterian Church of Canada. Published by Geo. Brown, Toronto." Second pastor of Knox Church, Toronto. Born in Scotland in 1788, and was, before coming to Canada, minister of St. George's Church, Paisley, and secretary of the Glasgow Colonial Missionary Society. He succeeded Rev. James Harris as pastor of Knox Church, Toronto, in 1844, and served till 1856, when he was appointed Professor of Evidences and Church History in Knox College. To Dr. Burns, Knox College, Toronto, is largely indebted for its extensive library. He died 19th Aug., 1869. Line engraving. Size 7 x 8. Head and shoulders. See 3523.

2515-19—Rectors of St. George's Church (Anglican), Toronto, 1844-1917—In 1843 St. James' Church organized the first mission district in Toronto, which subsequently became St. George's Parish. It was originally proposed to erect a church near John and King streets, but this site was abandoned, and in 1844 building began on land at the corner of John street and Stephanie place, given to the parish by Mr. and Mrs. D'Arcy Boulton. On 9th Nov., 1845, St. George's was opened for service. On St. Andrew's Day, 1853, it was consecrated by the late Bishop Strachan. It is built in the early English Gothic style, of white brick, now, however (1917), dingy and weatherbeaten. The clergy since the foundation of the parish have been as follows:—

2515—RUTTAN, REV. CHARLES—First rector St. George's Church, 1844-8—Was born in Cobourg, Ont., 23rd March, 1820. Received his education at Upper Canada College, Toronto, and the Theological School, Cobourg. After leaving St. George's Church he was at Paris, Hillier and Sydenham. His last charge was St. John's Church, Norway, which he resigned in 1896, in consequence of his declining years. Died in Toronto, Oct., 1900. His widow died here, 9th Nov., 1914. Photograph, colored. Size 3 x 4. Head and shoulders.

2516—LETT, REV. STEPHEN, LL.D., D.D.—Second rector St. George's Church, 1848-62; came to Canada in 1847 from Wicklow, Ireland, where he was born in 1815. He was educated at Trinity College, Dublin; ordained, and held his first curacy in Callan Church, Co. Kilkenny, Ireland. Dr. Lett introduced Christmas offerings all over Canada, as a Christmas present to the clergyman in each Anglican Church. Sunday school picnics, too, originated with him, and were first held in St. George's Sunday school. He was one of the founders of the Orphans' Home, Toronto. Died 3rd Oct., 1897. Photograph, colored. Size 3 x 4. Head and shoulders.

2517—FULLER, REV. THOMAS BROCK (Bishop)—Third rector St. George's Church, 1862-75—Born in the Garrison, Kingston, U.C., 1810, where his father, Capt. R. T. Fuller, of the 41st, was quartered. Major-General Sir Isaac Brock was his godfather. Ordained to the diaconate in 1833, engaged in missionary work for a time, and in 1841 became first rector of Thorold, Ont. He was one of the founders of the High School, the Agricultural Society and of the Mechanics' Institute in that place. When the Diocese of Niagara was formed, in 1875, Dr. Fuller was elected Bishop, and consecrated, 1st May. Died at Bishophurst, Hamilton, 17th Dec., 1884. Photograph, colored. Size 3 x 4. Head and shoulders.

2518—CAYLEY, REV. CANON, J.D.—Fourth rector St. George's Church, 1875-1911; eldest son of the late Hon. Wm. Cayley, came to Canada at an early age; was educated at Upper Canada College and Trinity University, Toronto; M.A., 1863; D.D., 1904. In 1860 ordained deacon, and three years later became rector of Whitby, Ont. Mr. Cayley took a deep interest in prohibition, was a councillor Trinity University, and a canon and precentor St. Alban's Cathedral, Toronto. Born in England, March, 1837; died at Muskoka, Ont., 20th August, 1911. Photograph, colored. Size 3 x 4. Head and shoulders.

2519—MOORE, REV. R. J., M.A.—Fifth rector St. George's Church, 1911-17—He is a Canadian of Irish descent; born at Kingston, Ont., in March, 1858; educated at Port Hope and Trinity College (M.A.), Toronto. He began his ministry in St. Catharines. From 1885-90 was curate of St. George's, Toronto, rector of St. Margaret's, which was built by him, 1890-1909, and on amalgamation of the two parishes became vicar of the former. In 1911 he succeeded the late Rev. J. D. Cayley, as rector. Mr. Moore was instrumental in establishing the Church Home (Anglican) for the Aged, Toronto, and is actively interested in social work in down-town districts of the city. Photograph, colored. Size 3 x 4. Head and shoulders.

2520-24—Rectors St. Paul's Church (Anglican), Bloor St., Toronto, 1846-1917—In 1842, Rev. Alexander Sanson (late Canon Sanson, of Little Trinity) built an unpretentious place of worship—the first St. Paul's—in Yorkville, as a mission of the York Mills Church. It was designed by Mr. John G. Howard and opened "for performance of Divine service" on 12th June, 1842, continuing as a branch of York Mills until 1846, when it was made a separate parish. In 1860 a stone church of Gothic architecture was erected, designed by E. Radford, who modelled it after one he had built in England. Additions and alterations were made on this building from time to time, until in 1909 the site for a new church was purchased, and in September of the following year its foundation stone laid by the late Hon. S. H. Blake. The opening and consecration took place on 30th Nov., 1914, on, to quote Archbishop Matheson, Primate of Canada, "one of the finest, most stately parish churches in the world."

2520—MACKENZIE, REV. J. G. DELHOSTE, M.A.—Acting rector St. Paul's Church, 1846-55—Born at St. Ann's Garrison, Bridgetown, Island of Barbadoes, 25th April, 1822, his father at that time being in command of a company of H. M. 1st West India Regiment. Educated at Upper Canada College, Toronto, in 1838 winning the Lieut.-Governor's prize. From 1843-4 filled position of classical master, Diocesan Theological College, Cobourg, and in 1845 ordained deacon. In conjunction with his duties at St. Paul's, he carried on a private school; held first M.A. degree conferred by Trinity College; appointed inspector of Grammar Schools, Province of Ontario, 1868. Died 4th March, 1873. Photograph, colored. Size 4 x 5. Head and shoulders.

2521—JOHNSON, REV. WILLIAM A.—Rector St. Paul's Church, 1555—Son of Col. John Johnson, C.B.; was born in India in 1813. Educated in England; received a commission in army, which he resigned at an early age to come to Canada. Mr. Johnson was only acting rector of St. Paul's for the year subsequent to the retirement of Rev. J. G. D. Mackenzie. From 1856-1880 was rector of St. Phillip's, Etobicoke, the charge including St. John's Chapel, Weston. Founded at Weston the Preparatory English Church Training School, which in 1880 removed to Port Hope, and is now Trinity College School. Died December. 1880. Dr. Jukes Johnson, of Toronto, is a son of Rev. W. A. Johnson. Photograph, colored. Size 4 x 5. Head and shoulders.

2522—GIVINS, REV. SALTERN — Rector St. Paul's Church, 1856-79—He was born in York (Toronto), 1809, third son of Col. James Givins, who was aide to Brock at the taking of Detroit, 16th Aug., 1812. Previous to filling the rectorship of St. Paul's Church, Bloor street, Toronto, Mr. Givins for nineteen years was missionary at Tyendenaga, on the Bay of Quinte. He died at Colborne, Ont., 30th October, 1880. Photograph, colored. Size 3 x 4. Head and shoulders.

2523—DES BARRES. REV. T. CUTLER — Rector St. Paul's Church, 1879-99—Great-grandson of Col. J. F. W. Des Barres, Governor of Cape Breton, 1784-7, and founder of Sydney; was born at Guysboro, N.S., in 1832; educated there and at King's College, Windsor, N.S. Before entering the ministry engaged in business in New York and Halifax. Ordained, 1860, by Dr. Cronyn, first Bishop of Huron. Was at Pictou, N.S., Clinton, St. Thomas and Brockville, Ont., before coming to St. Paul's, Toronto. Died 1907. Photograph, colored. Size **4 x 5. Head and shoulders.**

2524—CODY, REV. H. J., M.A., LLD.—Rector St. Paul's Church, 1907-17—His birthplace was Embro, Ont., 1868. He was educated at Galt Collegiate Institute and Toronto University, his career at the latter being most brilliant; B.A., gold medal in Classics, first class honors in Mental and Moral Philosophy, etc., 1889, and the following year, M.A. Ordained deacon, 1893, and priest, 1894; appointed canon St. Alban's Cathedral, Toronto, 1903, and later Archdeacon of York. He was elected Bishop of Nova Scotia in 1904, but declined the preferment; he also declined the principalship of Wycliffe College, Toronto. Ven. Archdeacon Cody was acting rector of St. Paul's, 1899-1907. **Photograph, colored. Size 4 x 5.** Head and shoulders.

2525—BREYNTON—"John Breynton, D.D., Etat 78, Chaplain in the Royal Navy, 1742, and the first Rector of St. Paul's, Halifax, Nova Scotia. Painted by L. F. Abbott. Engraved by W. Barnard." He was chaplain of one of H.M. ships at the Siege of Louisburg, 1745. In 1752 was sent to Halifax to assist Mr. William Tutty, first missionary at St. Paul's Church, and was licensed by the Lord Bishop of London "to perform the office of a priest in the Province of Nova Scotia." Mr. Breynton was appointed first rector of St. Paul's in 1759, and in recognition of his valuable services received honorary degree of D.D., 1771. The Sunday school of St. Paul's Church, Halifax, founded in 1783 by Dr. Breynton, is the oldest on the American continent. He resigned his rectorship in 1790. Line engraving. Size 11 x 13. Head and shoulders.

2526—HILLS, RT. REV. GEORGE, D.D., 1816-95—First Bishop of Columbia—Born at Egthorne, Kent, Eng.; eldest son of Rear-Admiral Hills. He received his education at the University of Durham, where he successively took the degrees of B.A., M.A., B.D., and D.D. Admitted to the diaconate, 1839, and later became priest; was incumbent of St. Mary's, Leeds, and of Great Yarmouth, Norfolk, in 1850 receiving the appointment of Honorary Canon of Norwich Cathedral. Through the munificence of Miss (Baroness) Burdett-Coutts, a bishopric and two archdeaconries were endowed in Columbia, and Rev. George Hills was selected as Missionary Bishop to Victoria. Consecrated Bishop of Columbia in Westminster Abbey, 24th Feb., 1859, and arrived in the West in 1860. He labored zealously in the distant West, travelled continuously from post to post by canoe, Hudson's Bay steamboat, or on horseback. He described himself on his solitary journeys as "a man with stout country shoes, corduroy trousers, a colored woollen shirt, a leather strap around his waist, and an axe upon his shoulders, driving a mule or horse laden with packs of blankets, a tent, bacon, a sack of flour, a coffee pot, a kettle and frying pan." In 1866 Vancouver Island was united to the mainland, and the two colonies were known as "British Columbia." The Bishop set up his cathedral in Victoria. He resigned in 1892 and returned to England, where his death took place, 10th Dec., 1895. Engraved on stone. Size 7 x 9. Head and shoulders.

2527—McEVAY, THE MOST REV. FERGUS PATRICK—Fourth Archbishop of Toronto, 1908-11—Educated in Canada and the United States; ordained priest, 1882. Served as parish priest at Fenelon Falls, and subsequently became rector of St. Peter's Cathedral, Peterboro, and Chancellor of the Diocese. He was transferred to Hamilton, becoming rector of St. Mary's Cathedral there in 1889. Held Bishopric of London, Ont., 1899-1908, in the latter year being appointed Archbishop of Toronto. He was born in Lindsay, 1852, and died in Toronto, 10th May, 1911. Water color. Size 4 x 5. Head and shoulders.

2528—McNEIL, THE MOST REV. NEIL—Fifth Archbishop of Toronto, 1912-17—He was born in Hillsborough, N.S., 27th Nov., 1852. Studied philosophy and theology in Rome, Rector of Antigonish, 1884-91. In 1895 he proceeded to the western coast of Newfoundland, then a barren field, and after nine years in the vicariate, it was changed to a bishopric, and Father McNeil became first Bishop of St. George's. When the rearrangement of the Church provinces of British Columbia took place a few years ago, his Lordship Bishop McNeil was sought out by Rome to face the difficulties involved in the reorganization of the Church in a new diocese. He became Archbishop of Vancouver, January, 1910, and was installed Archbishop of Toronto, 22nd Dec., 1912. Photograph, colored. Size 4 x 5. Head and shoulders.

2529—POWER, RT. REV. MICHAEL, D.D.—First Roman Catholic Bishop of Toronto, 1842-7—Son of William Power, of Halifax, N.S. Born there, 17th Oct., 1804. Ordained a priest, 1827, and appointed Vicar-General of the Diocese of Montreal in 1839. The Diocese of Kingston was divided in 1841, and Father Power named first bishop with permission to choose the city and title of his See. He was consecrated 8th May, 1842, and took up his residence in Toronto. He founded St. Michael's Cathedral, Toronto, and the Loretto Community. During the siege of typhus fever, Bishop Power was untiring in relief work. He contracted the malady while administering the last rites of the Church to a poor woman at the immigrant sheds, Toronto, and, after a few days' illness, died 1st Oct., 1847. Photograph, colored. Size 4 x 5. Head and shoulders.

2530—LYNCH, THE MOST REV. JOHN JOSEPH—First Archbishop of Toronto, 1870-88—Born near Clones, Ireland, 1816. Entered Lazarist College at Castleknock in 1835, and in June, 1843, was ordained deacon and priest. For a year he labored in Texas; appointed President St. Mary's Lazarist College in Missouri, established College of the Holy Angels, Niagara Falls, N.Y., and in 1860 on resignation of Bishop Charbonnel, became third Bishop of Toronto. In December, 1869, he attended the Vatican Council at Rome, and the following March was consecrated Archbishop of Toronto, in the Pope's private chapel. He was always intensely interested in missionary work and enterprise. During his administration of the diocese, some of the principal events were the establishment of Loretto Convent, St. Joseph's Convent and De La Salle Institute. Died at Toronto, 12th May, 1888. Photograph, colored. Size 3 x 4. Head and shoulders.

2531—O'CONNOR, THE MOST REV. DENNIS, C.S.B.—Third Archbishop of Toronto, 1899-1908—Born in Township of Pickering, Ont., 28th March, 1841; educated in St. Michael's College, Toronto, and College of Annonay, France. He was ordained to the priesthood, 1863, and acted as professor in St. Michael's College from that year until 1870, when he became President of Sandwich College. In 1888 he was created a D.D. by the Pope; appointed third Bishop of London in succession to Bishop Walsh, and in 1899 appointed Archbishop of Toronto. He died 30th June, 1911. Photograph, colored. Size 3 x 3. Head and shoulders.

2532—JENNINGS, REV. JOHN, D.D.—Pastor of United Presbyterian Church, Toronto—He was born in Glasgow, Scotland, Oct., 1814; attended St. Andrew's University and University of Edinburgh, and in addition to his course in theology, studied medicine, as he purposed laboring in a foreign field. In 1838 he was appointed missionary to Canada by the United Presbyterian Church of Cupar, and the following year inducted pastor of the United Presbyterian congregation in Toronto, which for a time met in the March (Lombard) Street Baptist Chapel, and later in the M. E. Church, Richmond street. A new church was erected in 1848, corner Bay and Richmond streets. Dr. Jennings continued as minister until 1874, when he resigned. In acknowledgment of his labors and several works on theological and university subjects, the University of New York conferred on him the degree of D.D., the first degree given to a Canadian minister. For many years he was a member of the Senate of Toronto University and Upper Canada College. His death took place in Toronto, 25th Feb., 1876. Water color. Size 3 x 4. Head and shoulders.

2533—STARK, REV. MARK YOUNG, A.M.—Born at Dunfermline, Scotland, 9th November, 1799; educated in France, Germany and Scotland, taking his A.M. degree at Glasgow University. Entered Established Church of Scotland in 1824, after which he refused an offer to take orders in the Church of England. Came to Canada in 1832, was first minister of Ancaster and Dundas, moderator of the last Synod of the Church of Scotland in Canada, and first moderator of the Free Church Synod. Died at Dundas, Ont., 24th January, 1866, after more than 30 years' ministry there. Water color from portrait in possession of his son, Robert Stark. Toronto. Size 4 x 5. Head and shoulders.

2534—RINTOUL, REV. WILLIAM, M.A.—First minister St. Andrew's Presbyterian Church, Toronto, 1831-4—Records of old St. Gabriel Street Presbyterian Church, Montreal, state that Mr. Rintoul was born 30th Oct., 1797, in Kincardine, Perthshire, Scotland, although some writers claim that he was a native of Clackmannanshire. He received his M.A. at Edinburgh University, and in 1830 was appointed by the Glasgow Colonial Society to St. Andrew's Church, York (Toronto). He was the first to preach in the church, corner Church and Adelaide streets, 19th June, 1831. Remained here three years, then becoming missionary agent. In 1835 became minister of Streetsville. Filled the position of Professor of Hebrew and Biblical Literature, Knox College, Toronto, and later accepted a call to St. Gabriel Street Presbyterian Church, Montreal. In September, 1851, he died at Trois Pistoles, Que. Water color from an oil portrait in Knox College, Toronto. Size 6 x 7. Head and shoulders. See 3429, 3531.

2535—CHARBONNEL, THE RT. REV. ARMAND, 1802-91—Water color. Size 5 x 7. Half length. See 249.

2536—WALSH, THE MOST REV. JOHN, D.D.—Second Archbishop of Toronto, 1889-98. He decided his vocation lay in the mission field, and, accordingly, came to Canada in 1852 from Ireland. The following autumn he entered the Grand Seminary of Montreal as a student of the Diocese of Toronto. He was ordained priest, 1854, appointed, 1855, to Brock Mission, bordering on Lake Simcoe; given charge of St. Mary's, Toronto, in 1857; rector St. Michael's Cathedral, 1859, and in 1862 was made Vicar-General of the Diocese. Five years later his consecration as Bishop of Sandwich took place. Bishop Walsh, who removed the episcopal residence from Sandwich to London, visited every mission in his diocese, reorganized clergy and built churches, the chief of which is St. Peter's Cathedral, London, Ont. A brief from Rome, 27th August, 1889, nominated him Archbishop, his consecration being celebrated in November. Some marks of progress in the Church during his archbishopric were the erection of Sunnyside Chapel, Toronto, the renovation of St. Michael's Cathedral, and the encouragement of students for the priesthood. Archbishop Walsh was born in Ireland, 23rd May, 1830, and died at Toronto, 1898. Photograph, colored. Size 3 x 5. Head and shoulders.

2537-2718—Representative steamers of the Canadian Great Lakes, River St. Lawrence, etc., 1909-1917. All these pen drawings were made from pencil drawings, prints, sketches, photos, daguerreotypes and pictures in other forms, in possession of J. Ross Robertson.

2537—"ACCOMMODATION," 1809—This steamer, the first to ply on the St. Lawrence, was 81 feet long, built at Montreal by John Molson, and plied between Montreal and Quebec. She was popular, and although slow, was well patronized. First passage, Montreal to Quebec, took 66 hours. During the War of 1812-15 she carried British troops up the St. Lawrence from Quebec. Pen drawing. Size 5 x 7.

2538—"CAR OF COMMERCE," 1815—This steamer of about 200 tons burden and 100 feet long was built at Montreal in 1815, and plied between Montreal and Quebec in conjunction with the "Accommodation." She was owned by a syndicate, including Hon. John Molson and Adam Macnider. She was dismantled in 1821, her cabin surviving for the greater part of a century as a summer house on the Macnider estate, Cote St. Lawrence, Montreal. Pen drawing. Size 5 x 7.

2539—"FRONTENAC," 1816-1837—She was 170 feet long and 700 tons gross, built at Finkle's Point, Ernestown, on Bay of Quinte, by Teabout & Chapman, for a syndicate of Kingston, Niagara, Queenston, York and Prescott owners at a cost of $20,000. Capt. James McKenzie commanded the "Frontenac," the first steamer to enter the harbor at York (Toronto). She plied between Prescott and York, was damaged at Niagara, 1837, and broken up a few months later. Pen drawing. Size 5 x 7.

2540—"ONTARIO," 1817-32—Built either at Ogdensburg, N.Y., or Sackett's Harbor, and launched in April, 1817. She was the first American steam vessel for open lake work, and plied between Ogdensburg and Lewiston, taking ten days for round trip. About 1832 she was sent to Oswego and broken up. Pen drawing. Size 5 x 7.

2541—"QUEEN CHARLOTTE," 1818—This steamer was 150 tons register, built at Ernestown, north shore of Bay of Quinte, and plied from the Carrying Place, in Prince Edward County, to Prescott. At this point the Indians and Indian traders carried their canoes and merchandise from the Bay of Quinte to Lake Ontario. The "Queen Charlotte" was commanded by Capts. Dennis and Gildersleeve, and was broken up at Cataraqui Bay, near Kingston, U.C. Pen drawing. Size 5 x 7.

2542—"WALK IN THE WATER," 1818-21—Lake Erie's first steamer— 135 feet long and 338 tons gross. She was built at the mouth of Scajaguada Creek, Black Rock, N.Y., on Niagara River, by Noah Brown, plied between Black Rock and Detroit, and was wrecked at Buffalo, Nov. 1st, 1821. She was very popular with Windsor and Chatham people. Pen drawing. Size 5 x 7.

2543—"QUEENSTON," 1825—This steamer of 350 tons was built at Queenston, U.C., in 1824-5. The Hon. Robert Hamilton, a prominent merchant of Niagara, was the owner, and the vessel was sailed by Capt. Whitney. She plied between Niagara, York (Toronto), Hamilton and Prescott, frequently carrying troops, and was a favorite steamer with York people. Pen drawing. Size 5 x 7.

2544—"CANADA," 1826—This steamer, of English Channel packet model and 250 tons burden, was built near Toronto in 1826 by Capt. Hugh Richardson, and plied between Toronto and Niagara, with the exception of one season, when she ran between Oswego and Kingston. She was wrecked at Oswego, N.Y., 1837, when commanded by Capt. Nat Johnson. Pen drawing. Size 5 x 7.

2545—"MARTHA OGDEN," 1826—She was a sidewheel steamer of 120 tons, commanded by Capt. Estes, and was built at Sackett's Harbor, N.Y. She plied between York (Toronto), Niagara and the head of the lake (Hamilton). Pen drawing. Size 5 x 7.

2546—"WATERLOO," 1827—This steamer was a small American side-wheeler, built near Ogdensburg, N.Y. She traded on the St. Lawrence River, in the vicinity of Brockville, Clayton, Gananoque and Ogdensburg, and was a popular boat for excursions between Canadian and American ports. Pen drawing. Size 5 x 7.

2547—"GREAT BRITAIN," 1830—This steamer of 700 tons was built at Prescott in 1830 for Sir John Hamilton, and plied between Kingston, Niagara and Hamilton under command of Capt. J. Whitney. She was a great favorite with immigrants into the new province of Upper Canada, and her design marked a revolution in lake shipping. She had double engines, one on either side. Remained in the service until about 1842. Pen drawing. Size 5 x 7.

2548—"IROQUOIS," 1831—This steamer of 100 tons burden and 70 feet in length was built at Prescott in 1831, and plied between Prescott and Dickinson's Landing, on the St. Lawrence. She was of scow model, and propelled by a stern wheel, but was not a successful venture, and was soon broken up. Pen drawing. Size 5 x 7.

2549—"UNITED STATES," 1831-42—This vessel of 450 tons was built at Ogdensburg, N.Y., by William Capes, of New York, for the St. Lawrence Steamboat Co., in imitation of "Great Britain." She made her first trip on July 4th, 1832, and plied between Ogdensburg and Lewiston. She was broken up at Oswego in 1842. In Rebellion of 1837-8 the "Patriots" seized her at Morristown and ran her down the St. Lawrence to Prescott, where they landed. On her return journey to Ogdensburg she was seized by the U. S. Government. Pen drawing. Size 5 x 7.

2550—"JOHN BY," 1832—This steamer of 100 tons was built at Kingston in 1832, and plied on the Bay of Quinte and Rideau Canal, and later between Toronto and Hamilton, under the command of Capt. Kerr. She had a stern paddle wheel, but this means of propulsion was not satis-factory. She was wrecked near Port Credit, Ont. The "John By" was named after the colonel of that name, chief engineer of the Rideau Canal during its construction. Pen drawing. Size 5 x 7.

2551—"WILLIAM IV.," 1832—This steamer of 450 tons was built at Gananoque, and plied between Toronto and Prescott for many years. She was commanded at different periods by Capts. McDonald, Paynter, Jones, John Cowan and Hilliard, and finally became a towboat, and was broken up at Garden Island, opposite Kingston, U.C. Pen drawing. Size 5 x 7.

2552—"RAPID," 1834—Built at Prescott, Ont., in 1834, by a New York builder named Sanford, on the pontoon principle, with two cigar-shaped hulls and paddle wheels between them. She was unable to stem the current of the St. Lawrence River, and was broken up, her engines being trans-ferred to the "Oakville," completed that same year. The "Oakville" plied between Toronto and Hamilton under Capt. James Mills. Pen drawing. Size 5 x 7.

2553—"BYTOWN," 1835-50—Steamer of 150 tons burden and 120 feet in length, built at Kingston in 1835; plied between Kingston and Bytown (Ottawa), by way of the Rideau Canal, taking 28 hours for the journey. The "Bytown" also made voyages between Kingston and Montreal, being on that route in 1844. She went out of commission about 1850. Pen drawing. Size 5 x 7.

2554—"TRAVELLER," 1835-43—This steamer of 352 tons burden was built at Niagara in 1835, and plied on Lake Ontario under Capt. James Sutherland, her route being Hamilton, Toronto, Port Hope, Cobourg, Rochester and Prescott. She carried troops in the "Patriot" Rebellion, 1837-8, was bought by the Government, and in 1843, sold, becoming a towboat. Pen drawing. Size 5 x 7.

2555—"EXPERIMENT," 1837-60—Built at Niagara, and plied between Hamilton and Toronto under Captains Dick and Wheeler. Later she navigated the Upper St. Lawrence. On Nov. 12, 1838, in the Patriot Rebellion, she was at Prescott, and a cannon shot from her killed Solomon Foster, steersman of "United States," which the Patriots had seized. She afterwards became a ferry between Kingston and Wolfe Island. Her register was 150 tons. Pen drawing. Size 5 x 7.

2556—"CAROLINE," 1837—Built on the Hudson River, by Commodore Vanderbilt. She was bought by Wm. Wells, of Buffalo, and brought to Niagara River, via Erie Canal, and was used by the Canadian rebels as a supply steamer for their forces on Navy Island, above the Falls. The British officer suspected her mission, and decided to capture and destroy her. Lieut. Andrew Drew (Admiral), with a Loyalist force, captured the vessel, set her on fire and sent her over the Falls, Dec. 24th, 1837. Pen drawing. Size 5 x 7.

2557—"JOHN MUNN," 1838—This steamer, of almost 400 feet length over all, was built at Montreal for a syndicate, including Hon. John Molson, and plied between Montreal and Quebec, but her great size rendered her unprofitable, and she was scrapped in the fifties. Her engine is still (1917) in commission in the Monadnock Mills, Claremont, N.Y. Pen drawing. Size 5 x 7.

2558—"ST. LAWRENCE," 1839—This steamer, 180 feet long, was built at Oswego in 1839 for an American company of shipowners, and plied on the St. Lawrence River and on Lake Ontario between Oswego, Niagara, Toronto and Kingston, under command of Capt. J. C. Van Cleeve until 1847. Some time afterwards she was broken up on Washington Island, near Clayton, N.Y. Pen drawing. Size 5 x 7.

2559—"CITY OF TORONTO," 1840-63—"RACINE," 1863—"ALGOMA," 1864-87—This steamer, the first "City of Toronto," which plied between Toronto and Niagara, from 1841-63, was built at Niagara, 1840, and rebuilt at Detroit in 1863, and renamed the "Racine." In 1864 she was sold and renamed the "Algoma," plying between Collingwood and Fort William as one of the Lake Superior Royal Mail Line. E. M. Carruthers, who later was lessee of the Queen's Wharf, Toronto, bought her to run between Lake Superior ports till 1872. Scrapped about 1888. Pen drawing. Size 5 x 7.

2560—STR. "ALGOMA," 1864-1887—"CITY OF TORONTO," 1840-63—"RACINE," 1863—This steamer, the first "City of Toronto," which plied between Toronto and Niagara, from 1841-63, was built at Niagara, 1840, rebuilt at Detroit in 1863, and renamed the "Racine." In 1864 she was sold and renamed the "Algoma," plying between Collingwood and Fort William as one of the Lake Superior Royal Mail Line. E. M. Carruthers, who later was lessee of the Queen's Wharf, Toronto, bought her to run between Lake Superior ports. In 1888 she was broken up and sold for scrap. Pen drawing. Size 5 x 7.

2561—"NIAGARA," 1840—"SOVEREIGN," 1843-59—This steamer of 475 tons was built at Niagara, 1840, by Niagara Harbor and Dock Co., for Hon. John Hamilton, of the Royal Mail Line. She ran between Toronto and Kingston under Capt. Sutherland, and was originally the "Niagara." Renamed "Sovereign," 1843, under Capt. Elmsley. Displaced by "Passport," 1851, and used as an extra boat up to 1856, when she was laid up at east side of Rees' Wharf, foot of Simcoe street, Toronto, and dismantled. Her hull remained till about 1859, when it was scrapped. Pen drawing. Size 5 x 7.

2562—"VAN DALIA," 1841—"MILWAUKEE," 1850—Pioneer propeller upon the Great Lakes—91 feet long, measured 138 tons, and built by Sylvester Doolittle, of Oswego, for Capt. J. C. Van Cleve and partners. Capt. Rufus Hawkins was her first commander. She plied between Oswego, Toronto and Buffalo. About 1850 she was enlarged to 350 tons measurement and renamed "Milwaukee." Pen drawing. Size 5 x 7.

2563—"PRINCESS ROYAL," 1841-1843—This steamer of 500 tons was built at Niagara in 1841 for the Royal Mail Line, and plied between Kingston, Toronto and Niagara, 1841-1852, Capt. J. Dick being one of her commanders. In 1853 she plied between Toronto and Rochester, N.Y. She was afterwards dismantled and became a tow barge. Pen drawing. Size 5 x 7.

2564—"CHIEF JUSTICE ROBINSON," 1841—This steamer of 400 tons was built at Niagara, 1841, for Capt. Hugh Richardson. Her bow of ploughshare shape was so designed to cut the waves more easily. She plied between Toronto and Niagara, Hamilton and Presqu'isle, frequently running all winter and landing passengers on the ice when Toronto harbor was frozen. Subsequently she was sold, her engine eventually being put into a new steamer, "Marine City." Pen drawing. Size 5 x 7.

2565—"PRINCE OF WALES," 1842—This iron steamer of 200 tons was built at Kingston in 1842 for Hon. John Hamilton, and had the engine of the "Sir James Kempt." She was commanded by Capts. Clark, Hamilton, Chrysler and Kelly. Up to 1855 was in active service on Bay of Quinte, going out of commission about the date of her Royal namesake's visit to Canada, 1860. Pen drawing. Size 5 x 7.

2566—"WELLAND," 1842-56—A steamer of 300 tons burden, and 140 feet long, the first of the name, was built at Bath, on the Bay of Quinte, 1842, and completed at St. Catharines. She was owned by J. Romain & Co., and had various routes, principally along the north shore of Lake Ontario, between Kingston and Toronto, and on the Bay of Quinte. Destroyed by fire in 1856. Pen drawing. Size 5 x 7.

2567—H. M. S. "MOHAWK," 1842—This gunboat of 150 tons claimed with the "Prince of Wales" the distinction of being the first iron steamer on the lakes, having been built at Kingston in 1842. She cruised on Lake Erie and Lake Huron under the command of Lieuts. Tyssen and R. Herbert, R. N. She was broken up in the early fifties. Pen drawing. Size 5 x 7.

2568—"LADY OF THE LAKE," 1843—"QUEEN CITY," 1853-55—Built at Oswego in 1843 for the American Steamboat Co., and plied between Toronto and Niagara, and later between Kingston and Cape Vincent, under Capt. Seymour. From 1853 onwards, under the new name, "Queen City," she plied between Toronto and Hamilton, running all the year round. On Jan. 22, 1855, she was totally destroyed by fire at Brown's Wharf, Toronto. Her register was 450 tons. Pen drawing. Size 5 x 7.

2569—"ADMIRAL," 1843—This popular steamer of 400 tons was built at Niagara. She ran between Oswego and Hamilton, calling at Toronto, and connected with the Royal Mail Line steamers. Her captain, Wm. Gordon, a salt water sailor of the old school, fitted her out as a topsail schooner, with a four-pounder cannonade on the forecastle head. In 1850 she ran between Toronto and Niagara, in 1852 between Toronto and Rochester, and was burned at Brown's Wharf, Toronto, June 10th, 1853. Pen drawing. Size 5 x 7.

2570—H. M. S. "CHEROKEE," 1843—This wooden gunboat of 700 tons burthen was built at Kingston, 1843-4, and used by Government as a cruiser between Kingston, Toronto and Niagara. She carried eighteen guns, six and nine-pounders. Commanded by Capt. Davis, R.N. Later taken to Halifax, bought by Capt. Gaskin and E. M. Yenwood, of Kingston, and plied as a mail packet between Halifax and St. John's. Brought back to Lake Ontario and dismantled in Deadman's Bay, Kingston. Pen drawing. Size 5 x 7.

2571—U. S. GUNBOAT "MICHIGAN," 1843—LATER "WOLVERINE"— An early iron steamer, built at Pittsburg, assembled at Erie, Pa., and launched Dec. 5th, 1843; still in service. She is 164 feet long and 27 feet beam, and draws 11 feet. Originally armed with the single 18-pounder stipulated by treaty between Britain and the U.S. Now carries six sixes and two one-pounders. Renamed "Wolverine." Pen drawing. Size 5 x 7.

2572—"ECLIPSE," 1843—This steamer of 400 tons was built at Niagara for Capt. James Sutherland, and plied between Hamilton and Toronto in connection with the Royal Mail Line. Christened the "Commerce," she was renamed "Eclipse" on account of breaking the record between Toronto and Niagara on her trial trip. She became a schooner in the fifties. Pen drawing. Size 5 x 7.

2573—"MAID OF THE MIST," 1846—The first "Maid of the Mist," built 1846, to run below Niagara Falls, and Joel Robinson's "little red skiff" are given in this sketch. They were contemporary. The "Maid" afterwards sank at her dock. From drawings by Hon. Peter A. Porter, Niagara Falls, N.Y. Pen drawing. Size 5 x 7.

2574—"MAID OF THE MIST," 1854—Built in 1854 to run as a ferry below the Falls of Niagara, under command of Capt. Baily. Proving unprofitable, she was in 1861 run down the Niagara River through the Whirlpool Rapids to Queenston, making the trip with no mishap except losing her funnel. She was piloted by Joel Robinson, the veteran ferryman. Later, as the "Maid of Orleans," plied between Quebec and the Island of Orleans. She was eventually burned. Pen drawing. Size 5 x 7.

2575—"MAID OF THE MIST" (CANADIAN)—Built at Niagara Falls, Ont., 1884—71 feet long and of 62 tons gross. Flying the American flag forward and the British flag aft, she plies between the Canadian and American shores with sight-seeing passengers. Between 1861 and 1884 there was no steamboat; people were ferried across the river in yawl boats. Pen drawing. Size 5 x 7.

2576—"MAID OF THE MIST" (AMERICAN), 1892—This steamer, 75 feet long, and of about 65 tons gross, was built at Niagara Falls, N.Y., and plies (1917) on the Niagara River, just below the Falls, between the American and Canadian shores. She flies the British flag forward and the American flag aft, and covers the same route as her Canadian consort, but in the opposite direction. Pen drawing. Size 5 x 7.

2577—"BRITISH QUEEN," 1846—This steamer, of about 250 tons register, was built at Montreal, and plied between Lachine and Prescott on the St. Lawrence River, connecting with lake steamers completing the route from Montreal to Niagara. She was commanded by Capt. Chamberlain. Went out of commission in the fifties. Pen drawing. Size 5 x 7.

2578—"CASPIAN," 1846—An iron steamer of 957 tons gross and 177 feet long, built in Kingston in 1846, still in commission for the Richelieu and Ontario Navigation Co. between Kingston, Belleville and Bay of Quinte ports. She was one of the pioneer iron steamers on the Great Lakes. Pen drawing. Size 5 x 7.

2579—"PASSPORT," 1847—"PICTON," 1900-1907—This iron steamer of 500 tons was launched at Niagara early in 1847, having been built by the Niagara Dock Co. for Hon. John Hamilton. In the service of the Royal Mail Line, Canadian Navigation Co., and Richelieu and Ontario Navigation Co., she plied Lake Ontario and the St. Lawrence River for sixty years. Renamed "Picton" in 1900, and turned into a tow barge in 1907, after being seriously damaged by fire at Toronto. Pen drawing. Size 5 x 7.

2580—"CATARACT," 1847-74—This steamer of 577 tons burden was built at Clayton, N.Y., for the Ontario and St. Lawrence Steamboat Co., and plied between Toronto, Oswego and Montreal under Capts. J. C. Van Cleve, R. B. Chapman, A. D. Kilby and H. N. Throop. In 1871 she was bought by a Canadian syndicate. She was dismantled and her machinery was placed in the steamer "Cumberland," 1874. Pen drawing. Size 5 x 7.

2581—"MAGNET," 1847—"HAMILTON," 1895—An iron steamer of 500 tons, launched at Niagara, July 3, 1847; built by Niagara Dock Co. for Capt. Sutherland and Mr. Gunn, of Niagara, from materials imported from England. She plied for 60 years between Hamilton and Montreal in service of the Royal Mail Line, Canadian Navigation Co., and Richelieu and Ontario Navigation Co. Renamed "Hamilton," 1895, continuing in service on the St. Lawrence. Pen drawing. Size 5 x 7.

2582—"COMET," 1849—"MAYFLOWER," 1851-57—About 170 feet long and 300 tons register, built at Hay Bay, Ont. Commanded by Capts. Taylor and O'Connor, and plied between Kingston, Toronto and Hamilton. Her boiler exploded at Oswego, April 21, 1851, killing eight persons, injuring many and wrecking the vessel. She was repaired, renamed "Mayflower," and plied between Hamilton and Cape Vincent; seriously damaged through striking the Cataraqui Bridge, Kingston, and in 1857 sunk in collision with another vessel. Pen drawing. Size 5 x 7.

2583—"ATLANTIC" (AMERICAN), 1849-52—This steamer, 1,150 tons register and 267 feet long, was built at Newport, Lake Erie, in 1849, and plied between Buffalo and Detroit. Her record was remarkable for her time—16½ hours for the 270 miles. On Aug. 20, 1852, she was rammed off Long Point by the "Ogdensburg" and sunk with the loss of 131 lives and $36,000 in a safe of the American Express Co. This was recovered four years later. Pen drawing. Size 5 x 7.

2584—TINNING'S CIGAR BOAT, 1849—This curious experiment in the pontoon principle was built by Mr. R. Tinning, the wharfinger, at Toronto in 1849, and consisted of three cigar-shaped hulls covered by a deck and equipped with side wheels and an engine. She plied between the city and the island, but was a failure. In 1850 she was dismantled and used as a temporary bridge over the Don River while the regular bridge, damaged by a flood, was being repaired. Pen drawing. Size 5 x 7.

2585—"NEW ERA," 1849—"EMPRESS," 1864-70—This steamer of about 170 feet length and 250 tons register was built at Kingston by O. S. Gildersleeve, and plied between Kingston and Montreal. In 1853-57 she was one of the Royal Mail line on that route. In 1864 she plied between Toronto and Niagara under the new name "Empress." Later in 1864 she was on the Dorchester-Cobourg route. She was burned at Kingston about 1870. Pen drawing. Size 5 x 7.

29

2586—"HIGHLANDER," 1850-71—The second of the name, this steamer of 250 tons register, was built at Montreal in 1850, and plied between that port and Hamilton for three years. Later she had various routes, Toronto to Hamilton, Toronto to Rochester, Toronto to Cape Vincent, and Rochester to Port Hope. She became a towboat and was burned at Garden Island, 1871. Pen drawing. Size 5 x 7.

2587—"CHAMPION," 1850-80—This steamer of 350 tons register was built at Montreal in 1850, and plied principally between Montreal, Toronto, Lewiston and Hamilton, in the service of the Royal Mail Line, and Canadian Navigation Co., and Richelieu and Ontario Navigation Co. From 1853-56 she was on the route between Toronto and Cape Vincent, and in 1880 was broken up. Pen drawing. Size 5 x 7.

2588—"OCEAN WAVE," 1850-53—The steamer, of 300 tons burden, was built at Montreal about 1850, and was on the night of April 30, 1853, the scene of a terrible disaster. While coming up Lake Ontario, near the Duck Islands, 20 miles west of Kingston, she took fire and burned to the water's edge. Thirteen passengers and fifteen members of the crew lost their lives. Pen drawing. Size 5 x 7.

2589—"CITY OF HAMILTON," 1851—This steamer of 250 tons burthen was built at Hamilton, Ont., and plied between that place and Toronto, calling at Wellington Square (Burlington), Bronte, Oakville and Port Credit. Capt. John Gordon, one of the best-known mariners on Lake Ontario, commanded her. Pen drawing. Size 5 x 7.

2590—"ARABIAN," 1851—The Royal Mail Line purchased her in 1853 and placed her on the route between Hamilton, Toronto and Kingston, under Capt. Colcleugh. Later she ran between Hamilton, Toronto and Prescott, under Capt. Sclater, and in the sixties Capt. Thomas Leach commanded her. She was 350 tons register, and was built at Niagara in 1851. Pen drawing. Size 5 x 7.

2591—"NOVELTY," 1852—"CORA LINN," 1860—She was 150 tons, built at Kingston, U.C., in 1852, and plied between Kingston and Bay of Quinte ports under Capt. Chas. Bonter. Her name was changed to "Cora Linn;" 1860, and after continuing on the Bay of Quinte route for some years she was sent down the St. Lawrence. Totally wrecked in collision with another steamer near Coteau du Lac during the sixties. Pen drawing. Size 5 x 7.

2592—"LORD ELGIN," 1852-64—This propeller of 600 tons burden was built in Montreal in 1852 for Hooker, Jacques & Co., and plied with passengers and freight between Montreal and Lake Ontario ports. She did a large immigrant passenger trade. In 1864 she was one of the American Steamboat Co.'s fleet of four steamers giving a daily service between Toronto, Oswego and Montreal. Soon afterwards she was taken down the St. Lawrence and became a barge. Pen drawing. Size 5 x 7.

2593—"WELLAND," 1853—This steamer of 300 tons register, the second of the name, was built at St. Catharines, in 1853, for Capt. Donaldson. She was 184 feet long and 22 feet wide, and plied between Toronto and St. Catharines and Toronto and Niagara with passengers and freight. Pen drawing. Size 5 x 7.

2594—"PEERLESS," 1853-61—An iron vessel of 400 tons burden, built near Glasgow, Scotland, for Capt. Thos. Dick, of Toronto. She was launched Jan. 6th, 1853, and arrived in Lake Ontario, June, 1853. Her speed was 21 knots, and she was the fastest steamer on the lakes when running between Toronto and Niagara. In 1861 she was sold to the American Government, and was lost in a collision with the steamer "Star of the South" off Cape Hatteras, 2nd Nov., 1861. Pen drawing. Size 5 x 7.

2595—"KALOOLAH," 1853—"COLLINGWOOD," 1857-60—This steamer, it is claimed, was built in Detroit and bought by Charles Thompson, of Toronto in 1853, for the route between Dunnville and Sault Ste. Marie. She was bought by Collingwood owners and renamed "Collingwood" in 1857. En route to Fort William with the Canadian Red River Expedition, July, 1857, she ran on a low, rocky island two miles from the harbor of Michipicoten. She was refloated, but in 1860 was wrecked off Southampton. Pen drawing. Size 5 x 7.

2596—"GEORGE MOFFATT," 1853-66—This steamer, 350 tons, 45 feet long, was built at Chatham, 1853, and for a brief period plied between Chatham and Montreal with passengers and freight under Capt. W. G. Patton. Her route was later shortened from Hamilton to Montreal, calling at way ports. A fine steamer with walnut decks, she was totally wrecked off Raby's Head, near Oshawa, Lake Ontario, 1866. Pen drawing. Size 5 x 7.

2597—"BANSHEE," 1854—A steamer of 400 tons, built at Montreal in 1854. She plied between Toronto and Montreal in the service of the Royal Mail Line, her usual route being between Montreal and Prescott. Badly damaged in collision with the "Empress" off the docks near Kingston, 1864. Continued in passenger trade, however, until the eighties, when she was partially dismantled and became a tug on Coteau Lake. Pen drawing. Size 5 x 7.

2598—"EUROPA," 1854—This steamer of 500 tons was built at Hamilton, Ont., 1854, and plied between Hamilton, Toronto and Oswego. In that year the Great Western Railway sent a large amount of freight to Toronto, prior to the building of the Toronto branch, by the "Europa," and this led to the building of the two G. W. R. steamers, the "Canada" and "America," for freight and passengers. Pen drawing. Size 5 x 7.

2599—"ZIMMERMAN," 1854-63—This steamer of 500 tons measurement was launched at Niagara, May 6th, 1854, having been built by L. Shickluna for Oliver T. Macklem, of Chippawa. She was named for Samuel Zimmerman, railway magnate, who was killed in Desjardins disaster, 1857. The steamer plied between Toronto and Niagara under Captains James Dick and D. Milloy, making the journey in two hours. She was destroyed by fire at Niagara, Aug. 21, 1863. Pen drawing. Size 5 x 7.

2600—"CLIFTON," 1854-67—This steamer of about 200 tons was built at Chippawa by Oliver T. Macklem in 1854 for Buffalo-Niagara route. She plied between Collingwood and Owen Sound in 1863, in connection with the Northern Ry. from Toronto. Capt. W. H. Smith then commanded her. Prior to this date she was engaged in traffic from Sarnia. Her engines were taken out and placed in the "Frances Smith," 1867. Pen drawing. Size 5 x 7.

2601—SAILING SHIP "CITY OF TORONTO," 1855-56—This vessel, 168 feet long, and of 1,000 tons burden, was built by Messrs. Hayes Bros. & Co., in their shipyard on Front st., opposite Queen's Hotel, Toronto; launched April 3, 1855, and sailed from Toronto for Liverpool in August, with passengers and a cargo of walnut. She was intended for the timber trade between Quebec and Liverpool. In the autumn of 1856 she was totally wrecked on the coast of Nova Scotia. Pen drawing. Size 5 x 7.

2602—"INKERMAN," 1855-57—A propeller of 600 tons burden, built at Kingston, U.C., in 1855, and plied between Montreal and Toronto with passengers and freight. She had a Crimean musket, with fixed bayonet, for a bowsprit. Her boiler blew up at Upton & Brown's Wharf, Toronto, May 29th, 1857, completely destroying the vessel and killing the entire crew and one passenger who was on board. Pen drawing. Size 5 x 7.

2603—"BOWMANVILLE," 1856-66—Steamer of 400 tons burden; was built at Bowmanville by Capt. Charles Perry, of Toronto, and plied between Hamilton and Montreal, calling at way ports with passengers and freight. She was wrecked after about ten years of service. In 1861 the "Bowmanville" made a special trip to Quebec with excursionists to see the "Great Eastern." Pen drawing. Size 5 x 7.

2604—"KINGSTON," 1855-72—"BAVARIAN," 1873—THEN "ALGERIAN" —The steamer was of 456 tons, and built at Montreal for Royal Mail Line and Canadian Navigation Co.; she plied between Toronto and Montreal. On September 7th, 1860, brought the Prince of Wales (Edward VII.) to Toronto from Cobourg, and a week later took him down the St. Lawrence to Montreal. Wrecked in the St. Lawrence, 1872, she was rebuilt and renamed "Bavarian," but in 1873 was burned near Bowmanville with great loss of life. She was rebuilt as the "Algerian," and in 1875 was bought by the R. and O. Co. Pen drawing. Size 5 x 7.

2605—"CANADA," 1855-61—This steamer of 700 tons was built at Niagara by Great Western Railway Co. in 1854. Commenced running between Hamilton, Toronto and Oswego, July 16, 1855, under Capt. C. E. Willoughby. The "Canada" and her sister ship, "America," gave a daily service, and were sold to the American Government for transport purposes in 1861-2. Pen drawing. Size 5 x 7.

2606—"AMERICA," 1855-61—This steamer of 700 tons was built at Niagara by Great Western Railway Co. in 1854, and commenced running between Hamilton, Toronto and Oswego, July 16, 1855, under Capt. J. Masson. She and her sister ship, "Canada," gave a daily service. These two vessels were the palatial steamers of the lake while in commission. They were sold to the U.S. as transports in 1861-2. Pen drawing. Size 5 x 7.

2607—"PHOENIX," 1856-67—Built at Montreal and placed on the Ottawa River route, between Ottawa and Point Anne, in 1856 by Capt. Sheppard, of Montreal. In 1864 she was bought by the Ottawa River Navigation Co., and plied between Ottawa and Montreal until 1867. Then passed into the business of towing rafts on the St. Lawrence River. Her measurement was about 200 tons. Pen drawing. Size 5 x 7.

2608—"MONARCH," 1856—The "Monarch," a freight and passenger steamer running between Hamilton, Toronto and Montreal, was built at Kingston by James D. Shaw and Capt. Sinclair. She cost $40,000, and was 700 tons gross. In her first season in a storm on Lake Ontario the "Monarch" was wrecked, 29th Nov., 1856, and went ashore on the lake side of Toronto Island, south of Privat's Hotel, near and west of the present eastern entrance to the harbor. Pen drawing. Size 5 x 7.

2609—"JENNY LIND," 1858—The second of the name, her predecessor built in 1855 having had a very short career, was built at Montreal in 1858. She plied between Toronto and Montreal, being chartered by the Royal Mail Line in 1859, and continued on the route during the sixties. One of several steamers chartered to convey the Prince of Wales during his visit to Canada in 1860. Pen drawing. Size 5 x 7.

2610—"PLOUGHBOY," 1858—Royal Mail steamer on Lake Huron and Georgian Bay, built 1857-8. She was of 500 tons burden. On July 1st, 1859, a party, among whom were Hon. (Sir) John A. Macdonald, Hon. John and Mrs. Ross, left Toronto on an excursion to Sault Ste. Marie. At Collingwood they took the steamer "Ploughboy." Shortly before arrival at Lonely Island, Georgian Bay, an accident happened to the machinery, making it necessary to shut off steam. After drifting before the gale for some time, the anchor caught bottom and held fast until the "Canada" from

Owen Sound took the distressed vessel in tow, landing her safely at Collingwood. The "Ploughboy," subsequently known as the "Parks," was burned in 1870. Pen drawing. Size 5 x 7.

2611—"PROVINCIAL," 1858-69—This steamer was built for freighting purposes. In 1858 she was dismantled, and from 1860-69 served as club-house for the Royal Canadian Yacht Club, being moored near the east side of Rees' Wharf at the foot of Simcoe street. In the winter of 1869 the "Provincial" broke away from her moorings and was frozen in the bay, becoming a wreck, which subsequently was blown up by order of the corporation. Pen drawing. Size 5 x 7.

2612—"LADY ELGIN," 1860—A favorite with passengers going be-tween Chicago and ports on Lake Michigan and Lake Huron. On Sept. 8th, 1860, in collision with the schooner "Augusta," a sailing vessel of the type shown in background of this picture, she was sunk 16 miles north of Chicago. The collision occurred at night, and of 400 persons on board only 98 were rescued. Among those who perished was Mr. Herbert Ingram, founder and proprietor of the London (England) Illustrated News. Pen drawing. Size 5 x 7.

2613—"MONTREAL," 1860-1904—This vessel of 519 tons register was built by Gilbert, of Montreal, to ply between Montreal and Quebec, and bought by the Richelieu and Ontario Company in 1875. She was replaced by a new "Montreal," built at Sorel, Que., in 1904, on similar lines, but of much greater size—332 feet long and 4,282 tons gross. The first "Mont-real" was lost in a snowstorm, 29th Nov., 1853, and the second burned in the St. Lawrence, 26th June, 1857. Pen drawing. Size 5 x 7.

2614—"BAY OF QUINTE," 1861—This steamer of 250 tons register and 150 feet in length was built at Kingston in 1861 for Henry Gildersleeve, and plied between Kingston and Belleville in opposition to the "Cora Linn." She eventually became a rafting tug in the fleet of Hiram Calvin, on Garden Island, and was broken up. Pen drawing. Size 5 x 7.

2615—"HER MAJESTY," 1863—A propeller of nearly 1,000 tons burden, and 185 feet long, one of the largest vessels of her kind on Lake Ontario at the time of her launching. She was built by L. Shickluna for Capt. Perry at St. Catharines in 1863, and plied between Toronto and Montreal with passengers and freight. Made occasional voyages to Upper Lakes, and was finally engaged in the Gulf of St. Lawrence trade. Pen drawing. Size 5 x 7.

2616—"GRECIAN," 1863-70—Built on the Clyde in 1863—175 feet long, 400 tons register—and put together at Montreal for Canadian Navigation Co. She plied between Hamilton, Toronto and Montreal, and in 1870 was wrecked on Split Rock, above the Cascade Rapids, St. Lawrence River. A battery of artillery, under Major Sandom, was on board. All were saved. Capt. C. Hamilton, of Kingston, commanded her. Pen drawing. Size 5 x 7.

2617—STEAM YACHT "ROSAMOND," R.C.Y.C., 1885-95—The sixty-foot pleasure craft was one of the early steam members of the Royal Canadian Yacht Club fleet. She was built for W. J. Walton, of Hamilton, about 1885, and later bought by Captain J. T. Matthews for a Toronto syndicate com-posed of R. L. Patterson, Joshua Beard, M. McConnell, David Walker, and Alderman Mitchell. Cruised on Lake Ontario, with Toronto as head-quarters, for ten years, when she was sold and taken to the St. Lawrence River. Pen drawing. Size 5 x 7.

2618—"QUEEN VICTORIA," 1864-1880—This steamer, of about 300 tons burden, built in Montreal, was placed on the Ottawa River route be-tween Montreal and Ottawa, by the Ottawa River Navigation Co., in 1864. Remained in commission on the Ottawa route until 1880, when she was sold, and soon afterwards broken up. Pen drawing. Size 5 x 7.

2619—"LETTER B," 1864-69—LATER THE "CHICORA"—This drawing, from a photograph, shows the well-known excursion steamer as the "Letter B," a blockade runner during American Civil War. Painted an indefinite grey, with no cabins or upper works, the smoke from her long, slender funnels was almost all that was left to catch the eyes of Northern cruisers. In sacrificing tophamper, two fully-rigged lower masts were retained. Auxiliary equipment of sails was considered essential for ocean-going steamers at this time. The name "Letter B" was a hint to the blockaders to "Let Her Be." Sister ships were called "Let Her Go" and "Let Her Rip." Pen drawing. Size 5 x 7.

2620—"CHICORA," 1869-1917—This iron steamer, 221 feet long, 931 tons gross, was built at Liverpool, England, in 1864. After a career as a blockade runner in the American War, as the "Letter B," she was brought to the Upper Lakes in 1869, and altered, plying between Collingwood and Chicago. The Niagara Navigation Co. began business in 1878, and from that time until the present (1917) the "Chicora," the company's first vessel, has been in service. Pen drawing. Size 5 x 7.

2621—"CORINTHIAN," 1864—She was a steel plated steamer of 350 tons, built at Kingston in 1864. Capt. Crysler commanded her, and she plied between Port Hope, Cobourg, Charlotte and Colborne on what was known as the Rochester route. In 1870 the "Corinthian" belonged to the Canadian Navigation Co.'s Royal Mail Line, plying between Hamilton and Montreal, under Capt. Dunlop, for several seasons. Pen drawing. Size 5 x 7.

2622—"CITY OF TORONTO II."—The second steamer of the name, 202 feet long, of 600 tons burden, built at Niagara in 1864 for Capt. Milloy, of Toronto, by Louis Shickluna to replace the burned "Zimmerman." She plied regularly between Toronto and Lewiston, N.Y. In the Fenian Raid of 1866 she carried the Queen's Own to Port Colborne. In 1882 she was totally destroyed by fire at Port Dalhousie, Ont. Pen drawing. Size 5 x 7.

2623—"ROTHESAY CASTLE," 1864—"SOUTHERN BELLE," 1875-1891—This noted steamer was a blockade runner during American Civil War. Built on Clyde, 1864, bought by Andrew Heron and Capt. Thos. Leach in 1866, and brought to Lake Ontario, running between Toronto, Niagara and Hamilton. She was later sold to New Brunswick Government, and partly burned at Shediac, N.B., in 1874, but was rebuilt and brought to Toronto as the "Southern Belle." She was wrecked on boilers of the "Monarch," near the Eastern Gap, Toronto, Aug. 17th, 1875, but was refloated and ran between Toronto and Hamilton until 1891. Pen drawing. Size 5 x 7.

2624—"SOUTHERN BELLE" (EX-"ROTHESAY CASTLE"), 1875-91—This picture shows the "Rothesay Castle" after she reappeared on Lake Ontario. She had been burned at Shediac, N.B., in 1874, and was rebuilt and renamed "Southern Belle." After her return to Lake Ontario she plied between Toronto and Hamilton, Niagara and Buffalo in connection with the Canada Southern Railway, remaining in service until dismantled in 1891. Pen drawing. Size 5 x 7.

2625—STR. "OSPREY," 1864-1878—This steamer, 175 feet long, of about 800 tons burden, built at Sorel, 1864, for use as an armed cruiser in American War, but her owners were unable to effect the sale of her for that purpose. She then plied between Hamilton and Montreal with passengers and freight. Bought by Aeneas Mackay, 1867, and made a voyage to Halifax from Lake Ontario. Returned to the Hamilton-Montreal route, and continued on it until 1876; then laid up, and in 1878 destroyed by fire. Pen drawing. Size 5 x 7.

2626—"BOHEMIAN," 1865—"PRESCOTT," 1905—This steamer of 380 tons register was built by Cantin, of Montreal, about 1865, and plied on the St. Lawrence River between Kingston and Montreal in the service of the Richelieu and Ontario Navigation Co. She was rebuilt at Montreal in 1892, and in 1905 was renamed "Prescott." She went out of commission in 1913. Pen drawing. Size 5 x 7.

2627—"QUEBEC," 1865—This iron steamer of 3,498 tons gross was built by Le Mas at Sorel, Que., in 1865, and rebuilt in 1907. She is still (1917) in service, and belongs to the Richelieu and Ontario Company's fleet. Her route has been on the St. Lawrence River between Montreal and Quebec. Pen drawing. Size 5 x 7.

2628—"WAUBUNO," 1865-1879—This steamer of 180 tons, and 100 feet long, was built at Port Robinson, 1865, and brought to the Georgian Bay in 1867 by Jas. H. and William Beatty, of Parry Sound. She plied between Collingwood and Thunder Bay for the Great Northern Transit Co., with passengers and freight. On Nov. 22, 1879, she was lost with all on board —70 persons—while endeavoring to reach Parry Sound from Collingwood. Next year her capsized hull was discovered near the Haystacks Islands, Georgian Bay, but no bodies were recovered. Pen drawing. Size 5 x 7.

2629—"SPARTAN," 1865—"BELLEVILLE," 1905—An iron steamer 200 feet long and of 1,233 tons gross, built at Montreal, 1865, by Gilbert, and rebuilt at Kingston, 1905, when she was renamed "Belleville." She plies between Toronto and Montreal in the service of the Richelieu and Ontario Navigation Co., calling at Bay of Quinte ports in addition to the harbors on the north shore of Lake Ontario, and is still (1917) in commission. Pen drawing. Size 5 x 7.

2630—TUG "W. T. ROBB," 1866-90—This tug was 120 feet long and was built at Dunnville by Geo. Hardison for Senator McCallum to tow timber rafts on Lake Erie. One of her rafts is shown astern of her in the picture. Capt. Wm. Hall, of Toronto, bought her and she towed rafts from Toronto to Prescott. She carried troops in the Fenian Raid, June, 1866, from Dunnville and Port Colborne to Fort Erie: later lay in Toronto harbor: was beached at Victoria Park, 1890, and finally burned. Pen drawing. Size 5 x 7.

2631—"FRANCES SMITH," 1867—"BALTIC," 1888—Built at Owen Sound, Ont., 1867, of 833 tons register. She plied between Collingwood and Fort William as one of the "Lake Superior Line" or "Pioneer Route," along with the "Cumberland" and "Chicora." She was destroyed by fire at Collingwood, Sept. 5th, 1895. At that time she was known as the "Baltic," having been rebuilt and renamed. Pen drawing. Size 5 x 7.

2632—"CANADA," 1867—"ST. IRENEE." 1905—This steamer of 2,094 tons gross, and 258 feet long, was built at Sorel, Que., in 1867, and is still (1917) employed in the service of the Richelieu and Ontario Navigation Co. on the River St. Lawrence, between Montreal and the Saguenay River. She was rebuilt in 1905. Pen drawing. Size 5 x 7.

2633—"NORSEMAN," 1868—"NORTH KING," 1891—This steamer of 422 tons, 175 feet long, was built by Cantin at Montreal in 1868, for Gildersleeve, of Kingston. She was rebuilt at that place in 1891, and renamed "North King." The Richelieu and Ontario Navigation Co. are her present owners. Her route has been between Toronto and Rochester, and later between Kingston and Oswego and Rochester. Pen drawing. Size 5 x 7.

2634—"UNION," 1868-92—"SAGUENAY," 1892-1917—This river steamer of 720 tons was built by Brunet, of Quebec, as the "Union" in 1868, and renamed the "Saguenay" in 1892. She plies on the St. Lawrence River between Quebec and the ports on the Saguenay River as part of the fleet of the Richelieu and Ontario Navigation Company. Pen drawing. Size 5 x 7.

2635—"HASTINGS," 1868-90—"EURYDICE," 1890—"DONELLY," 1906 —Of 286 tons burden, this steamer was built at Montreal in 1868, and brought west to Lake Ontario and renamed the "Eurydice." She ran on passenger and excursion routes out of Toronto until about 1906, when she was refitted as a wrecking steamer, renamed "Donelly," by Donelly Wrecking Co., of Kingston. Pen drawing. Size 5 x 7.

2636—"TROIS RIVIERES," 1869-1917—This steamer, 219 feet long and 1,449 tons gross, was built at Sorel, Que., in 1869, and rebuilt there in 1910. She is owned by the Richelieu and Ontario Navigation Co., and plies between Montreal and Quebec. Pen drawing. Size 5 x 7.

2637—"CORSICAN," 1870—Of 478 tons register, built in Gilbert's shipyard, Montreal, Que., 1870, plying on Lake Ontario and the St. Lawrence River between Toronto and Montreal in the service of the Canadian Navigation Co. up to 1875. She was then taken over by the Richelieu and Ontario Navigation Company. Pen drawing. Size 5 x 7.

2638—"PIERREPONT," 1871-1917—A steamer of 252 tons gross and 123 feet long, built at Kingston, Ont., and still in commission as a ferry for passengers, horses and freight between Kingston and the adjacent islands in the St. Lawrence. Between 1880 and 1890 she plied as an excursion steamer between Toronto, Sunnyside and the Humber. On account of her shovel-like form she has been very successful as an ice-breaker. Pen drawing. Size 5 x 7.

2639—"CARMONA" ("MANITOBA"), 1871-1904—This steamer of 590 tons, and 175 feet long, was built at Thorold, 1871, and plied on Lake Huron and Georgian Bay in connection with the G.T.R. from Sarnia. She was originally the "Manitoba," of the Beatty line out of Sarnia. Later, with the Cambria, she plied between Owen Sound and Sault Ste. Marie for the C.P.R. In 1890 she ran from Toronto to Lorne and Grimsby Parks. In 1893 made daily trips to Rochester, and in 1898 was on Toronto-Thousand Island route. Demolished at Port Dalhousie, 1904. Pen drawing. Size 5 x 7.

2640—"CITY OF OTTAWA," 1871—This steamer was 220 feet long, 1,529 tons gross, and was built at Buffalo, N.Y., and known as "India." She was bought by Montreal and Lake Erie Steamship Co., of Toronto, renamed, and ran between Montreal and Cleveland, Ohio. Pen drawing. Size 5 x 7.

2641—"JAPAN,"—"CITY OF HAMILTON," 1871—This propeller, the second steamer of the name, was originally the "Japan," built at Buffalo, N.Y. She is 220 feet long and 1,574 tons gross and plies between Montreal and Cleveland, being owned by the Montreal and Lake Erie Steamship Co., Limited, Toronto (Canada Steamship Lines). Pen drawing. Size 5 x 7.

2642—"CUMBERLAND," 1871-77—This steamer of about 750 tons, and 150 feet long, was built at Port Robinson, on the Welland Canal, in 1871, and plied between Collingwood and Lake Superior ports until wrecked on Isle Royale, Lake Superior, 1877. She was named for the late F. W. Cumberland, one of her owners. Pen drawing. Size 5 x 7.

2643—PROPELLER "OCEAN," 1872-1904—This propeller was 140 feet long, 350 tons register, built in 1872 at Port Dalhousie, by Captain Andrews, for Sylvester Neelon, of St. Catharines. She carried passengers and freight between Montreal and Chicago, and was bought in 1890 by W. A. Geddes, of the Custom House Wharf, foot of Yonge street, Toronto. She ran between Hamilton, Toronto and Montreal, and was destroyed by fire at Port Dalhousie in 1904. Pen drawing. Size 5 x 7.

2644—PROPELLER "ALMA MUNRO," 1873—This propeller was built at Port Dalhousie in 1873 and was 580 tons. She ran between Montreal and Chicago, calling at Toronto and places east of Toronto with passengers and freight. Pen drawing. Size 5 x 7.

2645—"EMPRESS," 1873—Built at Ottawa as the "Peerless." Rebuilt at Montreal, 1886. First owned by the Ottawa River Navigation Co., and later by the Central Railway Co. of Canada. She ran between Ottawa and Montreal. The "Empress' was 185 feet long; 678 tons gross. Pen drawing. Size 5 x 7.

2646—"CAMPANA," 1881—ORIGINALLY THE "NORTH"—Built in Glasgow, Scotland, August, 1873, by Messrs. Aitken and Mansell, her port of register being Buenos Aires. In 1881 she was brought to Canada for service on the lakes, and renamed the "Campana." The Quebec Steamship Company purchased her in 1895 from Messrs. A. M. Smith and others, of Toronto, took her to Montreal in two sections, and had her put together to run on the St. Lawrence route between Montreal and Pictou, N.S. The "Campana," on June 17th, 1909, went ashore a few miles below Quebec. She broke in two, the break occurring at the place the last join had been made. As the "North" the gross register of this iron twin screw steamer was 1,285 tons, and as the "Campana," 1,681 tons. Pen drawing. Size 5 x 7.

2647—"PERSIA," 1873—This propeller of 392 tons register was built by Melancthon Simpson for James Morris at St. Catharines, 1873, and plied between St. Catharines and Montreal with passengers and freight. Capt. John Scott commanded her for thirty years. She is employed as a barge on the St. Lawrence. Pen drawing. Size 5 x 7.

2648—"ONTARIO," 1874—This propeller of about 600 tons burden, was one of the Beatty line of steamers hailing from Sarnia, plying on Lake Huron, Georgian Bay, Lake Superior to Fort William and Duluth, in connection with the Grand Trunk Railway. She later belonged to the North-West Transportation Co., was sold and run as a pulp barge, and in August, 1899, went to pieces at Michipicoten Island, Lake Superior. Pen drawing. Size 5 x 7.

2649—"QUEBEC," 1874—This propeller of about 600 tons burden was one of the Beatty line of steamers plying between Sarnia and Duluth in connection with the Grand Trunk Railway. Belonged subsequently to the North-West Transportation Co. She sank in the Sault River, was raised and sold to a company in the States, renamed the "Spinner," and is now a tramp barge known as the "Helen C." Pen drawing. Size 5 x 7.

2650—PROPELLER "ASIA," 1874-1882—This steamer of about 600 tons burden was built at St. Catharines in 1874, and carried passengers and freight between Windsor and Duluth, calling at way ports in connection with the Grand Trunk, Great Western and Canada Southern Railways. She was lost in the great storm of Sept. 14, 1882, near Bustard Island, Georgian Bay, all of the 80 persons on board except two passengers perished. Pen drawing. Size 5 x 7.

2651—PROPELLER "ZEELAND," 1875-81—This vessel was built for Captain Edward Zeeland, of Hamilton, in 1875, from the hull of the burned steamer "City of Chatham," and ran between Hamilton, Toronto and Kingston, with passengers and freight. Her tonnage was 500 gross. On November 7th, 1881, she was lost with sixteen persons off Long Point in Lake Ontario. Pen drawing. Size 5 x 7.

2652—"NORTHERN BELLE," 1875-1898—This steamer of 290 tons register was built at Marine City, Mich., in 1875, under the name of "Gladys." She was brought to Collingwood, Ont., by Capt. Dan Cameron for the Great Northern Transit Co., completed there and named "Northern Belle." She plied between Collingwood and Sault Ste. Marie, and was destroyed by fire at Byng Inlet, 1898. Pen drawing. Size 5 x 7.

2653—"EMPRESS OF INDIA," 1876 — "EMPRESS" — "ARGYLE" — "FRONTIER," 1914—This steamer was 185 feet long and 700 tons gross, built by Wm. Jamieson at Mill Point, Bay of Quinte, 1876, and plied between Toronto and Niagara and St. Catharines for A. W. Hepburn, of Picton, 1883-93. She was rebuilt at Picton, 1899, and renamed the "Empress," and later the "Argyle," and still later the "Frontier." In after years she became the property of the Argyle Steamship Co., of Toronto, and is now running on Detroit River. Pen drawing. Size 5 x 7.

2654—"J. W. STEINHOFF," 1876—"QUEEN CITY," 1899-1917—This steamer, 120 feet long, built at Chatham in 1876, plied on Lake Huron until 1881 when she was burned. Rebuilt, she continued on the Upper Lakes until 1889. She was then bought by Alderman Thomas Davies, of Toronto, and placed on the Victoria Park route, and was engaged on this and excursion routes until 1899, when her name was changed to "Queen City." Now engaged in Owen Sound excursion trade. Pen drawing. Size 5 x 7.

2655—"CAROLINA," 1877—"MURRAY BAY," 1915—She is 251 feet long, 969 tons gross. Built at Wilmington, Del., 1877. Bought by Richelieu and Ontario Navigation Co., and brought to Canada 1893. Plied on the St. Lawrence between Montreal and Saguenay River. Renamed the "Murray Bay." Still (1917) running. Pen drawing. Size 5 x 7.

2656—"UNITED EMPIRE," 1882—"SARONIC," 1900-1916—This fine propeller of 2,000 tons burden and 252 feet long, was built at Sarnia in 1882, and was the pride of the famous Beatty line, carrying passengers and freight from Sarnia to Fort William and Lake Superior ports. About 1900 she was purchased by the Northern Navigation Co. and renamed "Saronic." She was badly burned at Sarnia, Dec. 15th, 1915, and destroyed by fire at Cockburn Island, Aug. 20th, 1916. Pen drawing. Size 5 x 7.

2657—"ATLANTIC," 1882—This propeller of 391 tons register was built at Owen Sound in 1882, and plied between Collingwood and Sault Ste. Marie in conjunction with the "Baltic," "Pacific" and "Northern Belle" of the Great Northern Transit Company. She was destroyed by fire off the Pancakes, Georgian Bay, 1903. Pen drawing. Size 5 x 7.

2658—"CHICOUTIMI," 1882-1900—This steamer of 110 tons was built at Quebec and plied on the St. Lawrence River, and also on Lake Huron for several seasons before being placed on the Toronto-Victoria Park route by Mr. Thomas Davies in 1889. She was commanded by Captains Parkinson and Jennings, and was burned in Toronto harbor in 1900. Pen drawing. Size 5 x 7.

2659—"QUEEN CITY," 1885—"ONGIARA," 1890—This ferry steamer, 90 feet long and of 98 tons gross, was built at Toronto as the "Queen City" in the excursion and ferry trade around Toronto harbor. She was renamed "Ongiara" in 1890, and used by the Niagara Navigation Co. as a tender on the Niagara River, transferring steamer passengers between Queenston and Lewiston. In 1912 she was bought by Patrick McSherry and placed on harbor towing at Toronto, at which she is still engaged. Pen drawing. Size 5 x 7.

2660—"CIBOLA," 1887-1895—This steel steamer, 260 feet long and of 739 tons register, was built at the Rathbun yards, Deseronto, in 1887, her plates having been sent out from Glasgow, Scotland. She plied between Toronto and Niagara until destroyed by fire at the latter place in 1895. One life was lost in her destruction. Her steel hull was afterwards towed to Toronto and broken up. Pen drawing. Size 5 x 7.

2661—"LAKESIDE," 1888-1917—This steamer is 121 feet long and 348 tons gross, and was built at Windsor, Ont., by Lane. She ran one season on Lake Erie under Capt. Wigle. Bought by Lakeside Navigation Co., of Toronto, and run by them between Toronto and St. Catharines in opposition to "Empress of India." Chartered by St. Catharines, Grimsby and Toronto Navigation Co., for same route, 1892. She ran between Toronto and Port Dalhousie until 1908; bought by M. J. Hogan, of Port Colborne, and converted into a towing barge. Pen drawing. Size 5 x 7.

2662—"ROSEDALE," 1888-1917—This steamer, of 1,507 tons gross, 246 feet long, was built at Sunderland, Eng., in 1888, and employed in the grain trade from the head of the lakes to Kingston. Messrs. Hagarty, Crangle & Co., of Toronto, were the original owners, and in 1915 she was sold to the Rosedale Co., of Hamilton. The "Rosedale" was the first vessel to take a cargo through from Montreal to Chicago without unloading between ports. Pen drawing. Size 5 x 7.

2663—"GREYHOUND," 1888—"LINCOLN," 1900—"PREMIER," 1904—This passenger steamer, 130 feet long and of 337 tons gross, was built at Hamilton by Melancthon Simpson for W. G. Gooderham and the Lorne Park Navigation Co., and plied on the Toronto, Lorne Park, Grimsby and Port Dalhousie excursion route. In 1900 she was renamed "Lincoln," and plied between Toronto and Port Dalhousie. Soon afterwards she was bought by the St. Joe Island and Sault Line, Ltd., placed on Lake Superior and Georgian Bay routes from Sault Ste. Marie and renamed "Premier." Pen drawing. Size 5 x 7.

2664—"MACASSA," 1888-1917—This steamer, 155 feet long and 529 tons gross, was built by Hamilton & Co., on the Clyde, at Glasgow, Scotland, for Hamilton Steamboat Co. She crossed the Atlantic with Capt. Hardy in command and ran continuously between Toronto and Hamilton. She was rebuilt at Collingwood, 1905, and is owned by Niagara Navigation Company. Pen drawing. Size 5 x 7.

2665—"MODJESKA," 1889-1917—This steamer is 178 feet long and 678 tons gross, was built at Glasgow for the Hamilton Steamboat Co. by Napier, Shanks & Bell. She crossed the Atlantic under her own steam and ran between Toronto and Hamilton continuously. In 1913 the Niagara Navigation Co. purchased her. Pen drawing. Size 5 x 7.

2666—"SOVEREIGN," 1889—This steamer of 303 tons was the second of the name, the first having been built at Niagara in 1840, and until 1843 known as the "Niagara." The steamer given was built by White, at Montreal, for Ottawa River Navigation Co., and ran between Ottawa and Montreal, under Captain Wm. Sheppard. Pen drawing. Size 5 x 7.

2667—"CITY OF MIDLAND," 1890—This steamer of 974 tons gross and 176 feet long was built at Owen Sound, Ont., in 1890 for the Northern Navigation Company, and plied between Collingwood and Sault Ste. Marie, via Georgian Bay ports, with passengers and freight. Burned at Collingwood, 17th March, 1916. Pen drawing. Size 5 x 7.

2668—"COLUMBIAN," 1892-1917—This twin screw steel steamer is 488 tons gross, and was built at Chester, Pa., for the Richelieu and Ontario Navigation Co. She plies between Kingston and Montreal. The passengers going through from Toronto to Montreal transfer from the large steamers at Prescott, Ont. Pen drawing. Size 5 x 7.

2669—"GARDEN CITY," 1892-1917—This steamer is 177 feet long and 401 tons register, and was built at the Bertram Shipyards, Toronto, the owners being the Niagara, St. Catharines & Toronto Navigation Co., Limited, and her route, a daily run, is from Toronto to Port Dalhousie. Pen drawing. Size 5 x 7.

2670—"CITY OF COLLINGWOOD," 1893-1905—This large propeller, 212 feet long, was built at Owen Sound and launched May 3, 1893. She was destroyed by fire, with the loss of three lives, at Collingwood, June 19, 1905. Her route was between Collingwood and Chicago, with calls at north shore ports on the Georgian Bay, Sault Ste. Marie and Mackinac. Originally owned by the North Shore Navigation Co., or "Black Line," she became one of the Northern Navigation Co.'s fleet in 1897. Pen drawing. Size 5 x 7.

2671—"CHIPPEWA," 1893—This steel passenger steamer, 380 feet long, and of 1,514 tons gross, was built at Hamilton in 1893 by Mr. Wm. Hendrie, of the Hamilton Bridge Co., for the Niagara Navigation Co., and has plied between Toronto and Niagara very successfully for over twenty years. Pen drawing. Size 5 x 7.

2672—"MAJESTIC," 1895-1915—The "Majestic" was a well-known steamer, 209 feet long, 1,073 tons register; was built at Collingwood, and ran from Sarnia to Sault Ste. Marie for the Northern Navigation Co. She was burned at Point Edward, near Sarnia, Ont., December 15th, 1915. Pen drawing. Size 5 x 7.

2673—"CORONA," 1896-1917—This steamer, 270 feet long and 1,274 tons gross, was built at the Bertram Shipyards, Toronto, for the Niagara Navigation Co., to run on Toronto and Niagara route. A fine picture of the launching of this steamer, 23rd May, 1896, is on another screen in this collection. Pen drawing. Size 5 x 7.

2674—KNAPP'S ROLLER BOAT, 1897—She was a tubular craft, 125 feet long and 25 feet in diameter outside. Her engines were set on roller bearings at either end and imparted a revolving motion to the hull, the engines and projecting platforms remaining stationary. The craft once attained a speed of seven knots for a short period on Toronto Bay, but never became a practical success. After an attempt being made to turn her into a tow barge, she was laid up at the Polson yards and abandoned. Pen drawing. Size 5 x 7.

2675—"TORONTO," 1899-1917—This steamer is 269 feet long and 2,779 tons gross, was built at Toronto for Richelieu and Ontario Navigation Co., her route being Toronto to Prescott, calling at Charlotte for Rochester, N.Y., and Kingston, Ont. Pen drawing. Size 5 x 7.

2676—"GERMANIC," 1899—This steamer of 1,014 tons gross, and 184 feet long, was built at Collingwood, Ont., in 1899 for the Ontario Navigation Company, and plied between Collingwood and Sault Ste. Marie. Burned in the spring of 1917. Pen drawing. Size 5 x 7.

2677—"KINGSTON," 1901-17—This steamer, the third of the name, was 288 feet long and 2,925 tons gross. Built at Toronto in 1901 for the Richelieu and Ontario Navigation Co. Her route is Toronto to Prescott, calling at Charlotte, N.Y., and Kingston, Ont. Pen drawing. Size 5 x 7.

2678—"TURBINIA," 1904—Built at Hebburn-on-Tyne—250 feet long, 1,064 tons gross—and brought across the Atlantic to give a service between Toronto and Hamilton in opposition to the "Macassa" and "Modjeska." After the first season she plied in fruit trade between New York and West Indies. Returning to Lake Ontario she ran in conjunction with her former competitors, and in 1913 she was bought by Niagara Navigation Co., and plied between Toronto, Hamilton and Niagara. She was the first turbine steamer on the Great Lakes, and the fastest—26 knots. Pen drawing. Size 5 x 7.

2679—"CAYUGA," 1907-1917—This steamer was built in 1907 at the Canadian Shipbuilding Co.'s yards, Toronto, for the Niagara Navigation Co. She is 305 feet long and 2,196 tons gross, and runs between Toronto, Niagara and Lewiston, N.Y. Pen drawing. Size 5 x 7.

2680—"EMPRESS OF FORT WILLIAM," 1908-16—Built at Newcastle-on-Tyne, and carried coal, grain and ore for Canada Steamship Lines, Limited, on Great Lakes and St. Lawrence River. In 1915 she was sent to England on time charter, under Capt. W. D. Shepherd, of Aberdeen. She was destroyed by a German mine off Dover, in the English Channel, 27th Feb., 1916, when going to the assistance of the P. and O. liner "Maloja," also mined. Pen drawing. Size 5 x 7.

2681—"HAMONIC," 1909—This steamer, 349 feet long, and of 5,265 tons gross, was built by the Collingwood Shipbuilding Co. in 1909 for the Northern Navigation Co., and plies between Sarnia and Port Arthur. She has passenger equipment equal to that of one-class ocean liners and freight capacity equal to that of many ocean carriers. Named after the late H. C. Hammond, Toronto, who was president of the Northern Navigation Co. at the time. Pen drawing. Size 5 x 7.

2682—"DALHOUSIE CITY," 1911-1917—This steamer, 199 feet long and 1,256 tons gross, was built at Collingwood, Ont., for Mackenzie, Mann & Co., Limited. She plies between Toronto and Port Dalhousie, and makes connection with trains east and west to and from New York and other American ports. Pen drawing. Size 5 x 7.

2683—"NORONIC," 1913—This steamer, 362 feet long, and of 6,905 tons gross, was built at Port Arthur, Ont., 1913, by the Western Drydocks and Shipbuilding Co. for the Northern Navigation Co., and carries (1917) passengers and freight between Sarnia and Duluth and intervening ports. She is as well equipped as a trans-Atlantic liner. Pen drawing. Size 5 x 7.

2684—"PORT DALHOUSIE," 1913-16—This steamer, 250 feet long, and of 1,744 tons register, and valued at $200,000, was built at Newcastle-on-Tyne in 1913, and brought to the Great Lakes for the bulk freight trade by her owner, Capt. R. A. McLelland, manager of the Forwarders Co., Kingston, Ont. She sailed from Pictou, N.S., for England, in January, 1916. On March 19th she was torpedoed by a German submarine while at anchor and sank, drowning five of her crew. Pen drawing. Size 5 x 7.

2685—"SIR JOHN COLBORNE," 1831—This steamer, the first on Lake Simcoe, was built at Holland Landing in 1831 by a joint stock company of retired army officers and other settlers in Simcoe County. She made her first voyage, a circuit of the lake, in 1832, and for a few years made bi-weekly trips from Holland Landing. From a description by Mrs. Joseph Beaver, Toronto, 1916, who as a child saw the "Colborne" on her first voyage down the Holland River. Pen drawing. Size 5 x 7.

2686—"PETER ROBINSON," 1834-54—This steamer was the second on Lake Simcoe. She was built at Holland Landing in 1833, and launched in 1834, and named after her principal shareholder, the late Hon. Peter Robinson. She plied on Lake Simcoe until about 1854, Orillia being her headquarters in her later years. Pen drawing. Size 5 x 7.

2687—"BEAVER," 1845-55—This steamer, about 70 feet in length, was built in 1845 at Thompsonville, on Lake Simcoe, by Capt. Laughton and

Charles Thompson, and plied between Barrie and other Lake Simcoe ports for about ten years. She was laid up at Barrie during the 50's and sunk, the present G.T.R. station covering her remains. Pen drawing. Size 5 x 7.

2688—"MORNING," 1849—Built by Charles Thompson at Holland Landing in 1849. Her length was about 80 feet. She plied on Lake Simcoe in connection with the Northern Railway from 1853 onwards; was commanded by Capt. Bell in 1854, and by Capt. Isaac May in 1860. Capt. McDougall was another of her commanders. The "Morning" was finally sunk at Belle Ewart. Pen drawing. Size 5 x 7.

2689—"J. C. MORRISON," 1855-57—The finest in her time on Lake Simcoe; 150 feet long; launched at Belle Ewart in 1855 for the Ontario, Simcoe and Huron Railway Co. (later the Northern). She cost $60,000. She was named after the late Judge Morrison, president of the railway. On Aug. 4th, 1857, she was totally destroyed by fire at Barrie, Ont. Pen drawing. Size 5 x 7.

2690—"EMILY MAY," 1861—"LADY OF THE LAKES," 1874—She was 151 feet long, built at Orillia, in 1861, for Capt. Isaac May, one of the best-known mariners in Ontario. She was first christened the "Emily May," after a daughter of the captain, but was renamed in 1874 by Capt. Moe as "The Lady of the Lakes," her route being Barrie, Orillia and other Lake Simcoe ports daily. She was finally dismantled and sunk at Belle Ewart. Pen drawing. Size 5 x 7.

2691—"IDA BURTON," 1863-75—This steamer, 80 feet in length, was built at Barrie, on Lake Simcoe, by George Burton, and plied between Barrie and Washago under Capt. Mark Burton, carrying passengers and freight until railway extensions rendered her trade unprofitable. She was laid up about 1875, sunk later, and used as a wharf at Orillia, Ont. Pen drawing. Size 5 x 7.

2692—"FAIRY," 1863—"CARRIE ELLA," 1870-8—A screw steamer, 75 feet long, built by Thompson Smith at Barrie, to ply between Orillia and Washago, on Lake Couchiching, in connection with the stage line to Gravenhurst, before the railway reached Muskoka. She was later rebuilt by D. L. Sanson, of Orillia, and renamed "Carrie Ella." She was commanded by Capt. Peter Lyons, and later by his son, Capt. O. H. Lyons, of Barrie. Pen drawing. Size 5 x 7.

2693—"ENTERPRISE," 1874-1905—This steamer, 100 feet long and of 300 tons, originally the schooner "Couchiching," of Rama, was built at Longford Mills, Lake Simcoe, 1868, and was sailed by Capt. O. H. Lyons, of Barrie. Converted into a steamer in 1874, she plied until sunk at the G.T.R. Wharf, Jackson's Point, 1905. Pen drawing. Size 5 x 7.

2694—SECOND HORSE BOAT—TORONTO ISLAND FERRY, 1845—Louis Privat came to Toronto, 1844, and leased the Island residence of Lord Sydenham, then owned by the Hon. Peter McGill, and called it the Peninsula Hotel. He built a scow-like craft with paddle, which was set in motion by two horses around a circular treadmill. Peter, popularly known as Louis, Privat, his brother, ran the boat, which plied between Maitland's Wharf, at the foot of Church street, and the wharf in front of the Peninsula Hotel, west of the present eastern entrance to the harbor. A picture of the first horse boat, "Sir John of the Peninsula," is not extant. Pen drawing. Size 5 x 7.

2695—HORSE BOAT "PENINSULA PACKET," 1849-51—This Island ferry boat, 60 feet long and 23 feet beam, was made from the hull of a small steamer which formerly ran on Niagara River below Queenston. It was called the "Peninsula Packet." L. J. Privat substituted three horses on a treadmill for her engines, and ran her between Maitland's Wharf, foot of Church street, and the wharf in front of his hotel on the Island, up to the summer of 1851, when the steamer "Victoria" succeeded her. Pen drawing. Size 5 x 7.

2696—"VICTORIA," 1850—The "Victoria" was built in 1850 for Island purposes by L. J. Privat, who inaugurated the Island service. She ran from Robert Maitland's wharf, foot of Church street, to Privat's Peninsula Hotel, on the Island, west of present eastern entrance, for at that time the Island was a peninsula. The steamer was operated by Privat himself from 1850-53 and for George Tate, of the Grand Trunk Railway, from 1853-5. As early as 1835, however, a steamer plied between Toronto and the Island. Pen drawing. Size 5 x 7.

2697—"ISLAND QUEEN," 1843—This small ferry steamer of 70 tons register, called the "Island Queen," was built in 1843 at Kingston, and in 1855 was used as a ferry between Toronto and the Island. Pen drawing. Size 5 x 7.

2698—"FIREFLY"—Built at Toronto about 1855. Plied as ferry to and from the Island, and did towing work on Toronto Bay under Capt. Robt. Moodie and Capt. Thos. Graham (later chief of the Toronto Fire Department). Pen drawing. Size 5 x 7.

2699—"BOUQUET," 1866-80—The "Bouquet" was built in 1866 by Thomas Saulter as a Toronto Island ferry boat, and was run by his brother, Captain James Saulter, a mariner. She ran from Maitland's Wharf, foot of Church street, to Centre Island. Pen drawing. Size 5 x 7.

2700—"ADA ALICE," 1868-1915—This steamer, 66 feet long and 60 tons gross, was built at Port Dalhousie, 1868; rebuilt there 1879. Brought by Toronto Ferry Co., about 1893, to Toronto Bay, and there operated for over twenty years. Owned by Wm. Davies Co., Toronto. Pen drawing. Size 5 x 7.

2701—"ST. JEAN BAPTISTE," 1878—"SADIE," 1885—"SHAMROCK," 1897-1905—Built at Quebec as the "St. Jean Baptiste," and brought to Toronto Bay by John Turner in 1878. Ran at first from Tinning's Wharf to Hanlan's Point. Rebuilt at Oakville, Ont., 1885, and renamed "Sadie." Sold to Doty Ferry Co. and later to Toronto Ferry Co. Rebuilt by latter as a double-ender and renamed the "Shamrock." Burned and dismantled in 1905. She was 154 tons. Pen drawing. Size 5 x 7.

2702—"LUELLA," 1880-1917—This steamer is 66 feet long and 38 tons gross. Built at Toronto, 1880, and in continuous use as a ferry on Toronto Bay for over thirty-five years, running to Centre Island and The Lakeside Home for Little Children at the Lighthouse Point. Belonged to Doty Ferry Co. and Toronto Ferry Co., and now owned by the latter company. She was provided with a "ram" stem for cutting a passage through the ice in spring and fall. Pen drawing. Size 5 x 7.

2703—"CANADIAN," 1882—"THISTLE," 1897-1906—This steamer, first of the "double-enders" in the Toronto ferry service, was 122 feet long and measured 230 tons. She was built by John Alexander Glindinning at the foot of Lorne street, Toronto, in 1882. She was renamed "Thistle" in 1897. In 1906, having outlived her usefulness, her machinery was taken out and she was set on fire and destroyed. Pen drawing. Size 5 x 7.

2704—"JOHN HANLAN," 1884-1916—A well-known steamer, 71 feet long and 37 tons gross, built by Abbey, at Port Dalhousie, 1884. She was bought by Lawrence Solman and leased to the Toronto Ferry Co., and has been in service on Toronto Bay for thirty years. Pen drawing. Size 5 x 7.

2705—"MASCOTTE," 1886-1901—This steamer was 70 feet long and 49 tons gross. Built at Toronto, 1886, by Wm. Redway, with a "ram" bow for icebreaking purposes. She was unsuccessful as an icebreaker, but the shape of the bow made her very speedy. Ran to the Island from Brock street wharf as a steamer of the Doty Ferry Co. and Toronto Ferry Co. fleet. Sunk at Oakville, 1901, and broken up. Pen drawing. Size 5 x 7.

2706—"PRIMROSE," 1890-1916—This steamer, 140 feet long and 189 tons gross, was built at Toronto for Doty Ferry Co., and was bought by Toronto Ferry Co. She ran from Yonge street and Bay street to Centre Island and Hanlan's Point. The "Mayflower" and "Trillium" ferry steamers on Toronto Bay are of the same design. Pen drawing. Size 5 x 7.

2707—"A. J. TYMON," 1892—"OJIBWAY"—JASMINE," 1912—This steamer, 112 feet long, 298 tons gross, was built at Toronto in 1892, from the original W. M. Alderson, and christened "A. J. Tymon," after her owner. She was rebuilt at Sorel, Que., after plying successively on Lake Ontario, Georgian Bay and the St. Lawrence River. Renamed "Ojibway." She returned to Toronto as an Island ferry, and was called "Jasmine," 1912. Pen drawing. Size 5 x 7.

2708—"ALGOMA," 1883-85—This steamer, of 2,377 tons register, was built at Whiteinch, on the Clyde, for the Canadian Pacific Railway, in 1883. She plied between Owen Sound and Fort William, on Lake Superior, and was lost, with about forty persons, off Rock Harbor, Isle Royale, Lake Superior, in 1885. Pen drawing. Size 5 x 7.

2709—"ATHABASCA," 1883-1917—This steamer, 298 feet long and 2,784 tons gross, was built at Kelvinhaugh, on the Clyde, near Glasgow, Scotland, in 1883, for the Canadian Pacific Railway, and was rebuilt at Collingwood, Ont., 1910. She plies (1917) between Owen Sound and other Georgian Bay ports and Fort William with passengers and freight. Pen drawing. Size 5 x 7.

2710—"ALBERTA," 1883-1917—Built at Whiteinch, on the Clyde, near Glasgow, Scotland, for the Canadian Pacific Railway, in 1883, and rebuilt at Collingwood, Ont., in 1911. She is 309 feet long and registers 2,829 tons gross, and plies (1917) from Owen Sound and other Georgian Bay ports to Fort William with passengers and freight. Pen drawing. Size 5 x 7.

2711—"MANITOBA," 1889-1917—This steamer, 303 feet long and 2,616 tons gross, was built in Great Britain, the parts being brought out and put together at Owen Sound in 1889 for the Canadian Pacific Railway. She plies (1917) between Owen Sound and other Georgian Bay ports and Fort William with passengers and freight. Pen drawing. Size 5 x 7.

2712—"ASSINIBOIA," 1907-1917—This steamer, 336 feet long and 3,880 tons gross, was built at Govan, on the left bank of the Clyde, near Glasgow, Scotland, for the Canadian Pacific Railway. She plies (1917) between Port McNicoll and Fort William with passengers and freight. Pen drawing. Size 5 x 7.

2713—"KEEWATIN," 1907-1917—This steamer, 336 feet long and 3,856 tons gross, was built at Govan, on the left bank of the Clyde, near Glasgow, Scotland, for the Canadian Pacific Railway. As a passenger vessel and freighter the "Keewatin" plies (1917) between Port McNicoll and Fort William. Pen drawing. Size 5 x 7.

2714—FIRST R. C. Y. C. LAUNCH "ESPERANZA," 1881-95—A steam yacht, 55 feet long, used as a ferry between the Island Club House of the Royal Canadian Yacht Club and city landings at foot of Yonge and York streets. The launch, for the sole use of the members of the club and their guests, was succeeded in 1895 by the "Hiawatha." Pen drawing. Size 5 x 7.

2715—SECOND R. C. Y. C. LAUNCH "HIAWATHA," 1895-1917—This launch, 56 feet long and 46 tons gross, was built at the Bertram Shipyards, Toronto. It is used as committee boat and as a ferry between the Island Club House of the Royal Canadian Yacht Club and city landings at Yonge and York streets. Pen drawing. Size 5 x 7.

2716—THIRD R.C.Y.C. LAUNCH "KWASIND," 1912-17—This launch is 71 feet long and 47 tons gross, and was built by the Polson Shipbuilding Co., Toronto, for ferry service in connection with Royal Canadian Yacht Club, between the Island Club House and city landings at Yonge and York streets. Pen drawing. Size 5 x 7.

2717—"W. GRANT MORDEN," 1914—This steamer, built in Port Arthur, Ont., 1914, is the largest bulk freighter, Canadian or American, on fresh water. She is 635 feet long and of 15,000 tons burden, and broke all records by carrying 476,000 bushels of wheat through the "Soo" Canal, November, 1915. She is owned by the Canada Steamship Lines, Limited, Toronto. Pen drawing. Size 5 x 7.

2718—CAR FERRY "ONTARIO NO. 2," 1915—Built at the Polson yards, Toronto, for the G.T.R.; was, when launched, the largest vessel of any kind on Lake Ontario. She is 318 feet long and of 5,567 tons gross. The first car ferry, Ontario No. 1, was also built at Toronto in 1907, measuring 421 tons less than No. 2. Both vessels carry loaded coal cars from Charlotte, N.Y., to Cobourg, Ont., and do an extensive passenger trade. Pen drawing. Size 5 x 7.

2719—WINNIPEG, MAN., 1881—Showing the east and west sides of Main street—With key. Lithograph. Sizes (three pictures), east side, 5 x 94; west side, 5 x 70; west side, continued, 5 x 65.

2720—HUDSON'S BAY CO.'S STR, "BEAVER," 1835-88—The historic "Beaver" was the first steamer to round the Horn into the Pacific. She was launched 2nd May, 1835, on the Thames at London, England, and the following August left London in charge of Capt. David Home, anchoring off Fort Vancouver in April, 1836. For many years she was in the service of the Hudson's Bay Company, and from 1863-70 was employed by the British Government in surveying western waters. She was wrecked July 26th, 1888, at Prospect Point, Vancouver. Pen drawing. Size 5 x 7.

2721—MILLOY, CAPT. PETER—A mariner who sailed a number of large schooners which plied between different ports on Lake Ontario. He was born in Oban, Scotland, 1819, resided at Niagara, and died 5th Nov., 1855, in Brantford, Ont. Water color, from a portrait in possession of Mrs. Harvey, of Niagara. Size 3 x 4. Head and shoulders.

2722—MILLOY, CAPT. DUNCAN—He resided in Niagara, and was one of the most popular captains of his day on Lake Ontario, commanding for years the steamers "City of Toronto" and "Zimmerman," which ran between Toronto and Niagara. He was born in Oban, Scotland, and died at Niagara, 20th Oct., 1871. Water color, from a portrait in possession of Mrs. Harvey, of Niagara. Size 3 x 4. Head and shoulders.

2723—MILLOY, NICHOL—His birthplace was Oban, Scotland, 1832; emigrated to Canada, and became agent of the Royal Mail Steamer Line. His office was on Front street east, Toronto, next the American Hotel. Died in Toronto, January, 1874. Water color, from a portrait in possession of Mrs. Harvey, of Niagara. Size 3 x 4. Head and shoulders.

2724—MILLOY, DONALD—Born at Oban, Scotland, 1836. For many years he resided in Toronto, he and his brother, Neil, leasing the Yonge street wharf. His death occurred in Toronto, 1907. Water color, from a portrait in possession of Mrs. Harvey, Niagara. Size 3 x 4. Head and shoulders.

30

2725—MILLOY, NEIL—Born in Oban, Scotland, 1839; came to Canada at an early age, and for a number of years was the lessee of Yonge street wharf, Toronto, in conjunction with his brother, Donald Milloy. His death took place in Toronto, 3rd March, 1878. Water color, from a portrait in possession of Mrs. Harvey, of Niagara. Size 3 x 4. Head and shoulders.

2726—MILLOY, CAPT. WILLIAM A.—Son of Captain Duncan Milloy; was born in 1852, and died 27th April, 1905. He was for a number of years captain of the steamer "City of Toronto," running between Toronto and Niagara, the steamer which his father had sailed. Water color, from a portrait in possession of Mrs. Harvey, of Niagara. Size 3 x 4. Head and shoulders.

2727—MILLOY, ALEXANDER, 1822-1899—Born in Kintyre, Argyleshire, Scotland, and came to Canada in 1830. In 1840 he entered the Montreal office of the old Royal Mail Line of steamers, which ran between Montreal and Hamilton, acting as agent of that line for many years. He was in 1895 appointed traffic manager of the Richelieu and Ontario Navigation Co., the successors of the old Royal Mail Line. His death took place in Montreal. Water color, from a portrait in possession of Mrs. Harvey, of Niagara. Size 3 x 4. Head and shoulders.

2728—HUDSON'S BAY CO.'S STEAMER "LABOUCHERE," 1858-66— A paddle wheel steamer, 680 tons register, 181 h.p., with a speed on her trial trip of 10 knots. Named after Rt. Hon. H. Labouchere, Secretary of State for the Colonies, 1855-8. She was built at Sunderland, Eng., 1858, and arrived at Victoria, V.I., 31st January following, in command of Capt. J. F. Trivett. She made many trading voyages to the company's post on northern coast of British Columbia and to Alaska. En route from San Francisco to Victoria the "Labouchere" was lost near Point Reyes, 1st April, 1866. Pen drawing. Size 5 x 7.

2729—WHARF AT EXHIBITION PARK, TORONTO, 1880—Built in 1878 as a landing place for steamers conveying visitors to the Fair Grounds. Railway facilities, however, made rapid strides, and opposition becoming so great, the boat service was discontinued and the wharf abandoned. Facing the water front is seen the old Main Building in the Exhibition Grounds. Water color from original drawing by W. T. Smedley for "Picturesque Canada." Size 5 x 7.

2730—STEPHEN, SIR GEORGE, BART. (LORD MOUNT STEPHEN) —In 1850 he came to Canada, entering into business partnership in Montreal with his brother, William Stephen. From 1876-81 was president of the Bank of Montreal, and in the latter year became president of the Canadian Pacific Railway, from which he retired in 1888. For his services in connection with building the road he was in 1886 created a baronet. He, with Lord Strathcona, gave a large sum for the erection of the Royal Victoria Hospital, Montreal. He also aided materially the Barnardo Home movement, Aberdeen Royal Infirmary, and King Edward's Hospital Fund. In 1891 Sir George Stephen was raised to the peerage with the title of Lord Mount Stephen, from a high peak in the Rockies which had been called after Mr. Stephen when he was president of the C.P.R. He was born in 1831, at Dufftown, Scotland. Photogravure from portrait by Frank Holl, R. A. Colored. Size 5 x 7. Three-quarter length. This photogravure, along with a number of others in the Collection, was presented to Mr. J. Ross Robertson by Mr. Robert Glasgow, of Toronto.

2731—DRIVING THE GOLDEN SPIKE TO COMMEMORATE COMPLETION OF THE C.P.R.—On 7th Nov., 1885, the scene in picture was enacted, when Hon. Donald A. Smith (Lord Strathcona) drove the last spike—one of gold—in the rails of the newly constructed road from Montreal to the Pacific. The place, near the Columbia River, is now (1917)

Craigellachie, in Eagle Pass, about 350 miles west of Vancouver, B.C. A cairn has been erected, marking the spot where the spike was driven. 1, Hon. Donald Smith (Lord Strathcona). 2, William (Sir) Van Horne. 3, Sandford (Sir) Fleming. 4, William Stephen, brother of George Stephen (Lord Mount Stephen). 5, John McTavish, land commissioner of the C.P.R. This group was surrounded by a concourse of working men. Photogravure, colored. Size 4 x 6.

2732—STRACHAN, JOHN, 1778-1867—First Anglican Bishop of Toronto—Photogravure from painting in Department of Education, Toronto. Size 5 x 7. Half length. See 252, 2805, 3199.

2733—GALT, SIR ALEXANDER TILLOCH, 1817-93—Son of John Galt, founder of the Canada Company—He was born at Chelsea, London, Eng., and educated in England. Came to Canada as a lad, entering the service of the British and American Land Co. (Eastern Townships), which, under his management, was placed on a firm business footing. Mr. Galt was one of the first advocates for establishment of railways in Canada. He entered Parliament in 1849, dropped out of politics for some years, and was again elected. He became Minister of Finance in the Cartier-Macdonald Administration; was actively engaged in the Confederation movement, being one of the commissioners sent to England in 1865 to confer with the Imperial Government. He was High Commissioner in Great Britain, 1880-83; refused decoration of C.B. Photogravure from a photograph. Size 5 x 7. Three-quarter length.

2734—BULLER, CHARLES, 1806-48—Born in Calcutta, his father being in the revenue department of the East India Company's service. Educated at Harrow, and under tutorship of Thomas Carlyle; later at Edinburgh University and Trinity College, Cambridge (B.A., 1828). Sat for West Looe, Cornwall, in Parliament, 1830-1, voting for the first Reform Bill and for the extinction of his own constituency. Called to Bar at Lincoln's Inn, 1831. On passing of Reform Bill of 1832, elected to Liskeard. In 1838 came to Canada as chief secretary to Lord Durham, Gov.-General; the celebrated Durham report on Canada was mainly written by Buller. Appointed to post of Judge Advocate-General, 1846. Refused Privy Councillorship. Became Chief Poor Law Commissioner, and in 1848 carried through several short bills reforming existing enactments relating thereto. His death took place in London. Photogravure from an engraving by E. Scriven. Size 5 x 7. Head and shoulders.

2735—VAN HORNE, SIR WILLIAM, 1843-1915—Noted capitalist and railway president. Photogravure, colored. Size 4 x 6. See 2740.

2736—STRATHCONA, RT. HON. THE BARONESS—Wife of Lord Strathcona and Mount Royal—She was Isabella Hardisty, daughter of Richard Hardisty, of the Hudson's Bay Company, whom Donald Smith (Lord Strathcona) succeeded at Esquimaux Bay, Labrador. On 9th March, 1853, she married Mr. Smith. Notwithstanding her retiring and unostentatious nature, Lady Strathcona ably assisted her husband in his many acts of benefaction for his fellow-men. She always exercised gracious hospitality and was highly esteemed by all who knew her. With her daughter, she subscribed liberally towards McGill University, and, amongst other funds, contributed largely to the Queen Alexandra Fund for the relief of unemployed of Great Britain. In 1903 she was presented to the King and Queen. Lady Strathcona's death took place in London, Eng., 12th Nov., 1913. Photogravure, colored. Size 4 x 6. Three-quarter length, sitting.

2737—HUSKISSON, WILLIAM, 1770-1830—Native of Warwickshire, Eng. For several years lived in Paris, where he became private secretary to the British Ambassador; returned to England on recall of Embassy, 1792. Under-Secretary at War, 1795-1801. In 1808 took large share in re-arrangement of relations between Bank of England and the Treasury. Published pamphlet on "Depreciation of the Currency," which earned for him the reputation of being the first financier of the age. Treasurer of Navy and Board of Trade. Obtained select committee to inquire into relations between employers and employes, and, as a result, an act was passed which regulated relations between capital and labor for forty years. On Canning's death, 1827, succeeded him in Colonial Office. Died as result of an accident. It was he who introduced bill for admission of Canadian wheat into Britain on payment of fixed duty of 5s per quarter, in place of existing unsatisfactory sliding scale of duties. Speeches on silk trade and shipping interest brought him favorable notice. Photogravure from painting by Rothwell, in the National Portrait Gallery. Size 5 x 7. Half length.

2738—CUNARD, SIR SAMUEL, BART., 1787-1865—Founder of the Great Steamship Company—Son of Abraham Cunard, a merchant of Philadelphia, who, after the Revolutionary War, settled in Halifax. Samuel Cunard commenced his business life in a merchant's office. In time he became agent in Halifax of the East India Company, and carried mail, in sailing vessels, between Canada and the States. He contemplated in the early thirties a trans-Atlantic steam line, which later became an accomplished fact. In 1839 Cunard received from the Admiralty a contract for the first steam mail service between Great Britain and America, and in the same year he, with Mr. George Burns, of Glasgow, and Mr. David MacIver, of Liverpool, established the British and North American Royal Mail Steam Packet Company. Mr. Cunard was alert and intelligent, a keen observer and a man of affairs. In 1846 he was elected a Fellow of the Royal Geographical Society, and in 1859 Her Majesty Queen Victoria was pleased to confer upon him a baronetcy in recognition of the services he had rendered by establishing the Cunard line of steamers. Photogravure from a photograph. Size 5 x 7. Head and shoulders.

2739—STRATHCONA AND MOUNT ROYAL, RT. HON. SIR DONALD ALEXANDER SMITH, BARON—Born in Forres, Scotland, Aug. 6th, 1820, and educated there. In 1838 came to Canada; entered service of Hudson's Bay Co. Stationed on Labrador Coast for many years. Afterwards served in North-west, in the development of which he had a large part. Became a chief factor of the company, and, subsequently, resident governor and chief commissioner in Canada. Appointed Dec., 1869, by the Dominion Government, special commissioner to inquire into insurrection at the Red River Settlement. On the organization of Manitoba as a province sat in the Legislature for Winnipeg and St. John. Returned for Selkirk in House of Commons and afterwards for Montreal West. Appointed High Commissioner for Canada in London, 1896, a post he retained until his death. Indissolubly connected with the history of railway development in the Dominion. Raised and maintained, at his own expense, the Strathcona Horse, which did excellent service in Boer War. Lord Strathcona took a great interest in education, and was the founder of a university annex for women in Canada—the Royal Victoria College. Died in London, Eng., Jan. 21st, 1914. Photogravure from a photograph by Lafayette. Size 4 x 6. Head and shoulders. See 2744.

2740—VAN HORNE, SIR WILLIAM, 1843-1915—President Canadian Pacific Railway—His birthplace was Will County, Ill. He entered service of Illinois Central Railway as telegraph operator in 1857. In 1881, after serving on various roads in the States, appointed general manager of the

Canadian Pacific Railway, subsequently becoming vice-president, president, and chairman of the Board of Directors. He was interested in many financial concerns; had several model farms in Selkirk, Man., for raising live stock. As a connoisseur in Japanese and Chinese art work, and a collector of paintings, Sir William was well known. In 1894 created a K.C.M.G.; opposed the Taft-Fielding reciprocity agreement with the States, 1911. Photogravure from painting by Wyatt Eaton. Size 5 x 7. Half length, sitting. See 2735.

2741—GALT, JOHN—Founder of Guelph and Goderich, U.C.—Born in Irvine, Ayrshire, Scotland, 1779. Engaged in business in London, Eng., for a time. Appointed agent in England for some of the principal Canadians who had claims to urge for losses incurred during the War of 1812-14. As commissioner of the Canada Company, in 1827, visited Shade's Mills (present Galt) to open up a road from there to the lands of the company in the neighborhood of what is now Guelph. The city of Galt was named after his by Mr. William Dickson, an old school friend. Mr. Galt came to Canada first in 1824, and was here again from 1826 to 1829. He died in England in 1839. Author of "Laurie Todd," "The Annals of Our Parish," and other works. Sir Alexander Tilloch Galt and Judge Sir Thomas Galt were sons. Photogravure from the portrait by Irvine in the Chateau de Ramezay, Montreal. Size 5 x 7. Half length.

2742—CRAWFORD, ISABELLA VALANCY—Born near Dublin, Ireland, Christmas Eve, 1850, the daughter of a physician. In 1858 the family removed to Canada, settling first at Paisley, and later near Peterboro. In the late seventies, Miss Crawford and her mother came to Toronto, the daughter contributing verses to the newspapers. In 1884 Miss Crawford published a small paper-covered volume of poems, "Old Spookses' Pass, Malcolm's Katie, and Other Poems," which was received by the public with indifference. The poetess died in 1887. In 1905 a collection of her poems, edited by Mr. J. W. Garvin, appeared and had a good reception. Photogravure from the portrait in possession of Mr. E. S. Caswell, Toronto. Size 5 x 6. Head and shoulders.

2743—DORION, SIR ANTOINE AIME, 1818-91—Educated at Nicolet College; called to the Bar of Lower Canada, 1842. Sat in Legislature as member for Montreal, 1854-61. In 1858 formed an administration with George Brown. Provincial Secretary in Sandfield Macdonald Government, 1862, and the following year succeeded Sicotte as Attorney-General. From 1873-4 was Minister of Justice. Chief Justice, 1874-91. Opposed Confederation, and in February, 1865, made a telling speech against it. Died, 1891. Photogravure from photograph, oval. Size 4 x 5.

2744—STRATHCONA AND MOUNT ROYAL, RT. HON. SIR DONALD ALEXANDER SMITH, BARON—At eighteen years of age and late in life—Photogravure, colored (oval) from a miniature, and photogravure, colored, from a photograph. Both, head and shoulders. Size 4 x 5 and 4 x 6, respectively. See 2739.

2745—LYMBURNER, ADAM, 1746-1836—He came to Canada about 1776, settling at Quebec, where he carried on the business of his brother. For many years he was a member of the Executive Council. Mr. Lymburner was sent to England in 1789 to represent the views of the British-Canadians and a portion of the French population in Quebec, requesting constitutional changes. The bill regarding the division of Quebec into two provinces was introduced, 7th March, 1791, and on the 23rd Lymburner addressed the House of Commons, pleading for a total repeal of the Quebec Act, in his strong opposition to the bill. On 14th May the act became law. Mr. Lymburner died in London, Eng. Photogravure. Size 5 x 6. Three-quarter length, sitting.

2746—HALIBURTON, JUDGE THOMAS CHANDLER, 1796-1865—Author of "The Clockmaker, or Sayings and Doings of Sam Slick, of Slickville." Photogravure from an engraving in the Dominion Archives, Ottawa. Size 5 x 7. Head and shoulders. See 2211.

2747—TORONTO BOARD OF TRADE—Members in 1891—With key. Photograph. Size 16 x 40.

2748—FLEMING, SIR SANDFORD, C.E., 1827-1915—"One of the builders of Canada"—Photogravure from a photograph. Size 5 x 7. Head and shoulders. See 2826.

2749—COSBY—"Phillips Cosby, Esqr., Admiral of the Red Squadron—Pub'd by J. Gold, 103 Shoe Lane, London, Decr., 1805. Robinson, pinxt. Ridley, Sculp." Born in Nova Scotia about 1727. In 1745 he entered the navy, and in 1755 was in the fleet under Boscawen; at Louisburg, 1758, and Quebec the following year. Said to have been specially attached as naval aide-de-camp to Wolfe. From 1771-8 was Receiver-General of St. Kitts, B.W.I. Accompanied Arbuthnot to North America, 1779. Subsequently went to the Mediterranean as third in command of the fleet under Lord Hood. Became Admiral, 1799. Died in Bath, Eng., 1808. Line engraving. Size 4 x 5. Head and shoulders, oval.

2750—FRASER, SIMON, 1776-1862—An official and explorer of the North-West Company—Early in life he came to Canada from New York State. He joined the North-West Company in 1792, and ten years later became a partner. In 1805 he was selected for the work of penetrating the Rockies, the same year establishing the posts, Rocky Mountain House and Fort Macleod; the latter was the first fur-trading post built in British Columbia. At that time what is now northern British Columbia was known as New Caledonia. In 1808, Fraser, with Stuart, Quesnel, and a party of voyageurs and Indians, explored to its mouth the river bearing his name. He established, in all, four forts in New Caledonia, thus securing for his company a firm hold on the territory. In 1811 he was promoted to the charge of the Red River Department. For his services in the cause of exploration Fraser was offered knighthood, but declined. He retired from the fur trade about the time of the amalgamation of the Hudson's Bay and North-West Companies. Photogravure. Size 5 x 7. Half length.

2751—BEGBIE, SIR MATTHEW BAILLIE, 1819-94—First judge in British Columbia—He was born in Edinburgh, Scotland; educated at Cambridge; called to the English Bar in 1844. He arrived in British Columbia, as first judge, in November, 1858. Strictly speaking, although the office was judicial, Judge Begbie was instructed to lend assistance in framing laws and other legal business. In the spring of 1859 he journeyed to the upper Fraser, establishing law, order, and a code of justice in the colony. His administration of justice was fearless and direct. No region was too remote for his justice. Until his death Sir Matthew filled a commanding place in British Columbia affairs. He was Chief Justice of British Columbia, 1870-94, and Judge of the Admiralty District of B.C., 1891-4. In 1875 received knighthood. His death took place in 1894. Photogravure. Size 5 x 7. Half length.

2752—HENRY, ALEXANDER—Known as the Elder, to distinguish him from his nephew, who was in the employ of the North-West Company. Born in New Jersey, 1739. At the age of twenty-one entered the fur trade in Canada. In 1761 left Montreal on a trading expedition to Michilimackinac, and in 1775 penetrated the Far West. Coasting up the east side of Lake Winnipeg, he was joined by Pond, and later by Joseph and Thomas Frobisher, Montreal fur traders. Went to Europe for the first time in

1776, and had an opportunity of describing his adventures to Marie Antoinette. Ultimately settled at Montreal as a merchant. Disposed of his privileges in the Indian country to the North-West Company, becoming a dormant partner, and continuing as such until 1796. Appointed King's auctioneer for the district of Montreal, 1812, holding the position until his death, April 4th, 1824, at Montreal. His "Travels and Adventures" were published in New York, 1807. Photogravure from engraving. Size 5 x 7. Head and shoulders, oval.

2753—MACKENZIE, SIR ALEXANDER, 1755-1820—First white man to cross the Rocky Mountains—Emigrated to Canada in his youth. Entered service of North-West Company as a clerk, later becoming a partner. From 1781-9 he traded with the Indians of Lake Athabasca, in the latter year leaving Fort Chippewayan, on the south shore of the lake (removed in 1820 to the north shore) for a perilous journey of exploration. He discovered the river since bearing his name, and traced it from its source to its entrance into the Arctic Ocean. In 1792 Mackenzie led another exploring party westward to the Pacific. He established a North-West post on the Great Slave Lake and one on Peace River. On his return to England in 1801 he published his "Voyages from Montreal Through the Continent of North America, 1789 and 1793." He was knighted in 1802; represented Huntingdon County in Legislature of Lower Canada. The explorations of Sir Alexander Mackenzie gave impetus to other explorers, and other traders received encouragement to open new regions in the far distant parts of Canada. Photogravure from painting by Sir T. Lawrence. Size 5 x 7. Head and shoulders, oval.

2754—RYERSON, REV. EGERTON—First principal of Victoria College, Cobourg, C.W. Photogravure from painting by J. W. L. Forster. Size 5 x 7. Half length, sitting. See 2755.

2755—RYERSON—"Revd. Egerton Ryerson—Painted by Gush. Engraved by Dean." Born in the township of Charlotteville, in the London district (now Norfolk County, Ont.), U.C., 1803, the son of Colonel Joseph Ryerson, a U.E. Loyalist. Entered the Wesleyan ministry in 1825, and later founded the "Christian Guardian," of which he became editor. In 1833 sent as delegate to the Wesleyan Conference in England, and succeeded in bringing about a union between it and the Methodist Episcopal Church in Canada. Appointed first principal of Victoria College, Cobourg, C.W., in 1841, and Chief Superintendent of Education for Upper Canada three years later. He was the founder of an excellent system of Public school instruction. Died in Toronto, 1882. Line engraving. Size 4 x 5. Head and shoulders. See 2754.

2756—JENKINS, REV. JOHN, D.D., LL.D.—Pastor St. Paul's Presbyterian Church, Montreal, 1863-81—Ordained to the ministry of the Wesleyan Methodist Church in 1837. Went to India as a missionary, and later became minister of St. James' Church, Montreal. In 1863 he succeeded Rev. Dr. Snodgrass as pastor of St. Paul's Presbyterian Church, an offshoot of the St. Gabriel Street Church. Dr. Jenkins was born and educated in England. Painted by W. Gush, Esq. Engraved by J. Cochran. Size 4 x 5. Head and shoulders.

2757—GRANT, GEORGE MONRO, D.D., 1835-1902—Principal of Queen's University, Kingston, Ont.—He was an eminent Presbyterian divine, a well-known author and lecturer. A Nova Scotian by birth, he was educated at the University of Glasgow; entered the ministry in his native province, his first appointment being a mission field near Pictou. Here he roused the people to erect a church. He removed to Prince Edward Island, where, through his efforts, another church was built, near Charlottetown. In 1863 he became pastor of St. Matthew's (St. Mather's), Halifax. He accompanied Sandford (Sir) Fleming as his secretary to British Columbia, 1872. "From Ocean to Ocean" gives an account of the expedition. Again in 1883 Principal Grant travelled West with Sir Sandford, who had been asked by the directors of the C.P.R. to penetrate the Rockies by the Kicking Horse, Rogers and Eagle Passes. In 1876 Dr. Grant was sent as a delegate to the General Assembly of the Church of Scotland, and the following year offered the principalship of Queen's, which institution was brought through his efforts to the front rank of Canadian universities. Photogravure from the "Life," by W. L. Grant and C. F. Hamilton. Size 5 x 7. Head and shoulders, in profile.

2758—**HEARNE, SAMUEL,** 1745-1792—First European to penetrate to the Arctic Ocean from the interior. Photogravure from an engraving in the Dominion Archives, Ottawa. Size 5 x 7. Half length, oval. See 31.

2759—**McLOUGHLIN, DR. JOHN,** 1784-1857—Great leader of Hudson's Bay Company in Oregon—A Canadian, born at Riviere du Loup, Que., and educated in Canada and Scotland. He studied medicine in Edinburgh, joined the North-West Company as a young man. He was in charge of Fort William when the amalgamation of the North-West and Hudson's Bay Companies took place, and although strongly opposed to it, when accomplished, threw in his lot with the latter. He induced James (Sir) Douglas to take service with the Hudson's Bay, built Fort Vancouver, 1824, and, it is said, did more than any other man to strengthen the company's fur trade on the Pacific coast. He was a born ruler, feared as well as loved by employes and Indians. It is worthy of note that during his regime no Indian wars took place. He was known as the "Great White Eagle," "Good Old Doctor," and the "Father of Oregon." In time immigrants began to arrive on the Columbia. The company did not approve the aid given by McLoughlin to these settlers, many of whom were in need, and he was instructed to desist. Rather than accede, McLoughlin retired in 1845, his resignation taking effect in 1846. The remainder of his life was spent in Oregon City. Photogravure from portrait by Savannah. Size 5 x 7. Head and shoulders.

2760—**BEVERLEY HOUSE**—Hall and Stairway. Water color. Size 5 x 6.

2761—**BEVERLEY HOUSE, TORONTO**—North-east corner John and Richmond streets—The oldest portion of the house was built by D'Arcy Boulton, eldest son of Judge Boulton, some time about the War of 1812. In its early days it was merely a small brick cottage, and up to 1820 was the only building in the square bounded by John, Simcoe, Richmond and Queen streets. Boulton occupied the dwelling until 1816, when it came into possession of Attorney-General (Chief Justice) Robinson. He added a wing to the west, then raised the entire building, putting on a verandah and building stables. Thus the modest cottage of early days became the handsome home which remained until recent years. Beverley House was used as a temporary residence by Poulett Thomson (Lord Sydenham), Governor-General, 1839-41. On the death of Sir John Beverley Robinson and his widow, it was taken over by their son, the late Christopher Robinson, K.C. In 1912 the old mansion was demolished to make way for the new Methodist Book Room building. Water color. Size 5 x 7.

2762—**BEVERLEY HOUSE**—View of Drawing-room. Water color. Size 5 x 6.

2763-2769—**St. Paul's (Presbyterian) Church, Hamilton, Ont.**—Exterior and interior views.

2763—**FIRST ST. ANDREW'S CHURCH (ST. PAUL'S), HAMILTON, C.W.**—In November, 1833, a congregation, named St. Andrew's, was formed in Hamilton in connection with the Church of Scotland. Rev. Alexander Gale was inducted minister. The church, a frame building, stood on the south side of Main st., now (1917) the north-west corner of James and Jackson, and was opened for worship in the summer of 1834. Two or three times the building was enlarged, and in 1854 removed to a lot on the south-west corner of Charles and Jackson sts. On the completion of the present Gothic structure, on the old site, the frame building was sold to the German Catholics of Hamilton. The first meeting to discuss founding Queen's University was held in St. Andrew's Church. Water color. Size 4 x 6.

2764—MAIN PORTAL, ST. PAUL'S CHURCH, HAMILTON, ONT.— This doorway, one of the five exits of the church, faces James street. It is of Gothic design, in harmony with the stateliness of the general archi-tecture of St. Paul's. Water color. Size 4 x 6.

2765—INTERIOR VIEW OF ST. PAUL'S CHURCH, HAMILTON, ONT., 1917—During 1909-10 alterations were made in the interior of the church. In order to provide chancel space and accommodation for the organ and choir, formerly in the east gallery, an extension westward was made, and, without changing the Gothic interior, additional seating space for one hundred persons was also acquired. Water color. Size 5 x 6.

2766—CHAPEL AND BELFRY, ST. PAUL'S CHURCH (PRESBY-TERIAN), HAMILTON, ONT.—The chapel, an idea which originated with the present pastor, Rev. D. R. Drummond, D.D., was built in 1909-10, and has been found most useful in connection with church meetings and mid-week services. It has a seating capacity of a hundred persons. Above the chapel is shown the belfry (designed by Mr. Frank Darling, of Toronto), and the old bell, which was placed in the primitive frame church, St. Andrew's (St. Paul's) in 1834, and for a time used as a town bell as well as a kirk bell. Water color. Size 2 x 4.

2767—COMMUNION TABLE AND PULPIT FRONT, ST. PAUL'S CHURCH, HAMILTON, ONT.—They are of dark oak, beautifully carved in effective designs. In the background, above the chancel, may be seen the screen, modelled after that of Salisbury Cathedral in England. Water color. Size 4 x 6.

2768—ST. PAUL'S (FORMERLY ST. ANDREW'S) PRESBYTERIAN CHURCH, HAMILTON, ONT.—This edifice, of Gothic design, was erected on the original site of the old frame church of 1834, and opened 7th March, 1857, by Rev. Dr. Mathieson, of Montreal. Owing to financial and other circumstances the church was closed from 1st Oct., 1871, until 1st Sept., 1872. In May, 1873, the name was changed to 'St. Paul's." Later in the year the building was sold to the Baptists, but a release was secured in 1878. Extensive alterations and improvements were made in the church and Sunday school in 1909-10, so that they now rank with the finest in Hamilton. With Rev. D. R. Drummond, D.D., who has been pastor since 1905, originated the plan of using the different floor levels for various rooms, and also the idea of a chapel and belfry for the old bell of St. Andrew's, 1834. Water color. Size 4 x 6.

2769—SOUTH PORCH AND CHIMES IN ST. PAUL'S CHURCH, HAMILTON, ONT.—The eleven bells composing the chimes, were installed in November, 1906, at a cost of $6,500. The donors were various friends and members of St. Paul's, including the Sunday school, who gave the "Children's Bell." Water color. Size 4 x 6.

2770—DRUMMOND, REV. D. R., D.D.—Pastor St. Paul's Church, Hamilton, 1906-17—Of Scottish descent; born near Almonte, Lanark County, Ont., July 9th, 1868. Educated at Almonte High School and Queen's University, where he had a distinguished career; graduated 1889 (gold medal in classics; M.A.), and three years later took degree of B.D., winning Leitch Memorial Scholarship No. 2, the only travelling scholarship connected with the theological faculty. After a post-graduate course in philosophy and English, went to Edinburgh, where he attended theological classes. On returning to Canada was ordained to the pastorate of Russeltown, Que., 1894; in 1897 succeeded Rev. J. A. Macdonald (of the Toronto Globe) as pastor of Knox Church, St. Thomas, remaining there until his removal to Hamilton, where he has since ministered successfully; acted as chaplain at the Niagara Military Camp. At various periods just subsequent to his ordination supplied the pulpit of New St. Andrew's, Toronto, with great acceptance to the congregation. Water color. Size 3 x 4. Head and shoulders.

2771—BURNETT, REV. ROBERT—Pastor St. Andrew's Church, Hamilton, 1853-70—He was born at Horndean, Scotland, 18th June, 1823; came to Canada in 1851. As an eloquent, scholarly preacher, skilled in church law, Mr. Burnett was well known. He had also a provincial reputation as a horticulturist. Through his efforts steps were taken to build a new church, opened 7th March, 1857 (since 1873 known as St. Paul's), and during his pastorate of St. Andrew's work on missionary lines was carried on in the eastern part of Hamilton, resulting in the opening of St. John's Church, Wentworth street north. Mr. Burnett ministered in Pictou, N. S., for five years. His death took place in Milton, Ont., 13th August, 1889. Water color. Size 3 x 4. Head and shoulders.

2772—INTERIOR VIEW OF GREENOCK CHURCH, ST. ANDREW'S, N.B.—A gallery, extending along the two sides and one end of the building, is supported by ten pillars of solid bird's-eye maple; the facing of the gallery is of solid mahogany and bird's-eye maple, finished in panel work of artistic design. In each of the four corners of the high ceiling is a large Scotch thistle, emblematic of the native land of many of the first settlers of St. Andrew's. No nails were used in the construction of the pulpit, which is of the same materials as the gallery facing. To procure the mahogany required for the church, a vessel was sent to Honduras, W.I., and the maple was obtained in Charlotte County, N.B. Water color. Size 4 x 6.

2773—GREENOCK CHURCH (PRESBYTERIAN), ST. ANDREW'S, N.B.—Erected in colonial design, by Christopher Scott, a wealthy Scotsman, and completed in 1824. In memory of his birthplace—Greenock—Mr. Scott caused to be carved on the end of the tower facing the harbor an oak tree in full leaf, a bit of the heraldry of his native town. When the church was dedicated Rev. Dr. Davidson, of Edinburgh, grandfather of the present (1917) Archbishop of Canterbury, presented it with a pulpit Bible and a communion service. The latter is still in use. Water color. Size 4 x 6.

2774—CLENCH, LIEUT.-COL. RALFE, 1762-1828—Founder of one of the oldest families in the Niagara District—At the time of the American Revolution, 1775, he joined the Royal Standard as cadet in the 42nd Regiment; later served in the 8th, or King's Regiment, in Butler's Rangers and 1st Lincoln Militia. Fought with the 1st Lincolns at Queenston Heights. First Judge of Niagara District Court, and Registrar of the Surrogate Court for 1827. Member of the House of Assembly, 1801, 1805, 1813. Col. Clench married Elizabeth Johnson, granddaughter of Sir William Johnson and Molly Brant. Silhouette taken in 1827, the only known picture. Size 2 x 3.

2775—PRESENTATION TO R.M.S. "EMPRESS OF IRELAND"—This handsome timepiece of Irish bog oak, with works manufactured in Ireland, was "Presented to R.M.S. Empress of Ireland by Irishmen of the cities of Quebec, Montreal, Ottawa and Toronto. A token of esteem and respect to Sir Thomas G. Shaughnessy, President, 1906." The presentation was made on the completion of the first voyage of the "Empress" across the Atlantic. She was built at Glasgow by the Fairfield Company, and launched in the summer of 1906. In a collision with the Norwegian collier "Storstad," east of Father Point, in the St. Lawrence, she was sunk, with a loss of a thousand lives, May 29th, 1914. The clock went down with the vessel. Water color. Size 5 x 7.

2776—HOUSE OF REFUGE, TORONTO—Broadview avenue, overlooking the Don Flats—Built about 1875 and use as a House of Refuge for ten years. It then became a Smallpox Hospital, continuing as such until 1894. On 25th September, of that year, by order of the corporation, the building was burned. The site is now (1917) in a direct line from Nos. 459-65, east side of Broadview. Water color. Size 5 x 7.

2777—THOMAS, WILLIAM—Well known Toronto engineer and architect in the fifties. Water color from marble bust in possession of Mrs. Cyrus Thomas, Boston, Mass. Size 4 x 5. See 2782.

2778—WILKES, REV. HENRY—"Revd. H. Wilkes, D.D., Montreal Engraved by J. Cochran from a photograph"—Born in Birmingham, Eng., in 1805, and educated in Scotland. In 1820 came to Canada, engaging in business in Montreal for six years. Studied for the ministry at Glasgow University and at Dr. Wardlaw's Theological Academy. Licensed as an evangelist in 1832; ordained to the pastorate of Albany Street Church, Edinburgh, the following year. Began his Canadian ministry in 1836, following the Rev. Richard Miles as pastor of the first Congregational Church—Zion—in Montreal. Also served as corresponding agent in the Canadas for the Colonial Missionary Society, in connection with the Congregational Union of England and Wales. Dr. Wilkes died, 17th Nov., 1886. He has been called "the patriarch and apostle of Congregationalism in this country." Line engraving. Size 5 x 6. Half length, sitting.

2779—WALKEM, CHARLES—Born Jan. 12th, 1805, at Botusfleming, on the borders of Cornwall and Devon, Eng.; educated at Stonehouse, Plymouth. When the trigonometrical survey of Ireland was ordered by the Government Mr. Walkem was one of those chosen to carry out the project, afterwards coming to Canada to assist in settling the boundary between Canada and the United States. Given military rank as Royal Surveyor, with status of Major in the Royal Engineers. Remained in the service until 1870, when the Imperial troops were removed from this country. He was then employed in connection with the Imperial Government properties by the Canadian Government. His death occurred at Kingston, Ont., 17th Aug., 1883. Water color. Size 3 x 4. Head and shoulders.

2780-95—City Engineers, Toronto, 1840-1912.

2780—YOUNG, THOMAS—City Engineer, Toronto, 1840-2—An Englishman by birth. Came to Canada in 1836 and engaged in his profession as architect and surveyor, locating on Hospital (Richmond) street. The earliest pictures of King street, Toronto (Nos. 262 and 3262), in this collection, and that of the Houses of Parliament, Front street west, 1835 (No. 1060), were done by him. Mr. Young, who was the first City Engineer of Toronto, was succeeded by Mr. John G. Howard. Water color from original drawing by Mr. Edward Copping, for forty years Inspector of Buildings, Toronto. Size 3 x 4. Head and shoulders.

2781—HOWARD, JOHN G.—City Engineer, Toronto, 1843-52 and 1854. Water color. Size 3 x 4. Head and shoulders. See 835, 837, 841, 846, 3660.

2782—THOMAS, WILLIAM—City Engineer, Toronto, 1853—A prominent Toronto architect in the fifties. Associated also with Mr. John G. Howard (City Engineer, 1843-52, and 1854) as Civil Engineer. Architect of St. Lawrence Hall, various churches, and the jail of 1858. Mr. Thomas was born in 1800, in Stroud, Gloucestershire; his death occurred Dec. 25th, 1860. Water color from portrait in possession of his daughter, the late Miss Helena Thomas. Size 3 x 4. Head and shoulders. See 2777.

2783—KINGSFORD, WILLIAM—City Engineer, Toronto, 1855. Water color. Size 3 x 4. Head and shoulders. See 1026.

2784—HARRISON, THOMAS H.—City Engineer, Toronto, 1856—Prior to his appointment as City Engineer, in succession to William Kingsford, he was connected with the Surveying Department of the Corporation. Mr. Harrison held office for only one year, and was succeeded by Mr. Thomas Booth. Water color from original drawing by Mr. Edward Copping. Size 3 x 4. Head and shoulders.

2785—BOOTH, THOMAS—City Engineer, Toronto, 1857-8—For some years prior to his appointment as City Engineer Mr. Booth was connected with the Surveying Department of the Corporation. Was succeeded as Engineer by Mr. Alfred Brunel. Water color from original drawing by Mr. Edward Copping. Size 3 x 4. Head and shoulders.

2786—BRUNEL, ALFRED—City Engineer, Toronto, 1859-60—Born in 1818, of French descent. From 1844-50 was employed on various public works in Canada. Assistant engineer, Northern Railway, 1852, and superintendent, 1853-6. Alderman for St. George's Ward, Toronto, 1857-9 and 1861-2. At the time of the Trent Affair, in 1861, and the Fenian Raid, 1866, took an active part in organizing the 10th Royals; resigned his command as lieut.-colonel in 1871. In 1862 he entered the Government service, being appointed a "special commissioner" to enquire into the working of Customs ports." Became Inspector of Customs Ports and of Excise and Canals, 1863; Commissioner of Inland Revenue, 1871. Died, April 17th, 1887. Water color. Size 3 x 4. Head and shoulders.

2787—BENNETT, JOSEPH H.—City Engineer, Toronto, 1861-71—Born in England, 1809; well known in engineering circles in Toronto, where he died, 23rd July, 1878. Succeeded as Engineer of the Corporation by, Charles W. Johnston. Water color from portrait in possession of Mr. Bennett's niece, Mrs. David Moore, Qu'Appelle, Sask. Size 3 x 4. Head and shoulders.

2788—JOHNSTON, CHARLES W.—City Engineer, Toronto, 1871-5—Born at Taunton, Somersetshire, Eng., 1822, and educated there. During the potato famine of 1849 he was employed by the British Government to superintend extensive works (planned to give work to the starving people) in County Waterford, Ireland. Came to Canada in the sixties, and, after resigning the office of City Engineer, settled on a farm near Aspdin, Muskoka. One of the founders of the first log church in the Aspdin Mission—St. Mary's Church (Anglican), and for several years was a warden. Mr. Johnston died, 27th March, 1892. Water color. Size 3 x 4. Head and shoulders.

2789—SHANLY, FRANK—City Engineer, Toronto, 1875-80. Water color. Size 3 x 4. Head and shoulders. See 496.

2790—BROUGH, REDMOND JOHN—City Engineer, Toronto, 1881-3—Born in Toronto, Aug. 10th, 1946. First attended the Model Grammar School, under Mr. G. R. R. Cockburn, going to Upper Canada College when Mr. Cockburn became principal of that institution. A graduate of Toronto University. Mr. Brough died in Toronto, July 21st, 1883, as a result of an accident entailed when he was engaged on City Engineering work. Water color. Size 3 x 4. Head and shoulders.

2791—SPROATT, CHARLES—City Engineer, Toronto, 1883-90—Born in Toronto, June 21st, 1835; received his education at Upper Canada College and served his apprenticeship in engineering under Mr. Kivas Tully. Employed as an engineer by the Grand Trunk Railway when nineteen years of age. For some years resident engineer, Toronto, Grey & Bruce Railway at Orangeville. Later chief engineer Georgian Bay & Wellington Railway, completing the building of this road. In 1882 the firm of Gossage, Sproatt &

Thompson, land surveyors, was formed, with offices in the West. In addition to being a civil engineer, Mr. Sproatt was a Dominion and Provincial Land Surveyor. He died at Innisfail, Alta., Dec., 1895. Water color. Size 3 x 4. Head and shoulders.

2792—JENNINGS, WILLIAM TINDAL—City Engineer, Toronto, 1890-1 —Born in Toronto in 1846, son of Rev. Dr. John Jennings, minister of Bay Street (United) Presbyterian Church, 1839-74. Began his career as an engineer in the service of the Great Western Railway, and in the early days of the C.P.R. was engaged in exploratory survey work on that road. Advised the Government in the building of the graving dock at Esquimalt and the dock at Halifax. A member of the Institute of Civil Engineers, and past president of the Canadian Society of Civil Engineers. Mr. Jennings' death occurred 24th Oct., 1906, at Lansing, Mich. Water color. Size 3 x 4. Head and shoulders.

2793—CUNINGHAM, GRANVILLE C.—City Engineer, Toronto, 1891-2—A native of Edinburgh, Scotland, where he was born, April 27th, 1847. In 1870 went to Honduras to take charge of railway construction work, afterwards coming to Canada, where he also had charge of several railway construction works. In 1889 appointed Deputy City Engineer, Toronto, and two years later, City Engineer. Chief engineer Montreal Street Railway Company, 1892, and manager, 1893. Mr. Cuningham went to England in 1897, taking up tramway work in Birmingham. Later became manager and engineer of the London Central Railway, which was opened by King Edward VII. Still (1917) resides in London, where he is consulting engineer. Water color. Size 3 x 4. Head and shoulders.

2794—KEATING, E. H.—City Engineer, Toronto, 1892-8—Well known architect and engineer; born in Halifax, N.S., 7th Aug., 1844. Educated at the Free Church Academy there, and at Dalhousie College. Studied his profession under Geo. Whiteman, C.E., Provincial Government Engineer, and Sir Sandford Fleming, chief engineer Intercolonial Railway. Made surveys of early Nova Scotia railways, and from 1873-91 was City Engineer of Halifax. Resigned in the latter year to accept a similar position in Duluth, Minn., but in 1892 returned to Canada to become City Engineer of Toronto. General manager of the Toronto Street Railway, 1898-1904. Died June 17th, 1912. Water color. Size 3 x 4. Head and shoulders.

2795—RUST, CHARLES H.—City Engineer, Toronto, 1898-1912—Born Dec. 25th, 1852, at Great Waltham, Essex, Eng.; educated at Brentwood Grammar School, Essex. Subsequently entered auditor's department of the Great Western Railway, London, remaining there until 1872, when he came to Canada with his parents. Engaged in farming for a time, then taking up survey work with the Ontario & Quebec Railway. In 1877 entered the service of the Department of Works, Toronto, eventually becoming City Engineer. In May, 1912, he resigned the latter position to become City Engineer and Water Commissioner for Victoria, B.C. Water color. Size 3 x 4. Head and shoulders.

2796—HARRIS, ROLAND C.—Commissioner of Works and City Engineer, Toronto—He was born at Lansing, Ont., 26th May, 1875; educated in Toronto. After some years' experience in newspaper, bank and contracting work, he in 1899 entered the City Commissioner's Department. The Property Department was separated from the Assessment Department in 1904 and placed under the direction of the City Architect, under whom Mr. Harris served, the following year becoming Commissioner of Property. He was in 1910 given the title of Property and Street Commissioner, holding this office until June, 1912, when he was appointed to his present position. Water color. Size 3 x 4. Head and shoulders. See 3516.

2797—GALE, REV. ALEXANDER, 1800-54—First Presbyterian minister in Hamilton, C.W. Water color. Size 3 x 4. Head and shoulders. See 245.

2798—BLOCKHOUSE, ST. ANDREW'S. N.B.—Still standing at the head of the main street; one of three blockhouses built during the War of 1812, and used for military purposes at the time of the Fenian trouble. The other two blockhouses have been torn down. Water color. Size 5 x 7.

2799—FORT TIPPERARY, ST. ANDREW'S, N.B.—Built during the War of 1812, on a commanding site overlooking Passamaquoddy Bay. It served as a military post down to the time of the Fenian trouble. In 1902 Sir Thomas (Baron) Shaughnessy obtained possession of the property and removed the old buildings, erecting a handsome summer home on the site of the Fort. Lord Shaughnessy has retained the name, "Fort Tipperary," for his residence, and has also rebuilt the ramparts and remounted the old guns. Water color. Size 5 x 7.

2800—MATTHEWS, PETER, 1786-1838—Active in Rebellion of 1837— He saw service during the War of 1812-15 as a member of the Brock Volunteers. In the township of Pickering, where his father, a U.E.L., settled after the Revolutionary War, Matthews took a prominent part in public affairs, and in Rebellion of 1837 played a part as a supporter of William Lyon Mackenzie. He was tried for treason at Toronto, and, with Samuel Lount, hanged in the Court House yard, northeast corner of King and Toronto sts., 12th April, 1838. The scaffold stood on the north, or Court street side of the yard, directly in rear of No. 66 King street east, about 150 feet east of the east line of Toronto street. Water color from portrait in possession of Mrs. O. B. Sheppard, Toronto, granddaughter of John Montgomery, of Rebellion fame. Size 3 x 4. Head and shoulders.

2801—KERR, CAPT. ROBERT—Well known lake mariner in the early days—He was born at Kellswater, County Antrim, Ireland, March 11th, 1807. When a young man, emigrated to Canada, and for forty years commanded various vessels on the Great Lakes, sailing as far east as the Gulf of St. Lawrence. Captain Kerr's death took place in Toronto, March 3rd, 1876. Water color. Size 3 x 4. Head and shoulders.

2802—KERR, ROBERT, JR.—A prominent railway man—Son of Capt. Robert Kerr; born in Toronto, March 3rd, 1845; educated at Upper Canada College. In 1860 served in regular U.S. army, and in 1861 was in No. 3 Co., Q.O.R. Joined the Northern Railway, 1866, becoming traffic manager in 1884. Afterwards joined the C.P.R.; appointed general freight and passenger agent of the Western lines at Winnipeg. In 1899 was passenger and traffic manager of the whole system, resigning in 1910. His death took place in Toronto, Dec. 9th, 1916. Water color. Size 3 x 4. Head and shoulders.

2803—THOMAS, REV. RICHARD TUTIN—Pastor Northern Congregational Church, Toronto, 1867-9—Born at Royal Leamington Spa, Eng., Feb. 20th, 1842. Came to Canada with his parents; went to Upper Canada College, and later studied for the ministry. His first charge was that of the newly organized Northern Congregational Church (a Sunday school and services had, however, been conducted by members of Zion congregation since 1858); but he was not ordained until January, of the following year, when the new church was finished. In 1869 Mr. Thomas left Canada for England, where he held various pastorates. For some years he was agent in England for the French-Canadian Missionary Society. His death occurred in 1895. Mr. William Thomas, father of the subject of this note, was a well-known engineer and architect in Toronto in the early days. Water color. Size 3 x 4. Head and shoulders.

2804-10—**Principals and Rectors, Home District (Toronto) Grammar School, 1807-1900**—To date it has been impossible to obtain portraits of Rev. Samuel Armour, M.A., principal, 1823-5; Rev. Duncan MacAuley, 1834-6, and Mr. Charles N. B. Cosens, 1836-8.

2804—**STUART, REV. GEORGE O'KILL, D.D**—Principal Home District Grammar School, York (Toronto), 1807-12. Water color. Size 3 x 4. Head and shoulders. See 2513, 3198.

2805—**STRACHAN, REV. JOHN, D.D. (BISHOP)**—Principal Home District Grammar School, York (Toronto), 1812-23. Water color. Size 3 x 4. Head and shoulders. See 252, 2732, 3199.

2806—**PHILLIPS, REV. THOMAS, D.D.**—Principal Home District Grammar School, 1825-30—An Englishman, born 1781, and a graduate of Queen's College, Cambridge, 1805. Succeeded Rev. Samuel Armour, a Scotsman and a graduate of Glasgow University, as principal of the Grammar School. Previous to coming to Canada Dr. Phillips taught at Whitchurch, Herefordshire, Eng. In the Grammar School at York he made many changes in the text-books used, introducing those in vogue at Eton. Appointed vice-principal of Upper Canada College and Royal Grammar School, established in 1828, and which carried on the work of the Home District Grammar School in the building of the latter institution until removed in January, 1831, to the new Upper Canada College, Russell Square. Dr. Phillips resigned his position at U.C.C. in 1834 to take charge of the Anglican Church at Weston. His death occurred at Weston, 1849. Water color. Size 3 x 4. Head and shoulders.

2807—**CROMBIE, MARCUS CHRISTOPHILUS**—Principal Toronto Grammar School, 1838-53—When Upper Canada College removed to its new quarters in Russell Square, the work of the Grammar School was left in confusion, no provision having been made for the conduct of classes in the old building. Work was, however, resumed in May, 1834, when Rev. Duncan MacAuley was appointed to the principalship. He, in turn, was succeeded by Mr. Charles N. B. Cosens, who came from England in 1835. Mr. Cosens subsequently joined the staff of Upper Canada College, and was succeeded by Mr. Crombie, an Irishman, born at Dungiven, County Londonderry, in 1800. He was educated at Foyle College, Londonderry, coming to Canada in 1821, and settling first in Montreal, where he successfully carried on a private school. In 1836 appointed head master Royal Grammar School, Picton, where he remained until his appointment at York. Died December, 1853. Water color from portrait in possession of the Crombie family. Size 3 x 4. Head and shoulders.

2808—**HOWE, MICHAEL C., LL.D.**—Principal Toronto Grammar School, 1854-63—Born in 1818, in the County of Tipperary, Ireland. A graduate of Trinity College, Dublin, where he occupied the room which the poet, Oliver Goldsmith, had had during his residence at Trinity. Subsequent to his graduation Mr. Howe was offered the principalship of a college in India by Rev. Alex. Duff, D.D., but declined it. Principal of the Royal Belfast Academical Institution for a time. Came to Canada in 1851, and was appointed head master of Cayuga Grammar School; for a short time held a similar post in the Galt Grammar School. In 1866 removed to Australia, where he taught in Melbourne, afterwards becoming principal of the Newington College, New South Wales. There he died in 1884. Water color from original portrait belonging to the late Mrs. Howe. Size 3 x 4. Head and shoulders.

2809—**WICKSON, REV. ARTHUR A., LL.D.**—Rector Toronto Grammar School, 1863-72—Born in London, Eng., Dec. 9th, 1825, son of Mr. James Wickson, sr. Came to Canada with his parents in 1834. Had a brilliant career at Upper Canada College and later at Toronto University, winning a gold medal in classics and the Duke of Wellington Scholarship, and taking degrees of B.A., M.A. and LL.B. Studied for the Congregational ministry; became classical lecturer in the Congregational College (then in Toronto; but afterwards removed to Montreal). For some years registrar of Toronto University. and at the same time classical tutor in that institution. In addition to his work as rector of the Grammar School he was matriculation examiner for medical students, and spent much of his time in giving private lessons. Nervous prostration, brought on by overwork, necessitated his resignation from the rectorship at Easter, 1872. Dr. Wickson then went to Europe, eventually settling in London, Eng., where he died, July 26th, 1913. Water color from portrait in possession of his son, Mr. Paul Wickson, Paris, Ont. Size 3 x 4. Head and shoulders.

2810—MACMURCHY, ARCHIBALD, M.A.—Rector Toronto High School and Principal Jarvis Street Collegiate Institute, Toronto, 1872-1900—Born at Stewartfield, Kintyre, Argyleshire, Scotland, in 1832, came to Canada in 1840. Took his B.A. at Toronto University with first-class honors in mathematics and silver medal, 1861, M.A., 1868. Subsequent to teaching in the first Public School opened in Collingwood in 1854, he attended the Normal School in Toronto, and afterwards joined the staff of the Provincial Model School. In 1858 he was appointed mathematical master in Toronto Grammar School, holding that appointment until his promotion to the rectorship. Was at Ridgeway, 1866, as a private in the University Company. Author of several text books in Arithmetic, Hand Book on Canadian Literature, editor of Canadian Educational Monthly. Died 27th April, 1912. Water color from portrait in possession of his son, Mr. Angus MacMurchy, Toronto. Size 3 x 4. Head and shoulders.

2811-17—Home District (Toronto) Grammar School—Jarvis Street Collegiate Institute—1807-1917.

2811—HOME DISTRICT SCHOOL—A small, one-storey building, of stone, afterwards clap-boarded, attached to the modest frame residence of Rev. George O'Kill Stuart, at the southeast corner of George and King streets. Here, on April 16th, 1807, Dr. Stuart opened the first Public school in York. In 1813 the school was removed to a barn at the southeast corner of King and Yonge streets, classes being conducted here until 1816, when the "Old Blue School" was erected. Water color. Size 4 x 6.

2812—OLD BLUE SCHOOL—Centre "Block D"—Bounded by Church, Hospital (Richmond), New (Jarvis), and Newgate (Adelaide) streets, Toronto. Water color. Size 4 x 6. See 929.

2813—OLD GRAMMAR SCHOOL—Near corner Nelson, formerly New (Jarvis), and March, afterwards Stanley (Lombard) streets—In 1829 the "Old Blue School" was removed from its original site, in the centre of "Block D,'" to its easterly boundary. The building was repainted, improved and fitted up for the use of Upper Canada College. When U.C.C. removed to its own quarters in Russell Square, January, 1831, classes were discontinued in the old Grammar School; but were resumed in 1834, and continued there until January, 1864, when the institution removed to Dalhousie street. Water color. Size 4 x 6.

2814—TORONTO GRAMMAR SCHOOL, DALHOUSIE STREET—In January, 1864, the Grammar School removed from Nelson (Jarvis) and Stanley (Lombard) street to a small structure on the east side of Dalhousie street, just north of Gould, and in the rear of the residence of Dr. Wickson, then rector of the institution. In 1870 the school removed temporarily to the former King's College, Queen's Park. Water color. Size 4 x 6.

2815—OLD KING'S COLLEGE, QUEEN'S PARK—Used as a temporary Grammar School, 1870-71. Water color. Size 4 x 6. See 273.

2816—TORONTO HIGH SCHOOL—In 1871 an Act was passed providing that hereafter Grammar Schools should be known as High Schools, and the newly completed Toronto High School, formerly the Toronto Grammar School, and now (1917) Jarvis Street Collegiate Institute, was occupied 15th of September of that year. Since its erection additions have been made at various times. Water color. Size 4 x 6.

2817—JARVIS STREET COLLEGIATE INSTITUTE—As it stands in 1917—Since its erection as the Toronto High School in 1871, several additions have been made to the original structure. On the occasion of the one hundredth anniversary of the founding of the school, in 1907, a suitably inscribed tablet was placed in the front of the building. Water color. Size 4 x 6.

2818—GAMBLE, JOSEPH CLARKE, 1808-1902—Prominent lawyer and promoter of the Toronto and Lake Huron Railway. Water color. Size 3 x 4. Head and shoulders, oval. See 3227.

2819—HALIFAX, N.S., FROM DARTMOUTH COVE—View looking southwest, 1828—With key. Size 12 x 18. Original water color from which was made "View of Halifax from Dartmouth Cove," frontispiece second volume of Haliburton's "Historical and Statistical Account of Nova Scotia," printed and published at Halifax by Joseph Howe in 1829. Haliburton, in his preface to the first volume, refers to the view as follows:—"For the correct and beautiful view of Halifax, prefixed to the second volume, I am indebted to a lady of that place whose name I regret I have not permission to mention, but who enhanced the value of this embellishment by the very friendly manner in which it was communicated to me."
Note.—The artist has taken artistic license in depicting the northern part of the town, as the portion from the Citadel to the north (that is to the right) has been compressed or condensed so that it is difficult to scale the picture relatively in that direction.

2820—MEETING PLACE OF PARLIAMENT IN QUEBEC, 1792—To the left of picture is shown the rear of residence of the Roman Catholic Bishops of Quebec, erected by Bishop St. Valier. The building was used as Parliament House in 1792, the sittings of the first Canadian Parliament being held in the portion of building on extreme left. Towards the right is Chateau St. Louis, burned in 1834, after which Lord Durham, Governor-General of Canada, 1838, had the ruins removed and erected on the site Durham Terrace. Greatly enlarged and improved under Lord Dufferin's administration, it now bears his name, and from this fine promenade, under shadow of the Citadel, may be had a magnificent view of the St. Lawrence and opposite shore. The artist has in picture lessened the distance between Chateau St. Louis and the Bishop's Palace. The former stood near the site of Chateau Frontenac, and the latter on the vacant space beyond Mountain Hill and the present post office. Water color by H. Bunnett, 1888. Size 6 x 9.

2821—PLAINS OF ABRAHAM, QUEBEC—Wolfe's Cove in the distance—The Plains or Heights of Abraham received their name from Abraham Martin, who away back in 1635 was given land in the vicinity by the Company of New France. The centre tract became known as Abraham's Plains, from the fact that it was utilized by Martin as pasture fields. The site of the engagement of 13th Sept., 1759, has been built over, but land adjoining is used as a public park, on the western side of which, ascent was made from beneath the cliff (the point is still, 1917, known as Wolfe's Cove) to the place of battle. Lithograph in color. Size 6 x 8. See 1826.

31

2822—BARRACKS, ST. JOHN'S, C.E., 1846—Looking north from the Richelieu River—The view shows:—1-2, Old stables, now demolished; the site is covered with the new cavalry stables. 3, South barrack block. 4, Originally the hospital, later married men's quarters, and now occupied by men in training for active service. The small building adjoining is the dead house. 5, Officers' quarters. All the buildings except 1 and 2 are still standing as in 1846. The mounds shown are the old ramparts, now levelled, only the ditch remaining. A fence running to the water's edge replaces them. Water color. Size 5 x 10.

2823—CAPE DIAMOND, QUEBEC—The view is from one of the coves a little east of Wolfe's Cove. With the disappearance of the timber trade the buildings shown mostly fell into decay and have since been removed to make way for the Transcontinental Railway. On the farther side of Cape Diamond stands the Citadel of Quebec (not visible in picture). Photograph. Size 5 x 11.

2824—FIRST PARLIAMENT OF QUEBEC, 1792—Held in residence of R.C. Bishops—The opening of the first session of the first Parliament of Quebec took place on 17th December, 1792, the House on this occasion sitting in the episcopal palace erected by Bishop St. Valier at the top of Mountain Hill. The chapel, 30 x 60 ft., was converted into a legislative assembly chamber. As the members were unaccustomed to Parliamentary procedure there was some confusion, which, however, was overcome through those present having a knowledge of French and English. In the absence in England of Lord Dorchester, Sir Alured Clark, Lieutenant-Governor, opened the House. Print in water color from the original painting by M. Huot in the Legislative Assembly Chamber, Parliament Buildings, Quebec. Size 11 x 23.

2825—FIRST PARLIAMENT, QUEBEC, 17TH DECEMBER, 1792—, Key to—Note:—The artist, in his work, was able to obtain authentic portraits of the members whose names are followed by an "x."

2826—FLEMING, SIR SANDFORD, C.E.—Born at Kirkcaldy, Fifeshire, Scotland, 1827, and educated there; studied surveying and engineering; came to Canada, 1845; Chief Engineer Intercolonial Railway; appointed in 1871 Engineer-in-Chief in connection with Pacific Railway surveys. Mr. Fleming was one of the founders of the Canadian (Royal) Institute, Toronto. He was created a Companion of the Order of St. Michael and St. George, 1877, and in 1897 became a Knight Commander of the same order. He carried on at his own expense an examination of Newfoundland to ascertain the possibility of building a railway across the island. This resulted in the road built and operated by Messrs. Reid. He interested himself in universal or Cosmic time, and in 1878-9 wrote several pamphlets on the matter. Sir Sandford, "one of the builders of Canada," died at his home in Ottawa, July 22nd, 1915. Photo from life. Size 8 x 10. Three-quarter length, sitting. See 2748.

2827—BOURGET, 1799-1885—"Ignace Bourget, Eveque de Montreal, Assistant au Throne Pontifical. Llanta. Im Lemercier, Paris." Bishop of Montreal, 19th April, 1840, and in 1862 created a Roman Count and Assistant at the Pontifical throne. Lithograph. Size 8 x 12, three-quarter length. See 321.

2828—LANDING OF CHAMPLAIN AT QUEBEC, 3RD JULY, 1608— In the early autumn of 1607 the colony at Port Royal, N.S., was recalled to France, and in the following year De Monte, who had had his patent for trading privileges in Canada and Acadia renewed for a year, decided after consultation with Champlain, that Quebec would be an excellent place for a settlement. On 13th April, 1608, Champlain sailed from Honfleur, France, in Le Don de Dieu, with a party of twenty-eight, arriving at

Tadousac, 3rd June, and at Quebec, 3rd July. On disembarking, land at the base of the cliff was cleared, and here a "habitation" fort and stores were erected. Thus was the old city of Quebec founded and the power of France, in the formation of this new colony, formally established in North America. The portraits on each side of the picture are painted into the border. That facing the spectator's left hand is Jacques Cartier. The other is Montcalm. Print in water color from the original painting by Henri Beau, in the Legislative Council Chamber, Parliament Buildings, Quebec. Size 14 x 24.

2829—**QUEEN ST., FREDERICTON, N.B.,** 1835—With key—In 1785 Governor Carleton changed the name of St. Anne, N.B., to that of Fredericton, and in that year five main streets, parallel to the River St. John, were laid out in the town, one of which was Queen street. To-day (1917) it is the chief street in the city, with shops and many public buildings. Water color by W. M. Moxon. Size 6 x 14.

2830—**QUEBEC**—A modern view from the Lower Town—With key. Photograph, colored. **Size 7 x 9.**

2831—**"A PERSPECTIVE VIEW OF THE TOWN AND FORTIFICATIONS OF MONTREAL IN CANADA,** D. Pomarade, Sculp."—From the River St. Lawrence, 1760—With key. The Montreal of to-day (1917) from Berri street on the east to McGill street on the west, is represented in the picture. Engraving. Size 6 x 8.

2832—**RAMPARTS, QUEBEC**—Overlooking the St. Lawrence—The view is taken from Rampart street, near the back of the Hotel Dieu Hospital. Standing out prominently in centre of the background are the new grain elevators. To the right the spire of Laval University is shown, and at the extreme right is the lower end of the block of houses on Hamel street. Photograph. Size 5 x 11.

2833—**PLACE D'ARMES, MONTREAL, QUE.,** 1807—This historic square, near which the founders of Ville Marie (Montreal) first encountered the Iroquois, is surrounded by many and varied interests of the city's life. In the centre of the square, now known as Place d'Armes, stands a statue of Maisonneuve. With key. Water color by G. Horne Russell, R.C.A., 1897, from original by R. Dillon. Size 10 x 14.

2834—**OLD WINDMILL, POINT ST. CHARLES**—At entrance to present Lachine Canal—This picturesque bit of masonry was built about 1805. After having performed years of service grinding corn, it was abandoned for mercantile purposes, used as a morgue and later demolished. The buildings in background of picture are on the south side of Commissioners' street, named after the commissioners who had charge of the demolition of the fortifications around Montreal. These old French fortifications were of stone in bastioned form, with several gate exits. Water color by H. Bunnett. Size 7 x 7.

2835—**LITTLE CHAMPLAIN ST., QUEBEC**—Along the base of the cliffs. Photogravure, colored. Size 6 x 8. See 1933.

2836—**NOTRE DAME ST., MONTREAL,** 1832—With key. Matthews, lith. Drawn by J. Duncan. Lithograph. Size 10 x 15.

2837—**"MODERN STREET VIEW OF POINT LEVI AND QUEBEC IN DISTANCE**—Published by Adolphus Bourne, Montreal, Canada, 1874. J. Duncan, del. C. G. Crehen, chromo"—With key. Cote du Passage, Point Levi, 1843, with Quebec in the distance, is here shown. The name "La Cote" was formerly "La Route du Passage," that is, the hill or road leading from the crossing or ferry to Quebec. The trip was made in large wooden canoes, strong enough to resist ice, somewhat like whaleboats, but not so high in the gunwale. These were followed by boats propelled by live horse-power, and eventually steam. All the dwellings and stores in the picture were destroyed by fire in 1876. Lithograph in color. Size 10 x 14.

2838—**NEAR DARTMOUTH, N.S.**—View in 1846—In the vicinity of Dartmouth, on the east side of Halifax Harbor, the marine scenery is very fine. At one time the Dartmouth Lakes, commencing within a mile of the town, were a favorite resort of sportsmen. The town itself was founded in 1750, burned soon afterwards, and later reoccupied by New Englanders. Water color. Size 5 x 7.

2839—**STORMY DAY IN OLD QUEBEC**—Scene on Fabrique St., 1890—The church in centre background is the Basilica, raised to that dignity in 1874. The first mass was said in it on Christmas Day, 1650, the steeple begun in 1674, and in 1849 the square tower built. The houses to left of picture are on the north side of Fabrique street, and are shown, with one exception, as they are to-day (1917). The second building from the church (marked "X") was occupied in 1810 by Sir Isaac Brock. About 1901 it was demolished and replaced by a building containing two shops which reached to the same height as the neighboring houses. Water color by Walter Baker. Size 6 x 7.

2840—**DRINKING FOUNTAIN, THE GORE, HAMILTON**—Until 1860 the Gore was simply a grass plot; but in that year an iron fence was put up, flower beds laid out, and various other improvements made. Set in the heart of the city, the Gore is still a place of rest for the passerby. The fence and gates at the four corners have been removed. Water color from original drawing by F. B. Schell, for "Picturesque Canada," 1880. Size 5 x 5.

2841—**SERVICE IN A MENNONITE CHURCH**—In the Canadian West —As early as 1525 the views now held by the Mennonites were advocated in Zurich, Switzerland, and they soon spread to surrounding countries. In Holland, Menno Simons, a Roman Catholic priest, dissatisfied with his Church, espoused and expounded the new teaching, and his followers came to be known as Mennonites. In 1783-8 many of the sect emigrated to Russia, to escape military service, the Empress Catharine having offered liberal inducements, including exemption from military service. In 1870 these special privileges were withdrawn and the Mennonites again emi-grated, many going to Southern Manitoba, where they settled in village communities, as was their custom in the old world. The village com-munity is now, however, almost a thing of the past, and the Mennonites farm in much the same way as their Canadian neighbors. Many of the younger generation have left the older settlements to take up homesteads in Saskatchewan. Water color from original drawing by W. T. Smedley, for "Picturesque Canada," 1880. Size 5 x 5.

2842—**QUEBEC**—"View of the Esplanade and Fortifications of Quebec, 1832. R. A. Sproule, Del. C. G. Crehen, Chromo. Published by Adolphus Bourne, Montreal, Canada, 1874"—The Esplanade, covering an area of over an acre, bounded on the west by the city walls, and extending from St. Louis to Kent gates, was, in 1832 and later, used as a drill and parade ground. To the right of the picture is the Jesuit Church, formerly the Church of the Congregation of Notre Dame de Quebec. Some of the resi-dences shown still (1917) remain, while others have given place to more modern buildings. The well in the background is still there, but without beam or lever for raising the water. Lithograph in color. Size 10 x 15.

2843—**QUEBEC**—"View of Quebec from Point Levis, 1832. R. A. Sproule, Del. C. G. Crehen Chromo. Published by Adolphus Bourne,

451

Montreal, Canada, 1874." The picture is taken, not from Point Levis, as given in the original title: but from Indian Cove, farther west up the river, on the Levis side of the St. Lawrence, and near the present graving dock. The view shows the Citadel-crowned rock of Quebec and prominent buildings of the city. Lithograph in color. Size 10 x 15.

2844—LITTLEHALES, MAJOR E. B. (subsequently Sir Edward Baker Baker)—Military secretary to Governor Simcoe during the period of his residence in Canada. Was an excellent official of the Crown, as well as of Governor Simcoe, in preparing plans and obtaining information respecting the newly-settled country, the affairs of which his chief was called upon to administer. He was also an author of some repute, being the writer of the "Journal of an Exploring Excursion from Niagara to Detroit," first given to the public in 1834, though the expedition took place in 1793. He returned to England on the recall of Simcoe, and in 1801 became Under-Secretary of the Military Department in Ireland, which position he held until 1820. In 1802 Lieutenant-Colonel Littlehales was created a baronet, and by royal license in 1817 assumed the surname of Baker in lieu of Littlehales, on inheriting the property of Ranston, in Dorsetshire. Facsimile reproduction of oil painting in possession of his grand-niece, Mrs. A. M. Fitzgerald Dalton, of Guildford, Eng. Size 13 x 16. Half length. See 186.

2845—ST. GABRIEL ST. PRESBYTERIAN CHURCH, MONTREAL—First Protestant church in that city—Rev. John Bethune, a retired chaplain of the 84th Regiment, commenced Presbyterian services in Montreal in 1786. He was succeeded by Rev. John Young. In 1792 St. Gabriel St. Church, a quaint little building 60 x 48, on the northeast corner of St. Gabriel and St. James streets, was opened, with Rev. John Young as first pastor. A new roof was put on the church in 1809 and a steeple and bell added. Later a gallery was built. The building continued in use until 1886, the last service being held on the morning of 19th Sept., and the following Sunday full services were held in the congregation's new home, St. Catherine street, east of Phillip's Square. For some time previous to the erection of the old St. Gabriel St. Church, which was demolished in 1903, to make room for an extension to the Court House, Presbyterians of Montreal worshipped in the Church of the Recollet Fathers, a privilege which was much appreciated. Water color by Holdstock. Size 7 x 9.

2846—CENTRAL PRESBYTERIAN CHURCH, GALT, ONT.—With the Grand River in the foreground—On July 26th, 1880, Principal Caven, of Knox College, Toronto, laid the corner-stone of the church, which is situated at the northeast corner of Queen's Square. The prevailing style of architecture is Gothic, and a particularly graceful spire rises above the stately pile. There is also a fine set of chimes, the bells of which were presented by different members of the congregation. At the southwest corner of Queen's Square is Knox Church, the spire of which may be seen. The buildings to the left of the picture, and which are across the street from the front of Central Church, are still (1917) standing, and are used as shops. The high structure to the right is the old Queen's Arms Hotel, since demolished to make way for the building of the Young Men's Christian Association, facing directly on Queen's Square. It is the east side of Central Church that is shown. Water color from original drawing by F. B. Schell, for "Picturesque Canada." Size 5 x 6.

2847—WINNIPEG FROM ST. BONIFACE FERRY LANDING—St. Boniface, on the banks of the Red River, opposite Winnipeg, was founded in 1818. A trolley line now (1917) connects the town, which has risen to considerable importance, with Winnipeg. Water color from original drawing by F. B. Schell, for "Picturesque Canada," 1880. Size 5 x 7.

2848—HOW THE SUSPENSION BRIDGE WAS BEGUN—The first over the Niagara River—In 1848 Mr. Charles Ellet built the first suspension bridge over the river. He offered $5 reward to anyone who would get a string across it, and the next windy day all the boys on the American side were kiting. One landed his kite across the river, and received the reward. The first iron successor to the string was a wire cable. To this was suspended a wire basket, in which two persons could cross, the basket being attached to an endless rope, worked by a windlass on each bank. The basket-bridge was an excellent auxiliary in the building of the first suspension bridge. Water color. Size 5 x 7.

2849—"VIEW OF THE MARKET PLACE AND CATHOLIC CHURCH, UPPERTOWN, QUEBEC, 1832. R. A. Sproule, Del. C. G. Crehen, Chromo. Published by Adolphus Bourne, Montreal, Canada, 1874."—With key—The old Market Square was in bygone days a busy place with habitants' wives selling farm produce to frequenters of the market, and here in old times stood the pillory, for the punishment of thieves and perjurers. Now (1917) the space is planted in grass and has public pathways in the form of a Roman cross. The Basilica or Roman Catholic Cathedral (left of picture) faces upon the square. Mass was said for the first time in the old church, Christmas, 1650. In 1849 a square stone tower was erected. Lithograph in color. Size 10 x 14.

2850—QUEBEC—"View of the Place d'Armes, Quebec, 1832. Published by Adolphus Bourne, Montreal, Canada, 1874"—With key—The Place d'Armes, which adjoins the Chateau Frontenac and Dufferin Terrace, was used from the days of the French occupation and until the Champs de Mars was formed, as a military parade ground. To-day (1917) it is partially covered with shade trees, and in the centre is an ornamental fountain, erected as a monument to the founders of the Christian religion in New France. It was the second parade ground, the first having been on the Place Royale. Lithograph in color. Size 10 x 15.

2851—STEAMBOAT WHARF, MONTREAL, 1832—Showing Commissioner's street and the Harbor front—In 1832 Montreal was made a port of entry and a line of substantial wharves commenced. The "Queen," shown in picture, was a market steamer, which brought people with their produce from near-lying parishes, noted for their vegetable and fruit gardens. The gas lamp stood in centre of Custom House Square, in old days a market place, and which in 1611 was named La Place Royale by Champlain. On 18th May, 1892, this name was reconferred on petition of the Antiquarian Society of Montreal. Matthews, lith. Drawn on stone by J. Duncan. Size 10 x 15.

2852—"POSITION OF PIERS', HOWE'S & MABURY'S BOATS coming in at the last regatta held at Halifax, 26th September, 1838. Ide C. Beamis, Jr., del. T. Moore's Lithography, Boston"—With key. This race for first-class sailing boats, which took place on Halifax Harbor, Thursday, 20th Sept., 1838, not 26th, as given on picture, and which was an engraver's error, was one of the most notable and exciting sailing competitions held at Halifax in the old days, and was long remembered by sportsmen. Eight boats started, the fastest of these being W. B. T. Piers' schooner "Victoria," 32½ feet keel, 12 feet beam, which had just been built at Bedford by Henry Moseley, as a service boat for Piers' grist mill at that place; Postmaster John Howe's new schooner "Mary," and Mabury's (Black's) new cutter "Mary Ann," which was sailed by navy men. There was a steady northerly breeze. As the boats neared the winning mark, the old receiving ship "Pyramus," off the naval yard, and which had to be rounded, the "Mary Ann" was leading slightly, with the "Mary" close alongside, and the "Victoria" very close hauled a couple of lengths astern. The "Victoria," by clever handling, was enabled to round the "Pyramus" first and won the prize of $100. The event created such interest that the lithograph shown was published. The view was taken from Halifax Naval Yard, looking east-northeast towards Dartmouth. Lithograph. Size 8 x 15.

2853—MAIN STREET, WINNIPEG, 1880—Showing from Ryan's boot and shoe store to Portage avenue, on the west side, and a part of the east side. Water color from original drawing by F. B. Schell, for "Picturesque Canada." Size 5 x 7.

2854—McGILL ST., CORNER FORTIFICATION LANE, MONTREAL— The old No. 52 McGill street, built 1810, was at different times variously used. In 1842 the lower portion was fitted up by the Unitarians as a place of worship, and, again, a woodenware shop was kept here by one Lamouche. The doorway to right of picture was site of first American Presbyterian Church in Montreal, opened 1st December, 1826. On the old-time corner at McGill street and Fortification lane stands (1917) the office building of the Richelieu & Ontario Navigation Co., occupied by the Canada Steam-ships Lines. Water color by Walter Baker. Size 7 x 8.

2855—THE BIG TREE—Stanley Park, Vancouver, B.C., 1912—Stanley Park, 960 acres in extent, and almost entirely surrounded by the sea, is one of Vancouver's chief attractions. It is practically virgin forest, although here and there the underbrush has been cleared for picnickers, and miles of good roads have been made. The giant tree to the right of the picture, the biggest of the big trees in the park, is now in a state of decay, being simply a hollow stump in which a pair of horses can stand easily. Reproduction, in color, of original drawing by Harold Copping. Size 6 x 8.

2856—PARLIAMENT BUILDINGS, VICTORIA, B.C.—From the Old Indian Reserve—The Provincial Buildings, which comprise the Parliament House, Provincial Museum and Library, and Government Offices, are of grey stone, and present a very handsome appearance. They are situated on Belleville street, near James' Bay. Surmounting the dome is a statue of Captain Vancouver, Pacific coast explorer, while in front of the buildings stands a monument commemorating Sir James Douglas, Governor of Van-couver Island, 1851-64, and of British Columbia, 1858-64. Reproduction, in color, from original drawing by Harold Copping. Size 6 x 8.

2857—HOT SULPHUR SPRINGS, BANFF, ALTA.—On the southern slope of Sulphur Mountain are the sulphur springs, the uppermost of which is situated nine hundred feet above the Bow River, and the water has made a strange yellow streak down the side of the moun-tain. The springs, which possess medicinal properties, and the dry, in-vigorating air of the mountains attract many visitors to Banff, which in winter is increasingly popular as a playground, affording facilities for ice-boating on Lake Minnewanka, skating, ski-ing, snowshoeing and toboggan-ing. In summer there is excellent rowing and canoeing on the picturesque Bow River. Reproduction, in color, from original drawing by Harold Copping. Size 5 x 8.

2858—REAR OF GREY NUNNERY, MONTREAL—The nuns are said to have received their name at first in hatred for leading inhabitants of Montreal were maliciously disposed towards them. The order was founded in 1747 by Madame d'Youville, who by letters patent dated 3rd June, 1753, was legally authorized to establish the community. The sheds in picture have been removed and the buildings are used as warehouses fronting Normandin street, formerly the courtyard of the nunnery, which faced on the present Youville Square, and was outside the old French fortifications. In 1861, property bounded on the south by Dorchester street, and on the north by St. Catherine street, was purchased, and in 1870 the present large stone building was erected. The Grey Nuns not only carry on hospital work, but care for the infirm, aged and insane of both sexes. Water color by H. Bunnett. Size 4 x 5.

2859—CONVENT AND CHURCH OF THE RECOLLETS, MONTREAL —The view shows the rear, on Recollet street side, of the buildings, which faced on Notre Dame street. In the Church of the Recollet Fathers the Anglicans of Montreal held services from 1764 to 1789, and Presbyterians (afterwards St. Gabriel St. Church), in 1791-2. It was also the first parish church for the Irish Catholics of Montreal, from 1830 to 1837. The property was demolished in 1866, and the site is now (1917) covered by the wholesale mercantile district of Montreal. Water color by H. Bunnett. Size 5 x 5.

2860—SASKATCHEWAN PARLIAMENT BUILDINGS, REGINA—In the course of erection—When the Provinces of Saskatchewan and Alberta were created from the North-West Territories in 1915, Regina, which had been the seat of government for the Territories, was chosen as the capital of Saskatchewan. In 1912 the new Parliament Buildings were opened—a stately greystone pile, on Lake Wascana. Lake Wascana—half a mile broad at its widest part, and seven miles long—was formed by damming up Wascana, or Pile-o-Bones Creek. Not far from the Parliament Buildings are the headquarters of the North-west Mounted Police. Reproduction, in color, of original drawing by Harold Copping. Size 6 x 8.

2861—VANCOUVER FROM THE HARBOR, 1912—As late as 1886 Vancouver consisted simply of two dozen rickety shacks in the forest. In the early summer of that year the embryo city began to grow at an amazing rate; but in July fire, sweeping down from the forests, destroyed every house save one. Out of the ashes has grown the present picturesquely situated and populous Pacific city. Reproduction, in color, of original drawing by Harold Copping. Size 6 x 8.

2862—WHEATFIELDS OF MANITOBA, 1912—Prairie land in Western Canada—The Province of Manitoba raises every year millions of bushels of wheat on its prairie lands. Spring sets in early; the summer heat causes the grain to ripen quickly, and as there is little rain at harvest time, crops are gathered in without fear of wetting. At times, in order to accomplish the cutting speedily, work is carried on at night. Of Manitoba it has been written, "Softly the shadows of prairie land wheat, Ripple and riot adown to her feet." The wheatfields of this province and of the other wheat-growing provinces of the Canadian West are a beautiful sight, either early in the season when they appear like the great green sea, or later, when ready for harvest, they are a mass of red gold. Reproduction in color of original drawing by Harold Copping. Size 5 x 7.

2863—INDIAN BURIAL GROUND—The artist has here depicted a group of heathen Blackfoot graves on a lonely stretch of prairie land. When mission work was begun among the Blackfoot tribe the missionaries found a sun and moon worshipping people, who, unlike many other tribes, did not believe in a beneficent Spirit or a "Happy Hunting Ground." To them the future after death meant "sad, ceaseless wanderings near the scenes amongst which they had passed their lives." For many years the missionaries labored without making any apparent impression on their red-skinned brethren; but there are now, however, many earnest Christians amongst the Blackfeet. Reproduction, in color, from original drawing by Harold Copping. Size 6 x 8.

2864—FISH MARKET, VANCOUVER, 1912—Showing the "Mosquito Fleet"—The fleet, which is manned by Japanese fishermen, consists of a number of small, gaudily painted, but shabby gasoline launches, with quaint cabins. Fishing is one of the principal industries of British Columbia. In the canneries are many Chinese—working under white overseers—but the actual fishing is done largely by the Japanese, who are thoroughly familiar with the British Columbia coast. Reproduction, in color, of original drawing by Harold Copping. Size 6 x 8.

2865—**SHORE OF KOOTENAY LAKE**—The lake, sixty miles in length. is an expansion of the Kootenay River, between the Purcell and Selkirk Mountains. The scenery in the vicinity of the lake is very lovely. and along its shores and in adjacent valleys numerous fruit farms are to be found. The word "Kootenay," it is said, signifies in the Indian tongue, "Water People." Reproduction, in color, of original drawing by Harold Copping. Size 5 x 8. See 2881.

2866—**METROPOLITAN CHURCH, TORONTO,** 1870-1917—It was built in 1870 to succeed Adelaide Street Methodist Church, north-east corner Toronto and Adelaide streets. The land on which the Metropolitan is situated, "McGill Square," bounded by Bond, Shuter, Church and Queen streets, was part of the estate of Capt. John McGill, who served with the Queen's Rangers under Simcoe. The Metropolitan Church, a graceful building of modern Gothic architecture, is said to resemble St. George's, Sheffield, Eng. Since erection many alterations and improvements have been made. To the left of the church, in picture, may be seen Bond street, and a short distance to the rear, St. Michael's (R. C.) Cathedral. Water color from original drawing by F. B. Schell, for "Picturesque Canada," 1880. Size 5 x 6.

2867—**CALEDONIA, C.W.,** 1863—View from Seneca Hill, on the east side of the Grand River—The village, which is in Haldimand County, Ont., although now included in the limits of one municipality, may be said to consist of two villages, or even three—Caledonia proper, on the north side of the river; South Caledonia, on the south side, straight opposite, and Seneca, about a mile from the Caledonia Bridge, eastward, down the river. on the north side. The principal points shown are: 1. Argyle Street Presbyterian Church. 2. Sutherland Street Presbyterian Church. 3. Town Hall. 4. Scott's Foundry. 5. Roper's Block. 6. Grand River road, Caledonia to Cayuga. 7. Grand River. Drawing in water color from old print. Size 4 x 7.

2868—**WINNIPEG IN 1912**—View from Union Bank Building—Prior to 1870 Winnipeg was merely a trading post of the Hudson's Bay Company. It was incorporated in November, 1873. The completion of the C.P.R. in 1885 gave a wonderful impetus to the Prairie City, which is now (1917), through its growth and expansion, one of the leading cities of Canada. Across the Red River is the town of St. Boniface, seat of the Roman Catholic Archbishop of Manitoba. Reproduction, in color, of original drawing by Harold Copping. Size 6 x 8.

2869—**DOUKHOBOR HOUSE**—Near Veregin, Sask., 1912—The typical Doukhobor house consists of a low framework of wood—very often of slight poles cut from nearby poplar bluffs. This framework is plastered thickly with mud, worked up to the proper consistency with water and chopped straw or hay. The resulting thick walls are whitewashed. outside and inside, and, in some cases, the frames of the doors and windows are rudely carved. Weeds grow in profusion on the poles of the roof, which are covered with a double layer of sods. The furniture is of the most primitive character. Reproduction, in color, of original drawing by Harold Copping. Size 6 x 8.

2870—PAUL, A BLACKFOOT INDIAN—The Blackfeet are considered the best looking of the North American Indian tribes, and belong to the Algonquin Confederacy. They are now (1917) settled on three reservations in Alberta and one in northwest Montana, about half being on each side of the international boundary. Reproduction, in color, of original drawing by Harold Copping. Size 5 x 8. Head and shoulders.

2871—BLACKFOOT CHILD—Seen by the artist on an Alberta Reservation—For many years there have been schools among the Blackfeet. The girls, in addition to being educated in the ordinary sense of the term, are instructed in the rudiments of housekeeping and domestic requirements. The boys also are taught to become useful members of the community, and they have been encouraged to take up agriculture. The pupils are not influenced to live the life of the white man; but rather to return to their people. Thus they exert an influence on the older generation. Often, on returning home, however, they intermarry with Pagan Indians and fall back into the old customs of the tribe; but, though progress has been slow, it has, nevertheless, been real. There is a Blackfoot Home and Hospital near Calgary, Alta. Reproduction, in color, from original drawing by Harold Copping. Size 5 x 8. Head and shoulders.

2872—TYPICAL DOUKHOBOR WOMAN OF THE WEST—When the Doukhobors first emigrated to Canada it was the women who built the new homes, the men having gone to work on railroad construction. Much of the field labor is done by the women, who are also clever in the domestic arts of spinning, weaving and sewing. Reproduction, in color, of original drawing by Harold Copping. Size 6 x 8. Head and shoulders.

2873—MOUNT CAVELL—Named in memory of the martyred Edith Cavell—Situated in Jasper Park, Alberta, 12½ miles from the town of Jasper, and west of the Whirlpool River, six miles above its junction with the Athabaska River. It was named by the Geographic Board of Canada to perpetuate the memory of Miss Edith Cavell, the heroic English nurse, executed in Belgium by the Germans, Oct. 12th, 1915, for harboring allied soldiers and aiding them to escape. An excellent trail has been cut from the C.N.R., giving easy access to the isolated, snowclad peak, which rises to a height of 11,033 feet above the sea level. Water color. Size 6 x 12.

2874—MOUTH OF COBOURG HARBOR, 1880—The town, on the north shore of Lake Ontario, has borne several names. The appellation —Hamilton—was changed to Coburg, in honor of the Prince of Coburg-Gotha, and the spelling was afterwards amplified. The foreground shows the commodious harbor, with the lighthouse, since replaced by a finer structure. The town is shown in the background. Water color from original drawing by H. Fenn, for "Picturesque Canada." Size 5 x 7. See 1731.

2875—LAKE LOUISE—"The Lake in the Clouds"—Nestling near the base of glacier-clad Mount Victoria, at a height of over 5,600 feet above sea level, is Lake Louise, especially lovely because of the varying green tints it shows in different lights and from different points of view. Brilliant wild flowers abound in the neighborhood. Higher up the forest-clad mountain side is Mirror Lake—so called from its wonderful reflections—and still higher is tiny Lake Agnes. A fine cascade falls from the latter to Mirror Lake. Reproduction, in color, of original drawing by Harold Copping. Size 5 x 7.

2876—KITCHEN GARDEN AT VEREGIN, SASK.—In the Doukhobor country—In these gardens are grown a great variety of herbs and vegetables, the Doukhobors being vegetarians. The strange sect sprang up among the peasantry on the southern frontier of Russia in the eighteenth century. Like the Mennonites, they object to military service, and their tenets, meeting with disfavor in Russian Government circles, they were for long subject to persecution, and many were exiled to Siberia. In 1898 permission was granted them to emigrate, and in that year many came to Canada, Tolstoy and others having raised funds to send them to the new land. Settlements were formed in Manitoba and Saskatchewan and community villages organized, with Veregin as headquarters. Recently large numbers have gone as far west as British Columbia. The Doukhobors (Spirit-Wrestlers—a term originally applied in derision), while not readily assimilating, have, through their industry, become exceedingly prosperous since coming to the Dominion. In things temporal and spiritual their leader is Peter Veregin, who exercises a remarkable influence over the people and who, at the time of their first migration to Canada, was an exile in Siberia. Reproduction, in color, of original drawing by Harold Copping. Size 6 x 8.

2877—**NAOMI, PAUL'S WIFE**—Blackfoot Reservation, Alberta, 1912. Reproduction, in color, from original drawing by Harold Copping. Size 5 x 8. Head and shoulders.

2878—**NORTH SASKATCHEWAN RIVER AT EDMONTON**—The North Saskatchewan (Saskatchewan being an abbreviation of the Cree, Kisiskatchewan, meaning "rapid stream") takes its rise in the Rocky Mountains, in a small lake near Mount Forbes. A little east of Prince Albert it joins the South Saskatchewan and flows into Lake Winnipeg, whence it emerges as the Nelson, pouring its waters into Hudson's Bay, Edmonton, an important fur trading post of the early days, and now the capital of the Province of Alberta, is situated on the banks of the North Saskatchewan, to which it owes its prestige. Reproduction, in color, of original drawing by Harold Copping. Size 6 x 9.

2879—**MOON CHUTE, NEAR BALA**, 1912—The waters of the three lakes of the Muskoka district—the playground of Ontario—find their way to Georgian Bay through the Moon and Muskosh Rivers. The latter, which falls into Bala Bay, on the west side of Lake Muskoka, receives the waters of the Moon. Canoeists, in order to go down the Moon River from Bala, have to make a portage at the chute shown in picture. It is a naturally picturesque spot, with tossing waters over a rocky bed, and surrounded by banks of rock crowned with pine. The real nature-lover can find here all he desires. Reproduction, in color, of original drawing by Harold Copping. Size 6 x 8.

2880—**HOUSES OF PARLIAMENT, OTTAWA**, 1912—Overlooking the Ottawa River. Reproduction, in color, of original drawing by Harold Copping. Size 6 x 8. See 1901, 1907.

2881—**KOOTENAY LAKE**—A picturesque bit of lake and shore. Reproduction, in color, of original drawing by Harold Copping. Size 6 x 8.

2882—**COLLINGWOOD HARBOR, NOTTAWASAGA BAY**—From the northwest, looking southeast—With key—Mr. Joel Underwood, an American, was the nominal owner of the land on which Collingwood's first buildings were erected. The place had its beginning in 1852-3 when selected as a terminal of the Ontario, Simcoe and Huron Union Railway, and was incorporated as a town under a local act of the Canadian Legislature, 10th June, 1857. Thus it did not pass through the "village" stage. In that year the first regular line of steamboats, in connection with the railway, was begun. To-day (1917) Collingwood holds a prominent place in the manufacturing and shipping interests of Ontario. Water color from original drawing by Schell and Hogan, for "Picturesque Canada," 1880. Size 4 x 7.

2883—**QUEBEC FROM CHATEAU FRONTENAC**—As seen in the winter of 1912—A magnificent panoramic view may be had from Dufferin Terrace on the margin of which is Chateau Frontenac, the exact site of Chateau St. Louis. In foreground of picture is the Champlain monument, erected to the memory of the founder of Quebec, and unveiled 21st Sept., 1898, by Lord Aberdeen, Governor-General of Canada. Reproduction, in color, of original drawing by Harold Copping. Size 6 x 8.

2884—**BOW RIVER**—The Bow, which rises in the White Goat Range of the Rocky Mountains, together with its many tributaries, adds much to the scenery of the Rocky Mountains National Park. On its emergence from the park it is harnessed to supply energy for transmission to Calgary and other places, to be used for municipal, commercial and industrial purposes. The waters of the Bow are also used in irrigating the Alberta "Dry Belt," many thousands of acres of otherwise useless land having thus been made fertile. Reproduction, in color, of original drawing by Harold Copping. Size 5 x 8.

2885—**GLEICHEN, ALTA.,** 1912—This thriving little place on the C.P.R., fifty-five miles southeast of Calgary, is in an irrigated farming district. The intake of the irrigation system of the Southern Alberta Land Company, which commenced work in 1907, is on the Bow River, twenty-five miles west of Gleichen, a town owning its water and sewerage works. Sixteen thousand cubic yards of concrete were required to put in the dam and intake. The tendency in irrigated districts is to carry on mixed farming, so that the area under cultivation is small, and, therefore, more thickly populated Reproduction, in color, from original drawing by Harold Copping. Size 6 x 8.

2886—**OAK HALL MINES SMELTER, NELSON, B.C.**—"The Old Smelter," as it was known, was completed in 1895, and from time to time was altered to suit it for the treatment of the peculiarly mixed ores (containing gold, silver, copper and lead) obtained from the Silver King and other mines in the district. In 1907 the owners of the properties fell into financial difficulties and the smelter was closed. In September, 1911, the works were fired by an incendiary, and now nothing remains of the "Old Smelter" save a tall chimney, which, at the time it was built, was said to be the largest copper stack on the continent. Reproduction, in color, of original drawing by Harold Copping. Size 6 x 8.

2887—**CASCADE MOUNTAIN, BANFF**—The town of Banff, nestling in the valley of the Bow, it at an altitude of 4,500 feet above sea level, while Cascade Mountain, composed for the most part of grim reddish rocks, with the lower slopes clothed in places with firs. The mountain derives its name from a stream which takes a leap of two thousand feet down the mountain side. While of considerable volume, the height from which it falls makes the stream appear hardly more than a thread against the dark rocks. Snowfilled gullies score the top and sides of the mountain. Reproduction, in color, from original drawing by Harold Copping. Size 5 x 8.

2888—**CAPILANO CANYON**—Near Vancouver, B.C.—Fed by the mountain snows, the Capilano River rushes, clear and pure, along its way, through the narrow, rocky gorge it has worn for itself. The scenery is surpassingly lovely. It is from the Capilano that the city of Vancouver receives its water supply. Reproduction, in color, of original drawing by Harold Copping. Size 6 x 8.

2889—**SCUGOG IN 1853**—On an island in Lake Scugog—The construction of the mill dam at Lindsay turned Scugog Township into an island, which in 1856 became a separate municipality. The view shows:—1,

Mason & Phillips' Hotel. 2 and 3, William Sexton's sawmill. 4, Wm. Ross' mill. 5, Thos. Paxton & Co.'s sawmill. 6, The "Woodman," first steamboat to run from Port Perry to Lindsay. 7, West end Lake Scugog. Water color, from an engraving in the Anglo-American Magazine, 1854. Size 3 x 6.

2890—S. S. "PRUSSIAN"—A Royal Mail steamer of 3,030 tons gross, 500 h.p., built for the Allan Company in 1869 by Robert Steele, of Greenock, Scotland. In the picture the vessel is shown in the Gulf of St. Lawrence, on its way to Quebec, September, 1871. Original pencil drawing by G. Harlow White. Size 3 x 5.

2891—FULL-RIGGED SAILING SHIP—Awaiting repairs at Levis, August 12th, 1876. Original pencil drawing by G. Harlow White. Size 4 x 6.

2892—LEVIS, OPPOSITE QUEBEC—Showing the old buildings partly overhanging the cliff, August 16th, 1876. Original pencil drawing by G. Harlow White. Size 4 x 6.

2893—LEVIS, FROM THE HEIGHTS, AUGUST 16TH, 1876—Showing the Roman Catholic Parish Church of Notre Dame, as well as the square tower of the Presbyterian Church. Original pencil drawing by G. Harlow White. Size 3 x 6.

2894—PICTURESQUE STREAM NEAR ETCHEMIN—Point Levi, Aug., 1876. Original pencil drawing by G. Harlow White. Size 3 x 6.

2895—ALONG THE LEVIS SHORE AT QUEBEC—A riverside view at Indian Cove, August 5th, 1876. Original pencil drawing by G. Harlow White. Size 4 x 6.

2896—HEIGHTS OF LEVIS, AUGUST, 1876—As viewed from the Plains of Abraham, and showing the Grand Trunk Railway terminals at the head of the bay on the Levis shore of the St. Lawrence. Point Levis is on the south shore of the St. Lawrence, opposite Quebec. Beyond the town is a lofty plateau, and it was on this line of heights that Wolfe located the batteries with which he attacked Quebec in 1759. Original pencil drawing by G. Harlow White. Size 4 x 6.

2897—INDIAN COVE, QUEBEC—Showing a spot, three miles from Levis, as it appeared in the summer of 1876. Original pencil drawing by G. Harlow White. Size 4 x 6.

2898—OLD DWELLINGS AT POINT LEVI, OPPOSITE QUEBEC, AUGUST, 1876—A short cut, forming a detour from the Upper Town, is shown in the centre of the foreground. Original pencil drawing by G. Harlow White. Size 3 x 6.

2899—POINT LEVI, AUGUST 25TH—By the side of the St. Lawrence—Above the Grand Trunk Railway station. Original pencil drawing by G. Harlow White. Size 4 x 6.

2900—VIEW OF THE ROCKY BED OF A SMALL STREAM NEAR ETCHEMIN, AUGUST, 1876—Original pencil drawing by G. Harlow White. Size 4 x 6.

2901—POINT LEVI, QUEBEC—View of the shore, Aug. 8th, 1876. Original pencil drawing by G. Harlow White. Size 4 x 6.

2902—MILL SITE OF THE EARLY DAYS ON THE RIDEAU—Original pencil drawing by G. Harlow White, July, 1876. Size 3 x 6.

460

2903—**NORTH VIEW OF OTTAWA RIVER**—From the Library of Parliament, July, 1876—The library, with its handsome pinnacle and vane, is on the right, and on the left is shown the tower of the main building in which the House of Commons meets. In the fire which took place 4th Feb., 1916, the library escaped, but was deluged by water, and the tower for the most part was undamaged. Original pencil drawing by G. Harlow White. Size 3 x 6.

2904—**OTTAWA RIVER. JULY, 1876**—A north-west view, showing the towers of the Dominion Legislative Buildings. Original pencil drawing by G. Harlow White. Size 3 x 6.

2905—**LIBRARY OF PARLIAMENT, OTTAWA, JULY, 1876**—A north view. Original pencil drawing by G. Harlow White. Size 3 x 5.

2906—**OTTAWA RIVER, JULY, 1876**—Showing lumbermen's homes, built of logs and slabs, about three miles from the city. The "tawny Ottawa," which flows through the capital, was known to the early French voyageurs as the Grand River. Although only a tributary to the mighty St. Lawrence, it has been compared in volume to the Danube. Original pencil drawing by G. Harlow White. Size 3 x 6.

2907—**PIONEER HOME ON THE RIDEAU, JULY, 1876**—About a mile from the Dominion capital. Original pencil drawing by G. Harlow White. Size 4 x 6.

2908—**OTTAWA RIVER, JULY, 1876**—Showing an old mill site, with the home of the owner of the mill adjoining. Original pencil drawing by G. Harlow White. Size 4 x 6.

2909—**OLD SAWMILL ON THE RIDEAU RIVER, JULY, 1876**—The Rideau is a beautiful stream, flowing from the south and plunging over a rocky ledge in double, curtain-like falls into the Ottawa, about a mile from the Parliament Buildings. Original pencil drawing by G. Harlow White. Size 3 x 6.

2910—**RIDEAU RIVER, JULY, 1876**—Near Billings' Bridge, two miles south of Ottawa. In the centre of the background is seen the residence of Mr. Billings, on the Osgoode road. Original pencil drawing by G. Harlow White. Size 3 x 6.

2911—**CITY OF HULL, JULY, 1876**—Opposite Ottawa, from below the timber slides in Hull, and on the north side of the river—The crib of square timber in the foreground has just shot down over the first slide south, about fifteen feet from the present offices of the Eddy Paper Company. Original pencil drawing by G. Harlow White. Size 3 x 6.

2912—**OTTAWA RIVER**—North side, showing a row of log buildings in the old town as they stood in July, 1876. Original pencil drawing by G. Harlow White. Size 3 x 6.

2913—**OLD-TIME SAWMILL ON BREWERY CREEK, JULY 29TH, 1876**—Brewery Creek runs into the Ottawa, just below Gilmore's steam mill. Original pencil drawing by G. Harlow White. Size 4 x 6.

2914—**LAKE ONTARIO, NEAR PORT HOPE, JULY, 1876**—The town lies to the left, and the high range of land shown to the north of it is Monkey Mountain. Original pencil drawing by G. Harlow White. Size 3 x 6.

2915—**KINGSTON, ONT., AUGUST, 1876**—From Point Frederick, or Navy Island. Original pencil drawing by G. Harlow White. Size 3 x 6.

2916—THOUSAND ISLES, JULY, 1876—A picturesque spot in the group, which is situated in an expansion of the St. Lawrence at its emergence from Lake Ontario. The archipelago consists of over one thousand five hundred woody and rocky islets, widely famed for their beauty. Original pencil drawing by G. Harlow White. Size 3 x 6.

2917—PORT HOPE, AUG., 1876—On the north shore of Lake Ontario— Depicting the harbor, to the left, and the lighthouse, to the right. The spire of the Anglican Church is also seen. Port Hope is built on the site of the Indian village of Cockingomink, and is some sixty miles east of Toronto. Original pencil drawing by G. Harlow White. Size 3 x 6.

2918—KINGSTON, ONT., AUGUST, 1876—South view from Battery Place on the water front—The City Hall, and tower and steeple of St. George's Church (Anglican Cathedral) are shown. For a time Kingston was the capital of Upper Canada. Original pencil drawing by G. Harlow White. Size 3 x 6.

2919—BROCKVILLE, ONT., JULY, 1876—View from the St. Lawrence River—The town is situated on the left bank of the St. Lawrence, one hundred and twenty-five miles south-west of Montreal, and is now a port of entry and call for the St. Lawrence steamers. In the early days the little settlement was known as "Snarlingtown," because of the quarrelsome nature of some of its inhabitants. It later became Elizabethtown, and was finally named Brockville by Major-General Sir Isaac Brock. Original pencil drawing by G. Harlow White. Size 3 x 6.

2920—POINT LEVI SHORE, AUGUST 4TH, 1876—Bordering on the St. Lawrence, opposite Quebec. Original pencil drawing by G. Harlow White. Size 3 x 6.

2921—PRESCOTT, GRENVILLE COUNTY, ONT., AUG., 1876—On the shore of the St. Lawrence, fifty-seven miles east of Kingston. A short distance below the town is Windmill Point, where stands a lighthouse, originally the ruins of an old stone windmill in which a number of "Patriots" established themselves in the Rebellion of 1837, only to be driven out with heavy loss. Original pencil drawing by G. Harlow White. Size 3 x 6.

2922—AURORA BOREALIS (NORTHERN LIGHTS)—As seen by George Harlow White, March, 1873, in Oro Township, Simcoe County, Ont. Original pencil drawing by G. Harlow White. Size 3 x 6.

2923—RURAL SCENE IN THE TOWNSHIP OF ORO, 1872—Near Shanty Bay. Original pencil drawing by G. Harlow White. Size 3 x 5.

2924—STORM CONQUERED PINE, ORO, FEBRUARY, 1873—Original pencil drawing by G. Harlow White. Size 3 x 5.

2925—LOG CHOPPER'S HUT—Oro Township, April, 1874. Original pencil drawing by G. Harlow White. Size 3 x 5.

2926—ORO, FEBRUARY, 1873—A scene depicting the reign of King Winter in Oro Township. Original pencil drawing by G. Harlow White. Size 3 x 4.

2927—MAKING PINE SHINGLES IN ORO, FEBRUARY, 1873—Curtis, an Oro farmer, is hard at work. The shingle-block is shown ready for riving and cutting. Original pencil drawing by G. Harlow White. Size 3 x 5.

2928—HOMESEEKER'S CLEARING—Oro Township, July, 1873. Original pencil drawing by G. Harlow White. Size 3 x 5.

2929—CAMP OF HARLOW WHITE, ORO TOWNSHIP, SIMCOE COUNTY, JANUARY, 1873—Original pencil drawing by G. Harlow White. Size 3 x 5.

2930—HOME IN SHANTY BAY, ORO TOWNSHIP, 1872—About 1830 Col. Edward George O'Brien was commissioned by the Government to act as agent for the location of negro immigrants in Oro Township, and became a settler there, living in a pretty log cottage at Shanty Bay. On the erection of Simcoe into a county he removed to Toronto with his family. Lucius R. O'Brien, the well-known Canadian artist, was a son of the founder of Shanty Bay. Original pencil drawing by G. Harlow White. Size 3 x 6.

2931—SHANTY BAY, SIMCOE COUNTY—Six miles from Barrie, Ont., on the shore of Lake Simcoe. Original pencil drawing by G. Harlow White. Size 3 x 6.

2932—ROSIE POINT—Near Shanty Bay, Simcoe County, 1872. Original pencil drawing by G. Harlow White. Size 3 x 5.

2933—ORO TOWNSHIP, 1872—Showing a primitive log bridge, near Shanty Bay. Original pencil drawing by G. Harlow White. Size 3 x 5.

2934—"OUR CHICKEN SHANTY"—On a farm in Oro Township. Original pencil drawing by G. Harlow White. Size 3 x 5.

2935—FOREST SHADE, NEAR ORO, JULY, 1873—Original pencil drawing by G. Harlow White. Size 3 x 5.

2936—SNOWBOUND IN MIDWINTER—On Mr. Curtis' farm, Oro Township, January, 1873. Original pencil drawing by G. Harlow White. Size 3 x 5.

2937—SNOW-CLAD PINE STUMP, ORO TOWNSHIP, JANUARY, 1873 —Original pencil drawing by G. Harlow White. Size 3 x 5.

2938—OLD-TIME BARN—On the farm of Mr. Polk, in Oro Township, as it was in 1873. Original pencil drawing by G. Harlow White. Size 3 x 5.

2939—CORDUROY ROAD ON THE SECOND CONCESSION OF ORO TOWNSHIP IN THE SPRING OF 1873—Original pencil drawing by G. Harlow White. Size 3 x 5.

2940—WOODLAND CREEK, ORO TOWNSHIP, 1872—Original pencil drawing by G. Harlow White. Size 3 x 6.

2941—ORO TOWNSHIP, WHEN EVENING FALLS—Showing a picturesque spot sixteen miles from Barrie. as it was in 1872. The name, "Oro," is of African origin, and at one time the Government founded a colored colony in Oro Township. The project, however, was not very successful. During Governor Sir John Colborne's regime many British officers, retired on half pay by the Government of Upper Canada, settled in the township along the beautiful north shore of Lake Simcoe. Settlements of English and Scotch also figure prominently in the early history of the district. Original pencil drawing by G. Harlow White. Size 3 x 5.

2942—PICTURESQUE STREAMLET NEAR ETCHEMIN, AUGUST 16th, 1876—Etchemin is a little village, five miles from Levis, on the south shore of the St. Lawrence. The French name for the river is Bruyante, from the noise it makes before easterly gales. The village is known also as New Liverpool. Original pencil drawing by G. Harlow White. Size 3 x 6.

2943—**WINTER SCENE IN ORO, 1873**—Showing the last of a pine. Original pencil drawing by G. Harlow White. Size 3 x 5.

2944—**ORO, 1873**—A sheltered spot on a creek in the woods. Original pencil drawing by G. Harlow White. Size 3 x 5.

2945—**AT PLAY IN A LOG PILE, ORO, SEPTEMBER, 1872**—The logs are piled ready for burning after clearing the farm land. Original pencil drawing by G. Harlow White. Size 3 x 5.

2946—**ORO TOWNSHIP, FEBRUARY, 1873**—After a storm, showing the logs and upturned roots of trees scattered about on a Muskoka farm. Original pencil drawing by G. Harlow White. Size 3 x 5.

2947—**CLEARING THE LAND**—At one of Oro Township's isolated homes, in the winter of 1872. Original pencil drawing by G. Harlow White. Size 3 x 5.

2948—**WORKING UNDER DIFFICULTIES**—Making pine shingles by hand with a draw knife, in Oro Township, Simcoe County, February, 1873. Original pencil drawing by G. Harlow White. Size 3 x 5.

2949—**SEVERN BRIDGE, SEPTEMBER, 1873**—Where rock abounds. A sketch of one of many parts of Muskoka, showing the burnt country and hardwood trees destroyed by fire. Original pencil drawing by G. Harlow White. Size 3 x 5.

2950—**SPARROW LAKE, SEPTEMBER, 1873**—A marshy spot on the east shore. Sparrow Lake is an extension of the Severn River, in Muskoka, south of the Muskoka Lakes. Original pencil drawing by G. Harlow White. Size 3 x 6.

2951—**COTEAU DU LAC, OR ST. IGNACE, AUGUST 1ST, 1876**—On the River St. Lawrence, three miles from Coteau Landing and thirty-six miles south-west of Montreal. Original pencil drawing by G. Harlow White. Size 3 x 6.

2952—**ORILLIA, 1872**—On the west shore of Lake Couchiching (at the northern extremity of Lake Simcoe)—To the right is the town park, on the north-west point of the bay. Original pencil drawing by G. Harlow White. Size 3 x 5.

2953—**SAWMILL AT WASHAGO, SEPTEMBER, 1873**—A quaint old mill at the outlet of Lake Couchiching into the River Severn. Original pencil drawing by G. Harlow White. Size 3 x 5.

2954—**BASKET MAKING AT THE CHIPPAWA ENCAMPMENT AT RAMA, LAKE COUCHICHING, AUGUST, 1874**—There is a reservation here, occupied by the remnant of a once numerous tribe. Original pencil drawing by G. Harlow White. Size 3 x 5.

2955—**LAKE COUCHICHING, SEPTEMBER, 1873**—Showing a bit of marsh in an inlet off the lake. Original pencil drawing by G. Harlow White. Size 3 x 5.

2956—**LAKE COUCHICHING, OCTOBER, 1872**—Showing the south-west point of Chief Island, from the "Ida Burton." This beautiful Simcoe County lake is about twelve miles long, and is connected with Lake Simcoe by a channel, known as the "Narrows." Original pencil drawing by G. Harlow White. Size 3 x 5.

2957—**RAMA, SEPTEMBER, 1876**—Showing the Chippawa camp in the early autumn. Original pencil drawing by G. Harlow White. Size 3 x 6.

32

2958—RAMA, SEPTEMBER, 1876—Preparing the evening meal at the Chippawa camp at Rama, on Lake Couchiching, seven miles north-west of Orillia, the reservation of the last of the Ojibway Indians, who at one time were very numerous in the locality. Original pencil drawing by G. Harlow White. Size 3 x 6.

2959—LAKE COUCHICHING, OCTOBER, 1872—From Washago, Simcoe County, Ont.—An Indian summer scene. Original pencil drawing by G. Harlow White. Size 3 x 5.

2960—WASHAGO, SEPTEMBER, 1872—The road leading to Washago, a village in Simcoe County, Ont., at the outlet of Lake Couchiching into the Severn River, twelve miles from Orillia. Original pencil drawing by G. Harlow White. Size 3 x 5.

2961—HOME BY THE WAYSIDE, SEPTEMBER, 1873—A view on the high road from Washago to Gravenhurst. Original pencil drawing by G. Harlow White. Size 3 x 5.

2962—LONGFORD, SIMCOE COUNTY, AUGUST, 1875—South side of Lake St. John. Original pencil drawing by G. Harlow White. Size 3 x 5.

2963—LONELY SPOT NEAR SEVERN BRIDGE, SEPTEMBER, 1873—Severn Bridge is a picturesque little village in Ontario County, Ont., four miles from Sparrow Lake. Original pencil drawing by G. Harlow White. Size 3 x 5.

2964—QUEBEC, FROM POINT LEVIS, AUGUST, 1876—The wharf and store of the Quebec Warehouse Company at Levis is shown in the foreground. The high building on the point of Quebec is Laval University. Original pencil drawing by G. Harlow White. Size 3 x 6.

2965—NORTH-WEST CORNER OF THE OLD CHAMPLAIN MARKET PLACE, QUEBEC, 1876—The market stands between Little Champlain street and the St. Lawrence, near the wharves of the river steamers. Original pencil drawing by G. Harlow White. Size 4 x 6.

2966—SHIP BEACHED AT HIGH TIDE AT BEAUPORT—Across the bay from Quebec, August 11th, 1876—Here many a ship which has outlived its usefulness, has been beached at high tide, to be stripped of all that remains on it of any value, and then to be set on fire and burned for the sake of the old metal that may remain. Original pencil drawing by G. Harlow White. Size 4 x 6.

2967—TWIN-FACED MONUMENT IN MEMORY OF WOLFE AND MONTCALM—Erected in the Governor's Garden at Quebec in 1827-8. The idea of erecting a memorial to the two generals who died so bravely while contending for the possession of Canada for their respective countries, originated with Lord Dalhousie, then Governor-General of Canada. The monument is strictly classical in its proportions, and on the front of the sarcophagus is carved a Latin inscription, the translation of which is: "Valor gave them a common death, history a common fame, and posterity a common monument." Original pencil drawing by G. Harlow White. Size 3 x 6. See 1819, 2078.

2968—VIEW FROM THE RAMPARTS, NEAR LAVAL UNIVERSITY, QUEBEC—As the scene appeared, August 7th, 1876, looking over the fortification wall and a portion of the Lower Town. Original pencil drawing by G. Harlow White. Size 3 x 6.

2969—OLD HOUSES AT CAP BLANC, QUEBEC—On the Quebec side of the river, under the cliff, about midway from the Lower Town to Wolfe's Côve. Original pencil drawing by G. Harlow White, Aug. 3rd, 1876. Size 3 x 6.

2970—QUEBEC—From the beach at Levis, as it appeared, August 5th, 1876—The picture represents that part of the city east of the ferry landing, at low water. Original pencil drawing by G. Harlow White. Size 3 x 5.

2971—LAVAL UNIVERSITY, QUEBEC, AUGUST, 1876—The Seminary was founded in 1663 by Mgr. de Montmorency Laval, the first Roman Catholic Bishop of Canada (Quebec). The original building was destroyed by fire in 1701. In 1852 the university received its royal charter and thereupon became known as Laval. The library, with the exception of that of the Dominion Parliament at Ottawa, is the largest in Canada, and contains valuable MSS. pertaining to the early history of the country. There is also a valuable art gallery in connection with the historic seat of learning. The view is from Mountain Hill; in the distance is seen the dome of the Customs House, and a portion of the Laurentians is shown rising in the rear of Beauport. The water between is that part of the St. Lawrence which expands into a bay just beyond the mouth of the St. Charles. Original pencil drawing by G. Harlow White. Size 4 x 6.

2972—MONUMENT ERECTED IN MEMORY OF WOLFE—By the British army, on the Plains of Abraham, Que., in 1849, on the exact spot where Wolfe died in 1759—In 1913 the National Battlefields Commission had the monument rebuilt in granite instead of limestone, on the old site, but on a raised foundation. The new pillar is an exact replica of the old, and shows three bronzes, one bearing the inscription, "Here died Wolfe victorious," the second, placed by the British troops when the original broken column was replaced by the stone pillar in 1849, and the third giving the details of the 1913 rebuilding. Original pencil drawing by G. Harlow White. Size 4 x 6.

2973—VALLEY OF THE ST. CHARLES, QUE.—The River St. Charles, first named by Jacques Cartier, in 1535, the St. Croix, takes its rise in Stoneham Township and flows into the St. Lawrence at Quebec. The Indians call this river "Cubir Coubat," because of its windings and meanderings. Original pencil drawing by G. Harlow White. Size 3 x 6.

2974—HOPE HILL, QUEBEC, AUGUST, 1876—Near the head of the hill, on the northern face of the ramparts, stood the first of the two purely British gates of Quebec. It was erected in 1786 by Col. Henry Hope, Commandant of the Forces and Administrator of the Province of Canada. In 1823 it was altered, and again in 1832. In 1874 it was demolished. Original pencil drawing by G. Harlow White. Size 3 x 6.

2975—NARROWING OF THE SEVERN RIVER—Below Sparrow Lake, September, 1873. Original pencil drawing by G. Harlow White. Size 3 x 5.

2976—LAKE OF BAYS, JULY, 1875—An outlet into the south branch of the Muskoka River. Original pencil drawing by G. Harlow White. Size 3 x 6.

2977—LAKE OF BAYS—Entrance to the North Bay, coming from the Portage to Peninsular Lake, south branch of the Muskoka River. Original pencil drawing by G. Harlow White. Size 3 x 5.

2978—AFTERNOON QUIETUDE, TRADING LAKE, JULY 26TH, 1875—Trading Lake is a small body of water, separated from Lake of Bays by a narrows, some two, or three and a half miles long. Original pencil drawing by G. Harlow White. Size 3 x 6.

2979—LAKE OF BAYS, JULY, 1875—A bay near the outlet of the lake. Original pencil drawing by G. Harlow White. Size 3 x 6.

2980—LAKE OF BAYS, 27TH JULY, 1875—Looking west from about the centre of the lake, near Blow Point. Original pencil drawing by G. Harlow White. Size 3 x 6.

2981—JOYS OF CAMP LIFE—Trading Lake, July 27th, 1875. Original pencil drawing by G. Harlow White. Size 3 x 5.

2982—LAKE OF BAYS, JULY 27TH, 1875—Rocks and ripples on North Bay, Lake of Bays. Original pencil drawing by G. Harlow White. Size 3 x 5.

2983—CHIEF ISLAND, LAKE OF BAYS, JULY, 1875—The lake is a curiously formed sheet of water on the Muskoka River, near Baysville, dotted with a number of islands. On its bay-indented shores are forests of pine and hardwood. For a number of years it was known as Trading Lake, possibly because the Indians had a trading post on Bigwin Island, or it may have been that it was confused with the real Trading Lake, just east of it. Original pencil drawing by G. Harlow White. Size 3 x 6.

2984—HAMLET ON THE BAY SHORE NEAR PENETANGUISHENE, SEPTEMBER, 1876—Original pencil drawing by G. Harlow White. Size 3 x 6.

2985—SAWMILL NEAR PENETANGUISHENE, SEPTEMBER, 1876— On an inlet of Lake Huron, forty miles north of Barrie. Original pencil drawing by G. Harlow White. Size 3 x 6.

2986—AT THE OLD MILL, PENETANGUISHENE, SEPTEMBER, 1876—Original pencil drawing by G. Harlow White. Size 3 x 6.

2987—PENETANGUISHENE, SEPT., 1876—Original pencil drawing by G. Harlow White. Size 3 x 6.

2988—EAST RIVER, AUGUST, 1875—Four miles north of Huntsville, on the east side. The river flows into Vernon Lake. Original pencil drawing by G. Harlow White. Size 3 x 6.

2989—BIG EAST RIVER, AUGUST, 1875—A timber jam four miles from the mouth of the Big East River, near where the Government Colonization road crosses. It is now all cleared land. Original pencil drawing by G. Harlow White. Size 3 x 6.

2990—EAST RIVER, AUGUST, 1875—Showing the timber locked and jammed on the river. Original pencil drawing by G. Harlow White. Size 3 x 6.

2991—EAST RIVER—A timber jam some miles from the outlet of the East River, August, 1875. Original pencil drawing by G. Harlow White. Size 3 x 5.

2992—HOME OF COL. MATTHEW ELLIOTT—On the River road, below Amherstburg—Matthew Elliott, who had served in the Revolutionary War, was granted 2,500 acres of land in Malden Township by the British Government. With a number of slaves from Virginia, he took up his residence in Canada, below the site of the present Amherstburg, and there the erection of his homestead was immediately begun. Col. Elliott, who was first Superintendent of Indian Affairs in Western Ontario, was an Irishman, educated for the priesthood. He was a personal friend of Brock and Proctor, and at the old Elliott home Brock first met Tecumseh. At eighty years of age Col. Elliott commanded the Indians at the assault on Fort Niagara, 1813. The house, the present (1917) site of which is Elliott's Point, near where the Detroit River empties into Lake Erie, is in ruins, as are also the slave quarters. The property is owned by W. C. Webber, of Detroit, Mich. Water color. Size 4 x 6.

2993—TRENTON, ONT., 1871—A town on the Trent River—The view shows (1) S. S. Young's block. (2) Aberdeen Hotel, now the King George. (3) The James Bros.' workshop. (4) W. D. Matthew's elevator. (5) Rathbun boarding house. (6) Boom piers. (7) Gilmour & Co.'s upper office. Bunker Hill in distance. (8) Boom of logs rafted for floating to Rathbun & Co.'s, Deseronto. Water color. Size 5 x 14.

2994—SOLDIERS' MONUMENT AT AMHERSTBURG, ONT.—It stands at the entrance of Christ Church (Anglican) graveyard, Gore street, and was erected by the inhabitants of Amherstburg "In memory of Thomas McCurtan, Samuel Holmes, Edwin Miller and Thomas Symonds, of H.M. 32d Regt. of Foot, and of Thomas Parish, of the St. Thomas Volunteer Cavalry, who gloriously fell in repelling a band of Brigands from Pelee Island, third of March, 1838." Towards the end of February, 1838, some hundreds of Patriots took possession of Point Pelee Island, belonging to Canada, about thirty-five miles south-east of Amherstburg and eighteen from the mainland. A few British regulars had come from Lower Canada, and they, with Canadian militia, crossed the ice from the mainland to the island. A sharp encounter ensued, which resulted in considerable loss to the invaders, who soon retired to the States. There was comparative quiet on the western frontier for a time after this event. Water color. Size 5 x 5.

2995—BAILEY'S SHANTY, HUNTSVILLE, JULY, 1875—The shanty was built by Alexander Bailey for trading with the Indians. It is on the river between Vernon and Fairy Lakes, half a mile from Huntsville. Original pencil drawing by G. Harlow White. Size 3 x 6.

2996—HUNTSVILLE, ONT., 1875—Centre of present town, on the south side of the Muskoka River. Original pencil drawing by G. Harlow White. Size 3 x 5.

2997—HUNTSVILLE, AUGUST, 1875—A one-time home which occupied a spot in the centre of the site on which Huntsville is now built. Original pencil drawing by G. Harlow White. Size 3 x 6.

2998—THROUGH THE FOREST—Showing a corduroy bridge on the Chaffey road, north of Huntsville, August, 1875. Original pencil drawing by G. Harlow White. Size 3 x 6.

2999—SHADES OF NIGHT IN THE FOREST, HUNTSVILLE, JULY, 1874—The town of Huntsville is charmingly situated between Vernon and Fairy Lakes, two of the chain of lakes on the Muskoka River. Original pencil drawing by G. Harlow White. Size 3 x 5.

3000—MUSKOKA, OCTOBER 16TH, 1872—Autumn among the hills of Macaulay Township. Original pencil drawing by G. Harlow White. Size 3 x 5.

3001—MUSKOKA CLEARING, AUGUST, 1875—Part of the present town of Huntsville is built on this site. Original pencil drawing by G. Harlow White. Size 3 x 6.

3002—PIONEER HOME IN HUNTSVILLE, AUGUST, 1875—Built by an early northland pioneer. Original pencil drawing by G. Harlow White. Size 3 x 6.

3003—BEAVER MEADOW IN THE HUNTSVILLE DISTRICT, JULY, 1875—Original pencil drawing by G. Harlow White. Size 3 x 5.

3004—HUNT'S SHANTY, JULY 21, 1875—G. L. Hunt owned the land and built this log house on the west side of the Muskoka River, now the site of the town of Huntsville. Original pencil drawing by G. Harlow White. Size 3 x 6.

3005—**FALLEN BRIDGE**—Crossing a creek north of Huntsville, July, 1875. Original pencil drawing by G. Harlow White. Size 3 x 6.

3006—**GLIMPSE OF FOREST AND STREAM**—On the Chaffey road, north of Huntsville, August, 1875. Original pencil drawing by G. Harlow White. Size 3 x 5.

3007—**BRIDGE OVER THE MUSKOKA RIVER**—Near Huntsville, August, 1875. Original pencil drawing by G. Harlow White. Size 3 x 6.

3008—**SYLVAN WALK**—Glimpse of a forest road between Bracebridge and Huntsville, July 25th, 1875. Original pencil drawing by G. Harlow White. Size 3x 5.

3009—**INTERIOR OF A SETTLER'S SHANTY NEAR HUNTSVILLE**— Original pencil drawing by G. Harlow White. Size 3 x 5.

3010—**BRUCE MINES, ALGOMA**—On the north shore of Lake Huron, opposite the east end of the Island of St. Joseph. Pencil drawing by George Harlow White, from original by Mr. Fleming (afterwards Sir Sandford) of the C.P.R. survey service. Size 3 x 5.

3011—**NEPIGON RIVER, THUNDER BAY DISTRICT**—View looking toward Nepigon Bay, 1876. This river, which issues from the south-east side of Lake Nepigon, is the largest stream flowing into Lake Superior. Original pencil drawing by G. Harlow White. Size 3 x 5.

3012—**MOOSE MOUNTAIN**, 1876—Nepigon Bay, Lake Superior. Original pencil drawing by G. Harlow White. Size 3 x 5.

3013—**SAULT STE. MARIE, ONT.**, 1876—On St. Mary's Strait, where Lake Simcoe flows into Lake Huron, at the boundary line of Canada and the United States. Original pencil drawing by G. Harlow White. Size 3 x 5.

3014—**ENTRANCE TO THUNDER BAY**—The bay is at the head of Lake Superior and is surrounded by high headlands and islands, forming such a well protected harbor that an ordinary sail boat can safely ride at anchor there in any gale. The shores are rich in silver and copper. Original pencil drawing by G. Harlow White. Size 3 x 5.

3015—**LAKE SHEBANDOWAN**, 1876—This lake is situated forty-five miles west of Thunder Bay, at the head of Lake Superior. Original pencil drawing by G. Harlow White. Size 3 x 5.

3016—**TORONTO, JUNE**, 1871—Showing the Northern Railway wharf and elevator and the waterfront at the foot of Brock street (Spadina ave.) The Island is seen to the right. Original pencil drawing by G. Harlow White. Size 3 x 5.

3017—**TORONTO BAY AND CITY, AUGUST**, 1876—A view from the centre of the Bay, looking west—Note the sandbar south of Queen's Wharf entrance, on the left, and the Northern Elevator, on the Bay front. The spire of St. James' Cathedral is also shown. Original pencil drawing by G. Harlow White. Size 3 x 6.

3018—**NIAGARA FALLS, CANADIAN SIDE**, 1871—From the River road—About fourteen miles from the point at which the Niagara River enters Lake Ontario, the rushing waters fall over an almost perpendicular precipice, some one hundred and sixty feet in height. By the interposition of two islands the river is separated into three falls, the Great Horseshoe on the Canadian side, and those of Fort Schlosser and Montmorency (the latter so called because of its nearness in size to the fall of that name in Quebec) on the American side. Original pencil drawing by G. Harlow White. Size 3 x 5.

3019—**ENTRANCE TO FAIRY LAKE, JULY,** 1875—On a branch of the Muskoka River, near Huntsville. Several islands add to the beauty of the charming bit of water. Original pencil drawing by G. Harlow White. Size 3 x 6.

3020—**FAIRY LAKE, JULY,** 1875—Looking east and down the river from the mouth of the Muskoka River. Original pencil drawing by G. Harlow White. Size 3 x 6.

3021—**FAIRY LAKE, JULY 21ST,** 1875—A view of the east end of the lake. Original pencil drawing by G. Harlow White. Size 3 x 6.

3022—**FAIRY LAKE, JULY 25TH,** 1875—Looking south from the centre of the lake—The log house of Mr. Chaffey is seen on the left. Original pencil drawing by G. Harlow White. Size 3 x 5.

3023—**FAIRY LAKE, JULY,** 1875—A rocky spot on the shore, near the east end of the lake. Original pencil drawing by G. Harlow White. Size 3 x 5.

3024—**SEVERN RIVER, SEPTEMBER,** 1873—Where the shadows fall— A beautiful spot on the Severn. This river flows through some charming country between Simcoe County and Muskoka. The even tenor of its way is varied by a number of rapids and falls. Original pencil drawing by G. Harlow White. Size 3 x 6.

3025—**FAIRY LAKE, AUGUST,** 1875—At the extreme east end of the lake near the entrance to Peninsular Creek. Original pencil drawing by G. Harlow White. Size 3 x 6.

3026—**WHERE BOATING IS A PLEASURE**—On the main expanse of Fairy Lake, July, 1875. Original pencil drawing by G. Harlow White. Size 3 x 6.

3027—**FAIRY LAKE, JULY,** 1875—Sunshine and shadow on a bay in the lake. Original pencil drawing by G. Harlow White. Size 3 x 6.

3028—**FAIRY LAKE, JULY,** 1875—A view of the whole lake from near the west end. In the background is the township of Brunel. Original pencil drawing by G. Harlow White. Size 3 x 5.

3029—**FAIRY LAKE, JULY,** 1875—A secluded bay near the east end of the lake. Original pencil drawing by G. Harlow White. Size 3 x 6.

3030—**FAIRY LAKE, TOWNSHIP OF BRUNEL, AUGUST,** 1875—A bay at the east end of the lake. Original pencil drawing by G. Harlow White. Size 3 x 5.

3031—**UTTERSON, AUGUST,** 1875—On the Inland River, between Bracebridge and Huntsville. Original pencil drawing by G. Harlow White. Size 3 x 5.

3032—**FALLS ON INDIAN RIVER, AUGUST,** 1874—Indian River is a winding stream connecting Lake Muskoka and Lake Rosseau. Original pencil drawing by G. Harlow White. Size 3 x 6.

3033—**MARY LAKE, AUGUST 9TH,** 1875—This lake is a pretty little island-studded bit of water in the Lake of Bays district, near Port Sydney. Original pencil drawing by G. Harlow White. Size 3 x 5.

3034—MARY LAKE, AUGUST, 1875—Showing the islands and bluffs near the south end of the lake. Original pencil drawing by G. Harlow White. Size 3 x 5.

3035—MARY LAKE, AUGUST, 1875—An outlet of the lake—Showing an island close to the mouth of the Muskoka River. Original pencil drawing by G. Harlow White. Size 3 x 6.

3036—MARY LAKE, AUGUST, 1875—The west end of the lake, at the point where the Colonization road reaches its waters. Original pencil drawing by G. Harlow White. Size 3 x 6.

3037—MARY LAKE, AUGUST, 1875—Where the Muskoka River enters at head of lake. Original pencil drawing by G. Harlow White. Size 3 x 6.

3038—MARY LAKE, AUGUST 9TH, 1875—Another bit of landscape, near the south end of the lake. The Ontario Government Colonization road is shown running about east from Utterson to Mary Lake. Original pencil drawing by G. Harlow White. Size 3 x 5.

3039—MARY LAKE, AUGUST, 1875—A view of the shore line. Original pencil drawing by G. Harlow White. Size 3 x 6.

3040—MARY LAKE, AUGUST, 1875—Showing Port Sydney, a village on Mary Lake—From the Utterson River, south end of Lake Muskoka, three miles from Utterson. Mary Lake empties into the north branch of the Muskoka River. Original pencil drawing by G. Harlow White. Size 3 x 5.

3041—WINTER SCENE NEAR BARRIE—Looking towards the southeast, in the winter of 1870. Original pencil drawing by G. Harlow White. Size 3 x 5.

3042—COVES IN KEMPENFELDT BAY—Near Barrie, 1872. Original pencil drawing by G. Harlow White. Size 3 x 5.

3043—HOME OF HARLOW WHITE—On the north shore of Kempenfeldt Bay, near Barrie, 1876. Original pencil drawing by G. Harlow White. Size 3 x 6.

3044—LAKE SIMCOE, 1872—View on the north shore, five miles from Barrie. Original pencil drawing by G. Harlow White. Size 3 x 5.

3045—LAKE SIMCOE—Where nature reigns—A pretty spot on the north shore of Lake Simcoe, near Barrie, 1872. Original pencil drawing by G. Harlow White. Size 3 x 5.

3046—"WOODLANDS," SHANTY BAY—A private summer residence, five and a half miles from Barrie, on the north side of Kempenfeldt Bay, Lake Simcoe. It was built by Mr. Richard Powers and subsequently occupied by the late Mr. Dugald Crawford, of Toronto, and others. It is now the summer residence of Mr. Frederic Nicholls, of Toronto. Original pencil drawing by G. Harlow White. Size 3 x 6.

3047—YELLOWHEAD PASS, B.C., 1876—Showing Yellowhead Lake, five miles west of the summit of the Pass. Original pencil drawing by G. Harlow White. Size 3 x 5.

3048—MOUNT MILTON—From Albreda Lake, Rocky Mountains. This lake is situated near the head of the waters of the North Thompson River, and is twenty-five miles south of Tete Jeune Cache, at the summit of the pass of the waters of the Fraser River to those of the North Thompson. Original pencil drawing by G. Harlow White, Oct., 1876. Size 3 x 5.

3049—SALMON COVE, B.C., OCTOBER, 1876—Situated on the Nass River, a stream emptying into Observatory Inlet, and forty-five miles north-east of Prince Rupert. It is a salmon canning centre. It was at Salmon Cove that Captain George Vancouver, R.N., set up his observatory in 1793 to correct his positions in the neighborhood, and to ascertain the rates of his chronometers. Original pencil drawing by G. Harlow White. Size 3 x 4.

3050—SOUTH SASKATCHEWAN RIVER, OCTOBER, 1876—A typical scene on one of Canada's great rivers. The Saskatchewan takes its rise in a small lake near Mount Forbes in the Rockies. Original pencil drawing by G. Harlow White. Size 3 x 5.

3051—LYTTON, B.C.—Towering Heights—A scene depicting the old Caribou road between Lytton and Ashcroft, B.C., October, 1876. Original pencil drawing by G. Harlow White. Size 3 x 4.

3052—YELLOWHEAD LAKE, B.C., 1876—A few miles west of the summit of Yellowhead Pass, near the sources of the Fraser. Original pencil drawing by G. Harlow White. Size 3 x 4.

3053—YALE, B.C., 1876—An old British Columbia trading town on the Fraser River, finely situated on a bench at the foot of the mountains, at the head of navigation of the Lower Fraser. Original pencil drawing by G. Harlow White. Size 3 x 5.

3054—THOMPSON RIVER, ROCKY MOUNTAINS, OCTOBER, 1876— A bend in the river above Lytton, B.C.—A typical view. Original pencil drawing by G. Harlow White. Size 3 x 4.

3055—NORTH THOMPSON RIVER, B.C., OCTOBER, 1876—In its mountain home, just above its junction with the Clearwater River. Original pencil drawing by G. Harlow White. Size 3 x 5.

3056—SAVONA'S FERRY, B.C., OCTOBER, 1876—The Ferry, now only a small village, is situated near the outlet of Kamloops Lake, and is twenty-five miles west of Kamloops. Original pencil drawing by G. Harlow White. Size 3 x 5.

3057—PEACE RIVER, OCTOBER, 1876—At Fort Dunvegan, a Hudson's Bay post in the Peace River country, two hundred and fifty miles north-west of Edmonton, consisting of the company's office and a few dwellings. Original pencil drawing by G. Harlow White. Size 3 x 5.

3058—JASPER LAKE, OCTOBER, 1876—This lake is an expansion of the Athabasca River, and is situated two hundred and twenty-five miles west of Edmonton. It is very deep and one of the most beautiful in the Western country. Original pencil drawing by G. Harlow White. Size 3 x 5.

3059—SKEENA RIVER, B.C., OCTOBER, 1876—Showing Port Essington, a small fishing town—The mountains are seen in the background. On the authority of Dr. Ridley, the late Bishop of Caledonia, Skeena is an adaptation of "K'shian," the Tsimshian name for the river, meaning a "divide." The Skeena was known to the traders of 1787 or thereabouts, as Ayton's River. In July, 1793, its estuary and neighborhood were examined by the master of the "Discovery," Mr. Whidbey, who, concluding that the stream was unimportant, did not explore it further than the Raspberry Islands (so named by him). Original pencil drawing by G. Harlow White. Size 3 x 5.

3060—**ROBSON PEAK, OCTOBER,** 1876—This is the highest peak in the Canadian Rockies, being 11,700 feet above the sea level. It is situated on the Fraser River, fifteen miles north-east of Tete Jeune Cache. Original pencil drawing by G. Harlow White. Size 3 x 5.

3061—**OLD HOUSES AT OTTAWA**—On the shore of the river, a short distance from the city, July, 1875. Original pencil drawing by G. Harlow White. Size 3 x 6.

3062—**NORTH THOMPSON RIVER, B.C., OCTOBER,** 1876—Mountain fastnesses at the confluence of the Muddy (Mad) River and the North Thompson. Original pencil drawing by G. Harlow White. Size 3 x 5.

3063—**ROCKY MOUNTAINS**—Showing the point at which the Athabasca River issues from the mountains, sixty miles west of Edson, a divisional point on the Grand Trunk Pacific Railway. Original pencil drawing by G. Harlow White. Size 3 x 5.

3064—**HOMATHCA RIVER, NOVEMBER,** 1876—Below the defile, near the head of Bute Inlet, and looking towards the Pacific Ocean—The river takes its rise in a small British Columbia lake and flows in a southerly direction, emptying into Bute Inlet in the Strait or Gulf of Georgia. Original pencil drawing by G. Harlow White. Size 3 x 5.

3065—**A CENTURY OF YACHTS ON LAKE ONTARIO,** 1795-1911— Including many famous vessels of the Royal Canadian Yacht Club, Toronto —These are exact drawings of representative craft of different periods in the history of lake sailing, beginning with the "King's Yacht," mentioned by the Duke de Rochefoucauld de Liancourt in 1795, and ending with the "Patricia," winner of the Yacht Racing Union International trophy, 1912. The dates given with each name refer to the first appearance of each yacht. Water color on pencil drawing by C. H. J. Snider. Size 12 x 54.

3066—**ROYAL CANADIAN YACHT CLUB FLAGS,** 1914—Including officers' flags and club ensign. Water colors. Size (each) 2 x 3. See 3067.

3067—**TORONTO YACHT CLUB FLAGS,** 1853—This club was formed in 1852 as the Toronto Boat Club, with T. J. Robertson as captain and J. B. Jones as lieutenant. In July, 1853, it was decided to change the name of the Toronto Yacht Club. Subsequently it became the Canadian Yacht Club, and in 1854 permission was obtained through the Governor-General, Sir Edmund W. Head, from her Majesty Queen Victoria's Secretary of State to use the term Royal. It was incorporated under its new name, "The Royal Canadian Yacht Club," in 1868, and ten years later the Admiralty permitted the members to wear, on board their respective vessels, the blue ensign of her Majesty's fleet, with a crown on the fly. Water colors. Size (each) 2 x 3. See 3066.

3068—**VERNON RIVER, JULY,** 1875—A well wooded bank between Vernon and Fairy Lakes. Original pencil drawing by G. Harlow White. Size 3 x 6.

3069—**LAKE VERNON, JULY,** 1875—Showing a small bay in the main body of the lake, a mile and a half from Huntsville. Original pencil drawing by G. Harlow White. Size 3 x 5.

3070—**CLEARING AT THE EAST END OF LAKE VERNON**—Original pencil drawing by G. Harlow White. Size 3 x 5.

3071—**ASHORE AT AN OUTLET OF LAKE VERNON, JULY,** 1875— Lake Vernon is a large and beautiful lake in Muskoka district, near Hoodstown, having water connections with Fairy and Peninsular Lakes and Lake of Bays. Original pencil drawing by G. Harlow White. Size 3 x 6.

3072—**VERNON LAKE, JULY, 1875**—The north side of the lake, where the east branch of the Muskoka River enters it. Original pencil drawing by G. Harlow White. Size 3 x 6.

3073—**VERNON RIVER, JULY, 1875**—Where Huntsville now stands. Original pencil drawing by G. Harlow White. Size 3 x 6.

3074—**VERNON RIVER, AUGUST, 1875**—A bay on the stream, about a mile from Huntsville. Original pencil drawing by G. Harlow White Size 3x6.

3075—**LAKE VERNON, JULY, 1875**—Depicting the west end. Original pencil drawing by G. Harlow White. Size 3 x 5.

3076—**VERNON RIVER, JULY, 1875**—Shadows long and cool—between Vernon and Fairy Lakes. Original pencil drawing by G. Harlow White. Size 3 x 6.

3077—**VERNON RIVER, JULY 22ND, 1875**—Near the old Indian farm, where the river leaves the lake. Original pencil drawing by G. Harlow White. Size 3 x 6.

3078—**CANOEING ON LAKE VERNON, JULY, 1875**—A favorite Muskoka pastime. Original pencil drawing by G. Harlow White. Size 3 x 5.

3079—**LAKE VERNON, JULY, 1875**—A sheltered bay on the lake, on the north branch of the Muskoka River. Original pencil drawing by G. Harlow White. Size 3 x 6.

3080—**SPARROW LAKE, SEPTEMBER, 1873**—The lake, which is fourteen miles north of Orillia, near Severn Station, is a beautiful sheet of water, sometimes called "one of the gems of the Highlands" of Muskoka. Original pencil drawing by G. Harlow White. Size 3 x 5.

3081—**VERNON LAKE, JULY 29th., 1875**—A bay on the south shore. Original pencil drawing by G. Harlow White. Size 3 x 6.

3082—**VERNON RIVER, AUGUST 3rd, 1875**—A stretch of river near Huntsville. Original pencil drawing by G. Harlow White. Size 3 x 6.

3083—**VESPRA**—A fringe of young pines on the shore of Lake Simcoe, May, 1874. Original pencil drawing by G. Harlow White. Size 3 x 6.

3084—**MIDSUMMER SCENE**—In the Township of Vespra, Simcoe County, August, 1872. Original pencil drawing by G. Harlow White. Size 3 x 5.

3085—**PICTURESQUE LUMBER MILL AT CRAIGHURST, 1872**—Craighurst, thirteen miles from Barrie, was originally known as Morrison's Corners, receiving the latter name from a pioneer settler, James Morrison, who kept the first tavern at the settlement, and built the first mill there. He was also the originator of the line of stages along the Penetanguishene road. The place was subsequently named Craighurst, after the Craig family, who settled in the district in 1821. Original pencil drawing by G. Harlow White. Size 3 x 5.

3086—**VESPRA IN SPRINGTIME**—A group of young pines, May, 1874. Original pencil drawing by G. Harlow White. Size 3 x 6.

3087—**VESPRA TOWNSHIP, SIMCOE COUNTY**—From the Penetanguishene road, August, 1872. Original pencil drawing by G. Harlow White. Size 3 x 5.

3088—FLESHERTON, GREY COUNTY—On a branch of the Beaver River, showing the old lumber mills to the right, July, 1875. Original pencil drawing by G. Harlow White. Size 3 x 5.

3089—EUGENIA, JULY, 1875—A busy afternoon at the lumber mill. Original pencil drawing by G. Harlow White. Size 3 x 6. See 3090.

3090—EUGENIA, JULY, 1875—When work is over at the lumber mill, Original pencil drawing by G. Harlow White. Size 3 x 4. See 3089.

3091—OVERLOOKING THE OTTAWA RIVER, JULY 31ST, 1876— The view shows a storehouse of the early days at Bytown (Ottawa). Original pencil drawing by G. Harlow White. Size 3 x 3.

3092—HEAD OF EUGENIA FALLS, JULY, 1875—The scene has vastly changed since the artist visited it. Dams have been thrown across the country near the falls, to create a lake, some 2,000 acres in area, and containing over a thousand million gallons of water at maximum depth. The plant at Eugenia was the second constructed by the Ontario Hydro Commission. Original pencil drawing by G. Harlow White. Size 3 x 6.

3093—FOREST SCENE NEAR EUGENIA, GREY COUNTY, JULY, 1875—Eugenia is a pretty little village on the Beaver River, five miles from Flesherton. Original pencil drawing by G. Harlow White. Size 3 x 5.

3094—FALLS OF MONTMORENCY, QUE.—View from the easterly side, showing the greater portion of the Falls. Aug. 21st, 1876. Original pencil drawing by G. Harlow White. Size 4 x 6.

3095—CHAUDIERE FALLS, QUE., AUGUST 18TH, 1876—Near the mouth of the Chaudiere River. Original pencil drawing by G. Harlow White. Size 3 x 6.

3096—CHAUDIERE FALLS—A north view of the falls, July, 1876. Original pencil drawing by G. Harlow White. Size 3 x 6.

3097—FALLS OF MONTMORENCY, QUE.—From below and from the western side of the cataract—These falls are higher than those at Niagara, being more than two hundred and fifty feet in height, although only about fifty feet wide, and are situated on the Montmorenci River, some nine miles from Quebec. About two miles farther along the river banks is a strange formation, known as "the natural steps," being a series of layers of limestone, each about a foot thick, and going back for half a mile, rising to a height of nearly twenty feet. These steps have been since submerged as the result of the construction of a dam, just below them. Original pencil drawing by G. Harlow White. Size 3 x 6.

3098—FALLS ON THE CHAUDIERE RIVER, QUE., AUGUST 18TH, 1876—These falls, which are about one hundred and fifty feet high, are eight miles from Quebec. Original pencil drawing by G. Harlow White. Size 3 x 6.

3099—CHAUDIERE RIVER, JULY, 1876—Showing the centre fall, with islands to the west. Original pencil drawing by G. Harlow White. Size 3 x 6.

3100—A BIT OF SHORE—The town of Meaford is in Grey County, Ont., at the mouth of Big Head River, in Georgian Bay, twenty-two miles from Collingwood. Original pencil drawing by G. Harlow White. Size 3 x 6.

3101—MEAFORD, ONT.—Moonlight on the Georgian Bay, near Meaford—Georgian Bay is on the north-east part of Lake Huron and is separated from the main body of the lake by a peninsula called Cabot Head, and by the Manitoulin Island. This drawing was made from a boat in the centre of the bay. Original pencil drawing by G. Harlow White. Size 3 x 6.

3102—LOG HOUSE NEAR BARRIE, 1872—On the Little Lake road, which runs to Little Lake, about three miles from Barrie, in the Township of Vespra. Original pencil drawing by G. Harlow White. Size 3 x 5.

3103—BARRIE, SEPT., 1872—The old Town Hall, facing south on Collier street—The town fire engine is depicted as coming out on the street, and the Haymarket is seen to the east of the hall. Original pencil drawing by G. Harlow White. Size 3 x 5.

3104—OLD EPISCOPAL CHURCH, BARRIE, ONT., JUNE, 1874—It was a wooden structure, now demolished, and stood north of Lally's residence, opposite the court house. Original pencil drawing by G. Harlow White. Size 3 x 5.

3105—BARRIE IN SPRINGTIME—From the west end of Kempenfeldt Bay, 1874—The logs floating near the shore were for the Durham sawmills, on the west end of the bay, between Barrie and Allandale. Original pencil drawing by G. Harlow White. Size 3 x 5. See 3109.

3106—BARRIE, ONT.—View from Kempenfeldt Hill, on the Penetang and Lake Shore road—Kempenfeldt Bay is in the background to the south. The roadway runs west into Barrie. Original pencil drawing by G. Harlow White. Size 3 x 5.

3107—A SETTLER'S HOME, MAY, 1872—Simcoe County, near Little Lake. Original pencil drawing by G. Harlow White. Size 3 x 5.

3108—HUMBLE ABODE IN SIMCOE COUNTY—Home of a Simcoe County pioneer as it appeared in 1872. Original pencil drawing by G. Harlow White. Size 3 x 5.

3109—BARRIE, SIMCOE COUNTY—On the north shore of Kempenfeldt Bay, June, 1874—Barrie was originally a portage, dating back to the eighteenth century or earlier. To the right, or west of the picture, is shown the outskirts of the town. The first spire to the east is that of the Anglican Church, the second that of the Methodist. Original pencil drawing by G. Harlow White. Size 3 x 6. See 3105.

3110—BARRIE WELCOMES LORD DUFFERIN—Scene at the old wharf, July 25th, 1874, when Lord Dufferin, then Governor-General of Canada, visited Barrie on board the steamer "Emily May," docking at the old wharf, which was situated below the present post-office. Original pencil drawing by G. Harlow White. Size 3 x 5.

3111—PLEASANT WALK TO GRAVENHURST, SEPTEMBER, 1873—Gravenhurst, in the Township of Morrison, is a pretty town on the rising ground between Gull and Muskoka Lakes, in the midst of some of the loveliest scenery of the district. Original pencil drawing by G. Harlow White. Size 3 x 5.

3112—GULL LAKE—Near Gravenhurst, August, 1875—A sequestered spot. Original pencil drawing by G. Harlow White. Size 3 x 6.

3113—LAKE MUSKOKA, OCTOBER, 1872—Near the "Narrows," three miles from Gravenhurst. Original pencil drawing by G. Harlow White. Size 3 x 6.

3114—LAKE MUSKOKA, OCTOBER 13TH, 1875—A view from Gravenhurst, Ont. Original pencil drawing by G. Harlow White. Size 3 x 5.

3115—LAKE MUSKOKA, NEAR THE NARROWS, AUGUST, 1875—Three miles from Gravenhurst. Original pencil drawing by G. Harlow White. Size 3 x 6.

3116—MUSKOKA NARROWS, OCTOBER, 1872—Entrance to Gravenhurst Bay—The island on the left belongs to Colonel George T. Denison, Toronto. Original pencil drawing by G. Harlow White. Size 3 x 5.

3117—CHATTING BY THE WAY—A home on the high road from Washago to Gravenhurst, August, 1875. Original pencil drawing by G. Harlow White. Size 3 x 6.

3118—SPARROW LAKE, SEPTEMBER, 1873—Depicting the outlet of the lake. Original pencil drawing by G. Harlow White. Size 3 x 5.

3119—MUSKOKA RIVER, OCTOBER, 1872—A view of its quiet waters near Bracebridge. Original pencil drawing by G. Harlow White. Size 3 x 5.

3120—FALLS OF THE MUSKOKA RIVER, NEAR BRACEBRIDGE, ONT., OCTOBER, 1872—These falls are now harnessed and furnish electric power and light for Bracebridge and Gravenhurst. Original pencil drawing by G. Harlow White. Size 3 x 5.

3121—SOUTH FALLS, OCTOBER, 1872—Near Bracebridge. Original pencil drawing by G. Harlow White. Size 3 x 5.

3122—NORTH FALLS, OCTOBER, 1872—A little above Bracebridge. Original pencil drawing by G. Harlow White. Size 3 x 5.

3123—NORTH FALLS, OCTOBER, 1872—At the east end of Bracebridge. Original drawing by G. Harlow White. Size 3 x 5.

3124—OLD ROAD BETWEEN BRACEBRIDGE AND GRAVENHURST—Near South Falls, October, 1872. Original pencil drawing by G. Harlow White. Size 3 x 5.

3125—MUSKOKA RIVER, OCTOBER, 1872—Logs delayed in their course, jammed by rocks. Original pencil drawing by G. Harlow White. Size 3 x 6.

3126—MUSKOKA RIVER, OCTOBER, 1872—Rushing on its journey—The river takes its rise in a cedar swamp on the highlands separating the waters of the Ottawa from those of the Georgian Bay, and flows through a well wooded country into that bay. Original pencil drawing by G. Harlow White. Size 3 x 5.

3127—HOMES ALONG THE BANKS OF THE MUSKOKA RIVER—Near Huntsville, July, 1875. Original pencil drawing by G. Harlow White. Size 3 x 5.

3128—INDIAN SUMMER SCENE ON THE MUSKOKA RIVER, OCTOBER, 1872. Original pencil drawing by G. Harlow White. Size 3 x 5.

3129—MUSKOKA RIVER, AUGUST, 1875—Near South Falls. Original pencil drawing by G. Harlow White. Size 3 x 6.

3130—NORTH FALLS, OCTOBER, 1872—A lowering scene at the foot of the falls. Original pencil drawing by G. Harlow White. Size 3 x 6.

3131—**EDGE OF NORTH FALLS**—A view in October, 1872. **Original** pencil drawing by G. Harlow White. Size 3 x 5.

3132—**SOUTH FALLS, AUGUST. 1875**—In their rocky abode. Original pencil drawing by G. Harlow White. Size 3 x 3.

3133—**MUSKOKA RIVER, AUGUST, 1875**—A solitary pool in the rocks. Original pencil drawing by G. Harlow White. Size 3 x 6.

3134—**PIONEER SETTLEMENT NEAR ORILLIA, 1872.** Original pencil drawing by G. Harlow White. Size 3 x 6.

3135—**CHAUDIERE FALLS**—From Victoria Island, looking due west, 1876—Hull is shown on the right, and to the left is that part of Ottawa formerly known as Mechanicsville. Original pencil drawing by G. Harlow White. Size 3 x 6.

3136—**MUSKOKA RIVER, AUGUST, 1875**—A rocky approach on the shore of the river near South Falls. Original pencil drawing by G. Harlow White. Size 3 x 6.

3137—**SOUTH FALLS, AUGUST, 1875**—Showing the lowest cascade— Near Bracebridge, Victoria County, Ont., on the north branch of the Muskoka River. The falls were formerly known as Grand Falls. Original pencil drawing by G. Harlow White. Size 3 x 6.

3138—**NORTH FALLS, BRACEBRIDGE, OCTOBER 13TH, 1872**—Lumber mills have destroyed the effectiveness of these falls. Original pencil drawing by G. Harlow White. Size 3 x 5.

3139—**OWEN SOUND, FROM THE SOUTH-EAST, AUGUST, 1874**— Showing the Sydenham River and Owen Sound Bay—The spire on the right is St. Mary's Roman Catholic Church, while the steeple in the centre is that of the Anglican Church. The foreground is the east side of the town, now built up. Owen Sound, the capital of Grey County and a port of entry, was originally known as Sydenham. The Sound, which is twelve miles long from the town to its mouth, is the best harbor on Lake Huron, and throughout its entire length is completely sheltered on both sides. It is navigable for the largest vessels on the lake. Original pencil drawing by G. Harlow White. Size 3 x 6. See 3140.

3140—**OWEN SOUND**—From the south, July 20th, 1875—Showing the Sydenham River in the foreground—The steeple of Knox Church is seen to the left, and the tower in the centre is that of the Fire Department. The building with the cupola to the left is the Town Hall. Original pencil drawing by G. Harlow White. Size 3 x 5. See 3139.

3141—**ROCK FORMATION EAST OF OWEN SOUND**—Looking down the valley to the west, August, 1874. Original pencil drawing by G. Harlow White. Size 3 x 5.

3142—**SYDENHAM RIVER, 1874**—A peaceful scene in summer, showing the river and the town of Owen Sound. Original pencil drawing by G. Harlow White. Size 3 x 6.

3143—**WOOD GATHERERS ON THE ROADWAY NEAR INGLIS FALLS, JULY, 1875**—Original pencil drawing by G. Harlow White. Size 3 x 5.

3144—**LOOKING TOWARDS INGLIS FALLS**—A roadway leading south from Owen Sound, July, 1875. Original pencil drawing by G. Harlow White. Size 3 x 5.

3145—SYDENHAM RIVER, AUGUST, 1874—A bend in the stream. Original pencil drawing by G. Harlow White. Size 3 x 6.

3146—INGLIS FALLS, AUGUST, 1874—On the Sydenham River, three miles from the town of Owen Sound—The picture also shows the flour and woollen mills. Original pencil drawing by G. Harlow White. Size 3 x 6.

3147—ROCKY RIDGES NEAR OWEN SOUND—The town of Owen Sound is bounded on the east and west sides by ridges of rock. The picture shows a bit of rocky ground, as seen by the artist, in the summer of 1874. Original pencil drawing by G. Harlow White. Size 3 x 6.

3148—BARRIE, ONT., 1872—Looking towards Allandale. Original pencil drawing by G. Harlow White. Size 3 x 5.

3149—NIAGARA'S WATERS, 1872—Showing the Horseshoe Falls, from the Canadian side. Original pencil drawing by G. Harlow White. Size 3 x 5.

3150—ROCKS AT OWEN SOUND—Another view of rocky ground at Owen Sound, to the west of the town. Original pencil drawing by G. Harlow White. Size 3 x 5.

3151—RAPIDS OF SYDENHAM RIVER—The river, which rises in a small lake in Holland Township, Grey County, flows through a picturesque valley and empties into the Sound. The scene depicted is about a mile from Inglis Falls. Original pencil drawing by G. Harlow White. Size 3 x 6.

3152—SYDENHAM RIVER—Just below Inglis Falls, July, 1875. Original pencil drawing by G. Harlow White. Size 3 x 6.

3153—ONTARIO GOVERNMENT DREDGER—At work in 1875 near the mouth of the Sydenham River, Owen Sound, where the C.P.R. elevators stood before being destroyed by fire. Original pencil drawing by G. Harlow White. Size 3 x 5.

3154—POTTAWATEAMIE RIVER, AUGUST 14TH, 1874—In its forest home—The river enters Owen Sound Bay at Owen Sound. Original pencil drawing by G. Harlow White. Size 3 x 5.

3155—SYDENHAM RIVER, AUGUST, 1874—A pastoral scene—Crossing a creek up the river. Original pencil drawing by G. Harlow White. Size 3 x 6.

3156—RUSTIC BRIDGE—Over a creek near the outskirts of Owen Sound, August, 1874. Original pencil drawing by G. Harlow White. Size 3 x 5.

3157—ROCKS EAST OF OWEN SOUND, AUGUST, 1874—Original pencil drawing by G. Harlow White. Size 3 x 6.

3158—BARRIE SHORE, 1870—Looking across Kempenfeldt Bay from Allandale. Kempenfeldt Bay is an arm of Lake Simcoe. Original pencil drawing by G. Harlow White. Size 2 x 5.

3159—OWEN SOUND BAY, AUGUST, 1874—With Georgian Bay in the background. Original pencil drawing by G. Harlow White. Size 3 x 6.

3160—ROCKS AT OWEN SOUND—Looking upward from the valley to the west. Original pencil drawing by G. Harlow White. Size 3 x 6.

3161—SYDENHAM RIVER, AUGUST, 1874—View of the river running south and to the left. Original pencil drawing by G. Harlow White. Size 3 x 6.

3162—WOODLAND STREAM NEAR OWEN SOUND, JULY, 1875—Original pencil drawing by G. Harlow White. Size 3 x 5.

3163—OUTLET OF POTTAWATEAMIE RIVER, 1874—With the Georgian Bay in the distance. Original pencil drawing by G. Harlow White. Size 3 x 5.

3164—MONTREAL, 1876—On the St. Lawrence, from the east point of St. Helen's Island, on the left of the picture—The view shows the towers of Notre Dame and the spire of Christ Church Cathedral (Anglican) on the left. The mountain is in the background. Original pencil drawing by G. Harlow White. Size 3 x 6. See 3167.

3165—MOUNT ROYAL, MONTREAL, AUGUST, 1876—At its highest point Mount Royal is seven hundred and fifty feet above the level of the St. Lawrence, and was once volcanic. From the summit a magnificent view is obtained of the country round about. The beautiful St. Lawrence may be traced for an immense distance, while the southern view is bounded by a long range of mountains in New York State. Original pencil drawing by G. Harlow White. Size 3 x 6.

3166—LACHINE RAPIDS, JULY, 1876—Showing a schooner going through the canal locks—The falls, which are situated between Lachine and Montreal, present a scene of wild grandeur and are a source of great attraction to tourists. Original pencil drawing by G. Harlow White. Size 3 x 6.

3167—MONTREAL, 1876—From the winding road leading to the summit of Mount Royal—The reservoir is shown in the foreground. The two church towers are those of Notre Dame, and to the west is seen the Church of St. Patrick; further west is Christ Church Cathedral. On the west (right side of the drawing) is also shown Victoria Bridge. Original pencil drawing by G. Harlow White. Size 3 x 6. See 3164.

3168—AMONG THE THOUSAND ISLANDS—Showing the near bank of the River St. Lawrence as the scene appeared in July, 1876. Original pencil drawing by G. Harlow White. Size 3 x 6.

3169—LACHINE, QUE., AUG., 1876—At the foot of Lake St. Louis, about eight miles from Montreal and a favorite summer resort of holiday seekers from the latter city—This picturesque town was given its name by Champlain in 1613. In 1689 the town of that time was destroyed by the Iroquois, when two hundred of the inhabitants were burnt at the stake. Original pencil drawing by G. Harlow White. Size 3 x 6.

3170—PENINSULAR LAKE, LONDON TOWNSHIP, JULY, 1875— View of the west end. Original pencil drawing by G. Harlow White. Size 3x6.

3171—CENTRE OF PENINSULAR LAKE, JULY, 1875—The lake is a curiously formed sheet of water east of Huntsville, on the Muskoka River. It is three miles long and a mile and a half wide, and is one of a series of lakes in the district, including Lake of Bays, Fairy Lake, Mary Lake, and Lake Vernon. A point of land cuts this body of water in two, hence the name. In the background is seen the Township of Brunel. Original pencil drawing by G. Harlow White. Size 3 x 6.

3172—PENINSULAR LAKE, JULY, 1875—From a portage between Peninsular Lake and Lake of Bays. Original pencil drawing by G. Harlow White. Size 3 x 6.

3173—BRACEBRIDGE, OCTOBER, 1872—Original pencil drawing by G. Harlow White. Size 3 x 5. See 3174.

33

3174—BRACEBRIDGE, VICTORIA COUNTY, OCTOBER, 1872—A Muskoka village as seen from North Falls—The town is beautifully situated on the northern branch of the Muskoka River. Original pencil drawing by G. Harlow White. Size 3 x 6. See 3173.

3175—A FOREST HOME NEAR BRACEBRIDGE, SEPTEMBER, 1872— Original pencil drawing by G. Harlow White. Size 3 x 5.

3176—LAKE KAUSHESHEBOGAMOG, SEPTEMBER, 1873—Central view of the lake. Original pencil drawing by G. Harlow White. Size 3 x 6.

3177—LAKE KAUSHESHEBOGAMOG, SEPTEMBER, 1873—A dangerous spot on the west end of the lake. Original pencil drawing by G. Harlow White. Size 3 x 5.

3178—LAKE KAUSHESHEBOGAMOG, SEPTEMBER, 1873—Bays and inlets on the south side of the lake. Original pencil drawing by G. Harlow White. Size 3 x 5.

3179—BARRIE—In Bleak December—Looking south, in 1870. Original pencil drawing by G. Harlow White. Size 2 x 5.

3180—LAKE KAUSHESHEBOGAMOG, SEPTEMBER, 1873—Lake of the many channels. Original pencil drawing by G. Harlow White. Size 3 x 5.

3181—LAKE KAUSHESHEBOGAMOG, SEPTEMBER, 1873—At its outlet—The waters of the lake empty into the Severn River, in the Township of Morrison, Muskoka. Original pencil drawing by G. Harlow White. Size 3 x 5.

3182—WHITE, GEORGE HARLOW, R.C.A.—Born in England in 1817; educated at the Charterhouse School, London. Came to Canada about 1870, remaining here for several years. In 1877 he returned to his native land, and in 1884 was elected a member of the Royal Canadian Academy. His death occurred in 1888. White's landscapes are noted for their perspicuous and delicate touch, and are becoming very rare. Photograph, colored. Size 4 x 5. Head and shoulders.

3183—J. B. BOUSTEAD STEAM FIRE ENGINE—Built at Seneca Falls, N.Y., by the Silsby Co., in 1871. It was stationed in the Yonge street hall, north of College, until 1877, when the water-works pressure being largely increased, the continuous use of steam fire engines became unnecessary. The old engine was subsequently reconstructed at Seneca Falls, with a new boiler, engine and other parts, and stationed in one of the fire halls until 1910. It is now (1917) beyond repair and is stored in the Yorkville avenue hall. Photograph, colored. Size 5 x 8.

3184—KNOX COLLEGE, TORONTO, 1917—South side St. George street—In 1906 the Board of Knox College resolved that a new college building was necessary; in 1910 plans were called for, and two years later the corner-stone of the present seminary was laid. The style of architecture is Collegiate Gothic. Around three sides of a quadrangle are the connected buildings, of Credit Valley grey sandstone, with Indiana limestone trimmings. The dedicatory services were held 29th September, 1915.

DINING HALL AND TOWER, KNOX COLLEGE—From St. George street—One hundred and sixty students can be comfortably accommodated in the dining hall, which, with its oak-beamed roof, high Gothic windows and heavy oak wainscotting, presents a handsome interior. Photogravure. Size 5 x 8.

VIEW OF ENTRANCE HALL, KNOX COLLEGE—This central hall, with its vaulted Gothic roof and fan leaf tracery, is said to be the beauty spot of the entire group of buildings. Photogravure. Size 4 x 5.

INTERIOR OF THE GOTHIC CHAPEL, KNOX COLLEGE—On the south side of the entrance hall—The beautifully carved pulpit was the gift of the Misses Caven, in honor of their mother, wife of the late Principal Caven. Mr. J. Ross Robertson presented a carved chair and communion table, made from oak beams taken from the old Crown Court Presbyterian Church, London, Eng. The organ and woodwork were given by Dr. J. A. Macdonald and friends whom he had interested outside the province. Photogravure. Size 5 x 7.

LIBRARY, KNOX COLLEGE—Known as the Caven Library, and erected in memory of the late Principal Caven. The reading-room is of noble proportions—90 feet long and 40 feet wide. In the stackroom there is accommodation for 75,000 volumes, and in the reading-room are shelves for many more. Photogravure. Size 4 x 5.

FRONT DOORWAY OF KNOX COLLEGE—Opening out upon the university grounds—The building, facing the university lawn, is divided into two, the central part, between the library and chapel, dropping to a lower elevation. This gives the appearance of a gateway to the quadrangle. Photogravure. Size 5 x 7.

COMMON ROOM, KNOX COLLEGE—A quaint bit of the vaulted tower entrance way. Photogravure. Size 5 x 5.

THE CLOISTER, KNOX COLLEGE—Traversing the quadrangle, so as to obtain protected communication from the academic to the residence portion of the building. It is one storey in height, and through traceried windows on either side may be seen the attractive quadrangle. Photogravure. Size 4 x 5.

TOWER, KNOX COLLEGE—At the west end of the cloister is the massive tower, which faces on St. George street. Photogravure. Size 5 x 7.

CORNER OF THE QUADRANGLE, KNOX COLLEGE—Showing part of East House and Chapel—Running along the southern side of the quadrangle, from the central tower to the chapel, are the dormitories, known as West House, Centre House and East House, and having accommodation for 104 students. Photogravure. Size 5 x 5.

KNOX COLLEGE, 1917—As seen from the University Campus—In the centre of picture is the St. George street tower, over the entrance to the quadrangle. As university buildings, these are considered, both in the interior and exterior, the finest of the kind in Canada. Photogravure. Size 5 x 8.

3185—GROUP OF FIREMEN AND J. B. BOUSTEAD STEAM FIRE ENGINE—In front of Yonge street hall, 1874—With key. The "J. B. Boustead" was built at Seneca Falls, N.Y., 1871. Until 1877 it was stationed at the Yonge street hall. Subsequently rebuilt, but now (1917) beyond further service, it is stored in the Yorkville avenue hall. Photograph, colored. Size 6 x 10.

3186-92—Toronto Fire Department, 1838-1917 — A volunteer fire company was first organized in York (Toronto) in 1826, Mr. Carfrae, jr., acting as captain. Subsequently additional units were formed. In 1838, however, the various fire companies then in existence were entirely reorganized, and Mr. T. D. Harris appointed chief engineer of the brigade.

3186—HARRIS, THOMAS D.—Chief Engineer of the Fire Brigade, 1838-41. Water color. Size 3 x 4. Head and shoulders. See 590.

3187—BEARD, ROBERT—Engineer of the Fire Brigade, 1842-46 and 1848-50—Born in Manchester, Eng., 1807; came to Canada as a child, receiving his education here. He was captain of the hook and ladder company for a time, and appointed assistant engineer of the brigade in 1838. From 1839-41 Mr. Beard acted as councilman for St. Lawrence Ward, of which he subsequently became alderman. His death took place in Toronto, 14th Aug., 1882. Water color. Size 3 x 4. Head and shoulders.

3188—ASHFIELD, JAMES—Chief Engineer of the Fire Brigade, 1851-77, and Chief of the Fire Department, 1877-89—In May, 1839, he became a member of the Toronto Fire Brigade, which at that time consisted of five companies of from thirty to forty members each, all volunteers. He was elected captain in 1846, and chief engineer, 1851. On his retirement from active duty he became purchasing officer. Died 15th June, 1890, in Toronto. In 1877 the brigade was divided, with a chief for the brigade and also one for the department. Mr. Ashfield was chief of the latter, and Richard Ardagh of the former. After Ashfield's death a reorganization took place, with Ardagh as chief of the Fire Department. Water color on print. Size 3 x 4. Head and shoulders.

3189—ARDAGH, RICHARD—Chief of the Fire Brigade, 1877-89, and of the Fire Department, 1889-95—He came to Canada with his parents when but six months old, having been born in Thurles, Tipperary, Ireland, 1832. In 1847 he entered the brigade, soon became captain, and in 1866 was appointed deputy chief. On the division of the brigade, 1877, Mr. Ardagh became chief. His death took place 27th Jan., 1895, as a result of injuries received at the Globe fire early in the month, when he had to jump from a burning ledge to the ground, forty-five feet below. Water color on print. Size 3 x 4. Head and shoulders.

3190—GRAHAM, THOMAS—Chief of the Fire Department, 1895-99 —His birthplace was Wicklow, Ireland, 1832. He came to Canada with his parents in 1847. Before joining the Fire Brigade he was a sailor on the lakes, and for a time engineer on the ferry steamer "Fire Fly," which ran to Toronto Island in the late fifties. Mr. Graham became a member of the brigade in 1860, as a volunteer, subsequently was appointed deputy chief of the department, and then chief. His death took place 29th April, 1911. Water color. Size 3 x 4. Head and shoulders.

3191—THOMPSON, JOHN—Chief of the Fire Department, 1899-1915— Born 24th June, 1848, County Antrim, Ireland. Joined the Toronto Fire Department, January, 1876, and the following year was appointed foreman. In 1883 he became district chief, and deputy in 1895. Mr. Thompson still (1917) resides in Toronto. Water color on print. Size 3 x 4. Head and shoulders.

3192—SMITH, WM. J.—Chief of Fire Department, 1916—Born in Toronto, June 17th, 1856. For a time served in the navy and on the lake boats, but in March, 1876, joined the Fire Department, being first attached to hook and ladder No. 1, located at Court street station. In 1883 transferred to No. 7 hose at Wilton avenue, and four years later promoted to foreman (captain) of No. 9 station, Dundas street. Served at various halls until his appointment as district chief, with headquarters at No. 4 station, Berkeley street. Transferred to headquarters, Adelaide street, 1914, and on Feb. 26th, 1915, appointed acting deputy chief, with headquarters at No. 2 station, Portland street. On April 16th, 1915, made acting chief, and Jan. 12th, 1916, Chief of Fire Department. Water color on print. Size 3 x 4. Head and shoulders.

3193—KNOX COLLEGE, TORONTO, 1844—Where the first classes were held—The college was founded by the Presbyterian (Free) Church of Canada, and work begun under Rev. Henry Esson, of St. Gabriel Street Church, Montreal, and Rev. Andrew King, a delegate from the Free Church of Scotland. The first session was opened 5th Nov., 1844, with fourteen students, in the home of Mr. Esson, on James street, the college proper consisting of one room, with a long table, two wooden benches and a few chairs. Water color. Size 5 x 7.

3194—SECOND HOME OF KNOX COLLEGE—Adelaide street west, Toronto—Rev. Henry Esson, A.M., removed from James street to 79 Adelaide street west, between York and Simcoe, and for a time classes were held there. In 1845 the Synod confirmed the appointment of Dr. Robert Burns, of Paisley, Scotland, as professor of theology, Rev. Andrew King having been appointed professor of divinity, pro tem. The following year the college became known as "Knox." Mr. Esson's house was subsequently occupied by the late J. J. Vickers, and is now (1917) No. 172 Adelaide street west. Water color. Size 4 x 5.

3195—THIRD HOME OF KNOX COLLEGE, TORONTO—North side Front street, between York and Bay—From 1848-55 the college occupied three dwelling houses, called the Ontario Terrace, on the north side of Front street, between York and Bay. On the removal of Knox to Elmsley Villa, these buildings became Swords' Hotel, under the proprietorship of P. Swords. The site is now (1917) Queen's Hotel. Water color. Size 5 x 5.

3196—FOURTH HOME OF KNOX COLLEGE, TORONTO—N.W. corner Grosvenor and St. Vincent streets—Instead of building a new college, as recommended by the Synod in 1854, Elmsley Villa, which had been the residence of Lord Elgin in Toronto, while he was Governor-General, was purchased. Aid was received from the Free Church of Scotland and also from the Irish Presbyterian Church. The building, to which a wing was added to the west for dormitories, was used by Knox from 1855-75. Grosvenor St. Presbyterian Church (formerly Central) stands on the site in 1916. The college was incorporated 1858. Water color. Size 5 x 7.

3197—FIFTH HOME OF KNOX COLLEGE, TORONTO—Spadina avenue, north of College street—On 3rd April, 1874, the corner-stone was laid, and in October, 1875, the college removed from Elmsley Villa to the pile of buildings shown in picture. They were commodious, with ample class-room space, chapel, library and students' rooms, and accommodated about eighty students. The late Dr. Warden, Principal Caven and other friends of Knox were untiring in their efforts to collect funds for the erection of the buildings, which in 1915 were vacated for the new college on St. George street. The old building is at present (1917) the "Spadina Military Hospital." Knox College was the first purely theological college on this continent to receive the power of conferring degrees in theology. Water color. Size 5 x 6.

3198-3204—Rectors St. James' Church (Cathedral), York and Toronto, 1803-1917.

3198—STUART, REV. GEORGE O'KILL—Rector (first) St. James' Church, York (Toronto), 1803-12—As early as 1801 Mr. Stuart was missionary at York, without, however, any permanent building as a place of worship. The Anglican Church—St. James'—was begun in 1803 and opened early in 1807. Water color. Size 3 x 4. Head and shoulders. See 2513.

3199—STRACHAN, RT. REV. BISHOP JOHN, D.D.—Rector St. James' Church, York (Toronto), 1812-47—Despite his elevation to the Episcopate in 1839 Dr. Strachan continued for some years as rector of St. James'. Water color. Size 3 x 4. Head and shoulders. See 252, 2732.

3200—GRASETT, REV. HENRY JAMES, D.D.—Rector St. James' Cathedral, Toronto, 1847-82, and first dean, 1867. Water color. Size 3 x 4. Head and shoulders. See 275.

3201—DUMOULIN REV. J. P. (BISHOP)—Rector St.. James' Cathedral, 1882-96—He was born in Dublin, Ireland, 1834; ordained deacon, 1862, and priest the following year. Mr. DuMoulin had charge of various parishes until 1875, in that year becoming rector of St. Martin's, Montreal. Came to Toronto in 1882; rector and canon St. James' Cathedral; sub-dean St. Alban's. In May, 1896, he was elected third Bishop of Niagara (declined Bishopric of Algoma in 1872). Bishop DuMoulin attended the Pan-Anglican Congress in London, Eng., 1908, and in July of that year was presented to King Edward and Queen Alexandra. Received degree of M.A. from Lennoxville, and D.C.L. from Trinity University, Toronto. Wrote "The Eternal Law." Died at Hamilton, Ont., 29th March, 1911. Water color. Size 3 x 4. Head and shoulders.

3202—SULLIVAN, RT. REV. EDWARD—Rector St. James' Cathedral, Toronto, 1896-99—Born at Lurgan, Ireland, 18th Aug., 1832, a graduate of Trinity College, Dublin. Came to Canada in 1858, and in that year was ordained deacon, the following year becoming priest. He was appointed missionary bishop in the township of London, where he labored until 1862. He then became assistant at St. George's Church, Montreal. Went to Chicago in 1868 as rector of Trinity Church, but returned to Montreal in 1878. There he remained until his elevation to the Episcopate as Bishop of Algoma, June, 1882. In a missionary diocese he was truly a missionary bishop. Bishop Sullivan resigned his See to become rector of St. James' Cathedral, Toronto. He was D.C.L. of Dublin, and D.D. of Trinity University, Toronto. His death took place 6th Jan., 1899. Water color. Size 3 x 4. Head and shoulders.

3203—WELCH, REV. EDWARD A., M.A., D.C.L.—Rector St. James' Cathedral, Toronto—Son of Rev. Andrew Welch; born at Orpington, Eng., Aug. 22nd, 1860; educated at King's College, London. Proceeded to Cambridge in 1879, and took his B.A., 1882. He was ordained deacon in 1884; became curate of St. Paul's, Haggerston. Domestic chaplain to the Bishop of Durham, and rector of Venerable Bede's church at Gateshead. He held the latter living up to the time of his appointment as Provost and Vice-Chancellor of Trinity University, Toronto, 1895. Four years later he was appointed rector of St. James' Cathedral, an office that carries with it the position of canon and sub-dean of St. Alban's Cathedral. Through his efforts the affiliation of Trinity College and the Provincial University was largely due. Canon Welch returned to England in 1909 to become Vicar of Wakefield. Water color. Size 3 x 4. Head and shoulders.

3204—PLUMPTRE, REV. H. P., M.A.—Rector St. James' Cathedral, Toronto, 1909—His birthplace was Nonington, Kent, Eng., 24th Oct., 1870. Educated at Harrow and Trinity College, Oxford (M.A.); became curate of Faringdon, Berks., in 1895, and from 1897-1901 was chaplain and lecturer at Wycliffe Hall, Oxford. Came to Canada, and for a time acted as Dean of Wycliffe College, later becoming assistant rector St. George's, Montreal, and while there was vice-president of the Montreal Cricket Club. He returned to England, but came again to Canada, 1909, and since that time has been rector of St. James' Cathedral, canon and sub-dean St. Alban's Cathedral, Toronto. Water color. Size 3 x 4. Head and shoulders.

3205-08—Corporation Counsel, Toronto, 1888-1917—

3205—MEREDITH, HON. SIR WILLIAM R.—Corporation Counsel, Toronto, 1888-94—He was called to the Ontario Bar in 1861, for many years practising his profession in London, Ont. In 1875 he was created Q.C. by the Ontario Government, and subsequently by the Marquis of Lorne. Mr. Meredith in 1872 became a member of the Ontario Legislature, at once taking a firm stand on the side of workingmen; was one of the first advocates of manhood suffrage. He fought for a ballot in Separate schools and against undue clerical influence in educational matters. In 1894 raised to Bench as Chief Justice of Common Pleas, Ontario; appointed a member of the Commission for the Revision of the Provincial Statutes; knighted 1896. His Lordship as a young man served as officer for some time in the London Light Infantry. He still (1917) resides in Toronto. Water color. Size 3 x 4. Head and shoulders.

3206—FULLERTON, JAMES S., K.C.—Corporation Counsel, 1894-1909 —Of Irish parentage, born 3rd April, 1848, at South Dorchester, Ont. Educated in Galt and Toronto. He was called to the Bar in 1877, taking 2nd, 3rd and 4th year scholarships at Osgoode Hall. In 1889 he was created Q.C. (now K.C.) by the Earl of Derby. Succeeded Sir Wm. Meredith as Corporation Counsel, and at the present time (1917) is associate counsel with Messrs. Robinette, Godfrey & Phalen, Toronto. Water color. Size 3 x 4. Head and shoulders.

3207—DRAYTON, HENRY L. (SIR), K.C.—Corporation Counsel, 1910-12—Born in Kingston, Ont., 1869, son of P. H. Drayton, who came to Canada with the 16th Rifles of England. In 1891 he was called to the Ontario Bar; created a K.C., 1908. Counsel to the Railway Committee of the Ontario Legislature, 1902; appointed County Crown Attorney for the County of York, 1904, and in 1912 became Chief Commissioner, Board of Railway Commissioners for Canada. Sir Henry (1917) resides at Ottawa. Photograph, colored. Size 3 x 4. Head and shoulders.

3208—GEARY, G. REGINALD—Corporation Counsel, Toronto, 1912-17. Water color. Size 3 x 4. Head and shoulders. See 398.

3209-16—Toronto Fire Fighting Department, 1826-61—The Toronto Fire Brigade was first formed in 1826, and improved in 1831, when the Fireman's Hall in Church street was built. There were two engines in commission. In 1835-7 a third engine was procured and a hook and ladder company formed. In 1848 a hose company was in operation, and by 1855 there were six engines, with the hose and hook and ladder companies. In 1861 the first steam engine was installed and the hand-brake engines passed out.

3209—ENGINE COMPANY NO. 1, "PHOENIX"—This engine was stationed from 1855 in west division of Court Street Fire Hall, old Mechanics' Institute, late Police Court building, now (1917) occupied as headquarters of City Ambulance Department. The first No. 1, called "York," was a goose-neck engine, and was until 1854 in Fireman's Hall, west side of Church street, south of St. Andrew's Church. The picture shows the second engine, a "piano" pattern, built by Perry, of Montreal. It was sold to the village of Oakville in 1860. Drawing, in water color. Size 4 x 7.

3210—ENGINE COMPANY NO. 2, "RESCUE"—This engine was stationed in centre division of Court Street Fire Hall. In 1852-3 the first No. 2, known as "Toronto," a "goose-neck," installed in 1831, was sold and a "piano" pattern bought by William Marks, of Temperance street, and name changed to "Rescue." In 1861, when hand-brake engines were discarded, this company resigned and engine was sold to a country town. A boys' hose company was attached in 1856-8, with Geo. McConkey as captain, and J. Ross Robertson 1st lieutenant. Drawing, in water color. Size 4 x 7.

3211—**ENGINE COMPANY NO. 3, "BRITISH AMERICA"**—In 1837 the British America Insurance Company presented a "fore and aft" engine to the city. It was called "British America," No. 3. It was from 1837-55 housed in Fireman's Hall, Church street, south of St. Andrew's Church, and in 1855 was moved to centre division of Bay street hall on south-east corner of Temperance street. It was presented 20 years ago to the York Pioneers for exhibit at the National Exhibition. Drawing, in water color. Size 5 x 7.

3212—**ENGINE COMPANY NO. 4, "VICTORIA"**—The first No. 4, built in 1842, was a "goose-neck," but in 1848 it was replaced by a "piano" pattern, built by Perry, of Montreal. Its station was always in a hall in the rear of St. Patrick's Market, Queen street west, north side, near John. About 1858 the station house was in a frame building on the south side of Queen street, west of John, on site of present No. 6 Hose Station. Drawing, in water color. Size 4 x 7.

3213—**ENGINE COMPANY. NO. 5, "DELUGE"**—This engine, built in 1852 by Perry, of Montreal, was "piano" pattern, and was stationed in Berkeley street hall, situated in rear of a row of brick buildings on n.w. corner of King and Berkeley streets. The entrance was from Berkeley street. This picture was made from an excellent drawing in color by Wm. Gough, a branchman of the company, and which is now (1917) in the department at headquarters, Adelaide street west. Drawing, in water color. Size 4 x 7.

3214—**ENGINE COMPANY NO. 6, "PROVINCIAL"**—This engine was presented to the city in 1852 by the Provincial Insurance Company—long since gone out of existence. It was a "fore and aft," built by Alfred Perry, of Montreal. When the hand-brake engines went out of use this engine was returned to the insurance company. It was stationed in the south division of the Bay street building. The Hercules Hook and Ladder Company No. 2 ceased operations, and was turned into a fire company in order to work this engine. Drawing, in water color. Size 4 x 7.

3215—**HOOK AND LADDER COMPANIES, TORONTO**—The first Hook and Ladder Company No. 1 was stationed in 1831 in the Church street hall, south of St. Andrew's Church, on the s.w. corner of Church and Adelaide streets. This hall was also occupied in its centre and south divisions by "York" No. 1 and "Toronto" No. 2 engines till 1855. The Hook and Ladder Company No. 1 was in the north division of the hall. In 1845 a second company, known as "Hercules" No. 2, was formed and stationed in the south division of the Bay street hall, but this company later became a fire company to take charge of No. 6 "Provincial." Drawing, in water color. Size 4 x 7.

3216—**TORONTO HOSE COMPANY NO. 1, "NIAGARA"**—All the engines in Toronto, from 1831, had hand-drawn hose reels, with from 500 to 750 feet of leather hose, for rubber hose was then unknown. In the latter part of 1849 a hose company, called "Niagara" No. 1, was organized and was stationed in the north division of the Bay street hall, s.e. corner of Temperance. It was disbanded when steam engines were introduced and hose sections of the brigade formed. For years it was known as the Jackson Hose Company, from the name of its captain, James Jackson, a china merchant, King street west. Drawing, in water color. Size 4 x 7.

3217-20—**Principals Knox College, Toronto, 1857-1917**—

3217—**WILLIS, REV. MICHAEL, D.D., LL.D.**—Principal of Knox College, 1857-70—Born at Greenock, Scotland, in 1798, the son of a burgher minister. Became pastor of Renfield Street Church, Glasgow. After the disruption of 1843 in Scotland, Dr. Willis came to Canada as a deputy of the Free Church, and for the session 1845-6 taught theology in the recently established Knox College, at that time held on Adelaide street, Toronto. Appointed Professor of Theology in 1847, and Principal of Knox, 1857. Water color from portrait in Knox College. Size 3 x 4. Head and shoulders.

3218—CAVEN, REV. WILLIAM, D.D., LL.D.—Principal Knox College, 1873-1904—Of Covenanting stock, ancestors of his having been amongst the "Wigton Martyrs." Emigrated to Canada with his father, from whom he received his early education. Studied for the ministry in the Hall of the United Presbyterian Church, at London, Ont., under Rev. Wm. Proudfoot. Became pastor of St. Mary's and Downie. In 1866 appointed Professor of Exegetical Theology and Biblical Criticism in Knox College. Born in Kirkcolm, Wigtonshire, Scotland, in 1830. Died in Toronto, 1904. Water color from portrait in possession of his daughters, the Misses Caven, Toronto. Size 3 x 4. Head and shoulders.

3219—MACLAREN, REV. WILLIAM, D.D., LL.D.—Principal Knox College, 1905-8—Principal Maclaren was the first Canadian-born principal of Knox, his birthplace having been Torbolton, near Ottawa. Prepared for the ministry in the College of which he afterwards became head, and held pastorates at Amherstburg, Ont., Boston, Mass., Belleville, Ont., and Knox Church, Ottawa. In 1873 he was appointed to the staff of Knox College, as Professor of Systematic Theology. Born in 1828. His death occurred in Toronto, 1909. Water color from portrait in Knox College. Size 3 x 4. Head and shoulders.

3220—GANDIER, REV. ALFRED, D.D., LL.D.—Principal Knox College, 1908—A son of the manse; born in Hastings County, 1861, and educated at Queen's University, Kingston (B.A., gold medallist in philosophy and in history and English literature, 1884; M.A., 1887), and Edinburgh University (B.D., 1889). In 1889 ordained to the pastorate of Brampton, Ont. Resigned in 1893 to accept charge of Fort Massey Church, Halifax. Pastor St. James' Square Presbyterian Church, Toronto, 1901-8. Lectured on Apologetics in Knox College, 1902-8. Declined Professorship of Systematic Theology in Halifax Presbyterian College, 1903. Water color from original portrait. Size 3 x 4. Head and shoulders.

3221—ROBERTSON, J. ROSS—First Lieutenant of the Boys' Hose Company, Toronto—This juvenile company was attached in 1856-8 to the Rescue Fire Engine No. 2, Court street hall. George McConkey was captain. They attended day fires, and on 24th May, when the firemen's procession took place, the boys were much in evidence in their uniform. Mr. Robertson, son of the late Mr. John Robertson, a prominent Toronto merchant of the early days, was born in Toronto, Dec. 28th, 1841. He was educated at Upper Canada College, and at this time edited the College Times (later the Boys' Times). Served on the staff of the Toronto Leader, and in 1864 became city editor of the Globe. Mr. Robertson was one of the founders of the Daily Telegraph, 1866, and ten years later established The Evening Telegram, of which he is still sole proprietor. Water color. Size 3 x 5. Three-quarter length.

3222-5—Medical Officers of Health, Toronto, 1883-17.

3222—CANNIFF, DR. WILLIAM—Medical Officer of Health, Toronto, 1883-91—Of U.E. Loyalist descent; born at Canniffton, Ont., 1829. Studied his profession at Toronto School of Medicine, in United States and England. First practised in Belleville; called to the Chair of Pathology in Medical Faculty of Victoria College; afterwards Professor of Surgery. Later Sub-Dean of the Medical School, and served on the staff of the Toronto General Hospital. During the Crimean War did duty in the Royal Artillery; with the American army on the Potomac, and also served in Fenian Raid. In 1867 formed the Canadian Medical Association at Quebec. Author of "A History of the Early Settlement of Upper Canada" and "The Medical Profession in Upper Canada." Dr. Canniff died at Belleville, October 18th, 1909. Water color from portrait in possession of his daughter, Mrs. R. A. L. Gray, Toronto. Size 3 x 4. Head and shoulders.

3223—ALLEN, DR. NORMAN—Medical Officer of Health, Toronto, 1891-3—Born January 3rd, 1865, at Millbrook, Ont.; seventh son of Ven. Archdeacon T. W. Allen. Educated privately at Millbrook and at Trinity University, Toronto (M.D., C.M., 1885). Fellow Trinity Medical School; M.R.C.S. (Eng.), 1886. Dr. Allen still (1917) practises his profession in Toronto. Water color. Size 3 x 4. Head and shoulders.

3224—SHEARD, DR. CHARLES—Medical Officer of Health, Toronto, 1893-1910—Born in Toronto, Feb. 15th, 1857, son of Joseph Sheard, Mayor of Toronto, 1871-2. Educated at Upper Canada College and Trinity University, Toronto (M.B., 1878). Fellow Trinity Medical College, and M.R.C.S. (Eng.). Professor of Physiology, Trinity Medical College, 1882-1905, and of Preventive Medicine, Toronto University, 1905-11. For many years successfully practised his profession in the city of his birth. President Canadian Medical Association, 1892; of Ontario Health Officers' Association, 1896, and Chairman Provincial Board of Health, 1909. Still (1917) resides in Toronto. Water color. Size 3 x 4. Head and shoulders.

3225—HASTINGS, DR. CHARLES J. C. O.—Medical Officer of Health, Toronto, 1910-16—A York County man by birth, of Irish origin. Educated at Toronto and Hamilton Collegiate Institutes; M.D., C.M. (Victoria University), 1885. Acting Medical Health Officer of Toronto in 1885. Licentiate of King's and Queen's College of Physicians, Ireland, 1886. Senior physician Grace Hospital, Toronto, and a senator of Toronto University, elected in 1906. A promoter of Canadian Public Health Association, and in 1916, President. Author of many valuable papers, including "Race Suicide; the Great Problem of the Day." Still (1917) serves as Medical Officer of Health. Water color. Size 3 x 4. Head and shoulders.

3226—MEETING OF TORONTO CITY COUNCIL, 1896—Mayor Fleming in the chair—With key. Photograph, colored. Size 8 x 20.

3227-33—City Solicitors, Toronto, 1840-1917—

3227—GAMBLE, JOSEPH CLARKE, K.C.—City Solicitor, 1840-63—Of U.E. Loyalist stock; born in Kingston, U.C., 1808; studied law and was called to the Bar in Trinity Term, 1832. In 1840 became a Bencher, and in 1867, Q.C. Drew the charter of the British America Assurance Co. in 1833, and was solicitor to the company until his decease. Promoter Toronto & Huron Railway Co. Died, Nov. 23, 1902, and at his decease was the oldest lawyer in actual practice in Ontario. Water color. Size 3 x 4. Head and shoulders. See 2818.

3228—ROBINSON, HON. JOHN BEVERLEY—City Solicitor, 1864-80. Water color. Size 3 x 4. Head and shoulders. See 374, 425, 1006.

3229—McWILLIAMS, WM. G.—City Solicitor, 1880-88—Born at Mount Vernon, Brantford, in 1840. Received his education at Oberlin Academy, Oberlin, Ohio, and Toronto University. Prior to entering the service of the city as assistant to Hon. John Beverley Robinson (City Solicitor, 1864-80), was a member of the firm of Clarke, McWilliams & Foster. Mr. McWilliams' death occurred in 1907. Water color. Size 3 x 4. Head and shoulders.

3230—**BIGGAR, CHARLES R. W.**—City Solicitor, 1888-94—Born at Murray Bay, Ont., 1847; eldest son of James Lyons Biggar, M.P. Educated at Victoria College and Grammar School, Cobourg, Ont., and Toronto University (B.A., 1869; M.A., 1873). Called to the Bar, 1873. Served as City Solicitor jointly with Hon. John Beverley Robinson, 1874-6, becoming sole Solicitor in 1888. Created Q.C. in 1890. A member of the firm of Biggar & Burton. Died in Toronto, 16th Oct., 1909. Water color. Size 3 x 4. Head and shoulders.

3231—**CASWELL, THOMAS**—City Solicitor, 1894-1905—A native of Ontario; born, 1849. Studied law, and for a time was a partner in the firm of Caswell, Cameron & Cleary, later being associated with Mr. St. John, some-time Speaker of the Ontario Legislature. Entered the service of the Corporation of Toronto, 1888, and in 1894 succeeded Mr. C. R. W. Biggar as City Solicitor. Died at Warrenpoint, Ireland, June 9th, 1905. Water color. Size 3 x 4. Head and shoulders.

3232—**CHISHOLM, WILLIAM CRAIG**—City Solicitor, 1905-9—Eldest son of His Honor Judge Chisholm. Born at Port Hope, Ont., Aug. 20th, 1864; educated at Port Hope High School and Toronto University (B.A., 1885). Called to the Bar, 1888, and appointed K.C., 1908. In 1891 became Assistant City Solicitor, and in 1905 Solicitor, resigning to go into general practice as a member of the legal firm of Watson, Smoke & Smith. Water color. Size 3 x 4. Head and shoulders.

3233—**JOHNSTON, WILLIAM**—City Solicitor, 1909-17—A native of Morrisburg, Ont.; educated there and at Toronto University (B.A., 1883; LL.B., with honors, 1891). Called to the Bar in 1891 and first practised at Athens, Ont. In 1903 appointed Assistant City Solicitor, and six years later Solicitor. Water color. Size 3 x 4. Head and shoulders.

3234—**INDIANS PREPARING BIRCH BARK MAP FOR PROF. HIND**—In charge of the Expedition on the Labrador Peninsula, 1861—Before reaching the first gorge of the Moisie the Hind Expedition fell in with Domenique, chief of the Montagnais of the Moisie River, and his family en route to the coast. He and his adopted son, Michel, a Nasquapee, made for the guidance of the Expedition a map of the river, portages and old Montagnais route, showing where the Ashwanipi River took its rise and began its long course to Hamilton Inlet. Oil by William G. R. Hind, artist, Canadian Government Expedition to Labrador. Size 11 x 16.

3235—**ROMAN CATHOLIC PROCESSION OF INDIANS AT SEVEN ISLANDS**—On the Labrador Peninsula, 1861—The picture shows a Sunday evening procession from the Mission Chapel at Seven Islands, marching towards the cross in background. As soon as the assembly started the women began a chant in which the men soon joined. On reaching the cross the priest entered a temporary chapel, chanted a short service, and, after singing a hymn, the gathering returned again to the Mission Chapel for the customary priestly blessing. Chromo lithograph from drawing by William Hind, artist, Canadian Government Expedition to Labrador. Size 5 x 8.

3236—**THIRD RAPID ON THE MOISIE RIVER**—Labrador Peninsula, 1861—In 1861 the Canadian Government Expedition for the exploration of the Labrador Peninsula, started from the mouth of this river, called the "Great River" of the Montagnais Indians, on north shore of Gulf of St. Lawrence, east of the Bay of Seven Islands. The river is noted for salmon fisheries, and there are many rapids and, consequently, portages, from the mouth to its rise, about 150 miles north in the highlands of eastern Quebec. Chromo lithograph from drawing by William Hind, artist, Canadian Government Expedition to Labrador. Size 5 x 8.

3237—**SECOND GORGE OF THE MOISIE RIVER**—On the Labrador Peninsula, 1861—On June 20th the Canadian Government Expedition passed this gorge without difficulty, notwithstanding the rapid current, which increases greatly as the river is ascended. The scenery at the entrance to the second gorge is most impressive, with rocks rising to a great height above the river. Chromo lithograph from drawing by William Hind, artist, Canadian Government Expedition to Labrador. Size 5 x 8.

3238—**HIND EXPEDITION CROSSING MOSQUITO LAKE**—On the Labrador Peninsula, 1861—To reach Lake Nipsis from Trout Lake Prof. Hind and his party had to pass through four sheets of water and their connecting rivers, having to carry everything over the portages which separated them. The lakes had no Indian names, and on account of the number of mosquitoes there, the first lake was named Mosquito Lake by the expedition. In order to protect themselves from the insects, the canoeists were compelled to cover their heads and faces. Chromo lithograph from drawing by William Hind, artist, Canadian Government Expedition to Labrador. Size 5 x 8.

3239—**COURT HOUSE AND S.W. BASTION, FORT GARRY**—The Council of the Northern Department of Rupert's Land passed, 3rd June, 1835, a resolution "That a grant of £300 be made towards the expense of building a gaol about to be erected at Red River Settlement, and in aid of other public works in progress there." The building shown in picture was subsequently erected outside the fort and for many years used as a court house and gaol. In 1882 it was demolished when the walls, bastions and buildings inside Fort Garry were razed. Water color. Size 4 x 5.

3240—**SEVEN OAKS MONUMENT, WINNIPEG, MAN.**—For years rivalry had existed between the North-west Company and the Hudson's Bay. This rivalry and fur trading contest assumed a new form when Lord Selkirk determined to establish his colony, under the auspices of the latter company, on the banks of the Red River. Robert Semple, who had been sent out as Governor by Lord Selkirk, arrived at Fort Douglas in 1816. The Nor'westers had determined to attack the settlement. On 17th June two Cree Indians, who had escaped from the invaders, warned Gov. Semple that Fort Douglas would be attacked. Peguis, Chief of the Swampy Indians, also waited on the Governor, offering the aid of his tribe. An encounter took place on the afternoon of 19th June, about a mile from the fort. The half-breeds surrounded the Hudson's Bay people, who had arms, but no ammunition with them, and soon despatched the party. In all twenty-one persons, including Governor Semple, were killed. The monument at Seven Oaks was erected in 1891 by the Manitoba Historical Society, to the memory of those who were massacred there. Drawing, in water color. Size 4 x 6.

3241—**SOUTH-WEST BASTION, FORT VICTORIA**—A Hudson's Bay Post—The site of the fort, the foundation of the future city of Victoria, B.C., was selected in 1841 by Mr. James Douglas (afterwards Sir James, K.C.B.), and other officers of the Hudson's Bay Company. Building commenced in 1843. For a time all hands had to live in the fort, as the Indians were not to be trusted. Only a few were admitted at a time when they came for trading purposes. The two bastions, at the north-east and south-west corners respectively, were intended to overawe the Indians in case they committed offences, and were used in firing salutes on special occasions. The post was known first as Fort Albert, then as Fort Victoria, and finally became Victoria. In 1862 the city was incorporated, and on 24th Nov., 1864, the fort demolished and the lots advertised for sale. The present (1917) site of the north-east bastion is Government and Bastion streets, Victoria, and that of the south-west bastion (shown in picture), Wharf and Broughton streets. Water color. Size 5 x 7.

3242—A MONTAGNAIS INDIAN TAKING HIS SQUAW TO BURIAL— On the Labrador Peninsula, 1861—He is taking his squaw, who has died some distance from the burying-ground, to her last resting place, to lie with her body east and west—head to the west, the land of the happy hunting grounds. The grave is generally about three feet deep, and a small birch bark hut is built over it. When a woman is buried her paddles and her wooden dishes are placed in the lodge. Chromo lithograph from drawing by William Hind, artist, Canadian Government Expedition to Labrador. Size 5 x 7.

3243—SCENE FROM OJIA-PI-SI-TAGAN, OR TOP OF THE RIDGE PORTAGE—On the Labrador Peninsula, 1861—From this summit "The Top of the Ridge Lake" may be seen, surrounded by peaked mountains of a great height. The Canadian Government Expedition found the highest point of the portage path to be 800 feet above the lake, or about 1,460 feet above the sea. In the foreground is shown the capture of a caribou by a couple of Montagnais (Mountaineer) Indians. Chromo lithograph from drawing by William Hind, artist, Canadian Government Expedition to Labrador. Size 5 x 8.

3244—SEAL HUNTING IN THE GULF OF ST. LAWRENCE—Labrador Peninsula, 1861—In his "Explorations in Labrador," Prof. Henry Youle Hind states that "the Gulf of St. Lawrence forms the winter quarters of a vast number of seals, who come through the Straits of Belle Isle from Davis' Strait and the North Atlantic in November." Seals have been the chief cause of wars between the Montagnais and Esquimaux of the Labrador Peninsula. In 1857 the skins brought from four to twelve dollars apiece. Chromo lithograph from drawing by William Hind, artist, Canadian Government Expedition to Labrador. Size 5 x 8.

3245—BUFFALO HERD ON THE WESTERN PRAIRIES, 1863—A scene on the south branch of the Saskatchewan River, not far from the Qu'Appelle Valley—The herd is here shown in repose, far from the Plain Crees and other Indians and half-breed skilled hunters, whose favorite sport was "bringing in the buffalo," to be wantonly slain in pounds erected for the purpose. These pounds consisted of a circular fence, 120 feet broad, constructed of the trunks of trees laced together with withes, and braced by outside supports. At the present time there are in Canada about 2,500 buffalo, including those in park enclosures and the herd of wild buffalo near Fort Smith, Slave district. It is almost impossible, however, to estimate the number of wild buffalo. Each month the Government receive reports concerning numbers, and is thus enabled to issue a report annually. Drawing, in water color, by William G. R. Hind. Size 4 x 7.

3246—FOURTH RAPID OF THE MOISIE RIVER—Labrador Peninsula 1861—At the foot of this rapid, in their descent of the Moisie in July, 1861, a number of the Hind party were in danger of being swamped. When almost two-thirds of the way across, the canoe entered the swell of the rapid, and the water came over the sides of the craft. By dint of hard paddling, however, the bow touched the rocks just in time and the canoe was hauled in. Chromo lithograph from drawing by William Hind, artist, Canadian Government Expedition to Labrador. Size 5 x 8.

3247—MONTAGNAIS INDIAN—With his luggage—Crossing the portage of the Moisie (Misteshipu) River, on the Labrador Peninsula, 1861. The artist of the Hind Expedition thought the undulating surroundings a picturesque setting for the Montagnais and asked him to pose for a sketch. Oil by W. G. R. Hind, artist, Canadian Government Expedition to Labrador. Size 11 x 16.

3248—BUNGES INDIANS OF MANITOBA, 1863—A sub tribe of the Crees—They lived on the Assiniboine River at the western limit of Manitoba. The Crees, an important Algonquin tribe, ranged north-eastward to the vicinity of Hudson's Bay, and north-westward almost to Athabasca Lake. The Bunges were a fine looking, tall, well built race, and were like the Crees, nomadic, living by hunting and fishing. The lower picture represents an encampment of the Bunges with tepees and Qu'Appelle carts. Oil by W. G. R. Hind, brother of Prof. Henry Youle Hind. Size 15 x 18.

3249—PORTAGE ON THE MOISIE (MISTESHIPU) RIVER—On the Labrador Peninsula, 1861—A party of luggage-bearers of the Hind Expedition are here shown on one of the old and well-worn portage paths of the Moisie River, which for centuries has been a leading line of communication from the interior of Labrador to the coast. Bringing up the rear is a Montagnais Indian. The scenery along the Moisie is wild and picturesque. Oil by W. G. R. Hind, artist, Canadian Government Expedition to Labrador. Size 7 x 11.

3250—HIND, WILLIAM, G. R.—A well-known artist in Canada—Born at Nottingham, Eng., 12th June, 1833. Studied art in London and on the Continent. At the age of nineteen came to Toronto, where he held classes in drawing for two years. He returned to England, but in 1861 again came to Canada to join his brother, Prof. Henry Youle Hind, as artist in the Labrador Expedition for the purpose of making sketches and water color drawings of scenery and Indian life. In 1863-4 and also in the early seventies he was in Manitoba and British Columbia. During the latter part of his life he resided in different parts of New Brunswick. Many of the pictures in this collection, the Indian views particularly, were made by Hind. He died at Sussex, N.B., 1888. Portrait by the artist. Size 4 x 6. Head and shoulders.

3251—INDIAN WINDING SHEET—On the Labrador Peninsula, 1861— The winding sheet, thought to be absolutely essential, was generally procured before death took place. This squaw has just obtained one for her husband, whose end was expected at sunset. As she walked to the boat his eyes rested for a moment upon her and upon his shroud, and then turned towards the setting sun. The woman took her place in the craft and the party put away from shore. Chromo lithograph from drawing by William Hind, artist, Canadian Government Expedition to Labrador. Size 5 x 8.

3252—RUINS OF PRINCE OF WALES' FORT—As they stand to-day (1917) at the mouth of the Churchill River. Water color. Size 5 x 6. See 2368, 2384.

3253—RED RIVER CARTS—Since 1801, when the first Red River cart was made in the North-westers' fort at Pembina, the model has been continually in use all over the North-west. Being of wood and repairable with wood and shagamappi (raw hide cord), hunters and freighters could build or repair anywhere on the trails where wood existed. Where there was no wood, buffalo bones were used, and Moose Jaw city derives its name from the place where a "white man mended his cart with a moose jawbone." The picture shows a procession or festival of lighter built carts used by native women in travelling. The wheels had twelve spokes, not eight, as in picture. On hunting or freighting trails, one such covered cart would be seen in a long string of heavily laden carts, the cargo of which was protected by raw buffalo bull hides over the rails flat. When camping in a hostile or horse thieving country the carts were unhitched in a circle around the ponies during the night. Under the cart, with a leather lodge thrown over it, travellers rested or slept. The cart, with wheels off and lashed to the body and covered with a waterproof hide or oil sheet, made a raft to cross streams. Oil by W. G. R. Hind, 1862-63. Size 4 x 8.

3254—DOMENIQUE, A MONTAGNAIS CHIEF, AND HIS FAMILY— On the Labrador Peninsula, 1861—They were on their way in June, 1861, from a winter camp at Ashwanipi Lake to Seven Islands, just west of the mouth of the Moisie (Moisic). After passing the last gorge of the river on the downward journey Domenique met the Hind party and spent a day or two in camp near by. While sojourning here this picture was made. Oil by William Hind, artist, Canadian Government Expedition to Labrador. Size 11 x 16.

3255—DOG TRAIN OF THE NORTH-WEST—In the winter of 1863— These trains were used all over the North-west, and were very much in evidence in the fifties and sixties. The dogs hauled either carrioles or sledges, which were made of thin pieces of board ten feet long and fourteen inches wide. The teams were used by travellers for carriage of mails and goods, attached to the sledge by buffalo thongs. Oil by W. G. R. Hind. Size 7 x 9.

3256—INDIANS OF NEW BRUNSWICK—Malecites or Etchimins— Several explanations of the name Malecite have been given. According to Chamberlain it is from their Micmac name, Malisit, "broken talkers." The Malecites belong to the Abnaki group of the Algonquin stock. J. A. Maurault distinguishes between them and the Etchimin, but adds that "the remnants of this tribe and the Etchimin are called at the present day Malecites." The earliest recorded notice of the tribe is in Champlain's narrative of his voyage in 1604, when the country along the banks of the St. John River was in their possession. Fort La Tour was built on this river early in the 17th century and became the rallying point of the tribe. They intermarried with French settlers, thus forming a close alliance, and causing them to become enemies of the New England settlers. After the country fell into the hands of the English, repeated disputes arose between them and the Malecites in regard to lands, until 1776. The tribe was never numerous, and although some went into Nova Scotia and Quebec, the greater part remained in New Brunswick. Water colors by W. G. R. Hind. Size (each) 4 x 5. Head and shoulders.

3257—VISIT TO OTELNE, A NASQUAPEE, IN HIS LODGE—Labrador Peninsula, 1861—Prof. Henry Youle Hind and his brother, during their stay at Seven Islands in July, 1861, visited Otelne, the Tongue, in his lodge. It was constructed of birch bark, the pieces being stitched together with caribou sinews. On this occasion, doubtless in honor of the visitors, it accommodated about twenty-five persons. Like the Montagnais, the Nasquapees speak a dialect of the Cree. Chromo lithograph from drawing by William Hind, artist, Canadian Government Expedition to Labrador. Size 5 x 8.

3258—OTELNE, THE TONGUE, AND ARKASKE, THE ARROW—Two Nasquapee Indians on the Labrador Peninsula, 1861—After the visit of Prof. Henry Youle Hind and his brother to Otelne's lodge in July, 1861, the latter came with Arkaske to their tent to be sketched. Otelne, who is seated to the left of picture, is described as "a very handsome Indian," and Arkaske, to the right, "resembles him in most particulars." Chromo lithograph from drawing by William Hind, artist, Canadian Government Expedition to Labrador. Size 5 x 8.

3259—DUCK SHOOTING IN THE NORTH-WEST, 1863—A party of travellers, accompanied by William G. R. Hind, in the autumn of 1863, were attracted to this spot on the prairie, within four miles of Plum Creek, Oak Lake. Bits of marshland here proved a veritable paradise for the hunter, hundreds of ducks flocking to these spots every September. Members of the party brought back, besides a score of ducks, a number of pelicans on this occasion. Drawing, in water color, by W. G. R. Hind. Size 4 x 7.

3260—RESTING AT THE GRAND PORTAGE OF THE MOISIE RIVER —On the Labrador Peninsula, 1861—The scene is a striking one. It represents the luggage bearers of the Canadian Government Expedition after a steep climb of a mile and a half around the Grand Portage at the first rapids on the River Moisie. Chromo lithograph from drawing by William Hind, artist, Canadian Government Expedition to Labrador. Size 5 x 8.

3261—DOMENIQUE, A MONTAGNAIS CHIEF, AND HIS FAMILY— On the Moisie (Moisic), Labrador Peninsula, 1861—As he was seen canoeing in the vicinity of the first gorge of the river, near the camp of the Hind Expedition in June, 1861, before they made an ascent of the passage. Domenique, with his family, had wintered at Ashwanipi Lake, near what is now (1917) the southern boundary of Ungava, and were on their way to Seven Islands, where it was expected a priest would visit in July. Oil by William Hind, artist, Canadian Government Expedition to Labrador. Size 11 x 16.

3262—DUNKESWELL PARISH CHURCH (ST. NICHOLAS), DEVON, ENG.—It is about two miles south of Dunkeswell Abbey Church (Holy Trinity), built by Mrs. and the Misses Simcoe in 1842. The parish church, which is of ancient date, was partly rebuilt in 1817, and entirely rebuilt and enlarged about 1868. It is a cruciform structure with nave, chancel, short transepts and north and south aisles. The roof is of oak, as are also the pews. The tower was also rebuilt in 1868 and two additional bells put up, making fifteen in all. The Misses Simcoe were greatly interested in the work of the parish. On 27th January, 1850, Rev. John Blackmore, A.M., rector of Culmstock, in Devon, an esteemed friend of the family, preached Mrs. Simcoe's memorial sermon in this church. Pen drawing, colored, from a sketch made in 1800 by Mrs. Simcoe at Wolford, Devon. Size 9 x 14. See 3277.

3263—KING'S HEAD INN, BURLINGTON BAY—From the south-east —This tavern, or inn, stood near the present filtering basins of the Hamilton Water-works, and north of the pumping house. It was two miles south of the Burlington Canal, 200 feet from the bay shore, and faced north or north-westerly. In connection with the King's Head Inn and its situation, "Topographical Description of Upper Canada" says: "At the head of Lake Ontario there is a smaller lake, within a long beach, of about five miles, from whence there is an outlet to Lake Ontario, over which there is a bridge. At the south end of the beach is the King's Head, a good inn, erected for the accommodation of travellers, by order of his Excellency Major-General Simcoe, the Lieutenant-Governor. It is beautifully situated at a small portage which leads from the head of a natural canal connecting Burlington Bay with Lake Ontario, and is a good landmark." The building was burned by the Americans in 1812. Pen drawing, colored, from a sketch by Mrs. Simcoe. Size 6 x 12. See 3278.

3264—MRS. SIMCOE IN WELSH DRESS—Water color from a miniature at Wolford, Devon. Size 5 x 6. Head and shoulders. See 3275.

3265—SIMCOE, GENERAL JOHN GRAVES, FIRST LIEUTENANT-GOVERNOR, UPPER CANADA, 1792-96—From original crayon drawing at Wolford, Devon. Size 4 x 5. Head and shoulders. See 161, 406, 3370.

3266—ASCENSION OF KING GEORGE IV., 29TH JAN., 1820—Proclamation in connection with the ascension of George IV., King of Great Britain and Ireland (1820-30), which was read 3rd May, 1820, on the steps of the Legislative Buildings, east end of Palace street (now Front), and at the foot of the present (1917) Berkeley, which in those days was called Parliament street. The proclamation is signed by Samuel Smith, whose second term as Administrator of Upper Canada lasted from 8th March, 1820-29th June, 1820. Original. Size 12 x 15.

3267—HEMBURY FORT—On site of old Roman encampment, near Wolford, Devon, was the home of Admiral Graves. His wife, who was Elizabeth Posthuma Gwillim's aunt, cared for the child after her mother's death. Miss Gwillim spent her girlhood days at Hembury Fort, and it was here she met in 1782 her future husband, Colonel Simcoe. Etching on copper and in color, by Owen Staples, from a drawing by Mrs. Simcoe. Size 3 x 4.

3268—SIMCOE, CAPTAIN JOHN KENNAWAY, R.N.—Second son of Rev. H. A. Simcoe, and grandson of General Simcoe. Born 1825; married in 1867, Mary, second daughter of Col. Basil Jackson, of the late Royal Staff Corps, and in that year retired from the navy. Justice of the Peace for Devon. Inherited Wolford from his father. Died at Wolford, 1891. His widow still (1917) resides there. From a photograph at Wolford. Size 3 x 5. Head and shoulders.

3269—COLE, MRS. F. C. (LYDIA H. SIMCOE)—Granddaughter of Governor Simcoe, and fourth daughter of the Rev. Henry Addington Simcoe, by his first wife. She was born in 1832, and married in 1861 the Rev. Francis C. Cole, of Greywell, England. Her death occurred in March, 1914. This portrait is made from one taken on Mr. and Mrs. Cole's golden wedding day, 3rd Oct., 1911. Size 3 x 4. Head and shoulders.

3270—BUCKERALL PARISH CHURCH, DEVON, ENG.—In the spring of 1782 Lieut.-Colonel Simcoe met Miss Gwillim at Hembury Fort, the home of her aunt, Mrs. Samuel Graves. They shortly afterwards became engaged, and on the 30th December were married, the ceremony being performed by Rev. Thomas Rosskilly in Buckerall Parish Church. Admiral and Mrs. Graves were witnesses. Pen sketch, colored, from the original drawing. Size 8 x 12.

3271—SIMCOE, REV. HENRY ADDINGTON—Third son of Governor Simcoe, was born at Plymouth in 1800, educated at Oxford, ordained in Church of England, and from about 1826 served in the curacy of Egloskerry with Tremaine in Cornwall, and in 1846 became vicar. Died at Penheale Manor, near Launceston, 1868. From original crayon drawing at Wolford, Devon. Size 3 x 5. Head and shoulders.

3272—MURAL MEMORIAL IN ST. ANDREW'S CHURCH, COTTER-STOCK, ENG.—Erected to the memory of Capt. John Simcoe, R.N., father of Gen. Simcoe, first Lieut.-Governor of Upper Canada. The arms depicted are those of the Simcoe family as in 1759, and the ship shown is the "Pembroke" man-o'war, 60 guns, of which Capt. John Simcoe was commander in 1757. On board this vessel his death from pneumonia took place 15th May, 1759. Pen drawing for J. Ross Robertson, by Marcus Holmes, Oundle, England. Size 11 x 17.

3273—WAR BETWEEN AUSTRIA AND FRANCE—Proclamation issued by Lieut.-Governor Simcoe, 25th May, 1792, warning British subjects in Upper Canada from participating in the war commenced by Austria against France in the early days of the French Revolution, while Louis XVI. was still alive, but a prisoner. The term "The Most Christian King" (Le Roi tres Chretien) was a title borne by the Kings of France, and dates back to the time of Clovis, the latter half of the fifth century, and was probably conferred by one of the church councils. Original manuscript. Size 15 x 18.

3274—H.M.S. "PEMBROKE," 60 GUNS, BUILT 1757—In that year Capt. John Simcoe, R.N., father of Gen. John Graves Simcoe, was commander, and Mr. James Cook, afterwards the celebrated navigator, master of the "Pembroke." In 1758 the "Pembroke" sailed in a small fleet with Admiral Boscawen to serve under Major-Gen. Amherst in recapturing Louis-

34

burg. After the capitulation of Louisburg the "Pembroke" was sent with other ships to harass the French in the Gulf of St. Lawrence. In the spring of 1759 she formed part of Admiral Durrell's squadron to the St. Lawrence, and while on this expedition, Capt. John Simcoe died, 15th May, when the ship was off Anticosti. The "Pembroke" was at the bombardment of Quebec. Pen drawing by C. H. J. Snider, of Toronto, from an engraving, 1760. Size 11 x 14.

3275—SIMCOE, MRS. JOHN GRAVES (Elizabeth Posthuma Gwillim), only child of Lieut.-Colonel Thomas Gwillim, was born in 1766 at Whitchurch, in Herefordshire. She married in 1782 Lieut.-Colonel Simcoe, accompanying him to Canada in 1792. Incidents of life in Quebec and in the old Province of Upper Canada are related by Mrs. Simcoe in a diary which she kept from a few days prior to her departure from the homeland until she again arrived in London, 16th October, 1796. The family home was at Wolford, Devon, where Mrs. Simcoe died, 17th January, 1850. From original crayon drawing at Wolford, Devon. Size 5 x 6. Head and shoulders. See 3264.

3276—GWILLIM, LIEUTENANT-COLONEL THOMAS—Father of Mrs. Simcoe—Served in Canada, and was one of the three majors of brigade of General Wolfe at Quebec, 1759. He died in 1766, while his regiment was stationed at Gibraltar. From a crayon drawing. Size 3 x 5. Head and shoulders.

3277—DUNKESWELL PARISH CHURCH (ST. NICHOLAS)—Interior view, before restoration. Pen drawing, colored, from a sketch by Miss Harriet Simcoe, daughter of Governor Simcoe. Size 9 x 13. See 3262.

3278—KING'S HEAD INN, BURLINGTON BAY—From the north-west —Showing the sign on which the head of George III. was painted by Lieut. Pilkington, who was much amused when Governor Simcoe laughingly suggested that he ought to leave "one example of sign painting in Canada." Pen drawing, colored, from a sketch by Mrs. Simcoe. Size 9 x 13. See 3263.

3279—"OLD COURT," NEAR ROSS, HEREFORDSHIRE—Birthplace of Elizabeth Posthuma Gwillim (Mrs. Simcoe), and home of her mother, Elizabeth Spinckes. On the death of her parents Elizabeth Gwillim inherited "Old Court" and all it contained. Etching on copper and in color, by Owen Staples, from a drawing by Mrs. Simcoe. Size 3 x 5.

3280—DE LONGUEUIL, DOWAGER BARONESS (MARIE FLEURY D'ESCHAMBAULT)—Of noble French family—She married the third Baron de Longueil, Charles Jacques Le Moyne, who died on active military service in 1755. In 1770 the Baroness married a second time, Hon. William Grant, Receiver-General of the Province of Canada. Water color from an oil in possession of her great-great-granddaughter, Mrs. Rushton Fairclough, Stanford University, Cal. Size 3 x 5. Half length.

3281—DE LONGUEUIL, MARIE CHARLES JOSEPH DE MOYNE— Fourth Baroness in her own right, daughter and sole inheritor of the third Baron, who was killed at Lake St. Sacrement encounter, Sept., 1755. In 1781 she married Captain David Alexander Grant, of the 94th Regiment, nephew of the Receiver-General. She lived on the family property, St. Helen's Island, opposite Montreal. The Baroness was a much-loved person in her family, being known as the "Mimi" Baronne. She died at Montreal in 1841. Water color from an oil in possession of her great-granddaughter, Mrs. Arklay Fergusson, Ethiebeaton, Scotland. Size 3 x 5. Head and shoulders.

497

3282—"OLD COURT," NEAR ROSS, HEREFORDSHIRE, ENG.—While motoring through England in 1911, Mr. J. Ross Robertson and party visited "Old Court," where, in 1766, Elizabeth Posthuma Gwillim (Mrs. John Graves Simcoe) was born. This photo, taken on the occasion, shows, from left to right: Prof. Irving H. Cameron, M.B., Miss Jennie Holland, Mrs. J. Ross Robertson and Mr. J. Ross Robertson. Size 4 x 6.

3283—YORK HARBOR, 1793—With a glimpse of the shore, near the Old Fort. Sepia reproduction from a drawing by Mrs. Simcoe, in the King's Library, British Museum, London, Eng. Size 5 x 11.

3284—CREDIT RIVER—Near York, 1796—The Credit River empties into Lake Ontario, thirteen miles west of Toronto. Sepia reproduction from a drawing by Mrs. Simcoe in the King's Library, British Museum, London, Eng. Size 4 x 7.

3285—PLAYTER'S BRIDGE—First bridge over the Don River, foot of Winchester street, 1794—It was a butternut tree, with a pole fastened through the branches by Capt. George Playter, an early settler of York. Sepia reproduction from a drawing by Mrs. Simcoe, in the King's Library, British Museum, London, Eng. Size 4 x 7.

3286—CASTLE FRANK—On the Don River, York—Home of Governor Simcoe. In 1794 Gov. Simcoe built Castle Frank as a summer residence and named it after his son Francis Gwillim. It was in the woods, on the brow of a steep, high bank, overlooking the valley of the Don, at a point just beyond the fence, now the northern boundary of St. James' Cemetery. The building was not occupied permanently by the Governor and his family, but many excursions were made there, and week-ends spent by the friends, who enjoyed pleasant hours in the little settlement during Simcoe's Administration. In 1829 this quaint little structure was accidentally burned. Sepia reproduction from a drawing by Mrs. Simcoe, in the King's Library, British Museum, London, Eng. Size 4 x 7.

3287—THE GARRISON, YORK, 1796—Showing the first houses in the fort, and magazine on shore. Sepia reproduction from a drawing by Mrs. Simcoe, in the King's Library, British Museum, London, Eng. Size 4 x 7.

3288—BRIDGE OVER THE DON RIVER, YORK, 1796—It is impossible to identify the precise location of this bridge, but it is said to have been near Castle Frank Hill. Sepia reproduction from a drawing by Mrs. Simcoe, in the King's Library, British Museum, London, Eng. Size 4 x 7.

3289—CHARLOTTEVILLE—At Long Point, 1795—Lieutenant-Governor Simcoe proposed to found there a military establishment to aid in the defence of the new Province of Upper Canada, for he claimed that at Long Point was "the only good roadstead on Lake Erie" and "admirably adapted for settlements." Here he laid out a site for Government Buildings, calling it "Charlotte Villa," in honor of Queen Charlotte. The township of Charlotteville, surveyed afterwards, fronts on Long Point Bay, Lake Erie. Lord Dorchester strongly objected to this founding of a military settlement. In 1812 Fort Norfolk was built at Charlotteville, but nothing except the trenches remains. Sepia reproduction from a drawing in the King's Library, British Museum, by Lieut. Pilkington, and copied by Mrs. Simcoe. Size 4 x 7.

3290—BASS ISLAND—West end of Lake Erie, 1795. Sepia reproduction from a drawing in the King's Library, British Museum, by Lieut. Pilkington, and copied by Mrs. Simcoe. Size 4 x 7.

3291—**POINT AU BODET, QUE.,** 1792—On the north shore of Lake St. Francis, in the Seigniory of Monsieur de Longueuil, and a little east of the cove in which is the boundary line between the Provinces of Quebec and Ontario. Sepia reproduction from a drawing by Mrs. Simcoe in the King's Library, British Museum, London, England. Size 4 x 7.

3292—**KERR, ELIZABETH (BRANT)**—Born in 1796, youngest daughter of Joseph Brant (Thayendanegea), and a woman of charming and dignified manners. She lived for some time with her brother, Capt. John Brant, at Brant House, Burlington. It was her custom, on special occasions, to dress in Indian costume befitting her rank, and she so appeared at Government House balls and on similar occasions. In 1828 she married Col. William Johnson Kerr, who led the Indians at the battle of Beaver Dams, 24th June, 1813. Died April, 1845. Miniature from original in possession of Mrs. Donald Kerby, Morden, Man., granddaughter of Elizabeth Kerr. Size 2 x 2. Head and shoulders.

3293—**NEAR THE THOUSAND ISLANDS,** 1792—View of one of the many picturesque spots in the largest collection of river islands in the world. These islands, about fifteen hundred in number, are situated at the emergence from Lake Ontario, of the St. Lawrence in an expansion known as the Lake of the Thousand Isles. Sepia reproduction from a drawing by Mrs. Simcoe at Wolford, Devon. Size 3 x 7.

3294—**BRANTFORD (MOHAWK VILLAGE)**—On the Grand River, 1793—Showing Council House and church—After the Revolutionary War a great part of the Mohawks and a number of Indians from the other five tribes, withdrew to Canada, where the Six Nations subsequently received grants of land on the Bay of Quinte and Grand River. On the latter place was situated "Brant's Village"—(Brantford). In 1785, through the effort of Joseph Brant (Thayendanegea), a wooden church, that shown in the picture, was erected near Brantford, where was placed the first "church-going bell" that ever tolled in Upper Canada. The Council House was the building in which meetings and councils were held. Sepia reproduction from a drawing in the King's Library, British Museum, by Lieut. Pilkington and copied by Mrs. Simcoe. Size 4 x 7.

3295—**MURRAY, SIR GEORGE,** 1759-1819—"George Murray, Esqr., Rear-Admiral of the White Squadron. H. R. Cook, Sculp. Published Septr. 30, 1807, by J. Gold, 103 Shoe Lane, Fleet Street." Murray's services in the navy began about 1772, when he joined the "Panther," on the Newfoundland Station. In 1792 he was appointed to the "Triton," frigate, in which Governor Simcoe and his family sailed for Canada in October of that year. Vice-Admiral 1809; K.C.B. 1815. Line engraving. Size 3 x 4. Head and shoulders, oval.

3296—**THE BASILICA, QUEBEC**—Facing the old Market Square— Erected 1647; raised to the dignity of a Basilica in 1874. Etched by B. Magill; published by H. L. Everett. Size 8 x 11.

3297—**QUEENSTOWN, OR LOWER LANDING,** 1792—Then, as now, Queenstown was almost opposite Lewiston, the Lower Landing on the American shore. Sepia reproduction from a drawing by Mrs. Simcoe in the King's Library, British Museum, London, England. Size 4 x 7.

3298—**NIAGARA FALLS**—From the Canadian side, 1793—From a water color by Mrs. Simcoe, at Wolford, Devon. Size 4 x 7. See 3300.

3299—**QUEEN'S RANGERS' HUTS, QUEENSTOWN, U.C.,** 1792—In that year the Rangers were stationed at Queenstown (Queenston), where they built the huts shown in the picture. From a pen drawing by Mrs. Simcoe, at Wolford, Devon. Size 4 x 7.

3300—NIAGARA FALLS—From Canadian side, 1792. From a water color by Mrs. Simcoe, at Wolford, Devon. Size 3 x 7. See 3298.

3301—WHIRLPOOL RAPIDS, NIAGARA, 1793—From a pen drawing by Mrs. Simcoe, at Wolford, Devon. Size 4 x 7.

3302—TENTS OF MRS. SIMCOE IN CAMP, QUEENSTOWN (QUEENSTON), U.C., 1793—The picture gives Mrs. Simcoe's camp on the mountain, near Queenstown, where, owing to the illness of her son, Francis Gwillim, she spent July, 1793. From a pen drawing by Mrs. Simcoe, at Wolford, Devon. Size 4 x 7.

3303—NAVY HALL, NIAGARA, 1792—Sepia reproduction from a drawing by Mrs. Simcoe, in the King's Library, British Museum, London, Eng. Size 4 x 7. See 1269.

3304—MRS. GILBERT TICE'S HOUSE, QUEENSTOWN (QUEENS-TON), U.C., 1795—Mrs. Tice, at whose home Mrs. Simcoe spent part of the summer of 1795, was the wife of Captain Gilbert Tice, a U.E.L., who settled in Niagara about 1786. From a pen drawing by Mrs. Simcoe, at Wolford, Devon. Size 4 x 7.

3305—COOTE'S PARADISE, BURLINGTON BAY, 1796—At this date the marsh between the head of Burlington Bay and Dundas, was known as Coote's Paradise, from the fact that Capt. Coote, a keen sportsman, formerly of the 8th Regiment of Foot, spent a great deal of his time there shooting ducks. In 1826 an Act was passed incorporating a company with authority to construct a canal from Burlington Bay to the village of Coote's Paradise (Dundas). This work became known as the Desjardins Canal. Sepia reproduction from a drawing by Mrs. Simcoe, in the King's Library, British Museum, London, Eng. Size 4 x 7.

3306—LAKE ONTARIO AND ORIGINAL ENTRANCE TO BURLING-TON BAY, 1796—Up to 1792 Burlington Bay was known as Geneva Lake, or Macassa Bay, when by proclamation the name was changed. The picture is the only one known of the original entrance to the bay at the extreme north end of the beach. It was almost landlocked in 1796. Sepia reproduction from a drawing by Mrs. Simcoe in the King's Library, British Museum, London, Eng. Size 4 x 7. See 3307.

3307—ORIGINAL ENTRANCE TO BURLINGTON BAY, 1795—Sepia reproduction from a drawing by Mrs. Simcoe, in the King's Library, British Museum, London, Eng. Size 4 x 7. See 3306.

3308—WATERFALL NEAR BURLINGTON BAY, 1794—Sepia reproduction from a drawing by Mrs. Simcoe, in the King's Library, British Museum, London, Eng. Size 4 x 7.

3309—BURLINGTON BAY—A view from the King's Head Inn, 1796. Sepia reproduction from a drawing by Mrs. Simcoe, in the King's Library, British Museum, London, Eng. Size 4 x 7.

3310—MOUTH OF THE WELLAND RIVER—At Chippawa, U.C., 1795. Sepia reproduction from a drawing by Mrs. Simcoe, in the King's Library, British Museum, London, Eng. Size 4 x 7.

3311—SPRAY OF THE FALLS OF NIAGARA—As seen from Chippawa River. Sepia reproduction from a drawing by Mrs. Simcoe, in the King's Library, British Museum, London, Eng. Size 4 x 7.

3312—**FORT CHIPPAWA, U.C.,** 1795—On the Welland River—Fort Chippawa was built by the British to protect their portage at this point. The fort stood at the mouth of the Chippawa Creek, or river (called the Welland by proclamation, July, 1792). On the 5th July, 1814, the Battle of Chippawa was fought between the Americans and British, and after persistent fighting and clever manoeuvring on each side, the latter were compelled to retreat until their entrenchments below Chippawa were reached. Sepia reproduction of a drawing by Mrs. Simcoe, in the King's Library, British Museum, London, Eng. Size 4 x 7.

3313—**FORT ERIE, COUNTY OF WELLAND,** 1795—A glimpse of the lake and beach—Fort Erie is in Welland County, on Lake Erie. It was first fortified during the French occupation, and greatly strengthened during the War of 1812. Since then it has gone gradually to decay, and has long been dismantled. Sepia reproduction from a drawing by Mrs. Simcoe, in the King's Library, British Museum, London, Eng. Size 4 x 7.

3314—**SIMCOE, MRS. JOHN KENNAWAY**—The "Lady of the Manor" at Wolford, Devon—Daughter of the late Col. Basil Jackson, of Glewstone Court, Herefordshire, and an officer of the late Royal Staff Corps. She married in 1867, Capt. John Kennaway Simcoe, R.N., grandson of General Simcoe. Captain Simcoe died in 1891, and Mrs. Simcoe has the life interest in the estate of Wolford. Photograph (1911). Size 4 x 6. Three-quarter length.

3315—**CARLETON, GUY, FIRST BARON DORCHESTER**—Governor-General of Canada, Sept. 12th, 1791-Dec. 15th, 1796—Served in America, 1758-62, and from 1766-70 was Acting-Governor of Quebec. Returned to England, 1770. Advocated the passing of the Quebec Act, and in 1775 returned as Governor of the Province of Quebec; in December of that year successfully defending Quebec against the American invaders under Arnold and Montgomery. As Governor he resided in Quebec, 1786-91, and as Governor-General from 1793 till 1796. He was born in Strabane, Island, 1724; created first Baron Dorchester, 1786, and died in 1808. Engraved by A. H. Ritchie. Size 3 x 4. Head and shoulders.

3316—**DORCHESTER, LADY (MARIA HOWARD)**—Younger daughter of the Earl of Effingham—During Sir Guy Carleton's (Baron Dorchester) stay in England, 1770-74, she became his wife, accompanying him to Canada after the passing of the Quebec Act. From a copy of a miniature in England. Size 4 x 5. Head and shoulders, oval.

3317—**BUST OF COL. HON. JOHN SIMCOE MACAULAY, R.E.—** "Presented to Mrs. Macaulay by the Gentlemen Cadets of the 1st Academy, Woolwich." John Simcoe Macaulay, eldest son of Dr. James Macaulay, of the Queen's Rangers, was born 1791, and named in honor of Governor Simcoe, who was his godfather. Col. Macaulay married a daughter of Chief Justice Elmsley, and resided at Elmsley Villa, near Yonge and Grosvenor sts., Toronto, on the outskirts of the Chief Justice's property. Elmsley Villa was known as Government House in Lord Elgin's day, and in the fifties was purchased for occupancy by Knox College. The bust is at Langstone Court, Exmouth, Devon, where two daughters of Col. John Simcoe Macaulay still (1917) reside. Photo. Size 6 x 8. See 985, 1668.

3318—**GOVERNMENT GRIST MILL, APPANEE (NAPANEE) RIVER** —On the left bank of the river, just below the Falls—It was set up on the 25th May, 1786, and the grinding of wheat was begun a year later. It is said that the Ross Grist Mill, in operation until a few years ago in Napanee, Ont., occupied approximately the site of the original grist mill. Sepia reproduction, from a drawing by Mrs. Simcoe, in the Royal Library, British Museum, London, England. Size 4 x 7.

3319—**COLLIER**—"Sir George Collier, Knt.—Vice-Admiral of the Blue, Blood, sc. Published Octr. 31st, 1814, by Joyce Gold, Naval Chronicle office, 103 Shoe Lane, London." Sir George was senior officer at Halifax, July, 1776 to 1779, and in 1780 commanded the "Canada" man-of-war. Stipple engraving. Size 3 x 4. Head and shoulders, oval.

3320—**COLLIER, LADY (ELIZABETH FRYER)**—Second wife of Sir George Collier. Lady Collier, who married Sir George in 1781, was a personal friend of Mrs. Simcoe. Sir Joshua Reynolds, pinxt. S. W. Reynolds, sculp. Line engraving. Size 4 x 5. Half length.

3321—**KINGSTON, U.C.**, 1794—With key—Three pictures of Kingston were made by Mrs. Simcoe, this one, from the water front, bearing date 1794. It shows the principal houses and the steeple and belfry of the first Protestant Church, built 1790-3, and known from 1820 as St. George's. Sepia reproduction from a drawing by Mrs. Simcoe, in the King's Library, British Museum, London, Eng. Size 4 x 7.

3322—**TWENTY-MILE CREEK**, 1796 (JORDAN, ONT.)—Twenty-Mile Creek runs into Twenty-Mile Pond before it reaches the lake. Jordan, Ont., is situated three miles from the lake shore, on high ground, having on its left a deep valley through which flows the "Twenty-Mile Creek." Sepia reproduction from a drawing by Mrs. Simcoe, in the King's Library, British Museum, London, England. Size 4 x 7.

3323—**FIFTEEN-MILE CREEK**, 1794—St. Catharines, Ontario (formerly known as "The Twelve"), is near the Fifteen, which is not actually occupied by the site of any place. Sepia reproduction from drawing by Mrs. Simcoe, in the King's Library, British Museum, London, Eng. Size 4 x 7.

3324—**HEAD OF BIG CHUTE, near GLOUCESTER POOL**—The Big Chute has been developed by the Simcoe Power, Light and Railway Company, and for many years there has been a lumberman's dam at this point. At the right side of the river, going down stream, in the neighborhood of the Big Chute, there is considerable indentation caused by the dams raising the water. This indentation was not apparent in 1793. Sepia reproduction from a drawing in the King's Library, British Museum, London, Eng., by Lieut. Pilkington and copied by Mrs. Simcoe. Size 4 x 7.

3325—**McLEAN'S BAY**—At the outlet of Sparrow Lake. Sepia reproduction from a drawing in the King's Library, British Museum, London, Eng., by Lieut. Pilkington, and copied by Mrs. Simcoe. Size 4 x 7.

3326—**SPARROW LAKE**—The chute, two or three miles below McLean's Bay, has been considerably affected by dams built on the Ragged Rapids, to such an extent, in fact, that it is no longer navigable by steamers. Sepia reproduction from a drawing in the King's Library, British Museum, London, Eng., by Lieut. Pilkington, and copied by Mrs. Simcoe. Size 4 x 7.

3327—**LITTLE CHUTE**—Near the entrance to Gloucester Pool. Sepia reproduction from a drawing in the King's Library, British Museum, London, Eng., by Lieut. Pilkington, and copied by Mrs. Simcoe. Size 4 x 7.

3328—**GLOUCESTER POOL, SEVERN RIVER**—Gloucester Pool is an enlargement of the Severn River, five miles from its mouth—The Severn empties into Georgian Bay at Port Severn on the east side of the bay at its southern extremity. Civilization has so completely altered the aspect of this landscape that it is a difficult matter after a hundred years to identify places. Sepia reproduction from a drawing in the King's Library, British Museum, by Lieut. Pilkington, and copied by Mrs. Simcoe. Size 4 x 7.

3329—McDONALD'S RAPIDS—Below Sparrow Lake and Ragged Rapids—McDonald's Rapids have been almost obliterated by blasting done by the Dominion Government and by the town's power dam at the Ragged Rapids, but Mr. G. H. Hale, of Orillia, says that in his recollection the principal cascade of McDonald's Rapids was as shown in this picture. Sepia reproduction from a drawing in the King's Library, British Museum, London, Eng., by Lieut. Pilkington, and copied by Mrs. Simcoe. Size 4 x 7.

3330—RESIDENCE OF COL. FRANCIS BABY, WINDSOR, C.W.—Near the corner of Church and Sandwich streets, about forty feet from the street—In 1812 the location was the farm of Col. Francis Baby, who was member of the Executive and Legislative Councils, and later Adjutant-General of Militia, Lower Canada. The orchard, a part of the farm, was where the Battle of Windsor was fought on the morning of 4th Dec., 1838. The old dwelling, a storey and a half frame house, with weather-beaten sideboards, was demolished in the mid-seventies. The site on Sandwich street is now (1917) occupied by the Scott wholesale grocery, British American Brewery and the Frederick Stearns Laboratory. Water color. Size 4 x 5.

3331—ST. JOHN'S CHURCH (ANGLICAN), SANDWICH, ONT.—As rebuilt in 1872—Previous to 1796 occasional religious services were held in a little Indian meeting house, facing the Indian trail, now (1917) called Huron street, where the present church stands. A small log building was put up in 1796, and Richard Pollard, then a layman, held services therein. Later he became first rector of St. John's. The first church, built of logs and ripped boards, was destroyed 13th Sept., 1813, by Gen. Harrison's men, the Kentucky Horse, and rebuilt in 1818. The body of the church was reconstructed of brick in 1872, the windows and interior being made more modern. This is the church of to-day. A mural tablet to the memory of Hon. Alexander Grant, Administrator U.C., 1805-6, was some years ago placed in St. John's. Rev. D. H. Hind, son of Prof. Henry Youle Hind, was rector from 1887 until his death in 1916. Water color. Size 5 x 6.

3332—MALDEN, OR AMHERSTBURG, IN 1860—A town with an historic past—It is in the Township of Malden, Essex County, on the Detroit River, and in 1812-15 was the western outpost of the old Province of Upper Canada, now Ontario. It was laid out in 1796, and early the following year Fort Amhertsburg was begun. By some, the group of houses outside the fort, to the south, was for a time called Malden, but there does not appear to have been any Fort Malden in the early days. The second fort was known by both names, and the third, built after the Rebellion of 1837, bore the name Fort Malden. The picture gives an extensive view of the river, southward, with Elliott's Point to the left, and Bois Blanc Island, now a public park, on the right. Looking to the right on the island is the lighthouse and blockhouse battery, erected 1812. In that year a blockhouse was also erected at the upper end of the shipyard, and in 1838 there were two put up on the water front. From 27th Sept. 1813-1st July, 1815, Amherstburg was occupied by American troops, the British having partly destroyed it before their retreat. On the restoration of peace, however, it again fell into British possession. Water color. Size 4 x 7.

3333—CHRIST CHURCH, AMHERSTBURG, 1809-1917—Situated at Ramsey street, at the south end of the town—The first missionary to Amherstburg was Richard Pollard, 1792-1802, who in the latter year became first rector of the Parish of Sandwich. Although it has been impossible to ascertain the exact date Christ Church was built, as early as 1809 Adoniram Masonic Lodge, No. 18, attended service here. It is of red brick, with a porchway added in 1852. The steeple was burned in 1893 and rebuilt the same year. This old place of worship, with the exception of a few alterations, appears as it did in the early days of the nineteenth century. Water color. Size 5 x 5. See 3334.

3334—CHRIST CHURCH, AMHERSTBURG, U.C.—Interior view—The pulpit, communion table and lectern, which were originally of walnut, have been replaced by brass. In 1874, during the incumbency of Rev. T. C. Des Barres, afterwards rector of St. Paul's Church, Toronto, a transept and chancel was built. In 1912 the false ceiling was taken out, exposing the original roof, which members of Christ Church consider quaint and unique. The pews and furniture were also replaced. Water color. Size 3 x 6. See 3333.

3335—GUELPH, C. W., 1862—On the River Speed, in Wellington County, Ontario—It was founded in 1827 by John Galt, secretary of the Canada Company, and named after the Royal Family of Great Britain. The view is from the Grand Trunk Railway tracks at the south side of the town, looking north up Lower Wyndham street—With key. Water color on print. Size 4 x 10.

3336—GUELPH, U.C., 1840—From the hill below the Water Tower— With key. The City of Guelph, on the Speed River, was named in honor of the Royal House of Brunswick. In April, 1827, Mr. John Galt, secretary of the Canada Company, and Dr. Dunlop, walked through the rain to the site chosen for Guelph, losing their way en route. They had a large maple tree cut down, and, the doctor producing a flask of whiskey, they drank prosperity to the City of Guelph. In 1828 settlers began to arrive in large numbers and houses were put up in all directions. Guelph, now a flourishing city, is built almost entirely of limestone quarried in the vicinity, and is picturesquely situated upon a number of hills. Water color from a drawing by Miss Neeve, an early resident of the Royal City. Size 9 x 13.

3337—BARRACKS AT SANDWICH, U.C.—They were built during the War of 1812-14, and in 1867 demolished to make room for the Sandwich Public school on Bedford street. This in turn was succeeded by a modern building, known as "The General Brock Public School," opened in September, 1915. The dock to the right of the picture was the "Henry Kennedy Dock," in Sandwich Bay, which went out of existence about forty years ago. The buildings shown on the opposite side of the Detroit River, near Fort Wayne (not in picture), were the Cooper Smelting Works. These, too, are no longer to the fore. The American side of the river was at that time known as Springwells, Mich. It is now (1917) a part of the City of Detroit. The Essex County Historical Society, at the suggestion of Mr. Frederick Neal, Sandwich, marked the premises a few years ago with a suitable tablet. Water color. Size 3 x 7.

3338—"MARCH OF INTELLECT"—School in Adelaide, visited Decr., 1845. Teacher, Mr. St. Leger. Sketched at the time. W. E." This quaint old picture shows the interior of a primitive school in the Township of Adelaide, Middlesex County, in 1845. William Elliott, afterwards County Judge of Middlesex, was in the early forties appointed a District Superintendent of Schools, and it was on the occasion of one of his visits to this "hall of learning" that he made the sketch. It was presented by Judge Elliott to Sir George W. Ross, who in turn gave it to the late Lachlan McCorkindale, of Toronto. From the latter's family it was obtained by J. Ross Robertson in 1913. As a relic of old times it is of great interest. Colored cartoon. Size 6 x 8.

3339—RESIDENCE OF HENRY DE BLAQUIERE, DUNDAS STREET, WOODSTOCK, ONT.—The cottage stood on the north side of Dundas street, and was erected in 1838 by Thomas Spunner Short. Subsequently it was purchased by Henry de Blaquiere, and in 1903 demolished to make room for the residence of Mr. James Hay. Photograph, colored. Size 5 x 7.

3340—WILKINSON HOMESTEAD, CHIPPAWA ST., SANDWICH, C.W. —Built immediately after the War of 1812 by Col. (Hon.) John A. Wilkinson, who brought the material for the house from Montreal. The quaint old dwelling is now (1917) owned by Miss Fanes Nelson, a descendant of the Colonel. He had served in the British army during the Peninsular Campaign, and was sent to Canada to take part in the War of 1812. From 1828-35 he was member for Essex, in the Legislature of Upper Canada. Photograph, colored. Size 5 x 6.

3341—METHODIST CHURCH, SWITZERVILLE, C.W.—Home of the first Methodist Conference in Canada—This church is in the village of Switzerville, six miles from Napanee, in Lennox County. It was built in 1826, of frame, and in it was held the first Methodist Conference and the first ordination service in Canada. The farewell tea meeting, held previous to removing to the new brick church in Switzerville, was held 20th Jan., 1892. Water color. Size 5 x 7.

3342—COL. (HON.) JAMES BABY'S RESIDENCE, SANDWICH, U.C. Built in 1790 for the North-west fur trade—The house, which stands halfway up the hill at the corner of Russell and Mills streets, is about 40 x 50 ft. in size, two and a half storeys high, with a three-foot stone wall cellar the size of the house. Frederick Neal, the Sandwich historian, in his work, "The Township of Sandwich, Past and Present," writes that the frame work of the building was filled with bricks and mortar and that the beams and sheeting, as well as sills of doors and windows, are of warnut. In the large hallway, which was the trading room, was hung an iron hook, still there, from which were suspended massive scales capable of weighing 2,000 pounds of furs. At the Battle of the Thames, 5th Oct., 1813, Col. Baby, commanding the Kent Militia, was taken prisoner, and returned to Sandwich with General Harrison, who occupied this house as his headquarters. In 1905 Dr. W. J. Beasley purchased the property, and now (1917) resides in the old homestead. The Essex County Historical Society in 1908 placed on the north side of the house, next to Mill street, coming up from the river, a bronze tablet bearing the following inscription: "This dwelling was erected about 1790 by the Hon. James Baby, Legislative Councillor. The headquarters of Gen. Hull when he invaded Canada in 1812. Subsequently occupied by Gen. Brock, Col. Proctor and Gen. Harrison." Water color. Size 5 x 6.

3343—TALBOT, COLONEL THOMAS, 1771-1853—Founder Talbot Settlement, Township of Dunwich. Born at Malahide, near Dublin, Ireland. In May, 1783, he received a commission as ensign in the 66th Regiment of Foot, and in September of the same year became lieutenant. Joined 24th Regiment at Quebec, and soon after Governor Simcoe's arrival in Canada, became his private and confidential secretary. In 1796 he was appointed lieut.-colonel of the 5th Foot, which had been stationed at Niagara during his period on Simcoe's staff, and three years later commanded the second battalion in Holland. Took up permanent residence in Canada in 1803, receiving a grant of 5,000 acres in the Township of Dunwich, County of Middlesex. During his residence in Canada, Col. Talbot occasionally visited England, and it was on his last visit, in 1851, that he met the companion of his early youth, Arthur Wellesley, then Duke of Wellington. It is a coincidence that they died within a few months of each other, the "Iron Duke" passing away 14th September, 1852, and the "Founder of the Talbot Settlement" on 6th Feb., 1853. Water color. Size 3 x 5. Head and shoulders.

3344—DUNDAS WRECK—"View of the accident on the G. W. Railway, near Dundas, on the morning of the 19th March, 1859. From a sketch taken on the spot lithographed and published by H. Gregory, Hamilton,

C.W." Where the accident happened between Copetown and Dundas, Ont., a ravine had been filled in. Heavy rains undermined and washed it away, causing a hole 100 yards long by 50 feet deep. In the early morning darkness, for the disaster took place at 2.30, the engineer did not see the gap, and the train dashed over the embankment. Seven persons were killed, amongst whom was Alexander Baird, locomotive superintendent, and several injured. Size 8 x 13.

3345—A DIVISION COURT AT MONO MILLS, SIMCOE COUNTY, 1855 —Exterior of Court House—This old log dwelling had for twenty-five years been the dwelling of George McManus, clerk of the Mono Mills Court, and subsequently clerk of the 8th Division Court of the County of Simcoe. When he moved into a substantial brick house, his former home became the Court House. 1. The man on horseback was James McLaughlin, a farmer and prominent resident. 2. Robert Keenan, a merchant of Keenansville, nine miles distant. He was a genial Irishman, and is here seen presenting the case, with authority, to attentive listeners. Water color from a sketch by Lucius O'Brien, R.C.A. Size 3 x 5. See 3346-7.

3346—INTERIOR OF COURT HOUSE, MONO MILLS, SIMCOE CO., 1855—The apartment shown had been the principal room in the old home of Mr. George McManus, and had been divided along one side to keep the crowd at a respectful distance from the judge and the bar. 1. Judge Gowan (Sir James R. Gowan, Senator). 2. Lucius O'Brien, artist. 3. Mr. George McManus, clerk of the court. 4. John Haffey, bailiff of the court, tendering the oath to a witness. 5. Thomas Jackson, a resident of Mono Mills. 6. Alex Hamilton, a witness making oath. 7. Rev. John Fletcher, Anglican clergyman at Mono Mills. 8. James Darragh, an old settler, comfortably hanging over the bar. Water color from a sketch by Lucius O'Brien, R.C.A. Size 5 x 6.

3347—JURY DELIBERATING UPON A CASE AT MONO MILLS, SIMCOE CO., 1855—The jury of five, summoned by Judge Gowan, had stowed themselves in a corner of the room. When the case was closed a difficulty presented itself in that there was no other room to which they could retire. Thereupon Judge Gowan told them to deliberate out of doors, charging them on their honor not to speak to anyone until their return. With one consent, and with wonderful foresight, the jury betook themselves to the orchard. In about the time required to eat half a dozen apples apiece and fill their pockets, they returned, giving verdict in favor of the defendant. Water color from a sketch by Lucius O'Brien, R.C.A. Size 4 x 5.

3348—ORILLIA, ON LAKE COUCHICHING, C.W.—With key—View from Cedar Island, looking west, August, 1864. In the picture only about one-third of the buildings in the town at the time are shown. Doubtless those appearing are all that would be visible from the point at which the picture was made. The Indian name for the locality of Orillia was Me-che-kuh-neeg, or "narrows dividing two lakes." Water color by Captain W. H. Grubbe. Size 7 x 20.

3349—NAVAL AND MILITARY ESTABLISHMENT AT PENETAN-GUISHENE, U.C., 1818—The view, with key, is an excellent one of the harbor—Towards the close of the War of 1812 a naval establishment was proposed for Penetanguishene. It was broken up 10th March, 1815, revived three years later as a naval and military depot, and in the early fifties finally reduced. Lieut. Bayfield, who became Admiralty Surveyor in 1817, made his headquarters in Penetanguishene for some time. In 1846 Rev. A. W. H. Rose stated with regard to the place: "Penetanguishene is situated at the bottom of a bay, extremely shallow on one side, and is a small military and naval station, the latter force consisting of two iron war steamers of about sixty horse power each." Water color from original in possession of Prof. J. Watson Bain, Toronto. Size 6 x 26.

3350—HISTORIC HOUSE NEAR CHATHAM, U.C.—Built in 1797 by John McGregor, and still (1917) standing, on lot 3, River road, Harwich Township. Here the first mail was distributed and the first courts held for the district. McGregor succeeded Thomas Clark as owner of a grist mill on the north bank of what became known as McGregor's Creek, a little south-west of the house. Prior to the War of 1812 the mill was burned by the Indians, but later rebuilt. The old house, which stands just outside the Corporation of Chatham, is used as a barn on the McGregor farm, occupied by a descendant of the family. Water color. Size 5 x 6.

3351—HOME OF DUNCAN McGREGOR, CHATHAM, U.C., 1825— Situated in front and north of the old building in which the first courts for the district were held. For many years Duncan McGregor occupied the house and farm attached. Later it was owned by D. A. Wilcox and is now (1917) in possession of Mrs. J. E. McIntyre, daughter of the latter. The ravine to the east of the house on the north bank of McGregor Creek is, it is said, where Tecumseh camped in the early part of October, 1813. Photograph, colored. Size 4 x 6.

3352—CHATHAM, C.W., 1860—A view of King street west—with key. Water color from photograph. Size 6 x 10.

3353—CRYSLER'S HOUSE, 1855—Near this spot the Battle of Crysler's Farm took place on 11th November, 1813, between the British and American forces. The land was given by the Crown to Ludwick Aeker and John Killam, who sold it to John Crysler. From time to time it fell into different hands until purchased by Abram Van Allen, father of William Van Allen, the present owner. In the old house, which stood on the northeast corner of lot 13, first concession of Williamsburg, County Dundas, were placed the killed and wounded in the battle. In 1855 the chimney and foundation were all that remained of the building, and these, too, were removed in the late seventies. A monument erected by the Canadian Parliament to the memory of those who fell stands near the eastern line of lot 12, some distance east of the Van Allen home. Historians have given several spellings of the word "Crysler," the commonly accepted form being "Chrystler." In all deeds and mortgages, however, for over a hundred years it is spelled "Crysler," and descendants of the family to-day use that spelling. Water color from a drawing by Lossing. Size 4 x 7.

3354—OLD STONE CHURCH, SACKSVILLE, ONT.—Known as Christ Church (Anglican), built about 1806 by the U.E. Loyalists, assisted by Rev. Richard Pollard, first missionary to Amherstburg, 1792-1802. The waters of Lake Erie have washed away a portion of the old parish graveyard surrounding the church, which has not been used for nearly half a century. Expenditure has been made, without success, in the effort to stay the ravages of the lake waters. A modern frame church has been built further inland. The present (1917) rector is Rev. W. J. Connor, of Colchester. Water color from a photo by W. D. McKay, Kingsville, 1913. Size 4 x 6.

3355—BATTLE GROUND OF THE THAMES, OR MORAVIANTOWN —On the morning of the 5th October, 1813, a battle was fought here between the British and Indian forces under General Proctor and the celebrated Shawanoe (a sub-tribe of the great Algonquin nation) chief, Tecumseh, and the American forces under General Harrison. The scene of the battle was on the right of the River Thames, at the Indian village of Moraviantown. The result was disastrous to the British troops. Gen. Proctor, seeing that he would be hemmed in by Harrison's army, retreated; Tecumseh was killed; and so the day was lost. After the battle the Indians removed to the opposite side of the river. In 1836 they were induced to surrender a large portion of their land, about six miles square, for an annuity of one hundred and fifty pounds. Old Moraviantown was in the Township of Zone, Kent County, but the present Moraviantown, across the river, is in the Township of Orford. The site of the old village is now occupied by cultivated farms, and there are on the north side of the river a few graves, where the early Indians had their burying-ground. Water color. Size 5 x 6.

3356—BATTLE OF CRYSLER'S FARM, 11TH NOV., 1813—Monument to the memory of those who fell there—The engagement took place near the farm of a Canadian settler named Crysler, not far from the head of the Long Sault Rapids. About noon on 11th November the battle commenced, General Boyd commanding the American force of some 1,800 in three columns, including a regiment of dragoons, and Colonel Morrison commanding 800 British. The latter formed his line in the open fields, and Boyd, who had landed at Cook's Point, about half a mile below the monument shown in picture, advanced with his force. About half-past two the action became general, and, after a stubbornly contested fight, ended in victory for the British. A monument erected by the Canadian Parliament stands on lot 12, first concession of Williamsburg, County Dundas, on land given for the purpose to the Government by Abram Van Allen, whose son now occupies the old Crysler farm. The inscription reads: "In honour of the brave men who fought and fell in the victory of Crysler's farm on the 11th November, 1813, this monument was erected by the Canadian Parliament, 1895." It is built of Canadian granite, and stands in a commanding position, 60 feet above the St. Lawrence. Photograph, colored. Size 6 x 10.

3357—BIRTHPLACE OF TECUMSEH, OR TECUMTHA, CHIEF OF THE SHAWANOE TRIBE—The village of Piqua, on the north side of the Mad River, a few miles west of Springfield, Ohio. This was the ancient Piqua, the seat of the Piqua clan of the Shawanoe tribe, a name signifying "a man formed out of the ashes." Near the river stood a rude fort of logs and surrounded by a stockade, outside of which were grouped huts and wigwams of the inhabitants. In this village Tecumseh was born in 1768. Water color. Size 3 x 6.

3358—TECUMSEH, OR TECUMTHA—A celebrated Indian chief and statesman of the Shawanoe tribe—He was born in 1768 at Piqua, on the banks of the Mad River (a tributary of the Ohio), about seven miles below the present Springfield. His father was a chief of the Kiscopoke, and his mother a member of the Turtle band, both clans of the Shawanoe tribe, a sub-tribe of the Algonquins. The name Tecumseh, or more properly speaking, "Tecumtha," according to the native pronunciation, means "a panther springing upon its prey." He was engaged in many incursions into Kentucky, formed the project of uniting the Western Indians against the Americans, the former, under Tecumseh's brother, the "Prophet," being defeated at Tippecanoe, 7th Nov., 1811. In 1812 he joined the British, obtained the rank of Brigadier-General; was at the capture of Detroit in August of that year, and in the Battle of Moraviantown, or the Thames, 5th Oct., 1813, was killed. The battle was lost through the retreat of the British General Proctor. The spot where the great Indian warrior fell is marked by a tablet, erected by the citizens of Thamesville, 1911. This portrait is from a pencil sketch by Pierre le Dru, a French trader. Lossing says he found the sketch in possession of Le Dru's son at Quebec, 1848, and was permitted to copy it. The dress, however, is from a drawing which

Lossing saw in Montreal in the summer of 1858, made at Malden after the surrender of Detroit, where the Indians celebrated that event by a grand feast. In the uniform Tecumseh appears as a Brigadier-General of the British army. His burial place is unknown. Water color by Owen Staples. Size 6 x 8. Head and shoulders.

3359—GRAND TRUNK BRIDGE ACCIDENT AT GEORGETOWN, 1864 —The disaster occurred Feb. 9th, 1864, on the Grand Trunk Railway, within the first ten years of its operation in Western Canada. The train had left Georgetown; when within four hundred yards of the bridge which crosses the River Credit near the town, an axle-tree broke, the last two cars became detached and went over the bridge into the river, a distance of 120 feet. Three were killed, the conductor and two passengers. Water color. Size 6 x 10.

3360—CHATHAM, U.C., 1854—Looking north-east from above the Rankin Dock—With key. Governor Simcoe in 1793 wrote Secretary Dundas, proposing London as the seat of Government for Upper Canada. He also stated that he had chosen a site to be called Oxford, the present Woodstock, and one which in all probability would become the capital of the Lower District, called Chatham. These places, on the Canadian Thames, corresponded to places of the same names on the Thames in England. Chatham is historic in the War of 1812-15, for on 3rd September, 1813, Tecumseh crossed the bridge over the creek dividing the military reserve from the town-site, and, with his warriors, encamped on the ground now known as Tecumseh Park. One of the finest buildings in Western Ontario—Harrison Hall—is in Chatham. It is occupied by city and county offices, and is called after Hon. Robert Alexander Harrison, Chief Justice of Ontario. This thriving centre was first settled in 1827, and in 1895 incorporated as a city. Water color. Size 5 x 9.

3361—"THE POPLARS," WOODSTOCK, ONT., 1837-1917—The de Blaquiere Homestead—Residence of Charles de Blaquiere, eldest son of the Hon. P. B. de Blaquiere, and father of the present Lord de Blaquiere, of Bath, England. The house is situated about one and a half miles east of Woodstock, on Governor's road. It was purchased by the late Henry Huntingford, by whom it was sold to George McPherson, the present owner. When Charles de Blaquiere was appointed postmaster of Woodstock, he removed to the Post-office building, north-west corner Dundas and Wellington streets. The old homestead is still (1917) standing, though greatly changed since the de Blaquiere time. Photograph, colored. Size 4 x 6.

3362—TABLET MARKING SPOT WHERE TECUMSEH FELL—The great Shawanoe chief, with his Indian followers, fought in the battle between the Americans, under Harrison, and the British, under Proctor, near Moraviantown, October, 1813. The latter, through indecision and retreat, lost the day. The tablet to Tecumseh's memory bears the following inscription: "Here on October 5, 1813, was fought the Battle of the Thames, and here Tecumseh fell. Erected by the Citizens of Thamesville, A.D. 1911." Water color from photograph. Size 4 x 5.

3363—TECUMSEH STONE, AMHERSTBURG, ONT.—On the north-west corner of Mr. Simon Fraser's lawn, midway from Dalhousie street and the Detroit River, on Gore street—From this stone, Tecumseh, the noted Indian chief and statesman, made speeches to his warriors, and here also he denounced General Proctor in retreating before the Americans under General Harrison. The stone, which has been erected on a cement base, stands to-day (1917) as a memorial of a hundred years ago. Water color. Size 4 x 6.

3364—**GARRETT, LIEUT., OF THE 49TH REGIMENT**—He served in Ireland in 1806, and in 1808 received a commission in the 49th Regiment; was at the Battle of Queenston Heights and the bearer of the last order of Gen. Brock a few minutes before that officer's death; was present at the Battles of Fort George and Stoney Creek. He was ordnance storekeeper at Fort George for several years, retiring in 1850. Water color from the oil painting in Niagara Historical Museum. Size 9 x 11. Half length.

3365—**LISGAR, SIR JOHN YOUNG, BARON, GOVERNOR-GENERAL OF CANADA, 1869-72**—Born in Bombay, 1807; educated at Eton and Corpus Christi College, Oxford. In 1831 entered Parliament, and ten years later became Lord of the Treasury; Secretary of the Treasury, 1844-6. Chief Secretary for Ireland, 1852-5, and Lord High Commissioner of the Ionian Islands, 1855-9. Went to New South Wales in 1861 as Governor-General; came to Canada in December, 1868, as Administrator, and the following February became Governor-General of the Dominion. His death occurred in 1876. Stipple engraving. Size 5 x 6. Head and shoulders, oval.

3366—**PRINCE, COL. JOHN**—Prominent in the Western District—He was a barrister from Cheltenham, Eng., settling at "Park Farm," near Sandwich, U.C., in 1833. As a sportsman and lover of agriculture he soon became known in the district. On the outbreak of the Rebellion he was appointed colonel, taking an active part in military affairs, as well as political, having been in 1836 returned for Essex, which place he represented also in the United Parliament. Although criticized severely for his action in summarily shooting prisoners after the Battle of Windsor, December, 1838, the colonel was wholly acquitted of the charges against him in connection with the matter. In 1860 he was appointed Judge of the District of Algoma, where he spent the remaining ten years of his life. Colonel Prince was the father of Capt. Prince, Chief Constable of Toronto, 1859-73. Water color. Size 3 x 4. Head and shoulders.

3367—**BARRIE, ONT., 1867-8**—View taken from the east—The several buildings shown are: 1. Northern Railway station. 2. E. S. Meeking's hotel. 3. Double house, in which Crown Attorney J. R. Cotter and the late Canon Morgan resided (the late Dalton McCarthy also lived there at one time. 4. Trinity Church Sunday School. 5. Late George Plaxton's residence. 6. Northern Railway freight sheds. Water color. Size 4 x 6.

3368—**MARKET DAY, HAMILTON, 1878**—Hamilton's market is one of the finest in the Dominion. It is conveniently situated in the centre of the city, so that everyone has the opportunity of "going to market"—in fact, the habit is generally practised by householders. Points of interest surrounding the scene in picture are:—1, First Municipal Building, built 1839, clock tower added 1872, torn down and present building erected in 1888; 2, Mechanics' Institute, replaced by Public Library Building, now transformed into "Arcade" departmental store; 3, Old sheds, present meat market on site; 4, Stinson Bank occupied this building prior to removal to Hughson street, now a store, with Stinson estate offices on upper floor; 5, The Spectator, founded in 1849, was here in 1878—until 1884. Now (1917) Parke & Parke, drugs, and apartments above. Water color, from original drawing by W. T. Smedley, for "Picturesque Canada." Size 5 x 6.

3369—**CRYSTAL PALACE, HAMILTON, C.W.**—Built in 1860 on a block of twenty-two acres purchased by the city for Fair Grounds. It was erected on the north-east corner of the block, and opened by the Prince of Wales (King Edward VII.) on his visit to Hamilton. The building was used for exhibition purposes until 1890, sold and removed the following year. Portions of it form the Caledonia Exhibition Buildings. A remnant of the old Fair Grounds is now (1917) Victoria Park, Hamilton, bounded by King, Florence, Sophia and Locke streets. In 1863-64 the Crystal Palace was used as a barracks by the Battery of Royal Artillery stationed in the city. Water color. Size 5 x 8.

3370—SIMCOE, JOHN GRAVES, 1752-1806—First Lieutenant-Governor of Upper Canada, 1792-6. Miniature in water color. Size 2½ x 3. Head and shoulders. See 161, 406, 3265.

3371—McGILL, REV. ROBERT, D.D.—Noted Presbyterian Minister in Upper and Lower Canada—He was a native of Ayrshire, Scotland, ordained and chosen by the Glasgow Presbytery to take charge of the Presbyterian Church at Niagara, where he arrived in the summer of 1829. During his pastorate a new church was built, the St. Andrew's of to-day. He commenced the publication of the Canadian Christian Examiner in 1839, a paper which vindicated the principles and asserted the rights of his church. Mr. McGill was given the degree of D.D. by the University of Glasgow, in 1853. He had in 1845 succeeded Dr. Black as pastor of St. Paul's Church, Montreal, continuing until 1856. His death took place on 4th February of that year. Dr. McGill has been described as an able preacher, a systematic organizer and a born leader. Lithograph by Endicott & Co., New York. Size 12 x 13. Head and shoulders.

3372—SIMCOE MARRIAGE CERTIFICATE FROM REGISTER OF BUCKERALL PARISH CHURCH, DEVON, ENG.—Col. Simcoe first met Miss Gwillim, the lady of his choice, while visiting at the home of his godfather, Admiral Samuel Graves, Hembury Fort, in the spring of 1782. Miss Gwillim was a niece of Mrs. Graves. On 30th December, 1782, their marriage was solemnized by the curate of the parish, Rev. Thomas Roskilly, Admiral and Mrs. Graves being the witnesses. Photographic reproduction.

3373—MITCHELL, JAMES—Judge of London District, 1819-43. From a caricature in possession of his grandson, Chas. E. Macdonald, Toronto. Water color. Size 4 x 7. Full length. See 3374.

3374—MITCHELL, JUDGE JAMES, 1778-1852—A pioneer settler of Long Point, U.C.—Born in Aberdeen, Scotland, and educated at the University in that city. Came to Long Point Settlement early in the 19th century. The first Grammar school for the London district was started on his farm in 1807, and he taught it until 1819. He took an active part in the War of 1812, as captain of the 1st Regiment of Norfolk Militia, and in 1817 was appointed a commissioner to inquire into property forfeited to the Crown by certain British subjects who assisted the Americans during the war. Was Master of the Masonic Lodge at Long Point. Made Judge of the London district in 1819, which position he held for twenty-four years. Water color from portrait in possession of his grandson, Charles E. Macdonald, barrister, Toronto. Size 3 x 5. Head and shoulders. See 3373.

3375—TOWN HALL AND MARKET, BARRIE, ONT., 1880—View from the south side of Collier street, looking northeast—Points of interest shown are:—1, Residence built by the late Henry Dougall, and afterwards occupied by the late Dr. Hamilton; 2, St. Mary's R. C. Church; 3, Town Hall and Market Building; 4, Simcoe County Jail. Barrie was incorporated as a "town" in 1850, "without any municipal organization," however. At the beginning of 1854 it sent a representative separately from Vespra Township to the County Council; but it was not until 1871 that it became a town in the ordinary sense of the word, with Robert Simpson as first mayor. The town takes its name from Commodore Barrie, who commanded a British naval squadron at Kingston during the War of 1812. Water color from original drawing by Schell and Hogan, for "Picturesque Canada." Size 5 x 7.

3376—WAKEFIELD, WILLIAM, 1802-73—Well-known Toronto auctioneer. Oil, by Berthon. Size 5 x 6. Head and shoulders. See 988.

3377—INDIAN CHIEFS AT SARNIA, 1860—The right hand figure, the shorter and older man, was old Shawanoe, aide-de-camp to Tecumseh in 1812. The Sarnia Public Library has in its possession a flag which was given to Shawanoe by the British Government in 1812. His descendants have two silver medals, one presented to Shawanoe at the close of the War of 1812-14, and the other presented on the occasion of King Edward's (Prince of Wales') visit to Sarnia in 1860. Water color, from original in possession of A. C. Pousette, M.D., Sarnia. Size 4 x 6.

3378—MASONIC CERTIFICATE OF JOHN LAUCHLIN (SOUTAR JOHNNIE), AND TRESS OF HIGHLAND MARY'S HAIR—John Lauchlin, a shoemaker of Ayr, Scotland, was a member of Newton St. James Lodge, and in 1806 became an honorary member and tyler of Lodge Ayr St. Paul's, his son, John Lauchlin, then being R.W. Master. The elder man died in 1819. It is said that he was the original of Burns' Soutar Johnnie, in "Tam o' Shanter." Within the Burns Monument grounds near Ayr are two statues of Tam o' Shanter and Soutar Johnnie, the work of James Thom, a self-taught sculptor of unusual talent. Mary Campbell is the Highland Mary celebrated in the poet's "Flow Gently, Sweet Afton."

3379—CHURCH OF NOTRE DAME DE LOURDES, MONTREAL—Corner St. Denis and St. Catharine streets—Built in 1874 to commemorate the Apparition of the Virgin to the peasant girl, Bernadette Soubirons, in a grotto, near Lourdes, France. It is after the Byzantine and Renaissance style of architecture, and is designed to express in visible form the Dogma of the Immaculate Conception of the Virgin Mary. The church was planned by Napoleon Bourassa, Canadian painter and architect, and contains many well executed frescoes by him. It is of noble proportions, the dome being 90 feet high and the total length 102 feet. Lithograph. Size 12 x 14.

3380—ST. PAUL'S CHURCH (ANGLICAN), TORONTO, 1842-61—The First Building, Bloor St. E.—It was a long, low wooden structure, with a squat, square tower, "near the toll gate on Yonge street." The steeple shown in picture was designed by Mr. J. G. Howard, and under his direction was, with the assistance of friends, erected in one day. The opening services of St. Paul's were held 12th June, 1842. Up to 1850 the church was enlarged three times to accommodate the increasing congregation. The building was, with the exception of the spire, removed to the north side of Bloor street west. A new St. Paul's, a Gothic stone edifice, was erected in 1861 on the first site; the old church, which remained as a chapel of ease and Sunday school, finally developing into the Church of the Redeemer. The present St. Paul's (third), Bloor street east, was on 30th November, 1913, opened and consecrated. Original pencil drawing by John G. Howard, architect, Toronto, 1842. Size 8 x 8.

3381—OLD MILL ON THE HUMBER RIVER, TORONTO—In 1833-4 a wooden mill had been erected by Thomas Fisher, an Englishman, who came to Canada in 1819. In 1835, however, he sold out to Wm. Gamble, and two years later Mr. Gamble erected a stone mill, the walls of which still (1917) remain. It was for many years an important business centre in York County. In the fifties trade was diverted by the opening up of railway systems, and in 1858 the mills were finally closed. Water color. Size 5 x 7.

3382—SHERBROOKE, QUE.—With key. Water color from original drawing by F. B. Schell, for "Picturesque Canada," 1880. Size 5 x 5.

35

3383—KEY TO TORONTO'S THIRD JAIL—Palace St. (Front East), Foot of Berkeley—The large stone structure which opened at the bidding of this key was entirely encircled by a stone wall twelve feet high. From 1840-60 it was used as a jail, afterwards occupied by a safe manufacturing company, and later purchased by the Consumers' Gas Company, who erected new buildings on the site.

3384—BYRON, ADMIRAL JOHN—Governor of Newfoundland, 1769-72. Grandfather of Lord Byron, the great English poet. Born in 1723; entered the navy, and was a midshipman on the "Wager" with Anson. Wrecked off the coast of South America, 1741. The narrative of the wreck, published by Byron on his return to England, was said to be one of the most interesting works of the kind in the language. Commanded the "Dolphin" and "Tamar" in a voyage of discovery in the South Sea, 1764-6. In 1778 he obtained command of a fleet destined to operate against the French in the West Indies, and fought an undecisive battle against D'Estaing off Grenada, July, 1779. Promoted to the rank of Vice-Admiral in that year. Died 1786. Line engraving. Size 4 x 5. Head and shoulders.

3385—BROWN, HON. GEORGE, 1818-80—Water color. Size 9 x 13. Full length. See 475, 969.

3386—ARBUTHNOT—"Marriott Arbuthnot, Esq., Admiral of the Blue Squadron. Rising, pinxt. H. R. Cook, sculp. Published April 30, 1810, by J. Gold, No. 103 Shoe Lane, London." Born in 1711; entered the navy and in 1747 became a post-captain. Vice-admiral in 1779, obtaining the chief command on the American station; blockaded by Count D'Estaing in New York harbor. In 1780 co-operated with Sir Henry Clinton in the capture of Charleston, S.C. Admiral of the Blue, 1793. His death occurred in London, Eng., January 31st, 1794. Size 3 x 4. Line engraving. Head and shoulders, oval.

3387—PULPIT AND SOUNDING BOARD, ST. JAMES' CHURCH, TORONTO, and St. Margaret's, Scarboro—When the primitive Church of St. James was reconstructed in 1818, Governor Gore presented this bit of furniture, which stood half-way up the centre aisle on the right side. It remained in the church until 1830, St. James' in that year being replaced by a stone building. The pulpit and sounding board were then presented to St. Margaret's Church, Scarboro, the first Anglican place of worship in the township—on south side of Kingston road, and afterwards, when the highway was straightened, on the north side. When St. Margaret's was burned in 1903 the pulpit, with other furnishings, was destroyed. Water color. Size 4 x 6.

3388—THE ST. GEORGE ACCIDENT ON THE G.T.R.—Happened 27th Feb., 1889, about six o'clock in the afternoon—The train, a Chicago express, was coming from the west. Just before crossing the creek at the village of St. George, three miles from Harrisburg, the tire of one of the driving wheels came off, causing the train to go off the track when it struck the bridge. The engine, baggage car and smoking car reached the east side of the bridge safely, but in so doing they broke up the track and the day coach (1) went over the bridge. The parlor car (2) hung half over, and the other half went down with the dining car (3). Fourteen people were killed and thirty-five injured. The bridge was seventy feet high. Mr. George Margetts, who had charge of the dining car, went over with the wreck, but was saved. He is now (1917) chief steward of the York Club, Toronto. Water color. Size 6 x 8.

3389—AMHERST, GENERAL JEFFERY, 1717-97—From original silhouette taken at Quebec, 21st July, 1759. Size 9 x 13. Full length. See 1691.

3390-8—**Arms of Provinces of Canada**—The arms of the provinces of the Dominion are in a sense territorial arms. There is in each a device indicating fealty to Britain, and this device has reference to the sovereignty of the Motherland. At Confederation Ontario, Quebec, Nova Scotia and New Brunswick formed the Dominion of Canada. By Royal Warrant of 26th May, 1868, these provinces were granted coats-of-arms, and, although other provinces have since joined the Dominion, each having a distinct "coat," the official and authorized arms of Canada are comprised of those of the original provinces placed "quarterly" on a shield.

3390—**QUEBEC**—The Royal Warrant of 26th May, 1868, describes the arms of Quebec thus: "On the fess gules, between two fleur-de-lis in chief, azure, and a sprig of three leaves of Maple, slipped, vert, in base; a lion passant guardant Or." The fleur-de-lis upon a golden ground, in the upper third of the shield, denotes the French origin and early sovereignty of the province. The fess, or central portion of shield, shows a gold lion like that in the Royal Arms, placed on a red ground, and indicates the King's sovereignty in the Province of Quebec. Below the lion "in base" are three green maple leaves with stalks conjoined, like those of Ontario—green symbolizing spring. The similarity of the maple leaves in the Ontario and Quebec "coats" connects old Upper and Lower Canada, from which the Dominion takes its name. Water color. Size 6 x 8.

3391—**NOVA SCOTIA**—In 1621 James I. gave to Sir William Alexander a grant of land in North America, comprising practically what is now Nova Scotia, New Brunswick and Prince Edward Island. The arms of the province, given by Royal Warrant, 26th May, 1868, are: "Or on a fess wavy azure, between three thistles proper, a salmon naiant argent." On the golden shield are three thistles in their natural colors. The wavy fess is blue and bears a silver salmon in the act of swimming—an allusion to the fishing industry and blue waters of the winding rivers of Nova Scotia—New Scotland—as they flow towards the sea. Water color. Size 6 x 8.

3392—**NEW BRUNSWICK**—In 1784 New Brunswick, which had been included in the territory granted by James I. to Sir William Alexander in 1621, became a separate province. Royal Warrant for its arms was given 26th May, 1868, and in heraldic language they are: "Or, on waves, a lymphad or ancient galley with oars in action, proper, on a chief gules, a lion passant guardant Or." On the chief is a gold lion on red, indicating the sovereignty of the King, and doubtless also alluding to the Duchy of Brunswick. On the shield, the ground color of which is gold, is shown an ancient galley on waves, both in their natural colors. The oars in the water are described as being "in action." The galley is an heraldic allusion to the shipbuilding of New Brunswick in early days. Water color. Size 6 x 8.

3393—**PRINCE EDWARD ISLAND**—Discovered by Jacques Cartier, and by him called "Isle St. Jean"—The island was in 1763 ceded to Britain by France, and in 1770 separated from Nova Scotia. In honor of Prince Edward, Duke of Kent, the name was changed in 1799, and in 1873, as Prince Edward Island, came into the Dominion. The blazon of its arms, given by Royal Warrant, 30th May, 1905, designates it as: "Argent, on an island, vert, to the sinister an oak tree fructed, to the dexter thereof three oak saplings sprouting, all proper. On a chief gules a lion passant guardant, Or." The silver shield suggests the bright waters surrounding the island, on which are appropriately grouped a sturdy oak and saplings. The lion, gold on a red ground, forms the territorial arms of the sovereign. The large oak, with acorns ready to drop, typifies the coming of Prince Edward Island permanently under British rule, and the three saplings under the shadow of the larger tree bear out the motto "The Small Beneath the Great." Water color. Size 6 x 8.

3394—**ONTARIO**—By Royal Warrant, 26th May, 1868, Ontario was granted a coat-of-arms—"Vert, a sprig of three leaves of Maple, slipped, Or; on a chief argent, the Cross of St. George." That is, the shield is green; the sprig of maple leaves, slipped, indicate that each with a stalk are joined together. The tincture is of the autumn leaf, gold. The chief holds the Cross of St. George. The first use of the maple leaf in Canada was in 1860 at the reception of the Prince of Wales (Edward VII.) in Toronto. On Feb. 27th, 1909, a second Royal Warrant gave Ontario a crest, supporters and motto. Crest—"Upon a wreath of the colors, a bear passant sable." On the crest-wreath of green and silver is shown a black bear, and the supporters on the dexter side, a moose, and on the sinister side, a deer. Translated the motto is "As loyal she began, so loyal she remains." Water color. Size 8 x 8. See 542.

3395—**BRITISH COLUMBIA**—So named by Queen Victoria in 1858; came into the Dominion in 1871, and by Royal Warrant, dated 31st March. 1906, the badge of the colony, which had previously been the crown and wreath, was changed to the arms shown in picture—"Argent, three bars wavy, azure, issuant from the base a demi sun in splendor, proper. On a chief, the Union device, charged in the centre point with an antique crown, Or." The chief contains the Union Jack, the territorial sign of British sovereignty. At the intersection of the crosses is a gold crown, the form of which in heraldry is called "antique," and its use here signifies that British Columbia was in the past a Crown colony. On the base of the shield is the upper half of the sun. The ground is silver, representing the sea, and upon it are three bars wavy across the shield—waves rolling in on a rocky shore. Translated, British Columbia's motto is, "Brightness without setting," alluding to the loyalty and prosperity of the people of the province. As originally laid out the Union Jack was placed in the base of the shield, but at the suggestion of Ottawa, approved of by the College of Heralds, the national device was placed in the chief, and the setting sun and white wavy bars in the base. The crest and supporters are generally used by the province, but so far (1917) no warrant has been approved, and the matter is still under advisement. Water color. Size 6 x 8.

3396—**MANITOBA**—In 1870 the Prairie Province came into the Dominion, and, by Royal Warrant of 10th May, 1905, was granted arms: "Vert, on a rock, a buffalo, statant, proper. On a chief argent the Cross of St. George." The Cross of St. George on a silver field is here the territorial insignium of the King. The "field" of the escutcheon is green, emblematic of the virgin soil of the western part of Manitoba, where the wheat region begins; the eastern portion is rocky and broken. The buffalo, standing still, and the rock are in their natural colors. To science the buffalo is known as the "Bos Americanus," or American Ox; it is really the bison, though described as the buffalo in the blazon of shield. In this province is grown the wheat known as "Manitoba No. 1 hard," which, on account of its power to resist moisture, has a world-wide reputation. Water color. Size 6 x 8.

3397—**ALBERTA**—When Saskatchewan was made a province, Alberta, to the west, was also established. The name was given in 1882, when the Marquis of Lorne was Governor-General of Canada. He married Princess Louise Carolina Alberta, whose name was derived from that of her father, Prince Consort. Thus the province perpetuates the name of both. The blazon of Alberta's arms is, perhaps, more symbolic than heraldic. In the Royal Warrant, dated 30th May, 1907, they are thus described: "Azure, in front of a range of snow mountains, proper, a range of hills, vert; in base a wheatfield surmounted by a prairie proper; on a chief argent, a St. George's Cross." The Cross of St. George, on a silver ground, is represented on the chief. In the foreground of shield is a field of golden grain, unreaped, in its natural color. Beyond are the green foothills, and in the distance are the snow-capped Rockies. Water color. Size 6 x 8.

3398—SASKATCHEWAN—It was originally one of the Northwest Territories; created a province, 1st Sept. 1905. The grant of arms was by Royal Warrant, 25th Aug., 1906, and reads: "Vert, three garbs in fess, Or; on a chief of the last, a lion passant guardant, gules." This is the only example in provincial coats-of-arms where the "territorial" lion is not gold, and is doubtless given in red so that the ground color of the chief and of the shield will not clash, as they would if one were red and the other green. The field, green, indicates the verdure of the prairie land, and on it are shown three sheaves of golden grain, arranged as a fess would be placed across the shield. Saskatchewan is doubtless the greatest wheat-growing area in Canada, the natural fertility of its soil being aided by the great depth of frost penetration in winter. Water color. Size 6 x 8.

2399—McGILL, HON. PETER (McCUTCHEON)—Mayor of Montreal 1840-2. A Scotsman by birth. Came to Canada in 1809; engaged in mercantile pursuits in Montreal. He was chairman of the first railroad company established in Canada—the St. Lawrence and Champlain, and from 1834-60 held office as President of the Bank of Montreal. He was also a member of the first Legislative Council under the Union. Mr. McGill's surname was originally McCutcheon, but in order to inherit the property of his uncle, Hon. Peter McGill, of Toronto, he adopted the name of his relative. Original silhouette, taken at Saratoga, 26th August, 1841. Size 6 x 9. Full length.

3400-2—Clerks, House of Assembly, Lower Canada, 1792-1841.

3400—PHILLIPS, SAMUEL—Clerk, House of Assembly, L. C., 1792-1808. His death occurred Aug. 6th, 1808. Silhouette. Size 3 x 4.

3401—LINDSAY, WILLIAM ROBERT—Clerk, House of Assembly, L. C., 1808-29—A prominent Quebec merchant, commonly called William Lindsay, Jr. Born in London, Eng., May 10th, 1761. Appointed Assistant Clerk of the House of Assembly, L. C., Jan. 21st, 1793, and Clerk, 1808, retiring from that office in 1829. His death took place Jan. 11th, 1834. Water color from portrait in possession of his great-grandson, Col. Crawford Lindsay, Quebec. Size 3 x 4. Head and shoulders.

3402—LINDSAY, WILLIAM BURNS, SR.—Clerk, House of Assembly, L. C., 1829-41—Prior to his appointment as Clerk of the Legislative Assembly, L. C., Mr. Lindsay had been teller in the Bank of Montreal, Quebec. In 1841 he was appointed Clerk of the Legislative Assembly of United Canada. Died May 15th, 1862. Water color, from portrait in possession of his grandson, Col. Crawford Lindsay, Quebec. Size 3 x 4. Head and shoulders. See 3410.

3403-6—Clerks House of Assembly, Upper Canada, 1792-1840.

3403—MACDONELL, ANGUS—Clerk, House of Assembly, U. C., 1792-1800—Mr. Macdonell, first Clerk of the U. C. House of Assembly, was the son of Allan Macdonell, captain in the 84th Royal Highland Emigrant Regiment. A barrister-at-law; sat in the Assembly for Durham, Simcoe, and the East Riding of York; Treasurer of the Law Society, 1801-4. Drowned when the schooner "Speedy" was lost near Presqu' Isle, Oct. 7th, 1804. Silhouette. Size 3 x 4.

3404—McLEAN, DONALD—Clerk, House of Assembly, U.C., 1801-13—Succeeding Angus Macdonell, came Donald McLean, who fell while gallantly opposing the landing of the Americans at York, April 27th, 1813.

Mr. McLean was one of the early pew-holders in St. James' Church (Cathedral), Toronto. His son, Lieut. A. H. McLean, of the 41st Regiment, was aide-de-camp to Proctor, and, as colonel, served in the Rebellion of 1837. Silhouette. Size 3 x 4.

3405—POWELL, GRANT—Clerk, House of Assembly, U. C., 1813-27—Donald McLean, who lost his life in the defence of York, April 27th, 1813, was succeeded by Grant Powell, son of William Dummer Powell, Chief Justice of Upper Canada. Grant Powell was born May 4th, 1779. Appointed Clerk of the House of Assembly, U. C., May 18th, 1813; judge of District Court for the Home District, U. C., 1818; and Clerk of the Legislative Council, Upper Canada, May 4th, 1827. Also acted as medical officer for the troops from time to time. He died in June, 1838. Water color. Size 3 x 4. Head and shoulders.

3406—FITZGIBBON, COL. JAMES—Clerk, House of Assembly, U. C., 1827-40—Water color. Size 3 x 4. Head and shoulders. See 1217.

3407—GREAT SEAL OF CANADA—Authorized for use by the Government of the Dominion of Canada at the time of Confederation. The seal was designed and executed by Messrs. Wyon, Regent street, London, and is five inches in diameter. H. M. Queen Victoria is shown, seated under a Gothic canopy, crowned, and wearing the robe and collar of the Garter, and holding a sceptre in the right hand, and the orb in the left. Underneath is a shield bearing the arms of the United Kingdom, and in minor compartments on each side are suspended, on oak trees, shields bearing the Coats of Arms of the four confederating Provinces. The shield of Ontario shows a sprig of maple, and on the chief the Cross of St. George. Quebec bears two fleurs-de-lis and a sprig of maple, and on a fess a lion of England. Nova Scotia bears three thistles, and on a wavy fess a salmon. New Brunswick shows an antique ship, and on a chief a lion of England. The translation of the Latin superscription is, "Victoria, by the Grace of God, of the British Isles, Queen, Defender of the Faith—The Seal in Canada." The Great Seal is attached to all important documents executed by the Dominion Government, and, like the Great Seal of England, conveys the Royal authority to all documents to which it is attached. In addition, each Province has its own seal. The only change which takes place in the Great Seal proper is in the inscription surrounding it, and the insertion of the figure of the reigning sovereign. From original at Ottawa.

3408—GREAT SEAL OF CANADA—The seal here given shows the figure of Edward VII. and the arms of the four Provinces forming the Dominion in 1867. The translation of the superscription is: "Edward VII., by the Grace of God, of the United Kingdom of Great Britain and Ireland, and of the British Dominions Beyond the Seas, King, Defender of the Faith, Emperor of India—the Seal in Canada." When a sovereign dies the seal becomes the personal property of the Secretary of State. From original at Ottawa.

3409—GREAT SEAL OF CANADA—The seal shown is that in use at the present time (1917). The figure of George V. and the arms of the four Provinces forming the Dominion at the time of Confederation are given. Translated, the superscription reads: "George V., by the Grace of God, of the United Kingdom of Great Britain and Ireland, and of the British Dominions Beyond the Seas, King, Defender of the Faith, Emperor of India—the Seal of Canada." From original at Ottawa.

3410-11—Clerks of Assembly, United Canada, 1841-67.

3410—LINDSAY, WILLIAM BURNS, Sr.—Clerk of Assembly, United Canada, 1841-62. Water color from portrait in possession of his grandson, Col. Crawford Lindsay, Quebec. Size 3 x 4. Head and shoulders. See 3402.

3411—**LINDSAY, WILLIAM BURNS, Jr.**—Clerk House of Assembly, United Canada, 1862-7—Appointed assistant law clerk and English translator for the Assembly of United Canada, 1841. In 1845 he was called to the bar of Lower Canada, and on the death of his father, in 1862, succeeded him as Clerk of the Legislative Assembly of United Canada. Clerk of the House of Commons from Confederation until 1872. Died Sept. 2nd, 1872. Water color from portrait in possession of his son, Col. Crawford Lindsay, Quebec. Size 3 x 4. Head and shoulders. See 3419.

3412-14—**Clerks, Legislative Assembly, Ontario, 1867-1917.**

3412—**GILLMOR, COL. CHARLES TOD**—Clerk, Legislative Assembly, Ontario, 1867-91—Born in Balligrass, Sligo, Ireland, 1819; came to Canada, 1858. Entered the office of Sheriff Jarvis, remaining there until 1867, when he became first Clerk of the Ontario Legislative Assembly. Appointed ensign in Sligo militia, July 10th, 1839. Gazetted ensign in 3rd Battalion, Toronto militia, Jan. 24th, 1862. Transferred in 1863 to 2nd Battalion, Queen's Own. Gazetted captain of the 7th Company, known as the old Civil Service Company, 20th May, 1864. Served on Canadian frontier in 1865 (the concluding year of the American Civil War). Served as major in Fenian Raid, at Ridgeway. Appointed colonel of Queen's Own, 1st June, 1866. Col. Gillmor's death occurred in Toronto, Jan. 3rd, 1892. Water color. Size 3 x 4. Head and shoulders.

3413—**CLARKE, COL. CHARLES**—Clerk, Legislative Asssmbly, Ontario, 1892-1906—Born in Lincoln, Eng., Nov. 28th, 1826. Came to Canada in 1844, and for a time engaged in farming. Afterwards took up newspaper work. Elected to the Local Legislature for Centre Wellington, 1871, sitting for that constituency until 1887, when he was elected for East Wellington, which he represented until 1891. Speaker of the Provincial House, 1880-6. On his retirement from the Speaker's chair he became chairman of the Public Accounts Committee, resigning to become Clerk of the House. Organized the Elora Rifle Company. Became senior major of the 30th Battalion on its formation, 1866. Served in Fenian Raid. Lieutenant-colonel, 1871. Author of "Sixty Years in Upper Canada." His death took place, April 6th, 1909. Water color. Size 3 x 4. Head and shoulders.

3414—**SYDERE, A. H.**—Clerk, Legislative Assembly, Ontario, 1907-17—Born at Wymondham, Norfolk, Eng., June 15th, 1841. In 1844 he came to Canada with his parents, who settled in Elgin Co., Ont. Educated at St. Thomas and London Grammar Schools and by private tuition. Barrister, 1865, but never practised his profession. Entered Ontario public service, 1867. Prior to his appointment to his present (1917) post as Clerk of the Provincial Legislature, January, 1907, he was Clerk Assistant. Has compiled several indices relating to Parliamentary procedure. Water color. Size 3 x 4. Head and shoulders.

3415—**HAMILTON, HON. GEORGE**—Founder of the City of Hamilton—He was born at Queenston, U.C., second son of Hon. Robert Hamilton. In 1812 he removed to Burlington Bay, where in all probability the massing of men and military stores during the war laid the foundation of a permanent settlement. In 1813 George Hamilton laid out his farm in village lots, thus forming the nucleus of the city, incorporated as such, 1st Jan., 1847. He was a member of the Provincial Legislature and Legislative Council. His death occurred at Hamilton, 1836. Water color. Size 4 x 6. Half length.

3416—**ROBINSON, CHRISTOPHER, K.C.**—Consulting Corporation Counsel, Toronto, 1868-1905—He was born at Beverley House, Toronto, 21st Jan., 1828, third son of Hon. Sir John Beverley Robinson; called to the Bar in 1850. In 1885 he was elected a Bencher of the Law Society of

Upper Canada, in the same year acting as leading counsel for the Crown in the prosecution of Riel at Regina, and later represented the Dominion Government in the arbitration with the Canadian Pacific Railway. In the Behring Sea arbitration at Paris, 1893, between Britain and the States, Mr. Robinson was retained on behalf of the British Government, and in recognition of his services was offered knighthood, which, however, he declined. Before the Supreme Court and the Privy Council he was recognized as leader of the Canadian Bar. Owing to his special ability and intimate knowledge of civic affairs he had a permanent retainer from the Corporation of Toronto up to the time of his death in October, 1905. Water color from a portrait in possession of his son, Mr. Christopher C. Robinson, Toronto. Size 3 x 4. Head and shoulders.

3417—DUNN, COL. ALEXANDER ROBERTS—The only Canadian at Balaclava—Son of Hon. John Henry Dunn, Receiver-General of Upper Canada; he was born, 1833, in the family residence at the head of Catharine (Richmond) street, Toronto. Entered the army and from the beginning had a distinguished career. Awarded the Victoria Cross for his bravery in the Crimea. In 1858 the Hundredth Prince of Wales Royal Canadian Regiment was raised, partly through his instrumentality, and he was gazetted its first major, later succeeding Baron de Rottenburg as lieutenant-colonel. Finding an inactive life irksome, he requested a transfer to a command in India, and as colonel of the 33rd Regiment, accompanied General Napier (afterwards Lord Napier of Magdala) in the expedition against King Theodore of Abyssinia. While out shooting deer during a halt at Senafe, in that country, January, 1868, he was killed by a sudden explosion of his rife. Water color from oil in Upper Canada College, Toronto. Size 3 x 4. Head and shoulders.

3418—ESSON, REV. HENRY—An early professor of Knox College, Toronto—Born at Deeside, Aberdeenshire, Scotland, 1793; received his education at Marischal College, Aberdeen. Came to Canada as a young man, and from 1817-22 was assistant pastor of St. Gabriel Street Presbyterian Church, Montreal. In the latter year he became minister of the church, in succession to Rev. J. Somerville, who had held the pastorate for twenty years. When a Presbyterian theological college (subsequently designated Knox College) was founded in Toronto, 1844, Mr. Esson was appointed Professor of Literature and Science, and on November 5th, the first session of the infant seminary was opened in Mr. Esson's residence on James street. The reverend professor's death occurred 11th May, 1853. In 1835 he preached the first sermon of the St. Andrew's Society in Montreal. Water color from original portrait in Knox College, Toronto. Size 3 x 4. Head and shoulders.

3419-22—Clerks, House of Commons, 1867-1917.

3419—LINDSAY, WILLIAM BURNS, JR.—Clerk. House of Commons, 1867-72. Water color from portrait in possession of his son, Col. Crawford Lindsay, Quebec. Size 3 x 4. Head and shoulders. See 3411.

3420—PATRICK, ALFRED, C.M.G.—Clerk, House of Commons, 1873-1880—Entered the service of the House of Assembly, Upper Canada, Jan. 13th, 1827. At the Union of Upper and Lower Canada, 1841, was appointed Clerk of Committees; Chief Clerk of Controverted Elections, 1850. Deputy Clerk Assistant, 1858; Joint Clerk Assistant, 1863; sole Clerk Assistant at Confederation, and Clerk of the House of Commons, Jan. 21st, 1873, resigning from that office, Nov. 30th, 1880. Mr. Patrick was born at Kingston, U.C., 1811; educated at York (Toronto) under tutorship of Dr. (Bishop) Strachan, and afterwards at Cazenovia Seminary, New York State. Author of a digest of "Precedents or Decisions on U.C. Controverted Election Cases from 1828 to 1841." Water color. Size 3 x 4. Head and shoulders.

3421—BOURINOT, SIR JOHN GEORGE, K.C.M.G.—Clerk, House of Commons, 1880-1902—Born at Sydney, C.B., Oct. 24th, 1838—the son of Senator John Bourinot. Educated at Trinity University, Toronto, afterwards engaging in newspaper work. Editor of the Halifax Reporter, 1861. Reporter in the Dominion Senate, 1868. In 1873 he was appointed Second Assistant Clerk of the House of Commons; First Assistant Clerk, 1876, and Clerk, 1880, in succession to Alfred Patrick. Knighted, 1898. His death occurred Oct. 13th, 1902. Water color. Size 3 x 4. Head and shoulders.

3422—FLINT, THOMAS B.—Clerk, House of Commons, 1902-17—Born at Yarmouth, N.S., April 28th, 1847; educated at Mount Allison University (B.A., 1867; M.A., 1872; D.C.L., hon., 1903), and Harvard University (LL.B., 1871). Studied law, subsequently practising his profession at Yarmouth. Appointed a Commissioner of the Superior and County Courts, 1873; High Sheriff of Yarmouth, 1884-7. Assistant Clerk, Nova Scotia Assembly, 1887-91. Represented the place of his birth in the House of Commons, 1891-1902. Appointed Clerk of the House of Commons, Nov. 11th, 1902, as successor to Sir John Bourinot, and still (1917) holds the positon. Water color. Size 3 x 4. Head and shoulders.

3423—CANADIAN PROVINCES CONFEDERATION MEDAL—Obverse and reverse—The Confederation of the British Provinces of North America, formerly known as Upper and Lower Canada, Nova Scotia and New Brunswick, into the Dominion of Canada, 1867, was commemorated by the Canadian Government by a medal. The medal, which was executed by Messrs. Wyon of Regent st., London, is three inches in diameter, and bears on the obverse a portrait of H.M. Queen Victoria, who honored Mr. Wyon with sittings for the purpose. The portion of her dress visible is ornamented with a rich border of rose, thistle and shamrock. The reverse shows an allegorical group of figures representing Britannia giving the charter of Confederation to the four Provinces. Each figure is distinguished by appropriate emblems. Ontario (U.C.) carries a sheaf of grain and a sickle; Quebec (L.C.) holds a paddle and wears a fleur de lis, indicating her French origin; Nova Scotia holds a mining spade, and New Brunswick, a timber axe. The medal, struck in gold, was presented to Queen Victoria, and a large number were struck for general distribution.

3424-7—Clerks, Legislative Assembly, Quebec, 1867-1917.

3424—MUIR, GEORGE MANLY—Clerk, Legislative Assembly, Quebec, 1867-79—Mr. Muir was born at Amherstburg, Ont., 1807. Studied law, and practised his profession until his appointment as Clerk of the Provincial Assembly. He was a liberal benefactor of the Good Shepherd Convent of Quebec, and at his own expense erected a small convent for the Order at St. Pierre de Charlesbourg. Resigned from the Clerkship, May 31st, 1879. His death took place in 1882. Water color. Size 3 x 4. Head and shoulders.

3425—DELORME, LOUIS—Clerk, Legislative Assembly, Quebec, 1879-92 —Mr. Delorme, who had represented St. Hyacinthe, Que., in the House of Commons from 1870 to 1878 was appointed to the Clerkship on the resignation of Mr. George Manly Muir. He was by profession a barrister. Born at Montreal, 1824; died in the city of his birth, 1895. Water color. Size 3 x 4. Head and shoulders.

3426—DESJARDINS, Lt.-COL. LOUIS GEORGES—Clerk, Legislative Assembly, Quebec, 1892-1911—Born at St. Jean Port Joli, P. Q., May 12th, 1849. Educated at Levis College. Editor and co-proprietor with the late Hon. J. Israel Tarte of "Le Canadien." Sat in the Quebec Legislature for Montmorency, 1881-90. First returned to the House of Commons for Montmorency, 1890, resigning in 1892. Served during the Fenian Raids (medal). Holds long service decoration. Author of several works of a political character. Still (1917) resides in Quebec. Water color. Size 3 x 4. Head and shoulders.

3427—GEOFFRION, LOUIS PHILIPPE, K.C.—Clerk, Legislative Assembly, Quebec, 1912-17—The present (1917) Clerk of the Quebec Legislature was born at Varennes, P.Q., Feb. 24th, 1875; educated at Colleges of Varennes and L'Assomption, and at Laval University. Called to the Bar, 1897, practising his profession in Montreal from 1897 to 1903. Private secretary to Sir Lomer Gouin, 1903-12, when he was appointed Clerk of the Legislature and Clerk of the Crown in Chancery. Water color. Size 3 x 4. Head and shoulders.

3428—SHEA, REV. FATHER JOHN JOSEPH—Born in Toronto, March, 1837. Pursued his studies at St. Michael's College, Toronto, at St. Hyacinthe, and at the Grand Seminary, Montreal, where he completed his theological training. Returning to Toronto, he was ordained by Bishop Charbonnel, and was the first native of Toronto to enter the Roman Catholic priesthood. Afterwards stationed at Streetsville, Oshawa and Brockton, and from May, 1861, to September, 1863, was assistant rector of St. Michael's Cathedral. For a short time before his death, which occurred on Oct. 30th, 1888, he was parish priest at Dixie. Water color. Size 3 x 4. Head and shoulders.

3429—RINTOUL, REV. WILLIAM, M.A.—Professor of Hebrew and Biblical Literature, Knox College, Toronto. Water color from portrait in Knox College. Size 3 x 4. Head and shoulders. See 2534, 3531.

3430—MONTCALM, LOUIS JOSEPH, MARQUIS DE—A famous French general, born at the Chateau de Candiac, near Nimes, France, 29th Feb., 1712; served in various campaigns in France and the Netherlands, and in 1756 was sent to defend the French colonies in North America. Montcalm captured Fort William Henry in 1757, repulsed the British, under Abercrombie, at Ticonderoga the following year, and in July, 1759, repelled Wolfe's attack on Quebec. On 13th September, however, he was mortally wounded at the capture of the capital. Reproduced from colored photo of original oil in possession of Marquis de Montcalm, Chateau d'Aveze, le Vigan, Gard, France. Size 3 x 4. Half length.

3431—VIEW OF NEW GLASGOW, N.S.—With key. Water color from original drawing by Schell and Hogan, for "Picturesque Canada," 1880. Size 5 x 7.

3432—SNOW FIGHTING ON TORONTO, GREY AND BRUCE RAILWAY—Near Owen Sound, March, 1875—With key—The scene shows a train hauled by two engines being dug out of drifts near Berkeley, a few miles from Owen Sound. Many prominent railway officials and men of Owen Sound were on the train. Photograph, colored, from original in possession of Mr. Edmund Wragge, Toronto. Size 7 x 10.

3433—McMASTER, CAPT. WM. FENTON, 1822-1907—In uniform as captain of the Toronto Naval Brigade. Water color from portrait in possession of his daughter, Mrs. Hertzberg, Toronto. Size 3 x 6. Full length. See 1114.

3434—ABITATION DE QUEBEC, 1608-20—In 1608, the year of the founding of Quebec, a "sort of compromise between a mediaeval castle and a backwoods stockade" was erected by Champlain. The structure, which was of wood and earth, had a drawbridge, ditch and courtyard, with platforms for cannon and loopholes for musketry. With additions and improvements, this rude fortification served the colony until 1620, when the first Fort St. Louis was begun. Water color from engraving in "Voyages de Champlain." With key. Size 4 x 5.

3435—FORT ST. LOUIS, QUEBEC, 1620-47—To replace the "Abitation de Quebec," Champlain commenced to erect the first Fort St. Louis on the crest of the rock, but the work proceeded very slowly because of the scarcity of labor and lack of material. When Champlain was leaving for France in 1624 he urged the inhabitants to continue the work of construction; but on his return two years later he found that no progress had been made. He therefore had the walls levelled to their foundations, and recommenced building, this time on a larger scale. In July, 1629, Quebec fell into the hands of Sir David Kirke, and for the first time the English flag floated over the fortress of the city. By the Treaty of St. Germain-en-Laye, Fort St. Louis was restored to the French in 1632, and in 1633 Champlain was again appointed Governor of New France, taking over the command of Quebec from De Caen in May of that year, and occupying the fort until his death in 1635. Water color. Size 4 x 6.

3436—CHATEAU ST. LOUIS, QUEBEC, 1647-94—Montmagny, who succeeded Champlain as Governor of New France, built the first stone fort. In 1647 he laid the foundation of the first Chateau St. Louis, within the boundaries of the fort of the name. The Chateau was demolished in 1694 by Frontenac, who had written to the King that it was so rotten and shaky it was a miracle that he had not been buried under it, and that the walls of the fort were in ruins. Water color. Size 3½ x 6.

3437—CHATEAU ST. LOUIS, QUEBEC, 1694-1834—In 1693 Frontenac, then Governor of New France, rebuilt Fort St. Louis, which, with the Chateau, was in a ruinous condition. The latter was demolished the following year, and a new building, having a second storey, was begun on the old foundations, with the addition of a wing. Later another wing was added, and thus the Chateau remained, with only slight further repairs, until the days of the British regime. Water color on print from original water color, made in 1804, by Wm. Morrison, Jr., and given by Judge Black, of Quebec, to the late Sir James M. LeMoine. Size 3½ x 6.

3438—CHATEAU ST. LOUIS, QUEBEC—From the land, or courtyard side—Under British rule the structure began by Frontenac in 1694 was restored and another storey added, the building then being known, erroneously, as the New Chateau. Haldimand Castle, the foundation stone of which was laid by Governor Haldimand in May, 1784, and which was used for public receptions and social functions (the original Chateau proving inadequate to the growing needs of the ancient capital), became known as the Old Chateau. In January, 1834, the relic of the days of French supremacy was destroyed by fire, and the name, Chateau St. Louis, given to the building of Haldimand's time. This, too, has been removed to make way for the present (1917) Chateau Frontenac. Struck with the commanding position of the site of the original Chateau, Lord Durham, in 1838, had the ruins removed and erected there what afterwards became known as Durham Terrace, now included in Dufferin Terrace. Water color on print from enlargement printed March, 1881, in the Canadian Illustrated News, from original line engraving by Smillie, in Bourne's "Picture of Quebec," published 1829. Size 4 x 6.

3439—CHATEAU ST. LOUIS, QUEBEC—From the front side, facing the St. Lawrence. The view shows the Chateau as it appeared from the completion of its restoration in 1811 until its destruction by fire, January, 1834. Water color on print. Size 4 x 6.

3440—**SHARON TEMPERANCE BAND**—With key—It was organized in 1820, and attained a high standard of excellence. At the time of the Fenian Raid some of the members left Sharon to assemble at Newmarket, en route to Toronto. Others left Canada during the gold rush to California, and full membership was never regained. At meetings, entertainments and excursions this old-time band never failed to render familiar, popular airs such as "Swanee River" and "The Mocking Bird." When the photograph, of which this is a colored reproduction, was made, the bandsmen were all about twenty years of age. Size 6 x 8.

3441—**BRIDGE, ELORA**—Spanning the Irvine River near its junction with the Grand—The first bridge, consisting of long timbers projecting from either bank and supported by braces from the rock below, was built 1847-8. There was no pier. Later, the timbers not being considered safe, an arch top of planks nailed together was added; but this "bow and string bridge" did not stand the weather, and the stone pier was built in 1867. Some years later the woodwork, as shown in picture, was put up. This, in turn, was replaced in February, 1886, by the steel bridge now (1917) in use. The River Irvine was named after the town of Irvine, Ayrshire, Scotland, birthplace of William Gilkison, who in 1832 founded Elora. Water color from original drawing by F. B. Schell, for "Picturesque Canada." Size 5 x 7.

3442—**SKULL OF MONTCALM, IN URSULINE CHAPEL, QUEBEC**— Montcalm, fatally wounded at Quebec, was assisted back to the city, where he died on the morning of 14th September, 1759. A shell had exploded in the Chapel of the Ursuline Convent during the siege, causing an excavation in the ground beneath, and here, after cleaning out the excavation to make a grave, the body of the French General was buried that evening by torch-light. In 1833, when the south wall of the chapel was undergoing repairs, Sister Dube, of the convent, who as a little girl had attended Montcalm's funeral with her father, pointed out the exact location of the grave. In removing the skeleton, the skull became detached. It was given to the chaplain of the institution as a precious relic, and now (1917) is preserved in a glass case. Photograph, colored. Size 3½ x 4.

3443—**ARTILLERY BARN, FORT MALDEN, AMHERSTBURG**—Con-structed in 1812, and still (1917) in excellent condition. The lower storey is of solid stone, the upper of wood and of the old kind of frame work. It is now the property of W. S. Falls, manager of Molsons Bank, Amherstburg, and is used as a horse stable. Water color. Size 4 x 6.

3444—**TRAFALGAR CASTLE**—A palatial residence near Whitby, C.W. —In 1859-61 Mr. Nelson Gilbert Reynolds, first Sheriff of Ontario County after its separation from the Home District in 1853, erected on rising ground half a mile from the centre of Whitby, this residence of white brick and stone dressings, in Elizabethan order of architecture. It stood in the centre of 150 acres of ground and overlooked Whitby harbor and Lake Ontario. In 1875 the building was sold and turned into the Ontario Ladies' College. Sheriff Reynolds was born near Cookstown, Ireland, 1814, and died in Whitby in 1881. The corner-stone of the residence was laid by Mr. Reynolds' six-year-old son, now Mr. G. N. Reynolds, of Toronto. Water color from print. Size 4 x 6.

3445—**MOY HOUSE, WINDSOR, U.C.**—Built in 1797 by Angus Mackin-tosh, on farm lot No. 93, 1st concession, Sandwich (Windsor was separated from the Township of Sandwich in 1854). Mr. Mackintosh, who inherited the estate belonging to the Earldom of Moy, and who was a factor of the Hudson's Bay Company, resided in this old dwelling until 1830. In 1912 the Moy house was demolished and the property, along with the Davis farm nearby, was sold in city lots and avenues. Water color. Size 4 x 6.

3446—**FIRST COURT HOUSE IN WENTWORTH COUNTY**—Built in 1816 on lot 52, 1st concession of Ancaster, just south of the present town of Dundas. Prisoners were confined in the building, which was far from being safe, and sittings of the Gore District Court, Quarter Sessions and Surrogate Court were held therein. After many years it was removed to the estate of the late George Rolph, the property being (1917) owned by J. D. Pennington. The picture shows the building as it now appears, the material having been removed piece by piece and re-erected on its present foundation. From original water color by Mrs. M. H. Holmstead, formerly of Dundas. Size 5 x 8.

3447—**OBSERVATION CAR**—Used by H.R.H. Prince of Wales (King Edward VII.) at official inauguration of Victoria Bridge, Montreal, 1860. The car, which had been specially built for the occasion by the Grand Trunk Railway, was open on all four sides, the roof being supported simply by wooden pillars. It was used by the Prince on the occasion of his laying the last stone and clinching the last rivet, which was of silver, in the Victoria Tubular Bridge, August 25th, 1860. The first stone for the first pier was laid July 22nd, 1854, a number of prominent people taking part in the ceremony. Water color. Size 5 x 7.

3448—**TUG ROBB AT FORT ERIE DOCK, JUNE, 1866**—She left Dunnville in charge of Capt. Lockie McCallum (afterwards Senator McCallum), of the Dunnville Naval Brigade, and was joined at Port Colborne by Capt. Richard S. King (Colonel), of the Welland Canal Field Battery. About eighty of the Battery were taken on board and the tug proceeded to Fort Erie, where she is shown in picture, pointing up the river, looking towards Lake Erie. On disembarking, the troops marched down for patrol work to Black Creek, the boat following along the shore. The Fenians were in retreat at the time, and a number of prisoners were taken. They were afterwards sent to Brantford. Subsequently the Robb lay for some time in Toronto Harbor, was beached at Victoria Park, 1890, and finally burned. It is to be noted that guns are shown on the boat. In this particular the picture is incorrect, for the Field Batttery were acting as infantry, the guns being at Hamilton. Water color from engraving in Harper's Weekly. Size 5 x 8.

3449—**TRINITY CHURCH (ANGLICAN), MOORE**—Second Anglican Church in Lambton County—In 1835 the congregation was organized and the building erected in 1842. It stood in the Sutherland Settlement, between Courtwright and Mooretown, on the farm now (1917) owned by Mr. J. H. Kittermaster, manager of the Lambton Loan and Investment Company. The old church was demolished many years ago, and in 1868 a new one built in the village of Moore, on the St. Clair River. The communion service of Trinity Church was presented by John Ruskin. Water color from a pen drawing by Grace Sutherland, daughter of Thomas Sutherland, founder of the church, and wife of the elder Dr. Johnston, of Sarnia. Size 4 x 6.

3450—**FORT MALDEN BARRACKS**—Amherstburg, Essex Co., Ont.—The original Fort Amherstburg (Malden), a wooden structure, with loop-holes for the rifles, was erected in 1797. In 1813 it was abandoned and destroyed by the British, but after the war of 1812-15 some of the buildings were replaced, that shown in the picture being one. It is of brick, with stone foundations—situated on the west front of the old fort grounds—and is still in a good state of preservation. The propery is a part of the J. R. Park estate, Amherstburg. Water color. Size 2 x 6.

3451—**HAND FIRE ENGINE, HALIFAX, 1813**—These hand pumps, as they were also called, were manned by two rows of men at the brake-handles, and supplied by water placed, by means of hand buckets, in the tank at base of the pump. The buckets, shown beside the engine, were usually of leather with rope handles covered with leather. For some years after the introduction of steam fire engines in Halifax improved hand engines were used. From "Acadian Recorder," Halifax. Water color. Size 3 x 4.

GOVERNMENT HOUSE, ROSEDALE, TORONTO—Exterior and Interior Views—The exterior is designed in the French chateau style, Louis XVI. period, and is constructed of Credit Valley stone. The grounds, drives and courts, being designed in the same style, form a harmonious setting for the buildings. The front facade faces south, the main entrance driveway leading from Roxborough drive, with a circular outer court connected by a stone bridge, and a fore court immediately in front of the building, the side entrance being from Douglas drive on the west. The fore court is connected with a broad terrace extending the full length of the residence on the east side overlooking the Ravine. Continued alongside the main drive and around the courts is a handsome stone balustrade, with electric light standards at intervals on the pedestals. On Nov. 1st, 1915, the buildings and grounds were completed, and were occupied by Col. the Hon. Sir John S. Hendrie on 15th November. The French chateau style, Louis XVI. period, is continued in the interior in the grand hall and stairways, the drawing and reception rooms and the ballroom, and the furniture of these apartments has all been designed in that period. The State dining-room is Jacobean in style, and the royal suite and apartments on the upper floor are in the Adam style. The building and terraces were designed by Mr. Frank R. Heakes, Provincial · Government architect, and carried out under his supervision.

3452—HENDRIE, COL. HON. SIR JOHN S.—Lieutenant-Governor of Ontario, appointed Sept. 25th, 1914—At his desk at Government House. Water color on print. Size 8 x 10. Half length.

3453—DETAIL OF WALL OF GRAND HALL—West side, looking north. The walls are of marble, with panels inset with blue Laurentian marble. The floor is of tessellated marble, with variegated colors in the border. Water color on print. Size 8 x 10.

3454—RECEPTION-ROOM—Designed in Louis XVI. period, including the furniture, rug and electric fixtures. Woodwork and ceilings are finished in ivory, the high light in the wood carvings taken out in gold. The walls are panelled in rose-colored silk and the draperies and Donegal rug are in soft harmonizing tints. The furniture is finished in gold, upholstered with Petit Point tapestry. Onyx is used for the top of the centre table and the consoles on the wall. The electric fixtures are of ormolu gold and crystals. Water color on print. Size 8 x 10.

3455—MONTREUIL WINDMILL, SANDWICH, U.C.—Built about 1815 by Mr. Montreuil, a miller by trade, on his farm, Lot 97, Sandwich East, above the present (1917) town of Walkerville. When the wind was steady the mill ground 100 bushels of wheat every 24 hours, and it is said that some of the best flour on the Detroit River was made here. Until 1852 it was in operation, and for years afterwards the old windmill's round bulk was a picturesque and familiar landmark on the banks of the Detroit River. In the mid-seventies it was demolished. Water color. Size 4 x 6.

3456—OLD COUNTY TREASURER'S OFFICE, SANDWICH, ONT.— Bedford and Sandwich streets—A small brick building, which was used as a District and County Treasurer's office during the administration of Mr. George Bullock, 1850-58. During the War of 1812-14 it did service as a saloon, and later became a harness and saddlery shop. Water color. Size 4x7.

3457—SIDE OF THE DRAWING-ROOM—With bay window opposite the entrance from reception-room, and overlooking the terrace, lawn and Ravine to the east—The room and electric fixtures have been designed to harmonize with the reception-room. The color scheme is ivory and grey, the wood and plaster work being finished in ivory and the walls panelled in oyster grey silk. The furniture is upholstered in grey tapestry, and the rug is of grey and rose. Water color on print. Size 8 x 10.

3458—GRAND HALL—Looking south and towards the main corridor and main entrance. Water color on print. Size 8 x 10.

3459—GOVERNMENT HOUSE—View from the south-west, showing the approach from Douglas drive on the west, and the fore court and bridge connecting it with the outer court. In the foreground, on the bank, is the rock garden, with rustic stone steps and pathway leading down under the bridge to the ravine on the east. Beyond the fore court is the east terrace, overlooking the Ravine, with the flag staff at the south-east corner. Water color on print. Size 8 x 10.

3460—GOVERNMENT HOUSE, ROSEDALE, TORONTO—Main approach from Roxborough drive, to the south—The view shows the roadway, walk and stone balustrade overlooking the Ravine and extending round the circular or outer court, across the bridge to the fore court and around the terrace on the east side. Water color on print. Size 8 x 10.

3461—GRAND HALL, OR ATRIUM—Showing the north end, the marble staircase in the centre, the entrances to the ballroom at the sides, and the galleries, with their marble and bronze balconies, on the upper floors. The atrium is designed in Louis XVI. period, finished in marble (from the quarries near Bancroft, Hastings County, Ont.), extending the full height of the building and terminating in a groined ceiling. The centre portion of the ceiling is of obscured glass, illuminated at night by electric lights. Water color on print. Size 8 x 10.

3462—BALLROOM—Looking south toward the entrances from the corridor adjoining the main hall, and showing the balconies of the grand staircase, overlooking the ballroom; also the alcove on the east side. At the opposite end of the room is an alcove with a raised dais, to be used on State occasions. The apartment is designed in Louis XVI. period, with old ivory and grey as the color scheme. The panels on the walls are in soft greys, painted in imitation of silk, while the draperies are in Rose du Barry. The electric fixtures are finished in ormolu gold and crystals. Water color on print. Size 8 x 10.

3463—HOME OF THE RED MAN, BRUCE MINES, 1862—This town was active in the days of fifty years ago, when the Bruce, Wellington and Huron Copper Bay Mines were working. Competition, however, with American mines, the output of which is large and the working expenses less, put the Canadian industries out of business, and they are now practically abandoned. The Indians shown in the picture are Objibways, whose wigwams were to be found in those days along the north shores of Lakes Huron and Superior. These wigwams were simple in construction. A few poles were set up, meeting at the top, in the form of a cone, covered with bark, and with branches spread within for a mattress. The drawing was made a short distance from the town, at the edge of the wood. Water color from print. Size 5 x 7.

3464—HOME OF HON. JAMES CROOKS, WEST FLAMBORO, U.C.— The Crooks residence was situated at the eastern limit of Flamboro village, on the north side of the Dundas and Waterloo road. In 1884 it was removed, and the property purchased by the late John Weir, who erected on the site a brick residence, which is still (1917) standing. Hon. James Crooks was a prominent Niagara merchant, who subsequently settled at Flamboro, where he operated grist and paper mills. Water color. Size 5 x 7.

3465—ALCOVE ON EAST SIDE OF BALLROOM—The mirrors were taken from the old Government House on Simcoe street. Water color on print. Size 8 x 10.

3466—DRAWING-ROOM—Looking north—The French casement windows on either side of the mantelpiece open on to the Fountain Terrace. Water color on print. Size 8 x 10.

3467—GOVERNMENT HOUSE—View from the western approach, from Douglas drive, showing the walk to the side entrance and the rose garden and pergola at the north end of the rose garden, screening the lower part of the servants' wing. Water color on print. Size 8 x 10.

3468—GOVERNMENT HOUSE—View from circular court to the south of the building, showing the approach to the fore court over the bridge, the rock garden and pathway to the rose garden on the west, and the terrace to the east of the house. Water color on print. Size 8 x 10.

3469—FIREPLACE, STATE DINING-ROOM—Over the fireplace, which is of Caen stone, richly carved, may be seen the Arms of the Province of Ontario, and to the left of the picture is the oil painting, by Berthon, of Sir Peregrine Maitland, Lieut.-Governor of Upper Canada, 1818-28. Water color on print. Size 8 x 10.

3470—MORNING-ROOM—Finished in oak and designed in Victorian period, with corresponding furniture. The lower part of the mantel is of marble, while the upper part is finished in bronze. The casement windows open on to the Fountain Terrace on the east side of the building. Water color on print. Size 8 x 10.

3471—U.S. STEAMER "MICHIGAN"—On June 1st, 1866, the Fenians left Black Rock and crossed the Niagara River in three scows, towed by two tugs. They landed on the Canadian side and marched to Fort Erie, which they took possession of, then marching back and camping over night on the Newbigging Farm, just below Bridgeburg. Next morning they took a circuitous route to the Limestone Ridge, on the Ridge road, at Ridgeway, and about 2 p.m. met the British troops. Retiring to Fort Erie, they encountered the Dunnville Naval Brigade, and Col. King's Welland Battery, and a sharp engagement on the streets of the village ensued. A number of prisoners were taken by the Fenians and held for a few hours at the old Fort Erie. A tug and scow attempted to land near the old fort, but the scow was caught in the current and carried down to the G.W.R.R. dock. There the Fenians got on board and attempted to land at Black Rock; but the Buffalo tug "Harrison" stopped them and handed the scow over to the U.S. steamer "Michigan" (shown in picture), which held the raiders on the river for several days, awaiting instructions from Washington, and finally landed them at Black Rock. Water color from an old print. Size 4 x 6.

3472—PARIS, C.W., 1853—From Governor's Road, southeast of the town—With key. In 1828 Paris was founded by Hiram Capron, from Vermont, who bought a thousand acres of land at "the forks of the Grand River." A public meeting was called in 1836 for the purpose of naming the place, and Capron suggested it be called Paris "for shortness, and because there was so much gypsum in the neighborhood." To-day (1917) Paris, in Brant County, is a thriving manufacturing town. Water color, from engraving in the Anglo-American Magazine, 1854. Size 4 x 7.

3473—SIR JOHN HENDRIE'S WRITING-ROOM—Designed in Victorian period, in harmony with the morning-room adjoining it. The woodwork is of oak. Water color on print. Size 8 x 10.

3474—STATE DINING-ROOM—Designed in Jacobean style, with harmonizing furniture. The walls are panelled in fumed oak, with rich carvings in frieze and over the heads of the doors. The massive ceiling is of plaster, with beams richly decorated in blue, silver and gold to harmonize with the carpet, which is a deep blue color. The electroliers are finished in oxidized silver. As in the old Government House on Simcoe street, the walls of the State dining-room are hung with portraits of past Lieutenant-Governors of Ontario. Reading from left to right the portraits shown are those of Sir Francis Bond Head, Poulett Thomson (Lord Sydenham), Sir Gordon Drummond, Sir Peregrine Maitland and Sir John Colborne. (Lord Seaton). Water color on print. Size 8 x 10.

3475—GOVERNMENT HOUSE—East court and terrace and corner of palmroom, overlooking the Ravine. Water color on print. Size 8 x 10.

3476—PATHWAY OF STONE—From the Ravine, and under the bridge leading to the steps of the rock garden. Water color on print. Size 8 x 10.

3477—MAIN CORRIDOR—Designed in Louis XVI. period—It extends the full width of the building, from east to west, and is panelled in oak. Here, as in the State dining-room, hang portraits of past Lieutenant-Governors of the province. At the extreme right of the picture is the oil, by A. Dickson Patterson, of Sir George Airey Kirkpatrick, Lieutenant-Governor, 1892-7. Water color on print. Size 8 x 10.

3478—BREAKFAST ROOM—Or private dining-room—With windows overlooking the rose garden and pergola. The apartment, which is designed in the Adam period, is furnished in mahogany, with ivory and green as the color scheme. The electrolier is in antique silver. Water color on print. Size 8 x 10.

3479—NORTH SYDNEY, C. B.—The view, taken from Chapel Hill, northeast of the town, shows:—1, Roman Catholic Church; 2, Entrance to the Harbor; 3, Hills Bordering the North-west Arm (formerly called the Sandwich River) of Sydney Harbor; 4, Point Edward, four miles from Sydney and a mile and a half from North Sydney; 5, Wharf of the General Mining Association, now (1917) the Nova Scotia Steel and Coal Company, where the coal from Sydney Mines was shipped. Water color from original drawing by Schell and Hogan, for "Picturesque Canada," 1880. Size 5 x 7.

3480—BILLIARD-ROOM—In Jacobean style—The wainscoting of the walls is panelled in fumed oak, surmounted by a richly colored frieze in plaster, with the Tudor rose in relief. Suede cloth of a garnet shade drapes the windows. The mantel is of Caen stone. Water color on print. Size 8 x 10.

3481—PALM ROOM—Overlooking the east terrace—The Victorian period is here exemplified. The walls are executed in Caen stone and the floor is of composition marble. The furniture is of grey oak and the window hangings of soft grey silk. Water color on print. Size 8 x 10.

3482—BEDROOM USED BY H.R.H. DUKE OF CONNAUGHT—Designed in the Adam style, with ivory and King's blue as the color scheme. Water color on print. Size 8 x 10.

3483—BEDROOM USED BY H.R.H. THE LATE DUCHESS OF CONNAUGHT—Designed in the Adam style—The color scheme is ivory and turquoise blue. Water color on print. Size 8 x 10.

36

3484—BOUDOIR USED BY H.R.H. DUCHESS OF CONNAUGHT—Designed in the Adam style, with decorations and furniture in Chase Chippendale. Ivory, blue and canary is the color scheme. Water color on print. Size 8 x 10.

3485—SIR JOHN HENDRIE'S ROOM—The apartment is done in ivory and grey. Water color on print. Size 8 x 10.

3486—LADY HENDRIE'S ROOM—In the Adam style—Ivory, grey and mauve are the colors used here. Water color on print. Size 8 x 10.

3487—BLUE PARLOR—On the first floor, in centre of the building, overlooking the grounds to the south. Adam period is the design used in the furnishings, while the color scheme is ivory and blue. It was in this apartment that his Excellency the Duke of Devonshire signed the Conscription Bill, Aug. 28th, 1917. Water color on print. Size 8 x 10.

3488—CABINET CHAMBER, HOUSE OF PARLIAMENT, QUEBEC—In this chamber, which is rather a handsome room, are held the meetings of the Government of Quebec during the sessions of the Legislature. Here the Cabinet deliberates and lays down the policy to be followed in all matter in connection with the government of the province. The Premier sits at the head of the table, and on the right the members of the Government. Water color. Size 7 x 9.

3489—HENDRIE, LADY—Wife of Sir John Hendrie, present (1917) Lieutenant-Governor of Ontario, and daughter of the late P. R. Henderson, of Kingston, Ont. Lady Hendrie was president of the Queen Victoria Memorial Statue Committee, 1902, and in 1905 was elected vice-president of the Women's Wentworth Historical Society. Active in the various forms of war work in connection with the present war. Water color. Size 5 x 8. Full length.

3490—HENDRIE, COL. HON. SIR JOHN S.—Lieutenant-Governor, Ontario. Appointed Sept. 25th, 1914. Water color. Size 5 x 8. Full length. See 431.

3491—HENDRIE, MISS ENID STRATHEARN—Only daughter of the (1917) Lieutenant-Governor of Ontario, Sir John Strathearn Hendrie. Miss Hendrie was born in Hamilton, Ont., and received her education in Canada, England and France. Water color. Size 6 x 8. Half length, sitting.

3492—COUNCIL CHAMBER, CITY HALL, QUEBEC—The new City Hall was erected in 1894-5, facing the Basilica, and on the site of the old Jesuits' College. It is a handsome building, of mixed style of architecture, with Norman predominating. The stone used in construction was brought from different quarries in the province. In the hall are the Council Chamber, Office of the Civic Administration, Recorder's Court, and Central Police and Fire Stations. Along the front of gallery in the Council Chamber are shown in picture shields containing names of ex-mayors of the city. These have been removed. And, on the west wall, are shields bearing dates of the discovery of Canada and foundation of Quebec. The Mayor's chair is at the west end. The lithograph portraits which can be seen in picture are: 1, Prince of Wales in 1860; 2, Queen Victoria; 3, Queen Alexandra, and, 4, King Edward. Water color on print. Size 8 x 10.

3493—LEGISLATIVE COUNCIL CHAMBER, HOUSE OF PARLIAMENT, QUEBEC—The Legislature consists of two branches, the Legislative Council and Legislative Assembly. The picture shows the meeting place of the former, whose members are appointed for life by the Lieut.-Governor. On the right of the Speaker's chair (left of spectator) is the portrait of Hon. Mr. Turgeon, present (1917) Speaker, and on the other side is that of Hon. Mr. De Boucherville, a former Speaker, and from

1874-8 Premier of Quebec. Over the throne is "The Landing of Champlain," by Henri Beau. The first Legislative Council of Quebec met in the Chateau St. Louis, 1775, having been established by the Act of 1774. Water color on print. Size 8 x 10.

3494—BLOCKHOUSE AND OFFICERS' QUARTERS, FORT EDWARD, WINDSOR, N.S.—The order to erect the Fort at Pisiquid, as the place was known to the French, was given on March 12th, 1749, by Governor Cornwallis to Capt. John Gorham. Dissatisfaction was rampant among the Acadians, and it was to combat this state of affairs that the work of defence was built. The officers' quarters are now (1917) used as a golf clubhouse; for several years after the fire of 1897 the building was used as a dwelling. The blockhouse is also still standing. Water color. Size 6 x 10.

3495—LEGISLATIVE ASSEMBLY CHAMBER, HOUSE OF PARLIAMENT, QUEBEC—The Parliament House and Departmental Buildings are on St. Louis street, or, as it is here called—Grande Allee. The sessions of the Legislature are opened and closed by his Honor the Lieut.-Governor of the province, who also sanctions bills passed by both branches of the Legislature. The handsomely furnished Legislative Assembly Chamber in which the members, elected every five years or oftener, meet, is shown. At the north-west end are the Speaker's chair and that of the Clerk of the House, and in the gallery is a painting of Canada's first Parliament, 17th December, 1792. Water color on print. Size 8 x 10.

3496—PICTON, U.C., 1830—View from the hilltop, south of harbor—The picture shows: 1, Anglican Church of St. Mary Magdalene; 2, Miller's warehouse and dock; 3, Striker's Inn (known in 1815 as Clute's Inn); 4, Chuckery Hill; 5, Brick Kiln Point; 6, Gray's storehouse and dock; 7, Old Danforth road, used 1812-15 by the military (this part of Picton, 1917, is called Bridge street); 8, Building said to have been used for meetings of the Masonic Lodge; 9, Townsend's Point, a mile north-east of Picton; 10, Storehouse and dock. Water color from original by Captain Downs, in possession of Prince Edward's Lodge, A.F.& A.M., Picton, Ont. Size 5 x 7.

3497—HENDRIE, WILLIAM—Pioneer of railway cartage system in Canada—Born in Glasgow, Scotland, Nov., 1831; educated at Glasgow High School. Came to Canada, 1854, obtaining a position in the Great Western general freight office at Hamilton. With John Shedden introduced the railway cartage system in Canada, 1885. Built Wellington, Grey and Bruce Ry., and Hamilton and Northwestern Ry. Chief promoter Hamilton Bridge Works, 1895. Mr. Hendrie's death took place in 1906. Water color from portrait in possession of his widow, Mrs. Hendrie, by Sir George Reid, F.R.S.A., Edinburgh. Size 8 x 10. Three-quarter length, sitting.

3498—PICTON, ON THE BAY OF QUINTE, 1880—From the north-west, on west high bank of harbor—Key: 1. Residence of late Philip Low, K.C. 2. Church of St. Mary Magdalene (Anglican). 3. Court House and jail. 4. Warehouse used by strs. Alexandra, Bay of Quinte and Utica. 5. Residence on south side of Bridge street. 6. Str. Alexandra. 7. Str. St. Helen. 8. Str. Bay of Quinte. 9. Dock and warehouse used by strs. St. Helen and Hero. 10. Lumber yard and warehouse. 11. Hill south of harbor. Water color, from original drawing by F. B. Schell, for "Picturesque Canada." Size 5 x 7.

3499—RIDEAU HALL, OTTAWA—As the home of Canada's Governor-General appears in 1917. Water color on print. Size 6 x 8. See 1890.

3500—WALLS OF PARLIAMENT BUILDINGS, OTTAWA—In process of demolition after the fire of February 3rd, 1916—Huge scaffolds were erected on all sides of the walls, valued at $2,000,000, and the stone work removed piece by piece, note being taken of the relative position of each stone, in the event of its being again used. With the exception of the library, the entire building was taken down preliminary to re-erection. The architectural lines of the old are preserved in the new structure, but the building and its tower will be higher. Photograph, colored. Size 4 x 9.

3501—INTERIOR OF THE COMMONS CHAMBER, HOUSES OF PARLIAMENT, OTTAWA, 1916—In the centre may be seen the Speaker's chair and dais, with Press Gallery directly above. The public galleries ran around the four sides of the chamber, which in the great fire of Feb. 3rd, 1916, was completely destroyed. On the night of the fire, fortunately, very few people were in the galleries, and only about fifty members in the chamber. The ceiling was glass with crosswise beams, light cherry color, and walls a neutral green tint. The woodwork in the galleries was Canadian pine, varnished, having become by long use darker than the ordinary pine so coated, and the columns and bases were of marble, nearly white, with upper portieres, white and grey. Photograph, colored. Size 7 x 9.

3502—PERILOUS UNDERTAKING BY FARINI—Carrying a man across the Niagara River—Signor Farini (William Hunt), a rival of the celebrated Blondin, is shown crossing the Niagara River on a tightrope, with a man named Mullin strapped on his back. They had gone but a few feet when it was discovered that the tackling of the rider was out of order, necessitating a return to shore; a second attempt was, however, successful. At the first parallel guy they stopped to rest and Mullin dismounted; another halt was made near the centre of the rope, and here Farini, motioning for the "Maid of the Mist" to come nearer, suspended himself by the arms and turned a somersault. After a short rest the two men returned to the American side. Water color from sketch by H. Ingraham, taken from the Clifton House balcony, August 29th, 1860. Size 5 x 9.

3503—PORT PERRY IN 1853—With Scugog Lake and Island in the background—The view shows:—1, Bigelow store; 2, McMichael's store; 3, James Squire, merchant tailor; 4, Whitaker and Crandell; 5, Charles S. Jewett, boots and shoes; 6-7, William White, steam planing mill; 8, Steamer "Woodman"; 9, Water street. Water color from an engraving in the Anglo-American Magazine, 1854. Size 4 x 7.

3504—NEW MACE, HOUSE OF COMMONS, CANADA, 1917—It replaces the original Mace of the House of Commons of the Dominion, destroyed by fire 3rd February, 1916, and was presented by three distinguished London gentlemen—Colonel the Right Hon. Sir Charles Cheers Wakefield, Lord Mayor, and the Sheriffs of London, George Alexander Touche, Esq., M.P., and Samuel George Shead, Esq. Their names are inscribed on the foot of the staff. The ensign is of solid silver mercurial gilt, fashioned on lines similar to the English mace. The head is vase-shaped, supported by four ornamental brackets and surmounted by a crown, indicating the Royal authority. The staff is divided at intervals by two spiral fluted knops, and the entire length is richly chased. On the head of the staff, beneath the crown, are three beavers in relief, immortalizing the industrious habits of Canada. This symbol of authority, made by the Goldsmiths and Silversmiths Company, Regent street, London, will, when the new Parliament Buildings are completed at Ottawa, be placed on the table in the Commons Chamber. From original, which is almost five feet in length.

3505—OLD ANCHOR AT HOLLAND LANDING—A relic of the War of 1812-15—The anchor was destined for a ship on the stocks at Penetanguishene, in those days an important naval station. It was forged in Chatham dockyard, England, and arrived at Quebec late in 1814. In charge of Capt. Samuel Brock, a distant relative of Gen. Sir Isaac Brock, it was taken up the St. Lawrence to Montreal by batteau, then by road to Kingston, and again by batteau to York. Captain Brock had contracted to carry it as far as the Holland River, whence it was to be shipped by batteau to Pene-tanguishene; but ere it reached its destination peace was declared. A messenger, despatched from York to notify Capt. Brock that the anchor need be carried no farther, overtook the party at Holland Landing. The anchor was immediately hoisted off the sled and the men returned to York. In 1870 the ancient relic was removed from its original resting place and taken to the Holland Park, where it still (1917) remains. Water color. Size 4 x 6.

3506—COBOURG, C.W., 1854—From Weller's Hill, west of Factory Creek—The key shows: 1. Victoria College, Seminary street, now (1916) University ave., facing College st. 2. Sydney Smith's block of stores. 3. St. Peter's Church, facing south on north side of King street. 4. North American Hotel, Division street. 5. Steamer dock, foot of Division street. 6. Butler's storehouse. 7. Factory Creek, which ran through centre of town. 8. Shore line west of creek. 9. "Buck House," built by Elijah Buck. 10. "Brooklands," residence of Judge Boswell. 11. Archdeacon Bethune's Theological Seminary. Water color. Size 4 x 6. See 1731.

3507—CITADEL, HALIFAX, N.S., FROM CAMP HILL—Looking east, 1782—The defences of Halifax originally consisted of a wooden palisade and blockhouses. About 1778 Citadel Hill was first regularly fortified, and the works of the present fortress were commenced by Edward, Duke of Kent, who during his sojourn at Halifax had a residence on the slope of the hill. (1) The Citadel, showing old octagonal blockhouse on summit. (2) St. George's Tavern, near the "Willow Tree" on northern slope of Camp Hill. (3) Highway leading from Halifax to Windsor. (4) Northern slope of Camp Hill, summit of which is not in picture. (5) Soldiers of troops encamped on Camp Hill. (6) The Common, where the troops exercised. It was in the hollow between Citadel Hill and Camp Hill. Water color on print, from India ink drawing by Dr. T. B. Akins, in Provincial Museum, Halifax, after engraving published in London, after drawing by Lieut.-Col. Edward Hicks, H.M. 70th Regiment of Foot. Size 4 x 6.

3508—WILLIAMS, HENRY BURT, 1813-64—Originator of Omnibuses in Toronto—Came to Canada from England, via Albany, N.Y., in 1837. He was for a short time in the Commissariat Department, then commenced business as a cabinetmaker. In 1849 he started a 'bus line from St. Lawrence Market and from the corner of King and Yonge streets, to the Red Lion Hotel, Yorkville, continuing the business until 1862, when he sold out to the Street Railway Company, having carried on an opposition busi-ness for a year. Died in Toronto, January, 1884. Mr. H. H. Williams, of Toronto, is a son of Mr. H. B. Williams. Water color. Size 3 x 4. Head and shoulders.

3509—EARLY TORONTO LOCOMOTION—In 1849 Mr. H..B. Williams, cabinet-maker, 140 Yonge street, Toronto (the location would now, 1917, be opposite Eaton's), started a line of four omnibuses from St. Lawrence Market, and from the corner of King and Yonge streets, to the Red Lion Hotel, Yorkville (present location 749-63). The first 'bus, that in picture, was built in Mr. Williams' shops. It was a six-passenger vehicle, had mov-able windows, but could be closed in with leather curtains. The fare was the old English sixpence, and the line, which ran every ten minutes from both ends, at once became popular. Yonge street in those days was a macadamized road, and in wet weather was often in a deplorable condition. Water color. Size 3 x 4.

3510—'BUS OF 1850—In 1850 Mr. Williams built four larger 'busses, ten-passenger vehicles. When horse cars came into operation he had the gear of his 'busses narrowed to fit and run on the street railway track. He continued in opposition to the railway for a time, selling out to the com-pany in 1862. Water color. Size 3 x 4.

3511—SCHREIBER, SIR COLLINGWOOD—Prominent Canadian Engineer—Born in Colchester, Essex, Eng., Dec. 14th, 1831. Came to Canada in 1852. For the ensuing four years he served as assistant engineer on the Toronto and Hamilton Railway, and from 1856-60, while a member of the firm of Fleming, Ridout & Schreiber, was superintending engineer on the Toronto Esplanade. Superintending engineer on the rebuilding of the Northern Railway, 1860-63. Served in various railroad engineering capacities in the Maritime Provinces. In 1880 succeeded Sir Sandford Fleming as chief engineer of the Canadian Pacific Railway. Also chief engineer and general manager of Government Railways, holding the three positions until 1892. A member of Royal Commission on Railways, 1886. In 1892 appointed Chief Engineer and Deputy Minister of Railways and Canals. Appointed general consulting engineer to the Dominion Government and chief engineer of the western division of the Grand Trunk Pacific Railway from Winnipeg to Prince Rupert, 1905. Received knighthood Jan. 1st, 1916. Sir Collingwood (1917) resides in Ottawa. Water color. Sizes 3 x 4. Head and shoulders.

3512—SCHREIBER, WILFRED CHARLES—Born in Essex, Eng., 25th Jan., 1836, son of Rev. Thomas Schreiber. Educated by tutors. Came to Canada, 1845. In 1853 was employed, under his brother (Sir) Collingwood Schreiber, on the staff of the Hamilton and Toronto Railway as picketman. in 1864 entered the service of the Northern Railway, and when the Grand Trunk absorbed that road removed to London, Ont., as purchasing agent. Severed his connection with the G.T.R. in 1897. His death took place at Petrolea, Ont., June 4th, 1903. Water color from portrait in possession of his brother, Sir Collingwood Schreiber, Ottawa. Size 3 x 4. Head and shoulders.

3513-17—City Commissioners, Toronto, 1871-1917.

3513—CARR, JOHN—City Commissioner, Toronto, 1871-2—Sepia. Size 3 x 4. Head and shoulders. See 378, 591, 752.

3514—COATSWORTH, EMERSON, Sr.—City Commissioner, Toronto, 1872-1903—Born in Yorkshire, Eng., July 25th, 1825. In 1852 came to Toronto. Alderman for St. David's Ward, 1872. Until his appointment as City Commissioner he carried on business as a builder and contractor; built the first Berkeley Street Methodist Church in 1857. Was City Commissioner until his death, May 8th, 1903. From 1861-2 served as captain in the 10th Royals. Sepia from portrait in possession of his son, Judge Coatsworth. Size 3 x 4. Head and shoulders.

3515—FLEMING, R. J.—City (Assessment and Property) Commissioner, Toronto, 1903-5—In 1903, after the death of Mr. Coatsworth, the office of City Commissioner was abolished and the work taken over by the Property Commissioner. Sepia. Size 3 x 4. Head and shoulders. See 390, 3571.

3516—HARRIS, R. C.—City (Property) Commissioner, Toronto, 1905-12 —Sepia. Size 3 x 4. Head and shoulders. See 2796.

3517—CHISHOLM, DANIEL—City (Property) Commissioner, Toronto, 1912-17—He was born in Kingston, Ont., 1859, a son of Daniel Chisholm, an official of the old Royal Mail Line of steamers. The Property Commissioner came to Toronto in 1872, and in later years became engaged in general commission business. From 1903-12 he was Alderman for Ward One, Toronto. Sepia. Size 3 x 4. Head and shoulders.

3518—MORRISON, HON. JOSEPH CURRAN—Advocated and assisted in promotion of Ontario, Simcoe and Huron Railway, and for several years was president of directorate, in succession to Hon. Henry John Boulton. Water color. Size 3 x 4. Head and shoulders. See 946.

3519—**PROVINCIAL FAIR, TORONTO, 1852**—View of Agricultural Hall, Show Grounds and Floral Hall—The grounds, oblong in shape, comprised, exclusive of the horse parade, about seventeen acres. They were divided almost equally into two parts by a winding, shallow ravine, through a portion of which a stream ran. The southern half was clear of trees and the northern prettily wooded. Each side of the Agricultural Hall was divided into compartments, in which were the exhibits of wheat, flour and vegetables. In the centre of the building stood a large table 50 x 6 ft., on which were tastefully arranged dairy products. The interior decorations of the Floral Hall were simple and effective, and the introduction of a fountain, in active play during the Exhibition, was pleasing and attractive. Many florists in Toronto and vicinity sent in plants and flowers, and gardens and greenhouses of Toronto were represented in the exhibits. Water colors. Size (each) 5 x 7.

3520—**THE HOMESTEADERS**—A ray of romance brightens the life of the "Rider of the Plains." Lithograph, in color, from original oil painting by Paul Wickson, Paris, Ont. Size 8 x 13.

3521—**"YOUR COUNTRY CALLS"**—The recruiting sergeant on his rounds, calling for men in the Northwest. Lithograph, in color, from original oil painting by Paul Wickson, Paris, Ont., 1915. Size 7 x 14.

3522-6—**Pastors, Knox (Presbyterian) Church, Toronto, 1820-1917.**

3522—**HARRIS, REV. JAMES**—First Pastor, Knox Church, Toronto, 1820-44—In the autumn of 1820 the first Presbyterian congregation in York (Toronto) was organized by the Rev. James Harris, of Belfast, Ireland. Mr. Harris was ordained pastor, 10th July, 1823, by a committee of the Presbytery of Brockville, and continued in the charge until his retirement from the active ministry in 1844. At this time—the year of the Disruption of the Presbyterian Church in Canada, many members of St. Andrew's who sympathized with the Free Church united with Mr. Harris' old congregation, which then became known as Knox Church. Mr. Harris removed to Eglinton, where he spent his last years. He was born in 1793, and died Sept. 14th, 1873. Sepia from portrait in Knox Church, Toronto. Size 3 x 4. Head and shoulders.

3523—**BURNS, REV. ROBERT. D.D.**—Second Pastor, Knox Church, Toronto, 1844-56—Sepia from portrait in Knox Church. Size 3 x 4. Head and shoulders. See 2514.

3524—**TOPP, REV. ALEXANDER, D.D.**—Third Pastor, Knox Church, Toronto, 1858-79—Born near Elgin, Scotland, April 1st, 1815; educated at Elgin Academy and afterwards at Aberdeen University. On being licensed, was appointed assistant pastor of Elgin parish church, and a few months later pastor. When the Scottish Disruption of 1843 took place Mr. Topp, with the greater part of his congregation, seceded. In 1852 he removed to Free Roxburgh Church, Edinburgh, remaining there for six years. In 1858 accepted a call from Knox congregation, Toronto, in succession to Dr. Burns—the pulpit of Knox having been vacant for two years. Moderator of the General Assembly of the Presbyterian Church in Canada, 1868 (the first instance of a unanimous nomination to that office by the various presbyteries of the church), and again in 1876. Received the degree of D.D. from Aberdeen University, 1870. One of the promoters of the Home for Incurables, Toronto. Died Oct. 8th, 1879. Sepia from portrait in Knox Church, Toronto. Size 3 x 4. Head and shoulders.

3525—**PARSONS, REV. HENRY M., D.D.**—Pastor, Knox Church, Toronto, 1880-1900—Son of Rev. Isaac Parsons; born at East Haddam, Conn. Nov. 13th, 1828. Studied at Williston Seminary, Easthampton, Mass., and at Yale, graduating from the latter institution in 1848. Taught at Lynn, Conn., for two years,and at Richmond Academy, Richmond, Va., for one year. Graduated from the Connecticut Theological School (now Hartford Theological Seminary), Windsor Hill, 1854, and was ordained Nov. 15th of that year. Assistant to Rev. Samuel Osgood, D.D., First Congregational Church, Springfield, Mass., later succeeding Mr. Osgood as pastor. In 1874 became pastor of the Union Church, Boston. After four years there he accepted the pulpit of Olivet Congregational Church in the same city. In 1877 accepted a call to Lafayette Presbyterian Church, Buffalo, N.Y., remaining there until his coming to Knox. On resigning from the active ministry, 1900, made Pastor Emeritus of Knox Church. His death occurred in Toronto, Jan. 14th, 1913. Sepia from portrait in Knox Church. Size 3 x 4. Head and shoulders.

3526—WINCHESTER, REV. ALEXANDER B.—Pastor Knox Church, Toronto, 1900-1917—Born at Peterhead, Aberdeenshire, Scotland, in 1858. Came to Canada with his parents, settling in Woodstock, Ont. Educated at Manitoba College, graduating in 1887. Volunteered for mission work in North China, but in 1889 returned to Canada on account of ill-health. Subsequently pastor of St. Andrew's Church, Berlin, Ont. Organized and superintended a mission to the Chinese in British Columbia. 1892. Still (1917) occupies the pulpit of Knox. Sepia from original portrait. Size 3 x 4. Head and shoulders.

3527—HOME AGAIN AFTER TWO YEARS "SOMEWHERE IN FRANCE"—The Canadian hero returns with the Victoria Cross. Lithograph, in color, from original oil painting by Paul Wickson, Paris, Ont., 1916. Size 7 x 14.

3528—THE FIRST-BORN IN THE SETTLEMENT—An eventful incident in the life of the Canadian Northwest. Lithograph, in color, from original oil painting by Paul Wickson, Paris, Ont., 1912. Size 9 x 13.

3529—"A VIEW OF THE BRIDGE BUILT OVER THE RIVER MASKE-NONGE. by order of General Haldmand, in 1782—By James Peachey, 1783"—It was situated twenty-four miles above Three Rivers, near the mouth of the Maskinonge, where it flows into Lake St. Peter, and was on the line of the highway between Quebec and Montreal. During his stay in Canada Haldimand, who was Governor 1778-84, brought about many improvements which benefited the country, including the building of roads, canals and bridges. The bridge shown in picture was rebuilt many years ago. Water color. Size 13 x 20.

3530—BOULTON, WILLIAM SOMERVILLE, C.E., 1830-60—He was born in York (Toronto), educated at Cobourg, Ont., and Upper Canada College, Toronto. In 1848 he went to England with his mother (his father. Rev. Wm. Boulton, having died in 1834): studied for his profession at King's College, London. Returning to Canada, he took up construction work on the Grand Trunk Railway, and in the summer of 1855 surveyed the shores of Georgian Bay. Later he became a partner with Col. Dennis. engineer and surveyor, and undertook a good deal of Government work. Afterwards Mr. Boulton returned to the service of the Grand Trunk, and had charge of two sections near St. Mary's, Ont. About 1859 he visited England with a view to obtaining engineering work there, and having prospects in connection with Mont Cenis tunnel (constructed 1857-70, seven miles in length), he decided to bring his family from Canada. En route from England was lost at sea when the Hungarian foundered off Cape Sable, Feb. 19th, 1860. Water color from portrait by W. Lockwood, 1853, in possession of his daughter, Miss D. C. Boulton, Toronto. Size 5 x 6. Half length.

535

3531-8—Pastors, St. Andrew's Presbyterian Church, Toronto, 1831-1917.

3531—RINTOUL, REV. WILLIAM—Pastor, St. Andrew's Church, 1831-4. Sepia. Size 3 x 4. Head and shoulders. See 2534, 3429.

3532—LEACH, REV. WM. TURNBULL—Pastor, St. Andrew's Church, 1835-42. Sepia. Size 3 x 4. Head and shoulders. See 2510.

3533—BARCLAY, REV. JOHN—Pastor, St. Andrew's Church, 1842-70. Sepia. Size 3 x 4. Head and shoulders. See 2512.

3534—MACDONNELL, REV. D. J.—Pastor, St. Andrew's Church, 1870-96. A native of Bathurst, N. B.; born 1843; educated at Glasgow, Edinburgh, and at Queen's, Kingston. Ordained in Edinburgh June 14th, 1866, and in 1870 came to Canada as pastor of St. Andrew's, where he remained until his death, Feb. 19th, 1896. Sepia. Size 3 x 4. Head and shoulders.

3535—McCAUGHAN, REV. W. J.—Pastor, St. Andrew's Church, 1897-8. Born at Moycraig, Ballycastle, County Antrim, Ireland, Dec. 4th, 1859. Educated at the Coleraine Institute, matriculating at McGee College, Londonderry. In 1879 became senior master at Erdington Collegiate School near Birmingham. Took his theological course at the Free Church College, Edinburgh. Ordained Jan. 1st, 1884. Pastor successively of Wellington street congregation, Ballymena, and of Mount Pottinger Church, Belfast. From the latter charge he was called to St. Andrew's, Toronto, in succession to Rev. D. J. Macdonnell. Mr. McCaughan was inducted here March 25th, 1897. In October of the following year he resigned to accept the pastorate of the Third Presbyterian Church, Chicago. In 1907 called to the Cooke Memorial Church, Belfast, Ireland. Died July 31st, 1910, from injuries received through jumping from an upper window of the burning Belfast Hotel in which he and his wife were guests. Sepia. Size 3 x 4. Head and shoulders.

3536—BLACK, REV. ARMSTRONG, D.D.—Pastor St. Andrew's Church, 1899-1904. Born at Newcastleton. Roxburghshire, Scotland. Studied at the University of Edinburgh and in the Divinity Hall of the United Presbyterian Church. In 1875 he was ordained to the charge of Waterbeck, Dumfries-shire. Two years later went to Palmerston Place Church, Edinburgh, but because of the strain imposed upon him in this important position, he accepted a call to Kilcreggan, on the River Clyde. In 1896 he proceeded to Egremont, a suburb of Liverpool, Eng., remaining there until 1899. On leaving St. Andrew's, Toronto, he returned to England, and is now (1917) engaged in ministerial work at St. Leonard's-on-the-Sea. Sepia. Size 3 x 4. Head and shoulders.

3537—BROWN, REV. T. CRAWFORD—Pastor, St. Andrew's Church, 1905-15. Born 1874, at Richmond, Ont. Matriculated in 1896; B.A. of Queen's, 1900, and M.A., 1902, with first class honors in Political Economy, Mental and Moral Philosophy. Also a double gold medallist in Philosophy, and winner of first scholarship in Political Economy, as well as scholarships for general proficiency, Apologetics and Hebrew. Took post-graduate course in Edinburgh University. First assistant to late Rev. Sir James Cameron Lees, St. Giles' Cathedral, Edinburgh, until coming to St. Andrew's, Toronto. Chaplain of the 48th Highlanders, Toronto, since 1907. Sepia. Size 3 x 4. Head and shoulders.

3538—EAKIN, REV. THOMAS, Ph.D.—Pastor, St. Andrew's Church, 1915-17. An Irishman, having been born in Magherafelt, Derry, Ireland; received his early education at Moneymore. Graduated from University of Toronto, B.A., 1896; M.A., 1897; Ph.D., 1905. Graduate in Theology of Knox College, Toronto. From 1899-1905 Mr. Eakin was minister of St. Andrew's Church, Guelph, in the latter year becoming lecturer in Semitic languages and literature in University College, Toronto, and later was associate professor. Resigned this chair in 1912. Sepia. Size 3 x 4. Head and shoulders.

3539—PROVINCIAL FAIR, TORONTO, 1852—Plan of Grounds—This Exhibition, the seventh of the series which commenced at Toronto in 1846, was held in the "fields" at the north end of William street, above Queen. Simcoe was then south of Queen, but in later years William street, north of Queen, was changed to Simcoe street. Simcoe street and Dummer street (now William) are shown at the south end of the plan. The entrance was at the "office," about the site of the old Erskine Presbyterian Church. The grounds were bounded on the east by College avenue; the western boundary was a short distance west of Dummer street. The northern boundary was the Toronto Cricket Grounds, College street, and the Caer Howell Pleasure Grounds, just north of the present Hydro building in the Avenue. Note the several buildings—the Fruit, Dairy and Floral Hall and the Mechanics' Building. The Horse Park was at the west in fields belonging to Mrs. Boulton, of The Grange. After 1857 the Fairs were held alternately in Toronto, Kingston, Hamilton and London. The Fair of 1878 was the last year of the Provincial Exhibition held under the auspices of the Provincial Agricultural Association, and it was succeeded by the present National Exhibition, now held yearly in Toronto. The only pictures extant of the Toronto grounds and buildings are those which appeared in the Canadian Journal of October, 1852, published by the Canadian Institute, Toronto, and from which this plan and No. 3519 are reproduced. Size 7 x 9.

3540—"A VIEW OF THE BRIDGE BUILT OVER RIVIERE DE LOUP, by order of General Haldimand, in 1780—By James Peachey 1785"—It was twenty-two miles above Three Rivers, and crossed Riviere du Loup en haut, or Upper Riviere du Loup, now (1917) known as Louiseville, a thriving little town in Maskinonge County, Que. This bridge, rebuilt many years ago, was on the line of highway between Quebec and Montreal. Water color. Size 13 x 20.

3541-54—Collectors of Customs, Toronto, 1801-1917.

3541—ALLAN, LT.-COL. WILLIAM—Collector of Customs, York (Toronto), 1801-28—York was in 1801 made a customs port, and Col. William Allan, who on 25th August of that year, was appointed Collector, established the first Customs House on the east side of Frederick street, south of King. Mr. Allan was postmaster until 1827. He was the father of the late Hon. G. W. Allan. Water color. Size 3 x 4. Head and shoulders. See 610, 941.

3542—SAVAGE, GEORGE—Collector of Customs, York (Toronto), 1828-35—On his appointment as successor to Col. Allan, Mr. Savage announced that for customs purposes he had "temporarily established an office in part of the premises fronting on Duke street occupied by Mr. Columbus." Mr. Savage was a well-known figure in York, and in his position as Collector of Customs exercised praiseworthy vigilance. His death occurred Sept. 9th, 1835. Water color. Size 3 x 4. Head and shoulders.

3543—CARFRAE, THOMAS—Collector of Customs, Toronto, 1835-40— Mr. Carfrae, who was descended from a Huguenot family, was born in Edinburgh, Scotland, Nov. 17th, 1796. He was a prominent citizen of Toronto in the early days, and was the originator of the Potter's Field, or, to give it its official title, "The York General, or Strangers' Burying Ground," incorporated, January 30th, 1826. He was actively interested in the militia, becoming major in the Royal Provincial Artillery. Alderman for St George's Ward, 1834-5. Mr. Carfrae died June, 1844. Water color from portrait in possession of his grand-daughter, Mrs. G. A. McVicar, Toronto. Size 3 x 4. Head and shoulders. See 3604.

3544—MANAHAN, ANTHONY—Collector of Customs, Toronto, 1841-2—
He was born in Ireland; emigrated in the early thirties to Trinidad, afterwards coming to Canada. In 1836 he represented Hastings in the Legislature, and in 1841 became member for Kingston in the United Parliament.
Three years later, however, Mr. Manahan, who in the meantime had been
appointed Collector of Customs at York, retaining the position until April,
1842, was defeated by John A. (Sir) Macdonald as member for Kingston.
Water color from portrait in possession of his grandson, A. M. LeMoine,
Bradevelt, N.J.. Size 3 x 4. Head and shoulders.

3545—KELLY, WILLIAM MOORE—Collector of Customs, Toronto,
1842-3—Born in County Mayo, Ireland, in 1810, and came to Canada as a
young man. On the establishment in 1860 of the Ontario Reformatory
for Boys, at Penetanguishene, Mr. Kelly was appointed warden, holding
the position until the late seventies. He was also a captain in the militia.
His death took place at Penetanguishene, July 20th, 1896. Water color
from portrait in possession of his nephew, A. M. LeMoine, Bradevelt, N.J.
Size 3 x 4. Head and shoulders.

3546—STANTON, ROBERT—Collector of Customs, Toronto, 1843-9—
Appointed to succeed Mr. Kelly. Born June 6th, 1794, at St. John's, L.C.,
son of Wm. Stanton, who for many years served in military and civil
capacities in both Upper and Lower Canada. Robert Stanton was one of
the first pupils enrolled at the Home District Grammar School, established
by Rev. Geo. O'Kill Stuart, in 1807. On August 19th, 1826, he was appointed
King's Printer for U.C.; succeeded Charles Fothergill as editor and publisher of the Upper Canada Gazette and Weekly Register. The second
title of the paper was, however, changed by Mr. Stanton to the U. E.
Loyalist. His death took place in Toronto, Feb. 25th, 1866. Water color
from portrait in possession of Mrs. A. H. Walker, Toronto. Size 3 x 4.
Head and shoulders.

3547—MEUDELL, WILLIAM F.—Collector of Customs, Toronto,
1850-58—Mr. Meudell was born in Poole, Eng., Jan. 8th, 1800, and came
to Canada in 1832. In 1858 he was transferred from Toronto to Belleville, Ont., where he died, Jan. 10th, 1885. In the interim between the
resignation of Mr. Robert Stanton and the appointment on January 1st,
1850, of Mr. Meudell, Mr. William Pring acted as Collector. Water color
from portrait in possession of Mr. Meudell's daughter, Mrs. Anderson,
Belleville, Ont. Size 3 x 4. Head and shoulders.

3548—SPENCE, ROBERT—Collector of Customs, Toronto, 1858-68—A
native of Ireland, born in 1801. In early life immigrated to Canada,
settling in the town of Dundas, where he was successively auctioneer,
schoolmaster and editor of the Dundas Warder. Elected to represent
North Wentworth in the Parliament of United Canada in 1854, in the
Hincks-Morin Government, and had the honor of becoming a Cabinet
Minister before he sat a week in the House. Postmaster-General in the
McNab-Morin administration, and also in the Tache-Macdonald Ministry.
Withdrew from public life in 1857. Mr. Spence held the position of Col-
lector of Customs for the port of Toronto from 1858 until his death,
Feb. 26th, 1868. Water color. Size 3 x 4. Head and shoulders.

3549—SMITH, JAMES EDWARD—Collector of Customs, Toronto, 1868-
79—Subsequent to the death of Mr. Spence, and until Nov. 5th, 1868, Mr.
Thomas C. Scott, surveyor, acted as temporary Customs Collector. Mr.
Smith was then appointed. He was born in Cheshire, Eng., 1831, coming
to Canada about 1840. Partner in the firm of Smith & Miller, wholesale
grocers. Councillor for St. John's Ward, 1857-58; Alderman, 1859-67 and

1869-70; Mayor of Toronto, 1867-8. Also connected with the British Empire Life Assurance Co. Died March, 1892, in Toronto. Water color from portrait in possession of his son, Mr. W. Assheton Smith, Toronto. Size 3 x 4. Head and shoulders. See 380.

3550—DOUGLAS, JOHN—Collector of Customs, Toronto, 1879-81 and 1888-91—Born in Edinburgh, Scotland, March 19th, 1826, and educated in the Edinburgh public schools. In 1854 he came to Canada, and in that year was appointed to the Toronto Customs; Surveyor of the port in 1876. Although acting Collector twice, Mr. Douglas was never appointed to the office permanently. Superannuated from the public service in 1905. Water color from portrait in possession of his son, Mr. J. C. Douglas, Toronto. Size 3 x 4. Head and shoulders.

3551—PATTON, JAMES—Collector of Customs, Toronto, 1881-8—Born at Prescott, C.W., June 10th, 1824, and educated at Upper Canada College. Commenced the study of law in 1840 under Hon. J. Hillyard Cameron, Q.C. Entered King's College (Toronto University), in 1843. Called to the Bar in 1845, and practised his profession in Barrie, Ont., where he began the publication of the Barrie Herald. In 1855 inaugurated, with several other members of the legal profession, the Upper Canada Law Journal. Elected for the Saugeen Division (Counties of Bruce, Grey and North Simcoe) in 1856. Made a Bencher of the Law Society in 1858, and Vice-Chancellor Toronto University in 1860. Died Oct. 11th, 1888. Water color. Size 3 x 4. Head and shoulders.

3552—SMALL, JOHN—Collector of Customs, 1891-1909—Mr. Small was a grandson of Major John Small, who came from England in 1793. The Collector was born in Toronto in 1831, and educated at the Home District Grammar School and Upper Canada College. In 1855 he became taxing officer of the Court of the Queen's Bench, holding the position until 1882. In the latter year he was elected to the House of Commons to represent East Toronto, continuing to serve the constituency until 1891. Sat in the City Council of Toronto as Alderman for St. Lawrence Ward, 1877-9. Died 18th Feb., 1909. Water color. Size 3 x 4. Head and shoulders.

3553—BERTRAM, JOHN H.—Collector of Customs, 1909—Born at Lindsay, Ont., April 10th, 1872; educated in Toronto; engaged in the hardware business with the firm of Bertram & Co. Appointed hardware appraiser H.M. Customs, Toronto, Sept. 22nd, 1900; Surveyor of Customs, Sept. 1st, 1904, and Collector, Feb. 19th, 1909. Mr. Bertram still (1917) holds that position. Water color. Size 3 x 4. Head and shoulders.

3554—For Future Collector of Customs.

3555-9—City Treasurers, Toronto, 1834-1917.

3555—McCORD, ANDREW T.—City Chamberlain, 1834-72, and City Treasurer, 1872-4—Born in Belfast, Ireland, July 12th, 1805; emigrated to Canada about 1830, and was engaged in mercantile business for some years. Received appointment, July, 1834, as City Chamberlain in succession to Matthew Walton, who had filled the position since the incorporation of Toronto the previous March. In 1872 the office of City Chamberlain became known as City Treasurer. Mr. McCord died in 1881. Water color. Size 3 x 4. Head and shoulders.

3556—HARMAN, SAMUEL BICKERTON—City Treasurer, 1874-88. Water color. Size 3 x 4. Head and shoulders. See 381, 1008, 3568.

3557—COADY, RICHARD T.—City Treasurer, 1888-1914—A native of Toronto, of Irish parentage; educated at Model and Grammar Schools, here, After engaging in commercial life for a time, he entered the service of the City of Toronto, as accountant in the Treasury Department, 1873. Made chief accountant and assistant treasurer, Nov., 1877. In 1888 he succeeded S. B. Harman, K.C., as City Treasurer. Made several trips to England in connection with the city's finances, and in 1909 was the guest of the Lord Mayor of London. Died, September, 1914. Water color. Size 3 x 4. Head and shoulders.

3558—PATTERSON, JOHN—City Treasurer, 1914-16—Mr. Patterson was born in Toronto, Sept. 17th, 1848, and educated here. For a time he was in the employ of the firm of Virtue & Yorston; entered the service of the corporation in 1872. Died Feb. 23rd, 1916. Water color. Size 3 x 4. Head and shoulders.

3559—BRADSHAW, THOMAS—Commissioner of Finance and City Treasurer, 1916—Has held various financial posts; assistant actuary North American Life Assurance Co.; on the organization of the Imperial Life Assurance Company of Canada, January, 1898, he was appointed secretary and actuary, and, subsequently, managing director and vice-president. In 1911 ceased his connection with the insurance business to become a partner in A. E. Ames & Co.,stock brokers, retiring to accept his present (1917) appointment. One of the founders of the Metropolitan Bank (since absorbed by the Bank of Nova Scotia). Secretary-treasurer Canadian Life Assurance Officers' Association. Author of "Essential Features of Life Assurance Organization," "Investments of Canadian Life Offices," and, in collaboration with Mr. Frank Sanderson, of "Actuarial Tables." Born in Manchester, Eng., 1868; educated at Manchester Grammar School, and came to Canada, 1879. Water color. Size 3 x 4. Head and shoulders.

3560-7—Temple of "The Children of Peace" at Sharon, Ont.

3560—OLD MUSIC HALL—The first church of the Children of Peace, afterwards known as the Music Hall, was built at Sharon in 1819. It was forty feet square at the base, sixteen feet high, one-storey. Each of the four sides had a doorway and two windows. Until 1892 the building stood, when it was torn down and the lot sold, the ground now (1917) being owned and cultivated by Mr. Richard Wayling. Water color. Size 3 x 4.

3561—AN ENTRANCE TO THE TEMPLE—In the centre of each side of the Temple was built a doorway, as a symbol that people from the north, south, east and west were welcomed on equal and same footing. Water color. Size 2 x 3.

3562—INTERIOR OF TEMPLE—Showing a part of the ground floor where the outer and inner square of pillars surround the altar or ark. Water color. Size 4 x 4.

3563—TEMPLE AT SHARON, ONT., 1825-1917—A three-storey structure, 75 feet in height, surmounted by a gilded ball bearing the word "Peace." The first storey was the auditorium, the second a music gallery. and the third a dome. The evening service was held 29th Oct., 1831. Fifteen times a year the temple was intended to be used, but never at any time for Sunday worship. On the first Friday in September an illumination took place, when the building presented a beautiful appearance as the light shone from windows and spires. The three storeys represented the Trinity, the square base signified dealing on the square with all men, and the doorway on each side welcomed people from all quarters on equal footing. The entrances had the same number of windows on either side, symbolizing the light of the Gospel being shed alike on all assembled in the building. To-day the temple, fallen into disuse, stands in the quaint hamlet of Sharon, as an interesting reminder of the happy, contented people, unique in their faith, who in the bygone worshipped within its walls. Water color. Size 5 x 6.

3564—THE ALTAR, OR ARK—In the centre of the ground floor, surrounded bv an outer and inner square of pillars, stood this unique little structure. It had a high curved roof, tiny windows and open doors, through which one could see a Bible resting on a crimson cushion. The Children of Peace took an entire year to make the Ark, choosing the beautiful inlaid walnut with care, and putting it together exquisitely. At each corner there rested little lamps of pure gold. These and the Bible were long ago taken by vandals. Water color. Size 4 x 4.

3565—MEETING HOUSE—Near the temple, and closer to the main street of Sharon, stood this commodious colonnaded building, 100 x 50 ft. It was commenced in 1834 and finished in 1842. Sunday services were held here, and in the upstairs room band rehearsals and Sunday school classes. In the Meeting House was also held the special Christmas service at five o'clock in the morning, when the house was lighted by a candle placed in each window, both above and below. The Children of Peace worshipped here until August, 1886. In 1913 the building was demolished and the site is now (1917) occupied by the residence of Mr. Ramsay. Water color. Size 4½ x 6½.

3566—INTERIOR OF MEETING HOUSE—The ceiling, the corner of which joined the walls in graduated curves, was supported by polished pillars of pine. Both doors and windows, colonial in architecture, were of oak. In the Meeting House was placed in 1848 the third pipe organ, built by Richard Coates. The services each Sunday began with an organ voluntary, followed by a band selection before the usual prayers and sermon by David Willson. The different feasts celebrated by the Davidites were held in this building as well as special Christmas services. Water color. Size 3 x 4.

3567—INTERIOR OF STUDY—This building, erected in 1829, and opened in September of that year, was, like the Meeting House, surrounded by a colonnade of pillars. The body of the building was 16 ft. by 8 ft., one storey high, shaped not unlike a Chinese pagoda. In the roof were twelve small spires. Later, a pipe organ, with three barrels attached—the second built by Mr. Coates—was installed. It was a great acquisition, for old-time ballads as well as hymns were amongst the tunes, thirty in all. The Davidite women in those early days carefully dressed the organ with white muslin curtains and blue ribbons, carrying out the idea in the window hangings so that the little study had a pleasing effect. In the centre stood a little wood stove which ornamented as well as heated the building. Water color. Size 4 x 4.

3568-72—Assessment Commissioners, Toronto, 1873-1917.

3568—HARMAN, SAMUEL BICKERTON—Assessment Commissioner, Toronto, 1873-4. Water color. Size 3 x 4. Head and shoulders. See 381, 1008, 3556.

3569—RIDOUT, SAMUEL G.—Assessment Commissioner, Toronto, 1876 —Born in York (Toronto), 1819, son of Samuel Ridout, sheriff of the Home District, 1815-27. Entered as attorney-at-law in Trinity Term, 1862. Prior to becoming Assessment Commissioner was Deputy Registrar of Deeds for the County of York. Died in Toronto, 1876. Water color. Size 3 x 4. Head and shoulders.

3570—MAUGHAN, NICHOLAS—Assessment Commissioner, Toronto, 1877-97—Came to Canada with his parents in 1832. Settled eventually in Eglinton, now (1917) a par' of the city of Toronto, and for many years was engaged in the building and contracting business. In 1869 moved into Toronto, and three years later became identified with the Assessment Department, receiving the Commissionership in 1877. Mr. Maughan was born in Northumberland, Eng., 1822. He died December, 1900. Water color. Size 3 x 4. Head and shoulders.

3571—FLEMING, ROBERT J.—Assessment Commissioner, Toronto, 1897-1905. Water color. Size 3 x 4. Head and shoulders. See 390, 3515.

3572—FORMAN, JAMES C.—Assessment Commissioner, Toronto, 1905-17—Born in Toronto, 1851. Educated in the city of his birth, and at an early age engaged in mercantile life; entered the service of the corporation as clerk in 1874. Still (1917) holds the position of Commissioner. Mr. Forman assisted in preparing the new Ontario Assessment Act. Water color. Size 3x 4. Head and shoulders.

3573—McDONALD, HON. DONALD, 1816-79—Assistant Commissioner of the Canada Company. Eldest son of Alexander McDonald, of Invernessshire, Scotland, and a descendant of an old Highland family, members of which served under Wolfe at Quebec. Came to Canada in 1817; educated at Upper Canada College, Toronto. Served in Rebellion of 1837. In 1858 Mr. McDonald was elected a member of the Legislative Council of Upper Canada, and continued to hold that position until Confederation, after which he was called to the Senate by proclamation. His death occurred in Toronto in 1879. Water color from a portrait in possession of his son, Charles E. Macdonald, Toronto. Size 4 x 5. Head and shoulders.

3574—GIVINS, MISS MAUDE A. A.—Miss Givins, who was born in London. Ont., is the youngest daughter of the late Judge James Givins, of that city, and a granddaughter of Colonel James Givins. Superintendent of Indian Affairs. The greater part of her life was spent at the old homestead, Toronto, where she lived with her aunt, Miss Cecil Givins. She was educated in London and Toronto, and still (1917) resides in the latter city, Water color. Size 3 x 4. Head and shoulders.

3575-8—City Surveyors, Toronto, 1843-1917.

3575—HOWARD, JOHN G.—City Surveyor, Toronto, 1843-54. Water color. Size 3 x 4. Head and shoulders. See 835, 837, 841, 846, 3660.

3576—SANKEY, MATTHEW VILLIERS—City Surveyor, Toronto, 1888-1905—The post of City Surveyor, left vacant in 1854 by the resignation of Mr. Howard, was not filled until Dec. 24th, 1888, when Mr. Villiers Sankey received the appointment. Mr. Sankey was born at Brookeboro, County Fermanagh, Ireland, Oct. 3rd. 1854: educated at Portora Royal School, Enniskillen, and in 1872 passed his examinations for the India Civil Service. On coming to Canada he entered the firm of Wadsworth, Unwin & Brown, afterwards becoming a partner. Mr. Sankey, who laid out the new rifle ranges in Toronto, was an authority on military matters, and supplied the Government with special maps, particularly of the Toronto and Niagara districts. He was a major in the Queen's Own Rifles: commanded the Corps of Guides. Resigned his post as City Surveyor, Jan. 20th, 1905. On July 10th, of that year, while engaged on engineering work near Kenora, Mr. Sankey met death by drowning. Water color. Size 3 x 4. Head and shoulders.

3577—UNWIN, CHARLES—City Surveyor, Toronto, 1905-10. Water color. Size 3 x 4. Head and shoulders. See 787.

3578—**LEMAY, TRACY D.**—City Surveyor, Toronto, 1910—Born June 5th, 1884, at Paddock Wood, Kent, Eng.; educated at Tonbridge School, Kent. Qualified as professional associate, Surveyors' Institution of Great Britain and Ireland, 1904; Fellow of Surveyors' Institution, 1905. In July, 1907, came to Canada, and in 1909 was admitted as a member of the Association of Ontario Land Surveyors. Appointed City Surveyor of Toronto, Nov., 1910, and still (1917) holds the position. Water color. Size 3 x 4. Head and shoulders.

3579—**ST. JOHN'S CHURCH, YORK MILLS**—Frame building, erected 1816—Shortly after Rev. John Strachan (Bishop) became rector of St. James' Church, York (Toronto), he held missionary services at York Mills once a month, in a small log house near the present St. John's Church. This house was in 1816 replaced by the oblong frame building shown, which was erected on land given by Mr. Joseph Sheppard and his wife for a church and burying ground. The remains of the building are to be found (1917) at Lansing, Ont., as a part of some farm buildings. Water color on print. Size 4 x 5.

3580—**BARREL ORGAN, ST. JOHN'S CHURCH, YORK MILLS**—This unique old instrument, with three barrels containing ten tunes each, was made by Bell and Ludgate, of London, Eng. It stands in the gallery of the church and is used to play a voluntary at the end of the Sunday services, when Mr. John Squire, who in 1913 celebrated his fiftieth year as sexton of St. John's, vigorously turns the handle. The organ is said to be the only one of its kind in a church in Canada. Water color on print. Size 3 x 6.

3581—**INTERIOR ST. JOHN'S CHURCH, YORK MILLS,** 1917. Water color on print. Size 6 x 9.

3582—**ST. JOHN'S CHURCH, YORK MILLS, 1844-1917**—York Mills was placed under the charge of a missionary in 1824. It became a rectory in 1840, and three years later the corner-stone of the new church was laid, the opening services being held 11th June, 1844, by Bishop Strachan. The old-fashioned high pews were removed many years ago, and from time to time alterations and improvements have been made transforming the dull, dingy church into a place of brightness. There are several memorials in the church, including two beautiful windows to the memory of the late Canon Osler and Mrs. Osler, and to Mr. Robert Leeder, a former church warden. Rev. Richard Ashcroft has been rector since 1900. Generations of worshippers have come and gone since St. John's, which celebrated its centennial 1st December, 1916, had its beginning in a forest clearing overlooking Yonge street, near Toronto. Water color on print. Size 6 x 7.

3583-5—**Commissioners of Parks, Toronto, 1879-1917.**

3583—**CHAMBERS, JOHN**—Commissioner of Parks, Toronto, 1879-1907 —Born in Canterbury, Eng., Nov. 11th, 1850; educated at the National and Grammar schools, Faversham, Kent. In 1871 he came to Canada; took charge of the florist and nursery business of the late James Fleming, Toronto. In 1878 Mr. Chambers was engaged by the City Council to lay out the then new Exhibition Grounds, and the following year, appointed Commissioner of Parks. His death took place Sept. 1st, 1913. Water color from portrait in possession of his son, C. E. Chambers, Toronto. Size 3 x 4. Head and shoulders.

3584—**WILSON, JAMES**—Commissioner of Parks, Toronto, 1908-11— Born in the city of Quebec, April 9th, 1850, and as a young man joined the staff of the Engineering Department of the Grand Trunk Railway at Montreal. Prior to coming to Toronto as Commissioner of Parks, May, 1908, he was superintendent of the Queen Victoria Niagara Falls Park. His death occurred in Toronto, October, 1911. Water color from portrait in possession of Mrs. Wilson, Toronto. Size 3 x 4. Head and shoulders.

3585—**CHAMBERS, CHARLES E.**—Commissioner of Parks, Toronto, 1912—Son of Mr. John Chambers, first, Commissioner of Parks. Born in Toronto, Sept. 25th, 1874, and educated in the Public schools of his native city. Entered the service of the corporation in 1890, being employed from that date until 1900 in the Parks Department. He was in the City Clerk's office, 1900-07, and from 1907 to 1912 served as chief clerk of the Parks Department. Appointed Commissioner of Parks, March 19th, 1912, and still (1917) holds the position. Water color. Size 3 x 4. Head and shoulders.

3586—**SCOTT, HUGH,** 1828-1912—A well-known underwriter; born at Kingston, C.W., but removed to Toronto at an early age, and for a time engaged in mercantile pursuits. In 1858 the firm of Scott and Walmsley was established. Mr. Thomas Walmsley, who died in Toronto, 28th March, 1912, was associated with Mr. Scott from boyhood up to the time of the latter's death. After the partners passed away a joint stock company was formed, known as Scott & Walmsley, Limited, with Mr. Joseph Walmsley as president. Mr. Scott was a promoter of the mutual system of fire insurance, and a member of the "Canada First Party." He was also one of the founders of the Monetary Times. Water color. Size 4 x 5. Head and shoulders.

3587—**NICOL, DR. WILLIAM BULMER**—Dean of Medical Faculty, Toronto University—He was a descendant of a Scottish family of Norman extraction; born in Stockwell, Middlesex, Eng., 11th Nov., 1812; educated at Christ's College, Cambridge. Arrived in Canada, 1836, and at once commenced practice at Bowmanville. During the Rebellion of 1837-8 he was surgeon of the Northumberland Battalion of Militia. Dr. Nicol removed to Toronto in 1842, and, the following year, received a commission from Sir Charles Medcalfe as Professor of Materia Medica, King's College, continuing to hold the position when that institution was merged into the University of Toronto. He became in 1845 a member of the U.C. Medical Board. For his attention to the immigrants afflicted with cholera in 1849 he received the thanks of the Government. Dr. Nicol's death took place in Toronto, 24th Dec., 1886. Water color from portrait in possession of his son, George B. Nicol, Toronto. Size 3 x 4. Head and shoulders.

3588—**JAMES, CHARLES CANNIFF**—Dominion Commissioner of Agriculture, 1912-16—Born at Napanee, Ont., 1863. Educated at Napanee High School and Victoria University (B.A. and gold medallist in Natural Science, 1883; M.A. 1886). From 1883-6 he was assistant master in Cobourg Collegiate Institute; professor of chemistry, Ontario Agricultural College, Guelph, 1886-91. In June, 1891, appointed Deputy Minister of Agriculture and Secretary of the Bureau of Industries, Ontario. Senator Toronto University; Fellow Royal Society of Canada; made C.M.G. in 1911. Author of various works on agriculture and the early history of Upper Canada. Died June 23rd, 1916. Water color, from portrait in possession of Mrs. James. Size 3 x 4. Head and shoulders.

3589—**HILLIER, MRS. GEORGE (CAROLINE GIVINS)**—Eldest daughter of Col. James Givins, for many years Superintendent of Indian Affairs. She was born at the old homestead, North road (Givens street), Toronto; married Captain (Col.) George Hillier, at that time aide-de-camp to Sir Peregrine Maitland, Lieut.-Governor of U.C., 1818-28. Mrs. Hillier went to England with her husband, and later accompanied him to the different stations at which his regiment, the 74th, was quartered. Col. Hillier died in India, and his widow removed to England, where her death took place, in London, at the age of ninety-four. Water color from portrait in possession of her niece, Miss M. A. A. Givins, Toronto. Size 3 x 4. Half length.

3590—**FLEMING, JOHN,** 1836-76—Provincial Land Surveyor and Draughtsman—He was a son of Andrew Greig Fleming, of Kirkcaldy, Fifeshire, Scotland; born and educated there. Came to Canada as a youth.

37

He accompanied Prof. Henry Youle Hind on his Canadian Red River and Assiniboine and Saskatchewan expeditions of 1857-8, acting as assistant surveyor and making the sketches utilized in Hind's report. Mr. Fleming, who was a younger brother of the late Sir Sandford Fleming, died in Toronto. Many of his pictures, especially those in connection with the Hind expeditions, are to be seen in this collection. Water color. Size 3 x 4. Head and shoulders.

3591—SPENCER WOOD—Home of the Lieutenant-Governors of Quebec —-Altered in 1901, on the occasion of the visit of T.R.H. the Duke and Duchess of Cornwall and York (George V. and Queen Mary). Water color on print. Size 6 x 9. See 1948.

3592—"SALT PLAINS, SLAVE RIVER—Captn. Back, R.N., August 5th, 1833. Engraved by E. Finden. Published by John Murray, London, 1836." The Salt Plains are on the Salt River, which is a tributary of the Slave River. The former is twelve milles below Fort Smith. The plains, which are a resort of all voyageurs in search of salt, contain many salt springs which in summer deposit salt, crystalized in the form of cubes. The springs are twenty-two miles from the mouth of the river. Engraving printed in color. Size 4 x 6.

3593—"INTERVIEW WITH THE ESQUIMAUX OF THE THLEWEE-CHODEZETH—Captn. Back, R.N., July 28th, 1834 Engraved by E. Finden. Published by John Murray, London, 1836." Captain George Back and his party are here depicted meeting with some Esquimaux, who, fearing at first that the white strangers were enemies, were in a state of alarm; but on Captain Back's landing alone, without visible weapon, and crying "Peace," in their own tongue, they were reassured, and threw down their spears, subsequently giving the explorers valuable information. The men, who were well-knit and atheltic, and of average stature, did not, as did the Esquimaux farther west, wear lip and nose ornaments. Neither were they tattooed, although the women favored this mode of adornment. Engraving printed in color. Size 4 x 6.

3594—"THUNDER STORM NEAR POINT OGLE—Captn. Back, R.N., August 8th, 1834. Engraved by E. Finden. Published by John Murray, London, 1836." Point Ogle, at the mouth of Back's River—where it falls into the Arctic Ocean, was named by Capt. Back (discoverer of the river) in honor of Sir Charles Ogle, Admiral of the Fleet in 1857. Engraving printed in color. Size 4 x 6.

3595—"CROSSING LAKE AYLMER (3 HS. A.M.)—Captn. Back, R.N., June 25th, 1834. Engraved by E. Finden. Published by John Murray, London, 1836." Lake Aylmer lies north of the eastern extremity of Great Slave Lake. It drains through Clinton, Colden and Artillery Lakes, and the Lockhart River into Great Slave Lake. Engraving printed in color. Size 4 x 6.

3596—"PORTAGE IN HOARFROST RIVER—Captn. Back, R.N., August 19th, 1833. Engraved by E. Finden. Published by John Murray, London, 1836." The Hoarfrost River flows southward into Great Slave Lake, entering the lake on the north shore, thirty-five miles from the eastern extremity. Engraving in color. Size 4 x 6.

3597—"ANDERSON'S FALL, HAHELDESSA RIVER—Captn. Back, R.N.. September 26th, 1834. Engraved by E. Finden. Published by John Murray, London, 1836." The Haheldessa is the Indian name for the Lockhart River, which falls into the extreme eastern end of Great Slave Lake. Anderson's Falls, twenty miles from the mouth of the river, were named by Capt. Back, after Capt. Anderson, of the Royal Artillery. Engraving printed in color. Size 4 x 6.

3598—"ESQUIMAUX WOMAN OF THE THLEWEECHODEZETH— ESQUIMAUX MAN OF THE THLEWEECHODEZETH—Captn. Back, R.N., July 28th, 1834. Engraved by E. Finden. Published by John Murray, London, 1836." Thleweechodezeth is the Indian for Great Fish River, now known as Back's River. The Esquimaux referred to by Capt. Back in his "Narrative of the Arctic Land Expedition, 1833-5," were found on the banks of the river, near its mouth. Engraving printed in color. Size 7 x 10. Head and shoulders (in each case).

3599—SENATE CHAMBER, HOUSES OF PARLIAMENT, OTTAWA— Before the great fire of Feb., 1916—The seating arrangements and general appearance was different from the Commons. Red was the prevailing shade, in carpet, upholstery and hangings. At the base of the walls ran a strip of turkey red, then above a wide space of a neutral mauve, surmounted by a combination of green and gold. Opening and closing ceremonies of Parliament were conducted by the Governor-General in the Senate Chamber, which was completely destroyed, but, fortunately, many valuable paintings of Canadian historic interest, in the outer galleries, were removed before the fire reached the side of the buildings in which the chamber was situated. Photograph, colored. Size 7 x 9.

3600—WILLSON, DAVID, 1778-1866—Founder of the "Children of Peace"—He was born of Irish parentage, in Duchess County, N.Y. Before emigrating to Canada in 1801 he was engaged on a sailing vessel plying between New York and the West Indies. On arriving in Toronto he applied for and obtained a Crown grant in East Gwillimbury. He became a member of the "Friends," but entertaining views not considered orthodox by the society was dismissed. Then began the sect known as the "Children of Peace," with David Willson as leader. They differed from the Quakers in that they were fond of music and did not conform to a particular style of dress. In 1814 the first church was built, afterwards known as the Music Hall, and in 1825 the Temple at Sharon was commenced. A brass band was formed and a school organized, and the society, noted for its morality and honesty of purpose, grew and thrived until Mr. Willson's death. It then began to decline, and finally became extinct. Revival meetings were unknown with the Davidites, as they were sometimes called. David Willson, who gave his services free, was their only minister. Water color. Size 3 x 4. Head and shoulders.

3601—JARVIS, MRS. F. W. (CAROLINE SKYNNER)—Born in England, July 22nd, 1826. Eight years later came to Canada with her father, John Skynner, R.N., Lydney, Gloucestershire, and settled at Clarkson, Ont. In 1856 she married Frederick W. Jarvis, sheriff of the County of York, and from that time until her death, May 10th, 1916, resided in Toronto. Water color. Size 3 x 4. Head and shoulders.

3602—RAMSAY, A. G.—A Scotsman; born in Edinburgh, 1830. Came to Canada in 1859, from Glasgow, where he was associated with the Scottish Amicable. From 1859 to 1899, when he retired from active business, Mr. Ramsay was connected with the Canada Life Assurance Company, first as manager, and eventually as president and managing director. Elected to the presidency in 1875, and held office continuously until the time of his retirement. His death occurred December 19th, 1915. Water color from portrait in possession of his daughter, Mrs. H. Crawford Scadding, Toronto. Size 3 x 4. Head and shoulders.

3603—DICK, CAPTAIN JAMES—A well-known early mariner of the Great Lakes—Born in Islay, Scotland, 1820. Educated for the navy, his uncle, Sir Thomas Dick, being at that time Admiral of the Blue. Later decided to enter the merchant service and sailed several times around the world. Came to Canada in 1845, and, leaving the merchant service, sailed the Great Lakes. His vessel, the "Rescue," was the first steamer to carry mail for the Hudson's Bay Company up Lake Superior. Assisted Sir Simon Dawson in the construction of the "Dawson Road," building the boats required. Later Captain Dick was appointed Government Inspector of Marine and Fisheries, holding the post for many years. His death took place Jan. 11th, 1894. Water color from portrait in possession of his daughter, Mrs. G. A. McVicar, Toronto. Size 3 x 4. Head and shoulders.

3604—CARFRAE, THOMAS—In his uniform of major in the Royal Provincial Artillery. Water color from portrait in possession of his granddaughter, Mrs. G. A. McVicar, Toronto. Size 5½ x 6. Three-quarter length. See 3543.

3605—COX, HON. GEORGE A.—Born at Colborne, Ont., in 1840, and educated at the Public and Grammar schools there; early in life he entered the service of the Montreal Telegraph Company. In 1858 he removed to Peterboro, Ont., where he remained for thirty years, taking an active interest in the municipal, educational and commercial activities of the city, being elected to the office of Mayor for seven terms. In 1878 he became President of the Midland Railway of Canada, holding the position until 1884, when the railroad was absorbed by the G.T.R. He was for a long period identified with many financial concerns, and from 1900-14 was President of the Canada Life Assurance Company. Called to the Senate in 1896, and died in Toronto, Jan. 16th, 1914. Photograph, hand-colored. Size 4 x 5. Head and shoulders.

3606—WATER WHEEL ABOVE THE WHIRLPOOL, NIAGARA—At Colt's Point, on the Canadian side—At this point a double-track railway ran down the bank to the water's edge, with two small passenger cars, one on each track, connected by a cable, and operated ordinarily by gravity. Under the floor of each car was a large tank, and sufficient water was added to or taken from these tanks to start the cars in motion on the incline, one going up as the other went down. Occasionally, however, when the cars, filled with tourists, reached the centre of the incline they would balance nicely, remaining stationary. It was this emergency that the water wheel was designed to overcome. A large reservoir, fed from a nearby stream, was maintained near the wheel; a valve, when opened, released the water, which started the wheel in motion, and the necessary power to rescue the tourists from their plight was secured. The old incline railway was destroyed about 1893 by a landslide. Water color, from original drawing by M. Nimmo Moran, for "Picturesque Canada," 1880. Size 4 x 7.

3607—ENGLISH CATHEDRAL, QUEBEC—West of Place d'Armes, on the site of the ancient church and convent of the Recollets, this cathedral was built at the suggestion of Right Rev. Jacob Mountain, first Anglican Bishop of Quebec, and consecrated in 1804. It is a plain, substantial structure, without pretensions to architectural beauty. The mural monuments, however, are very fine. This is believed to be the only cathedral on the continent containing the colors of a British regiment of the line, for therein are the historic colors of the 69th, deposited with ceremonial when Prince Arthur in 1870 presented the regiment with a new set. Lithograph, in color. Size 5 x 8.

3608—INTERIOR OF ENGLISH CATHEDRAL, QUEBEC—Containing many evidences of the past, of wide historic interest, the interior of the cathedral is very striking. The chancel window, to the memory of Dr. Jehoshaphat Mountain, third Bishop of Quebec, is rich in design and coloring, representing the Baptism, Transfiguration and Ascension of Christ. A silver Communion Service, of exquisite workmanship, together with altar cloth and hangings of the desk and pulpit, were presented by George III. Amongst the monuments is one of marble, surmounted by a bust of Rt. Rev. Jacob Mountain, first Bishop of Quebec, at whose suggestion the church was built. Overhanging the chancel may be seen the remains of two old and tattered flags, the former colors of the 69th Regiment, deposited in the cathedral in 1870, when H.R.H., Prince Arthur presented the regiment with new colors. In the north gallery (left of picture) is the Governor-General's pew, with the Royal Arms at the front. Amongst leading clergy to occupy the pulpit have been the Archbishop of Canterbury, Dean Stanley, and Archdeacon Farrar, besides many American bishops. Photograph, colored. Size 8 x 10.

3609—CREASE, GEN. A. R. V., R. E.—Born at Ince Castle, Cornwall, Eng., 1827; entered the army in 1846. In winter of 1855-6 served in Crimea, and was second in command of the Engineers with the Turkish contingent; commanded Royal Engineers during the last four months of the occupation of Kertch by the Allies. Also served with Central India Field Force, commanding the 21st Company of Royal Engineers during summer of 1858; present at capture of Gwalior, for which he received medal with clasps. Commanded Royal Engineers in South Africa, 1881-5, retiring from the army in that year. Acting Lieutenant-Governor of Guernsey, 1877. Was in Canada at various times, when he made many views of the country. Died at St. Leonards-on-the-Sea, Eng., Oct. 9th, 1892. Water color from portrait in possession of his son, Anthony H. Crease, Toronto. Size 3 x 4. Head and shoulders.

3610—WELLER, WILLIAM, 1799-1863—Came to Canada from Potsdam, N.Y., in early life, and for a short time lived at Toronto and Prescott, eventually making his home in Cobourg, where he was Mayor, 1850-51 and 1863, and where he died. For many years he was engaged in the stage business, and from 1829 to 1856 operated a line "eastward" from Toronto. The service was discontinued after the opening of the Grand Trunk Railway. In the winter of 1840 Weller drove Mr. Poulett Thomson (Lord Sydenham) from Toronto to Montreal—a distance of 360 milles—in thirty-five hours and forty minutes. Water color. Size 3 x 4. Head and shoulders.

3611—ST. GEORGE'S CHURCH, "THE ROUND CHURCH," HALIFAX, N.S.—As it appeared in 1814—This wooden church, of unusual architectural form, being circular in shape, was erected on Brunswick st. by the Church of England congregation, once Lutheran, which had formerly worshipped in the older St. George's (the Little Dutch Church). The corner-store was laid 10th April, 1800, by Gov. John Wentworth, and the first service held 19th July, 1801, although the church was not completed until 1812. Rev. George Wright was the first rector of the new church. St. George's Parish was formally set apart in 1827. The church records are complete since 1759, with the exception of the years 1814-18, which have been lost. The building is still (1917) in use. View looking northwestward towards Dartmouth, from a water color, rather poorly drawn, by a lady of Halifax. name unknown. Size 4 x 5.

3612—DUNLOP, DR. WILLIAM—Born 1795, at Greenock, Scotland, Served as regimental surgeon in Canada in the War of 1812-15, and afterwards in India, where he edited a paper. On account of ill-health was forced to return to Scotland, living for a time in Edinburgh, and giving a course of lectures in Medical Jurisprudence there. Later went to London, where he was engaged in journalistic work. In 1826 came again to Canada, this time in the service of the Canada Company. Represented Huron in first and second Parliaments after the union, but resigned in 1846. Chairman of a Select Committee of the Legislative Assembly, 1841, to report on the petition of Robert Gourlay. At a meeting of the adherents of the Church of Scotland, held at York, March 3rd, 1830, it was Dr. Dunlop who moved that immediate steps be taken to erect a place of worship and for the calling of a minister. The doctor also served in the rebellion of 1837, as colonel of the Huron Invincibles. Took part in cutting down the first tree on the site of the present town of Guelph. Was a frequent contributor, under the nom de plume of Colin Ballantyne, to Blackwoods. His death occurred June 29th, 1848. Lithograph. Size 4 x 6. Full length, sitting.

3613—**HARPER, JOHN,** 1806-88—Builder and Architect, Toronto—His birthplace was Belfast, Ireland. In 1823 he came to Canada with his parents, locating at York, where he built quite a number of residences. He superintended in part the construction of the General Hospital, Gerrard street, the Toronto Asylum, the new Garrison and St. Michael's Cathedral, and had charge also of the erection of the present post-office on Adelaide street. Mr. Harper was a member of the City Council for St. Andrew's Ward, 1834-6. Water color from portrait in possession of his grandson, E. W. Harper, Toronto. Size 3 x 4. Head and shoulders.

3614—**HUCKETT, WILLIAM J.**—First Engineer Ontario Simcoe and Huron Railway—He was born in London, Eng., 1st July, 1820, came to America with his parents in 1832. Mr. Huckett, who was master mechanic of the Ontario, Simcoe and Huron Railway, now (1917) the Northern Division of the Grand Trunk, acted as engineer on the "Toronto," in taking the first passenger train from Toronto to Machell's Corners (now Aurora), 16th May, 1853. Some years later he entered the service of an American company. His death took place in Kansas City, December, 1904. Water color from portrait in possession of his granddaughter, Mrs. E. M. Hansell, Kansas City. Size 3 x 4. Head and shoulders.

3615—**"ROSELANDS"**—A quaint cottage of early Toronto—The residence of Samuel Ridout, Sheriff of the Home District, 1815-27. It stood facing Queen street, one hundred and seventy feet back from the roadway, and between Sherbourne and Seaton streets (the latter being then simply a lane), with carriage entrance by Seaton. The house, which was of logs, clapboarded, was pulled down in the eighties and replaced by a row of houses. Facing Seaton street, however, still (1917) remains the old back kitchen of "Roselands." Water color. Size 4 x 6.

3616—**EASTWOOD, JOHN**—Founder of the village of Todmorden—Mr. Eastwood, who was born in Todmorden, Yorkshire, Eng., Nov. 17th, 1792, came to Canada in 1815. At first he resided at Drummondville, engaging in trade between Buffalo and Niagara. Later entered into partnership with Colin Skinner, proprietor of a grist mill on the Don. The building was converted into a paper mill, and it is said that the first paper made in Upper Canada was turned out here. The Crooks mill at Flamboro, however, also claimed that distinction. In 1836 Mr. Eastwood, along with Mr. Wm. Cawthra, was alderman for St. Lawrence Ward, Toronto. His son, Colin Eastwood, resides in Denver, Col. His death occurred at the age of sixty-five. Water color. Size 3 x 4. Head and shoulders.

3617—**TOWN CLOCK, HALIFAX, N.S.**—Eastern Glacis of Citadel Hill —This quaint clock, one of the most familiar old landmarks in Halifax, still (1917) rings the hours and quarter hours. It was erected about 1802, jointly by the garrison and the town, the merchants of Halifax raising a subscription towards the object. The lower part of the building is square and has been used as keeper's quarters, a guard house, etc., while the tower itself is semi-round (actually octagonal) with a dome-shaped roof, originally covered with copper. The clock was managed by the garrison until the departure of the Imperial troops from Halifax, when it was transferred to the city. In the background of picture is shown Citadel Hill, with the storm drum-staff. Water color on print. Size 8 x 10.

3618—ROTUNDA OR BAND HOUSE AT PRINCE'S LODGE—Bedford Basin, near Halifax—Built on the grounds adjoining Prince's Lodge, summer residence of Edward, Duke of Kent, during his sojourn in Halifax. These grounds, improved and beautified by the Duke, were a part of the estate of Sir John Wentworth. Nothing but the foundation of the lodge now (1917) remains. The rotunda, however, is in good repair. The railway passes between it and the site of the lodge. Water color on print. Size 6 x 10.

3619—DALHOUSIE COLLEGE (FIRST BUILDING), HALIFAX—North end of the Grand Parade—Founded in 1818 by the Earl of Dalhousie. The original endowment was derived from funds collected at Castine, Me., during its occupation by the British in 1812-14. In the low wing shown on the left hand (west) side of picture the old Halifax Mechanics' Institute had its room and museum from 1831-68. The corresponding wing on the right hand (east) side was in the thirties occupied by a Classical Academy for Boys. College classes were held in the centre portion until the college occupied the entire building. After unsuccessful efforts to unite with King's, Dalhousie College went into operation in 1838, with Rev. Thomas McCulloch, D.D., as first principal. The institution was closed in 1845 and reopened in 1863 under the principalship of Rev. James Ross, D.D., and with Presbyterian support. About 1887 the city purchased the building, which was demolished and present City Hall built on site. Some years ago new college buildings were erected at Studley, Halifax. Water color on print. Size 5 x 7.

3620—ST. MATTHEW'S PRESBYTERIAN CHURCH, HALIFAX, N.S. —This old landmark, s.w. corner Hollis and Prince sts., was erected about 1751, and was the oldest Protestant Dissenting meeting-house in Canada. For some time it was known as Mather's Church, the first minister being Rev. Aaron Cleaveland, great-great-grandfather of President Grover Cleveland. In 1787 the pulpit was erected, and in 1812 the building enlarged and the steeple built into the roof. The building was destroyed by fire 1st Jan., 1857, and the present St. Matthew's Church erected on Pleasant st., 1858. Water color on print from a model built to a scale, in Provincial Museum, Halifax, showing exterior, and interior furnishings of buildings in its later years. The older form of building is seen in No. 52 of this Collection. Size 7 x 7.

3621—TEAM FERRY "SHERBROOKE"—Running from Halifax to Dartmouth, N.S., in the early days—In 1752 John Connor, of Dartmouth, was granted the exclusive right to run a ferry between Halifax and Dartmouth; but up to 1816 the ferry boats were propelled by oarsmen. On Nov. 8th of that year the "Sherbrooke" made her first trip. She really consisted of two boats, or hulls, united by a platform, with a paddle between the boats. The deck was surrounded by a roundhouse, in which was a large cogwheel, arranged horizontally. Eight or nine horses were attached to iron stanchions coming down from the wheel, and, as the horses moved round, the wheel, by means of connecting gear, revolved the paddle. Water color on print from "Acadian Recorder." Size 5 x 7.

3622—PLEASANT ST.—Looking north from Morris St., Halifax, N.S., 1838—With key. From water color by William Eagar. Size 5 x 7.

3623—PRINCE'S LODGE, BEDFORD BASIN, NEAR HALIFAX—Summer residence of Edward, Duke of Kent—With key. The lodge was built on land originally granted to Capt. William Foy, first Provost Marshal of the province, and which, in time, came into possession of Sir John Wentworth, Governor of Nova Scotia, 1792-1808. He had a small summer residence called "Friar Lawrence's Cell." When Prince Edward came to Halifax in 1794 Wentworth turned over his estate to him, and the Prince enlarged or rebuilt the wooden building, which he called "The Lodge," at the same time beautifying the grounds and building a rotunda or bandstand and a Chinese summer house. Near "The Lodge" was a barrack and guardhouse, which subsequently became the Rockingham Inn. When the Duke left Halifax, Sir John Wentworth resumed possession of the estate, which afterwards passed through several hands. "The Lodge" eventually became ruinous, and now (1917) only the foundation remains. From water color, owned by Mr. William Y. Gray, of "Prince's Lodge." Size 6 x 9.

3624—GARRISON CHAPEL—TRINITY CHURCH—HALIFAX, N.S.— This church, corner of Brunswick and Cogswell sts., was built in 1846 for the use of the garrison of Halifax, which had hitherto worshipped at St. Paul's and other churches. It was used for this purpose till the Imperial troops left Halifax in 1905-6, and was then transferred to the congregation of Trinity Church (which had been erected in 1866, and was thereupon sold and became a theatre). In 1912 a parish hall was added at the west end (shown as the transverse structure), otherwise the building is as left by the military. Within are a number of mural tablets, chiefly commemorative of military men. Water color on print. Size 8 x 9.

3625—ST. PAUL'S CHURCH, HALIFAX, N.S., 1916— The Nave, looking towards the Chancel—In 1868 the wings shown on extreme right and left, beyond the second row of columns, were added, and the chancel built in 1872. The remainder of church, except the pews, is the original structure and design. The mural tablets and hatchments about the galleries are laden with the history of Nova Scotia from early times, and the many memorials, including the chancel and other windows, the communion table, pulpit, lectern and font, enhance the beauty of St. Paul's. Beneath the church are twenty vaults, the resting place of many notable men, governors, chief justices, bishops, military and naval personages of note. The Royal Arms on gallery were placed there in 1812, and in the chancel the old colors of the 66th Princess Louise Fusiliers, which belonged to one of the first Halifax militia regiments, were deposited in 1903. Water color on print. Size 8 x 10.

3626—PRINCE OF WALES' TOWER, POINT PLEASANT, HALIFAX —This old fort, known technically and locally as a Martello Tower, was built about 1808, and was one of a series of such towers built about that period, erected at Fort Clarence, George's Island (1812), Mauger's Beach (Sherbrooke Tower, begun 1814, completed 1828, and since the latter date used as a lighthouse) and York Redoubt. All have long since been demolished, except the one in Point Pleasant Park, which occupies the extremity of the peninsula on which the city lies, and at Mauger's Beach. The former is built of "ironstone" with extremely thick walls, and once carried guns on its upper platform. It is a prominent landmark, but for many years has been entirely obsolete for defensive purposes. Water color on print. Size 7 x 9.

3627—FERRY SLIP, FOOT OF GEORGE ST., HALIFAX, 1838— Looking eastward—With key. From water color, by William Eagar. Size 5 x 7.

3628—"LITTLE DUTCH CHURCH" (OLD ST. GEORGE'S), HALIFAX N.S.— A small, quaint wooden structure (originally 29 x 20 feet) at the northeast corner of Brunswick and Gerrish sts., begun in 1756 as a Lutheran Church by German settlers who were locally called "Dutch." The first service was held in 1758, and two years later the steeple erected. On 23rd March, 1761, the church was dedicated by Dr. Breynton under the name "St. George's." Soon the Church of England form of service was followed. When the present St. George's was opened in July, 1801, the "Little Dutch" or "Chicken-Cock Church," as it was often called, because of the gilded weather-cock on its spire, ceased to be used for services. Water color on print. Size 8 x 10.

3629—**ST. MARY'S R. C. CATHEDRAL, HALIFAX, N.S.,** 1838—With key—The corner stone of the church, on Spring Garden road, was laid by Bishop Burke, 24th May, 1820, and the opening services held 1829. Halifax became a Roman Catholic diocese in 1842, and the Metropolitan See of the three Maritime Provinces in 1852. The cathedral was enlarged and modernized under Archbishop Connolly, and the old front with square tower replaced by a granite facade and spire in the florid Gothic style. It is one of the finest ecclesastical buildings in Halifax. From water color by William Eagar. Size 4 x 6.

3630—**KENT, EDWARD, DUKE OF,** 1767-1820—Commander-in-Chief of H.M. Forces in British North America. Water color from original oil painting on panel by J. Weaver, in Legislative Library, Halifax. Size 5 x 7. Full length.

3631—**GRAY, JOHN**—First President Bank of Montreal—A native of Scotland; came to Canada and engaged for many years as a general merchant in Montreal. He was largely interested in real estate, and a part of Mount Royal Cemetery belonged to him. First treasurer of the first Montreal Waterworks, incorporated 1801. On the foundation of the Bank of Montreal in 1817, by an association of merchants, he became president of the institution, holding office until 1820. Mr. Gray's death occurred 18th September, 1829, at Montreal. Water color from original portrait in possession of Mrs. Walter Lawson, Halifax, a granddaughter of John Gray. Size 7 x 9. Head and shoulders, oval.

3632—**ST. GEORGE'S CHURCH, "THE ROUND CHURCH," HALIFAX, N.S.,** 1916—The Duke of Kent was interested in its erection, and he seems to have had a predilection for the classic style of architecture in the round form, evidenced also in the town clock and the rotunda at the "Prince's Lodge," Halifax. Water color on print. Size 8 x 10. See 3611, 3628.

3633—**WELSFORD-PARKER MONUMENT, HALIFAX, N.S.**—In St. Paul's Cemetery—Erected in 1860 by the people of Halifax in memory of two brave Nova Scotians who fell in the Crimean War—Major Augustus F. Welsford, 97th Regiment, a native of Halifax, and Capt. William B. C. A. Parker, 77th Regiment, born at Lawrencetown, near Halifax, both of whom were killed at the storming of the Redan in 1855. The monument consists of a freestone arch, surmounted by a lion cut in stone by George Lang, a notable local stonecutter of the time. St. Paul's Cemetery is the oldest burying ground in Halifax, and was used as a general burial place for all denominations from the settlement in 1749. The title remained with the Crown until 1794, when it was granted to St. Paul's Church. It was closed for burials about 1845. Water color on print. Size 8 x 10.

3634—**PROVINCE BUILDING, HALIFAX, N.S.**—Begun in 1811 and first occupied by the Legislature in February, 1819. It is of freestone, designed on classical lines, and occupies the site of Governor Cornwallis' first small, one-storey residence, of 1749, which was replaced by a larger Governor's house about 1758-9. In the present building are the Chambers of the Legislative Council and the Assembly, the Legislative Library, and various governmental offices. An anteroom contains the old oak tables around which Cornwallis' first Council sat in 1749, and in the hall is a tablet commemorating the first Assembly, which met 22nd October, 1758. Water color on print. Size 7 x 10. See 3643.

3635—**HALIFAX FROM FORT NEEDHAM**—Looking southeast about 1782—With key. Water color on print, from India ink drawing by Dr. T. B. Akins, in Provincial Museum, Halifax, after engraving published in London, after drawing by Lieut.Col. Edward Hicks, H.M. 70th Regiment of Foot. Size 4 x 8.

3636—ST. PAUL'S CHURCH, SOUTH END OF GRAND PARADE, HALIFAX, N.S.—View looking southwestward, 1916—This church, of Royal foundation, having been built at the expense of the Crown (George II.), and by moneys granted to his Majesty in this province for use of the Government, is the oldest Protestant church in Canada and the first building used as a Protestant cathedral in the country. It was formally opened 2nd Sept., 1750, by Rev. Wm. Tutty, missionary of the S.P.G. The first rector was Rev. Dr. John Breynton. St. Paul's Parish was constituted by Legislature in August, 1758. The church plate, of Queen Anne's period, which had been used at Annapolis Royal, was transferred to Halifax in 1759, and other fine pieces added. In 1762 the first organ was installed. The chime of three bells, which are still used, was presented by A. Belcher in July, 1812, and the present tower and steeple were erected the same year. The wings were added in 1868, and the chancel built in 1872. For genealogists the records of the Parish of St. Paul are a very valuable source of information. Water color on print. Size 7 x 9.

3637—NORTH BRITISH AND HIGHLAND SOCIETIES' PICNIC, 15TH AUG., 1842—At "Prince's Lodge," near Halifax—The picture shows a part of the rear of the old lodge, in the grounds of which these organizations held joint picnics for some years. The North British Society was instituted at Halifax, 26th March, 1768, and was the first national and patriotic association formed there. It is still (1917) one of the strongest and most influential societies in the city. On 31st May, 1838, the Highland Society was founded at Halifax by means of a commission from the Highland Society of London, Eng. About 1883 it became defunct. Water color from an old woodcut. Size 4 x 8.

3638—HALIFAX, N.S., 1782—View looking northwest from near Point Pleasant Battery—With key. Water color on print from India ink drawing by Dr. T. B. Akins, in Provincial Museum, Halifax, after engraving published in London, after drawing by Lieut.-Col. Edward Hicks, H.M. 70th Regiment of Foot. Size 5 x 8.

3639—LEGISLATIVE COUNCIL CHAMBER, PROVINCE BUILDING, HALIFAX, N.S.—With key. The Legislative Council of Nova Scotia has met here since the opening of the Province Building in Feb., 1819. The room is finely proportioned, with heavy, elaborately ornamented cornice, and applied stucco work about the doors, windows and mantelpieces. In this room have taken place many notable gatherings, and here the remains of the late Sir John Thompson, Premier of the Dominion, 1892-5, lay in State in 1895. In the Council Chamber may be seen the finest collection of full-length portraits in the province, including those of several British sovereigns and of men prominent in the making of Nova Scotia's history. The Royal Arms on the canopy over the State chair are of the period of George III. Water color on print. Size 8 x 10.

3640—GOVERNMENT HOUSE, HALIFAX, N.S.—Here all the Lieutenant-Governors of Nova Scotia have resided since 1805. The mansion, which is of freestone, was begun in 1800, in the time of Sir John Wentworth, and, although occupied five years later, it was not finished until in, or shortly after, 1807. The main facade faces Hollis street; but for many years the Pleasant street entrance has been the principal one. Prior to the erection of the mansion shown in the picture the Governors resided in a wooden structure on the site of the present (1917) Province Building. Water color on print. Size 8 x 10.

3641—BALLROOM, GOVERNMENT HOUSE, HALIFAX, N.S.—View looking east—The apartment is shown with tables set for a State banquet in honor of T.R.H. the Duke and Duchess of Cornwall and York (King George V. and Queen Mary) in 1901. Hon. A. G. Jones was Lieutenant-Governor of Nova Scotia at the time. The ballroom is on the ground floor at the north end of the main building, which was begun in 1800. In the right foreground is the main entrance from the hallway, and at the right far corner is a smaller door leading to anterooms and the Governor's office. The small pictures seen on the walls are portraits of Governors and other prominent men of the province. The collection was begun by Hon. A. G. Jones. Water color on print. Size 8 x 10.

3642—LEGISLATIVE ASSEMBLY CHAMBER, PROVINCE BUILDING, HALIFAX, N.S., 1916—View looking west—With key. In this apartment the Assembly has met since February, 1819. It was originally like the Legislative Council Chamber and had long, red-covered benches, running lengthwise, for the members, and two galleries for the public at the west and east ends. The Speaker's Chair was at the west end. About 1888 the room was entirely changed, the members' floor being made semi-circular in form, with the Speaker's Chair at the north side, and a gallery for the public erected above. Water color on print. Size 8 x 10.

3643—PROVINCE BUILDING, HALIFAX, N.S.,—Perspective view from the northeast—With key. The original of this picture was drawn and etched by J. E. Woolford, and published at Halifax in 1819. It was the first etching made in Nova Scotia, and hangs to-day (1917) in the Recorder office, Halifax. Size 5 x 7. See 3634.

3644—ST. JOHN'S CHURCH, LUNENBURG, N.S.—This church, the third Protestant church in Canada, was built in 1754, at the expense of the Government. The frame of the building was first put together in Boston. Rev. Jean Baptiste Morreau, formerly a Roman Catholic priest, was the first minister. He came to Halifax in 1749, and in 1753 accompanied the German settlers to Lunenburg, when the town was founded. Other notable early ministers were Rev. Baulus Bryzelius, at one time a Lutheran clergyman, and Rev. Peter De La Roche, of Geneva, who was "Cure of Lunenburg" in 1771. The corner-stone of the new tower was laid in July, 1840. The parish records of St. John's, which begin with a baptism in 1753, are most interesting. Water color. Size 6 x 8.

3645—WEDD, WILLIAM, M.A., LL.D.—First Classical Master, Upper Canada College—Born at Boughton, near Maidstone, Kent, Eng., Feb. 19th, 1825. Came to Canada in 1832, and entered U.C.C. four years later; head boy, 1843. Graduated, with honors, from Toronto University in 1848, and after a brief period in the law office of Chancellor Blake, joined the staff of Upper Canada College as Third Classical Master, eventually becoming First Classical Master. His retirement took place in 1891. As the oldest living graduate of Toronto University, he subsequently had the degree of LL.D. (honoris causa) conferred upon him by his Alma Mater. Mr. Wedd still (1917) resides in Toronto. Water color. Size 3 x 4. Head and shoulders.

3646—BOULTON, REV. WILLIAM—Second Classical Master, Upper Canada College, Toronto, 1829-34—Youngest son of Hon. Mr. Justice Boulton; born at Kingston, U.C., 1st Dec., 1805. He took his degree at Queen's College, Oxford, and soon afterwards was ordained to the curacy of Cadbury, Devonshire. He also acted as undermaster at Blundell's School, Tiverton, described in "Lorna Doone," where a cousin, Dr. Anthony Boulton, was second master. On the appointment of Rev. Wm. Boulton to the first staff of Upper Canada College he came to this country with his wife, daughter of Capt. Henry Carew, R.N. Mr. Boulton's death took place 1st May, 1834. From original silhouette in possession of Miss Cronin, Toronto. Size 3 x 4. Head and shoulders.

3647—MAYNARD, REV. GEORGE, M.A.—Second Classical and First Mathematical Master, U.C.C.—Born near Bristol, Eng., 1805, the son of a British army officer. An honor graduate of Caius College, Cambridge, and one of the Wranglers of his final year. Came to Canada to take the Second Classical Mastership at Upper Canada College, as successor to Rev. Wm. Boulton, who died in 1834. In 1838 was appointed First Mathematical Master, in succession to Mr. Dade, holding that position until 1856. In addition to his work at the College, he served for a time as curate at St. James' Cathedral, under Dr. (Bishop) Strachan, and later was curate at St. Paul's Church, Bloor street. Subsequent to his resignation from U. C. C., he, for a short time, conducted a private school for boys in Dr. Hodder's old house on Simcoe street. His death occurred in Toronto, 1878. Water color. Size 3 x 4. Head and shoulders.

3648—BAKER, ALFRED, M.A.—Second Mathematical Master and a House Master, U.C.C., 1872-75—Born and educated in Toronto; B.A., University of Toronto, 1869 (gold medallist for mathematics); M.A., 1878. He was successively principal of Vienna, Perth and Oshawa High Schools before joining the staff of Upper Canada College. He was registrar of Toronto University from 1881-87, in the latter year becoming professor of mathematics, which position he still (1917) holds; president Royal Society of Canada, 1915-16. Professor Baker has edited works on trigonometry, statics and dynamics, and has issued publications on geometry. Water color. Size 3 x 4. Head and shoulders.

3649-57—Principals Upper Canada College, 1830-1917—

3649—HARRIS, REV. JOSEPH H., D.D.—Principal Upper Canada College, 1830-8—Born in England, 1800; educated at University of Cambridge, where he was Fellow of Clare Hall. Came to Canada on being appointed principal of the recently founded Upper Canada College, and took a large part in the actual organization of that institution. In 1838 he resigned the principalship to accept the living of Tor Mohun, Devonshire, Eng. His death occurred at his residence, "Sorel," Torquay, 1881. Water color. Size 3 x 4. Head and shoulders.

3650—McCAUL, REV. JOHN, LL.D.—Principal Upper Canada College, 1839-43—An Irishman, having been born in Dublin, March 7th, 1807. Graduated from Trinity College, Dublin, with highest honors, winning the gold medal for classics and the Berkeley Greek medal (B.A., 1824; M.A., 1828). Remained at Trinity as Examiner in Classics until his appointment to U.C.C. Ordained to the Anglican diaconate, 1831; priest, 1833; LL.B. and LL.D. (by examination) two years later. In 1843 resigned the principalship of Upper Canada College to become vice-president of Toronto University and Professor of Classical Literature, Logic, Rhetoric and Belles Lettres. President of the University, 1849-1880. Author of many valuable works on classical subjects. Died in Toronto, 1887. Water color. Size 3 x 4. Head and shoulders.

3651—BARRON, F. W.—Principal Upper Canada College, 1843-56— Born at Norwich, Eng., 1810; educated there and at Cambridge. Almost immediately after his arrival in Canada was appointed to a mastership at U. C. C. Subsequently became principal of that institution, resigning after thirteen years, because of ill-health, and removing to Gore's Landing. Afterwards head master of Cobourg Grammar School. Elected Master of St. Andrew's Lodge (Masonic) in 1852, holding office until 1855. For many years a member of the Royal Canadian Yacht Club. Died 2nd February, 1886. Water color from portrait by Egerton Baines, in possession of his son, Judge Barron, Stratford, Ont. Size 3 x 4. Head and shoulders.

3652—STENNETT, REV. WALTER, M.A.—Principal Upper Canada College, 1857-61—A native of Kingston. Had a distinguished career at U.C.C. and King's College (Toronto University). B.A., 1847; M.A., 1854. Ordained to the Anglican diaconate, and in 1847 was appointed curate at

Holy Trinity Church, Toronto. In 1846 became third classical master at Upper Canada College, and, three years later, second classical master. In 1861 appointed to the incumbency of Christ Church, Keswick, and on the elevation of his father-in-law, Dr. Bethune, to the Bishopric of Toronto, succeeded him as rector of Cobourg. Died February 25th, 1889. Water color from original portrait by G. T. Berthon, in Upper Canada College. Size 3 x 4. Head and shoulders.

3653—COCKBURN, G. R. R., M.A.—Principal Upper Canada College, 1861-81. Water color from portrait by A. Dickson Patterson, in Upper Canada College. Size 3 x 4. Head and shoulders. See 629, 966.

3654—BUCHAN, JOHN MILNE, M.A.—Principal Upper Canada College, 1881-5—Born in Lockport, N. Y., March 16th, 1842, but was brought to Upper Canada by his parents in infancy. Educated at the Grammar School, Hamilton, and Toronto University. Subsequent to graduating from the latter institution, he was appointed head master of the recently organized Hamilton High School. From 1873-81 served as High School Inspector. His death occurred July 19th, 1885. Water color from portrait by G. A. Reid, in Upper Canada College. Size 3 x 4. Head and shoulders.

3655—DICKSON, GEORGE, M.A.—Principal Upper Canada College, 1885-95—Of Scottish parentage; born in 1846 at Carrick Mills, Markham, Ont. Received his education at Richmond Hill and Whitby Grammar Schools, and at Victoria University, Cobourg. (B.A., 1872; M.A., 1878). Assistant master Chatham High School, 1868-9; master Woodstock College, 1870-71. Assistant master Hamilton Collegiate Institute, 1872-3, and head master, 1873-85. In 1907 founded St. Margaret's College (Ladies'), Toronto, and held the presidency until his death, March 21st, 1910. One of the founders of "The Canadian Educational Monthly." Co-editor, with G. Mercer Adam, of "A History of Upper Canada College." Water color. Size 3 x 4. Head and shoulders.

3656—PARKIN, GEORGE ROBERT, M.A., C.M.G.—Principal Upper Canada College, 1895-1902—Born at Salisbury, Westmoreland Co., N. B., in 1846. Qualified for the teaching profession at the Normal School, St. John, N. B. After teaching for a time he entered the University of New Brunswick (Douglas gold medal; science prizeman; B.A., 1868; M.A., 1873). Head master Bathurst (N. B.) Grammar School, 1868-72, subsequently taking a special course in classics and history at Oxford; secretary of the Oxford Union under the presidency of Mr. (Premier) Asquith. After a period of travel returned to Canada and became principal of Fredericton Collegiate. Toured Canada and the Australian Colonies in the interests of Imperial Federation. Special correspondent in Canada for the London Times. LL.D., 1894. Author of various works bearing on Imperialism. Water color. Size 3 x 4. Head and shoulders.

3657—AUDEN, HENRY W., M.A.—Principal Upper Canada College, 1903-17—Born at Wellingborough, Eng., 1867; son of Prebendary Auden. Educated at Shrewsbury School, at Christ's College, Cambridge (M.A., scholar and prizeman; Porteous gold medal for Latin prose; Bell University Scholarship; first-class Classical Tripos, Part I., 1889; second-class Classical Tripos, Part II., 1890), and at Marburg University. From 1891 to 1903 was Sixth Form master and librarian, Fettes College, Edinburgh. Editor of various classical editions for Cambridge University Press and Macmillan's; general editor Blackwood's Classical Series. Author, in conjunction with A. E. Taylor, of "A Minimum of Greek." Resigned from the principalship of U.C.C., 1917. Water color. Size 3 x 4. Head and shoulders.

3658—DE LA HAYE, JEAN DU PETITPONT—French Master, U.C.C., Toronto—He was born at St. Malo, France, 1799, and educated at the College of St. Servan. On 1st Sept., 1829, Mr. De la Haye was appointed

French Master, Upper Canada College, which was opened 8th January, 1830, his service extending over a period of twenty-seven years. After leaving the college he resided at Claireville, Ont. His death took place 3rd December, 1872. Water color from portrait by Berthon, in possession of Mr. De la Haye's grandson, Mr. J. M. De la Haye, Toronto. Size 3 x 4. Head and shoulders.

3659—ST. REMY, EDMOND J. LE LIEVRE—French Master, U.C.C., Toronto, 1852-60—Son of an emigre nobleman, the trusted negotiator between the Royal Families of France and Great Britain. He was born in London, Eng., 11th Dec., 1810, and came to Canada in 1837, when he served against Mackenzie in the Rebellion of that year. For several years Mr. St. Remy taught in New York, returning to Canada in 1845. He assisted Mrs. St. Remy in her school in Toronto for a time, was French master in the Ontario College for Boys at Picton for two years, and subsequently head of the Junior Department of the Kingston Grammar School. His death took place in 1882. Water color from a portrait in possession of his daughter, Miss E. St. Remy, Portsmouth, Ont. Size 3 x 4. Head and shoulders.

3660—HOWARD, JOHN G.—Drawing Master, Upper Canada College, Toronto, 1833-39—Mr. Howard, who came to this country in 1832, was appointed by Sir John Colborne in March, 1833, to teach perspective, planning and surveying in Upper Canada College. In 1839 he became first drawing master. Improvements were made to the central building of the college, from his plans, and also to the front grounds in the erection of new gates and gas lamps. Mr. Howard, who presented High Park to the Corporation of Toronto, died in 1890. Water color from portrait in Upper Canada College. Size 3 x 4. Head and shoulders. See 835, 837, 841, 846, 2781.

3661—BARRETT, DR. MICHAEL, M.A.—First English Master and Science Master, U.C.C., Toronto, 1866-84—A son of Michael Barrett, barrister; born in London, Eng., 16th May, 1816; educated at Caen, Normandy and King's College, Toronto; B.A., University of Toronto, 1849, and M.A., 1853. In 1855 he received his degree of M.D., subsequently founding the Ontario Medical College for Women. Died in Toronto, 26th Feb., 1887. Water color. Size 3 x 4. Head and shoulders.

3662—DADE, REV. CHARLES, M.A.—Mathematical Master, U.C.C., Toronto, 1829-38—At the University of Cambridge Mr. Dade obtained the high wrangler's degree in the Mathematical Tripos. He was elected a fellow of Gonville and Caius College immediately after obtaining his degree in 1825, and while at Cambridge gained the Member's Prize for Latin Prose Dissertation. Valuable papers on "Law of Storms," "Meteorology of Toronto," and other subjects, were written by Mr. Dade. He was much interested in farming and returned to his farm on resigning his mastership at Upper Canada College. Mr. Dade was born at Yarmouth, Eng., 20th June, 1802, and died at Georgetown, Ont., May, 1872. In the churchyard at the latter place a number of his pupils erected, some years after his death, a monument to his memory. Water color from portrait in possession of Mrs. C. R. Dade, Calgary, Alta. Size 3 x 4. Head and shoulders.

3663—MARTLAND, JOHN—Second Classical Master and Head of Boarding House, U.C.C., 1862-91—He was educated at Sedbergh Grammar School and Queen's College, Oxford (B.A. and M.A.) He declined the principalship of Upper Canada College in 1885, and two years later helped, with Hon. T. B. Pardee, to place the college on a firm financial basis and suggested having $100,000 kept as a contingency fund. Mr. Martland's memory has been perpetuated by his Old Boys in the establishment of the "John Martland Scholarship." He was born in Blackburn, Eng., 1828, and died there in 1901. Water color. Size 3 x 4. Head and shoulders.